LEGAL PROTECTION
OF THE
ENVIRONMENT

By

Craig N. Johnston
Professor
Lewis & Clark College

William F. Funk
Professor
Lewis & Clark College

Victor B. Flatt
Professor
University of Houston

AMERICAN CASEBOOK SERIES®

Mat # 40242994

American Casebook Series and West Group are trademarks registered in the U.S. Patent and Trademark Office.

© 2005 Thomson/West
      610 Opperman Drive
      P.O. Box 64526
      St. Paul, MN 55164–0526
      1–800–328–9352

ISBN 0–314–15266–0

 *TEXT IS PRINTED ON 10% POST CONSUMER RECYCLED PAPER*

To my wife, Jane, and children, Michael, Alison and Dan

To my wife Renate

and

For Oscar

*

Preface

There is too much environmental law to be captured in any one book or course. Thus, every environmental law book must make choices about what to cover and what not to cover, what to emphasize and what not to emphasize. This book tries to cover the broad range of federal environmental law—the law that protects the environment.

It emphasizes a small number of federal statutes:

- the National Environmental Policy Act (NEPA), because it continues to play a major role in governing how federal agencies must act when they affect the environment, and it generates a significant amount of litigation brought by environmental groups;

- the Clean Water Act (CWA), the Clean Air Act (CAA), and the Resource Conservation and Recovery Act (RCRA), because they are the trinity of federal regulatory statutes that are intended to protect the water, the air, and the ground, respectively, from polluting activities;

- the Comprehensive Environmental Response, Compensation and Liability Act (CERCLA or Superfund), because it is a relatively unique remedial statute and one that has had massive impacts on the management of hazardous wastes; and

- the Endangered Species Act, because it is the most uncompromising federal environmental statute, has raised a number of problems in its implementation, and generates a large amount of litigation.

Most of these statutes have enforcement provisions by which governmental authorities or citizens can enforce the statutory or regulatory requirements on violators. This will be another area of emphasis.

This is a lot, so there must be things that are left out. Primarily what is left out is discussion of the theoretical and policy issues that underlie environmental statutes and their implementation in regulations. The authors are not averse to those issues, but the focus of this book is to portray the current status of environmental law. The introductory chapter will provide a short introduction to the primary theoretical and policy issues, but an in-depth appraisal we leave to an upper level course.

This book also limits its coverage of the constitutional, administrative, and common law aspects of environmental law as separate areas of study. Again, these are important, and the introductory chapter provides material on those subjects, but we leave fuller discussion of these matters to courses in constitutional law, administrative law, and torts.

Nevertheless, each of these subjects, and especially administrative law, can become inextricably intertwined with substantive environmental law, the practice of which almost invariably involves the work of administrative agencies. Consequently, in the course of the various chapters on different environmental law topics there will be some substantial exposure to these topics.

Acknowledgments

We would like to acknowledge Devra Davis, who has allowed us to use an excerpt from "When Smoke Ran Like Water." We would also like to acknowledge Chris Grady and Charles Irvine for their research assistance.

*

Summary of Contents

Page

Preface v
Acknowledgments vii
Table of Cases xix

Chapter 1. Introduction 1
  I. Introduction 1
  II. Some Perspectives on Environmental Law 2
  III. The Constitution and Environmental Law 35
  IV. Administrative Law Issues 69

Chapter 2. NEPA 82
  I. Introduction to NEPA 82
  II. Overview of NEPA and the NEPA Process 83
  III. Is an EIS Required? 91
  IV. Is the EIS Adequate? 112
  V. State Environmental Policy Acts 125
  VI. The Effects of NEPA 127

Chapter 3. The Clean Water Act 130
  I. The NPDES Program 130

Chapter 4. Clean Air Act 213
  I. The Problem of Air Pollution 213
  II. The Clean Air Act—Overview 232
  III. The Clean Air Act and the Control of "Criteria Pollutants" ... 234
  IV. The Clean Air Act—Direct Controls on Sources 281
  V. Clean Air Act—Prevention of Significant Deterioration and Related Requirements 321
  VI. The Clean Air Act—General Enforcement and Permits for Regulated Stationary Sources 340
  VII. Clean Air Act—Regulation of Hazardous Air Pollution ... 367
  VIII. The Clean Air Act—Mobile Sources 372
  IX. The Clean Air Act—Acid Deposition Control and the Use of Market Based Controls 381

Chapter 5. Resource Conservation and Recovery Act 389
  I. Overview and Jurisdiction 389
  II. The Regulatory Program 408

Chapter 6. Regulatory Enforcement 422
  I. Enforcement 422

Page

Chapter 7. Comprehensive Environmental Response, Compensation and Liability Act ---------------------------------- **518**
  I. CERCLA --- 518

Chapter 8. Protection of Particular Natural Resources ------- **592**
  I. The Endangered Species Act of 1973 ------------------------- 592
  II. Protecting Wetlands -- 656
  III. The Surface Mining Control and Reclamation Act of 1977 ------ 704

APPENDIX --- 727
GLOSSARY OF ACRONYMS --- 763
INDEX -- 767

Table of Contents

                                                                        Page

PREFACE --- v
ACKNOWLEDGMENTS --- vii
TABLE OF CASES -- xix

Chapter 1. Introduction --- **1**
  I. Introduction -- 1
  II. Some Perspectives on Environmental Law ---------------------------- 2
       A. History of Environmental Law --------------------------------- 2
       B. Types of Regulations -- 6
       C. Theoretical Issues --- 10
            i. Public Goods -- 11
                Notes and Comments ------------------------------------ 13
            ii. Cost/Benefit Analysis -------------------------------- 15
                Notes and Comments ------------------------------------ 20
            iii. Risk Analysis -------------------------------------- 20
                Notes and Comments ------------------------------------ 23
            iv. The Polluter Pays Principle ------------------------- 24
            v. Sustainable Development ----------------------------- 24
            vi. The Precautionary Principle ------------------------ 26
            vii. Environmental Ethics ----------------------------- 30
                Notes and Comments ------------------------------------ 32
            viii. Environmental Justice --------------------------- 32
                Notes and Comments ------------------------------------ 35
  III. The Constitution and Environmental Law ------------------------- 35
       A. Authority for Environmental Laws --------------------------- 35
           Hodel v. Virginia Surface Mining and Reclamation Association,
             Inc. -- 39
           Hodel v. Indiana -------------------------------------- 42
           Notes and Comments -------------------------------------- 46
       B. Constitutional Limitations on Environmental Laws --------- 48
            1. Tenth Amendment ------------------------------------- 48
            2. The Eleventh Amendment ----------------------------- 49
            3. The Takings Clause --------------------------------- 50
                Notes and Comments ------------------------------------ 53
       C. Constitutional Limitations on State Laws ----------------- 54
            1. The Supremacy Clause ------------------------------- 54
            2. The Dormant Commerce Clause ----------------------- 56
       D. Constitutional Limitations on Bringing Lawsuits --------- 58
           Lujan v. Defenders of Wildlife --------------------------- 59
           Notes and Comments -------------------------------------- 69
  IV. Administrative Law Issues ------------------------------------- 69
       A. Rulemaking -- 70

Page

IV. Administrative Law Issues—Continued
    B. Adjudication 71
    C. Presidential Oversight 72
    D. Judicial Review 73
        1. Obtaining Review 73
            a. Preclusion of Review 73
            b. APA Requirements for Review 74
                i. Zone of Interests 74
                ii. Finality 75
                iii. Exhaustion of Administrative Remedies 77
            c. Common Law Requirements for Review 78
                i. Issue Exhaustion and Waiver 78
                ii. Ripeness 78
        2. The Scope of Judicial Review 79

Chapter 2. NEPA **82**
  I. Introduction to NEPA 82
  II. Overview of NEPA and the NEPA Process 83
  III. Is an EIS Required? 91
    A. Is it a Major Action? 91
      Kleppe v. Sierra Club American Electric Power System v. Sierra Club 92
      Notes and Questions 100
    B. Is it Federal? 101
      Winnebago Tribe of Nebraska v. Ray 101
      Notes and Questions 105
    C. Does it Significantly Affect the Quality of the Human Environment 106
      Grand Canyon Trust v. Federal Aviation Administration 107
      Notes and Questions 111
  IV. Is the EIS Adequate? 112
    A. Environmental Effects 112
      Robertson v. Methow Valley Citizens Council 114
      Notes and Questions 121
    B. Alternatives Consideration 121
    C. Mitigation 123
      Robertson v. Methow Valley Citizens Council 123
  V. State Environmental Policy Acts 125
  VI. The Effects of NEPA 127

Chapter 3. The Clean Water Act **130**
  I. The NPDES Program 130
    A. Jurisdiction 131
        1. Addition of a Pollutant 132
            Catskill Mountains Chapter of Trout Unlimited, Inc. v. City of New York 132
            Notes and Questions 135
        2. Navigable Waters 138
            Idaho Rural Council v. Bosma 139
            Notes and Questions 141
        3. Point Source 143

Page

I. The NPDES Program—Continued
United States v. Plaza Health Laboratories, Inc. 143
Notes and Questions 148
B. The Federal/State Relationship 150
1. How States Become Authorized 151
Natural Resources Defense Council, Inc. v. EPA 152
Notes and Questions 156
2. EPA Oversight 157
Natural Resources Defense Council, Inc. v. U.S. EPA 158
Questions and Notes 161
C. Substantive Standards 162
1. Technology–Based Standards 163
Weyerhaeuser Co. v. Costle 164
Questions and Notes 171
2. Water Quality–Based Requirements 178
a. How Water Quality Standards are Set 178
Notes and Questions 180
b. How Water Quality Standards are Implement-
ed for Point Sources 182
Arkansas v. Oklahoma 184
Questions and Notes 189
D. Other Water Quality–Based Programs Under the CWA 192
1. § 401 Certifications 192
PUD No. 1 of Jefferson County v. Washington Dept. of
Ecology 193
Questions and Notes 200
2. Sections 208 and 319 202
3. The TMDL Program 203
Pronsolino v. Nastri 205
Notes and Questions 211

Chapter 4. Clean Air Act **213**
I. The Problem of Air Pollution 213
II. The Clean Air Act—Overview 232
III. The Clean Air Act and the Control of "Criteria Pollutants" ... 234
A. What is a Criteria Pollutant? 234
Natural Resources Defense Council, Inc. v. Train 234
Notes and Questions 238
B. How is a National Ambient Air Quality Standard Estab-
lished? 239
Whitman v. American Trucking Associations, Inc. 249
Commonwealth of Massachusetts v. United States Environmen-
tal Protection Agency 255
C. How are the National Ambient Air Quality Standards
Met?—State Implementation Plans 255
Natural Resources Defense Council, Inc. v. Train 256
Train v. Natural Resources Defense Council, Inc. 257
1. What about the transport of criteria pollutants? .. 259
Appalachian Power Company v. Environmental Protec-
tion Agency 260
Notes and Questions 274
Environmental Protection Agency 274
Notes and Questions 277

Page

III. The Clean Air Act and the Control of "Criteria Pollutants"—Continued

D. What happens when the states don't meet the NAAQS—Non-compliance 277

Whitman v. American Trucking Associations, Inc. 280

IV. The Clean Air Act—Direct Controls on Sources 281

A. Stationary sources 281

Notes and Questions 284

Lignite Energy Council v. U.S. Environmental Protection Agency 284

B. New Source Review—What about existing sources? (An exercise in the administrative process) 288

1. New Source Review 289

2. Application to Existing Sources 289

Wisconsin Electric Power Company v. Reilly 290

Notes and Questions 298

Chevron, U.S.A., Inc. v. Natural Resources Defense Council, Inc. 299

Wisconsin Electric Power Company v. Reilly 307

Notes and Comments 314

United States v. Ohio Edison Company 317

Notes and Questions 319

V. Clean Air Act—Prevention of Significant Deterioration and Related Requirements 321

A. The Core Program 321

Alabama Power Company v. Costle 321

B. Air Quality Related Values and Visibility Protection 328

Central Arizona Water Conservation District v. United States Environmental Protection Agency 329

VI. The Clean Air Act—General Enforcement and Permits for Regulated Stationary Sources 340

A. What is required for a state permit program to be approved? 342

Public Citizen, Inc. v. United States Environmental Protection Agency 342

B. Federal Overfiling—Federal Enforcement above and beyond the state 351

Alaska Department of Environmental Conservation v. Environmental Protection Agency 351

VII. Clean Air Act—Regulation of Hazardous Air Pollution 367

A. History of the regulation of HAP–the change to technology based standards 367

B. Health Based Standards Remain 371

VIII. The Clean Air Act—Mobile Sources 372

IX. The Clean Air Act—Acid Deposition Control and the Use of Market Based Controls 381

A. SO_2 Emission Limitation Program 382

B. NOx Emission Limitation Program 384

C. The Use of Market Based Trading Systems 385

Chapter 5. Resource Conservation and Recovery Act 389

I. Overview and Jurisdiction 389

A. What is a "Solid Waste"? 390

Page

I. Overview and Jurisdiction—Continued
    American Mining Congress v. U.S. EPA ------------------------------- 392
    Notes and Questions --- 398
  B. What is a "Hazardous Waste"? ---------------------------------- 404
    Notes and Questions --- 406
II. The Regulatory Program -- 408
  A. Generator Requirements --- 408
    Notes and Questions --- 412
  B. Requirements for Treatment, Storage and Disposal Facilities (TSDs) --- 412
    Notes and Questions --- 420

Chapter 6. Regulatory Enforcement ----------------------------------- **422**
  I. Enforcement -- 422
    A. Investigations --- 422
    B. Enforcement Options -- 424
      1. EPA–Lead Civil Actions in Court -------------------------- 425
        Weinberger v. Romero–Barcelo ------------------------------ 425
        Questions and Notes -- 431
        United States v. The Municipal Authority of Union Township -- 432
        Questions and Notes -- 438
      2. Administrative Enforcement ------------------------------- 439
        Southern Pines Associates v. United States --------------- 439
        Questions and Notes -- 442
        Questions and Notes -- 453
      3. Criminal Enforcement -------------------------------------- 455
        United States v. Weitzenhoff -------------------------------- 456
        Questions and Notes -- 464
    C. Federalism Issues in the Enforcement Context -------------- 465
        Harmon Industries, Inc. v. Browner ----------------------- 466
        Questions and Notes -- 470
    D. Citizen Suits --- 472
      1. Notice --- 473
      2. Standing -- 474
        Friends of the Earth v. Laidlaw Environmental Services --- 474
        Questions and Notes -- 479
      3. The *Gwaltney* Doctrine -------------------------------------- 483
        Gwaltney of Smithfield, Ltd., v. Chesapeake Bay Foundation, Inc. --- 483
        Questions and Notes -- 490
        Friends of the Earth, Inc. v. Laidlaw Environmental Services --- 494
        Questions and Notes -- 499
      4. The Effect of Prior Governmental Enforcement Actions -- 502
      5. Attorney Fees -- 504
        Hensley v. Eckerhart -- 505
        Buckhannon Board and Care Home, Inc. v. West Virginia Department of Health and Human Resources --- 508
        Questions and Notes -- 515

Page

Chapter 7. Comprehensive Environmental Response, Compensation and Liability Act **518**
 I. CERCLA 518
  A. Overview and Jurisdiction 518
  B. EPA Response 521
   1. Liable Parties 522
    a. Owner/Operator Liability 523
     i. Ownership Liability 523
      New York v. Shore Realty Corp. 523
      Notes and Questions 524
     ii. Operator Liability 527
      United States v. Bestfoods 527
      Notes and Questions 533
    b. Arrangers for Disposal or Treatment 537
     United States v. Wade 538
     Notes and Questions 540
   2. Scope of Liability 543
    United States v. Chem–Dyne Corp. 543
    O'Neil v. Picillo 547
    Notes and Questions 550
   3. Defenses 552
    Notes and Questions 557
   4. A Quick Overview of the Cleanup Process 560
   5. Settlement 564
    United States v. Cannons Engineering Corp. 569
    Notes and Questions 575
  C. Private Party Cost–Recovery and Contribution 575
   Bedford Affiliates v. Sills 577
   Cooper Industries, Inc. v. Aviall Services, Inc. ... 579
   Notes and Questions 585

Chapter 8. Protection of Particular Natural Resources **592**
 I. The Endangered Species Act of 1973 592
  A. Outline of the Act 593
  B. Section 4 593
   1. Listing 594
    a. Endangered or Threatened 594
     Notes and Comments 595
    b. "A Significant Portion of its Range" 597
     Defenders of Wildlife v. Norton 597
     Notes and Comments 600
    c. "Species" includes "subspecies" 600
    d. "Species" includes Distinct Population Segments 601
     National Association of Home Builders v. Norton 602
     Notes and Comments 608
   2. Critical Habitat 610
   3. Recovery 613
   4. The Procedures 613
    Notes and Comments 615
  C. Section 7 616
   1. The Affirmative Obligation 617

Page

I. The Endangered Species Act of 1973—Continued
    2. The Procedural Requirements ------------------------- 618
      Thomas v. Peterson ------------------------------------ 620
      Lane County Audubon Society v. Jamison ------------ 624
      Newton County Wildlife Association v. Rogers ----------- 628
      Questions and Comments --------------------------------- 629
    3. The Substantive Requirements -------------------------- 631
      Gifford Pinchot Task Force v. United States ------------- 632
      Notes and Comments ------------------------------------- 635
    4. Exemptions -- 636
      Notes and Comments ------------------------------------- 638
  D. Section 9 --- 639
    Babbitt v. Sweet Home Chapter of Communities for a Great Oregon --- 639
    Notes and Questions -- 651
  E. Section 10 --- 653
  F. Section 11 --- 655
II. Protecting Wetlands -- 656
  A. Section 404 of the Clean Water Act ------------------------ 657
    1. What Waters are Covered? ----------------------------- 658
      United States v. Riverside Bayview Homes, Inc. ---------- 659
      Notes and Comments ------------------------------------- 663
      Solid Waste Agency of Northern Cook County v. United States Army Corps of Engineers -------------------------- 664
      Notes and Comments ------------------------------------- 673
    2. What Activities are Covered? -------------------------- 676
      National Mining Association v. U.S. Army Corps of Engineers -- 678
      Notes and Comments ------------------------------------- 681
    3. Exceptions from the Permit Requirement ----------- 684
    4. The 404 Permit --------------------------------------- 684
      a. The 404(b)(1) Guidelines and the Public Interest Review --- 686
        Fund for Animals, Inc. v. Rice --------------------------- 689
        Notes and Comments ------------------------------------- 695
      b. General Permits and Alternative Procedures -- 696
        i. Nationwide Permits --------------------------- 696
        ii. Other General Permits and Letters of Permission --- 698
        Notes and Comments ------------------------------------- 700
  B. The Swampbuster Program ------------------------------- 701
III. The Surface Mining Control and Reclamation Act of 1977 ------ 704
  A. Background -- 704
  B. SMCRA's Provisions --- 708
    Notes and Comments --- 710
  C. Issues --- 711
    1. Federalism Issues ------------------------------------- 711
      Haydo v. Amerikohl Mining, Inc. ---------------------- 713
      Molinary v. Powell Mountain Coal Company ------------- 716
      Notes and Comments ------------------------------------- 720
    2. Mountaintop-removal/Valley fill mining ------------- 720
      Notes and Comments ------------------------------------- 724
    3. Enforcement Issues ----------------------------------- 724

                                                           Page
APPENDIX-- 727
GLOSSARY OF ACRONYMS-- 763
INDEX -- 767

Table of Cases

The principal cases are in bold type. Cases cited or discussed in the text are roman type. References are to pages. Cases cited in principal cases and within other quoted materials are not included.

Abbott Laboratories v. Gardner, 387 U.S. 136, 87 S.Ct. 1507, 18 L.Ed.2d 681 (1967), 76, 79

Aceto Agr. Chemicals Corp., United States v., 872 F.2d 1373 (8th Cir.1989), 525, 543

Acker v. E.P.A., 290 F.3d 892 (7th Cir. 2002), 77

ACORN v. Edwards, 81 F.3d 1387 (5th Cir. 1996), 53

Adams Fruit Co., Inc. v. Barrett, 494 U.S. 638, 110 S.Ct. 1384, 108 L.Ed.2d 585 (1990), 536

Ailor v. City of Maynardville, Tennessee, 368 F.3d 587 (6th Cir.2004), 500

Air Brake Systems, Inc. v. Mineta, 357 F.3d 632 (6th Cir.2004), 76

Akzo Coatings, Inc. v. Aigner Corp., 30 F.3d 761 (7th Cir.1994), 585

Alabama Power Co. v. Castle, 636 F.2d 323, 204 U.S.App.D.C. 51 (D.C.Cir. 1979), 136, 278, **321**

Alabama Rivers Alliance v. F.E.R.C., 325 F.3d 290, 355 U.S.App.D.C. 390 (D.C.Cir.2003), 201

Alabama–Tombigbee Rivers Coalition v. Department of Interior, 26 F.3d 1103 (11th Cir.1994), 594

Alaska Dept. of Environmental Conservation v. E.P.A., 540 U.S. 461, 124 S.Ct. 983, 157 L.Ed.2d 967 (2004), 77, **351,** 444

Alaska, Dept. of Environmental Conservation v. United States E.P.A., 244 F.3d 748 (9th Cir.2001), 444

Alcan Aluminum Corp., United States v., 892 F.Supp. 648 (M.D.Pa.1995), 552

Alcan Aluminum Corp., United States v., 990 F.2d 711 (2nd Cir.1993), 551

Alcan Aluminum Corp., United States v., 964 F.2d 252 (3rd Cir.1992), 521, 541, 551

Alcan Aluminum Corp., United States v., 315 F.3d 179 (2nd Cir.2003), 526, 552

Alexander v. Choate, 469 U.S. 287, 105 S.Ct. 712, 83 L.Ed.2d 661 (1985), 33

Alexander v. Sandoval, 532 U.S. 275, 121 S.Ct. 1511, 149 L.Ed.2d 517 (2001), 33

Allsteel, Inc. v. United States E.P.A., 25 F.3d 312 (6th Cir.1994), 77, 443

Alsea Valley Alliance v. Evans, 161 F.Supp.2d 1154 (D.Or.2001), 594

American Forest and Paper Ass'n v. United States E.P.A., 137 F.3d 291 (5th Cir. 1998), 162

American Min. Congress v. United States E.P.A., 907 F.2d 1179, 285 U.S.App.D.C. 173 (D.C.Cir.1990), 400

American Min. Congress v. United States E.P.A., 824 F.2d 1177, 263 U.S.App.D.C. 197 (D.C.Cir.1987), **392**

American Paper Institute, Inc. v. United States E.P.A., 890 F.2d 869 (7th Cir. 1989), 162

American Petroleum Institute v. United States E.P.A., 906 F.2d 729, 285 U.S.App.D.C. 35 (D.C.Cir.1990), 400

American Petroleum Institute v. United States E.P.A., 216 F.3d 50, 342 U.S.App. D.C. 159 (D.C.Cir.2000), 402

American Wildlands v. Browner, 260 F.3d 1192 (10th Cir.2001), 182, 189

Amoco Production Co. v. Village of Gambell, AK, 480 U.S. 531, 107 S.Ct. 1396, 94 L.Ed.2d 542 (1987), 431

A & N Cleaners and Launderers, Inc., United States v., 854 F.Supp. 229 (S.D.N.Y. 1994), 557

A & N Cleaners and Launderers, Inc., United States v., 788 F.Supp. 1317 (S.D.N.Y. 1992), 557

Appalachian Power Co. v. E.P.A., 249 F.3d 1032, 346 U.S.App.D.C. 38 (D.C.Cir.2001), **260**

Appalachian Power Co. v. E.P.A., 208 F.3d 1015, 341 U.S.App.D.C. 46 (D.C.Cir. 2000), 76

Arizonans for Official English v. Arizona, 520 U.S. 43, 117 S.Ct. 1055, 137 L.Ed.2d 170 (1997), 492

Arkansas v. Oklahoma, 503 U.S. 91, 112 S.Ct. 1046, 117 L.Ed.2d 239 (1992), **184**

Association of Battery Recyclers, Inc. v. United States E.P.A., 208 F.3d 1047, 341 U.S.App.D.C. 78 (D.C.Cir.2000), 398, 401

Association of California Water Agencies v. Evans, 386 F.3d 879 (9th Cir.2004), 516, 517

Association of Pacific Fisheries v. E.P.A., 615 F.2d 794 (9th Cir.1980), 136, 172

Association to Protect Hammersley, Eld, and Totten Inlets v. Taylor Resources, Inc., 299 F.3d 1007 (9th Cir.2002), 137

Atlantic States Legal Foundation, Inc. v. Pan American Tanning Corp., 993 F.2d 1017 (2nd Cir.1993), 493

Atlantic States Legal Foundation, Inc. v. Stroh Die Casting Co., 116 F.3d 814 (7th Cir.1997), 491, 493

Atlantic States Legal Foundation, Inc. v. Tyson Foods, Inc., 897 F.2d 1128 (11th Cir.1990), 438, 493

Atlantic States Legal Foundation, Inc. v. United Musical Instruments, United StatesA., Inc., 61 F.3d 473 (6th Cir. 1995), 492

Auer v. Robbins, 519 U.S. 452, 117 S.Ct. 905, 137 L.Ed.2d 79 (1997), 142, 212

Avoyelles Sportsmen's League, Inc. v. Marsh, 715 F.2d 897 (5th Cir.1983), 677

Axel Johnson, Inc. v. Carroll Carolina Oil Co., Inc., 191 F.3d 409 (4th Cir.1999), 585

Babbitt v. Sweet Home Chapter of Communities for a Great Oregon, 515 U.S. 687, 115 S.Ct. 2407, 132 L.Ed.2d 597 (1995), 150, **639**

Bangor, City of v. Citizens Communications Co., 2004 WL 483201 (D.Me.2004), 557

BASF Wyandotte Corp. v. Costle, 598 F.2d 637 (1st Cir.1979), 172

Bedford Affiliates v. Sills, 156 F.3d 416 (2nd Cir.1998), 557, **577**

Bell Petroleum Services, Inc., Matter of, 3 F.3d 889 (5th Cir.1993), 551

Bennett v. Spear, 520 U.S. 154, 117 S.Ct. 1154, 137 L.Ed.2d 281 (1997), 69, 75, 76, 81, 472

Bersani v. United States E.P.A., 850 F.2d 36 (2nd Cir.1988), 687

Bestfoods v. Aerojet–General Corp., 173 F.Supp.2d 729 (W.D.Mich.2001), 534

Bestfoods, United States v., 524 U.S. 51, 118 S.Ct. 1876, 141 L.Ed.2d 43 (1998), **527**

B.F. Goodrich v. Betkoski, 99 F.3d 505 (2nd Cir.1996), 536

Biodiversity Legal Foundation v. Babbitt, 943 F.Supp. 23 (D.D.C.1996), 596

Biodiversity Legal Foundation v. Badgley, 309 F.3d 1166 (9th Cir.2002), 615

Bliss, United States v., 667 F.Supp. 1298 (E.D.Mo.1987), 541

Blum v. Stenson, 465 U.S. 886, 104 S.Ct. 1541, 79 L.Ed.2d 891 (1984), 517

Boomer v. Atlantic Cement Co., 309 N.Y.S.2d 312, 257 N.E.2d 870 (N.Y. 1970), 4

Borden Ranch Partnership v. United States Army Corps of Engineers, 261 F.3d 810 (9th Cir.2001), 682

Bowles v. Seminole Rock & Sand Co., 325 U.S. 410, 65 S.Ct. 1215, 89 L.Ed. 1700 (1945), 81, 142

BP Exploration & Oil, Inc.(93–3310) v. United States E.P.A., 66 F.3d 784 (6th Cir.1995), 172

Brace, United States v., 41 F.3d 117 (3rd Cir.1994), 702

Bragg v. Robertson, 72 F.Supp.2d 642 (S.D.W.Va.1999), 721, 722

Bragg v. Robertson, 83 F.Supp.2d 713 (S.D.W.Va.2000), 722

Bragg v. West Virginia Coal Ass'n, 248 F.3d 275 (4th Cir.2001), 713, 722

Browning–Ferris Industries of Illinois, Inc. v. Ter Maat, 195 F.3d 953 (7th Cir. 1999), 535

Buckhannon Bd. and Care Home, Inc. v. West Virginia Dept. of Health and Human Resources, 532 U.S. 598, 121 S.Ct. 1835, 149 L.Ed.2d 855 (2001), **508**

Burlington, City of v. Dague, 505 U.S. 557, 112 S.Ct. 2638, 120 L.Ed.2d 449 (1992), 517

C & A Carbone, Inc. v. Town of Clarkstown, N.Y., 511 U.S. 383, 114 S.Ct. 1677, 128 L.Ed.2d 399 (1994), 57

Calvert Cliffs' Coordinating Committee, Inc. v. United States Atomic Energy Commission, 449 F.2d 1109, 146 U.S.App.D.C. 33 (D.C.Cir.1971), 82, 90

Cannon v. University of Chicago, 441 U.S. 677, 99 S.Ct. 1946, 60 L.Ed.2d 560 (1979), 33

Cannons Engineering Corp., United States v., 899 F.2d 79 (1st Cir.1990), **569**

Cannons Engineering Corp., United States v., 720 F.Supp. 1027 (D.Mass.1989), 571

Carson–Truckee Water Conservancy Dist. v. Clark, 741 F.2d 257 (9th Cir.1984), 617

Carter–Jones Lumber Co. v. Dixie Distributing Co., 166 F.3d 840 (6th Cir.1999), 537

Catellus Development Corp. v. United States, 34 F.3d 748 (9th Cir.1994), 542

Catron County Bd. of Com'rs, New Mexico v. United States Fish & Wildlife Service, 75 F.3d 1429 (10th Cir.1996), 616

Catskill Mountains Chapter of Trout Unlimited, Inc. v. City of New York, 273 F.3d 481 (2nd Cir.2001), **132**

CDMG Realty Co., United States v., 96 F.3d 706 (3rd Cir.1996), 526

Center for Biological Diversity v. Badgley, 2001 WL 844399 (D.Or.2001), 596

Center for Biological Diversity v. Norton, 240 F.Supp.2d 1090 (D.Ariz.2003), 611

Center for Biological Diversity v. Norton, 262 F.3d 1077 (10th Cir.2001), 517

Center for Biological Diversity v. Rumsfeld, 198 F.Supp.2d 1139 (D.Ariz.2002), 636

Centerior Service Co. v. Acme Scrap Iron & Metal Corp., 153 F.3d 344 (6th Cir. 1998), 585

Central Arizona Water Conservation Dist. v. United States E.P.A., 990 F.2d 1531 (9th Cir.1993), **329**

Chem–Dyne Corp., United States v., 572 F.Supp. 802 (S.D.Ohio 1983), 525, **543**

Chemical Mfrs. Ass'n v. Natural Resources Defense Council, Inc., 470 U.S. 116, 105 S.Ct. 1102, 84 L.Ed.2d 90 (1985), 173, 175

Chemical Waste Management, Inc. v. Hunt, 504 U.S. 334, 112 S.Ct. 2009, 119 L.Ed.2d 121 (1992), 56

Chemical Waste Management, Inc. v. United States E.P.A., 976 F.2d 2, 298 U.S.App.D.C. 54 (D.C.Cir.1992), 421

Chemical Waste Management, Inc. v. United StatesE.P.A., 869 F.2d 1526, 276 U.S.App.D.C. 207 (D.C.Cir.1989), 406

Chesapeake Bay Foundation, Inc. v. Gwaltney of Smithfield, Ltd., 890 F.2d 690 (4th Cir.1989), 491, 493

Chesapeake Bay Foundation, Inc. v. Gwaltney of Smithfield, Ltd., 844 F.2d 170 (4th Cir.1988), 491

Chester Residents Concerned for Quality Living v. Seif, 132 F.3d 925 (3rd Cir. 1997), 33

Chevron U.S.A., Inc. v. Natural Resources Defense Council, Inc., 467 U.S. 837, 104 S.Ct. 2778, 81 L.Ed.2d 694 (1984), 80, **299**

Chicago, City of v. Environmental Defense Fund, 511 U.S. 328, 114 S.Ct. 1588, 128 L.Ed.2d 302 (1994), 406

Christensen v. Harris County, 529 U.S. 576, 120 S.Ct. 1655, 146 L.Ed.2d 621 (2000), 133

Christiansburg Garment Co. v. Equal Employment Opportunity Commission, 434 U.S. 412, 98 S.Ct. 694, 54 L.Ed.2d 648 (1978), 515

Cipollone v. Liggett Group, Inc., 505 U.S. 504, 112 S.Ct. 2608, 120 L.Ed.2d 407 (1992), 54

Citizens Coal Council v. Norton, 330 F.3d 478, 356 U.S.App.D.C. 214 (D.C.Cir. 2003), 711

Citizens for a Better Environment v. Steel Co., 90 F.3d 1237 (7th Cir.1996), 492

Citizens for a Better Environment–California v. Union Oil Co. of California, 83 F.3d 1111 (9th Cir.1996), 504

Citizens to Preserve Overton Park, Inc. v. Volpe, 401 U.S. 402, 91 S.Ct. 814, 28 L.Ed.2d 136 (1971), 79

City of (see name of city)

Comfort Lake Ass'n, Inc. v. Dresel Contracting, Inc., 138 F.3d 351 (8th Cir. 1998), 493

Commonwealth of (see name of Commonwealth)

Como–Falcon Coalition, Inc. v. United States Dept. of Labor, 465 F.Supp. 850 (D.Minn.1978), 113

Concerned Area Residents for Environment v. Southview Farm, 34 F.3d 114 (2nd Cir.1994), 149

Control Data Corp. v. S.C.S.C. Corp., 53 F.3d 930 (8th Cir.1995), 585

Cooper Industries, Inc. v. Aviall Services, Inc., ___ U.S. ___, 125 S.Ct. 577, 160 L.Ed.2d 548 (2004), **579**

CPC Intern., Inc. v. Aerojet–General Corp., 777 F.Supp. 549 (W.D.Mich.1991), 531

Darby, United States v., 312 U.S. 100, 312 U.S. 657, 61 S.Ct. 451, 85 L.Ed. 609 (1941), 37

Deaton, United States v., 332 F.3d 698 (4th Cir.2003), 675

Deaton, United States v., 209 F.3d 331 (4th Cir.2000), 682

Defenders of Wildlife v. Administrator, E.P.A., 882 F.2d 1294 (8th Cir.1989), 652

Defenders of Wildlife v. Babbitt, 1999 WL 33537981 (S.D.Cal.1999), 596

Defenders of Wildlife v. Norton, 258 F.3d 1136 (9th Cir.2001), **597**

Department of Transp. v. Public Citizen, 541 U.S. 752, 124 S.Ct. 2204, 159 L.Ed.2d 60 (2004), 85

DiBiase Salem Realty Trust, United States v., 1993 WL 729662 (D.Mass.1993), 557

Dioxin/Organochlorine Center v. Clarke, 57 F.3d 1517 (9th Cir.1995), 189

Dolan v. City of Tigard, 512 U.S. 374, 114 S.Ct. 2309, 129 L.Ed.2d 304 (1994), 52

Donahey v. Bogle, 129 F.3d 838 (6th Cir. 1997), 536

Donovan v. Dewey, 452 U.S. 594, 101 S.Ct. 2534, 69 L.Ed.2d 262 (1981), 423

Douglas County v. Babbitt, 48 F.3d 1495 (9th Cir.1995), 616

Drummond v. United States, 324 U.S. 316, 65 S.Ct. 659, 89 L.Ed. 969 (1945), 471

Dubois v. Thomas, 820 F.2d 943 (8th Cir. 1987), 424

Eastern Enterprises v. Apfel, 524 U.S. 498, 118 S.Ct. 2131, 141 L.Ed.2d 451 (1998), 526

Edward Hines Lumber Co. v. Vulcan Materials Co., 861 F.2d 155 (7th Cir.1988), 525

E. I. du Pont de Nemours & Co. v. Train, 430 U.S. 112, 97 S.Ct. 965, 51 L.Ed.2d 204 (1977), 164

Environmental Defense Fund v. Tennessee Val. Authority, 468 F.2d 1164 (6th Cir. 1972), 113

Environmental Protection Agency v. California ex rel. State Water Resources Control Bd., 426 U.S. 200, 96 S.Ct. 2022, 48 L.Ed.2d 578 (1976), 171

E.P.A. v. National Crushed Stone Ass'n, 449 U.S. 64, 101 S.Ct. 295, 66 L.Ed.2d 268 (1980), 173

Ex parte (see name of party)

Federal Election Com'n v. Akins, 524 U.S. 11, 118 S.Ct. 1777, 141 L.Ed.2d 10 (1998), 69

Fleet Factors Corp., United States v., 901 F.2d 1550 (11th Cir.1990), 537

Florida Power & Light Co. v. Allis Chalmers Corp., 893 F.2d 1313 (11th Cir. 1990), 525, 542

Fogerty v. Fantasy, Inc., 510 U.S. 517, 114 S.Ct. 1023, 127 L.Ed.2d 455 (1994), 515

Fort Gratiot Sanitary Landfill, Inc. v. Michigan Dept. of Natural Resources, 504 U.S. 353, 112 S.Ct. 2019, 119 L.Ed.2d 139 (1992), 57

Foster v. United States, 922 F.Supp. 642 (D.D.C.1996), 558

Franklin v. Massachusetts, 505 U.S. 788, 112 S.Ct. 2767, 120 L.Ed.2d 636 (1992), 76

Franklin County Convention Facilities Authority v. American Premier Underwriters, Inc., 240 F.3d 534 (6th Cir.2001), 557

Friends of Earth, Inc. v. Laidlaw Environmental Services (TOC), Inc., 149 F.3d 303 (4th Cir.1998), 494

Friends of Milwaukee's Rivers v. Milwaukee Metropolitan Sewerage Dist., 382 F.3d 743 (7th Cir.2004), 504

Friends of the Earth, Inc. v. Gaston Copper Recycling Corp., 179 F.3d 107 (4th Cir. 1999), 481

Friends of the Earth, Inc. v. Gaston Copper Recycling Corp., 204 F.3d 149 (4th Cir. 2000), 481

Friends of the Earth, Inc. v. Laidlaw Environmental Services (TOC), Inc., 890 F.Supp. 470 (D.S.C.1995), 503

Friends of the Earth, Inc. v. Laidlaw Environmental Services (TOC), Inc., 528 U.S. 167, 120 S.Ct. 693, 145 L.Ed.2d 610 (2000), 69, 473, **474, 494**

Friends of the Earth, Inc. v. United States Army Corps of Engineers, 109 F.Supp.2d 30 (D.D.C.2000), 105

Friends of the Payette v. Horseshoe Bend Hydroelectric Co., 988 F.2d 989 (9th Cir. 1993), 695

Friends of Wild Swan, Inc. v. United States Fish and Wildlife Service, 945 F.Supp. 1388 (D.Or.1996), 596

Fund for Animals, Inc. v. Rice, 85 F.3d 535 (11th Cir.1996), **689**

Garcia v. San Antonio Metropolitan Transit Authority, 469 U.S. 528, 105 S.Ct. 1005, 83 L.Ed.2d 1016 (1985), 48

GDF Realty Investments, Ltd. v. Norton, 326 F.3d 622 (5th Cir.2003), 47

Georgia, State of v. Tennessee Copper Co., 206 U.S. 230, 27 S.Ct. 618, 51 L.Ed. 1038 (1907), 4

Gerber v. Norton, 294 F.3d 173, 352 U.S.App.D.C. 375 (D.C.Cir.2002), 654

Gibbs v. Babbitt, 214 F.3d 483 (4th Cir. 2000), 48

Gifford Pinchot Task Force v. United States Fish and Wildlife Service, 378 F.3d 1059 (9th Cir.2004), 631, **632**

Goe Engineering Co., Inc. v. Physicians Formula Cosmetics, Inc., 1997 WL 889278 (C.D.Cal.1997), 557, 558

Grand Canyon Trust v. F.A.A., 290 F.3d 339, 351 U.S.App.D.C. 253 (D.C.Cir. 2002), **107**

Guardians Ass'n v. Civil Service Com'n of City of New York, 463 U.S. 582, 103 S.Ct. 3221, 77 L.Ed.2d 866 (1983), 33

Gwaltney of Smithfield, Ltd. v. Chesapeake Bay Foundation, Inc., 484 U.S. 49, 108 S.Ct. 376, 98 L.Ed.2d 306 (1987), **483**

Hallstrom v. Tillamook County, 493 U.S. 20, 110 S.Ct. 304, 107 L.Ed.2d 237 (1989), 473

Hanly v. Kleindienst, 471 F.2d 823 (2nd Cir.1972), 107, 112

Hans v. Louisiana, 134 U.S. 1, 10 S.Ct. 504, 33 L.Ed. 842 (1890), 49

Harmon Industries, Inc. v. Browner, 191 F.3d 894 (8th Cir.1999), **466**

Haydo v. Amerikohl Min., Inc., 830 F.2d 494 (3rd Cir.1987), **713**

Hazardous Waste Treatment Council v. United States E.P.A., 886 F.2d 355, 280 U.S.App.D.C. 338 (D.C.Cir.1989), 421

Headwaters, Inc. v. Talent Irrigation Dist., 243 F.3d 526 (9th Cir.2001), 136, 139, 675

Heckler v. Chaney, 470 U.S. 821, 105 S.Ct. 1649, 84 L.Ed.2d 714 (1985), 424

Hensley v. Eckerhart, 461 U.S. 424, 103 S.Ct. 1933, 76 L.Ed.2d 40 (1983), **505**

Hodel v. Indiana, 452 U.S. 314, 101 S.Ct. 2376, 69 L.Ed.2d 40 (1981), **42**

Hodel v. Virginia Surface Min. and Reclamation Ass'n, Inc., 452 U.S. 264, 101 S.Ct. 2352, 69 L.Ed.2d 1 (1981), **39,** 48

Hunt v. Washington State Apple Advertising Com'n, 432 U.S. 333, 97 S.Ct. 2434, 53 L.Ed.2d 383 (1977), 58

Idaho Rural Council v. Bosma, 143 F.Supp.2d 1169 (D.Idaho 2001), **139**

ILCO, Inc., United States v., 996 F.2d 1126 (11th Cir.1993), 401

In re (see name of party)

James City County, Va. v. E.P.A., 12 F.3d 1330 (4th Cir.1993), 685

Johnson v. Director, Office of Workers' Compensation Programs, 183 F.3d 1169 (9th Cir.1999), 78

Kaiser Aetna v. United States, 444 U.S. 164, 100 S.Ct. 383, 62 L.Ed.2d 332 (1979), 51

Kalamazoo River Study Group v. Rockwell Intern., 3 F.Supp.2d 799 (W.D.Mich. 1998), 557

Kayser–Roth Corp., United States v., 272 F.3d 89 (1st Cir.2001), 534

Kelley v. E.P.A., 15 F.3d 1100, 304 U.S.App. D.C. 369 (D.C.Cir.1994), 536

Kennecott v. United StatesE.P.A., 780 F.2d 445 (4th Cir.1985), 173

Kentuckians for Commonwealth Inc. v. Rivenburgh, 317 F.3d 425 (4th Cir.2003), 658, 721, 722

Kerr–McGee Chemical Corp. v. Lefton Iron & Metal Co., 14 F.3d 321 (7th Cir.1994), 557

Kimbell Foods, Inc., United States v., 440 U.S. 715, 99 S.Ct. 1448, 59 L.Ed.2d 711 (1979), 550

Kleppe v. New Mexico, 426 U.S. 529, 96 S.Ct. 2285, 49 L.Ed.2d 34 (1976), 36

Kleppe v. Sierra Club, 427 U.S. 390, 96 S.Ct. 2718, 49 L.Ed.2d 576 (1976), **92**

Lane County Audubon Soc. v. Jamison, 958 F.2d 290 (9th Cir.1992), **624**

Lansford–Coaldale Joint Water Authority v. Tonolli Corp., 4 F.3d 1209 (3rd Cir. 1993), 536

League of Wilderness Defenders/Blue Mountains Biodiversity Project v. Forsgren, 309 F.3d 1181 (9th Cir.2002), 150

Lefebvre v. Central Maine Power Co., 7 F.Supp.2d 64 (D.Me.1998), 557

Leslie Salt Co. v. United States, 55 F.3d 1388 (9th Cir.1995), 438

Lignite Energy Council v. United States E.P.A., 198 F.3d 930, 339 U.S.App.D.C. 183 (D.C.Cir.1999), **284**

Lloyd A. Fry Roofing Co. v. United States Environmental Protection Agency, 554 F.2d 885 (8th Cir.1977), 443

Locke, United States v., 529 U.S. 89, 120 S.Ct. 1135, 146 L.Ed.2d 69 (2000), 55

Loggerhead Turtle v. County Council of Volusia County, Fla., 148 F.3d 1231 (11th Cir.1998), 652

Loggerhead Turtle v. County Council of Volusia County, Fla., 307 F.3d 1318 (11th Cir.2002), 516

Lopez, United States v., 514 U.S. 549, 115 S.Ct. 1624, 131 L.Ed.2d 626 (1995), 38

Louisiana–Pacific Corp. v. Asarco, Inc., 909 F.2d 1260 (9th Cir.1990), 536

LTV Steel Co., Inc., United States v., 118 F.Supp.2d 827 (N.D.Ohio 2000), 471

Lucas v. South Carolina Coastal Council, 505 U.S. 1003, 112 S.Ct. 2886, 120 L.Ed.2d 798 (1992), 51

Lujan v. Defenders of Wildlife, 504 U.S. 555, 112 S.Ct. 2130, 119 L.Ed.2d 351 (1992), **59,** 474

Lujan v. National Wildlife Federation, 497 U.S. 871, 110 S.Ct. 3177, 111 L.Ed.2d 695 (1990), 69, 75

Maine v. Taylor, 477 U.S. 131, 106 S.Ct. 2440, 91 L.Ed.2d 110 (1986), 56

Mall Properties, Inc. v. Marsh, 672 F.Supp. 561 (D.Mass.1987), 689

Mango, United States v., 199 F.3d 85 (2nd Cir.1999), 443

Marbled Murrelet v. Babbitt, 182 F.3d 1091 (9th Cir.1999), 516

Marbled Murrelet v. Babbitt, 83 F.3d 1060 (9th Cir.1996), 652

Markwardt v. City of Guthrie, 18 Okla. 32, 90 P. 26 (Okla.Terr.1907), 3

Marsh v. Oregon Natural Resources Council, 490 U.S. 360, 109 S.Ct. 1851, 104 L.Ed.2d 377 (1989), 83

Marshall v. Barlow's, Inc., 436 U.S. 307, 98 S.Ct. 1816, 56 L.Ed.2d 305 (1978), 423

Martin v. Reynolds Metals Co., 221 Or. 86, 342 P.2d 790 (Or.1959), 4

Matter of (see name of party)

McKittrick, United States v., 142 F.3d 1170 (9th Cir.1998), 655

Mead Corp., United States v., 533 U.S. 218, 121 S.Ct. 2164, 150 L.Ed.2d 292 (2001), 80, 133

Mesquite, City of v. Aladdin's Castle, Inc., 455 U.S. 283, 102 S.Ct. 1070, 71 L.Ed.2d 152 (1982), 495

Methow Valley Citizens Council v. Regional Forester, 833 F.2d 810 (9th Cir.1987), 121

Michigan, State of v. Thomas, 805 F.2d 176 (6th Cir.1986), 73

Miller v. Schoene, 276 U.S. 272, 48 S.Ct. 246, 72 L.Ed. 568 (1928), 53

Mississippi Commission on Natural Resources v. Costle, 625 F.2d 1269 (5th Cir.1980), 180

Mississippi River Revival, Inc. v. City of Minneapolis, Minn., 319 F.3d 1013 (8th Cir.2003), 500

Missouri, State of v. Holland, 252 U.S. 416, 40 S.Ct. 382, 64 L.Ed. 641 (1920), 37

Molinary v. Powell Mountain Coal Co., Inc., 125 F.3d 231 (4th Cir.1997), **716, 720**

Monsanto Co., United States v., 858 F.2d 160 (4th Cir.1988), 526, 541

Montana v. United States, 440 U.S. 147, 99 S.Ct. 970, 59 L.Ed.2d 210 (1979), 471

Morrison, United States v., 529 U.S. 598, 120 S.Ct. 1740, 146 L.Ed.2d 658 (2000), 38

Municipal Authority of Union Tp., United States v., 150 F.3d 259 (3rd Cir.1998), **432**

National Ass'n of Home Builders v. Babbitt, 130 F.3d 1041, 327 U.S.App.D.C. 248 (D.C.Cir.1997), 47

National Ass'n of Home Builders v. Norton, 340 F.3d 835 (9th Cir.2003), **602**

National Ass'n of Metal Finishers v. E.P.A., 719 F.2d 624 (3rd Cir.1983), 172, 177

National Credit Union Admin. v. First Nat. Bank & Trust Co., 522 U.S. 479, 118 S.Ct. 927, 140 L.Ed.2d 1 (1998), 75

National Lime Ass'n v. E.P.A., 233 F.3d 625, 344 U.S.App.D.C. 97 (D.C.Cir. 2000), 370

National Min. Ass'n v. United States Army Corps of Engineers, 145 F.3d 1399, 330 U.S.App.D.C. 329 (D.C.Cir. 1998), **678**

National Min. Ass'n v. United States Dept. of Interior, 70 F.3d 1345, 315 U.S.App. D.C. 133 (D.C.Cir.1995), 713, 720, 726

National Min. Ass'n v. United States E.P.A., 59 F.3d 1351, 313 U.S.App.D.C. 363 (D.C.Cir.1995), 371

National Solid Wastes Management Ass'n v. Alabama Dept. of Environmental Management, 910 F.2d 713 (11th Cir.1990), 56

National Wildlife Federation v. Coleman, 529 F.2d 359 (5th Cir.1976), 632

National Wildlife Federation v. E.P.A., 286 F.3d 554, 351 U.S.App.D.C. 42 (D.C.Cir. 2002), 78, 174

National Wildlife Federation v. Gorsuch, 693 F.2d 156, 224 U.S.App.D.C. 41 (D.C.Cir.1982), 130, 137

National Wildlife Federation v. Lujan, 950 F.2d 765, 292 U.S.App.D.C. 356 (D.C.Cir.1991), 710

National Wildlife Federation v. National Marine Fisheries Service, 254 F.Supp.2d 1196 (D.Or.2003), 636

Natural Resources Defense Council v. California Dept. of Transp., 96 F.3d 420 (9th Cir.1996), 720

Natural Resources Defense Council v. United States Dept. of the Interior, 113 F.3d 1121 (9th Cir.1997), 613

Natural Resources Defense Council, Inc. v. Costle, 568 F.2d 1369, 186 U.S.App.D.C. 147 (D.C.Cir.1977), 135

Natural Resources Defense Council, Inc. v. Texaco Refining and Marketing, Inc., 2 F.3d 493 (3rd Cir.1993), 493

Natural Resources Defense Council, Inc. v. Train, 545 F.2d 320 (2nd Cir. 1976), **234**, 238, **256**

Natural Resources Defense Council, Inc. v. United States E.P.A., 16 F.3d 1395 (4th Cir.1993), 181

Natural Resources Defense Council, Inc. v. United States E.P.A., 966 F.2d 1292 (9th Cir.1992), 136

Natural Resources Defense Council, Inc. v. United States E.P.A., 863 F.2d 1420 (9th Cir.1988), 174

Natural Resources Defense Council, Inc. v. United States E.P.A., 859 F.2d 156, 273 U.S.App.D.C. 180 (D.C.Cir. 1988), **152, 158**

Natural Resources Defense Council, Inc. v. United States E.P.A., 824 F.2d 1146, 263 U.S.App.D.C. 166 (D.C.Cir.1987), 368

Natural Resources Defense Council, Inc. v. United States E.P.A., 822 F.2d 104, 261 U.S.App.D.C. 372 (D.C.Cir.1987), 174

Needham, In re, 354 F.3d 340 (5th Cir. 2003), 675

Nevada Land Action Ass'n v. United States Forest Service, 8 F.3d 713 (9th Cir. 1993), 74

New Castle County v. Halliburton N United States Corp., 111 F.3d 1116 (3rd Cir. 1997), 585, 589

New Mexico Cattle Growers Ass'n v. United States Fish and Wildlife Service, 248 F.3d 1277 (10th Cir.2001), 613

Newton County Wildlife Ass'n v. Rogers, 141 F.3d 803 (8th Cir.1998), **628**

New York v. Burger, 482 U.S. 691, 107 S.Ct. 2636, 96 L.Ed.2d 601 (1987), 423

New York, State of v. General Elec. Co., 592 F.Supp. 291 (N.D.N.Y.1984), 521, 542

New York, State of v. Lashins Arcade Co., 91 F.3d 353 (2nd Cir.1996), 557

New York, State of v. Shore Realty Corp., 759 F.2d 1032 (2nd Cir.1985), 521, **523**

New York v. United States, 505 U.S. 144, Nuclear Reg. Rep. P 20553, 112 S.Ct. 2408, 120 L.Ed.2d 120 (1992), 49

Nollan v. California Coastal Com'n, 483 U.S. 825, 107 S.Ct. 3141, 97 L.Ed.2d 677 (1987), 52

North and South Rivers Watershed Ass'n, Inc. v. Town of Scituate, 949 F.2d 552 (1st Cir.1991), 504

North Carolina, State of v. F.E.R.C., 112 F.3d 1175, 324 U.S.App.D.C. 209 (D.C.Cir.1997), 201

Northernaire Plating Co., United States v., 670 F.Supp. 742 (W.D.Mich.1987), 521, 557

Northern Spotted Owl (Strix Occidentalis Caurina) v. Hodel, 716 F.Supp. 479 (W.D.Wash.1988), 595

Northwest Environmental Advocates v. City of Portland, 56 F.3d 979 (9th Cir.1995), 184

Norton v. Southern Utah Wilderness Alliance, 542 U.S. 55, 124 S.Ct. 2373, 159 L.Ed.2d 137 (2004), 75

No Spray Coalition, Inc. v. City of New York, 351 F.3d 602 (2nd Cir.2003), 136

Nurad, Inc. v. William E. Hooper & Sons Co., 966 F.2d 837 (4th Cir.1992), 526

Oakland Cannabis Buyers' Co-op., United States v., 532 U.S. 483, 121 S.Ct. 1711, 149 L.Ed.2d 722 (2001), 431

Oconomowoc Lake, Village of v. Dayton Hudson Corp., 24 F.3d 962 (7th Cir. 1994), 141

Ohio Edison Co., United States v., 276 F.Supp.2d 829 (S.D.Ohio 2003), **317**

Ohio Forestry Ass'n, Inc. v. Sierra Club, 523 U.S. 726, 118 S.Ct. 1665, 140 L.Ed.2d 921 (1998), 79

Ohio Valley Environmental Coalition v. Horinko, 279 F.Supp.2d 732 (S.D.W.Va. 2003), 180

OHM Remediation Services v. Evans Cooperage Co., Inc., 116 F.3d 1574 (5th Cir. 1997), 587

Oil, Chemical and Atomic Workers Intern. Union, AFL–CIO v. Department of Energy, 288 F.3d 452, 351 U.S.App.D.C. 199 (D.C.Cir.2002), 516

Olin Corp., United States v., 107 F.3d 1506 (11th Cir.1997), 47, 526

150 Acres of Land, United States v., 204 F.3d 698 (6th Cir.2000), 557, 558

O'Neil v. Picillo, 883 F.2d 176 (1st Cir. 1989), **547**

Oregon Natural Desert Ass'n v. Dombeck, 172 F.3d 1092 (9th Cir.1998), 200

Oregon Natural Resource Council v. Turner, 863 F.Supp. 1277 (D.Or.1994), 613

Oregon Natural Resources Council v. Daley, 6 F.Supp.2d 1139 (D.Or.1998), 596

Oregon Waste Systems, Inc. v. Department of Environmental Quality of State of Or., 511 U.S. 93, 114 S.Ct. 1345, 128 L.Ed.2d 13 (1994), 57

Overholt, United States v., 307 F.3d 1231 (10th Cir.2002), 464

Owen Elec. Steel Co. of South Carolina, Inc. v. Browner, 37 F.3d 146 (4th Cir.1994), 401

Pacific Coast Federation of Fishermen's Ass'n, Inc. v. National Marine Fisheries Service, 265 F.3d 1028 (9th Cir.2001), 631

Pacific Hide & Fur Depot, Inc., United States v., 716 F.Supp. 1341 (D.Idaho 1989), 558

Pacific Legal Foundation v. Andrus, 657 F.2d 829 (6th Cir.1981), 616

Palazzolo v. Rhode Island, 533 U.S. 606, 121 S.Ct. 2448, 150 L.Ed.2d 592 (2001), 53

Penn Cent. Transp. Co. v. City of New York, 438 U.S. 104, 98 S.Ct. 2646, 57 L.Ed.2d 631 (1978), 51

Pennsylvania v. Union Gas Co., 491 U.S. 1, 109 S.Ct. 2273, 105 L.Ed.2d 1 (1989), 50

Pennsylvania Coal Co. v. Mahon, 260 U.S. 393, 43 S.Ct. 158, 67 L.Ed. 322 (1922), 50

Pennsylvania, Dept. of Environmental Resources, Com. of v. E.P.A., 618 F.2d 991 (3rd Cir.1980), 174

Pennsylvania Federation of Sportsmen's Clubs, Inc. v. Hess, 297 F.3d 310 (3rd Cir.2002), 720

Pennsylvania Urban Development Corp. v. Golen, 708 F.Supp. 669 (E.D.Pa.1989), 587

Pfohl Brothers Landfill Site Steering Committee v. Allied Waste Systems, Inc., 255 F.Supp.2d 134 (W.D.N.Y.2003), 588

Philadelphia, City of v. New Jersey, 437 U.S. 617, 98 S.Ct. 2531, 57 L.Ed.2d 475 (1978), 56

Pinal Creek Group v. Newmont Min. Corp., 118 F.3d 1298 (9th Cir.1997), 585

Platt v. City of Waterbury, 72 Conn. 531, 45 A. 154 (Conn.1900), 3

Plaza Health Laboratories, Inc., United States v., 3 F.3d 643 (2nd Cir.1993), **143**

PMC, Inc. v. Sherwin–Williams Co., 151 F.3d 610 (7th Cir.1998), 589

Pneumo Abex Corp. v. High Point, Thomasville and Denton R. Co., 142 F.3d 769 (4th Cir.1998), 542

Power Engineering Co., United States v., 303 F.3d 1232 (10th Cir.2002), 471

Printz v. United States, 521 U.S. 898, 117 S.Ct. 2365, 138 L.Ed.2d 914 (1997), 49

Pronsolino v. Nastri, 291 F.3d 1123 (9th Cir.2002), **205**

Public Citizen, Inc. v. United States E.P.A., 343 F.3d 449 (5th Cir.2003), **342**

Public Interest Research Group of New Jersey, Inc. v. Hercules, Inc., 50 F.3d 1239 (3rd Cir.1995), 473

Public Interest Research Group of New Jersey, Inc. v. Magnesium Elektron, Inc., 123 F.3d 111 (3rd Cir.1997), 479

Public Interest Research Group of New Jersey, Inc. v. Powell Duffryn Terminals Inc., 913 F.2d 64 (3rd Cir.1990), 439, 480

Public Interest Research Group of New Jersey, Inc. v. Windall, 51 F.3d 1179 (3rd Cir.1995), 517

PUD No. 1 of Jefferson County v. Washington Dept. of Ecology, 511 U.S. 700, 114 S.Ct. 1900, 128 L.Ed.2d 716 (1994), 181, **193**

Puerto Rico Campers' Ass'n. v. Puerto Rico Aqueduct and Sewer Authority, 219 F.Supp.2d 201 (D.Puerto Rico 2002), 500

Pyramid Lake Paiute Tribe of Indians v. United States Dept. of Navy, 898 F.2d 1410 (9th Cir.1990), 617

Rancho Viejo, LLC v. Norton, 323 F.3d 1062, 355 U.S.App.D.C. 303 (D.C.Cir. 2003), 47

Rapanos, United States v., 339 F.3d 447 (6th Cir.2003), 675

Reading Co., Matter of, 115 F.3d 1111 (3rd Cir.1997), 589

Redwing Carriers, Inc. v. Saraland Apartments, 94 F.3d 1489 (11th Cir.1996), 537, 585

Reeves, Inc. v. Stake, 447 U.S. 429, 100 S.Ct. 2271, 65 L.Ed.2d 244 (1980), 57

Reilly Tar & Chemical Corp., United States v., 606 F.Supp. 412 (D.Minn.1985), 444

Riley v. St. Luke's Episcopal Hosp., 252 F.3d 749 (5th Cir.2001), 501

Riverside Bayview Homes, Inc., United States v., 474 U.S. 121, 106 S.Ct. 455, 88 L.Ed.2d 419 (1985), 138, **659**

Robertson v. Methow Valley Citizens Council, 490 U.S. 332, 109 S.Ct. 1835, 104 L.Ed.2d 351 (1989), 84, **114, 123**

Rock Island, Ill., City of, United States v., 182 F.Supp.2d 690 (C.D.Ill.2001), 472

Rohm and Haas Co., United States v., 790 F.Supp. 1255 (E.D.Pa.1992), 558

Ruckelshaus v. Sierra Club, 463 U.S. 680, 103 S.Ct. 3274, 77 L.Ed.2d 938 (1983), 516

Rumpke of Indiana, Inc. v. Cummins Engine Co., Inc., 107 F.3d 1235 (7th Cir. 1997), 587

Safe Air for Everyone v. Meyer, 373 F.3d 1035 (9th Cir.2004), 402

San Francisco BayKeeper, Inc. v. Tosco Corp., 309 F.3d 1153 (9th Cir.2002), 473, 500

Save Our Community v. United States E.P.A., 971 F.2d 1155 (5th Cir.1992), 677

Save the Bay, Inc. v. Administrator of Environmental Protection Agency, 556 F.2d 1282 (5th Cir.1977), 162

Scott v. City of Hammond, Ind., 741 F.2d 992 (7th Cir.1984), 204

Selkirk Conservation Alliance v. Forsgren, 336 F.3d 944 (9th Cir.2003), 636

Seminole Tribe of Florida v. Florida, 517 U.S. 44, 116 S.Ct. 1114, 134 L.Ed.2d 252 (1996), 50

Serafini, United States v., 706 F.Supp. 346 (M.D.Pa.1988), 558

Shell Oil Co. v. E.P.A., 950 F.2d 741, 292 U.S.App.D.C. 332 (D.C.Cir.1991), 81, 407

Sierra Club v. City of Little Rock, 351 F.3d 840 (8th Cir.2003), 516

Sierra Club v. E.P.A., 322 F.3d 718, 355 U.S.App.D.C. 258 (D.C.Cir.2003), 516

Sierra Club v. Glickman, 156 F.3d 606 (5th Cir.1998), 617

Sierra Club v. Hankinson, 939 F.Supp. 865 (N.D.Ga.1996), 386

Sierra Club v. Marsh, 816 F.2d 1376 (9th Cir.1987), 630

Sierra Club v. Morton, 405 U.S. 727, 92 S.Ct. 1361, 31 L.Ed.2d 636 (1972), 58

Sierra Club v. United States Army Corps of Engineers, 295 F.3d 1209 (11th Cir. 2002), 630

Sierra Club v. United States Fish and Wildlife Service, 245 F.3d 434 (5th Cir.2001), 613

Sierra Club v. Whitman, 268 F.3d 898 (9th Cir.2001), 424

Skidmore v. Swift & Co., 323 U.S. 134, 65 S.Ct. 161, 89 L.Ed. 124 (1944), 80, 133

Solid Waste Agency of Northern Cook County v. United States Army Corps of Engineers, 531 U.S. 159, 121 S.Ct. 675, 148 L.Ed.2d 576 (2001), 46, 139, **664**

South Dakota v. Dole, 483 U.S. 203, 107 S.Ct. 2793, 97 L.Ed.2d 171 (1987), 36

Southern Pines Associates by Goldmeier v. United States, 912 F.2d 713 (4th Cir.1990), **439**

South Florida Water Management Dist. v. Miccosukee Tribe of Indians, 541 U.S. 95, 124 S.Ct. 1537, 158 L.Ed.2d 264 (2004), 137, 677

Southwest Center for Biological Diversity v. Babbitt, 939 F.Supp. 49 (D.D.C.1996), 596

Speach, United States v., 968 F.2d 795 (9th Cir.1992), 464

Spirit of Sage Council v. Norton, 294 F.Supp.2d 67 (D.D.C.2003), 654

Sporhase v. Nebraska, ex rel. Douglas, 458 U.S. 941, 102 S.Ct. 3456, 73 L.Ed.2d 1254 (1982), 56

Staples v. United States, 511 U.S. 600, 114 S.Ct. 1793, 128 L.Ed.2d 608 (1994), 465

State of (see name of state)

Steel Co. v. Citizens for a Better Environment, 523 U.S. 83, 118 S.Ct. 1003, 140 L.Ed.2d 210 (1998), 69, 492

Strahan v. Coxe, 127 F.3d 155 (1st Cir. 1997), 653

Student Public Interest Research Group of New Jersey, Inc. v. Fritzsche, Dodge & Olcott, Inc., 759 F.2d 1131 (3rd Cir. 1985), 502

Sun Co., Inc. (R&M) v. Browning–Ferris, Inc., 124 F.3d 1187 (10th Cir.1997), 585, 589

Supporters to Oppose Pollution, Inc. v. Heritage Group, 973 F.2d 1320 (7th Cir. 1992), 504

Susquehanna Fertilizer Co. v. Malone, 73 Md. 268, 20 A. 900 (Md.1890), 3

Sylvester v. United States Army Corps of Engineers, 882 F.2d 407 (9th Cir.1989), 687

Tahoe–Sierra Preservation Council, Inc. v. Tahoe Regional Planning Agency, 535 U.S. 302, 122 S.Ct. 1465, 152 L.Ed.2d 517 (2002), 51

Taylor, United States v., 1993 WL 760996 (W.D.Mich.1993), 558

Tennessee Valley Authority v. Hill, 437 U.S. 153, 98 S.Ct. 2279, 57 L.Ed.2d 117 (1978), 592

Tennessee Valley Authority v. Whitman, 336 F.3d 1236 (11th Cir.2003), 443

Texans United for a Safe Economy Educ. Fund v. Crown Cent. Petroleum Corp., 207 F.3d 789 (5th Cir.2000), 502

Thomas v. Peterson, 753 F.2d 754 (9th Cir.1985), **620**

Thompson/Center Arms Co., United States v., 504 U.S. 505, 112 S.Ct. 2102, 119 L.Ed.2d 308 (1992), 149

3M Co. (Minnesota Min. and Mfg.) v. Browner, 17 F.3d 1453, 305 U.S.App. D.C. 100 (D.C.Cir.1994), 455

TIC Inv. Corp., United States v., 68 F.3d 1082 (8th Cir.1995), 542

Train v. Colorado Public Interest Research Group, Inc., 426 U.S. 1, 96 S.Ct. 1938, 48 L.Ed.2d 434 (1976), 135

Train v. Natural Resources Defense Council, Inc., 421 U.S. 60, 95 S.Ct. 1470, 43 L.Ed.2d 731 (1975), **257**

Trustees for Alaska v. E.P.A., 749 F.2d 549 (9th Cir.1984), 184

Umatilla Waterquality Protective Ass'n, Inc. v. Smith Frozen Foods, Inc., 962 F.Supp. 1312 (D.Or.1997), 140

Union of Needletrades, Indus. and Textile Employees, AFL–CIO, CLC v. United States I.N.S., 336 F.3d 200 (2nd Cir. 2003), 516

United Haulers Ass'n, Inc. v. Oneida–Herkimer Solid Waste Management Authority, 261 F.3d 245 (2nd Cir.2001), 57

United States v. ____ (see opposing party)

USA Recycling, Inc. v. Town of Babylon, 66 F.3d 1272 (2nd Cir.1995), 57

United Technologies Corp. v. Browning–Ferris Industries, Inc., 33 F.3d 96 (1st Cir.1994), 585, 588

Usery v. Turner Elkhorn Mining Co., 428 U.S. 1, 96 S.Ct. 2882, 49 L.Ed.2d 752 (1976), 526

Village of (see name of village)

Wade, United States v., 577 F.Supp. 1326 (E.D.Pa.1983), **538**

Ward, United States v., 618 F.Supp. 884 (E.D.N.C.1985), 521, 541

Washington Toxic Coalition v. EPA, No. 01–132C (W.D.Wash.2002), 630

Washington Wilderness Coalition v. Hecla Min. Co., 870 F.Supp. 983 (E.D.Wash. 1994), 140

Weinberger v. Romero–Barcelo, 456 U.S. 305, 102 S.Ct. 1798, 72 L.Ed.2d 91 (1982), **425**

Weitzenhoff, United States v., 35 F.3d 1275 (9th Cir.1993), **456**

Western Properties Service Corp. v. Shell Oil Co., 358 F.3d 678 (9th Cir.2004), 588

West Virginia Coal Ass'n v. Reilly, 728 F.Supp. 1276 (S.D.W.Va.1989), 721

Weyerhaeuser Co. v. Costle, 590 F.2d 1011, 191 U.S.App.D.C. 309 (D.C.Cir. 1978), **164**

Whitman v. American Trucking Associations, 531 U.S. 457, 121 S.Ct. 903, 149 L.Ed.2d 1 (2001), 6, **249, 280**

Wichita, Kansas, City of v. Trustees of APCO Oil Corp. Liquidating Trust, 306 F.Supp.2d 1040 (D.Kan.2003), 534

Wickard v. Filburn, 317 U.S. 111, 63 S.Ct. 82, 87 L.Ed. 122 (1942), 37

Willson v. Black–Bird Creek Marsh Co., 27 U.S. 245, 2 Pet. 245, 7 L.Ed. 412 (1829), 656

Wilshire Westwood Associates v. Atlantic Richfield Corp., 881 F.2d 801 (9th Cir. 1989), 520

Wilson, United States v., 133 F.3d 251 (4th Cir.1997), 674, 677

Winnebago Tribe of Nebraska v. Ray, 621 F.2d 269 (8th Cir.1980), **101**

Wisconsin Elec. Power Co. v. Reilly, 893 F.2d 901 (7th Cir.1990), **290, 307**

Wyoming Farm Bureau Federation v. Babbitt, 199 F.3d 1224 (10th Cir.2000), 655

Young, Ex parte, 209 U.S. 123, 28 S.Ct. 441, 52 L.Ed. 714 (1908), 50, 720

*

LEGAL PROTECTION OF THE ENVIRONMENT

*

Chapter 1

INTRODUCTION

I. INTRODUCTION

Environmental Law is law designed to protect the environment, and the plants and animals that rely on it, including us. In the scale of things, however, the law is a puny instrument to protect the environment. The environment is affected by so much that is not subject to human law. Nature itself alters the environment. A volcano erupts causing massive environmental effects, sometimes even worldwide. A hurricane visits devastation on a wide region.

Environmental degradation through human action is not just a modern phenomenon. Humans have been altering the environment since prehistoric times. Historians today believe that the inhabitants of Easter Island, who erected the great stone statutes, essentially destroyed their civilization through overgrazing. John Fenley and Paul Bahn, THE ENIGMAS OF EASTER ISLAND: ISLAND ON THE EDGE (2003). The desert of what is now Iraq was once the fertile crescent that gave birth to the earliest human civilizations but which was destroyed through water diversions and non-sustainable farming practices. Jared Diamond, GUNS, GERMS, AND STEEL (1997). Population density and civilization combine to place great stresses on natural resources both as a source of food, fiber, and minerals and as a repository for human-generated waste. Sometimes the harm to the environment may make life more difficult or less attractive for humans; sometimes the harm is more direct, causing disease or injury to humans.

Civilization also brings law, and one response to human-caused environmental harm is law designed to reduce or eliminate such harm. For law to be effective, however, it must exist within a regime that values and enforces law. In the United States "the rule of law" is an important public value, but even here the "law" sometimes seems to be subordinate to other values reflecting the exigencies of the time. In developing nations, law may be only a marginal concern. In the world-wide community, one may well ask whether international law is law at all.

II. SOME PERSPECTIVES ON ENVIRONMENTAL LAW

A. History of Environmental Law

There are two enduring threads in environmental law over the past two or three centuries. One focuses on protecting the environment in its natural state, whether for moral, esthetic, economic, or recreational purposes. The other focuses on protecting the health of humans, animals, and plants from the polluting effects of human activity.

The first thread itself has two distinguishable lines. From Thoreau's *Walden,* an 1854 paean to the natural world and the simple life, to John Muir's founding of the Sierra Club in 1892, the call of nature as a source of inspiration and spiritual awakening found many adherents, whom we today call Preservationists. Preservationism was responsible for the original creation of the national parks and various reserved federal lands. Today, Preservationism is reflected in the Wilderness Act, the Endangered Species Act, and the National Historic Preservation Act, among other laws. The counter to Preservationism was Conservationism, and its leading figure was Gifford Pinchot, the father of the United States Forest Service. The theme of Conservationism, in Pinchot's words, was "the greatest good of the greatest number in the long run." In his day, Conservationism strove to limit the use and development of federal natural resources so that they would not destroy the system that created and maintained them. Today we know this as sustainable development. While both Preservationism and Conservationism are "environmental," the two can conflict precisely because the one stresses non-use values and the other embraces use values.

Both Preservationism and Conservationism focused on federal (and to a lesser extent state) lands, both because private lands were more likely already developed and because the regulation of private lands by limiting development was viewed as raising constitutional difficulties. Until the second half of the Twentieth Century, however, most federal lands were not protected by any environmental laws or considerations. National Parks, then and now, constituted a relatively small amount of federal land. Rather, federal policy generally favored the development of "unused" public lands for homesteading, grazing, mining, and timbering. This policy is perhaps epitomized by the 1872 General Mining Act, still in effect today, that allows unreserved federal lands to be used for "hard rock" mining without any environmental controls and without having to pay any royalties to the federal government. Thus, both Preservationism and Conservationism were environmental counterweights to the development-without-restriction mentality of the past, and the widespread adoption of environmental laws to protect public lands is of very recent vintage.

Between the two movements, Conservationism was, as might be imagined, the more successful. Preservationism succeeded in those areas in which development was not generally perceived as likely or profitable. For example, wilderness areas principally were established in timber-poor, steep-slope areas where forestry, grazing, and mining appeared unwarranted. Although today the conflicts between the Endangered Species Act and development are obvious, they were not obvious at the time of its passage. Then, it was thought that the major threat to endangered species was hunting. Holly Doremus, *Adaptive Management, the Endangered Species Act, and the Institutional Challenges of "New Age" Environmental Protection*, 41 Washburn L.J. 50, 57 (2001). Where development or use was possible, Conservationism was the preferred environmental solution because it promised protection of the environment but economic use at the same time. For example, the Federal Land Policy and Management Act (FLPMA), which generally governs public lands, establishes a policy of multiple use and sustained yield that is to be accomplished through systematic planning. The National Forest Management Act likewise requires planning for the various National Forests so that they may support not only timber harvesting and grazing but also recreation and wildlife habitat. Even the National Parks, in which traditional economic development and use, such as silviculture, mining, and grazing, are prohibited, are today governed more by Conservationism ideals as the Parks become recreational venues for tourists.

As opposed to environmentalism, pollution control has a long history. Urbanization and the Industrial Revolution both had environmental impacts that were hard to miss. However, just as the impacts were generally felt locally, the solutions were local in nature. For example, smoke control ordinances were passed by cities in the 19th Century, so that by the turn of the century most large American cities had such ordinances. Similarly, the first water pollution problem related to the need to provide safe water for drinking, washing, and cooking, and in the 19th Century large American cities created municipal water supply systems. This development made flush toilets feasible, but it naturally led to the second water pollution problem: disposing of the wastes and waste water in a safe manner, which resulted in the building of sewer systems. These at least transported the wastes from the streets and yards of the cities to the rivers, lakes, and oceans. Unfortunately, these fresh water sources were usually the very sources from which municipalities obtained their drinking water. Health problems could be avoided, however, by treating drinking water through filtration and chlorination, thus reducing the incentive to treat the waste water itself.

State common law actions were also used to address pollution issues. Usually commercial interests adversely affected by air or water pollution in sufficient degrees to justify litigation brought nuisance actions for both air and water pollution. For example, in *Platt v. City of Waterbury*, 72 Conn. 531, 45 A. 154 (1900), the owners of a mill sued because the city disposed of sewage waste into the river making it unfit for the mill's purposes. The court found a nuisance and entered an injunction that within three years the city would have to remove the sewage from its waste water. In *Markwardt v. City of Guthrie*, 18 Okla. 32, 90 P. 26 (1907), a farmer sued a city for polluting a stream that he used for irrigating his crops and watering his livestock. The court held that such pollution can be a nuisance. Similarly, in *Susquehanna Fertilizer Co. v.*

Malone, 73 Md. 268, 20 A. 900 (1890), the owner of a hotel and rental properties brought suit against a nearby fertilizer company because the air emissions harmed his business; the court found that there was a nuisance. Later, plaintiffs also brought suits involving air pollution as trespass claims. *See, e.g., Martin v. Reynolds Metals Co.*, 221 Or. 86, 342 P.2d 790 (1959) (aluminum plant air emissions that poisoned cattle on plaintiff's land, making it unfit for raising livestock, deemed a trespass).

While air emissions especially could extend over greater distances, even crossing state and national boundaries, this did not mean that common law solutions, originally developed for local problems in state courts, could not still be applicable. For example, in *Georgia v. Tennessee Copper Co.*, 206 U.S. 230, 27 S.Ct. 618, 51 L.Ed. 1038 (1907), Georgia sued in the United States Supreme Court to enjoin the discharge of sulphur dioxide in Tennessee that became sulphuric acid in the atmosphere resulting in "wholesale destruction of forests, orchards, and crops" in Georgia. The Supreme Court found a public nuisance and enjoined the defendants from discharging the emissions. *See also Trail Smelter Case (United States v. Canada)*, Arbitral Tribunal, 1941, 3 UN Rep. Int'l Arb. Awards (1941) (an international tribunal citing American common law cases rendered a judgment that the smelter in Canada must modify its operations to reduce substantially its emissions of sulphur dioxide that were adversely affecting the environment in the United States).

There were, however, a number of shortcomings with common law solutions. The cost and difficulty of litigation, especially before the widespread use of class actions, made lawsuits for pollution infeasible unless the pollution caused serious economic harm to someone with enough resources to bring a case against a major industrial (or municipal) polluter. Unless a particular polluter was especially egregious, there could be a difficulty of proof as to the source of the pollution causing the injury. Even when the proof was there, the nature of the appropriate remedy was difficult. Courts struggled with the idea of closing down a major industrial facility when the cost of closing it down dwarfed the financial costs of the pollution injury. *See, e.g., Boomer v. Atlantic Cement Co.*, 26 N.Y.2d 219, 309 N.Y.S.2d 312, 257 N.E.2d 870 (1970) (refusing to enjoin unconditionally the operation of a cement company; instead conditioning an injunction on the payment of damages to plaintiffs for past and future injuries). Finally, these common law remedies all acted as "after-the-fact" remedies; they might act to stop or compensate for injuries once suffered, but they were not available to stop the injury from occurring in the first place.

Nonetheless, common law actions continue to play an important role in both environmental regulation and health and safety regulation. The general elimination of asbestos from the economy was not a result of state or federal regulation but the result of the dogged persistence of a small number of lawyers who first established in court the health effects of exposure to asbestos and the organized attempts by the asbestos industry to deny and cover up those effects. While tobacco products have certainly not been eliminated from the economy and federal and state regulation both play a role reducing their sales, the effect of lawsuits establishing product liability on tobacco companies for the harm caused by cigarettes has had perhaps the biggest impact on sales. From John Travolta in Civil Action to Julia Roberts in Erin Brockovic, the popular media have portrayed some of the effects of toxic tort litigation brought under traditional common law tort theories.

Some conservative think tanks have suggested that private enforcement of common law rights should substitute for government regulatory programs. *See generally* Terry Anderson and Donald Leal, FREE MARKET ENVIRONMENTALISM, Rev. Ed. (2001). When presented with the history of tort law's inadequacies, in particular with respect to air and water pollution, these organizations respond that the failure in these areas arises out of the lack of a property rights system for these media, which they maintain is the basis of effective tort law remedies. Therefore, they argue for the creation of property rights in air, water, and public resources, such as national forests, grazing lands, and even national parks. Others have suggested that these suggestions are unrealistic. *See, e.g.,* William Funk, *Free Market Environmentalism: Wonder Drug or Snake Oil?,* 15 Harv. J.L. Pub. Pol'y 511 (1992).

At the same time, other conservative think tanks have suggested that existing tort law has resulted in regulation by litigation, and they believe this is the worst form of regulation. *See, e.g.,* Kip Viscusi, Robert Hahn, and Robert Litan, REGULATION THROUGH LITIGATION (2002).

Whatever the ultimate result of this debate over the use of common law remedies as a substitute for government regulation, in the 1960s the consensus clearly was that the common law was not adequate. The year 1970 was a watershed in environmental law. On January 1, President Nixon signed into law the National Environmental Policy Act; on April 22, the nation celebrated the first Earth Day, a day of mass demonstrations in the nation's largest cities and its capital, and teach-ins at thousands of high schools and university campuses; the Environmental Protection Agency, the National Oceanic and Atmospheric Administration, and the Council on Environmental Quality all were created; and on the last day of the year, the Clean Air Act became law. The following years likewise saw a cascade of new environmental laws. The Federal Water Pollution Control Act, which we now call the Clean Water Act, was passed in 1972. In 1973 Congress passed the Endangered Species Act. In 1976, the Resource Conservation and Recovery Act, aimed primarily at controlling the disposal of hazardous wastes, became law; in 1977, the Surface Mining and Reclamation Act was adopted to regulate the effects of surface coal mining; and in 1980 the Comprehensive Environmental Response, Compensation and Liability Act was passed to clean up what had been the largely unregulated disposal of hazardous wastes on the land before 1976. The era of federal responsibility for and attention to the environment had arrived.

B. Types of Regulations

Government can regulate its own and private conduct in a variety of ways, and it can sometimes promote protection of the environment without "regulation" at all. Across the range of environmental laws, there is a broad array of regulatory methodologies.

Command-and-Control regulations are regulations that direct people to do certain specific things or prohibit them from doing certain specific things. Thus, the Clean Air Act's requirement for EPA to set maximum pollution emission limits on factories for certain types of pollutants results in command-and-control regulations applicable to those factories. Command-and-control regulations can take a variety of forms. For example, a pollution limit might be set on a **health-based** standard; that is, the emission standard is set on the basis of achieving a certain level of public health. Most of the early toxic pollutant regulatory requirements were supposed to be based on health concerns. Moreover, EPA is to set the primary National Ambient Air Quality Standards under the Clean Air Act at a level "requisite to protect the public health" "with an adequate margin of safety." 42 U.S.C. § 7409(b)(1). Such an approach ignores the costs involved in achieving this standard. *See Whitman v. American Trucking Ass'ns*, 531 U.S. 457, 121 S.Ct. 903, 149 L.Ed.2d 1 (2001).

This approach can be contrasted to the **technology-based** or **feasibility-limited** approaches. Under these approaches the regulation is set based upon what industry or a subset of industry can achieve in light of the present state of technology or of the economic abilities of the industry. Here the focus is more on costs rather than the health or environmental benefits of the regulation. For example, under the Clean Water Act, the general requirement for factories discharging toxic materials is that they use the "best available technology economically achievable." 33 U.S.C. § 1311(b)(2)(A). Similarly, new sources of pollution under the Clean Water Act must use "the best available demonstrated control technology." 33 U.S.C. § 1316(1). Perhaps what industry can attain under these approaches does not protect public health or the environment very well, or perhaps what industry can attain is greater than necessary to protect the public health or the environment. Technically, these standards ignore health and environmental considerations, although as we will see later, they may be motivated by health considerations. Under the Occupational Safety and Health Act, workers are to be protected from toxic materials so that "to the extent feasible, ... no employee will suffer material impairment of health or functional capacity...." 29 U.S.C. § 655(b)(5). Here, health concerns are not ignored, but health benefits are trumped by feasibility considerations. In this context, "feasibility" relates to the economic ability of an industry to continue in existence. In other words, a standard is not feasible if it would put an industry out of business. This does not mean that the standard might not put an individual company out of business.

Yet another approach is to set the requirement based upon a **balance of the benefits against the costs**. This can be done implicitly by prohibiting *unreasonable* risks to the health or environment, such as in the Federal Insecticide, Fungicide and Rodenticide Act's permitting requirement for pesticides, *see* 7 U.S.C. § 136a(c)(5)(C) & (D), or it can be done explicitly by requiring a cost-benefit analysis. For example, the Safe Drinking Water Act, after requiring that Maximum Contaminant Levels for drinking water be set "as close . . . as is feasible" to the level that will result in no anticipated adverse effects on health, 42 U.S.C. § 300g–1(b)(4) then authorizes EPA to reduce that protection to a level that "maximizes health risk reduction benefits at a cost that is justified by the benefits." 42 U.S.C. § 300g–1(b)(6)(A).

However the standard is derived, command-and-control regulations can specify that standard as either a **design standard** or as a **performance standard**. For example, an agency might specify a particular kind of equipment in a regulation, because the agency has determined that that type of equipment will achieve the performance required. This would be a design standard. Alternatively, the agency could specify in the regulation only the outcome required, such as a certain amount of pollution per hour, without specifying how that outcome is to be achieved. This is a performance standard. Especially when the statute requires either a technology basis or feasibility basis for the regulation, an agency will need to determine that a particular type of equipment does in fact exist and will in fact achieve a certain result in order for the standard to be feasible. At that point, the agency could merely specify that equipment as the regulatory requirement or set as the performance standard what that equipment actually achieves. There are benefits and detriments to each approach.

Performance standards provide the regulated entity more freedom in how to achieve the desired outcome, and concomitantly maximize economic efficiency by providing incentives to achieve the desired outcome at a lower cost than the particular means identified by the agency. Design standards, however, provide regulated entities enhanced certainty as to how to comply and usually make enforcement easier. Traditionally, environmental statutes did not specify whether regulations should be expressed as design standards or performance standards, but some more recent statutes, consistent with increased interest in enhancing regulatory efficiency, have specified the use of performance standards. *See, e.g.*, 42 U.S.C. § 300g–1(b)(4)(E)(Safe Drinking Water Act).

Most of the first generation of environmental laws utilized the command-and-control regulatory methodology. More recently, there is increasing interest in so-called "**second generation**" strategies. These have in common a desire to make environmental protection more efficient–achieving the same results at lower cost–and to create incentives for improving environmental enforcement beyond what the law may require. One form of second generation strategies involves **market-based** regulations, particularly what are known as "cap-and-trade" regulations. Market-based regulations refer to regulations that allow certain market concepts to operate within a more general regulatory environment in order to achieve greater efficiencies. Best-known are the cap-and-trade provisions of the Acid Rain Program of the Clean Air Act. 42 U.S.C. §§ 7651 et.seq. Under this program, rather than set limits for pollutants emitted at particular facilities, there is a nationwide "cap" on the amount of emissions of sulfur dioxide from coal-fired power plants, which is lower than the historical emissions. Facilities must have an allowance for each ton emitted and the number of allowances are set based upon the cap. The idea is that individual facilities may either reduce their emissions so that the allowances issued to them are sufficient to cover their emissions, or they may purchase allowances from other emitters, who do not need them because they have reduced their emissions below the amount for which they have allowances. Thus, those facilities that can reduce their emissions least expensively will do so, while those for whom it is more expensive will not. The result is, in theory, the most efficient reduction in emissions. Moreover, such a program can also create a spur to investment in environmental protection, because facilities that achieve reductions greater than required are able to sell their excess allowances to other facilities that may need them. Overall, the Acid Rain Program is considered a substantial success. *See, e.g.*, EPA, Acid Rain Program 2001 Progress Report (2002).

As a result of its success, there is an increasing tendency to use cap-and-trade and other trading systems in other situations. Whether they are appropriate in certain situations is, however, hotly debated. That is, when it does not matter where the pollutant is emitted, such as with greenhouse gases and to a large degree with precursors of acid rain, trading between different emitters, so long as the total emitted is reduced, may be efficient without adverse consequences. If, though, the pollutant emitted has locally undesirable effects, as is usually the case with particulates, smog precursors, and toxic pollutants, then allowing some facilities actually to increase their emissions, because elsewhere they will be decreased, can create local "hot spots." Thus, even if overall emissions are reduced, they may actually be increased in particular places, helping some people at the expense of others. *See generally* Jonathan Remy Nash and Richard L. Revesz, *Markets and Geography: Designing Marketable Permit Schemes to Control Local and Regional Pollutants*, 28 Ecology L.Q. 569 (2001). Moreover, depending upon the particulars of the cap-and-trade program, there may be substantial difficulties in enforcement. *See* Victor Flatt, *The Enron Story and Environmental Policy*, 33 Env. L.Rep. 10485, 10492 (2003).

Another form of second generation regulation involves individually tailored permits for facilities that address all their environmental impacts holistically, rather than trying to regulate each separate medium separately–air under the Clean Air Act, water under the Clean Water Act, etc. On the national level, EPA's Project XL (meaning "excel") is best known. It attempted to negotiate wide ranging permits that would also encourage efficiencies by having companies propose how they could maximize their environmental protection, perhaps trading greater than required protections in one area for reduced protections in another, where the sum was greater than otherwise would be obtained. Unlike the Acid Rain Program, Project XL is generally considered to have been a failure, and it has been discontinued. *See, e.g.*, Rena I. Steinzor, *Reinventing Environmental Regulation: The Dangerous Journey from Command to Self–Control*, 22 Harv. Envtl. L. Rev. 103 (1998). It was characterized by extremely high transaction costs–that is, the time and resources necessary for the companies to prove their case to EPA and for EPA to assure itself that the proposal would indeed be worthwhile–that made it impractical to use on a widespread basis. Another second generation initiative is to encourage companies to institute Environmental Management Systems (EMS), which hold the promise of liberating environmental performance from being considered a barrier to a company maximizing its profits to being viewed as one of the ways by which to measure a company's success. So far the track record for EMS's is mixed with both limited evidence that companies are adopting them or that their adoption in fact improves environmental performance. *See generally* Cary Coglianese and Jennifer Nash, ed., REGULATING FROM THE INSIDE: CAN ENVIRONMENTAL MANAGEMENT SYSTEMS ACHIEVE POLICY GOALS? (2001).

Yet another form of environmental regulation is through publicizing environmental information. This can be used to reward good performers and tar bad performers. EPA's Toxic Release Inventory, which publishes nationwide data about toxic releases to the environment, is the best known example of this type of regulation. *See* www.epa.gov/tri/. Companies that are reported to be the largest toxic polluters, whether nationally or locally, find themselves under some public and political pressure to clean up their act. California's Proposition 65 prohibits businesses from knowingly exposing persons to a chemical known to cause cancer or reproductive toxicity without first giving a warning. As a result businesses are required to post signs advising persons of their possible exposure to carcinogens. At least in theory, this is supposed to create an incentive for businesses to reduce their use of carcinogenic substances so that they will not lose business from customers repelled by their signs.

Whatever the effects of these second generation strategies, no one seriously imagines that they can replace command-and-control regulations entirely. Pragmatists see a role for them to the extent that they are helpful, but these strategies are no magic bullet.

In a federal system such as the United States, all of the above techniques of regulation could be used by states on their own or by the federal government. As discussed earlier, federal regulation is a relatively recent phenomenon, but it has effectively come to occupy the field. That is, while states are generally allowed to provide for *greater* environmental protection (as described below under pre-emption) than the federal government, for the most part they have not exceeded the federal requirements. Nevertheless, the role of states in environmental law remains central. This is due to the form that most of the major federal environmental laws take, which is known as **cooperative federalism**.

Under the cooperative federalism model, states administer the federal laws on a day-to-day basis under the general supervision of a federal agency, usually EPA. For example, under the Clean Air Act, the Act establishes the basic requirements that states must follow in order to administer the federal law, and EPA reviews and approves the state program to ensure that it meets the Act's requirements. As will be discussed later, the federal government cannot require states to administer these programs, but the federal government can attempt to induce states to participate by, for example, providing money to pay the cost of administering the program. If a state refuses to administer the program or if a state does not comply with the requirements of the program it has agreed to administer, then EPA is supposed to establish and administer a federal program for the state. States may see an advantage in administering the federal program, besides other inducements, simply because it means that the state, rather than the federal government will make the discretionary decisions within the federally mandated framework. Because there remains a large area for the exercise of discretion in the day-to-day administration, this relieves the state of being totally at the mercy of an omni-present federal agency. Under the cooperative federalism model, EPA oversees the performance of states, has the authority to disapprove certain of the state decisions, and generally retains a back-up enforcement authority to enforce the federal requirements in the state against polluters—at least in theory. In practice, the monitoring of states and the use of back-up enforcement authority is substantially burdened by resource limitations.

C. Theoretical Issues

It may seem obvious that when we perceive human-caused environmental harms we respond by passing laws to address those harms. It is well to recognize, however, that humans cause environmental harms not because we affirmatively want to harm the environment, but because there is some activity that appears to be valuable to those causing the harm.

Sometimes the harm to the environment caused by the otherwise valuable human activity may not be obvious. For example, who would have imagined that aerosol sprays in deodorant cans (as well as other uses of chlorofluorocarbons) could destroy the ozone layer, potentially paving the way for worldwide environmental disaster, or that lead put in gasoline to avoid engine knock could be a potential airborne poison? In these cases, establishing that an activity does harm the environment is the first step. This may not be easy, however, and there may be disputes over the causes of harm and the extent of the harm. There are those today who question the existence or extent of global warming and whether it is induced by human behavior, despite the overwhelming consensus of the scientific community that human activity is causing global warming.

Sometimes the harm to the environment is obvious, but the value of the activity to those engaged in it is much greater than the harm suffered by them. Maybe others suffer greater harms, but they are not the ones involved in the harming activity. For example, a factory may emit air pollutants as part of its industrial process, but the factory is engaged in making a profit for its owners, paying taxes to the local government, and providing wages to its employees. It views itself, and is viewed by many others, as engaging in a valuable activity. But how valuable is it? The persons downwind who suffer from the smell, particles, or poison from the emissions may not view the activity's value in the same light. Their focus is on their harm. But how great is their harm? Those who suffer the harm might like the activity stopped, but stopping the activity might mean forgoing an overall benefit to the community.

Economists, in particular, have in recent years been studying these issues with the asserted goal of improving environmental laws. That is, economic theory may help elucidate the incentives for why persons harm the environment, and it may help to inform us as to the best ways to overcome those incentives at the least cost to society.

i. Public Goods

One focus of economists has been on the public goods problem; that is, when resources are publicly owned, but all can use them, those resources tend to be overused. The environmental problems associated with public goods were described in a classic article by Garrett Hardin.

THE TRAGEDY OF THE COMMONS

Garrett Hardin.

Science 162 (1968).

The tragedy of the commons develops in this way. Picture a pasture open to all. It is to be expected that each herdsman will try to keep as many cattle as possible on the commons. Such an arrangement may work reasonably satisfactorily for centuries because tribal wars, poaching, and disease keep the numbers of both man and beast well below the carrying capacity of the land. Finally, however, comes the day of reckoning, that is, the day when the long-desired goal of social stability becomes a reality. At this point, the inherent logic of the commons remorselessly generates tragedy.

As a rational being, each herdsman seeks to maximize his gain. Explicitly or implicitly, more or less consciously, he asks, "What is the utility to me of adding one more animal to my herd?" This utility has one negative and one positive component.

1.   The positive component is a function of the increment of one animal. Since the herdsman receives all the proceeds from the sale of the additional animal, the positive utility is nearly + 1.

2.   The negative component is a function of the additional overgrazing created by one more animal. Since, however, the effects of overgraz-

ing are shared by all the herdsmen, the negative utility for any particular decision-making herdsman is only a fraction of -1.

Adding together the component partial utilities, the rational herdsman concludes that the only sensible course for him to pursue is to add another animal to his herd. And another.... But this is the conclusion reached by each and every rational herdsman sharing a commons. Therein is the tragedy. Each man is locked into a system that compels him to increase his herd without limit—in a world that is limited. Ruin is the destination toward which all men rush, each pursuing his own best interest in a society that believes in the freedom of the commons. Freedom in a commons brings ruin to all.

Some would say that this is a platitude. Would that it were! In a sense, it was learned thousands of years ago, but natural selection favors the forces of psychological denial. The individual benefits as an individual from his ability to deny the truth even though society as a whole, of which he is a part, suffers. Education can counteract the natural tendency to do the wrong thing, but the inexorable succession of generations requires that the basis for this knowledge be constantly refreshed....

In an approximate way, the logic of the commons has been understood for a long time, perhaps since the discovery of agriculture or the invention of private property in real estate. But it is understood mostly only in special cases which are not sufficiently generalized. Even at this late date, cattlemen leasing national land on the Western ranges demonstrate no more than an ambivalent understanding, in constantly pressuring federal authorities to increase the head count to the point where overgrazing produces erosion and weed-dominance. Likewise, the oceans of the world continue to suffer from the survival of the philosophy of the commons. Maritime nations still respond automatically to the shibboleth of the "freedom of the seas." Professing to believe in the "inexhaustible resources of the oceans," they bring species after species of fish and whales closer to extinction.

The National Parks present another instance of the working out of the tragedy of the commons. At present, they are open to all, without limit. The parks themselves are limited in extent—there is only one Yosemite Valley—whereas population seems to grow without limit. The values that visitors seek in the parks are steadily eroded. Plainly, we must soon cease to treat the parks as commons or they will be of no value to anyone.

What shall we do? We have several options. We might sell them off as private property. We might keep them as public property, but allocate the right to enter them. The allocation might be on the basis of wealth, by the use of an auction system. It might be on the basis of merit, as defined by some agreed-upon standards. It might be by lottery. Or it might be on a first-come, first-served basis, administered to long queues. These, I think, are all objectionable. But we must choose—or acquiesce in the destruction of the commons that we call our National Parks.

POLLUTION

In a reverse way, the tragedy of the commons reappears in problems of pollution. Here it is not a question of taking something out of the commons, but of putting something in—sewage, or chemical, radioactive, and heat wastes into water; noxious and dangerous fumes into the air; and distracting and unpleasant advertising signs into the line of sight. The calculations of utility are much the same as before. The rational man finds that his share of the cost of the wastes he discharges into the commons is less than the cost of purifying his wastes before releasing them. Since this is true for everyone, we are locked into a system of "fouling our own nest," so long as we behave only as independent, rational, free enterprisers.

The tragedy of the commons as a food basket is averted by private property, or something formally like it. But the air and waters surrounding us cannot readily be fenced, and so the tragedy of the commons as a cesspool must be prevented by different means, by coercive laws or taxing devices that make it cheaper for the polluter to treat his pollutants than to discharge them untreated. We have not progressed as far with the solution of this problem as we have with the first. Indeed, our particular concept of private property, which deters us from exhausting the positive resources of the earth, favors pollution. The owner of a factory on the bank of a stream—whose property extends to the middle of the stream—often has difficulty seeing why it is not his natural right to muddy the waters flowing past his door. The law, always behind the times, requires elaborate stitching and fitting to adapt it to this newly perceived aspect of the commons....

Notes and Comments

1. As Hardin indicates, one solution to a common resource problem is privatizing the resource. But even when the resource is one that commonly is privately held, such as land, there still are questions as to how to privatize the resource. The federal government gave away public lands to homesteaders in prior centuries. Those who demonstrated the desire to live on and farm the land were given the land. Many would consider the homesteading experiment a success from an economic and cultural perspective, but when Native American reservations were turned from common property into individual allotments, starting in 1887, the result was a disaster, which led to the repeal of that program in 1934.

2. The 1872 General Mining Act was another form of privatization. It was much like the idea of homesteading, except rather than give land to persons willing to live and farm it, this act gave land to persons who found "valuable minerals" on public land and were willing to develop it. Yet, this program is generally considered to be an environmental disaster, with the landowner solely concerned with maximizing his profit from mining and having no concern for the environment. The tragedy of the commons may have been averted, but this privatization destroys the resource even more surely than the commons described by Hardin. Why do you suppose that is?

Might it be the difference between a productive resource and an extractive resource?

3. Another way to privatize land, or resources on land, is simply to offer the public resource to the highest bidder. Timber sales and oil leases on public land are offered on this basis. Few believe that such "privatization" is likely to further environmental considerations, but these too could be characterized as extractive activities, not productive activities. Public grazing lands are also leased to ranchers for grazing cattle and sheep, but this privatized use of the lands has not resulted in the ranchers treating the lands in a sustainable manner. Why does this type of privatization not overcome the tragedy of the commons? Is it simply because the rancher does not own the land? As a practical matter, grazing permits for particular lands are almost invariably held by the same rancher indefinitely and are often considered rights that transfer with the rancher's own property.

4. Hardin's argument, based on economic concepts, which he says some might characterize as a platitude, can itself be challenged. In light of empirical research showing that traditional farming commons in fact were not overgrazed, other economist/lawyers have evolved a theory that cooperation with common goods can be as efficient as the free market with private goods in certain circumstances. *See, e.g.,* Robert C. Ellickson, ORDER WITHOUT LAW: HOW NEIGHBORS SETTLE DISPUTES (1991). What might be those certain circumstances—repeat players, close-knit societies, small groups? Are those circumstances transferable to larger political fields?

5. "Free Market Environmentalists" today argue in favor of privatizing federal forest and grazing lands, by selling them outright to the highest bidder, as a way of furthering environmental protection. They cite to Hardin's article for support of their position. What do you think? You might ask whether privately owned forest lands and privately owned grazing lands have fared better environmentally than public lands.

6. Hardin likens the National Parks to commons in that they are publicly owned and open to all, with the result that they are overused and in danger of being destroyed. National Parks too could be sold off to the highest bidder, perhaps to the Disney corporation, which could then run them like a theme park. Presumably, the new owner would run the Parks on a sustainable basis, making necessary investments and limiting use to the carrying capacity of the Parks. How do you suppose such an owner would do that? Would that be better than their present situation?

7. As Hardin notes, many of the commons today are not land-based and hence are not easily subjected to private ownership; you cannot fence air and water, and fisheries are not so easily reduced to ownership. Nevertheless, there are "water rights" that are a form of property, and regulatory experiments are being made in trying to address overfishing through assignment of fishing rights that could be bought and sold like other property, and theoretically would lead those having the rights not to overfish and destroy the value of their right.

8. Nevertheless, Hardin expected that "coercive laws or taxing devices" would be necessary where privatization was not a solution. Coercive laws generally mean government laws and regulations imposing limitations on what people can do and providing for punishments if people do not

comply with those limitations. Indeed, that is what most environmental law consists of.

ii. Cost/Benefit Analysis

Since the beginning of the modern environmental movement, there has been a companion movement to improve the quality of governmental regulations by having government regulators explicitly consider the costs and the benefits of their regulations and to consider alternative regulatory mechanisms to maximize the net benefit of regulations. Although the practice originated with President Nixon, who created EPA and signed NEPA and the Clean Air Act into law, President Carter was the first to institutionalize a regularized practice requiring agencies to assess significant regulations in terms of their costs and benefits and to identify the least burdensome alternative. President Reagan enlarged and expanded this requirement and placed responsibility for overseeing agencies' compliance in the Office of Information and Regulatory Affairs (OIRA) in the Office of Management and Budget (OMB). When President Clinton was elected 12 years later, he, in essence, continued the same requirements, and the second President Bush has continued the Clinton executive order imposing the requirements for agency cost-benefit analysis and OMB review. In other words, over the past 20 years the idea that agencies should engage in cost-benefit analyses has become a bi-partisan concept, even if its application may have differed between administrations.

According to the various executive orders, cost-benefit analyses should assess all costs and benefits of available regulatory alternatives, including the alternative of not regulating. Costs and benefits are to include both those that are quantifiable (to the maximum extent feasible) and those that are qualitative or non-quantifiable. Then, to the extent permissible by law, the agency should choose the alternative that maximizes the net benefits to society.

The following selection describes the process of cost-benefit analysis and the arguments made by those who support its use.

ECONOMICS, EQUITY, AND THE ENVIRONMENT
Stephen M. Johnson (2004).

II.   Cost-Benefit Analysis Process

The first step that an agency must take when preparing a cost-benefit analysis is to establish a baseline for the analysis by assessing what the world would look like without the proposed regulation. When the agency conducts the cost-benefit analysis, it will compare the costs and benefits of the proposed regulation (and other alternatives to that regulation) to that baseline. If more than one baseline is reasonable, and the analysis of costs and benefits will vary greatly depending on the selection of the baseline, the agency should calculate costs and benefits of the proposed rule against each of the reasonable baselines.

Once the agency has identified the baseline for analysis, it must calculate the *costs* of the proposed regulation (and alternatives). The "opportunity costs" of a proposed regulation should include the regulated community's compliance costs, the government's administrative costs for implementing the regulation, as well as other costs. The costs also include the costs of benefits that are foregone if the government adopts the regulation. Thus, the cost of banning a product includes the foregone net benefit of that product, taking into account any mitigation effects from substitutes for the product. Since the agency will be attempting to predict costs and outcomes that may or may not occur in the future, the agency should use probability estimates to assign a weight to costs or outcomes, depending on their likelihood.

The agency should also attempt to quantify the *benefits* of the regulation (and alternatives) in monetary terms, if possible, and use probability estimates to assign weights to the benefits, depending on their likelihood. In some cases, environmental regulations provide benefits that can be readily measured. For instance, when a regulation prevents damage to natural resources, it may be possible to measure the "use values" of those resources because there is a direct or indirect market for the resources. If the regulation prevents the destruction of thousands of fish in a commercial fishing region, the market value of the fish in the region can be directly measured. Similarly, while the market value of recreational fishing, hiking, or camping ... cannot be directly measured, their value is reflected in the prices of related goods that are directly traded in the market. Through the "revealed preference" method, economists can calculate the value of the recreational uses of those natural resources by examining the amount of money that was spent on fishing, hiking, and camping equipment, licensee travel to the region, and other goods and services related to the recreational use of the resources.

While market values can be directly or indirectly calculated for the "use values" of natural resources, it is much more difficult to calculate the monetary value of the "non-use values" ("passive use values") of natural resources, or the monetary value of many of the other benefits of environmental regulation because there is no market for many of those benefits. For instance, environmental regulations may reduce the potential number of cancer deaths, reduce the number of cases of asthma, prevent further pollution of a low-income community, protect endangered species, protect the peace and tranquility of a natural area, or provide a wide variety of other benefits. Since there is no market value for these benefits, agencies create artificial prices for the benefits by calculating what people would be "willing to pay" for the benefits, or "willing to accept" to give up the benefits.

There are two different methods that agencies normally use to calculate "willingness-to-pay" or "willingness-to-accept." The "hedonic price method" attempts to infer values for benefits from market behavior that can measured. For instance, the difference between the wages that are paid to persons who work in dangerous jobs and those who do not is often used to determine the amount of money that a worker would accept to face an increased risk of harm. That value is then used to determine the value of lives saved by regulations. The other method that agencies commonly use to determine "willingness-to-pay" or "willingness-to-accept" is "contingent valuation." In this approach, a cross-section of the population that would be affected by a proposed government action is surveyed to determine how much they would be willing to pay for benefits that would be impacted by the government's action. Agencies have used hedonic pricing and contingent valuation to establish the value of human life (ranging from $1.5 million to almost $6 million), the value of an episode of acute bronchitis ($45), an emergency visit to the hospital for asthma ($9,000), a single episode of shortness of breath ($5.30), protection of grey wolves ($8 billion), and preservation of bald eagles (more than $25 billion), as well as many other benefits.

While agencies have used hedonic pricing and contingent valuation to estimate values for a wide variety of benefits that are not directly or indirectly traded in the market, some benefits cannot be quantified in monetary terms. Nevertheless, agencies are required to identify, in cost-benefit analyses, the benefits that cannot be quantified. It is not clear, however, how the agency should weigh those benefits in the analysis.

When agencies calculate the costs and benefits of proposed regulations in cost-benefit analysis, they are examining costs and benefits that occur at different times. While costs are often incurred at the time that the regulation will be implemented, or shortly thereafter, to provide benefits that occur in the future, some costs might not arise until the future. Accordingly, as part of the cost-benefit analysis process, agencies *discount* future costs and benefits to present value for purposes of analysis. The discount rate is often an interest rate taken from financial markets, and OMB guidance recommends the use of a 7% discount rate. Thus, if a $1,000 cost will be incurred in 10 years, the present value of the cost, when discounted at a rate of 7%, will be $500.

* * *

III. ADVANTAGES OF COST-BENEFIT ANALYSIS

Supporters of cost-benefit analysis advocate the broader use of the process on several grounds. The primary argument in favor of cost-benefit analysis is an efficiency argument. When the government uses cost-benefit analysis to make decisions, supporters argue, the government will only impose costs on society when the benefits outweigh or justify the costs. Without cost-benefit analysis, supporters argue, the government has imposed restrictions on businesses that can cost billions of dollars for each life that they save. The billions of dollars that is spent to save one life, they argue, could be spent to save many more lives and provide many more benefits if the government utilized cost-benefit analysis. For instance, Professors Sunstein and Hahn argue that "better allocations of health care expenditures could save, each year, 60,200 additional lives at no additional cost...." Since there are limited resources that can be spent to protect human health and the environment, supporters argue, those resources should be used in the most efficient manner.

Supporters of cost-benefit analysis also criticize the high cost of regulations designed without cost-benefit analysis on the grounds that such regulations increase prices, reduce wages, and increase unemployment and poverty. Thus, they argue, regulation designed to protect health and the environment actually harms health.

Cost-benefit analysis advocates also contend that the process is more objective and transparent than the current regulatory process. Since the agency has to follow specific procedures and make decisions according to a readily identifiable standard, the agency is less likely to make arbitrary decisions or to make decisions that benefit politically favored groups. Similarly, supporters of cost-benefit analysis argue that the process makes agency decisionmaking transparent because it requires the agency to reveal all of its assumptions and uncertainties in language that the public, rather than merely toxicologists and biologists, can understand.

Defenders of cost-benefit analysis also argue that it is not merely an antiregulatory tool, and may even be used to support regulatory efforts by agencies. Professor Sunstein argues, for instance, that cost-benefit analysis has helped spur the removal of lead from gasoline and the elimination of chlorofluorocarbons (CFCs), and demonstrated that it was appropriate for EPA to reduce the acceptable level of arsenic in drinking water from 50 parts per billion. Similarly, a recent OMB report concluded that the health and social benefits of enforcing CAA regulations between 1992 and 2002 were five to seven times greater than the costs of complying with the rules.

––––––

Despite the bipartisan acceptance and arguments above in support of cost-benefit analysis, there is a rising critique of cost-benefit analysis from both practical and philosophical perspectives. Practically, studies have shown that the cost estimates for federal regulations, almost always based upon industry-supplied data, are invariably too high. *See* Frank Ackerman & Lisa Heinzerling, PRICELESS 37–39 (2004). This has the effect of suggesting that stricter regulations are less cost-effective than they actually are.

Numerous complaints have been raised regarding the methodology for valuing human life, or more accurately the benefits of regulations that reduce the risk of premature death. Many commentators have criticized the value assigned to a human life derived from studies of wage levels in risky industries, suggesting that the value is too low, because those studies do not adequately account for the lack of information about relative risks and the lack of job choices practically available to workers in these industries; they do not control for individuals' different attitudes toward risk, suggesting workers who choose riskier jobs do not place as great a premium on risk as the normal population; and they do not account for the difference between persons' willingness to accept and persons' willingness to pay, which numerous studies have found but which economists tend to discount. *See Id.*, at 75–81. And there are commentators who argue that the value of life assigned is too high because usually the premature death that is avoided is someone of advanced age and poor health—those most likely to be susceptible to environmental risks—who would only live for a few more years anyway. These commentators suggest a shift to valuing life-years, rather than simple life. A proposal by OIRA to use life-years, rather than the value of a whole life, which would reduce the monetary benefits of regulations that protect older persons, was withdrawn after a strong lobbying campaign by the American Association of Retired Persons. *See* Resources for the Future, Under Fire, EPA Drops the "Senior Death Discount," Tuesday, May 13, 2003, http://www.rff.org/rff/News/Coverage/2003/May/Under-Fire-EPA-drops-the-Senior–Death-Discount.cfm (visited on July 2, 2004).

Professors Ackerman and Heinzerling have suggested that what is really being measured by the so-called valuation of life is the value that people may perceive in living with reduced risk. That is, it is a benefit to live day-to-day feeling less afraid. This is a real value, but it is a different value than the value of a life itself. *See* Frank Ackerman & Lisa Heinzerling, *Pricing the Priceless: Cost–Benefit Analysis of Environmental Protection*, 150 U. Pa. L. Rev. 1553, 1564–1565 (2002).

Sometimes the difficulties in measuring costs or benefits results in simply not monetizing certain costs and benefits, but this too can create practical problems. For example, in 2002 the Bush administration's OMB reported to Congress that a Clinton administration initiated forest plan would impose $184 million in costs but only $219,000 in benefits. The costs reflected the value of the timber that would not be cut under the Clinton plan; the benefits would be costs the Forest Service would avoid by not having to build roads to get the timber out. In other words, OMB did not recognize *any* benefit in the non-monetized value of preserving uncut forest for habitat, recreation, and future generations. *See* PRICELESS, *supra*, at 6–7. And this is not an isolated example. *See, e.g.*, Richard W. Parker, *Grading the Government*, 70 U. Chi. L. Rev. 1345 (2003).

Beyond the practical objections to cost-benefit analysis as it is currently employed, there is also a significant philosophical objection to the attempt to monetize values that may not be appropriately monetized. For example, there are several commentators who argue that it is simply inappropriate to assign a value to human life. To bolster their argument they provide some examples where the valuation of human life simply seems improper. One noted example involves a study done by a famous Harvard cost-benefit proponent that concluded that government should subsidize smoking because the costs saved by government in pensions and health care resulting from premature deaths offset the value of the lives lost. Another example involved an attempt to value the costs and benefits of mitigating global warming. Using traditional valuation methods, lives in poor countries were only worth $100,000, while lives in rich countries were valued at $1.5 million. In other words, every American was worth 15 persons from Bangla Desh. *See* PRICELESS, *supra*, at 72–74.

The concept of discounting future costs and benefits also comes in for philosophical criticism when used for non-market values. For example, using OMB's preferred 7% discount rate, if the effect of a government required expenditure today is to prevent an unnecessary death in ten years, then it is not "cost effective" to impose any cost that is more than half of what a human life is worth. That is, lives in the future are discounted, as are other future benefits for the environment. Preserving nature for our children and our children's children generally does not pass the cost-benefit test.

Notes and Comments

1. The above discussion only scratches the surface of the debate over cost-benefit analysis. It is perhaps ironic that while environmentalists usually are critical of cost-benefit analyses, for the reasons described above, the basic analytical framework for cost-benefit analysis is identical to the decision structure mandated by the National Environmental Policy Act, fervently supported by environmentalists. As you will see later in this book, NEPA requires agencies to engage in an alternatives analysis for actions that may significantly affect the environment. That is, the agency compares what the effects of its proposed action and the reasonable alternatives would have on the environment in order to assess which alternative would achieve the desired result with the least adverse effect on the environment. Do you think environmentalists are not being consistent, or is there a principled basis for distinguishing between the environmental analysis and cost-benefit analysis?

2. It seems that many of the problems identified with cost-benefit analysis involve the difficulties or inappropriateness with trying to monetize certain values. Inasmuch as every executive order requiring cost-benefit analysis has only required quantification, as opposed to monetization, and then only to the extent feasible, why has there been such an attempt to assign dollar values to non-market and non-use values? One suggestion is that absent monetization, one would be comparing apples and oranges. Is it really so difficult to compare apples and oranges?

iii. Risk Analysis

Risk analysis is closely related to cost-benefit analysis and is a necessary prerequisite to it in the health and safety arena. Risk analysis is comprised of two parts: risk assessment and risk management. The former is supposed to determine what risk exists; the latter is supposed to decide what should be done about that risk. It is in the second step that cost-benefit comes into play. Once the risk assessment has determined the number of likely premature deaths from exposure to some chemical, the risk management decisionmaking process can determine how many premature deaths are acceptable. The following is a description of risk assessment.

RISK AND THE ENVIRONMENT: IMPROVING REGULATORY DECISION MAKING

A Report of the Carnegie Commission on Science,
Technology, and Government 76–78 (1993).

Risk assessment is a composite of established disciplines, including toxicology, biostatistics, epidemiology, economics, and demography. The goals of risk assessment are to characterize the nature of the adverse effects and to produce quantitative estimates of one or both of the following fundamental quantities: (1) the *probability* that an individual (a hypothetical or identified person) will suffer disease or death as a result of a specified exposure to a pollutant or pollutants; and (2) the *consequences* of such an exposure to an entire population (i.e., the number of cases of disease or death)....

The regulatory process is generally thought to encompass two elements, risk assessment and risk management. The distinction between these two components is important, though controversial. Risk assessment is usually conceived as the "Objective" part of the process, and risk management the subjective part. In risk assessment the analyst decides how big the problem is, while in risk management political decision makers decide what to do about the problem. The "conventional wisdom" (which some believe needs rethinking) stresses that risk management must not influence the processes and assumptions made in risk assessment, so the two functions must be kept conceptually and administratively separate.

Numerical estimates derived from risk assessment serve as inputs to several very different kinds of decisions, including (1) "acceptable risk" determinations (wherein action is taken if the risk exceeds some "bright line;" which can be zero); (2) "cost-benefit" determinations, where the risks reduced by a proposed action are translated into benefits (e.g., lives saved, life-years extended), expressed in dollar amounts, and compared to the estimated costs of implementing the action and some rule of thumb regarding how much cost it is wise to incur to achieve a given level of benefit (e.g., $10 million to save one additional life); and (3) "cost-effectiveness" determinations, where the action that maximizes the amount of risk reduction (not necessarily expressed in dollar terms) per unit cost is favored.

Since at least 1983 (with the publication of the National Research Council's "Redbook"), the dominant paradigm for risk assessment has been a sequential, four-step process:

- *Hazard identification*—in which a qualitative determination is made of what kinds of adverse health or ecological effects a substance can cause. Typically, agencies have focused on cancer as the effect that drives further analysis and regulation. So, for example, a typical hazard identification for vinyl chloride released from industrial facilities would involve the collection and critical analysis of short-term test-tube assays (for mutagenicity, etc.), of long-term animal assays (typically two-year rodent carcinogenicity tests), and of human epidemiologic data—either cohort studies (in which populations exposed to vinyl chloride are followed to assess whether their rates of any disease were significantly greater than those of unexposed or less-exposed populations) or case-control studies (which focus on victims of a particular disease to see whether they were significantly more likely to have been exposed to vinyl chloride than similar but disease-free individuals).

• *Exposure assessment*—in which a determination is made of the amounts of a substance to which a hypothetical person (usually the "maximally exposed individual") and/or the total population are exposed. To return to the vinyl chloride example, this part of risk assessment would bring to bear techniques of emissions characterization (how much vinyl chloride leaves the plant in a given time?), fate-and-transport analysis (how is the chemical dispersed in the atmosphere and transformed into other compounds?), uptake analysis (how much air do people breathe, both outdoors and indoors?), and demographic analysis (how many hours per day do people spend in various locations near the plant, and how long do they reside in one locale before moving away?).

• *Dose-response assessment*—in which an estimate is made of the probability or extent of injury at the exposure levels determined above, by quantifying the "potency" of the chemical in question. For vinyl chloride again, scientists would determine its carcinogenic potency by fitting the animal bioassay data (number of tumors produced at different exposure levels) to a mathematical model (usually one that is linear at low doses), and then transforming the resultant potency estimate for rodents into a human potency estimate through the use of a "scaling factor" (usually, a ratio of the body surface areas of the two species). Additionally, human epidemiologic data could be used to validate or supplant the animal-based potency estimate.

• *Risk characterization*—in which the results of the above steps are integrated to describe the nature of the adverse effects and the strength of the evidence and to present one or more "risk numbers." For example, EPA might say, "This vinyl chloride plant is estimated to produce up to 3 excess cases of liver cancer every 70 years among the 100,000 people living within 1 mile of the facility" or "the maximally exposed individual faces an excess lifetime liver cancer risk of 5.4×10^{-4}."

Risk assessment is essentially a tool for extrapolating from scientific data to a risk number. The tool is made up of a host of assumptions, which are an admixture of science and policy. Sometimes either science or policy predominates, but it is often difficult to get a broad consensus that this is so.

A view among some in industry and elsewhere is that risk assessment systematically overestimates risk and frightens the public: as they see it, the typical risk assessment takes a trivial emission source, pretends that people are pressed up against the fenceline of the source 24 hours a day for 70 years, gauges the toxicity of the pollutant released by exposing ultrasensitive rodents to huge doses in the laboratory, and then uses the most "conservative" dose-response model to estimate a risk to humans at the low ambient exposures of interest. The view of some in environmental and public interest groups, and elsewhere, is that risk assessment may often inherently underestimate the true magnitude of the problem, by ignoring complicating but salient factors, including synergies among exposures, vast variations in susceptibility among humans, and unusual exposure pathways (e.g., inhalation of steam in showers containing volatilized chemicals from contaminated water).

Because the science underlying most risk assessment assumptions is inconclusive, arguments over whether or not an assumption is scientifically valid often distill down to debates about whether it is better to err on the side of "false positives" (if there is an error, it will more likely be a false indication of danger) or "false negatives" (if there is an error, it will more likely be a false indication of safety). Those who might be harmed by the substance being assessed will generally favor false positives; those who would gain from the substance will generally favor false negatives.

Notes and Comments

1. As the selection suggests, risk assessment is usually described as an objective process, in the sense that scientists, rather than policy makers, are in charge of the process. However, as the selection also indicates, risk assessment requires those involved in the process to make a number of assumptions, and these assumptions are not themselves objective. They reflect what those utilizing them believe is appropriate to the circumstances. This often means that important, qualitative decisions are being made in a manner that is not very transparent. Concern about how these decisions are made is one of the reasons for an increased demand for peer review of scientific determinations that affect regulatory decisions. *See, e.g.,* Office of Management and Budget, Final Information Quality Bulletin for Peer Review, 70 Fed. Reg. 2664 (January 14, 2005).

2. An important part of risk assessments is establishing the dose/response relationship between the substance and the affected entity. Usually this is reflected as a dose/response curve, showing that at higher exposures (doses) the greater the response (e.g., the likelihood that cancer develops). For many toxic substances there is a threshold level, a level at which a substance that is harmful at some levels of exposure is no longer harmful. For example, iodine is a poison that can kill you, but a lack of any iodine in your system will result in health problems. For some substances, scientists can run tests that result in a "no observable effect level" (NOEL), sometimes phrased as "no observable adverse effect level" (NOAEL), that provides the basis for a threshold level. For carcinogens, however, generally there is no established NOEL or NOAEL. Instead, it is assumed that at very

low levels of exposure one's risk of cancer diminishes but never disappears. Moreover, it is further assumed that there is a linear (straight-line) relationship between exposure and contracting cancer. That is, if exposure is reduced by a factor of ten, then one's risk of contracting cancer is reduced by a factor of ten. These assumptions can then result in a finding that a very small exposure to a substance will still pose some risk of causing cancer, perhaps one in 10 million. But if a population of 280 million people were subject to this small exposure, this would suggest 28 persons would die from the exposure. This conclusion, however, would be driven by *assumptions*. A different assumption, for example, that at this exposure level there is *no* increased risk of cancer, would lead to a conclusion that no one would die from this exposure. While still a different assumption, that at this level the dose/response is higher, could lead to the conclusion that 100 persons might die from this exposure. None of these conclusions might be provable or disprovable. And one might be as reasonable as another, but each reflects an attitude of what position one should take in the absence of information.

iv. The Polluter Pays Principle

Earlier, in discussing the economic concept of public goods, it was noted that when people can use the commons, they do not bear the full cost of the harm they do to the commons. One theory of environmental laws is that they should impose the full cost of the pollution on the polluter. Then, the polluter receives the right price signals with respect to that pollution. Moreover, the notion that the polluter should pay for the harm it creates resonates even with non-economists.

Polluters can be made to pay in various ways. In theory, taxes could be levied on polluters calibrated to the cost of their pollution, but there are both technical difficulties in making that calibration and political difficulties in imposing taxes at all. Simply requiring polluters to spend money on pollution control equipment is a form of making them pay for their pollution. The Comprehensive Environmental Response, Compensation, and Liability Act (also known as Superfund) imposes a tort-like form of liability on persons whose hazardous substances are released to the environment.

v. Sustainable Development

The idea of sustainable development is a mantra of the modern environmental movement, and the term has been used particularly to describe the goals of international environmental law. It was enshrined in the Declaration of Principles of the United Nations Conference on Environment and Development (UNCED) in 1992. There is, however, no agreed upon definition. Nevertheless, a common description is "development that meets the needs of the present without compromising the ability of future generations to meet their own needs." World Commission on Environment and Development, Our Common Future 8 (1987). The devil, however, is in the details. No one is in favor of unsustainable development.

The difficulty is for the most part in determining what is sustainable, especially for non-renewable resources. In a sense, no use of a non-renewable resource is sustainable forever. By definition, the resource is finite. However, ever since Malthus, predictions of non-renewable resource depletion have turned out to be erroneous. For example, predictions that petroleum supplies would be used up by various dates have been notably in error. In the United States, the federal government predicted in the 1930s that domestic reserves would be exhausted in less than 15 years. In 1951 the government adjusted its prediction and said that domestic reserves would be exhausted by 1965. Julian Simon, *The Ultimate Resource 2* (1996). In 1970, a famous study entitled *Limits to Growth*, produced by a number of scientists under the name of the Club of Rome, predicted that oil resources would be exhausted by 1992. Donella Meadows, *et. al.*, *Limits to Growth* (1972). In 1987, Anne and Paul Ehrlich, scientists famous (or infamous) for their writings on the coming environmental crisis, predicted a worldwide oil crisis in the 1990s. Anne Ehrlich & Paul Ehrlich, *Earth* (1987). Today, the predictions continue with a recent issue of National Geographic publicizing the predictions of "some experts" that oil production is about to decline at any moment, or in 10 years, or in 35 years. Tim Appenzeller, *The End of Cheap Oil*, National Geographic 84, 90 (June 2004).

Others, however, read the data differently. Bjorn Lomborg, a Danish environmental officer who has become notorious for his conclusions that the environment is improving without regard to government environmental efforts, reported in 2001 that world oil reserves compared to annual production was higher than at any time prior to 1985. Bjorn Lomborg, *The Skeptical Environmentalist* 125 (2001). Moreover, he argued that the prophets of doom failed to recognize that throughout history, as a resource appeared to become more scarce, price signals motivated greater exploration for new discoveries, greater efficiencies in the use of the resource, as well as the development of substitutes for the now higher priced resource. If petroleum becomes too expensive, we will develop fuel cells. "Optimists," such as Lomborg, take comfort in the history of resource utilization, which seems to support their conclusion. In a famous showdown between "optimist" Julian Simon and "pessimist" Paul Ehrlich, Ehrlich bet Simon that the price of five mineral commodities would be higher in 1990 than in 1980. In fact, all five commodities were cheaper in 1990. *See* Lomborg, *supra*, at 136.

Nevertheless, even pessimists recognize that resources will not disappear; they will just become more expensive as the demand increases relative to the supply, and at a certain level the price might become prohibitive. To the extent that our way of life depends on the resources remaining relatively inexpensive, a significant price increase might jeopardize our way of life. The pessimists argue that we should take preventive measures today to avoid their predicted catastrophic effects of such price increases. If two-dollar a gallon gasoline seems expensive, imagine what $15 a gallon gasoline would do to our way of life. It is better to adopt practices today that will soften the blow that is bound to come, they say. And those practices are to reduce materialism, consumerism, and the never ending quest for growth. Not surprisingly, critics of materialism see sustainability as the hope for the future, while business and development interests see "sustainability" as a code word for opposing growth.

Sustainability perhaps has more meaning with respect to renewable resources, because it is here, especially with regard to worldwide fisheries and timber practices in much of the world that we find ready examples of non-sustainable practices. Even Lomborg concedes that there is overfishing of wild stocks and unsustainable deforestation in developing countries. Recognition of the problem, however, is only the beginning. Particularly in the developing world, suggestions by richer nations that resources should only be used sustainably are not taken kindly. In poorer nations the first demand is for basic necessities and then for some material goods, and this may place a higher priority on present-day needs than on those of future generations.

vi. The Precautionary Principle

Like sustainable development, the Precautionary Principle has become a fundamental principle of modern environmentalism, and it too is reflected in international legal documents, such as the 1992 Declaration of Principles by the United Nations Conference on Environment and Development. Again, however, there is no agreed upon definition of the principle, and the application of the principle in practice depends upon its definition. A generally liberal academic had the following to say about the principle.

CASS R. SUNSTEIN, THE PARALYZING PRINCIPLE

Regulation 32 (Winter 2002–2003).

All over the world, there is increasing interest in a simple idea for the regulation of risk: the Precautionary Principle. Simply put, the principle counsels that we should avoid steps that will create a risk of harm; until safety is established through clear evidence, we should be cautious. In a catchphrase: Better safe than sorry.

In ordinary life, pleas of this kind seem quite sensible. People buy smoke alarms and insurance. They wear seatbelts and motorcycle helmets, even if they are unlikely to be involved in an accident. Should rational regulators not follow the same approach as well? Many people believe so.

In many ways, the Precautionary Principle seems quite sensible, even appealing. To justify regulation, a certainty of harm should not be required; a risk, even a low one, may well be enough. It makes sense to expend resources to prevent a small chance of complete disaster; consider the high costs, pecuniary and otherwise, that are spent to reduce the risk of terrorist attack. On reasonable assumptions, the costs are worth incurring even if the probability of harm—in individual cases or even in the aggregate—is relatively low.

The Precautionary Principle might well be seen as a plea for a kind of regulatory insurance. Certainly the principle might do some real-world good, spurring us to attend to neglected problems. Nonetheless, the principle cannot be fully defended in those ways, simply because risks are on all sides of social situations. Any effort to be universally precautionary will be paralyzing, forbidding every imaginable step, including no step at all.

The Precautionary Principle enjoys widespread international support. But what does the principle mean or require? There are numerous definitions, and they are not all compatible with one another. We can imagine a continuum of understandings. At one extreme are weak versions to which no reasonable person could object; at the other extreme are strong versions that would appear to call for a fundamental rethinking of regulatory policy.

The most cautious and weak versions suggest, quite sensibly, that a lack of decisive evidence of harm should not be a ground for refusing to regulate. Regulation might be justified even if we cannot establish an incontrovertible connection between, say, low-level exposures to certain carcinogens and adverse effects on human health. Thus, the 1992 Rio Declaration states, "Where there are threats of serious or irreversible damage, lack of full scientific certainty shall not be used as a reason for postponing cost-effective measures to prevent environmental degradation."

The weak versions of the Precautionary Principle are unobjectionable and important. Every day, people take steps (and incur costs) to avoid hazards that are far from certain. We do not walk in moderately dangerous areas at night; we exercise; we buy smoke detectors; we buckle our seatbelts; we might even avoid fatty foods. Because the weak versions are sensible, I will not discuss them here. Instead, I will understand the principle in a strong way, to suggest that regulation is required whenever there is a possible risk to health, safety, or the environment, even if the supporting evidence is speculative and even if the economic costs of regulation are high. To avoid palpable absurdity, the idea of "possible risk" will be understood to require a certain threshold of scientific plausibility. To support regulation, no one thinks that it is enough if someone, somewhere, urges that a risk is worth taking seriously. But under the Precautionary Principle as I shall understand it, the threshold burden is minimal, and once it is met, there is something like a presumption in favor of stringent regulatory controls.

In 1982, the United Nations World Charter for Nature apparently gave the first international recognition to the strong version of the principle, suggesting that when "potential adverse effects are not fully understood, the activities should not proceed." The widely publicized Wingspread Declaration, from a meeting of environmentalists in 1998, is another example of the strong version:

When an activity raises threats of harm to human health or the environment, precautionary measures should be taken even if some cause and effect relationships are not established scientifically. In this context the proponent of the activity, rather than the public, should bear the burden of proof.

Unlike the weak version of the Precautionary Principle, the strong version is not limited to threats of serious or irreversible damage and reverses the burden of proof.

Belief in the strong version of the Precautionary Principle is not limited to any particular group. All over the world, the idea has been a staple of regulatory policy for several decades. In the United States, both Congress and the federal courts, without using the term explicitly, have built in a notion of precaution in some important cases, allowing or requiring regulation on the basis of conservative assumptions. The Precautionary Principle has played a significant role in international documents, to the point where it has become ubiquitous.

The most serious problem with the Precautionary Principle is that it offers no guidance—not that it is wrong, but that it forbids all courses of action, including inaction. To understand that point, it will be useful to anchor the discussion in some concrete problems:

* * *

- Genetic modification of food has become a widespread practice. But the risks involved are not known with precision. Some people fear that genetic modification will result in serious ecological harm and large risks to human health. Other people claim that genetic modification will have significant health benefits.

- Scientists are hardly in full accord about the dangers associated with global warming, but there is general agreement that global warming is occurring. It is possible that global warming will produce, by 2100, a mean temperature increase of 4.5 degrees C; that it will result in well over $5 trillion in annual monetized costs; and that it will also produce a significant number of deaths from malaria. The Kyoto Protocol would require most industrialized nations to reduce greenhouse gas emissions to between 92 and 94 percent of 1990 levels in an effort to reduce the degree of warming. Such reductions would impose substantial costs.

- Many people fear nuclear power on the ground that nuclear power plants raise various health and safety issues, including some possibility of catastrophe. But if a nation does not rely on nuclear power, it is likely to rely on fossil fuels, and in particular on coal-fired power plants. Such plants create risks of their own, including risks associated with global warming. China, for example, has relied on nuclear energy as a way of reducing greenhouse gases and other air pollution problems.

- There is a possible conflict between the protection of marine mammals and military exercises. The U.S. Navy, for example, engages in many such exercises, and it is possible that marine mammals are threatened as a result. Military activities in the oceans might well cause significant harm, but a decision to suspend those activities might also endanger military preparedness.

In those cases, what guidance does the Precautionary Principle provide? It is tempting to say that the principle calls for strong controls on ... genetic engineering of food, greenhouse gases, threats to marine mammals, and nuclear power. In all of those cases, there is a possibility of serious harms, and no authoritative scientific evidence suggests that the possibility is close to zero.

If the burden of proof is on the proponent of the activity or processes in question, the Precautionary Principle would seem to impose a burden of proof that cannot be met. Put to one side the question of whether the principle, so understood, is sensible; let us ask a more fundamental question: Is more stringent regulation really compelled by the Precautionary Principle?

The answer is that it is not. In most of the cases above, it should be easy to see that in its own way, stringent regulation would actually run afoul of the Precautionary Principle. The simplest reason is that such regulation might well deprive society of significant benefits, and for that reason produce risks and even deaths that would otherwise not occur. In some cases, regulation eliminates the "opportunity benefits" of a process or activity, and thus causes preventable deaths. If that is so, regulation is hardly precautionary.

The most familiar cases involve the "drug lag" produced by a highly precautionary approach to the introduction of new medicines and drugs into the market. If a government takes such an approach, it might protect people, in a precautionary way, against harms from inadequately tested drugs. But it will also prevent people from receiving potential benefits from those drugs. Is it "precautionary" to require extensive premarketing testing, or to do the opposite?

Or consider the case of genetic modification of food. Many people believe that a failure to allow genetic modification might well result in numerous deaths, and a small probability of many more. The reason is that genetic modification holds out the promise of producing food that is both cheaper and healthier, which would have large benefits in developing countries. Now the point is not that genetic modification will definitely have those benefits, or that the benefits of genetic modification outweigh the risks. The point is only that if the Precautionary Principle is taken literally, it is offended by regulation as well as by nonregulation.

Sometimes regulation would violate the Precautionary Principle because it would give rise to substitute risks in the form of hazards that materialize, or are increased, as a result of regulation. Consider nuclear power. It is reasonable to think that in light of current options, a ban on nuclear power will increase dependence on fossil fuels that contribute to global warming. If so, such a ban would seem to run afoul of the Precautionary Principle. Or consider the Environmental Protection

Agency's effort to ban asbestos, a ban that might well seem justified or even compelled by the principle. The difficulty, from the standpoint of that very principle, is that substitutes for asbestos also carry risks. Or return to possible risks to marine mammals from the U.S. Navy. Some people are concerned that efforts to eliminate those risks will endanger military preparedness, if only because of the rise of new administrative barriers to training exercises. In those circumstances, what is the appropriate approach, according to the Precautionary Principle?

vii. Environmental Ethics

For the most part, our discussion has centered on protecting the environment for the benefit of humankind. Whether the issue is risk regulation or sustainable development, the focus is on how to benefit people. Even within this framework there are clearly ethical issues. One of these is described as intergenerational equity. The idea is simple: that one generation should neither hoard to itself all the benefits nor impose on later generations all the costs. You can see how the sustainable development idea relates to this ethical concern. Another ethical issue is captured by the expression: environmental justice. It is described in more detail below, but in short it is concerned with avoiding the imposition of environmental harms disproportionately on the poor or on minority populations.

Beyond the human concern, however, is another issue–whether the environment should be protected not for our utilitarian concerns but for a broader ethical principle. Probably the best known statement of this principle was made in the following work.

A SAND COUNTY ALMANAC
Aldo Leopold
201–204 (1949).

THE LAND ETHIC

When god-like Odysseus returned from the wars in Troy, he hanged all on one rope a dozen slave-girls of his household whom be suspected of misbehavior during his absence.

This hanging involved no question of propriety. The girls were property. The disposal of property was then, as now, a matter of expediency, not of right and wrong.

Concepts of right and wrong were not lacking from Odysseus' Greece: witness the fidelity of his wife through the long years before at last his black-prowed galleys clove the wine-dark seas for home. The ethical structure of that day covered wives, but had not yet been extended to human chattels. During the three thousand years which have since elapsed, ethical criteria have been extended to many fields of conduct, with corresponding shrinkages in those judged by expediency only. . . .

The first ethics dealt with the relation between individuals; the Mosaic Decalogue is an example. Later accretions dealt with the relation between the individual and society. The Golden rule tries to integrate the individual to society; democracy to integrate social organization to the individual.

There is as yet no ethic dealing with man's relation to land and to the animals and plants which grow upon it. Land, like Odysseus' slave-girls, is still property. The land relation is still strictly economic, entailing privileges but not obligations.

The extension of ethics to this third element in human environment is, if I read the evidence correctly, an evolutionary possibility and an ecological necessity. It is the third step in a sequence. The first two have already been taken. Individual thinkers since the days of Ezekiel and Isaiah have asserted that the despoliation of land is not only inexpedient but wrong. Society, however, has not yet affirmed their belief....

An ethic may be regarded as a mode of guidance for meeting ecological situations so new or intricate, or involving such deferred reactions, that the path of social expediency is not discernible to the average individual. Animal instincts are modes of guidance for the individual in meeting such situations. Ethics are possibly a kind of community instinct in-the-making.

All ethics so far evolved rest upon a single premise: that the individual is a member of a community of interdependent parts. His instincts prompt him to compete for his place in that community, but his ethics prompt him also to co-operate (perhaps in order that there may be a place to compete for).

The land ethic simply enlarges the boundaries of the community to include soils, waters, plants, and animals, or collectively: the land.

This sounds simple: do we not already sing our love for and obligation to the land of the free and the home of the brave? Yes, but just what and whom do we love? Certainly not the soil, which we are sending helter-skelter downriver. Certainly not the waters, which we assume have no function except to turn turbines, float barges, and carry off sewage. Certainly not the plants, of which we exterminate whole communities without batting an eye. Certainly not the animals, of which we have already extirpated many of the largest and most beautiful species, A land ethic of course cannot prevent the alteration, management, and use of these 'resources', but it does affirm their right to continued existence, and, at least in spots, their continued existence in a natural state.

In short, a land ethic changes the role of *Homo sapiens* from conqueror of the land-community to plain member and citizen of it. It implies respect for his fellow-members, and also respect for the community as such.

In human history, we have learned (I hope) that the conqueror role is eventually self-defeating. Why? Because it is implicit in such a role that the conqueror knows, *ex cathedra,* just what makes the community clock tick, and just what and who is valuable, and what and who is worthless, in community life. It always turns out that he knows neither, and this is why his conquests eventually defeat themselves.

Notes and Comments

1.   Leopold's thesis, that we should consider plants and animals—in short, nature—to be part of the same community that includes humankind, has a potential alternative conclusion to the one Leopold draws. That is, if humankind is part of nature, then whatever we do is "natural." If we destroy plants and animals, it is no more unethical than if a volcano, asteroid, or earthquake destroyed plants and animals. Or are ethical considerations uniquely human? If so, does that suggest an unbridgeable gap between humans and the rest of nature?

2.   Leopold's ethical challenge is conspicuously agnostic. For those more religiously inclined, there can be a different ethical perspective. Historically, the focus has been on Genesis's reference to man having "dominion over the fish of the sea, and over the birds of the air, and over the cattle, and over all the earth, and over every creeping thing that creeps upon the earth." Genesis 1:26. This suggested that nature was man's for the taking; that it was there for man's benefit. More recently, scholars have argued that the Bible instead teaches that God enjoined man to be responsible for the environment; that God has made man the steward of the environment, responsible to God for the faithful execution of that duty. *See, e.g.,* John Copeland Nagle, *Playing Noah,* 82 U. MINN. L. REV. 1171 (1998); Chuck D. Barlow, *Why the Christian Right Must Protect the Environment: Theocentricity in the Political Workplace,* 23 B.C. ENVTL. AFF. L. REV. 781 (1996).

viii. Environmental Justice

As indicated above, the term "environmental justice" is used most often to describe concern with environmental harms being visited disproportionately on the poor and minority groups. In the 1980s a General Accounting Office report and a report by the Commission for Racial Justice of the United Church of Christ both found that the location of hazardous waste facilities were disproportionately found in black and Hispanic communities. These studies were then subjected to a number of criticisms. For example, the definition of a black or minority community was determined by the percentage of the population of the particular "community" exceeding the national average percentage of black or Hispanic residents. Thus, Staten Island, the "whitest" of the New York City boroughs, and the site of the largest solid waste site, was determined to be a minority community because 20% of its population is minority. Another criticism was that the studies did not show that the waste facilities were placed into existing minority communities, as opposed to the communities becoming minority communities through in-migration. *See, e.g.,* Vicki Been, *Locally Undesirable Land Uses in Minority Neighborhoods: Disproportionate Siting or Market Dynamics?,* 103 Yale L.J. 1383 (1994).

Notwithstanding the criticisms, there can be little question that poor people are more likely to suffer environmental harms than richer persons, just as they suffer worse housing, education, medical treatment, etc. And to the extent that the poor are disproportionately made up of minorities, minorities likewise will disproportionately bear the brunt of environmental problems. Moreover, to the extent that the political process can be used by affected persons to fight LULUs (locally unwanted land uses), those with the least political clout are the most likely to be the victims of LULU siting. Phrased as "environmental injustice" or "environmental racism," interest groups could perhaps hope to galvanize minority communities to use environmental laws and the political process to improve their situation.

For a while, a combination of environmental laws and Title VI of the Civil Rights Act of 1964 seemed like they might provide a handle to attack siting decisions that disproportionately affected minority communities. Title VI prohibits discrimination based on race, color, or national origin in any program receiving federal funds, and state agencies implementing the Clean Air Act, Clean Water Act, and other environmental statutes invariably receive federal funds to administer these laws under the cooperative federalism model. A person subject to discrimination under one of these programs can sue to enjoin the discrimination. That is, enforcement is not limited to the federal government enforcing the Act either through an injunction or withdrawing federal funds. *See Cannon v. University of Chicago*, 441 U.S. 677, 99 S.Ct. 1946, 60 L.Ed.2d 560 (1979). However, the Supreme Court has held that Title VI itself only prohibits *intentional* racial discrimination; it does not forbid disproportionate impacts. *See Alexander v. Choate*, 469 U.S. 287, 105 S.Ct. 712, 83 L.Ed.2d 661 (1985). Rarely, if ever, is the claim made that state officials have intentionally discriminated on the basis of race. Even if the suspicion is there, the proof is not. Rather, the claim is that the state official's decision has a disparate impact. Thus, at this point, Title VI provides little help.

There is, however, some authority for the idea that agencies can adopt regulations implementing Title VI that can go beyond prohibiting merely what the act itself prohibits. *See Guardians Assn. v. Civil Service Comm'n of New York City*, 463 U.S. 582, 103 S.Ct. 3221, 77 L.Ed.2d 866 (1983) (five justices in three separate opinions so indicated, but none of the opinions was joined by a majority of the Court). And indeed, agencies, including the EPA, have adopted regulations implementing Title VI that effectively prohibit discriminatory effects in its funded programs, even if the effect is unintentional. Consequently, minority persons who believed state environmental agencies' actions had the effect of disproportionately affecting them brought a number of suits alleging violations of EPA's regulations. *See, e.g., Chester Residents Concerned for Quality Living v. Seif*, 132 F.3d 925 (3d Cir. 1997), judgment vacated and case remanded, 524 U.S. 974, 119 S.Ct. 22, 141 L.Ed.2d 783 (1998) (mem.). In *Alexander v. Sandoval*, 532 U.S. 275, 121 S.Ct. 1511, 149 L.Ed.2d 517 (2001), however, the Supreme Court ruled that, while there is a private right of action directly under Title VI, there is no private right of action under an agency's Title VI regulations; these may be enforced only by the agency. Consequently, private suits under federal law trying to stop action receiving federal funds because of disparate effects on minority populations no longer may be brought.

While *Alexander v. Sandoval* did not directly rule on whether agencies may adopt regulations under Title VI that prohibit discriminatory effects without an intent to discriminate, the majority opinion stated that a finding of such a power would be "in considerable tension" with earlier decided cases. Nevertheless, that power is currently presumed to exist, and the agency regulations remain in effect, so that agencies may themselves enforce against discriminatory effects in programs they fund. Consequently, minority groups have filed Title VI complaints with EPA, requesting EPA to take enforcement action (or to deny approval to a particular state action because of the alleged discriminatory effects of the proposed state action). These have been notably unsuccessful. As of December 1, 2004, of the 118 complaints where action is completed, EPA has not found a single violation. *See* http://epa.gov/civilrights/docs/t6stdec012004.pdf (last visited on 2/23/2005). Perhaps not coincidentally, EPA's draft guidance on investigating administrative complaints published in June 2000 has never been finalized.

In 1994 President Clinton issued Executive Order 12898, Federal Actions to Address Environmental Justice in Minority Populations and Low–Income Populations. It continues in effect. The order required agencies to adopt an environmental justice strategy that identifies and addresses disproportionately high and adverse effects on minority and low-income populations. In addition, it requires agencies to conduct their programs in a manner that ensures such programs do not have the effect of excluding persons from the benefits of the programs because of their race, color, or national origin. Nevertheless, unlike Title VI, the executive order creates no private rights whatsoever and states that it is solely to improve the internal management of the executive branch. Consequently, like the regulatory reform executive orders discussed earlier in this chapter, courts will not consider whether agencies violate their requirements under the order.

This order has also had little to no effect on agencies' actions. Indeed, in 2004, the EPA Inspector General issued a scathing report on EPA's implementation of the order. In particular, it criticized the agency for not defining what a disproportionately high impact is or what is a minority or low-income community. The agency's response takes issue with the IG's report and suggests that the IG has misinterpreted the executive order:

> [T]he recommended OIG approach appears to be predicated on an intuitively reasonable but faulty interpretation of Executive Order 12898. The OIG recommended approach is premised on the commonly held notion, drawn from the Environmental Jus-

tice Movement's emergence from the Civil Rights Movement, that environmental justice can be achieved merely by identifying disproportionately high minority and low-income communities, and designating them as forming a "protected class." This approach fails to recognize that the Nation's environmental laws do not recognize race, ethnicity, or income as protected classes. To the contrary, those environmental laws are designed to address human health and environmental effects for all communities.

Memorandum, Agency Response to Recommendations Provided in the OIG Evaluation Report (June 7, 2004) (http://www.epa.gov/compliance/resources/publications/ej/ej_annual_project_reports.html, visited on July 8, 2004). In other words, EPA promotes environmental justice by assuring that all communities are protected, so there is no need to focus on minority and low-income groups.

Notes and Comments

1. It is easy to find fault with EPA's performance under either Title VI or Executive Order 12898. First, there is no specific funding for its environmental justice work. Probably more important, the task of determining who is responsible when poor and minority populations do not seem to benefit equally with others in America is, to say the least, daunting. And finally, why should we expect EPA to be any better in solving inequality with respect to environmental benefits than the rest of society is in solving inequality generally in America, especially when no environmental law provides them any particular tool? This seemingly hopeless job led some to criticize the Executive Order in the beginning as simply a political ploy to appeal to certain interest groups. *See, e.g.,* David Schoenbrod, *Environmental "Injustice" Is About Politics, Not Racism,* Wall St. J., Feb. 23, 1994, p. A21.

2. Nonetheless, even if the environmental justice movement has found the law an inhospitable partner, it is not without some successes in the political sphere. There are a number of cases where permits or siting permission have been denied, not on their face because of environmental justice issues, but because of the publicity and problems identified by an opposition movement motivated by environmental justice concerns. *See, e.g.,* Robert Holden and Tad Bartlett, *Leaving Communities Behind: the Evolving World of Environmental Justice,* 51 La. Bar J. 94 (August/September 2003)(telling the story of the proposed Shintech facility in Louisiana).

III. THE CONSTITUTION AND ENVIRONMENTAL LAW

A. Authority for Environmental Laws

As you have probably already learned in Constitutional Law, if not in high school, federal laws must find a basis in the Constitution. Unlike states, which have the inherent power to make all laws not prohibited by the Constitution, the federal government must be able to point to some constitutional provision as authority for laws passed by Congress. And there is no grant of authority in the Constitution for Congress to protect the environment. There are, however, a number of constitutional provisions that can provide a basis for environmental laws: the Commerce Clause, the Spending Clause, the Property Clause, and the Necessary and Proper Clause.

Probably the least problematic of these is the Property Clause, Article IV, Section 3, cl. 2: "The Congress shall have power to dispose of and make all needful rules and regulations respecting the territory or other property belonging to the United States." Not only is the textual authorization broad, but the Supreme Court has also read it broadly. *See Kleppe v. New Mexico*, 426 U.S. 529, 96 S.Ct. 2285, 49 L.Ed.2d 34 (1976) (upholding the Wild Free–Roaming Horses and Burros Act and concluding that Congress has "complete power" over federal lands). Consequently, any federal law regarding what happens on United States' property stands on strong constitutional foundations. Examples would include the National Forest Management Act, 16 U.S.C. §§ 1601 *et seq.*, and the Federal Land Policy and Management Act, 43 U.S.C. §§ 1701 *et seq.*, that govern the uses of lands owned by the federal government and managed by, respectively, the United States Forest Service and the Bureau of Land Management. Another example would be the provision of the Endangered Species Act that makes it unlawful to maliciously damage or destroy any endangered plant on lands under federal jurisdiction, 16 U.S.C. § 1538(a)(2)(B).

The Spending Clause is also broad. Article I, Section 8, cl. 1 provides that "Congress shall have the power to lay and collect taxes ... to pay the debts and provide for the common defence and general welfare of the United States." In other words, Congress can spend money for any purpose that furthers the general welfare of the United States. As yet, no court has found any expenditure not included within that authorization.

An important aspect of the spending power, however, is the ability to place conditions on expenditures. For example, states receive substantial sums of money from the federal government for the purpose of building highways, but there can be conditions on states receiving those funds beyond the simple requirement that they be used for building highways. One condition is that they cannot use those funds to build a highway through a park unless there is no feasible and prudent alternative route and plans minimize the adverse environmental impact on the park. 23 U.S.C. § 138. A condition of a different type is that the state will lose a portion of its highway funds if it does not maintain an adequate state implementation plan under the Clean Air Act. 42 U.S.C. § 7509(b)(1). In other words, a state may be induced to take certain actions it would not otherwise do by offering it money on the condition that it take those actions. There is a limit to such inducement, however. In *South Dakota v. Dole*, 483 U.S. 203, 107 S.Ct. 2793, 97 L.Ed.2d 171 (1987), the Supreme Court said that in order for a condition to be constitutional, (a) the condition itself must further the general welfare—but that, of course, is a very broad concept; (b) the condition must be unambiguous–the state must be on clear notice that by accepting the funds it is agreeing to the condition; (c) the condition must be related in some way to the reason the funds are being given to the state—in *Dole* the condition that states impose a minimum drinking age of 21 in order to receive all their federal highway funds was related because a higher drinking age meant less highway deaths; (d) the condition may not require the state to violate any constitutional provision; and (e) the condition must not be unduly coercive—in *Dole* the failure to impose the minimum drinking age would only result in the loss of a fairly small percentage of the state's highway funds and hence was not too coercive. Although these limitations on conditional spending can raise questions—especially with regard to the degree of necessary relationship between the condition and the federal spending and the point at which inducement becomes prohibited coercion—the courts have not invalidated any spending conditions in more than a half century.

The Necessary and Proper Clause together with the Treaty Clause can also provide a basis for congressional action. The Treaty Clause, Article II, Section 2, Cl. 2, states that the President makes treaties with the advice and consent of the Senate; the Necessary and Proper Clause, Article I, Section 8, Cl. 18, states that Congress can make all laws necessary and proper "for carrying into execution . . . all other powers vested by this Constitution in the Government of the United States, or in any Department or Officer thereof." In *Missouri v. Holland*, 252 U.S. 416, 40 S.Ct. 382, 64 L.Ed. 641 (1920), the Supreme Court upheld the Migratory Bird Treaty Act against a challenge that it was beyond Congress's powers. Earlier lower court opinions had found such an act beyond Congress's Commerce Clause powers, but then the United States entered into a treaty with Canada to protect migratory birds. The Court said that Congress could enact legislation to carry into execution the United States' duties under that treaty, even absent any other constitutional basis for the legislation.

Undoubtedly, the Commerce Clause is the most important source of authority for environmental laws—it is the articulated basis for the Clean Air Act, the Clean Water Act, and the various laws dealing with hazardous wastes and substances. The history of the interpretation of the Commerce Clause reflects periods of expansive interpretation followed by more restrictive interpretation. The restrictive approach of the Supreme Court at the beginning of the New Deal in the early 1930s gave way to the "modern" approach by the 1940s. This modern approach is exemplified by the cases of *United States v. Darby*, 312 U.S. 100, 61 S.Ct. 451, 85 L.Ed. 609 (1941), and *Wickard v. Filburn*, 317 U.S. 111, 63 S.Ct. 82, 87 L.Ed. 122 (1942). In those cases, the Court held that the Commerce Clause authorized Congress to regulate (a) the channels of interstate commerce—meaning Congress could regulate the means by which commerce is carried interstate, such as highways, rail lines, airspace, navigable waters, the and the broadcast spectrum; (b) the instrumentalities of interstate commerce—meaning what crosses state lines as part of commerce; and (c) activities that have a substantial effect on interstate commerce. Moreover, in order to determine whether activities would have a substantial effect on interstate commerce, Congress is allowed to aggregate a large number of small activities. Thus, in *Wickard*, Congress could regulate a farmer's production of 239 bushels of wheat in excess of the allowed amount, because if Congress could not regulate that farmer's small amount, it would not be able to regulate all other farmers' small amounts, which in aggregate would amount to such a substantial amount of wheat that it would have a meaningful effect on the interstate market in wheat.

For more than a half century, after the adoption of the modern approach, no federal statute was found unconstitutional as beyond Congress's Commerce Clause power. Some believed that meaningful limits on federal power under the Commerce Clause had ceased to exist. In recent Supreme Court cases, however, the Court has established that there is a limit. In *United States v. Lopez*, 514 U.S. 549, 115 S.Ct. 1624, 131 L.Ed.2d 626 (1995), the Court found unconstitutional the Gun Free School Zones Act, which made it a federal crime to possess a firearm within 500 feet of a school. And *United States v. Morrison*, 529 U.S. 598, 120 S.Ct. 1740, 146 L.Ed.2d 658 (2000), held unconstitutional the Violence Against Women Act's provisions authorizing civil suits against persons who commit acts of violence motivated by gender. In these, what-might-be-called, "post-modern" cases, the Court did not change the tests it had established in *Darby* and *Wickard*; indeed, it reaffirmed them, but it did clarify how activities might have a substantial effect on interstate commerce and, in particular, when activities with small impacts could be aggregated to reach a substantial effect.

In *Lopez*, the government argued that guns in schools would impact the quality of education; the lessened quality of education would affect national skills and productivity, resulting in a substantial effect on interstate commerce. In *Morrison*, it argued that gender-motivated violence affected medical bills, insurance costs, and persons' willingness to travel in interstate commerce. The Court rejected aggregation in these contexts. It noted that all the earlier cases had involved regulation of economic activity, and it suggested that the modern cases recognized the reality of a national economic marketplace, so that as a practical matter even local economic activities would invariably be linked directly to that national economy, thereby authorizing federal regulation. However, in *Lopez* and *Morrison* the Court said that the local activities were not economic or commercial in nature and were simply local criminal activity traditionally dealt with by state law. To allow aggregation of all the direct and indirect effects of local criminal activity, in order to show substantial effect on interstate commerce, would effectively remove any limit on federal legislative authority and would create a general, federal police power. This would be inconsistent with the constitutional design.

The question for us is how this case law affects environmental law. The constitutional authority for only one environmental law has been decided by the Supreme Court, and that was before the post-modern Commerce Clause cases. In 1981 the Supreme Court decided a pair of cases challenging various provisions of the Surface Mining Control and Reclamation Act, 30 U.S.C. §§ 1201 *et seq.*

HODEL v. VIRGINIA SURFACE MINING AND RECLAMATION ASSOCIATION, INC.

Supreme Court of the United States, 1981.

452 U.S. 264, 101 S.Ct. 2352, 69 L.Ed.2d 1.

Justice MARSHALL delivered the opinion of the Court.

These cases arise out of a pre-enforcement challenge to the constitutionality of the Surface Mining Control and Reclamation Act of 1977 (Surface Mining Act or Act).... In these appeals, we consider whether Congress, in adopting the Act, exceeded its powers under the Commerce Clause of the Constitution.... We conclude that in the context of a facial challenge, the Surface Mining Act does not suffer from any of these alleged constitutional defects, and we uphold the Act as constitutional.

I

A

The Surface Mining Act is a comprehensive statute designed to "establish a nationwide program to protect society and the environment from the adverse effects of surface coal mining operations." * * * Section 501 establishes a two-stage program for the regulation of surface coal mining: an initial, or interim regulatory phase, and a subsequent, permanent phase. The interim program mandates immediate promulgation and federal enforcement of some of the Act's environmental protection performance standards, complemented by continuing state regulation. Under the permanent phase, a regulatory program is to be adopted for each State, mandating compliance with the full panoply of federal performance standards, with enforcement responsibility lying with either the State or Federal Government.

Section 501(a) directs the Secretary to promulgate regulations establishing an interim regulatory program during which mine operators will be required to comply with some of the Act's performance standards, as specified by § 502(c). Included among those selected standards are requirements governing: (a) restoration of land after mining to its prior condition; (b) restoration of land to its approximate original contour; (c) segregation and preservation of topsoil; (d) minimization of disturbance to the hydrologic balance; (e) construction of coal mine waste piles used as dams and embankments; (f) revegetation of mined areas; and (g) spoil disposal....

Section 501(b) directs the Secretary to promulgate regulations establishing a permanent regulatory program incorporating all the Act's performance standards....

B

On October 23, 1978, the Virginia Surface Mining and Reclamation Association, Inc., an association of coal producers engaged in surface coal mining operations in Virginia, 63 of its member coal companies, and 4 individuals [*sic*] landowners filed suit in Federal District Court seeking declaratory and injunctive relief against various provisions of the Act. . . .

II

On cross-appeal, appellees argue that the District Court erred in rejecting their challenge to the Act as beyond the scope of congressional power under the Commerce Clause. They insist that the Act's principal goal is regulating the use of private lands within the borders of the States and not, as the District Court found, regulating the interstate commerce effects of surface coal mining. Consequently, appellees contend that the ultimate issue presented is "whether land as such is subject to regulation under the Commerce Clause, i. e. whether land can be regarded as 'in commerce.' " In urging us to answer "no" to this question, appellees emphasize that the Court has recognized that land-use regulation is within the inherent police powers of the States and their political subdivisions, and argue that Congress may regulate land use only insofar as the Property Clause grants it control over federal lands.

We do not accept either appellees' framing of the question or the answer they would have us supply. The task of a court that is asked to determine whether a particular exercise of congressional power is valid under the Commerce Clause is relatively narrow. The court must defer to a congressional finding that a regulated activity affects interstate commerce, if there is any rational basis for such a finding. This established, the only remaining question for judicial inquiry is whether "the means chosen by [Congress] must be reasonably adapted to the end permitted by the Constitution." The judicial task is at an end once the court determines that Congress acted rationally in adopting a particular regulatory scheme. . . .

Thus, when Congress has determined that an activity affects interstate commerce, the courts need inquire only whether the finding is rational. Here, the District Court properly deferred to Congress' express findings, set out in the Act itself, about the effects of surface coal mining on interstate commerce. Section 101(c) recites the congressional finding that

> "many surface mining operations result in disturbances of surface areas that burden and adversely affect commerce and the public welfare by destroying or diminishing the utility of land for commercial, industrial, residential, recreational, agricultural, and forestry purposes, by causing erosion and landslides, by contributing to floods, by polluting the water, by destroying fish and wildlife habitats, by impairing natural beauty, by damaging the property of citizens, by creating hazards dangerous to life and property by degrading the quality of life in local communities, and by counteract-

ing governmental programs and efforts to conserve soil, water, and other natural resources."

The legislative record provides ample support for these statutory findings.... In light of the evidence available to Congress and the detailed consideration that the legislation received, we cannot say that Congress did not have a rational basis for concluding that surface coal mining has substantial effects on interstate commerce....

The denomination of an activity as a "local" or "intrastate" activity does not resolve the question whether Congress may regulate it under the Commerce Clause. As previously noted, the commerce power "extends to those activities intrastate which so affect interstate commerce, or the exertion of the power of Congress over it, as to make regulation of them appropriate means to the attainment of a legitimate end, the effective execution of the granted power to regulate interstate commerce." This Court has long held that Congress may regulate the conditions under which goods shipped in interstate commerce are produced where the "local" activity of producing these goods itself affects interstate commerce. Appellees do not dispute that coal is a commodity that moves in interstate commerce. Here, Congress rationally determined that regulation of surface coal mining is necessary to protect interstate commerce from adverse effects that may result from that activity. This congressional finding is sufficient to sustain the Act as a valid exercise of Congress' power under the Commerce Clause.

Moreover, the Act responds to a congressional finding that nationwide "surface mining and reclamation standards are essential in order to insure that competition in interstate commerce among sellers of coal produced in different States will not be used to undermine the ability of the several States to improve and maintain adequate standards on coal mining operations within their borders." The prevention of this sort of destructive interstate competition is a traditional role for congressional action under the Commerce Clause. In *United States v. Darby*, the Court used a similar rationale to sustain the imposition of federal minimum wage and maximum hour regulations on a manufacturer of goods shipped in interstate commerce. The Court explained that the statute implemented Congress' view that "interstate commerce should not be made the instrument of competition in the distribution of goods produced under substandard labor conditions, which competition is injurious to the commerce and to the states from and to which the commerce flows." The same rationale applies here to support the conclusion that the Surface Mining Act is within the authority granted to Congress by the Commerce Clause.

Finally, we agree with the lower federal courts that have uniformly found the power conferred by the Commerce Clause broad enough to permit congressional regulation of activities causing air or water pollution, or other environmental hazards that may have effects in more than one State....

In sum, we conclude that the District Court properly rejected appellees' Commerce Clause challenge to the Act....

HODEL v. INDIANA

Supreme Court of the United States, 1981.

452 U.S. 314, 101 S.Ct. 2376, 69 L.Ed.2d 40.

Justice MARSHALL delivered the opinion of the Court.

This appeal, like *Hodel v. Virginia Surface Mining & Reclamation Assn., Inc.*, also decided today, involves a broad constitutional challenge to numerous important provisions of the Surface Mining Control and Reclamation Act of 1977. Many of the specific provisions attacked in this case, however, differ from the "steep-slope" provisions that were the primary focus of the challenge in *Virginia Surface Mining*. The United States District Court for the Southern District of Indiana ruled that the provisions of the Act challenged here are unconstitutional and permanently enjoined their enforcement. We noted probable jurisdiction, and we now reverse.

I

A

... Several of the challenged sections of the Act are known collectively as the "prime farmland" provisions. These sections establish special requirements for surface mining operations conducted on land that both qualifies as prime farmland under a definition promulgated by the Secretary of Agriculture and has historically been used as cropland.... A permit for surface coal mining on such lands may be granted only if the mine operator can demonstrate its "technological capability to restore such mined area, within a reasonable time, to equivalent or higher levels of yield as nonmined prime farmland in the surrounding area under equivalent levels of management...." The operator must also show that it can "meet the soil reconstruction standards" for prime farmland.... Furthermore, § 519(c)(2) provides that upon its completion of mining activities on prime farmland, a mine operator can have its performance bond released only on a showing that soil productivity "has returned to equivalent levels of yield as nonmined land of the same soil type in the surrounding area under equivalent management practices...."

Also challenged here are some of the Act's more general provisions that are applicable throughout the country. These include § 515(b)(3), which requires restoration of mined land to its approximate original contour, and the directive in § 515(b)(5) that surface mine operators remove topsoil separately during mining activities and preserve it for use during reclamation if it is not to be replaced immediately on the backfill area of the mining cut. Section 508 requires applicants for surface coal mining permits to submit proposed reclamation plans specifying the intended postmining use of the land and the method by which that use will be achieved. In addition, §§ 522(a), (c), (d) require States wishing to assume permanent regulatory authority over surface coal mining to establish an administrative procedure for determining whether particular lands are unsuitable for some or all kinds of surface mining. Section 522(e) proscribes mining activity within 100 feet of roadways and cemeteries or within 300 feet of public buildings, schools, churches, public parks, or occupied dwellings. Finally, the Act's procedures for collecting proposed civil penalties contained in § 518(c) are also drawn into question here....

II

The District Court gave two rationales for its decision on the Commerce Clause issue. The court first held that the six "prime farmland" provisions are beyond congressional power to regulate interstate commerce because they are "directed at facets of surface coal mining which have no substantial and adverse effect on interstate commerce."
...

With respect to the other 15 substantive provisions which apply to surface mining generally, the District Court reasoned that the only possible adverse effects on interstate commerce justifying congressional action are air and water pollution and determined that these effects are adequately addressed by other provisions of the Act. The court therefore concluded that these 15 provisions as well as the 6 prime farmland provisions "are not directed at the alleviation of water or air pollution, to the extent that there are [any] such effects, and are not means reasonably and plainly adapted to [the legitimate end of] removing any substantial and adverse effect on interstate commerce." We find both of the District Court's rationales untenable....

In our view, Congress was entitled to find that the protection of prime farmland is a federal interest that may be addressed through Commerce Clause legislation.... More important, the court below incorrectly assumed that the relevant inquiry under the rational-basis test is the volume of commerce actually affected by the regulated activity. This Court held in *NLRB v. Fainblatt*, 306 U.S. 601, 606, 59 S.Ct. 668, 671, 83 L.Ed. 1014 (1939), that "[t]he power of Congress to regulate interstate commerce is plenary and extends to all such commerce be it great or small." The pertinent inquiry therefore is not how much commerce is involved but whether Congress could rationally conclude that the regulated activity affects interstate commerce.

Against this background, we have little difficulty in concluding that the congressional finding in this case satisfies the rational-basis test. The Senate considered information from the Interagency Report about the prime farmland acreage that might be affected by surface coal mining....

In our judgment, the evidence summarized in the Reports mandates the conclusion that Congress had a rational basis for finding that surface coal mining on prime farmland affects interstate commerce in agricultural products. As we explained in *Stafford v. Wallace*, 258 U.S. 495, 521, 42 S.Ct. 397, 403, 66 L.Ed. 735 (1922):

> Whatever amounts to more or less constant practice, and threatens to obstruct or unduly to burden the freedom of interstate commerce is within the regulatory power of Congress under the commerce clause, and it is primarily for Congress to consider and decide the fact of danger and meet it. This court will certainly not substitute its judgment for that of Congress unless the relation of the subject to interstate commerce and its effect upon it are clearly non-existent.

The court below improperly substituted its judgment for the congressional determination.

We also conclude that the court below erred in holding that the prime farmland and 15 other substantive provisions challenged by appellees are not reasonably related to the legitimate goal of protecting interstate commerce from adverse effects attributable to surface coal mining. The court incorrectly assumed that the Act's goals are limited to preventing air and water pollution. As we noted in *Hodel v. Virginia Surface Mining & Reclamation Assn., Inc.*, Congress was also concerned about preserving the productive capacity of mined lands and protecting the public from health and safety hazards that may result from surface coal mining. All the provisions invalidated by the court below are reasonably calculated to further these legitimate goals.

For example, the approximate-original-contour requirement in § 515(b)(5) is designed to avoid the environmental and other harm that may result from unreclaimed or improperly restored mining cuts. . . .

Congress adopted the Surface Mining Act in order to ensure that production of coal for interstate commerce would not be at the expense of agriculture, the environment, or public health and safety, injury to any of which interests would have deleterious effects on interstate commerce. Moreover, as noted in *Hodel v. Virginia Surface Mining & Reclamation Assn., Inc.*, the Act reflects the congressional goal of protecting mine operators in States adhering to high performance and reclamation standards from disadvantageous competition with operators in States with less rigorous regulatory programs. The statutory provisions invalidated by the District Court advance these legitimate goals, and we conclude that Congress acted reasonably in adopting the regulatory scheme contained in the Act.[17] * * *

Justice REHNQUIST, concurring in the judgment in both *Hodel v. Virginia Surface Mining and Reclamation Assn., Inc.* and *Hodel v. Indiana*.

---

17. Appellees contend that a number of the specific provisions challenged in this case cannot be shown to be related to the congressional goal of preventing adverse effects on interstate commerce. This claim, even if correct, is beside the point. A complex regulatory program such as established by the Act can survive a Commerce Clause challenge without a showing that every single facet of the program is independently and directly related to a valid congressional goal. It is enough that the challenged provisions are an integral part of the regulatory program and that the regulatory scheme when considered as a whole satisfies this test.

* * * It would be a mistake to conclude that Congress' power to regulate pursuant to the Commerce Clause is unlimited. Some activities may be so private or local in nature that they simply may not be *in* commerce. Nor is it sufficient that the person or activity reached have *some* nexus with interstate commerce. Our cases have consistently held that the regulated activity must have a *substantial* effect on interstate commerce. Moreover, simply because Congress may conclude that a particular activity substantially affects interstate commerce does not necessarily make it so. Congress' findings must be supported by a "rational basis" and are reviewable by the courts. In short, unlike the reserved police powers of the States, which are plenary unless challenged as violating some specific provision of the Constitution, the connection with interstate commerce is itself a jurisdictional prerequisite for any substantive legislation by Congress under the Commerce Clause.

In many ways, the Court's opinions in these cases are consistent with that approach. In both the *Virginia* and *Indiana* cases, the Court exhaustively analyzes Congress' articulated justifications for the exercise of its power under the Commerce Clause and concludes that Congress' detailed factual findings as to the effect of surface mining on interstate commerce are sufficient to justify the exercise of that power. Though there can be no doubt that Congress in regulating surface mining has stretched its authority to the "nth degree," our prior precedents compel me to agree with the Court's conclusion. I therefore concur in the judgments of the Court.

There is, however, a troublesome difference between what the Court does and what it says. In both cases, the Court asserts that regulation will be upheld if Congress had a rational basis for finding that the regulated activity affects interstate commerce. . . . In my view, the Court misstates the test. As noted above, it has long been established that the commerce power does not reach activity which merely "affects" interstate commerce. There must instead be a showing that regulated activity has a *substantial effect* on that commerce. . . .

In sum, my difficulty with some of the recent Commerce Clause jurisprudence is that the Court often seems to forget that legislation enacted by Congress is subject to two different kinds of challenge, while that enacted by the States is subject to only one kind of challenge. Neither Congress nor the States may act in a manner prohibited by any provision of the Constitution. Congress must show that the activity it seeks to regulate has a substantial effect on interstate commerce. It is my uncertainty as to whether the Court intends to broaden, by some of its language, this test that leads me to concur only in the judgments.

The Chief Justice [Burger], concurring in both cases.

I agree largely with what Justice Rehnquist has said about ... the gradual case-by-case expansion of the reach of the Commerce Clause.

I agree fully with his view that we often seem to forget the doctrine that laws enacted by Congress under the Commerce Clause must be based on a substantial effect on interstate commerce. However, I join the

Court's opinions in these cases ... because in them the Court acknowledges and reaffirms that doctrine.

* * *

Notes and Comments

1. The opinions for the Court in both *Lopez* and *Morrison* were authored by then Chief Justice Rehnquist. In *Lopez* he took care to enshrine the point in his concurrence in the two *Hodels* that there must be a *substantial* effect on commerce in order to justify federal regulation under the third doctrinal test, not just *some* effect. In *Morrison* he made clear that congressional findings that an activity has a substantial effect on commerce are subject to serious judicial review and are not presumed valid. Both these points modify slightly the Court's earlier discussion in the *Hodels* but would not change the outcomes. More broadly, however, Rehnquist as Chief Justice writing for the Court in *Lopez* and *Morrison* also brought home his earlier statement as an Associate Justice that "some activities may be so private or local in nature that they simply may not be *in* commerce." Do *Lopez* and *Morrison* raise any question about the continued applicability of the two *Hodels* or whether the theory underlying them would be applied to uphold other environmental laws?

2. In a recent Supreme Court environmental case this concern with federal regulation of local activities under the Commerce Clause led the Court, in another opinion by Chief Justice Rehnquist, to interpret the Clean Water Act narrowly to avoid the constitutional question whether the Act more broadly interpreted would exceed Congress's power under the Commerce Clause. *See Solid Waste Agency of Northern Cook County v. U.S. Army Corps of Engineers*, 531 U.S. 159, 121 S.Ct. 675, 148 L.Ed.2d 576 (2001).

3. There are, of course, a number of environmental laws that regulate economic activity in ways that the *Lopez* and *Morrison* Courts would find fully within the traditional realm of federal regulation. For example, the Federal Insecticide, Fungicide, and Rodenticide Act, 7 U.S.C. §§ 136 *et seq.*, regulates the sale and use of pesticides; the Toxic Substances Control Act, 15 U.S.C. §§ 2601 *et seq.*, regulates the manufacture, sale, and disposal of chemicals that present an unreasonable risk of injury to health or the environment. The mobile source provisions of the Clean Air Act, 42 U.S.C. §§ 7521–7590, regulate what pollution controls new motor vehicles must have in order to be sold. In other words, these laws are directed at economic activity, albeit for the purpose of protecting the environment and public health and safety.

4. The Clean Water Act can probably avoid this line of cases altogether, because by its terms the CWA applies to "waters of the United States," which the Supreme Court has now interpreted to mean either navigable waters or waters somehow connected to or affecting those navigable waters. Navigable waters are themselves channels of interstate commerce and so can be regulated and protected without any showing of a substantial effect on interstate commerce. *But see* William Funk, *The Court, the Clean Water Act, and the Constitution:* SWANCC *and Beyond*, 31 ELR 10741 (2001)(arguing that because the CWA's purposes and effects do not involve protection of navigation or commerce by water, neither the navigability of the waters nor

the cases upholding federal regulation of waters as channels of interstate commerce should be relevant to the constitutionality of the CWA).

5. There are a number of post-*Lopez* or *Morrison* cases from the courts of appeals in which persons challenged the constitutionality of various environmental laws. *None* of those challenges has yet been successful. For example, in *United States v. Olin Corp.*, 107 F.3d 1506 (11th Cir. 1997), Olin challenged the constitutionality of the Comprehensive Environmental Response, Compensation and Liability Act, which makes persons liable for the clean up of hazardous substances that have been released to the environment. Olin argued that the disposal of hazardous substances at its site was not economic activity and the release did not affect interstate commerce. The Eleventh Circuit applied *Lopez* and found that the disposal of hazardous substances by companies on their sites was an economic activity and that, even if Olin's release itself did not affect interstate commerce, there was ample evidence that releases of hazardous substances in the aggregate did affect interstate commerce.

6. The Endangered Species Act has probably raised the most constitutional questions. Certain aspects of the ESA are clearly within Congress's power. For example, a major portion of the ESA's protections involves federal actions themselves or private actions on federal lands. Neither would raise a serious constitutional issue. Moreover, some of the ESA protections are undoubtedly authorized by the Commerce Clause. For example, the ESA regulates the importation of endangered species or their parts. Also, the ESA protects some species which are commercial in nature, such as salmon. The particular cases that may present problems involve protections on private lands of wildlife that has no commercial value. As of this writing, however, no cases involving such wildlife have held the Act unconstitutional as applied to them. In *Rancho Viejo, LLC v. Norton*, 323 F.3d 1062 (D.C. Cir. 2003), the court upheld the constitutionality of the ESA with respect to its protection of the Arroyo Southwestern Toad, a toad that lives only in California. In *GDF Realty Investments, Ltd. v. Norton*, 326 F.3d 622 (5th Cir. 2003), the court upheld the Act as applied to four spiders and two beetles that only live underground in two counties in Texas. In *National Ass'n of Home Builders v. Babbitt*, 130 F.3d 1041 (D.C. Cir. 1997), the court upheld the Act as applied to the Delhi Sands Flower–Loving Fly, that only lives in two counties in California. While these three cases all found the protection of these exotic species within the Commerce Clause power of Congress, they did not agree on how the Clause authorized this protection. For example, the *Rancho Viejo* court rested its analysis on the fact that the activity threatening the toad, and precluded by the ESA, was itself activity affecting interstate commerce– a residential housing development. The *GDF Realty* court, however, expressly rejected such a basis for its decision, finding instead that the ESA was an economic regulatory scheme because it protects biodiversity generally, and the total destruction of biodiversity would have a substantial effect on interstate commerce. Even if the destruction of a particular, non-commercial species would only have a de minimis effect on interstate commerce, to allow it to avoid regulation would enable the wholesale destruction of biodiversity one species at a time. In the *National Ass'n of Home Builders* case, there was no majority opinion, with one judge using an analysis similar to the *GDF Realty* court, one judge using an analysis similar to the *Rancho Viejo*

court, and one judge dissenting, arguing that the ESA could not constitutionally protect the Delhi Sands Flower–Loving Fly. *See also Gibbs v. Babbitt,* 214 F.3d 483 (4th Cir. 2000)(upholding ESA as applied to red wolves on the basis that taking wolves was itself an economic activity because, invariably, the taking was done to protect farmers' property and, alternatively, on the basis that Congress can protect an endangered species in order to return its numbers to a place where harvest of that species would have economic value).

B. Constitutional Limitations on Environmental Laws

Even if a matter is otherwise within the power of Congress to make law, there may be constitutional limitations on the exercise of that power. There are three constitutional limitations particularly applicable to environmental law: the Tenth Amendment, the Eleventh Amendment, and the Takings Clause of the Fifth Amendment.

1. Tenth Amendment

The Tenth Amendment reserves those powers not delegated to the United States to the States and to the people. The judicial construction of the Tenth Amendment, like much of the Constitution, has varied over time, sometimes providing real constraints on congressional action and at other times providing virtually no restriction. A Tenth Amendment issue has arisen in two distinct circumstances: one is where the federal law interferes with the way a state would like to regulate something, and the claim is that interference with a traditional state prerogative violates the Tenth Amendment; the other is where the federal law directly regulates a state or an entity of a state. In the former context, the Court has been fairly consistent in denying Tenth Amendment claims, holding that so long as Congress is acting within its Article I powers, the fact that it interferes with a historical state prerogative does not violate the Tenth Amendment. *See, e.g., Hodel v. Virginia Surface Mining and Reclamation Ass'n,* 452 U.S. 264, 101 S.Ct. 2352, 69 L.Ed.2d 1 (1981)(in a portion of the opinion edited from version earlier in this chapter). Thus, in these kinds of cases, the decision as to whether something is within Congress's constitutional power ends the analysis.

The second circumstance itself has two dimensions: (1) when the federal law regulates everyone who engages in certain activities, and a state or state entity happens to be one of those persons; and (2) when the federal law requires a state or state entity to act essentially as an agent of the federal government to carry out federal policy. The former situation is governed by the case of *Garcia v. San Antonio Metropolitan Transit Authority,* 469 U.S. 528, 105 S.Ct. 1005, 83 L.Ed.2d 1016 (1985). *Garcia* involved a federal law mandating minimum wages and overtime pay to any employee and whether those requirements could be enforced with respect to a municipal bus system. The Court held in this context that the Tenth Amendment was essentially tautological and had no independent force restricting laws otherwise within Congress's Commerce Clause power. In other words, the constitutional test is the same as when Congress regulates private entities. Therefore, federal laws may regulate states to the extent that they or their subdivsions engage in actions that have a substantial effect on interstate commerce. For example, federal laws might require state buildings to meet federal energy conservation requirements or prohibit state workers from harming federal endangered species.

The latter situation, however, when the federal law requires a state to act as an agent of the federal government to carry out federal policy, is governed by a different case: *New York v. United States*, 505 U.S. 144, 112 S.Ct. 2408, 120 L.Ed.2d 120 (1992). In this case, the Court found one part of the federal Low–Level Radioactive Waste Policy Amendments Act unconstitutional in light of the Tenth Amendment. That part effectively required states to adopt legislation to administer a federal program, or as the Court put it: the law commandeered the states to act as agencies of the federal government. That is, something may be subject to federal regulation under the Commerce Clause because of its substantial effect on interstate commerce, but the federal government may not accomplish that regulation simply by directing the states to adopt and administer the regulatory scheme on behalf of the federal government. A subsequent case, *Printz v. United States*, 521 U.S. 898, 117 S.Ct. 2365, 138 L.Ed.2d 914 (1997), made clear that the same prohibition exists when Congress attempts to commandeer state or local executive officials as well as when it commandeers state legislatures. In *New York*, nevertheless, the Court reaffirmed the constitutionality of the cooperative federalism model used by most environmental statutes, where the federal government provides that states may regulate the environment if their state plans are approved by EPA, but states are not required to so regulate. If they fail to adopt state plans that meet federal standards, then EPA adopts a federal plan that regulates the environment in the state in place of the state doing it. Thus, the state's decision to regulate according to the federal framework is voluntary and not required. Moreover, the court reiterated the ability of the federal government to provide funds to the states upon the condition that the states undertake certain activities. Again, however, because the state can refuse the funds (and thereby the conditions), the state's decision to regulate according to a federal framework is voluntary and not required.

2. The Eleventh Amendment

The Eleventh Amendment, passed to overrule an early Supreme Court decision that subjected a state to a suit in federal court brought by a citizen of another state, has been interpreted since 1890 generally to prohibit private suits against states in federal court. *See Hans v. Louisiana*, 134 U.S. 1, 10 S.Ct. 504, 33 L.Ed. 842 (1890). Despite its limited wording, the amendment was perceived as a constitutional recognition of state sovereign immunity from private law suits; it does not bar suits brought by the federal government against a state. While the Court has held that Congress can override that immunity under the powers granted to Congress in the Civil War Amendments, it was not clear whether

Congress could likewise overcome a state's sovereign immunity from private suits under its Article I powers. In 1989, a person sued Pennsylvania under the federal Comprehensive Environmental Response, Compensation and Liability Act for the costs of a hazardous waste cleanup, and the Supreme Court in a divided opinion held that CERCLA, enacted under Congress's Commerce Clause authority, could abrogate state sovereign immunity. *See Pennsylvania v. Union Gas Co.*, 491 U.S. 1, 109 S.Ct. 2273, 105 L.Ed.2d 1 (1989). However, seven years later the Court overruled *Union Gas* and held that Congress cannot abrogate state sovereign immunity under its Article I powers. *Seminole Tribe of Florida v. Florida*, 517 U.S. 44, 116 S.Ct. 1114, 134 L.Ed.2d 252 (1996). Thus, environmental statutes cannot generally authorize private suits, such as citizen suits or suits for compensation, like in CERCLA, against unconsenting states.

There is one major loophole around this prohibition. Early on, in *Ex parte Young*, 209 U.S. 123, 28 S.Ct. 441, 52 L.Ed. 714 (1908), the Court held that it did not violate state sovereign immunity for a private person to sue a state officer for injunctive relief, alleging the officer was violating the Constitution. This has subsequently been extended to suits alleging the state officer is violating federal law. Accordingly, if a state agency were polluting illegally under federal law, a person could sue the state official who heads the agency under a federal citizen suit provision for an injunction to stop the unlawful polluting.

As indicated earlier, state sovereign immunity does not bar EPA or the U.S. Department of Justice from suing states. Moreover, state sovereign immunity does not extend to local governments, so persons can generally sue municipalities and various forms of local government under citizen suit provisions.

3. The Takings Clause

The Fifth Amendment provides, among other things, that private property may not be taken for a public use without just compensation. This clause impacts environmental legislation because many environmental laws restrict what persons may do with their private property. They may not be able to develop their property in the ways they might wish because to do so would run afoul of one or more environmental laws. The issue then is whether that restriction on the use of their property "takes" their property. If an environmental law does "take" their property, the government must pay "just compensation"; the law is not enjoined as unconstitutional.

In a famous case, Justice Oliver Wendell Holmes declared that if a governmental regulation goes "too far," it will constitute a taking. *See Pennsylvania Coal Co. v. Mahon*, 260 U.S. 393, 43 S.Ct. 158, 67 L.Ed. 322 (1922). The question, of course, is how far is "too far." Over the years, the Court has developed a couple of *per se* tests; that is, if the circumstances fit these tests, then the regulation is a taking. If, however, neither of these circumstances apply, then the Court has directed that courts use one of two *ad hoc* tests, each of which balances a number of factors to determine whether the regulation goes too far and is a taking.

One *per se* test is whether the government regulation authorizes the physical possession or permanent physical invasion of a person's property. For example, in *Kaiser Aetna v. United States*, 444 U.S. 164, 100 S.Ct. 383, 62 L.Ed.2d 332 (1979), the Court found that requiring Kaiser Aetna to open its marina to the public amounted to a taking. Another *per se* test asks whether the government regulation has totally deprived the landowner of all value in the land. If so, it is a taking. This might occur where a restriction to protect the environment precludes the landowner from developing the land in any way. *See Lucas v. South Carolina Coastal Council*, 505 U.S. 1003, 112 S.Ct. 2886, 120 L.Ed.2d 798 (1992).

The more common situation, especially in environmental law applications, is a restriction on the development of some portion of a person's land, such as a prohibition on filling a wetland or developing an area that is habitat for an endangered species. One question that arises in this situation is whether the restriction on a portion of a person's land should be viewed as a total deprivation of economic value of that portion of the land, and therefore a *per se* taking of that portion of the land, or whether it should be viewed as only a partial deprivation of the value of the entire parcel. The Supreme Court has seemed consistently to answer this question to say that one must judge the deprivation in light of the entire parcel, not just the affected portion of the parcel, in determining whether there has been a total deprivation triggering a *per se* taking. *See, e.g., Tahoe–Sierra Preservation Council, Inc. v. Tahoe Regional Planning Agency*, 535 U.S. 302, 122 S.Ct. 1465, 152 L.Ed.2d 517 (2002).

Absent the physical possession or invasion of property or the total deprivation of economic value of the property, courts are to use a multi-factored approach to determining whether a government restriction constitutes a taking. *Penn Central Transp. Co. v. City of New York*, 438 U.S. 104, 98 S.Ct. 2646, 57 L.Ed.2d 631 (1978), is the case generally cited for identifying those factors to be considered when a regulation generally restricts the use of property. The overall concern is to assure that the regulation does not force some people alone to bear burdens which, in all fairness and justice, should be borne by the public as a whole. Thus, the court is to consider the economic impact of the regulation, the extent to which the regulation has interfered with reasonable investment backed expectations, and the nature and character of the government action. An important consideration is whether the regulation provides a "reciprocity of advantage," a term that refers to the effects of a regulation, like zoning, that applies to all and both benefits and restricts at the same time.

When a government regulation does not just restrict the use of property but also imposes a condition on its use, there is an additional or alternative *ad hoc* test to be applied to the condition. This is common in local land use planning contexts, but it can also occur under federal environmental laws, such as regulations under the Clean Water Act requiring persons who wish to fill waters of the United States to obtain a permit conditioned on the person engaging in various mitigation activities. The Court has said that such conditions, or regulatory exactions, must meet two requirements to avoid being a taking. First, there must be an "essential nexus" between the legitimate state interest justifying the restriction and the effects of the condition. That is, the effect of the condition must further the state interest for imposing the restriction. For example, in *Nollan v. California Coastal Comm'n*, 483 U.S. 825, 107 S.Ct. 3141, 97 L.Ed.2d 677 (1987), California failed this test when it required beachfront property owners to provide an easement to the public across their beach as a condition of obtaining a building permit. The Court found no connection between the state interest in requiring a building permit and the creation of an easement for the public to walk on the beach. The second requirement for conditions is that there must be a "rough proportionality" between the impacts of the condition on the private property owner and the furtherance of the legitimate state interest. For example, in *Dolan v. City of Tigard*, 512 U.S. 374, 114 S.Ct. 2309, 129 L.Ed.2d 304 (1994), Tigard had required a hardware store to donate a portion of its property as a "greenway" for a floodplain to counter the effects of increased runoff from the proposed development and for a bike path to mitigate the effects of increased traffic that would be generated by the proposed development. The Court held that neither of these conditions were roughly proportionate. First, there was no basis for requiring the owner to deed some of its property to the city for flood control purposes, when merely preserving that portion of the property in an undeveloped state would fully serve the flood control purposes. Second, there was no evidence that the amount of increased traffic to be generated by the development bore any relation to what effect the bike path would have in terms of reducing traffic.

Under either the *Penn Central* or the *Dolan* tests, courts must apply rather malleable concepts to particular situations. As a result, the outcome of cases using these tests are sometimes difficult to predict and may turn more on the particular facts and the proclivities of the particular judges than a "rule of law" might find ideal. Probably what drives the outcome in these cases more than the phrasing of the test is the assignment of the burden of proof. A person seeking to establish a taking under the *Penn Central* test has the burden of proof to establish that a taking has occurred. Under the *Dolan* test, while the plaintiff land owner still has the overall burden of proof, the government has the burden of proof with regard to the essential nexus and rough proportionality of the condition. Thus, plaintiffs tend to fare better under the *Dolan* test than the *Penn Central* test.

It has long been understood that a property owner has no right to use property in a manner that creates either a private or public nuisance. Consequently, any government regulation that bars a person from creating a nuisance, no matter how great an impact that might have on the person's property, would not deprive the person of any property *right*, so no compensation would be due. A question arises whether, if a legislature enacts a law barring something that courts have not recognized as a nuisance but which the legislature believes is "nuisance-like," such a law would be viewed as comparable to a nuisance and therefore could avoid a takings claim. An earlier Supreme Court decision, *Miller v. Schoene*, 276 U.S. 272, 48 S.Ct. 246, 72 L.Ed. 568 (1928), suggested that it could, but the more recent *Lucas* case seemed to take a harder line on the ability of legislatures to define "new" nuisances.

Underlying the nuisance exception and the "reasonable investment backed expectations" factor in the *Penn Central* test is the concept of background principles of property law. That is, when a person obtains property, the person takes that property subject to the background principles of property law—such as the principle that no one has the right to create a nuisance. But does this mean that all existing statutory and regulatory provisions are part of the background principles when a person obtains property? If you buy property knowing that the Clean Water Act restricts the filling of waters of the United States, can you later sue for just compensation if it turns out that you cannot fill the waters on your property that you must fill in order to develop the property? A recent Supreme Court case, *Palazzolo v. Rhode Island*, 533 U.S. 606, 121 S.Ct. 2448, 150 L.Ed.2d 592 (2001), overturned a Rhode Island Supreme Court decision that a law in existence when a person obtains property necessarily becomes part of the background principles under which the person takes the property. Such a rule, the Court said, would divest the owner at the time the regulation came into existence of the ability to transfer the interest possessed prior to the regulation. Instead, the prior existence of the regulation would be considered in the weighing of the *Penn Central* factors, in particular in considering the extent of the person's *reasonable* investment backed expectations.

If a person believes that the federal government has "taken" his property, his suit for compensation generally must be filed in the United States Court of Federal Claims, which has exclusive jurisdiction over suits for just compensation if the amount involved exceeds $10,000. 28 U.S.C. § 1491. Appeals from this court go to the United States Court of Appeals for the Federal Circuit, a court of appeals with nationwide jurisdiction. Thus, generally speaking, federal district courts and the geographic courts of appeals do not play significant roles in the development of Takings law, whereas the Federal Circuit's decisions are of special importance.

Notes and Comments

1. While the Tenth Amendment imposes a limitation on the tools the federal government may use to effect its regulatory ends, most persons do not consider the restrictions to impose significant burdens. Most federal environmental statutes that involve states follow the cooperative federalism model approved by the Court, or involve the conditional use of federal funds, also approved by the Court. Nevertheless, there may be some statutes that were drafted before or in ignorance of *New York v. United States* that run afoul of it. For example, in *ACORN v. Edwards*, 81 F.3d 1387 (5th Cir.

1996), the court found one subsection of the Safe Drinking Water Act unconstitutional under *New York*. That subsection required each state to establish a program to assist school districts in testing for, and remedying, lead contamination in drinking water from coolers under their jurisdiction. Can you see why that would raise problems under *New York v. United States*?

2. Environmentalists normally want to interpret the Takings Clause narrowly, so that it has minimal effect. They fear that if government action that protects the environment results in having to pay just compensation, government will be less willing to take action that protects the environment. Of course, if a law requires a government agency to take certain action to protect the environment, the fact that such action might require payment of just compensation to a private landowner would provide no legal excuse for not taking that action. Moreover, at the federal level, normally the agency doing the regulation would not be financially responsible for payment of the just compensation; a different federal appropriation would be involved. Nevertheless, to the extent that environmentally protective actions might result in large numbers of awards of just compensation, there obviously would be political ramifications to those actions. To date, however, the number of awards under the Takings Clause has been minimal, occurring almost entirely in connection with restrictions on the filling of wetlands.

3. One could argue that the failure to pay just compensation liberally might result in a backlash against environmental regulations that impact private persons' use of their property. If landowners actually could receive compensation for environmentally protective action, they might be much more willing to take it. The Clean Water Act's regulation of wetlands and the Endangered Species Act's restrictions have been especially controversial precisely because they have so often seemed to thwart traditional development or resource utilization to the economic detriment of landowners.

C. Constitutional Limitations on State Laws

While states do not need to find authority in the U.S. Constitution to make laws to protect the environment, the Constitution does place limitations on what states may do. For example, the Takings Clause, discussed above as a limitation on federal action, applies to state action through the Fourteenth Amendment, using the same tests described above.

1. The Supremacy Clause

The Supremacy Clause declares that federal laws are the supreme law of the land, so that federal laws may preempt states from protecting their own environment in ways they believe proper. There are said to be three different types of preemption: (1) express preemption, where a statute expressly precludes a state from regulating; (2) implied preemption, where a federal statute so fills the field as to imply that there is no room for further state regulation (sometimes called "field preemption"); and (3) conflict preemption, where a state law stands as an obstacle to the fulfilling the purpose of the federal law. *See, e.g., Cipollone v. Liggett Group, Inc.,* 505 U.S. 504, 112 S.Ct. 2608, 120 L.Ed.2d 407 (1992). Most of the basic environmental laws, however, do not create an exclusive federal regime. Usually they explicitly allow states to provide greater protection than mandated by federal laws. Nevertheless, there are exceptions.

An example is the Clean Air Act's requirements for pollution controls on automobiles. In order to ensure that auto manufacturers are not made subject to differing requirements in each of the various states, the Clean Air Act makes the federal pollution requirement the exclusive requirement, generally precluding states from adopting their own requirements. At the time the Act was passed in 1970, California already imposed a requirement on cars sold in California, and southern California's air was particularly bad, so the Clean Air Act made an exception for California, grandfathering its ability to set a requirement stricter than the federal standard. Later, this exception was broadened, so that other states could impose the identical requirement as California. As a result, now car manufacturers essentially must produce two different kinds of cars, one that meets California's standards for sale in California and the other states that have adopted it, and one for the rest of the nation.

Another example is the Federal Insecticide, Fungicide, and Rodenticide Act's labeling provisions. In order to protect persons who might be exposed to pesticides, FIFRA allows EPA to regulate the labels and directions for pesticides. FIFRA then says that states "shall not impose or continue in effect any requirements for labeling or packaging in addition to or different from those required under this chapter." Thus, manufacturers are subject only to a uniform national requirement for labeling and packaging.

Despite these clear statements of preemption, questions still may arise under these provisions as to whether the effects of state law result in a "requirement in addition to or different from" the federal standard. A recurring question has been whether Congress intended to preclude tort actions for negligence or strict liability when it writes preclusion provisions like the one in FIFRA. In *Cippolone v. Liggett Group, Inc.*, the Court addressed a similar preemption provision governing cigarette labeling and held that common law actions were preempted. Subsequently, most circuits have applied the *Cippolone* reasoning to FIFRA's provision.

Determining field preemption is particularly difficult, because it involves a judicial inference of Congress's intent that must be derived from an overall sense of a statute. Where the matter involved is one traditionally regulated by the states, rather than the federal government, there is a presumption against field preemption, but ultimately the question is what Congress's purpose was. *See, e.g., United States v. Locke*, 529 U.S. 89, 120 S.Ct. 1135, 146 L.Ed.2d 69 (2000)(federal statutes governing requirements for ship construction and safe operation pre-empted field so that Washington could not require particular operating procedures by tankers in Puget Sound to protect against oil spills).

2. The Dormant Commerce Clause

The constitutional doctrine of the Dormant Commerce Clause is complicated, if only because there is no textual basis for it. The original justification, that the grant of power to regulate commerce among the states to the federal government operated to withdraw any state power to regulate commerce among the states, has been rejected, but the doctrine nevertheless lives on. At its most basic level it precludes states from discriminating against interstate commerce in favor of their own commerce or from discriminating against out-of-state interests in commerce. Thus, for example, Nebraska could not forbid the export out of state of its ground water. *Sporhase v. Nebraska, ex rel. Douglas*, 458 U.S. 941, 102 S.Ct. 3456, 73 L.Ed.2d 1254 (1982). Similarly, New Jersey could not prohibit the importation of solid waste into the state. *City of Philadelphia v. New Jersey*, 437 U.S. 617, 98 S.Ct. 2531, 57 L.Ed.2d 475 (1978). Such discrimination is permissible only if there is no other way of achieving a legitimate state purpose. *See Maine v. Taylor,* 477 U.S. 131, 106 S.Ct. 2440, 91 L.Ed.2d 110 (1986)(upholding ban on the importation of baitfish because of inability to separate baitfish with parasites from other baitfish). It is not a legitimate state purpose merely to protect in-state economic interests. Moreover, "a State may not accord its own inhabitants a preferred right of access over consumers in other States to natural resources located within its borders." *City of Philadelphia*, 437 U.S. at 627. If a state statute regulates in-state and out-of-state interests equally, the fact that out-of-state interests may be disproportionately affected does not itself create a violation of the Dormant Commerce Clause, although if the disproportionate effect is significant, courts are to weigh the legitimate state interests furthered by the regulation against the costs to interstate commerce. If the latter clearly outweigh the former, the regulation would be found in violation of the Dormant Commerce Clause.

In the environmental area, there have been recurring problems related to states and localities' attempts to regulate the transportation and disposal of solid and hazardous waste. In *City of Philadelphia* the Court said that states could not ban the importation of solid waste. In *National Solid Wastes Management Ass'n v. Alabama Dept. of Envtl. Mgmt.*, 910 F.2d 713 (11th Cir. 1990), the Eleventh Circuit reached the same conclusion with respect to hazardous waste. In *Chemical Waste Management, Inc. v. Hunt*, 504 U.S. 334, 112 S.Ct. 2009, 119 L.Ed.2d 121 (1992), the Supreme Court overturned Alabama's response to the Eleventh Circuit decision, a surcharge imposed on in-state disposal of hazardous waste generated in other states that was higher than the charge imposed on disposal of the same waste generated in state. Oregon attempted to get around the *Hunt* decision by justifying its higher charge for the disposal of out-of-state solid waste than for in-state waste on the basis that in-state waste producers already had to pay taxes and other charges to the state. Thus, the claim was that the higher out-of-state charge was merely compensatory. The Court did not accept this claim and rejected the charge. *Oregon Waste Systems, Inc. v. Department of*

Envtl. Quality of the State of Or., 511 U.S. 93, 114 S.Ct. 1345, 128 L.Ed.2d 13 (1994). In *Fort Gratiot Sanitary Landfill, Inc. v. Michigan Dept. of Natural Resources*, 504 U.S. 353, 112 S.Ct. 2019, 119 L.Ed.2d 139 (1992), the Court found that a county ban on disposal of out-of-county solid waste, even though it applied not only to out-of-state waste but also to in-state waste from outside the county, violated the Dormant Commerce Clause.

Some states and localities have responded to solid waste problems by supporting the construction of waste recycling centers, separating out recyclables and thereby reducing the total volume of solid waste. The problem is that these facilities are expensive, and many localities have attempted to subsidize them by enacting "flow control ordinances," laws that require all local solid waste to be brought to the local recycling center at which there is a "tipping fee" for the waste disposed of there. This creates a legal monopoly enabling the recycling center to charge an inflated price, thereby enabling recovery of the high cost of its construction and operation. Absent such a legal monopoly, the wastes would simply be brought to commercial waste disposal sites, because typically they charge less than the recycling centers. These laws have also been challenged under the Dormant Commerce Clause, and in *C & A Carbone, Inc. v. Town of Clarkstown*, 511 U.S. 383, 114 S.Ct. 1677, 128 L.Ed.2d 399 (1994), the Supreme Court held that the town's flow control ordinance discriminated against interstate commerce and therefore was unconstitutional. It discriminated against interstate commerce in two ways: first, it restricted persons from sending waste out of state for disposal at lower cost and, second, it raised the cost of out-of-state waste sent into the locality (because it would then have to be sent to the high-cost recycling center).

There are a large number of lower court cases involving Dormant Commerce Clause challenges to flow control ordinances and other local attempts to manage solid waste problems. Some seem to apply *Carbone* in a straightforward and liberal manner and therefore tend to find the local actions unconstitutional. Others read it narrowly to find distinguishing circumstances that will enable the state or local law to pass muster. For example, because localities have historically collected solid waste and garbage for their residents as a government service, some courts have been willing to let local governments monopolize the solid waste collection industry, including running the recycling centers without violating the Dormant Commerce Clause. *See, e.g., United Haulers Ass'n, Inc. v. Oneida–Herkimer Solid Waste Management Authority*, 261 F.3d 245 (2d Cir. 2001); *USA Recycling, Inc. v. Town of Babylon*, 66 F.3d 1272 (2d Cir. 1995). Localities are in the best position when they actually own the facility that discriminates, as opposed to acting as a government regulator. Supreme Court precedent provides an exception to the Dormant Commerce Clause restrictions when a state or locality acts as a market participant rather than a market regulator. *See, e.g., Reeves, Inc. v. Stake*, 447 U.S. 429, 100 S.Ct. 2271, 65 L.Ed.2d 244. 447 U.S. 429, 100 S.Ct. 2271, 65 L.Ed.2d 244 (1980). Thus, if a state or locality itself operates a landfill or recycling facility, it may as a market participant discriminate against out-of-state waste. Of course, if it acts merely as a market participant, it will not be able to require by law that everyone bring their waste to its facility, precisely what was required in *Carbone* in order to make the facility financially viable.

D. Constitutional Limitations on Bringing Lawsuits

In courses on Constitutional Law, you learn that Article III of the Constitution limits the jurisdiction of federal courts to "cases and controversies." Thus, in order for a federal court to hear a case, the case must meet the various tests that have been established in judicial decisions for determining whether it is a "case or controversy" within the meaning of Article III. One of the most important tests is whether a plaintiff has "standing" to bring a case. In order to have standing, a plaintiff must have suffered, or be about to suffer, injury caused by an allegedly unlawful action, and a court must be able to grant relief to redress or avoid the injury.

Many of the important recent standing cases have arisen in an environmental law context. A watershed case was *Sierra Club v. Morton*, 405 U.S. 727, 92 S.Ct. 1361, 31 L.Ed.2d 636 (1972). In that case, the Sierra Club brought a case against the Secretaries of Interior and Agriculture, alleging that their proposed approval of the development of a ski resort in the Sequoia National Forest adjacent to the Sequoia National Park would violate several environmental laws. The initial question before the Court, however, was whether the Sierra Club was entitled to obtain judicial review of the federal agencies' actions. While the Sierra Club was obviously interested in and concerned about development activities in wild areas in California, the Court held that such interest and concern were not sufficient to establish "standing"; the Sierra Club must suffer actual injury. However, the Court said, aesthetic or recreational injury would suffice. That is, if a member of the Sierra Club liked to walk in the woods where the development was scheduled to take place, the creation of a ski resort in place of a wild scenic area might injure the member's aesthetic or recreational experience. This would suffice to establish constitutional injury for purposes of standing.*

Subsequent to *Sierra Club v. Morton*, there have been a number of cases testing the limits of what kinds of injury will suffice for standing in environmental lawsuits. Probably the most significant of these cases was *Lujan v. Defenders of Wildlife*.

---

* Public interest and environmental groups can bring lawsuits on behalf of one or more of their members under the doctrine of "representational" standing. Under this doctrine, an association can sue in its own name on behalf of its members if: (1) one of its members would have standing to bring the action, (2) the lawsuit relates to the purposes of the organization, and (3) neither the claim asserted nor the relief requested requires the participation of indi- vidual members (which in practical terms means the action is not for damages, but is for declaratory or injunctive relief). *See Hunt v. Washington State Apple Advertising Comm'n*, 432 U.S. 333, 97 S.Ct. 2434, 53 L.Ed.2d 383 (1977). Thus, much public in- terest and environmental litigation requires these groups to find members who actually would suffer the injury requisite for stand- ing.

LUJAN v. DEFENDERS OF WILDLIFE

Supreme Court of the United States, 1992.
504 U.S. 555, 112 S.Ct. 2130, 119 L.Ed.2d 351.

JUSTICE SCALIA delivered the opinion of the Court with respect to Parts I, II, III–A, and IV, and an opinion with respect to Part III–B in which the CHIEF JUSTICE, JUSTICE WHITE, and JUSTICE THOMAS join.

This case involves a challenge to a rule promulgated by the Secretary of the Interior interpreting § 7 of the Endangered Species Act of 1973 (ESA), in such fashion as to render it applicable only to actions within the United States or on the high seas. The preliminary issue, and the only one we reach, is whether the respondents here, plaintiffs below, have standing to seek judicial review of the rule.

I

[The ESA, which is administered jointly by the Secretaries of Interior and Commerce, provides in § 7(a) that Federal agencies must consult with either the Secretary of Interior or Commerce before undertaking actions that might jeopardize the continued existence of any endangered species or threatened species. In 1978, the Fish and Wildlife Service (FWS) and the National Marine Fisheries Service (NMFS), on behalf of the Secretary of the Interior and the Secretary of Commerce respectively, promulgated a joint regulation stating that this obligation extends to Federal actions taken in foreign nations. In 1986, however, these agencies issued a revised regulation, reinterpreting the ESA, to limit the consultation obligation to Federal actions taken in the United States or on the high seas. Shortly thereafter, respondents, organizations dedicated to wildlife conservation causes, filed this action against the Secretary of the Interior, seeking a declaratory judgment that the new regulation is in error as to the geographic scope of this requirement of the ESA and an injunction requiring the Secretary to promulgate a new regulation restoring the initial interpretation. The District Court granted the Secretary's motion to dismiss for lack of standing, and the Eighth Circuit reversed.]

II

While the Constitution of the United States divides all power conferred upon the Federal Government into "legislative Powers," Art. I, § 1, "[t]he executive Power," Art. II, § 1, and "[t]he judicial Power," Art. III, § 1, it does not attempt to define those terms. To be sure, it limits the jurisdiction of federal courts to "Cases" and "Controversies," but an executive inquiry can bear the name "case" (the Hoffa case) and a legislative dispute can bear the name "controversy" (the Smoot–Hawley controversy). Obviously, then, the Constitution's central mechanism of separation of powers depends largely upon common understanding of what activities are appropriate to legislatures, to executives, and to courts.... One of those landmarks, setting apart the "Cases" and "Controversies" that are of the justiciable sort referred to in Article III ... is the doctrine of standing. Though some of its elements express merely prudential considerations that are part of judicial self-government, the core component of standing is an essential and unchanging part of the case-or-controversy requirement of Article III.

Over the years, our cases have established that the irreducible constitutional minimum of standing contains three elements: First, the plaintiff must have suffered an "injury in fact"—an invasion of a legally-protected interest which is (a) concrete and particularized[2] and (b) "actual or imminent, not 'conjectural' or 'hypothetical.' " Second, there must be a causal connection between the injury and the conduct complained of—the injury has to be "fairly ... trace[able] to the challenged action of the defendant, and not ... th[e] result [of] the independent action of some third party not before the court." Third, it must be "likely," as opposed to merely "speculative," that the injury will be "redressed by a favorable decision."

The party invoking federal jurisdiction bears the burden of establishing these elements. Since they are not mere pleading requirements but rather an indispensable part of the plaintiff's case, each element must be supported in the same way as any other matter on which the plaintiff bears the burden of proof, *i.e.*, with the manner and degree of evidence required at the successive stages of the litigation....

When the suit is one challenging the legality of government action or inaction, the nature and extent of facts that must be averred (at the summary judgment stage) or proved (at the trial stage) in order to establish standing depends considerably upon whether the plaintiff is himself an object of the action (or forgone action) at issue. If he is, there is ordinarily little question that the action or inaction has caused him injury, and that a judgment preventing or requiring the action will redress it. When, however, as in this case, a plaintiff's asserted injury arises from the government's allegedly unlawful regulation (or lack of regulation) of someone else, much more is needed. In that circumstance, causation and redressability ordinarily hinge on the response of the regulated (or regulable) third party to the government action or inaction—and perhaps on the response of others as well. The existence of one or more of the essential elements of standing "depends on the unfettered choices made by independent actors not before the courts and whose exercise of broad and legitimate discretion the courts cannot presume either to control or to predict," and it becomes the burden of the plaintiff to adduce facts showing that those choices have been or will be made in such manner as to produce causation and permit redressability of injury....

2. By particularized, we mean that the injury must affect the plaintiff in a personal and individual way.

III

We think the Court of Appeals failed to apply the foregoing principles in denying the Secretary's motion for summary judgment. Respondents had not made the requisite demonstration of (at least) injury and redressability.

A

Respondents' claim to injury is that the lack of consultation with respect to certain funded activities abroad "increas[es] the rate of extinction of endangered and threatened species." Of course, the desire to use or observe an animal species, even for purely aesthetic purposes, is undeniably a cognizable interest for purpose of standing. "But the 'injury in fact' test requires more than an injury to a cognizable interest. It requires that the party seeking review be himself among the injured." To survive the Secretary's summary judgment motion, respondents had to submit affidavits or other evidence showing, through specific facts, not only that listed species were in fact being threatened by funded activities abroad, but also that one or more of respondents' members would thereby be "directly" affected apart from their " 'special interest' in th[e] subject."

With respect to this aspect of the case, the Court of Appeals focused on the affidavits of two Defenders' members—Joyce Kelly and Amy Skilbred. Ms. Kelly stated that she traveled to Egypt in 1986 and "observed the traditional habitat of the endangered Nile crocodile there and intend[s] to do so again, and hope[s] to observe the crocodile directly," and that she "will suffer harm in fact as a result of [the] American ... role ... in overseeing the rehabilitation of the Aswan High Dam on the Nile ... and [in] develop [ing] ... Egypt's ... Master Water Plan." Ms. Skilbred averred that she traveled to Sri Lanka in 1981 and "observed th[e] habitat" of "endangered species such as the Asian elephant and the leopard" at what is now the site of the Mahaweli Project funded by the Agency for International Development (AID), although she "was unable to see any of the endangered species;" "this development project," she continued, "will seriously reduce endangered, threatened, and endemic species habitat including areas that I visited ... [, which] may severely shorten the future of these species;" that threat, she concluded, harmed her because she "intend[s] to return to Sri Lanka in the future and hope[s] to be more fortunate in spotting at least the endangered elephant and leopard." When Ms. Skilbred was asked at a subsequent deposition if and when she had any plans to return to Sri Lanka, she reiterated that "I intend to go back to Sri Lanka," but confessed that she had no current plans....

We shall assume for the sake of argument that these affidavits contain facts showing that certain agency-funded projects threaten listed species—though that is questionable. They plainly contain no facts, however, showing how damage to the species will produce "imminent" injury to Mss. Kelly and Skilbred. That the women "had visited" the areas of the projects before the projects commenced proves nothing. As we have said in a related context, " '[p]ast exposure to illegal conduct does not in itself show a present case or controversy regarding injunctive relief . . . if unaccompanied by any continuing, present adverse effects.' " And the affiants' profession of an "inten[t]" to return to the places they had visited before—where they will presumably, this time, be deprived of the opportunity to observe animals of the endangered species—is simply not enough. Such "some day" intentions—without any description of concrete plans, or indeed even any specification of when the some day will be—do not support a finding of the "actual or imminent" injury that our cases require.

Besides relying upon the Kelly and Skilbred affidavits, respondents propose a series of novel standing theories. The first, inelegantly styled "ecosystem nexus," proposes that any person who uses any part of a "contiguous ecosystem" adversely affected by a funded activity has standing even if the activity is located a great distance away. This approach, as the Court of Appeals correctly observed, is inconsistent with our opinion in [*Lujan* v.] *National Wildlife Federation*, [497 U.S. 871, 110 S.Ct. 3177 (1990),] which held that a plaintiff claiming injury from environmental damage must use the area affected by the challenged activity and not an area roughly "in the vicinity" of it. . . .

Respondents' other theories are called, alas, the "animal nexus" approach, whereby anyone who has an interest in studying or seeing the endangered animals anywhere on the globe has standing; and the "vocational nexus" approach, under which anyone with a professional interest in such animals can sue. Under these theories, anyone who goes to see Asian elephants in the Bronx Zoo, and anyone who is a keeper of Asian elephants in the Bronx Zoo, has standing to sue because the Director of AID did not consult with the Secretary regarding the AID-funded project in Sri Lanka. This is beyond all reason. . . . It is clear that the person who observes or works with a particular animal threatened by a federal decision is facing perceptible harm, since the very subject of his interest will no longer exist. It is even plausible—though it goes to the outermost limit of plausibility—to think that a person who observes or works with animals of a particular species in the very area of the world where that species is threatened by a federal decision is facing such harm, since some animals that might have been the subject of his interest will no longer exist. It goes beyond the limit, however, and into pure speculation and fantasy, to say that anyone who observes or works with an endangered species, anywhere in the world, is appreciably harmed by a single project affecting some portion of that species with which he has no more specific connection.

B.

Besides failing to show injury, respondents failed to demonstrate redressability. . . . Since the agencies funding the projects were not parties to the case, the District Court could accord relief only against the Secretary: He could be ordered to revise his regulation to require consultation for foreign projects. But this would not remedy respondents' alleged injury unless the funding agencies were bound by the Secretary's regulation, which is very much an open question. . . .

A further impediment to redressability is the fact that the agencies generally supply only a fraction of the funding for a foreign project. AID, for example, has provided less than 10% of the funding for the Mahaweli Project. Respondents have produced nothing to indicate that the projects they have named will either be suspended, or do less harm to listed species, if that fraction is eliminated. . . . [I]t is entirely conjectural whether the nonagency activity that affects respondents will be altered or affected by the agency activity they seek to achieve. There is no standing.

IV

The Court of Appeals found that respondents had standing for an additional reason: because they had suffered a "procedural injury." The so-called "citizen-suit" provision of the ESA provides, in pertinent part, that "any person may commence a civil suit on his own behalf (A) to enjoin any person, including the United States and any other governmental instrumentality or agency . . . who is alleged to be in violation of any provision of this chapter." The court held that, because § 7(a) requires interagency consultation, the citizen-suit provision creates a "procedural righ[t]" to consultation in all "persons"—so that *anyone* can file suit in federal court to challenge the Secretary's (or presumably any other official's) failure to follow the assertedly correct consultative procedure, notwithstanding their inability to allege any discrete injury flowing from that failure. To understand the remarkable nature of this holding one must be clear about what it does not rest upon: This is not a case where plaintiffs are seeking to enforce a procedural requirement the disregard of which could impair a separate concrete interest of theirs (*e.g.*, the procedural requirement for a hearing prior to denial of their license application, or the procedural requirement for an environmental impact statement before a federal facility is constructed next door to them).[7] . . . Rather, the court held that the injury-in-fact requirement had been satisfied by congressional conferral upon all persons of an abstract, self-contained, noninstrumental "right" to have the Executive observe the procedures required by law. We reject this view[8]

---

7. There is this much truth to the assertion that "procedural rights" are special: The person who has been accorded a procedural right to protect his concrete interests can assert that right without meeting all the normal standards for redressability and immediacy. Thus, under our case-law, one living adjacent to the site for proposed construction of a federally licensed dam has standing to challenge the licensing agency's failure to prepare an Environmental Impact Statement, even though he cannot establish with any certainty that the Statement will cause the license to be withheld or altered,

and even though the dam will not be completed for many years. (That is why we do not rely, in the present case, upon the Government's argument that, *even if* the other agencies were obliged to consult with the Secretary, they might not have followed his advice.) What respondents' "procedural rights" argument seeks, however, is quite different from this: standing for persons who have no concrete interests affected—persons who live (and propose to live) at the other end of the country from the dam.

8. . . . We do *not* hold that an individual cannot enforce procedural rights; he as-

We have consistently held that a plaintiff raising only a generally available grievance about government—claiming only harm to his and every citizen's interest in proper application of the Constitution and laws, and seeking relief that no more directly and tangibly benefits him than it does the public at large—does not state an Article III case or controversy. . . .

To be sure, our generalized-grievance cases have typically involved Government violation of procedures assertedly ordained by the Constitution rather than the Congress. But there is absolutely no basis for making the Article III inquiry turn on the source of the asserted right. Whether the courts were to act on their own, or at the invitation of Congress, in ignoring the concrete injury requirement described in our cases, they would be discarding a principle fundamental to the separate and distinct constitutional role of the Third Branch—one of the essential elements that identifies those "Cases" and "Controversies" that are the business of the courts rather than of the political branches. "The province of the court," as Chief Justice Marshall said in *Marbury v. Madison*, "is, solely, to decide on the rights of individuals." Vindicating the *public* interest (including the public interest in government observance of the Constitution and laws) is the function of Congress and the Chief Executive. The question presented here is whether the public interest in proper administration of the laws (specifically, in agencies' observance of a particular, statutorily prescribed procedure) can be converted into an individual right by a statute that denominates it as such, and that permits all citizens (or, for that matter, a subclass of citizens who suffer no distinctive concrete harm) to sue. If the concrete injury requirement has the separation-of-powers significance we have always said, the answer must be obvious: To permit Congress to convert the undifferentiated public interest in executive officers' compliance with the law into an "individual right" vindicable in the courts is to permit Congress to transfer from the President to the courts the Chief Executive's most important constitutional duty, to "take Care that the Laws be faithfully executed," Art. II, § 3. . . .

Nothing in this contradicts the principle that "[t]he ... injury required by Art. III may exist solely by virtue of 'statutes creating legal rights, the invasion of which creates standing.' " [But the cases in which this was said] involved Congress's elevating to the status of legally cognizable injuries concrete, *de facto* injuries that were previously inade-

---

suredly can, so long as the procedures in question are designed to protect some threatened concrete interest of his that is the ultimate basis of his standing. The dissent, however, asserts that there exist "classes of procedural duties ... so enmeshed with the prevention of a substantive, concrete harm that an individual plaintiff may be able to demonstrate a sufficient likelihood of injury just through the breach of that procedural duty." If we understand this correctly, it means that the government's violation of a certain (undescribed) class of procedural duty satisfies the concrete-injury requirement by itself, without any showing that the procedural violation endangers a concrete interest of the plaintiff (apart from his interest in having the procedure observed). We cannot agree. The dissent is unable to cite a single case in which we actually found standing solely on the basis of a "procedural right" unconnected to the plaintiff's own concrete harm. . . .

quate in law (namely, injury to an individual's personal interest in living in a racially integrated community and injury to a company's interest in marketing its product free from competition.) As we said in *Sierra Club v. Morton*, "[Statutory] broadening [of] the categories of injury that may be alleged in support of standing is a different matter from abandoning the requirement that the party seeking review must himself have suffered an injury." [I]t is clear that in suits against the government, at least, the concrete injury requirement must remain.

JUSTICE KENNEDY, with whom JUSTICE SOUTER joins, concurring in part and concurring in the judgment.

. . . While it may seem trivial to require that Mss. Kelly and Skilbred acquire airline tickets to the project sites or announce a date certain upon which they will return, this is not a case where it is reasonable to assume that the affiants will be using the sites on a regular basis, nor do the affiants claim to have visited the sites since the projects commenced. With respect to the Court's discussion of respondents' "ecosystem nexus," "animal nexus," and "vocational nexus" theories, I agree that on this record respondents' showing is insufficient to establish standing on any of these bases. I am not willing to foreclose the possibility, however, that in different circumstances a nexus theory similar to those proffered here might support a claim to standing. . . .

I also join Part IV of the Court's opinion with the following observations. As government programs and policies become more complex and far-reaching, we must be sensitive to the articulation of new rights of action that do not have clear analogs in our common-law tradition. Modern litigation has progressed far from the paradigm of Marbury suing Madison to get his commission, or Ogden seeking an injunction to halt Gibbons' steamboat operations. In my view, Congress has the power to define injuries and articulate chains of causation that will give rise to a case or controversy where none existed before, and I do not read the Court's opinion to suggest a contrary view. In exercising this power, however, Congress must at the very least identify the injury it seeks to vindicate and relate the injury to the class of persons entitled to bring suit. The citizen-suit provision of the Endangered Species Act does not meet these minimal requirements, because while the statute purports to confer a right on "any person . . . to enjoin . . . the United States and any other governmental instrumentality or agency . . . who is alleged to be in violation of any provision of this chapter," it does not of its own force establish that there is an injury in "any person" by virtue of any "violation."

The Court's holding that there is an outer limit to the power of Congress to confer rights of action is a direct and necessary consequence of the case and controversy limitations found in Article III. I agree that it would exceed those limitations if, at the behest of Congress and in the absence of any showing of concrete injury, we were to entertain citizen-suits to vindicate the public's nonconcrete interest in the proper administration of the laws. While it does not matter how many persons have been injured by the challenged action, the party bringing suit must show that the action injures him in a concrete and personal way. This requirement is not just an empty formality. It preserves the vitality of the adversarial process by assuring both that the parties before the court have an actual, as opposed to professed, stake in the outcome, and that "the legal questions presented ... will be resolved, not in the rarefied atmosphere of a debating society, but in a concrete factual context conducive to a realistic appreciation of the consequences of judicial action." In addition, the requirement of concrete injury confines the Judicial Branch to its proper, limited role in the constitutional framework of government....

JUSTICE STEVENS, concurring in the judgment.

Because I am not persuaded that Congress intended the consultation requirement in § 7(a)(2) of the ESA, to apply to activities in foreign countries, I concur in the judgment of reversal. I do not, however, agree with the Court's conclusion that respondents lack standing because the threatened injury to their interest in protecting the environment and studying endangered species is not "imminent." Nor do I agree with the plurality's additional conclusion that respondents' injury is not "redressable" in this litigation.

In my opinion a person who has visited the critical habitat of an endangered species, has a professional interest in preserving the species and its habitat, and intends to revisit them in the future has standing to challenge agency action that threatens their destruction. Congress has found that a wide variety of endangered species of fish, wildlife, and plants are of "aesthetic, ecological, educational, historical, recreational, and scientific value to the Nation and its people." Given that finding, we have no license to demean the importance of the interest that particular individuals may have in observing any species or its habitat, whether those individuals are motivated by aesthetic enjoyment, an interest in professional research, or an economic interest in preservation of the species....

The Court nevertheless concludes that respondents have not suffered "injury in fact" because they have not shown that the harm to the endangered species will produce "imminent" injury to them. I disagree. An injury to an individual's interest in studying or enjoying a species and its natural habitat occurs when someone (whether it be the government or a private party) takes action that harms that species and habitat. In my judgment, therefore, the "imminence" of such an injury should be measured by the timing and likelihood of the threatened environmental harm, rather than by the time that might elapse between the present and the time when the individuals would visit the area if no such injury should occur....

Although I believe that respondents have standing, I nevertheless concur in the judgment of reversal because I am persuaded that the Government is correct in its submission that § 7(a)(2) does not apply to activities in foreign countries....

JUSTICE BLACKMUN, with whom JUSTICE O'CONNOR joins, dissenting.

I part company with the Court in this case in two respects. First, I believe that respondents have raised genuine issues of fact—sufficient to survive summary judgment—both as to injury and as to redressability. Second, I question the Court's breadth of language in rejecting standing for "procedural" injuries. I fear the Court seeks to impose fresh limitations on the constitutional authority of Congress to allow citizen-suits in the federal courts for injuries deemed "procedural" in nature. I dissent.

... Were the Court to apply the proper standard for summary judgment, I believe it would conclude that the sworn affidavits and deposition testimony of Joyce Kelly and Amy Skilbred advance sufficient facts to create a genuine issue for trial concerning whether one or both would be imminently harmed by the Aswan and Mahaweli projects. In the first instance, as the Court itself concedes, the affidavits contained facts making it at least "questionable" (and therefore within the province of the factfinder) that certain agency-funded projects threaten listed species. The only remaining issue, then, is whether Kelly and Skilbred have shown that they personally would suffer imminent harm....

By requiring a "description of concrete plans" or "specification of when the some day [for a return visit] will be," the Court, in my view, demands what is likely an empty formality. No substantial barriers prevent Kelly or Skilbred from simply purchasing plane tickets to return to the Aswan and Mahaweli projects. This case differs from other cases in which the imminence of harm turned largely on the affirmative actions of third parties beyond a plaintiff's control....

The Court also concludes that injury is lacking, because respondents' allegations of "ecosystem nexus" failed to demonstrate sufficient proximity to the site of the environmental harm. To support that conclusion, the Court mischaracterizes our decision in *Lujan v. National Wildlife Federation*, as establishing a general rule that "a plaintiff claiming injury from environmental damage must use the area affected by the challenged activity." In *National Wildlife Federation*, the Court required specific geographical proximity because of the particular type of harm alleged in that case: harm to the plaintiff's visual enjoyment of nature from mining activities. One cannot suffer from the sight of a ruined landscape without being close enough to see the sites actually being mined. Many environmental injuries, however, cause harm distant from the area immediately affected by the challenged action. Environmental destruction may affect animals traveling over vast geographical ranges, see, *e.g., Japan Whaling Assn. v. American Cetacean Soc.*, 478 U.S. 221 (1986)(harm to American whale watchers from Japanese whaling activities), or rivers running long geographical courses, see, *e.g., Arkansas v. Oklahoma,* 503 U.S. 91 (1992)(harm to Oklahoma residents from wastewater treatment plant 39 miles from border). It cannot seriously be contended that a litigant's failure to use the precise or exact site where animals are slaughtered or where toxic waste is dumped into a river means he or she cannot show injury.

The Court also rejects respondents' claim of vocational or professional injury. The Court says that it is "beyond all reason" that a zoo "keeper" of Asian elephants would have standing to contest his government's participation in the eradication of all the Asian elephants in another part of the world. I am unable to see how the distant location of the destruction necessarily (for purposes of ruling at summary judgment) mitigates the harm to the elephant keeper. If there is no more access to a future supply of the animal that sustains a keeper's livelihood, surely there is harm. . . .

The Court concludes that any "procedural injury" suffered by respondents is insufficient to confer standing. It rejects the view that the "injury-in-fact requirement . . . [is] satisfied by congressional conferral upon *all* person of an abstract, self-contained, noninstrumental 'right' to have the Executive observe the procedures required by law." Whatever the Court might mean with that very broad language, it cannot be saying that "procedural injuries" *as a class* are necessarily insufficient for purposes of Article III standing.

Most governmental conduct can be classified as "procedural." Many injuries caused by governmental conduct, therefore, are categorizable at some level of generality as "procedural" injuries. Yet, these injuries are not categorically beyond the pale of redress by the federal courts. When the Government, for example, "procedurally" issues a pollution permit, those affected by the permittee's pollutants are not without standing to sue. Only later cases will tell just what the Court means by its intimation that "procedural" injuries are not constitutionally cognizable injuries. In the meantime, I have the greatest of sympathy for the courts across the country that will struggle to understand the Court's standardless exposition of this concept today.

The Court expresses concern that allowing judicial enforcement of "agencies' observance of a particular, statutorily prescribed procedure" would "transfer from the President to the courts the Chief Executive's most important constitutional duty, to 'take Care that the Laws be faithfully executed,' Art. II, sec. 3." In fact, the principal effect of foreclosing judicial enforcement of such procedures is to transfer power into the hands of the Executive at the expense—not of the courts—but of Congress, from which that power originates and emanates. . . .

It is to be hoped that over time the Court will acknowledge that some classes of procedural duties are so enmeshed with the prevention of a substantive, concrete harm that an individual plaintiff may be able to demonstrate a sufficient likelihood of injury just through the breach of that procedural duty. For example, in the context of the NEPA requirement of environmental impact statements, this Court has acknowledged "it is now well settled that NEPA itself does not mandate particular results [and] simply prescribes the necessary process," but "these procedures are almost certain to affect the agency's substantive decision." This acknowledgment of an inextricable link between procedural and substantive harm does not reflect improper appellate factfinding. It reflects nothing more than the proper deference owed to the judgment of a coordinate branch—Congress—that certain procedures are directly tied to protection against a substantive harm. . . .

Notes and Comments

1. The Court recognized that the citizen suit provision of the Endangered Species Act authorizes a lawsuit by "any person" to challenge action by any person violating the Act. How was it then that the Court held that Defenders of Wildlife could not bring the lawsuit? What does this say about persons later bringing lawsuits under the ESA's citizen suit provision?

2. The Court for a number of years seemingly was hostile to environmentalists, denying standing in other environmental cases besides *Defenders*. *See Lujan v. National Wildlife Federation*, 497 U.S. 871, 110 S.Ct. 3177, 111 L.Ed.2d 695 (1990)(lack of injury); *Steel Co. v. Citizens for a Better Environment*, 523 U.S. 83, 118 S.Ct. 1003, 140 L.Ed.2d 210 (1998)(lack of redressability). *Cf., Bennett v. Spear*, 520 U.S. 154, 117 S.Ct. 1154, 137 L.Ed.2d 281 (1997)(finding standing for "anti-environmentalists"). More recently, however, the cases have been more favorable for plaintiffs. *See Friends of the Earth, Inc. v. Laidlaw Environmental Services (TOC), Inc.*, 528 U.S. 167, 120 S.Ct. 693, 145 L.Ed.2d 610 (2000)(finding injury to plaintiffs from defendants' pollution without having to show that the pollution actually harmed the environment and finding a civil penalty adequate redressability). *Steel Company* and *Friends of the Earth* will be dealt with in more detail in the later section of the book dealing with citizen suits.

3. What if the defendant's allegedly unlawful action is the failure to file some report with a federal agency that is required by some environmental law? For example, persons with a National Pollution Discharge Elimination System (NPDES) permit under the Clean Water Act generally are required to file monthly Discharge Monitoring Reports (DMRs). What if the polluter fails to file the reports? Or, under the Emergency Planning and Community Right-to-Know Act, companies that discharge toxic materials into the environment are required to file an annual report as to the amount and nature of those discharges. These reports are then collated and published by EPA as the Toxics Release Inventory (TRI)(www.epa.gov/tri/). Could an environmental group sue a company that failed to file its required report? What would be its injury? While there is no Supreme Court case answering this direct question, the Supreme Court did answer a similar question in *Federal Election Comm'n v. Akins*, 524 U.S. 11, 118 S.Ct. 1777, 141 L.Ed.2d 10 (1998). In that case, a group failed to file an allegedly required campaign finance report with the FEC. An organization that tracked campaign finances and reported the information to its members sued the FEC to require the report to be filed. Over Justice Scalia's dissent (joined by Justices O'Connor and Thomas), the Court held that the plaintiff had suffered a particularized injury, rather than a generalized grievance, in not being able to access what would be important publicly available information.

IV. ADMINISTRATIVE LAW ISSUES

If you have already taken an administrative law course, this section of the chapter is just review. If you have not taken an administrative law course, this section is just an introduction to a subject that is a necessary one for anyone serious about environmental law. Administrative law is the law that governs agencies. Environmental law is law administered by agencies to protect the environment, so the law that governs agencies in administering environmental laws is essential not only to those in the agencies but also to those outside the agencies who wish to influence or challenge agency action.

A. Rulemaking

Normally, when Congress (or a state legislature) passes a law, it authorizes or requires an agency to administer the law. This is true of an environmental law like the Clean Air Act, for instance, that requires the Environmental Protection Agency to do certain things, or the National Forest Management Act that requires the Forest Service to manage national forests in certain ways. Usually this means that Congress requires or authorizes an agency to adopt **rules*** by which the statutory requirements will be implemented. For example, the Clean Air Act, among other things, requires EPA to adopt standards setting the minimum acceptable quality for the outdoor air with respect to pollutants that may adversely affect human health or the environment. Consequently, EPA has adopted a rule to protect human health with respect to carbon monoxide that allows no more than 9 parts per million (or 10 micrograms per cubic meter) in the air averaged over an eight-hour period. Similarly, the National Forest Management Act requires the Forest Service to adopt land and resource management plans for each national forest, and the Forest Service has adopted rules specifying what must be contained in those management plans.

The process by which these regulations are adopted is called **rulemaking**. The Administrative Procedure Act, 5 U.S.C. §§ 551 et seq., specifies certain procedures which agencies must follow as a general matter when they engage in rulemaking. *See* 5 U.S.C. § 553. The general procedures required by the APA are often supplemented or replaced by more specific procedural requirements in the particular statutes being implemented or in other statutes. For example, the Clean Air Act contains specific procedures supplementing the APA's provisions. *See* 42 U.S.C. § 7607(d). In addition, the Regulatory Flexibility Act imposes special requirements when regulations, especially those of EPA or the Occupational Safety and Health Administration, impact small businesses, organizations or governmental units. *See* 5 U.S.C. §§ 601 et seq. Nevertheless, the normal procedure required for rulemaking is that:

- An agency must provide the public notice in the Federal Register of its intent to engage in rulemaking; the Federal Register is a daily publication of the federal government, but today notice is additionally provided through publication on the internet.

* The term "rule" and the term "regulation" mean the same thing, and they can be used interchangeably.

- The agency must provide the public an opportunity to comment on the agency's proposed rulemaking; the opportunity to comment in writing is always provided; often the public is also given the opportunity to comment orally at a hearing before agency officials.

- The agency must provide the public with adequate information about the proposed rulemaking to allow for the public comment to be meaningful; normally this means that the agency publishes an actual proposed rule as well as information explaining what the rule does and why; in addition, factual information that is the basis for the rule must be made available to the public.

- The agency must consider the public comments, and when it issues its final rule, it must respond to the significant comments made.

An agency's failure to follow these procedural requirements, for example, by not providing adequate notice of what it proposes to do, may lead to a court setting aside the rule, if a person challenges it.

In addition to the procedural requirements imposed by statute, which generally are subject to judicial review, there are other procedural requirements imposed on federal agencies by presidential executive orders, most importantly E.O. 12866.

Rulemaking that may have a significant effect on the human environment is also subject to the National Environmental Policy Act, which imposes its own procedural requirements. As you will see later, NEPA's requirements are not limited to rulemaking; they apply to any federal action that may have a significant impact. And as you will see, NEPA's requirements are themselves modeled after the procedural requirements for notice-and-comment rulemaking.

B. Adjudication

Adjudication is the agency equivalent of judicial trials. Most agencies conduct adjudication in various contexts. For example, EPA can assess money penalties against persons who violate the Clean Air Act by bringing a case against them before an Administrative Law Judge. *See* 42 U.S.C. § 7413(d). An ALJ is technically an employee of the agency, but ALJs have special personnel protections to provide them a certain amount of independence from agency policymakers and enforcement officers. Sometimes the adjudications are before other agency employees who do not have even the special protections afforded ALJs. For example, EPA can assess money penalties of less than $25,000 under the Clean Water Act in an adjudication before an adjudicator other than an ALJ.

When an ALJ is the adjudicator, the APA's adjudication procedures are used, and they typically mirror those of a court trial. When an ALJ is not the adjudicator, the APA's procedures are not used. These proceedings tend to be more informal, and persons may not necessarily have the right to call witnesses or cross examine witnesses.

A common type of non-penalty adjudication involves permit applications. For example, under several environmental statutes persons must obtain permits before they are allowed to emit pollution. Normally the adjudication of a permit application does not involve ALJs and often is done only through written submissions. It is unlike penalty proceedings in that the agency acts only as an adjudicator, not as a party participant. Occasionally, however, a public interest group may intervene in the proceeding to oppose the permit application.

In administrative adjudication, after the ALJ or other adjudicator makes a decision, the losing party typically may appeal the decision to the head of the agency, or in the case of the EPA, to the Environmental Appeals Board, which has the power to review the initial decision de novo. The person who loses on the administrative appeal, other than the agency, may then normally seek judicial review of the agency decision. Where the agency enforcement officers brought an enforcement action that was denied on administrative appeal, they may not seek judicial review; the administrative appellate decision is the decision of the *agency* and therefore binds its enforcement officers.

C. Presidential Oversight

As mentioned earlier, beginning with President Nixon, presidents have increasingly moved to strengthen their oversight of agency regulatory activities, in particular with health, safety, and environmental regulations. The methodology of this oversight created by President Reagan has remained with little formal change over the years and different administrations. Under what is now Executive Order 12866, agencies must prepare an annual plan of their regulatory objectives and priorities and a list of all their planned significant regulatory activities for the year. The Office of Information and Regulatory Affairs (OIRA) in the Office of Management and Budget reviews the list for consistency with the President's priorities and policies, and informs the agency of any inconsistency.

Probably more importantly, the Order also imposes several requirements on agencies, other than independent regulatory agencies, with respect to "significant regulatory actions," which are defined as an action leading to a rulemaking that would have an effect of $100 million on the economy or would otherwise have a substantial effect on a number of listed values including the environment. The requirements include a mandate that, before proposed rules are proposed or final rules are adopted, agencies must submit the document and supporting cost-benefit analyses to OIRA for its review and comment. While OIRA does not have the authority actually to rewrite or veto the rules proposed by agencies, it does have a lot of power to influence agency outcomes, at least to the extent that Presidents want to support OIRA. OIRA also can influence agency actions pursuant to its authority under the Paperwork Reduction Act, 44 U.S.C. §§ 3501 *et seq.*, and under the Information Quality Act, 44 U.S.C. § 3516 note, both of which enable OIRA to impose further requirements on agency rulemakings and other actions.

One of the important differences between procedures imposed on agencies by the President through OIRA, as compared to procedures required by the APA or other statute, is that judicial review of the agencies' compliance is precluded. Each of the Executive Orders has specifically stated that they are an exercise of the internal management of the executive branch and are not intended to create any rights or benefits enforceable at law. Courts have respected this limitation and refused to review agency action under the orders. *See, e.g., State of Michigan v. Thomas*, 805 F.2d 176 (6th Cir. 1986).

Generally, OIRA has exercised its authority so as to be a brake on agency environmental rulemaking, and consequently its activities are viewed as detrimental by environmental groups and positive by business groups.

D. Judicial Review

Some environmental statutes have specific provisions governing judicial review of agency actions under the statute. *See, e.g.*, 42 U.S.C § 7607 (Clean Air Act). Others do not. When a statute does not itself provide for judicial review, a person may be able to obtain judicial review under the Administrative Procedure Act. Under the APA, courts may review agency actions to determine if they are contrary to statute, are arbitrary and capricious or an abuse of discretion, were adopted without complying with all procedural requirements, or, if the action was either formal rulemaking or adjudication, it was not supported by substantial evidence. 5 U.S.C. § 706(2). In addition, courts may review agency inaction in certain circumstances and compel agency action unlawfully withheld or unreasonably delayed. 5 U.S.C. § 706(1).

1. Obtaining Review

There are many hurdles to obtaining judicial review under the APA, even though the Supreme Court has said that there is a "presumption" of review of agency actions. Unless a plaintiff can overcome these hurdles, unlawful agency action may escape review. You have already met a constitutional requirement for review–standing. The APA contains several of its own, and the Court has imposed others as a matter of common law decisionmaking.

a. Preclusion of Review

The APA specifically precludes judicial review under the APA in two circumstances—when a statute precludes review and to the extent that the agency action was committed to agency discretion by law. In the environmental field there are not many statutes that preclude review under the APA, unless those statutes substitute their own review provisions. Moreover, there are few environmental statutes that commit agency decisionmaking to the agency's discretion. That is, the statutes constrain the agencies' discretion by indicating what factors should guide or govern the agencies' decisionmaking. However, an agency's decision whether or not to engage in enforcement actions against alleged violators is generally held to be inherently committed to agency discretion as prosecutorial discretion.

b.   APA Requirements for Review

i.   *Zone of Interests*

The APA provides that a person may obtain review under the APA only if a person suffers a "legal wrong" or is "adversely affected or aggrieved within the meaning of a relevant statute." 5 U.S.C. § 702. This is known as the "zone of interests" requirement.

If a person suffers "legal wrong" because of agency action, they are within the zone of interest of whatever law has been violated. A simple example is an agency action that limits a person's liberty or property interests. For instance, if the Corps of Engineers precludes a person from filling wetlands on his property under the Clean Water Act, and the person believes the agency action is unlawful under the CWA, then the person is said to suffer legal wrong under the CWA, and he can obtain judicial review of that action. However, if the Corps had granted a permit to a person to fill wetlands on his property, and an environmental organization believes that the permit violates the CWA, neither that organization nor its members suffers a legal wrong. Their liberty and property are not affected. Their interests may be adversely affected, but this implicates the second phrase in Section 702, not the first.

If a person does not suffer legal wrong because of an agency action, a person seeking judicial review of the action under the APA must be able to identify a statute that "arguably" protects the interest that the person is seeking to protect in bringing the lawsuit. For example, the environmental group upset about the filling of wetlands would need to show that their interest that is adversely affected–their interest in protecting the environment–is one that is arguably intended to be protected by the CWA. Normally, that is not difficult, but there are instances where there may be a problem. For instance, a group of ranchers tried to sue under the APA, asserting that the U.S. Forest Service had violated the National Environmental Policy Act (which does not have a judicial review provision) in adopting a Land and Resource Management Plan. In order to determine whether the ranchers could sue under the APA, however, the court first had to decide whether the interest they sought to protect—continued cattle grazing on U.S. Forest Service land—was an interest intended to be protected under NEPA. The court held that it was not. Rather, it said, "The purpose of NEPA is to protect the environment, not the economic interests of those adversely affected by agency decisions." *Nevada Land Action Ass'n v. U.S. Forest Service*, 8 F.3d 713 (9th Cir. 1993). Thus, even though the U.S. Forest Service may have violated NEPA, and the ranchers may have been harmed by the Plan, the ranchers were not able to obtain judicial review of the Plan, because they were not in the zone of interests protected by NEPA.

In determining the zone of interests, courts are to look to the particular provision involved in the case, not the statute generally. For example, in *Bennett v. Spear*, 520 U.S. 154, 117 S.Ct. 1154, 137 L.Ed.2d 281 (1997), where ranchers argued that the Fish & Wildlife Service had violated the Endangered Species Act, it was clear that the intent of the ESA generally was not to protect the interests of cattle grazing. However, the Court found that the ranchers were within the zone of interests of the particular ESA provision they alleged was violated, a requirement that the agency's decision reflect "the best scientific and commercial data available." This provision, the Court said, served not only "the ESA's overall goal of species preservation" but also the "avoid[ance of] needless economic dislocation produced by agency officials zealously but unintelligently pursuing their environmental objectives." It was the latter that was the interest claimed by the ranchers.

In any case, the zone of interests test is not intended to be especially rigorous, and the Supreme Court has emphasized that the plaintiff's interest need only be "arguably" within the zone of interests of the statute involved. *See, e.g., National Credit Union Admin. v. First Nat'l Bank & Trust Co.*, 522 U.S. 479, 118 S.Ct. 927, 140 L.Ed.2d 1 (1998). Thus, only where the interests of the plaintiff seem to have virtually no basis in the statutory provision involved is a court likely to find its claims outside the zone of interests.

ii. Finality

Only "final agency actions" are subject to judicial review under the APA. 5 U.S.C. § 704. In order for there to be a "final agency action," there must first be agency action. The APA defines "agency action" to "include[] the whole or a part of an agency rule, order, license, sanction, relief, or the equivalent thereof, or failure to act." 5 U.S.C. § 551(13). The Supreme Court has held that agency "programs" are not the type of discrete activities that are required for something to be an agency action within the meaning of the APA. *See Lujan v. National Wildlife Federation*, 497 U.S. 871, 110 S.Ct. 3177, 111 L.Ed.2d 695 (1990) ("land withdrawal review program" not itself subject to review, because it is not the product of an agency action, as opposed to particular actions that might occur under the program).

Norton v. Southern Utah Wilderness Alliance, 542 U.S. 55, 124 S.Ct. 2373, 159 L.Ed.2d 137 (2004), addressed what constitutes a "failure to act," such that the agency's failure to act might be final agency action subject to judicial review. There environmental groups claimed that the Bureau of Land Management had failed to protect wilderness study areas from destruction by off-road vehicles in violation of both its statutory mandate and its own land use plans. The Supreme Court said that this was in essence a challenge to the adequacy of the BLM's management of the wilderness study areas, and as such was not a challenge to the failure to take a particular, legally required discrete action. Only the failure to take one of the listed actions under the definition of "agency action" could qualify as a "failure to act" that would be subject to judicial review.

The purpose of the finality requirement in the term "final agency action" is to assure that agency proceedings are not interrupted by attempts to seek judicial review before the agency makes its final decision and that judicial review is based upon the authoritative agency decision, rather than some tentative determination. To carry out this purpose the Supreme Court has articulated a two-part test: "First, the action must mark the 'consummation' of the agency's decisionmaking process,—it must not be of a merely tentative or interlocutory nature. And second, the action must be one by which 'rights or obligations have been determined,' or from which 'legal consequences will flow.'" *Bennett v. Spear*, 520 U.S. 154, 178, 117 S.Ct. 1154, 1168, 137 L.Ed.2d 281 (1997). The second part of this test has also been phrased as requiring an impact that "is sufficiently direct and immediate" and has a "direct effect on ... day-to-day business.... The core question is whether the agency has completed its decisionmaking process, and whether the result of that process is one that will directly affect the parties." *Franklin v. Massachusetts*, 505 U.S. 788, 796–97, 112 S.Ct. 2767, 2773, 120 L.Ed.2d 636 (1992) (quoting from *Abbott Laboratories v. Gardner*, 387 U.S. 136, 152, 87 S.Ct. 1507, 1517, 18 L.Ed.2d 681 (1967)) This latter phraseology would appear to find "final" agency action when there is a real practical effect, even if the effect is not a legal one.

The distinction between a practical effect and a legal one can make a difference in at least two different situations. First, agencies often issue interpretive documents, opinion letters, guidance manuals, etc., intended to provide guidance to the public and direction to subunits in the agency. These documents, while technically "rules" under the APA, do not have legal force; they are merely advisory. They can, nevertheless, have tremendous practical effect. For example, the guidance may state that persons are deemed in violation of the law unless they take certain action that might be very expensive. Persons subject to that guidance, who believe it misinterprets the law, often would like to obtain judicial review. If, however, an action must have "legal consequences" or "determine rights or obligations," this guidance may not be final agency action. If an action need only have real, practical consequences, then the guidance probably would be final agency action. Thus, if an action must have legal consequences in order to be reviewable, the person faced with the guidance must choose whether to conform to what he believes is not a lawful interpretation of the law or to willfully violate the agency's guidance. The lower courts have not acted consistently in this situation. Sometimes they find a legal effect is required; sometimes they find a practical effect is sufficient. *See, e.g., Air Brake Systems, Inc. v. Mineta*, 357 F.3d 632 (6th Cir. 2004)(holding an interpretation letter non-final because of a lack of legal consequences); *Appalachian Power Co. v. EPA*, 208 F.3d 1015 (D.C. Cir. 2000)(holding a guidance document final because of its practical effects).

The second situation where a difference between a practical and legal effect is important in determining whether agency action is final and therefore reviewable commonly occurs in EPA enforcement. EPA believes that someone is violating one of the environmental laws that it enforces, so it issues a compliance order—an order directing the person to stop violating the law. The person receiving the order believes the order is unlawful. If the order has legal effect, it is clearly final agency action, but it may not be if it only has practical effect. EPA has successfully argued in a number of cases that its compliance orders do not have independent legal effect, because they merely restate the person's underlying legal duty. Again, the courts have not been totally consistent in deciding whether this is final agency action. *Compare, e.g., Acker v. EPA*, 290 F.3d 892 (7th Cir. 2002) (order that identified past violations and directed company to comply with law in the future not final action) *with Allsteel, Inc. v. EPA*, 25 F.3d 312, 315 (6th Cir. 1994)(holding an order to stop construction imposed legal obligations beyond those of the statute). Recently, however, the Supreme Court in dictum suggested that such orders should be final agency action. *Alaska Dept. of Environmental Conservation v. EPA*, 540 U.S. 461, 124 S.Ct. 983, 157 L.Ed.2d 967 (2004)(stressing the "practical and legal consequences (lost costs and vulnerability to penalties)" of EPA's order).

iii. Exhaustion of Administrative Remedies

Like the finality requirement, the doctrine of exhaustion is intended to keep courts from reviewing agency action until the agency has had a full opportunity to hear and consider a case and to correct its own errors. Originally this was a common law limitation on judicial review, and it continues to exist in non-APA cases. In cases brought under the APA, however, 5 U.S.C. § 704 creates a statutory exhaustion standard for determining whether an agency action is final. That is, an action is not final if a statute requires someone to exhaust their administrative remedies before obtaining judicial review, or if an agency by rule requires persons to exhaust their administrative remedies before going to court and the agency suspends its action pending the administrative review. For example, if an ALJ assesses an administrative penalty against a person in an EPA administrative enforcement action, the person may not immediately seek review of that decision in court, if EPA has required by rule that the person must first appeal to the Environmental Appeals Board and that the person need not pay the penalty until the appeal is finally decided.

Under common law exhaustion, a person must exhaust his administrative remedies whether or not the agency so requires by rule or suspends its action pending review, but there are also a number of exceptions to the general requirement to exhaust. An interesting question, not yet resolved by the courts, is whether those exceptions continue to apply under the APA when an agency requires exhaustion by rule.

c. Common Law Requirements for Review

Although the Administrative Procedure Act purports to state all the requirements for obtaining judicial review of agency action, the Supreme Court has accepted some common law limitations on judicial review as continuing to apply in APA cases, even though those limitations do not appear in the APA.

i. *Issue Exhaustion and Waiver*

Closely related to exhaustion doctrine in terms of their purpose and origin are the two closely related, if not overlapping, common law doctrines of issue exhaustion and waiver. Issue exhaustion requires that in order for a person to obtain judicial consideration of a particular legal claim, the person must have raised the issue before the agency. For example, a person might argue before an ALJ in an EPA enforcement action that the water he allegedly polluted was not water protected by the Clean Water Act, and losing there he might argue that point on appeal to the EPA Environmental Appeals Board. If he loses there, he could seek judicial review of that issue in court, but at this point he could not also argue that he did not actually pollute the water, because he had not argued that before the agency. This is similar to the judicial practice of not allowing persons to argue on appeal issues they did not raise in the initial trial.

The concept of waiver is similar but it has applied more often with regard to judicial review of rules, rather than judicial review of adjudications, where exhaustion issues usually apply. Courts have increasingly been willing to deny a person judicial review of certain issues in any agency rule, or to deny review of the rule altogether, if the person had not exercised their right to comment on the proposed rule during the rulemaking proceeding, or had not raised the issue to the agency that it was now raising to the court. Sometimes this requirement is specified by statute, *see, e.g.,* 42 U.S.C. § 7607(d)(7)(B)(requiring objections to a rule under the Clean Air Act to be raised before the agency as a prerequisite for judicial review). Other times, courts require it as a matter of common law in APA cases. *See, e.g., National Wildlife Federation v. EPA*, 286 F.3d 554, 562 (D.C. Cir. 2002). But *see* William Funk, Exhaustion of Administrative Remedies—New Dimensions Since *Darby*, 18 Pace Env. L. Rev. 1 (2000)(criticizing trend). If the plaintiff can show "exceptional circumstances" justifying review notwithstanding the general policy of allowing agencies the opportunity to consider issues in the first instance, courts may then allow review. *See, e.g., Johnson v. Director, Office of Workers' Compensation Programs*, 183 F.3d 1169 (9th Cir. 1999)(finding exceptional circumstances where the agency had already considered and decided the issue in an earlier setting).

ii. *Ripeness*

The most important common law limitation on obtaining judicial review is the ripeness doctrine. It overlaps with the doctrines of finality and exhaustion in that it is intended to assure that courts do not become involved in agency activities until it is appropriate. The case of *Abbott Laboratories v. Gardner*, 387 U.S. 136, 148, 87 S.Ct. 1507, 1515, 18 L.Ed.2d 681 (1967), provided the Supreme Court's classic statement of the rule: "The problem is best seen in a twofold aspect, requiring us to evaluate both the fitness of the issues for judicial decision and the hardship to the parties of withholding court consideration." More recently, in an environmental case, *Ohio Forestry Ass'n v. Sierra Club*, 523 U.S. 726, 733, 118 S.Ct. 1665, 1670, 140 L.Ed.2d 921 (1998), the Court reiterated the test with a slight variation: "we must consider: (1) whether delayed review would cause hardship to the plaintiffs; (2) whether judicial intervention would inappropriately interfere with further administrative action; and (3) whether the courts would benefit from further factual development of the issues presented." However stated, the test involves a balancing of the plaintiff's interest in obtaining review at this time against the court's and the agency's interests in awaiting review in a different context. In *Ohio Forestry*, for example, the plaintiffs challenged a provision in a forest plan that allegedly would allow the Forest Service to make timber sales involving clear cuts in inappropriate cases. The Court said this was not ripe for review, because it was not clear that any timber sales allowing such cuts would actually occur, because the agency might not allow clear cuts in the inappropriate circumstances, and, moreover, even if the Forest Service did make such a timber sale, the plaintiffs could then challenge the particular timber sale, so there was no hardship to plaintiff in waiting for an actual timber sale involving a clear cut.

2. The Scope of Judicial Review

Once a court determines to hear a case, the question becomes the nature of that review. The Administrative Procedure Act specifies a number of bases upon which a court should invalidate agency action, 5 U.S.C. § 706. In environmental cases, the most frequent bases argued are that the agency action was: arbitrary and capricious, contrary to statute or rule, or adopted without following all the required procedures.

For an agency action to be "arbitrary and capricious" in essence means that the agency did not act reasonably in light of its statutory authority and all the information the agency had before it. The court assesses the agency's explanation for the action and the factual basis the agency provides for the action. The court is supposed to be deferential to the agency's decision in light of the agency's expertise and the fact that Congress has delegated the decisionmaking to the agency, not the courts. Nonetheless, many agency actions are set aside because the court simply does not believe the agency's action makes sense in light of all the information the agency had. This type of review stems from the seminal case of *Citizens to Preserve Overton Park v. Volpe*, 401 U.S. 402, 91 S.Ct. 814, 28 L.Ed.2d 136 (1971), in which the Court held that the Secretary of Transportation's decision to authorize a highway through a park without any explanation, when the statute required avoidance of parks to the extent feasible and prudent, could not be found to be reasonable.

Sometimes a court will not set aside the agency action but merely remand it to the agency for a better explanation. In these cases, the plaintiff may only obtain delay in the agency action, rather than setting it aside forever.

Agencies have no inherent authority, so they must look to some statute for the authority for what they do. Invariably there are disputes over the meaning of their statutory authorities or limitations. When agencies interpret the statutes they administer or the regulations they promulgate, the Supreme Court has established some tests for how courts are to view those interpretations. First, to the extent that the court, using traditional methods of statutory construction, believes the meaning of the statute or regulation is clear, that is the end of the issue– the court simply announces its interpretation without regard to the agency's interpretation. Second, to the extent that the statute is ambiguous, and the agency's interpretation has the force of law (as, for example, a regulation would have), a court is to defer to any reasonable agency interpretation. *See United States v. Mead Corp.*, 533 U.S. 218, 121 S.Ct. 2164, 150 L.Ed.2d 292 (2001); *Chevron, USA, Inc. v. NRDC*, 467 U.S. 837, 104 S.Ct. 2778, 81 L.Ed.2d 694 (1984). Third, if the statute is ambiguous, and the agency's interpretation does not have the force of law (as an interpretive rule or policy statement would not), then a court is not to defer to the agency's interpretation, but it is to consider that interpretation in light of "the thoroughness evident in its consideration, the validity of its reasoning, its consistency with earlier and later pronouncements, and all those factors which give it the power to persuade, if lacking the power to control." *Skidmore v. Swift & Co.*, 323 U.S. 134, 65 S.Ct. 161, 89 L.Ed. 124 (1944). Sometimes, the deference commanded by *Chevron* is called "strong deference" and the respect suggested by *Skidmore* is called "weak deference." Many law review pages have been devoted to the distinctions between these two levels of review, and some have suggested that the alleged difference is more myth than reality, with courts invoking *Chevron* when they agree with the agency's interpretation and invoking *Skidmore* when they disagree. Whatever the truth of this debate, there is no question that lawyers expend a great deal of effort trying to convince courts that *Chevron* or *Skidmore* applies, depending upon which degree of deference aids their client. Usually this means that the agency is asserting *Chevron* should apply, so that the agency will receive maximum deference, whereas the private person challenging the agency's interpretation would rather have *Skidmore* apply. Which applies turns on whether the agency interpretation has the "force of law." The Supreme Court has made clear that legislative regulations, adopted after notice and comment, and formal adjudications under the APA both have the force of law. It has also said that informal guidance documents do not. However, the Court has eschewed drawing bright lines in this area, so there is considerable question as to what other agency interpretations have the force of law commanding *Chevron* deference. Finally, if the agency is interpreting its own regulation, to the extent it is not clear on its face, courts are to uphold the agency interpretation unless it is clearly erroneous. *Bowles v. Seminole Rock & Sand Co.* 325 U.S. 410, 65 S.Ct. 1215, 89 L.Ed. 1700 (1945). This is strong deference, whether or not the interpretation has the force of law.

The failure of an agency to comply with the procedural requirements for its action normally results in the invalidation of the agency action. If, for example, the agency does not provide adequate notice and comment before adopting a regulation, the regulation will likely be set aside. *See, e.g., Shell Oil Co. v. EPA*, 950 F.2d 741 (D.C. Cir. 1991)(holding so-called "mixture and derived from" rule invalid for not giving adequate notice of the issue). Moreover, challenges to agency action under the National Environmental Policy Act invariably involve a claim that the agency has failed to comply with the procedural requirements of NEPA, usually by not making the required Environmental Impact Statement. Similarly, challenges under the Endangered Species Act often involve a claim that an agency has not complied with the procedural requirement of Section 7 of the Act to consult with the Fish and Wildlife Service or NOAA Fisheries. *See, e.g., Bennett v. Spear*, 520 U.S. 154, 117 S.Ct. 1154, 137 L.Ed.2d 281 (1997).

Chapter 2

NEPA

I. INTRODUCTION TO NEPA

[A]ll agencies of the Federal Government shall . . . include in every recommendation or report on proposals for . . . major federal actions significantly affecting the quality of the human environment, a detailed statement . . . on the environmental impact of the proposed action."[1]

With these simple words, the U.S. Congress, with President Nixon's signature, ushered in the modern era of environmental law in 1969. Although the National Environmental Policy Act (or "NEPA") may have evolved into something different than was originally foreseen, it represented the collective concern over mounting environmental problems and an attempt to try to address those problems legislatively. It is conceptually distinct from pollution control laws, like the Clean Air Act, the Clean Water Act, and RCRA, in that it seeks not to control the discharge of pollution per se; but instead focuses on the environmental degradation that can result as a by-product of the actions of federal agencies, and those private activities which they can control or permit. It does this not by forcing an agency to take the most environmentally friendly decision, but by requiring federal agencies to consider the impact of their actions on the environment.

> "Congress did not establish environmental protection as an exclusive goal; rather, it desired a reordering of priorities, so that environmental costs and benefits will assume their proper place along with other considerations."[2]

Its impact on government action and the shape of our world has been far-reaching, and it has served as a model for other federal laws, and other environmental assessment laws the world over. The flexibility and breadth of such laws, which allows one to examine environmental impacts in whatever form they arise, can contribute to far more in-

---

1. National Environmental Policy Act of 1969, Pub. L. No. 91–190, Sec. 83 Stat. 852 (1970) (codified as 42 U.S.C. Sec. 4332 (2)(C)(i)(1988)).

2. *Calvert Cliffs' Coordinating Committee, Inc. v. U.S. Atomic Energy Commission,* 449 F.2d 1109, 1112 (D.C. Cir. 1971).

formed decision making but can also lead to extensive problems related to its very broad nature.

NEPA's ultimate effects are debated to this day, with many arguing that it is simply an opportunity for "no-growth NIMBYs[3]" to stop or slow down important needed projects, at great cost to the government and society[4]; while others argue that it gives a voice to environmental values that were not considered before and has changed our world for the betterment of humanity and the surrounding environment.[5] As you read this chapter, and learn more about NEPA and its process, try to determine which camp you think is most correct.

II. OVERVIEW OF NEPA AND THE NEPA PROCESS

NEPA does several things. "Section 101 sets forth the Act's basic substantive policy: that the federal government 'use all practicable means and measures' to protect environmental values."[6]

NEPA also creates the Council on Environmental Quality, or CEQ, which is to both coordinate the NEPA activities of other federal agencies and also promulgate regulations for NEPA implementation generally.[7] The C.E.Q. has been less active than was initially anticipated but still serves the important function of addressing questions of general NEPA implementation and coordination of NEPA requirements between agencies. As the primary federal agency charged with implementing NEPA's requirements, the C.E.Q.'s regulations "are entitled to substantial deference."[8] CEQ regulations and individual agency implementing regulations can be found at http://ceq.eh.doe.gov/nepa/nepanet.htm.

NEPA gives all federal agencies the authority to consider environmental impacts and to alter their actions to account for the environment and environmental impacts.[9] Students of administrative law will note the importance of this provision since federal agencies can only do or consider what Congress has directed. This provision allows federal agencies, which were generally created with one or a few specific purposes, such as building federal office buildings (GAO), leasing land for mineral exploration and extraction (BLM)[10], harvesting of trees (Forest Service), or constructing dams (U.S. Army Corps of Engineers), to temper these goals with appropriate environmental consideration.[11]

But by far the most important feature of NEPA, and one that received scant debate at the time of passage, is a procedural provision[12],

---

3. NIMBY is an acronym meaning "Not in my Back Yard" and usually refers to those persons who care only about preserving their own neighborhood at the expense of others. *See* Barry George Rabe, *Beyond NIMBY: Hazardous Waste Siting in Canada and the United States* Brookings Institution Press (1994).

4. *Id.*

5. *Id.*

6. *Calvert Cliffs', supra* n. 2.

7. 42 U.S.C. Sec. 4342

8. *Marsh v. Oregon Natural Res. Council*, 490 U.S. 360, 372, 109 S.Ct. 1851, 1858, 104 L.Ed.2d 377 (1989) (citations omitted).

9. 42 U.S.C. Sec. 4331(b).

10. 43 C.F.R. Sec. 3610.1–1

11. 42 U.S.C. Sec. 4331(b).

12. Although the point was hotly debated shortly after NEPA was passed, case law indicates that NEPA is primarily procedur-

that requires all agencies to list environmental impacts of any federal action that significantly affects the quality of the human environment.[13] The document prepared pursuant to this provision is known as an Environmental Impact Statement (EIS). The documentation an agency generates in determining whether an EIS is required, and in generating the EIS if mandated, in turn, creates the administrative record which can be used to determine whether an agency has fulfilled its NEPA obligations.

> "The sort of consideration of environmental values which NEPA compels is clarified in Section 102(2)(A)and (B). In general, all agencies must use a 'systematic, interdisciplinary, approach' to environmental planning and evaluation in decisionmaking which may have an impact on man's environment. In order to include all possible environmental factors in the decisional equation, agencies must identify and develop methods and procedures ... which will insure that presently unquantified environmental amenities and values may be given appropriate consideration in decisionmaking along with economic and technical considerations."[14]

Presumably, a consideration of the environmental impacts of a project also strengthens the information on environmental costs needed to do an analysis of the desirability of the project over all. Additionally, because the public is invited to participate, this creates an opportunity for public input on projects, and for better or worse, expands the time line for moving forward.

Federal actions (which will be explained more, *infra*) include federally sponsored projects, projects that are federally funded, and private projects that require federal approval or the granting of a federal permit in order to be completed. [15]

The procedural requirement of Section 102(c) gives rise to what is known as the NEPA process. This process includes the actions necessary to determine whether NEPA applies, the determination of whether an EIS is required, and the preparation of the EIS itself.

The NEPA process usually begins with the agency making a determination of whether the procedural requirements of NEPA are even applicable to the action under consideration.[16] By operation of other statutes, NEPA may not be applicable to certain actions. In 2003, for example, the Healthy Forests Initiative exempted certain significant logging projects from the NEPA process.[17] If the application of NEPA is made impossible by other circumstances, such as lack of agency discre-

al—that is, once the environmental impacts are 'considered,' the actual decision or action by the federal agency is discretionary. Robertson v. Methow Valley Citizens Council, 490 U.S. 332, 350–51, 109 S.Ct. 1835, 104 L.Ed.2d 351 (1989).

13. 42 U.S.C. § 4332(2)(C) (1988).

14. *Calvert Cliffs', supra* n. 2 at 1113.

15. For a discussion of the limits of what constitutes federal action, see William B. Ellis & Turner T. Smith, the Limits of Federal Responsibility and Control under the National Environmental Policy Act, 18 Envtl. L. 10055 (1988).

16. 42 U.S.C. Sec. 4332 (1988).

17. 16 U.S.C. § 6513(c) (2004).

tion to consider the environmental impacts, then NEPA is also not applicable.[18] As the court in the recent case of D.O.T. v. Public Citizen noted:

> "Also, inherent in NEPA and its implementing regulations is a "rule of reason," which ensures that agencies determine whether and to what extent to prepare an EIS based on the usefulness of any new potential information to the decisionmaking [sic] process. Where the preparation of an EIS would serve "no purpose" in light of NEPA's regulatory scheme as a whole, no rule of reason worthy of that title would require an agency to prepare an EIS."[19]

Assuming that NEPA is not inapplicable for one of these reasons, the determination must still be made if an EIS is to be prepared. In practice, the first step in this process is a preliminary analysis to determine whether significant impacts on the environment are likely to occur from a government action, and thus whether a document must be prepared to list and analyze those impacts and consider action alternatives.[20] This in turn depends on the meaning of these terms as defined by agency practice and case law over time. Some applicability decisions are obvious; some, less so.

Many agencies may make categorical determinations that certain actions that they take, particularly repetitive and/or routine actions, will never rise to the level of an action that will significantly affect the quality of the human environment.[21] These actions therefore will never trigger the EIS requirement.[22] These are known as categorical exclusions.[23] An agency usually adopts these categorical exclusions through the notice and comment process. For many agencies, these categorical exclusions form the majority of agency actions.

CATEGORICAL EXCLUSIONS FROM NEPA–FEDERAL HIGHWAY ADMINISTRATION
23 C.F.R. 771.119.

Sec. 771.117 Categorical exclusions.

(a) Categorical exclusions (CEs) are actions which meet the definition contained in 40 CFR 1508.4, and, based on past experience with similar actions, do not involve significant environmental impacts. They are actions which: do not induce significant impacts to planned growth or land use for the area, do not require the relocation of significant numbers of people; do not have a significant impact on any natural,

---

18. For instance, Congress might require a federal agency to take a particular action, such as building an office building in a particular style in a particular place [cite to implicit no NEPA], in which there are no alternatives to consider, or Congress might explicitly exempt certain activities from NEPA [cite-forest service sales].

19. *Department of Transportation v. Public Citizen*, 541 U.S. 752, 124 S.Ct. 2204, 2215, 159 L.Ed.2d 60 (2004).

20. 40 C.F.R. § 1501.3 (1993).

21. 40 C.F.R. Sec. 1508.4 (2005); *see also* 23 C.F.R. Sec. 771.115.

22. *Id.*

23. See 40 C.F.R. 1508.4

cultural, recreational, historic or other resource; do not involve significant air, noise, or water quality impacts; do not have significant impacts on travel patterns; and do not otherwise, either individually or cumulatively, have any significant environmental impacts.

(b) Any action which normally would be classified as a CE but could involve unusual circumstances will require the Administration, in cooperation with the applicant, to conduct appropriate environmental studies to determine if the CE classification is proper. Such unusual circumstances include:

(1) Significant environmental impacts;

(2) Substantial controversy on environmental grounds;

(3) Significant impact on properties protected by Section 4(f) of the DOT Act or section 106 of the National Historic Preservation Act; or

(4) Inconsistencies with any Federal, State, or local law, requirement or administrative determination relating to the environmental aspects of the action.

(c) The following actions meet the criteria for CEs in the CEQ regulation (Section 1508.4) and Sec. 771.117(a) of this regulation and normally do not require any further NEPA approvals by the Administration:

(1) Activities which do not involve or lead directly to construction, such as planning and technical studies; grants for training and research programs; research activities as defined in 23 U.S.C. 307; approval of a unified work program and any findings required in the planning process pursuant to 23 U.S.C. 134; approval of statewide programs under 23 CFR part 630; approval of project concepts under 23 CFR part 476; engineering to define the elements of a proposed action or alternatives so that social, economic, and environmental effects can be assessed; and Federal-aid system revisions which establish classes of highways on the Federal-aid highway system.

(2) Approval of utility installations along or across a transportation facility.

(3) Construction of bicycle and pedestrian lanes, paths, and facilities.

(4) Activities included in the State's "highway safety plan" under 23 U.S.C. 402.

(5) Transfer of Federal lands pursuant to 23 U.S.C. 317 when the subsequent action is not an FHWA action.

(6) The installation of noise barriers or alterations to existing publicly owned buildings to provide for noise reduction.

(7) Landscaping.

(8) Installation of fencing, signs, pavement markings, small passenger shelters, traffic signals, and railroad warning devices where no substantial land acquisition or traffic disruption will occur.

(9) Emergency repairs under 23 U.S.C. 125.

(10) Acquisition of scenic easements.

(11) Determination of payback under 23 CFR part 480 for property previously acquired with Federal-aid participation.

(12) Improvements to existing rest areas and truck weigh stations.

(13) Ridesharing activities.

(14) Bus and rail car rehabilitation.

(15) Alterations to facilities or vehicles in order to make them accessible for elderly and handicapped persons.

(16) Program administration, technical assistance activities, and operating assistance to transit authorities to continue existing service or increase service to meet routine changes in demand.

(17) The purchase of vehicles by the applicant where the use of these vehicles can be accommodated by existing facilities or by new facilities which themselves are within a CE.

(18) Track and railbed maintenance and improvements when carried out within the existing right-of-way.

(19) Purchase and installation of operating or maintenance equipment to be located within the transit facility and with no significant impacts off the site.

(20) Promulgation of rules, regulations, and directives.

(d) Additional actions which meet the criteria for a CE in the CEQ regulations (40 CFR 1508.4) and paragraph (a) of this section may be designated as CEs only after Administration approval. The applicant shall submit documentation which demonstrates that the specific conditions or criteria for these CEs are satisfied and that significant environmental effects will not result. Examples of such actions include but are not limited to:

(1) Modernization of a highway by resurfacing, restoration, rehabilitation, reconstruction, adding shoulders, or adding auxiliary lanes (e.g., parking, weaving, turning, climbing).

(2) Highway safety or traffic operations improvement projects including the installation of ramp metering control devices and lighting.

(3) Bridge rehabilitation, reconstruction or replacement or the construction of grade separation to replace existing at-grade railroad crossings.

(4) Transportation corridor fringe parking facilities.

(5) Construction of new truck weigh stations or rest areas.

(6) Approvals for disposal of excess right-of-way or for joint or limited use of right-of-way, where the proposed use does not have significant adverse impacts.

(7) Approvals for changes in access control.

(8) Construction of new bus storage and maintenance facilities in areas used predominantly for industrial or transportation purposes where such construction is not inconsistent with existing zoning and located on or near a street with adequate capacity to handle anticipated bus and support vehicle traffic.

(9) Rehabilitation or reconstruction of existing rail and bus buildings and ancillary facilities where only minor amounts of additional land are required and there is not a substantial increase in the number of users.

(10) Construction of bus transfer facilities (an open area consisting of passenger shelters, boarding areas, kiosks and related street improvements) when located in a commercial area or other high activity center in which there is adequate street capacity for projected bus traffic.

(11) Construction of rail storage and maintenance facilities in areas used predominantly for industrial or transportation purposes where such construction is not inconsistent with existing zoning and where there is no significant noise impact on the surrounding community.

(12) Acquisition of land for hardship or protective purposes; advance land acquisition loans under section 3(b) of the UMT Act. Hardship acquisition is early acquisition of property by the applicant at the property owner's request to alleviate particular hardship to the owner, in contrast to others, because of an inability to sell his property. This is justified when the property owner can document on the basis of health, safety or financial reasons that remaining in the property poses an undue hardship compared to others. Hardship and protective buying will be permitted only for a particular parcel or a limited number of parcels. These types of land acquisition qualify for a CE only where the acquisition will not limit the evaluation of alternatives, including shifts in alignment for planned construction projects, which may be required in the NEPA process. No project development on such land may proceed until the NEPA process has been completed.

(e) Where a pattern emerges of granting CE status for a particular type of action, the Administration will initiate rulemaking proposing to add this type of action to the list of categorical exclusions in paragraph (c) or (d) of this section, as appropriate.

[52 FR 32660, Aug. 28, 1987; 53 FR 11066, Apr. 5, 1988]

As can be seen from the list of categorical exclusions for the Federal Highway Administration, many of the activities do seem truly minor. Nevertheless, the procedural requirements of NEPA are always in effect for agency actions, unless precluded by law, and it is possible that certain actions that appear to meet the definition of categorical exclusions in reality might be an action that would have a significant affect on the quality of the human environment. If this is the case, the listing of an activity as a categorical exclusion is no defense for failure to prepare an EIS.

For actions that are not routine, but where it is not obvious if the action taken will result in a significant impact on the environment, an agency may often prepare what is known as an environmental assessment to assist in the applicability decision. The environmental assessment, or EA, analyzes the possibility of significant environmental impacts.[24]

If it is determined through the EA that the action has not been exempted from NEPA, but there are no significant impacts on the human environment, an agency issues a 'finding of no significant impact' or a FONSI.[25] Concurrent with the determination of a FONSI, an agency will usually present documentation as to why an impact statement is not necessary either in the form of the environmental assessment or a less formal explanation of the determination.[26] The environmental assessment or other documentation provides evidence of a critical procedural step in the process and also provides evidence for judicial review.

At this stage, an agency may alter the action with required mitigation to reduce the environmental impacts to a level below "significant." Looked at differently, the agency is merely proposing a different action that would not trigger the EIS requirement. If an agency takes this action, it will produce what is known as a "mitigated FONSI," or a finding of no significant impact given the proposed mitigation.

If the proposal is to go forward and the agency has determined that it is not excluded from NEPA, when significant environmental impacts are present, the agency must prepare an EIS. At this point an agency may also make a determination as to the jurisdiction of other agencies. It is possible that one project may require the action of more than one agency. Though the requirements of NEPA are always applicable to each agency's own action, it is possible for the agencies to coordinate their activities regarding EIS preparation, in order to avoid duplication. Usually one agency will take the lead, and is called the "lead agency."

To begin the EIS process, the agency issues a 'notice of intent' and determines the proper scope of impacts to be considered and the level of action alternatives that are to be explored.[27] This process is important because it determines not only the 'breadth' of environmental impacts, but also the presumed extent and reach of the project and its connections with other actions. An environmental impact statement must provide sufficient information for a decision maker to consider the environmental impacts of a project; and it must also examine alternatives to the action and mitigation measures that can be taken to limit the environmental impacts.[28] It is at this stage that other agencies and the public may be invited to assist the agency in determining the

---

24. 40 C.F.R. Secs. 1501.3, 1508.9.

25. 40 C.F.R. Sec. 1508.13.

26. 40 C.F.R. Sec. 1501.4(e).

27. 40 C.F.R. Secs. 1501.7, 1508.22.

28. 40 C.F.R. Secs. 1502.14–.16.

environmental impacts that may occur as well as alternatives and mitigation. This input into the process may be referred to as "scoping."[29]

After the scope of the impact statement is determined, the agency prepares the 'draft environmental impact statement' or DEIS, which is published in the Federal Register.[30] Public and other relevant agency comments on the DEIS are then considered and incorporated into the 'final environmental impact statement' or FEIS, which is also published in the Federal Register.[31] The agency must consider the FEIS before it takes action on a project. Occasionally, because of the discovery of new information or because of a realization that the FEIS is inadequate, an agency, of its own accord or under court order, may prepare a 'supplementary environmental impact statement' or SEIS.[32] All environmental impact statements, together with comments and responses, are filed with the Environmental Protection Agency and the CEQ.[33] An agency cannot take any action requiring the preparation of an EIS until at least 90 days after the publication of the DEIS in the Federal Register and 30 days after the publication of the FEIS in the Federal Register.[34]

These NEPA procedures are enforced through lawsuits under the Administrative Procedures Act (or APA).[35] The plaintiff or enforcing agency must allege that the government action was undertaken without the observance of the procedures that are required of NEPA. Typically these challenges fall into a few camps: 1) the agency didn't follow normal procedure in either documenting or analyzing the issue; 2) the agency did not prepare an EIS when it should have, an allegation that there was a significant impact on the human environment of a major federal action; or 3) the EIS itself was not adequate, in other words did not follow statutory requirements. NEPA is considered procedural, not substantive; that is, an agency does not have to take the "best" action for the environment.[36] However, it should be noted that if the agency ignores or undervalues environmental values, this could render its action subject to reversal for being arbitrary and capricious under the APA.

> "The reviewing courts probably cannot reverse a substantive decision on its merits, under Section 101, unless it be shown that the actual balance of costs and benefits that was struck was arbitrary or clearly gave insufficient weight to environmental values. But if the decision was reached procedurally without individualized consideration and balancing of environmental factors-conducted fully and in good faith-it is the responsibility of the courts to reverse."[37]

The consideration of environmental impacts is the method by which environmental protection was to be a made part of the mandate of every

29. 40 C.F.R. Sec. 1501.7.

30. 40 C.F.R. Secs. 1502.9(a), 1503.1, 1506.6.

31. 40 C.F.R. Secs. 1502.9(b), 1503.1, 1506.6.

32. 40 C.F.R. Sec. 1502.9 (c).

33. 40 C.F.R., Sec. 1506.9.

34. 40 C.F.R., Secs. 1506.1, 1506.10.

35. 5 U.S.C. Sec. 551 et seq.

36. *Calvert Cliffs Coordinating Committee, Inc. v. U.S. Atomic Energy Commission,* 449 F.2d 1109, 1112 (D.C. Cir. 1971) (citations omitted).

37. *Id.* at 1115.

federal agency.[38] Congress hoped to influence decision making of federal agencies by forcing them to analyze and publicize information about the environmental effects of actions.[39]

Analysis of NEPA's requirements reveals several questions for a federal agency: is there an action? Is it federal? Does it affect the quality of the human environment? What impacts are there? What alternative should be considered? What mitigation? Most of the remaining parts of the chapter explore these questions.

III. IS AN EIS REQUIRED?

As noted, *supra*, an EIS is to be prepared when there is a major federal action that will significantly affect the quality of the human environment. Assuming that the action is not outside the scope of NEPA by force of law or because it is a categorical exclusion, how is this determination made? In considering whether an action rises to the level of requiring an EIS, the agency must determine whether it is a major action, that is federal, and whether it will significantly affect the quality of the human environment. Sometimes this is obvious; sometimes less so. An agency may prepare an environmental assessment or other documentation to record its deliberations on these issues. But however the determination is presented procedurally, the agency must still find the answer to three questions.

A. Is it a Major Action?

NEPA specifies that the EIS be included in "every recommendation or report or proposals for legislation and other major Federal actions significantly affecting the quality of the human environment" that are performed by a federal agency.[40] The requirement that an EIS attach to proposals for legislation have been undercut by a CEQ regulation that states that the EIS requirement is not to attach to appropriations requests, the most common legislative proposal of a federal agency.[41] Instead, most of the controversy on NEPA application is in the second part that applies to "other major Federal actions."

Under NEPA, the term "action" has a fairly broad definition. Action is defined as anything carried out, funded, or approved by a federal agency. This last category especially can have a broad impact on the private sector if they must receive permits or leases from a federal agency, since that would constitute an approval by the agency. There are however, some gray areas. What about agency decisions *not* to take an action? Informal agency activities? Decisions not necessarily categorized as a proposal? Over time, court cases have helped to clarify when an agency activity is an "action" for purposes of NEPA, and when it is not. After reading the following case, see if you can discern a working test for this determination.

38. *Id.* at 1112.

39. 40 C.F.R., Sec. 1502.1.

40. 42 U.S.C. Sec. 4332(C).

41. 40 C.F.R. Sec. 1508.17.

KLEPPE v. SIERRA CLUB
AMERICAN ELECTRIC POWER SYSTEM
v. SIERRA CLUB

Supreme Court of the United States, 1976.

427 U.S. 390, 96 S.Ct. 2718, 49 L.Ed.2d 576.

Mr. Justice POWELL delivered the opinion of the Court.

Section 102(2)(C) of the National Environmental Policy Act of 1969 (NEPA) requires that all federal agencies include a detailed statement of environmental consequences known as an environmental impact statement "in every recommendation or report on proposals for legislation and other major Federal actions significantly affecting the quality of the human environment." 42 U.S.C. § 4332(2)(C). * * *

I

Respondents, several organizations concerned with the environment, brought this suit in July 1973 in the United States District Court for the District of Columbia. The defendants in the suit, petitioners here, were the officials of the Department and other federal agencies responsible for issuing coal leases, approving mining plans, granting rights-of-way, and taking the other actions necessary to enable private companies and public utilities to develop coal reserves on land owned or controlled by the Federal Government. Citing widespread interest in the reserves of a region identified as the "Northern Great Plains region," and an alleged threat from coal-related operations to their members' enjoyment of the region's environment, respondents claimed that the federal officials could not allow further development without preparing a "comprehensive environmental impact statement" under § 102(2)(C) on the entire region. They sought declaratory and injunctive relief. * * *

II

The record and the opinions of the courts below contain extensive facts about coal development and the geographic area involved in this suit. The facts that we consider essential, however, can be stated briefly.

The Northern Great Plains region identified in respondents' complaint encompasses portions of four States: northeastern Wyoming, eastern Montana, western North Dakota, and western South Dakota. There is no dispute about its richness in coal, nor about the waxing interest in developing that coal, nor about the crucial role the federal petitioners will play due to the significant percentage of the coal to which they control access. The Department has initiated, in this decade, three studies in areas either inclusive of or included within this region. The North Central Power Study was addressed to the potential for coordinated development of electric power in an area encompassing all or part of 15 States in the North Central United States. * * *

III

The major issue remains the one with which the suit began: whether NEPA requires petitioners to prepare an environmental impact statement on the entire Northern Great Plains region. * * *

As noted in the first sentence of this opinion, § 102(2)(C) requires an impact statement "in every recommendation or report on proposals for legislation and other major Federal actions significantly affecting the quality of the human environment." Since no one has suggested that petitioners have proposed legislation on respondents' region, the controlling phrase in this section of the Act, for this case, is "major Federal actions." Respondents can prevail only is there has been a report or recommendation on a proposal for major federal action with respect to the Northern Great Plains region. Our statement of the relevant facts shows there has been none; instead, all proposals are for actions of either local or national scope.

The local actions are the decisions by the various petitioners to issue a lease, approve a mining plan, issue a right-of-way permit, or take other action to allow private activity at some point within the region identified by respondents. Several Courts of Appeals have held that an impact statement must be included in the report or recommendation on a proposal for such action if the private activity to be permitted is one "significantly affecting the quality of the human environment" within the meaning of § 102(2)(C). See, E.g., Scientists' Institute for Public Information, Inc. v. AEC, 156 U.S.App.D.C. 395, 404–405, 481 F.2d 1079, 1088–1089 (1973); Davis v. Morton, 469 F.2d 593 (CA10 1972). The petitioners do not dispute this requirement in this case, and indeed have prepared impact statements on several proposed actions of this type in the Northern Great Plains during the course of this litigation. Similarly, the federal petitioners agreed at oral argument that§ 102(2)(C) required the Coal Programmatic EIS that was prepared in tandem with the new national coal-leasing program and included as part of the final report on the proposal for adoption of that program. Tr. of Oral Arg. 9. Their admission is well made, for the new leasing program is a coherent plan of national scope, and its adoption surely has significant environmental consequences.

But there is no evidence in the record of an action or a proposal for an action of regional scope. The District Court, in fact, expressly found that there was no existing or proposed plan or program on the part of the Federal Government for the regional development of the area described in respondents' complaint. It found also that the three studies initiated by the Department in areas either included within or inclusive of respondents' region that is, the Montana–Wyoming Aqueducts Study, the North Central Power Study, and the NGPRP were not parts of any plan or program to develop or encourage development of the Northern Great Plains. That court found no evidence that the individual coal development projects undertaken or proposed by private industry and public utilities in that part of the country are integrated into a plan or otherwise interrelated. These findings were not disturbed by the Court of Appeals, and they remain fully supported by the record in this Court.

Quite apart from the fact that the statutory language requires an impact statement only in the event of a proposed action, respondents' desire for a regional environmental impact statement cannot be met for practical reasons. In the absence of a proposal for a regional plan of development, there is nothing that could be the subject of the analysis envisioned by the statute for an impact statement. Section 102(2)(C) requires that an impact statement contain, in essence a detailed statement of the expected adverse environmental consequences of an action, the resource commitments involved in it, and the alternatives to it. Absent an overall plan for regional development, it is impossible to predict the level of coal-related activity that will occur in the region identified by respondents, and thus impossible to analyze the environmental consequences and the resource commitments involved in, and the alternatives to, such activity. A regional plan would define fairly precisely the scope and limits of the proposed development of the region. Where no such plan exists, any attempt to produce an impact statement would be little more than a study along the lines of the NGPRP, containing estimates of potential development and attendant environmental consequences. There would be no factual predicate for the production of an environmental impact statement of the type envisioned by NEPA.

IV

A

The Court of Appeals, in reversing the District Court, did not find that there was a regional plan or program for development of the Northern Great Plains region. It accepted all of the District Court's findings of fact, but concluded nevertheless that the petitioners "contemplated" a regional plan or program. The court thought that the North Central Power Study, the Montana–Wyoming Aqueducts Study, and the NGPRP all constituted "attempts to control development" by individual companies on a regional scale. It also concluded that the interim report of the NGPRP, then expected to be released at any time, would provide the petitioners with the information needed to formulate the regional plan they had been "contemplating." The Court therefore remanded with instructions to the petitioners to inform the District Court of their role in the further development of the region within 30 days after the NGPRP interim report issued; if they decided to control that development, an impact statement would be required.

We conclude that the Court of Appeals erred in both its factual assumptions and its interpretation of NEPA. We think the court was mistaken in concluding, on the record before it, that the petitioners were "contemplating" a regional development plan or program. It considered the several studies undertaken by the petitioners to represent attempts to control development on a regional scale. This conclusion was based on a finding by the District Court that those studies, as well as the new national coal-leasing policy, were "attempts to control development by individual companies in a manner consistent with the policies and procedures of the National Environmental Policy Act of 1969." But in context, that finding meant only that the named studies were efforts to gain background environmental information for subsequent application in the decisionmaking with respect to individual coal-related projects. This is the sense in which the District Court spoke of controlling development consistently with NEPA. Indeed, in the same paragraph containing the language relied upon by the Court of Appeals, the District Court expressly found that the studies were not part of a plan or program to develop or encourage development. See *supra*, at 2726.

Moreover, at the time the Court of Appeals ruled there was no indication in the record that the NGPRP was aimed toward a regional plan or program, and subsequent events have shown that this was not its purpose. The interim report of the study, issued shortly after the Court of Appeals ruled, described the effects of several possible rates of coal development but stated in its preface that the alternatives "are for study and comparison only; they do not represent specific plans or proposals." All parties agreed in this Court that there still exists no proposal for a regional plan or program of development. See Tr. of Oral Arg. 48.

Even had the record justified a finding that a regional program was contemplated by the petitioners, the legal conclusion drawn by the Court of Appeals cannot be squared with the Act. The court recognized that the mere "contemplation" of certain action is not sufficient to require an impact statement. But it believed the statute nevertheless empowers a court to require the preparation of an impact statement to begin at some point prior to the formal recommendation or report on a proposal. The Court of Appeals accordingly devised its own four-part "balancing" test for determining when during the contemplation of a plan or other type of federal action, an agency must begin a statement. The factors to be considered were identified as the likelihood and imminence of the program's coming to fruition, the extent to which information is available on the effects of implementing the expected program and on alternatives thereto, the extent to which irretrievable commitments are being made and options precluded "as refinement of the proposal progresses," and the severity of the environmental effects should the action be implemented.

The Court of Appeals thought that as to two of these factors the availability of information on the effects of any regional development program, and the severity of those effects the time already was "ripe" for an impact statement. It deemed the record unclear, however, as to the likelihood of the petitioners' actually producing a plan to control the development, and surmised that irretrievable commitments were being avoided because petitioners had ceased approving most coal-related projects while the NGPRP study was underway. The court also thought that the imminent release of the NGPRP interim report would provide the officials with sufficient information to define their role in development of the region, and it believed that as soon as the NGPRP was completed the petitioners would begin approving individual projects in the region, thus permitting irrevocable commitments of resources. It was for this reason that the court in its remand required the petitioners to report to the District Court their decision on the federal role with respect to the Northern Great Plains as a region within 30 days after issuance of the NGPRP report.

The Court's reasoning and action find no support in the language or legislative history of NEPA. The statute clearly states when an impact statement is required, and mentions nothing about a balancing of factors. Rather, as we noted last Term, under the first sentence of § 102(2)(C) the moment at which an agency must have a final statement ready "is the time at which it makes a recommendation or report on a *proposal* for federal action." *Aberdeen & Rockfish R. C. v. SCRAP*, 422 U.S. 289, 320, 95 S.Ct. 2336, 2356, 45 L.Ed.2d 191 (1975) (SCRAP II) (emphasis in original). The procedural duty imposed upon agencies by this section is quite precise, and the role of the courts in enforcing that duty is similarly precise. A court has no authority to depart from the statutory language and, by a balancing of court-devised factors, determine a point during the germination process of a potential proposal at which an impact statement should be prepared. Such an assertion of judicial authority would leave the agencies uncertain as to their procedural duties under NEPA, would invite judicial involvement in the day-to-day decisionmaking process of the agencies, and would invite litigation. As the contemplation of a project and the accompanying study thereof do not necessarily result in a proposal for major federal action, it may be assumed that the balancing process devised by the Court of Appeals also would result in the preparation of a good many unnecessary impact statements. * * *

V

Our discussion thus far has been addressed primarily to the decision of the Court of Appeals. It remains, however, to consider the contention now urged by respondents. They have not attempted to support the Court of Appeals' decision. Instead, respondents renew an argument they appear to have made to the Court of Appeals, but which that court did not reach. Respondents insist that, even without a comprehensive federal plan for the development of the Northern Great Plains, a "regional" impact statement nevertheless is required on all coal-related projects in the region because they are intimately related.

There are two ways to view this contention. First, it amounts to an attack on the sufficiency of the impact statements already prepared by the petitioners on the coal-related projects that they have approved or stand ready to approve. As such, we cannot consider it in this proceeding, for the case was not brought as a challenge to a particular impact statement and there is no impact statement in the record.[17] It also is

---

17. Petitioners lodged with this Court a copy of the massive six-volume impact statement on the projects in the Powder River Coal Basin, but it is not part of the record.

possible to view the respondents' argument as an attack upon the decision of the petitioners not to prepare one comprehensive impact statement on all proposed projects in the region. This contention properly is before us, for the petitioners have made it clear they do not intend to prepare such a statement.

We begin by stating our general agreement with respondents' basic premise that s 102(2)(C) may require a comprehensive impact statement in certain situations where several proposed actions are pending at the same time. NEPA announced a national policy of environmental protection and placed a responsibility upon the Federal Government to further specific environmental goals by "all practicable means, consistent with other essential considerations of national policy." § 101(b), 42 U.S.C. § 4331(b). Section 102(2)(C) is one of the "action-forcing" provisions intended as a directive to "all agencies to assure consideration of the environmental impact of their actions in decisionmaking." Conference Report on NEPA, 115 Cong.Rec. 40416 (1969). By requiring on impact statement Congress intended to assure such consideration during the development of a proposal or as in this case during the formulation of a position on a proposal submitted by private parties. A comprehensive impact statement may be necessary in some cases for an agency to meet this duty. Thus, when several proposals for coal-related actions that will have cumulative or synergistic environmental impact upon a region are pending concurrently before an agency, their environmental consequences must be considered together. Only through comprehensive consideration of pending proposals can the agency evaluate different courses of action.

Agreement to this extent with respondents' premise, however, does not require acceptance of their conclusion that all proposed coal-related actions in the Northern Great Plains region are so "related" as to require their analysis in a single comprehensive impact statement. * * *

Respondents conceded at oral argument that to prevail they must show that petitioners have acted arbitrarily in refusing to prepare one comprehensive statement on this entire region, and we agree. Tr. of Oral Arg. 67. The determination of the region, if any, with respect to which a comprehensive statement is necessary requires the weighing of a number of relevant factors, including the extent of the interrelationship among proposed actions and practical considerations of feasibility. Resolving these issues requires a high level of technical expertise and is properly left to the informed discretion of the responsible federal agencies. Cf. SCRAP II, 422 U.S., at 325–326, 95 S.Ct., at 2358–2359. Absent a showing of arbitrary action, we must assume that the agencies have exercised this discretion appropriately. Respondents have made no showing to the contrary.

Respondents' basic argument is that one comprehensive statement on the Northern Great Plains is required because all coal-related activity in that region is "programmatically," "geographically," and "environmentally" related. Both the alleged "programmatic" relationship and the alleged "geographic" relationship resolve, ultimately, into an argument that the region is proper for a comprehensive impact statement because the petitioners themselves have approached environmental study in this area on a regional basis. Respondents point primarily to the NGPRP, which they claim and petitioners deny focused on the region described in the complaint. The precise region of the NGPRP is unimportant, for its irrelevance to the delineation of an appropriate area for analysis in a comprehensive impact statement has been well stated by the Secretary:

"Resource studies (like the NGPRP) are one of many analytical tools employed by the Department to inform itself as to general resource availability, resource need and general environmental considerations so that it can intelligently determine the scope of environmental analysis and review specific actions it may take. Simply put, resource studies are a prelude to informed agency planning, and provide the data base on which the Department may decide to take specific actions for which impact statements are prepared. The scope of environmental impact statements seldom coincide with that of a given resource study, since the statements evolve from specific proposals for federal action while the studies simply provide an educational backdrop." Affidavit of Oct. 28, 1975, App. 191.

As for the alleged "environmental" relationship, respondents contend that the coal-related projects "will produce a wide variety of cumulative environmental impacts" throughout the Northern Great Plains region. They described them as follows: Diminished availability of water, air and water pollution, increases in population and industrial densities, and perhaps even climatic changes. Cumulative environmental impacts are, indeed, what require a comprehensive impact statement. But determination of the extent and effect of these factors, and particularly identification of the geographic area within which they may occur, is a task assigned to the special competency of the appropriate agencies. Petitioners dispute respondents' contentions that the interrelationship of environmental impacts is regionwide, and, as respondents' own submissions indicate, petitioners appear to have determined that the appropriate scope of comprehensive statements should be based on basins, drainage areas, and other factors. See Supra, at 2730–2731. We cannot say that petitioners' choices are arbitrary. Even if environmental interrelationships could be shown conclusively to extend across basins and drainage areas, practical considerations of feasibility might well necessitate restricting the scope of comprehensive statements.

In sum, respondents' contention as to the relationships between all proposed coal-related projects in the Northern Great Plains region does not require that petitioners prepare one comprehensive impact statement covering all before proceeding to approve specific pending applications. As we already have determined that there exists no proposal for regionwide action that could require a regional impact statement, the judgment of the Court of Appeals must be reversed, and the judgment of the District Court reinstated and affirmed. The case is remanded for proceedings consistent with this opinion.

So ordered.

Mr. Justice MARSHALL, with whom Mr. Justice BRENNAN joins, concurring in part and dissenting in part.

While I agree with much of the Court's opinion, I must dissent from Part IV, which holds that the federal courts may not remedy violations of the National Environmental Policy Act of 1969 (NEPA), 83 Stat. 852, 42 U.S.C. § 4321 Et seq. no matter how blatant until it is too late for an adequate remedy to be formulated. As the Court today recognizes, NEPA contemplates agency consideration of environmental factors throughout the decisionmaking process. Since NEPA's enactment, however, litigation has been brought primarily at the end of that process challenging agency decisions to act made without adequate environmental impact statements or without any statements at all. In such situations, the courts have had to content themselves with the largely unsatisfactory remedy of enjoining the proposed federal action and ordering the preparation of an adequate impact statement. This remedy is insufficient because, except by deterrence, it does nothing to further early consideration of environmental factors. And, as with all after-the-fact remedies, a remand for preparation of an impact statement after the basic decision to act has been made invites *post hoc* rationalizations, cf. *Citizens to Preserve Overton Park v. Volpe*, 401 U.S. 402, 419–420, 91 S.Ct. 814, 825, 28 L.Ed.2d 136 (1971), rather than the candid and balanced environmental assessments envisioned by NEPA. Moreover, the remedy is wasteful of resources and time, causing fully developed plans for action to be laid aside while an impact statement is prepared.

Nonetheless, until this lawsuit, such belated remedies were all the federal courts had had the opportunity to impose under NEPA. In this case, confronted with a situation in which, according to respondents' allegations, federal agencies were violating NEPA prior to their basic decision to act, the Court of Appeals for the District of Columbia Circuit seized the opportunity to devise a different and effective remedy. It recognized a narrow class of cases essentially those where both the likelihood of eventual agency action and the danger posed by nonpreparation of an environmental impact statement were great in which it would allow judicial intervention prior to the time at which an impact statement must be ready. The Court today loses sight of the inadequacy of other remedies and the narrowness of the category constructed by the Court of Appeals, and construes NEPA so as to preclude a court from ever intervening prior to a formal agency proposal. This decision, which unnecessarily limits the ability of the federal courts to effectuate the intent of NEPA, is mandated neither by the statute nor by the various equitable considerations upon which the Court relies.

I

The premises of the Court of Appeals' approach are not novel and indeed are reaffirmed by the Court today. Under § 102(2)(C) of NEPA, 42 U.S.C. § 4332(2)(C), "the moment at which an agency must have a final (environmtal [sic] impact) statement ready 'is the time at which it makes a recommendation or report on a Proposal for federal action.'" Ante, at 2728, quoting Aberdeen & Rockfish R. Co. v. SCRAP, 422 U.S. 289, 320, 95 S.Ct. 2336, 2356, 45 L.Ed.2d 191 (1975) (first emphasis added). Preparation of an impact statement, particularly on a complicated project, takes a considerable amount of time. Flint Ridge Dev. Co. v. Scenic Rivers Assn., 426 U.S. 776, 789 n. 10, 96 S.Ct. 2430, 2438, 49 L.Ed.2d 205 (1976); Sixth Annual Report, Council on Environmental Quality 639 (1975). Necessarily, if the statement is to be completed by the time the agency makes its formal proposal to act, preparation must begin substantially before the proposal must be ready. In this litigation, for instance, the federal petitioners assert that a statement on the region in which respondents are interested would take more than three years to complete. Brief for Federal Petitioners 28 n. 22. Accordingly, since it would violate NEPA for the Government to propose a plan for regional development of the Northern Great Plains without an accompanying environmental impact statement, if the Government contemplates making such a proposal at any time in the next three years it should already be working on its impact statement.

But an early start on the statement is more than a procedural necessity. Early consideration of environmental consequences through production of an environmental impact statement is the whole point of NEPA, as the Court recognizes. The legislative history of NEPA demonstrates that "(b)y requiring an impact statement Congress intended to assure (environmental) consideration During the development of a proposal...." Ante, at 2730 (emphasis added). Compliance with this duty allows the decisionmaker to take environmental factors into account when he is making decisions, at a time when he has an open mind and is more like to be receptive to such considerations. Thus, the final impact statement itself is but "the tip of an iceberg, the visible evidence of an underlying planning and decisionmaking process that is usually unnoticed by the public." Sixth Annual Report, Council on Environmental Quality 628 (1975).

Because an early start in preparing an impact statement is necessary if an agency is to comply with NEPA, there comes a time when an agency that fails to begin preparation of a statement on a contemplated project is violating the law. It is this fact, which is not disputed by the Court today, that was recognized by the Court of Appeals and that formed the basis of its remedy. * * *

Notes and Questions

1) Why is a regional impact statement important to the petitioners in this case? Would consideration of environmental impacts of individual leases

capture all of the impacts that might occur if every piece of federal land with coal in the region is leased?

2) Does the Court seem to indicate that there is "no federal action" for purposes of NEPA unless the federal agency charged with implementing NEPA believes there to be an "action?" What role does the Court's standard of review of the agency's actions play in such a case?

3) Justice Marshall disagrees with the majority's opinion to the extent that it does not allow the NEPA process to apply until the agency has taken some formal action. Is this a fair reading of the majority opinion? Does this turn NEPA into a *post hoc* rationalization? When does an "idea" become an action for purposes of NEPA?

B. Is it Federal?

Any action "potentially subject to federal control or responsibility" is considered a federal action for purposes of NEPA. 40 C.F.R. Sec. 1508.18. This can include federally controlled projects, federally funded projects, and federally permitted projects. Although this may seem straightforward in many ways, the way the federal control interacts with the project is critical to determining if an EIS is required. For instance, if a federal action includes the granting of a wetland fill permit under the Clean Water Act, sec. 404, is the "fill" alone to be examined to determine whether this is a major federal action that will "significantly affect the quality of the human environment," or should the entire project made possible by the fill be examined? This "scope of review" or "small handle" problem refers to the level of federal involvement in a larger private project. In some cases, agencies may have their own views or guidelines concerning the "scope" of the project that should be considered "federal" for purposes of triggering the EIS requirement. One of the most thorough examinations of this issue is the following case:

WINNEBAGO TRIBE OF NEBRASKA v. RAY

United States Court of Appeals, Eighth Circuit, 1980.
621 F.2d 269.

BRIGHT, Circuit Judge.

Winnebago Tribe of Nebraska (the Tribe) appeals an order of the district court [FN1] denying its request for a permanent injunction to bar construction of a proposed power line running from Raun, Iowa, to Hoskins, Nebraska. The Tribe claims the district court erred in holding that the issuance of a permit to cross the Missouri River by the Army Corps of Engineers (Corps) was not a "major federal action" within the meaning of the National Environmental Policy Act of 1969 (NEPA), 42 U.S.C. §§ 4321–47 (1976).

* * *

I. Background.

Appellee Nebraska Public Power District (NPPD) began planning construction of a 345 KV transmission line from Raun, Iowa, to Hoskins, Nebraska, in 1975. The proposed line would cross the Missouri River 150 feet south of an Omaha Public Power District (OPPD) line and run through the Winnebago Indian Reservation. In the fall of 1977, NPPD informed the Tribe and the Bureau of Indian Affairs of its intent.

On July 13, 1978, appellee Iowa Public Service Company (IPS), a joint venturer with NPPD in this project, applied to the Corps for a permit to cross the Missouri River, as required by 33 U.S.C. § 403 (1976) (originally enacted as Rivers and Harbors Appropriation Act of March 3, 1899, ch. 425, § 10, 30 Stat. 1151) (hereinafter section 10). Before granting the permit, the Corps prepared an environmental effect assessment on the impact of the river-crossing portion of the line (approximately 1.25 miles out of 67 miles). The assessment concluded that an environmental impact statement was not required because "(t) here are no significant environmental impacts associated with this project." The assessment did not mention any possible adverse effect on bald eagles, a protected species.[2] The Corps granted the section 10 permit on January 10, 1979.

On April 30, 1979, the Tribe filed the present suit alleging noncompliance with NEPA and seeking to enjoin construction pending compliance. * * * The trial court ruled that the assessment properly considered only the river-crossing portion of the line, because the scope of the federal permit was limited to this area and the federal government was not funding the project. * * *

II. Analysis.

Section 102(2)(C) of NEPA, 42 U.S.C. § 4332(2)(C) (1976), requires that the relevant federal agency prepare an EIS for "major federal actions significantly affecting the quality of the human environment." Initially, the agency determines whether the proposed action triggers the EIS requirement. See Minnesota Public Interest Research Group v. Butz, 498 F.2d 1314, 1319–20 (8th Cir. 1974) (en banc) (MPIRG I). In MPIRG I, supra, this court set forth the standard for judicial review of an agency's threshold determination not to prepare an EIS:

To upset an agency determination not to prepare an impact statement, it still must be shown that the agency's determination was not reasonable under the circumstances. This will require a showing that the project could significantly affect the quality of the human environment. Save Our Ten Acres v. Kreger, (472 F.2d 463, 466 (5th Cir. 1973)). We therefore hold that review of an agency's determination not to prepare an impact statement should be measured by its reasonableness in the

---

2. See Bald Eagle Protection Act, 16 U.S.C.A. §§ 668–668d (1974 & West Supp. 1979); Migratory Bird Treaty Act, 16 U.S.C.A. §§ 703–712 (1974 & West Supp. 1979), 50 C.F.R. § 10.13 (1978); Endangered Species Act of 1973, 16 U.S.C.A. §§ 1531–43 (1974 & West Supp.1979), 50 C.F.R. § 17.11 (1978).

circumstances, not as to whether it was arbitrary, capricious, an abuse of discretion, or otherwise not in accordance with law. (MPIRG I, supra, 498 F.2d at 1320 (footnote omitted); accord, Monarch Chemical Works, Inc. v. Thone, 604 F.2d 1083, 1087–88 (8th Cir. 1979).)

* * *

The Tribe claims that the administrative record is deficient in three respects: (1) it ignores sixty-five miles of the sixty-seven mile transmission line; (2) it does not consider certain viable alternatives; and (3) it does not contemplate potential harm to bald eagles. We deal with these claims in the order presented.

A. Failure to Consider the Entire Project.

(3) The Tribe alleges that the administrative record should have considered environmental impacts posed by the entire transmission line, rather than just the river-crossing portion. Appellant's claim presents two related issues: (a) whether the Corps wields such control and responsibility over the entire project that nonfederal segments must be included in the assessment; and (b) assuming limited federal involvement, whether the Corps nevertheless must consider the impacts of nonfederal segments as secondary effects of the proposed action.

The Tribe notes initially that the power line will not be constructed without the section 10 permit. In light of "but for" veto power, the Tribe argues, the Corps wields sufficient control over the entire project to require project-wide environmental analysis. Factual or veto control, however, must be distinguished from legal control or "enablement." See NAACP v. Medical Center, Inc., 584 F.2d 619 (3d Cir. 1978) (Medical Center); Atlanta Coalition on the Transportation Crisis, Inc. v. Atlanta Regional Commission, 599 F.2d 1333 (5th Cir. 1979) (Atlanta Coalition).

In "enablement" cases federal action is a legal condition precedent to accomplishment of an entire nonfederal project. Medical Center, supra, 584 F.2d at 632–33; Atlanta Coalition, supra, 599 F.2d at 1345–47. Thus, for example, the federal statute at issue in Greene County Planning Board v. FPC, 455 F.2d 412 (2d Cir.), cert. denied, 409 U.S. 849, 93 S.Ct. 56, 34 L.Ed.2d 90 (1972), required the Federal Power Commission to assure that the entire project was "best adapted" to a comprehensive environmental plan before licensing construction of a power line. See also Cady v. Morton, 527 F.2d 786 (9th Cir. 1975) (the federal grant of Indian coal leases was the legal condition precedent for the strip mining project); Davis v. Morton, 469 F.2d 593 (10th Cir. 1972) (ninety-nine year lease of Indian lands was legal condition precedent to entire development project). The statute at issue in this case is far narrower and cannot be construed as a grant of legal control over the entire project.[3]

---

3. Section 10 does not contain the type of broad mandate present in the Federal Power Commission Act. Compare Greene County Planning Board v. FPC, supra, 455 F.2d at 423. The Corps' jurisdiction under section 10 governs nonfederal actions only to the extent they "affect the course, condition, capacity or location of (navigable wa-

The court in Medical Center, supra, identified three factors helpful in determining whether "but for" or factual control requires project-wide analysis: (1) the degree of discretion exercised by the agency over the federal portion of the project; (2) whether the federal government has given any direct financial aid to the project; and (3) whether "the overall federal involvement with the project (is) sufficient to turn essentially private action into federal action." Id. at 629 (citation omitted). In Medical Center, the agency had little or no discretion, there was no direct federal aid, and the court found the federal involvement insufficient.

In the present suit, while the Corps has broad discretion to consider environmental impacts (see Zabel v. Tabb, 430 F.2d 199 (5th Cir. 1970), cert. denied, 401 U.S. 910, 91 S.Ct. 873, 27 L.Ed.2d 808 (1971)), that discretion must be exercised within the scope of the agency's authority. As noted above, the Corps' jurisdiction under section 10 extends only to areas in and affecting navigable waters. See United States v. Sexton Cove Estates, Inc., 526 F.2d 1293, 1299 (5th Cir. 1976); Weiszmann v. District Engineer, United States Army Corps of Engineers, 526 F.2d 1302, 1304 (5th Cir. 1976); United States v. Joseph G. Moretti, Inc., 526 F.2d 1306 (5th Cir. 1976). As the Third Circuit observed in United States v. Stoeco Homes, Inc., 498 F.2d 597, 607 (3d Cir. 1974):

The federal environmental protection statutes did not * * * by their terms enlarge the jurisdiction of the Army Corps of Engineers under the Rivers and Harbors Appropriation Act of 1899. If there is no such jurisdiction environmental protection is still a matter primarily of state concern.

Thus, the Corps' discretion under section 10 does not dictate project-wide review.[4]

The factors remaining for consideration under Medical Center are the presence of direct federal funding and the degree of federal involvement. There has been no direct or even indirect federal funding for this project. Cf. Ely v. Velde, 451 F.2d 1130 (4th Cir. 1971) (Law Enforcement Assistance Administration involvement in and funding for a state prison amounts to major federal action). As for federal involvement, the fact that part of the line will cross the Winnebago Reservation does not suffice to turn this essentially private action into federal action.[5] Federal

---

ters) * * *." United States v. Sexton Cove Estates, Inc., 526 F.2d 1293, 1299 (5th Cir. 1976). See Weiszmann v. District Engineer, United States Army Corps of Engineers, 526 F.2d 1302, 1304 (5th Cir. 1976); United States v. Joseph G. Moretti, Inc., 526 F.2d 1306 (5th Cir. 1976).

4. Contrary to the Tribe's claim, the Corps' amended regulations do not appear to make the grant of a section 10 permit a per se major federal action. See 44 Fed.Reg. 38,292, 38,294, 38,307–12 (1979) (to be codified in 33 C.F.R. s 230.6(e) and Appendix

B to 33 C.F.R. § 230). Moreover, new Council on Environmental Quality regulations, 43 Fed.Reg. 55,978 (1978) (to be codified in 40 C.F.R. ss 1500–08), as well as amended Corps of Engineers regulations, 44 Fed.Reg. 38,292 (1979) (to be codified in 33 C.F.R. § 230), postdate the assessment here and do not apply. See 43 Fed.Reg. 56,002 (1978) (to be codified in 40 C.F.R. § 1506.12).

5. Cf. Citizens Committee for the Hudson Valley v. Volpe, 425 F.2d 97, 106 (2d Cir.), cert. denied, 400 U.S. 949, 91 S.Ct. 237, 27 L.Ed.2d 256 (1970) (Corps required

law allows the state to condemn this land for any public purpose in the same manner as land owned in fee. 25 U.S.C. § 357 (1976). Thus, we conclude that the Corps did not have sufficient control and responsibility to require it to study the entire project.

The Tribe also notes that an agency must consider secondary or indirect impacts in determining whether there are any significant impacts upon the environment. See 40 C.F.R. § 1500.6(b) (1978). Appellant argues that the administrative record does not reflect consideration of a secondary effect of granting the permit namely, building the remainder of the line. If, however, appellant's position were correct, then an EIS for a properly segmented portion of highway would have to consider impacts of subsequent segments as well. A careful reading of the Council on Environmental Quality Guidelines, 40 C.F.R. § 1500.8(a)(3)(ii)(1978),[6] leads us to reject appellant's contention as erroneous. Completion of the nonfederal aspects of this single project does not constitute a secondary or indirect effect of the federal action.

Notes and Questions

1) What role does the agency's own construction of the Act play in the determination of the scope of the project?

2) Would the outcome of this case have been different if there had been two river crossings? Three?

3) Is it dispositive to simply consider whether the project as a whole can go forward in substantially the same form without the federal permit? In such a case, would the environmental impacts of the federal action be major if the action could substantially occur without any federal involvement?

———

In *Friends of the Earth v. U.S. Army Corps*[42], the D.C. federal district court found that the Corps permitting of casinos in Mississippi coastal water required a consideration of all upland impacts because the entire casino was "federal." The court noted that the Corps own regulations, issued after *Winnebago,* required the Corps to consider all impacts if the "environmental consequences of the larger project are essentially prod-

to prepare project-wide EIS now because both Congress and the Secretary of Transportation later will have to approve other portions of the state expressway project).

6. 40 C.F.R. § 1500.8(a)(3)(ii) provides in part:

> (ii) Secondary or indirect, as well as primary or direct, consequences for the environment should be included in the analysis. Many major Federal actions, in particular those that involve the construction or licensing of infrastructure investments (e. g., highways, airports, sewer systems, water resource projects, etc.), stimulate or induce secondary ef-

fects in the form of associated investments and changed patterns of social and economic activities. Such secondary effects, through their impacts on existing community facilities and activities, through inducing new facilities and activities, or through changes in natural conditions, may often be even more substantial than the primary effects of the original action itself. For example, the effects of the proposed action on population and growth may be among the most significant secondary effects.

42. 109 F.Supp.2d 30 (D.D.C. 2000)

ucts of the Corps permit action."[43] In distinguishing *Winnebago* the court stated that "here, by contrast [to *Winnebago*], the agency's jurisdiction encompasses the heart of the development projects–the permitting of the floating casinos themselves."[44]

C. Does it Significantly Affect the Quality of the Human Environment

Once the scope of the "federal action" is ascertained, it must be determined whether it is one that "significantly affects the quality of the human environment." In some ways, this is similar to the question concerning which part of the action is federal, only here the question is expanded to whether the "federal" part of the action is one that will have a significant effect. In implementing regulations, the term "significant" is to be defined in context. 40 C.F.R. Sec. 1508.27. The intensity of the impact will be judged relative to the context and the total input is also to be considered. This regulatory provision echoes similar determinations in case law. The reason for this definition was explained in the *Hanly* case:

> "In the absence of any Congressional or administrative interpretation of the term, we are persuaded that in deciding whether a major federal action will "significantly" affect the quality of the human environment the agency in charge, although vested with broad discretion, should normally be required to review the proposed action in the light of at least two relevant factors: (1) the extent to which the action will cause adverse environmental effects in excess of those created by existing uses in the area affected by it, and (2) the absolute quantitative adverse environmental effects of the action itself, including the cumulative harm that results from its contribution to existing adverse conditions or uses in the affected area. Where conduct conforms to existing uses, its adverse consequences will usually be less significant than when it represents a radical change. Absent some showing that an entire neighborhood is in the process of redevelopment, its existing environment, though frequently below an ideal standard, represents a norm that cannot be ignored. For instance, one more highway in an area honeycombed with roads usually has less of an adverse impact than if it were constructed through a roadless public park. See, e.g., Citizens to Preserve Overton Park v. Volpe, 401 U.S. 402, 91 S.Ct. 814, 28 L.Ed.2d 136 (1971).

> Although the existing environment of the area which is the site of a major federal action constitutes one criterion to be considered, it must be recognized that even a slight increase in adverse conditions that form an existing environmental milieu may sometimes threaten harm that is significant. One more factory polluting air and water in an area zoned for industrial use may represent the straw that breaks the back of the environmental camel. Hence the absolute, as

---

43. *Id.* at 40. **44.** *Id.*

well as comparative, effects of a major federal action must be considered."[45]

Recall that the EIS requirement only attaches to "major federal actions that significantly affect the quality of the human environment." In such a case, why is it important that the agency consider effects of multiple, inter-related actions? Cumulative impacts? It should be noted that when inter-related and/or cumulative impacts of piecemeal actions are considered individually, the incremental changes taken by an agency may not rise to the level of a major federal action. This issue is explored in the following case:

GRAND CANYON TRUST v. FEDERAL AVIATION ADMINISTRATION

United States Court of Appeals, District of Columbia Circuit, 2002.
290 F.3d 339.
As Amended Aug. 27, 2002.

Opinion for the Court filed by Circuit Judge ROGERS.

ROGERS, Circuit Judge:

The Grand Canyon Trust petitions for review of the decision of the Federal Aviation Administration ("FAA") approving the federal actions necessary to allow the city of St. George, Utah, to construct a replacement airport near Zion National Park. The Trust challenges the adequacy of the FAA's environmental assessment under § 102(2)(C) of the National Environmental Policy Act of 1969 ("NEPA"), 42 U.S.C. § 4332(C) (1970), and the FAA's conclusion that there would be no significant environmental impacts from the project necessitating preparation of an environmental impact statement under NEPA. Focusing on the noise impacts on the Park, the Trust principally contends that the FAA failed adequately to consider the cumulative impact on the natural quiet of the Park and instead addressed only the incremental impact of the replacement airport. We grant the petition.

I.

In 1995, the FAA began working with the City of St. George, Utah, to determine the feasibility of continuing use of the existing airport as compared to development of a new airport at a new site. A growing retirement community and projected air-traffic demand was outstripping the capacity of the existing airport, which could not be expanded due to geographic constraints. Three sites in addition to a no-action alternative were examined. In response to comments on a draft environmental assessment, the FAA conducted a Supplemental Noise Analysis on the potential noise impacts of the replacement airport on Zion National Park ("the Park"). The Park is located approximately 25 miles northeast of St. George and the preferred replacement airport alternative.

---

45. *Hanly v. Kleindienst,* 471 F.2d 823, 830–31 (2d Cir. 1972).

The FAA concluded that the noise impacts on the Park from the replacement airport would be negligible and insignificant. On January 30, 2001, the FAA approved the final environmental assessment, concluding that an environmental impact statement was unnecessary, and issued the record of decision, setting forth actions, determinations, and approvals that will allow St. George to construct the replacement airport. It is the determination underlying this record of decision, that the proposed action will not significantly affect the environment of the Park, that the Trust challenges.

II.

The essential disagreement between the parties is whether the FAA was required in its environmental assessment to address more than the incremental impact of the replacement airport as compared to the existing airport. NEPA requires federal agencies to prepare an environmental impact statement ("EIS") for "every ... major Federal action significantly affecting the quality of the human environment." 42 U.S.C. § 4332(2)(C). An environmental assessment ("EA") is made for the purpose of determining whether an EIS is required. *See* 40 C.F.R. § 1508.9. "If *any* 'significant' environmental impacts might result from the proposed agency action then an EIS must be prepared *before* agency action is taken." *Sierra Club v. Peterson,* 717 F.2d 1409, 1415 (D.C.Cir. 1983) (*"Peterson"*).

An agency decision that an EIS is not required may be overturned "only if it was arbitrary, capricious or an abuse of discretion." *Sierra Club v. United States Dep't of Transportation,* 753 F.2d 120, 126 (D.C.Cir.1985) (*"Transportation"*). Under the long-established standard in this circuit, the court reviews an agency's finding of no significant impact to determine whether:

First, the agency [has] accurately identified the relevant environmental concern. Second, once the agency has identified the problem it must have taken a 'hard look' at the problem in preparing the EA. Third, if a finding of no significant impact is made, the agency must be able to make a convincing case for its finding. Last, if the agency does find an impact of true significance, preparation of an EIS can be avoided only if the agency finds that the changes or safeguards in the project sufficiently reduce the impact to a minimum.

Id. at 127; *see also Maryland–Nat'l Capital Park and Planning Comm'n v. U.S. Postal Serv.,* 487 F.2d 1029, 1040 (D.C.Cir.1973).

The Trust does not dispute that the FAA properly defined the relevant environmental concern of noise impacts from aircraft on the Park. Rather, the Trust contends that the FAA cannot be said to have taken a "hard look" at the problem when it considered only the incremental impacts of the replacement airport and not the total noise impact that will result from the relocated airport. The Trust notes that the EA does not address the cumulative impact in light of other air flights over the Park, air tours in or near the Park, and reasonably foreseeable future aircraft activity and airport expansions that will contribute to the cumulative noise impact on the Park. Indeed, the EA's statement on cumulative impact is, in full: "There are no known factors that could result in cumulative impacts as a result of the proposed St. George Replacement Airport." Further, the Trust notes, the FAA's Supplemental Noise Analysis disregards cumulative impacts. The FAA responds that it adequately considered the cumulative impact when it compared noise impacts associated with the replacement airport with the no-action alternative of continued use of the existing airport. It rejects the Trust's position that it was required in an EA to compare the project to an environmental baseline of natural quiet and to consider the total impact of aircraft noise on the Park.

The issue dividing the parties is settled by regulations promulgated by the Council on Environmental Quality ("CEQ") to implement NEPA and by case law applying those regulations.* "The CEQ regulations, which ... are entitled to substantial deference, impose a duty on all federal agencies." *Marsh v. Oregon Natural Res. Council,* 490 U.S. 360, 372, 109 S.Ct. 1851, 1858, 104 L.Ed.2d 377 (1989) (citations omitted); *see also Citizens Against Burlington, Inc. v. Busey,* 938 F.2d 190, 200 (D.C.Cir.1991). The CEQ regulations define each term within NEPA's requirement of an EIS for "every ... major Federal action[ ] significantly affecting the quality of the human environment." 42 U.S.C. § 4332(2)(C); 40 C.F.R. § 1502.3. The term "significantly" is defined as those actions "with individually insignificant but cumulatively significant impacts. Significance exists if it is reasonable to anticipate a cumulatively significant impact on the environment." 40 C.F.R. § 1508.27(b)(7). "Cumulative impact," in turn, is defined as:

> the impact on the environment which results from the incremental impact of the action when added to other past, present, and reasonably foreseeable future actions regardless of what agency (Federal or non-Federal) or person undertakes such other actions. Cumulative impacts can result from individually minor but collectively significant actions taking place over a period of time.

40 C.F.R. § 1508.7. Although federal agencies have discretion to decide whether a proposed action "is significant enough to warrant preparation of an EIS," the court owes no deference to the FAA's interpretation of NEPA or the CEQ regulations because NEPA is addressed to all federal agencies and Congress did not entrust administration of NEPA to the FAA alone. *Citizens Against Rails-to-Trails v. Surface Transportation Board,* 267 F.3d 1144, 1150 (D.C.Cir.2001); *see Amfac Resorts, LLC v. United States Dep't. of Interior,* 282 F.3d 818, 835 (D.C.Cir.2002); *cf. Al-Fayed v. CIA,* 254 F.3d 300, 307 (D.C.Cir.2001).

The courts, in reviewing whether a federal agency has acted arbitrarily and capriciously in finding no significant environmental impact,

---

* Neither party challenges the regulatory authority of the CEQ, and hence we have no occasion to question the binding effect of the regulations on the FAA. *See City of Alexandria v. Slater,* 198 F.3d 862, 866 n. 3 (D.C.Cir.1999).

have given effect to the plain language of the regulations. While the factual settings differ in some respects from the instant case, the consistent position in the case law is that, depending on the environmental concern at issue, the agency's EA must give a realistic evaluation of the total impacts and cannot isolate a proposed project, viewing it in a vacuum. For example, in *Coalition on Sensible Transportation v. Dole,* 826 F.2d 60 (D.C.Cir.1987) (*"Dole"*), this court stated that the CEQ regulations on cumulative impact "provide a distinct meaning to the concept" separate and apart from the notion of improper segmentation of agency action. *Id.* at 70. Noting that the regulatory definition of cumulative impact specifies that the " 'incremental impact of the action' [at issue]" must be considered " 'when added to other past, present, and reasonably foreseeable future actions,' " *id.* (quoting 40 C.F.R. § 1508.7), the court observed that, consistent with the regulation and purpose of NEPA, "[i]t makes sense to consider the 'incremental impact' of a project for possible cumulative effects by incorporating the effects of other projects into the background 'data base' of the project at issue." *Id.* at 70–71. The point, the court stated, was to provide in the EA "sufficient [information] to alert interested members of the public to any arguable cumulative impacts involving [ ] other projects." *Id.* at 71. * * *

The FAA, in finding that the St. George replacement airport would have no significant impact on the environment of the Park, concluded that "there is little discernable increased noise intrusion to the Park" from the proposed replacement airport as compared to the existing airport, and that "the increase in noise levels that would result from the development of a replacement airport is negligible [because] aircraft traffic will increase even if the replacement airport is not constructed." The FAA's analysis appears principally in a Supplemental Noise Analysis attached to the EA, and proceeds on the basis of a comparison of the noise impacts from predicted air traffic at the existing airport and predicted air traffic at the larger replacement airport. * * *

The FAA's noise analysis in the EA, including the Supplemental Noise Analysis, may, in fact, be a splendid incremental analysis, but it fails to address what is crucial if the EA is to serve its function. While, as the FAA stresses, the EA is not intended to be a lengthy document, *see* 40 C.F.R. § 1508.9(a)(1), it must at a minimum address the considerations relevant to determining whether an EIS is required. NEPA regulations require that an agency consider cumulative impacts and the FAA's EA fails to address the total noise impact that will result from the replacement airport. * * * Comments on the draft EA called the FAA's attention to the need to consider mitigation measures in view of the results of the study of noise-annoyance to persons in the Park; the EA does not respond and provides no analysis of the 2% to 9% or the 4% to 15% level of annoyance shown in the NPS study. Yet, as the FAA was aware, the NPS had identified Zion National Park as among the nine national parks of "highest priority" for attention to noise impact on their natural quiet from overflights. *See U.S. Department of the Interi-*

or/National Park Service, Report on Effects of Aircraft Overflights on the National Park System: Report to Congress (July, 1995). Comments also expressed concern about the total impacts of noise on the Park and on Park visitors, yet the EA contains no analysis of the impact of 54 daily flights in 2008 and 69 in 2018 associated with St. George.

* * *

The analysis in the EA, in other words, cannot treat the identified environmental concern in a vacuum, as an incremental approach attempts. Although the replacement airport may contribute only a 2% increase to the amount of overflights near or over the Park, there is no way to determine from the FAA's analysis in the EA whether, deferring to the FAA's expert calculations, a 2% increase, in addition to other noise impacts on the Park, will "significantly affect" the quality of the human environment in the Park. At no point does the FAA's EA aggregate the noise impacts on the Park. The analysis in the EA does not address the accumulated, or total, incremental impacts of various man-made noises, such as the 250 daily aircraft flights near or over the Park that originate at, or have as their destination, airports other than that in St. George. Neither does the EA consider in any manner the air tours near and over the Park originating from the St. George airport. Nor does the EA address the impact, much less the cumulative impact, of noise in the Park as a result of other activities, such as the planned expansions of other regional airports that have flights near or over the Park. Without analyzing the total noise impact on the Park as a result of the construction of the replacement airport, the FAA is not in a position to determine whether the additional noise that is projected to come from the expansion of the St. George airport facility at a new location would cause a significant environmental impact on the Park and, thus, to require preparation of an EIS.

* * *

Accordingly, we grant the petition without reaching the Trust's contention that an EIS is required because the project is "highly controversial," 40 C.F.R. § 1508.27(b)(4); *Fund for Animals v. Frizzell*, 530 F.2d 982, 988 n. 15 (D.C.Cir.1976). We remand the case because the record is insufficient for the court to determine whether an EIS is required. On remand, the FAA must evaluate the cumulative impact of noise pollution on the Park as a result of construction of the proposed replacement airport in light of air traffic near and over the Park, from whatever airport, air tours near or in the Park, and the acoustical data collected by NPS in the Park in 1995 and 1998 mentioned in comments on the draft EA.

* * *

Notes and Questions

1) Should an agency be required to prepare an environmental impact statement because a project is "highly controversial?" What would be the

benefit of such a requirement? If an agency did always prepare an EIS for projects that were "highly controversial" would they then avoid the type of preliminary litigation which invariably accompanies a decision not to prepare an impact statement for highly controversial projects? Would this save time and effort in the long run?

2) What impact will information about total noise in Zion National Park have on the decision to allow construction of a replacement airport for St. George, Utah? Particularly if the total noise after construction would only be 2% greater? Might it matter if the 2% increase is concentrated in a particular time period? Geographic area? Can we know this information without a more detailed environmental analysis?

––––––

The CEQ guidelines determining whether an action "significantly affects the quality of the human environment" are in agreement with early case law implementing NEPA. Recall that, *Hanly v. Kleindienst*,[46] addressed "significant" this way:

> "[W]e are persuaded that in deciding whether a major federal action will 'significantly' affect the quality of the human environment [should analyze] (1) the extent to which the action will cause adverse environmental harm in excess in excess of those created by existing uses in the area affected by it, and (2) the absolute quantitative adverse environmental effects of the action itself."

Is the holding in *Grand Canyon* consistent with *Hanly*?

IV. IS THE EIS ADEQUATE?

If it is determined that an EIS must be prepared, the focus shifts to what the EIS should contain. Both Section 102(2)(c) of NEPA and the CEQ regulations at 40 C.F.R., part 1502 specify what the EIS is to contain.

The EIS is to include a cover sheet, summary, table of contents, a statement of the purpose and need for the proposed action, a description of the proposed action and alternatives to the proposed action. It must also include a description of the affected environment, a description of the environmental consequences of each proposed and alternative action, and a description of the means to mitigate identified consequences. Each of the substantive requirements is necessary for a true "consideration" of environmental effects to occur. By requiring a comparison of environmental effects and ease of mitigation of the proposal and other alternative scenarios, the EIS allows the decision maker to know exactly what is gained and lost by the proposal.

A. Environmental Effects

Since complex proposals may have many effects, the determination of the "environmental consequences" of an action is no easy task.

––––––
46. 471 F.2d 823, 830 (2d Cir. 1972).

According to the statute, the agency must consider direct and indirect effects and cumulative effects as well. Environmental impacts include impacts that are ecological, aesthetic, historical, cultural, economic, and social.[47] One early NEPA case summarized the breadth of these impacts under NEPA.

"The environmental concerns courts have expressed in these cases may be classified into four somewhat overlapping categories. The first regards what might be termed health and public safety. Courts have examined a project's potential effect on the quality of air and water, the noise level of the community, and the capacity of existing or proposed sewage and solid waste facilities. Relevant as well is whether the project will affect the local crime rate, present fire dangers, or otherwise unduly tap police and fire forces in the community. The second category involves consideration of the project's impact on social services, such as the availability of schools, hospitals, businesses, commuter facilities, and parking. Apart from its impact on a community's services, a project may alter the character of the area in which it locates—the third category. Conformance to local zoning ordinances, harmonization with proximate land uses, and a blending with the aesthetics of the area are concerns relevant to this category. The final category involves consideration of the project's impact on the community's development policy. Relocation of a federal facility from a downtown to a suburban location, for example, might contribute to urban blight and decay. Neighborhood stability and growth are values which have been found to be cognizable under NEPA."[48]

The EIS has also become the preferred document for a consideration of environmental justice issues. The Council on Environmental Quality has published a guidance document to assist agencies in incorporating environmental justice considerations in their NEPA documents.

Because the considered effects can be so broad, once an EIS is required, agencies tend to make them over-inclusive rather than under-inclusive. The failure to consider any environmental impact may render the EIS deficient under NEPA. To assist in the determination of impacts and other considerations, agencies are to engage in a process called "scoping."[49] The so-called "lead agency" (the agency that is to take the lead in preparation of the EIS if more than one agency is involved) is to invite comment on the scope of effects to be considered from any affected Federal, State, or local agency, and any affected Indian tribe.[50] Any other interested persons may contribute as well. The scoping announcement is in the Federal Register, and an agency may, but is not required to, have

47. 40 C.F.R. Sec. 1508.8(b); *EDF v. TVA*, 468 F.2d 1164, 1174 (6th Cir. 1972), aff'd, 492 F.2d 466 (1974).

48. *Como–Falcon Coalition, Inc. v. United States Dept. Labor*, 465 F.Supp. 850, 859 (D. Minn. 1978), *aff'd and modified*, 609 F.2d 342 (8th Cir. 1979), *cert. denied*, 446 U.S. 936, 100 S.Ct. 2154, 64 L.Ed.2d 789 (1980).

49. 40 C.F.R., Sec. 1507.3(c).

50. 40 C.F.R., Sec. 1501 *et seq.*

a scoping hearing.[51] Generally, the scoping process will result in a determination of the extent of actions to be considered, the range of alternatives to be analyzed, and of course, the environmental effects that are to be examined.

Nevertheless, sometimes not all environmental impacts can be determined ahead of time. Is an EIS inadequate if it fails to identify environmental impacts that cannot yet be determined? Even if it is not legally inadequate, can the agency make an informed decision? The following case addresses these questions.

ROBERTSON v. METHOW VALLEY CITIZENS COUNCIL

Supreme Court of the United States, 1989.
490 U.S. 332, 109 S.Ct. 1835, 104 L.Ed.2d 351.

Justice STEVENS delivered the opinion of the Court.

* * *

I

The Forest Service is authorized by statute to manage the national forests for "outdoor recreation, range, timber, watershed, and wildlife and fish purposes." 74 Stat. 215, 16 U.S.C. § 528. See also 90 Stat. 2949, 16 U.S.C. § 1600 *et seq.* Pursuant to that authorization, the Forest Service has issued "special use" permits for the operation of approximately 170 Alpine and Nordic ski areas on federal lands.

The Forest Service permit process involves three separate stages. The Forest Service first examines the general environmental and financial feasibility of a proposed project and decides whether to issue a special use permit. See 36 CFR § 251.54(f) (1988). Because that decision is a "major Federal action" within the meaning of NEPA, it must be preceded by the preparation of an Environmental Impact Statement (EIS). 42 U.S.C. § 4332. If the Service decides to issue a permit, it then proceeds to select a developer, formulate the basic terms of the arrangement with the selected party, and issue the permit. The special use permit does not, however, give the developer the right to begin construction. See 36 CFR § 251.56(c) (1988). In a final stage of review, the Service evaluates the permittee's "master plan" for development, construction, and operation of the project. Construction may begin only after an additional environmental analysis (although it is not clear that a second EIS need always be prepared) and final approval of the developer's master plan. This case arises out of the Forest Service's decision to issue a special use permit authorizing the development of a major destination Alpine ski resort at Sandy Butte in the North Cascade Mountains.

Sandy Butte is a 6,000–foot mountain located in the Okanogan National Forest in Okanogan County, Washington. At present Sandy

---

51. 40 C.F.R., Sec. 1501.7.

Butte, like the Methow Valley it overlooks, is an unspoiled, sparsely populated area that the District Court characterized as "pristine." In 1968, Congress established the North Cascades National Park and directed the Secretaries of the Interior and Agriculture to agree on the designation of areas within, and adjacent to, the park for public uses, including ski areas. 82 Stat. 926, 930, 16 U.S.C. §§ 90, 90d–3. A 1970 study conducted by the Forest Service pursuant to this congressional directive identified Sandy Butte as having the highest potential of any site in the State of Washington for development as a major downhill ski resort.

In 1978, Methow Recreation, Inc. (MRI), applied for a special use permit to develop and operate its proposed "Early Winters Ski Resort" on Sandy Butte and an 1,165–acre parcel of land it had acquired adjacent to the National Forest. The proposed development would make use of approximately 3,900 acres of Sandy Butte; would entice visitors to travel long distances to stay at the resort for several days at a time; and would stimulate extensive commercial and residential growth in the vicinity to accommodate both vacationers and staff.

In response to MRI's application, the Forest Service, in cooperation with state and county officials, prepared an EIS known as the Early Winters Alpine Winter Sports Study (Early Winters Study or Study). The stated purpose of the EIS was "to provide the information required to evaluate the potential for skiing at Early Winters" and "to assist in making a decision whether to issue a Special Use Permit for downhill skiing on all or a portion of approximately 3900 acres of National Forest System land." A draft of the Study was completed and circulated in 1982, but release of the final EIS was delayed as Congress considered including Sandy Butte in a proposed wilderness area. When the Washington State Wilderness Act of 1984 was passed, however, Sandy Butte was excluded from the wilderness designation, and the EIS was released.

The Early Winters Study is a printed document containing almost 150 pages of text and 12 appendices. It evaluated five alternative levels of development of Sandy Butte that might be authorized, the lowest being a "no action" alternative and the highest being development of a 16–lift ski area able to accommodate 10,500 skiers at one time. The Study considered the effect of each level of development on water resources, soil, wildlife, air quality, vegetation, and visual quality, as well as land use and transportation in the Methow Valley, probable demographic shifts, the economic market for skiing and other summer and winter recreational activities in the Valley, and the energy requirements for the ski area and related developments. The Study's discussion of possible impacts was not limited to on-site effects, but also, as required by Council on Environmental Quality (CEQ) regulations, see 40 CFR § 1502.16(b) (1987), addressed "off-site impacts that each alternative might have on community facilities, socio-economic and other environmental conditions in the Upper Methow Valley." As to off-site effects, the Study explained that "due to the uncertainty of where other public and private lands may become developed," it is difficult to evaluate off-site impacts, and thus the document's analysis is necessarily "not site-specific . . ."

The effects of the proposed development on air quality and wildlife received particular attention in the Study. In the chapter on "Environmental Consequences," the first subject discussed is air quality. As is true of other subjects, the discussion included an analysis of cumulative impacts over several years resulting from actions on other lands as well as from the development of Sandy Butte itself. The Study concluded that although the construction, maintenance, and operation of the proposed ski area "will not have a measurable effect on existing or future air quality," the off-site development of private land under all five alternatives—including the "no action" alternative—"will have a significant effect on air quality during severe meteorological inversion periods." The burning of wood for space heat, the Study explained, would constitute the primary cause of diminished air quality, and the damage would increase incrementally with each of the successive levels of proposed development. The Study cautioned that without efforts to mitigate these effects, even under the "no action" alternative, the increase in automobile, fireplace, and wood stove use would reduce air quality below state standards, but added that "[t]he numerous mitigation measures discussed" in the Study "will greatly reduce the impacts presented by the model."

* * *

In its discussion of adverse effects on area wildlife, the EIS concluded that no endangered or threatened species would be affected by the proposed development and that the only impact on sensitive species was the probable loss of a pair of spotted owls and their progeny. With regard to other wildlife, the Study considered the impact on 75 different indigenous species and predicted that within a decade after development vegetational change and increased human activity would lead to a decrease in population for 31 species, while causing an increase in population for another 24 species on Sandy Butte. Two species, the pine marten and nesting goshawk, would be eliminated altogether from the area of development.

In a comment in response to the draft EIS, the Washington Department of Game voiced a special concern about potential losses to the State's largest migratory deer herd, which uses the Methow Valley as a critical winter range and as its migration route. The state agency estimated that the total population of mule deer in the area most likely to be affected was "better than 30,000 animals" and that "the ultimate impact on the Methow deer herd could exceed a 50 percent reduction in numbers." The agency asserted that "Okanogan County residents place a great deal of importance on the area's deer herd." In addition, it explained that hunters had "harvested" 3,247 deer in the Methow Valley area in 1981, and that, since in 1980 hunters on average spent $1,980 for each deer killed in Washington, they had contributed over $6 million to the State's economy in 1981. Because the deer harvest is apparently proportional to the size of the herd, the state agency predicted that "Washington business can expect to lose over $3 million annually from reduced recreational opportunity." The Forest Service's own analysis of the impact on the deer herd was more modest. It first concluded that the actual operation of the ski hill would have only a "minor" direct impact on the herd, but then recognized that the off-site effect of the development "would noticeably reduce numbers of deer in the Methow [Valley] with any alternative." Although its estimate indicated a possible 15 percent decrease in the size of the herd, it summarized the State's contrary view in the text of the EIS, and stressed that off-site effects are difficult to estimate due to uncertainty concerning private development.

Ultimately, the Early Winters Study recommended the issuance of a permit for development at the second highest level considered—a 16–lift ski area able to accommodate 8,200 skiers at one time. On July 5, 1984, the Regional Forester decided to issue a special use permit as recommended by the Study. In his decision, the Regional Forester found that no major adverse effects would result directly from the federal action, but that secondary effects could include a degradation of existing air quality and a reduction of mule deer winter range. He therefore directed the supervisor of the Okanogan National Forest, both independently and in cooperation with local officials, to identify and implement certain mitigating measures.

Four organizations (respondents) opposing the decision to issue a permit appealed the Regional Forester's decision to the Chief of the Forest Service. See 36 CFR § 211.18 (1988). After a hearing, he affirmed the Regional Forester's decision. Stressing that the decision, which simply approved the general concept of issuing a 30–year special use permit for development of Sandy Butte, did not authorize construction of a particular ski area and, in fact, did not even act on MRI specific permit application, he concluded that the EIS's discussion of mitigation was "adequate for this stage in the review process."

Thereafter, respondents brought this action under the Administrative Procedure Act, 5 U.S.C. §§ 701–706, to obtain judicial review of the Forest Service's decision. Their principal claim was that the Early Winters Study did not satisfy the requirements of NEPA, 42 U.S.C. § 4332. With the consent of the parties, the case was assigned to a United States Magistrate. See 28 U.S.C. § 636(c). After a trial, the Magistrate filed a comprehensive written opinion and concluded that the EIS was adequate. Specifically, he found that the EIS had adequately disclosed the adverse impacts on the mule deer herd and on air quality and that there was no duty to prepare a "worst case analysis" because the relevant information essential to a reasoned decision was available. In concluding that the discussion of off-site, or secondary, impacts was adequate, the Magistrate stressed that courts apply a "rule of reason" in evaluating the adequacy of an EIS and "take the uncertainty and speculation involved with secondary impacts into account in passing on the adequacy of the discussion of secondary impacts."

* * *

Concluding that the Early Winters Study was inadequate as a matter of law, the Court of Appeals reversed. *Methow Valley Citizens Council v. Regional Forester*, 833 F.2d 810 (CA9 1987). The court held that … if the agency had difficulty obtaining adequate information to make a reasoned assessment of the environmental impact on the herd, it had a duty to make a so-called "worst case analysis." Such an analysis is " 'formulated on the basis of available information, using reasonable projections of the worst possible consequences of a proposed action.' *Save our Ecosystems* [*v. Clark,*] 747 F.2d [1240], at 1244–45 (CA9 1984) (quoting 46 Fed.Reg. 18032 (1981))."

* * *

II

Section 101 of NEPA declares a broad national commitment to protecting and promoting environmental quality. 83 Stat. 852, 42 U.S.C. § 4331. To ensure that this commitment is "infused into the ongoing programs and actions of the Federal Government, the act also establishes some important 'action-forcing' procedures." 115 Cong.Rec. 40416 (remarks of Sen. Jackson). See also S.Rep. No. 91–296, p. 19 (1969) U.S.Code Cong. & Admin.News 1969 p. 2751; *Andrus v. Sierra Club,* 442 U.S. 347, 350, 99 S.Ct. 2335, 2337, 60 L.Ed.2d 943 (1979); *Kleppe v. Sierra Club,* 427 U.S. 390, 409, and n. 18, 96 S.Ct. 2718, 2730, and n. 18, 49 L.Ed.2d 576 (1976). Section 102 thus, among other measures "directs that, to the fullest extent possible … all agencies of the Federal Government shall—

* * *

"(C) include in every recommendation or report on proposals for legislation and other major Federal actions significantly affecting the quality of the human environment, a detailed statement by the responsible official on—

"(i) the environmental impact of the proposed action,

"(ii) any adverse environmental effects which cannot be avoided should the proposal be implemented,

"(iii) alternatives to the proposed action,

"(iv) the relationship between local short-term uses of man's environment and the maintenance and enhancement of long-term productivity, and

"(v) any irreversible and irretrievable commitments of resources which would be involved in the proposed action should it be implemented." 83 Stat. 853, 42 U.S.C. § 4332.

The statutory requirement that a federal agency contemplating a major action prepare such an environmental impact statement serves NEPA's "action-forcing" purpose in two important respects. See *Baltimore Gas & Electric Co. v. Natural Resources Defense Council, Inc.,* 462 U.S. 87, 97, 103 S.Ct. 2246, 2252, 76 L.Ed.2d 437 (1983); *Weinberger v.*

Catholic Action of Hawaii/Peace Education Project, 454 U.S. 139, 143, 102 S.Ct. 197, 201, 70 L.Ed.2d 298 (1981). It ensures that the agency, in reaching its decision, will have available, and will carefully consider, detailed information concerning significant environmental impacts; it also guarantees that the relevant information will be made available to the larger audience that may also play a role in both the decisionmaking process and the implementation of that decision.

Simply by focusing the agency's attention on the environmental consequences of a proposed project, NEPA ensures that important effects will not be overlooked or underestimated only to be discovered after resources have been committed or the die otherwise cast. See *ibid.; Kleppe, supra,* 427 U.S., at 409, 96 S.Ct., at 2729. Moreover, the strong precatory language of § 101 of the Act and the requirement that agencies prepare detailed impact statements inevitably bring pressure to bear on agencies "to respond to the needs of environmental quality." 115 Cong.Rec. 40425 (1969) (remarks of Sen. Muskie).

Publication of an EIS, both in draft and final form, also serves a larger informational role. It gives the public the assurance that the agency "has indeed considered environmental concerns in its decisionmaking process," *Baltimore Gas & Electric Co., supra,* 462 U.S., at 97, 103 S.Ct., at 2252, and, perhaps more significantly, provides a springboard for public comment, see L. Caldwell, Science and the National Environmental Policy Act 72 (1982). Thus, in this case the final draft of the Early Winters Study reflects not only the work of the Forest Service itself, but also the critical views of the Washington State Department of Game, the Methow Valley Citizens Council, and Friends of the Earth, as well as many others, to whom copies of the draft Study were circulated. See Early Winters Study, Appendix D. Moreover, with respect to a development such as Sandy Butte, where the adverse effects on air quality and the mule deer herd are primarily attributable to predicted off-site development that will be subject to regulation by other governmental bodies, the EIS serves the function of offering those bodies adequate notice of the expected consequences and the opportunity to plan and implement corrective measures in a timely manner.

The sweeping policy goals announced in § 101 of NEPA are thus realized through a set of "action-forcing" procedures that require that agencies take a " 'hard look' at environmental consequences," *Kleppe,* 427 U.S., at 410, n. 21, 96 S.Ct., at 2730, n. 21 (citation omitted), and that provide for broad dissemination of relevant environmental information. Although these procedures are almost certain to affect the agency's substantive decision, it is now well settled that NEPA itself does not mandate particular results, but simply prescribes the necessary process. See *Strycker's Bay Neighborhood Council, Inc. v. Karlen,* 444 U.S. 223, 227–228, 100 S.Ct. 497, 499–500, 62 L.Ed.2d 433 (1980) *(per curiam); Vermont Yankee Nuclear Power Corp. v. Natural Resources Defense Council, Inc.,* 435 U.S. 519, 558, 98 S.Ct. 1197, 1219, 55 L.Ed.2d 460 (1978). If the adverse environmental effects of the proposed action are adequately identified and evaluated, the agency is not constrained by

NEPA from deciding that other values outweigh the environmental costs. See *ibid.; Strycker's Bay Neighborhood Council, Inc., supra,* 444 U.S., at 227–228, 100 S.Ct., at 499–500; *Kleppe, supra,* 427 U.S., at 410, n. 21, 96 S.Ct., at 2730, n. 21. In this case, for example, it would not have violated NEPA if the Forest Service, after complying with the Act's procedural prerequisites, had decided that the benefits to be derived from downhill skiing at Sandy Butte justified the issuance of a special use permit, notwithstanding the loss of 15 percent, 50 percent, or even 100 percent of the mule deer herd. Other statutes may impose substantive environmental obligations on federal agencies, but NEPA merely prohibits uninformed—rather than unwise—agency action.

* * *

III

The Court of Appeals also concluded that the Forest Service had an obligation to make a "worst case analysis" if it could not make a reasoned assessment of the impact of the Early Winters project on the mule deer herd. Such a "worst case analysis" was required at one time by CEQ regulations, but those regulations have since been amended. Moreover, although the prior regulations may well have expressed a permissible application of NEPA, the Act itself does not mandate that uncertainty in predicting environmental harms be addressed exclusively in this manner. Accordingly, we conclude that the Court of Appeals also erred in requiring the "worst case" study.

In 1977, President Carter directed that CEQ promulgate binding regulations implementing the procedural provisions of NEPA. Exec. Order No. 11991, 3 CFR 123 (1977 Comp.). Pursuant to this Presidential order, CEQ promulgated implementing regulations. Under § 1502.22 of these regulations—a provision which became known as the "worst case requirement"—CEQ provided that if certain information relevant to the agency's evaluation of the proposed action is either unavailable or too costly to obtain, the agency must include in the EIS a "worst case analysis and an indication of the probability or improbability of its occurrence." 40 CFR § 1502.22 (1985). In 1986, however, CEQ replaced the "worst case" requirement with a requirement that federal agencies, in the face of unavailable information concerning a reasonably foreseeable significant environmental consequence, prepare "a summary of existing credible scientific evidence which is relevant to evaluating the . . . adverse impacts" and prepare an "evaluation of such impacts based upon theoretical approaches or research methods generally accepted in the scientific community." 40 CFR § 1502.22(b) (1987). The amended regulation thus "retains the duty to describe the consequences of a remote, but potentially severe impact, but grounds the duty in evaluation of scientific opinion rather than in the framework of a conjectural 'worst case analysis.' " 50 Fed.Reg. 32237 (1985).

The Court of Appeals recognized that the "worst case analysis" regulation has been superseded, yet held that "[t]his rescission . . . does not nullify the requirement ... since the regulation was merely a codification of prior NEPA case law." 833 F.2d, at 817, n. 11. This conclusion, however, is erroneous in a number of respects. Most notably, review of NEPA case law reveals that the regulation, in fact, was not a codification of prior judicial decisions. See Note, 86 Mich.L.Rev. 777, 798, 800–802, 813–814 (1988). The cases cited by the Court of Appeals ultimately rely on the Fifth Circuit's decision in *Sierra Club v. Sigler,* 695 F.2d 957 (1983). *Sigler,* however, simply recognized that the "worst case analysis" regulation codified the "judicially created principl[e]" that an EIS must "consider the probabilities of the occurrence of any environmental effects it discusses." *Id.,* at 970–971. As CEQ recognized at the time it superseded the regulation, case law prior to the adoption of the "worst case analysis" provision did require agencies to describe environmental impacts even in the face of substantial uncertainty, but did not require that this obligation necessarily be met through the mechanism of a "worst case analysis." See 51 Fed.Reg. 15625 (1986). CEQ's abandonment of the "worst case analysis" provision, therefore, is not inconsistent with any previously established judicial interpretation of the statute.

* * *

Notes and Questions

1) Can an agency adequately consider environmental impacts in the absence of a worst case scenario? Would the requirement of a worst case scenario improve the agency's ability to consider the environmental impacts? If so, should it not be included?

2) After this case, could a worst case analysis ever be required in an EIS?

B. Alternatives Consideration

The inclusion and analysis of alternatives to the proposed action is also a critical part of the EIS. Reasonable alternatives are to be considered, and an agency must always analyze a "no-action" alternative. The breadth of the alternatives to be considered can certainly affect the desirability of the proposed action. For instance, in the *Methow* case, *supra,* what kind of alternatives should be considered with respect to the proposed ski resort? In its alternatives analysis, is the forest service to examine only alternatives regarding the size of the proposed ski resort? The possibility of expanding ski resorts in other areas? Examine all possible recreational activities, such as bowling? Read the following from the Court of Appeals decision in *Methow Valley Citizens Council v. Regional Forester:*[52]

"To be adequate, an environmental impact statement must consider every reasonable alternative. *Friends of Endangered Species v. Jant-*

---

52. 833 F.2d 810, 815 (1987), *rev'd in part,* 490 U.S. 332, 109 S.Ct. 1835, 104 L.Ed.2d 351 (1989). Although the decision of the court of appeals was reversed in part, its discussion of alternative analysis stands.

zen, 760 F.2d 976, 988 (9th Cir.1985); *California v. Block,* 690 F.2d at 766–67; *Adler v. Lewis,* 675 F.2d 1085, 1097 (9th Cir.1982) ("this court has held the alternatives discussion to be subject to 'reasonableness.' "); *Save Lake Washington v. Frank,* 641 F.2d 1330, 1334 (9th Cir.1981); *Lange v. Brinegar,* 625 F.2d 812, 818 (9th Cir.1980) ("The discussion of alternatives in an E.I.S. statement is subject to a construction of reasonableness."). An EIS is rendered inadequate by the existence of a viable but unexamined alternative. *Citizens for a Better Henderson,* 768 F.2d at 1057 (citations omitted). Furthermore, even if an alternative requires "legislative action", this fact "does not automatically justify excluding it from an EIS." *City of Angoon v. Hodel,* 803 F.2d 1016, 1021 (9th Cir.1986) (footnote omitted), *cert. denied,* 484 U.S. 870, 108 S.Ct. 197, 98 L.Ed.2d 148 (1987). Thus, the range of alternatives considered must be sufficient to permit a reasoned choice. *Life of the Land v. Brinegar,* 485 F.2d 460, 472 (9th Cir.1973), *cert. denied,* 416 U.S. 961, 94 S.Ct. 1979, 40 L.Ed.2d 312 (1974).

Here the Forest Service's purpose—to provide a "winter sports opportunity"—is broadly framed in terms of service to the public benefit. It is not, *by its own terms,* tied to a specific parcel of land. *Compare City of Angoon,* 803 F.2d at 1021; *Trout Unlimited,* 509 F.2d at 1286. There appears no tenable reason for the Forest Service to be wedded exclusively to the development of Sandy Butte. Thus it should have appeared obvious that investigation was warranted to determine whether the development of winter sports opportunities could be pursued at alternative sites.[7]

Appellants have offered evidence suggesting that other sites may be well suited for the type of recreational development envisioned by the Forest Service. Unlike Sandy Butte, the sites discussed by the appellants are not adjacent to land owned by defendant MRI, but under the directive given to the Forest Service in its manual,[8] that fact does not preclude consideration of other reasonable alternatives. Moreover, since we find it reasonable to assume that expansion of existing ski areas would have less environmental impact than would the construction of an entirely new ski area,[9] while possibly achiev-

---

7. The Forest Service's final EIS listed four alternatives, including their preferred course of action, in addition to the alternative of "no action" mandated by statute. Yet all four of the "action" alternatives required development of Sandy Butte. No consideration was given in the EIS to ways of achieving the Forest Service's goal through other options, such as the expansion of existing downhill ski areas in other parts of Washington State.

8. The manual provides in relevant part that

A permit shall not be granted simply to provide a commercial profit-making oppor-

tunity. The Forest Service is not required to accommodate a desire of an individual applicant. A real public service or other justification must be evident . . . to show at least that the use meets a public need and will not conflict with National Forest objectives, programs or purposes.

Forest Service Manual § 2710.3.

9. In *Coalition for Canyon Preservation v. Bowers,* 632 F.2d 774, 778 (9th Cir.1980), the defendants intended to construct a new four-lane highway which would pass through parkland in plaintiffs' town. The EIS was held to be deficient because it failed to consider the alternative of improving a comparable net increase in the total capacity of skiers served,[10] such alternatives might have been appropriate for investigation.

This court, however, would not require that the Forest Service explore an unreasonably broad range of alternatives. Rather, the range "need not extend beyond those [alternatives] reasonably related to the purposes of the project." *Trout Unlimited,* 509 F.2d at 1286 (citations omitted). Thus, the Forest Service should more clearly articulate its goal, specifically identifying the market and geographic pool of skiers targeted. This will provide a clear standard by which it can determine which alternatives are appropriate for investigation and consideration in its EIS. In its present state, the EIS's discussion of alternatives to the proposed action is inadequate as a matter of law."

C. Mitigation

An EIS must also discuss how the proposed environmental impacts can be mitigated. The consideration of mitigation measures, particularly their ease and costs, assists in analyzing what the real environmental impacts of an action are. In *Methow,* the Supreme Court indicated that the level of specificity required for mitigation measures would depend on the scope of the project itself. Larger projects or programmatic undertakings may identify more generic mitigation, while more specifically tailored proposals would require the inclusion of more specific mitigation measures. Importantly, the Supreme Court made clear in *Methow* that mitigation measures do not have to be completely specified or identified at the time an action is taken.

ROBERTSON v. METHOW VALLEY CITIZENS COUNCIL

Supreme Court of the United States, 1989.

490 U.S. 332, 109 S.Ct. 1835, 104 L.Ed.2d 351.

[for more detailed facts, reread the case excerpt, *supra*]

* * *

In its discussion of air-quality mitigation measures, the EIS identified actions that could be taken by the county government to mitigate the adverse effects of development, as well as those that the Forest Service itself could implement at the construction stage of the project.

ing and widening a two-lane highway already in existence. This court stated that "the alternative ... was both reasonable and obvious, and that therefore the EIS is deficient.... The use of a narrower than four-lane road is made even more obvious by the possibility that parkland would thereby [be] spared." *Id.* at 784 (citations omitted). *See California v. Block,* 690 F.2d 753, 767 (9th Cir.1982) ("In the absence of an alternative that looks to already developed areas for future resource extraction and use, the ... decisional process ends its inquiry at the beginning.").

10. For example, one of the existing ski areas in Washington State has plans in motion to expand into a destination ski resort. A 1981 development report prepared for the Mission Ridge ski area details an intended expansion of the facility to accomodate an additional 3,900 SAOT, to make its total capacity 6,500 SAOT.

The Study suggested that Okanogan County develop an air quality management plan, requiring weatherization of new buildings, limiting the number of wood stoves and fireplaces, and adopting monitoring and enforcement measures. In addition, the Study suggested that the Forest Service require that the master plan include procedures to control dust and to comply with smoke management practices.

* * *

The court [of appeals] held that the Forest Service could not rely on " 'the implementation of mitigation measures' " [with respect to] the EIS' treatment of air quality. Since the EIS made it clear that commercial development in the Methow Valley will result in violations of state air-quality standards unless effective mitigation measures are put in place by the local governments and the private developer, the Court of Appeals concluded that the Forest Service had an affirmative duty to "develop the necessary mitigation measures *before* the permit is granted." *Id.,* at 819 (emphasis in original) (footnote omitted). The court held that this duty was imposed by both the Forest Service's own regulations and § 102 of NEPA. *Ibid.* It read the statute as imposing a substantive requirement that " 'action be taken to mitigate the adverse effects of major federal actions.' " *Ibid.* (quoting *Stop H–3 Assn. v. Brinegar,* 389 F.Supp. 1102, 1111 (Haw.1974), rev'd on other grounds, 533 F.2d 434 (CA9), cert. denied, 429 U.S. 999, 97 S.Ct. 526, 50 L.Ed.2d 610 (1976)). For this reason, it concluded that "an EIS must include a thorough discussion of measures to mitigate the adverse environmental impacts of a proposed action." 833 F.2d, at 819. The Court of Appeals concluded by quoting this paragraph from an opinion it had just announced:

" 'The importance of the mitigation plan cannot be overestimated. It is a determinative factor in evaluating the adequacy of an environmental impact statement. Without a complete mitigation plan, the decisionmaker is unable to make an informed judgment as to the environmental impact of the project—one of the main purposes of an environmental impact statement.' " *Id.,* at 820 (quoting *Oregon Natural Resources Council v. Marsh,* 832 F.2d 1489, 1493 (CA9 1987), rev'd, 490 U.S. 360, 109 S.Ct. 1851, 104 L.Ed.2d 377).

* * *

To be sure, one important ingredient of an EIS is the discussion of steps that can be taken to mitigate adverse environmental consequences. The requirement that an EIS contain a detailed discussion of possible mitigation measures flows both from the language of the Act and, more expressly, from CEQ's implementing regulations. Implicit in NEPA's demand that an agency prepare a detailed statement on "any adverse environmental effects which cannot be avoided should the proposal be implemented," 42 U.S.C. § 4332(C)(ii), is an understanding that the EIS will discuss the extent to which adverse effects can be avoided. See D. Mandelker, NEPA Law and Litigation § 10:38 (1984). More generally, omission of a reasonably complete discussion of possible mitigation measures would undermine the "action-forcing" function of NEPA. Without such a discussion, neither the agency nor other interested groups and individuals can properly evaluate the severity of the adverse effects. An adverse effect that can be fully remedied by, for example, an inconsequential public expenditure is certainly not as serious as a similar effect that can only be modestly ameliorated through the commitment of vast public and private resources. Recognizing the importance of such a discussion in guaranteeing that the agency has taken a "hard look" at the environmental consequences of proposed federal action, CEQ regulations require that the agency discuss possible mitigation measures in defining the scope of the EIS, 40 CFR § 1508.25(b) (1987), in discussing alternatives to the proposed action, § 1502.14(f), and consequences of that action, § 1502.16(h), and in explaining its ultimate decision, § 1505.2(c).

There is a fundamental distinction, however, between a requirement that mitigation be discussed in sufficient detail to ensure that environmental consequences have been fairly evaluated, on the one hand, and a substantive requirement that a complete mitigation plan be actually formulated and adopted, on the other. In this case, the off-site effects on air quality and on the mule deer herd cannot be mitigated unless nonfederal government agencies take appropriate action. Since it is those state and local governmental bodies that have jurisdiction over the area in which the adverse effects need be addressed and since they have the authority to mitigate them, it would be incongruous to conclude that the Forest Service has no power to act until the local agencies have reached a final conclusion on what mitigating measure they consider necessary. Even more significantly, it would be inconsistent with NEPA's reliance on procedural mechanisms—as opposed to substantive, result-based standards—to demand the presence of a fully developed plan that will mitigate environmental harm before an agency can act. Cf. *Baltimore Gas & Electric Co.,* 462 U.S., at 100, 103 S.Ct., at 2254 ("NEPA does not require agencies to adopt any particular internal decisionmaking structure").

We thus conclude that the Court of Appeals erred, first, in assuming that "NEPA requires that 'action be taken to mitigate the adverse effects of major federal actions,' " 833 F.2d, at 819 (quoting *Stop H–3 Assn. v. Brinegar,* 389 F.Supp., at 1111), and, second, in finding that this substantive requirement entails the further duty to include in every EIS "a detailed explanation of specific measures which *will* be employed to mitigate the adverse impacts of a proposed action," 833 F.2d, at 819 (emphasis supplied).

* * *

V. STATE ENVIRONMENTAL POLICY ACTS

By its terms, the National Environmental Policy Act only applies to the actions of federal agencies. Activities controlled by other governmental entities or by private parties that do not require federal action will not be encompassed by NEPA. Recognizing this as a gap in environmental protection, many states have implemented similar acts at the state level. Though many state statutes bear some variation of the name "state environmental policy act," their operations may be wildly divergent. Because of this divergence, there is not really even agreement on which states have the so-called "little NEPAs," with one law review article claiming that there were 25 such statutes and another suggesting that there were only sixteen.[53] The states of Minnesota, Washington, New York, and California are often described as having the strongest state environmental policy acts, though other states have stringent requirements as well.[54] Generally, some state environmental policy acts may be more restrictive than NEPA because they often require more procedures of mandate certain actions based on findings of significant environmental impacts.

"The California Environmental Quality Act (CEQA), for example, provides that "[e]ach public agency shall mitigate or avoid the significant effects on the environment of projects that it carries out or approves whenever it is feasible to do so." The law does not absolutely prohibit government agencies from taking actions that have significant effects on the environment. Instead, it provides that "[i]f economic, social, or other conditions make it infeasible to mitigate one or more significant effects on the environment of a project, the project may nonetheless be carried out or approved at the discretion of a public agency if the project is otherwise permissible under applicable laws and regulations." Similarly, the New York State Environmental Quality Review Act (SEQRA) requires government agencies, "to the maximum extent practicable," to minimize or avoid environmental impacts, taking into consideration social, economic, and other considerations. These substantive limitations are similar to the limitations imposed on the EPA and the U.S. Army Corps of Engineers when those agencies review applications for permits to develop wetlands under the Clean Water Act.

Minnesota's environmental review law goes even further and provides that[n]o state action significantly affecting the quality of the environment shall be allowed, nor shall any permit for natural resources management and development be granted, where such action or permit has caused or is likely to cause pollution, impairment, or destruction of the air, water, land or other natural resources located within the state, so long as there is a feasible and prudent alternative consistent with the reasonable requirements of the public health, safety, and welfare.

Washington takes a more moderate approach. The Washington State Environmental Protection Act broadly allows, but does not require,

53. Cole, et al., *Prospects for Health Impact Assessments in the United States ...*, 29 J.Health Pol., Policy, and Law 1153, 1162 (2004); Cliff Rechtschaffen, *Advancing Environmental Justice Norms*, 37 U.C. Davis L. Rev. 95, 120 (2003).

54. Cole, *supra*, at 1162.

government agencies to deny or condition the approval of a project based on the environmental impacts of the project."[55]

Though other states may have some form of an environmental policy act, many are extremely limited. For example, the state of Georgia's environmental policy act does not apply to permitting and therefore doesn't reach many actions that can affect the environment.[56]

VI. THE EFFECTS OF NEPA

As can be seen in the foregoing discussion, the procedures required to implement the NEPA can be cumbersome and time-consuming. In an effort to avoid successful court challenges, many agencies "throw in the kitchen sink," providing long and detailed analyses of any possible environmental effects. Some believe that this does not promote the purposes of NEPA, since the crush of information may make it difficult for agencies and the public to really focus in on the most important problems.[57] Given the state of the EISs, many persons have raised the question of whether the NEPA is worth all of this delay and cost. Do we thus have "too much" environmental analysis? One of the authors of this textbook has argued that the problem may be that we have too little, that, in particular, by failing to consider the environment as broadly as necessary to include such issues as risk allocation and environmental philosophy, agencies often run into opposition which is harder to understand and address.[58]

46 Hastings Law Journal 85

November, 1994

THE HUMAN ENVIRONMENT OF THE MIND: CORRECTING NEPA IMPLEMENTATION BY TREATING ENVIRONMENTAL PHILOSOPHY AND ENVIRONMENTAL RISK ALLOCATION AS ENVIRONMENTAL VALUES UNDER NEPA

Victor B. Flatt
[footnotes omitted]

* * *

The real cause of the gap in environmental understanding between those who conduct a cost benefit analysis using environmental impacts from the NEPA process and those who oppose the project on environmental grounds is that NEPA has not been routinely construed broadly

---

55. Stephen Johnson, *NEPAs and SEPAs in the Quest for Environmental Justice*, 30 Loy. L.A. L. Rev. 565, 598 (1997)

56. Ga. Code Ann. 12–16–3.

57. *See generally*, Bradley Karkkainen, Toward a Smarter NEPA: Monitoring and Managing Government's Environmental Performance, 102 Colum. L. Rev. 903, 904 (2002).

58. Victor B. Flatt, *The Human Environment of the Mind* ..., 46 Hastings L. J. 85, 113 (1998).

enough to allow for a consideration of all of the environmental impacts that concern society. Specifically, NEPA has not been construed as requiring consideration of environmental risk allocation and values associated with risk aversion, nor has it been construed as requiring an analysis of the value derived from holding and supporting a certain environmental philosophy.

When certain impacts on environmental values, such as environmental risk allocation and environmental philosophy, are not routinely considered under NEPA. but are of concern to society as a whole, this initial cost-efficient determination of project feasibility is lost with respect to these impacts. Allowing consideration of environmental risk allocation and environmental philosophical values would make NEPA more efficient. As one commentator stated with respect to the PANE Courts refusal to consider psychological distress. '[t]his consideration would ... allow the public to inform the agency of the publics willingness to accept a particular risk.' Michael A. Christofeno, Note, Psychological Distress Under NEPA, 19 Val. U. L. Rev. 899, 923 (1985).

Without consideration of these values, there will be projects. which may have effects on environmental philosophy or risk allocation values, that will proceed against a wall of public opposition and that may ultimately derail them. However, because these values are not presently considered or even acknowledged under NEPA, the opposition based on these values will not be well articulated, leaving a proponent of a project unsure of how to proceed to successfully address environmental concerns and complete the project. The opposition may take the form of a different environmental concern that a project proponent will address with massive expenditures for mitigation only to find that this was not the real concern at all, thus, leading to economic waste. Moreover, the proponents of the project may never spend resources to address or mitigate the real environmental concern; consequently, the opposition will remain stalwart.

If the opposition is finally successful in stopping a project, economic waste has occurred in gauging the depths of opposition that should have stopped a project before it even started. NEPA has been criticized for allowing too much delay to consider environmental problems, but many of these 'problems' mask concern about environmental risk allocation or an impact on environmental philosophy

Even if there is little public opposition, as long as there is any legal challenge to a project, the project could be derailed and economic waste may occur, if environmental risk allocation or environmental philosophical values are affected. It is easy to suppose that some judges, like the general public, appreciate the value of environmental philosophy and risk allocation and may through NEPA delay, prohibit, or seem hostile to a project for these reasons. Since these values have not been explicitly recognized and considered under NEPA, the basis of the judicial action may not be expressed forthrightly. Just as in cases of general opposition to government actions, this 'hidden' or 'masked' judicial opposition prevents a project's proponent from addressing or considering the true environmental costs, leading to frustration and expense in NEPA litigation. It also incurs an indirect cost to the judiciary in terms of loss of institutional respect. Directly acknowledging these values will help restore that institutional trust.

If environmental risk allocation and environmental philosophy were explicitly considered under NEPA, then they could be addressed at low cost. The proponents of an action would have a clearer understanding of what values would be affected by a project and whether the project as presented or modified is viable, without the initial expenditure of large sums of money to address phantom environmental concerns. Even if environmental philosophical concerns or risk allocation values were not immediately clear, they would come into focus early in the project, allowing proper mitigation or abandonment of the project at a far lower cost than now exists.

Environmental risk allocation and environmental philosophy are the only major environmental values not to be considered under NEPA. Though values other than environmental ones may be at play in time use of NEPA, as these values are incorporated into the NEPA decision-making process, the use of NEPA merely as a delay tactic will decline. This will bring NEPA procedure more in line with its legislative intent and will make the NEPA process more cost-effective.

* * *

In 2002, the Bush administration undertook a review of NEPA and the NEPA process to analyze its strengths and weaknesses. That report stressed that agencies should try sharing information better (perhaps through the use of technology); that there should be more mechanisms for collaboration; and that the CEQ could do more to strengthen effective NEPA compliance among some agencies, particularly with respect to determining categorical exclusions and Environmental Assessments.[59]

Though the criticism of NEPA has grown more in recent years, and its operation has been suspended for certain activities (such as leasing by the Forestry Department), it remains an important aspect of federal actions, and through permitting, to private activities. The agency or lawyer ignores its application at great risk. In complying with NEPA, procedure is critically important, and, experience generally shows that a willingness to compromise on the proposal or action can go a long way towards forestalling delay and expense.

---

59. NEPA Task Force Report to the Council on Environmental Quality, *Modern-* *izing NEPA Implementation*, http://ceq.eh.doe.gov/ntf/report/index.html.

Chapter 3

THE CLEAN WATER ACT

I. THE NPDES PROGRAM

The modern Clean Water Act ("CWA") assumed its current shape with the passage of the Federal Water Pollution Control Act of 1972, 33 U.S.C. § 1251 *et seq.*, Pub. L. 92–500 ("FWPCA"). In Section 101 of the new law, Congress announced that the statute's objective is to "restore and maintain the chemical, physical, and biological integrity of the Nation's waters." 33 U.S.C. § 1251(a). It further proclaimed several ambitious goals, including: (a) achieving by 1983, wherever attainable, a level of water quality that protects fish and wildlife and provides for recreation in and on the water (this is the so-called "fishable/swimmable" goal); and (b) eliminating, by 1985, all discharges of pollutants into the navigable waters. Id.

As we will see, we have fallen far short of these goals. Indeed, the statute never really contemplated that they would be met. As Judge Wald has pointed out,

> ... [I]t is one thing for Congress to announce a grand goal, and quite another for it to mandate full implementation of that goal. Read as a whole, the Clean Water Act shows not only Congress' determined effort to clean up our polluted lakes and rivers, but also its practical recognition of the economic, technological, and political limits on total elimination of all pollution from all sources.

National Wildlife Federation v. Gorsuch, 693 F.2d 156, 178 (D.C. Cir. 1982). While the CWA aspires to the achievement of water quality standards that will meet its fishable/swimmable aspirations, its regulatory gaps have virtually ensured that this has not and will not come to pass for many of our waters. And as to the "no discharges" goal, the CWA simply contains no mandates that have ever, or are ever likely to, lead to the achievement of that objective.

Do not be dismayed, however. As distinguished an observer as Professor Oliver Houck has lauded the CWA as possibly our most successful environmental statute. Houck, TMDLs IV: The Final Frontier, 29 Envt. L. Rep. 10469 (Aug. 1999). Despite our growing population and economy, our Nation's waters are, generally speaking, significantly cleaner than they were when the FWPCA was first passed in 1972. Id. Undoubtedly, the CWA deserves credit for this.

We begin our detailed study of the CWA with the National Pollutant Discharge Elimination System ("NPDES") program, which is the major mechanism through which the statute seeks to control water pollution. In a nutshell, the CWA contemplates that those who discharge pollutants into our waterways will be regulated under a permit system that imposes both technology- and, where necessary, water quality-based requirements. In theory, the technology-based requirements ensure that discharger will attain aggressive levels of pollutant-reduction that are uniform within each category of dischargers. The water quality-based requirements serve as a safety-net pursuant to which more aggressive controls will be required in situations in which the technology-based requirements may not result in the desired level of stream quality.

Before we focus on the substantive standards of the NPDES program, however, we consider some important preliminary matters: jurisdiction and the federal/state relationship.

A. Jurisdiction

Section 301(a) is the jurisdictional trigger for both the NPDES program under § 402 and the "dredge and fill" program under § 404 of the Act (this latter program is also known as the "wetlands" program, despite the fact that its scope transcends wetlands). Section 301(a) prohibits the "discharge of any pollutant" except as in conformance with several other sections of the Act, including §§ 402 and 404. In turn, Section 402 allows either EPA or the relevant State (depending upon whether the State is authorized to implement the program) to issue NPDES permits containing the relevant substantive requirements. (Likewise, Section 404 allows either the Corps of Engineers or—less often—the relevant State to issue permits for discharges of "dredged or fill material." We will consider this program in chapter 8, below.)

Section 502 defines the key statutory terms. Most significantly, Section 502(12) defines the term "discharge of a pollutant" to include "any addition of any pollutant to navigable waters from any point source." Thus it can be seen that there are three key elements of NPDES (and § 404) jurisdiction: there must be (1) an addition of a pollutant to (2) navigable waters (3) from a point source. If any one of these elements is missing, there is no NPDES (or § 404) jurisdiction. At the same time, note that if these three elements are present, no discharge can occur except as in compliance with the statutory sections listed in § 301(a). At least on the face of the statute, there is no de minimis exception. All discharges of pollutants are forbidden in the absence of a required permit.

In the NPDES world, classic examples of regulated dischargers include industrial facilities and sewage treatment plants that discharge contaminated wastewater into our rivers through outfall pipes. In these and other similar situations, there is typically little or no doubt as to whether the Act's jurisdictional elements are satisfied. As will be seen below, however, there has been much litigation defining the boundaries of these jurisdictional terms, and many important issues remain unresolved. As such, our focus will be on the uncertain boundaries of NPDES jurisdiction. At the same time, however, the reader should not lose sight of the fact that in many cases the existence of these elements is a foregone conclusion.

1. Addition of a Pollutant

While the phrase "addition of a pollutant" is not defined under the statute, Section 502(6) states that "the term 'pollutant' means dredged spoil, solid waste, incinerator residue, sewage, garbage, sewage sludge, munitions, chemical wastes, biological materials, radioactive materials, heat, wrecked or discarded equipment, rock, sand, cellar dirt and industrial, municipal, and agricultural waste discharged into water...." 33 U.S.C. § 1362(6). While this definition is framed as an exclusive one ("the term 'pollutant' means ..."), the breadth of some of its terms (e.g., "industrial, municipal and agricultural waste") results in there usually being little doubt as to whether pollutants are present in any offending discharges. As will be seen below, however, the question whether a particular point source is adding a pollutant has given rise to repeated litigation, often in the context of either dams or diversion projects that transfer water from one waterway to another. Consider the following case:

CATSKILL MOUNTAINS CHAPTER OF TROUT UNLIMITED, INC. v. CITY OF NEW YORK

United States Court of Appeals, Second Circuit, 2001.
273 F.3d 481.

WALKER, JR., Chief Judge:

Since before World War II, New York City has operated Schoharie Dam and Reservoir in the Catskill Mountains, to provide drinking water for New York City. Water is diverted south from the Schoharie Reservoir ("the Reservoir") through the Shandaken Tunnel ("the Tunnel") for several miles and released into Esopus Creek ("the Creek"), which in turn empties into Ashokan Reservoir. The transfer of water from the Reservoir to Esopus Creek and Ashokan Reservoir facilitates its delivery to New York City for use as drinking water.

Absent the tunnel, water leaving the Reservoir would flow north in Schoharie Creek, join the Mohawk River, and flow into the Hudson River. Water from Esopus Creek, on the other hand, makes its way southeast to the Hudson by way of Ashokan Reservoir. Schoharie Reservoir and Esopus Creek are hydrologically connected only insofar as both are tributaries of the Hudson. Under natural conditions, water from the Schoharie Reservoir would never reach Esopus Creek.

On March 31, 2000, [Catskill Mountains Chapter of Trout Unlimited, Inc. and other environmental groups ("Catskill")] filed a complaint ... alleging that the City, as owner and operator of the Schoharie Reservoir and Shandaken Tunnel, was in violation of 33 U.S.C. § 1311(a), which prohibits "the discharge of any pollutant" unless those discharges are conducted in accordance with a duly issued discharge permit. Catskill alleged that the Tunnel discharges pollutants in the form of "suspended solids," "turbidity," and heat into Esopus Creek. They alleged that the suspended solids and turbidity are the result of earth-disturbing activities within the Reservoir's watershed that produce fine, red-clay sediments in the Reservoir. They further alleged that the discharges cause the Creek to violate state water quality standards for turbidity and temperature. Esopus Creek, Catskill contended, is naturally clearer and cooler than the water entering it from the Tunnel and supports "one of the premier trout fishing streams in the Catskill Region."

As we have noted, the CWA prohibits, unless otherwise allowed by permit, "the discharge of any pollutant," 33 U.S.C. § 1311(a), which the Act defines to mean "any addition of any pollutant to navigable waters from any point source," 33 U.S.C. § 1362(12). The statute does not define "addition." The City argues that the release of water from Schoharie Reservoir into Esopus Creek is not an "addition," citing *National Wildlife Federation v. Gorsuch,* 693 F.2d 156 (D.C.Cir.1982), and *National Wildlife Federation v. Consumers Power Co.,* 862 F.2d 580 (6th Cir.1988), both of which accorded substantial deference to the EPA's position that the CWA's discharge permit requirement does not apply to discharges from dams. Catskill counters that the *Gorsuch* and *Consumers Power* courts accorded unjustified deference to the EPA's interpretation of "addition," that the cases are distinguishable on their facts, and that the City's conduct here qualifies as an "addition" under the plain meaning of that word....

[The court first noted that the *Gorsuch* and *Consumers Power* courts' determinations that EPA's interpretation of "addition" was entitled to *Chevron* deference had been undermined by the Supreme Court's more recent opinions in *Christensen v. Harris County,* 529 U.S. 576 (2000) ("*Christensen*"), and *United States v. Mead Corp.,* 533 U.S. 218 (2001) ("*Mead*"). The court noted that *Christensen,* in particular, stands for the proposition that interpretations announced in informal policy statements—which was the only context in which EPA had spoken here—do not have the force of law and, thus, do not merit *Chevron* deference. As a consequence, the court determined that EPA's interpretation of "addition" was entitled to only *Skidmore* deference, meaning that the court would follow it only to the extent that it found it persuasive. *Skidmore v. Swift & Co.,* 323 U.S. 134, 140 (1944).]

The EPA's position, upheld by the *Gorsuch* and *Consumers Power* courts, is that for there to be an "addition," a "point source must *introduce* the pollutant into navigable water from the outside world." *Gorsuch,* 693 F.2d at 165 [(emphasis in original)]. We agree with this view provided that "outside world" is construed as any place outside the particular water body to which pollutants are introduced. Given that understanding of "addition," the transfer of water containing pollutants from one body of water to another, distinct body of water is plainly an addition and thus a "discharge" that demands an NPDES permit.

Both *Gorsuch* and *Consumers Power* essentially involved the recirculation of water, without anything added "from the outside world." Such recirculation, they concluded, could not be an "addition." In *Gorsuch,* water was released from a reservoir through a dam to the stream below. Plaintiffs complained that such a release amounted to a regulated discharge under the Act, requiring a permit. The reservoir above the dam and the stream below, at least arguably, were sufficiently the "same" water that the release might not be considered an "addition"; nothing was introduced to the water that was not, in some sense, already there. See 693 F.2d at 74–75.

In *Consumers Power,* the defendant had withdrawn water from Lake Michigan, along with some surprised fish, for hydroelectric power generation. The water and fish were then returned to the Lake after passing through hydroelectric generators, which puréed some of the fish. The court found that returning the fish to the Lake, albeit in a different form, was not an "addition" because the fish had already been there. *See* 862 F.2d at 586. Indeed, the court concluded that "[t]he water which passes through the [defendant's hydropower works] never loses its status as water of the United States." *Id.* at 589. The navigable water was recirculated, but nothing was added. The Sixth Circuit therefore also concluded that the releases from the defendant's hydropower works were not "introduced from the outside world." *See id.* at 586. . . .

The *Gorsuch* and *Consumers Power* decisions comport with the plain meaning of "addition," assuming that the water from which the discharges came is the same as that to which they go. If one takes a ladle of soup from a pot, lifts it above the pot, and pours it back into the pot, one has not "added" soup or anything else to the pot (beyond, perhaps, a *de minimis* quantity of airborne dust that fell into the ladle). In requiring a permit for such a "discharge," the EPA might as easily require a permit for Niagra Falls (sic).

The present case, however, strains past the breaking point the assumption of "sameness" made by the *Gorsuch* and *Consumers Power* courts. Here, water is artificially diverted from its natural course and travels several miles from the Reservoir through Shandaken Tunnel to Esopus Creek, a body of water utterly unrelated in any relevant sense to the Schoharie Reservoir and its watershed. No one can reasonably argue that the water in the Reservoir and the Esopus are in any sense the "same," such that "addition" of one to the other is a logical impossibility. When the water and the suspended sediment therein passes from the Tunnel into the Creek, an "addition" of a "pollutant" from a "point source" has been made to a "navigable water," and the terms of the statute are satisfied.

Given the ordinary meaning of the CWA's text ..., we cannot accept the *Gorsuch* and *Consumers Power* courts' understanding of "addition," at least insofar as it implies acceptance of ... a "singular entity" theory of navigable waters, in which an addition to one water body is deemed an addition to all of the waters of the United States.... Such a theory would mean that movement of water from one discrete water body to another would not be an addition even if it involved a transfer of water from a water body contaminated with myriad pollutants to a pristine water body containing few or no pollutants. Such an interpretation is inconsistent with the ordinary meaning of the word "addition."

* * *

Notes and Questions

1.　The CWA is typical of most environmental statutes in that it is subject to two different numbering systems. Every section of the CWA has two section numbers: its Clean Water Act section number, which is based on the section numbers Congress used when it passed the Federal Water Pollution Control Act of 1972, and the U.S.C. section numbers West gave the law when it inserted it into the United States Code. In this book, we will primarily use the CWA section numbers (e.g. § 301 of the CWA) instead of the U.S.C. section numbers (e.g., 33 U.S.C. § 1311). The vast majority of practitioners, and most courts, do the same. Having said that, however, we note that the *Catskill* court and several other of the early decisions in this book use the U.S.C. section numbers. While this may cause some confusion at first, the student will quickly become adept at using both systems.

2.　What were the pollutants at issue in *Catskill*? Heat is on the statutory list, but what about "suspended solids" and "turbidity"? If the real pollutant at issue is a "fine, red-clay sediment," does that qualify? The definition includes rock and sand. Should it be read to therefore also include clay and other forms of dirt (beyond "cellar dirt")?

3.　Section 501(a) of the CWA gives EPA the power to issue such regulations as it deems necessary to carry out its functions under the statute. Pursuant to this authority, EPA has promulgated its own definitions of the terms "pollutant" and "point source." See 40 C.F.R. § 122.2 (we will address the "navigable waters" construct below). EPA's definitions track, but are not identical to, those in the statute. For example, EPA's regulatory definition of "pollutant" varies from the statutory definition only in that it adds "filter backwash" and excludes radioactive materials that are regulated under the Atomic Energy Act. Are these revisions reasonable interpretations of the statutory definitions, or simply alterations thereof? Relying on some legislative history that was precisely on point, in *Train v. Colorado Public Interest Group*, 426 U.S. 1, 25, 96 S.Ct. 1938, 48 L.Ed.2d 434 (1976), the Supreme Court found that EPA acted properly in concluding the radioactive materials exclusion was consistent with the statutory definition. To the extent that any of the regulatory definitions constitute changes, however, they beg the question of whether EPA has the authority to make them. See also 40 C.F.R. § 122.3(a) (exempting discharges incidental to the normal operation of a vessel). In *Natural Resources Defense Council, Inc. v. Costle*, 568 F.2d 1369 (D.C. Cir. 1977) ("*NRDC v. Costle*"), EPA argued that it could exempt agricultural point sources from the scope of the NPDES program, despite the fact that, at the time, there was no statutory basis for such an exemption. (EPA did not argue that it was interpreting any statutory language). The D.C. Circuit squarely rejected EPA's position, finding that "[t]he wording of the statute, legislative history, and precedents are clear: the EPA Administrator does not have the authority to exempt categories of point sources from the permit requirements of § 402." 568 F.2d at 1377. In a subsequent Clean Air Act case, however, the same D.C. Circuit seemed to limit *NRDC v. Costle*, holding that EPA has the implied authority to create de minimis exceptions to the permitting requirements under that statute. *Alabama Power Co. v. Costle*, 636 F.2d 323, 360 (D.C. Cir. 1979). In *Natural Resources Defense Council, Inc. v. U.S. EPA*, 966 F.2d 1292, 1306 (9th Cir. 1992), the Ninth Circuit allowed for the possibility of such a showing under the CWA, but found that it EPA had not met the de minimis standard in that case.

4. It is worth reiterating that the definition of "pollutant" contains no regulatory thresholds or de minimis exceptions. While *Alabama Power* may stand for the proposition that EPA has the implied authority to create de minimis exclusions, EPA does not appear to have ever invoked this potential authority. Thus, as it currently stands every addition of pollutants is covered under the Act, regardless of quantity or concentration, assuming the other jurisdictional requirements also are met.

5. One context in which the presence of a statutory pollutant is increasingly being litigated relates to the application of pesticides or herbicides to waterways for purposes of bug or weed control. In one case, the City of New York was applying pesticides to control the spread of the West Nile Virus. *No Spray Coalition, Inc. v. City of New York*, 351 F.3d 602 (2d Cir. 2003). In another, an irrigation district in Oregon was applying an herbicide to control the growth of weeds in its irrigation canals. *Headwaters, Inc. v. Talent Irrigation District*, 243 F.3d 526 (9th Cir. 2001). Are these types of materials "pollutants" within the meaning of the CWA? Interestingly, in the wake of *Headwaters*, which held that the CWA applied (the *No Spray* court remanded the issue to the lower court), EPA issued an "interim guidance" indicating its view that the application of pesticides and/or herbicides in accordance with the Federal Insecticide, Fungicide, and Rodenticide Act, 7 U.S.C. § 136 *et seq.* (FIFRA), does not require an NPDES permit. See 68 Fed. Reg. 48385 (2003). The primary basis for EPA's conclusion is that when these materials are applied in accordance with FIFRA, they are not "chemical wastes" because they are being applied for their intended purpose. *Id.* at 48388. How does EPA's interpretation change the framework for judicial review? Is it persuasive, within the meaning of *Skidmore*? If materials that are being applied for their intended purpose cannot qualify as "chemical waste," should it matter whether they are applied in accordance with FIFRA, given that (a) FIFRA was passed after the FWPCA in 1972 (by three days), and (b) neither statute refers to the other?

6. Another issue concerning the definition of "pollutant" involves what is meant by the phrase "biological materials." Clearly, this term encompasses, for example, the fish remains that fish processors generate as waste materials. See, e.g., *Association of Pacific Fisheries v. EPA*, 615 F.2d 794 (9th Cir. 1980). But what about living mussels introduced into a waterway to

promote mussel harvesting? See *Association to Protect Hammersly, Eld and Totten Inlets v. Taylor Resources, Inc.*, 299 F.3d 1007, 1016 (9th Cir. 2002) ("*APHETI*") (concluding that "[i]t would be anomalous to conclude that living shellfish sought to be *protected* under the Act are, at the same time, 'pollutants' the discharge of which may be *proscribed* by the Act"); but see *Consumers Power*, 862 F.2d at 585 ("under the CWA, live fish would be just as much a pollutant as a mixture of live and dead fish"). If you agree with *APHETI*, should this same logic apply to the invasive species contained in the ballast water discharges of trans-oceanic shippers? Does the CWA distinguish between these two scenarios?

7.   Were you convinced by the *Catskill* court's distinction between *Gorsuch* and *Consumers Power*, on the one hand, and the situation before it? One of the pollutants at issue in *Gorsuch* was sediment. Although these sediments would have moved downstream even absent the dam, the impact that they had on the river system was greater because they were discharged in short spikes rather than gradually making their way downstream. *National Wildlife Federation v. Gorsuch*, 693 F.2d 156, 164 (D.C. Cir. 1982). Should the adversity of this non-natural impact result in a determination that a pollutant has been added? As we will in chapter 8, this same issue comes up in the context of determining whether "fallback" (e.g., the soil that falls off of excavation equipment when one is engaged in earth-moving within a wetland) should be deemed to trigger the application of § 404 jurisdiction. As suggested by *Catskill* court's ladle analogy, the *Gorsuch* court's approach may continue predominate in the NPDES realm even in the post-*Christensen/Mead* era. In the recent Supreme Court case of *South Florida Water Management District v. Miccosukee Tribe of Indians*, 541 U.S. 95, 124 S.Ct. 1537, 1545, 158 L.Ed.2d 264 (2004) ("*Miccosukee*"), the Tribe conceded that pumping polluted water within the same water body could not constitute the addition of a pollutant. Would you have made the same concession? If you believe the *Gorsuch* result will survive *Christensen* and *Mead*, would you assume the same of *Consumers Power*? Does *APHETI* have any bearing on this question?

8.   What about the other prong of the *Catskill* court's distinction? Do you agree that an interpretation that would allow water to be transferred from a very contaminated waterway into a pristine one would be "inconsistent with the ordinary meaning of the word 'addition?' " In *Miccosukee*, the Government weighed in on this issue more heavily than ever before, arguing in favor of what it now terms the "unitary waters" theory. As explained by the Court:

> The "unitary waters" argument focuses on the Act's definition of a pollutant discharge as any addition of any pollutant to navigable waters from any point source. § 1362(12). The Government contends that the absence of the word "any" prior to the phrase "navigable waters" in § 1362(12) signals Congress' understanding that NPDES permits would not be required for pollution caused by the engineered transfer of one "navigable water" into another. . . .

124 S.Ct. at 1543–1544. The Government also noted that requiring permits in the context of engineered diversions might affect thousands of water diversions, particularly in the western States. Id. at 1544–45. Despite these arguments, the Court declined to rule on the issue, noting that neither the

water district nor the Government had raised the issue either before the Court of Appeals or in their briefs respecting the petition for certiorari. Id. at 1545. The Court thus remanded this issue to the Eleventh Circuit, together with some factual issues regarding whether the two waterways in that case were in fact separate. Id. at 1545 and 1547. If you were sitting on the Eleventh Circuit upon remand, would you be persuaded by the Government's arguments regarding the "unitary waters" theory? How much deference would they be due? If EPA were to promulgate a legislative rule implementing its view, would you defer under *Chevron*?

9.   In *Catskill*, New York also argued that, in order for there to be an "addition," the point source must create the pollutant, not just be a conduit through which the pollutant enters the relevant waters. The court rejected this argument, noting that even in the prototypical industrial setting, it is the pipe that is the point source, not the factory itself.

2.   Navigable Waters

Section 502((7) defines the term "navigable waters" to mean "the waters of the United States." In the absence of further statutory edification, EPA stepped into the breach by defining "waters of the United States" to mean:

(a) All waters which are currently used, were used in the past, or may be susceptible to use in interstate or foreign commerce, including all waters which are subject to the ebb and flow of the tide;

(b) All interstate waters, including interstate "wetlands;"

(c) All other waters such as intrastate lakes, rivers, streams (including intermittent streams), mudflats, sandflats, "wetlands," sloughs, prairie potholes, wet meadows, playa lakes, or natural ponds the use, degradation, or destruction of which would affect or could affect interstate or foreign commerce . . . ;

(d) All impoundments of waters otherwise defined as waters of the United States under this definition;

(e) Tributaries of waters identified in paragraphs (a) through (d) of this definition;

(f) The territorial sea; and

(g) "Wetlands" adjacent to waters (other than waters that are themselves wetlands) identified in paragraphs (a) through (f) of this definition.

Waste treatment systems, including treatment ponds or lagoons designed to meet the requirements of CWA . . . are not waters of the United States. . . .

40 C.F.R. § 122.2.

This rule, together with the Corps' equivalent rule at 33 C.F.R. § 328.3, has been subject to frequent litigation, including trips to the Supreme Court in *United States v. Riverside Bayview Homes, Inc.*, 474

U.S. 121, 106 S.Ct. 455, 88 L.Ed.2d 419 (1985) (*"Riverside Bayview"*) (wetlands adjacent to navigable waters are "navigable waters"), and *Solid Waste Agency of Northern Cook County v. U.S. Army Corps of Engineers*, 531 U.S. 159, 121 S.Ct. 675, 148 L.Ed.2d 576 (2001) (*"SWANCC"*) (isolated ponds are not). We leave much of this discussion for our study of the "wetlands" program in chapter 8, because it is in that context that the outer bounds of the statutory waters have most often been tested. As an introductory matter, however, it is important to make at least two *SWANCC*-related points. First, if the isolated ponds in *SWANCC* are not "navigable waters" for purposes of the wetlands program (and *SWANCC* tells us they are not), then neither are they "navigable waters" for purposes of NPDES jurisdiction; that is, if they may be filled with fill material, so also may they be filled with sewage or industrial waste. This is so because, again, the jurisdictional terms under §§ 402 and 404 are the same: an addition of a pollutant to the navigable waters, from a point source. It all comes from Section 301, which is the jurisdictional underpinning of both permit programs.

Second, it is worth noting that EPA's definition of "waters of the United States" includes non-navigable tributaries and even, at least in some cases, intermittent streams. Even post-*SWANCC*, the courts generally have upheld these assertions of jurisdiction. See, e.g., *Headwaters, Inc. v. Talent Irrigation District*, 243 F.3d 526, 533–534 (9th Cir. 2001) (non-navigable irrigation canals). We will return to these issues in chapter 8.

Another "navigable waters" issue that comes up frequently in the NPDES realm involves discharges into groundwater that has a hydrologic connection to a nearby surface water. Consider the following decision:

IDAHO RURAL COUNCIL v. BOSMA

United States District Court, D. Idaho, 2001.

143 F.Supp.2d 1169.

WINMILL, Chief Judge.

In 1994, the Defendants ("Bosmas") established a substantial dairy operation ("Grand View Dairy" or "the dairy") in an area near Bliss, Idaho, which is directly upgradient from farms operated by the Butler and Walker families. The Butlers and the Walkers are members of Plaintiff Idaho Rural Council ("IRC"), an Idaho non-profit corporation with approximately 500 members throughout Idaho.

[Among other allegations, IRC alleged that wastewater from several of the dairy's holding ponds and an irrigation pond seeped into the groundwater and thereby into nearby springs. The dairy disputed whether, even if true, this constituted a violation of the CWA.]

. . . The courts which have considered the issue generally agree that waters of the United States do not include isolated, nontributory groundwater, and that discharges of pollutants into such groundwater are not subject to CWA regulation. The courts are split, however, on the issue of whether the discharge of pollutants into groundwater which find their way into and affect the waters of the United States are subject to CWA regulation. . . .

One view is that Congress intended to regulate the discharge of any pollutants that could affect surface waters of the United States, whether it reaches the surface water directly or through groundwater. The rationale supporting this conclusion is simple and persuasive: "since the goal of the CWA is to protect the quality of surface waters, any pollutant which enters such waters, whether directly or through groundwater, is subject to regulation by NPDES permit." [*Washington Wilderness Coalition v. Hecla Mining Co.*, 870 F.Supp. 983, 990 (E.D.Wa.1994)]. Stated even more simply, whether pollution is introduced by a visible, above-ground conduit or enters the surface water through the aquifer matters little to the fish, waterfowl, and recreational users which are affected by the degradation of our nation's rivers and streams.

On the other hand, the Court is mindful of other decisions concluding that the CWA does not regulate the discharge of pollutants into any groundwaters, even where it ultimately affects the surface water. Those courts reach this conclusion based largely upon the legislative history of the CWA. They point out that Congress, in other provisions of the CWA, clearly included groundwater when they intended to do so, and that Congress considered "ground waters" to be a category of waters distinct from "navigable waters." [*Umatilla Waterquality Protective Assoc., Inc. v. Smith Frozen Foods, Inc.*, 962 F.Supp. 1312, 1318 (D.Or.1997)]. They also rely upon the legislative history of the CWA, which indicates that Congress specifically chose not to regulate groundwater, largely because "the jurisdiction regarding groundwaters is so complex and varied from State to State." *Id.* (quoting from S.Rep. No. 414, 92d Cong., 1st Sess. 73 (1971), U.S.Code Cong. & Admin. News 1972, pp. 3668, 3749. Finally, they attach significance to the fact that the "EPA has offered no formal or consistent interpretation of the CWA that would subject discharges to groundwater to the NPDES permitting requirement." *Id.*

The Court agrees that this interpretive history establishes that Congress, in enacting the [CWA], concluded that it would not attempt the general regulation of discharges to groundwater. However, Congress's decision not to comprehensively regulate groundwater as part of the CWA, does not require the conclusion that Congress intended to exempt ground water from all regulation—particularly under circumstances where the introduction of pollutants into the groundwater adversely affects the adjoining surface waters. In short, the interpretive history of the CWA only supports the unremarkable proposition with which all courts agree—that the CWA does not regulate "isolated/nontributary groundwater" which has no affect on surface water. It does not suggest that Congress intended to exclude from regulation discharges into hydrologically connected groundwater which adversely affect surface water.

For these reasons, the Court finds that the CWA extends federal jurisdiction over groundwater that is hydrologically connected to surface waters that are themselves waters of the United States. This does not mean, however, that the plaintiff's burden is light. As Judge Van Sickle explained in *Washington Wilderness Coalition:*

> Plaintiffs must still demonstrate that pollutants from a point source affect surface waters of the United States. It is not sufficient to allege groundwater pollution, and then to assert a general hydrological connection between all waters. Rather, pollutants must be traced from their source to surface waters, in order to come within the purview of the CWA.

Id. Whether IRC can make this showing remains to be seen. However, the Court finds, for purposes of the Bosma's summary judgment motion, that the CWA regulates discharges from the Grand View Dairy into the groundwater where there exists a hydrological connection with [nearby springs], and such discharges can be traced from their source to those springs. . . .

* * *

Notes and Questions

1. Why weren't the holding and irrigation ponds "waters of the United States" themselves? Does this seem like a reasonable result? Are there any drawbacks to this approach?

2. The parties in *Bosma* agreed that the dairy was a point source. This may have been due to the fact that the statutory definition of "point source" specifically includes "concentrated animal feeding operation[s]" ("CAFOs"). See CWA § 502(14).

3. The most surprising aspect of the groundwater issue is how unsettled it is. Were you persuaded by the *Bosma* court's analysis? Does EPA's definition of "waters of the United States" speak to this issue? If not, should its silence be dispositive? Or does it simply leave in place an ambiguity that EPA can then resolve through administrative interpretation? If EPA were to amend its rule to specifically include hydrologically-linked groundwater, would that interpretation pass muster under *Chevron*? Is the statutory definition of "navigable waters" ambiguous in this regard? Can it reasonably be interpreted to encompass these groundwaters? In *Riverside Bayview*, which we will consider at length below, the Supreme Court—in a *Chevron* analysis—relied on the hydrologic link between adjacent wetlands and their nearby surface waters in upholding the Corps' assertion of jurisdiction over those adjacent wetlands. Does that suggest that the Court would do likewise in this context? *Cf. Village of Oconomowoc Lake v. Dayton Hudson Corp.*, 24 F.3d 962, 966 (7th Cir. 1994), *cert. denied*, 513 U.S. 930, 115 S.Ct. 322, 130 L.Ed.2d 282 (1994) (disagreeing with the *Bosma* result, but noting that "[b]y amending its regulations, EPA could pose a harder question").

4. If one reads EPA's definition of "water of the United States" as being ambiguous on this point, keep in mind that any EPA interpretation of that regulation (if initially offered as other than a litigating position) would

be controlling unless it were plainly erroneous or inconsistent with the regulation. *Auer v. Robbins*, 519 U.S. 452, 461, 117 S.Ct. 905, 137 L.Ed.2d 79 (1997); *Bowles v. Seminole Rock & Sand Co.*, 325 U.S. 410, 414, 65 S.Ct. 1215, 89 L.Ed. 1700 (1945). This doctrine—which is alternately referred to as *Seminole Rock* or *Auer* deference—raises two immediate questions in this context: (1) has EPA ever opined on this issue in a fashion that should give rise to deference; and (2) if it has done so, was it interpreting the statute or, alternatively, was it interpreting its regulation. On the first point, EPA spoke at length on the issue of whether discharges to hydrologically-linked groundwaters should be jurisdictional in the preamble to its proposed new CAFO rules in 2001. 66 Fed. Reg. 2960 (2001). There, EPA said that it was "restating that the Agency interprets the [CWA] to apply to discharges of pollutants from a point source via ground water that has a direct hydrologic connection to surface water." Id. at 3015. It further offered an extensive "legal basis" for its interpretation, and noted at least five prior instances in which it had offered consistent interpretations. Id. at 3015–3018. In the final rule, however, EPA distanced itself from this interpretation, eliminating its proposed control program and stating that "[n]othing in this rule shall be construed to expand, diminish, or otherwise affect the jurisdiction of the [CWA] over discharges to surface water via groundwater that has a direct hydrologic connection to surface water." 68 Fed. Reg. 7176, 7216–7217 (2003). Where does this leave us?

5. On the second point raised in the prior note, it is worth at least noting an oddity inherent in the juxtaposition of the various deference doctrines. If the court were to determine that the position advanced in EPA's proposed rule were a reasonable interpretation of an ambiguous rule, it would apply the relatively strong deference contemplated under *Seminole Rock* (although there would then also be a question as to whether the regulation, as interpreted, was consistent with the statute—which would pose a *Chevron* issue). Alternatively, if the court concluded that EPA were interpreting the statute, it would at best be entitled to the much weaker *Skidmore* deference. In other words, if an agency speaks informally, it will get a higher form of deference if it can argue that it is interpreting its own rule, rather than the statute. Justice Scalia, who believes that even informal pronouncements should get *Chevron* deference, bemoaned this dynamic in his dissent in *Mead*:

> . . . [T]he majority's approach will have a perverse effect on the rules that do emerge, given the principle (which the Court leaves untouched today) that judges must defer to reasonable agency interpretations of their own rules. Agencies will now have high incentive to rush out barebones, ambiguous rules construing statutory ambiguities, which they can then in turn further clarify through informal rulings entitled to judicial respect.

533 U.S. at 246 (citations omitted).

6. The *Bosma* court followed *Washington Wilderness Coalition* in requiring the plaintiffs to demonstrate that the defendants' pollutants had in fact migrated through the groundwater into the nearby surface waters. Does this requirement seem appropriate? What if the plaintiffs could demonstrate that some of the defendants' pollutants would inevitably make their way into

the surface waters, even if it might take years? Can you argue that even less should be required?

3. Point Source

This requirement that the discharge be from a "point source" has historically been the most important jurisdictional dividing line under the CWA. As discussed in the case below, Congress sought to distinguish between discrete conveyances of pollutants, which were to be governed under the NPDES program, and contaminated runoff, which was to be addressed under the largely non-regulatory rubric of § 209 (later supplemented by § 319). In effectuating this framework, Congress defined the term "point source" to mean "any discernible, confined and discrete conveyance, including but not limited to any pipe, ditch, channel, tunnel, conduit, well, discrete fissure, container, rolling stock, concentrated animal feeding operation, or vessel or other floating craft, from which pollutants are or may be discharged." 33 U.S.C. § 1362(14). Note that while this definition requires a discrete conveyance, the list of examples set forth is framed non-exclusively ("including but not limited to . . ."). In its implementing rules, EPA maintains the non-exclusive orientation and adds only one further example ("landfill leachate collection system[s]") to the list. 40 C.F.R. § 122.2.

Not surprisingly, the indeterminate nature of these definitions has led to litigation over sources of pollution that are not on these lists. For example, should earth-moving equipment (e.g., bulldozers, backhoes and plows) qualify as a point source? If not, Section 404 will be rendered inapplicable to most wetlands-destroying activities. What about sumps or surface impoundments that overflow during periods of heavy rain? While the following case arises in an usual factual context, the majority and dissenting opinions highlight the tensions that arise in confronting these issues:

UNITED STATES v. PLAZA HEALTH LABORATORIES, INC.

United States Court of Appeals, Second Circuit, 1993.
3 F.3d 643.

PRATT, Circuit Judge:

[Geronimo Villegas was co-owner and vice president of Plaza Health Laboratories, Inc., a blood-testing laboratory in Brooklyn, New York. At least twice between April and September 1988, Villegas took containers of numerous vials of human blood from his business to his condominium in Edgewater, New Jersey. Once there, Villegas either put the containers in the river or, on one occasion, placed them at low tide within a crevice that separated the condominium complex from the river. This crevice was below the high-water line.

In May of that year, a group of eighth graders on a field trip discovered numerous glass vials containing human blood along the shore.

Some of the vials had washed up on the shore; many were still in the water. Some were cracked, although most remained sealed with stoppers in solid-plastic containers or ziplock bags. That afternoon, New York City workers recovered approximately 70 vials from the area. Four months later, a maintenance worker at Villegas's condominium discovered a plastic container holding blood vials wedged between rocks in the bulkhead. New Jersey authorities retrieved numerous blood vials from the bulkhead later that day. Ten of the retrieved vials contained blood infected with the hepatitis-B virus. All of the vials recovered were eventually traced to Plaza Health Laboratories.

After being convicted of knowingly discharging pollutants from a "point source" without a permit under the CWA, Villegas appealed, arguing that the definition of "point source" does not include discharges that result from the individual acts of human beings.]

* * *

Human beings are not among the enumerated items that may be a "point source". Although by its terms the definition of "point source" is nonexclusive, the words used to define the term and the examples given ("pipe, ditch, channel, tunnel, conduit, well, discrete fissure", etc.) evoke images of physical structures and instrumentalities that systematically act as a means of conveying pollutants from an industrial source to navigable waterways.

In addition, if every discharge involving humans were to be considered a "discharge from a point source", the statute's lengthy definition of "point source" would have been unnecessary. It is elemental that congress does not add unnecessary words to statutes. Had congress intended to punish any human being who polluted navigational waters, it could readily have said: "any person who places pollutants in navigable waters without a permit is guilty of a crime."

The [CWA] generally targets industrial and municipal sources of pollutants, as is evident from a perusal of its many sections. Consistent with this focus, the term "point source" is used throughout the statute, but invariably in sentences referencing industrial or municipal discharges.

This emphasis was sensible, as "[i]ndustrial and municipal point sources were the worst and most obvious offenders of surface water quality. They were also the easiest to address because their loadings emerge from a discrete point such as the end of a pipe." David Letson, Point/Nonpoint Source Pollution Reduction Trading: An Interpretive Survey, 32 Nat.Resources J. 219, 221 (1992).

Finally on this point, we assume that congress did not intend the awkward meaning that would result if we were to read "human being" into the definition of "point source". Section 1362(12)(A) defines "discharge of a pollutant" as "any addition of any pollutant to navigable waters from any point source". Enhanced by this definition, § 1311(a) reads in effect "the addition of any pollutant to navigable waters from any point source by any person shall be unlawful". But were a human being to be included within the definition of "point source", the prohibition would then read: "the addition of any pollutant to navigable waters from any person by any person shall be unlawful", and this simply makes no sense. As the statute stands today, the term "point source" is comprehensible only if it is held to the context of industrial and municipal discharges.

The legislative history of the CWA ... confirms the act's focus on industrial polluters. Congress required NPDES permits of those who discharge from a "point source". The term "point source" ... was intended to function as a means of identifying industrial polluters—generally a difficult task because pollutants quickly disperse throughout the subject waters. The senate report for the 1972 amendments explains:

> In order to further clarify the scope of the regulatory procedures in the Act the Committee had added a definition of point source to distinguish between control requirements where there are specific confined conveyances, such as pipes, and control requirements which are imposed to control runoff. The control of pollutants from runoff is applied pursuant to section 209 and the authority resides in the State or other local agency.

S.Rep. No. 92–414, reprinted in 1972 U.S.C.C.A.N. 3668, 3744.

We find no suggestion either in the act itself or in the history of its passage that congress intended the CWA to impose criminal liability on an individual for the myriad, random acts of human waste disposal, for example, a passerby who flings a candy wrapper into the Hudson River, or a urinating swimmer....

[T]he cases that have interpreted "point source" have done so in civil-penalty or licensing settings, where greater flexibility of interpretation to further remedial legislative purposes is permitted, and the rule of lenity does not protect a defendant against statutory ambiguities. *See, e.g., Avoyelles Sportsmen's League, Inc. v. Marsh*, 715 F.2d 897, 922 (5th Cir.1983) ("point source" includes bulldozing equipment that discharged dredged materials onto wetland).

In sum, ... § 1362(14) of the CWA does not expressly recognize a human being as a "point source"; nor does the act make structural sense when one incorporates a human being into that definition. The legislative history of the act adds no light to the muddy depths of this issue, and cases urging a broad interpretation of the definition in the civil-penalty context do not persuade us to do so here, where congress has imposed heavy criminal sanctions....

We accordingly conclude that the term "point source" as applied to a human being is at best ambiguous.

In criminal prosecutions the rule of lenity requires that ambiguities in the statute be resolved in the defendant's favor. In other words, we cannot add to the statute what congress did not provide....

Since the government's reading of the statute in this case founders on our inability to discern the "obvious intention of the legislature" to include a human being as a "point source", we conclude that the criminal provisions of the CWA did not clearly proscribe Villegas's conduct and did not accord him fair warning of the sanctions the law placed on that conduct. Under the rule of lenity, therefore, the prosecutions against him must be dismissed.

OAKES, Circuit Judge, dissenting:

I begin with the obvious, in hopes that it will illuminate the less obvious: the classic point source is something like a pipe. This is ... because pipes and similar conduits are needed to carry large quantities of waste water, which represents a large proportion of the point source pollution problem.... Because not all pollutants are liquids, however, the statute and the cases make clear that means of conveying solid wastes to be dumped in navigable waters are also point sources. *See, e.g.,* 33 U.S.C. § 1362(14) ("rolling stock," or railroad cars, listed as an example of a point source); *Avoyelles Sportsmen's League, Inc. v. Marsh,* 715 F.2d 897, 922 (5th Cir.1983) (backhoes and bulldozers used to gather fill and deposit it on wetlands are point sources).

What I take from this look at classic point sources is that, at the least, an organized means of channeling and conveying industrial waste in quantity to navigable waters is a "discernible, confined and discrete conveyance." The case law is in accord: courts have deemed a broad range of means of depositing pollutants in the country's navigable waters to be point sources. See, e.g., *Rybachek v. EPA,* 904 F.2d 1276 (9th Cir.1990) (placer mining; sluice box from which discharge water is redeposited in stream is point source, despite provisions protecting some mining activities); *Sierra Club v. Abston Constr. Co.,* 620 F.2d 41, 45 (5th Cir.1980) (spill of contaminated runoff from strip mine, if collected or channeled by the operator, is point source discharge); *United States v. Earth Sciences, Inc.,* 599 F.2d 368, 374 (10th Cir.1979) (same)....

In short, the term "point source" has been broadly construed to apply to a wide range of polluting techniques, so long as the pollutants involved are not just humanmade, but reach the navigable waters by human effort or by leaking from a clear point at which waste water was collected by human effort....

Nonetheless, the term "point source" sets significant definitional limits on the reach of the [CWA]. Fifty percent or more of all water pollution is thought to come from nonpoint sources. S.Rep. 99–50, 99th Cong., 1st Sess. 8 (1985). So, to further refine the definition of "point source," I consider what it is that the Act does not cover: nonpoint source discharges.[2]

Nonpoint source pollution is, generally, runoff: salt from roads, agricultural chemicals from farmlands, oil from parking lots, and other

---

2. The cases and commentators all seem to assume that all water pollution is either point source pollution or nonpoint source pollution.

substances washed by rain, in diffuse patterns, over the land and into navigable waters. The sources are many, difficult to identify and difficult to control. Indeed, an effort to greatly reduce nonpoint source pollution could require radical changes in land use patterns which Congress evidently was unwilling to mandate without further study. The structure of the statute—which regulates point source pollution closely, while leaving nonpoint source regulation to the states under the Section 208 program—indicates that the term "point source" was included in the definition of discharge so as to ensure that nonpoint source pollution would not be covered. Instead, Congress chose to regulate first that which could easily be regulated: direct discharges by identifiable parties, or point sources.

This rationale for regulating point and nonpoint sources differently . . . helps define what fits within each category. Thus, Professor Rodgers has suggested, "[t]he statutory 'discernible, confined and discrete conveyance' . . . can be understood as singling out those candidates suitable for control-at-the-source." 2 Rodgers, Environmental Law: Air and Water § 4.10 at 150 (1986). And, as Professor Rodgers notes, "[c]ase law confirms the controllability theory, adding to it a responsibility component, so that 'point sources' are understood both as sources that can be cleaned up and as sources where fairness suggests the named parties should do the cleaning." Id.

. . . Villegas did not dispose of the materials on land, where they could be washed into water as nonpoint source pollution. Rather, he carried them, from his firm's laboratory, in his car, to his apartment complex, where he placed them in a bulkhead below the high tide line. I do not think it is necessary to determine whether it was Mr. Villegas himself who was the point source, or whether it was his car, the vials, or the bulkhead: in a sense, the entire stream of Mr. Villegas' activity functioned as a "discrete conveyance" or point source. The point is that the source of the pollution was clear, and would have been easy to control. . . .

Villegas' method may have been an unusual one for a corporate officer, but it would undermine the statute . . . to regard as "ambiguous" a Congressional failure to list an unusual method of disposing of waste. I doubt that Congress would have regarded an army of men and women throwing industrial waste from trucks into a stream as exempt from the statute . . . A different reading would encourage corporations perfectly capable of abiding by the [CWA's] requirements to ask their employees to stand between the company trucks and the sea, thereby transforming point source pollution (dumping from trucks) into nonpoint source pollution (dumping by hand). . . .

My colleagues also suggest that the statute is sufficiently ambiguous that the rule of lenity requires resolving the ambiguity in Villegas' favor. However, . . . I do not think the [CWA] is ambiguous with respect to an individual physically disposing of medical wastes, in quantity, directly into navigable waters, by means of a controllable, discrete conveyance and course of action. As the Supreme Court has noted,

> [b]ecause the meaning of language is inherently contextual, we have declined to deem a statute 'ambiguous' for purposes of lenity merely because it was possible to articulate a construction more narrow than that urged by the Government.... Instead we have always reserved lenity for those situations in which a reasonable doubt persists about a statute's intended scope even after resort to "the language and structure, legislative history, and motivating policies" of the statute.

Moskal v. United States, 498 U.S. 103, 108 (1990).

... I think it plain enough that Congress intended the statute to bar corporate officers from disposing of corporate waste into navigable waters by hand as well as by pipe. Further, ... this is not a case in which the defendant had no fair warning that his actions were illegal. No compliance attorney here could have struggled with the difficulty of deciding whether this was activity for which a permit should be sought, as might be the case in a factory dealing with runoff that arguably was channeled and thereby transformed from nonpoint to point source pollution; rather, an attorney asked to advise Villegas whether his activity was permissible might say that there was as yet no case law indicating that such activity was point source pollution under the [CWA], but that such a view was certainly consistent with the Act and that the behavior would almost certainly be proscribed by that Act or some other.

Notes and Questions

1. Mr. Villegas did not dispute whether the blood vials were "pollutants" under the CWA. Would you have conceded this issue?

2. What exactly is the holding in *Plaza Health*? Would the court's approach allow individual homeowners to discharge sewage into rivers through pipes or ditches without fear of liability under the CWA? Would it, as Judge Oakes seemed to be concerned, allow industrial employees to discharge dioxin by the handful (presumably wearing gloves)? If not, how can this situation be distinguished from that of Mr. Villegas? Could a private individual discharge handfuls of paint thinner without fear of liability? If you think she can't do this under the CWA, what would you do about the litterer who tosses a gum wrapper off a bridge? Does the CWA distinguish between these two situations? If either both or neither of these individuals must be deemed to have committed a felony under the statute, how would that affect your analysis?

3. In *Earth Sciences* (cited by the dissent in *Plaza Health*), the defendant maintained several sumps (lined excavations) on the banks of a creek in Colorado to capture runoff from its mining activities. These sumps overflowed during a period of unusually high snow melt, spilling leachate into the creek. The court found that the sumps qualified as point sources despite the absence of a ditch or other conveyance between the sumps and the adjoining creek:

Despite the large capacity (168,000 gallons for the reserve sump) we view this operation as a closed circulating system to serve the gold extraction process with no discharge. When it fails because of flaws in the construction or inadequate size to handle the fluids utilized, with resulting discharge, whether from a fissure in the dirt berm or overflow of a wall, the escape of liquid from the confined system is from a point source. Although the source of the excess liquid is rainfall or snow melt, this is not the kind of general runoff considered to be from nonpoint sources under the [CWA].

599 F.2d at 374. Similarly, in *Concerned Area Residents for the Environment v. Southview Farm*, 34 F.3d 114, 118 (1994) ("*Southview Farms*"), the Second Circuit held that an irrigation system qualified as a point source where it sprayed liquid manure onto a field in such quantities that the manure directly flowed into a stream. Do you agree with these analyses? If not, would you find jurisdiction in a situation in which a sewage treatment plant cut off its pipe such that its effluent landed a foot before the river bank, from which it then immediately flowed into the river? If you agree with *Earth Sciences* and *Southview Farms*, would you also find jurisdiction in a situation in which a golf course applies partially-treated sewage effluent to its fairways, with the result being that some of the pollutants are later carried into streams when it rains? What should be the operative principle in these types of cases?

4. In *Plaza Health*, the Second Circuit distinguished the cases the government had cited (including *Earth Sciences*) at least in part based on the fact that those earlier cases had arisen in a civil setting. Similarly in *Southview Farms*, Judge Oakes (now writing for a unanimous panel) distinguished *Plaza Health* as having been a criminal case which thus triggered the rule of lenity. 34 F.3d at 118. These distinctions may be too facile. In *United States v. Thompson/Center Arms Co.*, 504 U.S. 505, 112 S.Ct. 2102, 119 L.Ed.2d 308 (1992), a plurality of the Supreme Court applied the rule of lenity in a civil case involving a gun tax. Writing for the plurality, Justice Souter responded to the dissent's argument to the contrary in the following terms:

> Justice Stevens contends that lenity should not be applied because this is a "tax statute," rather than a "criminal statute." But this tax statute has criminal applications, and we know of no other basis for determining when the essential nature of a statute is "criminal." Surely, Justice Stevens cannot mean to suggest that in order for the rule of lenity to apply, the statute must be contained in the Criminal Code. Justice Stevens further suggests that lenity is inappropriate because we construe the statute today " 'in a civil setting,' " rather than a "criminal prosecution." The rule of lenity, however, is a rule of statutory construction whose purpose is to help give authoritative meaning to statutory language. It is not a rule of administration calling for courts to refrain in criminal cases from applying statutory language that would have been held to apply if challenged in civil litigation.

504 U.S. at 517 n.10. Many lower courts have applied lenity in the context of civil penalty actions. This, of course, raises the question whether there is sufficient ambiguity to give rise to lenity concerns in situations like those

present in *Earth Sciences* and *Southview Farms* (or, in any Circuit other than the Second, even *Plaza Health*-type situations). How would you resolve these issues?

5. In *Babbitt v. Sweet Home Chapter of Communities for a Great Oregon*, 515 U.S. 687, 703–704 n.18, 115 S.Ct. 2407, 132 L.Ed.2d 597 (1995), the Supreme Court made clear that agencies can eliminate lenity concerns by promulgating rules that resolve statutory ambiguities. Should EPA revise its regulatory definition of "point source" to address the issues posed in some or all of these cases? If EPA were to do revise its definition to indicate that humans may qualify as point sources, would that solve the "*Plaza Health* problem" (assuming you think the result in that case is problematic)?

6. In response to *NRDC v. Costle* (discussed in the notes following *Catskill*, above), Congress amended the definition of "point source" to specifically exclude "agricultural stormwater discharges and return flows from irrigated agriculture." 33 U.S.C. § 1362(14). In *Southview Farms*, the Second Circuit deemed these exemptions inapplicable in that case because (1) even those discharges that occurred on rainy days were not the result of (but merely coincided with) the rainfall; and (2) the spraying of the manure was at volumes that were well beyond the agronomic rates that could be beneficial to crop production. 34 F.3d at 120–123.

7. In *League of Wilderness Defenders v. Forsgren*, 309 F.3d 1181 (9th Cir. 2002), the court found that the aerial application of insecticides from a plane satisfied the "point source" requirement.

B. The Federal/State Relationship

When Congress revamped its approach to pollution control in the early 1970s, it had a decision to make: Should it turn these new programs entirely over to the newly-created EPA, or should it give the States the option of staying involved in significant ways. Congress chose the latter option, setting up a federal/state model that has come to be known as "cooperative federalism." Although Congress first created this model when it passed the Clean Air Act in 1970, we will address it in the most depth here in our discussion of the NPDES program, and will then only touch on some differences that apply under the Clean Air Act and the Resource Conservation and Recovery Act (RCRA) when we turn our attention to those statutes.

One of the express policies of the CWA is to "recognize, preserve, and protect the primary responsibilities of States to prevent, reduce, and eliminate pollution. . . ." 33 U.S.C. § 1251(b). Congress implemented this policy in two main ways. First, it empowered the States to assume primary responsibility for the day-to-day implementation of the NPDES program. 33 U.S.C. § 1342(b). And second, it reserved to the States the primary role in establishing water quality standards. 33 U.S.C. § 1313. We will address the second of these roles when we consider the water quality-based mandates of the Act. Presently, we will consider how EPA and the States work together in implementing the NPDES program.

Taking part in this scheme of "cooperative federalism" is optional on the part of the States. If a particular State chooses not to do so, EPA will administer the program within that jurisdiction. Currently, 45 of the 50 States are authorized to administer most elements of the NPDES program. http://cfpub2.epa.gov/npdes/statestats.cfm. The District of Columbia and U.S. territories such as Puerto Rico and Guam also are eligible to seek authorization status, see 33 U.S.C. § 1362(3), although only the Territory of the Virgin Islands is currently authorized. Additionally, Section 518(e) authorizes EPA to treat Indian tribes as States for NPDES purposes if they demonstrate the ability to carry out the program.

There are two steps to understanding how the cooperative federalism scheme works. First, assuming a given State opts to participate, one must understand what the State must do to become "authorized" to implement the NPDES program. And second, one must learn how EPA exercises oversight authority in authorized States.

1. How States Become Authorized

Section 402(b) establishes the minimum requirements a State must meet if it chooses to become "authorized" as the primary implementer of the NPDES program within its boundaries. Under this provision, EPA must approve a given State's application for authorization if it finds that it meets the relevant requirements. These include the ability to issue permits that will meet the same substantive standards that would apply if EPA were acting as the permit-issuer. 33 U.S.C. § 1342(b)(1). They also include requirements relating to the State's investigatory powers, the involvement of both the public and EPA in State permit-issuance processes, and the State's ability to bring enforcement actions. 33 U.S.C. § 1342(b)(2), (3) and (7). It should be noted these requirements constitute federal "floors," not federal "ceilings;" that is, the States are free to go beyond these minimum requirements in any respects. Indeed, Section 510 of the CWA sets forth an express non-preemption clause, indicating that, except as expressly provided, nothing in the Act should be read as limiting the States' ability to adopt or enforce more stringent standards.

Section 304(i) specifically charged EPA with writing rules fleshing out § 402(b)'s authorization requirements. EPA has done so in 40 C.F.R. Part 123. These rules track the statutory requirements by requiring the States to issue permits containing the same technology-and water quality-based requirements as would apply if EPA were issuing the permits. 40 C.F.R. § 123.25(15). Additionally, they set minimum requirements State must meet regarding public involvement in the permit issuance process and, to a lesser extent, the enforcement realm. 40 C.F.R. §§ 123.25(27)-(32) and 123.27(d), respectively. And third, EPA requires the States to have both civil and criminal enforcement powers, although it does not require these powers to be equivalent to those which it possesses under the CWA. 40 C.F.R. § 123.27.

Certain aspects of these rules were challenged in the following case:

NATURAL RESOURCES DEFENSE COUNCIL, INC. v. EPA

United States Court of Appeals, District of Columbia Circuit, 1988.

859 F.2d 156.

Because of Congress's desire to "recognize, preserve, and protect the primary responsibilities and rights of States to prevent, reduce, and to eliminate pollution," 33 U.S.C. § 1251(b), the CWA provides for state assumption of the NPDES permit program. Id. § 1342(b). It specifies some prerequisites to states' assuming permitting responsibilities, id., authorizes the Administrator to supplement them, id. §§ 1361(a), 1314(i)(2), and requires him to approve a state's application once satisfied that these standards have been met, id. § 1342(b)....

1. *Regulatory Uniformity and State Autonomy.* Petitioners challenge two regulations implementing the Act's provisions on state assumption of the permit program. Citizens for a Better Environment (CBE) attacks the standards for minimum public participation at the state level. NRDC complains of the absence of state authority to impose a given maximum penalty. Both protests rest on the assumption that congressional emphasis on uniformity was directed to procedural as well as substantive standards, and that as a result federal requirements respecting public participation and penalties must be mirrored on the state level.

Uniformity is indeed a recurrent theme in the Act, a direct manifestation of concern that the permit program be standardized to avoid the "industrial equivalent of forum shopping" and the creation of "pollution havens" by migration of dischargers to areas having lower pollution standards. The desired uniformity, however, is spoken of almost exclusively in relation to effluent limitations. Moreover, Congress' quest for homogeneity is in tension with its independent emphasis on state autonomy, which ... is enshrined in the Act as the basic policy to "recognize, preserve, and protect the primary responsibilities and rights of States," and is the very foundation of the permit program....

In fashioning its guidelines on both participation and penalties, EPA endeavored to reconcile the competing objectives of regulatory uniformity and state autonomy by establishing a floor for citizen participation and state enforcement authority, while ensuring that states have the maximum possible independence. We are fully mindful of the rule that an agency is entitled to special deference when it harmonizes competing policies.... *Chevron U.S.A. v. NRDC*, 467 U.S. 837, 845 (1984)....

2. *Public Participation.* CBE assails on two grounds EPA's regulations specifying the minimum level of public participation that states must afford. CBE first claims that the regulations are inadequate because they do not include all of the protections built into the federal permit program. Alternatively, it contends that they fail to provide any meaningful right.

The requirement of public participation in efforts to control water pollution is established in the congressional declaration of policy and goals of the Act:

> Public participation in the development, revision, and enforcement of any regulation, standard, effluent limitation, plan, or program established by the Administrator or any State under this chapter shall be provided for, encouraged, and assisted by the Administrator and the States. The Administrator, in cooperation with the States, shall develop and publish regulations specifying minimum guidelines for public participation in such processes.[27]

The statutory text does not, however, elaborate on the extent of public participation contemplated by Congress. The legislative history of the Act repeatedly echoes the desire "that its provisions be administered and enforced in a fishbowl-like atmosphere." CBE asserts that in Section 1365, which governs citizen suits, Congress spelled out the elements of the public participation envisioned....[30]

As CBE insists, Congress considered the citizen suit provision to be of dual importance, serving both as a method of prodding the agency, and as a backup means of enforcing the Act. On the other hand, Congress also expressed reservations about potential abuses of citizen suits.... Nowhere in either the Act or its legislative history is there any express statement that the provisions of Section 1365 extend to states, nor do we find persuasive any equivocal intimation in that direction. It would have been very easy for Congress to say so if that was what it had in mind....

Finally, we note that EPA maintains that "[n]othing in the Act or its legislative history indicates that Congress intended that states be required to provide identical rights to those Congress specified for citizens in Federal court." Because we have found that Congress has not directly addressed the precise question at issue, and determined that "the agency's answer is based on a permissible construction of the statute, we defer to EPA's reading." [Citing *Chevron*]. We therefore hold that state-level citizen suits are not commanded by the Act, and find no impropriety in the Administrator's failure to require state programs to afford them.

CBE asks that, should we decide that state public participation specifications need not match the federal requirements, we hold that the present regulations are incapable of producing meaningful public involvement. We decline this invitation. The pertinent regulations read:

27. 33 U.S.C. § 1251(e). Section 1342(b)(3), (7) makes this requirement a prerequisite for state assumption of the permit program.

30. As characterized by CBE, the participation requisite at the state level would allow citizens to "(1) initiate an enforcement action against polluters in state court; (2) intervene as of right in any enforcement action brought by the state; (3) initiate an action in state court against an enforcement agency for failure to perform a nondiscretionary duty; and (4) recover litigation costs for participating in enforcement." Compare 33 U.S.C. § 1365 (1982). CBE demands as well access to information and judicial review of state-issued permits.

Any state administering a program shall provide for public participation in the State enforcement process by providing either: (1) Authority which allows intervention as of right in any civil or administrative action ... by any citizen having an interest which is or may be adversely affected; or (2) Assurance that the State agency or enforcement authority will: (i) Investigate and provide written responses to all citizen complaints ...; (ii) Not oppose intervention by any citizen when permissive intervention may be authorized by statute, rule, or regulation; and (iii) Publish notice of and provide at least 30 days for public comment on any proposed settlement of a State enforcement action.

40 C.F.R. § 123.27(d) (1987).

We might be somewhat more hospitable to CBE's claim, especially with regard to the second option, were it not for two statements by EPA in interpreting the regulations. First, in promulgating the regulations and again in its brief before this court, the agency indicated that the first option—provision of intervention as of right—called for state intervention rights similar to those accorded by the federal rules....

More importantly, however, EPA asserted at oral argument that the second option, to the extent that it is based on a state's agreement not to oppose permissive intervention, will not be available in states that do not provide some means of intervention. This interpretation is critical to our decision to uphold the agency. Were the second option open where permissive intervention is impossible, public participation would be limited to that flowing from the state's agreement to respond to citizen complaints and to entertain citizen comments on proposed settlements of state enforcement actions—rights dismissed by the Seventh Circuit as "no more than a legalistic articulation of a common courtesy and hardly ... satisfaction of the EPA's statutory duty to issue regulations promoting public participation in state enforcement." *Citizens for a Better Environment v. EPA*, 596 F.2d 720, 726 (7th Cir. 1979).

With this caveat, however, we conclude that the regulations, as interpreted, provide meaningful and adequate opportunity for public participation consistent with the statutory mandate....

3. *Maximum Penalties.* Section 1319 ... specifies the penalties assessable on the federal level.... Civil penalties for permit violations are "not to exceed $25,000 per day for each violation." 33 U.S.C. § 1319(d).

States are required to have "adequate authority" "[t]o abate violations of the permit or the permit program, including civil and criminal penalties and other ways and means of enforcement." § 1342(b)(7). The Administrator was charged with the responsibility of fashioning guidelines defining the minimum enforcement provisions deemed adequate. Pursuant to this mandate, the Administrator promulgated the regulations here in question, which require state authority

[t]o assess or sue to recover in court civil penalties and to seek criminal remedies, including fines, as follows: (i) Civil penalties ... shall be assessable in at least the amount of $5,000 a day for each violation....

40 C.F.R. § 123.27(3).

Petitioner NRDC contends that these regulations are invalid because they do not compel the states to provide authority to levy the maximum penalties assessable in federal enforcement programs.

Throughout its consideration of the Act, Congress reiterated the important role penalties play in enforcement of water pollution standards, and emphasized the need for substantial penalties, for example:

> [S]anctions under existing law have not been sufficient to encourage compliance.... Therefore, the Committee proposes to increase significantly the penalties.... [I]f the timetables established throughout the Act are to be met, the threat of sanction must be real, and enforcement provisions must be swift and direct.

In this articulation of congressional purpose, coupled with the congressional expectation that states would bear the primary enforcement burdens of the Act, NRDC would find a mandate for state ability and willingness to assess the federally required maximum penalties.

This challenge by NRDC exposes the same logical infirmity flawing the attack leveled by CBE. It presumes an unexpressed congressional intent that state requirements must mirror the federal ones, a presumption inconsistent with the elements of the statutory scheme limiting operation of the provisions to enforcement efforts at the national level and explicitly empowering the Administrator to set the prerequisites for state plans. Nothing in the Act or its legislative history supports a reduction of the Administrator's discretion to activity purely ministerial, ... and the Administrator's conclusion to the contrary is eminently reasonable.

The rationale EPA offers for its disinclination to adopt the statutory maxima also buttresses this conclusion. The proposed regulations would have required the states to exert enforcement authority virtually identical with the federal, including the same levels of minimum and maximum fines. In final structure, however, the regulations, changed largely in response to state comments, reflect the balancing of uniformity and state autonomy contemplated by the Act:

> The Agency has determined that it is necessary to set specific minimum levels of fines and penalties which States must have the authority to recover in order to ensure effective State enforcement programs. Without such minimum levels, EPA would often be forced to take its own enforcement action in approved States because the State action imposed inadequate penalties. Such EPA action, while available as a backup, is not intended to be relied upon as the prime enforcement mechanism in approved States. Accordingly, the Agency has set minimum levels of fines and penalties. However, it has

reduced the levels below those available to EPA based on the large volumes of comments from states requesting such relief.

We will not disturb this reasonable accommodation of manifestly competing interests, and consequently we uphold the agency's penalty regulations.

* * *

Notes and Questions

1. Section 402(b) compels EPA to approve State programs meeting the minimum requirements established therein. Additionally, as previously mentioned, Section 510 expressly preserves the ability of the States to establish more stringent standards if they so choose. In accordance with these provisions, EPA's authorization regulations confirm that they do not preclude States from adopting or enforcing more stringent requirements or from operating a program with a broader scope of coverage. 40 C.F.R. § 123.1(i). EPA will never disapprove a State program because it is too strict. Indeed, it lacks the power to do so. If a State program has a broader scope of coverage than required (if, for example, a State requires permits for runoff from nonpoint sources), EPA views those broader requirements as being effective solely as a matter of State law. 40 C.F.R. § 123.1(i)(2).

2. What was the distinction that the *NRDC* court drew between effluent limitations, on the one hand, and the public participation and enforcement matters raised by CBE and NRDC, on the other? Reread § 402(b). Is there a statutory basis for this distinction? What policy reasons might Congress have had for requiring uniformity in the former realm but not in the others? In support of its argument that state-level citizen suits were required, CBE cited §§ 101(e), 402(b)(3) and (7), and 505. Do you agree with the court's conclusions regarding the effect of these provisions? If EPA had compelled the States to provide for state-level citizen suits as a precondition to authorization, would either the States or Industry have been able to resist this requirement?

3. Exactly what public participation rights did EPA require States seeking authorization to provide citizens in the enforcement process? Does this mandate seem reasonable in light of the policy directives in § 101(e)? What is the effect of requiring States not to oppose motions for permissive intervention? Was the court justified in relying on the explanatory statement EPA made at oral argument? What did the court suggest it would have done if EPA had only mandated that States respond to citizen complaints and entertain citizen comments on proposed settlements? Do you agree with the court's suggestion on this point?

4. Strangely, the *NRDC* court never mentioned that citizens have a federal cause of action against alleged violators under § 505(a)(1), even in authorized States. Does the availability of this federal cause of action change your view regarding the significance of EPA's having declined to compel the States to provide for state-level citizen suits?

5. As we will see in chapter 6, EPA has an array of administrative, civil judicial and criminal enforcement options available to it under § 309 of the CWA. These authorities apply even in authorized States. See 33 U.S.C.

§ 1342(i). Despite this ongoing federal authority, and in line with § 402(b)(7), EPA has required States to have both civil and criminal penalty authorities as a precondition to receiving authorization. As indicated by that portion of the *NRDC* decision addressing civil penalties, EPA has not required the States to have equivalent penalty authorities. Nor has it required the States to have any administrative enforcement powers; that is, EPA does not mandate that States have the power to compel compliance and/or impose fines without having to go the court. As seen in 40 C.F.R. § 123.37(3), EPA requires the States to have *either* the right to assess penalties or to seek them in court.

6. What does it mean to require that civil penalties be "assessable in at least the amount of $5,000 a day?" Why was NRDC dissatisfied with this requirement? Why were its arguments unavailing? What explanation did EPA offer for declining to require more? Were you persuaded? Do you agree that EPA's explanation at least passes *Chevron* muster? How should the fact that EPA retains enforcement authority in authorized States factor into this analysis?

2. EPA Oversight

Upon authorization, the relevant State takes the lead role in the day-to-day implementation of the NPDES program. It issues the permits, receives the dischargers' monitoring reports (known as "discharge monitoring reports" or "DMRs"), undertakes most inspections and, in the event of noncompliance, initiates most enforcement actions.

This is not to say, however, that EPA becomes inert after approving a given State's program. Instead, EPA shifts into an oversight mode. This oversight has some aspects that are discharger-specific and others that are more programmatic. With respect to specific dischargers, section 402(d)(1) specifically requires each State to transmit to EPA a copy of each permit application, and to provide EPA with a copy of any draft permit. Section 402(d)(2) precludes the State from issuing the permit if within 90 days EPA objects to it as being "outside the guidelines and requirements of the [Act]." Thus, EPA can effectively "veto" State permits. EPA also has an ongoing role in overseeing compliance matters. The State must keep EPA abreast of any instances of noncompliance. 40 C.F.R. § 123.45. Additionally, EPA retains its full investigatory powers under § 308 and its full enforcement powers under § 309. See, e.g., 33 U.S.C. § 1342(i). Accordingly, while EPA tends to defer to the States on most enforcement matters, this is largely a matter of EPA self-restraint. It has the statutory ability to step in and take the enforcement lead in particular cases if it so chooses.

On a more programmatic level, EPA can and does review how the State is implementing its program. This includes but transcends patterns that may be evident in how the State handles numerous permitting or enforcement matters. Additionally, for example, EPA will want to ensure that the State has an appropriate inspection strategy. It will also want to ensure that the State does not alter its program such that it no longer meets the authorization requirements. EPA has the ability to revoke State authorization if it finds that the State program, or the State's administration thereof, no longer meets the relevant requirements. 33 U.S.C. § 1342(c)(3).

We will now consider a second excerpt from the *NRDC* case. This excerpt addresses the scope of the power that EPA reserved to itself to veto State permits. As we will see, EPA has essentially reserved the ability to second-guess any and all decisions made by the States in issuing permits. One might wonder why EPA views this prerogative as being so important. The answer inheres in both the nature of the decisions that are made by permit-issuers, and the legal effect of those decisions, once made. While many of the decisions made in issuing a particular permit are straightforward (e.g., imposing the appropriate technology-based requirements in situations in which EPA has previously established the standards for that industry through rulemaking), others are much more judgmental. These include, for example, setting the appropriate water quality-based requirements (see 40 C.F.R. § 122.44(d)) and establishing the appropriate frequency for the monitoring and reporting requirements (see 40 C.F.R. § 122.44(i)). Less commonly (but as discussed in the following case), they can also include setting the appropriate technology-based limits in situations in which EPA has not previously set them.

The importance of these decisions (and thus, in EPA's view, of its oversight) is due to § 402(k), which creates what is referred to as a "permit shield." To paraphrase, that provision indicates that, for most purposes, compliance with an NPDES permit is deemed to be compliance with the CWA; the permit is conclusively presumed to contain all of the relevant requirements imposed under the Act. Even if the CWA or EPA's regulations otherwise contemplate that a discharger should be subject to additional or more stringent requirements, those requirements will be inapplicable if they are omitted or weakened in the discharger's permit. This, obviously, underscores the importance of ensuring that the permit "gets it right."

In this context, consider the following excerpts from the *NRDC* opinion:

NATURAL RESOURCES DEFENSE COUNCIL, INC. v. U.S. EPA

United States Court of Appeals, District of Columbia Circuit, 1988.

859 F.2d 156.

[EPA promulgated 40 C.F.R. § 123.44(c), specifying six types of permit defects that would justify the exercise of its veto power. Industry challenged two of these, including subsection 6, in which EPA asserted its authority to veto a proposed permit if, in the absence of formally promulgated effluent limitations, the proposed permit fails in EPA's judgment to comport with the Act or regulations promulgated thereunder.]

In Industry's view, the sole basis for rejecting a proposed permit by virtue of improper effluent limits is if those limits are set pursuant to formally promulgated effluent limitations guidelines under section 1314(b). That section requires EPA to promulgate, pursuant to formal notice-and-comment rulemaking, guidelines ... to be used in setting effluent limits in particular permits....

Industry argues that these § 1314(b) guidelines are the "guidelines and requirements" referred to in § 1342(d). The agency may not, in Industry's view, reject permits based on noncompliance with effluent guidelines unless those limitations are set pursuant to § 1314....

Although it is consistent with some fragments of the statutory language, Industry's interpretation ultimately proves too much, and thus must be rejected as inconsistent with the structure of the Act. Section 1342(a)(1) requires EPA, in approving permits in the absence of formally promulgated effluent limitations guidelines, to exercise its best professional judgment (BPJ) as to proper effluent limits. When issuing permits according to its BPJ, EPA is required to adhere to the technology-based standards set out in § 1311(b). This is so despite the fact that EPA has not yet rigorously defined these standards through notice-and-comment rulemaking.

States issuing permits pursuant to § 1342(b) stand in the shoes of the agency, and thus must similarly pay heed to § 1311(b)'s technology-based standards when exercising their BPJ. Thus, notwithstanding Industry's contrary assertions, States are required to compel adherence to the Act's technology-based standards regardless of whether EPA has specified their content pursuant to § 1314(b). Accordingly, EPA contends that it may veto state permits that, in its estimation, fail to comply with § 1311's dictates.

In response, Industry asserts that even if a State must use its best professional judgment to comply with the § 1311(b) standards, its substantive decisions as to what constitutes BAT, BPT, et al., are subject to EPA veto only if inconsistent with nationally promulgated guidelines. In other words, EPA's interpretation of what § 1311(b) requires becomes an independent requirement of the Act only when determined pursuant to § 1314(b). Industry argues that its interpretation preserves Congress' intentional balance of federalism and uniformity: While state-issued permits must comply with formally promulgated national guidelines, in the absence of such guidelines ad hoc federal judgments cannot trump their ad hoc state counterparts. Under a contrary view, Industry contends, EPA would be able to roam freely, unconstrained by standards and at liberty to reject state-issued permits.

The battle lines are thus sharply drawn. Unfortunately, the express terms of § 1342(d) do not provide a ready answer to the interpretive question before us. The crucial language, "guidelines and requirements," fails conclusively to support either side's view....

Industry's reading of the legislative history focuses broadly on Congress' intent that States play the primary role in administering the

Act. As to that general proposition there can be no reasonable doubt. But the general, pro-federalism thrust of the statutory regime does not manifest itself in the legislative history in helpfully specific ways as to the issue at hand: whether in the absence of formally promulgated effluent limitations guidelines, EPA can veto state permits on the basis of inadequate effluent limits....

As to the scope of the veto authority, it is ultimately unhelpful to fall back to general principles of federalism, for those principles, however important to our polity, do not answer the specific question at hand. Contrary to Industry's unflattering characterizations, EPA's oversight of state permits is not ad hoc, nor is the agency's discretion unfettered. The requirement articulated in section 1342(a)(1) that the factors listed in sections 1311 and 1314 be considered operates as a significant check on the agency's discretion.

In sum, the Act envisions a significant role for the States in its administration, but nothing in the legislative history indicates Congress' intent on the issue at hand. Contrary to Industry's assertions, EPA's discretion is constrained under the Act; so long as the agency exercises its veto power "judiciously," the veto regulations are not at odds with Congress' view of abiding principles of federalism. And it goes without saying that we are not confronted, in this global challenge to EPA's regulations, with a specific action by federal authorities that is seen by Industry as riding roughshod over the felt interests of a particular State. Finally, we cannot but observe that Industry is in the odd role of seeking to carry on a reverse sort of parens patriae role, attending to the interests of the several States, when the States themselves have not seen fit (at least in litigation) to call the veto regulation into question. Like Congress itself, the States have been silent on the point.

Next, we consider the structure of the Act. Industry points out that the Act is premised on shared state and federal authority, and that the veto regulations, in authorizing ad hoc federal rejection of state permits, gut this carefully crafted structure....

But, again, the fact that the structure of the Act envisions that States will play a primary role under the Act does not mean that the agency's veto regulations go beyond what the statute permits. For, as we have seen, the Act undeniably provides some veto authority; the question is how much (or by what standard the authority is to be exercised). Industry can point to nothing in the Act that would reasonably lend itself to delimiting the bounds of the veto authority.... Absent such a showing, relying on the pro-federalism bent of the Act's structure does not, for reasons already stated, get us very far in resolving a highly specific question of statutory interpretation. Moreover, the veto regulations are not, as Industry would have it, "totally at odds with the principles of federalism embodied in the statute." Congress could not have intended, as Industry prefers, in all cases for state judgments about the proper conditions for permits to take precedence; the very presence of veto authority over individual permits belies this rather hard view of federalism principles.

EPA, on the other hand, mounts what seem to us more persuasive arguments based on the statute's structure. First, nowhere in the Act is there an indication that Congress intended that promulgation of ... effluent limitations guidelines would be a precondition for vetoing state permits. . . .

In addition, EPA argues that Industry's position may lead to results that would violate the Act. . . . Under Industry's view, . . . until EPA has promulgated national guidelines setting forth its view of § 1311(b)'s technology-based requirements, the agency is powerless to supplant a state permitting authority's judgment of whether a particular permit meets the technology-based standards. From this, as EPA emphasizes, States would be able (under Industry's view) to approve permits that plainly violate section 1311(a)—the Act's bedrock prohibition of pollutant discharges—and the federal authority must nonetheless stand helplessly aside, awaiting the uncertain coming of national effluent limitations guidelines. Cf. S. Beckett, Waiting for Godot.

This is the sort of situation (although admittedly stated in the extreme) that the Act's veto provision ... was designed to address. EPA persuasively argues that ... section 1342(d)'s veto authority provides considerable evidence that Congress intended federal minima (even if crafted on the basis of BPJ) to take precedence. In short, the several States are to be centrally involved in the Act's administration, but their involvement is to be in the achievement of federal goals. By virtue of Congress' policy decision to allow EPA to approve federal permits based on the Administrator's best professional judgment, it is consonant with that policy to allow a similar power with respect to vetoing state permits. Rejection of a state permit in the latter situation represents no more an ad hoc judgment than approval of a federal permit in the former.

[The court went on to conclude that, at a minimum, EPA's interpretation of its veto authority was reasonable and, thus, to be upheld under *Chevron*.]

Questions and Notes

1. Section 402(a)(1) itself does not use the term "best professional judgment." Instead, it requires EPA, when issuing permits before the relevant national standards have been set, to impose such conditions as it "determines are necessary to carry out the provisions of the [Act]." In its implementing regulations, EPA interpreted this as requiring a case-by-case determination pursuant to which the permit issuer is to try to anticipate what the national standards will be when they emerge. 40 C.F.R. § 125.3(c)(2). Elsewhere, EPA denominates this a "best professional judgment" (or "BPJ") determination. See, e.g., 40 C.F.R. § 125.3(a)(2)(i)(B). Elsewhere still, it requires authorized States to undertake this analysis when issuing permits. See 40 C.F.R. §§ 122.44(a)(1) and 123.25(a)(15).

2. Do you agree that section 402(d)(2) is unclear at to whether EPA may veto permits when it disagrees with a State's BPJ determination? If so, why didn't the court resolve the ambiguity by resort to the pro-federalism policies expressed in § 101(b)? What did the court mean when it said that Industry's argument "prove[d] too much?" Do you agree? Might there have been countervailing environmental benefits if the court had accepted Industry's position?

3. Might the court have viewed the issue in *NRDC* differently if the States had been the ones challenging EPA's regulations? Should Industry even have had standing to raise this challenge?

4. While section 402(d) empowers EPA to veto State permits, it does not on its face compel EPA to veto even blatantly deficient permits. Section 402(e) goes so far as to allow EPA to waive its review authority with respect to categories of point sources. See also 40 C.F.R § 123.24(d). As alluded to in *NRDC* (with the citation omitted), the legislative history suggests that Congress intended EPA to use its veto authority "judiciously." Should courts be able to review EPA decisions regarding whether to veto state permits? When thinking about this question, keep in mind what happens after EPA's decision. If EPA declines to veto, the State then makes a final decision on the permit, which would then be subject to challenge (by either citizens and/or the applicant) in State court. EPA requires the States, as a precondition to authorization, to provide such a right of review. 40 C.F.R. § 123.30. If EPA vetoes a State permit, on the other hand, the State has the option either of revising the permit to meet EPA's objection or of having the permit issuance decision revert to EPA. See 33 U.S.C. § 1342(d)(4). How should these dynamics affect the availability of federal review regarding EPA's veto decisions? Compare *Save the Bay, Inc. v. Administrator of EPA*, 556 F.2d 1282 (5th Cir. 1977) (denying review in the federal Courts of Appeal regarding EPA's decision not to veto a State-issued permit, but suggesting that district court review might be available in at least some situations), and *American Paper Institute, Inc. v. U.S. EPA*, 890 F.2d 869 (7th Cir. 1989) (denying Court of Appeals review of an EPA veto where the State ultimately issued a permit meeting EPA's concerns). Is State court review adequate in these contexts? Is EPA's decision whether to veto a "final agency action?" If EPA's decision not to veto a State permit may be reviewable in some cases, by what standards would that decision be judged?

5. As mentioned in the prior note, EPA requires the States to allow for judicial review of their permitting decisions as a precondition to authorization. While this requirement was not challenged in *NRDC*, its legality may be open to question. In *American Forest and Paper Ass'n v. U.S. EPA*, 137 F.3d 291 (5th Cir. 1998), the Fifth Circuit held that EPA cannot impose authorization requirements beyond those contemplated in § 402(b). It rejected EPA's argument that Section 304(i) allows it to supplement those requirements. Id. at 297–298. Read these two provisions. Do you agree with the Fifth Circuit? If so, do you find any basis in § 402(b) for the judicial review requirement contained in 40 C.F.R. § 123.30?

C. Substantive Standards

Sections 402(a) requires EPA, when it issues NPDES permits, to ensure that they comply with specified sections of the Act, including

§§ 301, 306 and 307. As contemplated in § 402(b), EPA's regulations require authorized States to do the same. See 40 C.F.R. §§ 122.44 and 123.25. Sections 301, 306 and 307 establish a series of technology-based requirements applicable to various categories of dischargers. Additionally, Section 301(b)(1)(C) requires permit issuers to establish more stringent requirements where necessary to ensure compliance with water quality standards. Seen in this light, the statute is best viewed as taking a technology-first approach; that is, it relies on technology-based standards as a first resort in trying to achieve the statute's water quality goals. It does not entirely forsake a water quality-based approach, however. Instead, it relegates this approach to backup status, to be used when technology-based standards may not by themselves achieve compliance with water quality standards.

1. Technology–Based Standards

The CWA imposes different technology-based standards on different types of dischargers. Industrial dischargers who discharge directly into our nation's waters (referred to as "direct dischargers") are subject to one set of requirements. We will focus primarily on these standards below. Sewage treatment plants (generally referred to as "publicly owned treatment works" or "POTWs") are subject to another set of standards. See 33 U.S.C. § 1311(b)(1)(B). Industrial dischargers who discharge into sewage treatment systems (referred to as "pretreaters") are subject to yet a third set of standards. See 33 U.S.C. § 1317(b) and (c).

Within the realm of direct dischargers, the CWA distinguishes between existing and new dischargers. For existing dischargers, the CWA established a phased approach pursuant to which dischargers were first required to install the best practicable control technology ("BPT") by 1977, 33 U.S.C. § 1311(b)(1), and then the best available control technology that is economically achievable ("BAT") by 1983. Congress twice extended the timeline by which BAT had to be achieved, eventually settling on 1989 as the final deadline. See 33 U.S.C. § 1311(b)(2). New dischargers, by contrast, have to comply with what is, at least in theory, an even more demanding technology-based standard, the "best available demonstrated control technology" ("BADT"), which is sometimes alternatively referred to as the "new source performance standard" ("NSPS"). See 33 U.S.C. § 1316(a) and (b).

The CWA was ambiguous on the question of who was supposed to set some of these standards. Section 304(b) clearly contemplated that EPA would establish "effluent limitation guidelines" that would inform the establishment of the actual effluent limitations. It did not clearly indicate, however, who would set the actual limitations that applied to individual dischargers. Instead, Section 301(b) merely indicated that the relevant standards were to "be achieved." This begged the question whether the States were bound to apply uniform standards established by EPA on an industry-by-industry basis, or, alternatively, whether they (the States) were in charge of setting the actual effluent limitations, with

EPA's guidelines to serve as a mere reference point in their analysis. Resolving a split in the Circuits, the Supreme Court resolved this issue in *E.I. du Pont v. Train*, 430 U.S. 112, 97 S.Ct. 965, 51 L.Ed.2d 204 (1977), holding that EPA has the power to set industry-by-industry effluent limitations.

Although the following case addresses the BPT requirements that have now largely been displaced by the BAT requirements, we include it because it contains one of the best discussions of some of the fundamental issues involved in the establishment of technology-based standards:

WEYERHAEUSER CO. v. COSTLE

United States Court of Appeals, Dist. of Columbia Circuit, 1978.

590 F.2d 1011.

McGOWAN, Circuit Judge:

To make paper from trees is an old art; to do it without water pollution is a new science. In papermaking, logs or wooden chips must be ground up or "cooked" in one of several processes until only cellulose pulp is left. The pulp is bleached and made into various types and grades of paper. The cooking solutions and wash water that are left contain a variety of chemicals produced during "cooking" and other processes, including acids and large quantities of dissolved cellulose-breakdown products. Indeed, in some pulping processes, more of the wood is discarded in the waste water than is used to make paper. EPA has selected three parameters for measuring the pollutant content of the industry's effluent, all of which have been used extensively in this and other industries' measurements: total suspended solids (TSS), biochemical oxygen demand (BOD), and pH. TSS reflects the total amount of solids in solution, while BOD reflects the amount of biodegradable material in solution, and pH measures the acidity of the solution.

EPA has divided this segment of the industry into 16 subcategories, and further subdivided it into 66 subdivisions, for the purposes of its rulemaking effort.... [O]f the 16 subcategories in the whole industry, only three the three that use some form of the "sulfite process" have evoked particularized challenges. The reaction of sulfite mill operators stems from the limitations' greater economic impact on them. That impact in turn results from the fact that the sulfite process creates one of the highest pollution loads of any industrial process, and certainly the highest within the pulping industry....

Some of the paper mills that must meet the effluent limitations under review discharge their effluents into the Pacific Ocean. Petitioners contend that the ocean can dilute or naturally treat effluent, and that EPA must take this capacity of the ocean ("receiving water capacity") into account in a variety of ways.[40] They urge what they term "common

---

40. Some petitioners contend that EPA should have taken receiving water capacity into account in setting pollutant parameters. They argue that the Agency should

sense," *i.e.*, that because the amounts of pollutant involved are small in comparison to bodies of water as vast as Puget Sound or the Pacific Ocean, they should not have to spend heavily on treatment equipment, or to increase their energy requirements and sludge levels, in order to treat wastes that the ocean could dilute or absorb.[41]

EPA's secondary response to this claim was that pollution is far from harmless, even when disposed of in the largest bodies of water. As congressional testimony indicated, the Great Lakes, Puget Sound, and even areas of the Atlantic Ocean have been seriously injured by water pollution. . . . In the main, however, EPA simply asserted that the issue of receiving water capacity could not be raised in setting effluent limitations because Congress had ruled it out. . . .

The earliest version of the [FWPCA] was passed in 1948 and amended five times before 1972. Throughout that 24 year period, Congress attempted to use receiving water quality as a basis for setting pollution standards. At the end of that period, Congress realized not only that its water pollution efforts until then had failed, but also that reliance on receiving water capacity as a crucial test for permissible pollution levels had contributed greatly to that failure. *EPA v. State Water Resources Control Board*, 426 U.S. 200, 202 (1976).

Based on this experience, Congress adopted a new approach in 1972. Under the Act, "a discharger's performance is . . . measured against strict technology-based effluent limitations specified levels of treatment to which it must conform, rather than against limitations derived from water quality standards to which it and other polluters must collectively conform." *Id.* at 204–05.

This new approach reflected developing views on practicality and rights. Congress concluded that water pollution seriously harmed the

not have considered BOD as such a parameter because the ocean has so much dissolved oxygen that wastes with high BOD have negligible impact and that it should not have considered pH as a parameter because ocean salts buffer waste acidity. Other petitioners contend that EPA should have taken receiving water capacity into account in subcategorization. They argue that ocean-discharging plants are in a wholly different stance from other plants and should be in a separate subcategory. It is also urged that EPA should be forced to give variances for ocean-discharging plants. Finally, the argument for taking receiving water capacity into account is sometimes couched in terms of an environmental balancing test: since there is no environmental "credit" for preventing discharges that the oceans could treat, and there is an environmental "debit" for the air pollution and sludge disposal problems incident to treatment, the balance should tilt in favor of ocean-discharging plants. We regard all the contentions as equivalent in their crucial component that Congress intended to let EPA take receiving water capacity into account.

41. Apart from this simple "common sense" version of the argument, there is a more sophisticated economic version called the "optimal pollution" theory. This economic theory contends that there is a level or type of pollution that, while technologically capable of being controlled, is uneconomic to treat because the benefit from treatment is small and the cost of treatment is large. *See generally* W. Baxter, People or Penguins: The Case for Optimal Pollution (1974). These economic theories are premised on a view that we have both adequate information about the effects of pollution to set an optimal test, and adequate political and administrative flexibility to keep polluters at that level once we allow any pollution to go untreated. As discussed in this section, it appears that Congress doubted these premises.

environment, and that although the cost of control would be heavy, the nation would benefit from controlling that pollution. Yet scientific uncertainties made it difficult to assess the benefits to particular bodies of receiving water. Even if the federal government eventually could succeed at the task at which had failed for 24 years and thus could determine benefits and devise water quality standards, Congress concluded that the requisite further delay was too long for the nation to wait.

Moreover, by eliminating the issue of the capacity of particular bodies of receiving water, Congress made nationwide uniformity in effluent regulation possible. Congress considered uniformity vital to free the states from the temptation of relaxing local limitations in order to woo or keep industrial facilities. In addition, national uniformity made pollution clean-up possible without engaging in the divisive task of favoring some regions of the country over others.

More fundamentally, the new approach implemented changing views as to the relative rights of the public and of industrial polluters. Hitherto, the right of the polluter was pre-eminent, unless the damage caused by pollution could be proven. Henceforth, the right of the public to a clean environment would be pre-eminent, unless pollution treatment was impractical or unachievable. The Senate Committee declared that "(t)he use of any river, lake, stream or ocean as a waste treatment system is unacceptable" regardless of the measurable impact of the waste on the body of water in question. Legislative History at 1425 (Senate Report). The Conference Report stated that the Act "specifically bans pollution dilution as an alternative to waste treatment." *Id.* at 284. This new view of relative rights was based in part on the hard-nosed assessment of our scientific ignorance: "we know so little about the ultimate consequences of injection of new matter into water that (the Act requires) a presumption of pollution ..." *Id.* at 1332 (remarks of Sen. Buckley). It also was based on the widely shared conviction that the nation's quality of life depended on its natural bounty, and that it was worth incurring heavy cost to preserve that bounty for future generations.

The Act reflects the new approach in a number of provisions.... [I]ts goal was *zero* discharge of pollutants by 1985, section 101(a), *not* discharges at acceptable or tolerable levels for receiving water.... In only one limited instance, thermal pollution, is receiving water capacity to be considered in relaxing standards, and the section allowing such consideration was drafted as a clear exception. Section 316(a). Otherwise, receiving water quality was to be considered only in setting "*more stringent*" standards than effluent limitations otherwise would prescribe. Section 301(b)(1)(C) of the Act (emphasis added).

The Act was passed with an expectation of "mid-course corrections," Legislative History, at 175 (statement of Sen. Muskie), and in 1977 Congress amended the Act, although generally holding to the same tack set five years earlier. Notably, during those five years, representatives of the paper industry had appeared before Congress and urged it to Change the Act and to incorporate receiving water capacity as a consideration. Nonetheless, Congress was satisfied with this element of the statutory scheme. Except for a provision specifically aimed at discharges from "publicly owned treatment plants," section 301(h) of the Act, it resolved in the recent amendments to continue regulating discharges into all receiving waters alike.[49]

Our experience with litigation under the Act, and particularly with this case, emphasized the weight of Congress' policies. Even without receiving water capacity as an issue to delay it, EPA was late in promulgating these regulations. We have wrestled with the problem of weighing technological imponderables and can understand the greater difficulties that would have arisen if he receiving water issues involving even greater imponderables had also been involved. . . .

Petitioners also challenge EPA's manner of assessing two factors that all parties agree must be considered: cost and non-water quality environmental impacts. They contend that the Agency should have more carefully balanced costs versus the effluent reduction benefits of the regulations, and that it should have also balanced those benefits against the non-water quality environmental impacts to arrive at a "net" environmental benefit conclusion. Petitioners base their arguments on certain comments made by the Conferees for the Act, and on the fact that the Act lists non-water quality environmental impacts as a factor the Agency must "take into account."

In order to discuss petitioners' challenges, we must first identify the relevant statutory standard. Section 304(b)(1)(B) of the Act identifies the factors bearing on [BPT] in two groups. First, the factors shall

> include consideration of the total cost of application of technology in relation to the effluent reduction benefits to be achieved from such application,

and second, they

> shall also take into account the age of equipment and facilities involved, the process employed, the engineering aspects of the application of various types of control techniques, process changes, non-water quality environmental impact (including energy requirements), and such other factors as the Administrator deems appropriate(.)

The first group consists of two factors that EPA must compare: total cost versus effluent reduction benefits. We shall call these the "comparison factors." The other group is a list of many factors that EPA must

---

49. Further support for this interpretation may be found in section 304 of the Act. This provision requires EPA in setting limitations to balance cost and "effluent reduction benefits." Although the section specifies other factors to be considered as well, none relates to the effect of regulation on the treated or receiving waters. The phrase "effluent reduction benefits" avoids any suggestion that receiving water quality is an issue. Effluent reduction occurs whenever less effluent is discharged, i.e., whenever a plant treats its wastes before discharge, and the same degree of reduction occurs whether the discharge is into a small stream or the Pacific Ocean.

"take into account:" age, process, engineering aspects, process changes, environmental impacts (including energy), and any others EPA deems appropriate. We shall call these the "consideration factors." Notably, section 304(b)(2)(B) of the Act, which delineates the factors relevant to setting [BAT], tracks the [BPT] provision before us except in one regard: in the [BAT] section, All factors, including costs and benefits, are consideration factors, and no factors are separated out for comparison.

Based on our examination of the statutory language and the legislative history, we conclude that Congress mandated a particular structure and weight for the [BPT] comparison factors, that is to say, a "limited" balancing test.[52] In contrast, Congress did not mandate any particular structure or weight for the many consideration factors. Rather, it left EPA with discretion to decide how to account for the consideration factors, and how much weight to give each factor. [Therefore,] we conclude that, on the one hand, we should examine EPA's treatment of cost and benefit under the [BPT] standard to assure that the Agency complied with Congress' "limited" balancing directive. On the other hand, our scrutiny of the Agency's treatment of the several consideration factors seeks to assure that the Agency informed itself as to their magnitude, and reached its own express and considered conclusion about their bearing. More particularly, we do not believe that EPA is required to use any specific structure such as a balancing test in assessing the consideration factors, nor do we believe that EPA is required to give each consideration factor any specific weight.

Our conclusions are based initially on the section's wording and apparent logic. By singling out two factors (the comparison factors) for separate treatment, and by requiring that they be considered "in relation to" each other, Congress elevated them to a level of greater attention and rigor. Moreover, the comparison factors are a closed set of two, making it possible to have a definite structure and weight in considering them and preventing extraneous factors from intruding on the balance.

By contrast, the statute directs the Agency only to "take into account" the consideration factors, without prescribing any structure for EPA's deliberations. As to this latter group of factors, the section cannot logically be interpreted to impose on EPA a specific structure of consideration or set of weights because it gave EPA authority to "upset" any such structure by exercising its discretion to add new factors to the mix.... So long as EPA pays some attention to the congressionally specified factors, the section on its face lets EPA relate the various factors as it deems necessary.

52. Senator Muskie described the "limited" balancing test:

The modification of subsection 304(b)(1) is intended to clarify what is meant by the term "practicable". *The balancing test between total cost and effluent reduction benefits* is intended to limit the application of technology only where the additional degree of effluent reduction is *wholly out of proportion* to the costs of achieving such marginal level of reduction for any class or category of sources.

Legislative History, at 170 (emphasis added).

Consequently, we must review the comparison factors to determine if EPA weighed them through the "limited" balancing test as intended by Congress. On the other hand, we may review the consideration factors only to determine if EPA was fully aware of them and reached its own express conclusions about them. Since the two type of factors are separate, we divide our discussion accordingly.

a.

Petitioners ... challenge the [cost-benefit] analysis for the sulfite sector, contending that EPA used an "overall" instead of an "incremental" method of balancing, and that its figures on the cost of [BPT] for the dissolving sulfite subcategory were underestimates....

... [EPA] assessed the costs of internal and external effluent treatment measures, not only for the industry, but also for each subcategory. This included a separate cost assessment for the sulfite subcategories. An economic analysis was prepared to determine the impact of the costs on the industry. It found that the industry as a whole would readily absorb the cost of compliance with [BPT], estimated at $1.6 billion. Out of 270 mills employing 120,000 people, eight mills would likely be closed and 1800 people laid off. The Agency noted that the impact on the three heavily polluting sulfite subcategories would be the greatest. Of less than 30 sulfite mills, three would probably close, resulting in 550 people being laid off.

Against these costs, EPA balanced the main effluent reduction benefit: overall 5,000 fewer tons per day of BOD discharged into the nation's waters. EPA refined this balance by calculating the cost per pound of BOD removed for each subcategory. Although sulfite mills must make large investments in waste treatment facilities, the cost-benefit balance is favorable for the limitations on these mills, because of the large volume of waste they produce and thus the greater treatment efficiency.

Petitioners' first contention is that EPA not only should have calculated the overall cost-benefit balance, but also should have made an "incremental" calculation of that balance. More precisely, they contend that EPA must undertake to measure the costs and benefits of each additional increment of waste treatment control, from bare minimum up to complete pollution removal.... [T]hey point to Senator Muskie's description of cost-benefit balancing, which suggests a focus on the "additional degree" or "marginal" amount of effluent reduction....

... While EPA has no discretion to avoid cost-benefit balancing for its [BPT] standards, it does have some discretion to decide how it will perform the cost-benefit balancing task. "(E)ven with [BPT], the cost of compliance was not a factor to be given primary importance," [*American Iron & Steel Inst. v. EPA*, 526 F.2d 1027, 1051 (3d Cir. 1975)], and, as such, cost need not be balanced against benefits with pinpoint precision. A requirement that EPA perform the elaborate task of calculating incremental balances would bog the Agency down in burdensome proceedings on a relatively subsidiary task. Hence, the Agency need not on its own undertake more than a net cost-benefit balancing to fulfill its obligation under section 304.

However, when an incremental analysis has been performed by industry and submitted to EPA, it is worthy of scrutiny by the Agency, for it may "avoid the risk of hidden imbalances between cost and benefit." *Id.* at 1076 n. 19 (Adams, J., concurring). If such a "hidden imbalance" were revealed here, and if the Agency had ignored it, we might remand for further consideration. But in this case the incremental analysis proffered by industry showed that the last and most expensive increment of BOD treated in sulfite mills cost less than $.15 per pound of BOD removed, which is below the average cost of treatment in most of the industry's subcategories. We would be reluctant to find that EPA had ignored a "hidden imbalance" when the most unfavorable incremental cost-benefit balance that is challenged falls well within the range of averages for the industry as a whole. . . .

b.

"(N)on-water quality environmental impact(s) (including energy requirements)" are among the "consideration factors" listed in section 304, and are the sole factors of that kind on which petitioners premise a challenge to the limitations. . . . [T]he Act does not specify a particular structure for EPA's treatment of the consideration factors but instead leaves the Agency with discretion in deciding how they will be "taken into account." In exercising that discretion, it is clear that EPA devoted considerable attention to assessing environmental impact and adequately set forth its conclusions with respect thereto. Most crucially, . . . EPA developed estimates of the new energy demands for the industry as a whole about 2.4% of the industry's total energy use and for each industry subcategory. For the sulfite subcategories, with their higher waste loads requiring greater waste treatment, the figure was an 18% increase in energy demand. EPA also developed estimates of the sludge disposal problem, which is the reverse side of effluent reduction benefit, because the waste that is removed from effluent must be disposed of as sludge. We are consequently convinced that EPA took adequately into account the environmental impacts of its regulations.

Petitioners assert, however, that we must impose on EPA a further and special requirement to engage in environmental balancing. They cite allegedly dramatic examples of negative environmental impacts from the air pollution and sludge disposal incident to waste treatment, and contend that EPA failed to give these enough "weight" in the balance. . . .

Congress' intent in passing this legislation was obviously not to minimize the importance of protecting the environment . . . Rather, Congress was resolved to rely on EPA's own internal structure and personnel attitudes to ensure that the net result of all of its programs would be a substantially enhanced natural environment. . . .

That Section 304 requires EPA to "take into account" non-water quality environmental impacts, therefore, reflects several concerns apart from a fear that the Agency will have an inadequate commitment to protection of the air and land. Perhaps most important, if these factors were not listed, EPA arguably would have no authority to temper its effluent regulations when its own conclusion was that such tempering was needed to protect the land and air. While committing the Agency to lead a comprehensive attack on water pollution, Congress did not intend that attack to prevent the Agency from realizing its other environmental goals....

Thus, since Congress intended EPA's internal structure to protect the non-water environment, the judicial function is completed when we have assured ourselves that EPA expressly considered the probable environmental impacts of its regulations. As we have noted, EPA fully investigated the environmental impacts, and thereby fulfilled this aspect of its statutorily mandated duty.

Questions and Notes

1. As the D.C. Circuit suggests, one of the reasons Congress moved to a technology-first approach in 1972 was the perceived failure of earlier water quality-based approaches. The Supreme Court characterized this shift in the following terms:

> ... [T]he Amendments are aimed at achieving maximum "effluent limitations" on "point sources".... Such direct restrictions on discharges facilitate enforcement by making it unnecessary to work backward from an overpolluted body of water to determine which point sources are responsible and which must be abated.

EPA v. California ex rel State Water Resources Control Board, 426 U.S. 200, 204, 96 S.Ct. 2022, 2024, 48 L.Ed.2d 578 (1976). What other justifications does the D.C. Circuit cite for the shift? Taken together, are these arguments persuasive? Professor Houck has cited the action-forcing nature of this approach as a principal reason for the CWA's success. See, e.g., Houck, Recent Developments Under the Clean Water Act NPDES Program (Feb. 5, 1991).

William Pedersen levels at least three attacks on technology-based approaches. First, he argues that, "by imposing the same requirements on similar plants everywhere they run the risk of regulating too little to meet water quality goals in some areas and more than necessary in others." Pedersen, Turning the Tide on Water Quality, 15 Ecology L.Q. 69, 82 (1988). In the latter instance, he maintains, the result is requirements that are "strict beyond any rational link to environmental improvements." Id. at 83. Pedersen also argues that technology-based requirements are inefficient because they do not rationally allocate the costs of reaching the desired level of pollutant-reduction:

> ... Only rarely will the costs of restricting pollutant X in industry A to a specified level–as calculated by rulemaking immersed in the details of determining the proper technology-based controls for that industry—equal the costs of restricting pollutant X to the level specified by a

similarly parochial rulemaking for industry B. Whenever these costs differ, the efficiency of pollution control for a given body of water will suffer to the extent that the overall reduction target could be met by substituting low-cost reductions at a plant in one industry for high-cost reductions at a plant in another.

Id. And third, Pedersen laments what he perceives as the illogic of an approach that requires EPA to learn so much about so many categories of industry:

> EPA has implemented "uniform" effluent standards since 1972, issuing separate technology-based control requirements for each of 500 different industries. Each guideline has required a major and expensive rulemaking. Most of the effort was spent on exploring, for EPA's education, details of the costs and achievable reductions for various technologies in the industry under consideration at the time the guideline was being developed. That knowledge had only short-term value; it quickly became outdated with economic changes and the advance of technology. Moreover, the process demanded that EPA develop expertise in an impossibly wide variety of fields, duplicating knowledge already acquired by the industries involved. EPA's resources would have produced for more permanent social return had they been invested in expanding our understanding of the effects both of discharges on water quality and of water quality on health and welfare.

Id. at 85 (footnotes omitted). On balance, how would you evaluate the advantages and disadvantages of technology-based approaches?

2. What was the statutory basis for the D.C. Circuit's conclusion that EPA need not take receiving water capacity into account? Did the mills have any statutory language supporting their positions? What were their positions, precisely? Was this a case in which the statutory language permitted only one reading, or was there any room for interpretive leeway under *Chevron*? Put another way, if EPA had chosen to subcategorize based on receiving water capacity, might the court have upheld that position?

3. The D.C. Circuit's analysis of the "comparison factors" and the "consideration factors," and their relative roles in the establishment of BPT and BAT has been embraced by other Circuits. See, e.g., *National Ass'n of Metal Finishers v. EPA*, 719 F.2d 624, 664 (3d Cir. 1983) ("*NAMF*") (in determining BPT, EPA must compare costs and benefits at least to the extent of applying the "wholly disproportionate" test); *Association of Pacific Fisheries v. EPA*, 615 F.2d 794, 805 and 817–818 (9th Cir. 1980) ("*Pacific Fisheries*") (applying the "wholly disproportionate" test to BPT, but indicating that EPA need not compare costs and benefits in determining BAT), and *BP Exploration & Oil, Inc. v. U.S. EPA*, 66 F.3d 784, 796, *reh'g den.* (6th Cir. 1995) ("*BP Exploration*") (EPA has discretion to determine how much weight to give the BAT factors, because they are all consideration factors). In *NAMF*, the court did determine that EPA was required to do an incremental analysis in applying the "wholly disproportionate" test. 719 F.2d at 664; but see *BASF Wyandotte Corp. v. Costle*, 598 F.2d 637, 656 (1st Cir. 1979) (agreeing fully with *Weyerhaueser* on this score).

4. Note that the D.C. Circuit upheld EPA's BPT determination in *Weyerhaueser* despite EPA's concession that it might result in the closure of

3 out of 30 sulfite mills. This is consistent with *EPA v. National Crushed Stone Ass'n*, 449 U.S. 64, 83, 101 S.Ct. 295, 307, 66 L.Ed.2d 268 (1980), in which the Supreme Court concluded that "Congress anticipated that [BPT] would cause economic hardship and plant closings." In *NAMF*, the court upheld EPA's BPT determination despite the Agency's projection that it would result in the closing of 20% of the electroplating job shops, with a corresponding loss of 10,000 jobs. 719 F.2d at 663.

5. BPT has little ongoing significance. By 1989 existing sources were to move to BAT for virtually all pollutants. See 33 U.S.C. § 1311(b)(2)(A), (C), (D) and (F); but see 33 U.S.C. § 1311(b)(2)(A) (setting a lesser second-level standard for so-called "conventional pollutants," such as BOD, pH, and suspended solids). Again, the acronym "BAT" is shorthand for the "best available technology" that is "economically achievable." 33 U.S.C. § 1311(b)(2)(A). Perhaps obviously, BAT is more demanding than BPT. In *Kennecott v. U.S. EPA*, 780 F.2d 445 (4th Cir. 1985), the court described the difference between the two standards in the following terms:

> ... EPA defines BPT as "the average of the best existing performance by plants of various sizes, ages and unit processes within each industrial category or subcategory. This average is not based upon a broad range of plants within an industrial category or subcategory, but is based upon performance levels achieved by exemplary plants." *EPA v. Nat'l Crushed Stone Ass'n*, 449 U.S. 64, 76 n. 15, 101 S.Ct. 295, 303 n. 15, 66 L.Ed.2d 268 (1980), quoting 39 Fed.Reg. 6580 (1974).
>
> In the second stage, Congress directed EPA to set an even more stringent standard, basing effluent limitations on [BAT]. [BAT] reflects the intention of Congress to use the latest scientific research and technology in setting effluent limits, pushing industries toward the goal of zero discharge as quickly as possible. In setting BAT, EPA uses not the average plant, but the optimally operating plant, the pilot plant which acts as a beacon to show what is possible.

780 F.2d at 448; see also *Chemical Manuf. Ass'n v. NRDC*, 470 U.S. 116, 155, 105 S.Ct. 1102, 1123, 84 L.Ed.2d 90 (1985) (Marshall, J., dissenting).

6. Section 304(b)(2) essentially establishes a two-step procedure for establishing BAT. First, § 304(b)(2)(A) requires EPA to identify "the degree of effluent reduction attainable through the application of the best control measures and practices achievable." And second, § 304(b)(2)(B) requires EPA, in determining the "best measure and practices available," to "take into account the age of the equipment and facilities involved, the process employed, the engineering aspects of the application of various types of control techniques, process changes, the cost of achieving such effluent reduction, non-water quality environmental impact (including energy requirements), and such other factors as [EPA] deems appropriate." Consistent with these provisions, the courts have required EPA to demonstrate that the relevant technology is both technologically available and economically achievable for the industry as a whole (although not for each individual plant). See, e.g., *Pacific Fisheries*, 615 F.2d at 816–820. As indicated in *Weyerhaueser*, however, the factors in § 304(b)(2)(B) track the BPT factors, but they are all "consideration factors." What does "economically achievable" for the industry mean? Presumably, EPA can impose standards here

that cause just as many closures as its BPT standards (subject to the availability of the § 301(c) variance, discussed in n.11 below). But must it? See *National Wildlife Federation v. EPA*, 286 F.3d 554, 564–565 (D.C. Cir. 2002) (EPA did not act arbitrarily and capriciously in determining that a technology was not economically achievable where it would result in four plant closures, lost shipments of $1.3 billion, and 4,800 lost jobs). Under what circumstances, if any, should EPA be able to settle for less than the "best" technology (here referring solely to technology's ability to remove pollutants) that meets both of the above requirements (i.e., it is technologically available and economically achievable)? Does the fact that EPA can consider non-water quality impacts and "such other factors as [it] deems appropriate" suggest that it has the discretion to select something less than the "best" (again, just technologically speaking) technology? If so, how much? Compare *BP Exploration*, 66 F.3d at 796 ("the CWA's requirement that EPA choose the 'best' technology does not mean the chosen technology must be the best pollutant removal"), and *NRDC v. U.S. EPA*, 863 F.2d 1420, 1426 (9th Cir. 1988) ("[t]he legislative history of the Act supports our conclusion that EPA should not delay requiring technologically feasible limitations as BAT in order to wait for precise cost figures").

7. As mentioned new sources are required to meet an even higher standard: the "best available demonstrated control technology" ("BADT"). 33 U.S.C. § 1316(a)(1). The statute defines the term "new source" to encompass any source, the construction of which is commenced after the date of the proposal of any new source standards for that industrial category. 33 U.S.C. § 1316(a)(2). EPA's rules do three interesting things. First, they define the term "source" to include "building[s]," "structure[s]" and "installations," thus indicating that an existing facility may sometimes be treated as a new source to the extent that, for example, new buildings with discharge points are being added. 40 C.F.R. § 122.2. Second, they establish criteria governing the circumstances under which this should be so. 40 C.F.R. § 122.29(b)(1). And third, they clarify that a source that commences construction while a proposed new source standard is pending will no longer be treated as a new source if EPA fails to adopt a final standard within 120 days of the proposal. Id.; see also 33 U.S.C. § 306(a)(1) and (b)(1)(B). On the last of these points, compare *NRDC v. U.S. EPA*, 822 F.2d 104, 112–114 (D.C. Cir. 1987), and *Pennsylvania Dept. of Nat. Res. v. EPA*, 618 F.2d 991, 999 (3d Cir. 1980).

8. As to the BADT standard itself, Section 306(a)(1) requires EPA to select a zero discharge standard, "where practicable." Beyond that, Section 306(b)(1)(B) merely requires EPA to "take into consideration the cost of achieving such effluent reduction, and any non-water quality environmental impact and energy requirements." Even though the phraseology of this latter subsection is not fundamentally different from that fleshing out the BAT standard in § 304(b)(1)(B), EPA often finds that new sources, collectively, can afford to incorporate higher levels of technology. Can you venture a guess as to why this might be so?

9. EPA generally does not set "design standards," requiring the use of particular technologies. Instead, it sets "performance standards," determining how much pollutant-reduction the relevant technologies would achieve and requiring the dischargers to achieve those levels however they see fit.

See, e.g., *Pacific Fisheries*, 615 F.2d at 814. Additionally, it should be noted that, for each individual discharger, the permit issuer (whether EPA or the State) translates EPA's effluent limitation guidelines into specific permit conditions, adjusting for variables such as water usage and rates of production.

10. The CWA provides a few limited relief valves from the above-described technology-based schemes. See, e.g., 33 U.S.C. § 301(c), (g) and (n). The two most significant of these are probably the "fundamentally different factors" ("FDF") variance in § 301(n) and what we will call the "affordability variance" in § 301(c). To best understand the FDF variance, one must consider how technology-based standards are set. In setting these standards, EPA (or its contractor) studies the types of plants in each relevant industry, develops a "model plant," and then uses that model plant as a reference point in determining what levels of pollutant reduction a given level of control technology would achieve, and how much it would cost the industry to incorporate that technology. However, not every plant in that industry will resemble the model plant EPA uses in its analysis. If the differences are great, a given plant may have to expend much more money than EPA anticipated to incorporate the relevant technology (e.g., to buy more land to have room for the surface impoundments that EPA factored in to its wastewater treatment assumptions), or may even be unable to do so (e.g., if the neighbors won't sell the land). The Supreme Court further explained this logic in *Chemical Manuf. Ass'n v. NRDC*, 470 U.S. 116, 105 S.Ct. 1102, 84 L.Ed.2d 90 (1985):

> ... An FDF variance does not excuse compliance with a correct requirement, but instead represents an acknowledgment that not all relevant factors were taken sufficiently into account in framing that requirement originally, and that those relevant factors, properly considered, would have justified—indeed, required—the creation of a subcategory for the discharger in question. As we have recognized, the FDF variance is a laudable corrective mechanism, "an acknowledgement (sic) that the uniform ... limitation was set without reference to the full range of current practices, to which the Administrator was to refer." *EPA v. National Crushed Stone Assn.*, 449 U.S. 64, 77–78 (1980). It is, essentially, not an exception to the standard-setting process, but rather a more fine-tuned application of it.

Id. at 130, 105 S.Ct. at 1110. EPA first developed the FDF variance without express statutory authorization. Do you agree with its logic? After the Supreme Court essentially blessed EPA's variance in a series of opinions (including *National Crushed Stone* and *Chemical Manuf.*), Congress codified it in the Water Quality Act Amendments of 1987. See 33 U.S.C. § 1311(n). At the same time, Congress placed some interesting restrictions on its use. Take a careful look at § 301(n). What do you think of the limits contained therein? What, in particular, do you think of the effect of § 301(n)(6), which indicates that the discharger must comply with the nationally-uniform effluent limitations while its request for an FDF variance is pending?

11. Section 301(c) essentially creates a temporary variance that applies if an individual cannot afford the upgrade from BPT to BAT. The Supreme Court explained this variance in *National Crushed Stone*:

A § 301(c) variance ... creates for a particular point source a BAT standard that represents for it the same sort of economic and technological commitment as the general BAT standard creates for the class. As with the general BAT standard, the variance assumes that [BPT] has been met by the point source and that the modification represents a commitment of the maximum resources economically possible to the ultimate goal of eliminating all polluting discharges. No one who can afford the best available technology can secure a variance.

Id. at 74–75, 101 S.Ct. at 302. Thus, while it is clear that the imposition of the imposition of BPT can result in plant closings, the imposition of BAT should not. EPA can set the standard at levels that would otherwise put plants out of business, but individual facilities can avoid this effect by showing that they: (1) have made the maximum use of technology within their economic capability, and (2) have made "reasonable further progress" in going beyond BPT. 33 U.S.C. § 1311(c), *National Crushed Stone*, 449 U.S. at 75, 101 S.Ct. at 303.

12. One of the great, unspoken weaknesses of the CWA is that there are no clear requirements for EPA to update the technology-based standards for each industry as technology improves. Instead, the statute appears to vest EPA with wide, perhaps even unfettered, discretion in this regard. See, e.g, 33 U.S.C. §§ 304(b) (requiring EPA to update its effluent limitation guidelines for BPT and BAT "if appropriate") and 306(b)(1)(B) (requiring EPA to update it NSPSs "from time to time"). Compare 42 U.S.C. § 7412 (d)(6) (requiring EPA to update its technology-based standards for air toxics at least every 8 years). As a result, many of EPA's technology-based standards under the CWA have become stale over time.

A Brief Note on the Requirements for Other Categories of Dischargers

As alluded to earlier, the CWA has other control programs relating to different categories of dischargers. Two of the most prominent of these are the programs relating to publicly owned treatment works ("POTWs") and those industrial dischargers who discharge not directly into the nation's waters, but rather into POTW systems (alternately referred to as "pretreaters" or "indirect dischargers").

Section 301(b)(1)(B) requires POTWs to meet effluent limitations based on "secondary treatment." This actually requires a two-step process, involving both "primary" and "secondary" treatment. EPA has described these processes in laymen's terms as follows:

[In primary treatment,] screens and sedimentation tanks are used to remove most materials that float or will settle. Primary treatment removes about 30 percent of carbonaceous biochemical oxygen demand from domestic sewage.

[Secondary treatment relies on bacteria to consume] the organic parts of the waste. It is accomplished by bringing together waste, bacteria, and oxygen in trickling filters or in the activated sludge process. This treatment removes floating and settleable solids and about 90 percent of the oxygen-demanding substances and suspended solids. Disinfection is the final stage of secondary treatment. See http://environment.about.com/cs/glossary/a/glossary_index.htm. EPA has established numeric standards for secondary treatment at 40 C.F.R. § 133.102.

Under the 1972 version of the CWA, POTWs were required to eventually move to a higher degree of treatment referred to as "tertiary treatment." Congress, however, repealed this requirement in 1981. It should be noted, however, that some States require tertiary treatment as a matter of State law. It should also be noted that, like direct industrial dischargers, POTWs are subject to the edicts of § 301(b)(1)(C) in that their permits must contain more stringent requirements (i.e., more stringent than secondary treatment) where necessary to meet water quality standards.

Pretreaters are governed under § 307(b) through (e). In general, these provisions require EPA to subject pretreaters to technology-based requirements that are analogous to those which would apply if they were discharging directly into the waterways: the pretreatment standards for existing sources are to be akin to BAT, and the pretreatment standards for new sources are to be comparable to BADT. See, e.g., *National Ass'n of Metal Finishers v. EPA*, 719 F.2d 624, 633 and 644 (3d Cir. 1983). There are several differences, however, between the pretreatment and NPDES programs. First, pretreaters are not required to have NPDES permits. Instead, they are deemed not to be "dicharg[ing] ... pollutants," within the meaning of § 301(a), because their discharges, at least as a preliminary matter, are into POTW systems instead of the nation's waters. See 40 C.F.R. § 122.2 (definition of "discharge of a pollutant"). Because they do not receive permits, pretreaters are regulated directly under the pretreatment standards: Section 307(d) simply states that it shall be unlawful for any pretreater to operate in violation of any such standard.

Second, the pretreatment program has some twists that are not present in the NPDES realm. One of these imposes two additional prohibitions (beyond the need to comply with the categorical standards): specifically, it prohibits pretreaters from discharging any pollutants that will either "pass through" the POTW or "interfere" with its operation. 33 U.S.C. § 1317(b); see also 40 C.F.R. § 403.5. The first of these prohibitions is most relevant for those pretreaters who are in an industry with respect to which EPA has not yet set categorical standards. The second, perhaps obviously, is intended to ensure that the pretreater doesn't discharge anything that will interfere with the POTW's ability to do its primary job, which is to treat sewage.

The other twist worth mentioning is potential availability of what are called "removal credits." The basic idea here that a pretreater should be able to able to have its own treatment requirements relaxed if it can convince the POTW to remove some of its pollutants for it. See 33 U.S.C. § 1317(b), and 40 C.F.R. § 403.7. Under this framework, for example, ten pretreaters who discharge into the same POTW system might band together to convince the POTW to incorporate an additional treatment technology so that they may all be subject to reduced requirements. Indeed, they may even pay for the POTW's upgrade. In this manner, they may be able to take advantage of some economies of scale. The soft underbelly of the removal credits program, however, is that the POTW's sewage sludge may thereby become contaminated with heavy metals or other toxic substances. As a result of this threat, EPA has developed sewage sludge standards that POTWs must meet if they are to take part in the removal credits program. See 40 C.F.R. Part 503.

Last, and perhaps most significantly, the primary regulatory overseer under the pretreatment program is neither EPA nor the States, but rather the local POTWs. See, e.g., 40 C.F.R. § 403.8(f). In general, pretreaters are thus subject to subject to less-demanding monitoring requirements, fewer inspections, and less significant penalties where violations occur.

The pretreatment program is often criticized. See, e.g., Houck, Ending the War: A Strategy to Save America's Coastal Zone, 47 Md. L. Rev. 358 (1988). At the same time, there does not seem to be any likelihood of significant change any time soon.

2. Water Quality–Based Requirements

a. How Water Quality Standards are Set

The CWA's statutory provisions addressing the establishment of water quality standards are straightforward but bare bones. Section 303(c) requires the States to develop such standards, and notes that they are to consist of both the designated uses of the waters and the water quality criteria necessary to protect those uses. It further requires that "[s]uch standards shall be established taking into account [the waters'] use and value for public water supplies, propagation of fish and wildlife, recreational purposes, and agricultural, industrial and other purposes, also taking into consideration their use and value for navigation." Section 303(c) also requires the States to review their water quality standards at least every three years to see if they need revision, and to submit any proposed revisions to EPA.

EPA has three authorities that are relevant to the standard-setting process. First, Section 304(a) tasks EPA with developing "criteria for water quality accurately reflecting the latest scientific knowledge" regarding adverse effects of pollutants. These criteria serve as guidance to the States for the standards-setting process. Second, EPA has an oversight role which requires it to review any State standards or any revisions to those standards. 33 U.S.C. § 1313(c)(1)-(3). If EPA finds that any such standards do not meet the requirements of the Act, Section 303(c)(3) indicates that EPA is to specify the deficiencies and give the relevant State an opportunity to cure them. If the State fails to do so, Section 303(c)(4) provides that EPA is to promulgate a federal water quality standard for that water body. And third, as previously mentioned, Section 501 gives EPA the authority "to prescribe such regulations as are necessary to carry out [its] functions under this chapter."

The last relevant statutory provisions are the Act's goal and policy statements in Section 101. As mentioned at the beginning of this chapter, § 101(a) establishes that the primary objective of the Act is "to restore and maintain the chemical, physical, and biological integrity of the Nation's waters." And Section 101(a)(2) provides that, pending the complete cessation of all polluting discharges, it is "the national goal that wherever attainable, an interim goal of water quality which provides for the protection and propagation of fish, shellfish and wildlife and provides for recreation in and on the water shall be achieved by July 1, 1983."

Relying on § 501, EPA has written regulations fleshing out how it will judge State standard submissions. These regulations have several key components. First, they essentially require the States to designate for each water all of the uses specified in § 101(a)(2) (i.e., "fishable/swimmable") that qualify as either "existing uses" or that are "attainable" in that waterway. They do this by: (a) requiring the States to conduct a "use attainability analysis" (UAA) if they designate or have designated uses that do not include all of the uses specified in § 101(a)(2); and (b) precluding the States from removing any "existing use," which is defined as any use which has been attained in the relevant water body at any point since 1975. See 40 C.F.R. §§ 131.3(e) and 131.10(g), (h) and (j). In effect, the UAA requirement creates a rebuttable presumption that all of the § 101(a)(2) uses are attainable in all waters unless the State demonstrates otherwise. In order to justify leaving a § 101(a)(2) use off the list, the State must show both that it is not an "existing use" and that it meets one of several other narrow requirements, e.g., that imposing controls more stringent than the statute's technology-based requirements would result in substantial and widespread economic and economic and social impact. 40 C.F.R. § 131.10(g)

Second, EPA's regulations reiterate the CWA's command that the States adopt criteria to protect the designated uses. They elaborate on the nature of this requirement as follows:

> Such criteria must be based on sound scientific rationale and must contain sufficient parameters or constituents to protect the designated use. For waters with multiple use designations, the criteria shall support the most sensitive use.

40 C.F.R. § 131.11(a). Consistent with § 304(a), EPA has developed a series of suggested water quality criteria to assist the States in the standards-setting process. Its latest efforts in this regard are reflected in a document referred to as EPA's "Gold Book" of suggested criteria. EPA, Quality Criteria for Water (1986). While these criteria are not binding on the States, EPA may require the States to justify any less

stringent criteria. *Mississippi Commission on Natural Resources v. Costle*, 625 F.2d 1269 (1980) (*"Mississippi Commission"*).

It may help the student to think of the designated uses and the criteria set to protect them, collectively, as "traditional" water quality standards. Together, they should in theory result in standards that protect many aquatic uses. One problem with this approach, however, is that States tend to be very general in their specification of "designated uses." Beyond alluding to the general goals of § 101, EPA's Water Quality Handbook states only that "States should designate aquatic life uses that appropriately address biological integrity." As a result, States often designate uses with a fairly broad brush (e.g., designating a particular stream as "fishable"), which may or may not result in the establishment of criteria that are protective of all species of flora and fauna in a particular aquatic ecosystem.

Partly in response to this concern, EPA requires the States to augment the level of protection afforded by traditional water quality standards by adopting what is referred to as an "antidegradation" policy. See 40 C.F.R. § 131.12(a)(1)-(3). The court in *Ohio Valley Environmental Coalition v. Horinko*, 279 F.Supp.2d 732 (S.D.W.V. 2003) (*"Horinko"*), recently provided an excellent summation of these provisions and their effect:

> . . . These three provisions establish what are commonly referred to as three "tiers" of antidegradation protection. Tier 1 applies to all waters, and requires that existing water uses be protected. 40 C.F.R. § 131.12(a)(1). Tier 2 applies to high quality waters, defined as waters "[w]here the quality of the waters exceed levels necessary to support propagation of fish, shellfish, and wildlife and recreation in and on the water." *Id.* § 131.12(a)(2). In Tier 2 waters, water *quality* (as opposed to uses) "shall be maintained and protected" unless the State finds, after a process of public participation, "that allowing lower water quality is necessary to accommodate important economic or social development in the area in which the waters are located." *Id.* This process of public participation and a finding of economic or social necessity is known as Tier 2 review. Tier 3 applies to high quality waters that "constitute an outstanding National resource, such as waters of National and State parks and wildlife refuges and waters of exceptional recreational or ecological significance." *Id.* § 131.12(a)(3). In Tier 3 waters, "water quality shall be maintained and protected," with no exception for economic or social necessity. *Id.* . . .

Id. at 740 (emphasis in original).

Notes and Questions

1. As we will see, EPA sets nationally-applicable air quality standards under the Clean Air Act. Why do you think Congress chose to have the States set the relevant standards on a water-body by water-body basis under the CWA? Why do you think that Congress chose the two-pronged approach

of designating uses and then setting criteria to protect those uses. Why didn't Congress just require the States to set standards according to the most-demanding uses such as, for example, drinking water consumption?

2. Again, EPA can reject a State's standards if it finds that they do not meet the requirements of the Act. 33 U.S.C. § 1313(c)(3); see also *Mississippi Commission*, 625 F.2d at 1278 (upholding EPA's decision to reject a Mississippi standard). This is not to say, however, that EPA will invariably reject State standards that are significantly less protective than EPA's suggested criteria. In *NRDC v. EPA*, 16 F.3d 1395 (4th Cir. 1993), for example, the court upheld EPA's decision to approve Maryland and Virginia's dioxin standards despite the fact that they allowed dioxin concentrations nearly 1,000 times greater than EPA's suggested criteria. The court found that EPA did not act arbitrarily and capriciously in determining that, despite this disparity, the standards were scientifically defensible and protective of beneficial uses. Id. at 1405–1406.

3. Traditionally, States often have adopted narrative criteria in lieu of numeric ones. Common narrative criteria have included such statements as "no toxic pollutants in toxic amounts" and "no aesthetically displeasing conditions." In 1987, Congress limited this practice by requiring that the States adopt numerical criteria for toxic pollutants, where available. See 33 U.S.C. § 1313(c)(2)(B).

4. Although Section 303(c) speaks of water quality standards consisting of both designated uses and the criteria necessary to protect them, the Supreme Court has held that, at least in some situations, a designated use may be treated as a fully effective water quality standard, even if the relevant State has not set a criterion to protect it from a given risk. *PUD No. 1 of Jefferson County v. Washington Dept. of Ecology*, 511 U.S. 700, 713–718, 114 S.Ct. 1900, 1910–1912, 128 L.Ed.2d 716 (1994) (*"Jefferson County"*). We will return to this issue when we consider this case, below.

5. Another problem posed by traditional water quality standards is that, even in situations in which the States may divide water bodies such as rivers into segments (usually by river mile), they tend to treat such segments as homogeneous ecosystems, instead of as complex systems they are, setting a single criterion for each pollutant for that segment. While such a criterion may make sense for the middle of the water column, it may make little sense for any associated wetlands. It also may ignore other issues such as, for example, temperature stratification or the accumulation of some pollutants (e.g., heavy metals or dioxin) in river sediments. With prompting by EPA, some States have begun to address some of these concerns. It has proven to be a slow process, however, and EPA has been reluctant to push very hard.

6. In 1983, EPA acknowledged that there was no explicit requirement for an antidegradation policy in the CWA. It indicated its view, however, that the policy "is consistent with the spirit, intent, and goals of the Act, especially the clause" ... restore and *maintain* the chemical, physical and biological integrity of the Nation's waters (§ 101(a).... EPA, Questions and Answers on Antidegradation, p. 1 (1983) ("Questions and Answers") (emphasis in original), available at www.epa.gov/waterscience/ library/wqstandards/antidegqa.pdf. Congress embraced this policy in 1987, specifically requiring that at least certain water-quality based effluent limitations con-

form with it. See 33 U.S.C. § 1313(d)(4)(B); see also *Jefferson County*, 511 U.S. at 705, 114 S.Ct. at 1905–1906.

7. As alluded to above, one purpose of the antidegradation policy is to fill in gaps that may be present under the "traditional" water quality standards. Tier 1 does this by requiring the States to protect all "existing uses" regardless of whether they are reflected in the relevant water quality standards. EPA explains in the Questions and Answers document:

> No activity is allowable under the antidegradation policy which would partially or completely eliminate any existing use whether or not that use is designated in a State's water quality standards.... Species that are in the water body and which are consistent with the designated use (i.e., not aberrational) must be protected, even if not prevalent in number or importance. Nor can activity be allowed which would render the species unfit for maintaining the use. Water quality should be such that it results in no mortality and no significant growth or reproductive impairment of resident species.... An existing aquatic community composed entirely of invertebrates and plants, such as may be found in a pristine alpine stream, should still be protected whether or not such stream supports a fishery....

Questions and Answers, p. 3. What is the regulatory significance of this guidance document?

8. As indicated in *Horinko*, Tiers 2 and 3 provide higher levels of protection for those water bodies that are cleaner than necessary to protect existing uses. The basic idea is to keep pristine waters pristine. As a policy matter, does this requirement make sense? Why are we interested in protecting water quality independent of any desire to protect the "uses" of those waters, broadly defined to include the health of all resident species, flora and fauna? Can one argue that we should be directing new growth to these areas, where there is excess assimilative capacity?

9. There are many unresolved questions regarding the effect of the antidegradation policy in certain contexts. These include, for example: (1) How does it apply in situations in which a water body supported a use in 1975 (again, a use will be deemed to be an "existing use" if it existed on or after that date), but where the use was impaired at that time? Does the state have to provide the use will full protection, or only the level to which it was protected in 1975?; (2) How does the policy apply to existing pollutant loadings from individual plants that have remained unchanged, but where the uses may now be impaired by, for example, the combined effect of that load and those from other sources that may or may not be more difficult to control?; and (3) How does it apply, more generally, to loadings from nonpoint sources (e.g. sediment in stormwater runoff)? On this last point, compare Questions and Answers, at p.6, with *American Wildlands v. Browner*, 260 F.3d 1192 (10th Cir. 2001).

b. How Water Quality Standards are Implemented for Point Sources

Section 301(b)(1)(c) of the CWA indicates that permits must ensure compliance with water quality standards. EPA has three separate regulatory provisions implementing this requirement. First, 40 C.F.R.

§ 122.4(d) precludes the issuance of any permit "when the imposition of conditions cannot ensure compliance with the applicable water quality requirements of all affected States." Second, 40 C.F.R. § 122.4(i) specifically precludes the issuance of permits to new sources if their discharges will cause or contribute to water quality standard violations. It further requires these would-be sources to make specific showings, as a precondition to receiving a permit, if the relevant water body already exceeds a standard, and if the State has performed what is called a "pollutant loads allocation" for the relevant pollutant. See 40 C.F.R. § 122.4(i). And finally, 40 C.F.R. § 122.44(d) requires permit issuers to determine whether any permit applicant's discharge "will cause, have the reasonable potential to cause, or contribute to an excursion above any State water quality standard, including State narrative criteria for water quality." If so, the permit must include conditions ensuring compliance with those standards. Id.

Permit issuers, including both the States and EPA, implement these requirements with varying degrees of rigor. In best-case situations, they will essentially undertake what is called "total maximum daily load" ("TMDL") analysis, whether or not they do so under the formal auspices of the TMDL program. Since the TMDL program transcends point source discharges, we reserve full consideration of it for a few more pages. For present purposes, it is sufficient to note that, in performing this type of analysis, the permit issuer will first determine how much of the particular pollutant the relevant water body can assimilate on a daily basis without violating the relevant standard. Narrowly speaking, this is the actual TMDL. More broadly speaking, however, the TMDL analysis moves on to consider all of the inputs (both point and nonpoint) of the relevant pollutant into that water body. The permit issuer will then divide up the maximum daily load among all of these sources, in theory determining each source's "fair share" of a compliant load. Since many States have no effective regulatory programs relating to non-point sources, and EPA has none, in many cases the State must essentially assume all known nonpoint source loads as a given, and divide up the rest of the rest of the available allotment among the point source contributors.

As one might imagine, however, this is a resource-intensive process. Indeed, laying the scientific groundwork for establishing a TMDL for even a single pollutant on a single river may in some cases cost hundreds of thousands of dollars. Not surprisingly, many permit issuers are loath to engage in that kind of analysis in the context of individual permit applications. As a result, they tend to take one of two potential shortcuts. First, some permit issuers analyze the impacts of the applicant's proposed discharge in isolation in determining its impact on water quality; that is, they model the impact of the applicant's discharge on water quality standards, without taking into account other sources of the same pollutant. Perhaps obviously, such an approach does not serve the regulatory prohibition on discharges that *contribute* to violations of water quality standards. Second, some permit issuers rely on narrative prohibitions to the exclusion of numeric requirements (although some also use them to supplement such requirements). A typical permit condition of this type might simply state that "no wastes shall be discharged ... which will violate [water quality standards]." See, e.g., *Northwest Environmental Advocates v. City of Portland*, 56 F.3d 979, 985 (9th Cir. 1995), *reh'g den.*, 74 F.3d 945, *cert. den.* 518 U.S. 1018, 116 S.Ct. 2550, 135 L.Ed.2d 1069 (1996) (*"City of Portland"*).

There is scant case law regarding the legal propriety of these shortcuts. The Ninth Circuit has issued two opinions touching on these matters. First, in *Trustees for Alaska v. Environmental Protection Agency*, 749 F.2d 549, 557 (9th Cir. 1986), it held that regulators have an obligation to establish numeric water quality-based permit conditions, where feasible. And second, in *City of Portland*, it held that citizens may enforce narrative permit conditions of the type described above in citizen suits under § 505. 56 F.3d at 986–990.

The following Supreme Court opinion addresses the effect of § 301(b)(1)(C) on dischargers in upstream States in situations in which their discharges may pose water quality concerns in downstream States:

ARKANSAS v. OKLAHOMA

Supreme Court of the United States, 1992.

503 U.S. 91, 112 S.Ct. 1046, 117 L.Ed.2d 239.

Justice STEVENS delivered the opinion of the Court.

In 1985, the City of Fayetteville, Arkansas, applied to the EPA, seeking [an NPDES] permit for the City's new sewage treatment plant.... [EPA issued] a permit authorizing the plant to discharge up to half of its effluent ... into an unnamed stream in northwestern Arkansas. That flow passes through a series of three creeks for about 17 miles, and then enters the Illinois River at a point 22 miles upstream from the Arkansas–Oklahoma border.

Respondents challenged this permit before the EPA, alleging, inter alia, that the discharge violated the Oklahoma water quality standards. Those standards provide that "no degradation [of water quality] shall be allowed" in the upper Illinois River, including the portion of the River immediately downstream from the state line.

Following a hearing, the [ALJ] concluded that the Oklahoma standards would not be implicated unless the contested discharge had "something more than a mere *de minimis* impact" on the State's waters. He found that the discharge would not have an "undue impact" on Oklahoma's waters and, accordingly, affirmed the issuance of the permit.

On a petition for review, the EPA's Chief Judicial Officer ["CJO"] first ruled that [§ 301(b)(1)(c)] "requires an NPDES permit to impose any effluent limitations necessary to comply with applicable state water quality standards." He then held that the Act and EPA regulations offered greater protection for the downstream State than the ALJ's "undue impact" standard suggested. He explained the proper standard as follows:

> "[A] mere theoretical impairment of Oklahoma's water quality standards—i.e., an infinitesimal impairment predicted through modeling but not expected to be actually detectable or measurable—should not by itself block the issuance of the permit. In this case, the permit should be upheld if the record shows by a preponderance of the evidence that the authorized discharges would not cause an actual *detectable* violation of Oklahoma's water quality standards." (Emphasis in original).

On remand, the ALJ made detailed findings of fact and concluded that the City had satisfied the standard set forth by the [CJO]. Specifically, the ALJ found that there would be no detectable violation of any of the components of Oklahoma's water quality standards. The [CJO] sustained the issuance of the permit.

Both the petitioners (collectively Arkansas) and the respondents in this litigation sought judicial review. Arkansas argued that the [CWA] did not require an Arkansas point source to comply with Oklahoma's water quality standards. Oklahoma challenged the EPA's determination that the Fayetteville discharge would not produce a detectable violation of the Oklahoma standards.

The Court of Appeals did not accept either of these arguments. The court agreed with the EPA that the statute required compliance with Oklahoma's water quality standards, and did not disagree with the Agency's determination that the discharges from the Fayetteville plant would not produce a detectable violation of those standards. Nevertheless, relying on a theory that neither party had advanced, the Court of Appeals reversed the Agency's issuance of the Fayetteville permit. The court first ruled that the statute requires that "where a proposed source would discharge effluents that would contribute to conditions currently constituting a violation of applicable water quality standards, such [a] proposed source may not be permitted." Then the court found that the Illinois River in Oklahoma was "already degraded," that the Fayetteville effluent would reach the Illinois River in Oklahoma, and that that effluent could "be expected to contribute to the ongoing deterioration of the scenic [Illinois R]iver" in Oklahoma even though it would not detectably affect the River's water quality.

IV

The parties have argued three analytically distinct questions concerning the interpretation of the [CWA]. First, does the Act require the EPA, in crafting and issuing a permit to a point source in one State, to apply the water quality standards of downstream States? Second, even if the Act does not require as much, does the Agency have the statutory authority to mandate such compliance? Third, does the Act provide, as the Court of Appeals held, that once a body of water fails to meet water quality standards no discharge that yields effluent that reach the degraded waters will be permitted?

In this case, it is neither necessary nor prudent for us to resolve the first of these questions. In issuing the Fayetteville permit, the EPA assumed it was obligated by both the Act and its own regulations to ensure that the Fayetteville discharge would not violate Oklahoma's standards. As we discuss below, this assumption was permissible and reasonable and therefore there is no need for us to address whether the Act requires as much. . . .

Our decision not to determine at this time the scope of the Agency's statutory *obligations* does not affect our resolution of the second question, which concerns the Agency's statutory *authority*. Even if the [CWA] does not require the Fayetteville discharge to comply with Oklahoma's water quality standards, the statute clearly does not limit the EPA's authority to mandate such compliance.

Since 1973, EPA regulations have provided that an NPDES permit shall not be issued "[w]hen the imposition of conditions cannot ensure compliance with the applicable water quality requirements of all affected States." 40 CFR § 122.4(d); *see also* 40 CFR § 122.44(d) (1991). Those regulations—relied upon by the EPA in the issuance of the Fayetteville permit—constitute a reasonable exercise of the Agency's statutory authority.

Congress has vested in the Administrator broad discretion to establish conditions for NPDES permits. Section 402(a)(2) provides that for EPA-issued permits "[t]he Administrator shall prescribe conditions for such permits to assure compliance with the requirements of [§ 402(a)(1)] and *such other requirements as he deems appropriate*." 33 U.S.C. § 1342(a)(2) (emphasis supplied). Similarly, Congress preserved for the Administrator broad authority to oversee state permit programs: "No permit shall issue . . . if the Administrator . . . objects in writing to the issuance of such permit as being outside the guidelines and requirements of this chapter." 33 U.S.C. § 1342(d)(2).

The regulations relied on by the EPA were a perfectly reasonable exercise of the Agency's statutory discretion. The application of state water quality standards in the interstate context is wholly consistent with the Act's broad purpose, "to restore and maintain the chemical, physical, and biological integrity of the Nation's waters." 33 U.S.C. § 1251(a). Moreover, . . . § 301(b)(1)(C) expressly identifies the achievement of state water quality standards as one of the Act's central objectives. The Agency's regulations conditioning NPDES permits are a well-tailored means of achieving this goal.

Notwithstanding this apparent reasonableness, Arkansas argues that our description in [*International Paper Co. v. Ouellette*, 479 U.S. 481 (1987),] of the role of affected States in the permit process and our characterization of the affected States' position as "subordinate," *see* [479 U.S. at 490–491], indicates that the EPA's application of the Oklahoma standards was error. We disagree. Our statement in *Ouellette* concerned only an affected State's input into the permit process; that input is clearly limited by the plain language of § 402(b). Limits on an affected State's direct participation in permitting decisions, however, do not in any way constrain the EPA's authority to require a point source to comply with downstream water quality standards.

... Arkansas emphasizes that § 510 preserves [state authority to adopt more demanding pollution-control standards] only as it is applied to the waters of the regulating State. Even assuming [this] is correct, ... that section only concerns state authority and does not constrain the EPA's authority to promulgate reasonable regulations requiring point sources in one State to comply with water quality standards in downstream States.

For these reasons, we find the EPA's requirement that the Fayetteville discharge comply with Oklahoma's water quality standards to be a reasonable exercise of the Agency's substantial statutory discretion.

V

The Court of Appeals construed the [CWA] to prohibit any discharge of effluent that would reach waters already in violation of existing water quality standards. We find nothing in the Act to support this reading.

Although the Act contains several provisions directing compliance with state water quality standards, see, e.g., 33 U.S.C. § 1311(b)(1)(c), the parties have pointed to nothing that mandates a complete ban on discharges into a waterway that is in violation of those standards. The statute does, however, contain provisions designed to remedy existing water quality violations and to allocate the burden of reducing undesirable discharges between existing sources and new sources. *See, e.g.*, 33 U.S.C. § 1313(d). Thus, rather than establishing the categorical ban announced by the Court of Appeals—which might frustrate the construction of new plants that would improve existing conditions—the [CWA] vests in the EPA and the States broad authority to develop long-range, area-wide programs to alleviate and eliminate existing pollution. See 33 U.S.C. § 1288(b)(2).

To the extent that the Court of Appeals relied on its interpretation of the Act to reverse the EPA's permitting decision, that reliance was misplaced.

VI

The Court of Appeals also concluded that the EPA's issuance of the Fayetteville permit was arbitrary and capricious because the Agency misinterpreted Oklahoma's water quality standards. The primary difference between the court's and the Agency's interpretation of the standards derives from the court's construction of the Act. Contrary to the EPA's interpretation of the Oklahoma standards, the Court of Appeals read those standards as containing the same categorical ban on new discharges that the court had found in the [CWA]. Although we do not believe the text of the Oklahoma standards supports the court's reading

... , we reject it for a more fundamental reason—namely, that the Court of Appeals exceeded the legitimate scope of judicial review of an agency adjudication....

As discussed above, EPA regulations require an NPDES permit to comply "with the applicable water quality requirements of all affected States." 40 CFR § 122.4(d). This regulation effectively incorporates into federal law those state law standards the Agency reasonably determines to be "applicable." In such a situation, then, state water quality standards—promulgated by the States with substantial guidance from the EPA and approved by the Agency—are part of the federal law of water pollution control.

Two features of the body of law governing water pollution support this conclusion. First, we have long recognized that interstate water pollution is controlled by federal law. Recognizing that the system of federally approved state standards as applied in the interstate context constitutes federal law is wholly consistent with this principle. Second, treating state standards in interstate controversies as federal law accords with the Act's purpose of authorizing the EPA to create and manage a uniform system of interstate water pollution regulation.

Because we recognize that, at least insofar as they affect the issuance of a permit in another State, the Oklahoma standards have a federal character, the EPA's reasonable, consistently held interpretation of those standards is entitled to substantial deference. In this case, the [CJO] ruled that the Oklahoma standards—which require that there be "no degradation" of the upper Illinois River—would only be violated if the discharge effected an "actually detectable or measurable" change in water quality.

This interpretation of the Oklahoma standards is certainly reasonable and consistent with the purposes and principles of the [CWA]. As the [CJO] noted, "unless there is some method for measuring compliance, there is no way to ensure compliance." Moreover, this interpretation of the Oklahoma standards makes eminent sense in the interstate context: if every discharge that had some theoretical impact on a downstream State were interpreted as "degrading" the downstream waters, downstream States might wield an effective veto over upstream discharges.

The EPA's application of those standards in this case was also sound. On remand, the ALJ scrutinized the record and made explicit factual findings regarding four primary measures of water quality under the Oklahoma standards: eutrophication, aesthetics, dissolved oxygen, and metals. In each case, the ALJ found that the Fayetteville discharge would not lead to a detectable change in water quality. He therefore concluded that the Fayetteville discharge would not violate the Oklahoma water quality standards. Because we agree with the [CJO] that these findings are supported by substantial evidence, we conclude that the Court of Appeals should have affirmed both the EPA's construction of the regulations and the issuance of the Fayetteville permit....

In sum, the Court of Appeals made a policy choice that it was not authorized to make. Arguably, as that court suggested, it might be wise to prohibit any discharge into the Illinois River, even if that discharge would have no adverse impact on water quality. But it was surely not arbitrary for the EPA to conclude—given the benefits to the River from the increased flow of relatively clean water and the benefits achieved in Arkansas by allowing the new plant to operate as designed—that allowing the discharge would be even wiser. It is not our role, or that of the Court of Appeals, to decide which policy choice is the better one, for it is clear that Congress has entrusted such decisions to [EPA].

Questions and Notes

1. As mentioned above, we will put off detailed consideration of the TMDL program for a few more pages because it transcends point sources. It is worth noting, however, that in 1987 Congress prioritized in § 304(*l*) what is essentially a mini-TMDL program for toxic pollutants. Under that provision, States were required to identify the stream segments within their boundaries that were not meeting toxics-related water quality standards, to identify the point sources contributing to those problems, and to develop "individual control strateg[ies]" for those sources which would result in the achievement of those standards within three years. 33 U.S.C. § 1314(*l*). While conceptually identical to the TMDL program, Section 304(*l*) differs in that (a) it relates only to point sources, and (b) it has aggressive statutory deadlines. For a good example of a case involving the § 304(*l*) program at work, see *Dioxin/Organochlorine Center v. Clarke*, 57 F.3d 1517 (9th Cir. 1995).

2. EPA allows the States to establish what are referred to as "mixing zones" in their water quality standards. 40 C.F.R. § 131.13. These are best viewed as implementation devices designed to allow for the consideration of a water body's assimilative capacity in determining whether a particular discharge will cause or contribute to violations of water quality standards. The Tenth Circuit further explained this concept in *American Wildlands v. Browner*, 260 F.3d 1192 (10th Cir. 2001):

> ... Mixing zones are "areas where an effluent discharge undergoes initial dilution and are extended to cover the secondary mixing in the ambient water body. A mixing zone is an allocated impact zone where acute and chronic water quality criteria can be exceeded as long as a number of protections are maintained." EPA, Water Quality Standards Handbook § 5.1.1, at 5–5 (2d ed.1994). The protections that must be maintained include the absence of "toxic conditions to aquatic life," "objectionable deposits," "floating debris," "objectionable color, odor, taste, or turbidity," and substances resulting in "a dominance of nuisance species." Id. at 5–5 to 5–6. Mixing zones are allowable as a practical necessity because "[i]t is not always necessary to meet all water quality criteria within the discharge pipe to protect the integrity of the water body as a whole. Sometimes it is appropriate to allow for ambient concentrations above the criteria in small areas near outfalls." Id. § 5.1, at 5–1.

Id. at 1195. Typically, mixing zones are quite small (e.g. a radius of 100 feet). Some States have been known to abuse this concept, however, by establishing mixing zones that encompass long reaches of entire streams.

3. As also mentioned above, in the *City of Portland* case the Ninth Circuit held that citizens can enforce narrative water quality-based permit conditions. In responding to Portland's argument that these conditions are too vague to be enforceable, the court pointed out that:

> The plain language of CWA § 505 authorizes citizens to enforce *all* permit conditions. That section provides: "[A]ny citizen may commence a civil action . . . (1) against any person . . . who is alleged to be in violation of (A) an effluent standard or limitation under [the Clean Water Act]. . . ." 33 U.S.C. § 1365(a)(1)(A). An effluent standard or limitation includes "(2) an effluent limitation or other limitation under section 1311 . . . *or* (6) a permit or condition thereof. . . ." 33 U.S.C. § 1365(f)(2), (f)(6) (emphasis added). This language clearly contemplates citizen suits to enforce "a permit or condition thereof." Portland holds [an NPDES permit], and the water quality standards are conditions of its permit.

56 F.3d at 986 (emphasis in original). The court further reasoned that:

> . . . Congress recognized that water quality standards "often cannot be translated into effluent limitations. . . ." For example, certain water quality standards cannot be expressed quantitatively, such as those that apply in this case to bacterial pollution, aesthetic conditions, and objectionable matter (scum, oily sleek, foul odors, and floating solids). . . .
>
> By interpreting § 505 to exclude citizen suit enforcement of water quality standards that are not translated into quantitative limitations, Portland would have us immunize the entire body of qualitative regulations from an important enforcement tool. Such a result would be especially troubling in this case, because no effluent limitations cover the discharges from Portland's combined sewer overflows ("CSOs").

Id. at 989.

In dissent, Judge Kleinfeld bemoaned the illogic of allowing citizens to enforce narrative conditions:

> Water quality standards are a useful device for government enforcement authorities . . ., because they provide standards for effluent limitations and goals toward which enforcement should be aimed. They are too uncertain and amorphous, however, for use against specific polluters. Suppose, hypothetically, that a water quality standard allows for 100 units of a pollutant, upstream and non-point source polluters discharge 50 units, and the downstream discharger is permitted to discharge 50 units. If the upstream and non-point source polluters increase their discharge to 80 units, it does not automatically follow that the downstream discharger should be limited to 20. The burdens of so severe a limitation may exceed the burdens of the extra pollution, or enforcement efforts might more appropriately be directed at the other polluters. In the case at bar, the majority concedes that the social costs of filling the streets and basements of Portland with sewage, or spending between a half billion and $1.2 billion dollars on renovation, are the practical

> alternatives to tolerating violations of the water quality standards. A
> public authority might rationally decide that filling the streets and
> basements with sewage is worse than polluting the river with it, and
> that the citizens of Portland need several years to raise and spend the
> money necessary to avoid running the sewage into the streets, the
> basements, and the river.

Id. at 992. Is this lament primarily about the enforceability of narrative
conditions or the wisdom of allowing citizens to pursue enforcement in
situations in which governmental entities have chosen not to proceed? To
the extent that it is the former, can it be squared with the language of
§ 505(f)(6)? See also CWA § 309(d) (allowing EPA to pursue penalties for
any violation of permit conditions). To the extent that it is the latter, can it
be squared with the very existence of citizen suits?

What are the real world implications of *City of Portland*? If you were
representing a discharger, might the court's decision encourage you to seek
numeric water quality-based permit conditions? Why or why not?

4. Reread § 301(b)(1)(C). Do you agree with the Supreme Court that it
can reasonably be interpreted as requiring compliance with the water quality
standards of downstream States? What water quality standard was at issue
in *Arkansas v. Oklahoma*? What was the Illinois' actual status (in terms of
pollution)? Note that merely listing a river as a "Tier 3" water does not by
itself guarantee that river will never become degraded. Note also that the
fact that the Illinois became degraded (presumably after it was designated as
a Tier 3 water) did not prevent it from being entitled to that heightened
degree of protection.

5. Would EPA's regulation have required compliance with the Oklahoma standard even if that standard had been much more stringent than
anything contemplated in EPA's criteria (e.g., if it contained a narrative
prohibition on any discharges of treated or untreated human waste)? In
Ouellette, the Supreme Court had held that, while § 510 preserves State
common law claims, it only does so to the extent that those claims are based
on the common law of the State in which the discharge occurs. It held that
the plaintiffs in that case could not apply Vermont common law to a New
York facility's discharges into Lake Champlain. 479 U.S. at 495–496, 107
S.Ct. at 813–814. In reaching this conclusion, the Court reasoned that "[i]f a
New York source were liable for violations of Vermont law, that law could
effectively override both the permit requirements and the policy choices
made by the source State." Id. at 495, 107 S.Ct. at 813. Read § 510. Do you
agree with the result in *Ouellette*? Can you square the outcome in that case
with the result in Part IV of *Arkansas v. Oklahoma*?

6. What do you make of the discussion in Part V of the Court's
opinion? How do you square it with § 301(b)(1)(C), as interpreted by 40
C.F.R. § 122.4(i)? Was this a situation in which the Court likely was simply
unaware of EPA's regulation (which it did not cite)? Does the Court's
analysis effectively overrule that provision? Remember that EPA was the
permit issuer in *Arkansas v. Oklahoma* (Arkansas was unauthorized at the
time). How do you think EPA would square its permit issuance with
§ 122.4(i)?

7. Why, in Part VI, did the Court determine that EPA' interpretation of the Oklahoma antidegradation policy was entitled to deference? Do you think the Court would have applied the same deference with respect to an Oklahoma discharger? Imagine, for example, a different situation in which EPA is reading a State's ambiguous water quality standard more strictly than the State is. If EPA vetoed a permit that the State proposed to issue to an in-state discharger, and the dispute rose all the way to the Supreme Court, to whose interpretation of the relevant standard do you think the Court would defer, if anyone's?

8. What did you think of EPA's interpretation of the Oklahoma standard in *Arkansas v. Oklahoma*? If we know for certain (through modeling) that some of the pollution will get down to Oklahoma, won't it "contribute" to a violation of Oklahoma's non-degradation provision? Did EPA, with the Supreme Court's blessing, essentially create a de minimis exception to the antidegradation policy? Is such an exception necessary? Is it at least reasonable? Do you think the same approach would or should apply to numeric water quality standards? How would such an approach apply to a pollutant like dioxin, where the water quality standards of several States (and EPA's suggested criterion) are set at 0.013 parts per quadrillion, which is nearly 1,000 times below the level of detection?

9. What is the take-away principle from *Arkansas v. Oklahoma*? Is it clear that new or expanded discharges are prohibited if: (a) the river already violates the water quality standard for a given pollutant; and (b) the new or increased load will result in detectable increases of that pollutant? Can you argue that the holding in the case is limited to interstate scenarios; i.e, that even non-detectable additions may be prohibited if the discharger is discharging directly into the waters that already violate water quality standards?

D. Other Water Quality–Based Programs Under the CWA

We now turn our attention to four different aspects of the CWA that are designed to address water quality concerns, but which transcend the NPDES program. As we will see, the first and the last of these, Sections 401 and 303(d), overlap with the NPDES program in at least some of their applications. By contrast, the other two, §§ 208 and 319, address only nonpoint sources. Given their non-regulatory nature, we will treat them together and our consideration of them will be quite brief.

1. § 401 Certifications

Section 401(a) of the CWA requires any applicant for a Federal license or permit, if its activity will result in a discharge into the navigable waters, to provide the licensing or permitting authority with a certification from the State in which the discharge originates that the discharge will comply with several requirements of the CWA, most notably the water quality standard requirements under § 303. This provision has the effect of keeping the States in the forefront, vis-a-vis water quality concerns, even if they are unauthorized and hence are not issuing the relevant NPDES permits. Moreover, the § 401 certification requirement transcends the NPDES world, applying, for example, to

§ 404 permits issued by the Corps of Engineers under the wetlands program and licenses issued by the Federal Energy Regulatory Commission ("FERC") under the Federal Power Act, 16 U.S.C. § 791 et seq.

Consider the following decision:

PUD NO. 1 OF JEFFERSON COUNTY v. WASHINGTON DEPT. OF ECOLOGY

Supreme Court of the United States, 1994.

511 U.S. 700, 114 S.Ct. 1900, 128 L.Ed.2d 716.

JUSTICE O'CONNOR delivered the opinion of the Court.

Petitioners, [a city and a local utility district], propose to build the Elkhorn Hydroelectric Project on the Dosewallips River. If constructed as presently planned, the facility would be located just outside the Olympic National Park on federally owned land within the Olympic National Forest. The project would divert water from a 1.2–mile reach of the River (the bypass reach), run the water through turbines to generate electricity and then return the water to the River below the bypass reach.... [Because this project requires a FERC license, and because it] may result in discharges into the Dosewallips River, petitioners are ... required to obtain State certification of the project pursuant to § 401 of the CWA.

The water flow in the bypass reach, which is currently undiminished by appropriation, ranges seasonally between 149 and 738 cubic feet per second (cfs). The Dosewallips supports two species of salmon, Coho and Chinook, as well as Steelhead trout. As originally proposed, the project was to include a diversion dam which would completely block the river and channel approximately 75% of the River's water into a tunnel alongside the streambed. About 25% of the water would remain in the bypass reach, but would be returned to the original riverbed through sluice gates or a fish ladder. Depending on the season, this would leave a residual minimum flow of between 65 and 155 cfs in the River. Respondent undertook a study to determine the minimum stream flows necessary to protect the salmon and steelhead fisheries in the bypass reach. On June 11, 1986, respondent issued a § 401 water quality certification imposing a variety of conditions on the project, including a minimum stream-flow requirement of between 100 and 200 cfs depending on the season.

[After preliminary appeals in both the State administrative and judicial systems, the case reached the Washington Supreme Court. There, the court held that the State's antidegradation provisions] require the imposition of minimum stream flows. The court also found that § 401(d), which allows States to impose conditions based upon several enumerated sections of the CWA and "any other appropriate requirement of State law," authorized the stream flow condition....

The principal dispute in this case concerns whether the minimum stream flow requirement that the State imposed on the Elkhorn project is a permissible condition of a § 401 certification under the CWA. To resolve this dispute we must first determine the scope of the State's authority under § 401. We must then determine whether the limitation at issue here, the requirement that petitioners maintain minimum stream flows, falls within the scope of that authority.

. . . Petitioners concede that, at a minimum, the project will result in two possible discharges-the release of dredged and fill material during the construction of the project, and the discharge of water at the end of the tailrace after the water has been used to generate electricity. Petitioners contend, however, that the minimum stream flow requirement imposed by the State was unrelated to these specific discharges. . . .

If § 401 consisted solely of subsection (a), which refers to a state certification that a "discharge" will comply with certain provisions of the Act, petitioners' assessment of the scope of the State's certification authority would have considerable force. Section 401, however, also contains subsection (d), which expands the State's authority to impose conditions on the certification of a project. Section 401(d) provides that any certification shall set forth "any effluent limitations and other limitations . . . necessary to assure that any applicant" will comply with various provisions of the Act and appropriate state law requirements. The language of this subsection contradicts petitioners' claim that the State may only impose water quality limitations specifically tied to a "discharge." The text refers to the compliance of the applicant, not the discharge. Section 401(d) thus allows the State to impose "other limitations" on the project in general to assure compliance with various provisions of the CWA and with "any other appropriate requirement of State law." Although the dissent asserts that this interpretation of § 401(d) renders § 401(a)(1) superfluous, we see no such anomaly. Section 401(a)(1) identifies the category of activities subject to certification namely those with discharges. And § 401(d) is most reasonably read as authorizing additional conditions and limitations on the activity as a whole once the threshold condition, the existence of a discharge, is satisfied.

Our view of the statute is consistent with EPA's regulations implementing § 401. The regulations expressly interpret § 401 as requiring the State to find that "there is a reasonable assurance that the activity will be conducted in a manner which will not violate applicable water quality standards." 40 CFR § 121.2(a)(3) (1992). EPA's conclusion that activities-not merely discharges-must comply with state water quality standards is a reasonable interpretation of § 401, and is entitled to deference.

Although § 401(d) authorizes the State to place restrictions on the activity as a whole, that authority is not unbounded. The State can only ensure that the project complies with "any applicable effluent limitations and other limitations, under [33 U.S.C. §§ 1311, 1312]" or certain other provisions of the Act, "and with any other appropriate requirement of State law." 33 U.S.C. § 1341(d). The State asserts that the minimum stream flow requirement was imposed to ensure compliance with the state water quality standards adopted pursuant to § 303 of the CWA.

We agree with the State that ensuring compliance with § 303 is a proper function of the § 401 certification. Although § 303 is not one of the statutory provisions listed in § 401(d), the statute allows states to impose limitations to ensure compliance with § 301 of the Act. Section 301 in turn incorporates § 303 by reference. *See* 33 U.S.C. § 1311(b)(1)(C). As a consequence, state water quality standards adopted pursuant to § 303 are among the "other limitations" with which a State may ensure compliance through the § 401 certification process. This interpretation is consistent with EPA's view of the statute. *See* 40 CFR § 121.2(a)(3) (1992). Moreover, limitations to assure compliance with state water quality standards are also permitted by § 401(d)'s reference to "any other appropriate requirement of State law." We do not speculate on what additional state laws, if any, might be incorporated by this language. But at a minimum, limitations imposed pursuant to state water quality standards adopted pursuant to § 303 are "appropriate" requirements of state law. . . .

Having concluded that, pursuant to § 401, States may condition certification upon any limitations necessary to ensure compliance with state water quality standards or any other "appropriate requirement of State law," we consider whether the minimum flow condition is such a limitation. Under § 303, state water quality standards must "consist of the designated uses of the navigable waters involved and the water quality criteria for such waters based upon such uses." In imposing the minimum stream flow requirement, the State determined that construction and operation of the project as planned would be inconsistent with one of the designated uses of Class AA water, namely "[s]almonid [and other fish] migration, rearing, spawning, and harvesting. . . ."

Petitioners assert, however, that § 303 requires the State to protect designated uses solely through implementation of specific "criteria." According to petitioners, the State may not require them to operate their dam in a manner consistent with a designated "use"; instead, say petitioners, under § 303 the State may only require that the project comply with specific numerical "criteria."

We disagree with petitioners' interpretation of the language of § 303(c)(2)(A). Under the statute, a water quality standard must "consist of the designated uses of the navigable waters involved and the water quality criteria for such waters based upon such uses." 33 U.S.C. § 1313(c)(2)(A). The text makes it plain that water quality standards contain two components. We think the language of § 303 is most naturally read to require that a project be consistent with both components, namely the designated use and the water quality criteria. Accordingly, under the literal terms of the statute, a project that does not comply with a designated use of the water does not comply with the applicable water quality standards.

Consequently, pursuant to § 401(d) the State may require that a permit applicant comply with both the designated uses and the water quality criteria of the state standards. In granting certification pursuant to § 401(d), the State "shall set forth any ... limitations ... necessary to assure that [the applicant] will comply with any ... limitations under [§ 303] ... and with any other appropriate requirement of State law." A certification requirement that an applicant operate the project consistently with state water quality standards-i.e., consistently with the designated uses of the water body and the water quality criteria-is both a "limitation" to assure "compliance with ... limitations" imposed under § 303, and an "appropriate" requirement of State law.

EPA has not interpreted § 303 to require the States to protect designated uses exclusively through enforcement of numerical criteria. In its regulations governing state water quality standards, EPA defines criteria as "elements of State water quality standards expressed as constituent concentrations, levels, or narrative statements, representing a quality of water that supports a particular use." § 40 CFR 131.3(b) (1992)(emphasis added). The regulations further provide that "[w]hen criteria are met, water quality will generally protect the designated use." Ibid. Thus, the EPA regulations implicitly recognize that in some circumstances, criteria alone are insufficient to protect a designated use.

Petitioners also appear to argue that use requirements are too open-ended, and that the Act only contemplates enforcement of the more specific and objective "criteria." But this argument is belied by the open-ended nature of the criteria themselves. As the Solicitor General points out, even "criteria" are often expressed in broad, narrative terms, such as " 'there shall be no discharge of toxic pollutants in toxic amounts.' " Brief for United States 18. In fact, under the CWA, only one class of criteria, those governing "toxic pollutants listed pursuant to section 1317(a)(1)" need be rendered in numerical form. *See* 33 U.S.C. § 1313(c)(2)(B); 40 CFR § 131.11(b)(2) (1992).

Washington's Class AA water quality standards are typical in that they contain several open-ended criteria which, like the use designation of the River as a fishery, must be translated into specific limitations for individual projects. For example, the standards state that "[t]oxic, radioactive, or deleterious material concentrations shall be less than those which may affect public health, the natural aquatic environment, or the desirability of the water for any use." Similarly, the state standards specify that "[a]esthetic values shall not be impaired by the presence of materials or their effects, excluding those of natural origin, which offend the senses of sight, smell, touch, or taste." We think petitioners' attempt to distinguish between uses and criteria loses much of its force in light of the fact that the Act permits enforcement of broad, narrative criteria based on, for example, "aesthetics."

Petitioners further argue that enforcement of water quality standards through use designations renders the water quality criteria component of the standards irrelevant. We see no anomaly, however, in the State's reliance on both use designations and criteria to protect water quality. The specific numerical limitations embodied in the criteria are a convenient enforcement mechanism for identifying minimum water conditions which will generally achieve the requisite water quality. And, in most circumstances, satisfying the criteria will, as EPA recognizes, be sufficient to maintain the designated use. *See* 40 CFR § 131.3(b). Water quality standards, however, apply to an entire class of water, a class which contains numerous individual water bodies.... While enforcement of criteria will in general protect the uses of these diverse waters, a complementary requirement that activities also comport with designated uses enables the States to ensure that each activity-even if not foreseen by the criteria-will be consistent with the specific uses and attributes of a particular body of water.

Under petitioners' interpretation of the statute, however, if a particular criterion, such as turbidity, were missing from the list contained in an individual state water quality standard, or even if an existing turbidity criterion were insufficient to protect a particular species of fish in a particular river, the State would nonetheless be forced to allow activities inconsistent with the existing or designated uses. We think petitioners' reading leads to an unreasonable interpretation of the Act. The criteria components of state water quality standards attempt to identify, for all the water bodies in a given class, water quality requirements generally sufficient to protect designated uses. These criteria, however, cannot reasonably be expected to anticipate all the water quality issues arising from every activity which can affect the State's hundreds of individual water bodies. Requiring the States to enforce only the criteria component of their water quality standards would in essence require the States to study to a level of great specificity each individual surface water to ensure that the criteria applicable to that water are sufficiently detailed and individualized to fully protect the water's designated uses. Given that there is no textual support for imposing this requirement, we are loath to attribute to Congress an intent to impose this heavy regulatory burden on the States.

The State also justified its minimum stream flow as necessary to implement the "antidegradation policy" of § 303....

... The State of Washington's antidegradation policy ... provides that "[e]xisting beneficial uses shall be maintained and protected and no further degradation which would interfere with or become injurious to existing beneficial uses will be allowed." The State concluded that the reduced streamflows would have just the effect prohibited by this policy. The Solicitor General, representing EPA, asserts, and we agree, that the State's minimum stream flow condition is a proper application of the state and federal antidegradation regulations, as it ensures that an "existing instream water us[e]" will be "maintained and protected."

Petitioners also assert more generally that the CWA is only concerned with water "quality," and does not allow the regulation of water "quantity." This is an artificial distinction. In many cases, water quantity is closely related to water quality; a sufficient lowering of the water quantity in a body of water could destroy all of its designated uses, be it for drinking water, recreation, navigation or, as here, as a fishery. . . .

JUSTICE THOMAS, with whom JUSTICE SCALIA joins, dissenting.

. . . [A] State's authority under § 401(a)(1) is limited to certifying that "any discharge" that "may result" from "any activity," such as petitioners' proposed hydroelectric project, will "comply" with the enumerated provisions of the CWA; if the discharge will fail to comply, the State may "den[y]" the certification. . . . [33 U.S.C. § 1341(a)(1)].

The minimum stream flow condition imposed by respondents in this case has no relation to any possible "discharge" that might "result" from petitioners' proposed project. The term "discharge" is not defined in the CWA, but its plain and ordinary meaning suggests "a flowing or issuing out," or "something that is emitted." Webster's Ninth New Collegiate Dictionary 360 (1991). Cf. 33 U.S.C. § 1362(16) ("The term 'discharge' when used without qualification includes a discharge of a pollutant, and a discharge of pollutants"). A minimum stream flow requirement, by contrast, is a limitation on the amount of water the project can take in or divert from the river. That is, a minimum stream flow requirement is a limitation on intake-the opposite of discharge. . . .

The Court remarks that this reading of § 401(a)(1) would have "considerable force" were it not for what the Court understands to be the expansive terms of § 401(d). . . . According to the Court, the fact that § 401(d) refers to an "applicant," rather than a "discharge," complying with various provisions of the Act "contradicts petitioners' claim that the State may only impose water quality limitations specifically tied to a 'discharge. . . .' "

While the Court's interpretation seems plausible at first glance, it ultimately must fail. If . . . § 401(d) permits States to impose conditions unrelated to discharges in § 401 certifications, Congress' careful focus on discharges in § 401(a)(1)—the provision that describes the scope and function of the certification process—was wasted effort. The power to set conditions that are unrelated to discharges is, of course, nothing but a conditional power to deny certification for reasons unrelated to discharges. Permitting States to impose conditions unrelated to discharges, then, effectively eliminates the constraints of § 401(a)(1).

Subsections 401(a)(1) and (d) can easily be reconciled to avoid this problem. . . . [Secction] 401(a)(1) limits a State's authority in the certification process to addressing concerns related to discharges and to ensuring that any discharge resulting from a project will comply with specified provisions of the Act. It is reasonable to infer that the conditions a State is permitted to impose on certification must relate to the very purpose the certification process is designed to serve. Thus, while § 401(d) permits a State to place conditions on a certification to ensure compliance of the "applicant," those conditions must still be related to discharges. In my view, this interpretation best harmonizes the subsections of § 401. Indeed, any broader interpretation of § 401(d) would permit that subsection to swallow § 401(a)(1).

The text of § 401(d) similarly suggests that the conditions it authorizes must be related to discharges. The Court attaches critical weight to the fact that § 401(d) speaks of the compliance of an "applicant," but that reference, in and of itself, says little about the nature of the conditions that may be imposed under § 401(d). Rather, because § 401(d) conditions can be imposed only to ensure compliance with specified provisions of law—that is, with "applicable effluent limitations and other limitations, under section 1311 or 1312 of this title, standard[s] of performance under section 1316 of this title, ... prohibition[s], effluent standard[s], or pretreatment standard[s] under section 1317 of this title, [or] ... any other appropriate requirement[s] of State law"—one should logically turn to those provisions for guidance in determining the nature, scope, and purpose of § 401(d) conditions. Each of the four identified CWA provisions describes discharge-related limitations . . . . .

The final term on the list—"appropriate requirement[s] of State law"—appears to be more general in scope. Because this reference follows a list of more limited provisions that specifically address discharges, however, the principle ejusdem generis would suggest that the general reference to "appropriate" requirements of state law is most reasonably construed to extend only to provisions that, like the other provisions in the list, impose discharge-related restrictions. . . .

The Court adopts its expansive reading of § 401(d) based at least in part upon deference to [EPA's "conclusion"] that § 401(d) is not limited to requirements relating to discharges. . . .

... [T]he regulation to which the Court defers is hardly a definitive construction of the scope of § 401(d). On the contrary, the EPA's position on the question whether conditions under § 401(d) must be related to discharges is far from clear. Indeed, the only EPA regulation that specifically addresses the "conditions" that may appear in § 401 certifications speaks exclusively in terms of limiting discharges. According to the EPA, a § 401 certification shall contain "[a] statement of any conditions which the certifying agency deems necessary or desirable with respect to the discharge of the activity." 40 CFR § 121.2(a)(4) (1993). In my view, § 121.2(a)(4) should ... give the Court pause before it resorts to *Chevron* deference in this case.

... As an alternative to their argument that § 401(d) conditions must be discharge-related, petitioners assert that the state court erred when it sustained the stream flow condition under the "use" component of the State's water quality standards without reference to the corresponding "water quality criteria" contained in those standards. . . .

... A water quality standard promulgated pursuant to § 303 must "consist of the designated uses of the navigable waters involved and the water quality criteria for such waters based upon such uses." The Court asserts that this language "is most naturally read to require that a project be consistent with both components, namely the designated use and the water quality criteria. . . ."

The Court's reading strikes me as contrary to common sense. It is difficult to see how compliance with a "use" of a body of water could be enforced without reference to the corresponding criteria. . . .

The problematic consequences of decoupling "uses" and "criteria" become clear once the Court's interpretation of § 303 is read in the context of § 401. In the Court's view, a State may condition the § 401 certification "upon any limitations necessary to ensure compliance" with the "uses of the water body." Under the Court's interpretation, then, state environmental agencies may pursue, through § 401, their water goals in any way they choose; the conditions imposed on certifications need not relate to discharges, nor to water quality criteria, nor to any objective or quantifiable standard, so long as they tend to make the water more suitable for the uses the State has chosen. In short, once a State is allowed to impose conditions on § 401 certifications to protect "uses" in the abstract, § 401(d) is limitless.

. . . [W]hile respondents in this case focused only on the "use" of the Dosewallips River as a fish habitat, this particular river has a number of other "[c]haracteristic uses," including "[r]ecreation (primary contact recreation, sport fishing, boating, and aesthetic enjoyment)." Under the Court's interpretation, respondents could have imposed any number of conditions related to recreation, including conditions that have little relation to water quality. In *Town of Summersville*, 60 FERC P 61,291, p. 61,990 (1992), for instance, the state agency required the applicant to "construct . . . access roads and paths, low water stepping stone bridges, . . . a boat launching facility . . . , and a residence and storage building." These conditions presumably would be sustained under the [Court's approach]. In the end, it is difficult to conceive of a condition that would fall outside a State's § 401(d) authority under the Court's approach.

Questions and Notes

1. The jurisdictional trigger under § 401(a) is a "discharge" into the navigable waters. As Justice Thomas points out in his dissent, § 502(16) states that "the term 'discharge' when used without qualification includes a discharge of a pollutant, and a discharge of pollutants." This is the only definition in all of § 502 that uses the term "includes" instead of "means" in its prefatory clause. What were the relevant discharges in *Jefferson County*? What, if anything, should the term "discharge" include beyond point source additions to the navigable waters? Should it include the nonpoint pollution contained in stormwater runoff? In *Oregon Natural Desert Ass'n v. Dombeck*, 172 F.3d 1092 (9th Cir. 1998), the Ninth Circuit concluded that it does not. The court reasoned that:

> The terminology employed throughout the [CWA] cuts against ONDA's argument that the term "discharge" includes nonpoint source pollution like runoff from grazing. Neither the phrase "nonpoint source dis-

charge" nor the phrase "discharge from a nonpoint source" appears in the Act. Rather, the word "discharge" is used consistently to refer to the release of effluent from a point source. By contrast, the term "runoff" describes pollution flowing from nonpoint sources. The term runoff is used throughout [§ 208], describing urban wastewater plans, and [§ 304(f)], providing guidelines for identification of nonpoint sources of pollution. Section [401] contains no reference to runoff.

172 F.3d at 1098. The court responded to ONDA's argument that the court had to construe the term "discharge" as including nonpoint pollution in order to honor the nonexclusive orientation of § 502(16) in the following terms:

> Appellees ... argue that "discharge" may only be [broader than the term "discharge of pollutants"] if it includes releases from nonpoint sources. This is incorrect. "Discharge" is the broader term because it includes all releases from point sources, whether polluting or nonpolluting. The D.C. Circuit reached this conclusion in *National Wildlife Fed'n v. Gorsuch*, 693 F.2d 156 (D.C.Cir.1982). There, the court interpreted "discharge" in [§ 502(16)] of the Act to include the release from a point source of turbid water that did not contain any pollutant. This is the logical interpretation of [§ 502(16)] that comports with the structure and lexicon of the Clean Water Act.

Id. Are you persuaded?

2. FERC licenses have terms of up to 50 years. See, e.g., 16 U.S.C. § 799. It seems clear that relicensing at the end of such a term triggers the § 401 certification requirement. See 18 C.F.R. § 4.38(f)(7)(iii). Amendments during the life of such licenses have proven trickier. In *North Carolina v. FERC*, 112 F.3d 1175 (D.C. Cir. 1997), a divided D.C. Circuit held that an operator was not required to go through § 401 certification where it was seeking an amendment for the construction of an intake structure that would facilitate the withdrawal of 60 million gallons of water per day from a lake. Although the dam discharged water through its turbines, the court held that a "decrease in the volume of water passing through the dam turbines cannot be considered a 'discharge' as that term is defined in the CWA." 112 F.3d at 1188. Judge Wald dissented, arguing that "if a State must consent before a new discharge is introduced into its waters, then a change in that discharge must require new consent." 112 F.3d at 1196. In *Alabama Rivers Alliance v. FERC*, 325 F.3d 290 (D.C. Cir. 2003), by contrast, the same D.C. Circuit held that certification was required where a licensee sought an amendment to upgrade its turbine generators, and where the new generators would have increased the flow of oxygen-deprived water.

3. Turning now to *Jefferson County*, were you persuaded by the majority's analysis with respect to the interplay between § 401(a) and (d)? What were the strongest elements of the majority's analysis? What were those of the dissent? Given the closeness of the issues in this case, many observers thought the outcome would hinge upon whose side the Government took. Ultimately, the Government sided with the State of Washington. Do you agree that this was a situation in which *Chevron* deference was appropriate?

4. Assuming that § 401 only relates to point source discharges, and in light of *Jefferson County*, we may now see that § 401 adds four significant

elements to the control that States otherwise possess under the NPDES program:

— It applies in situations in some situations in which neither the NPDES program nor the § 404 program apply; i.e., where there is a discharge that does not involve an addition of pollutants (as in most FERC licensing scenarios);

— It ensures that unauthorized States will have the opportunity to protect their water quality in situations in which EPA is issuing NPDES permits;

— It gives the States (here, all of them) a similar oversight role in the context of § 404 permits; and

— In all of the above situations, it empowers the States to address not only the impact of the discharge, but also any water quality impacts associated with the rest of the applicant's activity.

It should be noted, however, that § 401 only *empowers* the States to protect their water quality interests, it does not *require* them to do so. Section 401(a) specifically provides that States will be deemed to have waived their § 401 prerogative if they do not take action upon a certification request "within a reasonable period of time (which shall not exceed one year)." EPA's regulations further flesh out this dynamic by (a) allowing States to affirmatively waive before the expiration of this period, and (b) giving the licensing or permitting agencies the authority to specify the default waiver period which, EPA indicates, should generally be 6 months. 40 C.F.R. § 121.16.

5. Section 401(d) specifically provides that any conditions established through the § 401 process shall become conditions of the relevant Federal license or permit. Any arguments about the merits of any decisions made by the States in the § 401 process may be raised only in State court.

6. Did you agree with the Court's analysis regarding the State's ability to establish conditions regarding compliance with the designated use? What did you think of the dissent's objections on this front? Note that the Washington Supreme Court had relied primarily on the State's antidegradation standards, whereas Justice O'Connor's opinion seems to treat them as a secondary ground supporting the Court's result. Does it make a difference which way one analyzes this issue? More broadly speaking, what are the implications of the Court's treatment of the second issue? How might it apply, for example, in the wetlands context?

2. Sections 208 and 319

The CWA contains two programs—besides the TMDL program— that encourage the States to address areawide water quality planning in a manner that addresses nonpoint pollution. The first of these, § 208, was created in 1972; the second, § 319, was enacted in 1987, in response to the perceived failure of § 208. Professor Robert Adler has provided a nice description of the basic structure and weaknesses of these programs:

Section 208 required ... identification of various categories of nonpoint source pollution, and development of "procedures and methods" to control those sources "to the extent feasible"—known typically as "best management practices" or "BMPs." Section 208, however, included no specific requirement to match the controls selected or implemented under the plan with what was necessary to attain or maintain [water quality standards ("WQS")], as determined through TMDLs or otherwise. Moreover, the requirement that BMPs be "feasible" suggests a technology-based rather than water quality-based approach to BMP selection. In other words, while requiring general nonpoint-source pollution control practices, the law included no numeric, water quality-based effluent limitations for nonpoint sources.

In 1987, Congress added a new program to address nonpoint source pollution (section 319). While requiring new lists of waters impaired by nonpoint sources of pollution, and new statewide plans to redress that pollution, section 319 adds little rigor to the Act's nonpoint source controls. The provision includes a general requirement that states develop new programs on a watershed-specific basis "to the maximum extent practicable." This requirement suggests the need for states to focus on specific water quality problems, including WQS violations, in individual watersheds. Aside from this vague admonition, however, section 319 did little to remedy the lack of a precise requirement for states to match specific management practices with the degree of control necessary (in combination with new and existing controls on point sources) to meet WQS. Moreover, although section 319 authorizes EPA to conduct listing and assessment if a state fails to do so, like section 208, it contains no express authority for EPA to prepare or implement a nonpoint source pollution control program if a state's program is nonexistent or inadequate.

Adler, Integrated Approaches to Water Pollution: Lessons from the Clean Air Act, 23 Harv. Envtl. L. Rev. 203, 227 (1999) (footnotes omitted).

While some States have utilized the federal dollars available under these programs to develop innovative nonpoint source control programs, the lack of any real federal teeth has limited the effectiveness of Sections 208 and 319. In essence, all EPA can do in the face of State inaction is to deny States the monies that would otherwise be available to implement these programs, and to undertake a modest amount of planning (but no implementation) itself under § 319.

3. The TMDL Program

On its face, Section 303(d)(1)(A) of the CWA requires the States to identify those waters for which BPT and secondary treatment are not stringent enough to achieve compliance with water quality standards. It also dictates that they "shall establish a priority ranking for such waters, taking into account the severity of the pollution and the uses to be made of such waters." This ranking sets the stage for the development of TMDLs, the establishment of which is addressed primarily in § 303(d)(1)(C). Under that provision, the States are required to establish, in accordance with their priority ranking, TMDLs for those pollutants identified by EPA as being suitable for such calculation. It further instructs that the "load shall be established at a level necessary to implement the applicable standards ... with seasonal variations and a margin of safety which takes into account any lack of knowledge concerning the relationship between effluent limitations and water quality." Not surprisingly, the States must submit these ranking lists and TMDLs to EPA for its approval. 33 U.S.C. § 1313(d)(2). If EPA disapproves a submittal, Section 303(d)(2) requires it to establish its own ranking and TMDLs within 30 days.

Despite the fact that § 303(d) has been in place since 1972, the TMDL program is still in its infancy. For many years, both the States and EPA essentially ignored its edicts. Then, in 1984, a citizens group was successful in establishing that EPA has a mandatory duty to take action even in situations in which a State (in that case, Indiana) had never submitted any TMDLs. In *Scott v. City of Hammond*, 741 F.2d 992, 998 (7th Cir. 1984), the Seventh Circuit indicated its willingness to treat Indiana's non-submittal as being the "constructive submission" of no TMDLs. Thus, the court determined, EPA had a non-discretionary duty under § 303(d)(2) to either approve or disapprove that implied determination. Id.

Shortly after *Hammond* was decided, EPA promulgated rules clarifying in somewhat more detail its view as to how the TMDL program should work. Importantly, it defined the term "total maximum daily load" to mean the sum of what it refers to as "wasteload allocations" for point sources, and "load allocations" for nonpoint sources. 40 C.F.R. § 130.2. In this way, EPA made clear that a TMDL is more than just an overall determination of the amount of the relevant pollutant that the relevant water body can assimilate without violating the relevant water quality standard; instead, it also involves an allocation of that gross amount among all known point and nonpoint sources. Additionally, EPA slightly narrowed the circumstances in which TMDLs are required by expanding the list of other requirements that can be utilized to render TMDLs unnecessary; whereas (as mentioned above) the statutory language focuses solely on BPT and secondary treatment, EPA's regulations indicate that TMDLs are unnecessary if compliance with water quality standards can be achieved through resort to any of the CWA's technology-based requirements, any more stringent State or local standards, and/or any other pollution control requirements, such as BMPs. 40 C.F.R. § 130.7(b)(1). Thus, in EPA's view, the TMDL program is to be utilized as a last resort if other regulatory approaches have failed to achieve compliance with water quality standards. At the same time, however, EPA's regulations require the States to demonstrate "good cause" for leaving any waters not meeting standards (referred to as "water quality limited segments") off the list. 40 C.F.R. § 130.7(b)(6)(iv).

These developments led at first to a trickle and eventually to a cascade of *Hammond*-type citizen suits in other states. In turn, most of these cases have resulted in either consent decrees or court orders establishing schedules pursuant to which either the States or EPA are developing either priority rankings or TMDLs.

Although nothing in § 303(d) establishes any enforceable requirements vis-a-vis nonpoint sources, the TMDL program is more threatening to those sources than §§ 208 and 319 in part because the very nature of the TMDL process encourages the States, in addressing situations in which the impairment is due to both point and nonpoint sources, to establish a "fair share" for each contributor, whether point or nonpoint. In turn, this dynamic encourages the States to develop mechanisms for ensuring that the nonpoint sources will not exceed their load allocations. Additionally, if the TMDL program applies to waters that are impaired entirely by nonpoint sources, the only way States can make progress is by developing mechanisms to ensure that nonpoint sources will abide by their loads.

In this last regard, consider the following case:

PRONSOLINO v. NASTRI

United States Court of Appeals, Ninth Circuit, 2002.
291 F.3d 1123.

BERZON, Circuit Judge.

* * *

In 1992, California submitted to the EPA a list of waters pursuant to § 303(d)(1)(A). Pursuant to § 303(d)(2), the EPA disapproved California's 1992 list because it omitted seventeen water segments that did not meet the water quality standards set by California for those segments. Sixteen of the seventeen water segments, including the Garcia River, were impaired only by nonpoint sources of pollution. After California rejected an opportunity to amend its § 303(d)(1) list to include the seventeen sub-standard segments, the EPA, again acting pursuant to § 303(d)(2), established a new § 303(d)(1) list for California, including those segments on it. California retained the seventeen segments on its 1994, 1996, and 1998 § 303(d)(1) lists.

California did not, however, establish TMDLs for the segments added by the EPA. Environmental and fishermen's groups sued the EPA in 1995 to require the EPA to establish TMDLs for the seventeen segments, and in a March 1997 consent decree the EPA agreed to do so. According to the terms of the consent decree, the EPA set March 18, 1998, as the deadline for the establishment of a TMDL for the Garcia River. When California missed the deadline despite having initiated public comment on a draft TMDL and having prepared a draft implementation plan, the EPA established a TMDL for the Garcia River....

The Garcia River TMDL for sediment is 552 tons per square mile per year, a sixty percent reduction from historical loadings. The TMDL allocates portions of the total yearly load among the following categories of nonpoint source pollution: a) "mass wasting" associated with roads; b) "mass wasting" associated with timber-harvesting; c) erosion related to road surfaces; and d) erosion related to road and skid trail crossings.

In 1960, appellants Betty and Guido Pronsolino purchased approximately 800 acres of heavily logged timber land in the Garcia River watershed. In 1998, after re-growth of the forest, the Pronsolinos applied for a harvesting permit from the California Department of Forestry ("Forestry").

In order to comply with the Garcia River TMDL, Forestry and/or the state's Regional Water Quality Control Board required, among other things, that the Pronsolinos' harvesting permit provide for mitigation of 90% of controllable road-related sediment run-off and contain prohibitions on removing certain trees and on harvesting from mid-October until May 1. The Pronsolinos' forester estimates that the large tree restriction will cost the Pronsolinos $750,000.

Larry Mailliard, a member of the Mendocino County Farm Bureau, submitted a draft harvesting permit on February 4, 1998, for a portion of his property in the Garcia River watershed. Forestry granted a final version of the permit after incorporation of a 60.3% reduction of sediment loading, a requirement included to comply with the Garcia River TMDL. Mr. Mailliard's forester estimates that the additional restrictions imposed to comply with the Garcia River TMDL will cost Mr. Mailliard $10,602,000.

On August 12, 1999, the Pronsolinos, the Mendocino County Farm Bureau, the California Farm Bureau Federation, and the American Farm Bureau Federation brought this action ... The Pronsolinos challenged the EPA's authority to impose TMDLs on rivers polluted only by nonpoint sources of pollution and sought a determination of whether the Act authorized the Garcia River TMDL.

The parties filed cross-motions for summary judgment. On August 6, 2000, the district court entered final judgment in favor of the EPA. The Pronsolinos timely filed this appeal.

Section 303(d)(1)(A) requires listing and calculation of TMDLs for "those waters within [the state's] boundaries for which the effluent limitations required by section [301(b)(1)(A)] and section [301(b)(1)(B)] of this title *are not stringent enough to implement any water quality standard* applicable to such waters." § 303(d) (emphasis added). The precise statutory question before us is whether, as the Pronsolinos maintain, the term "not stringent enough to implement ... water quality standard[s]" as used in § 303(d)(1)(A) must be interpreted to mean *both* that application of effluent limitations will not achieve water quality standards *and* that the waters at issue are subject to effluent limitations. As only waters with point source pollution are subject to effluent limitations, such an interpretation would exclude from the § 303(d)(1) listing and TMDL requirements waters impaired only by nonpoint sources of pollution.

The EPA ... interprets "not stringent enough to implement ... water quality standard[s]" to mean "not adequate" or "not sufficient ... to implement any water quality standard," and does not read the statute as implicitly containing a limitation to waters initially covered by effluent limitations. According to the EPA, if the use of effluent limitations will not implement applicable water quality standards, the water falls within § 303(d)(1)(A) regardless of whether it is point or nonpoint sources, or a combination of the two, that continue to pollute the water.

Whether or not the appellants' suggested interpretation is entirely implausible, it is at least considerably weaker than the EPA's competing construction. The Pronsolinos' version necessarily relies upon: (1) understanding "stringent enough" to mean "strict enough" rather than "thorough going enough" or "adequate" or "sufficient"; and (2) reading the phrase "not stringent enough" in isolation, rather than with reference to the stated goal of implementing "any water quality standard applicable to such waters." Where the answer to the question "not stringent enough for what?" is "to implement any [applicable] water quality standard," the meaning of "stringent" should be determined by looking forward to the broad goal to be attained, not backwards at the inadequate effluent limitations. One might comment, for example, about a teacher that her standards requiring good spelling were not stringent enough to assure good writing, as her students still used bad grammar and poor logic. Based on the language of the contested phrase alone, then, the more sensible conclusion is that the § 303(d)(1) list must contain any waters for which the particular effluent limitations will not be adequate to attain the statute's water quality goals.

Placing the phrase in its statutory context supports this conclusion. Section 303(d) begins with the requirement that each state "identify those waters within its boundaries...." § 303(d)(1)(A). So the statute's starting point for the listing project is a compilation of each and every navigable water within the state. Then, only those waters that will attain water quality standards after application of the new point source technology are excluded from the § 303(d)(1) list, leaving all those waters for which that technology will not "implement any water quality standard applicable to such waters." § 303(d)(1)(A). The alternative construction, in contrast, would begin with a subset of all the state's waterways, those that have point sources subject to effluent limitations, and would result in a list containing only a subset of that subset—those waters as to which the applicable effluent limitations are not adequate to attain water quality standards.

The Pronsolinos' contention to the contrary notwithstanding, no such odd reading of the statute is necessary in order to give meaning to the phrase "for which the effluent limitations required by section [301(b)(1)(A)] and section [301(b)(1)(B)] ... are not stringent enough." The EPA interprets § 303(d)(1)(A) to require the identification of any waters not meeting water quality standards only if specified effluent limitations would not achieve those standards. 40 C.F.R. § 130.2(j). If the pertinent effluent limitations would, if implemented, achieve the water quality standards but are not in place yet, there need be no listing and no TMDL calculation. *Id.*

So construed, the meaning of the statute is different than it would be were the language recast to state only that "Each State shall identify those waters within its boundaries ... [not meeting] any water quality standard applicable to such waters." Under the EPA's construction, the reference to effluent limitations reflects Congress' intent that the EPA focus initially on implementing effluent limitations and only later avert its attention to water quality standards. *See e.g.,* 1 *Legislative History* 171 ("The Administrator should assign secondary priority to [§ 303] to the extent limited manpower and funding may require a choice between a water quality standards process and early and effective implementation of the effluent limitation-permit program." (statement of Sen. Muskie, principal author of the CWA and the Chair of the Senate's Public Works Committee)).

Nothing in § 303(d)(1)(A) distinguishes the treatment of point sources and nonpoint sources as such; the only reference is to the "effluent limitations required by" § 301(b)(1). So if the effluent limitations required by § 301(b)(1) are "as a matter of law" "not stringent enough" to achieve the applicable water quality standards for waters impaired by point sources not subject to those requirements, then they are also "not stringent enough" to achieve applicable water quality standards for other waters not subject to those requirements, in this instance because they are impacted only by nonpoint sources....

The Pronsolinos' objection to this view of § 303(d) ... is, in essence, that the CWA as a whole distinguishes between the regulatory schemes applicable to point and non-point sources, so we must assume such a distinction in applying §§ 303(d)(1)(A) and (C). We would hesitate in any case to read into a discrete statutory provision something that is not there because it is contained elsewhere in the statute. But here, the premise is wrong: There is no such general division throughout the CWA.

Point sources are treated differently from nonpoint sources for many purposes under the statute, but not all. In particular, there is no such distinction with regard to the basic purpose for which the § 303(d) list and TMDLs are compiled, the eventual attainment of state-defined water quality standards. Water quality standards reflect a state's designated *uses* for a water body and do not depend in any way upon the source of pollution. *See* § 303(a)-(c).

Nor is there any other basis for inferring from the structure of the Act an implicit limitation in §§ 303(d)(1)(A) and (C). The statutory subsection requiring water quality segment identification and TMDLs, § 303(d), appears in the section entitled "Water Quality Standards and Implementation Plans," not in the immediately preceding section, CWA § 302, entitled "Water Quality Related Effluent Limitations." So the section heading does not suggest any limitation to waters subject to effluent limitations.

Additionally, § 303(d) follows the subsections setting forth the requirements for water quality standards, § 303(a)-(c)—which, as noted above, apply without regard to the source of pollution—and precedes the "continuing planning process" subsection, § 303(e), which applies broadly as well. Thus, § 303(d) is structurally part of a set of provisions governing an interrelated goal-setting, information-gathering, and planning process that, unlike many other aspects of the CWA, applies without regard to the source of pollution.

True, there are, as the Pronsolinos point out, two sections of the statute as amended, § 208 and § 319, that set requirements exclusively for nonpoint sources of pollution. But the structural inference we are asked to draw from those specialized sections—that no *other* provisions of the Act set requirements for waters polluted by nonpoint sources—simply does not follow. Absent some irreconcilable contradiction between the requirements contained in §§ 208 and 319, on the one hand, and the listing and TMDL requirements of § 303(d), on the other, both apply.

There is no such contradiction. Section 208 provides for federal grants to encourage the development of state "areawide waste treatment management plans" for areas with substantial water quality problems, § 208(a), (f), and requires that those plans include a process for identifying and controlling nonpoint source pollution "to the extent feasible." § 208(b)(2)(F). Section 319, added to the CWA in 1987, directs states to adopt "nonpoint source management programs"; provides grants for nonpoint source pollution reduction; and requires states to submit a report to the EPA that "identifies those navigable waters within the State which, without additional action to control nonpoint sources of pollution, cannot reasonably be expected to attain or maintain applicable water quality standards or the goals and requirements of this chapter." § 319(a)(1)(A). This report must also describe state programs for reducing nonpoint source pollution and the process "to reduce, to the maximum extent practicable, the level of pollution" resulting from particular categories of nonpoint source pollution. § 319(a)(1)(C), (D).

The CWA is replete with multiple listing and planning requirements applicable to the same waterways (quite confusingly so, indeed), so no inference can be drawn from the overlap alone. Nor are we willing to draw the more discrete inference that the § 303(d) listing and TMDL requirements cannot apply to nonpoint source pollutants because the planning requirements imposed by § 208 and § 319 are qualified ones— "to the extent feasible" and "to the maximum extent practicable"— while the § 303(d) requirements are unbending. For one thing, the water quality standards set under § 303 are functional and may permit more pollution than it is "feasible" or "practicable" to eliminate, depending upon the intended use of a particular waterway. For another, with or without TMDLs, the § 303(e) plans for attaining water quality standards must, without qualification, account for elimination of nonpoint source pollution to the extent necessary to meet those standards. § 303(e)(3)(F).

The various reporting requirements that apply to nonpoint source pollution are no more impermissibly redundant than are the planning requirements. Congress specifically provided that in preparing the § 319 report, states may rely on information from § 303(e), which incorporates the TMDLs. § 319(a)(2). Moreover, states must produce a § 319 report only once, but must update the § 303(d)(1) list periodically. § 319; § 303(d)(2). Also, the § 319 report requires the identification of a plan to reduce nonpoint source pollution, without regard to the attainment of water quality standards, while the plans generated using the § 303(d)(1) lists and TMDLs are guided by the goal of achieving those standards. § 319; § 303(d), (e).

Essentially, § 319 encourages the states to institute an approach to the elimination of nonpoint source pollution similar to the federally-mandated effluent controls contained in the CWA, while § 303 encompasses a water quality based approach applicable to all sources of water pollution. As various sections of the Act encourage different, and complementary, state schemes for cleaning up nonpoint source pollution in the nation's waterways, there is no basis for reading any of those sections—including § 303(d)—out of the statute.

There is one final aspect of the Act's structure that bears consideration because it supports the EPA's interpretation of § 303(d): The list required by § 303(d)(1)(A) requires that waters be listed if they are impaired by a combination of point sources and nonpoint sources; the language admits of no other reading. Section 303(d)(1)(C), in turn, directs that TMDLs "shall be established at a level necessary *to implement* the applicable water quality standards...." *Id.* (emphasis added). So, at least in blended waters, TMDLs must be calculated with regard to nonpoint sources of pollution; otherwise, it would be impossible "to implement the applicable water quality standards," which do not differentiate sources of pollution....

Nothing in the statutory structure—or purpose—suggests that Congress meant to distinguish, as to § 303(d)(1) lists and TMDLs, between waters with one insignificant point source and substantial nonpoint source pollution and waters with only nonpoint source pollution. Such a distinction would, for no apparent reason, require the states or the EPA to monitor waters to determine whether a point source had been added or removed, and to adjust the § 303(d)(1) list and establish TMDLs accordingly. There is no statutory basis for concluding that Congress intended such an irrational regime.

Looking at the statute as a whole, we conclude that the EPA's interpretation of § 303(d) is not only entirely reasonable but considerably more convincing than the one offered by the plaintiffs in this case.

The Pronsolinos finally contend that, by establishing TMDLs for waters impaired only by nonpoint source pollution, the EPA has upset the balance of federal-state control established in the CWA by intruding into the states' traditional control over land use. That is not the case.

The Garcia River TMDL identifies the maximum load of pollutants that can enter the Garcia River from certain broad categories of non-point sources if the river is to attain water quality standards. It does not specify the load of pollutants that may be received from particular parcels of land or describe what measures the state should take to implement the TMDL. Instead, the TMDL expressly recognizes that "implementation and monitoring" "are state responsibilities" and notes that, for this reason, the EPA did not include implementation or monitoring plans within the TMDL.

Moreover, § 303(e) requires—separately from the § 303(d)(1) listing and TMDL requirements—that each state include in its continuing planning process "adequate implementation, including schedules of compliance, for revised or new water quality standards" "for all navigable waters within such State." § 303(e)(3). The Garcia River TMDL thus serves as an informational tool for the creation of the state's implementation plan, independently—and explicitly—required by Congress.

California chose both *if* and *how* it would implement the Garcia River TMDL. States must implement TMDLs only to the extent that they seek to avoid losing federal grant money; there is no pertinent statutory provision otherwise requiring implementation of § 303 plans or providing for their enforcement.

Finally, it is worth noting that the arguments that the Pronsolinos raise here would apply equally to nonpoint source pollution controls for blended waters. Yet, as discussed above, Congress definitely required that the states or the EPA establish TMDLs for all pollutants in waters on § 303(d)(1) lists, including blended waters.

For all the reasons we have surveyed, the CWA is best read to include in the § 303(d)(1) listing and TMDLs requirements waters impaired only by nonpoint sources of pollution. Moreover, to the extent the statute is ambiguous—which is not very much—the substantial deference we owe the EPA's interpretation, under either *Chevron* or *Skidmore,* requires that we uphold the agency's more than reasonable interpretation. We therefore hold that the EPA did not exceed its statutory authority in identifying the Garcia River pursuant to § 303(d)(1)(A) and establishing the Garcia River TMDL, even though the river is polluted only by nonpoint sources of pollution.

Notes and Questions

1. The Ninth Circuit began its discussion with an extensive analysis (which we have edited out) regarding the level of deference it owed to EPA's interpretation that § 303(d) applies regardless of whether there are any point sources on the relevant river segment. While EPA's TMDL regulations never explicitly address this point, the court noted that they "focus on the

attainment of water quality standards, whatever the source of any pollution." 291 F.3d at 1132. As one example of this focus, the court cited EPA's definition of a TMDL as the "sum of the individual [wasteload allocations] for point sources and [load allocations] for nonpoint sources and natural background." 40 C.F.R. s 130.2(i). The court noted that "[n]o reason appears why, under this TMDL definition, the amount of either point source loads or nonpoint source loads cannot be zero." 291 F.3d at 1132. The court also noted that EPA had issued at least two directives interpreting its rules as requiring TMDLs for waterbodies impaired solely by nonpoint sources. Id. at 1132–1133. Citing *Auer v. Robbins*, 519 U.S. 452, 461, 117 S.Ct. 905, 137 L.Ed.2d 79 (1997) for the proposition that EPA's interpretation of its own rules was "controlling unless plainly erroneous or inconsistent with the regulation" (which we have elsewhere termed "*Seminole Rock* deference"), the court then appeared to conclude that EPA's regulations, as so understood, were entitled to *Chevron* deference. 291 F.3d at 1133. Interestingly, however (as reflected in the last paragraph of the opinion), the court then waffled, suggesting that EPA's interpretation was at least entitled to *Skidmore* deference. Id. at 1133 and 1134–1135. Which of these standards of deference do you think was appropriate?

2.   Putting aside issues of deference, were you persuaded by the court's interpretation of the "not stringent enough" formulation? Was the court's teaching-standards analogy a good one? What did you think of the Prosolinos' structural arguments? Were you satisfied by the court's response to those arguments? And finally, what did you make of the Prosolinos' federalism argument? As we will see when we address *SWANCC* (in chapter 8, below), this is an argument that generated some traction in that case.

3.   Note the quote from Senator Muskie in the *Pronsolino* opinion, which may at least partially explain EPA's extreme slowness in implementing the TMDL program. How much attention should agencies pay to Congressional admonitions such as this one, in situations where, as here, those admonitions are in no way reflected in the statutes themselves?

4.   In July 2000, EPA published a much more extensive set of TMDL rules that, among other things, expressly required TMDLs for waters polluted solely by nonpoint sources. 65 Fed.Reg. 43586 (July 13, 2000). Additionally, these new rules would have established time lines for the listing of waterways, the implementation of measures to implement the TMDLs, and the ultimate attainment of water quality standards. Id. They also would have required the States to develop implementation plans (including any necessary enforcement mechanisms) capable of providing "reasonable assurance" that their scheme would unfold as contemplated. Id. In the end, however, these rules never took effect. In 2001, the Bush Administration put them on hold until 2003. 66 Fed.Reg. 53044 (Oct. 18, 2001). And in 2003, it announced that it was withdrawing them altogether. 68 Fed.Reg. 13608 (March 19, 2003). While EPA simultaneously announced that it was still looking into the possibility of regulatory updates, most observers are not holding their breath.

Chapter 4

CLEAN AIR ACT

I. THE PROBLEM OF AIR POLLUTION

The following is an excerpt of chapter 1 from When Smoke Flows Like Water, by Devra Davis:

> Donora, Pennsylvania, was the kind of place where an adventurous three-year-old like my brother Marty could wander five miles away from home and never really be lost. He made front page headlines both times, "Runaway Marty Does It Again!" read the second one, but each time, somebody brought him back up the steep hills, around the curvy slag-lined, coal-paved roads, back to our house.
>
> All of us children roamed free. Behind my house was a barren stretch of caked, light brown earth the size of two football fields. At its edge, the smooth dusty ground sloped down, at an angle perfect for sliding, to some black ditches with iridescent pools of oily water at the bottom. After a few hours of playing with my friends in the fantastic cracks and crevices of this field, I usually found myself half a mile down the road, at my beloved grandmother Bubbe Pearl's house. She was always home, and her bedroom was perfumed with the smell of chicken soup.
>
> Nestled into the hillside inside a sharp horseshoe bend in the Monongahela River, Donora had sprung up around its metalworks and steel industry. In 1900, William Donner began building an iron mill alongside the fast-moving river, and enough immigrants showed up for jobs that the town was officially incorporated a year later. By midcentury it featured a church or two on most corners, an intense Little League system, and one of the best high-school football teams in the Valley. The main street ran for two blocks with no traffic light and was anchored at one end by the Fraternal Order of Eagles, the Masons, the Polish Falcons, the Sons of Croatia, and a bowling alley. An ice cream cone with two big scoops cost a nickel at Weiss' Drug Store, and at Niccolanco's, a single penny could buy a child's fortune in sugar: 5 Tootsie Rolls, 3 red-hot jawbreakers, or 10 of the smaller gumballs.

Nobody needed a clock. Dinner times, school recesses, and PTA meetings were announced by the shrieking mill whistles. When there was a fire, long blasts from the mill would signal what precinct of town the fire was in. Short blasts would indicate the street number. Any time a fire whistle went off, anyone who could stopped whatever he was doing to go help. The firemen were all volunteers.

Everybody in Donora either worked for "the world's largest nail mill," as the sign atop the factory gate announced, or worked to feed, clothe, fuel or take care of those who did.

* * *

Donora was a simple town, not pretty in any conventional sense, with cobblestone streets that snaked up and down hills so steep they had stairs instead of sidewalks. It was a young place, full of working people, few of them over 60—the sort of place where weeks would pass and nobody would die.

* * *

In the 1950s, the mills began to shut down, and Donora became a place to leave. Nobody spoke about what was happening. My family moved to Pittsburgh when I was ready to begin high school, searching, like half the town's families, for better opportunities. One day I came home from my college classes, dropped my books in the hall, and said to my mother, "Mom, was there *another* place called Donora?" I had never heard much discussion about where we came from. Now it had grabbed my attention in an unsettling way.

My mother had just put a kettle on to boil. "Why do you ask?" she said.

"Well there are several Allentowns, several Websters, a couple of Eagles. There's Pittsburg, Kansas, and Pittsburgh, Pennsylvania. So maybe there are a few Donoras?"

She moved into the kitchen and sat down on the bench next to the built-in white table. I followed her in, took a big breath, and continued to press. "I read in a book at school that in a town with the *same* name as ours, there was pollution. Was Donora polluted? Or was there *another* Donora?" I could not imagine that what I'd read had anything to do with where I'd grown up. I had never heard about our town being anything other than a wonderful place. I had never heard of pollution. The word sounded dirty, something to be ashamed of.

The whistle of the teakettle interrupted, and my mother got up to take the pot off the stove. At first I thought she was going to tell me about someplace else, another Donora somewhere. I was pretty sure of that, but then I could tell she was hesitating. Slowly she poured the steaming water into a small blue cup, dunking the tea bag in briefly. Without even asking if I wanted any, with a nod that commanded me to join her, she poured another blue cup of water, passed the same tea bag into it, and handed it to me. We sat across from each other with steaming teacups on the table between us. She sighed and finally replied, "Nobody knew from pollution then. That was just the way it was. We didn't think much about it.

"Remember all that grime we had on the cars, how we had to drive with the headlights on at three in the afternoon? How the sun didn't shine for days at a time? Remember how women always had their curtains hanging out to dry every week? A lot of us gave up on curtains altogether. Venetian blinds were better, because they could be wiped down. My mother's house had 36 windows and we were always washing them. By the time we got to the last one, the first was already soiled. They were never really clean." I had expected an explanation, but what she gave me was a reminiscence.

There in the sunny kitchen of our big house, ten years and thirty miles away from our old town, it felt like we were on another planet. Outside I could see the sunlight on the green grass. Bubbe Pearl had never made it out of Donora. She had once been famous for her strength the first woman in the Valley to hand-crank a Model T Ford. A legendary driver, she frequently drove the nine hours to Atlantic City with her five children beside her, long before there was a Pennsylvania Turnpike. Nobody ever passed her. But when I was growing up she kept her bed in her dining room because she could not make it up the stairs to a bedroom. She could never be more than a few steps away from an oxygen tank. Traveling beauticians regularly attended to her and to dozens of other women who were too sick to walk up and down the hills to the beauty parlor. When I was very young, I simply assumed that all blue-haired grannies stayed in bed, tethered to oxygen tanks.

"But they say people got really sick in Donora. Did people get sick?"

"Well, we used to say, That's not coal dust, that's gold dust. As long as the mills were working, the town was in business. That's what kept your Zadde and your father employed. Nobody was going to ask if it made a few people ill. People had to eat."

I shot her the kind of skeptical look that daughters have been giving mothers since time immemorial. "Look, today they might call it pollution," she sighed. "Back then it was just a living."

So Donora was famous, but no one ever talked about it. We lapsed into silence.

* * *

Every child in Donora knew how to make steel. You needed limestone, coal and iron ore. A pamphlet handed out at one of the Donora Steel & Wire Works' annual Open Houses explained that a normal day's operation required 45 carloads of iron ore, 40 cars of coke, 6 of limestone, and 6 of miscellaneous materials. Each day the plant burned as much coal as all the homes in Pittsburgh.

These ingredients regularly arrived via massive coal-fired barges snaking up the Monongahela River. Along the Donora side of the river, we could watch the barges rising through the intricate system of locks. Huge metal gates would open, the giant vessel would slowly move inside as if being swallowed by some gigantic whale, and then the gates would bellow with the crunching, creaking, groaning sounds of metal on metal as they majestically swept shut. The captain would tie up to the side of the lock with oily, blackened hawsers as thick as my leg, crossing them at bow and stern. The lockmaster and barge captain would wave a thumbs-up, and hundreds of thousands of gallons of muddy river water would surge into the lock. Then, with a movement that never ceased to amaze us, the ship would gradually inch upward, as though lifted by some phantom force, until it could float out the other side and continue its journey to the mills.

Other supplies came on long freight trains that ran along the river and right through the center of the string of furnaces, rolling mills and smelters. Still others came right out of the ground nearby. Cliffs of limestone were regularly sliced away with huge shovels, draglines and half-tracks. Family mines, some in people's backyards, yielded Appalachian coal from some of the richest seams in the world.

More than anything else, coal was essential to keeping Donora alive. It heated our homes and fired the massive furnaces and ovens of the mills. Mountainous piles of coal at the mills meant the town was in business. In addition to needing coal for the furnaces, steel making depended on a derivative of coal called coke. Coke was essentially coal with the greasy impurities baked out at hellish temperatures. The pure carbon that remained determined whether what came out of the blast furnace was iron or steel.

As a blacksmith hammers a piece of wrought iron to shape it, he must keep it hot so that it remains soft. In charcoal-fired forges like those in Donora, carbon solids and carbon monoxide remain in contact with the iron surface at relatively high temperatures. The hammered surface combines with small amounts of carbon (the iron is carburized) to create a new alloy. When it contains just one part per thousand of carbon, iron is not ordinary iron any more; it becomes steel. This small trace of carbon distributed throughout the dense mass of iron makes it stronger, so that it will take a better edge, build a stronger bridge, or support a taller building than almost any other material humans know how to make.

A coke oven was a pretty simple affair, a gigantic beehive about the size of a one-car garage, built in honeycomb fashion out of fired bricks. Coal was shoveled in and heated to intense temperatures; coke came out. The gases and smoke that are baked out of the coal are supposed to remain in the oven, but they do not. Seductively sweet aromatic hydrocarbons fill the air and ground nearby.

A commercial coking operation required a string of about eighteen ovens, called a battery. Like a great shark that has to keep moving to stay alive, a coke battery had to run all the time, at temperatures above 2,000 degrees Fahrenheit. The ovens had to be blocked shut to assure a constant, even temperature. If they ever cooled, they could not be restarted. This meant that once the oven was fired, hardy souls with a good tolerance for heat had to carefully stack bricks together over the opening. Folks who worked the ovens tended to be young.

* * *

By 1950, however, the mill in Donora had converted entirely to more modern blast furnaces. The center of the blast furnace is called the "dead man" because it is absolutely devoid of air: metal formed in this zone will have no bubbles to weaken it. The limestone served as a kind of sponge, to soak up the impurities. When cooked to the right point, the limestone and impurities floated to the top where they could be skimmed off as slag, leaving the heavier stuff that ultimately became steel to sink to the bottom.

On summer evenings, my family and I would sit in lawn chairs behind our house and watch the fiery spray and sparks coming off the blast furnace as it was topped off. Sluice gates from the furnace channeled the steaming, molten slag into waiting gondola cars shaped like giant teacups. The train was hauled, still smoking, to the dump, where the slag was poured off between the surrounding bluffs. The remaining white-hot liquid steel moved slowly on tracks to where it was poured from huge ladles into five-ton molds to make ingots. An ingot was about four men long and two men wide, red, hot, heavy and forbidding. They were then shipped on slow wheels to the rolling mill, where they went through gigantic rolling pins for stretching, soaking, coating, blooming, heat-treating and galvanizing, to produce the essentials of industrial life.

A few years before I was born, a steelworker fell into the ladle being used to draw off the molten brew, just as the furnace was being tapped. They said he'd been drinking, though how this was proved is beyond me. Not a single body part was recovered. They buried the bucket outside, near the blast furnace.

I loved the spectacular, sprawling fire that lit up the sky for miles. The night sky, glowing with molten metal from the furnaces, was a fiercely hypnotic sight. My cousin Mark remembers that people on their way to Pittsburgh would stop their cars on the other side of the river just to watch.

* * *

The greatest enemy of steel, oddly enough, is air. Oxygen is constantly trying to bind with metals like iron, to create that permanent orange layer better known as rust. Iron had to be painted with a film that contained metals like cadmium or lead to keep out the air. Even steel eventually succumbed to rusting unless it was galvanized. Once the ingots had been milled, stretched, rolled, or cut into sheets, slabs, girders or fences, they could be given a galvanic shield to protect them against air. This essentially meant plunging the steel into a bath of molten zinc at about 850 degrees. The zinc would bond to the surface of the steel, forming a series of layered zinc-iron alloys. When done properly, these alloy layers last for three or four decades.

During the violent work slowdowns and protests before World War I that gave rise to the big steelworkers union, Donora remained staunchly anti-union. (In 1919, it would be the only town to oppose the Homestead strike.) For being the consummate company town, Donora was rewarded with a zinc plant. The new zinc works was built in 1915 as one of the world's largest facilities; it stretched for forty acres along the river and was out of date the moment it opened. Its massive, horizontal coal-fired furnaces were already giving way to electrically powered plants that were less smoky and that did not create such quantities of toxic zinc fumes. The plant's smokestacks, moreover, were less than 150 feet tall, too short to propel their contents above the 600–foot hills around them. In 1933, after the plant had been firing for less than two decades, a Pennsylvania historian reported that bones from some old Indian graves had washed out of the hillside downwind of the zinc plant. What was coming out of the smokestacks had killed all the grass so that the dead could not stay buried.

Figure 1.1: Topological map of Donora mill area, with plumes from zinc mill

Working zinc was like coking, only worse. The zinc furnaces were so hot that you could see heat rising from them for miles, in rivers of distorted light like fun-house mirrors. At its peak, the Donora Zinc Works employed about 1500 men, who enjoyed an average workday of just three hours and yet received the highest wages in town, this in an era before unions had entered the plants. There was some difference of opinion about why this was. The workers themselves used to say it was because they were so efficient that they could fill the ovens in three hours with as much raw material as could be processed in an entire day. An historian of the town's pollution, Lynn Snyder, maintains that zinc workers worked a three-hour day because nobody could have tolerated more time than that in front of the red-hot furnaces. As soon as the furnaces were filled with the materials from which zinc would be cooked out, the workers were allowed to leave.

Most of the plant's employees had emigrated from parts of Spain where their families had produced zinc workers for generations. They did not mix much with the rest of the townsfolk. One fellow who had worked in a zinc plant commented to me, "I was the only one in the workforce who could read or speak English. Most of the workers were under 25. Few of them lasted very long." He described for me his last day in the plant: "Five guys had gone before me to shovel out the finished zinc. Each one of them keeled over, real sick, kinda pale, and nearly passed out. I was the sixth one in. I couldn't take it either. I left. Spent a week in bed and never returned." Not many ever made it to the age of 30 as zinc workers.

Zinc is one of those elements that the body needs in very small doses in certain forms, but that is poisonous in larger amounts and other forms. When bound with sugars in microdoses, zinc probably fights colds by killing rhinoviruses. But when combined with gases of sulfur, carbon, fluoride or nitrogen, zinc can be exceptionally dangerous. And it was not the only poison rising from those ovens. The smelting of zinc and the making of steel both use lots of flurospar, a rock made of crystals of fluoride tied with calcium. During smelting, fluorspar creates a penetratingly and corrosively toxic fluoride gas which can eat the gloss off light bulbs, etch normal glass, and scar the teeth of children. One investigator found that mottled teeth, characteristic of fluoride poisoning, was common among young people in the Valley. My father had teeth like that, spotted no matter what he did. We figured he simply hadn't brushed enough as a kid.

Fumes from the mills, coke ovens, coal stoves, and zinc furnaces were often trapped in the Valley by the surrounding hills. They gave us spectacularly beautiful sunsets and plenty of barren dirt fields to play on.

* * *

On calm, cloudless, dry nights, the air gives up its heat to the surrounding hillsides, and growing denser as it cools, flows downhill like water. Usually, the temperature within any column of air is cooler the higher you get. Where there are valleys, the colder air from the hills can create an inversion layer that keeps warmer air from rising. Hot air balloons fly because hot air is lighter than cold air. But when an inversion happens, balloons cannot fly, smoke cannot rise, and fumes, hot when released, cool and sink back to the ground, unable to dissipate.

October 26th, 1948, brought a massive, still blanket of cold air over the entire Monongahela Valley. All the gases from Donora's mills, its furnaces and stoves, were unable to rise above the hilltops and began to fill the homes and streets of the town with a blinding fog of coal, coke and metal fumes. At first, cars and trucks tried to creep along with their headlights lit, but by midday, traffic came to a standstill as drivers could no longer see the street. "I could not even see my hand at the end of my arm," recalls Vince Graziano, then a strapping young steelworker. "I actually could not find my way home. I got lost that day."

Later, Berton Roueche, *The New Yorker*'s distinguished medical writer, described it this way:

> The fog closed over Donora on the morning of Tuesday, October 26th. The weather was raw, cloudy, and dead calm, and it stayed that way as the fog piled up all that day and the next. By Thursday, it had stiffened adhesively into a motionless clot of smoke. That afternoon, it was just possible to see across the street. Except for the stacks, the mills had vanished. The air began to have a sickening smell, almost a taste.

Arnold Hirsh, a World War II veteran then just beginning his half-century as the town's leading attorney, watched the gathering fog from his Main Street office. "The air looked yellow, never like that before. Nothing moved. I went over to Seventh Street and stood at the corner of McKean, looking down towards the river, and you could just barely see the railroad tracks. Right there on the tracks was a coal-burning engine puffing away. It issued a big blast of black smoke that went up about six feet in the air and stopped cold. It just hung there, with no place to go, in air that did not move."

The sturdy people of Donora were not perturbed. On Friday afternoon, the town's annual Halloween parade took place under a spooky haze. Children's costumes appeared and disappeared in the mist as the parade moved the two blocks down Main Street. My mother remembers it as a ghastly sight, but it fit the occasion. "Of course we all went," she told me later. "This fog was heavy, but there was only one Halloween every year. Only this time we could not see much." People could barely see their own feet. Within days, nearly half the town would fall ill.

Donora did not abandon its routines easily. The high-school football team, the Dragons, practiced kickoffs in preparation for the next day's home game against their great rivals, the Monongahela Wildcats. Jimmy Russell, the head coach, had to yell "Kick!" so that the receiving team would know the ball was in the air. He had no idea that some players had taken advantage of the fog and left early.

The football game between Donora and Monongahela went off as scheduled. The entire town turned out for pep rallies and parades, with strutting drum majorettes leading the black-and-orange-uniformed marching band. The spectators often lost sight of the ball and could only guess from the referees'' whistles when to cheer. When Donora's star tight end, Stanley Sawa, was ordered by the public address system in midgame to "Go home! Go home now!" some in the stands thought it was a prank.

Still in his uniform, with his helmet in his hands, Sawa raced up and down the hills to his family's home at the bottom of 5th Street. Fifth Street was one of the many streets that were so steep they had stairs instead of sidewalks, where nobody ever tried to park a car because the brake would not hold. He dashed into the house.

"What's going on?" he huffed. "Why'd you make me leave the game?"

"It's your dad," a neighbor told him.

"What are you talking about?" Sawa demanded. "Where is he?"

"In there, with the doctor," came the reply. "It doesn't look good."

The elder Sawa, who earned his living lifting massive loads of coke and iron ore, had been brought home from the mill, short of breath, dizzy, thinking he only needed to lie down. By the time Stanley arrived home his father had already died.

Monongahela won the game, 27 to 7. Spectators leaving the field quickly learned that by 10:00 that morning, nine people had died. Within 24 hours the number would be up to eighteen.

Arnold Hirsh had tried to attend the game. "My brother Wallace and I decided we would walk up the Fifth Street steps. We had just gotten out of the service. He had been a lieutenant in the Navy, and I had been an infantry officer. We were both in as good shape as you could be. When we finally got to the top of those steps on our way to the game, we simply could not take another step. We did not say another word to each other. We could barely talk. We turned and headed straight home."

When they got there, they found their mother in distress. "My mother, who had not been well for years, just could not catch her breath," Hirsh recalled. Donora had eight doctors at the time, all of whom made regular house calls. This time, however, no one would come. "I called Doc Rongaus and he said that he just could not make it. He said, the whole town is sick. Even healthy fellas are dropping. Get your mother the hell out of town!" The Hirshes drove into the Allegheny Mountains, away from the fog. Arnold's mother had come to Donora in 1920 as a healthy teenage bride. Both of her parents, who lived elsewhere, survived to almost 100. By the time her two children were grown, she was an invalid with a weak heart and serious breathing difficulties. She died two years after the smog, having barely reached her fifties.

Doc Rongaus gave the same advice to anyone who would listen: Leave if you can. The firemen of Donora went from door to door delivering whiffs of oxygen from tanks to those who were stranded. One of the firemen, John Volk, remembered borrowing oxygen canisters from the Monongahela, Monessen and Charleroi fire departments. "There never was such a fog. You couldn't see your hand in front of your face, day or night. Hell, even inside the station the air was blue. I drove on the left side of the street with my head out the window, steering by scraping the curb."

When I visited him recently at an old age home, Doc Rongaus told me that folks who made it to Palmer Park seemed to recover. The park sat high on a hill and was one of the few green places near the town, probably because fumes from the mills did not regularly sweep over it. "My brother and I hauled women and children in horse-drawn wagons up to the park. Soon as we got them above the smog, they would get much better." Church ladies from nearby towns provided food and blankets to the involuntary campers.

Others shut themselves in. "I had an elderly aunt and uncle," Arnold Hirsh recalls, "who lived on the corner of Fourth and McKean, named Myerson. My aunt looked out the window and figured out that this was something pretty bad. She closed her doors and kept them closed. They had no problem at all. They just stayed inside for five days."

The folks who ran the mills stuck to their routine. The whistles that kept the daily rhythms of the town shrieked on schedule, and the shifts that kept the plants running 24 hours a day did not cease. Although many people whispered that the mills had put something strange into the air, the superintendent of the zinc works, Michael Neale, knew that his mill was doing nothing unusual. That weekend, the enormous volume of telephone calls created a five-hour wait before frantic relatives could speak to local residents. Roger Blough, then Chief Counsel of American Steel and Wire and later its CEO, finally reached Neale at 3:00 Sunday morning to tell him to "dead fire" the furnaces, without zinc ore. A zinc furnace, like a coke oven, cannot be allowed to stop; once cooled, it can never be restarted. Dead firing would protect the equipment while reducing the plant's emissions. Resentful of the interference and unconvinced there was a problem, Neale only complied after a group of company-hired chemists arrived at six that morning, some hours after he had received the order to reduce operations. He described this action as a gesture of concern for the community, not an admission of responsibility for the smog. As he later told the press, "the zinc works has operated for 32 years with no problem."

It was Walter Winchell, with that voice that resonated importance and certainty, who made Donora famous. "Good evening, America!" he said in his national radio broadcast that Saturday night. "The small, hard-working steel town of Donora, Pennsylvania is in mourning tonight, as they recover from a catastrophe. People dropped dead from a thick killer fog that sickened much of the town. Folks are investigating what has hit the area." But, he had already given the answer many would come to accept: it was a "killer fog," a freak of the weather, ultimately an act of G-d.

By the time the fog began to ebb that Sunday, the local funeral home had run out of caskets. Still, the Pittsburgh Post Gazette reported, "the citizenry maintained an attitude of outward calm which was surprising to observe. Here and there on the streets the youngsters continued their games of touch football and rode their bikes." Rains early on the morning of November 1 washed the skies of whatever had hit the town. By November 2, the zinc mill was once again running at full steam. The same work ethic that had kept the football team practicing, the marching band playing, and the cheerleaders cheering also kept the town from delaying getting back to work.

Photographs taken from same point at same time of day showing comparison of atmospheric pollution on different days.

**Figure 1.2: Photos taken from the same point at the same time of
day, showing comparison of pollution on different days**

* * *

The day after the funerals, Dr. Joseph Shilen, a county medical
official, filed a report with the Pennsylvania Secretary of Health
recommending that the zinc works be reopened. The incident, he
wrote, was unlikely to recur. Asked to investigate the smog, John J.
Blumfield, Deputy Head of Industrial Hygiene for the Public Health
Service, refused to do so, calling it "a one-time atmospheric freak."

What happened in Donora was not freakish, nor was it the first time that winds and weather combined with industrial fumes to kill so many that the deaths could hardly be counted. Neither Donorans nor many others knew that in 1930, in the Meuse Valley of Belgium, dozens of people had died within days in a smoky fog. Here too, the exact count was never tallied. Like Donora, the city of Liege sat on a series of steep hills around a river valley, surrounded by metal mills and smelters. The conditions were similar: heavy fogs, lots of fumes from the mills, and workers who depended absolutely on the mills to feed their families.

Some experts who studied the Liege disaster in 1936 warned of the consequences if a similar catastrophe were to befall a larger city. Given the size and age distribution of Liege's population, they calculated that if the same conditions ever hit London, over 4,000 would die in a single week. Nobody listened.

One Belgian investigator painstakingly demonstrated that fluoride gases were the likely cause of the devastation. Sulfur, he pointed out, in heavy doses leaves distinct marks on the linings of the lungs, but fluoride gases do not. They pass right into the bloodstream and attack the heart and other organs, without marring the nasal passages, throat or lungs. The lungs of those who died in Liege were clean. Nobody noticed.

* * *

For Donora, as for Liege, the important questions never got asked. Information critical to figuring out what went on remained hidden, sometimes in full view. As a result, the right things never got counted.

After the smog, a brief campaign erupted against the zinc mill, led by folks outside of Donora. Abe Celapino, a prosperous farmer and restaurant owner from across the bridge in Webster, whose cows and chickens had died, joined forces with the Monessen Daily Independent in calling for the mill to be relocated to a desert area. The editor-in-chief remarked that this might soon be unnecessary: the mill was creating its own desert area where it stood. Dr. Bill Rongaus, the only member of the Borough Council at the time who was not employed by the mills, pointed out that the zinc mill was likely to account for the sudden sickness. "There was fog in Monessen, too," he told the Donora Board of Health, "but it didn't kill people there the way this did. There's something in the air here that isn't found anywhere else." Celapino alleged that Michael Duda, a zinc worker and Borough Council member, had told him late one night in Celapino's restaurant, "I've got a darn good job and I'm going to keep it. I don't care what it kills."

In the month that followed, calls for major studies of the town were rebuffed by people who did not want to know the answer, and others who feared what it would ultimately mean for the town's workforce.

It was revealed that the town council and the Chamber of Commerce had requested advice from the Pennsylvania Department of Forests and Waters the previous March. A reply from Deputy Forester James Cornely was read to a community hearing just after the smog had cleared: "It is my belief that Donora could demand that smoke filters could be placed in the smoke stacks of the zinc plant; and if done in the right manner with the suggestions of a possible usable precipitate or residue being produced, the result might be satisfactory."

This was an early suggestion for what later became standard industry practice. The escaping fumes contained valuable metals and other materials that could be trapped and reused, netting the mills more money and the town less pollution. But the mill operators in Donora had no interest in such a device.

* * *

A Philadelphia chemist brought in to study the problem, Philip Sadtler, speculated that the toxin came directly from the mills. Within months of the disaster, he reported in *Chemical and Engineering News,* the journal of the American Chemical Society, that he had found over 1000 parts per million of fluoride in an air conditioning unit from Donora. Blood taken from those who died showed 12 to 25 times the normal levels of fluoride.

Their lungs, Doc Rongaus recalled some fifty years later, looked fine at autopsy. A report issued by the State of Pennsylvania corroborates his memory, especially in its description of the person identified as Case P:

> The evidence discloses that the larynx, trachea and bronchi of the first order were little affected. Apparently, the irritating agent was carried into the lung and exerted its primary effect upon the terminal bronchi, the bronchioles and the pulmonary parenchyma. However, the agent must have had a low irritating capacity since none of the cases exhibited a degree of hemorrhage, oedema, or necrotizing process commonly associated with the inhalation of lethal irritating substances. Analogy might be made here with certain war gases. Phosgene, for example, has little effect upon the upper respiratory tract. The finer bronchi and lungs undergo intense oedema and congestion during the acute phase of the poisoning.

In other words, the body's upper breathing system was not disturbed by whatever was in the air in Donora. Whatever killed these people slipped deeply and directly into the body, making a bloody swollen mess of the lower lungs, much like phosgene, a nerve gas used in World Wars I and II.

But the source of the poison was never identified. The lethal smog of Donora spawned an entire new academic profession, focusing on the study of humans exposed to polluted air. The Public Health Service was charged with analyzing, assessing, measuring and confirming what had happened. Donora was investigated to death not because so many studies were done but because the absence of definitive evidence of air pollution's harmfulness was taken as evidence of its safety.

The few investigators who warned that all this was not merely bad weather were dismissed. About a year after the inconclusive Public Health Service report was issued, a remarkably candid critique appeared in *Science* magazine, on January 20, 1950. Clarence A. Mills, a physician from the University of Cincinnati, had been trying for years to generate support for studying the conditions of the Monongahela Valley. He wrote that just two years before the disaster, there had been no interest in such research.

He asked, "Just what did their year's work, with a staff of 25 investigators show?"

The answer was pitifully little.

> The most valuable part of their year's work analysis of poison output from the steel and zinc plant stacks remains unused and unevaluated in their written reports. They spent months analyzing the valley air for poisons, but failed to calculate the concentrations probably present during the killing smog a year ago, when an inversion blanket clamped a lid down over the valley's unfortunate people. Had they made such calculation, they would have found that even one day's accumulation of the very irritating red oxides of nitrogen from the acid plant stacks would have caused concentrations almost as high as had been set as the maximum allowable for safety of factory workers exposed only for an 8–hour work day. At the end of 4 days of last year's blanketing smog, concentrations reached were probably more than four times higher than the 10 milligrams per cubic meter of air listed as the upper limits of safety! And the Donora people breathed the poisoned air not 8 hours a day but for 4 whole days.

Mills noted the eerie and tragic parallels between Donora and Liege, where nearly identical conditions created lethal brews involving low lying mill towns, zinc and steel fumes. And he challenged the claim that the Public Health Service had opened up a new field of inquiry, charging them with ignoring years of work by others.

> Let us hope that the Donora tragedy may prove such an object lesson in air pollution dangers that no industrial plant will feel safe in the future in pouring aloft dangerous amounts of poisonous materials. Let us hope that the Donora disaster will awaken people everywhere to the dangers they face from pollution of the air they must breathe to live. These 20 suffered only briefly, but many of the 6000 made ill that night will face continuing difficulties in breathing for the remainder of their lives. Herein lies the greater health danger from polluted air continuing

damage to the respiratory system through years of nonkilling exposure.

It has a strange ring to it, "years of nonkilling exposure."

* * *

The first medical experts into Donora after the smog conducted all the proper clinical tests on the twenty who died right away. Following traditional approaches, they looked into each of the vital organs and all the other tissues that could be stained and assembled. They looked at each slide, each x-ray one at a time, and never put them all together. No measurements were made of pollution in Donora until two months after the fatal smog had ended. As Mills noted, no effort was made to reconstruct what had gone on during the episode itself. Worse, the experts never looked at the survivors. If they had, they would have learned that in the month after the smog lifted, at least fifty extra people had died.

The notion of "extra" deaths may seem strange. As my mother says, you only get one chance to die. But epidemiologists can, and routinely do, predict the number of people who should die in any given population in any given time period, and thus can tell if a group of deaths is occurring that should not. These statistical patterns of dying are human lives with the tears removed, the literal bodies of evidence. In Donora, one of every three people got very sick during the weeklong smog. Even a decade later, the town's death rate was much higher than in surrounding towns. But no attempt was made to link these deaths to the smog, or to air quality in general.

* * *

Figure 1.3: Map of Donora Deaths

It was not merely a sudden bad break of weather. It was foggy then, but the Valley is foggy in fall today, and the fogs will continue for as long as warmer river water emits vapor into colder air. What killed the people in Donora was what many suspected but could never prove. Most of the deaths occurred in the parts of town that sat just under the plume that spewed within a half-mile circle of the zinc mill.

* * *

Donora is a different place now. After the big strikes in the fifties, the massive, inefficient mills shut down, leaving the town to cope with deteriorating schools and a crumbling tax base. Many of the men, unwilling to give up the homes they had so painstakingly built (or unable to sell them) began commuting 60 or even 100 miles a day to take jobs in other towns. The Monongahela, ever a poisonous brown, began to flow blue. "First they tore down the big plants," one resident recalls. "Then they built a McDonald's and no one came. So they boarded that up and built a parking lot. Now nobody parks there either." Main Street now has a single traffic light, a second one having been converted back to a four-way stop sign to save on maintenance. The former Hotel Donora, once home to dozens of bachelor millworkers and a temporary morgue during the smog, is a martial arts training center and occasional rooming house.

* * *

In 1998, just about the time of the 50th anniversary of the disaster, an earnest high-school student named Justin Shawley got a monument set up. The State Historical and Museum Commission erected a five foot square bronze plaque near the center of the former steel mill as a memorial to those who died. To mark the occasion, residents and local and state officials held a service at Our Lady of the Valley Catholic Church, one of Donora's few remaining houses of worship. The plaque says:

The 1948 Donora Smog

> *Major Federal clean air laws became a legacy of this environmental disaster that focused national attention on air pollution. In late October of 1948, a heavy fog blanketed this valley, and as the days passed, the fog became a thick, acrid smog that left about 20 people dead and thousands ill. Not until October 31 did the Donora Zinc Works shut down its furnaces, just hours before rain finally dispersed the smog.*

It is a touching monument. The fifty people who died in the month following the smog are nowhere counted. The thousands who died over the following decade are nowhere counted. And there is no counting of the thousands whom Clarence Mills called the "nonkilled" all those who went on to suffer in various poorly understood ways. Standing there by the ruins of the old mill, I thought I understood, just a little, what Sol Filler must have felt on revisiting Tereisenstadt: These people are well intentioned. They are trying to commemorate, to remember, to atone. But they are not trying hard enough.

Every single one of Bubbe Pearl's five children developed heart problems. None of their illnesses would ever be tied to where they grew up. They are not listed on any memorial to Donora's dead. My dazzling, athletic Uncle Len dropped dead at age 50 on a handball court in Southern California, years and miles away from the Monongahela River Valley. But he carried Donora with him in his heart, and in other body tissues as well. By the time my mother reached the same age, a decade later, coronary artery bypass operations were available to keep her alive. She needed three of them. Aunt Gert required only two.

Bubbe Pearl's tombstone sits in the lovely Jewish cemetery with its spectacular view of the river valley. When I was born she was still a fierce driver, but by the time my brother arrived, a year and half later, she had become an invalid. She did not die during the smog of 1948 either but only some two dozen heart attacks later. The attacks were so common that they became almost a ritual. The room would go quiet, and my mother, the baby of the family, would steady her own mother by the arm and steer her to the bed. The heavy, mottled-green, steel oxygen tank would be wheeled over, the valve turned on, and the gas mask pulled over Bubbe's nose and mouth. Her skin often matched the blue-white color of her hair.

Aunt Gert, the oldest sister, always had to leave the room, unable to stand by helplessly while her mother fought for air. Sometimes Bubbe would shriek "Oy vey!" But usually there was silence, and sighing. We would all wait for Dr. Levin. Dr. Levin always came, always calm, always sure. His arrival meant that everything would be all right.

The night she finally died, he did not come. I could not stop crying. I had seen her nearly die so many times, I was sure it was a mistake.

––––––

The story of Donora, Pennsylvania vividly illustrates the multiple, complex issues that we face with air pollution. Like other forms of environmental pollution that are covered in this book, air pollution may be invisible, but can also be deadly. It can kill immediately, or over a longer time. It can be made up of gases inherently poisonous to the human body, or it can consist of gases that are naturally occurring but that in large quantities pose danger. It can scar the lungs and scar the countryside.

Most importantly, it is not an intentionally created product, but instead a by-product of modern development, in this case, combustion of fossil fuels and the production of useful products made possible by such combustion. Since the exploitation of energy fuels economic expansion, it is also the story of jobs and livelihoods.

Though we know much more about the causes and effects of air pollution now than at the time of the Donora "killer fog," the basic issues of air pollution have not changed. We still grapple with both acutely toxic air pollutants, and most of our major metropolitan areas contain levels of common pollutants that are considered unhealthy. Our major causes of air pollution still come from combustion byproducts, and there is still discussion about the trade-off of clean air and jobs.

What is different today is that we have chosen as a society to address these problems directly through the Clean Air Act. The practice of environmental law that deals with air pollution is very much the story of the implementation and administration of this act. The Act has been amended several times, but importantly, one basic policy choice made originally in the 1970 version of the Act has remained constant–that is that all inhabitants of the United States should ideally be able to breathe clean air and not suffer health impairments due to air pollution. Though this still remains normatively true, it is also true that we still have unhealthful air pollution and political disagreements over the proper way to control air pollution. Like most of environmental law, the real complexities of air pollution control are in the administration of the law and not so much the law itself. It is at the agency level where decisions about safe levels of exposure, measurement and prediction about pollution, and the technology that is necessary to control it are made. It is also in this arena where some of the basic questions about the future of the Clean Air Act, and how closely it will hew to its original goals, are being debated. Therefore this chapter will deal extensively with the implementation of the law and the process that is used in that implementation. The practice of Environmental Law requires knowing whether the agency charged with administering the law is following the law substantively, and implementing it under the correct procedures. Before we can understand whether the agencies are in fact administering the Clean Air Act correctly, we must first understand the basics of the law itself.

II. THE CLEAN AIR ACT—OVERVIEW

The Clean Air Act of 1970 was a very ambitious environmental law that arose out of an increasing consciousness regarding air pollution, its harms, and causes, and an increasingly affluent society that sought to provide decent standards of living, including health protection, to all of its citizens.

The 1970 Act had three major parts. One part required the Administrator (of what was later to become the EPA) to set health based standards for all common ubiquitous pollutants, commonly referred to as the criteria pollutants. [1]These originally included Nitrogen Oxides, Sulfur Oxides, particulate matter, volatile organic compounds, carbon monoxide, and ozone. In small quantities, most of these pollutants are not harmful, and indeed some are necessary compounds in our atmosphere. However, in the amounts produced by our modern industrial society, with its heavy dependence on the combustion of fossil fuels, of which these compounds are byproducts, these air pollutants can cause immediate and chronic health problems.

The second major part of the 1970 Act dealt with how these health based standards were to be reached and enforced. The answer, then as now, was that the states were to establish State Implementation Plans, or SIPS, which provided the regulatory controls necessary to establish and maintain these health based standards promulgated by the Administrator.[2]

Finally the Act sought to intervene directly in pollution control by establishing technology or process standards for the control of pollution at its source. This in turn was divided into sections dealing with both stationary, industrial sources, such as power plants[3], and mobile sources, such as automobiles and trucks.[4]

---

1. 42 U.S.C. Sec. 7408 and 7409 (CAA secs. 108 and 109).

2. 42 U.S.C. Sec. 7410 (CAA, Sec. 110).

3. 42 U.S.C. Sec. 7411 (CAA, Sec. 111).

4. 42 U.S.C. Sec. 7521 (CAA Sec. 202).

In response to concerns that a uniform national standard failed to adequately protect areas of the country that had particularly pristine air, in 1977, the Clean Air Act was amended to prevent deterioration of particularly clean air areas.[5] This program, aptly named the Prevention of Significant Deterioration (or PSD) program, divided the country into three classes of air quality and then limited the amount of pollution that could be added to these areas in order to maintain that level.[6] In particular, national parks were to be set at the highest (or Class I) level.[7] These limits were to be enforced by doing preconstruction review of any major sources to ensure that the air pollution increment would not be exceeded.[8]

The Clean Air Act was last amended significantly in 1990. At that time, it was clear that many of the nation's urban areas had failed to meet the national ambient air quality standards set by the administrator, particularly for ground level ozone. The 1990 Act sought to impose compliance by mandating very particular requirements in those areas that failed to implement the ozone standards. These requirements were more stringent depending on the severity of the ozone problem.[9]

The 1990 amendments also created a program for establishing and trading increments of sulfur dioxide. Called the Acid Rain Trading provisions, this program was the most ambitious use of market trading devices for pollution control up until that time.[10]

The 1990 Amendments also created a permitting program, similar to that of the Clean Water Act, which required the permitting of all major sources of air pollution. The permitting system also required that the ultimate permitting agency harmonize all the CAA requirements applicable to one source.[11]

Making sense of all of the Clean Air Act requirements simultaneously has been a challenge for both the administrative agencies and the regulated community. Sources of air pollution may have to comply with technology or process standards that are applicable to all new sources of a particular type, to technology or process requirements applicable to all new or upgraded sources that have an effect on air quality of areas subject to the prevention of significant deterioration program, in addition to requirements that might be mandated by a state or the EPA under an applicable state implementation plan, which may or may not be subject to national controls based on severity of ozone air quality attainment. Though the permitting program has been of some assistance in harmonizing the myriad requirements for sources of air pollution, the state and federal executive branch agencies that administer the various

5. 42 U.S.C. Sec. 7470 (CAA Sec. 160).

6. 42 U.S.C. Sec. 7471–7473 (CAA Secs. 161–163).

7. 42 U.S.C. Sec. 7472 (CAA Sec. 162).

8. 42 U.S.C. Sec. 7475 (CAA 165).

9. 42 U.S.C. Sec. 7511 (CAA 181).

10. 42 U.S.C. Sec. 7651b (CAA Sec. 403).

11. 42 U.S.C. Sec. 7661a(5) (CAA Sec. 502(5)).

parts of the law have various philosophies of enforcement that make consistent application of requirements and ongoing improvement of air quality elusive. It is here where the real action in the Clean Air Act occurs. To practice or understand air pollution control requires an examination of how the agencies have and will administer the various parts of the Clean Air Act. We will explore these parts of the Act in turn.

As you read about the agency actions, challenges to those actions, and court rulings on the legality of those actions, keep in mind that agencies may have wide deference in how to administer certain laws, and that deference is directly related to the flexibility the legislation has granted them.[12] Thus, pay attention not only to your own interpretation of a statute, but also to whether an enforcing agency's interpretation is within the bounds of discretion committed to the agency for that statute. If it is, and the agency has followed proper procedure, it is that interpretation that becomes the hard and fast requirement. If not, the implementation must be challenged or negotiated until a legal status is reached. Remember also that requirements based on administrative action can be changed without changing the legislation as long as the interpretation is validly within the agency's discretion and proper procedure has been followed.

III.   THE CLEAN AIR ACT AND THE CONTROL OF "CRITERIA POLLUTANTS"

A.   What is a Criteria Pollutant?

The following case describes the program that seeks to control the most common air pollutants, also called criteria pollutants.

NATURAL RESOURCES DEFENSE COUNCIL, INC. v. TRAIN

United States Court of Appeals, Second Circuit, 1976.

545 F.2d 320.

Before SMITH, OAKES and MESKILL, Circuit Judges.

J. JOSEPH SMITH, Circuit Judge:

The Environmental Protection Agency, ("EPA"), and its Administrator, Russell Train, appeal from an order of the United States District Court for the Southern District of New York, Charles E. Stewart, Jr., Judge, in an action under § 304 of the Clean Air Act, as amended, 42 U.S.C. § 1857h–2(a), requiring the Administrator of the EPA, within thirty days, to place lead on a list of air pollutants under § 108(a)(1) of the Clean Air Act, as amended, 42 U.S.C. § 1857c–3(a)(1), ("the Act"). [Footnote omitted]. We affirm the order of the district court.

---

12. For instance, the states had great flexibility in 1970 in coming up with State Implementation plans to implement the National Ambient Air Quality Standards, but the 1990 amendments took away much of that discretion of the EPA's discretion to approve a state program where there were ozone attainment problems. 42 U.S.C. Sec. 7511.

The 1970 Clean Air Act Amendments provide two different approaches for controlling pollutants in the air. One approach, incorporated in §§ 108–110, 42 U.S.C. §§ 1857c–3 to c–5, provides for the publication of a list of pollutants adverse to public health or welfare, derived from "numerous or diverse" sources, the promulgation of national ambient air quality standards for listed pollutants,[2] and subsequent implementation of these standards by the states.

* * *

The relevant part of § 108 reads as follows:

(a)(1) For the purpose of establishing national primary and secondary ambient air quality standards, the Administrator shall within 30 days after December 31, 1970, publish, and shall from time to time thereafter revise, a list which includes each air pollutant

(A) which in his judgment has an adverse effect on public health or welfare;

(B) the presence of which in the ambient air results from numerous or diverse mobile or stationary sources; and

(C) for which air quality criteria had not been issued before December 31, 1970, but for which he plans to issue air quality criteria under this section.

Once a pollutant has been listed under§ 108(a)(1), §§ 109 and 110 of the Act are automatically invoked. [footnote omitted].

* * *

The EPA concedes that lead meets the conditions of §§ 108(a)(1)(A) and (B) that it has an adverse effect on public health and welfare, and that the presence of lead in the ambient air results from numerous or diverse mobile or stationary sources. The EPA maintains, however, that under § 108(a)(1)(C) of the Act, the Administrator retains discretion whether to list a pollutant, even though the pollutant meets the criteria of §§ 108(a)(1)(A) and (B). The EPA regards the listing of lead under § 108(a)(1) and the issuance of ambient air quality standards as one of numerous alternative control strategies for lead available to it. Listing of substances is mandatory, the EPA argues, only for those pollutants for which the Administrator "plans to issue air quality criteria." He may, it is contended, choose not to issue, i. e., not "plan to issue" such criteria, and decide to control lead solely by regulating emission at the source, regardless of the total concentration of lead in the ambient air. The Administrator argues that if he chooses to control lead (or other pollutants) under § 211, he is not required to list the pollutant under § 108(a)(1) or to set air quality standards.

* * *

2. 40 C.F.R. § 50.1(e) defines ambient air as "that portion of the atmosphere, external to buildings, to which the general public has access."

Section 108(a)(1) and the Structure of the Clean Air Act

Section 108(a)(1) contains mandatory language. It provides that "the Administrator shall ... publish ... a list ...." (Emphasis added.) If the EPA interpretation were accepted and listing were mandatory only for substances "for which (the Administrator) plans to issue air quality criteria ... ", then the mandatory language of § 108(a)(1)(A) would become mere surplusage. The determination to list a pollutant and to issue air quality criteria would remain discretionary with the Administrator, and the rigid deadlines of § 108(a)(2), § 109, and § 110 for attaining air quality standards could be bypassed by him at will. If Congress had enacted § 211 as an alternative to, rather than as a supplement to, §§ 108–110, then one would expect a similar fixed timetable for implementation of the fuel control section. The absence of such a timetable for the enforcement of § 211 lends support to the view that fuel controls were intended by Congress as a means for attaining primary air quality standards rather than as an alternative to the promulgation of such standards. [footnote omitted].

* * *

Because state planning and implementation under the Air Quality Act of 1967 had made little progress by 1970, Congress reacted by "taking a stick to the States in the form of the Clean Air Amendments of 1970...." Train v. Natural Resources Defense Council, 421 U.S. 60, 64, 95 S.Ct. 1470, 1474, 43 L.Ed.2d 731 (1975). It enacted § 108(a)(1) which provides that the Administrator of the Environmental Protection Agency "shall" publish a list which includes each air pollutant which is harmful to health and originates from specified sources. Once a pollutant is listed under § 108(a)(1), §§ 109 and 110 are to be automatically invoked, and promulgation of national air quality standards and implementation thereof by the states within a limited, fixed time schedule becomes mandatory.

The EPA contention that the language of § 108(a)(1)(C) "for which (the Administrator) plans to issue air quality criteria" is a separate and third criterion to be met before § 108 requires listing lead and issuing air quality standards, thereby leaving the decision to list lead within the discretion of the Administrator, finds no support in the legislative history of the 1970 Amendments to the Act. The summary of the provisions of the conference agreement furnished the Senate by Senator Muskie contain the following language:

> The agreement requires issuance of remaining air quality criteria for major pollutants within 13 months of date of enactment.

and

> Within the 13–month deadline, the Congress expects criteria to be issued for nitrogen oxides, fluorides, lead, polynuclear organic matter, and odors, though others may be necessary.[9]

9. Legislative History, Clean Air Amendments, Vol. 1 at 430, 432.

The section-by-section analysis of the National Air Standards Act of 1970 in the Senate Report on S. 4358, 91st Cong., 2d Sess., contains this language describing § 108 (formerly designated § 109):

> This new section directs the Secretary to publish (initially 30 days after enactment) a list of air pollution agents or combination thereof for which air quality criteria will be issued. He can add to the list periodically. The agents on the initial list must include all those pollution agents or combinations of agents which have, or can be expected to have, an adverse effect on health and welfare and which are emitted from widely distributed mobile and stationary sources, and all those for which air quality criteria are planned.
>
> Twelve months after such initial list is published, the Secretary must issue air quality criteria for those listed agents.
>
> The Secretary must also issue information on air pollution control techniques.
>
> This section continues in effect those air quality criteria and information on pollution control techniques published prior to this section.
>
> This section provides that such criteria and information shall be published in the Federal Register and be available to the public.[10]

The same Senate Report contains the following explicit language regarding §§ 108 and 109 (formerly § 109 and § 110):

> Air quality criteria for five pollution agents have already been issued (sulfur oxides, particulates, carbon monoxide, hydrocarbons, and photochemical oxidants). Other contaminants of broad national impact include fluorides, nitrogen oxides, polynuclear organic matter, lead, and odors. Others may be added to this group as knowledge increases. The bill would require that air quality criteria for these and other pollutants be issued within 13 months from enactment. If the (Secretary) subsequently should find that there are other pollution agents for which the ambient air quality standards procedure is appropriate, he could list those agents in the Federal Register, and repeat the criteria process.

* * *

While the literal language of § 108(a)(1)(C) is somewhat ambiguous, this ambiguity is resolved when this section is placed in the context of the Act as a whole and in its legislative history. The deliberate inclusion of a specific timetable for the attainment of ambient air quality standards incorporated by Congress in §§ 108–110 would become an exercise in futility if the Administrator could avoid listing pollutants simply by choosing not to issue air quality criteria. The discretion given to the Administrator under the Act pertains to the review of state implementation plans under § 110, and to § 211 which authorizes but does not mandate the regulation of fuel or fuel additives. It does not extend to the issuance of air quality standards for substances derived from specified

---

10. Legislative History, Clean Air Amendments, Vol. 1 at 454.

sources which the Administrator had already adjudged injurious to health.[13]

III

Judicial Interpretations

The Supreme Court in Union Electric Co. v. Environmental Protection Agency, 427 U.S. 246, 256, 96 S.Ct. 2518, 2525, 49 L.Ed.2d 474 (1976), referred to the 1970 Amendments of the Clean Air Act as "a drastic remedy to what was perceived as a serious and otherwise uncheckable problem of air pollution." In the same opinion the Court described the three-year deadline for achieving primary air quality standards as "central to the Amendments' regulatory scheme." Id. at 258, 96 S.Ct. at 2526. Previously the Court had referred to the attainment of the national air quality standards within three years from the date of approval of state implementation plans as "the heart of the 1970 Amendments." Train v. Natural Resources Defense Council, 421 U.S. 60, 66, 95 S.Ct. 1470, 1475, 43 L.Ed.2d 731 (1975). The EPA, the Court stated, "is plainly charged by the Act with the responsibility for setting the national ambient air standards."

* * *

The structure of the Clean Air Act as amended in 1970, its legislative history, and the judicial gloss placed upon the Act leave no room for an interpretation which makes the issuance of air quality standards for lead under § 108 discretionary. The Congress sought to eliminate, not perpetuate, opportunity for administrative foot-dragging. Once the conditions of §§ 108(a) (1)(A) and (B) have been met, the listing of lead and the issuance of air quality standards for lead become mandatory.

The order of the district court is affirmed.

545 F.2d 320, 9 ERC 1425, 7 Envtl. L. Rep. 20,004.

Notes and Questions

1. As the Second Circuit in *NRDC v. Train* makes clear, the CAA requires the Administrator to designate and regulate an air pollutant as a criteria pollutant if it has a negative impact on human health and comes from numerous and diverse sources. As noted in the case, at the time the 1970 CAA was passed, several pollutants were already identified as meeting this requirement. These pollutants: sulfur oxides, particulates, carbon monoxide, hydrocarbons and photochemical oxidants, as by-products of combustion (or incomplete combustion) of fossil fuels, easily meet the definition of a "criteria pollutant," as do other combustion by-products, such as nitrogen oxides and lead, which were added to the list. Could there be "criteria pollutants" that are not the byproducts or waste products of fossil fuel combustion? Is there any other process which puts significant harmful substances in the air from numerous and diverse sources?

---

13. South Terminal Corp. v. EPA, 504 F.2d 646, 654 (1st Cir. 1974), cited in the brief by Train, refers to the discretion of the Administrator in approving state implementation plans. It does not address itself to the issuance of air quality standards.

Chemical Reaction of Fossil Fuel Combustion

CxHy (such as propane $-$ C_3H_8) $+$ O_2 in the presence of Sulfur (S) impurities
Nitrogen (N) in the air

$=CO_2$ $+$ H_2O $+$ CO (from incomplete combustion of carbon) $+$ NO_2 $+$ SOx $+$ CxHy (remaining organic compounds from incomplete combustion of fuel) $+$ particulates (relatively large pieces of carbon that did not combust) $+$ energy

CO, NO_2, SOx, organic compounds, and particulates have all been designated as criteria pollutants. Ozone or photochemical oxidants, are formed from the reaction of Nitrogen Oxides with volatile organic compounds in the presence of sunlight and heat. In addition, when gasoline was leaded, the burning of gasoline also produced lead.

2. At the time the modern CAA was passed, it was the criteria pollutants that were considered to be the primary health risk to humans, and it is these pollutants that much of the CAA addresses. Though other dangerous air pollutants are also regulated (such as the hazardous air pollutants, *infra)*, in general they are not produced on the same scale as the criteria pollutants. Are there other substances that might qualify as a criteria pollutant? What about Carbon Dioxide (CO_2)? *See discussion infra.*

A more difficult question than what constitutes a criteria pollutant, is what level of that pollutant can be considered "safe."

B. How is a National Ambient Air Quality Standard Established?

Once criteria pollutants are determined, Section 109 requires the Administrator to determine what ambient level of these pollutants will ensure the safety of the public. The process of setting allowable ambient pollution levels requires studying health effects of air pollution, which is not a precise science. A general discussion of the health effects of the criteria pollutants follows:

The Clean Air Problem

Health effects

Ozone

Roughly one out of every three people in the United States is at a higher risk of experiencing problems from ground-level ozone.

- One group at high risk is active children because they often spend a large part of the summer playing outdoors.

- People of all ages who are active outdoors are at increased risk because, during physical activity, ozone penetrates deeper into the parts of the lungs that are more vulnerable to injury.

- People with respiratory diseases, including asthma, that make their lungs more vulnerable to ozone may experience health effects earlier and at lower ozone levels than other people.

- Though scientists don't yet know why, some healthy people are unusually sensitive to ozone. They may experience health effects at more moderate levels of outdoor exertion or at lower ozone levels than the average person.

- Ozone can irritate the respiratory system, causing coughing, throat irritation, and/or an uncomfortable sensation in the chest.

- Ozone can reduce lung function and make it more difficult to breathe deeply and vigorously. Breathing may become more rapid and shallow than normal. This may limit a person's ability to engage in vigorous activities.

- Ozone can aggravate asthma. When ozone levels are high, more people with asthma have attacks that require a doctor's attention or use of medication. One reason this happens is that ozone makes people more sensitive to allergens such as pets, pollen, and dust mites, which are common triggers of asthma attacks.

- Ozone can increase susceptibility to respiratory infections.

- Ozone can inflame and damage the lining of the lungs. Within a few days, the damaged cells are shed and replaced—much like the skin peels after a sunburn. Studies suggest that if this type of inflammation happens repeatedly over a long time period (months, years, a lifetime), lung tissue may become permanently scarred, resulting in permanent loss of lung function and a lower quality of life.

Particle Pollution (Particulates)

Particles smaller than 10 micrometers in diameter can cause or aggravate a number of health problems and have been linked with illnesses and deaths from heart or lung diseases. These effects have been associated with both short-term exposures (usually over a 24–hour period, but possibly as short as one hour) and long-term exposures (years).

- Sensitive groups for particle pollution include people with heart or lung disease, older adults (who may have undiagnosed heart or lung disease), and children.

- People with heart or lung diseases—such as congestive heart failure, coronary artery disease, asthma, or chronic obstructive pulmonary disease—and older adults are more likely to visit emergency rooms, be admitted to hospitals, or in some cases, even die. When exposed to particle pollution, people with heart disease may experience chest pain, palpitations, shortness of breath, and fatigue. Particle pollution has also been associated with cardiac arrhythmias and heart attacks.

- When exposed to particles, people with existing lung disease may not be able to breathe as deeply or vigorously as they normally would. They may experience symptoms such as coughing and shortness of breath. Healthy people also may experience these effects, although they are unlikely to experience more serious effects.

- Particle pollution also can increase susceptibility to respiratory infections and can aggravate existing respiratory diseases, such as asthma and chronic bronchitis, causing more use of medication and more doctor visits.

Carbon Monoxide (CO)

Carbon monoxide enters the bloodstream through the lungs and binds to hemoglobin, the substance in blood that carries oxygen to cells. It actually reduces the amount of oxygen reaching the body's organs and tissues.

- People with cardiovascular disease, such as angina, are most at risk. They may experience chest pain and other cardiovascular symptoms if they are exposed to carbon monoxide, particularly while exercising.

- People with marginal or compromised cardiovascular and respiratory systems (for example, individuals with congestive heart failure, cerebrovascular disease, anemia, chronic obstructive lung disease), and possibly young infants and fetuses, also may be at greater risk from carbon monoxide pollution.

- In healthy individuals, exposure to higher levels of carbon monoxide can affect mental alertness and vision.

Sulfur Dioxide (SO2)

Sulfur dioxide is an irritant gas that is removed by the nasal passages. Moderate activity levels that trigger mouth breathing, such as a brisk walk, are needed for sulfur dioxide to cause health effects.

- People with asthma who are physically active outdoors are most likely to experience the health effects of sulfur dioxide. The main effect, even with brief exposure, is a narrowing of the airways (called bronchoconstriction). This may cause wheezing, chest tightness, and shortness of breath. Symptoms increase as sulfur dioxide levels and/or breathing rates increase. When exposure to sulfur dioxide ceases, lung function typically returns to normal within an hour.

- At very high levels, sulfur dioxide may cause wheezing, chest tightness, and shortness of breath even in healthy people who do not have asthma.

- Long-term exposure to sulfur dioxide can cause respiratory illness, alter the lung's defense mechanisms, and aggravate existing cardiovascular disease. People with cardiovascular disease or chronic lung disease, as well as children and older adults, may be most susceptible to these effects.

(Source: EPA Brochure–Air Quality Index: A Guide to Air Quality and Your Health, EPA–454/K–03–002, August 2003.)

JOURNAL OF TOXICOLOGY: CLINICAL TOXICOLOGY
COPYRIGHT 2002 GALE GROUP INC.
ALL RIGHTS RESERVED.
COPYRIGHT 2002 MARCEL DEKKER, INC.

Saturday, June 1, 2002
ISSN: 0731–3810; Volume 40; Issue 4.

Poisons in the Air: A Cause of Chronic Disease in Children.
(AAPCC/WHO Symposium).

Monique Mathieu–Nolf
[Citations omitted]

FACTORS RELATED TO TOXIC EXPOSURE SEVERITY

Air pollutants are gaseous or in the form of particle suspension. Exposures are difficult to assess and to characterize because a mixture of pollutants is often involved. Epidemiological data indicate the association of acid aerosol levels with mortality and respiratory symptoms in children. The affect of this specific pollutant is not clear. The role of other pollutants such as ozone, nitrogen oxides, sulfur oxides, and fine particles produced by the same sources may also be significant.

The main factors influencing penetration and retention within the respiratory tract are solubility, particle size, concentration, reactivity of the pollutant, and pattern of ventilation.

Solubility

Gases that are highly soluble in water, like sulfur dioxide (SO_2), are almost totally extracted by the nose and pharynx, whereas the less soluble gases like nitrogen dioxide (NO_2), ozone, or nonsoluble gases like CO are less removed by the upper respiratory tract and penetrate deeper into the lung. Exercise, by increasing minute ventilation, increases the total quantity reaching the deep lung. Moderate to heavy exercise may also increase penetration of soluble gases in the deep lung, bypassing the nasal passage when oral breathing is used.

Particle Size

Particles, liquid droplets or solid particles, remain in suspension (aerosol). Among other factors related to child airway anatomy and rate of ventilation, the penetration of particles depends on their size. Particles larger than 10 [micro]m are filtered by the nose and nasopharynx and cleared within hours. Particles of less than 10 [micro]m are deposited on the tracheo bronchial tree. Particles of 1–2 [micro]m may reach the alveoli. Particles of less than 0.5 [micro]m are carried by gases to alveoli and impacted on the alveolar surfaces. They are cleared from the deep lung by macrophages within days or months.

Pollution by respirable particles is assessed through PM10, defined as particulate matter with an aerodynamic diameter equal, or less than a nominal 10 [micro]m. This parameter is used for ambient air quality surveillance.

Reactivity, Mechanisms of Action

The mechanisms by which inhaled gases and particles injure the lung are diverse and still not fully understood.

Oxidant Gases

Oxidant gases, like ozone, N[O.sub.2] and S[O.sub.2] cause inflammation of the respiratory tract and deep lung. Studies have investigated the putative mechanisms underlying the effects of N[O.sub.2], S[O.sub.2], ozone, and respirable particles. They suggest that exposure to these agents may lead to perturbation of the airway epithelium and the release of pro-inflammatory mediators from epithelial cells, which then activate inflammatory cells, such as eosinophils.

Organic Compounds

Organic compounds absorbed onto particles may also cause inflammation and act as initiators of cancer. Several epidemiological studies have demonstrated a clear association between episodes of outdoor air pollution and impaired lung function and infection of the lower and upper respiratory tracts.

Pattern of Ventilation

The amount of pollutants reaching the respiratory tract and the deep lung is directly related to the minute ventilation. A child's ventilation pattern differs from that of an adult, with a higher rate and tidal volume relative to weight. This may explain in part the special vulnerability of child to respiratory pollutants. Such a vulnerability to pollutants is much increased for asthmatic children and adolescents. It has been suggested that children with bronchial hyperresponsiveness and raised serum concentrations of total IgE are more vulnerable to the effects of air pollution, although they are not necessarily identified as such because they do not present with chronic respiratory symptoms.

Different studies conducted in Seattle area hospitals suggest that health effects among asthmatic children resulting from short-term changes in air pollution levels are an important public health problem. A London study reports a most significant association between consultations for childhood asthma and N[O.sub.2] levels in the outdoor air and between other lower respiratory disease consultations (bronchitis) and S[O.sub.2] levels.

POLLUTANTS OF SPECIAL CONCERN IN CHILDREN

Children are exposed to numerous air pollutants both outdoors and indoors. The concentration of many pollutants has been found to be greater indoors than outdoors. This is of special concern because children (especially infants and young children) spend most of their time indoors. Because of the large number of agents, we will not review every hazardous air contaminant, but will focus on the main outdoor and indoor nonbiological air pollutants for children.

As airborne lead has decreased with the extended use of unleaded gasoline throughout the world, the main outdoor pollutants of concern in children remain ozone, CO, N[O.sub.2], S[O.sub.2], and particles.

Aside from the numerous volatile or semi-volatile substances used in the household, the indoor air pollution resulting from combustion and biomass burning related to heating and cooking is of special concern and represents a major public health challenge in developing countries. It is estimated that approximately 50% of the world population and up to 90% of rural households in developing countries still rely on unprocessed biomass fuels in the form of wood, dung, and crop residues for heating and cooking. These are too often burnt indoors in open fires or poorly functioning stoves. The most important pollutants from combustion of domestic origin are particles (small particles less than 10 [micro]m in diameter and particularly less than 2.5 [micro]m), CO, nitrogen oxides, and sulfur oxides (principally from coal). To a lesser extent, formaldehyde (gas stoves, space heaters) and polyclic organic matter including benzo [a] pyrene (open fire) are other indoor air pollutants.

Ozone

Origin

Ozone comes from motor vehicle and industry emissions as a product of the reaction of certain sunlight radiations on nitrogen oxides and hydrocarbons. The highest levels are formed in the afternoon during the summer, a time when children are often playing outdoors.

Health Effects in Children

The clinical effects observed in children are acute or subacute and result in persistent manifestations as cough, upper respiratory tract irritation, pain on inspiration, airway inflammation, increased bronchial permeability, and decrements in pulmonary function.

These respiratory symptoms may be associated with headache, nausea, malaise, and difficulties to sustain exercise for vigorously exercising children.

Many studies suggest that moderate levels of ozone may affect lungs in healthy school children and in asthmatic children. Whereas admission rates for persons of all ages, including the elderly, increase following summertime ozone exposure, children less than two years old were observed to be at greater risk. In a cohort of 846 asthmatic children aged 4–9 years, Mortimer et al. reported children who had had a low birth weight or a premature birth showed the greatest responses to ozone. Moreover, it has been reported that decreased peak flow persists for more than one week and that repeated exposures may result in persistent airway hyperresponsiveness.

Long-term consequences of chronic exposure to ozone are not clearly established, but animal and epidemiological studies suggest long-term health effects. Some experimental animal and clinical toxicological evidence suggests ozone exposure acts synergistically with other pollutants and aeroallergens.

Airborne Particles, Sulfur Oxides, and Acid Aerosols

Origin

Particles, S[O.sub.x] and acid aerosols are a complex group of distinct pollutants that have common sources and usually vary in concentration.

The sulfur oxides come from the combustion of fuels as coal and petroleum. The composition of airborne particles is complex and variable, coming from numerous, natural and manmade sources, including the same combustion sources. Those include industrial and agricultural smoke, engine and car exhausts, and home heating fumes. Particles, sulfur oxides, and nitrogen oxides contribute to the formation of acid aerosols in the atmosphere. While increasing smoke stack heights may have lowered local ambient levels, the residence time of S[O.sub.x] and particles in the air have been increased, thereby promoting transformation to various particulate sulfate compounds, including acidic sulfates. These sulfate particles constitute a large fraction of the total mass of smaller particles (< 3 [micro]m in aerodynamic diameter).

Health Effects in Children

Epidemiological studies have consistently provided evidence of their adverse health effects. Clinical manifestations include acute respiratory symptoms, asthma, bronchitis, chronic cough, and chest illness. Particulates and S[O.sub.2] are implicated in acute morbidity and mortality. The toxicity of particulate matter depends on its chemical composition, which, for example, may include toxins like trace metals or hydrocarbons, and the size of particles, which determines the location of their deposit within the respiratory tract.

Daily fluctuations in PM10 levels (30–150 [micro]g/[m.sup.3]) have been shown to be related to acute respiratory hospital admissions in children, to school and kindergarten absences, to a decrement in peak flow rates in normal children, and to increased medication use in children with asthma.

Acid aerosols have been said to be the most important toxic component of PM10 toxicity. In a recent chamber exposure study, children with allergies or asthma show a positive association between symptoms and acid dose. The role of acid aerosols in respiratory toxicity attributable to particulates, however, has also been challenged.

Controversies surrounding such investigatory results have been explained partly by the relationship between toxic exposure and symptoms may be difficult to analyze, and also because asthmatics can manage their symptoms and pulmonary function with medication, thus blurring the relationship between toxic exposure and hospitalization rate.

It has been reported that health effects display a time lag, with weak same-day effects and stronger cumulative effects of air pollution on asthmatic children for both peak expiratory flow and symptoms. Epidemiological studies suggest a positive association between respiratory morbidity and mortality with particulate matter that has a diameter [less than or equal to] 10 [micro]m. Within the broader toxicological understanding of particulate matter, toxicity in asthmatic children has not yet been clearly established.

Nitrogen Oxides

Origin

Nitrogen oxides come from the combustion of fuels such as coal and petroleum. They are emitted outdoors, but also predominantly indoors, and particularly in those houses without flues for gas appliances.

Health Effects in Children

In the past, the epidemiological evidence for toxic effects of nitrogen oxides were considered inconclusive partly because of methodological problems. More recently evidence has been reported that N[O.sub.2] is associated with an increase in respiratory symptoms among the general population, particularly in children. Studies in asthmatic children have shown an airway hyperresponsiveness to N[O.sub.2] in a homelike environment. In children under 14 years of age, significant associations were demonstrated between daily personal exposure to N[O.sub.2] levels readily available in the domestic setting and chest tightness on the same day, breathlessness on exertion with a one-day lag, daytime and night-time asthma attacks on the same day and with a one-day lag time. Part of the discrepancy between the early and recent studies may be related to the fact that, in children, short-term peak levels of exposure are important to consider in relation to adverse respiratory effects associated with N[O.sub.2] exposure.

Carbon Monoxide

Origin

Carbon monoxide is a tasteless, odorless, colorless, nonirritating gas produced by the incomplete combustion of organic material. It is also produced endogenously in man. It is one of many ubiquitous contaminants of both outdoor and indoor environments. Outdoors CO is a result of emissions from transportation sources, primarily from motor vehicles and combustion gases. The indoor sources include unvented or defective gas, coal, wood and fuel stoves, fire places, kerosene space heaters, water heaters, barbecues, car exhaust from attached garage, and cigarette smoke. CO is probably the most insidious and dangerous indoor air pollutant, and is responsible for poisoning with high mortality rates and sequelae. Carbon monoxide is of special concern for children because it may be found in certain conditions in highly toxic amounts in the indoor air where children spend most of their time.

Health Effects in Children

Carbon monoxide is a major public health problem both in developed and developing countries. It is responsible for a significant percentage of all poisoning deaths.

The frequency of health problems associated with sublethal levels of CO is difficult to quantify. Not all cases of acute or subacute CO poisoning are reported or diagnosed, and complete up-to-date data are difficult to obtain in most developed countries, even more in developing countries. It has been estimated that over 40,000 emergency department visits occurred annually for acute CO poisoning in the United States. Children are frequently poisoned in homes or in the back of a car. In a study concerning 4902 patients hospitalized for CO poisoning, children under 15 years of age represented 23%. Moreover, 6% of these CO-poisoned patients were pregnant women, raising the problem of fetal intoxication.

Acute and Subacute Clinical Effects in Children

The symptoms of CO poisoning in adults are described well in the literature. Several series have shown that the clinical presentation of adults and older children are similar. It includes headache, nausea, vomiting, visual disturbances, dizziness, weakness, confusion, ataxia, syncope, seizures, lethargy, coma, and death.

Unfortunately, little information exists regarding CO poisoning in infants and small children. Many of the early manifestations of CO poisoning, such as headache, nausea, and blurred vision are difficult or impossible to observe in an infant.

We have performed a two-year prospective study comparing clinical manifestations and outcome in 140 children, aged newborn–14 years, and 774 adults with CO poisoning. Results showed that clinical manifestations in children differed from those in adults. Symptoms like headache, nausea, and coma were less frequent, whereas loss of consciousness, convulsions, and lethargy were more frequent in children than in adults. Neurological examination also showed differences, with fewer abnormal plantar responses and more flaccidity in children than in adults.

Long–Term Manifestations

Moderate to severe CO poisoning is known to be responsible for long-term manifestations and delayed neurological sequelae. These manifestations have also been described in children. It is difficult to determine the incidence of delayed neurological manifestations in a pediatric population particularly because some frequent manifestations like memory impairment are difficult to detect in an infant and may be overlooked. Several series have reported various rates of incidence. These long-term manifestations have been reported to be less frequent in children than in adults. The most frequently reported symptoms involve the so-called high cortical functions like memory impairment, personality alterations, signs of parietal dysfunction, and more rarely motor symptoms (hemiplegia, akinesia). Temporary cortical blindness and involuntary movements have also been reported. Further studies are needed to determine the long-term consequences of CO poisoning in children.

Fetus Intoxication

Experimental and clinical studies have demonstrated the toxic effects of CO exposure on the fetus during all stages of gestation. Fetal hypoxia is more pronounced than maternal tissue hypoxia, and the severity of fetal intoxication cannot be assessed solely by the maternal state. These effects include teratogenesis, neurological dysfunction, decreased birth weight, and increased risk of fetal death. Even at 40w CO concentration, some evidence has been reported concerning the contribution of CO to the association of ambient air pollution with reduced birth weight.

In our center, we surveyed all women intoxicated by CO during pregnancy. We found a four-fold increase in the relative risk of fetal death. In this series, where every woman was treated with hyperbaric oxygen, no increase in prematurity, fetal hypotrophy, or malformation rate could be detected compared with the general population. Long-term prospective surveillance of these children has been implemented in order to assess the neurological deterioration if it occurs later during child development.

CONCLUSION

Various factors related to age, physiologic maturity, and exposure patterns make children potentially more susceptible than adults to the adverse effects of air pollution. Besides acute manifestations, exposure during childhood may have long lasting effects and requires special follow-up.

Our own experience acquired through studies of CO exposure taught us how toxic manifestations may be different in children compared to adults. Special attention has to be given to the unique physiology and other qualities of the child in order to properly evaluate the clinical consequences of their toxic exposures. Such considerations emphasize the key roles of poison centers, clinical toxicologists, and pediatricians working in collaboration towards the identification, assessment, and surveillance of toxic risks from air pollution for children health and development.

———

Based on these findings and others like them, the EPA had the following ambient levels established for these pollutants as of 2004:

Criteria Air Pollutants	Allowable Exposure Primary standard*	CFR Section
Sulfur Dioxide	Annual: 0.030 ppm 24–hour: 0.14 ppm	40 CFR § 50.4 (a) 40 CFR § 50.4 (b)
Sulfur Dioxide	3–hour: 0.5 ppm * (secondary standard)	40 CFR § 50.5 (a)
Particulate Matter 10	Annual: 50 µg/m3 24–hour: 150 µg/m3	40 CFR § 50.6 (b) 40 CFR § 50.6 (a)
Particulate Matter 2.5	Annual: 15 µg/m3 24–hour: 65 µg/m3	40 CFR § 50.7 (a)(1) 40 CFR § 50.7 (a)(1)
Carbon Monoxide	8–hour: 9 ppm	40 CFR § 50.8 (a)(1)

Criteria Air Pollutants	Allowable Exposure Primary standard*	CFR Section
	1–hour: 35 ppm	40 CFR § 50.8 (a)(2)
Ozone	8–hour: .08 ppm	40 CFR § 50.10 (a)
	1–hour: 12 ppm	40 CFR § 50.9 (a)
Nitrogen Dioxide	Annual: 0.053 ppm	40 CFR § 50.11 (a)
Lead	Calendar Quarter: 1.5 Sg/m3	40 CFR § 50.12

Given the nature of these criteria pollutants, the various effects they can cause, and the different "at risk" populations, how does the EPA actually establish a "safe" level under Sec. 109? What factors can it consider? What evidence can it use? How much deference is given to its air quality modeling? How does this alter the legal strategies of parties who will be affected by the establishment of these standards? The following case answers some of these questions.

WHITMAN v. AMERICAN TRUCKING ASSOCIATIONS, INC.

Supreme Court of the United States, 2001.
531 U.S. 457, 121 S.Ct. 903, 149 L.Ed.2d 1.

I

Section 109(a) of the CAA, as added, 84 Stat. 1679, and amended, 42 U.S.C.§ 7409(a), requires the Administrator of the EPA to promulgate NAAQS for each air pollutant for which "air quality criteria" have been issued under § 108, 42 U.S.C. § 7408. Once a NAAQS has been promulgated, the Administrator must review the standard (and the criteria on which it is based) "at five-year intervals" and make "such revisions ... as may be appropriate." CAA § 109(d)(1), 42 U.S.C. § 7409(d)(1). These cases arose when, on July 18, 1997, the Administrator revised the NAAQS for particulate matter and ozone.

See NAAQS for Particulate Matter, 62 Fed.Reg. 38652 (codified in 40 CFR § 50.7 (1999)); NAAQS for Ozone, id., at 38856 (codified in 40 CFR §§ 50.9, 50.10 (1999)).

* * *

II

In Lead Industries Assn., Inc. v. EPA, supra, at 1148, the District of Columbia Circuit held that "economic considerations [may] play no part in the promulgation of ambient air quality standards under Section 109" of the CAA. In the present cases,the court adhered to that holding, 175 F.3d, at 1040–1041, as it had done on many other occasions. See, e.g., American Lung Assn. v. EPA, 134 F.3d 388, 389(C.A.D.C.1998); NRDC v. Administrator, EPA, 902 F.2d 962, 973 (C.A.D.C.1990), vacated in part on other grounds, NRDC v. EPA, 921 F.2d 326 (C.A.D.C.1991); American

Petroleum Institute v. Costle, 665 F.2d 1176, 1185 (C.A.D.C.1981). Respondents argue that these decisions are incorrect. We disagree ...

Section 109(b)(1) instructs the EPA to set primary ambient air quality standards "the attainment and maintenance of which ... are requisite to protect the public health" with "an adequate margin of safety." 42 U.S.C. § 7409(b)(1). Were it not for the hundreds of pages of briefing respondents have submitted on the issue, one would have thought it fairly clear that this text does not permit the EPA to consider costs in setting the standards. The language, as one scholar has noted, "is absolute." D. Currie, Air Pollution: Federal Law and Analysis 4–15 (1981). The EPA, "based on" the information about health effects contained in the technical "criteria" documents compiled under § 108(a)(2), 42 U.S.C. § 7408(a)(2), is to identify the maximum airborne concentration of a pollutant that the public health can tolerate, decrease the concentration to provide an "adequate" margin of safety, and set the standard at that level. No where are the costs of achieving such a standard made part of that initial calculation.

* * *

[1]   Even so, respondents argue, many more factors than air pollution affect public health. In particular, the economic cost of implementing a very stringent standard might produce health losses sufficient to offset the health gains achieved in cleaning the air—for example, by closing down whole industries and thereby impoverishing the workers and consumers dependent upon those industries. That is unquestionably true, and Congress was unquestionably aware of it. Thus, Congress had commissioned in the Air Quality Act of 1967 (1967 Act) "a detailed estimate of the cost of carrying out the provisions of this Act; a comprehensive study of the cost of program implementation by affected units of government; and a comprehensive study of the economic impact of air quality standards on the Nation's industries, communities, and other contributing sources of pollution." § 2, 81 Stat.505. The 1970 Congress, armed with the results of this study, see The Cost of Clean Air, S. Doc. No. 91–40 (1969) (publishing the results of the study), not only anticipated that compliance costs could injure the public health, but provided for that precise exigency. Section 110(f)(1) of the CAA permitted the Administrator to waive the compliance deadline for stationary sources if, inter alia, sufficient control measures were simply unavailable and "the continued operation of such sources is essential ... to the public health or welfare." 84 Stat. 1683 (emphasis added). Other provisions explicitly permitted or required economic costs to be taken into account in implementing the air quality standards. Section111(b)(1)(B), for example, commanded the Administrator to set "standards of performance" for certain new sources of emissions that as specified in § 111(a)(1) were to "reflec[t] the degree of emission limitation achievable through the application of the best system of emission reduction which (taking into account the cost of achieving such reduction) the Administrator determines has been adequately demonstrated." Section

202(a)(2) prescribed that emissions standards for automobiles could take effect only "after such period as the Administrator finds necessary to permit the development and application of the requisite technology, giving appropriate consideration to the cost of compliance within such period." 84 Stat. 1690. See also § 202(b)(5)(C) (similar limitation for interim standards); § 211(c)(2) (similar limitation for fuel additives); § 231(b) (similar limitation for implementation of aircraft emission standards).

Subsequent amendments to the CAA have added many more provisions directing, in explicit language, that the Administrator consider costs in performing various duties. See, e.g., 42 U.S.C. § 7545(k)(1) (reformulate gasoline to "require the greatest reduction in emissions ... taking into consideration the cost of achieving such emissions reductions"); § 7547(a)(3) (emission reduction for nonroad vehicles to be set "giving appropriate consideration to the cost" of the standards). We have therefore refused to find implicit in ambiguous sections of the CAA an authorization to consider costs that has elsewhere, and so often, been expressly granted. See Union Elec. Co. v. EPA, 427 U.S. 246, 257, and n. 5, 96 S.Ct. 2518, 49 L.Ed.2d 474 (1976). Cf. General Motors Corp. v. United States, 496 U.S. 530, 538, 541, 110 S.Ct. 2528, 110 L.Ed.2d 480 (1990) (refusing to infer in certain provisions of the CAA deadlines and enforcement limitations that had been expressly imposed elsewhere).

* * *

Their first claim is that § 109(b)(1)'s terms "adequate margin" and "requisite" leave room to pad health effects with cost concerns. Just as we found it "highly unlikely that Congress would leave the determination of whether an industry will be entirely, or even substantially, rate-regulated to agency discretion—and even more unlikely that it would achieve that through such a subtle device as permission to 'modify' rate-filing requirements," MCI Telecommunications Corp. v. American Telephone & Telegraph Co., supra, at 231, 114 S.Ct. 2223, so also we find it implausible that Congress would give to the EPA through these modest words the power to determine whether implementation costs should moderate national air quality standards. Accord, Christensen v. Harris County, 529 U.S. 576, 590, 120 S.Ct. 1655, 146 L.Ed.2d 621, n.* (2000) (SCALIA, J., concurring in part and concurring in judgment) ("The implausibility of Congress's leaving a highly significant issue unaddressed (and thus 'delegating' its resolution to the administering agency) is assuredly one of the factors to be considered in determining whether there is ambiguity" (emphasis deleted)). [footnote omitted]

The same defect inheres in respondents' next two arguments: that while the Administrator's judgment about what is requisite to protect the public health must be "based on [the] criteria" documents developed under § 108(a)(2), see § 109(b)(1), it need not be based solely on those criteria; and that those criteria themselves, while they must include "effects on public health or welfare which may be expected from the presence of such pollutant in the ambient air," are not necessarily limited to those effects. Even if we were to concede those premises, we still would not conclude that one of the unenumerated factors that the agency can consider in developing and applying the criteria is cost of implementation. That factor is both so indirectly related to public health and so full of potential for canceling the conclusions drawn from direct health effects that it would surely have been expressly mentioned in §§ 108 and 109had Congress meant it to be considered. Yet while those provisions describe in detail how the health effects of pollutants in the ambient air are to be calculated and given effect, see § 108(a)(2), they say not a word about costs.

* * *

We agree with the Solicitor General that the text of § 109(b)(1) of the CAA at a minimum requires that "[f]or a discrete set of pollutants and based on published air quality criteria that reflect the latest scientific knowledge, [the] EPA must establish uniform national standards at a level that is requisite to protect public health from the adverse effects of the pollutant in the ambient air." Tr. of Oral Arg. in No. 99–1257, p. 5. Requisite, in turn, "mean[s] sufficient, but not more than necessary." Id., at 7.

The EPA is to revisit the NAAQS standards every five years to determine if the same standards should still govern in the face of new evidence. This allows standards to be revisited not only based on scientific understanding, but provides a chance for political influences as well. Much concern has recently been expressed about the NAAQS for particulates, with special attention to small particulates. New evidence may continue to alter this standard for some time to come.[1]

The language of Lead Industries (which has been cited approvingly by the Supreme Court) and the language of American Trucking set out both permissible and impermissible exercises of agency discretion in the implementation of the Clean Air Act. The EPA *must* list a pollutant as a criteria pollutant if the EPA determines that it causes an adverse effect and is from numerous and diverse sources,[13] but it has some discretion as to where it sets the acceptable level of exposure requisite to protect the public health, though cost is not to be considered.[14] This does not mean, however, that the EPA will always list a pollutant that many feel is injurious, or that it will always set the standard at an exposure level that some scientific studies may support.

Based on its role as a greenhouse gas, contributing to global warming, and its presence from myriad and diverse sources, should Carbon Dioxide be considered a criteria pollutant under 42 U.S.C. Sec. 7408? If so, at what level should the ambient standard be set? At levels that

---

1. Greenwire, April 4, 2005, at http://www.eenews.net/Greenwire/ (Scientists urge EPA to toughen particulate standard).

13. 42 U.S.C. Sec. 7408 (CAA 108).

14. 42 U.S.C. Sec. 7409 (CAA 109).

existed before the industrial revolution? What if some amount of global warming is beneficial? What if it is only beneficial to some persons? Beneficial to the United States but not Bangladesh? We may have an answer to this question soon.

―――――

June 5, 2003

3 States Sue E.P.A. to Regulate Emissions of Carbon Dioxide
By KIRK JOHNSON

Carbon dioxide emissions from cars and power plants should be regulated as an air pollutant because they contribute to global warming, three Northeast states said yesterday in a federal lawsuit against the Environmental Protection Agency.

State officials in Connecticut, Maine and Massachusetts said the suit, filed in Federal District Court in Hartford, is the first time that any state has sued the government to compel action on climate change.

If the suit succeeds, the E.P.A. will be required to classify carbon dioxide as a "criteria pollutant," under the Federal Clean Air Act, and that would trigger, the state's lawyers say, a process of setting standards for allowable levels in the atmosphere, as the federal government now does for ozone, lead and sulfur dioxide and other gasses.

"Global warming is no longer some abstract threat—it's real and it's urgent," said Richard Blumenthal, attorney general of Connecticut. "Our lawsuit is a last resort."

An E.P.A. spokesman, David Deegan, said the agency was still studying the suit and would have no specific comment. But he said that President Bush and Christie Whitman, the E.P.A. administrator, had made their positions clear.

"The president and Administrator Whitman have said that carbon dioxide shouldn't be regulated as a pollutant; the science on it is more complex, and the answers are elusive right now," he said. "They support a flexible approach that will adjust for new information and technology."

Ms. Whitman resigned last month and is leaving her post at the end of this month. The White House has not yet nominated a successor.

The heart of the states' argument, legal experts said, comes down, to a certain extent, to semantics: what exactly constitutes a pollutant? When the Clean Air Act was passed in the 1970's, air pollution meant things would make people demonstrably sick. But as evidence of indirect consequences has grown—like the chemical combinations that form smog, for instance, or acid rain, which mainly affects aquatic life—the boundary of what is considered harmful has expanded.

The suit contends that while carbon dioxide does not pose a direct threat to human health, it has passed over the threshold of harm because of its role in global warming. The scientific evidence about the buildup of so-called greenhouse gases like carbon dioxide—and the long-term threats posed by climate upheaval on everything from emerging diseases to economics—are so firmly established, the states say, that the government has a responsibility to act.

"E.P.A. itself predicts that the problems associated with atmospheric warming will intensify in the years to come," said Steven Rowe, Maine's attorney general. "The agency has a legal duty to act now."

A spokesman for the Edison Electric Institute, a trade group that represents shareholder-owned electricity companies, said the suit, if it succeeds, would hurt the economy without achieving its desired results. Electric power plants and automobiles account for a majority of the carbon dioxide emissions in the nation.

The spokesman, Dan Riedinger, said there is currently no technological means of eliminating carbon dioxide from a power plant's smoke-stacks. Imposing atmospheric standards, he said, would force plants to switch from burning coal, which produces lots of carbon dioxide, to natural gas, which produces less. But that kind of shift, he said, could bring havoc to the nation's natural gas supply and delivery system.

"To be effective, any policy response to global warming must allow time for new technology," he said.

Many states are starting to address climate change concerns. This year, Gov. George E. Pataki of New York said he hoped to create a regional consortium of states, from Maine to Maryland, to work on the issue. New Hampshire has passed legislation regulating power plant emissions. California passed a law last year requiring reductions in carbon dioxide for automobiles.

"There's a lot of activity, and it's all building," said Ashok Gupta, the director of air and energy programs at the Natural Resources Defense Council, a New York-based conservation group. "At some point, we will be regulating carbon dioxide at power plants, if not in the whole economy. It's a question of when."

After the filing of this lawsuit, the EPA issued a memorandum denying a similar request to regulate carbon dioxide from mobile sources. In doing so, the EPA specifically rejected an earlier EPA determination from the Clinton administration stating that carbon dioxide is an "air pollutant" under the CAA. This memorandum overturning the prior interpretation, dated August 28, 2003, stated that "the CAA does not authorize EPA [sic] to regulate for global climate change purposes."[15] Since the claim of the northeastern states had referenced the earlier EPA determination, the states withdrew their lawsuit without prejudice, and instead challenged this administrative action in the D.C. Circuit.

<hr />

15. Memorandum from Robert Fabricant, EPA General Counsel to Marianne L. Horinko, Acting EPA Administrator, dated August 23, 2003 [on file with the author.]

COMMONWEALTH OF MASSACHUSETTS v. UNITED STATES ENVIRONMENTAL PROTECTION AGENCY

United States Court of Appeals
For the District of Columbia Circuit.

NON-BINDING STATEMENT OF ISSUES

The petitioners listed above propound the following issues in support of their petition:

1. Does the Environmental Protection Agency (EPA) have authority to regulate greenhouse gas emissions where the Clean Air Act expressly authorizes the agency to regulate the emission of any substances that endanger public health or welfare and where nothing in the Act or in any other statute takes away that authority when the substances at issue contribute to global warming?

2. Is EPA precluded from exercising its express authority to protect the public health or welfare by setting emissions standards for new motor vehicles and engines merely because the implementation of such standards may affect the fuel economy of the regulated vehicles?

3. Was EPA's decision to deny a petition that had sought the regulation of greenhouse gas emissions from new motor vehicles and engines arbitrary, capricious, an abuse of discretion, or otherwise not in accordance with law, where the agency relied on erroneous interpretations of law, failed to consider relevant statutory factors, and otherwise failed to comply with its statutory responsibilities?

———

This case went to oral argument on April 8, 2005.

As this book goes to press, the issue has not resolved. Nevertheless, beyond the substantive issue, the consideration of Carbon Dioxide as a criteria pollutant or as a mobile source pollutant that affects public health shows the importance of the procedural stance of the agency and the care needed to challenge agency determinations at the right time and in the right forum.

C. How are the National Ambient Air Quality Standards Met?—State Implementation Plans

The primary responsibility for enforcing the ambient air quality standards was left to each state. Each state was to ensure that all criteria air pollutants were controlled at levels below the NAAQS throughout the entire state. The states were to do this by creating plans to implement these standards—the State Implementation Plans (SIPs). The process is described in the following cases:

NATURAL RESOURCES DEFENSE
COUNCIL, INC. v. TRAIN

United States Court of Appeals, Second Circuit, 1976.

545 F.2d 320.

* * *

Once a pollutant has been listed under § 108(a)(1), §§ 109 and 110 of the Act are automatically invoked.[4] These sections require that for any pollutant for which air quality criteria are issued under § 108(a)(1)(C) after the date of enactment of the Clean Air Amendments of 1970, the Administrator must simultaneously issue air quality standards. Within nine months of the promulgation of such standards, states are required to submit implementation plans to the Administrator. § 110(a)(1). The Administrator must approve or disapprove a state plan within four months. § 110(a)(2). If a state fails to submit an acceptable plan, the Administrator is required to prepare and publish such a plan himself. § 110(c). State implementation plans must provide for the attainment of primary ambient air quality standards no later than three years from the

---

4. Section 109, 42 U.S.C. § 1857c–4 provides in relevant part:

SEC. 109. (a)(1) The Administrator

(A) within 30 days after the date of enactment of the Clean Air Amendments of 1970, shall publish proposed regulations prescribing a national primary ambient air quality standard and a national secondary ambient air quality standard for each air pollutant for which air quality criteria have been issued prior to such date of enactment; and

(B) after a reasonable time for interested persons to submit written comments thereon (but no later than 90 days after the initial publication of such proposed standards) shall by regulation promulgate such proposed national primary and secondary ambient air quality standards with such modifications as he deems appropriate.

(2) With respect to any air pollutant for which air quality criteria are issued after the date of enactment of the Clean Air Amendments of 1970, the Administrator shall publish, simultaneously with the issuance of such criteria and information, proposed national primary and secondary ambient air quality standards for any such pollutant. The procedure provided for in paragraph (1) (B) of this subsection shall apply to the promulgation of such standards.

(b)(1) National primary ambient air quality standards, prescribed under subsection (a) shall be ambient air quality stan-

dards the attainment and maintenance of which in the judgment of the Administrator, based on such criteria and allowing an adequate margin of safety, are requisite to protect the public health. Such primary standards may be revised in the same manner as promulgated.

Section 110, 42 U.S.C. § 1857c–5, provides in pertinent part:

SEC. 110. (a)(1) Each State shall, after reasonable notice and public hearings, adopt and submit to the Administrator, within nine months after the promulgation of a national primary ambient air quality standard (or any revision thereof) under section 109 for any air pollutant, a plan which provides for implementation, maintenance, and enforcement of such primary standard in each air quality control region (or portion thereof) within such State. In addition, such State shall adopt and submit to the Administrator (either as a part of a plan submitted under the preceding sentence or separately) within nine months after the promulgation of a national ambient air quality secondary standard (or revision thereof), a plan which provides for implementation, maintenance, and enforcement of such secondary standard in each air quality control region (or portion thereof) within such State. Unless a separate public hearing is provided, each State shall consider its plan implementing such secondary standard at the hearing required by the first sentence of this paragraph.

date of approval of a plan. § 110(a)(2)(A)(i). Extension of the three-year period for attaining the primary standard may be granted by the Administrator only in very limited circumstances, and in no case for more than two years. § 110(e).

* * *

TRAIN v. NATURAL RESOURCES DEFENSE COUNCIL, INC.

Supreme Court of the United States, 1975.

421 U.S. 60, 95 S.Ct. 1470, 43 L.Ed.2d 731.

* * *

I

Congress initially responded to the problem of air pollution by offering encouragement and assistance to the States. In 1955 the Surgeon General was authorized to study the problem of air pollution, to support research, training, and demonstration projects, and to provide technical assistance to state and local governments attempting to abate pollution. 69 Stat. 322. In 1960 Congress directed the Surgeon General to focus his attention on the health hazards resulting from motor vehicle emissions. Pub.L. 86—493, 74 Stat. 162. The Clean Air Act of 1963, 77 Stat. 392, authorized federal authorities to expand their research efforts, to make grants to state air pollution control agencies, and also to intervene directly to abate interstate pollution in limited circumstances. Amendments in 1965, § 101, 79 Stat. 992, and in 1966, 80 Stat. 954, broadened federal authority to control motor vehicle emissions and to make grants to state pollution control agencies.

The focus shifted somewhat in the Air Quality Act of 1967, 81 Stat. 485. It reiterated the premise of the earlier Clean Air Act 'that the prevention and control of air pollution at its source is the primary responsibility of States and local governments.' Ibid. Its provisions, however, increased the federal role in the prevention of air pollution, by according federal authorities certain powers of supervision and enforcement. But the States generally retained wide latitude to determine both the air quality standards which they would meet and the period of time in which they would do so.

The response of the State to these manifestations of increasing congressional concern with air pollution was disappointing. Even by 1970, state planning and implementation under the Air Quality Act of 1967 had made little progress. Congress reacted by taking a stick to the States in the form of the Clean Air Amendments of 1970, Pub.L. 91—604, 84 Stat. 1676, enacted on December 31 of that year. These Amendments sharply increased federal authority and responsibility in the continuing effort to combat air pollution. Nonetheless, the Amendments explicitly preserved the principle: 'Each State shall have the primary responsibility for assuring air quality within the entire geographic area comprising such State....' § 107(a) of the Clean Air Act, as added, 84 Stat. 1678, 42 U.S.C. § 1857c—2(a). The difference under the Amendments was that the States were no longer given any choice as to whether they would meet this responsibility. For the first time they were required to attain air quality of specified standards, and to do so within a specified period of time.

* * *

Within nine months after the Agency's promulgation of primary and secondary air quality standards, each of the 50 States was required to submit to the Agency a plan designed to implement and maintain such standards within its boundaries. § 110(a)(1) of the Clean Air Act, as added, 84 Stat. 1680, 42 U.S.C. § 1857c—5(a)(1). The Agency was in turn required to approve each State's plan within four months of the deadline for submission, if it had been adopted after public hearings and if it satisfied eight general conditions set forth in§ 110(a)[footnote omitted]. Probably the principal of these conditions, and the heart of the 1970 Amendments, is that the plan provide for the attainment of the national primary ambient air quality standards in the particular State 'as expeditiously as practicable but . . . in no case later than three years from the date of approval of such plan.' § 110(a)(2)(A). In providing for such attainment, a State's plan must include 'emission limitations, schedules, and timetables for compliance with such limitations'; it must also contain such other measures as may be necessary to insure both timely attainment and subsequent maintenance of national ambient air standards. § 110(a)(2)(B).

* * *

No one can doubt that Congress imposed upon the Agency and States a comprehensive planning task of the first magnitude which was to be accomplished in a relatively short time. In the case of the States, it was soon realized that in order to develop the requisite plans within the statutory nine-month deadline, efforts would have to be focused on determining the stringent emission limitations necessary to comply with national standards. This was true even though compliance with the standards would not be necessary until the attainment date, which normally would be three years after Agency approval of a plan. The issue then arose as to how these stringent limitations, which often could not be satisfied without substantial research and investment, should be applied during the period prior to that date.

* * *

We believe that the foregoing analysis of the structure and legislative history of the Clean Air Amendments shows that Congress intended to impose national ambient air standards to be attained within a specific period of time. It also shows that in §§ 110(e) and (f) Congress carefully limited the circumstances in which timely attainment and subsequent maintenance of these standards could be compromised. We also believe that Congress, consistent with its declaration that '(e)ach State shall have the primary responsibility for assuring air quality' within its boundaries, § 107(a), left to the States considerable latitude in determining specifically how the standards would be met. This discretion includes the continuing authority to revise choices about the mix of emission limitations. We therefore conclude that the Agency's interpretation of §§ 110(a)(3) and 110(f) was 'correct,' to the extent that it can be said with complete assurance that any particular interpretation of a complex statute such as this is the 'correct' one.

* * *

Section 110(a)(2)(H) does nothing more than impose a minimum requirement that state plans be capable of such modifications as are necessary to meet the basic goal of cleansing the ambient air to the extent necessary to protect public health, as expeditiously as practicable within a three-year period. The section in no way prevents the States from also permitting ameliorative revisions which do not compromise the basic goal. Nor does it, by requiring a particular type of revision, preclude those of a different type. As we have already noted, § 110(a)(3) requires the Agency to approve 'any revision' which is consistent with § 110(a)(2)'s minimum standards for an initial plan, and which the State adopted after reasonable public notice and hearing; no other restrictions whatsoever are placed on the Agency's duty to approve revisions. [footnote omitted.]

* * *

1.   What about the transport of criteria pollutants?

In addition to ensuring the attainment of the NAAQS in their own states, State Implementation Plans are also supposed to ensure that air pollution sources in one state do not "contribute significantly to nonattainment in, or interfere with maintenance by, any other State with respect to any such national.... ambient air quality standard."[16] In a federalized system, such a requirement is logical, but how is it be measured or enforced? Two parts of the Clean Air Act address this question. Section 126 (42 U.S.C. Sec. 7426) requires the EPA to take action against sources in other states that contribute to the degradation of another state's SIP. In 1990, Congress added sections 176A and 184, which authorize the EPA to set up a multi-state transport region to deal with the cumulative effects of transport.[17] Both methods have their drawbacks and as the following cases illustrate, depend on vigorous enforcement by the federal agency, since the agency's findings are again given great deference.

16. 42 U.S.C. Sec. 7410 (a)(2)(D)(i)(I) (CAA 110 (a)(2)(D)(i)(I)).

17. 42 U.S.C. Sec. 7506a and 7511c.

APPALACHIAN POWER COMPANY v. ENVIRONMENTAL PROTECTION AGENCY

United States Court of Appeals, District of Columbia Circuit, 2001.
249 F.3d 1032.

* * *

A. *Statutory Framework*

Under the Clean Air Act, the EPA promulgates national ambient air quality standards ("NAAQS") for criteria air pollutants, including tropospheric ozone. *See* 42 U.S.C. § 7409. The EPA then designates those areas of the United States that fail to meet the various NAAQS. 42 U.S.C. § 7407(d). States, in turn, are required to adopt state implementation plans ("SIPs") providing for the attainment of the NAAQS. 42 U.S.C. § 7410. The SIPs are submitted to the EPA for approval, and may be revised at the EPA's insistence if found to be inadequate to ensure maintenance of the NAAQS or public health. States that fail to comply with these requirements are subject to various sanctions and the imposition of a Federal Implementation Plan ("FIP"). 42 U.S.C. § 7509.

Much air pollution is a local or regional problem. Some pollution, however, is caused or augmented by emissions from other states. Emissions from "upwind" regions may pollute "downwind" regions. Several provisions of the CAA are designed to address such transboundary air pollution. In particular, section 110(a)(2)(D)(i)(I) of the Act requires states to prohibit emissions within the state in amounts that will "contribute significantly to nonattainment in, or interfere with maintenance by, any other State" of the NAAQS. 42 U.S.C. § 7410(a)(2)(D)(i)(I).

CAA section 126 provides a mechanism whereby downwind states may petition the EPA to directly regulate upwind sources of pollution. Under section 126(b), 42 U.S.C. § 7426(b), a downwind state "may petition the Administrator for a finding that any major source or group of stationary sources emits or would emit any air pollutant in violation" of CAA section 110(a)(2)(D). Once the EPA makes a section 126(b) finding, section 126(c) provides that:

it shall be a violation of this section and the applicable implementation plan in such State—

(1) for any major proposed new (or modified) source with respect to which a finding has been made under subsection (b) of this section to be constructed or to operate in violation [of this section or section 110], or

(2) for any major existing source to operate more than three months after such finding has been made with respect to it.

42 U.S.C. § 7426(c). The Administrator may allow the continued operation of existing sources beyond three months provided such sources comply with emission limitations and compliance schedules provided by the Administrator which "bring about compliance ... as expeditiously as practicable, but in no case later than three years after the date of such finding." *Id.*

At issue in this case is the extent of the EPA's authority to make findings and directly regulate sources in upwind states under section 126, and whether the EPA's section 126 rule was arbitrary and capricious or contrary to law.

B. The NOx SIP Call

In October 1998, the EPA issued a final rule calling upon twenty two states[1] and the District of Columbia to revise their ozone SIPs to address interstate **air pollution** (aka "interstate **transport**"). *See* Finding of Significant Contribution and Rulemaking for Certain States in the Ozone Transport Assessment Group Region for Purposes of Reducing Regional Transport of Ozone, 63 Fed. Reg. 57,356 (1998) ("*NOx SIP Call*"). Concluding that upwind states contribute significantly to ozone nonattainment problems in downwind states, the EPA required each jurisdiction to promulgate a new SIP to reduce NOx emissions. This "NOx SIP call" required states to reduce NOx emissions by the amount that could be accomplished by emission controls capable of reducing emissions at a cost of $2,000 or less per ton. Under the rule, revised SIPs were due by September 30, 1999, and SIP provisions covering stationary sources had to be implemented by May 1, 2003. Failure to submit an adequate NOx SIP by the deadline would result in implementation of a FIP by the EPA. In other words, if the states do not submit a plan for meeting their CAA obligations, the EPA will impose one of its own.

C. The Original Section 126 Rule–Conditional Findings

In August 1997, eight states submitted petitions requesting that the EPA find that stationary sources in upwind states contribute significantly to downwind air pollution. Specifically, the petitioning states sought findings pursuant to CAA section 126(b), 42 U.S.C. § 7426(b), that specified sources or categories thereof are the source of NOx emissions that contribute significantly to ozone nonattainment in the petitioning states in violation of CAA section 110(a)(2)(D). 42 U.S.C. § 7410(a)(2)(D). Each petition further sought to have the EPA implement direct federal regulation of stationary sources in upwind states, primarily electric generating facilities and fossil-fuel fired industrial boilers and turbines. Because the section 126 petitions raised many of the same issues as the NOx SIP call, and would require comparable emission reductions, the EPA coordinated its response to the section 126 petitions with the NOx SIP call rulemaking.

In a final rule published on May 25, 1999, the EPA determined that NOx emissions in twelve states and the District of Columbia contribute significantly to nonattainment of the one-hour ozone NAAQS in Connecticut, Massachusetts, New York, and Pennsylvania. Findings of Sig-

---

1. The states are Alabama, Connecticut, Delaware, Georgia, Illinois, Indiana, Kentucky, Maryland, Massachusetts, Michigan, Missouri, New Jersey, New York, North Carolina, Ohio, Pennsylvania, Rhode Island, South Carolina, Tennessee, Virginia, West Virginia, and Wisconsin.

nificant Contribution and Rulemaking on Section 126 Petitions for Purposes of Reducing Interstate Ozone Transport, 64 Fed. Reg. 28,250 (May 25, 1999) ("*May 1999 Rule*"). The twelve states are Delaware, Indiana, Kentucky, Maryland, Michigan, New Jersey, New York, North Carolina, Ohio, Pennsylvania, Virginia, and West Virginia.

Rather than make section 126 findings at that time, however, the EPA determined that it was appropriate to postpone such findings pending the resolution of the NOx SIP call process. Accordingly, the EPA issued a rule providing that the findings would automatically be deemed made with regard to sources from a given state should that state fail to comply with a NOx SIP call deadline. The EPA based this decision on the judgment that full compliance with the NOx SIP call would obviate the need for section 126 findings. Once made, the section 126 findings would require covered sources to come into compliance no later than May 1, 2003. Sources that failed to comply by that date would be required to cease operations.

D. Revised Section 126 Rule–Final Findings

Subsequent to the completion of the section 126 rulemaking, [2] this court issued two orders which caused the EPA to change course. First, on May 14, 1999 this court remanded the EPA's proposed revisions to the ozone NAAQS. *American Trucking Ass'ns v. EPA,* 175 F.3d 1027, *reh'g granted in part and denied in part,* 195 F.3d 4 (D.C.Cir.1999), *rev'd in part sub nom. Whitman v. American Trucking Ass'ns,* 531 U.S. 457, 121 S.Ct. 903, 149 L.Ed.2d 1 (2001). Second, this court issued an order staying the NOx SIP call deadline. *Michigan v. EPA,* No. 98–1497 (D.C.Cir. May 25, 1999) (order granting stay in part).

In response to these orders, the EPA revised the section 126 rule. Findings of Significant Contribution and Rulemaking on Section 126 Petitions for Purposes of Reducing Interstate Ozone Transport, 65 Fed. Reg. 2674 (Jan. 18, 2000) ("*Jan. 2000 Rule*"). In particular, the EPA made the requested findings of significant contributions, granting the relevant portions of the section 126 petitions and delinking the section 126 findings from compliance with the NOx SIP call. The EPA explained that it was "implementing the requirements of section 126 of the CAA in the absence of any currently effective requirement for upwind States to address the interstate pollution transport problems themselves." *Id.* at 2683. Instead, the EPA's new rule contained a provision to withdraw the relevant findings upon approval of a NOx SIP in accordance with the October 1998 NOx SIP call.

As with the NOx SIP call, the EPA considered both NOx emissions and the cost of control in determining which sources contribute significantly to downwind ozone nonattainment. Based upon its analysis of the cost of emissions controls, the EPA concluded that measures which can reduce NOx emissions for $2,000 or less per ton are highly cost-effective.

---

2. Although published on May 25, the initial section 126 rule was signed by the Administrator on April 30, 1999. *See May 1999 Rule,* 65 Fed. Reg. at 28,318.

May 1999 Rule, 64 Fed. Reg. at 28,299. The EPA then divided NOx emission sources into various categories and determined the level of emission reduction that would be highly cost-effective for each category. *Id.* at 28,300–01.

The section 126 rule also established an emission allowance "cap and trade" program, known as the Federal NOx Budget Trading Program. Under this program, originally outlined in the May 1999 rule, regulated sources are allocated tradeable NOx emission allowances and are prohibited from emitting more NOx than the amount of allowances held. If a facility emits more than its initial allowance allocation, it must purchase additional allowances from another facility, reduce its emissions, or cease operations. *Jan. 2000 Rule,* 65 Fed. Reg. at 2733.

To determine the initial allocations, the EPA established a NOx emission cap for each upwind state. Each state's cap is based upon expected emission reductions from highly cost-effective controls in that state as of 2007. *Id.* at 2698. Ninety-five percent of each state's cap is allocated proportionally among existing sources based upon each facility's heat input. Five percent of the cap is set aside for future, as-yet-unproposed sources. *Id.* at 2698–99. These initial allocations will apply for the 2003–07 time period. *Id.* at 2700. The EPA will issue revised allocations for the 2008–12 time period, and every five years thereafter. *Id.*

Since the issuance of the final section 126 rule, this Court has ruled on various challenges to the EPA's NOx SIP call. In *Michigan v. EPA,* 213 F.3d 663 (D.C.Cir.2000), we upheld the SIP call in most respects, remanding portions of the rule to the EPA. Of greatest relevance to these proceedings, we upheld the EPA's analyses of interstate transport of NOx emissions and its use of cost-effectiveness criteria in determining which upwind sources "contribute significantly" to nonattainment in downwind states. Subsequently, we entered an order amending the deadline for full implementation of NOx SIP revisions from May 1, 2003 to May 31, 2004. *Michigan v. EPA,* No. 98–1497, 2000 WL 1341477 (D.C.Cir. Aug. 30, 2000) (order denying motion to stay mandate pending petition for certiorari).

After the EPA published the final section 126 rule in January 2000, numerous groups petitioned this Court for review. Among the petitioners are a group of upwind states from the midwestern and southeastern United States ("MW & SE State Petitioners"); utilities and other operators of electric generating facilities ("Non–State Petitioners"); companies that operate non-electric generating/industrial facilities ("Non–EGU Petitioners"); and several individual companies that have facility-specific concerns ("Facility—Specific Petitioners"). A group of northeastern states ("NE State Petitioners") also petitioned for review alleging that the EPA's rule did not go far enough in controlling upwind NOx emissions. The northeastern states otherwise intervened in support of the EPA, as did a group of environmental organizations. The various petitions for review were consolidated into this case.

II. COMMON AND GENERAL ISSUES

* * *

Section 126 gives a state the right to petition the EPA to find "that any major source or group of stationary sources [in another state] emits or would emit any air pollutant in violation of the prohibition of" a subsection of § 110(a)(2)(D), the subsection here at issue. 42 U.S.C. § 7426(b). As we have noted, the ability of such a source or group of sources to operate is severely constrained once such a finding is made. 42 U.S.C. § 7426(c). The constraints in § 126(c) are triggered by the "prohibition" in whichever subsection of § 110(a)(2)(D) it is that § 126 cross-references. Section 110(a)(2)(D) provides that a state implementation plan ("SIP"), which describes how a state plans to comply with the National Ambient Air Quality Standards ("NAAQS"), must

(D) contain adequate provisions—

(i) prohibiting ... any source or other type of emissions activity within the State from emitting any air pollutant in amounts which will—

(I) contribute significantly to nonattainment in, or interfere with maintenance by, any other State with respect [to the NAAQS] or

(II) interfere with [various other] measures.

(ii) insuring compliance with the applicable requirements of sections 7426 [CAA § 126] and 7415 [CAA § 115] of this title (relating to interstate and international pollution abatement).

42 U.S.C. § 7410(a)(2)(D). Thus, prior to the 1990 Amendments, § 126 provided an avenue by which a state could compel the EPA to enforce emissions limitations upon a neighboring state the emissions from which contributed to its own nonattainment of the NAAQS. The EPA argues that § 126 should still be read to have this effect, notwithstanding the substitution of "(ii)" for "(i)" therein.

* * *

According to the petitioners' reading, the 1990 amendment of §§ 126(b) and (c) gave each state the right to compel enforcement against another state that fails to provide notice of new sources and took away their right to compel enforcement against a state that actually pollutes the complaining state's air. Even were we to assume that such a counterintuitive switch from substantive to procedural compliance could plausibly reflect congressional policy, the petitioners' reading would still be flawed. Section 126(b) permits a state to petition the EPA to find that "any major source or group of stationary sources emits or would emit any air pollutant in violation of the prohibition of section 7410(a)(2)(D)(ii) [CAA § 110(a)(2)(D)(ii)]." 42 U.S.C. § 7426(b). The notice requirement of § 126(a), to which the petitioners claim this reference ultimately points, binds states only to warn their neighbors of proposed new and modified sources; it does not restrict the behavior of sources or groups of sources, whose "violation" of § 110(a)(2)(D) is the predicate for a § 126(b) finding. *See id.* § 7426(a).

The petitioners' suggestion that the enactment of § § 176A and 184, 42 U.S.C. § § 7506a, 7511c, as part of the 1990 Amendments somehow mitigates these problems is without foundation. Those sections authorize the EPA to designate a multistate "transport region" in a case where one state's emissions affect another state's attainment of the NAAQS; for each such region, the EPA must convene a "transport commission," including officials from each state within the region, to advise the EPA Administrator. *Id.* The petitioners correctly describe these new sections as establishing, at least in part, a new approach to interstate air pollution. Because the Congress did not repeal § 126, however, this new approach was clearly not meant to be exclusive; and neither § 176A nor § 184 renders the change in § 126 from "(i)" to "(ii)" any less linguistically or substantively anomalous.

* * *

B. *The NOx SIP Call and § 126*

The Administrator of the EPA must require a state to revise its SIP "as necessary" whenever she finds such a plan "substantially inadequate to ... comply" with various requirements of the Act, including the requirement that the plan "contain adequate provisions" to prevent sources within a state from contributing significantly to any other state's nonattainment or nonmaintenance of the NAAQS. *Id.* § 7410(a)(2)(D)(i)(I), 7410(k)(5). Pursuant to this authority, in October 1998 the EPA issued a request for SIP revisions, or a "SIP call," that required 22 states and the District of Columbia to revise their SIPs in order to mitigate the interstate transport of ozone. *Michigan v. EPA*, 213 F.3d 663, 669 (D.C.Cir.2000) (explicating *NOx SIP Call*, 63 Fed. Reg. at 57,358–59). This court upheld the essential elements of the NOx SIP call in March 2000, although we remanded the rule for further proceedings with regard to three states and to certain types of sources. *Id.* at 695.

In August 1997, during the preparation of the NOx SIP call, eight states petitioned the EPA to find, pursuant to CAA § 126(b), that "major stationary sources or groups of sources" in specified states were contributing to the petitioning states' failure to meet the NAAQS for ozone. 42 U.S.C. § 7426(b). In the first of the two rules challenged here, the EPA announced that because it was "operating on basically the same set of facts" in making determinations under § 126 as it had when it issued the NOx SIP call—that is, facts showing that upwind sources contributed to downwind nonattainment of the NAAQS—it would eschew making formal findings under § 126. *May 1999 Rule*, 64 Fed. Reg. at 28,274/3, 28,275/2. Instead, the agency made the "affirmative technical determination" that sources in upwind states were contributing to nonattainment in downwind states, and provided that a formal finding to that effect under § 126 would be deemed to be made for such sources in a state if by May 1, 2000, EPA has not either (a) approved a state's

SIP revision to comply with the NOx SIP call or (b) promulgated implementation plan provisions meeting the [CAA] section 110(a)(2)(D)(i) requirements.

Id. at 28,275/2.

The EPA used this "automatic trigger mechanism," *Jan. 2000 Rule,* 65 Fed. Reg. at 2679/1, as part of a "coordinated approach" to the SIP call and the § 126 petitions, *May 1999 Rule,* 64 Fed. Reg. at 28,275/3: § 126 findings would be withheld until the conclusion of the SIP call, but would be entered automatically should a state's response to the SIP call be either unsatisfactory or untimely. May 1, 2000 was chosen as the date for triggering the § 126 finding because § 126(c) allows the EPA to permit sources found to contribute to another state's nonattainment to continue to operate for no more than three years after the date of such a finding. 42 U.S.C. § 7426(c). For findings made on May 1, 2000, the three-year clock would expire on May 1, 2003—the same date by which states were required to have implemented controls over sources of interstate ozone under the original NOx SIP call. *See NOx SIP Call,* 63 Fed. Reg. at 57,308/1.

* * *

The petitioners' primary argument, therefore, is that Title I of the Clean Air Act is animated by a commitment to "cooperative federalism" under which the EPA is to determine what level of air quality is required but must defer in the first instance to the judgments of the states regarding how to achieve that level. This principle, according to the petitioners, requires that a SIP call inviting states to respond to the problem of interstate transport be the preferred remedy, while direct federal regulation of sources, as authorized by § 126, must be a last resort reserved for cases in which states cannot or do not meet their SIP obligation.

* * *

The petitioners contend that the delay in the NOx SIP call deadline, because it did not affect the "Congress' clear preference" for state implementation decisions, should not have altered the EPA's determination that the SIP call takes precedence over § 126. The EPA, however, is obligated not only to give to § 110 a meaning that is consistent with *Train* and *Virginia,* but also reasonably to construe § 126. The EPA, which considers the two provisions to be "independent statutory tools to address the problem of interstate pollution transport" that the EPA may deploy either singly or in tandem, *Jan. 2000 Rule,* 65 Fed. Reg. at 2680/1, reasonably construes both provisions.

The EPA's view accords with the position of the Second Circuit which, in *Connecticut v. EPA,* was presented with the converse of the question before us: Do §§ 110 and 126 require the EPA to postpone its approval of SIP revisions pending its final action upon petitions for findings under § 126(b)? 656 F.2d at 906–08. Although the *Connecticut* court suggested that "§ 126(b) appears to have been primarily designed as a means for resolving interstate pollution disputes in situations where an SIP is not being revised," *id.* at 907—a dictum in some tension with the EPA's view that § 126 is "independent" of the SIP revision process—the Second Circuit's point was only that the EPA need not, upon receipt of a § 126 petition, suspend the SIP revision process. The court therefore concluded, properly we think, that "[a]s the substantive inquiry for decision is the same in both [§ 110 and § 126] proceedings, an argument that one proceeding must be completed as a prerequisite to a final decision in the other makes no sense." *Id.* at 907; *see also id.* at 908 n. 4 (quoting statement of H.R. Rep. No. 95–249, at 331, *reprinted in* 4 a Legislative History of the Clean Air Act Amendments of 1977, at 2798 (1978), that "the § 126(b) process is designed to provide an 'entirely alternative method and basis for preventing and abating interstate pollution'") (emphasis omitted).

* * *

C. *Significant Contribution*

Non–State Petitioners challenge the methodology by which EPA reached its findings of "significant contribution" to nonattainment of the "1–hour" ozone rule under § 126, 42 U.S.C. § 7426. EPA started with the two-step method that it had used in issuing the SIP call and that we upheld in *Michigan v. EPA,* 213 F.3d 663, 674–80 (D.C.Cir. 2000). As we explained there, EPA first performed computer modeling to determine whether a state's manmade NOx emissions perceptibly hindered a downwind state's attainment. *Id.* at 675. For any state exceeding EPA's threshold criteria, EPA then defined as "significant" those emissions that could be eliminated through application of "highly cost-effective" controls, namely measures costing no more than $2,000 per ton of NOx removed. *Id.* Similarly, EPA relied here on the statewide threshold findings made in the SIP call and then applied the same cost-effectiveness criterion to determine which sources to include. *See* Findings of Significant Contribution and Rulemaking on Section 126 Petitions for Purposes of Reducing Interstate Ozone Transport, 63 Fed. Reg. 56,292, 56,301/3 (proposed Oct. 21, 1998) (*"Oct. 1998 Rule"*).

As discussed above, *see supra* Part II.B, both the SIP call and the § 126 rulemaking are directly linked to the requirement under § 110(a)(2)(D)(i) that SIPs contain provisions prohibiting "any source or other type of emissions activity within the State from emitting any air pollutant in amounts which will ... contribute significantly to nonattainment...." § 110(a)(2)(D)(i), 42 U.S.C. § 7410(a)(2)(D)(i). But the necessary determinations are different in at least two material respects. First, whereas the SIP call exercise yielded a total amount of NOx cutback for each state, which the state was then free to achieve however it might, *see Michigan,* 213 F.3d at 687–88, here the mandate applies directly to sources. Second, whereas § 110(a)(2)(D)'s broad reference to "any source or other type of emissions activity" supported SIP call findings based on aggregate emissions from within each regulated state,

§ 126 demands that the significant contribution come from a "major source or group of *stationary* sources." 42 U.S.C. § 7426(b) (emphasis added).

The Non–State Petitioners argue that this latter distinction renders EPA's reliance on the SIP call findings inadequate; the findings based on *all* emissions can't determine whether stationary source emissions are sufficient. Instead of using those findings, petitioners argue, EPA needed first to make the more rigorous finding that the specified stationary sources within a given state *independently* met its threshold test for effect on downwind nonattainment.

Petitioners find support for their view of the statute in *Michigan,* where we said that the first step in EPA's § 110(a)(2)(D)(i) finding must show a *"measurable contribution"* to downwind nonattainment. 213 F.3d at 683–84. Here, EPA did not purport to satisfy such a standard on the basis of the covered stationary sources alone. Rather, it conceded, "[i]t is conceivable that modeling only the emissions from the section 126 sources would result in smaller ambient impacts downwind [compared to total man-made emissions], and.... those smaller impacts, if analyzed on the basis of the metrics and thresholds developed for State-wide [total man-made] emissions, may not exceed those thresholds." *May 1999 Rule,* 64 Fed. Reg. at 28,283/1.

EPA defended its approach both as a recognition of the fact that the ozone problem is due to the *accumulation* of emissions and as a sensible reconciliation of § 110(a)(2)(D)(i) and § 126. *See id.* at 28,282–83. On the need for some aggregation, of course, there can be no quarrel. Congress's use of the phrase "group of ... sources" plainly reflected a decision to act against sources whose emissions, while harmless individually, could become harmful when combined with others. And, given the relevant statutory provisions, it was reasonable for EPA to link its stationary source findings to the significance of a state's *total* NOx emissions. By speaking of stationary sources that emit pollutants "in violation of the prohibition of [§ 110(a)(2)(D)(i)]," Congress clearly hinged the meaning of § 126 on that of § 110(a)(2)(D)(i). EPA reasoned that if it treated any state's entire manmade emissions as the controlling aggregate for both purposes and found a "significant contribution," "then the State's section 126 sources *may be* subject to SIP controls." *Id.* at 28,282/3 (emphasis added). In other words, a source can be subject to § 126 controls only if it is at least *at risk* of being subject to SIP controls. The effect, of course, is to displace the discretion the state would enjoy in the SIP process under § 110(a)(2)(D)(i). But this displacement of state power seems not materially greater than is inherent in EPA's interpretation of § 126, which we uphold vis-à-vis the objections petitioners raised in their initial briefs. *See supra* Part II.B. EPA's current reading, to be sure, may not be the only possible or even the most compelling view of § 126. Perhaps the EPA could reasonably read it as petitioners would, and require that stationary sources as a whole independently satisfy some "meaningful contribution" test before they may be subject to § 126 findings. But given § 126's silence on what it means for a stationary source to violate § 110(a)(2)(D)(i), EPA's approach is at least reasonable, and therefore entitled to deference under *Chevron*.

* * *

In the present case Non–State Petitioners do not dispute that emissions from affected § 126 sources actually contribute to total man-made NOx emissions that, at the statewide aggregate level, meet the EPA criteria upheld in *Michigan*. The process here does not involve sweeping up individual sources that might well not be part of the problem at all. The concern that drove our discussion in *Michigan* is inapplicable.

* * *

A final challenge to the "contribution" findings is the Non–State Petitioners' argument that for four states (Indiana, Kentucky, Michigan and New York) EPA used *state*-based aggregations to find the contribution but then applied controls to sources in only *part* of each state. This is a reverse of what we struck down in *Michigan*: there extension from part to the whole, here, contraction from the whole to a part. EPA's explanation was that while the modeling was statewide, § 126 empowered it only to address sources named in the downwind states' petitions (which here they did by *area*). *See Jan. 2000 Rule,* 65 Fed. Reg. at 2685/1. Petitioners do not contest EPA's legal assumption, but simply say that the process invalidates the finding.

* * *

D. Emission Limitation Determinations

In order to allocate NOx emission allowances to individual sources, the EPA made state-by-state emission projections for 2007. The EPA based each state's NOx emission budget on projected 2007 heat input (or "utilization") for electric generating units ("EGUs") and projected 2007 emissions for non-electric generating, industrial facilities ("non-EGUs"). The projections were developed with computer models working off of "baseline" emissions and heat input data from 1995 and 1996. Various petitioners challenge the EPA's budget allocations as arbitrary and capricious. While we generally uphold the EPA's authority to make emission projections and set emission limitations accordingly, we do so only where the EPA adequately responded to comments and explained the basis for its decisions. Thus, although we uphold the EPA's use of the Integrated Planning Model ("IPM") as against the specific challenges forwarded by MW & SE Petitioners, we conclude that at least one application of the model is sufficiently unexplained that we must remand the EPA's IPM-derived growth factors for further explanation.

1. Standard of Review

Agency determinations based upon highly complex and technical matters are "entitled to great deference." *Public Citizen Health Research Group v. Brock,* 823 F.2d 626, 628 (D.C.Cir.1987); *see also Huls Am., Inc.*

v. Browner, 83 F.3d 445, 452 (D.C.Cir.1996) ("[W]e will give an extreme degree of deference to the agency when it 'is evaluating scientific data within its technical expertise.'" (citation omitted)). In a prior case named *Appalachian Power Co. v. EPA,* 135 F.3d 791, 802 (D.C.Cir.1998), we described statistical analysis as "perhaps the prime example" of an area of technical wilderness into which judicial expeditions are best limited to ascertaining the lay of the land. Although computer models are "a useful and often essential tool for performing the Herculean labors Congress imposed on EPA in the Clean Air Act," their scientific nature does not easily lend itself to judicial review.... [I]t is only when the model bears no rational relationship to the characteristics of the data to which it is applied that we will hold that the use of the model was arbitrary and capricious.

Id. at 802 (citation omitted).

Under this standard, the EPA has "undoubted power to use predictive models" so long as it "explain[s] the assumptions and methodology used in preparing the model" and "provide[s] a complete analytic defense" should the model be challenged. *Small Refiner Lead Phase–Down Task Force v. EPA,* 705 F.2d 506, 535 (D.C.Cir.1983) ("*SRLPTF*") (citations and internal quotation marks omitted). That a model is limited or imperfect is not, in itself, a reason to remand agency decisions based upon it.

Ultimately, ... we must defer to the agency's decision on how to balance the cost and complexity of a more elaborate model against the oversimplification of a simpler model. We can reverse only if the model is so oversimplified that the agency's conclusions from it are unreasonable.

Id.

2. The Integrated Planning Model

The MW & SE Petitioners contend that the EPA's emissions growth projections were arbitrary and capricious because they relied upon a computer model—the "IPM"—that underestimated growth rates for electric power generation in some upwind states. Several states, including North Carolina, submitted comments to the EPA arguing that they projected significantly greater growth in electric power generation than that predicted by the IPM.

Rather than address the specific complaints of each commenting state, the EPA defended its reliance upon the IPM on three broad grounds. First, all state NOx budget growth rates should be based upon the same methodology to ensure consistency in the NOx cap's application. *Responses to Significant Comments on the Proposed Findings of Significant Contribution and Rulemaking on Section 126 Petitions for Purposes of Reducing Interstate Ozone Transport* at 111 (April 1999) ("*April 1999 RTC*"). Second, the IPM "has received extensive comment, review, and revision over the past several years" during the NOx SIP call and other proceedings. *Id.; see also Appalachian Power,* 135 F.3d at

814–15 (upholding the EPA's use of the IPM). Third, the IPM "provides a reasonable forecast of State growth rates because it carefully takes into account the most important determinants of electricity generation growth that are facing the power industry today." *April 1999 RTC* at 112.

Given the highly deferential standard of review applied to such questions, and the EPA's clear authority to rely upon computer models in place of inconsistent, incomplete, or unreliable empirical data, the Agency's decision to rely upon the IPM, rather than the projections offered by individual states, was not arbitrary and capricious. *See Texas Mun. Power Agency v. EPA,* 89 F.3d 858, 870 (D.C.Cir.1996). In the EPA's judgment, the IPM offered a more comprehensive and consistent means of allocating emission allowances than sorting through the various state-specific projections. That the EPA's projections depend, in large part, on economic projections, rather than environmental factors, makes little difference. "[I]t is within the scope of the agency's expertise to make such a prediction about the market it regulates, and a reasonable prediction deserves our deference notwithstanding that there might also be another reasonable view." *Environmental Action, Inc. v. FERC,* 939 F.2d 1057, 1064 (D.C.Cir.1991). MW & SE State Petitioners may believe their projections are superior to the EPA's—and they may even be correct—but they have not proved their case.

* * *

E. *Regulation of "Future" Sources*

The section 126 rule establishes a NOx budget for each upwind state found to contribute significantly to nonattainment in the petitioning states. Ninety-five percent of this budget is allocated in the form of NOx emission allowances to existing sources. Five percent of each state's budget is set aside for future sources. In this fashion, the rule caps emissions on existing and proposed sources, as well as sources to be proposed and built in the future.

MW & SE State Petitioners challenge the EPA's authority to impose the NOx cap limits to future, as-yet-unproposed stationary sources under section 126. Petitioners argue that the statute does not authorize the EPA to regulate future sources, and that the EPA's contrary interpretation of section 126 is unreasonable. We disagree.

We review the EPA's interpretation under the two-part analysis established in *Chevron U.S.A. Inc. v. Natural Resources Defense Council, Inc.,* 467 U.S. 837, 104 S.Ct. 2778, 81 L.Ed.2d 694 (1984). "First, always," we must consider "whether Congress has directly spoken to the precise question at issue." An affirmative answer "is the end of the matter; for the court, as well as the agency, must give effect to the unambiguously expressed intent of Congress." *Id.* at 842–43, 104 S.Ct. 2778. If, on the other hand, "the statute is silent or ambiguous with respect to the specific issue," we must uphold "a reasonable interpretation made by the administrator of an agency." *Id.* at 843, 844, 104 S.Ct. 2778; *see also American Bus Ass'n v. Slater,* 231 F.3d 1, 4 (D.C.Cir.2000).

Under section 126(b) a downwind state "may petition the Administrator for a finding that any major source or group of stationary sources emits or would emit any air pollutant" in an amount which contributes significantly to nonattainment in the petitioning state. 42 U.S.C. § 7426(b). Once the EPA makes a section 126(b) finding, section 126(c) provides that:

> it shall be a violation of this section and the applicable implementation plan in such State—
>
> (1) for any major proposed new (or modified) source with respect to which a finding has been made under subsection (b) of this section to be constructed or to operate in violation [of this section or section 110], or
>
> (2) for any major existing source to operate more than three months after such finding has been made with respect to it.

Id. § 7426(c). The Administrator may allow the continued operation of existing sources beyond three months provided such sources comply with emission reductions provided by the Administrator to "bring about compliance . . . as expeditiously as practicable, but in no case later than three years after the date of such finding." *Id.*

Petitioners argue that the EPA's interpretation fails at the first step of *Chevron,* contending that section 126(c) authorizes the EPA to regulate existing and proposed sources but not future sources that are not as yet proposed. In petitioners' view, the enumeration of two classes of sources that may be controlled—"major existing sources" and "proposed new (or modified) sources"—precludes the EPA's authority over a third class of sources—"future as-yet-unproposed" sources. *Expressio unius est exclusio alterius.* Petitioners argue that irrespective of whether the EPA can make findings with regard to future, as-yet-unproposed sources, it is not empowered to prohibit their construction or limit their emissions under section 126(c).

We reject petitioners' contention that the statute unambiguously reflects congressional intent to limit the EPA to the two categories defined by petitioners. Section 126 is at least subject to the interpretation that Congress intended to authorize the regulation of emissions from future sources. Under section 126(b), the EPA may find that "any major source or group of stationary sources emits *or would emit*" pollution in violation of section 110. The inclusion of the future conditional phrase "would emit" arguably contemplates the EPA's intervention to prevent future emissions that would contribute significantly to nonattainment in downwind states. Similarly, as the EPA argues, section 126(c) explicitly bars the construction or operation of "any major new proposed sources." By barring the *construction* of those sources, the statute clearly contemplates the imposition of controls on at least some facilities that do not yet exist. These provisions, taken together, may not compel the regulation of future sources under section 126, but they do not unambiguously forbid it. At the least, they introduce sufficient ambiguity into the statutory scheme to prevent resolution of this issue under *Chevron* step one.

In the absence of an unambiguous expression of congressional intent in the plain language of the statute, we advance to the second step of the *Chevron* analysis to determine whether the EPA's interpretation of section 126 is a reasonable one. We conclude that it is. Prior to 1990, section 126(b) only authorized EPA findings that "a major source emits or would emit any air pollutant" which contributes significantly to nonattainment in a downwind state. 42 U.S.C. § 7426(b) (1977). The 1990 Clean Air Act Amendments expanded the scope of this provision by allowing EPA findings with regard to "any major source *or group of stationary sources.*" 42 U.S.C. § 7426(b) (1994) (emphasis added). Similarly, the EPA notes that the cross-referenced provision of the act, section 110(a)(2)(D)([i]) prohibits "type [s] of emissions activity" that contribute significantly. 42 U.S.C. § 7410(a)(2)(D)(i). Like section 126, section 110 confers authority based upon the kind of activity in question. It does not impose any temporal limit.

The statutory language allows the EPA to regulate facilities in upwind states as a class or category, e.g. all coal-fired power plants in North Carolina. If such facilities, as a class, contribute significantly to nonattainment in northeastern states, this is as true for as-yet-unbuilt plants as it is for existing ones. Therefore, the EPA argues, it is reasonable to include future sources in the "group of stationary sources" found to contribute significantly to downwind nonattainment under section 126(b). Indeed, it would be irrational to enable the EPA to make findings that a group of sources in an upwind state contribute to downwind nonattainment, but then preclude the EPA from regulating new sources that contribute to that same pollution. As the EPA explained in its Response to Comments:

> Once EPA has determined that the emissions from the existing sources in an upwind State already make a significant contribution to one or more petitioning downwind States, any additional emissions from a new source in that upwind State would also constitute a portion of that significant contribution, unless the emissions from that new source are limited to the level of highly effective controls.

April 1999 RTC at 39. The EPA's construction of section 126 avoids this result.

The language of section 126(c) does not make the EPA's interpretation an unreasonable one. Petitioners note that section 126(c) specifically identifies two classes of sources—"major existing sources" and "proposed new (or modified) sources"—and makes no mention of future, as-yet-unproposed sources. What petitioners ignore is that section 126(c), by its terms, defines what constitutes a violation of section 126. For a facility to violate the law, by definition it must either exist or be proposed. Future, as-yet-unproposed sources are not mentioned because unproposed, unbuilt facilities cannot themselves be in violation of anything. At the time they become subject to the section 126(c) limitation, however, they will either be an "existing" or "proposed new" source. That is to say, section 126(c) has no direct effect on plants that have yet to be proposed for the precise reason that they have not yet been proposed. This does not mean, however, that facilities proposed after the promulgation of the EPA's findings are exempt from section 126(c). Once they are proposed, they become part of the regulated class.

Perhaps it would be reasonable for the EPA to interpret the statute as urged by petitioners. Section 126 is arguably a stop-gap provision designed to protect downwind states from upwind pollution by empowering the federal government to take direct action against those specific upwind facilities which cause downwind harm. From a structural standpoint, this interpretation may seem intuitive: States regulate all emitters; the EPA only regulates those emitters shown to contribute significantly to downwind nonattainment despite the existence of a SIP. Yet however rational this alternative interpretation of the Clean Air Act may be, under *Chevron* step two, the EPA's interpretation controls so long as it is based upon a permissible construction of the statute. As we conclude that the EPA adopted a reasonable interpretation of section 126's somewhat ambiguous provisions, its interpretation is upheld.

Notes and Questions

As noted in the case, the very real problems with transport, particularly of ozone forming chemicals led to more specific measures to control them in the 1990 amendments. Nevertheless as the case also indicates, great uncertainty about tracing sources makes specific actions difficult under section 126, which is why the EPA tried to work more for a global solution. What happens when there is no effective control of out of state sources? What if, because of out of state pollution, a state has to enact stricter standards to meet the NAAQS? The effective failure of the EPA to regionally control ozone forming chemicals dealt setbacks to several states.

[Federal Register: January 26, 2001 (Volume 66, Number 18)]

[Notices]

ENVIRONMENTAL PROTECTION AGENCY

[GA47–200003; FRL–6936–9].

Adequacy Status of the Atlanta, GA, Submitted Ozone Attainment State Implementation Plan for Transportation Conformity Purposes; Withdrawal of Adequacy Finding

AGENCY: Environmental Protection Agency (EPA).

ACTION: Withdrawal of adequacy finding.

SUMMARY: EPA has decided to withdraw our finding of adequacy for the motor vehicle emissions budgets in the Atlanta, Georgia, ozone attainment SIP submitted on October 28, 1999. We are withdrawing our adequacy finding for several reasons. The United States Court of Appeals for the District of Columbia circuit decided on August 30,2000, that the implementation of the Nitrogen Oxides (NOX)State Implementation

Plan (SIP) Call rule could not be required before May 31, 2004. The emission levels in the Atlanta attainment SIP motor vehicle emissions budget for NOX were based in part on the assumption that transport of ozone recursors into Atlanta from upwind states would be addressed by May 2003 pursuant to EPA's NOX SIP Call. Further, the Georgia Environmental Protection Division (EPD)recently requested that EPA withdraw its adequacy determination of the Atlanta ozone attainment SIP motor vehicle emissions budgets. The notice of the adequacy determination that is being withdrawn was made on February 15, 2000, in a letter to the State and was published in the Federal Register on February 28, 2000.

DATES: The notice of adequacy is withdrawn as of January 26, 2001.

FOR FURTHER INFORMATION CONTACT: Kelly Sheckler (404–562–9042).

SUPPLEMENTARY INFORMATION:

Background

On February 15, 2000, EPA Region 4 sent a letter to the Georgia Environmental Protection Division stating that the motor vehicle emissions budgets for nitrogen oxides (NOX) and volatile organic compounds (VOCs) in the October 28, 1999, Atlanta ozone attainment SIP for 2003 were adequate for the purpose of transportation conformity. EPA published a notice in the Federal Register on February 28, 2000, [65 FR 10490] announcing that we had made an adequacy determination for the motor vehicle emissions budgets in Atlanta's attainment SIP. This finding was also announced on EPA's conformity website, http://www.epa.gov/oms/traq.

Transportation conformity is required by section 176(c) of the Clean Air Act. EPA's conformity rule requires that transportation plans, programs, and projects conform to SIPs and establishes the criteria and procedures for determining whether or not they do conform. Conformity to a SIP means that transportation activities will not produce new air quality violations, worsen existing violations, or delay timely attainment of the national ambient air quality standards.

EPA described the process for determining the adequacy of submitted SIP budgets in guidance (May 14, 1999, memo titled "Conformity Guidance on Implementation of March 2, 1999, Conformity Court Decision"). This guidance was used in making the adequacy determination on the motor vehicle emissions budgets contained in the attainment demonstration for Atlanta. The criteria by which EPA determines whether a SIP's motor vehicle emission budgets are adequate for conformity purpose are outlined in 40 CFR 93.118(e)(4). An adequacy review is separate from EPA's SIP completeness review, and it also should not be used to prejudge EPA's ultimate action to approve or disapprove the SIP. The SIP could later be disapproved for reasons unrelated to transportation conformity even though the budgets had been deemed adequate.

* * *

EPA believes that a consequence of the D.C. Circuit's order delaying the implementation date of the NOX SIP Call rule is that the budget submitted by Georgia can no longer be considered adequate for purposes of transportation conformity. This belief is based on the fact that the attainment demonstration relied on the expected reductions from the NOX SIP call in 2003, where as those reductions can not now be assumed prior to 2004.

Furthermore, on December 21, 2000, Georgia sent a letter withdrawing the motor vehicle emission budgets contained in the October 28, 1999, SIP submittal and asked that EPA not undertake any further consideration of these budgets until the State concludes the work necessary to submit a revised budget. The revised budget is expected to be based on the results of the recent study of vehicle speeds data, updated vehicle registration data, and modeling information relevant to the estimation of current and future motor vehicle emissions developed since submission of the previous budget. Based on these changes of fact and law, the parties filed a joint motion to the 11th Circuit to hold further proceedings on review of the adequacy determination in abeyance and for permission for EPA to withdraw the finding of adequacy. All parties in those proceedings have agreed that because it is not appropriate for the transportation agencies to rely upon the currently submitted budget for the purpose of making transportation conformity determinations, the stay entered by the Court on July 19, 2000, should remain in effect pending EPA's completion of the withdrawal action. On January 12, 2001, the court granted EPA the motion to withdraw the adequacy determination.

Consequently, EPA has decided to withdraw the February 15 adequacy determination. Even though adequacy determinations are not considered rulemaking subject to procedural requirements of the Administrative Procedures Act, EPA's policy is to provide a notice and comment period on adequacy determinations. However, we are not providing opportunity for comment on this withdrawal notice for two reasons. EPA is taking this action without prior notice and comment because adequacy determinations are not considered rulemaking subject to the procedural requirements of the Administrative Procedures Act. In addition, EPA does not believe further notice through EPA's conformity website is necessary in advance, since as a result of the stay issued by the court, the conformity determination made by USDOT on July 25, 2000, did not rely on the motor vehicle emission budgets submitted in the attainment SIP. Therefore, although EPA had found these budgets to be adequate, they were never used for transportation conformity purposes. Further, because of the delay in the NOX SIP Call implementation date, it is clear that the budgets can no longer be considered adequate, and Georgia has requested that EPA withdraw the adequacy determination. Consequently, further public comment would be unnecessary and not in the public interest. In this action, EPA is also withdrawing all statements and comments previously made in relation to its earlier determination of the adequacy of the budgets for transportation conformity purposes. The substance of the budgets and any revisions to them will be further reviewed by EPA as part of its final decision to approve or disapprove the 1-hour ozone attainment demonstration SIP for the Atlanta nonattainment area. This SIP was initially submitted to EPA on October 28, 1999, and was supplemented on January 31, 2000, and July 31, 2000. EPA will consider all of these submissions as well as all comments timely submitted as we decide whether to approve or disapprove the SIP.

EPA will announce the withdrawal of the adequacy determination on its conformity website at http://www.epa.gov/oms/traq.

List of Subjects in 40 CFR Part 52

Environmental protection, Air pollution control, Hydrocarbons, Ozone.

Dated: January 16, 2001.

A. Stanley Meiburg, Acting Regional Administrator, Region 4.

[FR Doc. 01-2169 Filed 1-25-01; 8:45 am]

Notes and Questions

1. Why was Georgia's SIP approval withdrawn? Is this "fair" to the State of Georgia? What can it do about out-of-state emissions?

2. At the time this book goes to press, the problem of interstate transport has not been resolved. However, new rules were announced in 2005 to reduce overall emissions of SOx and NOx through a trading system.[18] Whether this will reduce out-of-state spillover remains to be seen. The State of North Carolina became one of the first southern states to file a lawsuit under Sec. 126, claiming that it could not meet the NAAQS unless EPA acted to control out of state sources. Can the EPA effectively regulate out of state sources? What if the EPA won't act? Can it be forced to? Will failure to act ensure that the NAAQS program will not work? Will the states be under pressure from their own citizens if they try to control domestic sources without controlling out of state pollution? Such questions demonstrate the importance of agency discretion to the environmental process. It is unclear what efforts can be exerted to pressure action on this issue, but it will have to be resolved if states are ever to meet and maintain the NAAQS. The next section explores the general question of what is to happen if a state fails to meet the NAAQS.

D. What happens when the states don't meet the NAAQS— Non-compliance

As noted in *Train, supra,* the states were not very successful at addressing air pollution before the passage of the 1970 CAA amend-

---

18. With "Clear Skies" sidelined, the EPA sets new power plant standards, Dar-ren Samuelson, Greenwire, March 10, 2005. www.eenews.net/Greenwire.

ments. Unfortunately, though direct controls on pollution sources had some salutary effect on the situation, the state role in ensuring that the NAAQS be obtained through their state implementation plans did not work as expected after the 1970 Act either. Nevertheless, the EPA has only rarely stepped in to enforce a Federal Implementation Plan.

Over time, Congress has amended the CAA to include increasingly stringent requirements and guidelines for states that have not met the NAAQS in the air quality regions under their control. The Clean Air Act amendments of 1977 included particular requirements for states that had as yet failed to meet the NAAQS, including new technological controls on new sources going into non-attainment areas.[19] Though there was some improvement in the 1980s, significant problems still remained. Moreover, certain efforts to control pollution, such as severe restrictions on driving, were not politically palatable. Due to the continuing problems of the non-compliant areas, the 1990 Amendments sought to curtail the discretion of states even further by requiring that specific elements be included in areas that had failed to reach attainment. In particular, the requirements were specific to ozone non-attainment areas, carbon monoxide non-attainment areas, and particulate matter non-attainment areas.[20] For ozone, these requirements addressed the magnitude of the problem in particular areas by dividing the non-attainment regions into categories with more stringent requirements for the areas with the greatest non-attainment problems.

TABLE 1

Area class	Design value*	Primary standard attainment date**
Marginal	0.121 up to 0.138	3 years after November 15, 1990
Moderate	0.138 up to 0.160	6 years after November 15, 1990
Serious	0.160 up to 0.180	9 years after November 15, 1990
Severe	0.180 up to 0.280	15 years after November 15, 1990
Extreme	0.280 and above	20 years after November 15, 1990

* The design value is measured in parts per million (ppm).
** The primary standard attainment date is measured from November 15, 1990.

19. 636 F.2d 323, 349 (D.C.Cir. 1979).

20. See 42 U.S.C. Sec. 7511, 7512, and 7513 (CAA 181, 186, and 188).

Each area was also required to make progress reports and show actual progress and the ability to reach attainment in the time period specified.

In many ways, these 1990 amendments were more realistic about the problem and the timetable required for solutions. For instance, the Los Angeles air quality control region, considered to be the worst non-attainment area for ozone and characterized as "extreme" non-attainment at the time of the 1990 amendments, was required to adopt very stringent requirements on sources in the area. These included high offsets for new sources, special fuel requirements, and ability to directly control traffic flow.[21] However, attainment of the standard was not required until 2010.[22]

In addition, the 1990 amendments set forth possible sanctions for failing to meet the requirements of these non-attainment timetables.[23] Importantly, these included the possibility of cutting highway funds to an area if the area failed to stay on timetable.[24] Of equal import were restrictions on federal agency assistance with projects that would contribute to non-attainment.[25]

Nevertheless, as these dates have approached there has been a flurry of litigation about whether the states are in fact on track to meet their requirements through their SIPs, and what should be done if they do not. Despite some progress, environmental groups still do not believe that some states have made the choices necessary to come into compliance. And many criticize the EPA for approving plans that some complain are inadequate and thus fail to satisfy the demonstration of progress and the ultimate satisfaction of the standard. Because of the discretion given an agency in approving plans that are based on sometimes conflicting assumptions or studies, it is true that the EPA could be quite generous with its assumptions regarding the states' ability to reach the required goals in the required time period. Sanctions were assessed against the State of Georgia for failing to provide a method to bring the Atlanta area into compliance,[26] but no other area has yet faced the sanction of loss of federal highway dollars for road expansion. The hard choices required for cities to comply have even encouraged several congresspersons to propose statutory exemptions. These are emblematic of the concerns that healthful levels may never be achieved.

An additional issue with the increasingly specific hammer used by Congress in trying to bring all parts of the country into compliance is that it eliminates the advantage of regulatory flexibility. As noted in the chapter on the role of administrative law in the environmental process, generally large goals are set by Congress but implementation is left to

---

21. 42 U.S.C. Sec. 7511a (e) (CAA 182 (e)).

22. 42 U.S.C. Sec. 7511.

23. 42 U.S.C. Sec. 7509 (CAA 179).

24. 42 U.S.C. Sec. 7509 (b)(1).

25. 42 U.S.C. Sec. 7506 (CAA 176).

26. Janet L. Bozeman, *Project XL: Should it be Used to Wage War on Urban Sprawl*, 16 Ga. St. U. L. rev. 625, 639 (Spring 2000).

the agencies since they can more quickly change standards to recognize new realities in the problem or in the treatment. The CAA has a mechanism to allow the administrator to revisit the NAAQS every five years in case there is new or different evidence regarding the health effects of the criteria pollutants, such that it prompts alteration of the standard.[27]

For instance, the chart of ozone non-compliance areas, *supra*, is based on a NAAQS of .12 parts per million, over a one hour average. In 1997, under its mandate to revisit the NAAQS, and based on new evidence, the EPA revised the ozone standard downward. This was challenged in court, and in particular, it brings up the question of how the very specific requirements for ozone non-attainment are to be read with the new standards set out by the EPA.

For instance, what is the conflict addressed in the following excerpt from the Whitman case? Does the court resolve the seeming discrepancy correctly? Should Congress not have been so specific about mandated requirements to trigger compliance with the then current ozone standard? Was there any other way to ensure that the EPA and state agencies begin a realistic drive toward attainment?

WHITMAN v. AMERICAN TRUCKING ASSOCIATIONS, INC.

Supreme Court of the United States, 2001.
531 U.S. 457, 121 S.Ct. 903, 149 L.Ed.2d 1

* * *

Whatever effect may be accorded the gaps in Subpart 2 as implying some limited applicability of Subpart 1, they cannot be thought to render Subpart 2's carefully designed restrictions on EPA discretion utterly nugatory once a new standard has been promulgated, as the EPA has concluded. The principal distinction between Subpart 1 and Subpart 2 is that the latter eliminates regulatory discretion that the former allowed. While Subpart 1 permits the EPA to establish classifications for nonattainment areas, Subpart 2 classifies areas as a matter of law based on a table. Compare § 7502(a)(1) with § 7511(a)(1) (Table 1). Whereas the EPA has discretion under Subpart 1 to extend attainment dates for as long as 12 years, under Subpart 2 it may grant no more than 2 years' extension. Compare § § 7502(a)(2)(A) and (C) with § 7511(a)(5). Whereas Subpart 1 gives the EPA considerable discretion to shape nonattainment programs, Subpart 2 prescribes large parts of them by law. Compare § § 7502(c) and (d) with § 7511a. Yet according to the EPA, Subpart 2 was simply Congress's "approach to the implementation of the [old] 1–hour" standard, and so there was no reason that "the new standard could not simultaneously be implemented under ... subpart 1." 62 Fed.Reg. 38856, 38885 (1997); see also *id.*, at 38873 ("[T]he provisions of subpart 1 ... would apply to the implementation of the

---

27. 42 U.S.C. Sec. 7409(2)(B) (CAA 109 (2)(B)).

new 8–hour ozone standards''). To use a few apparent gaps in Subpart 2 to render its textually explicit applicability to nonattainment areas under the new standard utterly inoperative is to go over the edge of reasonable interpretation. The EPA may not construe the statute in a way that completely nullifies textually applicable provisions meant to limit its discretion.

The EPA's interpretation making Subpart 2 abruptly obsolete is all the more astonishing because Subpart 2 was obviously written to govern implementation for some time. Some of the elements required to be included in SIP's under Subpart 2 were not to take effect until many years after the passage of the CAA. See § 7511a(e)(3) (restrictions on "electric utility and industrial and commercial boiler[s]" to be "effective 8 years after November 15, 1990"); § 7511a(c)(5)(A) (vehicle monitoring program to "[b]egi[n] 6 years after November 15, 1990"); § 7511a(g)(1) (emissions milestone requirements to be applied "6 years after November 15, 1990, and at intervals of every 3 years thereafter"). A plan reaching so far into the future was not enacted to be abandoned the next time the EPA reviewed the ozone standard—which Congress knew could happen at any time, since the technical staff papers had already been completed in late 1989. See 58 Fed.Reg. 13008, 13010 (1993); see also 42 U.S.C. § 7409(d)(1) (NAAQS must be reviewed and, if appropriate, revised at least once every five years). Yet nothing in the EPA's interpretation would have prevented the agency from aborting Subpart 2 the day after it was enacted. Even now, if the EPA's interpretation were correct, some areas of the country could be required to meet the new, more stringent ozone standard in *at most* the same time that Subpart 2 had allowed them to meet the old standard. Compare § 7502(a)(2) (Subpart 1 attainment dates) with § 7511(a) (Subpart 2 attainment dates). Los Angeles, for instance, "would be required to attain the revised NAAQS under Subpart 1 no later than the same year that marks the outer time limit for attaining Subpart 2's one-hour ozone standard." Brief for Petitioners in No. 99–1257, p. 49. An interpretation of Subpart 2 so at odds with its structure and manifest purpose cannot be sustained.

We therefore find the EPA's implementation policy to be unlawful, though not in the precise respect determined by the Court of Appeals. After our remand, and the Court of Appeals' final disposition of these cases, it is left to the EPA to develop a reasonable interpretation of the nonattainment implementation provisions insofar as they apply to revised ozone NAAQS.

* * *

IV. THE CLEAN AIR ACT—DIRECT CONTROLS ON SOURCES

A. Stationary sources

Unlike the standard setting and implementation of the ambient air quality standards discussed above, direct controls on sources take a different tack for controlling air pollution. Instead of relying on states to determine the best way to reach ambient levels of air quality, source controls require the specific installation of equipment or process changes on the sources themselves. Though there are many arguments about the efficiency of such an approach, it has the virtue of certainty. In general, once the equipment or process is in place, it is easier to monitor and any benefits are measurable. With other plans which may use various methods for lowering pollution loading it may not be clear whether the plan's components are being enforced or are effective. Indeed, the enforceability and measurability of direct controls on sources marks an important innovation in the 1970 Act.

The direct source controls in the Clean Air Act for stationary sources first appeared in the New Source Performance Standards of Section 111. Later, specific source controls on stationary sources were added to prevent deterioration of air quality and to assist in speeding up the cleaning of air in area that were non-compliant. The statutes basically provide for a standard of source control such as "best available technology" or "lowest achievable emissions rate" to be established by the Administrator for all similar sources.

Sample Emissions Standards in Statute:

111(a)(1)—New Source Performance Standard (all new sources)

The term "standard of performance" means a standard for emissions of air pollutants which reflects the degree of emission limitation achievable through the application of the best system of emission reduction which (taking into account the cost of health and environmental impact and energy requirements) the Administrator determines has been adequately demonstrated.

112(d)(2)—Maximum Reduction–Hazardous Air Pollution (Hazardous Air Pollutant Sources)

Emission standards promulgate under this subsection and applicable to new or existing sources of hazardous air pollutants shall require the maximum degree of reduction in emissions of hazardous air pollutants subject to this section ... that the Administrator ... determines is achievable for new or existing sources.

112(d)(3)—Hazardous Air Pollutants—New and existing sources

The degree of reduction for new sources shall not be less than the emission control achieved in practice by best controlled similar sources. Emission standards for existing sources shall be less stringent than that for new sources, but shall not be less stringent than the average emission rate for the best performing 12% of existing sources or the average emission achieved by the best performing 5 sources.

165(a)(4)—BACT—(Best Available Control Technology) Preconstruction requirements

major emitting facilities on which construction is commenced—the proposed facility is subject to the best available control technology for each pollutant subject to regulation under this chapter emitted from, or which results from, such facility.

169(3)—BACT—definition (new sources subject to PSD regulation)

"Best available control technology" means an emission limitation based on the maximum degree of reduction of each pollutant ... which the permitting authority ... determines is achievable through application of production processes and available methods.

169A(g)(2)—BART—(Best Available Retrofit Technology) definition (existing sources contributing to visibility degradation)

Lists factors to consider when determining best available retrofit technology: costs of compliance, environmental impact of compliance, existing pollution control technology at use at the source, remaining useful life of the source, anticipate improvement in visibility from use of such technology.

171(3)—LAER—(Lowest Achievable Emission Rate) definition (new sources in non-attainment areas)

The term "lowest achievable emission rate" means for any source, that rate of emission which reflects (A) the most stringent emission limitation in that SIP for such class of source unless owner demonstrates that such limitations are not achievable, or (B) the most stringent emission limitation achieved in practice by such class of source, whichever is most stringent.

172(c)(1)—RACT—(Reasonably Available Control Technology) (Nonattainment plan provisions–existing sources)

Such plan provisions shall provide for the implementation of all reasonably available measures as expeditiously as practicable (including such reductions in emissions from existing sources, in the area as may be obtained through the adoption, at a minimum, of reasonably available control technology) and shall provide for attainment of the national primary ambient quality standards.

173(a)(2)—LAER—(Lowest Achievable Emissions Rate) Permit Requirements for a major stationary source to construct in a nonattainment area

The permit program required if this title shall provide that permits to construct and operate may be issued if—the proposed source is required to comply with the lowest achievable emission rate.

182(a)(2)(A)—Marginal Areas—Corrections to the SIP—RACT corrections—

For any Marginal Area the Administrator, at his discretion, shall submit a revision that includes provisions to correct the plan concerning reasonably available control technology.

182(b)—Moderate Areas—RACT corrections

shall make the same submissions as 182(a)

182(c)—Serious Areas—RACT corrections

shall make the same submissions as 182(b)

182(d)—Severe Areas—RACT corrections

shall make the same submission as 182(c)

183(e)(1)(A)—BACT—definition

The term "best available controls" means the degree of emissions reduction that the Administrator determines on the basis of technological and economic feasibility, health, environmental and energy impacts, is achievable through application of the most effective equipment, measures, processes, methods, system or techniques.

Notes and Questions

On their face, the differences between these requirements are subtle. Is cost to be considered? Can non-existent technology be made a standard under any of the source requirements in the Act? Which pollutants are to be covered and what about multiple pollutants? Some of these basic questions were answered in early court cases. Nevertheless, it is still only in the actual promulgation of these standards by the agency that effectiveness of the requirements and their effect on industries' bottom line come into play. For any source subject to these requirements close attention must be paid to both current source requirements and future changes or proposals. Because of the great discretion given the agency in making these determinations, it is at the agency level where the environmental lawyer must make her case.

LIGNITE ENERGY COUNCIL v. U.S. ENVIRONMENTAL PROTECTION AGENCY

United States Court of Appeals, District of Columbia Circuit, 1999.

198 F.3d 930.

Before: EDWARDS, Chief Judge, SILBERMAN and HENDERSON, Circuit Judges.

PER CURIAM:

Petitioners challenge EPA's new source performance standards for nitrogen oxides emissions from utility and industrial boilers. We conclude that EPA did not exceed its discretion under section 111 of the Clean Air Act in promulgating these standards, and therefore deny the petitions.

* * *

Fossil-fuel fired steam generating units ("boilers") emit nitrogen oxides (NOx), air pollutants that can cause deleterious health effects and contribute to the formation of acid rain. Section 111 of the Clean Air Act requires EPA to establish performance standards for the emission of NOx from newly constructed boilers; these "new source performance standards" are to be set at a level that

> reflects the degree of emission limitation achievable through the
> application of the best system of emission reduction which (taking

into account the cost of achieving such reduction and any nonair quality health and environmental impact and energy requirements) the Administrator determines has been adequately demonstrated.

42 U.S.C. § 7411(a)(1). In its 1990 Clean Air Act Amendments Congress specifically directed EPA to exercise its section 111 authority and establish new NOx standards that incorporate "improvements in methods for the reduction of emissions of oxides of nitrogen." 42 U.S.C. § 7651f(c)(1).

In response to these statutory mandates, EPA promulgated a rule lowering its NOx new source performance standards to .15 lb/MMBtu (pounds of NOx emitted per million BTU burned) for utility boilers [1] and .20 lb/MMBtu for industrial boilers. *See* 63 Fed.Reg. 49,442, 49,443 (1998) (to be codified at 40 C.F.R. pt. 60). These standards reflect the level of NOx emissions achievable by what EPA considers to be the "best demonstrated system" of emissions reduction: the use of selective catalytic reduction (SCR) in combination with combustion control technologies.[2] Petitioners' central claim is that EPA selected SCR as the basis for its NOx standards without properly balancing the factors that section 111 requires it to "take into account." Because section 111 does not set forth the weight that be should assigned to each of these factors, we have granted the agency a great degree of discretion in balancing them, *see, e.g., New York v. Reilly,* 969 F.2d 1147, 1150 (D.C.Cir.1992); EPA's choice will be sustained unless the environmental or economic costs of using the technology are exorbitant. *See National Asphalt Pavement Ass'n v. Train,* 539 F.2d 775, 786 (D.C.Cir.1976).

Petitioners argue that SCR is not the "best demonstrated system" under section 111 because the incremental cost of reducing NOx emissions is considerably higher with SCR than with combustion controls. Recent improvements in combustion controls will enable many boilers to attain emissions levels close to EPA's SCR-based standards; accordingly, petitioners assert that EPA should have based its standards on these less expensive technologies. However, in light of EPA's unchallenged findings showing that the new standards will only modestly increase the cost of producing electricity in newly constructed boilers, *see* 62 Fed.Reg. 36,948, 36,958 (1997) (proposed NOx revisions), we do not think that EPA exceeded its considerable discretion under section 111. Moreover, petitioners' argument stressing the comparable environmental merits of advanced combustion controls is to a certain extent self-defeating, since

1. To be precise, the emission standard for utility boilers is an output-based standard of 1.6 pounds of NOx emitted per megawatt-hour of electricity generated. However, as this output-based standard was intended by EPA to correlate with a .15 lb/MMBtu input-based standard, we refer to its input-based equivalent for simplicity's sake throughout this opinion. We reject petitioners' argument that EPA's decision to shift to an output-based standard for utility boilers unfairly "penalizes" the use of low-energy coals, like lignite; it would seem just

as easy to argue that an input-based standard "penalizes" high-energy fuels.

2. SCR is a "flue gas treatment technology"; it reduces NOx after combustion by injecting ammonia into the flue gas in the presence of a catalyst, breaking down NOx and producing nitrogen and water. In setting past standards, EPA had focused solely on combustion control technologies, which instead reduce NOx by suppressing its formation during the combustion process. *See* 62 Fed.Reg. 36,948, 36,949–50 (1997).

the new source performance standards set by EPA are not technology-forcing, and continuing advances in combustion control technologies will reduce the amount of NOx reduction that must be captured by the more expensive SCR technology.

It was also within EPA's discretion to issue uniform standards for all utility boilers, rather than adhering to its past practice of setting a range of standards based on boiler and fuel type. *See, e.g.,* 44 Fed.Reg. 33,580 (1979) (establishing varying NOx emissions standards for utility boilers). Petitioners recognize that EPA is not required by law to subcategorize—section 111 merely states that "the Administrator *may* distinguish among classes, types, and sizes within categories of new sources," 42 U.S.C. § 7411(b)(2) (emphasis added)—but argue that it was arbitrary and capricious for EPA to decline to do so. EPA explains that its change to uniform standards is justified by SCR's performance characteristics: Unlike the technologies on which past new source performance standards were based, flue gas treatment technologies like SCR limit NOx emissions after combustion, and the effectiveness of SCR is thus far less dependent upon boiler design or fuel type. Petitioners respond that there are reasons to expect SCR to perform less adequately on boilers burning high-sulfur coals, but EPA collected continuous emissions monitoring data on two high-sulfur coal-fired utility boilers that showed that the .15 lb/MMBtu standard was achievable, and supplemented this study with similar evidence from foreign utility boilers. EPA also considered petitioners' concerns about the impact of alkaline metals on the performance of the catalyst used in the SCR process, and concluded that such "catalyst poisoning" is not a significant problem in coal-fired boilers. *See* 63 Fed.Reg. at 49,445. Mindful of the high degree of deference we must show to EPA's scientific judgment, *see, e.g., Appalachian Power Co. v. EPA,* 135 F.3d 791, 801–02 (D.C.Cir.1998), we accept these determinations and sustain EPA's uniform standard for utility boilers.

Petitioners offer a broader challenge to EPA's .20 lb/MMBtu standard for industrial boilers, claiming that SCR is not "adequately demonstrated" for any coal-fired industrial boilers. EPA was unable to collect emissions data for the application of SCR to these boilers, but this absence of data is not surprising for a new technology like SCR, nor does it in and of itself defeat EPA's standard. Because it applies only to new sources, we have recognized that section 111 "looks toward what may fairly be projected for the regulated future, rather than the state of the art at present." *Portland Cement Ass'n v. Ruckelshaus,* 486 F.2d 375, 391 (D.C.Cir.1973). Of course, where data are unavailable, EPA may not base its determination that a technology is adequately demonstrated or that a standard is achievable on mere speculation or conjecture, *see, e.g., National Asphalt Pavement Ass'n,* 539 F.2d at 787, but EPA may compensate for a shortage of data through the use of other qualitative methods, including the reasonable extrapolation of a technology's performance in other industries. *See, e.g., Weyerhaeuser Co. v. Costle,* 590 F.2d 1011, 1054 n. 70 (D.C.Cir.1978).

EPA has done precisely that here, concluding from its study of utility boilers that SCR is "adequately demonstrated" and the .20 lb/MMBtu standard is "achievable" for coal-fired industrial boilers as well. Utility and industrial boilers are similar in design and both categories of boilers can attain similar levels of NOx emissions reduction through combustion controls, which means that SCR will be required to capture comparable quantities of NOx for both boiler types. While petitioners argue that SCR is less likely to be effective on industrial boilers because they have widely fluctuating load cycles, EPA has shown that SCR can be successfully applied to coal-fired utility boilers under a "wide range of operating conditions" including those analogous to the load cycles of industrial boilers. 63 Fed.Reg. at 49,444. We think that it was reasonable for EPA to extrapolate from its studies of utility boilers in setting an SCR-based new source performance standard for coal-fired industrial boilers. [3]

We also sustain EPA's application of the .20 lb/MMBtu standard to combination boilers, which simultaneously combust a mixture of fuels. The preexisting NOx emissions standards established a range of values for combustion boilers that varied by fuel type: while combination boilers burning natural gas with non-coal solid fuels (*e.g.,* wood) were subject to a .30 lb/MMBtu standard, the performance standards for combination boilers combusting coal with oil or natural gas were determined based upon the proportion of the boiler's total heat input provided by each fuel. *See* 51 Fed.Reg. 42,768, 42,790 (1986). It is difficult to understand petitioners' objection to the application of the industrial boiler standard to boilers burning natural gas and wood. A reduction of that standard from .30 to .20 lb/MMBtu is perfectly reasonable in light of the significant advances in NOx emissions technology since 1986; indeed, EPA studies show that wood-fired boilers can reach emissions levels far lower than .20 lb/MMBtu through the application of flue gas treatment technologies. And our conclusion that the .20 lb/MMBtu standard is achievable for boilers burning only coal necessarily defeats petitioners' objection that the industrial boiler standard is unreasonable as applied to combination boilers burning coal simultaneously with other fuels with *lower* NOx emissions characteristics.

Petitioners' final objection is to EPA's valuation of steam energy produced by "cogeneration facilities." EPA's adoption of an output-based standard for utility boilers raised the question of how to calculate the energy produced by these units, which generate thermal steam energy in addition to electrical energy. Steam energy produced by cogeneration

---

3. For similar reasons, we do not think that EPA's lack of data on domestic SCR applications to boilers burning lignite renders its standards unlawful. In assessing a new technology like SCR, EPA is not required to provide evidence of its application to boilers burning every type of coal from every geographical location. It is acceptable for EPA to extrapolate from the successful applications of SCR to domestic high-sulfur coal-fired boilers and to foreign boilers burning lignite.

facilities is exported for several different industrial uses; however, because of inefficiencies in transporting and converting steam, only a fraction of steam energy produced by cogeneration facilities is actually used in the industrial process. EPA resolved this problem by assigning a 50% credit for steam energy when determining a cogeneration unit's output. *See* 63 Fed.Reg. at 49,447. Petitioners describe this credit as an arbitrary and capricious "discounting" of steam energy's value, but it just as easily could be called a subsidy: The maximum efficiency for the conversion of steam to electrical energy is only 38%, and EPA's final rule justifies the 50% credit on the ground that it will *encourage* cogeneration. *Id.* In light of the difficulties that would attend calculating the useful energy of steam heat produced by cogeneration facilities on a unit-by-unit basis, we conclude that EPA's resolution of this issue was acceptable.

The petitions for review are denied.

So ordered.

———

In addition to performance standards for any new sources, both non-attainment and PSD areas require that new sources of air pollution meet additional operational and/or technological standards, which are specified through a "new source review" process. Though there are some technological controls that may apply to existing sources in non-compliant areas ("reasonably available control technology" on emissions from existing sources),[28] the requirements for new sources are generally greater and more expensive.

Though the most intensive controls were reserved for new sources in order to not be inequitable with older sources, it was assumed that eventually the older sources would become less economically feasible and would be phased out over time, thus producing major gains in cleaning the air. Congress recognized that if older sources were to make significant adjustments, they would in effect be like new sources, and thus should be required to install any technology required of such new sources. Thus, "new source review" applies not only to brand new sources but to certain modifications of old sources. Because of the large expense in the new source pollution control requirements, many existing sources wish to avoid modifications that trigger these requirements. Nevertheless, since many of these existing sources began operation almost fifty years ago, they must engage in often significant repairs and possible upgrades to continue functioning. This brings us to the section on New Source Review.

B. New Source Review—What about existing sources? (An exercise in the administrative process)

The Clean Air Act like all of our environmental laws is a story of the continuing evolution of administrative standards and enforcement. Al-

28. 42 U.S.C. Sec. 7502(c)(1) (CAA Sec. 172 (c)(1)).

though the CAA has gone through significant revisions since its inception, the main focus on setting the concentrations of air pollution to safe levels and protecting human health has not changed. What has changed is the way this is to be implemented. As noted in the introductory chapter on the role of administrative law, there can be huge differences in cost, methods and effects depending upon how the implementation of a law occurs.

The story of New Source Review and how and when it applies to existing sources is one of the most complicated and interesting of these stories, and it is still being written as this book goes to press. Note the interplay of policy decisions made by Congress and the president in the passage of this part of the law and then the policy decisions inherent in the executive control of the implementation of this law. Also note the importance of the administrative process to what we call environmental law.

The story of the NSR (in both PSD and non-attainment) illustrates very well that any real impacts in actual air pollution reduction depend greatly on how the public and stakeholders engage in the administrative process. If you do not learn this anywhere else in the book, it is important to know that environmental victories and thus environmental law itself is rarely about cases, but more about the inputs and outputs of the administrative process.

1. New Source Review

As we will see, all of the country's air-sheds are divided into attainment and non-attainment areas. The attainment areas are further classified by the amount that their air can be degraded going forward. This is known as the Prevention of Significant Deterioration or "PSD" program, and we will examine that more closely later in the chapter. Both non-attainment and PSD areas require that new sources of air pollution meet operational and/or technological standards, which are specified through a "new source review" process. These requirements, which are quite strict, can be very expensive. Additionally, there are separate technological and operational requirement that apply to all new sources of a certain size, regardless of where they are built. These requirements are known as the New Source Performance Standards, or NSPS. See *infra* 42 U.S.C. Sec. 7411.

2. Application to Existing Sources

Recognizing that sources already in operation at the time of the implementation of the CAA had not had the opportunity to consider the costs of the technological and operational controls, and believing that in time these sources would be a very small part of the air pollution problem as they were retired, the CAA exempted existing sources from both NSR and NSPS, thus the name "new" source review.

However, the lawmakers who put together the CAA also recognized that if an existing source underwent a significant upgrade that it might be produce more pollution and could more easily accommodate these technological controls.[29] Moreover, this could give it new life, and allow it to go on in perpetuity. Therefore the NSR and NSPS were also to apply to modifications of existing sources. So, for purposes of existing stationary sources of pollution that are altered in any way, the important question is whether the modification now requires that source to undergo NSR and/or NSPS.

The next case addresses this question:

WISCONSIN ELECTRIC POWER COMPANY v. REILLY

United States Court of Appeals, Seventh Circuit, 1990.
893 F.2d 901.

As Amended on Denial of Rehearing and Rehearing En Banc April 3, 1990.

Before CUDAHY and FLAUM, Circuit Judges, and GRANT, Senior District Judge. [*]

CUDAHY, Circuit Judge.

...In 1970, Congress enacted the Clean Air Act Amendments, Pub.L. No.91–604, 84 Stat. 1676, to establish minimum air quality standards that would regulate the emission of certain pollutants into the atmosphere. To this end, Congress instructed the EPA to develop National Ambient Air Quality Standards ("NAAQS") that would specify the maximum permissible concentration of air pollutants in different areas across the country.

In section 111 of the 1970 Amendments, Congress required the EPA to promulgate New Source Performance Standards ("NSPS") in order to regulate the emission of air pollutants from new sources. These standards addressed hourly rates of emission and, in addition to new sources, applied to modifications of existing facilities that created new or increased pollution. Indeed, section 111(a)(2) of the Act stated that NSPS would apply to any stationary source, the construction or modification of which is commenced after the publication of regulations (or, if earlier, proposed regulations) prescribing a standard of performance under this section which will be applicable to such source.

42 U.S.C. § 7411(a)(2) (emphasis supplied). Congress then defined "modification" as any physical change in, or change in the method of operation of, a stationary source which increases the amount of any air pollutant emitted by such source or which results in the emission of any air pollutant not previously emitted. 42 U.S.C. § 7411(a)(4) (emphasis supplied).

Subsequently, faced with only varying degrees of success in controlling pollution in different parts of the country, Congress enacted the

---

29. *Wisconsin Electric Power Co. v. Reilly*, 893 F.2d 901, 910 (7th Cir. 1990).

* The Honorable Robert A. Grant, Senior District Judge for the Northern District of Indiana, is sitting by designation.

Clean Air Act Amendments of 1977, Pub.L. No. 95–95, 91 Stat. 685 (codified at 42 U.S.C. §§ 7401–7642 (1982) ... Congress added a program for the Prevention of Significant Deterioration ("PSD"), concerned with increases in total annual emissions, to ensure that operators of regulated sources in relatively unpolluted areas would not allow a decline of air quality to the minimum level permitted by NAAQS. Air quality is preserved in this program by requiring sources to limit their emissions to a"baseline rate"; regulated owners or operators in areas that have attained NAAQS must obtain a permit before constructing or modifying facilities. 42 U.S.C.§ 7475(a)(1). Congress also essentially adopted its NSPS definition of "modification" for the PSD program. 42 U.S.C. § 7479(2)(C).

From this statutory framework, the EPA promulgated regulations for both the NSPS and PSD programs. In this case, its regulations concerning modifications are central. The EPA defines "modification" in substantially the same terms used by Congress:

> [A]ny physical or operational change to an existing facility which results in an increase in the emission rate to the atmosphere of any pollutant to which a standard applies shall be considered a modification within the meaning of section 111 [42 U.S.C. § 7411] of the Act.

40 C.F.R. § 60.14(a) (1988). To determine whether a physical change constitutes a modification for purposes of NSPS, the EPA must determine whether the change increases the facility's hourly rate of emission. 40 C.F.R. § 60.14 (1988). For PSD purposes, current EPA regulations provide that an increase in the total amount of emissions activates the modification provisions of the regulations. 40 C.F.R. § 52.21(b)(3) (1988).

Even at first blush, the potential reach of these modification provisions is apparent: the most trivial activities—the replacement of leaky pipes, for example—may trigger the modification provisions if the change results in an increase in the emissions of a facility. As a result, the EPA promulgated specific exceptions to the modification provisions:

> The following shall not, by themselves, be considered modifications under this part:
>
> (1) Maintenance, repair, and replacement which the Administrator determines to be routine for a source category ...
>
> (2) An increase in production rate of an existing facility, if that increase can be accomplished without a capital expenditure on that facility.
>
> (3) An increase in the hours of operation....

40 C.F.R. § 60.14(e) (1988) (NSPS program); see 40 C.F.R. § 52.21(b)(2)(iii) (1988) (PSD program). These regulations (and the statutes from which they derive) are the focal point of this case.

B. WEPCO's Proposed Life–Extension Project

WEPCO's Port Washington electric power plant is located on Lake Michigan north of Milwaukee, Wisconsin. The plant consists of five coal-fired steam generating units that were placed in operation between 1935 and 1950. Each generating unit has a design capacity of 80 megawatts, but the recent performance of some of the units has declined due to age-related deterioration of the physical plant.

WEPCO and its consultant, Bechtel Eastern Power Corporation, conducted a Plant Availability Study in 1983 to examine and assess the condition of the power plant. As a result of the Study, WEPCO concluded "that extensive renovation of the five units and the plant common facilities is needed if operation of the plant is to be continued." Letter from Thomas J. Cassidy, Executive Vice President of WEPCO, to Jacqueline K. Reynolds, Secretary to the Public Service Commission of Wisconsin, at 2 (July 8, 1987) [Cassidy Letter] (emphasis supplied). The Study noted that the air heaters on the first four units had deteriorated severely, while the rear steam drums in units 2 through 5 had experienced serious cracking.[1] Air heater deterioration prevented units 1 and 4 from operating at full capacity, while the potential for steam drum blowout required a reduction in pressure (and output) in units 2 and 3. The possibility of catastrophic failure (steam drum blowout) in unit 5 was so great that WEPCO shut down the unit completely. Id. at 1–5.

As a result of this Study, WEPCO submitted a proposed replacement program (which it termed a "life extension" project) to the Wisconsin Public Service Commission for its approval, as required by state law. Wis.Stat. § 196.49 (1987). WEPCO explained in its proposal that "[r]enovation is necessary to allow the Port Washington units to operate beyond their currently planned retirement dates of 1992 (units 1 and 2) and 1999 (units 3, 4 and 5) . . . [and that renovation would render the plant] capable of generating at its designed capability until year 2010. . . ." Cassidy Letter at 1–2. Among the renovations required were repair and replacement of the turbine-generators, boilers, mechanical and electrical auxiliaries and the common plant support facilities. Id. at 1. After preliminary review of the program, the Public Service Commission consulted the Wisconsin Department of Natural Resources (which then consulted EPA Region V) to determine whether WEPCO needed to obtain a PSD permit before commencing the repair and replacement program. David Kee, the Director of EPA Region V's Air and Radiation Division, then referred the matter to EPA Headquarters. See, e.g., 40 C.F.R. § 60.5 (1988) (discussing the EPA's procedures regarding determinations of construction or modification).

EPA staff members conferred with WEPCO representatives between March and September 1988 to gain additional information regarding the

---

1. Air heaters preheat combustion air to improve the efficiency of the steam generating units. Steam: Its Generation and Use 13–4 (1978) (Babcock & Wilcox). Steam drums separate saturated steam from water within the boiler.

proposed repair and replacement project. On September 9, 1988, EPA Acting Assistant Administrator Don R. Clay issued a memorandum in which he preliminarily concluded that the project would subject the plant to both NSPS and PSD requirements.

. . . Alleging that the EPA has misconstrued both the Clean Air Act and its own regulations, WEPCO appeals the EPA's final determination. We have jurisdiction to hear this appeal pursuant to 42 U.S.C. § 7607(b) (1982).

[The court then discussed the Standard of Review, applying Chevron deference.]

III. LIKE-KIND REPLACEMENT AND MODIFICATION UNDER THE ACT

A. The Underlying Statutory Framework

. . . We must first consider whether WEPCO's Port Washington replacement program constitutes a modification under the terms of the controlling statute, 42 U.S.C. section 7411(a)(4). Cf. Blue Chip Stamps v. Manor Drug Stores, 421 U.S. 723, 756, 95 S.Ct. 1917, 1935, 44 L.Ed.2d 539 (1975) (Powell, J., concurring) ("The starting point in every case involving construction of a statute is the language itself."). Section 7411(a)(4) defines modification as "any physical change . . . which increases the amount of any air pollutant emitted. . . . " 42 U.S.C. § 7411(a)(4). Both parts of this definition—any physical change and an increase in emissions—must be satisfied before a replacement will be considered a "modification."

1. Physical Change

Certainly, under the plain terms of the Act, WEPCO's replacement program constitutes a "physical change." WEPCO proposes to replace rear steam drums on units 2, 3, 4 and 5; each of these steam drums measures 60 feet in length, 50.5 inches in diameter and 5.25 inches in thickness. Clay Memorandum at 4. In addition, WEPCO plans to replace another major component, the air heaters, in units 1–4. To implement this four-year program, WEPCO will need to make the replacements by taking the units successively out of service for nine-month periods. Id. These steps clearly amount to a "physical change" in the Port Washington plant. See Butler, New Source Netting in Nonattainment Areas under the Clean Air Act, 11 Ecology L.Q. 343, 349–50 (1984) ("[T]he new source review requirements are triggered not only when an operator builds a new plant, but also whenever the operator installs or alters a piece of equipment in an existing plant and thereby increases emissions.") (emphasis supplied).

WEPCO does not dispute that its steam drum and air heater replacements will result in an altered plant. But WEPCO does assert that Congress did not intend for simple equipment replacement to constitute a physical change for purposes of the Clean Air Act's modification provisions:

The plain meaning of "modify" is "to change or alter" [Webster's New World Dictionary] or "to make basic or fundamental changes in." [Webster's Ninth New Collegiate Dictionary] Reflecting the plain meaning of this term, Congress provided that a facility (1) must undergo a physical or operational "change" before it is evaluated under the modification provision.... Thus, under the plain meaning of the Act, a unit should not be deemed "modified" as a result of replacement of equipment with equipment similar to that replaced. As in the case of Port Washington, such like-kind replacement does not "change or alter" the design or nature of the facility. Rather, it merely allows the facility to operate again as it had before the specific equipment deteriorated.

Petitioner's Brief at 32–33.

Chevron instructs us to rely more on congressional direction and on agency construction (pursuant to congressional delegation) than on glosses found in the dictionary. What WEPCO calls "plain" is anything but plain and takes the definition far beyond the words enacted by Congress. Chevron, 467 U.S. at 843–45, 104 S.Ct. at 2781–83; see generally, R. Anthony, Report to the Administrative Conference of the United States: Which Agency Interpretations Should Bind the Courts and the Public? (1989) (explaining Chevron approach). Thus, whether the replacement of air heaters and steam drums is a "basic or fundamental change" in the Port Washington plant is irrelevant for our purposes, given Congress's directions on the subject: "The term 'modification' means any physical change...." 42 U.S.C. § 7411(a)(4) (emphasis supplied). We follow Congress's definition of "modification"—not Webster's—when interpreting this term within the context of the Clean Air Act. Cf. Chevron, 467 U.S. at 861, 104 S.Ct. at 2790 ("[T]he meaning of a word must be ascertained in the context of achieving particular objectives....").

Nor can we find any support in the relevant case law for the narrow constructions of "modification" and "physical change" offered by WEPCO. The Supreme Court reported in Chevron that Senator Muskie, one of the principal supporters of the Clean Air Act, remarked: "A source ... is subject to all the nonattainment requirements as a modified source if it makes any physical change which increases the amount of any air pollutant...." 467 U.S. at 853, 104 S.Ct. at 2787 (quoting 123 Cong.Rec. 26847 (1977)) (emphasis supplied). And other courts considering the modification provisions of NSPS and PSD have assumed that "any physical change" means precisely that. See, e.g., National–Southwire Aluminum Co. v. EPA, 838 F.2d 835 (6th Cir.), cert. denied, 488 U.S. 955, 109 S.Ct. 390, 102 L.Ed.2d 379 (1988) (turning off pollution control equipment constitutes "physical change" and modification); Alabama Power Co. v. Costle, 636 F.2d 323, 400 (D.C.Cir.1979) ("[T]he term 'modification' is nowhere limited to physical changes exceeding a certain magnitude."); ASARCO Inc. v. EPA, 578 F.2d 319, 322 (D.C.Cir.1978) (NSPS applies to any stationary source that is "physically or operationally changed in such a way that its emission of any air pollutant increases.") (emphasis removed). Cf. United States v. Narragansett Improvement Co., 571 F.Supp. 688, 694–95 (D.R.I.1983) (replacement program not modification because, despite physical change, no increase in emissions).

Further, to adopt WEPCO's definition of "physical change" would open vistas of indefinite immunity from the provisions of NSPS and PSD. Were we to hold that the replacement of major generating station systems—including steam drums and air heaters—does not constitute a physical change (and is therefore not a modification), the application of NSPS and PSD to important facilities might be postponed into the indefinite future. There is no reason to believe that such a result was intended by Congress. The Clean Air Act Amendments were enacted to "speed up, expand, and intensify the war against air pollution in the United States with a view to assuring that the air we breathe throughout the Nation is wholesome once again." H.R.Rep. No. 91–1146, 91st Cong., 2d Sess. 1, 1, reprinted in 1970 U.S.Code Cong. & Admin.News 5356, 5356. In particular, the permit program established by the 1977 Amendments to the Clean Air Act represented a balance between "the economic interests in permitting capital improvements to continue and the environmental interest in improving air quality." Chevron, 467 U.S. at 851, 104 S.Ct. at 2786. The House echoed this theme in its Committee report: "[The compliance program is designed, in part,] to allow reasonable economic growth to continue in an area while making reasonable further progress to assure attainment of the [pollution-control] standards by a fixed date...." H.R.Rep. No. 294, 95th Cong., 1st Sess. 211, reprinted in 1977 U.S.Code Cong. & Admin.News 1077, 1290. A too restrictive interpretation of "modification" might upset the economic-environmental balance in unintended ways. Consistent with its balanced approach, Congress chose not to subject existing plants to the requirements of NSPS and PSD. Members of the House recognized that "[b]uilding control technology into new plants at time of construction will plainly be less costly then [sic] requiring retrofit when pollution control ceilings are reached." H.R.Rep. No. 294, 95th Cong., 1st Sess. 185, reprinted in 1977 U.S.Code Cong. & Admin.News at 1264. But Congress did not permanently exempt existing plants from these requirements; section 7411(a)(2) provides that existing plants that have been modified are subject to the Clean Air Act programs at issue here. As Judge Boggs, dissenting in National–Southwire, reasoned: "The purpose of the 'modification' rule is to ensure that pollution control measures are undertaken when they can be most effective, at the time of new or modified construction. [citation omitted.]

National–Southwire Aluminum Co. v. EPA, 838 F.2d 835, 843 (6th Cir.) (Boggs, J., dissenting), cert. denied, 488 U.S. 955, 109 S.Ct. 390, 102 L.Ed.2d 379 (1988). Judge Boggs argued that the shutting down of pollution control equipment in an existing plant should not be considered a modification because it would not afford the utility an opportunity for "effective placement of new control technology." Id. Here the record is silent on this point (although the point is important). How easy or difficult would be "the effective placement of new control technology" in these renovated units is not clear, but we do know that the project already contemplates replacement of steam drums, air heaters and other components; each unit would, therefore, in any event be shut down for nine months.

Our reading of the phrase "any physical change" is also consistent with another of the basic goals of the 1977 Amendments: technology-forcing. The legislative history suggests and courts have recognized that in passing the Clean Air Act Amendments, Congress intended to stimulate the advancement of pollution control technology. See, e.g., S.Rep. No. 91–1196, 91st Cong., 2d Sess. 17 (1970)("Standards of performance should provide an incentive for industries to work toward constant improvement in techniques for preventing and controlling emissions from stationary sources...."); Duquesne Light Co. v. EPA, 698 F.2d 456, 475(D.C.Cir.1983); Alabama Power, 636 F.2d at 372; ASARCO, 578 F.2d at 327; United States v. SCM Corp., 667 F.Supp. 1110, 1126–27 (D.Md.1987). The development of emissions control systems is not furthered if operators could, without exposure to the standards of the 1977 Amendments, increase production (and pollution) through the extensive replacement of deteriorated generating systems.

B. The EPA's Regulations

Although we have determined that WEPCO's repair and replacement program satisfies the modification provisions of the Clean Air Act Amendments, this is not the end of our inquiry. WEPCO's attack focuses primarily on EPA regulations, which in a number of respects are narrower than the statute. WEPCO argues that the EPA applied its regulations arbitrarily and capriciously to the Port Washington project.

1. Physical Change and the "Routine" Exception

EPA regulations define "modification" as "any physical or operational change to an existing facility which results in an increase in the emission rate to the atmosphere of any pollutant to which a standard applies." 40 C.F.R. § 60.14(a) (1988). To a major degree, this definition parallels 42 U.S.C. section 7411(a)(2), and it is unnecessary to repeat the analysis already applied to the statute. See supra III(A)(1). However, the EPA has, in addition, used its regulations to exempt a number of activities from the broader definition. The exemption that may be relevant here is accomplished by the following language:

The following shall not, by themselves, be considered modifications under this part:

(1) Maintenance, repair, and replacement which the Administrator determines to be routine for a source category....

340 C.F.R. § 60.14(e) (1988). See 40 C.F.R. § 52.21(b)(2)(iii).

WEPCO relies on this language to argue that, even if its repair and replacement program amounts to a physical change, it was specifically exempted by the regulations.

Again, we accord substantial deference to an agency's interpretation of its own regulations, especially with respect to technical and complex matters. Lyng v. Payne, 476 U.S. 926, 939, 106 S.Ct. 2333, 2341, 90 L.Ed.2d 921 (1986); Aluminum Co. of Am. v. Central Lincoln Peoples' Util. Dist., 467 U.S. 380, 390, 104 S.Ct. 2472, 2479, 81 L.Ed.2d 301 (1984). In this connection, to determine whether proposed work at a facility is routine, "EPA makes a case-by-case determination by weighing the nature, extent, purpose, frequency, and cost of the work, as well as other relevant factors, to arrive at a common-sense finding." Clay Memorandum at 3. The EPA considered all these factors in determining that the Port Washington project was not routine; first, the EPA observed that the nature and extent of the project was substantial: WEPCO proposed to replace sixty-foot steam drums (in units 2, 3, 4 and 5) and air heaters (in units 1, 2, 3 and 4) during successive nine-month outages at each unit. Id. at 4. Certainly, the magnitude of the project (as well as the down-time required to implement it) suggests that it is more than routine.

Further, the EPA points to WEPCO's admission in its application that "[work items] falling into the category of repetitive maintenance that are normally performed during scheduled equipment outages ... are not included in this application." Cassidy Letter at 1 (emphasis supplied). This admission suggests that WEPCO at first blush did not regard the repair and replacement project as ordinary or routine.

In addition, the EPA noted that far from being routine, the Port Washington project apparently was unprecedented: "WEPCO did not identify, and EPA did not find, even a single instance of renovation work at any electric utility generating station that approached the Port Washington life extension project in nature, scope or extent." Respondent's Brief at 44; see Clay Memorandum at 4 ("[T]his is a highly unusual, if not unprecedented, and costly project."). We surmise, although the record is silent, that the "case of first impression" character of the project may reflect historical practice in the electric utility industry of replacing old plants (at the expiration of their useful lives) with new plants, employing improved technologies and achieving improved efficiencies. This was the typical practice, rather than the mere extension of life of existing plants through massive like-kind replacements. Cf. Clay Memorandum at 4 ("[The Port Washington project's] purpose is to completely rehabilitate aging power generating units whose capacity has significantly deteriorated over a period of years, thereby restoring their original capacity and substantially extending the period of their utilization as an alternative to retiring them as they approach the end of their useful physical and economic life.").

* * *

The purpose, frequency and cost of the work also support the EPA's decision here. WEPCO admits that the plans for extensive renovation "represent a life extension of the units from their planned retirement dates," Cassidy Letter at 2–3 (emphasis supplied), and it recognizes that "the renovation work items included in this application are those that would normally occur only once or twice during a unit's expected life cycle." Id. at 1. Indeed, WEPCO reported that it had never previously replaced a steam drum or "header" of comparable size at any of its coal-fired electrical generating facilities. Clay Memorandum at 5. Further, the Port Washington renovation project will cost at least $70.5 million. Letter from John W. Boston, Senior Vice President of WEPCO, to Gary D. McCutchen, Chief New Source Review Section of the EPA, at 4 (May 19, 1988). These factors suggest that the project is not routine.

WEPCO urges that the EPA's conclusions are supported by neither the evidence nor the provisions of the Clean Air Act Amendments. WEPCO reasons that because any replacement project will presumably extend the life of a facility, the EPA's reliance on life extension as a factor in denying the "routine" nature of a project is overbroad. Petitioners' Brief at 44. Although perhaps persuasive on its face, WEPCO's analysis is ultimately wide of the mark. While it is certainly true that the repair of deteriorated equipment will contribute to the useful life of any facility, it does not necessarily follow that the repairs in question would extend the life expectancy of the facility. The need for some repairs along the line is a given in determining in the first instance the life expectancy of a plant. WEPCO cannot seriously argue that its units' planned retirement dates of 1992 (units 1 and 2) and 1999 (units 3, 4 and 5) did not take into account at least minor equipment repairs and replacements.[3] And WEPCO concedes that the Port Washington program will extend the life expectancy of the plant until 2010. The EPA concluded that the proposed project will increase the life expectancy of the Port Washington facility, and this conclusion was a factor in the finding that the work was not routine. These determinations were not arbitrary and capricious.

* * *

[The court goes on to examine the EPA's methods of calculating emissions for the PSD limit and concludes that these methods may be violative of the CAA].

* * *

We therefore affirm in part and vacate in part, remanding the cause to the EPA for further proceedings not inconsistent with this opinion.

Notes and Questions

1. Can repairs ever be "routine repair and maintenance" if they prolong the useful life of the facility? Could the court have ruled solely on

---

3. By WEPCO's own admission, "even a new facility could not operate normally but for a relatively short period of time ... [w]ithout any repair or replacement.... "Petitioner's Brief at 44. Because the plants were placed into service between 1935 and 1950—and because WEPCO ac-

knowledges that the life expectancy of these plants was approximately fifty years—it is clear that WEPCO included minor part repair and replacement in its calculations. Of course, the planned retirement dates appear to be merely estimates and do not seem to be binding.

that ground in the *Wisconsin Electric* Case? Is this an ambiguity in the statute subject to *Chevron* deference?

2. If the sole criteria for determining whether a "modification" occurs that subjects a source to NSPS and NSR is whether there is any increase in emissions, what is the baseline from which increases are to be measured? Is it one discrete source of emissions or is increase to be viewed with respect to the total emissions of the plant (including say another smokestack or fugitive emissions)? Whether a source can avoid NSR by offsetting increasing emissions at one part of a plant by reductions at another is a very important question. Such "offsets" or "bubbling" could allow a plant to increase production efficiencies by determining the best way to reach target reduction levels.

3. Also with respect to the proper "baseline," are emissions measurements to be taken from potential to emit or actual emissions?

The following case excerpts address these questions.

CHEVRON, U.S.A., INC.
v.
NATURAL RESOURCES DEFENSE COUNCIL, INC.

467 U.S. 837, 104 S.Ct. 2778, 81 L.Ed.2d 694.

Justice STEVENS delivered the opinion of the Court.

In the Clean Air Act Amendments of 1977, Pub.L. 95–95, 91 Stat. 685, Congress enacted certain requirements applicable to States that had not achieved the national air quality standards established by the Environmental Protection Agency (EPA) pursuant to earlier legislation. The amended Clean Air Act required these "nonattainment" States to establish a permit program regulating "new or modified major stationary sources" of air pollution. Generally, a permit may not be issued for a new or modified major stationary source unless several stringent conditions are met.[1] The EPA regulation promulgated to implement this permit requirement allows a State to adopt a plantwide definition of the term "stationary source."[2] Under this definition, an existing plant that contains several pollution-emitting devices may install or modify one

---

1. Section 172(b)(6), 42 U.S.C. § 7502(b)(6), provides:

"The plan provisions required by subsection (a) shall—

"(6) require permits for the construction and operation of new or modified major stationary sources in accordance with section 173 (relating to permit requirements)." 91 Stat. 747.

2. "(i) 'Stationary source' means any building, structure, facility, or installation which emits or may emit any air pollutant subject to regulation under the Act.

"(ii) 'Building, structure, facility, or installation' means all of the pollutant-emitting activities which belong to the same industrial grouping, are located on one or more contiguous or adjacent properties, and are under the control of the same person (or persons under common control) except the activities of any vessel." 40 CFR § § 51.18(j)(1)(i) and (ii) (1983).

piece of equipment without meeting the permit conditions if the alteration will not increase the total emissions from the plant. The question presented by these cases is whether EPA's decision to allow States to treat all of the pollution-emitting devices within the same industrial grouping as though they were encased within a single "bubble" is based on a reasonable construction of the statutory term "stationary source."

I

The EPA regulations containing the plantwide definition of the term stationary source were promulgated on October 14, 1981. 46 Fed.Reg. 50766. Respondents[3] filed a timely petition for review in the United States Court of Appeals for the District of Columbia Circuit pursuant to 42 U.S.C. § 7607(b)(1).[4] The Court of Appeals set aside the regulations. Natural Resources Defense Council, Inc. v. Gorsuch, 222 U.S.App.D.C. 268, 685 F.2d 718 (1982).

The court observed that the relevant part of the amended Clean Air Act "does not explicitly define what Congress envisioned as a 'stationary source, to which the permit program ... should apply,'" and further stated that the precise issue was not "squarely addressed in the legislative history." Id., at 273, 685 F.2d, at 723. In light of its conclusion that the legislative history bearing on the question was "at best contradictory," it reasoned that "the purposes of the nonattainment program should guide our decision here." Id., at 276, n. 39, 685 F.2d, at 726, n. 39.[5] Based on two of its precedents concerning the applicability of the bubble concept to certain Clean Air Act programs,[6] the court stated that the bubble concept was "mandatory" in programs designed merely to maintain existing air quality, but held that it was "inappropriate" in programs enacted to improve air quality. Id., at 276, 685 F.2d, at 726. Since the purpose of the permit program—its "raison d'être," in the court's view—was to improve air quality, the court held that the bubble concept was inapplicable in these cases under its prior precedents. Ibid. It therefore set aside the regulations embodying the bubble concept as contrary to law. We granted certiorari to review that judgment, 461 U.S. 956, 103 S.Ct. 2427, 77 L.Ed.2d 1314 (1983), and we now reverse.

* * *

3. National Resources Defense Council, Inc., Citizens for a Better Environment, Inc., and North Western Ohio Lung Association, Inc.

4. Petitioners, Chevron U.S.A. Inc., American Iron and Steel Institute, American Petroleum Institute, Chemical Manufacturers Association, Inc., General Motors Corp., and Rubber Manufacturers Association were granted leave to intervene and argue in support of the regulation.

5. The court remarked in this regard:

"We regret, of course, that Congress did not advert specifically to the bubble concept's application to various Clean Air Act programs, and note that a further clarifying statutory directive would facilitate the work of the agency and of the court in their endeavors to serve the legislator will." 222 U.S.App.D.C., at 276, n. 39, 685 F.2d, at 726, n. 39.

6. Alabama Power Co. v. Costle, 204 U.S.App.D.C. 51, 636 F.2d 323 (1979); ASARCO Inc. v. EPA, 188 U.S.App.D.C. 77, 578 F.2d 319 (1978).

In light of these well-settled principles it is clear that the Court of Appeals misconceived the nature of its role in reviewing the regulations at issue. Once it determined, after its own examination of the legislation, that Congress did not actually have an intent regarding the applicability of the bubble concept to the permit program, the question before it was not whether in its view the concept is "inappropriate" in the general context of a program designed to improve air quality, but whether the Administrator's view that it is appropriate in the context of this particular program is a reasonable one. Based on the examination of the legislation and its history which follows, we agree with the Court of Appeals that Congress did not have a specific intention on the applicability of the bubble concept in these cases, and conclude that the EPA's use of that concept here is a reasonable policy choice for the agency to make.

* * *

VI

As previously noted, prior to the 1977 Amendments, the EPA had adhered to a plantwide definition of the term "source" under a NSPS program. After adoption of the 1977 Amendments, proposals for a plantwide definition were considered in at least three formal proceedings.

In January 1979, the EPA considered the question whether the same restriction on new construction in nonattainment areas that had been included in its December 1976 Ruling should be required in the revised SIP's that were scheduled to go into effect in July 1979. After noting that the 1976 Ruling was ambiguous on the question "whether a plant with a number of different processes and emission points would be considered a single source," 44 Fed.Reg. 3276 (1979), the EPA, in effect, provided a bifurcated answer to that question. In those areas that did not have a revised SIP in effect by July 1979, the EPA rejected the plantwide definition; on the other hand, it expressly concluded that the plantwide approach would be permissible in certain circumstances if authorized by an approved SIP.

* * *

Significantly, the EPA expressly noted that the word "source" might be given a plantwide definition for some purposes and a narrower definition for other purposes. It wrote:

"Source means any building structure, facility, or installation which emits or may emit any regulated pollutant. 'Building, structure, facility or installation' means plant in PSD areas and in nonattainment areas except where the growth prohibitions would apply or where no adequate SIP exists or is being carried out." Id., at 51925.[28]

28. In its explanation of why the use of the "bubble concept" was especially appropriate in preventing significant deterioration (PSD) in clean air areas, the EPA

The EPA's summary of its proposed Ruling discloses a flexible rather than rigid definition of the term "source" to implement various policies and programs:

"In summary, EPA is proposing two different ways to define source for different kinds of NSR programs:

"(1) For PSD and complete Part D SIPs, review would apply only to plants, with an unrestricted plant-wide bubble.

"(2) For the offset ruling, restrictions on construction, and incomplete Part D SIPs, review would apply to both plants and individual pieces of process equipment, causing the plant-wide bubble not to apply for new and modified major pieces of equipment.

"In addition, for the restrictions on construction, EPA is proposing to define 'major modification' so as to prohibit the bubble entirely. Finally, an alternative discussed but not favored is to have only pieces of process equipment reviewed, resulting in no plant-wide bubble and allowing minor pieces of equipment to escape NSR regardless of whether they are within a major plant." Id., at 51934.

In August 1980, however, the EPA adopted a regulation that, in essence, applied the basic reasoning of the Court of Appeals in these cases. The EPA took particular note of the two then-recent Court of Appeals decisions, which had created the bright-line rule that the "bubble concept" should be employed in a program designed to maintain air quality but not in one designed to enhance air quality. Relying heavily on those cases,[29] EPA adopted a dual definition of "source" for nonattainment areas that required a permit whenever a change in either the entire plant, or one of its components, would result in a significant increase in emissions even if the increase was completely offset by reductions elsewhere in the plant. The EPA expressed the opinion that this interpretation was "more consistent with congressional intent" than the plantwide definition because it "would bring in more sources or modifications for review," 45 Fed.Reg. 52697 (1980), but its primary legal analysis was predicated on the two Court of Appeals decisions.

In 1981 a new administration took office and initiated a "Government-wide reexamination of regulatory burdens and complexities." 46 Fed.Reg. 16281. In the context of that review, the EPA reevaluated the

stated: "In addition, application of the bubble on a plant-wide basis encourages voluntary upgrading of equipment, and growth in productive capacity." Id., at 51932.

29. "The dual definition also is consistent with Alabama Power and ASARCO. Alabama Power held that EPA had broad discretion to define the constituent terms of 'source' so as best to effectuate the purposes of the statute. Different definitions of 'source' can therefore be used for different sections of the statute. . . .

"Moreover, Alabama Power and ASARCO taken together suggest that there is a distinction between Clean Air Act programs designed to enhance air quality and those designed only to maintain air quality. . . .

"Promulgation of the dual definition follows the mandate of Alabama Power, which held that, while EPA could not define 'source' as a combination of sources, EPA had broad discretion to define 'building,' 'structure,' 'facility,' and 'installation' so as to best accomplish the purposes of the Act." 45 Fed.Reg. 52697 (1980).

various arguments that had been advanced in connection with the proper definition of the term "source" and concluded that the term should be given the same definition in both nonattainment areas and PSD areas.

In explaining its conclusion, the EPA first noted that the definitional issue was not squarely addressed in either the statute or its legislative history and therefore that the issue involved an agency "judgment as how to best carry out the Act." Ibid. It then set forth several reasons for concluding that the plantwide definition was more appropriate. It pointed out that the dual definition "can act as a disincentive to new investment and modernization by discouraging modifications to existing facilities" and "can actually retard progress in air pollution control by discouraging replacement of older, dirtier processes or pieces of equipment with new, cleaner ones." Ibid. Moreover, the new definition "would simplify EPA's rules by using the same definition of 'source' for PSD, nonattainment new source review and the construction moratorium. This reduces confusion and inconsistency." Ibid. Finally, the agency explained that additional requirements that remained in place would accomplish the fundamental purposes of achieving attainment with NAAQS's as expeditiously as possible.

* * *

Statutory Language

The definition of the term "stationary source" in § 111(a)(3) refers to "any building, structure, facility, or installation" which emits air pollution. See supra, at 2784. This definition is applicable only to the NSPS program by the express terms of the statute; the text of the statute does not make this definition applicable to the permit program. Petitioners therefore maintain that there is no statutory language even relevant to ascertaining the meaning of stationary source in the permit program aside from § 302(j), which defines the term "major stationary source." See supra, at 2786. We disagree with petitioners on this point.

The definition in § 302(j) tells us what the word "major" means—a source must emit at least 100 tons of pollution to qualify—but it sheds virtually no light on the meaning of the term "stationary source." It does equate a source with a facility—a "major emitting facility" and a "major stationary source" are synonymous under § 302(j). The ordinary meaning of the term "facility" is some collection of integrated elements which has been designed and constructed to achieve some purpose. Moreover, it is certainly no affront to common English usage to take a reference to a major facility or a major source to connote an entire plant as opposed to its constituent parts. Basically, however, the language of § 302(j) simply does not compel any given interpretation of the term "source."

Respondents recognize that, and hence point to § 111(a)(3). Although the definition in that section is not literally applicable to the permit program, it sheds as much light on the meaning of the word "source" as anything in the statute.[footnote omitted]. As respondents point out, use of the words "building, structure, facility, or installation," as the definition of source, could be read to impose the permit conditions on an individual building that is a part of a plant. [footnote omitted]. A "word may have a character of its own not to be submerged by its association." Russell Motor Car Co. v. United States, 261 U.S. 514, 519, 43 S.Ct. 428, 429, 67 L.Ed. 778 (1923). On the other hand, the meaning of a word must be ascertained in the context of achieving particular objectives, and the words associated with it may indicate that the true meaning of the series is to convey a common idea. The language may reasonably be interpreted to impose the requirement on any discrete, but integrated, operation which pollutes. This gives meaning to all of the terms—a single building, not part of a larger operation, would be covered if it emits more than 100 tons of pollution, as would any facility, structure, or installation. Indeed, the language itself implies a "bubble concept" of sorts: each enumerated item would seem to be treated as if it were encased in a bubble. While respondents insist that each of these terms must be given a discrete meaning, they also argue that § 111(a)(3) defines "source" as that term is used in § 302(j). The latter section, however, equates a source with a facility, whereas the former defines "source" as a facility, among other items.

We are not persuaded that parsing of general terms in the text of the statute will reveal an actual intent of Congress. [footnote omitted]. We know full well that this language is not dispositive; the terms are overlapping and the language is not precisely directed to the question of the applicability of a given term in the context of a larger operation. To the extent any congressional "intent" can be discerned from this language, it would appear that the listing of overlapping, illustrative terms was intended to enlarge, rather than to confine, the scope of the agency's power to regulate particular sources in order to effectuate the policies of the Act.

Legislative History

In addition, respondents argue that the legislative history and policies of the Act foreclose the plantwide definition, and that the EPA's interpretation is not entitled to deference because it represents a sharp break with prior interpretations of the Act.

Based on our examination of the legislative history, we agree with the Court of Appeals that it is unilluminating. The general remarks pointed to by respondents "were obviously not made with this narrow issue in mind and they cannot be said to demonstrate a Congressional desire...." Jewell Ridge Coal Corp. v. Mine Workers, 325 U.S. 161, 168–169, 65 S.Ct. 1063, 1067–1068, 89 L.Ed. 1534 (1945). Respondents' argument based on the legislative history relies heavily on Senator Muskie's observation that a new source is subject to the LAER requirement.[35] But the full statement is ambiguous and like the text of § 173 itself, this comment does not tell us what a new source is, much less that it is to have an inflexible definition. We find that the legislative history as a whole is silent on the precise issue before us. It is, however, consistent with the view that the EPA should have broad discretion in implementing the policies of the 1977 Amendments.

* * *

Our review of the EPA's varying interpretations of the word "source"—both before and after the 1977 Amendments—convinces us that the agency primarily responsible for administering this important legislation has consistently interpreted it flexibly—not in a sterile textual vacuum, but in the context of implementing policy decisions in a technical and complex arena. The fact that the agency has from time to time changed its interpretation of the term "source" does not, as respondents argue, lead us to conclude that no deference should be accorded the agency's interpretation of the statute. An initial agency interpretation is not instantly carved in stone. On the contrary, the agency, to engage in informed rulemaking, must consider varying interpretations and the wisdom of its policy on a continuing basis. Moreover, the fact that the agency has adopted different definitions in different contexts adds force to the argument that the definition itself is flexible, particularly since Congress has never indicated any disapproval of a flexible reading of the statute.

Significantly, it was not the agency in 1980, but rather the Court of Appeals that read the statute inflexibly to command a plantwide definition for programs designed to maintain clean air and to forbid such a definition for programs designed to improve air quality. The distinction the court drew may well be a sensible one, but our labored review of the problem has surely disclosed that it is not a distinction that Congress ever articulated itself, or one that the EPA found in the statute before the courts began to review the legislative work product. We conclude that it was the Court of Appeals, rather than Congress or any of the decisionmakers who are authorized by Congress to administer this legislation, that was primarily responsible for the 1980 position taken by the agency.

POLICY

The arguments over policy that are advanced in the parties' briefs create the impression that respondents are now waging in a judicial forum a specific policy battle which they ultimately lost in the agency and in the 32 jurisdictions opting for the "bubble concept," but one

---

35. See supra, at 2787. We note that Senator Muskie was not critical of the EPA's use of the "bubble concept" in one NSPS program prior to the 1977 amendments. See ibid.

More importantly, that history plainly identifies the policy concerns that motivated the enactment; the plantwide definition is fully consistent with one of those con-

cerns—the allowance of reasonable economic growth—and, whether or not we believe it most effectively implements the other, we must recognize that the EPA has advanced a reasonable explanation for its conclusion that the regulations serve the environmental objectives as well. See supra, at 2789–2790, and n. 29; see also supra, at 2788, n. 27.

which was never waged in the Congress. Such policy arguments are more properly addressed to legislators or administrators, not to judges [footnote omitted].

In these cases, the Administrator's interpretation represents a reasonable accommodation of manifestly competing interests and is entitled to deference: the regulatory scheme is technical and complex, [footnote omitted]. The agency considered the matter in a detailed and reasoned fashion, and the decision involves reconciling conflicting policies. [Footnotes omitted]. Congress intended to accommodate both interests, but did not do so itself on the level of specificity presented by these cases. Perhaps that body consciously desired the Administrator to strike the balance at this level, thinking that those with great expertise and charged with responsibility for administering the provision would be in a better position to do so; perhaps it simply did not consider the question at this level; and perhaps Congress was unable to forge a coalition on either side of the question, and those on each side decided to take their chances with the scheme devised by the agency. For judicial purposes, it matters not which of these things occurred.

Judges are not experts in the field, and are not part of either political branch of the Government. Courts must, in some cases, reconcile competing political interests, but not on the basis of the judges' personal policy preferences. In contrast, an agency to which Congress has delegated policy-making responsibilities may, within the limits of that delegation, properly rely upon the incumbent administration's views of wise policy to inform its judgments. While agencies are not directly accountable to the people, the Chief Executive is, and it is entirely appropriate for this political branch of the Government to make such policy choices—resolving the competing interests which Congress itself either inadvertently did not resolve, or intentionally left to be resolved by the agency charged with the administration of the statute in light of everyday realities.

When a challenge to an agency construction of a statutory provision, fairly conceptualized, really centers on the wisdom of the agency's policy, rather than whether it is a reasonable choice within a gap left open by Congress, the challenge must fail. In such a case, federal judges—who have no constituency—have a duty to respect legitimate policy choices made by those who do. The responsibilities for assessing the wisdom of such policy choices and resolving the struggle between competing views of the public interest are not judicial ones: "Our Constitution vests such responsibilities in the political branches." TVA v. Hill, 437 U.S. 153, 195, 98 S.Ct. 2279, 2302, 57 L.Ed.2d 117 (1978).

We hold that the EPA's definition of the term "source" is a permissible construction of the statute which seeks to accommodate progress in reducing air pollution with economic growth. "The Regulations which the Administrator has adopted provide what the agency could allowably view as ... [an] effective reconciliation of these twofold ends...." United States v. Shimer, 367 U.S., at 383, 81 S.Ct., at 1560.

The judgment of the Court of Appeals is reversed.

It is so ordered.

* * *

WISCONSIN ELECTRIC POWER COMPANY v. REILLY

United States Court of Appeals, Seventh Circuit, 1990.

893 F.2d 901.

[The facts of this case are set out on page _____, infra.]

     2.   Increase in Emissions

Thus far, we have not had to address the important differences between the PSD and NSPS programs. At this point, however, the differences become crucial, because each program measures emissions in a fundamentally distinct manner.

     a.   NSPS Measurements

As previously noted, the EPA's NSPS program is concerned primarily with increases in emission rates, expressed in kilograms per hour of discharged pollutants. 40 C.F.R. § 60.14 (1988). The EPA compares the hourly emissions of the unit at its current maximum capacity to its potential emissions at maximum capacity after the change. Clay Memorandum at 9; see 40 C.F.R. § 60 App. C (1988)(providing complex formulae for determining emission rate change). In this calculation, the agency disregards the unit's maximum design capacity; this factor often sheds little light on the unit's actual current capacity to produce emissions.[5]

The EPA applied these procedures in examining the generating units at Port Washington. The EPA asked WEPCO to submit figures for the actual operations and emissions of each unit at the Port Washington plant for the years 1978 to 1987; the EPA then relied upon the 1987 figures to calculate the emissions baseline against which post-replacement emissions could be compared. WEPCO, however, challenged the EPA's acceptance of these preliminary baseline figures, arguing that units 1, 2, 3 and 4 were capable of operating at higher rates of production than those calculated by the EPA based upon the 1987 figures. WEPCO conducted five ten-hour tests at each unit to determine its maximum capacity. Upon reviewing the test results, the EPA agreed that units 2 and 3 could be operated at their design capacities, and it revised the baseline levels for these units. The agency concluded that because there would be no increase in production or emissions, NSPS would not apply to these units following the renovation project. Nonetheless, the EPA refused to alter the baseline levels for units 1 and 4, noting

---

5. Of course, if the unit is currently operating at maximum design capacity, there will be no difference between the measure of emissions at maximum design capacity and at current maximum capacity. Since the units at Port Washington were operating well below maximum design capacity (and unit 5 was completely shut down), that is not the case here.

that WEPCO's tests had not been conducted pursuant to the test protocol as required by the regulations and the Wisconsin State Implementation Plan (units 1 and 4 exceeded certain maximum allowable emission limits). Supplemental Determination at 8–9. Comparing these 1987 baseline levels to the maximum capacity of the plant after renovation, the EPA concluded that the renovation project would be subject to the provisions of NSPS.

WEPCO asks us to overturn the EPA's final ruling that the Port Washington project triggers NSPS. Specifically, WEPCO argues that, by using 1987 figures in determining the emissions baseline, the EPA failed to apply its own regulations:

> WEPCO asserts that these figures "reflected voluntary decisions by WEPC[O] regarding safety considerations (e.g., the 'zero' rate for Unit 5) and an electricity demand which did not require operation of the units at higher capacities." Petitioner's Brief at 15–16. WEPCO also posits that the EPA's refusal to compare representative pre-renovation emissions with actual post-renovation emissions is contrary to EPA regulations and amounts to an abuse of agency discretion.[6]

WEPCO's first assertion is easily dismissed. The EPA's choice of the 1987 figures was based entirely upon WEPCO's own data. And, when WEPCO complained that its own data did not reflect WEPCO's pre-renovation capabilities, the EPA permitted WEPCO to conduct new tests (pursuant to 40 C.F.R. § 60 App. C (1988)) that eventually resulted in the revision of the baselines for units 2 and 3.

WEPCO's second charge is far more substantial. WEPCO argues that NSPS regulations require the EPA to use a "representative" year in determining a baseline rate of emissions. The EPA disputes this claim, arguing that "[a]s to NSPS, there is no 'representative emissions' concept.... Rather ... the baseline emission rates for units 1–5 are determined by hourly maximum capacity just prior to the renovations."[7] Thomas Letter at 5.

---

6. As a preliminary matter, we note that WEPCO has not asked us to review the propriety of the NSPS regulations themselves. Indeed, we have no jurisdiction to conduct such an inquiry: 42 U.S.C. section 7607(b)(1) reserves such questions for the United States Court of Appeals for the District of Columbia Circuit. In this case, WEPCO simply requests that we consider whether the EPA properly applied these regulations to the Port Washington generating units. We have jurisdiction to undertake such an inquiry. 42 U.S.C. § 7607(b)(1).

7. The regulations themselves provide, in part:

(a) ... any physical or operational change to an existing facility which re-

sults in an increase in the emission rate to the atmosphere of any pollutant to which a standard applies shall be considered a modification....

(b) Emission rate shall be expressed as kg/hr of any pollutant discharged into the atmosphere for which a standard is applicable. The Administrator shall use the following to determine the emission rate:

(1) Emission factors as specified in the latest issue of "Compilation of Air Pollutant Emission Factors," EPA Publication No. AP–42, or other emission factors determined by the Administrator to be superior to AP–42 emission factors, in cases where utilization of emission factors demonstrate that the emission level resulting from the physi-

WEPCO's interpretation of the regulations, at first blush, seems sensible: since the regulations require that the manual emission tests and continuous monitoring systems be based upon the "representative performance" of the facility, the emission factor test approach must also be based upon "representative performance." 40 C.F.R. § 60.14 (1988); see 39 Fed.Reg. 36946, 36947(1974) (explaining provision).[8] Otherwise, the tests might reach inconsistent results, making the rate of emissions entirely dependent upon the type of test used by the facility. Hence, argues WEPCO, the EPA must examine the emission rates during a representative period, not 1987.

WEPCO's analysis, however, relies upon a flawed premise. WEPCO assumes that the phrase "representative performance of the facility" suggests that the EPA must choose a representative year. Read in context, however, the phrase refers generally to all the conditions of the test, not specifically to its timing:

> Tests shall be conducted under such conditions as the Administrator shall specify to the owner or operator based on representative performance of the facility. At least three valid test runs must be conducted before and at least three after the physical or operational change. All operating parameters which may affect emissions must be held constant to the maximum feasible degree for all test runs. 40 C.F.R. § 60.14(b)(2) (1988). Compare 40 C.F.R. § 52.21(b)(21)(ii) (1988) (PSD program) ("The Administrator shall allow the use of a different time period upon a determination that it is more representative of normal source operation.") (emphasis supplied). Put simply, section 60.14 ensures that the operator will not doctor testing conditions to produce favorable emission results. The EPA's explanation of its regulations, which of course is given deference, supports this interpretation: "According to the proposed regulation, each set of emission tests (using manual tests or continuous moni-

cal or operational change will either clearly increase or clearly not increase.

(2) Material balances, continuous monitor data, or manual emission tests in cases where utilization of emission factors as referenced in paragraph (b)(1) of this section does not demonstrate to the Administrator's satisfaction whether the emission level resulting from the physical or operational change will either clearly increase or clearly not increase, or where an owner or operator demonstrates to the Administrator's satisfaction that there are reasonable grounds to dispute the result obtained by the Administrator utilizing emission factors as referenced in paragraph (b)(1) of this section. When the emission rate is based on results from manual emission tests or continuous monitoring systems, the procedures specified in Appendix C of this part shall be used to determine whether an increase in emission rate has occurred. Tests shall be conducted under such conditions as the Administrator shall specify to the owner or operator based on representative performance of the facility. At least three valid test runs must be conducted before and at least three after the physical or operational change. All operating parameters which may affect emissions must be held constant to the maximum feasible degree for all test runs.

40 C.F.R. § 60.14 (1988).

8. The emission factor test is the only technique that can predict emission rates after renovations. Because the determination at issue here must be made before the renovations are undertaken, the EPA relied on this test in evaluating the Port Washington project.

tors) conducted before and after a physical or operational change would consist of at least three runs, and would be conducted under representative operating conditions." 39 Fed.Reg. 36946, 36947 (1974) (emphasis supplied). WEPCO has not argued that it conducted its own tests under unrepresentative conditions, nor has it challenged any other part of the test protocol.[9] And WEPCO does not claim that the tests were conducted during a period of operations that substantially differed from the normal operations of the deteriorated Port Washington plant. Further, the fact that the EPA permitted WEPCO to conduct additional emissions tests on the units (during which, presumably, WEPCO could maintain representative operating conditions) undermines WEPCO's assertion that the regulations were applied arbitrarily or capriciously.

b. PSD Measurements

Unlike NSPS, PSD is concerned with changes in total annual emissions, expressed in tons per year. The PSD regulations require preconstruction review of the construction or modification of major emitting facilities. These regulations define their key term—"major modification"—as "any physical change in or change in the method of operation of a major stationary source that would result in a significant[10] net emissions increase of any pollutant subject to regulation under the Act." 40 C.F.R. § 52.21(b)(2)(i) (1988) (footnote supplied).

Here the question is whether WEPCO's renovation project will result in "a significant net emissions increase" so as to trigger the "major modification" provision of the regulations and, as a result, PSD. To determine whether the project would result in an emissions increase, the EPA compared actual pre-renovation emissions with potential post-renovation emissions at the Port Washington plant. Specifically, the EPA first examined the two-year period of 1983 through 1984 as the pre-renovation baseline period, pursuant to 40 C.F.R. section 52.21(b)(21)(ii):

In general, actual emissions as of a particular date shall equal the average rate, in tons per year, at which the unit actually emitted the pollutant during a two-year period which precedes the particular date and which is representative of normal source operation. The Administrator shall allow the use of a different time period upon a determination that it is more representative of normal source operation. Actual emissions shall be calculated using the unit's actual operating hours, produc-

9. WEPCO does assert that the EPA improperly examined only the lowest hourly capacity achieved during the test periods. Even if the EPA had accepted the highest capacity tests, however, the rate of emissions of units 1, 4 and 5 still would have subjected those units to NSPS after the renovation. Further, the EPA acknowledges that there will be no difference between the rate of emissions of units 2 and 3 before and after the renovation, regardless of the chosen capacity level. See Letter from Walt Stevenson to Jack Farmer (Jan. 5, 1989)(summarizing Port Washington capacity tests). We therefore need not consider whether the Administrator may rely upon the lowest capacity level.

10. The regulations define "significant" in terms of threshold emissions increases of individual pollutants: for example, an increase of 40 tons per year of nitrogen oxides is a "significant" net emissions increase. See 40 C.F.R. § 52.21(b)(23) (1988).

tion rates, and types of materials processed, stored, or combusted during the selected time period. 40 C.F.R. § 52.21(b)(21)(ii) (1988) (emphasis supplied). Because Administrator Thomas determined that the discovery of cracks in the rear steam drums led to a more recent "source curtailment," he relied upon the data from earlier years, 1983 and 1984, as the baseline to determine whether the renovation would cause an increase in emissions. Thomas Letter at 5. WEPCO does not challenge this component of the EPA's calculation.

Second, the EPA calculated the actual emissions of the plant following completion of the project. Generally, in order to apply PSD, the regulations require the EPA to find an "increase in actual emissions from a particular physical change or change in method of operation." 40 C.F.R. § 52.21(b)(3)(i)(a) (1988) (emphasis supplied). The EPA reasoned, however, that because the source "ha[d] not yet begun operations following the renovation, 'actual emissions' following the renovation [were] deemed to be the source's 'potential to emit.'" Clay Memorandum at 7. In support of its reliance on WEPCO's potential to emit, the EPA pointed to the regulations: "For any emissions unit which has not begun normal operations on the particular date, actual emissions shall equal the potential to emit of the unit on that date." 40 C.F.R. § 52.21(b)(21)(iv) (1988).

WEPCO objects strenuously, and with good reason. In calculating the plant'spost-renovation potential to emit, the EPA bases its figures on round-the-clock operations (24 hours per day, 365 days per year) because WEPCO could potentially operate its facility continuously, despite the fact that WEPCO has never done so in the past. And the EPA has admitted that it "assumed that emissions increases at Port Washington would come not from an increase in emission rate, but rather from increases in production rate or hours of operation." Supplemental Determination at 9; see Clay Memorandum at 7–8. The EPA responds that WEPCO can avoid these maximum calculations simply by consenting to federally enforceable restrictions on production rates and hours of operation, but WEPCO declines to do so. Clay Memorandum at 8; see 40 C.F.R. §§ 52.21(b)(4), 52.21(b)(16) (1988).Thus, argues the EPA, it has no choice but to assume that the plant will be operated continuously.[11]

The first issue to be addressed is whether the EPA properly invoked the "potential to emit" concept in calculating the emissions increase. As explained above, the PSD regulations state that the EPA may rely upon a facility's potential to emit if the unit "has not begun normal operations on the particular date." 40 C.F.R. § 52.21(b)(21)(iv) (1988) (emphasis supplied). WEPCO argues that this phrase should be interpreted to

---

11. Despite WEPCO's protestations, we note initially that the EPA's refusal to apply the "production rate/hours of operation" exclusion was proper. 40 C.F.R. § 52.21(b)(2)(iii)(f) (1988). This exclusion— which states that "[a]physical change or change in the method of operation shall not include ... [a]n increase in the hours of operation or in the production rate," id.— was provided to allow facilities to take advantage of fluctuating market conditions, not construction or modification activity. See 45 Fed.Reg. 52676, 52704 (1980).

include only those units that have never been in operation, while the EPA urges that the phrase can be applied to both new and modified units.

The regulatory history of this phrase sheds little light on its proper interpretation. The EPA argues that it has always interpreted this phrase to include modified units; it asserts that its formulae for determining emissions increases have consistently assumed that "new or modified units" would be deemed to operate at maximum physical or federally enforceable levels. 45 Fed.Reg. 52676, 52718 (1980) (emphasis supplied). But the EPA's analysis here seems circular: in order to demonstrate that the Port Washington like-kind replacement project constitutes a modification, the EPA applies the potential to emit concept (to show an increase in emissions). And in order to apply the potential to emit concept to like-kind replacement, the EPA assumes that the plant is a "modified" unit. Although we accord great deference to an agency construing the statute it administers, Chevron, 467 U.S. at 844, 104 S.Ct. at 2782, and even more deference to an agency interpreting its own complex regulations, Aluminum Co. of Am. v. Central Lincoln Peoples' Util. Dist., 467 U.S. at 390, 104 S.Ct. at 2479, we cannot defer to agency interpretations that, as applied here, appear to assume what they seek to prove.[12]

We are also troubled by the EPA's assumption of continuous operations in calculating potential to emit at the Port Washington plant. Although we agree that the EPA cannot reasonably rely on a utility's own unenforceable estimates of its annual emissions,[13] we find no support in the regulations for the EPA's decision wholly to disregard past operating conditions at the plant. Indeed, Alabama Power Co. v. Costle,

---

12. In a supplemental filing pursuant to Seventh Circuit Rule 28(j), the EPA intimates that the First Circuit's recent decision in Puerto Rican Cement Co. v. EPA, 889 F.2d 292 (1st Cir.1989), permits the use of the potential to emit concept in similar circumstances. However, unlike the case at issue here, Puerto Rican Cement involved the construction of a new emissions unit at an existing source. Further, the First Circuit distinguished its holding from controversies having something in common with the one before us. One can imagine circumstances that might test the reasonableness of EPA's regulation. An electricity company, for example, might wish to replace a peakload generator—one that operates only a few days per year—with a new peak load generator that the firm could, but almost certainly will not, operate everyday.... Whatever the arguments about the "irrationality" of EPA's interpretation in such

circumstances, however, those circumstances are not present here.

Id. at 297–98.

13. The EPA argues that WEPCO can avoid the presumption of continuous operations simply by consenting to federally enforceable emission limits. However, the EPA has not brought to our attention a clear regulatory basis for its conclusion that the provision of this alternative justifies the assumption of continuous operation if the utility refuses to consent. And WEPCO may have legitimate reasons for declining to submit to federally enforceable emission limits: "[U]ncertainties about the the precise shape of future electricity peak demand might make the firm hesitate to promise EPA it will never increase actual emissions...." Puerto Rican Cement Co. v. EPA, 889 F.2d 292, 298 (1st Cir.1989).

636 F.2d 323 (D.C.Cir.1979), which contributes importantly to the EPA's current PSD program, suggests otherwise. There, the D.C. Circuit held, in part, that the EPA must "take [ ] into account the anticipated functioning of the air pollution control equipment designed into the facility" when calculating the facility's potential to emit. Id. at 353. More important for our purposes, however, was the court's discussion of a unit's potential to emit:

If the source has no actual emissions because it has yet to commence operating, its hypothetical, projected emissions are included in the baseline. If, however, the source is an established operation, a more realistic assessment of its impact on ambient air quality levels is possible, and thus is directed.Id. at 379 (emphasis supplied). The district court in United States v. Louisiana–Pacific Corp., 682 F.Supp. 1141 (D.Colo. 1988), relying on Alabama Power, recently reached the same conclusion:

The broad holding of Alabama Power is that potential to emit does not refer to the maximum emissions that can be generated by a source hypothesizing the worst conceivable operation. Rather, the concept contemplates the maximum emissions that can be generated while operating the source as it is intended to be operated and as it is normally operated. Of course, it is possible that a source could be operated without the control equipment designed into it or that a Konus heater could be operated so badly that the fire would go out. Yet, Alabama Power stands for the proposition that hypothesizing the worst possible emissions from the worst possible operation is the wrong way to calculate potential to emit.

Id. at 1158.

In sum, we certainly do not suggest that the EPA may never subject replaced units to the potential to emit concept under its regulations. The EPA may, if it wishes, undertake notice and comment procedures to apply the potential to emit concept to like-kind replacement. See 42 U.S.C. § 7607(d). But existing regulations do not seem to us to support such an application. We therefore believe that the EPA's reliance on an assumed continuous operation as a basis for finding an emissions increase is not properly supported. The EPA's determination that there has been a major modification for PSD purposes must be set aside.[14]

* * *

14. It appears that WEPCO never submitted pollutant-specific data to the EPA. Clay Memorandum at 7–8. Consequently, the EPA could not, at the time the matter was before it, conclude whether the renovated plant would cause a significant net emissions increase if it were operated under present hours and conditions. WEPCO should make such data available so that the EPA can determine on that basis whether the Port Washington plant will be subject to the PSD program.

Notes and Comments

1. Both Chevron and WEPCO turn to some extent on how much deference can be given to agency determinations. The more deferential *Chevron* deference (named after the case) will generally apply when an agency has exercised authority to alter a legal norm that has been given it by Congress. Note the language used in WEPCO:

> In sum, we certainly do not suggest that the EPA may never subject replaced units to the potential to emit concept under its regulations. The EPA may, if it wishes, undertake notice and comment procedures to apply the potential to emit concept to like-kind replacement. See 42 U.S.C. § 7607(d).[30]

2. In *Chevron,* the court noted that "The fact that the agency has from time to time changed its interpretation of the term "source" does not, as respondents argue, lead us to conclude that no deference should be accorded the agency's interpretation of the statute." Interestingly, this deference to the executive branch has had profound effects on environmental law. As most of government has been relatively balanced between the two major parties for the last thirty years, major policy changes in environmental statutes have been difficult. Thus, rather than making changes in the actual laws, many administrations have tried to influence the direction of environmental law through regulation. The implementation of a "bubble" concept, long favored by industry and certain economists, is an example of this. Given the high deference enunciated in *Chevron* this can allow a court to ignore underlying intentions of statutory language and focus instead on explicit terms.[31]

3. Do you see why industry might favor the "bubble" concept and why others may oppose it? Note the diagram of the plant below with 2 smokestacks. Assume both smokestack need repair and major changes to work at all, and that because they have been becoming less efficient with age, upgrading would increase pollution. If each smokestack was constdered a "source" under the statute, an increase in emissions of one upgraded smokestack, even if the other smokestack emission decreased dramatically, would trigger new source review, requiring pollution control equipment at great expense. This requires the plant to pay a lot of money for pollution control equipment or allow the plant to eventually cease operation altogether. Upgrading one smokestack of the factory would cost a great deal, even if overall emissions did not increase because of the phaseout of the second smokestack.

---

30. WEPCO, 893 F.2d at 918.

31. Though this may not always be true, given that the precise contours of

Chevron deference are still argued by our courts.

With "bubbling", the plant can do the same thing, but at no cost, because the total considered is the total of both smokestacks under one "bubble." But also notice that this "bubbled" factory would produce more pollution than the "unbubbled" factory, because the first factory would have triggered the imposition of pollution control devices which would have cut emissions overall drastically.

WITHOUT BUBBLE

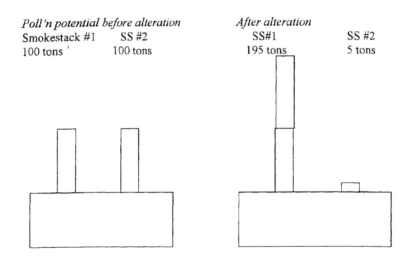

Poll'n potential before alteration   *After alteration*
Smokestack #1   SS #2   SS#1   SS #2
100 tons '   100 tons   195 tons   5 tons

WITH BUBBLE:

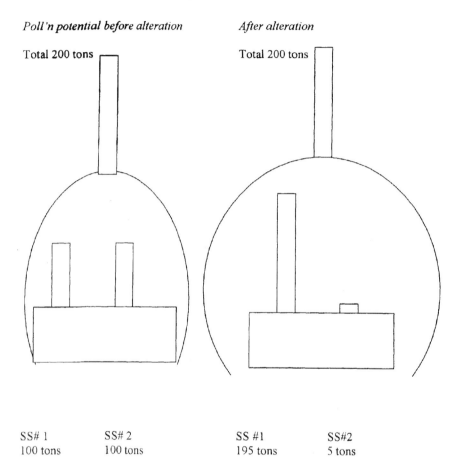

Poll'n potential before alteration

Total 200 tons

After alteration

Total 200 tons

SS# 1	SS# 2	SS #1	SS#2
100 tons	100 tons	195 tons	5 tons

4. Is a "bubble" concept consistent with phasing out heavily polluting sources over time? Does it allow an increase in efficiency which prolongs the life of a plant in such a way that it contravenes the purposes of the CAA? Is the statute ambiguous, thus allowing the agency to go either way? Could EPA decide to abandon the "bubble" concept and analyze each source separately for purposes of NSR and NSPS? Though "bubbling" is controversial, Congress did not statutorily alter the process in the 1990 CAA Amendments. Does this indicate the "wisdom" of Chevron deference?

———

The regulatory fight over new source review has heated up dramatically recently. The question in WEPCO, whether modifications at an existing plant can be considered "routine repair and maintenance" and thus exempt from new source review, has been at the heart of the dispute. The clearly opposing sides in this dispute provide the best example yet of the role of administrative law in environmental law. To better understand the actual administrative process, we have reproduced many of the actual documents and administrative steps that took place and are still taking place in the process in the Appendix. Keep in mind that while we have summarized many of these steps, that in an environmental law practice, it is up to the practitioner to follow, find, interpret, and react to administrative actions.

In the late 1990s the Clinton administration began aggressively enforcing new source review on existing sources and charged that many sources had illegally upgraded without adding the required pollution control equipment. Though there is disagreement as to the reason that this enforcement stance was taken at this time, many industry representatives believed it was an attempt by the administration to bring pressure on the states with significant NOx sources to come to the table and reach an agreement on the interstate movement of NOx that was affecting the ability of many states to reach ozone attainment. [see discussion of interstate effects of sources, *supra*.] In any event, it represented a dramatic change in EPA activity and provides a vivid example of the administrative flexibility in environmental enforcement and that effect on environmental law.

UNITED STATES v. OHIO EDISON COMPANY

United States District Court,
S.D. Ohio,
Eastern Division, 2003.
276 F.Supp.2d 829.

OPINION AND ORDER

SARGUS, District Judge.

This matter is before the Court following a trial to the Court on Plaintiffs' claims that Defendant Ohio Edison Company has violated the Clean Air Act ["CAA"], 42 U.S.C. § § 7401, *et seq.*, in connection with its operation of the W.H. Sammis Station, a coal-fired electric generating facility located in Jefferson County, Ohio. The Plaintiffs consist of the United States of America together with the States of Connecticut, New Jersey and New York. The Sammis Plant is owned by Pennsylvania Power Company, a wholly owned subsidiary of Defendant Ohio Edison which, in turn, is a wholly owned subsidiary of FirstEnergy Corporation of Akron, Ohio. The Court has jurisdiction over this action pursuant to 28 U.S.C. § 1331. Pursuant to Fed.R.Civ.P. 52(a), the Court makes the following Findings of Fact and Conclusions of Law based on the evidence adduced at trial.

I.

INTRODUCTION AND SUMMARY

A. Introduction

This case highlights an abysmal breakdown in the administrative process following the passage of the landmark Clean Air Act in 1970. For thirty-three years, various administrations have wrestled with and, to a great extent, have avoided a fundamental issue addressed in the Clean Air Act, that is, at what point plants built before 1970 must comply with new air pollution standards. The Clean Air Act requires plants constructed after 1970 to meet stringent air quality standards, but the Act exempts old facilities from compliance with the law, unless such sites undergo what the law identifies as a "modification." Decades later, the United States Environmental Protection Agency, together with the States of Connecticut, New Jersey and New York ask this Court to find that eleven construction projects undertaken between 1984 and 1998 on the seven electric generating units at the Sammis Plant constituted modifications, requiring Ohio Edison to bring the units into compliance with current ambient air quality standards.

By any standard, the enforcement of the Clean Air Act with regard to the Sammis Plant has been disastrous. From a public health perspective, thirty-three years after passage of the Act, the plant to this day emits on an annual basis 145,000 *tons* of sulphur dioxide, a pollutant injurious to the public health. From an employment perspective, Ohio Edison has chosen to meet other statewide and regional air quality standards by switching to out of state, low sulphur coal, a strategy which in conjunction with other utilities has caused a huge loss of coal mining and related jobs in Ohio.[1] From the standpoint of Ohio Edison, since 1970 the company has invested over $450 million to install pollution control devices on the Sammis units yet still fails to meet the new source pollution standards. Thirty-three years later, the air is still not clean, tens of thousands of jobs have been lost, and enforcement by the EPA has been highly inconsistent.

As is described in detail below, the original and current language of the Clean Air Act requires that an older plant undergoing a modification thereafter comply with new air quality standards. Regulations issued under the Clean Air Act by the U.S. EPA may not conflict with statutory language enacted into law by Congress. EPA regulations give further definition as to what types of projects are to be viewed as modifications which trigger the application of new air quality standards to an older facility. These statutory and regulatory definitions are at issue here.

This Court takes note of the fact that three decades after passage of the Clean Air Act the EPA finally moved, through this and several other lawsuits, to finally resolve this fundamental issue under the Act. While the law has always been clear, the enforcement strategies of the EPA have not. It is clear to this Court that at various times since 1970 officials of the EPA have been remiss in enforcing the law and clarifying its application to specific projects. For the reasons explained in Section III, I(H), *infra,* the Court finds that the EPA's failures in enforcement do not absolve Ohio Edison from liability under a law that has always been clear.

It is also evident from the record in this case that various electric utilities and industry organizations have sought within legal bounds to influence the conduct of the EPA. Given the enormous cost of retrofitting an older electric power plant with new pollution control devices, this strategy should not be unexpected in the democratic and administrative process. What should be unexpected and condemned, however, is an

---

1. In 1980, 14,638 coal miners were employed in Ohio mining high sulphur coal. By 2000, the number dropped to only 2,688. U.S. Census, 2000. During the same period, national coal production increased from 612 million tons to 1.12 billion tons. 2001 Annual Energy Review, U.S. Dept. of Energy.

agency unwilling to enforce a clear statutory mandate set forth in an act of Congress.

* * *

———

Because of the expense involved in installing upgraded pollution equipment as well as the liability now faced by companies that were or could be under investigation by a newly aggressive EPA, relief from these requirements moved to the top of the agenda of many affected businesses. The election of President George W. Bush, whose administration has extensive knowledge of and connections with the energy and electricity generating industries brought hope of relief. At least initially, it looked as if this faith might be rewarded. The Bush administration proposed amending the CAA to eliminate new source review altogether and instead focus on reducing NOx and mercury through a trading program. This proposal was known as the Clear Skies Initiative. When the passage of this proposal seemed doubtful, the administration moved to address the issue through rulemaking. The draft rule, dealing with routine repair and maintenance, was published on December 31, 2002. So you can see what federal register printed text looks like, this rule is reproduced in Appendix A. Review this proposed rule.

Notes and Questions

What is the main change proposed in these rules?

1. What does it mean if "the proposed annual maintenance, repair and replacement allowance for each source" is to be determined "by multiplying the replacement cost of the source by an annual maintenance, repair, and replacement allowance"?

2. Is this consistent with the statutory definition of modification?

3. Where is the statutory definition found?

For many persons, the changes suggested were beyond the agency's power. This became clear in the commenting period to which all rulemaking is subject. Several Environmental Law Professors, including one of the authors, submitted individual comments on the proposed rule. Two of these comments are reproduced in Appendix A.

1. What is the main thrust of these comments? Should comments to a rulemaking focus on legality or policy? What does the *Chevron* case indicate?

———

Based on the high number of comments, the EPA elected to hold public hearings. Public hearings may often add little more than written comments, and thus may have little effect on the outcome of the rule. Due to the fact that most persons do not read the Federal Register, nor receive individual notices of hearings, many of the speakers at public hearings will be organized by interest groups or industry. Nevertheless, the public hearing is an important part of the process, and may give an impression to the agency of apparent popularity of certain issues.

The final rule was published on October 27, 2003. You may find these rules at 68 Fed. Reg. 61248–61280. [search site: http://frwebgate.access.gpo.gov/cgi-bin/multidb.cgi]

1) As you read the final rule, did the comments you read earlier have any effect on the outcome?

2) In your opinion, is the rule likely to survive in this form? If you were to challenge the rulemaking, what would be the basis of your challenge?

3) If you were an existing source, what kind of upgrades would you be able to do without triggering new source review?

Again, strong criticism greeted the final rule. By specifying a percentage certain under which new source review would not be triggered, the legality was considered in doubt by some. What had been accomplished? Had the concerns of the existing sources been addressed?

Shortly after the publication of the final notice, the administration announced that it was not going to refer any suits under investigation for violation of New Source Review to the Justice Department, reasoning that it might be unwise to sue for violations (even past ones) if the standards were now different. The final rules were attacked in court immediately. The plaintiffs used the administration's change in the referral of cases to contend that a temporary restraining order should be issued. On December 24, 2003, a panel of the DC Circuit granted the temporary injunction, finding that the plaintiffs were likely to succeed on the merits, and that a delay would be harmful to them. The case was put on an expedited schedule, and at the time this book goes to print, is still undecided. What has certainly occurred is an unprecedented discussion of this issue. There were thousands of newspaper articles about this issue in the period between 1999 and the end of 2003. Any search of "routine repair and maintenance" on the web will return tens of thousands of hits as groups as diverse as the Electric power producers and Natural Resources Defense Council, as well as many states, sought to weigh in and have influence on the issue.

The Bush Administration also touted settlements of continuing prosecutions of past NSR violations.[32] Interestingly, many of the settlements may only require upgrades that may soon be mandated by the new rules governing transport.[33]

---

32. See, Ohio Edison reaches $1.1 billion NSR settlement, Darren Samuelson, Greenwire, March 18, 2005. www.eenews.net/Greenwire.

33. See, New utility regs will spur more pollution settlements, Darren Samuelson, Greenwire, March 16, 2005. www.eenews.net/Greenwire.

Even without a final resolution, this issue remains an important lesson in the role of the agency in altering the requirements of environmental law and also illustrates the administrative process and how and when it will be challenged in court and in the court of public opinion. It may be that even though the rulemaking is never enacted that the agency will still cease new prosecutions. Or this may spur a change in the statute itself. Either new source review could be eliminated as proposed in Clear Skies,[34] or they could be required of all sources, existing as well as new. Any major change in the Clean Air Act itself would almost certainly involve the control of greenhouse gases in one way or another as well. It is hard to predict if the law itself will ever change, but it is certain that new administrations will attempt to bring about favored policies through administrative change as much as they are able.

V.　CLEAN AIR ACT—PREVENTION OF SIGNIFICANT DETERIORATION AND RELATED REQUIREMENTS

A.　The Core Program

The 1977 amendments sought to address a problem that became clear with the original act. If states were only supposed to maintain an "ambient" standard of pollution that would protect human health, did this mean that clean air areas would get dirtier? Would the clean air areas be affected as industrial sources chose to move from already degraded industrial areas to pristine areas?

Thus, a primary feature of the first major amendment to the modern Clean Air Act was a provision to prevent already clean air areas from getting worse. How this was to be accomplished is discussed in the following cases:

ALABAMA POWER COMPANY v. COSTLE

United States Court of Appeals, District of Columbia Circuit, 1979.
636 F.2d 323.

* * *

B.　*The PSD Program Prior to the 1977 Amendments*

1) Genesis of PSD Program. Section 110 of the Act contained no explicit provision addressing potential deterioration of ambient air quality in those areas where ambient pollutant levels were lower than those mandated by primary and secondary NAAQS. EPA did not impose on the states any requirement to control new sources of pollution that posed no threat to ambient standards.

In 1972, the Sierra Club brought suit alleging that the Act required state plans to include measures to prevent the "significant deteriora-

---

34. A legislative Proposal of the Bush administration which does away with new source review for some pollutants, replacing it with a trading scheme.

tion" of air quality in those parts of the country where the ambient standards were being met. The District Court for the District of Columbia held that the Act's statement of purpose, contained in section 101(b)(1), imposed such an obligation. [footnote omitted]. On June 12, 1972, it issued a preliminary injunction directing the Administrator to disapprove state plans and to promulgate regulations where the plan failed to take the measures necessary to prevent such deterioration. This court affirmed. On June 11, 1973, the Supreme Court affirmed by an equally divided court. In response to the injunction, EPA disapproved all state plans in November, 1972, and in 1973, following the Supreme Court's action, the agency initiated rulemaking to incorporate PSD requirements into each state plan.

* * *

C.   Clean Air Act Amendments of 1977

The 1977 Amendments[35] maintain the basic structure of regulation of stationary sources through state plans, but made substantial changes in the requirements governing those plans. The Amendments provide for additional controls on existing sources to ensure protection of the ambient standards and visibility. Further, they establish strict requirements for major new sources to be located in areas where the national standards have not yet been attained ("non-attainment areas").

The central focus of this case is Part C of title I (sections 160–169) added to the Clean Air Act by the 1977 Amendments. Section 161 of the Act now provides an express directive that state plans include measures to prevent the significant deterioration of air quality in areas designated by the states under section 107(d)(1)(D) & (E) of the Act as having ambient air quality better than the applicable national primary or secondary ambient air quality standard, or for which there is insufficient data to make a determination of the air quality. An area so designated has commonly been referred to in the legislative history and in the literature that has developed as a "clean air area," a description often contrasted with the term "non-attainment area," which is defined by section 171(2) of the Act as an area that has been demonstrated to exceed an NAAQS for a given pollutant. [footnote omitted]. We wish to alert the reader that the phrase "clean air areas" is a generalization that may be confusing when employed in technical usages. A so-called clean air area for a given air pollutant may include an area that for the same pollutant would be classified as a non-attainment area if sufficient data existed. Further, since classification of areas is pollutant-specific, the same area may be a clean air area due to the air quality with respect to one pollutant, yet be a non-attainment area with respect to another pollutant. Finally, the areas of the country subject to regulation under the PSD provisions of the Act include areas other than those commonly referred to as clean air areas. With these caveats, which will be explained in greater detail as they become pertinent to our discussion, we will

35. Pub.L.No. 95–95, 91 Stat. 685, 42 U.S.C.§ 7401 et seq. (1978).

continue to use the term "clean air areas" as a shorthand expression where we do not feel the context calls for a more technical usage.

Under the provisions of the 1977 Amendments, areas subject to PSD regulation are divided into three classes; increments are set for each class; new major facilities to be located in such areas must meet technology-based emission limitations reflecting BACT; these facilities cannot commence construction if their emissions would cause or contribute to a violation of the applicable increments in a Class I, II or III area; and demonstrations that new facility emissions would not violate the applicable increments are to be based on both monitoring and diffusion modeling. The list of 19 major sources which emit, or have the potential to emit, 100 tons per year or more of any pollutant are subject to PSD review. In addition, any other source having the potential to emit 250 tons per year or more of any pollutant is also covered. As in the 1974 regulations, "modifications" of such major sources are also subject to PSD review. Section 165 of the Act tightens the requirement that must be included in state plans for the PSD preconstruction review and permitting of major new sources to be located in clean air areas. These stricter requirements include: (1) case-by-case determination of BACT rather than automatic application of NSPS; (2) requirements of air quality impact analyses performed in accordance with EPA regulations; (3) requirements for the protection of visibility in Class I areas even though Class I increments are met; and (4) provisions requiring public hearings in all cases instead of mere opportunity for written comment. Other changes in the 1974 regulations effected by the 1977 Amendments include provision for "variances" from Class I increments if stringent criteria are satisfied, and modification of the definition of "baseline." Congress also structured the program to minimize disruption, by exempting existing sources from the permit requirement of section 165 until "modifications" of those facilities increased emissions, and by phasing sources under construction into the program. In addition, section 166 directs EPA to develop within two years PSD programs for pollutants other than particulates and sulfur dioxide. EPA is not required to follow the "area classification" approach for these other pollutants, but implementation through a permit program is contemplated. [footnotes omitted].

* * *

The regulations require that each major stationary source and each modification covered by the regulations undergo a detailed preconstruction review and obtain a permit prior to the commencement of construction. The PSD review process contains a number of steps:

1) Control Technology Review. Each new major source must meet all applicable new source performance standards promulgated under section 111 of the Act, all emission standards for hazardous pollutants under section 112 of the Act, and all applicable state imple-

mentation plan requirements.[50] In addition, each such source must apply best available control technology (BACT) for sulfur dioxide and particulates unless emissions of that pollutant will be less than 50 tons per year, 1,000 pounds per day and 100 pounds per hour, whichever is most restrictive.[51]

2) Air Quality Review. At the time an application for a PSD permit is submitted, the owner or operator of the proposed source must demonstrate that allowable emissions from the source will not cause or contribute to a violation of any NAAQS or the applicable increments.[52] Estimates of ambient concentrations that must be provided in order to determine compliance with these requirements must "be based on the applicable air quality models, data bases, and other requirements" specified in EPA's modeling guidelines. The models described in these guidelines may be modified, or other models substituted, only after notice and opportunity for comment by the public, and written approval by the Administrator.[53]

* * *

4) Source Information. The PSD permit application must include, at a minimum, information on the location, design, and planned operating schedule of the proposed facility, a detailed construction schedule, and a description of the control technology that is proposed as BACT.[55] In addition, the applicant must provide an "analysis of impairment to visibility, soils, and vegetation" in the area, and an analysis of the air quality impacts of the expected growth associated with the proposed source.[56] Meteorological and topographical information on the air quality impacts and nature and extent of any growth in the locale of the proposed facility since August 7, 1977, must also be provided if requested by EPA or the state.

* * *

II. POTENTIAL TO EMIT

At the heart of the PSD provisions lies a definition that is jurisdictional in nature. We refer to the section 169(1) definition of "major emitting facility," which identifies sources of air pollution that are subject to the preconstruction review and permit requirements of section 165. The definition is not pollutant-specific, but rather identifies sources that emit more than a threshold quantity of any air pollutant. Once a source has been so identified, it may become subject to section 165's substantial administrative burdens and stringent technological control requirements for each pollutant regulated under the Act, even though the air pollutant, emissions of which caused the source to be classified as a "major emitting facility," may not be a pollutant for which NAAQS

---

50. 40 C.F.R. §§ 51.24(j)(1), 52.21(j)(1) (1978).

51. Id. at §§ 51.24(j)(2), 52.21(j)(2).

52. Id. at §§ 51.24(1), 52.21(1).

53. Id. at §§ 51.24(m)(1), 52.21(m)(1).

55. Id. at §§ 51.24(o), 52.21(o).

56. Id. at §§ 51.24(p), 52.21(p).

have been promulgated or even one that is otherwise regulated under the Act. As will become apparent from consideration of the ramifications of this definition, Congress's intention was to identify facilities which, due to their size, are financially able to bear the substantial regulatory costs imposed by the PSD provisions and which, as a group, are primarily responsible for emission of the deleterious pollutants that befoul our nation's air. Such facilities are defined in section 169(1) as those stationary sources of air pollutants from among 28 listed categories which "emit, or have the potential to emit" 100 tons per year or more of any air pollutant plus any other stationary source with the "potential to emit" 250 tons per year or more of any air pollutant. [footnotes omitted.]

EPA has interpreted the phrase "potential to emit" as referring to the measure of a source's "uncontrolled emissions" i.e., the projected emissions of a source when operating at full capacity, with the projection increased by hypothesizing the absence of air pollution control equipment designed into the source.[61] Yet, the language and comprehensive scheme of the statute reveal that an emitting facility is "major" within the meaning of section 169(1), only if it either (1) actually emits the specified annual tonnage of any air pollutant, or (2) has the potential, when operating at full design capacity, to emit the statutory amount. The purpose of Congress was to require preconstruction review and a permit before major amounts of emissions were released into the air. When determining a facility's potential to emit air pollutants, EPA must look to the facility's "design capacity" a concept which not only includes a facility's maximum productive capacity (a criterion employed by EPA) but also takes into account the anticipated functioning of the air pollution control equipment designed into the facility.

We are cognizant that in general a court defers to the interpretation of a new statute by the agency that is charged with putting it into effect, meshing the wheels, and that presumably has some awareness of the approaches of legislators particularly concerned with the legislation. However, we view our analysis of congressional intent, set forth above, as clearly discernible from section 169(1). We identify the following as indicators of legislative intent. Looking at language, we see that the first sentence provides that a major emitting facility (in enumerated categories) must "emit, or have the potential to emit" 100 tons per year of any air pollutant. Plainly, the pollutants that sources "emit" is a reference to some measure of actual emissions. However, under EPA's interpretation of "potential to emit," the actual emissions calculation called for by the verb "emit" would lose all significance. When potential emissions are calculated, as EPA provided, by assuming operation at full capacity, without any reduction to take into account the operation of the facility's air pollution control equipment, then potential emissions will always and inherently exceed actual emissions. Under our construction a meaning is given to the use of "emit" and "or," as applicable in those instances when for any reason, whether or not there is fault or accident, the

61. 40 C.F.R. §§ 51.24(b)(3), 52.21(b)(3) (1978).

"cleansing" equipment has not been operated, or has been operated at variance from design.[62]

For a wide angle lens on intent, we turn to the fact that Congress was fully aware that many major new sources of air pollution were already required by law to install and operate air pollution control equipment. The "new source performance standards" of section 111 of the Act, as well as provisions of existing state implementation plans, were the sources of such requirements. In this context one would require strong statutory evidence that Congress intended to approach the measurement of emissions in ignorance and disregard of the operation of pollution control equipment already required by law to be designed into a facility. All the statutory evidence points the other way.

The coverage of the 100 ton-per-annum threshold of the first sentence of section 169(1) extends to 28 categories of facilities. A look at these categories, and a further look at the legislative history[63] reveal that Congress was concerned with large industrial enterprises major actual emitters of air pollution. The draftsmen were of the view that certain small industrial facilities within these categories might actually and potentially emit less than the threshold amount. But the submissions of the parties establish that no operational industrial facility that could be described as within the listed categories would have the "potential to emit" less than the threshold amount if the operation of cleansing control equipment is totally discounted.

Congress was presumably also aware of the high rate of effectiveness with which control equipment eliminates pollutants from unprocessed industrial emissions. For example, at the time of the enactment of the PSD provisions, technology in operation was capable of eliminating over 99% of the particulate matter from emissions. Thus, a source with the potential according to EPA's "uncontrolled emissions" standard to emit 100 tons per annum of particulate matter would emit in actuality less than one ton per year. The record illustrates that the heating plant operating in a large high school or in a small community college would become "major" sources under such a test.[64] We have no reason to believe that Congress intended to define such obviously minor sources as "major" for the purposes of the PSD provision.

* * *

---

62. We are aware that the second sentence of section 169(1), which extends coverage of the term "major emitting facility" to "any other source with the potential to emit" 250 tons per year of any air pollutant, is not phrased in the disjunctive; the verb "emit" has not been included. Nevertheless, we are unpersuaded that Congress intended the disjunctive form of the first sentence to be mere surplusage. It may be that the "actual emissions" alternative should be read into the second sentence on the ground that Congress plainly included a parallel construction.

63. See notes 70 & 72, infra.

64. Cong.Rec. 512812 (July 19, 1976), LHA at 382.

* * *

Alabama Power sets out a good description of the reasons for, and the operation of, the PSD program. Additionally, the court overturns EPA's interpretation of "potential to emit" for a definition the court sees as mandated by Congress. By defining "potential to emit" as being governed by how a source works at normal operation (<u>with</u> pollution control equipment), the court defines the reach of PSD to large facilities.

The PSD program divides air quality control areas in attainment for each criteria pollutant into three classes. The class designation then determines how much additional pollution can ever be added to the ambient air in those air quality control regions. Class I areas are those that have, or should have, the most pristine air quality. All international parks, and the larger national parks, national monuments and wilderness areas are to be designated as Class I areas. 42 U.S.C. Sec. 7472. Any other attainment (or unclassifiable) areas are to be classified as Class II. 42 U.S.C. Sec. 7472. An area may be attainment (and Class II) for one or more of the criteria pollutants but be non-attainment for others. Class II areas may petition for reclassification as Class III (which allows a greater increment of pollution) upon action of state officials.In no case, can the national ambient air quality standard be exceeded for any criteria pollutant for which an area is already in attainment.

The increments allowed in each class under the PSD program are set out in the statute for sulfur dioxide and for particulates, and are created by regulation for the other criteria pollutants. See 42 U.S.C. Sec. 7473. The increments for each class area for sulfur dioxide and particulates follows:

Class I

Pollutant	**Max. allowable increase (mg/cubic meter)**
Particulate Matter:	
Annual geometric mean	5
Twenty-four-hour maximum	10
Sulfur Dioxide:	
Annual arithmetic mean	2
Twenty-four-hour maximum	5
Three-hour maximum	25

Class II

Pollutant	**Max. allowable increase (mg/cubic meter)**
Particulate Matter:	
Annual geometric mean	19
Twenty-four-hour maximum	37
Sulfur Dioxide:	
Annual arithmetic mean	20
Twenty-four-hour maximum	91
Three-hour maximum	512

Class III

Pollutant **Max. allowable increase (mg/cubic meter)**

Particulate Matter:
    Annual Geometric mean   37
    Twenty-four-hour maximum   75

Sulfur Dioxide:
    Annual arithmetic mean   40
    Twenty-four-hour maximum   182
    Three-hour maximum   700

As you can see, the PSD cap means that the total amount of additional pollution ever allowed is limited. Is the cap going to be stringently observed? What about pollution sources that do not undergo preconstruction review because they fall under the 100 ton or 250 ton threshold? Could they use up the increment? Is the increment amount monitored or is it based on previous calculations? What difference would it make?

Does this encourage major stationary sources to stake a claim for the increments as soon as possible? What happens if new information shows the loss of much of the increment? Can new sources 'purchase' increments from older sources?

B. Air Quality Related Values and Visibility Protection

The prevention of significant deterioration of "clean air areas" was an important addition to the Clean Air Act. It closed a "loophole" of sorts by maintaining clean air in areas that already had good air. This served the salutary purposes of both maintaining particularly pristine air areas (those designated Class 1), and also removed any major economic incentive to move polluting sources to cleaner air areas, which tended to be rural and away from the major job centers.

The Prevention of Significant Deterioration also shed light on other values associated with clean air that go beyond protection of health. A state is supposed to deny a PSD permit to any source that will have an effect on "air quality related values."[36] These "values" include visibility.[37] In addition, 1977 amendments also contained explicit protections for visibility in Class I areas, and provide that states must adopt long term strategies to remedy past impairment of visibility in these Class I areas.[38] The states are supposed to revise their SIPs to identify any major sources whose emissions cause or contribute to the visibility impairment.[39] Though there seems to be concern about visibility problems, particularly with respect to national treasures such as the Grand Can-

---

36. 42 U.S.C. Sec. 7475 (d)(2) (CAA 165 (d)(2)).

37. *Id.*

38. 42 U.S.C. Sec. 7491 (CAA Sec. 169A).

39. 42 U.S.C. Sec. 7491 (b)(2)(A).

yon, the phrasing of the statute does not specify how the state is to determine what sources are causing this impairment. Who bears the burden of persuasion in such cases? If a state does not wish to address this problem, can it hide behind the scientific uncertainty of determining specific sources? Is there any way around that for those who would seek to impose restrictions on these sources? Are these problems similar to the problems faced by states seeking to identify out-of-state pollution sources under sec. 126?

CENTRAL ARIZONA WATER CONSERVATION DISTRICT v. UNITED STATES ENVIRON-MENTAL PROTECTION AGENCY

United States Court of Appeals, Ninth Circuit, 1993.
990 F.2d 1531.

Water conservation district and irrigation districts petitioned for review of final rule issued by the Environmental Protection Agency (EPA) requiring 90% reduction in sulfur dioxide emissions at nearby electricity generating facility in order to improve winter average visibility at Grand Canyon National Park. The Court of Appeals, Goodwin, Circuit Judge, held that: (1) districts had constitutional and prudential standing; (2) final rule was legitimately promulgated under regulations directed at "reasonably attributable" visibility impairment, even if EPA was without authority to regulate "regional haze"; and (3) final rule was product of "reasoned decisionmaking" and would make "reasonable progress" toward preventing future, and remedying present, visibility impairment within meaning of Clean Air Act.

Petition denied.

* * *

I. BACKGROUND

This case involves regulations promulgated by EPA in an attempt to remedy, at least partially, visibility impairment at the Grand Canyon. In a final rule entitled "Approval and Promulgation of Implementation Plans: Revision of the Visibility FIP for Arizona," 56 Fed.Reg. 50,172 (1991) (codified at 40 C.F.R. § 52) ("Final Rule"), EPA required a 90% reduction in SO2 emissions at NGS, a power plant situated approximately twelve miles from the Grand Canyon, near Page, Arizona. The Final Rule limits SO2 emissions from NGS to 0.10 pound per million British thermal units (lb/MMBtu), with an estimated 7% winter average visibility improvement in the Grand Canyon. The estimated cost of the improvement, following an initial capital cost estimated at $430 million, is $89.6 million per year.

* * *

A. *Regulatory Framework*

1. *The Clean Air Act, Visibility Impairment, and the Grand Canyon*

In 1977, Congress substantially amended the Clean Air Act (the "Act"). Included in the 1977 amendments was section 169A, 42 U.S.C. § 7491, which declared "as a national goal the prevention of any future, and the remedying of any existing, impairment of visibility in mandatory class I Federal areas which impairment results from manmade air pollution." 42 U.S.C. § 7491(a)(1). Congress required EPA to promulgate regulations to assure "reasonable progress toward meeting th[is] national goal." 42 U.S.C. § 7491(a)(4). EPA was further directed to require each state with a class I Federal area to revise its state implementation plan ("SIP") "to contain such emission limits, schedules of compliance and other measures as may be necessary to make reasonable progress toward meeting the national goal." 42 U.S.C. § 7491(b)(2). Measures for achieving "reasonable progress" generally include best available retrofit technology ("BART")[4] and a long-term strategy. 42 U.S.C. § § 7491(b)(2)(A), (B). If an individual state fails to fulfill its obligations under the Act, EPA is directed to take such measures as are required to achieve "reasonable progress" pursuant to a federal implementation plan ("FIP") under section 110(c) of the Act. 42 U.S.C. § 7410(c)(1).

The Act defines class I Federal areas as international parks, national wilderness areas or memorial parks which exceed 5,000 acres in size, and national parks which exceed 6,000 acres in size. 42 U.S.C. § 7472(a). The Grand Canyon has been classified as a class I Federal area. *See* 44 Fed.Reg. 69,122 (1979). Congress recorded its concern with the visibility impairment at the Grand Canyon caused by NGS. *See* H.R.Rep. No. 294, 95th Cong., 1st Sess. 203–04 (1977) U.S.Code Cong. & Admin.News pp. 1077, 1282, 1283.

2. *EPA's 1980 Regulations*

In 1980, EPA promulgated visibility regulations under section 169A of the Act. 45 Fed.Reg. 80,084 (1980) (codified at 40 C.F.R. §§ 51.300–307). The regulations adopted a "phased approach to visibility protection." *Id.* at 80,085. Phase I was directed at controlling visibility impairment "that can be traced to a single existing stationary facility or small group of existing stationary facilities." *Id.* EPA refers to this type of impairment as "reasonably attributable" impairment. 45 Fed.Reg. 34,762, 34,779 (1980) (codified at 40 C.F.R. § 51). EPA deferred addressing other types of impairment such as "regional haze" for future phases

---

4. The regulations provide the following definition of BART:

Best Available Retrofit Technology (BART) means an emission limitation based on the degree of reduction achievable through the application of the best system of continuous emission reduction for each pollutant which is emitted by an existing stationary facility. The emission limitation must be established, on a case-by-case basis, taking into consideration the technology available, the costs of compliance, the energy and nonair quality environmental impacts of compliance, any pollution control equipment in use or in existence at the source, the remaining useful life of the source, and the degree of improvement in visibility which may reasonably be anticipated to result from the use of such technology.

40 C.F.R. § 51.301(c).

due to the heightened complexity and the scientific and technical limitations inherent in attempts to identify, measure, and control such broadscale visibility impairment. *See* 45 Fed.Reg. at 80,086; *see also id.* at 80,085 (defining regional haze as "widespread, regionally homogeneous haze from a multitude of sources which impairs visibility in every direction over a large area").

Generally, EPA's "Phase I" regulations require affected states to coordinate the development of SIPs with the appropriate Federal land managers, to develop programs to assess and remedy visibility impairment from new and existing sources, and to develop a long-term strategy to assure reasonable progress toward section 169A's national visibility goal. *See* 40 C.F.R. § § 51.300-.307. The regulations specifically require states to identify those existing sources "which may reasonably be anticipated to cause or contribute" to any visibility impairment which is "reasonably attributable to that existing stationary facility." 40 C.F.R. § 51.302(c)(4)(i). Once the source is identified, the affected state is required to take such measures as are required to attain "reasonable progress"; such measures generally include determination of emissions limitations for that source under BART and the development of a long-term strategy. 40 C.F.R. § § 51.302(c)(1), (2).

The regulations define the term "visibility impairment" as "any humanly perceptible change in visibility (visual range, contrast, coloration) from that which would have existed under natural conditions." 40 C.F.R. § 51.301(x). The term "reasonably attributable" is defined as "attributable by visual observation or any other technique the State deems appropriate." 40 C.F.R. § 51.301(s). The states, or EPA under § 7410(c), thus have broad discretion in determining how and whether impairment may be attributed to an individual source. *See* 45 Fed.Reg. at 80,094, 80,085.

B. *Prior Proceedings and the Rulemaking History*

In its implementation of Phase I, EPA required all states containing class I Federal areas to submit revised visibility SIPs within a nine-month period. Arizona was one of thirty-five states failing to submit a revised SIP to EPA. In 1982, the Environmental Defense Fund and other environmental groups brought a citizen suit against EPA to compel performance of the agency's nondiscretionary duty under 42 U.S.C. § 7410(c)(1)(A) to promulgate visibility FIPs when states fail to submit SIPs pursuant to the 1980 regulations. *See EDF v. Reilly,* No. C82–6850–RPA (N.D.Cal. Apr. 20, 1984). The parties reached a settlement agreement which the court approved in an April 20, 1984 consent decree. This consent decree required EPA to review existing SIPs for deficiencies and allow states to cure those deficiencies. If states remained deficient, the consent decree required EPA to issue visibility FIPs.

The Department of Interior subsequently certified the existence of visibility impairment in all class I Federal areas, and specifically declared NGS as a probable source of impairment at the Grand Canyon. Following this certification, the National Park Service ("Park Service") conducted the Winter Haze Intensive Tracer Experiment ("WHITEX"), a winter visibility attribution study. In part, WHITEX involved the release from NGS of a unique "tracer" gas, CD4; because CD4 is not found in the ambient air, its use "fingerprinted" NGS emissions when detected downwind.

In November 1987, EPA disapproved the SIPs of twenty-nine states, including Arizona, for failing to comply with the visibility regulations. *See* 52 Fed.Reg. 45,132, 45,133 (1987) (codified at 40 C.F.R. §§ 52, 81). Over the next few years, EPA further investigated visibility impairment at Grand Canyon and other class I Federal areas. While acting on many of the areas, EPA delayed action on the Grand Canyon to allow the Park Service time to analyze the data obtained from the WHITEX study. The Park Service issued an April 1989 draft report which attributed to NGS 70% of the sulfates in the Grand Canyon during the WHITEX experiment period. *See* William Malm et al., National Park Service Report on the Winter Haze Intensive Tracer Experiment, Draft Final Report (Apr. 7, 1989).

Relying on the Park Service's April 1989 draft report, EPA preliminarily attributed to NGS several episodes of winter-time visibility impairment at the Grand Canyon. *See* 54 Fed.Reg. 36,948, 36,951 (1989) (codified at 40 C.F.R. § 52). EPA solicited public comment on the merits of its preliminary attribution finding, and began the informal rulemaking process to determine the appropriate action to be taken. *Id.* In December 1989, the Park Service issued its final report on WHITEX. *See* William Malm et al., National Park Service Report on the Winter Haze Intensive Tracer Experiment, Final Report (Dec. 4, 1989).

SRP and others, including Petitioners, submitted comments severely criticizing the analyses, methodologies, and conclusions of the Park Service's reports. In response to the concerns raised about the Park Service's analysis of the WHITEX data, the National Research Council of the National Academy of Sciences ("NAS") was asked to evaluate the Park Service's WHITEX report and the other scientific evidence relevant to EPA's preliminary attribution. In its October 1990 report, the NAS confirmed that "at some times during the study period, NGS contributed significantly to haze" in the Grand Canyon. National Research Council, *Haze in the Grand Canyon: An Evaluation of the Winter Haze Intensive Tracer Experiment* 3, 37 (1990) [hereinafter *Haze in the Grand Canyon*]. NAS cautioned, however, that "aspects of the WHITEX data analysis preclude a quantitative determination of the exact fraction of the Grand Canyon haze problem that is attributable to NGS. These aspects are primarily related to problems with implementation and interpretation of multiple linear regression models." *Id.* at 37. Still, NAS acknowledged that Congress did not "require EPA to show a precise relationship between a source's emissions and all or a specific fraction of the visibility impairment within a Class I area." *Id.* at 5, 37.

* * *

In February 1991, EPA proposed to revise the FIP for Arizona to include emission limits under BART to address wintertime visibility impairment at the Grand Canyon reasonably attributable to NGS. *See* 56 Fed.Reg. 5,173 (1991) (codified at 40 C.F.R. § 52).

* * *

In the Final Rule, dated October 3, 1991, EPA issued its final determination that certain visibility impairment episodes at the Grand Canyon were "traceable to NGS and that NGS is a dominant contributor to certain visibility impairment episodes," and promulgated revisions to the Arizona visibility FIP to address the impairment. *Id.* The revisions adopted a regulatory approach consistent with the memorandum of understanding's proposal, reducing SO2 emissions 90% to a level of 0.10 lb/MMBtu. *Id.* EPA determined that this approach would more adequately achieve "reasonable progress" toward the national visibility goal under section 169A(b)(2) of the Act, 42 U.S.C. § 7491(b)(2), than would the alternative provided by BART analysis. *See* 56 Fed.Reg. at 50,177. As required by section 307(d) of the Act, EPA's action was "accompanied by a response to each of the significant comments, criticisms, and new data submitted in written or oral presentations during the comment period." 42 U.S.C. § 7607(d)(6)(B). EPA issued its responses in the regulation itself and in a supplementary ninety-one page document entitled "Response to Public Comments: Proposed Revisions to Arizona Visibility FIP for Navajo Generating Station" [hereinafter *Response to Public Comments*].

* * *

III. STANDARD OF REVIEW

The appropriate judicial review of the regulations at issue here is provided for in section 307(d) of the Act, 42 U.S.C. § 7607(d). In relevant part, section 307(d)(9) provides that a reviewing court may reverse any action of the Administrator found to be

> (A) arbitrary, capricious, an abuse of discretion, or otherwise not in accordance with law;

* * * * *

> (C) in excess of statutory jurisdiction, authority, or limitations, or short of statutory right; or

> (D) without observance of procedure required by law, if (i) such failure to observe such procedure is arbitrary or capricious, (ii) the requirement of paragraph (7)(B) has been met, and (iii) the condition of the last sentence of paragraph (8) is met.

42 U.S.C. §§ 7607(d)(9)(A), (C)–(D).

* * *

Review of EPA's actions under section 307(d) of the Act is guided by the appropriate deference given to an agency's interpretation of the statute Congress has entrusted it to administer. *Chevron U.S.A. Inc. v. NRDC, Inc.,* 467 U.S. 837, 843, 104 S.Ct. 2778, 2781, 81 L.Ed.2d 694 (1984) (where the Clean Air Act is either "silent or ambiguous with respect to the specific issue, the question for the court is whether the agency's answer is based on a permissible construction of the statute"). "Deference also guides our review of the Administrator's interpretation of EPA regulations if the interpretation is not unreasonable." *Citizens for Clean Air v. EPA,* 959 F.2d 839, 844 (9th Cir.1992); *see also Hawaiian Elec. Co. v. EPA,* 723 F.2d 1440, 1447 (9th Cir.1984) ("[W]hen EPA is interpreting its own regulations, it is entitled to even more deference."). Moreover, the Supreme Court has advised that "a reviewing court must generally be at its most deferential" when the agency is "making predictions, within its area of special expertise, at the frontiers of science." *Baltimore Gas & Elec. Co. v. NRDC, Inc.,* 462 U.S. 87, 103, 103 S.Ct. 2246, 2255, 76 L.Ed.2d 437 (1983). In such situations, this court is to "deter to the agency's interpretation of equivocal evidence, so long as it is reasonable." *NRDC, Inc. v. EPA,* 902 F.2d 962, 968 (D.C.Cir.1990), *vacated, in part, dismissed,* 921 F.2d 326 (D.C.Cir.), *certs. dismissed,* 498 U.S. 1075, 111 S.Ct. 806, 112 L.Ed.2d 865, *cert. denied,* 498 U.S. 1082, 111 S.Ct. 952, 112 L.Ed.2d 1040 (1991).

While this court should not defer to the agency where it "simply has not exercised its expertise," *Public Citizen Health Research Group v. Tyson,* 796 F.2d 1479, 1505 (D.C.Cir.1986),[8] courts are "extremely deferential to administrative agencies in cases involving technical rulemaking decisions." *New York v. Reilly,* 969 F.2d 1147, 1152 (D.C.Cir.1992); *see also id.* at 1150–51 ("We are particularly deferential when reviewing agency actions involving policy decisions based on uncertain technical information."); *Tyson,* 796 F.2d at 1505 ("[A]s long as Congress delegates power to an agency to regulate on the borders of the unknown, courts cannot interfere with reasonable interpretations of equivocal evidence.").

IV. DISCUSSION

A. *EPA's Statutory Authority to Promulgate the Final Rule*

Petitioners argue that in promulgating the Final Rule, EPA acted "in excess of statutory jurisdiction, authority, or limitations, or short of statutory right" under 42 U.S.C. § 7607(d)(9)(C). Petitioners claim that the Final Rule regulates "regional haze" when EPA's own regulations expressly defer regulation of that type of visibility impairment until future phases. *See* 45 Fed.Reg. at 80,086. We conclude that the Final

---

8. For instance, in *Motor Vehicle Manufacturers Association of United States, Inc. v. State Farm Mutual Automobile Insurance Co.,* 463 U.S. 29, 103 S.Ct. 2856, 77 L.Ed.2d 443 (1983), the Supreme Court found an agency ruling arbitrary and capricious where the agency had "entirely failed to consider an important aspect of the prob- lem." *Id.* at 43, 103 S.Ct. at 2867. *State Farm* shows that the "expertise model" does not necessarily mandate judicial deference, since the Court there took a "hard look" to ensure that the agency was in fact using its expertise in arriving at policy decisions.

Rule was legitimately promulgated under Phase I regulations directed at "reasonably attributable" visibility impairment.

* * *

EPA has acknowledged that "NGS is not the only source of visibility impairment" at the Grand Canyon, 56 Fed.Reg. at 50,177, and that regional haze also adversely affects visibility there. *Response to Public Comments* at 23. Nonetheless, these mere facts hardly mean that EPA is without statutory authority to remedy the impairment attributable to NGS. Even if the Final Rule addresses only a small fraction of the visibility impairment at the Grand Canyon, EPA still has the statutory authority to address that portion of the visibility impairment problem which is, in fact, "reasonably attributable" to NGS. Congress mandated an extremely low triggering threshold, requiring the installment of stringent emission controls when an individual source "emits any air pollutant which may reasonably be anticipated to cause or contribute to any impairment of visibility" in a class I Federal area. 42 U.S.C. § 7491(b)(2)(A). The National Academy of Sciences correctly noted that Congress has not required ironclad scientific certainty establishing the precise relationship between a source's emission and resulting visibility impairment:

> The phrase "may reasonably be anticipated" suggests that Congress did not intend to require EPA to show a precise relationship between a source's emissions and all or a specific fraction of the visibility impairment within a Class I area. Rather, EPA is to assess the risk in light of policy considerations regarding the respective risks of overprotection and underprotection.

Haze in the Grand Canyon at 5.

Acting in place of the state of Arizona pursuant to an FIP under 42 U.S.C. § 7410(c), EPA "stands in the shoes of the defaulting State, and all of the rights and duties that would otherwise fall to the State accrue instead to EPA." 54 Fed.Reg. at 36,952. EPA is therefore granted broad discretion in determining whether visibility impairment is "reasonably attributable" to a given source. *See* 40 C.F.R. § 51.301(s) (defining "reasonably attributable" as "attributable by visual observation *or any other technique the State deems appropriate*") (emphasis added). This broad, all-inclusive definition of the term "reasonably attributable" directly refutes Petitioners' argument that EPA is limited to addressing visibility impairment caused by a noticeable plume that is directly traceable to a given source through the use of visual observation or simple monitoring techniques.

We conclude that the technical, scientific record more than adequately supports EPA's reasonable conclusion that visibility impairment in the Grand Canyon is "reasonably attributable" to NGS. We defer to the agency's reasonable interpretation of its own regulations and statutory mandate. Its interpretation is most certainly consonant with Congress's apparent intent. For instance, in his introduction of the Conference Committee report to the House, Representative Henry Waxman stated:

> Protecting the Grand Canyon simply must become a normal business practice of the American industry ... [T]he Four Corners and Navajo powerplants can expect to retrofit with additional pollution controls to limit the vast deterioration in visibility which their plumes have caused.

> Impairment of visibility is the single most apparent impact air pollution has on the environment. It is our intent that aggressive steps be taken to reduce this eyesore which has defaced our grand vistas in the West.

123 Cong.Rec. 27,076 (1977) (statement of Rep. Waxman). EPA's interpretation of its authority to determine whether visibility impairment is "reasonably attributable" to NGS is entitled to deference from this court since the agency's " 'choice represents a reasonable accommodation of conflicting policies that were committed to the agency's care by the statute,' " which this court " 'should not disturb' " since it does not appear " 'from the statute or its legislative history that the accommodation is not one that Congress would have sanctioned.' " *Chevron,* 467 U.S. at 845, 104 S.Ct. at 2783 (quoting *United States v. Shimer,* 367 U.S. 374, 383, 81 S.Ct. 1554, 1560, 6 L.Ed.2d 908 (1961)).

B. *The Final Rule as the Product of "Reasoned Decisionmaking"*

Petitioners proffer various arguments that the Final Rule is not the product of "reasoned decisionmaking." They assert that EPA has acted arbitrarily and capriciously by overestimating the improvements in visibility expected from the Final Rule's emission controls at NGS, by purportedly failing to address criticisms to the scientific data and analyses on which it relied, and by allegedly ignoring certain evidence while placing undue reliance on other evidence. At bottom, however, Petitioners' real complaint appears to be that the Final Rule will most likely lead to minimal visibility improvement at the Grand Canyon while imposing a substantial financial burden on them. Nonetheless, we find unsupported Petitioners' legal claim that EPA acted arbitrarily and capriciously in promulgating the Final Rule. The Final Rule makes "reasonable progress" toward the national goal of remedying visibility impairment at the Grand Canyon, and is the product of reasoned decisionmaking.

1. *The Final Rule as "Reasonable Progress" toward the National Goal of Remedying Visibility Impairment at the Grand Canyon*

In reviewing whether the agency's action in promulgating the Final Rule was arbitrary and capricious, this court "is not to substitute its judgment for that of the agency." *State Farm,* 463 U.S. at 43, 103 S.Ct. at 2866. Instead, we inquire whether the agency has "examine[d] the relevant data and articulate[d] a satisfactory explanation for its action, including a 'rational connection between the facts found and the choice made.' " *Id.* (quoting *Burlington Truck Lines, Inc. v. United States,* 371 U.S. 156, 168, 83 S.Ct. 239, 245, 9 L.Ed.2d 207 (1962)). Our review is limited to "whether the agency considered the relevant factors and whether there has been a clear error of judgment." *NRDC, Inc. v. EPA,* 966 F.2d 1292, 1297 (9th Cir.1992) (citing *Citizens to Preserve Overton Park, Inc. v. Volpe,* 401 U.S. 402, 416, 91 S.Ct. 814, 823, 28 L.Ed.2d 136 (1971)). In this case, the relevant factors are provided by Congress's definition of "reasonable progress" in 42 U.S.C. § 7491(g)(1). Additionally, as the D.C. Circuit recently noted in discussing a similar provision of the Act, "[b]ecause Congress did not assign the specific weight the Administrator should accord each of these factors, the Administrator is free to exercise his discretion in this area." *New York v. Reilly,* 969 F.2d at 1150 (discussing 42 U.S.C. § 7411(a)(1)(C)).[10]

a. The "Reasonable Progress" Provisions

In the Act, Congress directed EPA to promulgate regulations to assure "reasonable progress toward meeting the national goal" of preventing future, and remedying existing visibility impairment in Class I federal areas like the Grand Canyon. *See* 42 U.S.C. § § 7491(a)(4), (a)(1), (b)(2), (b)(2)(B). Congress chose not to define the term "reasonable progress," but instead set forth several factors for the agency to consider:

> In determining reasonable progress there shall be taken into consideration the costs of compliance, the time necessary for compliance, and the energy and nonair quality environmental impacts of compliance, and the remaining useful life of any existing source subject to such requirements[.]

42 U.S.C. § 7491(g)(1). In promulgating the Final Rule, EPA relied on the "reasonable progress" provisions as its statutory authority. *See* 56 Fed.Reg. at 50,177 (noting that EPA adopts the "reasonable progress" provisions of section 169A(b)(2), 42 U.S.C. § 7491(b)(2) as the "legal rationale" for the Final Rule).

Generally, the Act and its regulations require the application of BART once it has been determined that visibility impairment is "reasonably attributable" to an existing source like NGS. *See* 42 U.S.C. § 7491(b)(2); 40 C.F.R. § 51.302(c)(4)(i). Under the unique circumstances of this case, however, EPA chose not to adopt the emission control limits indicated by BART analysis, but instead to adopt an emission limitations standard that would produce greater visibility improvement at a lower cost. Congress's use of the term "including" in § 7491(b)(2) prior to its listing BART as a method of attaining "reasonable progress" supports EPA's position that it has the discretion to adopt implementation plan provisions other than those provided by BART analyses in situations where the agency reasonably concludes that more "reasonable progress" will thereby be attained. Since the Act itself

---

10. Petitioners incorrectly suggest that EPA was required to engage in "cost-benefit" analysis. Congress has not required "cost-benefit" analysis in the Act. *Cf. American Textile Mfrs. Inst., Inc. v. Donovan,* 452 U.S. 490, 510, 101 S.Ct. 2478, 2491, 69 L.Ed.2d 185 (1981) ("When Congress has intended that an agency engage in cost-benefit analysis, it has clearly indicated such intent on the face of the statute.").

is ambiguous on the specific issue, we apply the Supreme Court's deferential standard from *Chevron* and hold that the agency's reliance on the "reasonable progress" provisions is a "permissible construction of the statute," 467 U.S. at 843, 104 S.Ct. at 2782, since "reasonable progress" is the overarching requirement that implementation plan revisions under 42 U.S.C. § 7491(b)(2) must address.

* * *

Petitioners further challenge as arbitrary and capricious EPA's estimate of the quantum of visibility improvement which the agency expects to result from imposition of the Final Rule's emission limits at NGS. In arriving at its estimate that the Final Rule "should improve the winter seasonal average visibility above the rim of the [Grand Canyon] approximately 7 percent," 56 Fed.Reg. at 50,180, EPA discussed the estimates of three studies: (1) the Park Service's WHITEX estimate of 14% improvement, (2) the NGSVS estimate of at most a 2% improvement, and (3) a modelling study, conducted by Douglas Latimer and submitted during the comment period, which estimated a range of 4 to 8% improvement. Petitioners contend that EPA arrived at its 7% estimate in an arbitrary and capricious manner because, they contend, EPA failed to consider and place in the administrative record a new report prepared by Latimer in which he allegedly reconsiders his previous estimate of visibility improvement, reducing it to 3 to 4%. Petitioners additionally claim that failure to put this new report in the administrative record constitutes an abuse of discretion. We find Petitioners' challenge both legally untenable and factually misleading.

First, the challenge is legally untenable because it relies on this court's consideration of evidence—the new Latimer report—which is not a part of the administrative record. In the Act, Congress explicitly and unambiguously provided that "the record for judicial review shall consist *exclusively*" of certain specifically enumerated categories of materials. 42 U.S.C. § 7607(d)(7)(A) (emphasis added). "Nothing in the statute or its legislative history indicates that a party or the agency may reopen the record by placing additional materials (other than those *required* by the statute and wrongfully omitted by EPA) in the docket after promulgation of the rule." *Lead Indus. Ass'n v. EPA*, 647 F.2d 1130, 1183 (D.C.Cir.), *cert. denied*, 449 U.S. 1042, 101 S.Ct. 621, 66 L.Ed.2d 503 (1980).[12] The new Latimer report was not included in the administrative record, nor was it required to be. EPA explains that the report was not directly related to NGS, but was instead submitted to EPA in the context of the GCVTC regional haze efforts under section 169B of the Act.

Additionally, Petitioners ignore the route for administrative and judicial review of "new information" and alleged "procedural errors" in

---

12. Petitioners' reliance on *Kent County v. EPA*, 963 F.2d 391 (D.C.Cir.1992) is misplaced because, unlike the Clean Air Act here, the statutory provision at issue in *Kent County* contained no special procedur- al provisions displacing general rules of administrative law governing the administrative record for judicial review. *Compare* 42 U.S.C. §§ 7607(d)(1), (d)(7)(A) *with* 42 U.S.C. § 9613(a).

the creation of the administrative docket that Congress created: 42 U.S.C. § 7607(d)(7)(B)'s mechanism for reconsideration by the agency. Petitioners have failed to move for reconsideration and are now trying to circumvent this congressionally mandated route by petitioning for direct judicial review. We therefore deny Petitioners' motion to supplement the administrative record and direct Petitioners to consult section 7607(d)(7)(B) in order to fashion their claim as a petition for reconsideration to EPA, as Congress had envisioned.

Second, even if this court were to consider Petitioners' argument on the merits, their challenge is misleading because Latimer himself indicates that Petitioners have misrepresented the statements and conclusions contained in his new report. We therefore reject Petitioners' argument that EPA has somehow acted arbitrarily or capriciously, or abused its discretion, through the manner in which it arrived at its estimate of visibility improvement.

V. CONCLUSION

In the final analysis, Petitioners simply adhere to a different interpretation of the rather disparate and equivocal scientific data in the record. While Petitioners may not be satisfied with EPA's responses, it is not EPA's duty to satisfy all of the concerns of potentially affected or aggrieved parties. EPA conducted an extensive and involved notice and comment period, and adequately met its statutory obligation of responding to significant comments and criticisms under 42 U.S.C. § 7607(d)(6)(B). Notwithstanding Petitioners' challenge, the Final Rule is the result of a site-specific informal rulemaking process that included virtually unprecedented cooperation between the governmental agency and the directly affected parties. *See generally* D. Michael Rappoport & John F. Cooney, *Visibility at the Grand Canyon: Regulatory Negotiations Under the Clean Air Act,* 24 Ariz.St.L.J. 627 (1992). Petitioners' arguments afford no reason for this court disruptively to interject itself into the picture. Because Congress delegated to EPA the power to "regulate on the borders of the unknown," this court will not interfere with the agency's "reasonable interpretations of equivocal evidence." *Public Citizen Health Research Group v. Tyson,* 796 F.2d at 1505. Even if this case highlights how hard it is to engage in "reasoned decisionmaking" in cases involving scientific uncertainty, EPA's actions in promulgating the Final Rule were reasonable and within the bounds of its statutory authority, and not arbitrary and capricious.

The Districts' petition for review and motion to supplement the administrative record are accordingly DENIED.

990 F.2d 1531, 143 P.U.R.4th 110, 61 USLW 2627, 36 ERC 1177, 23 Envtl. L. Rep. 20,678

The Court approved the EPA's direction of a particular source to make reductions to approve visibility at the Grand Canyon. But if the states appear to be identifying sources, does the EPA have any authority to step in? Is this approach to visibility unrealistic? Under § 169B, the

EPA has proposed a trading system to reduce haze, which was to be allowed if it created improvements beyond what could be obtained by the Best Available Retrofit Technology (BART) referenced in the preceding case. However, in CEED vs. EPA, the D.C. Circuit has invalidated those attempts by the EPA to force reductions on sources without the state making an individualized determination that the particular source affects visibility in a class 1 area. Given all of the uncertainty in tracing such effects, is it realistic to imagine any significant improvements in visibility under the current scheme?

VI. THE CLEAN AIR ACT—GENERAL ENFORCEMENT AND PERMITS FOR REGULATED STATIONARY SOURCES

Like other environmental laws, the full implementation of the Clean Air Act may be difficult if not supported by adequate administration and enforcement. The Clean Air Act is considered a cooperative statute in that the states and the federal government share responsibility for ensuring that it goes into effect. As discussed, *supra,* the states are to implement the ambient air quality standards by creating the SIPs. As noted in that discussion, the states were not always effective in doing so. Moreover, despite the failure of the states to ensure the attainment of the NAAQS, the EPA did not readily exercise its authority to implement Federal Implementation Plans in their place, despite a requirement for it to do so.

Additionally, the states are often given the primary authority to implement the other parts of the Act, such as the New Source Performance Standards and the Prevention of Significant Deterioration Program. But what is to ensure that they do so effectively? The public? The Clean Air Act does have a Citizen Suit enforcement provision, discussed generally *infra,* but courts have been reluctant to allow citizen enforcement actions as long as an agency is doing anything.[40] The federal government? As noted by one of the authors of this book,

> [W]ithout money, the threat of a true federal takeover largely disappeared, as the federal government could no longer afford the direct control of pollution compliance within most states.

> * * *

> Federal supervision of state enforcement was not as fail-safe a scheme as its proponents initially believed. The laws and standards were still there and they might be enforced with much energy from citizens. But all the laws on earth do not amount to much if they are not enforced, or if the enforcement lacks teeth. With the credible threat of a federal takeover removed, the states could go back to, or continue, their race to the bottom. Yet this time, they did not race with the laxity of laws, but with the lack of zeal of enforcement of

40. Victor Flatt, *A Dirty River Runs Through It* ... , 25 B. C. Envtl. L. Rev. 1, 3 (1998).

laws—a competition that is much more hidden and insidious, and one in which some states may not want to compete. [footnotes omitted].[41]

This failure of enforcement, particularly at the state level, was one of the reasons that Congress created the specific hammers in the 1970 Clean Air Act. The EPA's oversight failure may have led to the more specific legislative requirements for ozone non-compliance in the 1990 amendments. The 1990 amendments also added a permit feature to assist in providing information which could help with enforcement.

In 1990, Congress promulgated Title V of the CAA.[42] Title V of the CAA establishes a comprehensive permit program for stationary sources. It requires all major stationary sources of air pollution to obtain permits incorporating CAA requirements and establishes procedures for federal authorization of state-run Title V permit programs.[43] Title V permits do not impose additional requirements on sources but, to facilitate compliance, consolidate all applicable requirements in a single document.[44] By having all of the requirements in one place, the Permit Program was seen as an aid in compliance.

It was decided that the states should run the title V program much like they administered the NPDES program for water pollution sources. The CAA requires the EPA to determine that a state program meets all requirements of Title V and EPA's implementing regulations before granting full approval of the state's Title V program. The CAA establishes deadlines for states to meet in order to have delegation of the Title V program. States were required to submit proposed permit programs by November 1993.[45] The EPA had to either grant full approval or interim approval, or deny approval by November 1994.[46] EPA was to take over any state program that did not meet federal requirements and had not been granted interim approval by November 1995.[47] Additionally, EPA was to take over state permit programs that had been granted interim approval but did not qualify for full approval by November 1996.[48] This means that compliant programs were to be operating by November 1996. If a state program was not fully approved before the deadline, or if an interim approval expired without EPA granting full approval, EPA was directed to apply sanctions as outlined in section 7509(b).[49] If a state program is not approved two years after the date required for submission of such program, EPA was required to promulgate, administer, and enforce a program for that state.[50] Whenever EPA determined that a state was not adequately administering and enforcing a program in accordance with the requirements of the CAA, EPA was required to

41. Victor Flatt, *A Dirty River Runs Through It* . . . , 25 B. C. Envtl. L. Rev. 1, 3 (1998).

42. 42 U.S.C. Sec. 7661–7661e.

43. 42 U.S.C. Sec. 7661–7661f.

44. 42 U.S.C. Sec. 7661a(a).

45. 42 U.S.C. Sec. 7661a(d)(1).

46. 42 U.S.C. Sec. 7661a(d)(3).

47. 42 U.S.C. Sec. 7661a(d)(3).

48. 42 U.S.C. Sec. 7661a(g).

49. 42 U.S.C. Sec. 7661a(d)(2)(B).

50. 42 U.S.C. Sec. 7661a(d)(3).

provide notice to the state and apply any of the sanctions in section 7509(b) if the state did not correct the deficiency within 18 months.[51]

A. What is required for a state permit program to be approved?

Though the permit program may help with enforcement generally and provide information for citizen suits, much is still dependent on the agency wishing to enforce the laws in a particular way. New theories of "cooperative enforcement" were a hallmark of the early 90s, particularly in the states. This led to many audit provisions[52] that some claim are inconsistent with good enforcement. EPA's response has been more muted. During the Clinton administration, signals were given that state programs would be shut down if they were not consistent with EPA enforcement priorities, but that threat was never carried out. Despite the better, more specific laws we may have, much is still dependent on agency choice of enforcement. And if the federal agency is willing to go along with state enforcement that may be considered lax, given the deference that courts show to agency action, challenging such a decision is difficult. The following case further explores the requirements of the Title V permit program and illustrates the difficulty in challenging the EPA's approval of a state program.

PUBLIC CITIZEN, INC. v. UNITED STATES ENVIRONMENTAL PROTECTION AGENCY

United States Court of Appeals, Fifth Circuit, 2003.
343 F.3d 449.

* * *

In 1990, Congress enacted Title V for the CAA. Title V requires major stationary sources of air pollution, such as factories, to receive operating permits incorporating CAA requirements and establishes a procedure for federal authorization of state-run Title V permit programs. *See* 42 U.S.C. §§ 7661-7661f. Title V permits do not impose additional requirements on sources but, to facilitate compliance, consolidate all applicable requirements in a single document. *See* 42 U.S.C. § 7661a(a); *see also Virginia v. Browner*, 80 F.3d 869, 873 (4th Cir.1996) (Title V permit "is a source-specific bible for [CAA] compliance"), *cert. denied*, 519 U.S. 1090, 117 S.Ct. 764, 136 L.Ed.2d 711 (1997).

Congress directed the EPA to promulgate regulations establishing the minimum elements for a Title V operating permit program. Those minimum elements were to include certain requirements identified in the CAA. *See* 42 U.S.C. § 7661a(b) (articulating ten minimum elements for state programs).

---

51. 42 U.S.C. Sec. 7661a(i)(1).

52. Programs to allow regulated industry not to report violations of environmental laws if discovered pursuant to a good faith effort to investigate and improve compliance.

The CAA required each State to develop, and submit to the EPA for approval, an operating permit program that met the requirements of the Act and its regulations (Part 70—pursuant to the regulations implemented for the CAA). 42 U.S.C. § 7661a(d)(1). Section 502(d)(1) of the CAA, 42 U.S.C. § 7661a(d)(1), authorized the EPA to grant full approval to permit programs "to the extent" that the program met the CAA's requirements.

In the event a State was not eligible for full approval, but "substantially" met the minimum requirements, the CAA authorized the EPA to grant "interim approval". 42 U.S.C. § 7661a(g). On granting interim approval, the EPA had to identify deficiencies to be addressed before the program could receive full approval; the State was then required to revise and resubmit the program. *Id.* Interim approval could only last for two years and could not be renewed. *Id.*

Congress established firm deadlines for these processes. *See* 42 U.S.C. § 7661a. Pursuant to the statutory schedule: by November 1993, States were to submit proposed permit programs; by November 1994, the EPA had to either grant full or interim approval, or deny approval; by November 1995, the EPA was to take over state permit programs that did not meet federal requirements and had not been granted interim approval; and by November 1996, the EPA was to take over state permit programs that had been granted interim approval but did not qualify for full approval. In other words, compliant programs were to be operating no later than November 1996, six years after Title V became law. *See* 42 U.S.C. § 7661a(b), (d)(1), (d)(3), and (g).

If a program was not fully approved before the deadline, or if interim approval expired without the EPA's having granted full approval, the CAA mandated stiff sanctions, including exposure to financial penalties (*e.g.,* loss of highway funds). *See* 42 U.S.C. § 7661a(d)(2)(B) (incorporating 42 U.S.C. § 7509(b)). Moreover, the EPA would be required to implement a federal Title V permitting program in that State, pursuant to EPA regulations. *See* 42 U.S.C. § 7661a(d)(3).

After the EPA approved a State's Title V permit program, the EPA was to maintain an oversight role. The CAA provides that, whenever the EPA makes a determination that a State is not adequately administering and enforcing its permit program in accordance with Title V, it shall provide a notice of deficiency (NOD) to the State. 42 U.S.C. § 7661a(i)(1). If the State does not correct the deficiency within 18 months, it faces sanctions and, eventually, EPA takeover of its program. 42 U.S.C. § 7661a(i)(2), (4).

B.

The EPA issued regulations providing minimum requirements for state permit programs and, pursuant to those rules, began reviewing and authorizing state permit programs. It issued numerous interim approvals. Despite the statutory language that interim approval was to last only two years and could not be renewed, the EPA also extended those approvals for an additional ten months as the November 1996 deadline approached. *See* Operating Permits Program Interim Approval Extensions, 61 Fed.Reg. 56368 (31 Oct. 1996). It subsequently extended interim approval three times. *See* Extension of Operating Permits Program Interim Approvals, 62 Fed.Reg. 45732 (29 Aug. 1997); Extension of Operating Permits Program Interim Approval Expiration Dates, 63 Fed.Reg. 40054 (27 July 1998); Extending Operating Permits Program Interim Approval Expiration Dates, 65 Fed.Reg. 7290 (14 Feb. 2000).

The EPA was sued for doing so. *Sierra Club v. EPA*, No. 00–1262 (D.C.Cir.2000). As part of the settlement of that action, the EPA agreed: (1) to implement a federal permit program by 1 December 2001 in any State that did not have full approval; and (2) to take and respond by 1 December 2001 to public comments regarding deficiencies in state permit programs. *Id.* (Settlement Agreement). Regarding such public comments, it committed to respond on the merits to any claims of deficiency raised during the comment period and either issue an NOD or explain why it did not do so.

C.

In 1993, Texas submitted its Title V program to the EPA for approval. *See* Clean Air Act Final Interim Approval of Operating Permits Program; the State of Texas, 61 Fed.Reg. 32693 (25 June 1996). In 1996, the EPA granted interim approval to Texas' program. *See id.* The EPA identified numerous deficiencies in its approval notice that Texas was required to correct before it could obtain full approval. *See id.* at 32694–98; Clean Air Act Proposed Interim Approval for the State of Texas, 60 Fed.Reg. 30037 (7 June 1995). Subsequently, Texas submitted program revisions for the EPA's review.

Pursuant to the *Sierra Club* Settlement Agreement, the EPA published a Federal Register notice inviting public comments about Texas' program; Petitioners submitted comments in which they objected to full approval, based on their belief that Texas had not corrected all of the interim deficiencies and that additional deficiencies existed that had not been identified previously. The EPA determined, however, that Texas' revisions satisfactorily addressed the program deficiencies *identified during interim approval,* Clean Air Act Proposed Full Approval for Texas, 66 Fed.Reg. 51895 (11 Oct. 2001); accordingly, it granted Texas full approval in December 2001, Clean Air Act Full Approval of Texas Permits Program, 66 Fed.Reg. 63318 (6 Dec. 2001).

Regarding the deficiencies *not identified by the time of interim approval,* the EPA concluded that newly identified deficiencies did not prohibit full approval. It stated it would respond to those alleged deficiencies in a separate, then concurrently pending administrative proceeding. *Id.* at 63329–30. In January 2002, based upon the EPA's review of the public comments, it issued an NOD that identified six deficiencies. Notice of Deficiency for Clean Air Act Operating Permits Program; State of Texas, 67 Fed.Reg. 732 (7 Jan. 2002).

In February 2002, the EPA issued a response letter explaining its rationale for not issuing NODs for other deficiencies claimed by Petitioners. *See* Operating Permits Program; Notice of Location of Response Letters to Citizens Concerning Program Deficiencies in Texas, 67 Fed. Reg. 16374 (5 Apr. 2002). The response explained that the EPA agreed with Petitioners concerning some of the issues and was working with Texas to ensure its program was being implemented consistent with Title V; on other issues, it did not agree with Petitioners. EPA Responses to Citizen Comments on State Program Deficiencies (Texas) (21 Feb. 2002), *at,* http://www.epa.gov/air/oaqps/permits/response/.

II.

Petitioners seek review of two EPA final actions related to Texas' Title V operating permits program: (1) the 6 December 2001 full approval of the program; and (2) the 21 February 2002 decision not to issue NODs related to four aspects of the program. Texas has intervened in favor of the EPA, as have BP America, Inc., *et al.* (Industry Intervenors).

* * *

A.

Petitioners first maintain the EPA, in December 2001, had no authority to grant Texas' permit program full approval without finding that the program met the requirements of Title V and its implementing regulations. They further maintain that the EPA acted arbitrarily and capriciously in granting full approval because Texas had not corrected all deficiencies identified at interim approval.

1.

The first issue is a question of statutory interpretation governed by the *Chevron* standard. Under the EPA's interpretation of the statutory provisions governing interim and full approval, CAA § 502g, 42 U.S.C. § 7661a(g) (governing interim approval), provides an alternate path to full approval. Full approval would otherwise be governed by CAA § 502(d), 42 U.S.C. § 7661a(d), and would not be permitted when the EPA determined (as it did) that the program did not meet all of Title V's requirements. According to the EPA, if a State is granted interim approval, then to receive full approval it need only remedy deficiencies identified by the EPA *at the time of interim approval.*

Petitioners dispute this interpretation, contending that, when the EPA is aware of deficiencies, it may not fully approve a program (regardless of whether it becomes aware of the deficiencies *before or after* interim approval). According to Petitioners: there is but one path to full approval, that provided by CAA § 502d, 42 U.S.C. § 7661a(d); and only deficiency-free programs may be approved. Petitioners urge that the EPA's interpretation is contrary to the clear and unambiguous intent of

Congress; and, in the alternative, that the approval was arbitrary and capricious because it contradicts EPA regulations and memoranda.

* * *

On fully approving Texas' program, the EPA acknowledged this ambiguity, finding an "apparent tension" between the requirement that it grant full approval only to programs that meet minimum requirements and the requirement that it grant full approval to any program that has corrected interim deficiencies. 66 Fed.Reg. at 63319 ("Standing alone, § 502(d) appears to prevent EPA from granting a state operating permit program full approval until the state has corrected all deficiencies in its program no matter how insignificant, and *without consideration as to when* such deficiency was identified. Alternatively, § 502(g) appears to require that EPA grant a state program full approval if the state has corrected those issues that the EPA identified in the final [interim approval]." (emphasis added)).

Therefore, the EPA had to decide "whether Texas by virtue of correcting the deficiencies identified in the [interim approval was] eligible . . . for full approval, or whether Texas *must also* correct any new or recently identified deficiencies as a prerequisite to receiving full approval". *Id.* at 63319–20 (emphasis added). The EPA concluded:

> [T]he appropriate and more cohesive reading of the statute recognizes the EPA's authority to grant Texas full approval [where interim-approval deficiencies have been corrected] while working simultaneously with the state, in [the EPA's] oversight capacity, on any additional problems that were recently identified. To conclude otherwise would disrupt the current administration of the state program and cause further delay in Texas's ability to issue operating permits to major stationary sources.

Id. at 63320.

Because Congress did not unambiguously express its intent on this issue through the CAA, the EPA's interpretation is entitled to deference under *Chevron*. As a result, we must decide whether the EPA's interpretation is "based on a permissible construction of the [CAA]". *Chevron*, 467 U.S. at 843, 104 S.Ct. 2778.

We hold that it is. First, CAA § 502(g), 42 U.S.C. § 7661a(g), provides that, in the notice of final rulemaking granting interim approval, the EPA must "specify *the* changes that must be made before the program can receive full approval". (Emphasis added.) This suggests the interim-approval notice must identify all of the changes required for full approval, and the making of those specified changes (not all possible changes) triggers full approval.

Second, as the Second Circuit noted:

> [T]he EPA's interpretation comports with the timetable established by Congress, if not adhered to by the EPA. Under § 502(g), interim approval expires after two years and is not renewable. 42 U.S.C.

§ 7661a(g). Changes identified at the time of interim approval may require modifications of state statutes or regulations and, therefore, may be time consuming. *If a state were required, not only to make the changes identified at the start of interim approval but also to correct deficiencies arising during interim approval,* a state's efforts to receive full approval could be sabotaged by the identification of new deficiencies during or at the end of interim approval. Should these events occur it is doubtful whether the state could resubmit its plan for full approval since § 502(d) provides that any such submission must occur "[n]ot later than three years after November 15, 1990," 42 U.S.C. § 7661a(d)(1), and the statute does not otherwise authorize re-submission.

New York Pub. Interest Research Group, 321 F.3d at 329 (emphasis added).

Finally, the CAA provides a mechanism for correcting deficiencies in fully-approved programs—the NOD process (discussed in detail *infra*). Like the Second Circuit, "[w]e question whether Congress would have armed the EPA with this arsenal if it believed that every deficiency would be corrected during the interim approval period". *Id.* at 329. Moreover, the NOD process also applies to programs that have been granted interim approval, providing a means to correct deficiencies not identified at the time of interim approval. Thus, Congress provided processes for making corrections to programs once they initially enter the approval process and are given at least interim approval.

* * *

2.

Petitioners nonetheless contend that the EPA acted arbitrarily and capriciously in granting full approval to Texas because it had not corrected three of the deficiencies identified at interim approval. The EPA responds that it evaluated Texas' response to each deficiency and concluded that Texas had satisfactorily addressed the EPA's concerns.

We note that the EPA's determinations were based on detailed, technical evaluations of revisions to the Texas program to determine whether that program complied with the CAA and the EPA's regulatory scheme. Again, the EPA is entitled to a substantial deference in interpreting its regulations. *E.g., Marine Shale Processors v. EPA,* 81 F.3d 1371, 1384 (5th Cir.1996), *cert. denied,* 519 U.S. 1055, 117 S.Ct. 682, 136 L.Ed.2d 607 (1997).

* * *

The new source review (NSR) component of the CAA addresses preconstruction review for new and modified stationary sources of air pollution. All States must administer an EPA-approved program, commonly referred to as "minor NSR", that requires new sources and existing sources subject to modification to obtain a preconstruction authorization containing appropriate emission limitations and standards.

See 60 Fed.Reg. at 30039 (citing 40 C.F.R. § 70.2). Minor NSR permit terms and conditions are applicable requirements of the Act that must be incorporated into a Title V permit. *See id.*

The Title V and Part 70 provisions specify *what* Title V permits "shall include" but do not state *how* the items must be included. *See* 42 U.S.C. § 7661c(a) ("[e]ach permit issued under this subchapter shall include enforceable emissions limitations and standards ... and such other conditions as are necessary to assure compliance with applicable requirements of this chapter"); 40 C.F.R. § 70.6(a)(1) ("[e]ach permit issued under this part shall include [elements including emissions limitations and standards]").

* * *

b.

Next, Petitioners point to Texas' Audit Privilege Act as an interim-approval-identified deficiency that had not been corrected. They maintain the Audit Privilege Act prevents Texas from having adequate authority to enforce its permit program.

Title V includes, as one of its minimum elements, the requirement that the State have adequate authority to assure that sources comply with all applicable requirements and to enforce permits. 42 U.S.C. § 7661a(b)(5); *see also* 40 C.F.R. § 70.11(c) (penalties must be "appropriate to the violation"). Texas, through its Audit Privilege Act, provides for certain immunities and privileges associated with information obtained through an environmental audit of a facility. Tex.Rev.Civ. Stat. art. 4447cc.

In the EPA's interim approval notice for Texas, it noted its concern that the Audit Privilege Act might prevent Texas from having adequate enforcement authority. 61 Fed.Reg. at 32697. The EPA stated that, to qualify for full approval, Texas would be required to demonstrate that the Audit Privilege Act did not limit Texas' ability to adequately enforce and administer the operating permit program. *Id.*

In response, Texas amended the Audit Privilege Act. According to the EPA, these amendments: (1) eliminated the application of immunity and privilege provisions to criminal actions; (2) eliminated the application of immunity where a violation results in a serious threat to health or the environment, or where the violator has obtained a substantial economic benefit that gives it a competitive advantage; (3) clarified that the law would not sanction individuals who report violations of environmental laws to government agencies; and (4) clarified that the privilege does not impair access to information required to be made available under federal or state law. *See* 66 Fed.Reg. at 51903.

Petitioners concede that Texas has made these changes to its Audit Privilege Act since 1996, but insist that the law still: prevents Texas from having adequate enforcement authority; prevents it from being able to assess appropriate penalties; and improperly makes audit documents privileged. The EPA responds that it reasonably determined that limited immunity does not, *per se,* preclude States from possessing adequate enforcement authority.

i.

Concerning the adequacy of Texas' enforcement authority, Petitioners insist the Audit Privilege Act prevents Texas from being able to recover civil penalties for each violation of the Act because it has granted certain immunities. On the other hand, the EPA determined the immunities provided by Texas' Audit Privilege Act did not deprive Texas of adequate enforcement authority. It reasoned the Act does not: limit Texas' ability to seek declaratory or injunctive relief for violations disclosed by an audit; affect Texas' ability to pursue criminal sanctions, if appropriate; or preclude actions seeking penalties for serious violations. This determination was not arbitrary and capricious.

ii.

Regarding the Audit Privilege Act's impact on Texas' ability to impose appropriate penalties, Title V and Part 70 require that Texas have authority to recover penalties of up to $10,000 per day in an amount "appropriate to the violation". 40 C.F.R. § 70.11; *see also* 42 U.S.C. § 7661a(b)(5)(E). The EPA has interpreted these provisions to require that state law allow for the consideration of the penalty factors identified in CAA § 113(e), 42 U.S.C. § 7413(e): the violator's compliance history; the economic benefit of noncompliance; and the seriousness of the violation.

Petitioners note minor semantic differences between the federal penalty factors and those allowed consideration under the Audit Privilege Act. For example, Texas must be able to penalize violations resulting in substantial economic benefit; Texas' Audit Privilege Act provides an exception to immunity for violations that "have resulted in a significant economic benefit which gives the violator a clear advantage over its business competitors". Tex.Rev.Civ. Stat. Art. 4447cc § 10(d)(5). Notwithstanding minor variations, the EPA reasonably determined that Texas' statutory language allowed it to consider the appropriate factors in imposing punishments.

iii.

Petitioners assert Texas' Audit Privilege Act impermissibly makes audit documents privileged. The EPA responds that Texas addressed this concern by adding a section to the Audit Privilege Act that restored the authority of the State's employees, "[n]otwithstanding the privilege established under this Act" to "review information that is required to be available under a specific state or federal law...." Tex.Rev.Civ.Stat. art. 4447cc, § 9(b). The EPA determined this section restored Texas' authority to view any documents required to be collected, maintained, or reported under Title V, which it deemed sufficient to address the deficiency and for Texas to conduct both civil and criminal investigations. *See* 66 Fed.Reg. at 63329. This assessment was not arbitrary or capricious.

c.

Finally, Petitioners contend full approval was arbitrary and capricious because Texas has not demonstrated that it has adequate funding and personnel to administer a Title V program. 42 U.S.C. § 7661a(b)(4) requires States to so demonstrate, and Part 70 instructs that this demonstration must include a four-year estimate of program costs and a description of how the State plans to cover those costs. 40 C.F.R. § 70.4(b)(8)(v). The funding must be collected as a fee from owners and operators of Title V sources and must be sufficient to cover the cost of the Title V permit program, including: granting/denying permits; enforcing permits; emissions and ambient monitoring; preparing regulations and guidance; and modeling and tracking emissions. 42 U.S.C. § 7661a(b)(3)(A)(i)–(vi).

At the time of interim approval, the EPA identified as a deficiency Texas' failure to provide the four-year estimate. *See* 60 Fed.Reg. at 30044. Texas subsequently provided a four-year estimate of costs and its projection that fee revenues would exceed these costs. Texas estimated average annual costs of $34.3 million and revenues of $36.8 million for the four-year projection period.

Petitioners maintain that Texas has not corrected the deficiency because: this estimate includes an anticipated fee increase in 2003 (from $26 to $30 per ton) that the Texas agency staff stated it would recommend to the Commissioners of the Texas Natural Resources Conservation Commission; and, although costs of the program will increase, Texas has not budgeted for additional staff.

i.

Regarding the proposed increase, the EPA responds that it had no reason to believe an increase would not be adopted. Moreover, it notes that, if for some reason Texas did not adopt the recommended increases, it could then issue an NOD. This determination was not arbitrary or capricious.

ii.

Regarding Petitioners' assertion that the Texas agency faces a significant amount of work in the next few years which will increase costs, the EPA notes that Texas provided a spreadsheet identifying permitting tasks, the number of permitting actions in each category, and the number of staff members required to complete the tasks. It questioned Texas concerning certain items and was satisfied with Texas' explanations. This was not arbitrary or capricious.

3.

In sum, because the EPA's interpretation of these CAA provisions is a reasonable, and thus permissible, interpretation of the statute and because the EPA's determination that Texas corrected interim deficiencies was not arbitrary and capricious, Petitioners fail in their challenge to the EPA's decision to fully approve Texas' program.

* * *

B.　Federal Overfiling—Federal Enforcement above and beyond the state

Even though most of environmental law includes cooperative enforcement through which the federal government delegates primary enforcement authority to the states, the federal government still can retain significant control. In addition to revocation of a state's program for failure to follow delegated criteria (which it has rarely exercised), the EPA has also asserted that it has jurisdiction to directly enforce a law, even if the state chooses not to act. Generally, the courts have been deferential to the EPA's attempts to take direct enforcement actions if the EPA has been dissatisfied with the state action. Given the great difficulty and unlikelihood of the EPA directly taking over an entire program, this may be the only way to create a credible control on state discretion. The next case involves the EPA's decision to take a direct action on a permit specifying a technology standard under the Clean Air Act.

In addition to discussing the EPA's enforcement authority, this case also provides a discussion of how the general Clean Air Act requirements may be assumed by the states, and the factual issues that continually arise in determining what standard meets the technological requirements of NSPS and PSD for stationary sources. As you read the facts of the case, think about what position you would have taken had you been Teck Cominco. Is it financially logical to try to have the PSD requirement be the less expensive of two options? How do you convince the permitting agency of that option? What about the oversight capability? Could a compromise have been reached with the EPA earlier? Could political pressure have been brought to bear on the agency? Is it easier to bring pressure on a state agency rather than a federal one?

ALASKA DEPARTMENT OF ENVIRONMENTAL CONSERVATION v. ENVIRONMENTAL PROTECTION AGENCY

Supreme Court of the United States, 2004.
540 U.S. 461, 124 S.Ct. 983, 157 L.Ed.2d 967.

* * *

Justice GINSBURG delivered the opinion of the Court.

This case concerns the authority of the Environmental Protection Agency (EPA or Agency) to enforce the provisions of the Clean Air Act's (CAA or Act) Prevention of Significant Deterioration (PSD) program. Under that program, no major air pollutant emitting facility may be constructed unless the facility is equipped with "the best available control technology" (BACT). As added by § 165, 91 Stat. 735, and amended, 42 U.S.C. § 7475(a)(4). BACT, as defined in the CAA, means, for any major air pollutant emitting facility, "an emission limitation based on the maximum degree of [pollutant] reduction ... which the permitting authority, on a case-by-case basis, taking into account energy, environmental, and economic impacts and other costs, determines is achievable for [the] facility...." § 7479(3).

Regarding EPA oversight, the Act includes a general instruction and one geared specifically to the PSD program. The general prescription, § 113(a)(5) of the Act, authorizes EPA, when it finds that a State is not complying with a CAA requirement governing construction of a pollutant source, to issue an order prohibiting construction, to prescribe an administrative penalty, or to commence a civil action for injunctive relief. 42 U.S.C. § 7413(a). Directed specifically to the PSD program, CAA § 167 instructs EPA to "take such measures, including issuance of an order, or seeking injunctive relief, as necessary to prevent the construction" of a major pollutant emitting facility that does not conform to the PSD requirements of the Act. 42 U.S.C. § 7477.

In the case before us, "the permitting authority" under § 7479(3) is the State of Alaska, acting through Alaska's Department of Environmental Conservation (ADEC). The question presented is what role EPA has with respect to ADEC's BACT determinations. Specifically, may EPA act to block construction of a new major pollutant emitting facility permitted by ADEC when EPA finds ADEC's BACT determination unreasonable in light of the guides § 7479(3) prescribes? We hold that the Act confers that checking authority on EPA.

I

A

Congress enacted the Clean Air Amendments of 1970, 84 Stat. 1676, 42 U.S.C. § 7401 *et seq.,* in response to "dissatisfaction with the progress of existing air pollution programs." *Union Elec. Co. v. EPA,* 427 U.S. 246, 249, 96 S.Ct. 2518, 49 L.Ed.2d 474 (1976). The amendments aimed "to guarantee the prompt attainment and maintenance of specified air quality standards." *Ibid.;* D. Currie, Air Pollution § 1.13, p. 1–16 (1981) (summary of 1970 amendments). Added by the 1970 amendments, §§ 108(a) and 109(a) of the Act require EPA to publish lists of emissions that "cause or contribute to air pollution which may reasonably be anticipated to endanger public health or welfare," and to promulgate primary and secondary national ambient air quality standards (NAAQS) for such pollutants. 42 U.S.C. §§ 7408(a) and 7409(a); *Whitman v. American Trucking Assns.,* 531 U.S. 457, 462–463, 121 S.Ct. 903, 149 L.Ed.2d 1 (2001). NAAQS "define [the] levels of air quality that must be achieved to protect public health and welfare." R. Belden, Clean Air Act 6 (2001). The Agency published initial NAAQS in 1971, *Union Elec.,* 427 U.S., at 251, 96 S.Ct. 2518 (citing 40 CFR pt. 50 (1975)), and in 1985,

NAAQS for the pollutant at issue in this case, nitrogen dioxide. 40 CFR § 50.11 (2002).[1]

* * *

Section 165 of the Act, 42 U.S.C. § 7475, installs a permitting requirement for any "major emitting facility," defined to include any source emitting more than 250 tons of nitrogen oxides per year, § 7479(1). No such facility may be constructed or modified unless a permit prescribing emission limitations has been issued for the facility. § 7475(a)(1); see § 7479(2)(C) (defining "construction" to include "modification"). Alaska's SIP imposes an analogous requirement. 18 Alaska Admin. Code § 50.300(c)(1) (2003). Modifications to major emitting facilities that increase nitrogen oxide emissions in excess of 40 tons per year require a PSD permit. 40 CFR § 51.166(b)(23)(i) (2002); 18 Alaska Admin. Code § 50.300(h)(3)(B)(ii) (2003).

The Act sets out preconditions for the issuance of PSD permits. *Inter alia,* no PSD permit may issue unless "the proposed facility is subject to the best available control technology for each pollutant subject to [CAA] regulation ... emitted from ... [the] facility." 42 U.S.C. § 7475(a)(4). As described in the Act's definitional provisions, "best available control technology" (BACT) means:

> "[A]n emission limitation based on the maximum degree of reduction of each pollutant subject to regulation under this chapter emitted from or which results from any major emitting facility, which the permitting authority, on a case-by-case basis, taking into account energy, environmental, and economic impacts and other costs, determines is achievable for such facility through application of production processes and available methods, systems, and techniques.... In no event shall application of 'best available control technology' result in emissions of any pollutants which will exceed the emissions allowed by any applicable standard established pursuant to section 7411 or 7412 of this title [emission standards for new and existing stationary sources]." § 7479(3).

40 CFR § 51.166(b)(12) (2002) (repeating statutory definition). Alaska's SIP contains provisions that track the statutory BACT requirement and definition. 18 Alaska Admin. Code § § 50.310(d)(3) and 50.990(13) (2003). The State, with slightly variant terminology, defines BACT as "the emission limitation that represents the maximum reduction achievable for each regulated air contaminant, taking into account energy, environmental and economic impacts, and other costs." *Ibid.* Under the

---

1. Emissions levels for nitrogen dioxide, a regulated pollutant under the Act, are defined in terms of quantities of all oxides of nitrogen. R. Belden, Clean Air Act 47, n. 11 (2001). "The term nitrogen oxides refers to a family of compounds of nitrogen and oxygen. The principal nitrogen oxides component present in the atmosphere at any time is nitrogen dioxides. Combustion sources emit mostly nitric oxide, with some nitrogen dioxide. Upon entering the atmosphere, the nitric oxide changes rapidly, mostly to nitrogen dioxide." EPA, Prevention of Significant Deterioration for Nitrogen Oxides, 53 Fed.Reg. 40656 (1988). Nitrogen oxides are also termed "NOx."

federal Act, a limited class of sources must gain advance EPA approval for the BACT prescribed in the permit. 42 U.S.C. § 7475(a)(8).

CAA also provides that a PSD permit may issue only if a source "will not cause, or contribute to, air pollution in excess of any ... maximum allowable increase or maximum allowable concentration for any pollutant" or any NAAQS. § 7475(a)(3). Congress left to the Agency the determination of most maximum allowable increases, or "increments," in pollutants. EPA regulations have defined increments for nitrogen oxides. 40 CFR § 51.166(c) (2002). Typically, to demonstrate that increments will not be exceeded, applicants use mathematical models of pollutant plumes, their behavior, and their dispersion. Westbrook, Air Dispersion Models: Tools to Assess Impacts from Pollution Sources, 13 Natural Resources & Env. 546, 547–548 (1999).

Among measures EPA may take to ensure compliance with the PSD program, two have special relevance here. The first prescription, § 113(a)(5) of the Act, provides that "[w]henever, on the basis of any available information, [EPA] finds that a State is not acting in compliance with any requirement or prohibition of the chapter relating to the construction of new sources or the modification of existing sources," EPA may "issue an order prohibiting the construction or modification of any major stationary source in any area to which such requirement applies." 42 U.S.C. § 7413(a)(5)(A).[4] The second measure, § 167 of the Act, trains on enforcement of the PSD program; it requires EPA to "take such measures, including issuance of an order, or seeking injunctive relief, as necessary to prevent the construction or modification of a major emitting facility which does not conform to the [PSD] requirements." § 7477.

B

Teck Cominco Alaska, Inc. (Cominco), operates a zinc concentrate mine, the Red Dog Mine, in northwest Alaska approximately 100 miles north of the Arctic Circle and close to the native Alaskan villages of Kivalina and Noatak. App. to Pet. for Cert. 3a; Brief for Petitioner 8; Brief for Respondents 4. The mine is the region's largest private employer. Brief for Petitioner 9. It supplies a quarter of the area's wage base. *Ibid.* Cominco leases the land from the NANA Regional Corporation, an Alaskan corporation formed pursuant to the Alaska Native Claims Settlement Act, 85 Stat. 688, as amended, 43 U.S.C. § 1601 *et seq.* Brief for NANA Regional Corporation, Inc., as *Amicus Curiae* 1–2, 4.

In 1988, Cominco obtained authorization to operate the mine, a "major emitting facility" under the Act and Alaska's SIP.App. 106. The mine's PSD permit authorized five 5,000 kilowatt Wartsila diesel electric generators, MG–1 through MG–5, subject to operating restrictions; two of the five generators were permitted to operate only in standby status.

---

4. As enacted in 1977, § 113(a)(5) extended only to solid waste combustion and sources in nonattainment areas. See Title I, § 111(a), 91 Stat. 685. Congress extended § 113(a)(5) in 1990 amendments to the Act to cover attainment areas, and thus to encompass enforcement of PSD permitting requirements. Title VII, 104 Stat. 2672.

Ibid. Petitioner Alaska Department of Environmental Conservation (ADEC) issued a second PSD permit in 1994 allowing addition of a sixth full-time generator (MG–6), removing standby status from MG–2, and imposing a new operational cap that allowed all but one generator to run full time. *Ibid.*

In 1996, Cominco initiated a project, with funding from the State, to expand zinc production by 40%. Brief for Petitioner 5; Reply Brief for Petitioner 11, n. 9. Anticipating that the project would increase nitrogen oxide emissions by more than 40 tons per year, see *supra,* at 992, Cominco applied to ADEC for a PSD permit to allow, *inter alia,* increased electricity generation by its standby generator, MG–5.App. 107–108; App. to Pet. for Cert. 33a. On March 3, 1999, ADEC preliminarily proposed as BACT for MG–5 the emission control technology known as selective catalytic reduction (SCR),[5] which reduces nitrogen oxide emissions by 90%. App. 72, 108. In response, Cominco amended its application to add a seventh generator, MG–17, and to propose as BACT an alternative control technology—Low NOx [6]—that achieves a 30% reduction in nitrogen oxide pollutants. Brief for Respondents 5, and n. 1; App. 84.

On May 4, 1999, ADEC, in conjunction with Cominco's representative, issued a first draft PSD permit and preliminary technical analysis report that concluded Low NOx was BACT for MG–5 and MG–17. *Id.,* at 55–95. To determine BACT, ADEC employed EPA's recommended top-down methodology, *id.,* at 61:

> "In brief, the top-down process provides that all available control technologies be ranked in descending order of control effectiveness. The PSD applicant first examines the most stringent—or 'top'— alternative. That alternative is established as BACT unless the applicant demonstrates, and the permitting authority in its informed judgment agrees, that technical considerations, or energy, environmental, or economic impacts justify a conclusion that the most stringent technology is not 'achievable' in that case. If the most stringent technology is eliminated in this fashion, then the next most stringent alternative is considered, and so on." EPA, New Source Review Workshop Manual B2 (Draft Oct. 1990) (hereinafter New Source Review Manual); App. 61–62.[7]

Applying top-down methodology, ADEC first homed in on SCR as BACT for MG–5, and the new generator, MG17. "[W]ith an estimated reduction of 90%," ADEC stated, SCR "is the most stringent" technolo-

---

5. SCR requires injections of "ammonia or urea into the exhaust before the exhaust enters a catalyst bed made with vanadium, titanium, or platinum. The reduction reaction occurs when the flue gas passes over the catalyst bed where the NOx and ammonia combine to become nitrogen, oxygen, and water...." App. 71.

6. In Low NOx, changes are made to a generator to improve fuel atomization and

modify the combustion space to enhance the mixing of air and fuel. *Id.,* at 75.

7. Nothing in the Act or its implementing regulations mandates top-down analysis. See 42 U.S.C. § 7479(3); 40 CFR § 52.21(j) (2002). EPA represents that permitting authorities "commonly" use top-down methodology. Brief for Respondents 3.

gy. *Id.*, at 79. Finding SCR "technically and economically feasible," *id.*, at 65, ADEC characterized as "overstated" Cominco's cost estimate of $5,643 per ton of nitrogen oxide removed by SCR. *Id.*, at 113. Using Cominco's data, ADEC reached a cost estimate running between $1,586 and $2,279 per ton. *Id.*, at 83. Costs in that range, ADEC observed, "are well within what ADEC and EPA conside[r] economically feasible." *Id.*, at 84. Responding to Cominco's comments on the preliminary permit, engineering staff in ADEC's Air Permits Program pointed out that, according to information Cominco provided to ADEC, "SCR has been installed on similar diesel-fired engines throughout the world." *Id.*, at 102.

Despite its staff's clear view "that SCR (the most effective individual technology) [was] technologically, environmentally, and economically feasible for the Red Dog power plant engines," *id.*, at 103–104, ADEC endorsed the alternative proffered by Cominco. To achieve nitrogen oxide emission reductions commensurate with SCR's 90% impact, Cominco proposed fitting the new generator MG–17 and the six existing generators with Low NOx. *Ibid.*[8] Cominco asserted that it could lower net emissions by 396 tons per year if it fitted all seven generators with Low NOx rather than fitting two (MG–5 and MG-17) with SCR and choosing one of them as the standby unit. *Id.*, at 87. Cominco's proposal hinged on the "assumption . . . that under typical operating conditions one or more engines will not be running due to maintenance of standby-generation capacity." Ibid. If all seven generators ran continuously, however, Cominco's alternative would increase emissions by 79 tons per year. *Ibid.* Accepting Cominco's submission, ADEC stated that Cominco's Low NOx solution "achieve[d] a similar maximum NOx reduction as the most stringent controls; [could] potentially result in a greater NOx reduction; and is logistically and economically less onerous to Cominco." *Id.*, at 87–88.

On the final day of the public comment period, July 2, 1999, the United States Department of the Interior, National Parks Service (NPS), submitted comments to ADEC.App. to Pet. for Cert. 33a; App. 97, 108. NPS objected to the projected offset of new emissions from MG–5 and MG–17 against emissions from other existing generators that were not subject to BACT. Letter from John Notar, NPS Air Resources Division, to Jim Baumgartner, ADEC (June 2, 1999). Such an offset, NPS commented, "is neither allowed by BACT, nor achieves the degree of reduction that would result if all the generators that are subject to BACT were equipped with SCR." *Id.*, at 3. NPS further observed that the proposed production-increase project would remove operating restrictions that the 1994 PSD permit had placed on four of the existing generators—MG–1, MG–3, MG–4, and MG–5.App. to Pet. for Cert. 34a. Due to that alteration, NPS urged, those generators, too, became part of

---

8. Two generators already were fitted with a technology called Fuel Injection Timing Retard that results in a 20% to 30% reduction in nitrogen oxide emissions. App. 75–76, 86.

the production-expansion project and would be subject to the BACT requirement. *Ibid.*

Following NPS' lead, EPA wrote to ADEC on July 29, 1999, commenting: "Although ADEC states in its analysis that [SCR], the most stringent level of control, is economically and technologically feasible, ADEC did not propose to require SCR.... [O]nce it is determined that an emission unit is subject to BACT, the PSD program does not allow the imposition of a limit that is less stringent than BACT." App. 96–97. A permitting authority, EPA agreed with NPS, could not offset new emissions "by imposing new controls on other emission units" that were not subject to BACT. *Id.,* at 97. New emissions could be offset only against reduced emissions from sources covered by the same BACT authorization. *Id.,* at 285–286. EPA further agreed with NPS that, based on the existing information, BACT would be required for MG–1, MG–3, MG–4, and MG–5. *Id.,* at 97.

After receiving EPA comments, ADEC issued a second draft PSD permit and technical analysis report on September 1, 1999, again finding Low NOx to be BACT for MG–17. *Id.,* at 105–117. Abandoning the emissions-offsetting justification advanced in the May 4 draft permit, ADEC agreed with NPS and EPA that "emission reductions from sources that were not part of the permit action," here MG–1, MG–2, MG–3, MG–4, MG–5, and MG–6, could not be considered in determining BACT for MG–17. *Id.,* at 111; *id.,* at 199 (same).[9]

ADEC conceded that, lacking data from Cominco, it had made "no judgment ... as to the impact of ... [SCR] on the operation, profitability, and competitiveness of the Red Dog Mine." *Id.,* at 116. Contradicting its May 1999 conclusion that SCR was "technically and economically feasible," see *supra,* at——10, ADEC found in September 1999 that SCR imposed "a disproportionate cost" on the mine. App. 116. ADEC concluded, on a "cursory review," that requiring SCR for a rural Alaska utility would lead to a 20% price increase, and that in comparison with other BACT technologies, SCR came at a "significantly higher" cost. *Ibid.* No economic basis for a comparison between the mine and a rural utility appeared in ADEC's technical analysis.

EPA protested the revised permit. In a September 15, 1999, letter, the Agency stated: "Cominco has not adequately demonstrated any site-specific factors to support their claim that the installation of [SCR] is economically infeasible at the Red Dog Mine. Therefore, elimination of SCR as BACT based on cost-effectiveness grounds is not supported by the record and is clearly erroneous." *Id.,* at 127; see *id.,* at 138 (ADEC's

---

9. Rather than subject MG–1, MG–3, MG–4, and MG–5 to BACT, ADEC and Cominco "agreed to permit conditions that would require low NOx controls on MG–1, MG–3, MG–4, and MG–5, and emission limits that reflect the previous 'bubbled' limits. Under this approach, the permit would result in no increase in actual or allowable emissions from any of these engines and the installation of BACT would not be necessary for these four units." *Id.,* at 149. EPA found no cause to question this ADEC–Cominco agreement. *Ibid.*

record does not support the departure from ADEC's initial view that the costs for SCR were economically feasible).

To justify the September 1, 1999, permit, EPA suggested, ADEC could "include an analysis of whether requiring Cominco to install and operate [SCR] would have any adverse economic impacts upon Cominco specifically." *Id.,* at 127. Stating that such an inquiry was unnecessary and expressing "concerns related to confidentiality," Cominco declined to submit financial data. *Id.,* at 134. In this regard, Cominco simply asserted, without detail, that the company's "overall debt remains quite high" despite continuing profits. *Id.,* at 134–135. Cominco also invoked the need for "[i]ndustrial development in rural Alaska." *Id.,* at 135.

On December 10, 1999, ADEC issued the final permit and technical analysis report. Once again, ADEC approved Low NOx as BACT for MG–17 "[t]o support Cominco's Red Dog Mine Production Rate Increase Project, and its contributions to the region." *Id.,* at 208. ADEC did not include the economic analysis EPA had suggested. *Id.,* at 152–246. Indeed, ADEC conceded again that it had made "no judgment ... as to the impact of ... [SCR's] cost on the operation, profitability, and competitiveness of the Red Dog Mine." *Id.,* at 207. Nonetheless, ADEC advanced, as cause for its decision, SCR's adverse effect on the mine's "unique and continuing impact on the economic diversity of th[e] region" and on the venture's "world competitiveness." *Id.,* at 208. ADEC did not explain how its inferences of adverse effects on the region's economy or the mine's "world competitiveness" could be made without financial information showing SCR's impact on the "operation, profitability, and competitiveness" of the mine. *Id.,* at 207, 299. Instead, ADEC reiterated its rural Alaska utility analogy, and again compared SCR's cost to the costs of other, less stringent, control technologies. *Id.,* at 205–207.

The same day, December 10, 1999, EPA issued an order to ADEC, under §§ 113(a)(5) and 167 of the Act, 42 U.S.C. §§ 7413(a)(5) and 7477, prohibiting ADEC from issuing a PSD permit to Cominco "unless ADEC satisfactorily documents why SCR is not BACT for the Wartsila diesel generator [MG–17]." App. to Pet. for Cert. 36a. In the letter accompanying the order, the Agency stated that "ADEC's own analysis supports the determination that BACT is [SCR], and that ADEC's decision in the proposed permit therefore is both arbitrary and erroneous." App. 149.

On February 8, 2000, EPA, again invoking its authority under § § 113(a)(5) and 167 of the Act, issued a second order, this time prohibiting Cominco from beginning "construction or modification activities at the Red Dog mine." App. to Pet. for Cert. 49a. A third order, issued on March 7, 2000, superseding and vacating the February 8 order, generally prohibited Cominco from acting on ADEC's December 10 PSD permit but allowed limited summer construction. *Id.,* at 62a–64a. On April 25, 2000, EPA withdrew its December 10 order. App. 300; App. to Pet. for Cert. 6a. Once ADEC issued the permit, EPA explained, that order lacked utility. On July 16, 2003, ADEC granted Cominco a PSD permit to construct MG–17 with SCR as BACT. Letter from Theodore B. Olson, Solicitor General, to William K. Suter, Clerk of the Court (Aug. 21, 2003). Under the July 16, 2003, permit, SCR ceases to be BACT "if and when the case currently pending before the Supreme Court of the United States of America is decided in favor of the State of Alaska." ADEC, Air Quality Construction Permit, Final Technical Analysis Report, Permit No. 9932–AC005, Revision 2, p. 7.

* * *

III

A

Centrally at issue in this case is the question whether EPA's oversight role, described by Congress in CAA § § 113(a)(5) and 167, see *supra,* at—7, extends to ensuring that a state permitting authority's BACT determination is reasonable in light of the statutory guides. Sections 113(a)(5) and 167 lodge in the Agency encompassing supervisory responsibility over the construction and modification of pollutant emitting facilities in areas covered by the PSD program. 42 U.S.C. § § 7413(a)(5) and 7477. In notably capacious terms, Congress armed EPA with authority to issue orders stopping construction when "a State is not acting in compliance with any [CAA] requirement or prohibition ... relating to the construction of new sources or the modification of existing sources," § 7413(a)(5), or when "construction or modification of a major emitting facility ... does not conform to the requirements of [the PSD program]," § 7477.

The federal Act enumerates several "[p]reconstruction requirements" for the PSD program. § 7475. Absent these, "[n]o major emitting facility ... may be constructed." *Ibid.* One express preconstruction requirement is inclusion of a BACT determination in a facility's PSD permit. §§ 7475(a)(1) and (4). As earlier set out, see *supra,* at 993, the Act defines BACT as "an emission limitation based on the maximum degree of reduction of [a] pollutant ... which the permitting authority, on a case-by-case basis, taking into account energy, environmental, and economic impacts and other costs, determines is achievable for [a] facility." § 7479(3). Under this formulation, the permitting authority, ADEC here, exercises primary or initial responsibility for identifying BACT in line with the Act's definition of that term.

All parties agree that one of the "many requirements in the PSD provisions that the EPA may enforce" is "that a [PSD] permit contain a BACT limitation." Brief for Petitioner 34; see *id.,* at 22, 25 (same). See also Brief for Respondents 23. It is therefore undisputed that the Agency may issue an order to stop a facility's construction if a PSD permit contains no BACT designation.

EPA reads the Act's definition of BACT, together with CAA's explicit listing of BACT as a "[p]reconstruction requiremen[t]," to mandate not simply *a* BACT designation, but a determination of BACT faithful to the statute's definition. In keeping with the broad oversight role §§ 113(a)(5) and 167 vest in EPA, the Agency maintains, it may review permits to ensure that a State's BACT determination is reasonably moored to the Act's provisions. See *id.*, at 24. We hold, as elaborated below, that the Agency has rationally construed the Act's text and that EPA's construction warrants our respect and approbation.

BACT's statutory definition requires selection of an emission control technology that results in the "maximum" reduction of a pollutant "achievable for [a] facility" in view of "energy, environmental, and economic impacts, and other costs." 42 U.S.C. § 7479(3). This instruction, EPA submits, cabins state permitting authorities' discretion by granting only "authority to make *reasonable* BACT determinations," Brief for Respondents 27 (emphasis in original), *i.e.*, decisions made with fidelity to the Act's purpose "to insure that economic growth will occur in a manner consistent with the preservation of existing clean air resources," 42 U.S.C. § 7470(3). Noting that state permitting authorities' statutory discretion is constrained by CAA's strong, normative terms "maximum" and "achievable," § 7479(3),[12] EPA reads § § 113(a)(5) and 167 to empower the federal Agency to check a state agency's unreasonably lax BACT designation. See Brief for Respondents 27.

EPA stresses Congress' reason for enacting the PSD program—to prevent significant deterioration of air quality in clean-air areas within a State and in neighboring States. §§ 7470(3), (4); see *id.*, at 33. That aim, EPA urges, is unlikely to be realized absent an EPA surveillance role that extends to BACT determinations. The Agency notes in this regard a House Report observation:

"Without national guidelines for the prevention of significant deterioration a State deciding to protect its clean air resources will face a double threat. The prospect is very real that such a State would lose existing industrial plants to more permissive States. But additionally the State will likely become the target of "economic-environmental blackmail" from new industrial plants that will play one State off against another with threats to locate in whichever State adopts the most permissive pollution controls." H.R.Rep. No. 95–294, p. 134 (1977), U.S.Code Cong. & Admin.News 1977, 1077, 1213.

The House Report further observed that "a community that sets and enforces strict standards may still find its air polluted from sources in another community or another State." *Id.*, at 135, U.S.Code Cong. & Admin.News 1977, 1077, 1214 (quoting 116 Cong. Rec. 32909 (1970)). Federal agency surveillance of a State's BACT designation is needed, EPA asserts, to restrain the interjurisdictional pressures to which Congress was alert. See Brief for Respondents 33–34, 43; Brief for Vermont

12. Formulations similar to the BACT definition's "maximum degree of [pollutant] reduction ... achievable" appear in the Act's standards for new sources in non-attainment areas, 42 U.S.C. §§ 7501(3) and 7503(a)(2) ("lowest achievable emission rate") (internal quotation marks omitted), and its technology-based standard for hazardous emissions, § 7412(d)(2) ("maximum degree of reduction ... achievable").

et al. as *Amici Curiae* 12 ("If EPA has authority to ensure a reasonable level of consistency among BACT determinations nationwide, then every State can feel more confident about maintaining stringent standards without fear of losing its current industry or alienating prospective industry.").

The CAA construction EPA advances in this litigation is reflected in interpretive guides the Agency has several times published. See App. 268–269 (1983 EPA PSD guidance memorandum noting the Agency's "oversight function"); *id.,* at 274 (1988 EPA guidance memorandum stating EPA may find a BACT determination deficient if it is "not based on a reasoned analysis"); *id.,* at 281–282 (1993 guidance memorandum stating that "EPA acts to ensure that the state exercises its discretion within the bounds of the law" (internal quotation marks omitted); as to BACT, EPA will not intervene if the state agency has given "a reasoned justification for the basis of its decision" (internal quotation marks omitted)). See also Approval and Promulgation of Air Quality Implementation Plans; Commonwealth of Virginia—Prevention of Significant Deterioration Program, 63 Fed.Reg. 13797 (1998) (EPA will "review whether any determination by the permitting authority was made on reasonable grounds properly supported on the record, described in enforceable terms, and consistent with all applicable requirements"). We "normally accord particular deference to an agency interpretation of 'longstanding' duration," *Barnhart v. Walton,* 535 U.S. 212, 220, 122 S.Ct. 1265, 152 L.Ed.2d 330 (2002) (quoting *North Haven Bd. of Ed. v. Bell,* 456 U.S. 512, 522, n. 12, 102 S.Ct. 1912, 72 L.Ed.2d 299 (1982)), recognizing that "well-reasoned views" of an expert administrator rest on " 'a body of experience and informed judgment to which courts and litigants may properly resort for guidance,' " *Bragdon v. Abbott,* 524 U.S. 624, 642, 118 S.Ct. 2196, 141 L.Ed.2d 540 (1998) (quoting *Skidmore v. Swift & Co.,* 323 U.S. 134, 139–140, 65 S.Ct. 161, 89 L.Ed. 124 (1944)).

* * *

B

ADEC assails the Agency's construction of the Act on several grounds. Its arguments do not persuade us to reject as impermissible EPA's longstanding, consistently maintained interpretation.

ADEC argues that the statutory definition of BACT, § 7479(3), unambiguously assigns to "the permitting authority" alone determination of the control technology qualifying as "best available." Brief for Petitioner 21–26. Because the Act places responsibility for determining BACT with "the permitting authority," ADEC urges, CAA excludes federal Agency surveillance reaching the substance of the BACT decision. *Id.,* at 22–25. EPA's enforcement role, ADEC maintains, is restricted to the requirement "that the permit contain a BACT limitation." *Id.,* at 34.

Understandably, Congress entrusted state permitting authorities with initial responsibility to make BACT determinations "case-by-case." § 7479(3). A state agency, no doubt, is best positioned to adjust for local differences in raw materials or plant configurations, differences that might make a technology "unavailable" in a particular area. But the fact that the relevant statutory guides—"maximum" pollution reduction, considerations of energy, environmental, and economic impacts—may not yield a "single, objectively 'correct' BACT determination," *id.,* at 23, surely does not signify that there can be no *unreasonable* determinations. Nor does Congress' sensitivity to site-specific factors necessarily imply a design to preclude in this context meaningful EPA oversight under §§ 113(a)(5) and 167. EPA claims no prerogative to designate the correct BACT; the Agency asserts only the authority to guard against unreasonable designations. See 298 F.3d, at 821 ("the question presented is what requirements the *state* must meet," not what final substantive decision the State must make (emphasis in original)).[13]

Under ADEC's interpretation, EPA properly inquires whether a BACT determination appears in a PSD permit, Brief for Petitioner 34, but not whether that BACT determination "was made on reasonable grounds properly supported on the record," 63 Fed.Reg., at 13797. Congress, however, vested EPA with explicit and sweeping authority to enforce CAA "requirements" relating to the construction and modification of sources under the PSD program, including BACT. We fail to see why Congress, having expressly endorsed an expansive surveillance role for EPA in two independent CAA provisions, would then implicitly preclude the Agency from verifying substantive compliance with the BACT provisions and, instead, limit EPA's superintendence to the insubstantial question whether the state permitting authority had uttered the key words "BACT."

---

13. The dissent admonishes that "a statute is to be read as a whole." *Post,* at— 3 (quoting *King v. St. Vincent's Hospital,* 502 U.S. 215, 221, 112 S.Ct. 570, 116 L.Ed.2d 578 (1991)). We give that unexceptional principle effect by attending both to the unequivocal grant of supervisory authority to EPA in §§ 113(a)(5) and 167, and to the statutory control on permitting authorities' discretion contained in the BACT definition, 42 U.S.C. § 7479(3). It is, moreover, "a cardinal principle of statutory construction" that "a statute ought, upon the whole, to be so construed that, if it can be prevented, no clause, sentence, or word shall be superfluous, void, or insignificant." *TRW Inc. v. Andrews,* 534 U.S. 19, 31, 122 S.Ct. 441, 151 L.Ed.2d 339 (2001) (quoting *Duncan v. Walker,* 533 U.S. 167, 174, 121 S.Ct. 2120, 150 L.Ed.2d 251 (2001)). The Act instructs permitting authorities to identify the "best," "maximum" emission reduction technique, taking account of costs. 42 U.S.C. § 7479(3). The dissent does not

explain how that instruction can be construed as something other than a constraint on permitting authorities' discretion. Ultimately, the dissent recognizes the essential statutory requirement: selection of "the technology that can *best* reduce pollution within practical constraints." *Post,* at—4 (emphasis added).

Nor do we find enlightening Congress' inclusion of the word "determines" in the BACT definition. *Post,* at——2. Even under the dissent's view of the Act, state permitting authorities' BACT determinations are not "conclusiv[e] and authoritativ[e]." *Ibid.* (internal quotation marks and citation omitted). As the dissent develops at length, review of such BACT determinations may be sought in state court. *Post,* at———— 7–11; Alaska Stat. § 44.62.560 (2002). And EPA actions, of course, are subject to "the process of judicial review," see *post,* at—— 1, Congress empowered federal courts to provide, here in 42 U.S.C. § 7607(b)(1). See *supra,* at————16–17.

We emphasize, however, that EPA's rendition of the Act's less than crystalline text leaves the "permitting authority" considerable leeway. The Agency acknowledges "the need to accord appropriate deference" to States' BACT designations, Brief for Respondents 43, and disclaims any intention to " 'second guess' state decisions," 63 Fed.Reg., at 13797. Only when a state agency's BACT determination is "not based on a reasoned analysis," App. 274, may EPA step in to ensure that the statutory requirements are honored.[14] EPA adhered to that limited role here, explaining why ADEC's BACT determination was "arbitrary" and contrary to ADEC's own findings. *Id.*, at 149–150. EPA's limited but vital role in enforcing BACT is consistent with a scheme that "places primary responsibilities and authority with the States, backed by the Federal Government." S.Rep. No. 95–127, p. 29.

* * *

Nor do we find compelling ADEC's suggestion, reiterated by the dissent, that, if state courts are not the exclusive judicial arbiters, EPA would be free to invalidate a BACT determination "months, even years, after a permit has been issued." Brief for Petitioner 35; *post,* at————11–13. This case threatens no such development. It involves preconstruction orders issued by EPA, see *supra,* at——14, not postconstruction federal Agency directives. EPA itself regards it as "imperative" to act on a timely basis, recognizing that courts are "less likely to require new sources to accept more stringent permit conditions the farther planning and construction have progressed." App. 273 (July 15, 1988, EPA guidance memorandum). In the one instance of untimely EPA action ADEC identifies, the federal courts declined to permit enforcement to proceed. See *United States v. AM General Corp.,* 34 F.3d 472, 475 (C.A.7 1994) (affirming District Court's dismissal of an EPA-initiated enforcement action where EPA did not act until well after the facility received a PSD permit and completed plant modifications). EPA, we are confident, could not indulge in the inequitable conduct ADEC and the dissent hypothesize while the federal courts sit to review EPA's actions. Cf. *Walz v. Tax Comm'n of City of New York,* 397 U.S. 664, 678–679, 90 S.Ct. 1409, 25 L.Ed.2d 697 (1970); *Panhandle Oil Co. v. Mississippi ex rel. Knox,* 277 U.S. 218, 223, 48 S.Ct. 451, 72 L.Ed. 857 (1928) (Holmes, J., dissenting), overruled in part by *Alabama v. King & Boozer,* 314 U.S. 1, 8–9, 62 S.Ct. 43, 86 L.Ed. 3 (1941).

14. According to the Agency, "[i]t has proven to be relatively rare that a state agency has put EPA in the position of having to exercise [its] authority," noting that only two other reported judicial decisions concern EPA orders occasioned by States' faulty BACT determinations. Brief for Respondents 30, and n. 9 (citing *Allsteel, Inc. v. EPA,* 25 F.3d 312 (C.A.6 1994), and *Solar Turbines Inc. v. Seif,* 879 F.2d 1073 (C.A.3 1989)). EPA's restrained and moderate use of its authority hardly supports the dissent's speculation that the federal Agency will "displac[e]" or "degrad[e]" state agencies or relegate them to the performance of "ministerial" functions. *Post,* at __, ___-___. Nor has EPA ever asserted authority to override a state-court judgment. Cf. *post,* at——10. Preclusion principles, we note in this regard, unquestionably do apply against the United States, its agencies and officers. See, *e.g., Montana v. United States,* 440 U.S. 147, 99 S.Ct. 970, 59 L.Ed.2d 210 (1979).

In sum, EPA interprets the Act to allow substantive federal Agency surveillance of state permitting authorities' BACT determinations subject to federal court review. We credit EPA's longstanding construction of the Act and confirm EPA's authority, pursuant to § § 113(a)(5) and 167, to rule on the reasonableness of BACT decisions by state permitting authorities.

* * *

Affirmed.

Justice KENNEDY, with whom THE CHIEF JUSTICE, Justice SCALIA, and Justice THOMAS join, dissenting.

The majority, in my respectful view, rests its holding on mistaken premises, for its reasoning conflicts with the express language of the Clean Air Act (CAA or Act), with sound rules of administrative law, and with principles that preserve the integrity of States in our federal system. The State of Alaska had in place procedures that were in full compliance with the governing statute and accompanying regulations promulgated by the Environmental Protection Agency (EPA). As I understand the opinion of the Court and the parties' submissions, there is no disagreement on this point. Alaska followed these procedures to determine the best available control technology (BACT). EPA, however, sought to overturn the State's decision, not by the process of judicial review, but by administrative fiat. The Court errs, in my judgment, by failing to hold that EPA, based on nothing more than its substantive disagreement with the State's discretionary judgment, exceeded its powers in setting aside Alaska's BACT determination.

I

As the majority explains, the case begins with §§ 113(a)(5) and 167 of the Act. 42 U.S.C. §§ 7413(a)(5), 7477. These provisions give EPA authority to enforce "requirements" of the CAA. The meaning of the word "requiremen[t]," though, is not defined in these provisions. Other provisions of the Act must be consulted. All parties agree that the requirement in this case is the "preconstruction requiremen[t]" that a "major emitting facility" be "subject to the best available technology [BACT] for each pollutant subject to regulation under this chapter emitted from, or which results from, such facility." § 7475(a)(4). BACT, in turn, is defined as

"an emission limitation based on the maximum degree of reduction of each pollutant subject to regulation under this chapter emitted from or which results from any major emitting facility, which the permitting authority, on a case-by-case basis, taking into account energy, environmental, and economic impacts and other costs, determines is achievable for such facility through application of production processes and available methods, systems, and techniques...." § 7479(3).

The majority holds that, under the CAA, state agencies are vested with "initial responsibility for identifying BACT in line with the Act's definition of that term" and that EPA has a "broad oversight role" to ensure that a State's BACT determination is "reasonably moored to the Act's provisions." *Ante,* at————18–19. The statute, however, contemplates no such arrangement. It directs the "permitting authority"— here, the Alaska Department of Environmental Conservation (ADEC)— to "determine" what constitutes BACT. To "determine" is not simply to make an initial recommendation that can later be overturned. It is "[t]o decide or settle . . . conclusively and authoritatively." American Heritage Dictionary 495 (4th ed.2000). Cf. 5 U.S.C. § 554 ("to be determined on the record after opportunity for an agency hearing").

The BACT definition presumes that the permitting authority will exercise discretion. It presumes, in addition, that the BACT decision will accord full consideration to the statutory factors and other relevant and necessary criteria. Contrary to the majority's holding, the statute does not direct the State to find as BACT the technology that results in the "maximum reduction of a pollutant achievable for [a] facility" in the abstract. *Ante,* at——19 (internal quotation marks omitted). Indeed, for a State to do so without regard to the other mandatory criteria would be to ignore the words of the statute. The Act requires a more comprehensive judgment. It provides that the permitting authority must "tak[e] into account" a set of contextual considerations—"energy, environmental, and economic impacts and other costs"—to identify the best control technology "on a case-by-case basis." 42 U.S.C. § 7479(3). The majority reaches its narrow view of the scope of the State's discretion only by wresting two adjectives, "maximum" and "achievable," out of context. In doing so, it ignores "the cardinal rule that a statute is to be read as a whole." *King v. St. Vincent's Hospital,* 502 U.S. 215, 221, 112 S.Ct. 570, 116 L.Ed.2d 578 (1991).

To be sure, §§ 113(a)(5) and 167 authorize EPA to enforce requirements of the Act. These provisions, however, do not limit the States' latitude and responsibility to balance all the statutory factors in making their discretionary judgments. If a State has complied with the Act's requirements, §§ 113(a)(5) and 167 are not implicated and can supply no separate basis for EPA to exercise a supervisory role over a State's discretionary decision. The Court of Appeals for the Ninth Circuit had it altogether backwards when it reasoned that, "because neither Section 113(a)(5) nor Section 167 contains any exemption for requirements that involve the state's exercise of discretion," EPA had the authority to issue orders countermanding the State's BACT determination. 298 F.3d 814, 820 (2002). The question is not whether the two sections contain any exemption. Rather, it is about the nature of the Act's requirements and whether EPA has the authority to set aside a BACT determination when no requirement of the Act was violated in the first place. In affirming the judgment of the Court of Appeals, the majority repeats the same analytical error. See *ante,* at——24 ("We fail to see why Congress, having expressly endorsed an expansive surveillance role for EPA in two independent CAA provisions, would then implicitly preclude the Agency from verifying substantive compliance with [BACT] . . ."). When the statute is read as a whole, it is clear that the CAA commits BACT determinations to the discretion of the relevant permitting authorities. Unless an objecting party, including EPA, prevails on judicial review, the determinations are conclusive.

Here the state agency, ADEC, recognized it was required to make a BACT determination. It issued two detailed reports in response to comments by interested parties and concluded that Low Nitrogen Oxide (NOx) was BACT. The requirement that the agency weigh the list of statutory factors, study all other relevant considerations, and decide the technology that can best reduce pollution within practical constraints was met in full. As even EPA acknowledged, ADEC "provid[ed] a detailed accounting of the process." App. 286. This is not a case, then, where the state agency failed to have a BACT review procedure in place or altogether refused to apply the statute's formal requirements. EPA's only quarrel is with ADEC's substantive conclusion. In disagreeing with ADEC, EPA's sole contention, in the section of its order titled "Findings of *Fact*," is that "SCR is BACT." App. to Pet. for Cert. 30a, 34a (emphasis added). In addition, EPA does not allege that using Low NOx would violate other CAA requirements, such as the National Ambient Air Quality Standards, Alaska's Prevention of Significant Deterioration (PSD) increments, or other applicable emission standards, see 42 U.S.C. § 7475(a)(3). On this state of the record there is no deviation from any statutory "requirement." As a result, EPA has no statutory basis to invoke the enforcement authority of §§ 113(a)(5) and 167.

When Congress intends to give EPA general supervisory authority, it says so in clear terms. In addition to requiring EPA's advance approval of BACT determinations in some instances, 42 U.S.C. § 7475(a)(8), the statute grants EPA powers to block the construction or operation of polluting sources in circumstances not at issue here, §§ 7426(b), (c)(1), 7410(a)(2)(D)(i). Outside the context of the CAA, Congress likewise knows how to establish federal oversight in unambiguous language. See, *e.g.,* 42 U.S.C. § 1396a(a)(13)(A) (1994 ed.) (requiring, under the Medicaid Act, reimbursement according to rates that a "State finds, and makes assurances satisfactory to the Secretary [of Health and Human Services], are reasonable and adequate to meet the costs which must be incurred by efficiently and economically operated facilities"); *Wilder v. Virginia Hospital Assn.,* 496 U.S. 498, 110 S.Ct. 2510, 110 L.Ed.2d 455 (1990). No analogous language is used in the statutory definition of BACT.

EPA insists it needs oversight authority to prevent a "race to the bottom," where jurisdictions compete with each other to lower environmental standards to attract new industries and keep existing businesses within their borders. Whatever the merits of these arguments as a general matter, EPA's distrust of state agencies is inconsistent with the Act's clear mandate that States bear the primary role in controlling pollution and, here, the exclusive role in making BACT determinations.

In "cho[osing] not to dictate a Federal response to balancing sometimes conflicting goals" at the expense of "[m]aximum flexibility and State discretion," H.R.Rep. No. 95–294, p. 146 (1977), U.S.Code Cong. & Admin.News 1977, 1077, 1225, Congress made the overriding judgment that States are more responsive to local conditions and can strike the right balance between preserving environmental quality and advancing competing objectives. By assigning certain functions to the States, Congress assumed they would have a stake in implementing the environmental objectives of the Act. At the same time, Congress charged EPA with setting ambient standards and enforcing emission limits, 42 U.S.C. § 7475(a)(3), to ensure that the Nation takes the necessary steps to reduce air pollution.

The presumption that state agencies are not to be trusted to do their part is unwarranted in another respect: EPA itself said so. As EPA concedes, States, by and large, take their statutory responsibility seriously, and EPA sees no reason to intervene in the vast majority of cases. Brief for Respondents 30, n. 9; 57 Fed.Reg. 28095 (1992) ("States have been largely successful in ['administering and enforcing the various components of the PSD program'], and EPA's involvement in interpretative and enforcement issues is limited ... "). In light of this concession, EPA and *amici* not only fail to overcome the established presumption that States act in good faith, see Alden v. Maine, 527 U.S. 706, 755, 119 S.Ct. 2240, 144 L.Ed.2d 636 (1999) ("We are unwilling to assume the States will refuse to honor ... or obey the binding laws of the United States"), but also admit that their fears about a race to the bottom bear little relation to the real-world experience under the statute. See *ante,* at——36 ("We see no reason not to take EPA at its word").

* * *

For these reasons, and with all respect, I dissent from the opinion and the judgment of the Court.

VII.   CLEAN AIR ACT—REGULATION OF HAZARDOUS AIR POLLUTION

A.   History of the regulation of HAP–the change to technology based standards

The criteria pollutants have received the most attention under the Clean Air Act. These sources, which result primarily from combustion, are present in large quantities, and at least theoretically are not dangerous under a certain threshold—the National Ambient Air Quality Standards. There are other dangerous air contaminants however that may be produced on a smaller scale. These pollutants, many of them synthetic chemicals, can be hazardous or even toxic in very small quantities. Regulating these pollutants has been even more difficult than the regulation of the criteria pollutants.

The 1970 amendments to the Clean Air Act first established a strict regime for reducing emissions of these hazardous air pollutants

("HAP"). EPA was required to list as an HAP an air pollutant "which might reasonably have been anticipated to result in an increase in mortality or an increase in serious irreversible, or incapacitating reversible illness" 42 USCA 7412(a)(1), and once listed, to establish health based emission standards which provide an ample margin of safety to protect the public health. 42 USCA 7412(b)(1)(B). Substances listed as criteria pollutants were not considered under this category.

Just as with the setting of the NAAQS, the question of the EPA's ability to consider cost in standard setting arose early. In *Natural Resource Defense Council v. U.S. EPA*, 824 F2d 1146 (D.C.Cir. 1987), the NRDC argued that once EPA had concluded that the emission of vinyl chloride created an adverse health effect, even if it was unable to determine a safe threshold, Section 112 required EPA to establish a threshold of zero, which would effectively shut down the industry. The EPA disagreed and adopted a standard based solely on the level attainable by the best available control technology (BACT). The Court held that neither NRDC nor EPA were correct and remanded the case to EPA with instructions that EPA set a standard, which takes into account the effect the chosen emission standard has on health, in making the initial determination of what is "safe".

Effectively, the Court read Section 112 to require EPA to determine what is "safe" solely on the basis of risk to health at a particular emission level. However, the Court stated "safe" does not mean risk free but rather that the Administrator is to determine what is an acceptable risk to health. If the Administrator cannot find an acceptable risk at any level then he was to set the standard at zero emissions. Once the initial level was set, the Administrator was then required to set the appropriate standard at a level that ensures an ample margin of safety to protect the public. Only at this point was the Administrator free to take into account other factors, including technology and economics, in lowering the initial standard to the lowest feasible level.

This standard, which arguably followed Congress's intent, presented unusual problems for the EPA. Unlike the criteria pollutants, many of the HAPs might be harmful in extremely small doses, effectively banning certain chemicals that played an important part in [the economy]. Thus, despite litigation and pressure from Congress, between 1970 and 1990 the EPA identified only eight of the hundreds of hazardous air pollutants already listed by state agencies, and many of these were spurred by litigation against the agency. The first was asbestos, which was listed in 1971 with standards established in 1973. Later EPA listed benzene, beryllium, coke oven emissions, inorganic arsenic, mercury, radionuclide, and vinyl chloride.

In response to the NRDC case, in 1989, the EPA promulgated new standards for establishing national emission standards for hazardous pollutants that established a risk-based approach. This approach allowed the EPA to set the standard at a level that "(1) protects the greatest number of persons possible to a lifetime risk level no higher than 1 in 1 million and (2) limiting to no higher than 1 in 10 thousand the estimated risk that a person living near a plant would have if they were exposed for 70 years. In undertaking this analysis the EPA stated that it would first consider the extent of the estimated risk to an individual who is exposed for a lifetime; if it is less than 1 in 10 thousand that risk is acceptable. This is the maximum individual risk (MIR), which establishes the baseline. In setting the standard to ensure an ample margin of safety, EPA will then determine whether the risk is above or below that baseline. In this second step, EPA strives to provide protection to the greatest number of persons to an individual lifetime risk level no higher than 1 in 1 million. 54 Fed Reg 38,044 (1989).

In spite of passing new regulations defining how it would determine the appropriate threshold for a standard, the EPA continued to delay setting standards. As a result of the EPA's failure to act, in the 1990 CAA amendments Congress imposed a technology based regime with strict requirements that limited the agency's discretion and imposed short timelines for compliance. The regulatory model imposed on Hazardous Air Pollutants contrasted starkly with the models imposed on criteria pollutants (Congress required EPA to establish NAAQS which were to be achieved over several years through a variety of control mechanisms depending upon the severity of non-attainment) or the emissions trading programs that were established to reduce sulfur dioxide emissions. Instead, Congress set out a detailed and comprehensive plan that the EPA was required to implement in order to reduce emissions of hazardous air pollutants.

As a first step, rather than asking the EPA to develop a list, Congress itself listed 189 substances as hazardous air pollutants. Congress compiled the list from information furnished by companies in compliance with the Emergency Planning and Community Right to Know Act, 42 USC Section 1100 et. seq.[53]

The EPA was then required to review the list, either on its own initiative or in response to a petition,[54] on a continuous basis and was mandated to add a pollutant to the list if it presents or may present a threat of adverse human health affect or adverse environmental effect. See 42 USC Section 112 (b) (2). This effectively lowered the threshold for inclusion of a pollutant on the HCA list[55].

The EPA was then given 12 months (until November 15, 1991) to publish a list of the sources of the air pollutants.[56] The sources were

---

53. Information generated from the Super Fund Right to Know rule (SARA Section 313) indicated that more than 2.7 billion pounds of toxic air pollutants are emitted annually in the US.

54. Third parties were given the right to petition the EPA to have a pollutant added or removed from the list. Within 18 months of receipt of the petition, the EPA Administrator is required to either accept or deny the petition.

55. The EPA was no longer required to find that the pollutant caused a "serious" illness in humans.

56. Requiring the EPA to issue standards for each source rather than for each pollutant is another significant difference between the HAP program and the criteria pollutant program.

required to be classified as "major", i.e., a stationary source that emits 10 tons per year or more of any hazardous pollutant or 25 tons per year of any combination of hazardous air pollutants or "area," which includes all other stationary sources that emit hazardous air pollutants.[57]

Once sources were listed, Congress required a two-phase process. In Phase I, EPA was required to establish technological standards[58] *See National Lime Ass'n v. EPA,* 233 F.3d 625 (D.C.Cir. 2000) for each category of major sources and area sources that had been listed in accordance with the schedules established in sections (c) and (e). 42 USCA sect 7412(d)(1).

To ensure that there would be no delays in implementing controls, Congress stipulated that if the EPA failed to set a MACT standard for a major source within the specified time, each source in the category would be required to submit a Title V permit application.[59] The Title V permit was required to contain emission limitations that were determined on a case by case basis to be equivalent to the limitation that would apply to such source if an emission standard had been promulgated in a timely manner. 42 USC Section 7412(j)(5).

Congress established specific deadlines by which EPA was to promulgate the Maximum Achievable Control Technology (MACT) standards[60]: By 1992, the EPA was to issue MACT standards for the 40 most harmful HAPs, an additional 25% of the listed HAPs by 1994, an additional 25% by 1997 and the rest by 2000. In reality, by 1996 EPA had issued 17 MACT standards covering 29 major sources. 26 Envt Rept 1891 (1996).

57. In an attempt to remove impediments to speedy implementation Congress chose to set standards for a "source" rather than pollutant by pollutant).

58. Congress recognized that the previous law failed to work because of the reliance on "health based control" and substituted it for technology based controls in the 1990 version.

59. Of interest is the fact that Congress felt compelled to state that although the Administrator had discretion in how he developed the emission standards "there shall be no delay in the compliance date for any standard applicable to any source under subsection (i) of this section" as a result of the discretionary authority conveyed.

60. 42 USCA § 7412(d)(2) states that "Emissions standards promulgated under this subsection and applicable to new or existing sources of hazardous air pollutants shall require the maximum degree of reduction in emissions of the hazardous air pollutants subject to this section (including a prohibition on such emissions, where achievable) that the Administrator, taking into consideration the cost of achieving such emissions reduction, and any non-air quality health and environmental impacts and energy requirements, determines is achievable for new or existing sources in the category or subcategory to which such emission standard applies, through application of measures, processes, methods, systems or techniques including, but not limited to, measures which—

(A) reduce the volume of, or eliminate emissions of, such pollutants through process changes, substitution of materials or other modification,

(B) enclose systems or processes to eliminate emissions,

(C) collect, capture or treat such pollutants when released from a process, stack, storage or fugitive emissions point,

(D) are design, equipment, work practice, or operational standards (including requirements for operator training or certification) as provided in subsection (h) of this section, or are

(E) a combination of the above."

Congress also provided an incentive for companies to strive for early compliance. If a source had met 90% of the standard before it was required to do so, the source was given an additional six years to attain the final 10% compliance.

All major sources (new and existing[61]) were required to implement technology which provided the "maximum degree of reduction in emissions of the hazardous air pollutants," or MACT devices. In determining which devices could be required, the Administrator was invited to take into consideration the cost, any non-air quality health, environmental or energy impacts or requirements. 42 USCA Sect. 7412 (d) (2).

However, Congress effectively set the MACT as a floor or minimum control by requiring that any MACT deemed achievable for a new major source could not be less stringent than the emission control that is achieved in practice by the best controlled similar source" 42 USCA § 7412(d)(3). In contrast, the MACT standard for existing major sources was to be "less stringent than standards for new sources but not less stringent then the average emission limitation achieved by the best performing 12 percent of the existing sources or the average emission limitation achieved for the best 5 sources in a category with fewer than 30 sources." 42 USCA § 7412(3)(A) and (B).

With respect to area sources, i.e., all other sources that emit one of the listed Hazardous Pollutants, the Administrator was permitted to enact standards that provide for the use of generally available control technologies or management practices to reduce emissions. 42 USCA Section 7412(d)(5). Footnote: National Mining Association v. U.S. EPA, 59 F.3d 1351 (D.C.Cir. 1995).

B. Health Based Standards Remain

By focusing the EPA's attention on technology standards, Congress intended that the EPA would be able to quickly enunciate the applicable pollution control mechanisms, thereby effecting a noticeable reduction in emissions of HAPs. However, Congress did not eliminate the goal of health protection if the technology controls did not adequately do so. The 1990 Act directed the EPA to determine whether the MACT standards had worked in protecting health and required the EPA to report to Congress on any residual risk, which continued after application of MACT. The report would enable Congress to enact legislation before the Phase II requirements began. If Congress failed to enact legislation, Phase II would begin eight years after implementation of MACT standards. Congress has not enacted legislation to change the standard although the EPA and third parties have accumulated evidence that HAPs continue to pose a substantial health risk.

In Phase II, the EPA is to assess whether the MACT standards for a category of sources emitting a known, probable or possible carcinogen

---

61. Applying the Clean Air Act to existing sources was a new feature of the 1990 amendments.

reduced lifetime excess cancer risks to the most exposed population to less than one in one million. If not, the EPA is required to prepare standards that would address the residual risks created by emission of the particular HAP. This second phase is referred to as the "health based standards."

Changes in government have impacted the implementation of the HAP program since its inception. Most recently, under the George W. Bush Administration, the EPA has proposed regulating by a cap and trade approach rather than the technology approach specified in Sec. 112. This has been attacked* as illegal and unwise, but it shows the tremendous effect the administration also has on toxic air pollutants.

The 1990 amendments also show what can happen when the agency does not readily follow Congress's perceived direction. In each provision of the modern Hazardous Air Pollutant section, Congress constrained the Administrator's discretion by dictating what pollutants would be on the list, which sources would be subject to emission controls and the level of technology that would be required.

VIII. THE CLEAN AIR ACT—MOBILE SOURCES

Many of the criteria pollutants come from the exhaust of cars, trucks, and other mobile sources. Unlike stationary sources, the regulation of pollution from mobile sources does not lend itself well to state control. Most automobiles are in a nationwide market and can be transported easily. Thus, the CAA amendments of 1970 proposed a federal solution that was to require significant reductions in mobile source pollution within 5 years. These deadlines were later amended, but the national requirements have remained. With one exception, these requirements are uniform. Because it was seen as having a more intractable problem with mobile source pollution and had already begun regulating these sources before the passage of the 1970 CAA amendments, California has been allowed to create additional controls.

In addition, mobile source control can also be seen as encompassing controls on the fuel that will be used in the sources. The 1990 Amendments created fuel standards that had to be adopted depending on the severity of the ozone or Carbon Monoxide non-compliance problem in an area.

Though mobile sources have indeed become less polluting per unit of energy emitted over the last thirty years, the sheer growth in the volume of sources and miles traveled threatens to swamp the gains that have been made. Though states could regulate mobile sources indirectly through zoning or other transportation demand management techniques, most control of mobile sources comes through this section of the Clean Air Act. The following excerpt provides an excellent account of mobile source controls and the issues involved therein. Although the environmental lawyer may not routinely deal with mobile source con-

* Catherine A. O'Neill, Mercury, Risk, and Justice, 34 ELR 11070 (2004).

trols, with increased control on stationary sources, it is possible that the solution to truly clean air may only exist with reductions in mobile source emissions. Therefore, it is important to know the regulatory structure involved.

ENVIRONMENTAL LAWYER
FEBRUARY, 2000

Arnold W. Reitze, Jr.

[citations omitted].

ARTICLES

MOBILE SOURCE AIR POLLUTION CONTROL

The reduction of air pollution from mobile sources is a major goal of the Clean Air Act. The United States Environmental Protection Agency has interpreted the statute's requirements in thousands of pages of the Federal Register and through other guidance documents. Moreover, states regulate the use of vehicles and impose controls on their transportation systems to protect air quality....

The major regulated pollutants from motor vehicles are carbon monoxide (CO), nitrogen oxides (NOx), hydrocarbons (HC) or volatile organic compounds (VOCs), which are a chemically reactive subset of HC, and particulate matter (PM10) from diesel engines. VOCs and NOx react in the presence of sunlight to produce photochemical oxidants. Photochemical oxidants, which include ozone and a myriad of less easily identifiable air pollutants, are commonly known as smog.

In 1997, transportation sources in the United States were responsible for a large percentage of the nations total emissions, including: 76.6% of the CO emissions; 49.2% of the NOx; 39.9% of the VOCs; 23.0% of the PM10, 13.3% of the lead; and 6.8% of the S02 emissions. From 1988 to 1997, CO emissions from transportation sources in the United States decreased by twenty-five percent, and VOCs decreased by twenty-eight percent. Nitrogen oxide emissions from highway vehicles decreased eight percent from 1988 to 1997.

Other substances emitted from motor vehicles may be regulated as hazardous air pollutants (HAPs). Motor vehicles are responsible for the release of approximately twenty-one percent of the nation's HAP, although the percentages contributed in each state ranges from as much as fifty-five percent in Hawaii to as low as ten percent in Alabama. EPA estimates that HAP emissions from mobile sources decreased about sixteen percent from 1993 to 1996, primarily because of the shift to the use of reformulated gasoline. For the thirty HAPs that pose the most significant health risk, EPA estimates that mobile sources contribute thirty-one percent in rural areas and forty-five percent in urban areas.

In addition, motor vehicles are significant sources of stratospheric ozone-depleting substances because of the chemicals used in motor vehicle air conditioners.

Transportation sources also accounted for thirty-two percent of the United States carbon dioxide (CO2) emissions from fossil fuel consumption in 1997. CO2 is the leading cause of global warming. Each gallon of gasoline used by a motor vehicle results in the release of about twenty pounds of C02 (containing 5.47 pounds of carbon) into the atmosphere. Since 1984, C02 emissions from United States transportation sources have increased from 379.0 million metric tons (mmt) of carbon to 473.1 mmt in 1997. However, this tonnage increase represents just a 1.7% increase in the transportation share of the overall C02 emissions from total fossil fuel use over the same period of time. The worldwide contribution of emissions of global warming gases from motor vehicles is far more dramatic. Since 1950, the worldwide total of automobiles has increased from about 53 million to about 486 million in 1996, which has resulted in a decrease in the United States' percentage of the world's automobiles from 76.0% to 26.7%.

Today motor vehicles used in the United States emit significantly less pollution per mile traveled than the vehicles of the 1960s. As previously discussed, however, in 1997 transportation sources still accounted for over three-quarters of the CO, about two-fifths of the VOC, and about half of the NOx emissions in the United States. The improvements in emissions from mobile sources were made while annual vehicle miles traveled (VMT) increased. Since the 1970 CAA Amendments were enacted, annual VMT has increased from slightly under 1.100 trillion miles to 2.560 trillion miles in 1997. This increase in the use of motor vehicles helped nullify the reductions in exhaust emissions per VMT achieved through the use of air pollution controls. In addition, the increased size of the vehicle fleet reduced the overall effectiveness of evaporative controls. In 1970 there were 89.244 million automobiles and 14.211 million light trucks registered in the United States; in 1997 the number had increased to 129.749 million automobiles and 70.224 million light trucks.

These figures show that the mix of vehicles changed dramatically as sport utility vehicles (SUVs) and light-duty trucks (LDT) were used as substitutes for automobiles. In 1976 pickup trucks, vans and utility vehicles made up 19.8% of vehicle sales; that figure rose to 30.69% in 1998. The increased use of trucks and SUVs results in higher emissions and fuel efficiency that is significantly lower, than if consumers drove automobiles. The fuel economy of automobiles for the model year (MY) 1999 averages 28.3 miles per gallon (mpg), while MY 1999 LDT average 20.8 mpg. Fossil fuels used for transportation went from 8.38 quadrillion British Thermal Units or "quads" in 1950 to 16.04 quads in 1970 and then increased to 19.24 quads in 1977 and 21.80 quads in 1990. In 1998 the amount of fossil fuels used for transportation had climbed to 24.25 quads. This is an increase, for the 1988 to 1998 period, of 1.1% per year. Transportation used two-thirds of the petroleum consumed in the United

States in 1998. The reason that air quality in the United States has modestly improved despite substantial increases in vehicle miles traveled and in the size of the vehicle fleet is due to the development of technologies that have significantly reduced emissions per vehicle mile traveled.

* * *

C.   Exhaust Emissions

Exhaust emissions include unburned fuel and other HC, CO, and NOx. CO is a colorless, odorless, poisonous gas created from fuel combustion in an oxygen deficient environment resulting from an overly rich fuel mixture. The VOC component of HC and NOx are controlled primarily to prevent the formation of photochemical oxidants measured as ozone.In addition to their contribution to the creation of ozone, NOx react with water vapor to produce acid rain,and nitrous oxide is a greenhouse gas.

    1.   Control of Nitrogen Oxides From Motor Vehicles

Air is a mixture of gases, which is about seventy-eight percent nitrogen and about twenty-one percent oxygen by volume. Most NOx comes from the elemental nitrogen in the air which chemically reacts at high temperatures is used for combustion. When air is heated to over 1200–C (2192–F), nitrogen combines with oxygen to create nitric oxide, also called nitrogen oxide (NO). At temperatures above 1700–C (3092–F) the rate of NO formation increases significantly as shown by the following equation.

$$N_2 + O_2 \_ 2\,NO$$

Most of the nitrogen emissions from an internal combustion engine are in the form of NO. NO reacts instantly with oxygen at room temperature to form nitrogen dioxide (NO2).

$$2NO + O_2 \_ 2\,NO_2$$

NO2 is a criteria pollutant a pollutant controlled directly by the CAA. The NO2 then reacts with many substances. It combines with water to produce nitric acid (HNO3). It also reacts with ultraviolet light (hv) to produce ozone, as illustrated by the following chemical equations:

$$NO_2 + hv \_ NO + O$$

$$O + O_2 \_ O_3 + M$$

A major problem concerning the control of exhaust emissions is that, in general, increased air and combustion temperature decrease HC formation but increase NOx formation. The CO concentration in exhaust emissions is primarily a function of the air-to-fuel ratio. Increasing the supply of air decreases the supply of CO emissions. However, fuel rich mixtures and lower combustion temperatures will reduce NOx formation, but will increase CO and HC production. Thus, many vehicle manufacturers aim to reduce NOx formation during combustion and clean up the CO and HC emissions later in the vehicle's exhaust system.

Nevertheless, it should be emphasized that the relationship between HC, CO, and NOx formation is complex. Excess air usually increases NOx formation and reduces HC, however, the chemistry of combustion at various air-to-fuel ratios is quite complex.

Control strategies for NOx can be grouped into two categories: combustion controls and post-combustion controls. The principal post-combustion NOx control used in automobiles is the reduction catalyst discussed below. In contrast, combustion controls are aimed at adjusting the parameters of the burning of fuel to minimize NOx production. These include:

Combustion Temperature. A decrease in temperature reduces

NOx formation, but also decreases engine efficiency. Thus, more fuel is needed to do the same amount of work;

Air-to-Fuel Ratio. A very rich or very lean mixture reduces NOx formation, but a rich mixture increases HC and CO production and wastes fuel. A lean mixture may result in reduced performance;

Engine Speed (RPM). An increase in engine speed (RPM) will decrease NOx emissions;

Ambient Air Temperature. As ambient temperature decreases the intake air temperature decreases leading to decreased combustion temperatures and, thus, lower NOx emissions;

Humidity. Increased humidity in the intake air lowers NOx emissions.

2. Air-to-Fuel Ratio

Maximizing combustion efficiency, from an air pollution perspective, requires that all fuel be burned, and if this is achieved, the byproducts will be limited to heat, CO_2, water vapor, and nitrogen. This stoichiometric combustion results in no criteria air pollutants being released. The equation for complete combustion will vary depending upon the mix of combustible HC in the fuel.

* * *

III. Introduction to Legal Controls on Mobile Source Air Pollution

The technology for the control of motor vehicle emissions was driven by the legal requirements imposed on new vehicles by California and subsequently by the federal government. These legal developments will be examined in the material that follows.

* * *

The 1970 CAA Amendments provided the basic approach used today. Specifically, under the 1970 CAA Amendments:

> motor vehicle emissions were to be controlled primarily through improved technology mandated by the federal government for new vehicles (except for California); reduction of HC, CO, and NOx emissions from vehicles by ninety percent was targeted; and

the states could impose programs aimed at in-use vehicles to reduce the vehicle miles traveled or to keep in-use vehicles properly maintained.

In 1977, Congress again amended air pollution controls through the CAA Title II Amendments. The Title II Amendments:

postponed until MY 1980 the more stringent CO and HC standards;

relaxed the NOx emission standard from 0.4 gpm to 1 gpm for MY 1981 and thereafter;

allowed California to continue to have more stringent emissions standards, but nonattainment areas in other states could adopt California standards with EPA's approval;

modified the waiver for California to require the state's standards to be as protective of the public health and welfare as federal standards;

required inspection and maintenance ("I/M") programs in areas that are nonattainment for CO and O3;

added warranty and tampering provisions;

relaxed the standards applicable to vehicles sold at high altitudes;

softened testing requirements for small manufacturers;

tightened provisions concerning fuel additives;

relaxed lead additive requirements for small refineries;

ordered the administrator of the EPA (the Administrator) to set standards for heavy duty vehicles and motorcycles;

allowed refueling requirements to be imposed; and

allowed other pollutants that endangered public health or welfare to be regulated.

The 1970 CAA Amendments gave EPA the authority and responsibility to establish programs to provide for a ninety percent reduction by MY 1975 of HC and CO emissions that were allowable on 1970 MY cars and a ninety percent reduction by MY 1976 of NOx that was emitted from 1971 MY cars. To reach these goals, EPA established federal emission standards of 0.41 gpm for HC; 3.4 gpm for CO; and 0.4 gpm NOx. However, the achievement of the emissions reduction goals was delayed by EPA and Congressional actions between 1973 and 1990.

First, in 1973 EPA granted a one year postponement. The following year Congress postponed the reduction goals until 1977 (1978 for NOx) under the Energy Supply and Environmental Coordination Act (ESECA). Then in 1975, EPA granted another one year postponement. Congress again delayed implementation in 1977 when it amended the 1970 CAA Amendments to set new standards for MY 1978 79, 1980 and 1981 and all vehicles thereafter. Finally, in 1990, Congress set new emission standards under the 1990 CAA Amendments.

Under section 202 of the 1970 CAA, MY 1970 emissions were the baseline for determining the allowable CO and HC emissions for vehicles manufactured during or after MY 1975. For vehicles of MY 1976 and thereafter, the baseline for NOx emissions was MY 1971. The 1990 CAA Amendments include language similar to the 1970 CAA Amendments and use MY 1970 as the CO and HC baseline. The following chart illustrates the emissions baselines for HC, NOx, and CO; the NOx reduction is specified in a gpm standard without reference to a baseline. Pre–1990 Federal Exhaust Standards for Gasoline–Powered Light Vehicles in grams per mile (gpm):

MY		Hydrocarbons	/Carbon Monoxide	/Nitrogen Oxides
1968	1969	N/A	N/A	no standard
1970	1971	2.2	23.0	no standard
1972		3.4	39.0	no standard
1973	1974	3.4	39.0	3.0
1975	1976	1.5	15.0	3.1
1977	1979	1.5	15.0	2.0
1980		0.41	7.0	2.0
1981	1993	0.41	3 .4	1.0

B. Synopsis of the 1990 Clean Air Act Mobile Source Control Provisions

The 1990 CAA Amendments revised and tripled the size of the mobile source provisions in the 1970 CAA.The most significant new provisions impose:

more stringent controls on conventional vehicles;

new controls on gasoline and diesel fuels to reduce air pollution emissions; a program to encourage the development of "clean-fuel" vehicles; and more controls on mobile sources such as nonroad vehicles, trains, ships, and mobile equipment. Various provisions in subchapter I of the 1970 CAA Amendments make the states responsible for the establishment and enforcement of emission control strategies applicable to in-use vehicles that are incorporated in their SIPs. Since 1977, most states and the District of Columbia have been required to develop I/M programs for their air quality control regions that have non-attainment status for automotive related pollutants. Based on 1997 data, about 52.6 million people in the United States reside in an area where an air quality standard is violated. Over 47 million people live where the ozone standard is exceeded, and 9.1 million live where the CO standard is violated. Thus, most Americans who live in urbanized areas are subject to I/M programs. These I/M programs increased in stringency under the 1990 CAA Amendments for areas with a serious ozone nonattainment status or a moderate CO nonattainment status and a design value greater than 12.7 parts per million (ppm). In addition, other transportation control strategies are to be used to develop a transportation control plan that is part of the SIP.

* * *

In the 1990 CAA Amendments the standards for light-duty vehicles (LDV) and LDT became more stringent. Standards also were to be promulgated for motorcycles, heavy-duty engines (HDE), offroad vehicles, and marine engines. Emissions standards for heavy-duty vehicle engines have been less stringent than for LDV, but the 1990 CAA Amendments aimed to reduce the disparity. Emission standards apply to vehicles and engines for their useful life.

More stringent controls on LDV and LDT included new tailpipe emission limitations, new requirements for limiting emissions during cold temperature operation, and new requirements concerning the control of evaporative losses, including losses during refueling. There also are requirements for vehicles to have onboard diagnostic (OBD) capabilities in order to ensure that CAA requirements are met during the prescribed vehicle's life and to ensure compliance with the new warranty requirements, as well as provisions for the control of emissions from alternatively fueled vehicles.

Under the warranty provisions of section 207(a) and (b) coverage of major components, including the catalytic converter, was increased to 8 years or 80,000 miles, but the coverage for other minor emission components was reduced to 2 years or 24,000 miles. The warranty provisions were the only environmental issue decided in the U.S. House of Representatives by a contested floor vote. The warranty provisions included in the final bill were derived from the Sikorski–Green Amendment, which represented a compromise between service station owners and environmentalists.

A new section, 202(*l*), created a program to control hazardous air pollutants emitted from motor vehicles. The statute directed EPA to produce a study on the need to control such emissions and the means and measures for control. The section directs the agency to focus on emissions that pose the greatest risk to human health or about which there are significant uncertainties. Benzene, formaldehyde, and 1,3–butadiene are specifically to be regulated under section 211(k)(10)(C), and section 112(b)(1). EPA was directed to regulate under section 202(*l*)(2) to control hazardous emissions from motor vehicles to the greatest degree achievable by May 15, 1995. Benzene and formaldehyde are the only pollutants required to be regulated under section 202(*l*)(2). Fuels can be regulated under section 211(c).

IV.   Emission Standards After the CAA Amendments of 1990

* * *

New standards also were established for two categories of LDT those over 6000 GVWR and those under 6000 pounds GVWR but over 3750 pounds loaded vehicle weight (LVW). Final regulations issued June 5, 1991, set the Tier I NOx standard at 1.0 gpm for light-duty diesels and included a 0.08 gpm PM standard for 5/50,000 vehicles and a 0.10 gpm PM standard for 10/100,000 vehicles.

By 1999 EPA was to determine the need, cost, and feasibility of Tier 2 standards for 2004 and later MY gasoline and diesel-fueled LDV and LDT of 3750 pounds LVW or less. Tier 2 standards will apply for the extended useful life of ten years or 100,000 miles, whichever occurs first. The statute requires the Administrator to study whether emissions can be reduced to 0.125 gpm for NMHC, 1.7 gpm for CO, and 0.2 gpm for NOx.

On April 28, 1998, EPA announced the release of a Draft Tier 2 Study. The draft study examined three issues: (1) the need for further emission reductions to attain the ambient air standards; (2) the technical feasibility of meeting more stringent standards by MY 2004; and (3) the cost-effectiveness of such further reductions. The draft study included evidence that a need existed for further emission reductions, and that more stringent emission standards are technologically feasible and cost effective.

* * *

EPA subsequently proposed "Tier 2 Motor Vehicle Emission Standards and Gasoline Sulfur Control Requirements" on May 13, 1999. The proposed rule would impose more stringent emission requirements on automobiles, pickup trucks, mini-vans, and SUVs that are operated on any fuel. The cost of meeting the Proposed Rule is projected to be less than $100 per automobile and less than $200 per light truck. The Rule is to be phased in between 2004 and 2007 for automobiles and light trucks, but emission requirements for heavy LDT would be phased in during 2008 and 2009. The new NOx standard is an average of 0.07 gpm, which is significantly more stringent than the existing 0.4 gpm standard for automobiles and the 0.7 gpm for light trucks. The automotive industry however, seems to be supporting the new standard as achievable. The petroleum industry, however, is critical of the proposed rule's sulfur reduction requirement for fuel because of its costs and because of its applicability to areas of the country that are in compliance.

The day after the proposed rule appeared in the Federal Register, the U.S. Court of Appeals for the District of Columbia Circuit struck down the new NAAQS for ozone and for PM. On June 30, 1999, after the opinion was issued, EPA promulgated a clarification of the proposed Tier 2 rule to explain that the D.C. Circuit's opinion concerning the NAAQS for ozone and PM did not change EPA's proposed requirements for the Tier 2 program.

On December 21, 1999, President Clinton announced the issuance of a final rule to reduce dramatically the emissions from SUVs, mini-vans, vans, and LDT by tightening tailpipe emissions and by imposing more stringent standards on the sulfur content of gasoline. All classes of passenger vehicles beginning in 2004 must meet an average standard of 0.07 gpm for NOx emissions.

Vehicles under 6000 pounds will be phased in between 2004 and 2007. For heavier vehicles, including the heaviest LDT over 6000 pounds, the standard in 2004 will not exceed 0.6 gpm, which is more than a sixty percent reduction from the current standard. These vehicles are required to further decrease emissions between 2004 and 2007 to 0.2 gpm. By 2008, half of the vehicles are required to meet the 0.07 gpm standard, with the remaining vehicles complying by 2009. The heaviest passenger vehicles weighing between 8500 and 10,000 pounds have until 2008 to comply and have additional options for compliance.

In 2004, gasoline manufacturers cannot exceed the cap of 300 ppm of sulfur and must maintain an annual corporate average sulfur level of 120 ppm. In 2005, the corporate average requirement drops to 90 ppm and the refinery average will be 30 ppm. In 2006, the cap falls to 80 ppm. Small refiners and some western states have less stringent time criteria, but must comply with the 30 ppm average and 80 ppm cap by 2007.

EPA estimates that, as a result of these rules, projected emissions reductions of NOx will be 1.2 million tons annually in 2010, 2 million tons per year (tpy) by 2020, and nearly 3 million tpy by 2030. EPA estimates these standards will cost industry $5.3 billion, but will yield health and environmental benefits valued at $25.2 billion. The consumer cost is less than $1000 per car, $200 per each LDT, and under two cents per gallon of gas.

IX. The Clean Air Act—Acid Deposition Control and the Use of Market Based Controls

The problem of "acid rain" has been recognized for over thirty years. In both Europe and North America, the hydration of sulfur and nitrogen oxides created acids (sulfuric acid and nitric acid) that can then be deposited hundreds of mile from the source. This "acid rain" (though it is more likely dry deposition) can eat away at public monuments and buildings and can change the Ph of natural systems, killing both plants and animals. In North America, this problem was of particular concern to Canada, which believed that most of the acid production harming its environment originated in the United States.[62]

In response to this problem, in 1980, Congress passed the Acid Precipitation Act, which mandated a 10-year scientific, technological and economic study to examine the relationship between combustion of fossil fuels and the creation of acids and other pollutants. The National Acid Precipitation Assessment Program (NAPAP) was established to coordinate this study. NAPAP concluded that Sulfur Dioxide (SO_2) and Nitrogen Dioxide (NOx) are precursors to the formation of ozone. Once released into the atmosphere they can travel several hundred miles during which time they are chemically altered into ambient acidic sulfates and nitrates. NAPAP's studies indicated that the damage caused by these acidic depositions is large; it adversely affects water, vegetation, humans and visibility. Because the pollutants can travel long distances, the NAPAP research demonstrated that it was critical to develop region-

---

62. In fact, emissions in Ontario also contributed to acid deposition in areas of the United States. Nevertheless, it is proba- ble that most of the pollution went the other way.

al, even international, solutions to limit emissions of SO_2 and NOx into the atmosphere.

During the 1980's Canada continued to lobby the US government to develop an international approach to controlling these emissions. In 1991, Canada and the United States signed the Agreement on Air Quality in which both countries agreed on a "cap and trade" program.

In Canada, the federal government agreed to reduce, through provincial programs, SO_2 by 2.3 million tonnes and to establish a national cap on SO_2 emissions of 3.2 tonnes by the year 2000. Each province was assigned a specific limitation on SO_2 emissions, and the provinces were free to decide how to achieve the reduction needed to comply with the emission cap. Options included control options, process changes, changes in fuel source, energy conservation programs to reduce electric demand or back end control technologies such as controlling limits on sulfur content in heavy fuel oil. A central feature of the provincial program was "trading," in which the electric utilities were allocated a share of the "emission cap" and allowed to trade freely among their various power plants and generating plants within the province to meet their allocation.

In the United States, Congress met their commitments under the Agreement on Air Quality through the provisions of Title IV of the 1990 Clean Air Act. Rather than rely upon the states or specific source controls as they did in dealing with criteria pollutants, Congress adopted a national goal to reduce SO_2 emissions by 10 million tons below 1980 emission levels and reduce NOx by approximately 2 million tons below the 1980 levels. The regulatory scheme set out in Title IV is quite unique and reflected a radical departure for Congress. Rather than embroil Congress or the EPA in micromanaging how industry would comply, Congress translated the goal of "10 million ton reduction in SO_2 emissions" into a total cap that would be divided between each sulfur dioxide generating electric utility. Congress then set out a generous 20–year timetable for achieving this goal. Further, Congress gave the utilities a new tool by which to meet their targets, the trading of emissions.

A. SO_2 Emission Limitation Program

A "Cap and Trade" regulatory model is designed to give the regulated parties maximum flexibility in designing their solution to the limit established for them. This model had longed been hailed by economists for allowing the reduction of pollution at the lowest possible cost to the regulated industry. Environmental groups had long been suspicious of the theory, expressing concerns that it might be difficult to monitor, and that it would send the wrong message that it was "OK to pollute." The battle over the use of this emissions program was heated, but ultimately, its presence allowed the Republican Party and the first President Bush to agree to the 1990 Clean Air Act Amendments as a whole.

The adopted program works in the following way. Sources are all given an initial amount of pollutant that they can emit. They can reach this target in numerous ways. They are free to switch fuels, install control technology, change operations, replace facilities, retire facilities or trade their emission "credits or allowances" in order to ensure that their emissions, when accumulated, are within the allocation they received.

In Phase I, Congress identified the 110 electric utility plants that were thought to be the largest contributors to SO_2 and NOx emissions and allocated a specific number of "allowances" to them.[63] Each allowance was equivalent to 1 ton of SO_2 emissions. The number of allowances received was calculated on the basis of a baseline, which was calculated as the annual average quantity of British Thermal Units (Btus) produced in calendar years 1985, 1986 and 1987.[64] Then using this baseline, each unit was allowed to emit 2.5 pounds of SO_2 per British Thermal Unit (Btu) heat input. 2.5 lbs of emissions amounted to a significant reduction in the amount of SO_2 previously emitted by most of the utilities. By the end of 1995, each of these utilities was required to operate such that its emissions did not exceed the number of allowances it had been granted that year. In order to meet their cap, each utility was free to adopt a myriad of options as discussed above, including the right to purchase or sell emission allowances.

In Phase II, Congress required the EPA to allocate a specified number of allowances between the remaining 2,200 electric utility companies in the United States. The total number of allowances granted each year was determined based on the annual reduction in SO_2 emissions required to meet the stated goal of 10 million tons. Again, each allowance issued is equivalent to 1 ton of SO_2 emissions. Once granted, the utility is required to ensure that its emissions do not exceed its allowances. It can do this through a number of mechanisms including the purchase and sale of emission allowances.

New source emitters, i.e., new electric utility plants, were required to acquire allowances from the market in order to receive a permit to operate. In Phase II a certain number of allowances were set aside for new source emitters to purchase from the EPA. If additional allowances were required, the utility could go to the market and purchase them from other utilities.

The critical, and most innovative, element of this regulatory program was the creation of a market in pollution wherein "clean" utilities could make money selling excess allowances. The market was monitored through a permitting program. Each permit would specify the number of allowances a utility would be granted.[65] The application for a permit would detail how the utility would ensure that its emissions were within the allocated allowances. Failure to operate in compliance with the permit or the plan was punishable by significant penalties ($2,000 per ton in excess of allowed emissions); potential to require the utility to offset its SO_2 emissions by an equivalent amount in subsequent years;

63. 42 U.S.C. Sec. 7651b.

64. 42 U.S.C. Sec. 7651a(A).

65. 42 U.S.C. Sec. 7651g.

and an equivalent reduction in the allowances granted in subsequent years.

In order to accommodate new sources, Congress required the EPA to set aside 2.5% of emission allowances into a special allowance reserve and to offer them for sale at a price of $1,500.00. This sale was to be held on an annual basis. Congress also required the EPA to establish an annual auction. Specifically, in Phase I, the EPA was to set aside 150,000 tons per year and in Phase II this would be increased to 250,000 tons per year of SO_2 allowances for the auction. In addition to the allowances set aside by the EPA, utilities that had excess allowances were also free to submit them for sale at the auction. The auction was to be conducted on an annual basis. During the first few years the price received for credits was very low and there was very little trading activity. Since implementation of Phase II, however, trading activity has increased and the market is viable. In recent years, the price of an individual allowance has continued to rise, reflecting both the rise in demand for electric power, and the lowered total of emissions allowed.

B. NOx Emission Limitation Program

Both Canada and the United States agreed to limit the emissions of NOx in the Air Quality Agreement of 1991. The United States is obligated to reduce NOx emissions by approximately 2 million tons from 1980 levels. The emission reductions are expected to come from both stationary sources (electric utility plants) and mobile sources (motor vehicles). Unlike the regulatory program adopted for SO_2 emissions, the NOx emissions are controlled through a more traditional regulatory model under both Title IV(Acid Deposition) and Title II (Criteria Pollutants) of the Clean Air Act and a "cap and trade" program was not originally established.

Pursuant to Section 7651f, the EPA is required to establish the limitations for NOx emissions for two types of electric utility boilers: tangentially fired boilers are limited to 0.45/lb per mmBtu and (b) dry bottom wall-fired boilers are limited to 0.5lb/mmBtu. It is unlawful for either type of boiler to emit NOx in excess of these express limitations.

By 1997, the EPA was required to establish limits for other types of boilers. These limits are to be set based on the degree of reduction achievable through retrofit application of the best system of continuous emission reduction, taking into account (i) available technology, (ii) costs, (iii) energy and environmental impacts and (iv) a determination that the cost is comparable to the costs of NOx controls set by Congress in this section.[66]

However, if a utility does not think that it will be able to meet the emission limits, it can apply for an "alternative emission limit," which is to be granted if the EPA determines that the unit cannot meet the applicable limitation using low NOx burner technology. Units are not

---

66. 42 U.S.C. Sec. 7651f(d).

required to install any additional control technology beyond low NOx burner technology in order to comply with the limits imposed.

In 2005, the EPA moved to implement general reductions over the Eastern United States because of the particular problems governing interstate movement of NOx, and subsequent effects on ozone levels within states.

C. The Use of Market Based Trading Systems

As noted above, the truly revolutionary part of the Acid Rain Program was its use of trading mechanisms to achieve its overall goals. By most counts, the program has been a success. It has reduced the amount of Sulfur Dioxide produced at a far lower cost than was initially believed. Although the acidification of natural systems had proved to be a harder problem to address than first believed, the reductions in Sulfur Dioxide have produced important collateral health benefits. Nevertheless, the success of the Sulfur Dioxide trading program is not necessarily a recipe for future programs. There are many unique parts of the program which may not be able to be replicated in other programs.

The Enron Story and Environmental Policy[67]

* * *

Carol Rose categorized the tools used in the implementation of environmental policies.[68] These implementation devices are entitled "do nothing," "keepout," "rightway," or "property."[69] . . .

Our current environmental controls use all of these, either singly, or in combination.[70] However, all of these controls are not created equally. They have different effectiveness and different costs. Professor Rose's great contribution is to recognize what variables might affect the changing cost structure of each of these strategies, and to explore what those variables suggest about the employment of these various strategies.[71] Professor Rose characterized the variables as "system and administrative costs," "user costs," and "overuse or failure of strategy" cost.[72] The first cost is generally the cost to the government or regulated entity of the regulation itself. This can be seen as the cost to monitor and enforce. The second cost is the cost of equipment or other requirements, which is usually borne by the regulated party. The third is the cost that comes from the ineffectiveness of a strategy, or the loss due to commons overuse.

---

67. Victor Flatt, 33 ELR 10485 (2003) (reproduced in Enron Corporate Fiascoes and Their Implications (Foundation Press 2004)).

68. Rose, *supra* note 128, at 1.

69. *Id.*

70. For instance the Clean Air Act has "grandfather" provisions regarding existing stationary sources, "command and control"

in the New Source Performance Standards, and "market based strategies" in the Sulfur Dioxide trading system, designed to control acid deposition. See generally 42 U.S.C. Sec. 7401 et seq. (One could also note that with respect to climate change gases, the strategy appears to be "do-nothing.")

71. Rose, *supra* note 128, at 1.

72. *Id.* at 12.

In examining the various strategies, Professor Rose noted in particular that market based trading strategies, while significantly reducing costs to users, might significantly increase the costs of monitoring or enforcement.[73] This is because in a market system, each source must be individually monitored, and to achieve actual efficiencies, must be able to change and trade "outputs" instantaneously.[74] Professor Rose speculates that a market based control strategy might be an effective control of an environmental externality under extreme pressure because it could provide reductions at a lower cost to the polluter and with little loss due to failure of the program. But she also notes that in order to get effective reductions, enforcement is important and that this cost could be high. Thus, she concludes that market based control strategies would be best utilized under high environmental pressure because only control of such an extreme problem could provide enough of a benefit to justify the high cost of administration. . . .

Similarly, enforcement schemes that depend on an administration to monitor an overall "level" of desired environmental quality, which can be degraded from various and dispersed sources also present the difficulty of monitoring multiple sources simultaneously. Both the Clean Water Act (CWA) and the Clean Air Act (CAA) originally only required the maintenance of an ideal standard of cleanliness.[75] The states were supposed to ensure that this level was met. But without any mechanisms for compliance, any capacity to monitor, or any standards to govern, both provisions failed miserably.[76] The part of the modern CWA that still requires the maintenance of overall water quality whether technological or process controls work or not, the Total Maximum Daily Load program (TMDL), lay un-enforced for decades.[77]

The failure of this as a strategy was recognized by Congress as recently as 1990. Part of the 1990 CAA amendments altered the requirements for regulating hazardous air pollutants.[78] Prior to 1990, the administrator was supposed to set emissions limitations at the place which would adequately protect public health.[79] But in the case of hazardous air pollutants, many of which were carcinogenic, this was difficult to do in any principled manner. The administration was bogged down and only listed 8 pollutants in a twenty year period even though thousands more were clearly at issue.[80] Again, the certainty that came along with command and control regulation outweighed the supposed efficiencies that could come from a standard which allowed maximum flexibility but contained no mechanism or resources to enforce this mechanism.

73. *Id.* at 21.

74. *Id.* at 21–22.

75. Fredrick R. Anderson et al., Environmental Protection: Law and Policy 1, 375–76, 589–90 (3d ed. 1999).

76. *Id.*

77. *See generally Sierra Club v. Hankinson*, 939 F.Supp. 865 (N.D.Ga. 1996).

78. 42 U.S.C. § 7651(a) (2002).

79. Anderson, et al., *supra* note 161 at 1.

80. *Id.*

In such cases, it is not that inefficient regulation is eliminated, but that there is no regulation at all. Not because it is not necessary or required by law, but that it is impractical and difficult. This theory of environmental regulation and history of the success or failure of programs might suggest that our administrators would be wary of enforcement schemes that rely on monitoring of divergent, multiple sources simultaneously or that depend heavily on self regulation, but this is not the case.

The current administration, pointing to the success of market based regulation in controlling acid rain,[81] suggests that it can be replicated in many if not all areas, and that command and control regulation or direct emissions controls may be unnecessary.[82] A superficial glance at *only* the acid rain trading provision might support this theory.

The acid rain provisions that went into effect in 1990 allowed fossil-fueled power plants to control emissions of Sulfur Dioxide not just by installing particular required equipment, but by allowing them to try other control methods and to purchase and sell rights to pollute.[83] This allowed some companies to invest in expensive pollution control equipment because they could sell the additional "control" to other polluters. Similarly, some polluters could avoid purchasing expensive technology by purchasing the right to pollute from others who had installed higher than needed capacity due to the incremental nature of pollution control.[84] In terms of lowering the costs to the regulated parties, this program has worked remarkably well.[85]

Also of import is that it has happened without enormous administrative cost.[86] However, this does not provide evidence that we should eliminate command and control or totally rely on more market based control strategies. The Acid Rain Sulfur Dioxide trading program is somewhat unique among market based schemes, and unique in such a way that it would work well. Since the number of Sulfur Dioxide producers in the program is fairly small, they are similar types of entities, the trades are for relatively long time periods and the sources are already regulated, the cost of ensuring that the trades are complied with is small.[87] Only a few hundred reports have to be examined. This does not require an enormous expense and thus does not require that the government depend on self regulation for compliance.[88]

Of greater applicability might be the situation of states that have attempted to create trading programs for many if not all pollution

---

81. 42 U.S.C. § 7651(a) (2002).

82. Under the Acid Deposition Control Provision compliance has been an "unprecedented success (over 99%)." *Emissions Cap and Trade: A Basic Explanation & Results Under the Acid Rain Program*, at http://www.epa.gov/clearskies/emissions_cap_and_trade_3_14.pdf.

83. *Id.*

84. 42 U.S.C. § 7651(a).

85. Anderson, et al., *supra* note 161, at 1.

86. *See Emissions Cap and Trade: A Basic Explanation & Results Under the Acid Rain Program*, at http://www.epa.gov/clearskies/emissions_cap_and_trade_3_14.pdf.

87. Anderson, et al., *supra* note 161, at 1.

88. *Id.*

sources. So far, these programs have been disastrous. According to the EPA Inspector General, "state emissions programs to control air pollution are hobbled by a lack of adequate oversight from the EPA, lax enforcement, and bad emissions data."[89] The California RECLAIM program which attempted to trade Nitrogen Oxide emissions between stationary and mobile sources, has failed to meet its predicted pollution reductions from ten years ago, and was characterized by EPA's Region IX as having serious compliance problems.[90]

* * *

FINAL NOTE: The future of the Clean Air Act may well revolve around the increasing use of market trading schemes and the abandonment of "rightway" or technology control regimes. As we finish the Clean Air Act chapter it is important then to think through these questions in detail. After reading the foregoing excerpt, what is your opinion of the current proposal to replace new source performance standards and other technological controls with the widespread pollutant cap and trading program proposed in the Clear Skies Initiative? Are other amendments to the CAA called for? What would you suggest?

89. EPA Inspector General Calls on Agency to Improve Oversight of State Programs, 33 BNA Env't. Rep. 2142 (October 4, 2002). * * *

90. Trading Foes Hail EPA Region IX Report Criticizing RECLAIM Program, Inside EPA, November 22, 2002, p. 7.

Chapter 5

RESOURCE CONSERVATION
AND RECOVERY ACT

I. OVERVIEW AND JURISDICTION

We now turn our attention to the Resource Conservation and Recovery Act, more commonly known as "RCRA," 42 U.S.C. § 6901, et seq. RCRA took it basic statutory shape in 1976, when Congress converted what had previously been known as the Solid Waste Disposal Act into RCRA. Pub. L. No. 94–580, 90 Stat. 2795 (1976). From the outset, RCRA has had two major programs: Subtitle C, covering hazardous waste management; and Subtitle D, governing "solid waste" facilities that do not also handle hazardous waste. In 1984, Congress passed what to date has been its only set of comprehensive amendments to RCRA, the Hazardous and Solid Waste Amendments of 1984 ("HSWA"), Pub. L. No. 98–616, 98 Stat. 3224 (1984). Additionally, when Congress amended CERCLA in 1986, it simultaneously added a third major program to RCRA, Subtitle I, regulating those who store either petroleum or hazardous substances (other than hazardous waste) in underground storage tanks. Pub. L. No. 99–499, 100 Stat. 1615 (1986).

For purposes of this course, we will focus solely on Subtitle C, RCRA's hazardous waste provisions. Subtitle C governs those who generate, transport, or treat, store or dispose of hazardous waste. Although Congress created Subtitle C in 1976, it took EPA until May of 1980 to develop the regulations giving shape to the program. 45 Fed. Reg. 33119 (May 19, 1980). Hence, there was no effective hazardous waste regulatory program in place until that time.

Not surprisingly, the key jurisdictional trigger under Subtitle C is the term "hazardous waste." In order to understand which materials qualify as "hazardous wastes" under Subtitle C, students must familiarize themselves with the interrelationship between some key statutory and regulatory definitions. Section 1004(5) of RCRA defines the term "hazardous waste" as follows:

> The term "hazardous waste" means a solid waste, or combination of solid wastes, which because of its quantity, concentration, or physical, chemical, or infectious characteristics may—

(A) cause, or significantly contribute to an increase in mortality or an increase in serious irreversible, or incapacitating reversible, illness; or

(B) pose a substantial present or potential hazard to human health or the environment when improperly treated, stored, transported, or disposed of, or otherwise managed.

42 U.S.C. § 6903(5).

The first thing to note about this definition is that, in order to qualify as a hazardous waste, a material must first qualify as a "solid waste." Thus, as Judge Kenneth Starr (of Monica Lewinski fame) pointed out in the *American Mining Congress* case below, the universe of "hazardous wastes" under RCRA is a subset of the universe of "solid wastes." This latter term is also defined, in § 1004(27), as follows:

The term "solid waste" means any garbage, refuse, sludge from a waste treatment plant, water supply treatment plant, or air pollution control facility and other discarded material, including solid, liquid, semisolid, or contained gaseous material resulting from industrial, commercial, mining, and agricultural operations, and from community activities, but does not include solid or dissolved material in domestic sewage, or solid or dissolved materials in irrigation return flows or industrial discharges which are point sources subject to permits under section 1342 of Title 33, or source, special nuclear, or byproduct material as defined by the Atomic Energy Act of 1954, [42 U.S.C.A. § 2011 et seq.].

42 U.S.C. § 6903(27).

One could paraphrase the thrust of these two provisions as being that, subject to narrow exceptions, the term "hazardous waste" includes any discarded material that poses a substantial threat to human health or the environment when improperly managed. Seen in that light, the need for further regulatory explication is clear, particularly when one considers that Subtitle C contemplates a regulatory program backed up by both civil and criminal sanctions. In fact, Congress tasked EPA with establishing a more refined regulatory definition of those wastes which it deemed worthy of full-blown regulation under Subtitle C. See 42 U.S.C. § 6921. In this vein, EPA has promulgated complicated regulatory frameworks for determining both when materials qualify as "solid wastes" for purposes of Subtitle C, and when those same materials will also qualify as "hazardous wastes."

We will deal both of these constructs below. For now, it is important to understand that a material must meet the regulatory definitions of both of these terms in order be subject to the requirements of Subtitle C.

A. What is a "Solid Waste"?

The first thing to note is that a "solid waste" does not have to be solid. This much is clear from the statutory definition, which includes liquids and even "contained gaseous materials." Due to this dynamic, many practitioners refer to this first element of the jurisdictional test as simply involving whether the material is a "waste," deeming to term "solid" to be of no regulatory consequence.

EPA's regulatory definition of "solid waste" focuses on when EPA deems materials to have been "discarded." As we will see in the following case, EPA historically has defined the term "discarded" in a way that asserts jurisdiction over materials EPA deems to have been either "abandoned" or "recycled" in environmentally problematic ways. Additionally, EPA has identified some materials that it deems to be "solid wastes" simply because they are "inherently waste-like." See 40 C.F.R. § 261.2(a)(2)(iii) and (d).

By far the most controversial—and complicated—issue in all of RCRA involves EPA's assertion of jurisdiction over materials that are destined for recycling. The basic tensions underlying this controversy are obvious. Recently, EPA summarized its three historical arguments in favor of asserting jurisdiction in the following terms:

- The statute and the legislative history suggest that Congress expected EPA to regulate as wastes some materials that are destined for recycling.

- Many materials stored or transported prior to recycling present the same types of threats to human health and the environment as materials stored or transported prior to disposal. In fact, EPA found that recycling operations have accounted for a number of notorious damage incidents. For example, materials destined for recycling were involved in one-third of the first 60 filings under RCRA's imminent and substantial endangerment authority, and 20 of the first sites listed under CERCLA....

- Excluding all materials destined for recycling would allow materials to move in and out of the hazardous waste management system depending on what any person handling the material intended to do with it. This seems inconsistent with the mandate to track hazardous wastes and control them from "cradle to grave."

68 Fed.Reg. 61558, 61561–61562 (Oct. 28, 2003).

At the same time, subjecting certain types of recycling to regulation under Subtitle C may dramatically increase the cost of extracting further value from those materials. At the margin, it may encourage companies to buy new feedstock materials for their industrial processes rather than using recycled materials. At some level, of course, this undermines the "recovery" goal of the Resource, Conservation and *Recovery* Act (emphasis added).

How should EPA resolve this tension? How much flexibility does the statute allow it? The best way to understand these issues is by tracking their historical evolution. We begin with the following case, which (for reasons which will become clear) is referred to as "*AMC I*":

AMERICAN MINING CONGRESS v. U.S. EPA

United States Court of Appeals, District of Columbia Circuit, 1987.

824 F.2d 1177.

STARR, Circuit Judge:

RCRA is a comprehensive environmental statute under which EPA is granted authority to regulate solid and hazardous wastes....

Congress' "overriding concern" in enacting RCRA was to establish the framework for a national system to insure the safe management of hazardous waste. H.R.Rep. No. 1491, 94th Cong., 2d Sess. 3 (1976), U.S.Code Cong. & Admin.News 1976, pp. 6238, 6240, 6241....

... [Under Subtitle C], EPA is directed to promulgate regulations establishing a comprehensive management system. [42 U.S.C. § 6921]. EPA's authority, however, extends only to the regulation of "hazardous waste." Because "hazardous waste" is defined as a subset of "solid waste," *id.* § 6903(5), the scope of EPA's jurisdiction is limited to those materials that constitute "solid waste." That pivotal term is defined by RCRA as

> any garbage, refuse, sludge from a waste treatment plant, water supply treatment plant, or air pollution control facility *and other discarded material,* including solid, liquid, semisolid or contained gaseous material, resulting from industrial, commercial, mining, and agricultural operations, and from community activities....

42 U.S.C. § 6903(27) (emphasis added). As will become evident, this case turns on the meaning of the phrase, "and other discarded material," contained in the statute's definitional provisions.

EPA's interpretation of "solid waste" has evolved over time. On May 19, 1980, EPA issued interim regulations defining "solid waste" to include a material that is "a manufacturing or mining by-product and sometimes is discarded." 45 Fed.Reg. 33,119 (1980). This definition contained two terms needing elucidation: "by-product" and "sometimes discarded." In its definition of "a manufacturing or mining by-product," EPA expressly *excluded* "an intermediate manufacturing or mining product which results from one of the steps in a manufacturing or mining process and is typically processed through the next step of the process within a short time." *Id.*

In 1983, the agency proposed narrowing amendments to the 1980 interim rule. 48 Fed.Reg. 14,472 (1983). The agency showed especial concern over *recycling* activities. In the preamble to the amendments, the agency observed that, in light of the interlocking statutory provisions and RCRA's legislative history, it was clear that "Congress indeed intended that materials being recycled or held for recycling can be wastes, and if hazardous, hazardous wastes." *Id.* at 14,473. The agency also asserted that "not only can materials destined for recycling or being recycled be solid and hazardous wastes, but the Agency clearly has the authority to regulate recycling activities as hazardous management." *Id.*

While asserting its interest in recycling activities (and materials being held for recycling), EPA's discussion left unclear whether the agency in fact believed its jurisdiction extended to materials recycled in an industry's on-going production processes, or only to materials disposed of and recycled as part of a waste management program. In its preamble, EPA stated that "the revised definition of solid waste sets out the Agency's view of its jurisdiction over the recycling of hazardous waste ... Proposed section 261.6 then contains exemptions from regulations for those hazardous waste recycling activities that we do not think require regulation." *Id.* at 14,476. The amended regulatory description of "solid waste" itself, then, did not include materials "used or reused as effective substitutes for raw materials in processes using raw materials as principal feedstocks." *Id.* at 14,508. EPA explained the exclusion as follows:

> [These] materials are being used essentially as raw materials and so ordinarily are not appropriate candidates for regulatory control. Moreover, when these materials are used to manufacture new products, the processes generally are normal manufacturing operations.... The Agency is reluctant to read the statute as regulating actual manufacturing processes.

Id. at 14,488. This, then, seemed clear: EPA was drawing a line between discarding and ultimate recycling, on the one hand, and a continuous or ongoing manufacturing process with one-site "recycling," on the other. If the activity fell within the latter category, then the materials were not deemed to be "discarded."

After receiving extensive comments, EPA issued its final rule on January 4, 1985. 50 Fed.Reg. 614 (1985). Under the final rule, materials are considered "solid waste" if they are abandoned by being disposed of, burned, or incinerated; or stored, treated, or accumulated before or in lieu of those activities. In addition, certain recycling activities fall within EPA's definition. EPA determines whether a material is a RCRA solid waste when it is recycled by examining both the material or substance itself and the recycling activity involved. The final rule identifies five categories of "secondary materials" (spent materials, sludges, by-products, commercial chemical products, and scrap metal). These "secondary materials" constitute "solid waste" when they are disposed of; burned for energy recovery or used to produce a fuel; reclaimed; or accumulated speculatively. *Id.* at 618–19, 664.[1] Under the final rule, if a material

---

1. Under the final rule, a "use constituting disposal" is defined as direct placement on land of wastes or products containing or derived from wastes. A material is "accumulated speculatively" if it is accumulated prior to being recycled. If the accumulator can show that the materials feasibly can be recycled, and that during a one-year calendar period the amount of material recycled or transferred for recycling is 75% or more of the amount present at the beginning of the year, the materials are not considered solid wastes. A material is "reclaimed" if it is processed to recover a usable product, or if it is regenerated. *Id.*

constitutes "solid waste," it is subject to RCRA regulation *unless* it is directly reused as an ingredient or as an effective substitute for a commercial product, or is returned as a raw material substitute to its original manufacturing process.[2] *Id.* In the jargon of the trade, the latter category is known as the "closed-loop" exception. In either case, the material must not first be "reclaimed" (processed to recover a usable product or regenerated). *Id.* EPA exempts these activities "because they are like ordinary usage of commercial products." *Id.* at 619.

Petitioners, American Mining Congress ("AMC") and American Petroleum Institute ("API"), challenge the scope of EPA's final rule. Relying upon the statutory definition of "solid waste," petitioners contend that EPA's authority under RCRA is limited to controlling materials that are *discarded* or *intended for discard.* They argue that EPA's reuse and recycle rules, as applied to inprocess secondary materials, regulate materials that have not been discarded, and therefore exceed EPA's jurisdiction.

To understand petitioners' claims, a passing familiarity with the nature of their industrial processes is required.

Petroleum refineries vary greatly both in respect of their products and their processes.... In general, the refining process starts by "distilling" crude oil into various hydrocarbon streams or "fractions." The "fractions" are then subjected to a number of processing steps. Various hydrocarbon materials derived from virtually all stages of processing are combined or blended in order to produce products such as gasoline, fuel oil, and lubricating oils. Any hydrocarbons that are not usable in a particular form or state are returned to an appropriate stage in the refining process so they can eventually be used. Likewise, the hydrocarbons and materials which escape from a refinery's production vessels are gathered and, by a complex retrieval system, returned to appropriate parts of the refining process. Under EPA's final rule, this reuse and recycling of materials is subject to regulation under RCRA.

In the mining industry, primary metals production involves the extraction of fractions of a percent of a metal from a complex mineralogical matrix (i.e., the natural material in which minerals are embedded). Extractive metallurgy proceeds incrementally. Rome was not built in a day, and all metal cannot be extracted in one fell swoop. In consequence, materials are reprocessed in order to remove as much of the pure metal as possible from the natural ore. Under EPA's final rule, this reprocessed ore and the metal derived from it constitute "solid waste." What is more, valuable metal-bearing and mineral-bearing dusts are often released in processing a particular metal. The mining facility typically

---

2. Specifically, the final rule excludes materials recycled by being: "(1) [u]sed or reused as ingredients in an industrial process to make a product, *provided the materials are not being reclaimed;* or (2) [u]sed or reused as effective substitutes for commercial products; or (3) [r]eturned to the original process from which they are generated, without first being reclaimed." *Id.* (emphasis added). In the third category, the material must be returned to the original manufacturing process as a substitute for raw material feedstock, and the process must use raw materials as principal feedstocks.

recaptures, recycles, and reuses these dusts, frequently in production processes different from the one from which the dusts were originally emitted. The challenged regulations encompass this reprocessing, to the mining industry's dismay.

Because the issue is one of statutory interpretation, the principles enunciated in *Chevron U.S.A., Inc. v. NRDC,* 467 U.S. 837 (1984), and its progeny guide our inquiry. . . .

. . . Congress, it will be recalled, granted EPA power to regulate "solid waste." Congress specifically defined "solid waste" as "discarded material." EPA then defined "discarded material" to include materials destined for reuse in an industry's *ongoing* production processes. The challenge to EPA's jurisdictional reach is founded, again, on the proposition that in-process secondary materials are outside the bounds of EPA's lawful authority. Nothing has been *discarded,* the argument goes, and thus RCRA jurisdiction remains untriggered.

The first step in statutory interpretation is, of course, an analysis of the language itself. . . . Here, Congress defined "solid waste" as "discarded material." The ordinary, plain-English meaning of the word "discarded" is "disposed of," "thrown away" or "abandoned." Encompassing materials retained for immediate reuse within the scope of "discarded material" strains, to say the least, the everyday usage of that term.

. . . [Of course], a complete analysis of the statutory term "discarded" calls for more than resort to the ordinary, everyday meaning of the specific language at hand. For, "the sense in which [a term] is used in a statute must be determined by reference to the purpose of the particular legislation." *Burnet v. Chicago Portrait Co.,* 285 U.S. 1, 6 (1932). . . .

. . . RCRA was enacted in response to Congressional findings that the "rising tide of scrap, discarded, and waste materials" generated by consumers and increased industrial production had presented heavily populated urban communities with "serious financial, management, intergovernmental, and technical problems in the disposal of solid wastes." [42 U.S.C. § 6901(a)]. . . . Also animating Congress were its findings that "disposal of solid and hazardouse [sic] waste" without careful planning and management presents a danger to human health and the environment; that methods to "separate usable materials from solid waste" should be employed; and that usable energy can be produced from solid waste. *Id.* § 6901(b), (c), (d).

The question we face, then, is whether, in light of the National Legislature's expressly stated objectives and the underlying problems that motivated it to enact RCRA in the first instance, Congress was using the term "discarded" in its ordinary sense—"disposed of" or "abandoned"—or whether Congress was using it in a much more open-ended way, so as to encompass materials no longer useful in their original capacity though destined for immediate reuse in another phase of the industry's ongoing production process.

For the following reasons, we believe the former to be the case. RCRA was enacted, as the Congressional objectives and findings make clear, in an effort to help States deal with the ever-increasing problem of solid waste *disposal* by encouraging the search for and use of alternatives to existing methods of disposal (including recycling) and protecting health and the environment by regulating hazardous wastes. To fulfill these purposes, it seems clear that EPA need not regulate "spent" materials that are recycled and reused in an *ongoing* manufacturing or industrial process. These materials have not yet become part of the waste disposal problem; rather, *they are destined for beneficial reuse or recycling in a continuous process by the generating industry itself.*

The situation in this case thus stands in sharp contrast to that in *Riverside Bayview,* another post-*Chevron* case. There, the Corps of Engineers had defined "the waters of the United States" within the meaning of the Clean Water Act, 33 U.S.C. §§ 1311, 1362 (1972), to include "wetlands." Recognizing that it strained common sense to conclude that "Congress intended to abandon traditional notions of 'waters' and include in that term 'wetlands' as well," the Court performed a close and searching analysis of Congress' intent to determine if this counterintuitive result was nonetheless what Congress had in mind. *Id.* at 461–65. The Court based its holding (that the agency's expansive definition of "waters of the United States" was reasonable) on several factors: Congress' acquiescence in the agency's interpretation; provisions of the statute expressly including "wetlands" in the definition of "waters"; and, importantly, the danger that forbidding the Corps to regulate "wetlands" would defeat Congress' purpose since pollutants in "wetlands" water might well flow into "waters" that were indisputably jurisdictional. *Id.* at 465. Thus, due to the nature of the water system, the very evil that Congress sought to interdict—the befouling of the "waters of the United States"—would likely occur were the Corps of Engineers' jurisdiction to stop short of wetlands. *Riverside Bayview,* 106 S.Ct. at 463.

We are constrained to conclude that, in light of the language and structure of RCRA, the problems animating Congress to enact it, and the relevant portions of the legislative history, Congress clearly and unambiguously expressed its intent that "solid waste" (and therefore EPA's regulatory authority) be limited to materials that are "discarded" by virtue of being disposed of, abandoned, or thrown away. While we do not lightly overturn an agency's reading of its own statute, we are persuaded that by regulating in-process secondary materials, EPA has acted in contravention of Congress' intent. Accordingly, the petition for review is granted.

MIKVA, Circuit Judge, dissenting:

. . . Congress had broad remedial objectives in mind when it enacted RCRA, most notably to "regulat[e] the treatment, storage, transportation, and disposal of hazardous wastes which have adverse effects on the environment." 42 U.S.C. § 6902(4). The disposal problem Congress was combatting encompassed more than just abandoned materials. RCRA makes this clear with its definition of the central statutory term "disposal":

> the discharge, deposit, injection, dumping, spilling, leaking, or placing of any solid waste or hazardous waste into or on any land or water so that such solid waste or hazardous waste or any constituent thereof may enter the environment or be emitted into the air or discharged into any waters, including ground waters.

42 U.S.C. § 6903(3). This definition clearly encompasses more than the everyday meaning of disposal, which is a "discarding or throwing away." *Webster's Third International Dictionary* 654 (2d ed. 1981). The definition is *functional*: waste is disposed under this provision if it is put into contact with land or water in such a way as to pose the risks to health and environment that animated Congress to pass RCRA. Whether the manufacturer subjectively intends to put the material to additional use is irrelevant to this definition, as indeed it should be, because the manufacturer's state of mind bears no necessary relation to the hazards of the industrial processes he employs.

Faithful to RCRA's functional approach, EPA reasonably concluded that regulation of certain in-process secondary materials was necessary to carry out its mandate. The materials at issue in this case can pose the same risks as abandoned wastes, whether or not the manufacturer intends eventually to put them to further beneficial use. As the agency explained, "[s]imply because a waste is likely to be recycled will not ensure that it will not be spilled or leaked before recycling occurs." The storage, transportation, and even recycling of in-process secondary materials can cause severe environmental harm. Indeed, the EPA documented environmental disasters caused by the handling or storage of such materials. It also pointed out the risk of damage from spills or leaks when certain in-process secondary materials are placed on land or in underground product storage.

Moreover, the agency's action is carefully aligned with Congress' functional approach to problems of waste disposal. The agency is not seeking to regulate all recycled materials. Rather, it has promulgated a complicated scheme of different categories so as to regulate materials only when they present the same types of environmental risks RCRA seeks to correct. EPA stressed that "to determine if a secondary material is a RCRA solid waste when recycled, one must examine both the material and the recycling activity involved. A consequence is that the same material can be a waste if it is recycled in certain ways, but would not be a waste if it is recycled in other ways." Thus, the agency has sought to regulate these materials only when they present the risks Congress was combatting in RCRA....

... EPA has interpreted solid waste in a manner that seems to expand the everyday usage of the word "discarded." Its conclusion, however, is fully supportable in light of the statutory scheme and legislative history of RCRA. The agency concluded that certain on-site recycled materials constitute an integral part of the waste disposal problem. This judgment is grounded in the EPA's technical expertise and is adequately supported by evidence in the record. The majority nevertheless reverses the agency because it believes that the materials at issue "have not yet become part of the waste disposal problem." This declaration is nothing more than a substitution of the majority's own conclusions for the sound technical judgment of the EPA. The EPA's interpretation is a reasonable construction of an ambiguous statutory provision and should be upheld. . . .

Notes and Questions

1. The D.C. Circuit is the only Circuit that can hear pre-enforcement challenges to EPA's RCRA rules. 42 U.S.C. § 6976(a)(1); see also *Association of Battery Recyclers, Inc. v. U.S. EPA*, 208 F.3d 1047, 1052 (D.C. Cir. 2000). Perhaps obviously, this dynamic serves to underscore the importance of its rulings; barring Supreme Court review, when the D.C. Circuit speaks its determinations typically will be the final word on these issues.

2. As indicated in *AMC I*, EPA asserted it general regulatory power over "secondary materials" when they are recycled by being (1) used in a manner constituting disposal; (2) burned for energy recovery; (3) reclaimed; or (4) accumulated speculatively. 40 C.F.R. § 261.2(c). Leaving aside reclamation for the moment, can you understand why EPA is concerned about the other three forms of recycling? Can you think of problematic examples of each?

3. EPA's regulations define "reclaimed" in the following manner:

A material is "reclaimed" if it is processed to recover a usable product, or if it is regenerated. Examples are recovery of lead values from spent batteries and regeneration of spent solvents.

40 C.F.R. § 261.1(c)(4). Do you agree that the petroleum and mining materials in *AMC I* were being reclaimed? Were the practices at issue akin to the recovery of lead values from spent batteries?

4. It is worth noting that the *AMC I* court mischaracterized the "closed-loop" exclusion. EPA's regulations contain two distinct exceptions. First, as noted by the court, secondary materials generally avoid classification as "solid waste" if they are recycled by being reused as an ingredient or as an effective substitute for a commercial product, or are returned as raw material substitutes to the original process from which they were generated, without first being reclaimed. See 40 C.F.R. § 261.2(3). Beyond that, however, materials can still avoid regulation if they are reclaimed and returned to the original manufacturing process, so long as the reclamation process meets certain requirements, most notably that "[o]nly tank storage is involved, and the entire process through completion of reclamation is closed by being entirely connected with pipes or other comparable enclosed means of convey-ance." 40 C.F.R. § 261.4(a)(8). It is this latter exception that is known as the "closed-loop" exclusion. Do you agree with EPA's decision to create these exceptions?

5. Did you agree with the court's *Chevron* analysis? At one level, the disagreement between the majority and Judge Mikva seems to hinge upon

whether the courts should defer to EPA's determination regarding whether a particular management scenario for secondary materials indicates that those materials have "become part of the waste disposal problem." Should they? Would that allow EPA too much license to distort the otherwise ordinary meaning of "discarded?"

6. How would you characterize the effect of *AMC I* on EPA's regulatory construct? Does it affect EPA's ability to regulate recycling outside of the reclamation context? How great is its affect within the reclamation context? Interestingly, in a portion of the opinion we have edited out, the court addressed a number of statutory provisions which EPA had argued indicated Congress's support for an expansive definition of "discarded." One of them, § 3014, deals with the circumstances under which EPA should treat used oil as a hazardous waste. The court distinguished the effect of this provision in the following terms:

> Section [3014] addresses "used oil" collected by and utilized in the "oil recycling industry." Oil recyclers typically collect discarded used oils, distill them, and sell the resulting material for use as fuel in boilers. Regulation of those activities is likewise consistent with an everyday reading of the term "discarded." It is only when EPA attempts to extend the scope of that provision to include the recycling of *undiscarded* oils at petroleum refineries that conflict occurs.

824 F.2d at 1187 n.14 (emphasis in original). Does this affect your reading of *AMC I*?

7. Shortly after the D.C. Circuit issued its opinion in *AMC I*, EPA issued a proposed rule responding to the court's decision. There, EPA characterized the effect of the court's decision as follows:

> The court's decision does not affect the Agency's authority to regulate as hazardous wastes those secondary materials recycled in ways where the recycling activity itself is characterized by discarding as defined by the court. That is, manufacturing processes (or other types of recycling) involving an element of discard which do not involve secondary materials passing through a continuous, on-going manufacturing process remain within the Agency's jurisdiction.

53 Fed.Reg. 519, 520 (Jan. 8, 1988). More specifically, EPA asserted that the court's holding had no effect on its ability to regulate recycling where the reuse constitutes disposal, or involves either burning for energy recovery or speculative accumulation. Id. at 521–523. Additionally, EPA stated its belief that it continued to have jurisdiction over many forms of reclamation. In particular, it asserted that it still had the authority to regulate the reclamation of spent materials (e.g., spent solvents), because in its view they are by definition no longer directly usable in on-going manufacturing processes. Id. at 522. With respect to sludges and byproducts, by contrast, EPA asserted that it would determine, on a case-by-case basis, whether they were being re-utilized in an ongoing manufacturing process when it considered whether to "list" particular waste streams as hazardous waste. Id. at 523. It later articulated the factors that it would consider in making these determinations in the following terms:

(a) Whether the sludge or by-product is typically recycled on an industry-wide basis;

(b) whether the material is replacing a raw material and the degree to which it is similar in composition to the raw material; (c) the relation of the recovery practice to the principal activity of the facility; and (d) whether the secondary material is managed in a way designed to minimize loss, plus other relevant factors.

53 Fed.Reg. 33412, 35415 (Sept. 13, 1988).

8. For more than 10 years after *AMC I*, all of the case law in this area seemed to support EPA's narrow interpretation of the court's opinion and, consequently, its broad authority to assert regulatory jurisdiction over the recycling of secondary materials. Most notably, in *American Mining Congress v. U.S. EPA*, 907 F.2d 1179 (D.C. Cir. 1990) ("*AMC II*"), the D.C. Circuit addressed an industry challenge, based on *AMC I*, asserting that EPA could not regulate the petitioners' wastewater treatment sludge stored in surface impoundments, so long as they might at some point in the future reclaim some of the metals in the sludge. The court rejected the petitioners' plain meaning argument in the following terms:

Petitioners read *AMC* too broadly. *AMC*'s holding concerned only materials that are "destined for *immediate reuse* in another phase of the industry's ongoing production process," and that "have not yet become part of the waste disposal problem." Nothing in *AMC* prevents the agency from treating as "discarded" the wastes at issue in this case, which are managed in land disposal units that *are* part of wastewater treatment systems, which have therefore become "part of the waste disposal problem," and which are *not* part of ongoing industrial processes. Indeed, [we have] explicitly rejected the very claim that petitioners assert in this case, namely, that under RCRA, potential reuse of a material prevents the agency from classifying it as "discarded."

907 F.2d at 1186 (emphasis in original). Turning to the reasonableness of EPA's interpretation, the court concluded its analysis as follows:

. . . In this case, the agency determined that material placed in wastewater treatment surface impoundments where it is "capable of posing a substantial present or potential hazard to human health or the environment when improperly treated, stored, transported or disposed of, or otherwise managed," 40 C.F.R. § 261.11(a)(3), by leaching into the ground, is "discarded material," and hence a "solid waste." As the agency notes, because of their propensity to leak hazardous materials into the environment, surface impoundments are a central focus of RCRA's regime. In addition, Congress made clear in the legislative history of RCRA its concern to regulate hazardous materials in surface impoundments. In light of this evidence, we conclude that the agency's interpretation of "discarded" is both reasonable and consistent with the statutory purposes of RCRA.

Id. at 1187.

9. The case to which the *AMC II* court referred in the last sentence of the first indented quote in the prior note was *American Petroleum Institute v. U.S. EPA*, 906 F.2d 729 (D.C. Cir. 1990) ("*API I*"). The relevant portion of

that case involved an environmental attack on EPA's determination that it lost regulatory jurisdiction over a certain waste stream (referred to as "K061" waste) once it was delivered to a metals reclamation facility. Relying on *AMC I*, EPA contended that regulating the reclamation process "would be like directly regulating the industrial production of zinc from ore." Id. at 740 n.15. The court squarely rejected this logic:

> [*AMC I*] is by no means dispositive of EPA's authority to regulate K061 slag. Unlike the materials in question in *AMC*, K061 is indisputably "discarded" *before* being subject to metals reclamation. Consequently, it *has* "become part of the waste disposal problem"; that is why EPA has the power to require that K061 be subject to mandatory metals reclamation. *See* 53 Fed.Reg. 11,752–53 (recognizing this point). Nor does anything in *AMC* require EPA to cease treating K061 as "solid waste" once it reaches the metals reclamation facility. K061 is delivered to the facility not as part of an "*ongoing* manufacturing or industrial process" within "the generating industry," but as part of a mandatory waste treatment plan prescribed by EPA. As such, the resulting slag appears to remain within the scope of the agency's authority as "sludge from a *waste treatment plant*." 42 U.S.C. § 6903(27). . . .

Id. at 741 (emphasis in original).

10. Can the two *AMC* opinions be harmonized? Recall that in *AMC I*, the court resolved the issue at Step 1 of the *Chevron* analysis. When taken together, do these two opinions make clear where the D.C. Circuit views the plain meaning of the term "discarded" as ending, and where EPA's power to resolve any residual ambiguity begins?

11. As mentioned in note 1 above, other courts can consider the legality of EPA's RCRA rules only in enforcement actions. As a result, other Circuits don't hear nearly as many of these cases. During the 1990s, however, those that did so routinely upheld EPA's authority to regulate the materials at issue. In *United States v. Ilco, Inc.*, 996 F.2d 1126 (11th Cir. 1993), for example, the Eleventh Circuit upheld EPA's authority to deem the lead components of spent batteries "solid waste," despite the fact that the defendant was going to reclaim them at its lead smelting facility. And in *Owen Electric Steel Co. v. Browner*, 37 F.3d 146 (4th Cir. 1994), the Fourth Circuit held that EPA could regulate the slag produced by a steel mill in a situation in which the mill "cured" the material on the ground for six months prior to selling it for use as road bed material. Quoting from *AMC I*, the court concluded that "the fundamental inquiry in determining whether a by-product has been 'discarded' is whether the by-product is *immediately* recycled for use in the same industry; if not, then the by-product is justifiably seen as 'part of the waste disposal problem.' " Id. at 150 (emphasis in original).

12. In 2000, the tide turned again. First, in *Association of Battery Recyclers, Inc. v. U.S. EPA*, 208 F.3d 1047 (D.C. Cir. 1047) ("*Battery Recyclers*"), the D.C. Circuit rejected a new protocol EPA had developed for determining whether certain secondary materials derived from mineral processing qualified as "solid waste." If the materials were to be recycled back into the manufacturing process, EPA's new rule had made their potential status as waste hinge upon the method of interim storage: If the

materials were stored in tanks, containers, buildings, or on properly maintained pads, they would not be deemed wastes; alternatively, if they were stored in less environmentally sound ways, they would be deemed to be wastes. Id. at 1051. In a facial challenge, the D.C. Circuit rejected this approach, emphasizing that the length of the storage period was "of no consequence" according to the regulation. Most alarmingly, from EPA's perspective, the court harkened back to *AMC I* as the bellweather case within the Circuit. Moreover, it limited the "immediate reuse" language from that opinion by indicating that "immediate" in this context means "directly," not "at once." Id. at 1053. The court went on to distinguish *API I* as a case in which a waste was generated by one industry and reclaimed within another, id. at 1054, and *AMC II* as involving a situation in which it was unclear whether the materials would ever be reclaimed, id. at 1055.

13. In a second case from that year, the D.C. Circuit in *American Petroleum Institute v. U.S. EPA*, 216 F.3d 50 (D.C. Cir. 2000) ("*API II*"), considered whether certain oil-bearing wastes generated by the petroleum industry qualified as "solid waste" before they went through a CWA primary treatment system, even though that system would result in the recapture of some valuable oil. The court vacated EPA's determination that they did, finding EPA's conclusion that the wastewater treatment purpose predominated over the recycling purpose to be unsupported by the record. Id. at 57. Moreover, despite having previously noted that EPA should get deference on the question whether an industrial by-product is best characterized as discarded or an "in-process material," the court determined that EPA had not adequately explained why, even if the wastewater treatment purpose predominated, this would "compel the further conclusion that the wastewater has been discarded." Id. at 58.

14. In *Safe Air for Everyone v. Meyer*, 373 F.3d 1035 (9th Cir. 2004), the Ninth Circuit addressed the question whether bluegrass farmers who engage in the open burning of grass residues after harvest are burning "solid waste" for purposes of RCRA (the issue came up in the context of a citizen suit under § 7002(a)(1)(b), which requires only that the relevant material was a solid waste, not that it was a "hazardous waste" under Subtitle C). The court held that this practice did not involve either the treatment or disposal of agricultural waste, but rather the reuse of the residue in a continuous process of growing bluegrass. The crux of the court's analysis was as follows:

> ... [T]here is no dispute that the Growers realize farming benefits from reusing grass residue in the process of open burning. Safe Air did not present testimony challenging the Growers' contentions that: (1) grass residue offers nutrients to bluegrass fields; (2) burnt grass residue ash resulting from open burning helps fertilize bluegrass fields; (3) open burning reduces the incidence of weed, fungi, and insect infestation in bluegrass fields; and (4) open burning blackens bluegrass fields, which contributes to creating optimal conditions for the next bluegrass harvest. Safe Air dismisses these indisputable benefits as "incidental," but our view is necessarily controlled by RCRA's statutory language suggesting that materials must be "discarded" to be considered solid waste. Because there is undisputed evidence that the Growers reuse the grass residue in a continuous farming process effectively designed to produce

Kentucky bluegrass, there is no genuine issue of material fact as to whether grass residue is "discarded material." It is not. The bluegrass residue is not discarded, abandoned, or given up, and it does not qualify as "solid waste" under RCRA, based on its statutory definition of "solid waste" as "discarded material."

Id. at 1044–1045. Do you agree?

15.   In October of 2003, EPA proposed major revisions to its definition of "solid waste." 68 Fed.Reg. 61558 (Oct. 28, 2003). EPA already had withdrawn the specific rules the D.C. Circuit deemed invalid in *Battery Recyclers*. Despite having done so, however, it stated that it viewed *Battery Recyclers* "as creating an opportunity to re-examine its rules and interpretations and clarify whether they regulate certain materials that are not 'discarded.'" Id. at 61563. In short, the new proposal provides that "any material which is generated and reclaimed in a continuous process within the same industry . . . is not 'discarded' for purposes of Subtitle C, provided that the recycling process is 'legitimate.'" Id. If finalized, this new approach would go beyond any of the existing cases by allowing the reclamation to occur at other facilities, so long as they operate within the same industry. EPA explained its justification for this proposal in the following terms:

> . . . [P]rocesses and facilities that operate within the same industry are likely to use similar raw materials and process them in a similar manner. They are also likely to have expertise as to the types of secondary materials produced by their industry, their potential for recycling, and appropriate practices for managing such materials. For these practical reasons, EPA believes that the potential for environmental harm from de-regulating this type of recycling practice is likely to be relatively small compared to other types of recycling practices.

Id. at 61565. Moreover, the proposal would expand upon *Battery Recyclers* by defining the "continuous process" concept by reference to the "speculative accumulation" idea it already applies to secondary materials not requiring reclamation, see 40 C.F.R. § 261.2(c)(4); under this framework, the person accumulating the material must show that during a calendar year it recycled or transferred for recycling at least 75 percent of the material (by weight or volume) it had at the beginning of the year. Id. at 61576; see also 40 C.F.R. § 261.1(c)(8). Finally, EPA proposed a series of "legitimacy" criteria that it would use on a case-by-case basis to differentiate the permissible reclamation from what it views as "sham" recycling. The proposed criteria are as follows:

> 1.   The secondary material to be recycled is managed as a valuable commodity. Where there is an analogous raw material, the secondary material should be managed in a manner consistent with the management of the raw material. Where there is no analogous raw material, the secondary material should be managed to minimize the potential for releases into the environment.

> 2.   The secondary material provides a useful contribution to the recycling process or to a product of the recycling process and evaluating this criterion should include consideration of the economics of the recycling transaction. The recycling process itself may involve reclamation, or direct reuse without reclamation.

3. The recycling process yields a valuable product or intermediate that is: (i) Sold to a third party; or (ii) Used by the recycler or the generator as an effective substitute for a commercial product or as a useful ingredient in an industrial process.

4. The product of the recycling process: (i) Does not contain significant amounts of hazardous constituents that are not found in analogous products; and (ii) Does not contain significantly elevated levels of any hazardous constituents that are found in analogous products; and (iii) Does not exhibit a hazardous characteristic that analogous products do not exhibit.

Id. at 61583. Does this seem like an appropriate approach? Keeping in mind that this proposal has not been finalized, how would you advise industrial clients to proceed in light of the mixed messages provided in the case law to date? If you represented EPA, what types of cases would you recommend for either civil or criminal enforcement?

B. What is a "Hazardous Waste"?

If a given material qualifies as a "solid waste," the second step in determining whether Subtitle C applies is to determine whether it also qualifies as a "hazardous waste" within the regulatory meaning of that phrase. As mentioned above, Congress specifically contemplated that EPA would establish a regulatory construct for determining which wastes, within the broad statutory parameters of § 1004(5), were worthy of full-blown regulation under Subtitle C. 42 U.S.C. § 6921(a) and (b).

Section 3001(b) specifically contemplated that EPA would promulgate regulations "identifying the characteristics of hazardous waste, and listing particular hazardous wastes...." Consistent with this instruction, EPA created a two-pronged approach for determining which wastes are hazardous. 40 C.F.R. § 261.3(a). EPA listed certain waste streams as being per se hazardous. If a company generates one of these so-called "listed" wastes, it must treat it as a hazardous waste, regardless of the concentrations of any of the relevant contaminants in any particular batch of waste. Thus, for these wastes there is no need to test each batch; if they are on one of the lists, they are covered. Additionally, EPA identified four "characteristics" of hazardous waste: ignitability, corrosivity, reactivity and toxicity. These characteristics serve as a "catch-all" mechanism for waste streams that are not specifically listed; regardless of whether a particular waste stream is listed, it if exhibits one of these four characteristics it must be treated as a hazardous waste. For these waste streams, therefore, the generator must determine, on a case-by-case basis, whether a given batch of its waste exhibits one of the four characteristics. 40 C.F.R. § 262.11.

Broadly speaking, there are four categories of listed wastes. Some listed waste streams are industry-specific. These are denominated "K" series wastes, which means only that each waste stream is given a code number that begins with the letter "K" and is followed by three digits. They include, for example, wastewater treatment sludges from wood preserving processes that use creosote or pentachlorophenol (K001), and untreated process wastewater from the production of toxaphene (K098). Others are process specific, but involve industrial processes than transcend any one particular industry. These waste streams, which are known as "F" series wastes, include for example spent cyanide plating bath solutions from electroplating operations (F007).

In addition, there are two categories of chemical products which are deemed hazardous when they are discarded as commercial chemical products, off-specification by-products, or in soils or debris from the cleanup of any spills of either these products or by-products. "U" series wastes include such chemicals as mercury (U151) and methyl ethyl ketone (U159). "P" series wastes, which include such chemicals as dieldrin (P037) and sulfuric acid (P115), are considered acute hazardous wastes. The significance of their being deemed acutely hazardous lies in the effect it has on the amount a waste a given generator can generate without being considered a fully-regulated generator—a given entity will be deemed a fully-regulated generator if it generates more than 1 kilogram of acute hazardous waste per month. 40 C.F.R. § 261.5(e).

As mentioned, EPA has identified four "characteristics" which can render waste hazardous regardless of whether EPA has listed a particular waste stream: ignitability, corrosivity, reactivity and toxicity. For most liquids, the test of ignitability is whether the waste has a flash point of less than 60 C, using a specified test method. 40 C.F.R. §§ 261.21. For aqueous waste, the corrosivity test hinges on whether the material has a pH of less than or equal to 2 or greater than or equal to 12.5. 40 C.F.R. § 261.22(a). For reactivity, the standard test is whether the waste is normally unstable and readily undergoes violent change without detonating, whether it reacts violently with water or forms potentially explosive mixtures or generates toxic gases when mixed with water, or whether it is capable of detonation or explosive reaction under certain circumstances. 40 C.F.R. § 261.23.

EPA's toxicity characteristic attempts to determine whether toxic constituents may leach out of the relevant waste stream at harmful levels under typical landfill conditions. Perhaps obviously, this is due to the fact that if a given waste stream is deemed not to be hazardous waste, whoever generates it may send it to a standard municipal landfill. EPA has developed a test known as the "toxicity characteristic leachate procedure" (or "TCLP"), which is designed to mimic landfill conditions. If this test reveals that the toxic constituents would leach out at levels of concern under such conditions, the waste stream qualifies as a hazardous waste. The TCLP numbers (that is, the test results that trigger regulation) are generally 100 times the drinking water standards for the relevant constituents; for trichloroethylene, for example, the TCLP number is .5 mg/l, 40 C.F.R. § 261.24, whereas the "maximum concentration limit" under the Safe Drinking Water Act for that same chemical is .005 mg/l, 40 C.F.R § 141.61. This is due to the fact that EPA uses this "100 times" factor as a standard assumption as to how much dilution and attenuation would occur with respect to the relevant constituents between the point at which it leaches from the waste at the landfill and the point at which it reaches a potential drinking water source.

Finally, it is worth noting that listed wastes (but not characteristic wastes) are subject to three expansive principles that dramatically increase the scope of RCRA's regulatory net. First, they are subject to the "mixture rule," which provides that the mixture of a listed waste and any other solid waste is by definition a hazardous waste. 40 C.F.R. § 261.3(b)(2). Second, the "derived from" rule provides, in effect, that any solid waste generated from the treatment, storage or disposal of a listed waste is still a hazardous waste. 40 C.F.R. § 261.3(c)(2) and (d)(1). And third, EPA interprets two of its existing rules as indicating that any soils, groundwater or debris which have been contaminated by listed wastes must be treated as hazardous waste. See 40 C.F.R. § 261.3(c)(1) and (d)(2). The D.C. Circuit upheld this interpretation, known as the "contained in policy," in *Chemical Waste Management v. U.S. EPA*, 869 F.2d 1526 (D.C. Cir. 1989).

Notes and Questions

1. From the outset of the regulatory program, EPA has excluded household waste from the definition of "hazardous waste." 40 C.F.R. § 261.4(b). In the preamble underlying this regulation, EPA made clear that this was a "waste stream" exclusion, meaning that the exclusion also applied to any non-household entities that might transport, treat, store and/or dispose of this waste. 45 Fed.Reg. 33099 (May 19, 1980). In HSWA, the 1984 Amendments to RCRA, Congress codified this exclusion in § 3001(i) of RCRA. The existence of this exclusion means that a homeowner can take the paint thinner from her basement and pour it out in her backyard without violating RCRA or, for that matter, any other federal law (we are not recommending this). Yet if an industrial entity did the same thing, it would in all likelihood be committing a felony under RCRA, see 42 U.S.C. § 6928(d)(2). Does this distinction make sense?

2. While § 3001(i) made clear that municipal solid waste incinerators would not be deemed to be treating, storing or disposing of hazardous wastes if they received and burned only household hazardous wastes, the question arose as to whether these same facilities would be deemed to have generated a hazardous waste if the ash they generated through their incineration processes failed the TCLP. The Supreme Court ultimately addressed this question in *City of Chicago v. Environmental Defense Fund*, 511 U.S. 328, 114 S.Ct. 1588, 128 L.Ed.2d 302 (1994), holding that § 3001(i) plainly limits the exclusion to the incinerators' handling of the household waste itself and does not extend it to any ash generated through the process of incineration. This holding has major implications for these municipal incinerators. Prior to bringing the litigation that resulted in the Supreme Court's decision, EDF had done studies which indicated that incinerator fly ash fails the TCLP 80 to 90 percent of the time, and that bottom ash does so 20 to 25 percent of the time. Moreover, these incinerators collectively generate more than 8 million tons of ash per year. Read § 3001(i) carefully. Do you agree with the Supreme Court's determination? Would it matter to you whether EPA had interpreted the relevant statutory language one way or the other? In 1995,

EPA moved to mitigate the effect of the Court's holding at least somewhat by expressly allowing these facilities to mix their fly ash and bottom ash together before performing the required waste determination. 60 Fed.Reg. 6666 (Feb. 3, 1995).

3.   In *Shell Oil Co. v. EPA*, 950 F.2d 741 (D.C. Cir. 1991), the D.C. Circuit belatedly determined that EPA had provided inadequate notice and comment when it promulgated the mixture and derived-from rules in 1980. Concerned about the impacts of its ruling, however, the court suggested that EPA reenact the rules on an interim basis under the "good cause" exception to the notice and comment provisions of the APA, 5 U.S.C. § 553(b)(3)(B). EPA promptly did so. 57 Fed.Reg. 7628 (March 3, 1992). Congress later required EPA to revise the rule by 1994, but expressly provided that the interim rules would remain in effect until EPA acted. Pub. L. 102–389, 106 Stat. 1571, 1602–3 (1992). To make a long story short, EPA has yet to act despite a court order requiring it to have done so by April 30, 2000. Pending such action, its "interim" rules remain in effect.

4.   Although the derived-from rule provides that any wastes generated through the treatment of listed wastes are hazardous waste, it specifically recognizes the general proposition that any "materials that are reclaimed from solid wastes and that are used beneficially are not solid wastes and thus are not hazardous wastes...." 40 C.F.R. § 261.3(c)(2)(I).

5.   Generators of non-listed waste streams do not need to test every single batch of waste for every characteristic. Instead, EPA's rules allow them to either test or apply their "knowledge of the hazard characteristic of the waste in light of the materials or the processes used." 40 C.F.R. § 262.11(c).

6.   Many commentators have criticized EPA's regulatory definition of "hazardous waste." The mixture and derived-from rules have come under particular attack, with commentators alleging that they result in the over-regulation of materials posing little environmental risk. See, e.g., Pedersen, The Future of Federal Solid Waste Regulation, 16 Colum. J. Envtl. L. 109 (1991). Over the years, EPA has floated a variety of proposed methodologies to address these concerns. In 1992, for example, it suggested several potential approaches, three of which are worth highlighting. One approach, called the expanded characteristic option (or "ECHO"), would have expanded reliance on the TCLP by adding many new substances to the list that generators need to test for, with a corresponding decrease in the number of listed wastes. A second option would have identified concentration-based exit criteria at which listed wastes, if treated to the specified levels, would no longer be considered hazardous. And finally, a third option would have specified management practices that, if utilized, would have eliminated a given generator's need to manage a particular waste as hazardous. See generally, 57 Fed.Reg. 21450 (May 20, 1992). What do you think of these approaches? To date, EPA has yet to move forward with any of them. In the "contained-in" context, it does have a proposed rule pending that would conditionally exclude from the definition of hazardous waste disposable industrial wipes that are contaminated with hazardous solvents. 68 Fed.Reg. 65586 (Nov. 20, 2003).

II. THE REGULATORY PROGRAM

Subtitle C contains separate regulatory programs for those who generate, transport, and treat, store or dispose of hazardous waste. In EPA's regulations, the generator requirements are found in 40 C.F.R. Part 262, the transporter requirements in Part 263, and the treatment, storage and disposal ("TSD") requirements in Parts 264 and 265, as supplemented by the TSD permit requirements in Part 270.

In our discussion below, we will not try to provide comprehensive coverage of any of these programs. Instead, it is our aim to provide a brief overview of both the generator and TSD requirements, together with a problem in each area designed to (1) familiarize students with some of the basic issues that arise, and (2) provide them with some facility in working with the federal regulations. We will forgo any coverage of the transporter requirements, which are quite straightforward.

A. Generator Requirements

RCRA breaks generators of hazardous waste down into three categories, subject to widely varying degrees of regulation. In the highest category are the so-called "fully-regulated" generators. These generators, who will be the focus of our discussion below, are those who generate more than 1,000 kilograms of hazardous waste per month, or more than 1 kilogram of acute hazardous waste. See 40 C.F.R. §§ 262.34 and 261.5(f), respectively. In the 1980s, EPA estimated that these generators, while comprising only 2% of the generator universe, generate 99% of all hazardous waste. The next category down includes what EPA calls "small quantity generators" ("SQGs"), or those who generate between 100 and 1,000 kilograms of hazardous waste per month. SQGs are subject to a slightly relaxed set of requirements, as compared with the fully-regulated generators. For example, they can store their wastes for longer without qualifying as a TSD. 40 C.F.R. § 262.34(d). And finally, there are the so-called "conditionally-exempt generators" ("CEGs"). This category applies to those who generate less than 100 kilograms of hazardous waste per month (or less than 1 kilogram of acute hazardous waste). 40 C.F.R. § 261.5. To maintain the exemption, CEGs need only comply with a very limited set of requirements, including most notably never accumulating more than 1,000 kilograms at their facilities and sending their wastes to either hazardous waste facilities or approved solid waste facilities under Subtitle D. 40 C.F.R. § 261.5(g). Perhaps the best way to understand this favored treatment is to think of the CEGs as being more like households than they are like fully-regulated generators.

The threshold requirements stated in the above paragraph are aggregate totals, based on the total amount of all hazardous wastes that the particular generator generates at its entire facility each month. It should also be noted that one's generator status can vary from month-to-month depending on how much waste one generated during that particular month. Having said that, most generators decide that it is easiest to simply comply with the most demanding set of requirements to which it is commonly subject. For example, fully-regulated generators who store waste for any period of time are required to have "contingency plans," but small quantity generators who do the same are not. Compare 40 C.F.R. § 262.34(a)(4) and (d). Still, if a given generator hovers right around the 1,000 kg/month threshold from month to month, it would probably determine that it is in its best interest to keep its contingency plan in effect, even if it might not be required to do so during some particular months.

Turning more directly to the regulations that apply to fully-regulated generators, the first thing to note is that even these most-regulated generators are not required to have permits. Instead, they need only obtain what are referred to as "EPA identification numbers." 40 C.F.R. § 262.12. Because they don't have permits, RCRA generators are regulated directly under the relevant regulations, either 40 C.F.R. Part 262 or the State's equivalent regulations (in authorized States). This means that they need not go through the expensive process of acquiring a permit. It also means, however, that the lose the advantage of the so-called "permit shield." Compare 40 C.F.R. § 270.4.

There are five main requirements that apply to fully-regulated generators. First, like all generators (even CEGs), they must comply with the so-called "waste-determination" requirements; that is, they must determine whether a given waste stream is in fact hazardous waste. 40 C.F.R. § 262.11. Second, to the extent that they are going to store wastes on even a short-term basis, they must comply with the storage requirements set forth in 40 C.F.R. § 262.34 (which are the subject of our generator hypothetical, below). Third, when they send waste off-site, they must comply with the manifest and packaging requirements. See 40 C.F.R. Part 262, subpart B and § 262.30. Fourth, they must comply with certain record-keeping requirements. 40 C.F.R. Part 262, subpart D. And finally, they are subject to one additional requirement designed to implement RCRA's "land ban" program—they must identify the appropriate treatment standard that the waste is subject to under that program. See 40 C.F.R. § 268.7. (We will discuss the land ban program further below).

With this background, consider the following hypothetical:

A RCRA Generator Hypothetical

West Aerospace, Inc. ("West") does business in the State of Confusion, an unauthorized state under RCRA. The company manufactures aircraft parts and wings, and engages in metal finishing attendant thereto. Its hazardous waste activity records indicate that it generates more than 4,000 pounds of various hazardous wastes per month, including several "listed" spent solvents (F001, F002, F003 and F005), a listed stream of spent cyanide plating bath solutions (F007), and several waste streams waste streams that fail the TCLP. These latter streams include several paint wastes, strippers and contaminated fuels.

Bonnie Lee, an EPA inspector, recently visited the facility and made several findings. With respect to personnel training, she noted that the West employee who supervised the drum storage area, Billy Sunday, told her that when he started seven month ago, his boss had simply told him that he would teach him what he needed to know on an as-needed basis. Sunday further stated that he had received minimal training as time went along, and that he was unaware as to whether the company had a written personnel training plan or any other training records.

Lee also identified several issues with respect to drum storage. First, she found three containers of listed spent solvents in the drum storage area with lids that were ajar. The "accumulation date" labels on the outside of these drums indicated that no waste had been added to them in more than three weeks. Second, Lee noted that the "accumulation date" label on one of these drums indicated that the first wastes had been added to it 105 days before the inspection. And third, she observed an open drum of paint-and solvent-contaminated solids (cloths, rags, wipes, and debris) in a satellite accumulation area–the paint shop–that was not marked "hazardous waste" and did not have a marked accumulation date. The workers in the area conceded that some of these items had been used to clean up small spills of listed solvents.

As a courtesy, Lee left a copy of her inspection report at the facility. West's president, August West, has come to you seeking help in understanding the nature and significance of these alleged deficiencies. Consider the following regulations in formulating your advice.

40 C.F.R. Part 262, Subpart C—Pre–Transport Requirements

§ 262.34   Accumulation Time.

(a) Except as provided in paragraphs (d), (e), and (f) of this section, a generator may accumulate hazardous waste on-site for 90 days or less without a permit or without having interim status, provided that:

(1) The waste is placed:

     (i) In containers and the generator complies with subparts I, AA, BB and CC of 40 CFR part 265 . . .

(2) The date upon which each period of accumulation begins is clearly marked and visible for inspection on each container;

(3) While being accumulated on-site, each container and tank is labeled or marked clearly with the words, "Hazardous Waste"; and

(4) The generator complies with the requirements for owners or operators in subparts C and D in 40 CFR Part 265, with § 265.16, and with 40 CFR 268.7(a)(4).

(b) A generator who accumulates hazardous waste for more than 90 days is an operator of a storage facility and is subject to the requirements of 40 CFR Parts 264 and 265 and the permit requirements of 40

CFR Part 270 unless he has been granted an extension to the 90–day period....

(c)(1) A generator may accumulate as much as 55 gallons of hazardous waste or one quart of acutely hazardous waste listed in § 261.33(e) in containers at or near any point of generation where wastes initially accumulate, which is under the control of the operator of the process generating the waste, without a permit or interim status and without complying with paragraph (a) of this section provided he:

(i) Complies with §§ 265.171, 265.172, and 265.173(a) of this chapter; and

(ii) Marks his containers either with the words "Hazardous Waste" or with other words that identify the contents of the containers.

(2) A generator who accumulates either hazardous waste or acutely hazardous waste listed in § 261.33(e) in excess of the amounts listed in paragraph (c)(1) of this section at or near any point of generation must, with respect to that amount of excess waste, comply within three days with paragraph (a) of this section or other applicable provisions of this chapter. During the three day period the generator must continue to comply with paragraphs (c)(1)(i)-(ii) of this section. The generator must mark the container holding the excess accumulation of hazardous waste with the date the excess amount began accumulating.

40 C.F.R. Part 265, Subpart B—General Facility Standards

§ 265.16 Personnel Training.

(a)(1) Facility personnel must successfully complete a program of classroom instruction or on-the-job training that teaches them to perform their duties in a way that ensures the facility's compliance with the requirements of this part....

(2) This program must be directed by a person trained in hazardous waste management procedures, and must include instruction which teaches facility personnel hazardous waste management procedures ... relevant to the positions in which they are employed.

(3) At a minimum, the training program must be designed to ensure that facility personnel are able to respond effectively to emergencies by familiarizing them with emergency procedures, emergency equipment, and emergency systems....

(b) Facility personnel must successfully complete the program required in paragraph (a) of this section within six months after the effective date of these regulations or six months after the date of their employment or assignment to a facility, or to a new position at a facility, whichever is later....

(c) Facility personnel must take part in an annual review of the initial training required in paragraph (a) of this section.

(d) The owner or operator must maintain the following documents and records at the facility:

(1) The job title for each position at the facility related to hazardous waste management, and the name of the employee filling each job;

(3) A written description of the type and amount of both introductory and continuing training that will be given to each person filling a position listed under paragraph (d)(1) of this section;

(4) Records that document that the training or job experience required under paragraphs (a), (b), and (c) of this section has been given to, and completed by, facility personnel.

(e) Training records on current personnel must be kept until closure of the facility. . . .

40 C.F.R. Part 265, Subpart I—Use and Management of Containers

§ 265.173   Management of containers.

(a) A container holding hazardous waste must always be closed during storage, except when it is necessary to add or remove waste.

(b) A container holding hazardous waste must not be opened, handled, or stored in a manner which may rupture the container or cause it to leak.

Notes and Questions

1.   What violations can you be sure have been committed in the above hypothetical? Are there any potential violations with respect to which you would need further facts to make a final determination? Are the relevant regulations unclear regarding the regulatory significance of any of these facts? If so, what positions would you expect EPA to take, and what do you think its prospects for success would be?

2.   It is worth noting that one can generate a waste in perhaps unexpected ways. The term "generator" is defined in 40 C.F.R. § 260.10 to mean "any person . . . whose act or process first produces hazardous waste identified or listed in part 261 of this chapter *or whose act first causes a hazardous waste to become subject to regulation.*" (Emphasis added). Moreover, 40 C.F.R. § 262.11 requires any "person who generates a solid waste" to "determine if that waste is a hazardous waste." EPA has long interpreted these regulations as requiring, for example, one who cleans up contaminated soil to determine whether those materials qualify as hazardous wastes, regardless of when the original release occurred. The theory is that, by cleaning up the soil, the relevant party is generating a solid waste, and thus must perform the waste determination to determine whether it is hazardous.

B.   Requirements for Treatment, Storage and Disposal Facilities (TSDs)

Speaking generally, there are two types of TSDs under RCRA. Some facilities are in the business of treating, storing or disposing of other companies' hazardous waste. Think, for example, of Chemical Waste

Management's hazardous waste disposal facility in Emelle, Alabama. Others, however, are simply manufacturing facilities that have determined that it is in their financial interest to engage in some TSD activities attendant to their manufacturing processes. For example, many manufacturers store waste for longer than the 90–day grace period allotted to fully-regulated generators. Some eventually may reclaim some or all of the waste themselves, or others may treat their waste through a Clean Water Act treatment system and discharge some portion of the waste stream through an NPDES permit.

One common requirement that applies to all TSDs is that they must apply for a permit under § 3005(b) of the statute. See also 40 C.F.R. Part 270. Not all TSDs have final permits, however. When Congress created the permit requirement, Congress recognized that it would take EPA a while to issue permits to every TSD. Accordingly, Congress created a ''grandfathering'' mechanism pursuant to which facilities that were already treating, storing or disposing of hazardous waste were granted ''interim status'' to keep engaging in these activities until such time as EPA processed their permit applications.

To this day, more than half of all TSDs are operating under ''interim status.'' In 1984, Congress established deadlines by which EPA was required to process permit applications for various categories of TSDs, with the latest deadline expiring in 1992. 42 U.S.C. § 6925(c). This tactic failed, however, because all a given facility needed to do to retain interim status despite these deadlines was to apply for a final permit determination. Id. Hence, there was no real pressure on EPA to meet the deadlines. Moreover, since there has been a constant need for additional treatment capacity, and since new facilities cannot receive interim status, EPA has naturally tended to prioritize the issuance of permits to new facilities over the conversion of interim status facilities to fully-permitted status.

Beyond the permit requirement, EPA has two sets of regulations establishing the substantive standards for TSDs. The requirements for interim status facilities are found in 40 C.F.R. Part 265, and those for fully-permitted facilities are found in Part 264. The regulations are conceptually similar, though those for fully-permitted facilities are more stringent in some respects. In both contexts, there are some fairly generic standards that apply to all TSDs, such as personnel training, contingency planning, and record-keeping requirements. See, e.g., 40 C.F.R. Part 265, subparts B, C, D and E. Additionally, there are elaborate facility standard requirements for particular types of TSDs or TSD activities. These include specific standards for managing containers and for designing and operating specific types of units such as tank systems, surface impoundments, landfills and incinerators. See, e.g., 40 C.F.R. Part 265, subparts J, K, N and O.

Probably the most significant and expensive broadly applicable requirements in the TSD realm are those relating to groundwater monitoring, closure and post-closure, and financial responsibility. See, e.g., 40 C.F.R. Part 265, subparts F, G and H. We will use a second RCRA hypothetical to introduce the student to RCRA's groundwater monitoring and closure requirements:

A RCRA TSD Hypothetical

West Aerospace has another manufacturing facility in the State of Bliss (another "unauthorized" state), at which it operates a hazardous waste surface impoundment attendant to its electroplating processes. West's facility has "interim status" under RCRA.

Because West's property is on an incline, Pearly Baker, its environmental compliance manager assumed that the company could meet the requirements of Section 265.91 by installing one well immediately up the hill from the impoundment and three immediately on the downhill side. For several years, all went well. West sampled for all appropriate parameters twice a year and reported all results to EPA. Because Baker never heard anything in response from EPA, she eventually stopped reporting the results and merely entered them in her operating record. Last year, West first detected significant amounts of total organic halogen in two of its downgradient wells. Because West had never had any problems in the past, Baker attributed these results to sampling error. In the next sampling round, six months later, all four of West's wells showed significant concentrations of both total organic halogen and total organic carbon. Although the wastes West puts in the impoundment could have caused these results, Baker assumed that, because the upgradient well was contaminated, the contamination must be coming from an off-site location. Again, she noted these facts in her operating record, but did not report them to EPA.

Last month, West's insurance company reviewed West's monitoring data and informed Baker that it would decline to renew West's RCRA-based policies. In response, West decided it would close the surface impoundment. West's closure plan contemplates that it will "clean close" the impoundment, under 40 C.F.R. § 265.228(a)(1), by letting all of the liquids it cannot discharge into the river evaporate during the dry season, and then sending any remaining sludge to In Your Back Yard, an approved hazardous waste incineration facility. The dry season is at least three months away and the evaporation process would take another three months.

Yesterday, an EPA inspector showed up at West's facility and learned all of the above facts. While the inspector was there, Baker gave him a copy of West's closure plan and indicated that West would commence closure upon approval of the plan. The inspector comes to you, EPA lawyer extraordinaire, and wants to know what violations have been committed and what other implications these facts have under the relevant regulations. What do you tell him?

40 C.F.R. Part 265, Subpart F—Ground–Water Monitoring

§ 265.90 Applicability.

(a) Within one year after the effective date of these regulations, the owner or operator of a surface impoundment, landfill, or land treatment facility which is used to manage hazardous waste must implement a ground-water monitoring program capable of determining the facility's impact on the quality of ground water in the uppermost aquifer underlying the facility. . . .

(b) . . . [T]he owner or operator must install, operate, and maintain a ground-water monitoring system which meets the requirements of § 265.91, and must comply with §§ 265.92–265.94. This ground-water monitoring program must be carried out during the active life of the facility, and for disposal facilities, during the post-closure care period as well.

§ 265.91   Ground-Water Monitoring System.

(a) A ground-water monitoring system must be capable of yielding ground-water samples for analysis and must consist of:

(1) Monitoring wells (at least one) installed hydraulically upgradient (i.e., in the direction of increasing static head) from the limit of the waste management area. Their number, locations, and depths must be sufficient to yield ground-water samples that are:

(i) Representative of background ground-water quality in the uppermost aquifer near the facility; and

(ii) Not affected by the facility; and

(2) Monitoring wells (at least three) installed hydraulically downgradient (i.e., in the direction of decreasing static head) at the limit of the waste management area. Their number, locations, and depths must ensure that they immediately detect any statistically significant amounts of hazardous waste or hazardous waste constituents that migrate from the waste management area to the uppermost aquifer.

§ 265.92   Sampling and Analysis.

(a) The owner or operator must obtain and analyze samples from the installed ground-water monitoring system. The owner or operator must develop and follow a ground-water sampling and analysis plan. . . .

(b) The owner or operator must determine the concentration or value of the following parameters in ground-water samples in accordance with paragraphs (c) and (d) of this section:

(3) Parameters used as indicators of ground-water contamination:

(i) pH

(ii) Specific Conductance

(iii) Total Organic Carbon

(iv) Total Organic Halogen

(c)(1) For all monitoring wells, the owner or operator must establish initial background concentrations or values of all parameters specified in paragraph (b) of this section. He must do this quarterly for one year.

(d) After the first year, all monitoring wells must be sampled and the samples analyzed with the following frequencies:

(2) Samples collected to indicate ground-water contamination must be obtained and analyzed for the parameters specified in paragraph (b)(3) of this section at least semi-annually.

§ 265.93   Preparation, Evaluation, and Response.

(b) For each indicator parameter specified in § 265.92(b)(3), the owner or operator must calculate the arithmetic mean and variance, based on at least four replicate measurements on each sample, for each well monitored in accordance with § 265.92(d)(2), and compare these results with its initial background arithmetic mean. The comparison must consider individually each of the wells in the monitoring system, and must use the Student's t-test at the 0.01 level of significance to determine statistically significant increases (and decreases, in the case of pH) over initial background.

(c)(1) If the comparisons for the upgradient wells made under paragraph (b) of this Section show a significant increase (or pH decrease), the owner or operator must submit this information in accordance with § 265.94(a)(2)(ii).

(2) If the comparisons for downgradient wells made under paragraph (b) of this Section show a significant increase (or pH decrease), the owner or operator must then immediately obtain additional ground-water samples from those downgradient wells where a significant difference was detected, split the samples in two, and obtain analyses of all additional samples to determine whether the significant difference was a result of laboratory error.

(d)(1) If the analyses performed under paragraph (c)(2) of this Section confirm the significant increase (or pH decrease), the owner or operator must provide written notice to the Regional Administrator— within seven days of the date of such confirmation—that the facility may be affecting ground-water quality.

(2) Within 15 days after the notification under paragraph (d)(1) of this Section, the owner or operator must develop and submit to the Regional Administrator a specific plan, based on the outline required under paragraph (a) of this Section and certified by a qualified geologist or geotechnical engineer, for a ground-water quality assessment program at the facility.

(3) The plan to be submitted under § 265.90(d)(1) or paragraph (d)(2) of this Section must specify:

(i) The number, location, and depth of wells;

(ii) Sampling and analytical methods for those hazardous wastes or hazardous waste constituents in the facility;

(iii) Evaluation procedures, including any use of previously-gathered ground-water quality information; and

(iv) A schedule of implementation.

(4) The owner or operator must implement the ground-water quality assessment plan which satisfies the requirements of paragraph (d)(3) of this Section, and, at a minimum, determine:

(i) The rate and extent of migration of the hazardous waste or hazardous waste constituents in the ground water; and

(ii) The concentrations of the hazardous waste or hazardous waste constituents in the ground water.

(5) The owner or operator must make his first determination under paragraph (d)(4) of this Section as soon as technically feasible, and, within 15 days after that determination, submit to the Regional Administrator a written report containing an assessment of the ground-water quality.

§ 265.94   Recordkeeping and Reporting.

(a) Unless the ground water is monitored to satisfy the requirements of § 265.93(d)(4), the owner or operator must:

(2) Report the following ground-water monitoring information to the Regional Administrator:

(ii) Annually: Concentrations or values of the parameters listed in § 265.92(b)(3) for each ground-water monitoring well, along with the required evaluations for these parameters under § 265.93(b). The owner or operator must separately identify any significant differences from initial background found in the upgradient wells, in accordance with § 265.93(c)(1). During the active life of the facility, this information must be submitted no later than March 1 following each calendar year.

40 C.F.R. Part 265, Subpart G—Closure and Post–Closure

§ 265.111   Closure Performance Standard.

The owner or operator must close the facility in a manner that:

(a) Minimizes the need for further maintenance, and

(b) Controls, minimizes or eliminates, to the extent necessary to protect human health and the environment, post-closure escape of hazardous waste, hazardous constituents, leachate, contaminated run-off, or hazardous waste decomposition products to the ground or surface waters or to the atmosphere, and

(c) Complies with the closure requirements of this subpart, including, but not limited to, the requirements of §§ 265.197, 265.228, 265.258, 265.280, 265.310, 265.351, 265.381, 265.404, and 264.1102.

§ 265.112   Closure Plan; Amendment of Plan.

(a) Written plan. By May 19, 1981, or by six months after the effective date of the rule that first subjects a facility to provisions of this section, the owner or operator of a hazardous waste management facility must have a written closure plan. Until final closure is completed and certified in accordance with § 265.115, a copy of the most current plan must be furnished to the Regional Administrator upon request, including request by mail. . . .

(b) Content of plan. The plan must identify steps necessary to perform partial and/or final closure of the facility at any point during its active life. The closure plan must include, at least:

(1) A description of how each hazardous waste management unit at the facility will be closed in accordance with § 265.111; and

(2) A description of how final closure of the facility will be conducted in accordance with § 265.111. The description must identify the maximum extent of the operation which will be unclosed during the active life of the facility; and

(3) An estimate of the maximum inventory of hazardous wastes ever on-site over the active life of the facility and a detailed description of the methods to be used during partial and final closure, including, but not limited to methods for removing, transporting, treating, storing or disposing of all hazardous waste, identification of and the type(s) of off-site hazardous waste management unit(s) to be used, if applicable; and

(4) A detailed description of the steps needed to remove or decontaminate all hazardous waste residues and contaminated containment system components, equipment, structures, and soils during partial and final closure including, but not limited to, procedures for cleaning equipment and removing contaminated soils, methods for sampling and testing surrounding soils, and criteria for determining the extent of decontamination necessary to satisfy the closure performance standard; and

(5) A detailed description of other activities necessary during the partial and final closure period to ensure that all partial closures and final closure satisfy the closure performance standards, including, but not limited to, ground-water monitoring, leachate collection, and run-on and run-off control; and

(6) A schedule for closure of each hazardous waste management unit and for final closure of the facility. The schedule must include, at a minimum, the total time required to close each hazardous waste management unit and the time required for intervening closure activities which will allow tracking of the progress of partial and final closure. . . .

(c) Amendment of plan. The owner or operator may amend the closure plan at any time prior to the notification of partial or final closure of the facility. . . .

(1) The owner or operator must amend the closure plan whenever:

(i) Changes in operating plans or facility design affect the closure plan, or

(ii) There is a change in the expected year of closure, if applicable, or

(iii) In conducting partial or final closure activities, unexpected events require a modification of the closure plan.

(2) The owner or operator must amend the closure plan at least 60 days prior to the proposed change in facility design or operation, or no later than 60 days after an unexpected event has occurred which has affected the closure plan.... These provisions also apply to owners or operators of surface impoundments ... who intended to remove all hazardous wastes at closure, but are required to close as landfills in accordance with § 265.310.

(d) Notification of partial closure and final closure.

(1) The owner or operator must submit the closure plan to the Regional Administrator at least 180 days prior to the date on which he expects to begin closure of the first surface impoundment ..., or final closure if it involves such a unit, whichever is earlier....

§ 265.113   Closure; Time Allowed for Closure.

(a) Within 90 days after receiving the final volume of hazardous wastes, or the final volume of nonhazardous wastes if the owner or operator complies with all applicable requirements in paragraphs (d) and (e) of this section, at a hazardous waste management unit or facility, or within 90 days after approval of the closure plan, whichever is later, the owner or operator must treat, remove from the unit or facility, or dispose of on-site, all hazardous wastes in accordance with the approved closure plan. The Regional Administrator may approve a longer period if the owner or operator demonstrates that:

(1)(i) The activities required to comply with this paragraph will, of necessity, take longer than 90 days to complete ... ; and

(2) He has taken and will continue to take all steps to prevent threats to human health and the environment from the unclosed but not operating hazardous waste management unit or facility, including compliance with all applicable interim status requirements.

40 C.F.R. Part 265, Subpart K—Surface Impoundments

§ 265.228   Closure and Post-Closure Care.

(a) At closure, the owner or operator must:

(1) Remove or decontaminate all waste residues, contaminated containment system components (liners, etc.), contaminated subsoils, and structures and equipment contaminated with waste and leachate, and manage them as hazardous waste unless § 261.3(d) of this chapter applies; or

(2) Close the impoundment and provide post-closure care for a landfill under Subpart G and § 265.310, including the following:

(i) Eliminate free liquids by removing liquid wastes or solidifying the remaining wastes and waste residues;

(ii) Stabilize remaining wastes to a bearing capacity sufficient to support the final cover; and

(iii) Cover the surface impoundment with a final cover designed and constructed to:

(A) Provide long-term minimization of the migration of liquids through the closed impoundment;

(B) Function with minimum maintenance;

(C) Promote drainage and minimize erosion or abrasion of the cover;

(D) Accommodate settling and subsidence so that the cover's integrity is maintained; and

(E) Have a permeability less than or equal to the permeability of any bottom liner system or natural subsoils present.

(b) In addition to the requirements of Subpart G, and § 265.310, during the post-closure care period, the owner or operator of a surface impoundment in which wastes, waste residues, or contaminated materials remain after closure in accordance with the provisions of paragraph (a)(2) of this section must:

(1) Maintain the integrity and effectiveness of the final cover, including making repairs to the cover as necessary to correct the effects of settling, subsidence, erosion, or other events;

(2) Maintain and monitor the leak detection system in accordance with §§ 265.221(c)(2)(iv) and (3) of this chapter and 265.226(b) and comply with all other applicable leak detection system requirements of this part;

(3) Maintain and monitor the ground-water monitoring system and comply with all other applicable requirements of Subpart F of this part; and

(4) Prevent run-on and run-off from eroding or otherwise damaging the final cover. . . .

Notes and Questions

1. How would you respond to the questions posed by the EPA inspector? Can West still go through "clean closure?" If so, what would it entail? What are the implications of the requirement in 40 C.F.R. § 265.228 that the facility remove all contaminated subsoils?

2. It should be noted that EPA has the tools to require cleanup of contamination like that presented in the hypothetical if it deems it warranted. For interim status facilities, EPA can order "corrective action" under § 3008(h) of RCRA. For fully-permitted facilities, corrective action requirements are addressed in the relevant permits. See 40 C.F.R. §§ 264.100 and 264.101.

3. Note that the groundwater monitoring requirements do not apply to all TSDs. Rather, they only apply to those TSDs that manage wastes in surface impoundments, landfills, or land treatment facilities. 40 C.F.R. § 265.90(a).

4. TSDs can close individual units without closing their entire facilities. 40 C.F.R. § 265.112(b)(1). In fact, a given TSD can close all of its TSD units without closing its entire facility. Over the years, many TSDs (particularly manufacturers) have chosen to "revert" to generator status by ceasing all of their TSD activities. Thus, the student should not necessarily equate "closing" with the shutting down of a plant. It often means that a particular company has simply chosen to change its operations to an extent that alters its regulatory status.

5. RCRA's financial responsibility requirements have two main components. First, all TSDs must meet certain "financial assurance" requirements designed to ensure that they will have the necessary resources to implement their closure and (if applicable) post-closure plans. See, e.g., 40 C.F.R. §§ 265.142–265.146. Perhaps obviously, the goal here is to minimize the possibility that these RCRA facilities will require cleanup under other programs such as CERCLA. As a result, facilities have to estimate their projected closure and post-closure costs. 40 C.F.R. §§ 265.142 and 265.144. They then have to either pass a financial test indicating that these funds will be available, or set aside the requisite funds in some sort of bankruptcy-proof mechanism. See, e.g., 40 C.F.R. §§ 265.143 and 265.145. The second component of the financial responsibility requirements is that facilities have insurance designed to protect their neighbors. All TSDs must have coverage for what are termed "sudden accidental occurrences." See, e.g., 40 C.F.R. § 265.147(a). Additionally, land disposal facilities must have coverage for "nonsudden" occurrences as well. 40 C.F.R. § 265.147(b).

6. In passing HSWA in 1984, Congress created what is commonly referred to as the "land ban" program. See 42 U.S.C. § 6924(b)–(n). This program restricts the land disposal of hazardous wastes by requiring that they first be treated in accordance with standards set by EPA. 42 U.S.C. § 6924(m). The details of this program are far too complicated to be treated in an overview course. It is worth noting, however, that the D.C. has upheld the linchpins of EPA's implementation strategy. First, in *Hazardous Waste Treatment Council v. U.S. EPA*, 886 F.2d 355 (D.C. Cir. 1989), it upheld EPA's authority to generally require the "best demonstrated available technology" ("BDAT") as the relevant treatment standard. And second, in *Chemical Waste Management, Inc. v. U.S. EPA*, 976 F.2d 2 (1992), it affirmed EPA's authority generally to require that characteristic wastes be treated to BDAT even though they no longer qualify as hazardous wastes once they no longer exhibit the relevant characteristic. EPA's "land ban" regulations are found at 40 C.F.R. Part 268.

Chapter 6

REGULATORY ENFORCEMENT

I. ENFORCEMENT

As we have seen, the federal environmental statutes impose many binding legal requirements on regulated entities. Not surprisingly, these requirements are backed up by the threat of enforcement actions. Indeed, under most statutes the regulated entities operate under the supervision of three potential regulatory overseers. Using the Clean Water Act as an example, Section 309 gives the United States access to a broad range of enforcement powers, including the power to seek both civil and criminal sanctions. Section 402(i) indicates that these authorities apply even in authorized States. Additionally, as we have seen, Section 402(b)(7) requires States to provide their environmental agencies with similar powers as a precondition to authorization. And finally, Section 505 puts citizens on virtually the same footing as EPA, at least with respect to the ability to seek civil relief in court.

In the discussion below, we will focus primarily on the federal enforcement powers granted to EPA and citizens. While the precise contours of the State enforcement models may vary somewhat from what will be addressed below, the reader should rest assured that most of the principles discussed below will at least be relevant in State enforcement settings. Additionally, as the reader will soon see, we will focus primarily on the statutory dynamics of the Clean Water Act in our discussions in this chapter. This is due in significant part to the fact that there is much more enforcement case law under the CWA than there is under the other major command-and-control statutes. It will also serve to maintain some consistency in our discussions. Even more so in this context, however, the student should be assured that the relevant principles are more often than not directly applicable under the other statutes. While some differences will be noted, in most contexts the federal environmental laws have very similar statutory enforcement dynamics.

A. Investigations

The first step in any compliance oversight process involves compliance evaluation. Perhaps obviously, this requires access to the information necessary to evaluate a particular regulated entity's compliance status. Section 308 of the CWA provides a good example of the types of investigatory powers Congress typically vests in EPA. First, it gives EPA the power to compel point source operators to monitor their effluent, to maintain records, and to make such reports as EPA reasonably requires. 33 U.S.C. § 1318(a)(2)(A). Not surprisingly, EPA has established regulations on these fronts. The gist of these regulations is that permittees are required to monitor their discharges in accordance with specified protocols, and report the results of that monitoring monthly in what are called Discharge Monitoring Reports (or "DMRs"). See 40 C.F.R. § 122.41(j) and (*l*). Additionally, permittees must report all instances of noncompliance either within 24–hours (if they may endanger health or the environment) or, otherwise, at the time they submit their next DMRs, see 40 C.F.R. § 122.41(*l*)(6) and (7). They are also required to maintain copies of all relevant reports, including the underlying data, for at least three years. 40 C.F.R. § 122.41(j)(2). Permittees are subject to felony sanctions if they knowingly either fail to maintain or submit the required information, or if they submit false material statements. See 33 U.S.C. § 1319(c)(2) and (4).

Section 308 also gives EPA the power to inspect any premises in which an effluent source is located or in which any required records are maintained; it further expressly allows EPA to copy any relevant records, to inspect any monitoring equipment, and to sample any effluent. 33 U.S.C. § 1318(a)(2)(B). EPA's permit regulations elaborate on these requirements by compelling permittees to provide EPA (or an authorized State) with access to their facilities for any of the above purposes. Thus, the failure to do so constitutes a permit violation, subject to both civil and criminal enforcement.

Interestingly, EPA has never asserted the right to engage in warrantless inspections under any of the environmental statutes it administers. See, generally, *Donovan v. Dewey*, 452 U.S. 594, 101 S.Ct. 2534, 69 L.Ed.2d 262 (1981), and *New York v. Burger*, 482 U.S. 691, 107 S.Ct. 2636, 96 L.Ed.2d 601 (1987). As a practical matter, most regulated entities consent to EPA's inspections without requiring it to obtain a warrant. Even if a facility were to stand on its rights, the most that EPA would need to demonstrate to obtain a warrant for routine inspections would be something called "administrative probable cause." This requires only either one of two showings: (1) that EPA has "specific evidence of an existing violation," or (2) that "reasonable legislative or administrative standards for conducting an ... inspection are satisfied with respect to a particular [facility]." *Marshall v. Barlow's, Inc.*, 436 U.S. 307, 320, 98 S.Ct. 1816, 1824, 56 L.Ed.2d 305 (1978) (internal quotations omitted). Moreover, EPA can obtain such warrants from the courts in ex parte proceedings (that is, without the facility-owner being present). Given these dynamics, do you understand why most regulated entities consent to EPA's inspections? Under what circumstances, if any, would there be a tactical advantage to insisting upon a warrant? What might be the drawbacks of such an approach?

B. Enforcement Options

Once EPA learns that a particular facility has violated one of its regulatory programs, it must first determine whether to enforce and, if so, how. The decision as to whether to enforce is not as simple as one might think. Environmental violations may range from the relatively trivial (e.g., a facility submits a full and accurate DMR, but submits it one day late) to the very serious (e.g., a facility discharges highly toxic wastes into a small river without a permit). EPA surely wants the discretion to forgo enforcement completely with respect to relatively minor violations, especially in situations in which a facility otherwise has demonstrated its commitment to environmental compliance. In other cases, EPA may want to let the States take the enforcement lead, even with respect to relatively serious violations, in the interest of promoting harmony in the "cooperative federalism" scheme.

Under the CWA, Section 309(a) on its face appears to require EPA, upon a finding of violation, to bring some action to compel compliance if it determines, after 30–days notice, that the State "has not commenced an appropriate enforcement action." It does this by stating that, in such circumstances, EPA "shall issue an order requiring [the alleged violator] to comply ... or shall bring a civil action [under § 309(b)]." 33 U.S.C. § 1319(a)(1); see also § 1319(a)(3) (seemingly compelling EPA to either issue an order or file a court action, regardless of what the State does). Despite these formulations, however, the courts have been virtually unanimous in determining that EPA does not have a mandatory duty to bring enforcement actions in such situations. See, e.g., *Dubois v. Thomas*, 820 F.2d 943 (8th Cir. 1987) ("*Dubois*"), and *Sierra Club v. Whitman*, 268 F.3d 898 (9th Cir. 2001). In so holding, the courts have relied on both (1) the fact that nothing in these provisions explicitly requires EPA to make any findings as to a particular facility's compliance status; and (2) the Supreme Court's opinion in *Heckler v. Chaney*, 470 U.S. 821, 105 S.Ct. 1649, 84 L.Ed.2d 714 (1985), in which the Court determined that the Food and Drug Administration had the discretion not to bring an enforcement action under the Federal Food, Drug and Cosmetic Act, 21 U.S.C. § 301, et seq., despite statutory language indicating that violators "shall be imprisoned." See, e.g., *Dubois*, 820 F.2d at 946–950.

In those cases in which EPA does choose to enforce, it chooses between three basic approaches. First, EPA is empowered to seek both injunctive relief and penalties through the initiation of civil actions in federal court. See, e.g., 33 U.S.C. § 1319(b) and (d). Alternatively, it can essentially seek the same forms of relief administratively. As mentioned above, Section 309(a) of the CWA gives EPA the power to issue administrative orders compelling violators to comply with the statute. See 33 U.S.C. § 1319(a)(3). Additionally, in 1987 Congress gave EPA the related power to impose administrative penalties under § 309(g). Collectively, these two authorities constitute EPA's second basic enforcement pathway. And third, in many (but not all) noncompliance situations, EPA has the option of pursuing criminal sanctions. In general, EPA may purse felony sanctions in situations in which regulated entities have committed "knowing" violations. See, e.g., 33 U.S.C. § 1319(c)(2). As we will see, these formulations pose the issue of exactly what the violator must "know" in order to be criminally accountable.

In the pages below, we consider all three of these enforcement pathways. We will also consider the extent which prior State enforcement action may limit EPA's options.

1. EPA–Lead Civil Actions in Court

Not surprisingly, the environmental statutes give the Government the authority to seek judicial relief both compelling compliance and imposing penalties. Under the CWA, for example, Section 309(b) authorizes EPA, when faced with a violation, to seek either a permanent or temporary injunction. It also provides the court with "jurisdiction to restrain such violation and to require compliance." Additionally, Section 309(d) gives courts the authority to impose fines of up to $25,000 "per day for each violation" of the CWA. Despite this statutory language, the maximum fine for each violation has since been increased to $32,500 pursuant to the Federal Civil Penalties Inflation Adjustment Act, 28 U.S.C. § 2461 note. See 69 Fed.Reg. 7121 (Feb. 13, 2004).

On the injunctive relief front, one question that frequently arises relates to the degree of discretion the courts possess in fashioning relief under these provisions. Is the court, in any particular case, obligated to compel compliance even if such a decree might result in significant hardship to the defendant or others? If so, within what period of time must compliance be achieved? Consider the following case:

WEINBERGER v. ROMERO–BARCELO

Supreme Court of the United States, 1982.
456 U.S. 305, 102 S.Ct. 1798, 72 L.Ed.2d 91.

WHITE, Justice.

The issue in this case is whether the Federal Water Pollution Control Act ("FWPCA") requires a district court to enjoin immediately all discharges of pollutants that do not comply with the Act's permit requirements or whether the district court retains discretion to order other relief to achieve compliance....

For many years, the Navy has used Vieques Island, a small island off the Puerto Rico coast, for weapons training.... During air-to-ground training, however, pilots sometimes miss land-based targets, and ordnance falls into the sea. That is, accidental bombings of the navigable waters and, occasionally, intentional bombings of water targets occur....

In 1978, respondents, who include the Governor of Puerto Rico and residents of the island, sued to enjoin the Navy's operations on the island....

As the District Court construed the FWPCA the release of ordnance from aircraft or from ships into navigable waters is a discharge of pollutants, even though the EPA ... had not promulgated any regulations setting effluent levels or providing for the issuance of an NPDES permit for this category of pollutants. Recognizing that violations of the Act "must be cured," the District Court ordered the Navy to apply for an NPDES permit. It refused, however, to enjoin Navy operations pending consideration of the permit application. It explained that the Navy's "technical violations" were not causing any "appreciable harm" to the environment.[4] Moreover, because of the importance of the island as a training center, "the granting of the injunctive relief sought would cause grievous, and perhaps irreparable harm, not only to Defendant Navy, but to the general welfare of this Nation." The District Court concluded that an injunction was not necessary to ensure suitably prompt compliance by the Navy....

The Court of Appeals for the First Circuit vacated the District Court's order and remanded with instructions that the court order the Navy to cease the violation until it obtained a permit. Relying on *TVA v. Hill*, 437 U.S. 153 (1978), in which this Court held that an imminent violation of the Endangered Species Act required injunctive relief, the Court of Appeals concluded that the District Court erred in undertaking a traditional balancing of the parties' competing interests. "Whether or not the Navy's activities in fact harm the coastal waters, it has an absolute statutory obligation to stop any discharges of pollutants until the permit procedure has been followed and [EPA] ... has granted a permit...."

It goes without saying that an injunction is an equitable remedy. It "is not a remedy which issues as of course," *Harrisonville v. W.S. Dickey Clay Mfg. Co.*, 289 U.S. 334, 337–338 (1933), or "to restrain an act the injurious consequences of which are merely trifling." *Consolidated Canal Co. v. Mesa Canal Co.*, 177 U.S. 296, 302 (1900). The Court has repeatedly held that the basis for injunctive relief in the federal courts has always been irreparable injury and the inadequacy of legal remedies.

In exercising their sound discretion, courts of equity should pay particular regard for the public consequences in employing the extraordinary remedy of injunction. The grant of jurisdiction to ensure compliance with a statute hardly suggests an absolute duty to do so under any and all circumstances, and a federal judge sitting as chancellor is not mechanically obligated to grant an injunction for every violation of law.

---

4. The District Court wrote: "In fact, if anything, these waters are as aesthetically acceptable as any to be found anywhere, and Plaintiff's witnesses unanimously testified as to their being the best fishing grounds in Vieques." "[I]f the truth be said, the control of large areas of Vieques [by the Navy] probably constitutes a positive factor in its over all ecology. The very fact that there are in the Navy zones modest numbers of various marine species which are practically nonexistent in the civilian sector of Vieques or in the main island of Puerto Rico, is an eloquent example of res ipsa loquitur."

... Of course, Congress may intervene and guide or control the exercise of the courts' discretion, but we do not lightly assume that Congress has intended to depart from established principles....

In *TVA v. Hill*, we held that Congress had foreclosed the exercise of the usual discretion possessed by a court of equity. There, we thought that "[o]ne would be hard pressed to find a statutory provision whose terms were any plainer" than that before us. 437 U.S., at 173. The statute involved, the Endangered Species Act, required the District Court to enjoin completion of the Tellico Dam in order to preserve the snail darter, a species of perch. The purpose and language of the statute under consideration in *Hill*, not the bare fact of a statutory violation, compelled that conclusion. Section 7 of the Act requires federal agencies to "insure that actions authorized, funded, or carried out by them do not jeopardize the continued existence of [any] endangered species ... or result in the destruction or modification of habitat of such species which is determined ... to be critical." The statute thus contains a flat ban on the destruction of critical habitats.

It was conceded in *Hill* that completion of the dam would eliminate an endangered species by destroying its critical habitat. Refusal to enjoin the action would have ignored the [explicit provisions of the statute.] Congress, it appeared to us, had chosen the snail darter over the dam.... [O]nly an injunction could vindicate the objectives of the Act.

That is not the case here. An injunction is not the only means of ensuring compliance. The FWPCA itself, for example, provides for fines and criminal penalties. Respondents suggest that failure to enjoin the Navy will undermine the integrity of the permit process by allowing the statutory violation to continue. The integrity of the Nation's waters, however, not the permit process, is the purpose of the FWPCA....

This purpose is to be achieved by compliance with the Act, including compliance with the permit requirements. Here, however, the discharge of ordnance had not polluted the waters, and, although the District Court declined to enjoin the discharges, it neither ignored the statutory violation nor undercut the purpose and function of the permit system. The court ordered the Navy to apply for a permit.[9] It temporarily, not permanently, allowed the Navy to continue its activities without a permit.

In *Hill*, we also noted that none of the limited "hardship exemptions" of the Endangered Species Act would "even remotely apply to the Tellico Project." 437 U.S., at 188. The prohibition of the FWPCA against

9. The Navy applied for an NPDES permit in December 1979. In May 1981, the EPA issued a draft NPDES permit and a notice of intent to issue that permit. The FWPCA requires a certification of compliance with state water quality standards before the EPA may issue an NPDES permit. 33 U.S.C. § 1341(a). The Environmental Quality Board of the Commonwealth of Puerto Rico denied the Navy a water quali-ty certificate in connection with this application for an NPDES in June 1981. In February 1982, the Environmental Quality Board denied the Navy's reconsideration request and announced it was adhering to its original ruling. In a letter dated April 9, 1982, the Solicitor General informed the Clerk of the Court that the Navy has filed an action challenging the denial of the water quality certificate.

discharge of pollutants, in contrast, can be overcome by the very permit the Navy was ordered to seek. The Senate Report to the 1972 Amendments explains that the permit program would be enacted because "the Committee recognizes the impracticality of any effort to halt all pollution immediately." That the scheme as a whole contemplates the exercise of discretion and balancing of equities militates against the conclusion that Congress intended to deny courts their traditional equitable discretion in enforcing the statute.

Other aspects of the statutory scheme also suggest that Congress did not intend to deny courts the discretion to rely on remedies other than an immediate prohibitory injunction. Although the ultimate objective of the FWPCA is to eliminate all discharges of pollutants into the navigable waters by 1985, the statute sets forth a scheme of phased compliance. As enacted, it called for the achievement of [BPT by 1977] and [BAT by 1983]. This scheme of phased compliance further suggests that this is a statute in which Congress envisioned, rather than curtailed, the exercise of discretion.

The FWPCA directs the Administrator of the EPA to seek an injunction to restrain immediately discharges of pollutants he finds to be presenting "an imminent and substantial endangerment to the health of persons or to the welfare of persons." 33 U.S.C. § 1364(a). This rule of immediate cessation, however, is limited to the indicated class of violations. For other kinds of violations, the FWPCA authorizes the Administrator of the EPA "to commence a civil action for appropriate relief, including a permanent or temporary injunction, for any violation for which he is authorized to issue a compliance order...." 33 U.S.C. § 1319(b). The provision makes clear that Congress did not anticipate that all discharges would be immediately enjoined. Consistent with this view, the administrative practice has not been to request immediate cessation orders. "Rather, enforcement actions typically result, by consent or otherwise, in a remedial order setting out a detailed schedule of compliance designed to cure the identified violation of the Act." Brief for Petitioners 17. Here, again, the statutory scheme contemplates equitable consideration.

This Court explained in *Hecht Co. v. Bowles*, 321 U.S. 321 (1944), that a major departure from the long tradition of equity practice should not be lightly implied.... We do not read the FWPCA as foreclosing completely the exercise of the court's discretion. Rather than requiring a district court to issue an injunction for any and all statutory violations, the FWPCA permits the district court to order that relief it considers necessary to secure prompt compliance with the Act. That relief can include, but is not limited to, an order of immediate cessation.

The exercise of equitable discretion, which must include the ability to deny as well as grant injunctive relief, can fully protect the range of public interests at issue at this stage in the proceedings. The District Court did not face a situation in which a permit would very likely not issue, and the requirements and objective of the statute could therefore not be vindicated if discharges were permitted to continue. Should it become clear that no permit will be issued and that compliance with the FWPCA will not be forthcoming, the statutory scheme and purpose would require the court to reconsider the balance it has struck.

STEVENS, Justice, dissenting.

. . . Because the [FWPCA] does not specifically command the federal courts to issue an injunction every time an unpermitted discharge of a pollutant occurs, the Court today is obviously correct in asserting that such injunctions should not issue "automatically" or "mechanically" in every case. It is nevertheless equally clear that by enacting the [FWPCA] Congress channeled the discretion of the federal judiciary much more narrowly than the Court's rather glib opinion suggests. Indeed, although there may well be situations in which the failure to obtain an NPDES permit would not require immediate cessation of all discharges, I am convinced that Congress has circumscribed the district courts' discretion on the question of remedy so narrowly that a general rule of immediate cessation must be applied in all but a narrow category of cases....

Contrary to the impression created by the Court's opinion, the Court of Appeals did not hold that the District Court was under an absolute duty to require compliance with the FWPCA "under any and all circumstances," or that it was "mechanically obligated to grant an injunction for every violation of law." The only "absolute duty" that the Court of Appeals mentioned was the Navy's duty to obtain a permit before discharging pollutants into the waters off Vieques Island . . .

. . . The Court of Appeals' reasoning was correct in all respects. It recognized that the statute categorically prohibits discharges of pollutants without a permit. Unlike the Court, it recognized that the requested injunction was the only remedy that would bring the Navy into compliance with the statute on Congress' timetable.... The position of the Court of Appeals in effect was that the federal courts' equitable discretion is constrained by a strong presumption in favor of enforcing the law as Congress has written it. By reversing, the Court casts doubt on the validity of that position. This doubt is especially dangerous in the environmental area, where the temptations to delay compliance are already substantial.

The Court distinguishes *TVA v. Hill*, 437 U.S. 153, on the ground that the Endangered Species Act contained a "flat ban" on the destruction of critical habitats. But the statute involved in this case also contains a flat ban against discharges of pollutants into coastal waters without a permit....

It is true that in *TVA v. Hill* there was no room for compromise between the federal project and the statutory objective to preserve an endangered species; either the snail darter or the completion of the Tellico Dam had to be sacrificed. In the FWPCA, the Court tells us, the congressional objective is to protect the integrity of the Nation's waters, not to protect the integrity of the permit process. Therefore, the Court continues, a federal court may compromise the process chosen by Congress to protect our waters as long as the court is content that the waters are not actually being harmed by the particular discharge of pollutants.

On analysis, however, this reasoning does not distinguish the two cases. Courts are in no better position to decide whether the permit process is necessary to achieve the objectives of the FWPCA than they are to decide whether the destruction of the snail darter is an acceptable cost of completing the Tellico Dam. Congress has made both decisions, and there is nothing in the respective statutes or legislative histories to suggest that Congress invited the federal courts to second-guess the former decision any more than the latter.

A disregard of the respective roles of the three branches of government also tarnishes the Court's other principal argument in favor of expansive equitable discretion in this area. The Court points out that Congress intended to halt water pollution gradually, not immediately, and that "the scheme as a whole contemplates the exercise of discretion and balancing of equities." In the Court's words, Congress enacted a "scheme of phased compliance." Equitable discretion in enforcing the statute, the Court states, is therefore consistent with the statutory scheme.

The Court's sophistry is premised on a gross misunderstanding of the statutory scheme. Naturally, in 1972 Congress did not expect dischargers to end pollution immediately. Rather, it entrusted to expert administrative agencies the task of establishing timetables by which dischargers could reach that ultimate goal. These timetables are determined by the agencies and included in the NPDES permits; the conditions in the permits constitute the terms by which compliance with the statute is measured. Quite obviously, then, the requirement that each discharger subject itself to the permit process is crucial to the operation of the "scheme of phased compliance." By requiring each discharger to obtain a permit before continuing its discharges of pollutants, Congress demonstrated an intolerance for delay in compliance with the statute. It is also obvious that the "exercise of discretion and balancing of equities" were tasks delegated by Congress to expert agencies, not to federal courts, yet the Court simply ignores the difference.

The decision in *TVA v. Hill* did not depend on any peculiar or unique statutory language. Nor did it rest on any special interest in snail darters. The decision reflected a profound respect for the law and the proper allocation of lawmaking responsibilities in our Government. There we refused to sit as a committee of review. Today the Court authorizes free-thinking federal judges to do just that. Instead of requiring adherence to carefully integrated statutory procedures that assign to nonjudicial decisionmakers the responsibilities for evaluating potential harm to our water supply as well as potential harm to our national security, the Court unnecessarily and casually substitutes the chancellor's clumsy foot for the rule of law.

Questions and Notes

1. The phraseology of § 309(b) (quoted in *Romero-Barcelo*) is similar to that in the equitable relief provisions of other federal environmental statutes. See, e.g., 42 U.S.C. §§ 6928(a)(1) (RCRA) and 7413(b) (CAA).

2. How would you characterize the Court's holding in *Romero-Barcelo*? How did the Court distinguish *TVA v. Hill*? How did Justice Stevens respond? What aspects of the CWA did the Court cite as being supportive of its result? Are they persuasive? Do you think the Court would have reached the same result if the Navy's discharges had been causing clear harm to the waters? What if there had simply been more doubt about whether a permit would issue? What approach did Justice Stevens advocate? Under the majority's approach, does the fact that Congress forbade permitless discharges merit any weight in the equitable balancing process? Should it?

3. In the later case of *Amoco Production Co. v. Village of Gambell*, 480 U.S. 531, 107 S.Ct. 1396, 94 L.Ed.2d 542 (1987), the Supreme Court, while denying a rule of automatic injunction under the Alaska National Interest Lands Conservation Act, did state that:

> ... Environmental injury, by its nature, can seldom be adequately remedies by money damages and is often permanent or at least of long duration, *i.e.*, irreparable. If such injury is sufficiently likely, therefore, the balance of harms will usually favor the issuance of an injunction to protect the environment.

Id. at 545, 107 S.Ct. at 1404. Even more recently, in *United States v. Oakland Cannabis Buyers' Cooperative*, 532 U.S. 483, 121 S.Ct. 1711, 149 L.Ed.2d 722 (2001), the Supreme Court reversed a decision by the Ninth Circuit in which the latter court had held that the district court in that case had the discretion to decline to enjoin the Cooperative's ongoing distribution of marijuana in violation of the Controlled Substances Act:

> ... [T]he mere fact that the District Court had discretion does not suggest that the District Court, when evaluating the motion to modify the injunction, could consider any and all factors that might relate to the public interest or the conveniences of the parties, including the medical needs of the Cooperative's patients. On the contrary, a court sitting in equity cannot ignore the judgment of Congress, deliberately expressed in legislation. A district court cannot, for example, override Congress' policy choice, articulated in a statute, as to what behavior should be prohibited. "Once Congress, exercising its delegated powers, has decided the order of priorities in a given area, it is ... for the courts to enforce them when enforcement is sought." [*TVA v. Hill*], 437 U.S., at 194. Courts of equity cannot, in their discretion, reject the balance that Congress has struck in a statute. *Id.*, at 194–195. Their choice (unless there is statutory language to the contrary) is simply whether a particular means of enforcing the statute should be chosen over another permissible means; their choice is not whether enforcement is preferable to no enforcement at all. Consequently, when a court of equity exercises its discretion, it may not consider the advantages and disadvantages of nonenforcement of the statute, but only the advantages and disadvantages of "employing the extraordinary remedy of injunction," *Romero-Barcelo*, 456 U.S., at 311, over the other available methods of enforce-

ment. Cf. *id.,* at 316 (referring to "discretion to rely on remedies other than an immediate prohibitory injunction"). To the extent the district court considers the public interest and the conveniences of the parties, the court is limited to evaluating how such interest and conveniences are affected by the selection of an injunction over other enforcement mechanisms. . . .

Id. at 487–498, 121 S.Ct. at 1721–1722. How, if at all, should these cases affect the analysis under statutes such as the CWA?

Section 309(d) provides courts with a similar degree of discretion in the penalty imposition realm. First, it establishes the statutory range, which again, despite what § 309(d) says, should now be read as providing for penalties "not to exceed [$32,500] per day for each violation." See 69 Fed.Reg. 7121 (Feb. 13, 2004). Second, it dictates that, in determining the appropriate fine within that statutory range, the court shall consider

> the seriousness of the violation or violations, the economic benefit (if any) resulting from the violation, any history of such violations, any good-faith efforts to comply with the applicable requirements, the economic impact of the penalty on the violator, and such other matters as justice may require.

33 U.S.C. § 1319(d).

How should courts apply these factors? Consider the following case, which, despite its formal name, is commonly referred to as *"Dean Dairy:"*

UNITED STATES v. THE MUNICIPAL AUTHORITY OF UNION TOWNSHIP

United States Court of Appeals, Third Circuit, 1998.

150 F.3d 259.

Sloviter, Circuit Judge.

Appellant Dean Dairy Products, Inc., appeals the district court's imposition of a $4,031,000 civil penalty against it for Clean Water Act violations. Dean Dairy contends that the district court erred when it assessed the economic benefit Dean Dairy gained during the period of the Clean Water Act violations on the basis of Dean Dairy's "wrongful profits."

. . . Briefly stated, Dean Dairy, operating in Union Township, Belleville, Pennsylvania, is a wholly-owned subsidiary of Dean Foods, Inc., the country's largest milk processor. Since 1974 Dean Dairy's wastewater, a result of the production of sour cream, cottage cheese, yogurt and ice cream, has been discharged and treated by Union Township's [POTW]. . . .

Beginning in July 1989, Dean Dairy exceeded [its pretreatment limits]. Its wastewater, containing the impermissibly high levels of BOD and TSS, flowed from Union Township's POTW into the nearby Kishacoquillas Creek, which was damaged as a result. There is no dispute that because Dean Dairy issued monitoring reports to Union Township on a monthly basis, it had been aware of its violations since July 1989.

In 1994, the United States filed a civil enforcement action against Dean Dairy under the [CWA] for close to 1800 violations ... Following discovery, the United States moved for and was granted summary judgment on the issue of Dean Dairy's liability for the CWA violations. The action against the Municipal Authority of Union Township was settled and therefore the Authority is not a party to this appeal. Dean Dairy does not contest its liability for the violations. Its appeal is limited to the amount of the civil penalty imposed.

The district court found Dean Dairy liable for 1,754 violations ... between July 1989 and April 1994. It also found that Dean Dairy continued to violate [the relevant requirements] after the United States filed suit. Although Dean Dairy took certain steps to address the violations ... between 1991 and 1994, the district court found these efforts were belated and ineffective. It was only the construction of a $865,000 pretreatment system, which became operational in April 1995, that succeeded in reducing Dean Dairy's pollutants to permissible levels.

Important to the issue before us is that Dean Dairy considered various options to meet its permit obligations but, as the district court found, "it continued to produce at a volume which it recognized was very likely to generate [violations]. [Dean Dairy] chose not to reduce production volume because it viewed the concomitant reduction in earnings as too high a price to pay for compliance with the Clean Water Act."

Although the district court applied the six statutory factors a court must consider in assessing the appropriate penalty for a CWA violation, the appellant presents the case as if the court concentrated almost exclusively on the "economic benefit" factor. In fact, the district court made extensive findings of fact and issued conclusions of law on each of the six factors. The court noted that the history of Dean Diary's violations dated back to 1989, that the excessive discharges required the Pennsylvania Fish and Boat Commission to cease stocking fish in areas of the Kishacoquillas Creek, and that its two-year delay to take meaningful action to remedy the violations did "not speak highly of its good faith in this matter."

In connection with its evaluation of the economic benefit factor, ... the district court acknowledged that the parties had previously stipulated that Dean Dairy did not realize any economic benefit from delaying the capital investments necessary to achieve compliance.... This was due to the unusual fact that, by delaying the construction of the pretreatment plant, Dean Dairy was actually losing money because it was paying higher usage fees to the POTW for its increased volume. Thus, Dean Dairy did not reap an economic benefit by delaying the construction of the pretreatment plant. The court nevertheless found that Dean Dairy *did* realize an economic benefit during the period of the violations because it produced "at a volume above that which would have allowed it to operate within its IU permit."

In making the finding of economic benefit, the district court relied upon a document produced by Dean Dairy ... that outlined various options by which Dean Dairy could comply with its permit. The district court noted that Option #4 of that document indicated that Dean Dairy could drop PennMaid as a customer and thereby reduce the amount of wastewater generated. Dean Dairy recognized, however, that losing the revenues from PennMaid would result in a loss of earnings in the amount of $417,000 in fiscal year 1994.

In its opinion, the district court commented on [this information] as follows: "Production volume at Fairmont was higher in each year from 1989 to 1993 than it was in 1994, and, therefore, it is reasonable to believe that Fairmont gained at least $417,000 in earnings annually during the period of its violations. On this basis, the court concludes that between July 1989 and April 1994, Fairmont gained approximately $2,015,500 by violating its [pretreatment requirements]." The district court also determined that the figure should be doubled in order to provide a proper deterrent and punishment, and accordingly imposed a total penalty of $4,031,000.

Section 1319(d) of the [CWA] provides in pertinent part:

Any person who violates ... this title, or any permit condition or limitation ... shall be subject to a civil penalty not to exceed $25,000 per day for each violation. In determining the amount of a civil penalty the court shall consider the seriousness of the violation or violations, the economic benefit (if any) resulting from the violation, any history of such violations, any good-faith efforts to comply with the applicable requirements, the economic impact of the penalty on the violator, and such other matters as justice may require.

The statute does not define the term "economic benefit" used in this section. It is apparent, however, that the goal of the economic benefit analysis is to prevent a violator from profiting from its wrongdoing. In *United States v. Smithfield Foods, Inc.,* 972 F.Supp. 338, 348 (E.D.Va.1997), the district court explained that "[c]ourts use economic benefit analysis to level the economic playing field and prevent violators from gaining an unfair competitive advantage."

A similar rationale was also given by [EPA], which emphasized that the reason for considering economic benefit to a violator in assessing a CWA penalty is to remove or neutralize the economic incentive to violate environmental regulations. In a 1990 Manual to its BEN computer program, established to assist in the calculation of civil CWA penalties, the EPA explained:

An organization's decision to comply with environmental regulations usually implies a commitment of financial resources; both initially, in the form of a capital investment or one-time expenditure, and over time, in the form of annual, continuing expenses. These expenditures might result in better protection of public health or environmental quality; however, they are unlikely to yield any direct

economic benefit (i.e., net gain) to the organization. If these financial resources were not used for compliance, they presumably would
be invested in projects with an expected direct economic benefit to
the organization. This concept of alternative investment; that is, the
amount the violator would normally expect to make by not investing
in pollution control, is the basis for calculating the economic benefit
of noncompliance.... EPA uses the Agency's penalty authority to
remove or neutralize the economic incentive to violate environmental regulations. In the absence of enforcement and appropriate
penalties, it is usually in the organization's best economic interest to
delay the commitment of funds for compliance with environmental
regulations and to avoid certain other associated costs, such as
operating and maintenance expenses.

EPA BEN User's Manual I–6 (July 1990), *quoted in Friends of the Earth,
Inc. v. Laidlaw Envtl. Servs. (TOC), Inc.*, 890 F.Supp. 470 (D.S.C.1995)
("*Laidlaw I* ").

Few published cases discuss the "economic benefit" factor of the
Clean Water Act in any detail, and those that do are, in large part,
district court opinions. In *Laidlaw*, the court described economic benefit
as: "the after-tax present value of avoided or delayed expenditures on
necessary pollution control measures." 890 F.Supp. at 481. The theory is
that economic benefit "represents the opportunity a polluter had to earn
a return on funds that should have been spent to purchase, operate, and
maintain appropriate pollution control devices." *Id.*

This court has previously recognized that a violator's economic
benefit under the Clean Water Act may not be capable of ready determination. In *Public Interest Research Group of New Jersey, Inc. v. Powell
Duffryn Terminals Inc.*, 913 F.2d 64 (3d Cir.1990), we stated:

> Precise economic benefit to a polluter may be difficult to prove. The
> Senate Report accompanying the 1987 amendment that added the
> economic benefit factor to section 309(d) recognized that a reason-
> able approximation of economic benefit is sufficient to meet plain-
> tiff's burden for this factor.... The determination of economic
> benefit or other factors will not require an elaborate or burdensome
> evidentiary showing. Reasonable approximations of economic benefit
> will suffice.

Id. at 80 (citation omitted).

Because of the difficulty of determining the appropriate penalty
under the Clean Water Act, the court will accord the district court's
award of a penalty wide discretion, even though it represents an approximation. This was emphasized by the Supreme Court when it said, more
than a decade ago, "Congress [made the] assignment of the determination of the amount of civil penalties to trial judges.... Since Congress
itself may fix the civil penalties, it may delegate that determination to
trial judges. In this case, highly discretionary calculations that take into
account multiple factors are necessary in order to set civil penalties

under the Clean Water Act." *Tull v. United States,* 481 U.S. 412, 426–27 (1987).

Courts have applied different methods in determining the appropriate penalty for a Clean Water Act violation. Some courts have employed a "top down" approach in which the maximum possible penalty is first established, then reduced following an examination of the six "mitigating" factors. See, e.g., *Powell Duffryn,* 913 F.2d at 79.

Other courts have used a "bottom up" approach whereby the economic benefit a violator gained by noncompliance is established and adjusted upward or downward using the remaining five factors in § 1319(d). *See, e.g., Smithfield Foods,* 972 F.Supp. at 354. Because the statute does not prescribe either method, it appears that a court is free to use its discretion in choosing the appropriate method.

Had the district court in this case taken a "top-down" approach, it would have begun at the maximum penalty, which was approximately $45,825,000, based on the statutory penalty of $25,000 a day. Instead, the court applied the "bottom up" approach by determining Dean Dairy's economic benefit acquired through the Fairmont plant's production at a volume that resulted in more wastewater than permissible under its permit. These were knowing violations, as its own document demonstrated it was aware that if it had reduced its wastewater volume by reducing its production, it would have been in compliance with its IU permit.... [I]f Dean Dairy had reduced volume, it believed it would have lost PennMaid as a customer. Dean Dairy's own document prepared by Ron Crock, its controller, demonstrated that this loss of PennMaid would have had a negative impact of $417,000 per year. This was the basis on which the district court calculated Dean Dairy's economic benefit as $2,015,500, which when doubled, resulted in the penalty of $4,031,000. That penalty was barely 9% of the maximum statutory penalty to which Dean Dairy was subject.

It is not surprising that no published case has used this method of ascertaining a violator's economic benefit because it is the rare violator who actually loses money by delaying compliance with the law. Typically, a violator benefits economically by avoiding or delaying the construction of antipollution equipment that would have placed it in compliance with its permit. In *Smithfield Foods,* the court explained that, "[w]hen a company delays or avoids certain costs of capital and operations and maintenance necessary for compliance, the company is able to use those funds for other income-producing activities, such as investing that money in their own company." *Id.* at 349. Therefore, in that case, [the court found] "the avoided and/or delayed cost of compliance ... to be both the best and the appropriate method to determine how much money defendants made on the funds they did not spend for compliance." *Id.* at 349.

This case is unusual because Dean Dairy's delay in constructing a pretreatment plant was not beneficial to its "bottom line"; in effect, Dean Dairy was actually penalizing itself in failing to promptly build the pretreatment plant. Our general assumption of the reasonable capitalist went awry with this company.

There are methods other than the delayed or avoided capital expenditure for ascertaining economic benefit.... It is significant that neither the statute nor the case law supports the contention that the cost-avoidance method is the *only* permissible method of determining the amount a polluter has gained from violating the law....

In contrast to the situation in *Smithfield Foods,* the "cost-avoided" method of determining economic benefit is not a method that fits the facts that were presented to the district court because Dean Dairy did not profit by delaying its construction of the pretreatment plant. But it clearly gained *other* economic benefits by failing to adopt the method that was readily available. The wastewater from the Fairmont plant is created by the required daily cleaning of its vats and other processing equipment. A reduction of production would reduce the wastewater. Thus, if Dean Dairy wanted to avoid the cost entailed by the purchase of new equipment, it had the option of reducing volume.

The approach adopted by the district court is not in conflict with the CWA or basic economic principles. A violator who chooses to continue to violate its permit while experimenting with less costly remedies necessarily subjects itself to the surrender via penalty of any economic benefit it acquired. The fact that the violator has also penalized itself by failing to implement cost-effective methods that would have put it into compliance with its permit and thereby saved it money is certainly no basis to mitigate its penalty.

Requiring a company to reduce the amount of pollution it creates to comply with its permit is not unreasonable. As the court in *Tyson Foods* stated: "There was one simple and straightforward way for Tyson to avoid paying civil penalties for violations of the Clean Water Act: After purchasing the plant, Tyson could have ceased operations until it was able to discharge pollutants without violating the requirements of its ... permit. Tyson chose not to do this and it must now bear the consequences of that decision." 897 F.2d at 1141–42. Similarly, Dean Dairy chose neither what proved to be the economically sensible option (building the pretreatment facility) nor the alternative option of reducing the amount of wastewater produced. Accordingly, it must bear the consequences

We conclude that the district court's method of calculation of the penalty was within its discretion. We do not suggest that we have any dissatisfaction with the cost-avoided method of determining a violator's economic benefit in the usual case. However, under these unusual circumstances, we see no legally significant difference in measuring the economic benefit achieved by avoiding the costs of antipollution equipment, and the economic benefits achieved by failing to reduce the volume of pollution created. Both methods aim to recoup any benefits a violator gained by breaking the law and which gave the violator an advantage vis-a-vis its competitors. The penalty thus achieves the leveling of the playing field intended by Congress.

Questions and Notes

1. In *Tull*, the Supreme Court determined that the defendants in EPA civil judicial enforcement cases are entitled to request a jury trial on the issue of liability. At the same time, however, the Court concluded that Congress could constitutionally delegate to the court the responsibility to determine the appropriate penalty, assuming liability is found. 481 U.S. at 426–427. Given these dynamics, would you expect that many such defendants would seek a jury trial? Why or why not?

2. Does Section 309(d) require the courts to impose some penalty in every case in which liability is established? Interestingly, all three Circuits that have squarely addressed this question have concluded that it does, with only one of these decisions even drawing a dissenting opinion. See *Leslie Salt Co. v. United States*, 55 F.3d 1388 (9th Cir. 1995) (and cases cited therein). Reread § 309(d). Do you agree with this result? If so, what is the minimum fine a court could impose in response to a truly trivial violation?

3. As noted in the Third Circuit's opinion, the district court in *Dean Dairy* had taken pains to consider all of the § 309(d) factors before focusing in on the economic benefit as the key factor in its analysis. This was in accordance with other decisions indicating that district courts must at least consider all six of the statutory factors in their penalty analysis. See, e.g., *Atlantic States Legal Found., Inc. v. Tyson Foods, Inc.*, 897 F.2d 1128 (11th Cir. 1990).

4. The *Dean Dairy* identifies at least two related rationales for recapturing the economic benefit from violators: (1) it puts the violator back on a level economic playing field with its competitors who did whatever was necessary to comply with the law; and (2) it removes the economic incentive to violated environmental standards. A third, still-related rationale might include the simple desire to recapture ill-gotten gains. Should courts be required to recapture the economic benefit in all cases in which it is clear that the defendant did indeed enjoy such a benefit? Does § 309(d) mandate that result? Even if it doesn't, should the Courts of Appeal be more inclined to find an abuse of discretion in situations in which a district court has imposed a penalty that does not fully recapture the economic benefit?

5. What did you think of the "lost profits" approach to quantifying the economic benefit? Were there any costs in *Dean Dairy* that the defendant should perhaps have been able to use to offset some of the economic benefit, as calculated? Should defendants be able to subtract whatever sums they pay their lawyers in their defense of enforcement actions from what would otherwise be their economic benefit?

6. How should courts take factors such as "good faith" and "the economic impact ... on the violator" into account in assessing penalties? We will return to these questions when we address administrative enforcement.

7. Most of the pollution control statutes contain no statute-specific statute of limitations for civil penalty actions. As a result, the courts

have looked to the default five year federal statute of limitations for penalty actions found in 28 U.S.C. § 2462. See, e.g., *Public Interest Research Group of New Jersey, Inc. v. Powell Duffryn Terminals Inc.*, 913 F.2d 64, 73–76 (3d Cir. 1990).

2. Administrative Enforcement

Congress often provides EPA with administrative enforcement mechanisms it may use as an alternative to going to court. As mentioned, for example, the Clean Water Act gives EPA the power to issue unilateral orders requiring the recipients (typically referred to as "respondents") to comply with the law. 33 U.S.C. § 1319(a)(3). Additionally, Section 309(g) provides EPA with the authority to impose administrative fines for violations of the Act.

These authorities are significant in two respects. First, they may provide EPA with the advantage of speed–it is much easier to generate prompt compliance if all you have to do is order someone to comply, without any required discovery, hearings, or other procedural constraints. Second, they leave more power in EPA's hands, as opposed to in those of the courts. In the administrative realm, for example, EPA gets to make it own decisions about what steps are required to bring a violator into compliance, and as to how long it should take the violator to undertake them. If the respondent complies with the order, that's that.

Some statutes, such as RCRA, specifically provide respondents with the right to request an administrative hearing before the compliance order becomes final. See 42 U.S.C. § 6928(b). Others, such as the CWA, provide for no such hearing and are silent as to whether such respondents may seek judicial review before deciding whether or not to comply. See 33 U.S.C. §§ 1319(a)(3) and 1369(b). The following case addresses the effect of this silence on the question whether the recipients of these orders are entitled to what is referred to as "preenforcement" review of those orders:

SOUTHERN PINES ASSOCIATES v. UNITED STATES

United States Court of Appeals, Fourth Circuit, 1990.
912 F.2d 713.

ERVIN, Chief Judge:

Southern Pines is a Virginia limited partnership which owns 293.41 acres of land located in Chesapeake, Virginia. VICO has a contract with Southern Pines and has been involved in clearing and building upon 40 acres of the property.

On May 23, 1989, [EPA] issued a "Findings of Violation and Order for Compliance" to Southern Pines, informing the company that it had violated section 301(a) of the Clean Water Act by discharging fill material into wetlands without a permit. The order instructed Southern Pines to (1) "cease and desist all filling activities in the wetlands" at the site;

(2) "[c]ontact EPA within 5 working days" to discuss restoration of the areas; (3) implement a plan for restoration after EPA approval; and (4) submit written notice of intent to comply with the order. In a cover letter accompanying the order, EPA asked Southern Pines to provide information about the site for it to review in order to make a "final determination of the boundaries of the wetlands that fall under the jurisdiction of the Clean Water Act."

Upon receiving EPA's order, Southern Pines and VICO discontinued all work except logging which does not require a permit. . . .

On July 19, 1989, Southern Pines and VICO filed a complaint and a petition for a temporary restraining order. . . . They alleged that EPA's assertion of jurisdiction over the property created an actual controversy within the meaning of the Declaratory Judgment Act and argued that EPA lacks jurisdiction over the site because the wetlands on the property are not adjacent to any body of water.[1] The district court dismissed the case for lack of subject matter jurisdiction.

Southern Pines and VICO . . . argue that jurisdiction is proper under *Abbott Laboratories v. Gardner*, 387 U.S. 136 (1967), a case in which drug manufacturers challenged regulations promulgated by the Commissioner of Food and Drugs.

The Supreme Court held that judicial review was proper in *Abbott* because the Federal Food, Drug, and Cosmetic Act did not preclude review, and because the controversy was ripe for judicial resolution. However, the first question addressed by the Supreme Court in *Abbott* was whether "Congress by the Federal Food, Drug, and Cosmetic Act intended to forbid pre-enforcement review" of the regulation at issue in that case. The Court found that the statutory scheme did not preclude the action. The case before us today is distinguishable from *Abbott* because the statutory structure and history of the CWA provides clear and convincing evidence that Congress intended to exclude this type of action. We agree with the Seventh Circuit which recently held in *Hoffman Group, Inc. v. EPA*, 902 F.2d 567 (7th Cir.1990), that Congress "has impliedly precluded judicial review of a compliance order except in an enforcement proceeding."

In determining whether a statute precludes judicial review, we look not only to its language, but also to "the structure of the statutory scheme, its objectives, its legislative history, and the nature of the administrative action involved." *Block v. Community Nutrition Institute*, 467 U.S. 340, 345 (1984). The language, structure, objectives, and history of the CWA, persuade us that Congress intended to preclude judicial review.

---

1. The Act does not require Southern Pines to obtain a permit unless it is discharging fill materials into navigable waters. Navigable waters are "waters of the United States including the territorial seas." Waters of the United States include "wetlands adjacent to waters (other than waters that are themselves wetlands) . . . ." 40 C.F.R. § 230.3(s)(7) (1988).

The objective of the CWA is "to restore and maintain the chemical, physical, and biological integrity of the Nation's waters." 33 U.S.C. § 1251. To achieve this goal, the Act prohibits any discharge of dredge or fill materials into waters of the United States unless authorized by a permit issued by the Corps of Engineers pursuant to section 404 of the Act. 33 U.S.C. § 1311(a). Congress provided EPA with a choice of procedures for enforcing the Act. Section 309(a)(3) of the Act provides that when, on the basis of available information, the Administrator of EPA identifies a person in violation of the Act, the Administrator shall "either issue an order requiring such person to comply with [the Act], or he shall bring a civil action in accordance with subsection (b) of this section." In 1987, Congress added section 309(g) to the Act which provides that EPA may also assess administrative penalties against those who violate the Act or a permit issued under the Act. When EPA proceeds under section 309(g), the violator is entitled to a hearing before the agency, and the public is provided with an opportunity to comment. 33 U.S.C. § 1319(g)(2). Orders assessing administrative penalties are subject to judicial review. 33 U.S.C. § 1319(g)(8).

In this case, EPA issued a compliance order. A compliance order is a document served on the violator, setting forth the nature of the violation and specifying a time for compliance with the Act. 33 U.S.C. § 1319(a)(5)(A). If a violator fails to abide by that order, EPA may seek to enforce the order by bringing a suit in federal district court under section 309(b) of the Act. However, EPA need not issue a compliance order before bringing an action. The penalties for violating either the Act or a compliance order are the same. The court may issue an injunction to require compliance, and it may impose civil penalties of up to $25,000 per day for each violation of the Act, a permit, or a compliance order. 33 U.S.C. § 1319(d). The violator is subject to the same injunction and penalties whether or not EPA has issued a compliance order.[3]

The CWA is not the only environmental statute which allows EPA to issue pre-enforcement administrative orders. Both the Clean Air Act ("CAA"), 42 U.S.C. §§ 7401 et seq., and the Comprehensive Environmental Response, Compensation, and Liability Act (CERCLA), 42 U.S.C. §§ 9601 et seq., also provide for pre-enforcement agency action. The CAA, like the CWA, provides that EPA may issue a compliance order before bringing suit. Based upon the legislative history of the CAA, courts have found that Congress intended to preclude judicial review of compliance orders issued under the CAA. *See Union Electric Co. v. EPA*, 593 F.2d 299, 304 (8th Cir.), *cert. denied*, 444 U.S. 839; *Lloyd A. Fry Roofing Co. v. EPA*, 554 F.2d 885 (8th Cir.1977).

CERCLA allows the EPA to order that a site be cleaned up prior to bringing suit. 42 U.S.C. §§ 9604, 9606, 9607. Prior to 1986 courts held

3. Because the compliance order does not alter Southern Pines' and VICO's obligations under the Act, and EPA can bring a suit whether or not it issues an order, Southern Pines and VICO are not faced with any greater threat from EPA just because EPA seeks to negotiate a solution rather than to institute civil proceedings immediately.

that pre-enforcement remedial actions taken by the EPA under CERCLA were not subject to judicial review because litigation would interfere with CERCLA's policy of prompt agency response. *See, e.g., Wagner Seed Co. v. Daggett*, 800 F.2d 310, 315 (2d Cir.1986). In 1986 Congress added a provision to CERCLA which specifically precludes federal jurisdiction over pre-enforcement remedial action. 42 U.S.C. § 9613(h).

The structure of these environmental statutes indicates that Congress intended to allow EPA to act to address environmental problems quickly and without becoming immediately entangled in litigation. The CWA is not only similar in structure to the CAA and CERCLA, but its enforcement provisions were modeled after the enforcement provisions of the CAA. Considering this legislative history, the structure of these statutes, the objectives of the CWA, and the nature of the administrative action involved, we are persuaded that Congress meant to preclude judicial review of compliance orders under the CWA just as it meant to preclude pre-enforcement review under the CAA and CERCLA.

Southern Pines and VICO argue that this case does not involve pre-enforcement review because the compliance order is an "enforcement procedure." They also claim that this case should be distinguished from *Hoffman* because they are not merely contesting the extent of EPA's jurisdiction but are claiming that EPA totally lacks jurisdiction.

Southern Pines' action seeks pre-enforcement review because EPA has not yet sought penalties for any violation of the Act or its order. The cases discussing pre-enforcement review under the CAA and CERCLA concern action taken prior to the initiation of judicial proceedings. *See, e.g., Lloyd A. Fry Roofing Co.*, 554 F.2d 885.

We are also unpersuaded by Southern Pines' and VICO's attempt to distinguish this case from *Hoffman*. Allowing the parties to challenge the existence of EPA's jurisdiction would delay the agency's response in the same manner as litigation contesting the extent of EPA's jurisdiction. Southern Pines and VICO can contest the existence of EPA's jurisdiction if and when EPA seeks to enforce the penalties provided by the Act....

Questions and Notes

1. Do you agree that the CWA "provides clear and convincing evidence" that Congress intended to preclude preenforcement review? What were the statutory bases for the court's conclusion? Are they compelling? The court asserts that Southern Pines was subject to the same enforcement threat regardless of whether EPA had issued the compliance order. In reaching this conclusion, the Fourth Circuit implicitly assumed two things: (1) that those who violate compliance orders are subject to the same potential fines they would face absent the issuance of the order (i.e., if EPA went straight to court); and (2) that these respondents may raise the same substantive defenses in contesting the alleged violations that they could have raised if EPA had simply gone straight to court. Review § 309(d) and (g)(1) of the CWA in considering the first of these assumptions. Do you agree with the Fourth Circuit? If Southern Pines continued its filling activities after receiving the order, would EPA have had a basis for arguing for either

enhanced or additional fines for any continued filling activities? Did the order otherwise impose any obligations that could have led to separately finable offenses? Compare *Allsteel, Inc. v. U.S. EPA*, 25 F.3d 312, 315 (6th Cir. 1994).

2. With respect to the court's second assumption, the question is whether, for example, Southern Pines would have been able to raise its argument that EPA lacked jurisdiction over the site as a defense in an action seeking penalties for its disregard of the order. If it could not, it clearly would have been disadvantaged by EPA's having selected the administrative order route. This is so because, if EPA had gone straight to court (i.e., without issuing an order first), it would have had the burden of demonstrating jurisdiction to establish that Southern Pines had in fact violated the statute. In assuming that Southern Pines could test the legality of the order in an action seeking penalties for the violation thereof, the Fourth Circuit was following the general presumption of reviewability, as set forth in the APA. 5 U.S.C. § 701(a)(1); see also *Lloyd A. Fry Roofing Co. v. U.S. EPA*, 554 F.2d 885, 891 (8th Cir. 1977) (denying preenforcement review under the CAA, but noting that the respondent would be able to raise the same arguments if and when EPA went to court to enforce the order), and *United States v. Mango*, 199 F.3d 85 (1999) (allowing the defendant to challenge the legality of the relevant § 404 permit conditions in a criminal enforcement action for the violation thereof); *cf.* 33 U.S.C. § 1369(b)(2). Interestingly, however, in *Tennessee Valley Authority v. Whitman*, the Eleventh Circuit recently concluded that one who is alleged to have violated the requirements of a CAA order may not contest the legality of those requirements. 336 F.3d 1236, 1250, 1257 (11th Cir. 2003). Based on this conclusion, the court deemed the orders unconstitutional. Id. at 1260. What do you make of this approach?

3. The above notes raise questions about the legal effect of EPA's administrative orders. If we assume, though, that (a) these orders do "raise the stakes" in terms of the sanctions to which the respondents may be exposed, but that (b) the respondents will be able to contest the validity of these orders in any subsequent actions seeking penalties for the violation thereof, what are the policy dynamics hinging upon the availability of preenforcement review? What would the implications be for the Government (and the environment) if the recipients of these orders could forestall compliance by seeking judicial review in each and every case? On the other hand, what are the implications for companies like Southern Pines of denying preenforcement review? Absent such review, Southern Pines had two choices: It could either comply with the order or decline to do so. If Southern Pines had chosen to comply, when would it have had an opportunity to test EPA's assertion of jurisdiction? When considering this question, keep in mind that EPA's order not only required Southern Pines to cease all filling activities, but also ultimately to restore the areas that already had been filled. If, on the other hand, it had failed to comply, it may have faced the threat of increased penalties if EPA later established that the order was in fact lawful. Given this threat, a company in Southern Pines' position might decide to comply rather than risk this threat of penalties, even if it reasonably believed that the order was unlawful. From EPA's perspective, of course, this is part of the beauty of administrative orders: the respondents

may decide to forgo their right to a day in court because of the increased sanctions they may bear if the are ultimately proven to be in the wrong. From the respondents' perspectives, this chilling of their due process rights may feel like a violation of those rights. On this latter point, see *United States v. Reilly Tar & Chemical Corp.*, 606 F.Supp. 412 (D.Minn. 1985).

4. In addition to raising preclusion arguments of the type seen in *Southern Pines*, the Government has sometimes argued that its administrative orders do not constitute final agency actions within the meaning of the APA. While this argument may have some ongoing viability in contexts in which EPA's orders merely restate statutory commands, the Supreme Court has rejected it in situations in which the orders impose new legal obligations. In *Alaska Dept. of Env. Conservation v. Environmental Protection Agency*, 540 U.S. 461, 124 S.Ct. 983, 998–999, 157 L.Ed.2d 967 (2004) (*Alaska*), the Court went out of its way to resolve this question despite the Government's decision not to contest this issue at the Supreme Court level:

> In this Court, EPA agrees with the Ninth Circuit's [determination that EPA's order was a final agency action]. We are satisfied that the Court of Appeals correctly applied the guides we set out in *Bennett v. Spear*, 520 U.S. 154, 177–178 (1997) (to be "final," agency action must "mark the 'consummation' of the agency's decisionmaking process," and must either determine "rights or obligations" or occasion "legal consequences" (internal quotation marks omitted)). As the Court of Appeals stated, EPA had "asserted its final position on the factual circumstances" underpinning the Agency's orders, [*Alaska v. U.S. EPA*, 244 F.3d 748, 750 (9th Cir. 2001)], and if EPA's orders survived judicial review, Cominco could not escape the practical and legal consequences (lost costs and vulnerability to penalties) of any ADEC-permitted construction Cominco endeavored, *ibid.*

5. Finally, it is worth noting the result in *Alaska* indicates that EPA's orders under the CAA are now reviewable on a preenforcement basis in all situations in which they impose legal obligations beyond those specifically set forth in the statute. This is due to the fact that Congress amended that statute's judicial review provision in 1977 to specifically provide for review of all final agency actions. 42 U.S.C. § 7607(b). Thus, the statutory preclusion and final agency action issues are now convergent under the CAA.

In addition to providing for administrative compliance orders, most environmental statutes give the Government the authority to impose administrative penalties. In this context, some statutes, such as RCRA, provide EPA with the authority to impose the same penalties that it could seek if it went to court; i.e., up to $25,000 per day for each violation, 42 U.S.C. § 6928(a)(3) (adjusted to $32,500 pursuant to the Federal Civil Penalties Inflation Adjustment Act, 28 U.S.C. § 2461 note). Under that approach, EPA may impose administrative fines limited only by the overall number of violations in a particular case. Indeed, EPA can and does assess administrative penalties in excess of $1,000,000 in situations in which it determines that a violator has committed a large number of serious violations. Not surprisingly, given the seriousness of these enforcement actions, EPA is at least required to provide the respondent with the ability to request a hearing before an administrative law judge (ALJ) before the order becomes final. See 42 U.S.C. § 6928(b) and 40 C.F.R. Part 22.

Under other statutes, such as the CWA, Congress has placed overall caps on the penalty amounts EPA can trigger without going to court. Under that statute, for example, the largest fine EPA can impose administratively is $125,000, 33 U.S.C. § 1319(g)(2)(B) (adjusted to $162,500). If it wants to assess a fine of more than that, it has to go to court.

The CWA is also reflective of a recent trend of tiering the amount of administrative process required to the penalty amount EPA seeks to impose. If it seeks to impose a fine of greater than $25,000 (adjusted to $32,500) in one action, EPA must provide an APA-type hearing under Part 22. If it is willing to settle for less than that (and less than $10,000 per violation), an informal hearing before a "hearings officer" will suffice. See 33 U.S.C. § 1319(g)(2). This trend was further borne out in the 1990 amendments to the CAA, where Congress provided EPA with the authority to issue "field citations" in the amount of up to $5,000 (adjusted to $6,500), subject to a limited right of appeal as specified by EPA. 42 U.S.C. § 7413(d)(3). EPA has yet to write regulations implementing this program, however.

In the administrative penalty context, EPA (as opposed to a court) must determine the appropriate fine from within its statutory ranges. In general, the statutes require EPA to consider the same vague sorts of penalty factors that we saw in the judicial-penalties context. See, e.g., 33 U.S.C. § 1319(g)(3) and 42 U.S.C. § 6928(a)(3). Despite the imprecision in these criteria, EPA has an institutional interest in ensuring that like violations are treated in a similar fashion. Otherwise, sophisticated respondents would be able to research the fines paid in other cases and argue for a lowest-common-denominator approach. To further this objective, EPA has adopted "penalty policies" to guide its enforcement staff is determining the appropriate fines. Consider these excerpts from EPA's RCRA Civil Penalty Policy:

RCRA CIVIL PENALTY POLICY
Environmental Protection Agency, October 1990.

I. SUMMARY OF THE POLICY

The penalty calculation system established through EPA's RCRA Civil Penalty Policy consists of (1) determining a gravity-based penalty for a particular violation, from a penalty assessment matrix, (2) adding a "multi-day" component, as appropriate, to account for a violation's duration, (3) adjusting the sum of the gravity-based and multi-day components, up or down, for case specific circumstances, and (4) adding to this amount the appropriate economic benefit gained through non-compliance. More specifically, the Revised RCRA Civil Penalty Policy establishes the following penalty calculation methodology:

Penalty Amount = gravity-based component + multiday component + adjustments + economic benefit

* * *

Two factors are considered in determining the gravity-based penalty component:

- potential for harm; and

- extent of deviation from a statutory or regulatory requirement.

These two factors constitute the seriousness of a violation under RCRA, and have been incorporated into the following penalty matrix from which the gravity-based component will be chosen:

Matrix

Extent of Deviation From Requirement

Potential for Harm

	MAJOR	MODERATE	MINOR
MAJOR	$25,000 to 20,000	$19,999 to 15,000	$14,999 to 11,000
MODERATE	$10,999 to 8,000	$7,999 to 5,000	$4,999 to 3,000
MINOR	$2,999 to 1,500	$1,499 to 500	$499 to 100

The policy also explains how to factor into the calculation of the gravity component the presence of multiple and multi-day (continuing) violations. The policy provides that for days 2 through 180 of multi-day violations, multi-day penalties are mandatory, presumed, or discretionary, depending on the "potential for harm" and "extent of deviation" of the violations. For each day for which multi-day penalties are sought, the penalty amounts must be determined using the multi-day penalty matrix. The penalty amounts in the multi-day penalty matrix range from 5% to 20% (with a minimum of $100 per day) of the penalty amounts in the corresponding gravity-based matrix cells. Regions also retain discretion to impose multi-day penalties (1) of up to $25,000 per day, when appropriate under the circumstances, and (2) for days of violation after the first 180, as needed to achieve deterrence.

Where a company has derived significant savings or profits by its failure to comply with RCRA requirements, the amount of economic benefit from noncompliance gained by the violator will be calculated and added to the gravity-based penalty amount. The Agency has developed and made available to Agency personnel a computer model that can quickly and accurately calculate economic benefit—BEN.

After the appropriate gravity-based penalty amount (including the multi-day component) has been determined, it may be adjusted upward or downward to reflect particular circumstances surrounding the violation. Except in the unusual circumstances outlined in Section VIII the amount of any economic benefit enjoyed by the violator is not subject to adjustment. When adjusting the gravity-based penalty amount the following factors should be considered:

- good faith efforts to comply/lack of good faith (upward or downward adjustment);

- degree of willfulness and/or negligence (upward or downward adjustment);

- history of noncompliance (upward adjustment);

- ability to pay (downward adjustment);

- environmental projects to be undertaken by the violator (downward adjustment); and

- other unique factors, including but not limited to the risk and cost of litigation (upward or downward adjustment).

These factors (with the exception of (i) upward adjustment factors such as history of noncompliance, and (ii) the statutory downward adjustment factor reflecting a violator's good faith efforts to comply) should usually be considered after the penalty in the complaint has been proposed, i.e., during the settlement stage.

A detailed discussion of the policy follows. . . .

* * *

VI. DETERMINATION OF GRAVITY-BASED PENALTY AMOUNT

RCRA Section 3008(a)(3) states that the seriousness of a violation must be taken into account in assessing a penalty for the violation. The gravity-based component is a measure of the seriousness of a violation. The gravity-based penalty amount should be determined by examining two factors:

- potential for harm; and

- extent of deviation from a statutory or regulatory requirement.

A. Potential for Harm

The RCRA requirements were promulgated in order to prevent harm to human health and the environment. Thus, noncompliance with any RCRA requirement can result in a situation where there is a potential for harm to human health or the environment. Even violations such as recordkeeping violations create a risk of harm to the environment or human health by jeopardizing the integrity of the RCRA regulatory program. Accordingly, the assessment of the potential for harm resulting from a violation should be based on two factors:

- the risk of human or environmental exposure to hazardous waste and/or hazardous constituents that may be posed by noncompliance, and

- the adverse effect noncompliance may have on statutory or regulatory purposes or procedures for implementing the RCRA program.

1. Risk of Exposure

The risk of exposure presented by a given violation depends on both the likelihood that human or other environmental receptors may be exposed to hazardous waste and/or hazardous constituents and the degree of such potential exposure ...

2. Harm to the RCRA Regulatory Program

There are some requirements of the RCRA program which, if violated, may not be likely to give rise directly or immediately to a significant risk of contamination. Nonetheless, all regulatory requirements are fundamental to the continued integrity of the RCRA program. Violations of such requirements may have serious implications and merit substantial penalties where the violation undermines the statutory or regulatory purposes or procedures for implementing the RCRA program. Some examples of this kind of regulatory harm include:

- failure to comply with financial assurance requirements

- failure to submit a timely/adequate Part B application

- failure to respond to a formal information request

- operating without a permit or interim status

- failure to prepare or maintain a manifest

- failure to install or conduct adequate groundwater monitoring.

* * *

B. *Extent of Deviation From Requirement*

The "extent of deviation" from RCRA and its regulatory requirements relates to the degree to which the violation renders inoperative the requirement violated. In any violative situation, a range of potential noncompliance with the subject requirement exists. In other words, a violator may be substantially in compliance with the provisions of the requirement or it may have totally disregarded the requirement (or a point in between). In determining the extent of the deviation, the following categories should be used:

- MAJOR: the violator deviates from requirements of the regulation or statute to such an extent that most (or important aspects) of the requirements are not met resulting in substantial noncompliance.

- MODERATE: the violator significantly deviates from the requirements of the regulation or statute but some of the requirements are implemented as intended.

- MINOR: the violator deviates somewhat from the regulatory or statutory requirements but most (or all important aspects) of the requirements are met.

* * *

VII. Multiple and Multi-Day Penalties

A. Penalties for Multiple Violations

In certain situations, EPA may find that a particular firm has violated several different RCRA requirements. A separate penalty should be sought in a complaint and obtained in settlement or litigation for each separate violation that results from an independent act (or failure to act) by the violator and is substantially distinguishable from any other charge in the complaint for which a penalty is to be assessed. A given charge is independent of, and substantially distinguishable from, any other charge when it requires an element of proof not needed by the others. In many cases, violations of different sections of the regulations constitute independent and substantially distinguishable violations. . . .

It is also possible that different violations of the same section of the regulations could constitute independent and substantially distinguishable violations. For example, in the case of a firm which has open containers of hazardous waste in its storage area, 40 CFR § 265.173(a), and which also ruptured these or different hazardous waste containers while moving them on site, 40 CFR § 265.173(b), there are two independent acts. While the violations are both of the same regulatory section, each requires distinct elements of proof. In this situation, two counts with two separate penalties would be appropriate. For penalty purposes, each of the violations should be assessed separately and the amounts totalled.

Penalties for multiple violations also should be sought in litigation or obtained in settlement where one company has violated the same requirement in substantially different locations. An example of this type of violation is failure to clean up discharged hazardous waste during transportation, 40 CFR § 263.31. A transporter who did not clean up waste discharged in two separate locations during the same trip should be charged with two counts. In these situations the separate locations present separate and distinct risks to public health and the environment. Thus, separate penalty assessments are justified.

* * *

There are instances where a company's failure to satisfy one statutory or regulatory requirement either necessarily or generally leads to the violation of numerous other independent regulatory requirements. . . . In cases such as these where multiple violations result from a single initial transgression, assessment of a separate penalty for each distinguishable violation may produce a total penalty which is disproportionately high. Accordingly, in the specifically limited circumstances described, enforcement personnel have discretion to forego separate penalties for certain distinguishable violations, so long as the total penalty for all related violations is appropriate considering the gravity of the offense and sufficient to deter similar future behavior and recoup economic benefit.

B. *Penalties for Multi–Day Violations*

RCRA provides EPA with the authority to assess in administrative actions or seek in court civil penalties of up to $25,000 per day of non-compliance for each violation of a requirement of Subtitle C (or the regulations which implement that subtitle). This language explicitly authorizes the Agency to consider the duration of each violation as a factor in determining an appropriate total penalty amount. Accordingly, any penalty assessed should consist of a gravity-based component, economic benefit component, and to the extent that violations can be shown or presumed to have continued for more than one day, an appropriate multi-day component. The multi-day component should reflect the duration of the violation at issue, subject to the guidelines set forth in Section VII C., below.

* * *

C. *Calculation of the Multi–Day Penalty*

After the duration of the violation has been determined, the multi-day component of the total penalty is calculated, pursuant to the Multi–Day Matrix, as follows:

(1) Determine the gravity-based designations for the violation, e.g., major-major, moderate-minor, or minor-minor.

(2) Determine, for the specific violation, whether multi-day penalties are mandatory, presumed, or discretionary, as follows:

Mandatory multi-day penalties: Multi-day penalties are mandatory for days 2–180 of all violations with the following gravity-based designations: major-major, major-moderate, moderate-major.... Multi-day penalties for days 181+ are discretionary.

Presumption in favor of multi-day penalties: Multi-day penalties are presumed appropriate for days 2–180 of violations with the following gravity based designations: major-minor, moderate-moderate, minor-major. Therefore, multi-day penalties must be sought, unless case-specific facts overcoming the presumption for a particular violation are documented carefully in the case files. The presumption may be overcome for one or more days. Multi-day penalties for days 181+ are discretionary.

Discretionary multi-day penalties: Multi-day penalties are discretionary, generally, for all days of all violations with the following gravity-based designations: moderate-minor, minor-moderate, minor-minor.... The bases for decisions to impose or not impose any discretionary multi-day penalties must be documented in the case files.

(3) Locate the corresponding cell in the following Multi–Day Matrix. Multiply a dollar amount selected from the appropriate cell in the multi-

day matrix (or, where appropriate, a larger dollar amount not to exceed $25,000) by the number of days the violation lasted.

MULTI–DAY MATRIX OF MINIMUM
DAILY PENALTIES (in dollars)

Extent of Deviation

Potential for Harm

	MAJOR	MODERATE	MINOR
MAJOR	$5,000 to 1,000	$4,000 to 750	$3,000 to 550
MODERATE	$2,200 to 400	$1,600 to 250	$1,000 to 150
MINOR	$600 to 100	$300 to 100	$100

The dollar figure to be multiplied by the number of days of violation will generally be selected from the range provided in the appropriate multi-day cell. The figure selected should not be less than the lowest number in the range provided. . . .

VIII.   EFFECT OF ECONOMIC BENEFIT OF NONCOMPLIANCE

The Agency civil penalty policy mandates the recapture of any significant economic benefit of noncompliance that accrues to a violator. Enforcement personnel shall evaluate the economic benefit of noncompliance when penalties are calculated. A fundamental premise of the policy is that economic incentives for noncompliance are to be eliminated. If violators are allowed to profit by violating the law, there is little incentive to comply ... An economic benefit component should be calculated and added to the gravity-based penalty component when a violation results in "significant" economic benefit to the violator, as defined below.

* * *

It is generally the Agency's policy not to settle cases (i.e., the penalty amount) for an amount less than the economic benefit of noncompliance. However, the Agency civil penalty policy explicitly sets out three general [areas] where settling the total penalty amount for less than the economic benefit may be appropriate. The RCRA policy has added a fourth exception for cases where ability to pay is a factor. The four exceptions are:

- the economic benefit component consists of an insignificant amount (i.e., less than $2,500);

- there are compelling public concerns that would not be served by taking a case to trial;

- it is unlikely, based on the facts of the particular case as a whole, that EPA will be able to recover the economic benefit in litigation;

- the company has documented an inability to pay the total proposed penalty.

A. *Economic Benefit of Delayed Costs and Avoided Costs*

Compliance/enforcement personnel should examine two types of economic benefit from noncompliance in determining the economic benefit component:

- benefit from delayed costs; and

- benefit from avoided costs.

Delayed costs are expenditures which have been deferred by the violator's failure to comply with the requirements. The violator eventually will have to spend the money in order to achieve compliance. Delayed costs are the equivalent of capital costs ...

Avoided costs are expenditures which are nullified by the violator's failure to comply. These costs will never be incurred. Avoided costs include the usual operating and maintenance costs which would include any annual periodic costs such as leasing monitoring equipment....

* * *

IX. ADJUSTMENT FACTORS AND EFFECT OF SETTLEMENT

A. *Adjustment Factors*

* * *

The adjustment factors can increase, decrease or have no effect on the penalty amount obtained from the violator. Adjustments should generally be applied to the sum of the gravity-based and multi-day components of the penalty for a given violation. Note, however, that after all adjustment factors have been applied the resulting penalty shall not exceed the statutory maximum of $25,000 per day of violation....

Application of the adjustment factors is cumulative, i.e., more than one factor may apply in a case. For example, if the base penalty derived from the gravity-based and multi-day matrices is $109,500, and upward adjustments of 10% will be made for both history of noncompliance and degree of willfulness and/or negligence, the total adjusted penalty would be $131,400 ($109,500 + 20%).

For any given factor (except ability to pay and litigative risk) enforcement personnel can, assuming proper documentation, adjust the sum of the gravity-based and multi-day penalty components for any given violation up or down (1) by as much as 25% of that sum in ordinary circumstances or (2) from 26% to 40% of that sum, in unusual circumstances. Downward adjustments based on inability to pay or litigative risk will vary in amount depending on the individual facts present in a given case and in certain circumstances may be applied to the economic benefit component.

However, if a penalty is to achieve deterrence, both the violator and the general public must be convinced that the penalty places the violator in a worse position than those who have complied in a timely fashion. Moreover, allowing a violator to benefit from noncompliance punishes those who have complied by placing them at a competitive disadvantage. For these reasons, the Agency should at a minimum, absent the special circumstances enumerated in section VIII, recover any significant economic benefits resulting from failure to comply with the law. If violators are allowed to settle for a penalty less than their economic benefit of noncompliance, the goal of deterrence is undermined. Except in extraordinary circumstances, which include cases where there are demonstrated limitations on a respondent's ability to pay or very significant litigative risks, the final adjusted penalty should also include a significant gravity-based component beyond the economic benefit component.

* * *

Questions and Notes

1.   Note that EPA views its penalty policies as having relevance in both the judicial and administrative contexts. As it indicates in its introduction to the RCRA policy, in the judicial setting EPA may use the policy in framing its argument to the court as to the appropriate size of the penalty. While the court is not bound by the policy, it may find it a helpful way· of analyzing penalty matters. Moreover, note that EPA indicates that it will use the policy as a benchmark for analyzing potential settlements in both judicial and administrative penalty cases.

2.   Consider the following hypothetical:

Toymota, Inc., has a large manufacturing plant in the State of Bliss, an unauthorized State under RCRA. As part of it waste management activities, Toymota operates a hazardous waste surface impoundment and is thus regulated as a "TSD" (treatment, storage or disposal facility) under RCRA. Every year for the past ten years, it has purchased its required RCRA insurance from the same insurance company. Last year's policy expired on October 31. As it has done every year, Toymota applied for continuing coverage in June of last year. The insurance sale representative told Resteasy's corporate vice-president that there should be no problem.

In August, Resteasy applied for a loan to expand its production capacity. Because it was proposing to use its property as collateral for the loan,

Resteasy's lender asked it to hire a consultant to do an environmental assessment of the property. In late September, the consultant issued its report, indicating that some contamination had been found downgradient of the impoundment. Given how far the plume had migrated, the consultant surmised that the prior owner of the property likely had caused the contamination. The prior owner had used the impoundment during the pre-RCRA era.

On October 22, Toymota's insurance company informed it that it would not renew the required insurance. Since that time, Toymota has applied to more that 40 insurance companies seeking the necessary coverage. During a recent inspection, the VP told the EPA inspector about all of these events and indicated that she expected that the facility would obtain coverage within the next few weeks.

How should EPA respond? If it pursues an administrative penalty, what arguments will both sides make with regard to the appropriate penalty amount?

3. What do you think of EPA's effort to ensure consistent penalties? Is the policy likely to achieve this result? Do you think EPA could do better? If so, how? What do you think of the way in which EPA treats multi-day violations? What about the general manner in which it treats the adjustment factors? Do you agree that, in general, these factors should only be applied to the "gravity-based" portion of the fine? However you feel about that question, do you agree that the maximum adjustment, even in "unusual circumstances," for a factor such as "good faith efforts to comply" should be 40%?

4. In the interest of saving space, we have edited out the Penalty Policy's discussion of specific adjustment factors. There are, however, two points worth making about the "ability to pay" factor. First, EPA notes that this factor will result only in a downward adjustment; that is, EPA will never increase a company's fine over what the policy otherwise would contemplate because of that company's wealth. Do you agree with this approach? And second, EPA states that it "generally will not assess penalties that are clearly beyond the means of the violator." This latter point is subject to some express provisos: (1) the burden of demonstrating inability to pay is always on the respondent; (2) EPA will consider installment plans or delayed-payment schedules as a first resort before resorting to straight penalty reductions; and (3) EPA reserves the ability to impose fines that will put a company out of business where it has a long history of violations or where it is unable or refuses to correct the violations. Does this like an appropriate approach to these issues?

5. As mentioned, the recipients of administrative penalty orders commonly have the right to request at least some form of administrative hearing before the orders become final. See, e.g., 42 U.S.C. § 6928(b). Additionally, there is invariably a subsequent right of appeal to the courts, either under the environmental statute itself or under the APA. The courts review administratively-assessed penalties under the "abuse of discretion" standard of review. This standard is dictated either by the relevant environmental statute or by default under the APA. See, e.g., 33 U.S.C. § 1319(g)(8) and 5 U.S.C. § 706(2)(A).

6. The D.C. Circuit has determined that EPA's administrative penalty actions are subject to the same five-year statute of limitations (28 U.S.C. § 2462) that applies in the judicial realm. *3M Co. v. Browner*, 17 F.3d 1453 (D.C. Cir. 1994).

7. EPA has two other noteworthy policies that essentially act as addenda to its traditional penalty policies. First, EPA has created what it calls the "Final EPA Supplemental Environmental Projects Policy" (commonly known as the "SEP Policy"). 63 Fed. Reg. 24796 (May 1, 1998). Under this policy, EPA is willing to forgo portions of either judicial or administrative penalties if the relevant regulated entity agrees to perform environmentally beneficial projects that it is not otherwise legally required to perform. Not surprisingly, the SEP Policy has many conditions and caveats. Most notably, the environmental project that generates the reduction must have what EPA terms a "nexus" to the environmental concerns addressed by the requirements that were violated. Additionally, EPA insists that the violator must still pay a penalty reflecting at least the full economic benefit that it generated through its violative activities; this portion of the penalty cannot be mitigated by the SEP.

Second, EPA has developed what most people refer to as its "Environmental Audit Policy." 65 Fed. Reg. 19618 (April 11, 2000) (formally, if ponderously, entitled "Incentives for Self–Policing, Disclosure, Correction and Prevention of Violations"). Under this policy, EPA is willing to forgo penalties in situations in which regulated entities have voluntary programs in place to ferret out their own violations, where they do so, and where they notify EPA and promptly correct the problems. Perhaps obviously, the goal of the Audit Policy is to encourage regulatory self-policing in a world in which EPA and the States have limited inspection and enforcement resources. Here also, there are significant conditions and caveats. As under the SEP Policy, EPA will not waive the economic-benefit portion of the penalty; instead, only the gravity-based portion is in play. Additionally, the policy provides essentially no protection if corporate officials were either consciously involved in or willfully blind to the violations, or if the violation resulted in either serious environmental harm or an imminent and substantial endangerment. Outside of these situations, however, the Audit Policy contemplates broad penalty forgiveness if its conditions are met. Do you agree with EPA's decision to offer these incentives?

3. Criminal Enforcement

Most environmental statutes also provide the Government with the option of seeking criminal sanctions for at least some regulatory violations. Here again, the CWA is fairly typical of most pollution-control statutes. Section 309(c) establishes four categories of criminal violations: negligent violations, knowing violations, knowing endangerments, and knowing false statements. The first of these is a misdemeanor; the other three are felonies, with the most serious sanctions (fines of up to $250,000–or $1,000,000 for organizations–and jail terms of up to 15 years) for knowing endangerments.

By far the most significant legal issue in the area of environmental crimes relates to the mental state requirement for knowing violations:

What does one have to know, for example, in order to be convicted of "knowingly" violating one's NPDES permit? Do you just have to know the basic facts: e.g., that you are discharging less-than-fully-treated wastewater through a pipe into a waterway? Or do you have to also be aware of the legal significance of these facts? Consider the following case:

UNITED STATES v. WEITZENHOFF

United States Court of Appeals, Ninth Circuit, 1994.

35 F.3d 1275.

FLETCHER, Circuit Judge:

In 1988 and 1989 [Michael] Weitzenhoff was the manager and [Thomas] Mariani the assistant manager of the East Honolulu Community Services Sewage Treatment Plant ("the plant"), located not far from Sandy Beach, a popular swimming and surfing beach on Oahu. The plant is designed to treat some 4 million gallons of residential wastewater each day by removing the solids and other harmful pollutants from the sewage so that the resulting effluent can be safely discharged into the ocean. The plant operates under a permit issued pursuant to the [NPDES program], which established the limits on the Total Suspended Solids ("TSS") and Biochemical Oxygen Demand ("BOD")—indicators of the solid and organic matter, respectively, in the effluent discharged at Sandy Beach. During the period in question, the permit limited the discharge of both the TSS and BOD to an average of 976 pounds per day over a 30–day period. It also imposed monitoring and sampling requirements on the plant's management.

[As part of its treatment process, the plant generated something called "waste activated sludge" ("WAS").] From March 1987 through March 1988, the excess WAS generated by the plant was hauled away to another treatment plant, the Sand Island Facility. In March 1988, certain improvements were made to the East Honolulu plant and the hauling was discontinued. Within a few weeks, however, the plant began experiencing a buildup of excess WAS. Rather than have the excess WAS hauled away as before, however, Weitzenhoff and Mariani instructed two employees at the plant to dispose of it on a regular basis by pumping it from the storage tanks directly into the outfall, that is, directly into the ocean. The WAS thereby bypassed the plant's effluent sampler so that the samples taken and reported to Hawaii's Department of Health ("DOH") and the EPA did not reflect its discharge.

The evidence produced by the government at trial showed that WAS was discharged directly into the ocean from the plant on about 40 separate occasions from April 1988 to June 1989, resulting in some 436,000 pounds of pollutant solids being discharged into the ocean, and that the discharges violated the plant's 30–day average effluent limit under the permit for most of the months during which they occurred. Most of the WAS discharges occurred during the night, and none was reported to the DOH or EPA. DOH inspectors contacted the plant on several occasions in 1988 in response to complaints by lifeguards at Sandy Beach that sewage was being emitted from the outfall, but Weitzenhoff and Mariani repeatedly denied that there was any problem at the plant. In one letter responding to a DOH inquiry in October 1988, Mariani stated that "the debris that was reported could not have been from the East Honolulu Wastewater Treatment facility, as our records of effluent quality up to this time will substantiate." One of the plant employees who participated in the dumping operation testified that Weitzenhoff instructed him not to say anything about the discharges, because if they all stuck together and did not reveal anything, "they [couldn't] do anything to us."

Following an FBI investigation, Weitzenhoff and Mariani were charged in a thirty-one-count indictment with conspiracy and substantive violations of the [CWA]. At trial, Weitzenhoff and Mariani admitted having authorized the discharges, but claimed that their actions were justified under their interpretation of the NPDES permit....

Section 1311(a) of the CWA prohibits the discharge of pollutants into navigable waters without an NPDES permit. Section 1319(c)(2) makes it a felony offense to "knowingly violate [ ] section 1311, 1312, 1316, 1317, 1318, 1321(b)(3), 1328, or 1345 ..., or any permit condition or limitation implementing any of such sections in a permit issued under section 1342."

Prior to trial, the district court construed "knowingly" in section 1319(c)(2) as requiring only that Weitzenhoff and Mariani were aware that they were discharging the pollutants in question, not that they knew they were violating the terms of the statute or permit. According to appellants, the district court erred in its interpretation of the CWA and in instructing the jury that "the government is not required to prove that the defendant knew that his act or omissions were unlawful," as well as in rejecting their proposed instruction based on the defense that they mistakenly believed their conduct was authorized by the permit. Apparently, no court of appeals has confronted the issue raised by appellants.

As with certain other criminal statutes that employ the term "knowingly," it is not apparent from the face of the statute whether "knowingly" means a knowing violation of the law or simply knowing conduct that is violative of the law. We turn, then, to the legislative history of the provision at issue to ascertain what Congress intended.

In 1987, Congress substantially amended the CWA, elevating the penalties for violations of the Act. Increased penalties were considered necessary to deter would-be polluters. S.Rep. No. 50, 99th Cong., 1st Sess. 29 (1985). With the 1987 amendments, Congress substituted "knowingly" for the earlier intent requirement of "willfully" that appeared in the predecessor to section 1319(c)(2). The Senate report accompanying the legislation explains that the changes in the penalty provisions were to ensure that "[c]riminal liability shall ... attach to any person who is not in compliance with all applicable Federal, State and local requirements and permits *and causes* a POTW [publicly owned treatment works] to violate any effluent limitation or condition in any permit issued to the treatment works." *Id.* (emphasis added). Similarly, the report accompanying the House version of the bill, which contained parallel provisions for enhancement of penalties, states that the proposed amendments were to "provide penalties for dischargers or individuals who knowingly or negligently violate *or cause the violation of* certain of the Act's requirements." H.R.Rep. No. 189, 99th Cong., 1st Sess. 29–30 (1985) (emphasis added). Because they speak in terms of "causing" a violation, the congressional explanations of the new penalty provisions strongly suggest that criminal sanctions are to be imposed on an individual who knowingly engages in conduct that results in a permit violation, regardless of whether the polluter is cognizant of the requirements or even the existence of the permit

Our conclusion that "knowingly" does not refer to the legal violation is fortified by decisions interpreting analogous public welfare statutes. The leading case in this area is *United States v. International Minerals & Chem. Corp.*, 402 U.S. 558 (1971). In *International Minerals,* the Supreme Court construed a statute which made it a crime to "knowingly violate[ ] any ... regulation" promulgated by the ICC pursuant to 18 U.S.C. § 834(a), a provision authorizing the agency to formulate regulations for the safe transport of corrosive liquids. *Id.* at 559. The Court held that the term "knowingly" referred to the acts made criminal rather than a violation of the regulation, and that "regulation" was a shorthand designation for the specific acts or omissions contemplated by the act. *Id.* at 560–62. "[W]here ... dangerous or deleterious devices or products or obnoxious waste materials are involved, the probability of regulation is so great that anyone who is aware that he is in possession of them or dealing with them must be presumed to be aware of the regulation." *Id.* at 565.

This court followed *International Minerals* in *United States v. Hoflin,* 880 F.2d 1033 (9th Cir.1989), *cert. denied,* 493 U.S. 1083 (1990), when it held that knowledge of the absence of a permit is not an element of the offense defined by 42 U.S.C. § 6928(d)(2)(A), part of [RCRA]. *Id.* at 1039. "There can be little question that RCRA's purposes, like those of the Food and Drug Act, ' ... touch phases of the lives and health of people which, in the circumstances of modern industrialism, are largely beyond self-protection.' " *Id.* at 1038 (quoting *United States v. Dotterweich,* 320 U.S. 277, 280 (1943))....

Appellants seek to rely on the Supreme Court's decision in *Liparota v. United States,* 471 U.S. 419 (1985), to support their alternative reading of the intent requirement. *Liparota* concerned 7 U.S.C. § 2024(b)(1), which provides that anyone who "knowingly uses, transfers, acquires, alters, or possesses [food stamp] coupons or authorization cards in any manner not authorized by [the statute] or regulations" is subject to a fine or imprisonment. *Id.* at 420. The Court, noting that the conduct at issue did not constitute a public welfare offense, distinguished the *International Minerals* line of cases and held that the government must prove the defendant knew that his acquisition or possession of food stamps was in a manner unauthorized by statute or regulations. *Id.* at 432–33.

Subsequent to the filing of the original opinion in this case, the Supreme Court decided two cases which Weitzenhoff contends call our analysis into question. *See Ratzlaf v. United States,* 114 S.Ct. 655 (1994); *Staples v. United States,* 114 S.Ct. 1793 (1994). We disagree.

The statute in *Ratzlaf* does not deal with a public welfare offense, but rather with violations of the banking statutes. The Court construed the term "willfully" in the anti-structuring provisions of the Bank Secrecy Act to require both that the defendant knew he was structuring transactions to avoid reporting requirements and that he knew his acts were unlawful. The Court recognized that the money structuring provisions are not directed at conduct which a reasonable person necessarily should know is subject to strict public regulation and that the structuring offense applied to all persons with more than $10,000, many of whom could be engaged in structuring for innocent reasons. *Ratzlaf,* 114 S.Ct. at 660–62. In contrast, parties such as Weitzenhoff are closely regulated and are discharging waste materials that affect public health. The *International Minerals* rationale requires that we impute to these parties knowledge of their operating permit. This was recognized by the Court in *Staples.*

The specific holding in *Staples* was that the government is required to prove that a defendant charged with possession of a machine gun knew that the weapon he possessed had the characteristics that brought it within the statutory definition of a machinegun. But the Court took pains to contrast the gun laws to other regulatory regimes, specifically those regulations that govern the handling of "obnoxious waste materials." *See Staples,* 114 S.Ct. at 1798. It noted that the mere innocent ownership of guns is not a public welfare offense. *Id.* 1804. The Court focussed on the long tradition of widespread gun ownership in this country and, recognizing that approximately 50% of American homes contain a firearm, *id.* at 1801, acknowledged that mere ownership of a gun is not sufficient to place people on notice that the act of owning an unregistered firearm is not innocent under the law.

Staples thus explicitly contrasted the mere possession of guns to public welfare offenses, which include statutes that regulate " 'dangerous or deleterious devices or products or obnoxious waste materials,' " *id.* at 1800, and confirmed the continued vitality of statutes covering public welfare offenses, which "regulate potentially harmful or injurious items" and place a defendant on notice that he is dealing with a device or a substance "that places him in 'responsible relation to a public danger.' " *Id.* "[I]n such cases Congress intended to place the burden on the defendant to ascertain at his peril whether [his conduct] comes within the inhibition of the statute." *Id.* at 1798 (citations and internal quotations omitted).

Unlike "[g]uns [which] in general are not 'deleterious devices or products or obnoxious waste materials,' *International Minerals, supra* [402 U.S.], at 565, that put their owners on notice that they stand 'in responsible relation to a public danger[,]' *Dotterweich,* 320 U.S. at 281," *Staples,* 114 S.Ct. at 1800, the dumping of sewage and other pollutants into our nation's waters is precisely the type of activity that puts the discharger on notice that his acts may pose a public danger. Like other public welfare offenses that regulate ... the disposal of hazardous wastes [and] the undocumented shipping of acids ..., the improper and excessive discharge of sewage causes cholera, hepatitis, and other serious illnesses, and can have serious repercussions for public health and welfare.[7]

The criminal provisions of the CWA are clearly designed to protect the public at large from the potentially dire consequences of water pollution, and as such fall within the category of public welfare legislation. *International Minerals* rather than *Liparota* controls the case at hand. The government did not need to prove that Weitzenhoff and Mariani knew that their acts violated the permit or the CWA.

KLEINFELD, Circuit Judge, with whom Circuit Judges REINHARDT, KOZINSKI, TROTT, and T.G.NELSON join, dissenting from the order rejecting the suggestion for rehearing en banc.

... In my view, this is a case of exceptional importance, for two reasons. First, it impairs a fundamental purpose of criminal justice, sorting out the innocent from the guilty before imposing punishment. Second, it does so in the context of the [CWA]. This statute has tremendous sweep. Most statutes permit anything except what is prohibited, but this one prohibits all regulated conduct involving waters and wetlands except what is permitted. 33 U.S.C. § 1311(a). Much more ordinary, innocent, productive activity is regulated by this law than people not versed in environmental law might imagine.

The harm our mistaken decision may do is not necessarily limited to [CWA] cases. Dilution of the traditional requirement of a criminal state of mind, and application of the criminal law to innocent conduct, reduces the moral authority of our system of criminal law. If we use prison to achieve social goals regardless of the moral innocence of those we

---

7. In *Staples,* the Court also noted that the penalty attached to a violation of a criminal statute in the past has been a relevant factor in determining whether the statute defines a public welfare offense. The Court recognized that public welfare offenses originally involved statutes that provided only light penalties such as fines or short jail sentences, *see* 114 S.Ct. at 1802, but that modern statutes now punish public welfare offenses with much more significant terms of imprisonment. *E.g., International Minerals,* 402 U.S. 558 (ten years imprisonment if death or bodily injury results from violation); *United States v. Freed,* 401 U.S. 601, 609–10 (1971) (five years imprisonment for possession of unregistered grenade); *Hoflin,* 880 F.2d 1033 (two years imprisonment for certain violations of RCRA). While the *Staples* opinion expresses concern with this evolution of enhanced punishments for public welfare offenses, it refrains from holding that public welfare offenses may not be punished as felonies. *Staples,* 114 S.Ct. at 1804 (stating that the early cases suggest that public welfare offenses might not extend to felonies, but noting that "[w]e need not adopt such a definitive rule of construction to decide this case").

incarcerate, then imprisonment loses its moral opprobrium and our criminal law becomes morally arbitrary.

As the panel opinion states the facts, these two defendants were literally "midnight dumpers." They managed a sewer plant and told their employees to dump 436,000 pounds of sewage into the ocean, mostly at night, fouling a nearby beach. Their conduct, as set out in the panel opinion, suggests that they must have known they were violating their [NPDES] permit. But we cannot decide the case on that basis, because the jury did not. The court instructed the jury that the government did not have to prove the defendants knew their conduct was unlawful, and refused to instruct the jury that a mistaken belief that the discharge was authorized by the permit would be a defense. Because of the way the jury was instructed, its verdict is consistent with the proposition that the defendants honestly and reasonably believed that their NPDES permit authorized the discharges.

This proposition could be true. NPDES permits are often difficult to understand and obey. The EPA had licensed the defendants' plant to discharge 976 pounds of waste per day, or about 409,920 pounds over the fourteen months covered by the indictment, into the ocean. The wrongful conduct was not discharging waste into the ocean. That was socially desirable conduct by which the defendants protected the people of their city from sewage-borne disease and earned their pay. The wrongful conduct was violating the NPDES permit by discharging 26,000 more pounds of waste than the permit authorized during the fourteen months. Whether these defendants were innocent or not, in the sense of knowing that they were exceeding their permit limitation, the panel's holding will make innocence irrelevant in other permit violation cases where the defendants had no idea that they were exceeding permit limits. The only thing they have to know to be guilty is that they were dumping sewage into the ocean, yet that was a lawful activity expressly authorized by their federal permit.

The statute says "knowingly violate[s] ... any permit condition or limitation." "Knowingly" is an adverb. It modifies the verb "violates." The object of the verb is "any permit condition or limitation." ... Congress has distinguished those who knowingly violate permit conditions, and are thereby felons, from those who unknowingly violate permit conditions, so are not. The panel reads the statute as though it says "knowingly discharges pollutants." It does not. If we read the statute on the assumption that Congress used the English language in an ordinary way, the state of mind required is knowledge that one is violating a permit condition.

This approach has the virtue of attributing common sense and a rational purpose to Congress. It is one thing to defy a permit limitation, but quite another to violate it without realizing that one is violating it. Congress promulgated a parallel statute making it a misdemeanor "negligently" to violate a permit condition or limitation. 33 U.S.C. § 1319(c)(1)(A). If negligent violation is a misdemeanor, why would

Congress want to make it a felony to violate the permit without negligence and without even knowing that the discharge exceeded the permit limit? That does not make any sense. It would deter people from working in sewer plants, instead of deterring people from violating permits. All dischargers acting lawfully pursuant to a permit know that they are discharging pollutants. The presence or absence of that knowledge, which is the only mental element determining guilt under the panel's decision, has no bearing on any conduct Congress could have meant to turn into a felony. The only knowledge which could have mattered to Congress, the only knowledge which distinguishes good conduct from bad, is knowledge that the discharge violates the permit. That is what the statute says, "knowingly violates," not "knowingly discharges." There is no sensible reason to doubt that Congress meant what it said and said what it meant.

The panel reaches its surprising result in surprising ways. First, it says that the statute is ambiguous. . . . As explained above, a grammatical and sensible reading of the statute leaves no room for ambiguity. But for the sake of discussion, suppose that the statute is ambiguous, as the panel says. Then the rule of lenity requires that the construction allowing the defendant more liberty rather than less be applied by the courts. . . .

The panel . . . tries to bolster its construction by categorizing the offense as a "public welfare offense," as though that justified more aggressive criminalization without a plain statutory command. This category is a modernized version of "malum prohibitum." Traditionally the criminal law distinguishes between malum in se, conduct wrong upon principles of natural moral law, and malum prohibitum, conduct not inherently immoral but wrong because prohibited by law. Black's Law Dictionary 1112 (4th ed. 1951). To put this in plain, modern terms, any normal person knows murder, rape and robbery are wrong, and they would be wrong even in a place with no sovereign and no law. Discharging 6% more pollutants than one's permit allows is wrong only because the law says so. . . .

Staples reminds us that "offenses that require no *mens rea* generally are disfavored." 114 S.Ct. at 1797. *Mens rea* may be dispensed with in public welfare offenses, but the penalty is a "significant consideration in determining whether the statute should be construed as dispensing with *mens rea*." 114 S.Ct. at 1802. . . . If Congress makes a crime a felony, the felony categorization alone is a "factor tending to suggest that Congress did not intend to eliminate a *mens rea* requirement. In such a case, the usual presumption that a defendant must know the facts that make his conduct illegal should apply." 114 S.Ct. at 1804. In the case at bar, "the facts that make his conduct illegal" are the permit violations, not the discharges of pollutants. Discharge of pollutants was licensed by the federal government in the NPDES permit. Under *Staples,* it would be presumed, even if the law did not plainly say so, that the defendant would have to know that he was violating the permit in order to be guilty of the felony.

The panel cites *International Minerals* ... in support of its read-ing.... Because of the syntactically similar statute at issue in that case, it is the strongest authority for the panel's decision and raises the most serious question for my own analysis. It held that a shipper of sulfuric acid could be convicted of violating a statute applying to those who "knowingly violate[]" regulations governing shipments of corrosive liq-uids, regardless of whether he had knowledge of the regulations. *Interna-tional Minerals* expressly limits its holding to "dangerous or deleterious devices or products or obnoxious waste materials." 402 U.S. at 565. The Court distinguished materials not obviously subject to regulation:

> Pencils, dental floss, paper clips may also be regulated. But they may be the type of products which might raise substantial due process questions if Congress did not require ... *"mens rea"* as to each ingredient of the offense. But where, as here ..., dangerous or deleterious devices or products or obnoxious waste materials are involved, the probability of regulation is so great that anyone who is aware that he is in possession of them or dealing with them must be presumed to be aware of the regulation.

Id. at 564–65. *International Minerals* would have much persuasive force for *Weitzenhoff,* because of the grammatical similarity of the statute, if (1) the [CWA] limited pollutants to "dangerous or deleterious devices or products or obnoxious waste materials;" (2) the crime was only a misdemeanor; and (3) *Staples* had not come down this term. But all three of these conditions are contrary to fact. The pollutants to which the [CWA] felony statute applies include many in the "pencils, dental floss, paper clips" category. Hot water, rock, and sand are classified as "pollutants" by the Clean Water Act. *See* 33 U.S.C. § 1362(6). Discharg-ing silt from a stream back into the same stream may amount to discharge of a pollutant. For that matter, so may skipping a stone into a lake. So may a cafeteria worker's pouring hot, stale coffee down the drain. Making these acts a misdemeanor is one thing, but a felony is quite another, as *Staples* teaches.

The panel, finally, asserts that as a matter of policy, the [CWA] crimes "are clearly designed to protect the public at large from the dire consequences of water pollution." That is true, but the panel does not explain how the public is to be protected by making felons of sewer workers who unknowingly violate their plants' permits.... Sewage workers perform essential work of great social value. Probably nothing has prevented more infant mortality, or freed more people from cholera, hepatitis, typhoid fever, and other disease, than the development in the last two centuries of municipal sewer systems. Sewage utility workers perform their difficult work in malodorous and dangerous environments. We have now imposed on these vitally important public servants a massive legal risk, unjustified by law or precedent, if they unknowingly violate their permit conditions.

Nor is the risk of prison limited to sewage plant workers. It applies to anyone who discharges pollutants pursuant to a permit, and unknowingly violates the permit. The panel suggests that criminalizing this innocent conduct will protect the public from water pollution. It is at least as likely that the increased criminal risk will raise the cost and reduce the availability of such lawful and essential public services as sewage disposal. . . .

Questions and Notes

1.   In his dissent from the denial of the rehearing *Weitzenhoff*, Judge Kleinfeld concedes that the defendants must have known that they were violating their permit. Do you understand why he still thought the conviction needed to be reversed? Given the high degree of likelihood that a jury would have found awareness of illegality in this case, why do you think the Government at trial opposed a jury instruction that would have required such a finding?

2.   Congress, of course, can eliminate any doubt regarding the mental state requirements under a given statute by clearly specifying one standard or another. In some environmental contexts, for example, the courts have found that Congress has required awareness of illegality by using the term "willfully." See, e.g., *United States v. Overholt*, 307 F.3d 1231, 1245–1246 (10th Cir. 2002) (under the Safe Drinking Water Act). If Congress speaks clearly, that is the end of the matter, at least absent the potential due process problems alluded to in *International Minerals*. In *Weitzenhoff*, Judge Kleinfeld argues that the phase "knowingly violates" is clear. Do you agree? Can such a position be squared with *International Minerals*?

3.   If Congress uses ambiguous phraseology (e.g., "knowingly violates," or, if you prefer, "knowingly discharges pollutants"), one way to resolve such ambiguities might be through resort to statutory structure. In a pair of decisions under RCRA, for example, the Ninth Circuit relied on such structural arguments in holding that, while the Government need not prove that those who disposed of hazardous waste were aware that they did not have a permit to do so, to convict transporters it must prove that they were aware of the receiving facility's lack of a permit. Compare *Hoflin*, 880 F.2d at 1038 (applying 42 U.S.C. § 3008(d)(2)(A)), and *United States v. Speach*, 968 F.2d 795 (9th Cir. 1992) (applying subsection (d)(1)). Assuming that we can read the phrase "knowingly violates" to be ambiguous, does the structure of § 309 of the CWA provide any help?

4.   Another way to resolve ambiguity might be through the application of legislative history. What arguments of this type did the majority advance in *Weitzenhoff*? Were they persuasive?

5.   As Judge Kleinfeld points out, discharging illegal amounts of pollution does not fit the classic definition of a "malum in se" offense; rather, it would be characterized as a "malum prohibitum" offense. In the "regulatory crimes" context, the Supreme Court has fashioned an interpretive protocol to help resolve ambiguities involving mental-state requirements: If the regulatory regime criminalizes what the Court characterizes as "public welfare offenses," such as in *International Minerals*, the Court's default assumption is that Congress did not intend to require the Government to prove awareness of illegality. On the other hand, if the regime criminalizes what the Court considers "innocent conduct," as in *Liparota*, *Ratzlaf*, and

Staples, the Court's default assumption is that the statute requires proof that the defendant knew she was acting illegally. See generally *Staples v. United States*, 511 U.S. 600, 114 S.Ct. 1793, 128 L.Ed.2d 608 (1994). One commentator has described the circumstances in which the Court has applied these competing assumptions in the following terms:

> . . . The Court assumes that Congress meant to adopt the common law notion that felony convictions require proof of mens rea. Given that regulatory crimes were not taken from the common law, the Court determines the mens rea requirement by fitting the statute into one of two categories and applying the interpretive approach developed for each. Some statutes fit into the category of "public welfare offenses" (PWOs). These statutes address uncommon conduct that seriously threatens the community's health or safety. For such statutes, the Court interprets the mens rea requirement to be awareness of facts that make the conduct dangerous and uncommon. Such awareness is a kind of modern take on traditional mens rea: A person aware of engaging in a dangerous and uncommon activity is aware of wrongdoing if he or she does not take steps to determine the legally correct way of conducting the task. Non–PWO statutes regulate "innocent" conduct—that is, conduct that does not seriously threaten the community's health or safety, is common, or is both non-threatening and common. To ensure a mens rea requirement, the Court usually interprets these statutes to require proof that the defendant was aware the behavior was unauthorized by regulatory law in general. This is mens rea in the traditional sense because the person is aware of violating the law, even in a general sense, and it is morally wrong to violate legal authority knowingly.

Mandiberg, Fault Lines in the Clean Water Act: Criminal Enforcement, Continuing Violations, and Mental State, 33 Envt'l Law 173, 191–193 (2003) (footnotes omitted). Do you agree with the *Weitzenhoff* majority (and every other appellate court that has addressed the question) that the CWA is a proper context in which to apply the PWO doctrine? What legal objections does Judge Kleinfeld raise? What are his policy objections? Is it possible to apply one rule to defendants like Mr. Weitzenhoff and another to homeowners who may innocently add fill material to swampy areas without dreaming that the CWA might apply?

C. Federalism Issues in the Enforcement Context

We already have seen, in our discussion of the Clean Water Act, that States are required to have certain enforcement powers in order to become "authorized" to implement statutes such as the CWA, the CAA and RCRA. Despite that, however, it is clear that EPA retains the enforcement powers we have been addressing in this Chapter even in authorized States. Indeed, several of the relevant enforcement provisions specifically contemplate ongoing federal enforcement power, though they may condition its exercise in narrow ways, such as by requiring EPA to give authorized States advance notice and/or the opportunity to undertake an appropriate enforcement response. Compare 33 U.S.C. § 1319(a)(1), 42 U.S.C. § 6928(a)(2), and 42 U.S.C. § 7413(a)(1).

The more difficult issue involves EPA's ability to "overfile;" that is, to file a separate enforcement action relating to the same violations addressed by a State in situations in which either the State was unsuccessful or EPA deems its response to have been unsatisfactory. The following case is an example of the second of these two scenarios:

HARMON INDUSTRIES, INC. v. BROWNER

United States Court of Appeals, Eighth Circuit, 1999.
191 F.3d 894.

HANSEN, Circuit Judge.

Harmon Industries operates a plant in Grain Valley, Missouri, which it utilizes to assemble circuit boards for railroad control and safety equipment. In November 1987, Harmon's personnel manager discovered that maintenance workers at Harmon routinely discarded volatile solvent residue behind Harmon's Grain Valley plant. This practice apparently began in 1973 and continued until November 1987. Harmon's management was unaware of its employees' practices until the personnel manager filed his report in November 1987. Following the report, Harmon ceased its disposal activities and voluntarily contacted the Missouri Department of Natural Resources (MDNR). The MDNR investigated and concluded that Harmon's past disposal practices did not pose a threat to either human health or the environment. The MDNR and Harmon created a plan whereby Harmon would clean up the disposal area. Harmon implemented the clean up plan. While Harmon was cooperating with the MDNR, the EPA initiated an administrative enforcement action against Harmon in which the federal agency sought $2,343,706 in penalties. Meanwhile, Harmon and the MDNR continued to establish a voluntary compliance plan. In harmonizing the details of the plan, Harmon asked the MDNR not to impose civil penalties. Harmon based its request in part on the fact that it voluntarily self-reported the environmental violations and cooperated fully with the MDNR.

On March 5, 1993, while the EPA's administrative enforcement action was pending, a Missouri state court judge approved a consent decree entered into by the MDNR and Harmon. In the decree, MDNR acknowledged full accord and satisfaction and released Harmon from any claim for monetary penalties. MDNR based its decision to release Harmon on the fact that the company promptly self-reported its violation and cooperated in all aspects of the investigation. After the filing of the consent decree, Harmon litigated the EPA claim before an administrative law judge (ALJ). The ALJ found that a civil penalty against Harmon was appropriate in this case. The ALJ rejected the EPA's request for a penalty in excess of $2 million but the ALJ did impose a civil fine of $586,716 against Harmon. A three-person Environmental Appeals Board panel affirmed the ALJ's monetary penalty. Harmon filed a complaint challenging the EPA's decision in federal district court on June 6, 1997.

In its August 25, 1998, summary judgment order, the district court found that the EPA's decision to impose civil penalties violated [RCRA] and contravened principles of res judicata. The EPA appeals to this court.

[RCRA] permits states to apply to the EPA for authorization to administer and enforce a hazardous waste program. See 42 U.S.C. § 6926(b). If authorization is granted, the state's program then operates "in lieu of" the federal government's hazardous waste program. Id. The EPA authorization also allows states to issue and enforce permits for the treatment, storage, and disposal of hazardous wastes. Id. "Any action taken by a State under a hazardous waste program authorized under [the RCRA] [has] the same force and effect as action taken by the [EPA] under this subchapter." 42 U.S.C. § 6926(d). Once authorization is granted by the EPA, it cannot be rescinded unless the EPA finds that (1) the state program is not equivalent to the federal program, (2) the state program is not consistent with federal or state programs in other states, or (3) the state program is failing to provide adequate enforcement of compliance in accordance with the requirements of federal law. See 42 U.S.C. § 6926(b)....

Missouri, like many other states, is authorized to administer and enforce a hazardous waste program pursuant to the RCRA. Despite having authorized a state to act, the EPA frequently files its own enforcement actions against suspected environmental violators even after the commencement of a state-initiated enforcement action. The EPA's process of duplicating enforcement actions is known as overfiling. The permissibility of overfiling apparently is a question of first impression in the federal circuit courts....

The EPA contends that the district court's interpretation runs contrary to the plain language of the RCRA. Specifically, the EPA cites section 6928 of the RCRA, which states that:

(1) Except as provided in paragraph (2), whenever on the basis of any information the [EPA] determines that any person has violated or is in violation of any requirement of this subchapter, the [EPA] may issue an order assessing a civil penalty for any past or current violation, requiring compliance immediately or within a specified time period, or both, or the [EPA] may commence a civil action in the United States district court in the district in which the violation occurred for appropriate relief, including a temporary or permanent injunction.

(2) In the case of a violation of any requirement of [the RCRA] where such violation occurs in a State which is authorized to carry out a hazardous waste program under section 6926 of this title, the [EPA] shall give notice to the State in which such violation has occurred prior to issuing an order or commencing a civil action under this section.

42 U.S.C. § 6928(a)(1) and (2).

The EPA argues that the plain language of section 6928 allows the federal agency to initiate an enforcement action against an environmental violator even in states that have received authorization pursuant to the RCRA. The EPA contends that Harmon and the district court misinterpreted the phrases "in lieu of" and "same force and effect" as contained in the RCRA. According to the EPA, the phrase "in lieu of" refers to which regulations are to be enforced in an authorized state rather than who is responsible for enforcing the regulations. The EPA argues that the phrase "same force and effect" refers only to the effect of state issued permits. The EPA contends that the RCRA, taken as a whole, authorizes either the state or the EPA to enforce the state's regulations, which are in compliance with the regulations of the EPA. The only requirement, according to the EPA, is that the EPA notify the state in writing if it intends to initiate an enforcement action against an alleged violator.

An examination of the statute as a whole supports the district court's interpretation. The RCRA specifically allows states that have received authorization from the federal government to administer and enforce a program that operates "in lieu of" the EPA's regulatory program. 42 U.S.C. § 6926(b). While the EPA is correct that the "in lieu of" language refers to the program itself, the administration and enforcement of the program are inexorably intertwined.

The RCRA gives authority to the states to create and implement their own hazardous waste program. The plain "in lieu of" language contained in the RCRA reveals a congressional intent for an authorized state program to supplant the federal hazardous waste program in all respects including enforcement. Congressional intent is evinced within the authorization language of section 6926(b) of the RCRA. Specifically, the statute permits the EPA to repeal a state's authorization if the state's program "does not provide adequate enforcement of compliance with the requirements of" the RCRA. Id. This language indicates that Congress intended to grant states the primary role of enforcing their own hazardous waste program. Such an indication is not undermined, as the EPA suggests, by the language of section 6928. Again, section 6928(a)(1) allows the EPA to initiate enforcement actions against suspected environmental violators, except as provided in section 6928(a)(2). Section 6928(a)(2) permits the EPA to enforce the hazardous waste laws contained in the RCRA if the agency gives written notice to the state. Section 6928(a)(1) and (2), however, must be interpreted within the context of the entire Act. Harmonizing the section 6928(a)(1) and (2) language that allows the EPA to bring an enforcement action in certain circumstances with section 6926(b)'s provision that the EPA has the right to withdraw state authorization if the state's enforcement is inadequate manifests a congressional intent to give the EPA a secondary enforcement right in those cases where a state has been authorized to act that is triggered only after state authorization is rescinded or if the state fails to initiate an enforcement action. Rather than serving as an affirmative grant of federal enforcement power as the EPA suggests, we conclude that the notice requirement of section 6928(a)(2) reinforces the primacy of a state's enforcement rights under RCRA. Taken in the context of the statute as a whole, the notice requirement operates as a means to allow a state the first chance opportunity to initiate the statutorily-permitted enforcement action. If the state fails to initiate any action, then the EPA may institute its own action. Thus, the notice requirement is an indicator of the fact that Congress intended to give states, that are authorized to act, the lead role in enforcement under RCRA.

The "same force and effect" language of section 6926(d) provides additional support for the primacy of states' enforcement rights under the RCRA when the EPA has authorized a state to act in lieu of it. The EPA argues that the "same force and effect" language is limited to state permits because the words appear under a heading that reads: "Effect of State Permit." The EPA contends that the "same force and effect" language indicates only that state-issued permits will have the same force and effect as permits issued by the federal government. . . .

Regardless of the title or heading, the plain language of section 6926(d) states that "[a]ny action taken by a State under a hazardous waste program authorized under this section shall have the same force and effect as action taken by the [EPA] under this subchapter." 42 U.S.C. § 6926(d). In this context, the meaning of the text is plain and obvious. "Any action" under this provision broadly applies to any action authorized by the subchapter, and this language is not limited to the issuance of permits. The state authorization provision substitutes state action (not excluding enforcement action) for federal action. It would be incongruous to conclude that the RCRA authorizes states to implement and administer a hazardous waste program "in lieu of" the federal program where only the issuance of permits is accorded the same force and effect as an action taken by the federal government. Contrary to the EPA's assertions, the statute specifically provides that a "[s]tate is authorized to carry out [its hazardous waste program] in lieu of the Federal program . . . and to issue and enforce permits." 42 U.S.C. § 6926(b). Issuance and enforcement are two of the functions authorized as part of the state's hazardous waste enforcement program under the RCRA. Nothing in the statute suggests that the "same force and effect" language is limited to the issuance of permits but not their enforcement. . . .

Utilizing a sort of reverse plain language argument, the EPA contends that its approach is logically consistent with the framework of the RCRA. The EPA cites the statute's citizen suit provision for the proposition that limitations on a parties' right to act are expressly stated within the statute itself. Section 6972(b)(1)(B), provides that "if the [EPA] or State has commenced and is diligently prosecuting a civil or criminal action in a court of the United States or a State," then a private citizen suit is not permitted. Id. The EPA argues that if Congress had intended to limit the EPA's right to file an enforcement action, it would have expressly stated its intention as it did in the citizen suit context. We find the EPA's argument unpersuasive.... Section 6926 ... contains express language that establishes the primacy of states' enforcement rights once the EPA has granted a state authorization. The mere fact that Congress did not choose to employ the exact same language as contained in an unrelated part of the act does not detract from the plain language used in the state authorization section. Again, Congress provided that the state's program should operate in lieu of the federal program and that the state action should operate with the same force and effect as action taken by the EPA. We find the language contained in the state authorization section of the Act to be as unambiguous as the citizen suit provision....

Even assuming some ambiguity exists in the statutory language, the primacy of the states' enforcement rights, once the EPA has authorized a state to act, is illustrated further through the RCRA's legislative history.... The House Report states that although the "legislation permits the states to take the lead in the enforcement of the hazardous wastes [sic] laws[,] ... the Administrator [of the EPA] is not prohibited from acting in those cases where the state fails to act, or from withdrawing approval of the state hazardous waste plan and implementing the federal hazardous waste program pursuant to ... this act." [H.R.Rep. 1491, 94th Cong., 2nd Sess. 24, reprinted in 1976 U.S.C.C.A.N. 6262, 6269]. The House Report also states that the EPA, "after giving the appropriate notice to a state that is authorized to implement the state hazardous waste program, that violations of this Act are occurring and the state [is] failing to take action against such violations, is authorized to take appropriate action against those persons in such state not in compliance with the hazardous waste title." Id. at 6270. The House Report thus supports our interpretation of the statute—that the federal government's right to pursue an enforcement action under the RCRA attaches only when a state's authorization is revoked or when a state fails to initiate any enforcement action.

A contrary interpretation would result in two separate enforcement actions. Such an interpretation, as explained above, would derogate the RCRA's plain language and legislative history. Companies that reach an agreement through negotiations with a state authorized by the EPA to act in its place may find the agreement undermined by a later separate enforcement action by the EPA. While, generally speaking, two separate sovereigns can institute two separate enforcement actions, those actions can cause vastly different and potentially contradictory results. Such a potential schism runs afoul of the principles of comity and federalism so clearly embedded in the text and history of the RCRA....

* * *

Questions and Notes

1. Note that, technically speaking, *Harmon* did not involve an "overfiling" situation, because EPA filed its administrative action before Missouri undertook any formal enforcement response. Should this fact have influenced the court's analysis?

2. What did you think of the court's effort to "harmonize" the relevant subsections in §§ 3006 and 3008 (§§ 6926 and 6928 in U.S.C.-speak)? Can § 3006(b) bear the weight the court gave it? On the other hand, what did you think of EPA's attempt to avoid the effect of § 3006(d)? What did you make of EPA's argument based on § 7002 (§ 6972)? Does it seem plausible that Congress would have authorized citizens to proceed in the face of non-diligent State enforcement, while at the same time precluding EPA from doing so? At the same time, however, doesn't the House Report tend to support the *Harmon* court's result?

3. While *Harmon* constituted a bombshell when it first was issued, its long-term significance is open to question. The United States has continued to press what it believes to be its authority to overfile in appropriate cases. In a subsequent RCRA case, the Tenth Circuit expressly rejected the *Harmon* analysis, concluding that "[n]othing in the text of the statute suggests that [withdrawal of authorization] in a prerequisite to EPA enforcement or that it is the only remedy for inadequate enforcement." *United States v. Power Engineering Co.*, 303 F.3d 1232, 1238–1239 (10th Cir. 2002). Moreover, the "in lieu of" and "same force and effect" language the 8th Circuit relied on in *Harmon* is unique to RCRA. Both the Clean Water Act and the Clean Air Act, by contrast, appear to contain language that contemplates overfiling in at least some situations. See, e.g., 33 U.S.C. § 1319(g)(6)(A) (indicating narrow circumstances in which EPA may not overfile) and 42 U.S.C. § 7413(e) (stating that, in determining penalties, the court shall consider "payment by the violator of penalties previously assessed for the same violation"). Given these different statutory dynamics, it is perhaps unsurprising that what little post-*Harmon* case law there is tends to support EPA's ability to overfile under these other statutes. See, e.g., *United States v. LTV Steel Co., Inc.*, 118 F.Supp.2d 827 (N.D. Ohio 2000).

4. As a secondary basis for its decision (which we have edited out), the *Harmon* court found that EPA's action was barred by res judicata. In so holding, the 8th Circuit first noted that the Full Faith and Credit Act, 28 U.S.C. § 1738, required it to apply Missouri res judicata law to determine the preclusive effect to which the Missouri state court judgment was entitled. In performing the required "party identity" analysis, however, the court relied heavily on RCRA's "in lieu of" and "same force and effect" language in concluding that EPA is always in privity with authorized States when they act under RCRA. Other courts have rejected this approach, relying on *Drummond v. United States*, 324 U.S. 316, 318, 65 S.Ct. 659, 89 L.Ed. 969 (1945), and *Montana v. United States*, 440 U.S. 147, 154, 99 S.Ct. 970, 59 L.Ed.2d 210 (1979), for the proposition that the United States should not be bound by a prior judgment unless it had a "laboring oar" in the controversy. See, e.g., *Power Engineering*, 303 F.3d at 1240–1241.

5. Even if we assume that EPA has the power to overfile in most or all situations, that still leaves the question of the circumstances under which EPA should choose to exercise this authority. What policy dynamics did the *Harmon* court identify that might bear on this question? Did it seem like a complete list? In its guidance documents and its "Memoranda of Agreement" with the States, EPA generally does two things: first, it articulates what it believes to be its unfettered discretion in this area; but second, and most importantly, it states that it will only overfile in situations in which the

relevant State has failed to take what it terms "timely and appropriate" action. See, e.g., *United States v. City of Rock Island, Ill.*, 182 F.Supp.2d 690, 693 (C.D. Ill. 2001). In practice, this means that overfiling is a relatively rare phenomenon. Did you agree with EPA's decision to overfile in *Harmon?* Interestingly, despite EPA's decision to overfile, it did not pursue to case to the point of seeking Supreme Court review of the Eight Circuit's decision. Can you think of why this might be so?

D. Citizen Suits

One of Congress's most important innovations when it created the modern environmental statutes was the concept of citizen suits. The basic idea is very simple: if neither EPA nor the relevant State is enforcing the law appropriately, citizens can pursue alleged violators in federal court in their stead. Thus, it is often said that Congress has empowered these citizens to act as "private attorneys general," acting on the public's behalf. See, e.g., *Bennett v. Spear*, 520 U.S. 154, 165, 117 S.Ct. 1154, 137 L.Ed.2d 281 (1997).

It is important to note that in this section of the book we are distinguishing between actions under the citizen-suit provisions of the environmental laws, on the one hand, and challenges to environmental decisions under the Administrative Procedure Act. Assuming the elements of reviewability are present, citizens (and regulated entities) can use the APA to challenge a whole host governmental decisions made in the environmental context, such as those made in issuing rules, permits or administrative orders. Under the citizen suit provisions, by contrast, Congress typically has granted citizens two potential causes of action: one against regulated entities who are violating the relevant standards, and another against EPA where it has failed to perform a nondiscretionary duty. See, e.g., 33 U.S.C. § 1365(a)(1) and (2), respectively; see also *Bennett v. Spear*, 520 U.S. at 173–174, for a discussion of the difference between citizen suit and APA claims. Here, we will focus on one of these latter two causes of action—suits that citizens can bring under provisions such as § 505(a)(1) of the CWA against regulated entities who are alleged to be violating the applicable statutory or regulatory standards.

We begin by stressing the similarities between these citizen suits and EPA-lead civil judicial actions. If you read § 505(a) of the CWA, for example, you will see that, like EPA under § 309, citizens are entitled to seek both injunctive relief and penalties. In fact, Section 505(a) simply cross-references § 309(d) regarding the courts' authority to apply the appropriate fines. Thus, these suits can be seen as being very much like the EPA civil judicial-enforcement actions we considered at the beginning of this chapter: like EPA, citizens have to make their prima facie case by proving the relevant violations; once they do so, they are entitled to the same relief EPA would have been entitled to if it had brought the action. This, of course, is fully consistent with the notion that the citizens who bring these cases are fulfilling a quasi-public role–that of the private attorney general–rather than a purely private one. The nature of this undertaking is further underscored when one realizes that any penalties assessed in these actions are payable to the United States Treasury, not to the citizens themselves. See, e.g., *Friends of the Earth v. Laidlaw Environmental Services (TOC)*, 528 U.S. 167, 185,120 S.Ct. 693, 145 L.Ed.2d 610 (2000).

Despite these similarities, however, there are five key differences between citizen suits and EPA enforcement actions. The first four of these constitute additional hurdles that citizens must overcome in order to successfully prosecute their actions. These include: (1) the need to provide notice to EPA, the State and the alleged violator prior to bringing suit; (2) the requirement that citizens demonstrate that they have standing; (3) the need to overcome what we will loosely refer to as the "*Gwaltney* doctrine;" and (4) the fact that their suits are more likely to be barred by prior governmental enforcement actions.

Perhaps surprisingly, the fifth difference constitutes an area in which citizen enforcers are treated better than the Government is when it brings regulatory enforcement actions. If citizens are successful in bringing their claims, they are entitled to an award of attorney fees, to be paid by the defendant. See, e.g., 33 U.S.C. § 1365(d). EPA, by contrast, must bear its own legal costs. Compare, e.g., 33 U.S.C. § 1319 (containing no provision comparable to § 505(d)).

We will now consider all five of these differences, in varying degrees of detail. Keep in mind, however, that the similarities between governmental enforcement actions and citizen suits are in many ways more significant than the differences.

1. Notice

The environmental citizen suit provisions commonly require that the would-be plaintiff provide advance notice of its potential lawsuit to EPA, the State and the alleged violator, typically 60 days before filing suit. See, e.g., 33 U.S.C. § 1365(b)(1)(A). One idea behind these notice requirements is that it gives EPA and the State a window within which they may each decide whether to commence their own enforcement action, which in turn might render the citizen suit unnecessary.

The Supreme Court has determined that these notice requirements are jurisdictional, meaning that they cannot be waived and may be raised at any time during the relevant proceedings. Additionally, any suit filed without proper notice must be dismissed. *Hallstrom v. Tillamook County*, 493 U.S. 20, 110 S.Ct. 304, 107 L.Ed.2d 237(1989).

As contemplated under the statutes, see, e.g., 33 U.S.C. § 1365(b), EPA has developed rules fleshing out the notice requirements for each of the relevant statutes. See, e.g., 40 C.F.R. Part 135 (rules for the CWA and the Safe Drinking Water Act). While recognizing that any defects are fatal, the courts have been fairly generous in construing these requirements. See, e.g., *Public Interest Research Group of New Jersey, Inc. v. Hercules, Inc.*, 50 F.3d 1239 (3d Cir. 1995), and *San Francisco Baykeeper, Inc. v. Tosco Corp.*, 309 F.3d 1153 (9th Cir. 2002).

2. Standing

We already have touched on standing issues in Chapter 1, including consideration of *Lujan v. Defenders of Wildlife*, 504 U.S. 555, 112 S.Ct. 2130, 119 L.Ed.2d 351 (1992) (*"Defenders"*). We here revisit these matters, with a particular focus on the injury and causation questions that are likely to arise in citizens suits. We reserve discussion of yet another standing issue–whether citizens have standing to seek penalties that are payable to the Treasury–until our discussion of the *Gwaltney* doctrine, below.

In *Defenders*, we saw that the plaintiffs' "some day" intentions (to use Justice Scalia's phrase) to revisit sites half-way around the world were insufficient to demonstrate the type of "imminent" injury necessary to satisfy Article III. What kinds of showing do plaintiffs have to make in situations in which they live near the offending discharge? Consider the following case:

FRIENDS OF THE EARTH v. LAIDLAW ENVIRONMENTAL SERVICES

Supreme Court of the United States, 2000.
528 U.S. 167, 120 S.Ct. 693, 145 L.Ed.2d 610.

Justice GINSBURG delivered the opinion of the Court.

In 1986, defendant-respondent Laidlaw Environmental Services (TOC), Inc., bought a hazardous waste incinerator facility in Roebuck, South Carolina, that included a wastewater treatment plant. Shortly after Laidlaw acquired the facility, the South Carolina Department of Health and Environmental Control (DHEC) ... granted Laidlaw an NPDES permit authorizing the company to discharge treated water into the North Tyger River. The permit ... placed limits on Laidlaw's discharge of several pollutants into the river, including ... mercury, an extremely toxic pollutant. . . .

[From the outset, and despite several attempted technological fixes,] Laidlaw consistently failed to meet the permit's stringent 1.3 ppb (parts per billion) daily average limit on mercury discharges. The District Court later found that Laidlaw had violated the mercury limits on 489 occasions between 1987 and 1995.

On June 12, 1992, FOE filed this citizen suit against Laidlaw under § 505(a) of the [CWA], alleging noncompliance with the NPDES permit and seeking declaratory and injunctive relief and an award of civil penalties. Laidlaw moved for summary judgment on the ground that FOE had failed to present evidence demonstrating injury in fact, and therefore lacked Article III standing to bring the lawsuit.... After examining [the] evidence, the District Court denied Laidlaw's summary judgment motion, finding—albeit "by the very slimmest of margins"— that FOE had standing to bring the suit.

... The record indicates that after FOE initiated the suit, but before the District Court rendered judgment, Laidlaw violated the mercury discharge limitation in its permit 13 times.... The last recorded mercury discharge violation occurred in January 1995, long after the complaint was filed but about two years before judgment was rendered.

On January 22, 1997, the District Court issued its judgment. It found that Laidlaw had gained a total economic benefit of $1,092,581 as a result of its extended period of noncompliance with the mercury discharge limit in its permit. The court concluded, however, that a civil penalty of $405,800 was adequate in light of the guiding factors listed in 33 U.S.C. § 1319(d).... The court declined to grant FOE's request for injunctive relief, stating that an injunction was inappropriate because "Laidlaw has been in substantial compliance with all parameters in its NPDES permit since at least August 1992."

II

A

In *Lujan v. Defenders of Wildlife*, 504 U.S. 555, 560–561 (1992), we held that, to satisfy Article III's standing requirements, a plaintiff must show (1) it has suffered an "injury in fact" that is (a) concrete and particularized and (b) actual or imminent, not conjectural or hypothetical; (2) the injury is fairly traceable to the challenged action of the defendant; and (3) it is likely, as opposed to merely speculative, that the injury will be redressed by a favorable decision....

Laidlaw contends first that FOE lacked standing from the outset even to seek injunctive relief, because the plaintiff organizations failed to show that any of their members had sustained or faced the threat of any "injury in fact" from Laidlaw's activities. In support of this contention Laidlaw points to the District Court's finding, made in the course of setting the penalty amount, that there had been "no demonstrated proof of harm to the environment" from Laidlaw's mercury discharge violations.

The relevant showing for purposes of Article III standing, however, is not injury to the environment but injury to the plaintiff. To insist upon the former rather than the latter as part of the standing inquiry (as the dissent in essence does) is to raise the standing hurdle higher than the necessary showing for success on the merits in an action alleging noncompliance with an NPDES permit. Focusing properly on injury to the plaintiff, the District Court found that FOE had demonstrated sufficient injury to establish standing. For example, FOE member Kenneth Lee Curtis averred in affidavits that he lived a half-mile from Laidlaw's facility; that he occasionally drove over the North Tyger River, and that it looked and smelled polluted; and that he would like to fish, camp, swim, and picnic in and near the river between 3 and 15 miles downstream from the facility, as he did when he was a teenager, but would not do so because he was concerned that the water was polluted by Laidlaw's discharges. Curtis reaffirmed these statements in extensive deposition testimony. For example, he testified that he would like to fish in the river at a specific spot he used as a boy, but that he would not do so now because of his concerns about Laidlaw's discharges.

Other members presented evidence to similar effect. CLEAN member Angela Patterson attested that she lived two miles from the facility; that before Laidlaw operated the facility, she picnicked, walked, bird-watched, and waded in and along the North Tyger River because of the natural beauty of the area; that she no longer engaged in these activities in or near the river because she was concerned about harmful effects from discharged pollutants; and that she and her husband would like to purchase a home near the river but did not intend to do so, in part because of Laidlaw's discharges. CLEAN member Judy Pruitt averred that she lived one-quarter mile from Laidlaw's facility and would like to fish, hike, and picnic along the North Tyger River, but has refrained from those activities because of the discharges. FOE member Linda Moore attested that she lived 20 miles from Roebuck, and would use the North Tyger River south of Roebuck and the land surrounding it for recreational purposes were she not concerned that the water contained harmful pollutants. In her deposition, Moore testified at length that she would hike, picnic, camp, swim, boat, and drive near or in the river were it not for her concerns about illegal discharges. CLEAN member Gail Lee attested that her home, which is near Laidlaw's facility, had a lower value than similar homes located further from the facility, and that she believed the pollutant discharges accounted for some of the discrepancy. Sierra Club member Norman Sharp averred that he had canoed approximately 40 miles downstream of the Laidlaw facility and would like to canoe in the North Tyger River closer to Laidlaw's discharge point, but did not do so because he was concerned that the water contained harmful pollutants.

These sworn statements, as the District Court determined, adequately documented injury in fact. We have held that environmental plaintiffs adequately allege injury in fact when they aver that they use the affected area and are persons "for whom the aesthetic and recreational values of the area will be lessened" by the challenged activity. *Sierra Club v. Morton*, 405 U.S. 727, 735 (1972).

Our decision in *Lujan v. National Wildlife Federation*, 497 U.S. 871 (1990), is not to the contrary. In that case an environmental organization assailed the Bureau of Land Management's "land withdrawal review program," a program covering millions of acres, alleging that the program illegally opened up public lands to mining activities. The defendants moved for summary judgment, challenging the plaintiff organization's standing to initiate the action under the [APA]. We held that the plaintiff could not survive the summary judgment motion merely by offering "averments which state only that one of [the organization's] members uses unspecified portions of an immense tract of territory, on some portions of which mining activity has occurred or probably will occur by virtue of the governmental action." 497 U.S., at 889.

In contrast, the affidavits and testimony presented by FOE in this case assert that Laidlaw's discharges, and the affiant members' reasonable concerns about the effects of those discharges, directly affected those affiants' recreational, aesthetic, and economic interests. These submissions present dispositively more than the mere "general averments" and "conclusory allegations" found inadequate in *National Wildlife Federation*. Id., at 888. Nor can the affiants' conditional statements—that they would use the nearby North Tyger River for recreation if Laidlaw were not discharging pollutants into it—be equated with the speculative " 'some day' intentions" to visit endangered species halfway around the world that we held insufficient to show injury in fact in *Defenders of Wildlife*. 504 U.S., at 564.

Los Angeles v. Lyons, 461 U.S. 95 (1983), relied on by the dissent, does not weigh against standing in this case. In *Lyons*, we held that a plaintiff lacked standing to seek an injunction against the enforcement of a police chokehold policy because he could not credibly allege that he faced a realistic threat from the policy. 461 U.S., at 107, n. 7. In the footnote from *Lyons* cited by the dissent, we noted that "[t]he reasonableness of Lyons' fear is dependent upon the likelihood of a recurrence of the allegedly unlawful conduct," and that his "subjective apprehensions" that such a recurrence would even take place were not enough to support standing. Id., at 108, n. 8. Here, in contrast, it is undisputed that Laidlaw's unlawful conduct—discharging pollutants in excess of permit limits—was occurring at the time the complaint was filed. Under Lyons, then, the only "subjective" issue here is "[t]he reasonableness of [the] fear" that led the affiants to respond to that concededly ongoing conduct by refraining from use of the North Tyger River and surrounding areas. Unlike the dissent, we see nothing "improbable" about the proposition that a company's continuous and pervasive illegal discharges of pollutants into a river would cause nearby residents to curtail their recreational use of that waterway and would subject them to other economic and aesthetic harms. The proposition is entirely reasonable, the District Court found it was true in this case, and that is enough for injury in fact.

Justice SCALIA, with whom Justice THOMAS joins, dissenting.

Plaintiffs, as the parties invoking federal jurisdiction, have the burden of proof and persuasion as to the existence of standing. *Lujan v. Defenders of Wildlife*, 504 U.S. 555, 561 (1992) (hereinafter *Lujan*). The plaintiffs in this case fell far short of carrying their burden of demonstrating injury in fact. The Court cites affiants' testimony asserting that their enjoyment of the North Tyger River has been diminished due to "concern" that the water was polluted, and that they "believed" that Laidlaw's mercury exceedances had reduced the value of their homes. These averments alone cannot carry the plaintiffs' burden of demonstrating that they have suffered a "concrete and particularized" injury, *Lujan*, 504 U.S., at 560. General allegations of injury may suffice at the pleading stage, but at summary judgment plaintiffs must set forth "specific facts" to support their claims. Id., at 561. And where, as here, the case has proceeded to judgment, those specific facts must be " 'supported adequately by the evidence adduced at trial,' " *ibid*. In this case, the affidavits themselves are woefully short on "specific facts," and the vague allegations of injury they do make are undermined by the evidence adduced at trial.

Typically, an environmental plaintiff claiming injury due to discharges in violation of the Clean Water Act argues that the discharges harm the environment, and that the harm to the environment injures him. This route to injury is barred in the present case, however, since the District Court concluded after considering all the evidence that there had been "no demonstrated proof of harm to the environment," that the "permit violations at issue in this citizen suit did not result in any health risk or environmental harm," that "[a]ll available data . . . fail to show that Laidlaw's actual discharges have resulted in harm to the North Tyger River," and that "the overall quality of the river exceeds levels necessary to support . . . recreation in and on the water."

The Court finds these conclusions unproblematic for standing, because "[t]he relevant showing for purposes of Article III standing . . . is not injury to the environment but injury to the plaintiff." This statement is correct, as far as it goes. We have certainly held that a demonstration of harm to the environment is not enough to satisfy the injury-in-fact requirement unless the plaintiff can demonstrate how he personally was harmed. In the normal course, however, a lack of demonstrable harm to the environment will translate, as it plainly does here, into a lack of demonstrable harm to citizen plaintiffs. While it is perhaps possible that a plaintiff could be harmed even though the environment was not, such a plaintiff would have the burden of articulating and demonstrating the nature of that injury. Ongoing "concerns" about the environment are not enough, for "[i]t is the reality of the threat of repeated injury that is relevant to the standing inquiry, not the plaintiff's subjective apprehensions," *Los Angeles v. Lyons*, 461 U.S. 95, 107, n. 8. At the very least, in the present case, one would expect to see evidence supporting the affidavits' bald assertions regarding decreasing recreational usage and declining home values, as well as evidence for the improbable proposition that Laidlaw's violations, even though harmless to the environment, are somehow responsible for these effects. Plaintiffs here have made no attempt at such a showing, but rely entirely upon unsupported and unexplained affidavit allegations of "concern."

Indeed, every one of the affiants deposed by Laidlaw cast into doubt the (in any event inadequate) proposition that subjective "concerns" actually affected their conduct. Linda Moore, for example, said in her affidavit that she would use the affected waterways for recreation if it were not for her concern about pollution. Yet she testified in her deposition that she had been to the river only twice, once in 1980 (when she visited someone who lived by the river) and once after this suit was filed. Similarly, Kenneth Lee Curtis, who claimed he was injured by being deprived of recreational activity at the river, admitted that he had not been to the river since he was "a kid," and when asked whether the reason he stopped visiting the river was because of pollution, answered "no." As to Curtis's claim that the river "looke[d] and smell[ed] polluted," this condition, if present, was surely not caused by Laidlaw's discharges, which according to the District Court "did not result in any health risk or environmental harm." 956 F.Supp., at 602. The other affiants cited by the Court were not deposed, but their affidavits state either that they would use the river if it were not polluted or harmful (as the court subsequently found it is not), or said that the river looks polluted (which is also incompatible with the court's findings), ibid. These affiants have established nothing but "subjective apprehensions."

The Court is correct that the District Court explicitly found standing—albeit "by the very slimmest of margins," and as "an awfully close call." That cautious finding, however, was made in 1993, long before the court's 1997 conclusion that Laidlaw's discharges did not harm the environment. As we have previously recognized, an initial conclusion that plaintiffs have standing is subject to reexamination, particularly if later evidence proves inconsistent with that conclusion. Laidlaw challenged the existence of injury in fact on appeal to the Fourth Circuit, but that court did not reach the question. Thus no lower court has reviewed the injury-in-fact issue in light of the extensive studies that led the District Court to conclude that the environment was not harmed by Laidlaw's discharges.

Inexplicably, the Court is untroubled by this, but proceeds to find injury in fact in the most casual fashion, as though it is merely confirming a careful analysis made below. Although we have previously refused to find standing based on the "conclusory allegations of an affidavit" *Lujan v. National Wildlife Federation*, 497 U.S. 871, 888 (1990), the Court is content to do just that today. By accepting plaintiffs' vague, contradictory, and unsubstantiated allegations of "concern" about the environment as adequate to prove injury in fact, and accepting them even in the face of a finding that the environment was not demonstrably harmed, the Court makes the injury-in-fact requirement a sham. If there are permit violations, and a member of a plaintiff environmental organization lives near the offending plant, it would be difficult not to satisfy today's lenient standard.

Questions and Notes

1. Justice Ginsburg was surprisingly non-specific about which injuries of which affiants provided the requisite standing. Several of the affiants indicated that they were forgoing activities such as hiking, picnicking and camping near the North Tyger River as a result of their concerns about the discharges. If the affiants had engaged in these activities, how would Laidlaw's discharges of mercury have adversely affected them? Does it matter whether they could see or smell the offending discharges? If they could not, should it be enough if they merely "knew" the pollutants were there? See *Public Interest Research Group of New Jersey, Inc. v. Magnesium Elektron, Inc.*, 123 F.3d 111, 121 (3d Cir. 1997) (a pre-*Laidlaw* case denying standing in this situation because "absent a showing of tangible injury to the River or its immediate surroundings, PIRG's members are no less 'concerned

bystanders' than any other citizen who takes an interest in our environment"). Is *Magnesium Elektron* still good law in light of *Laidlaw*?

2. Ms. Lee attested that she believed that Laidlaw's discharges had adversely affected her property value. Should courts accept these assertions at face value? Does *Laidlaw* stand for the proposition that they must do so?

3. Perhaps the most Constitutionally-significant injuries in *Laidlaw* were those articulated by the affiants who said that they would like to fish, swim or wade in the River, but were afraid to do so in light of the defendant's discharges. What is the essence of the disagreement between the majority and the dissent with respect to these injuries? How should courts determine the reasonableness of the plaintiffs' concerns? Put another way, how much pollution should courts require to be present in water before they recognize that those who forgo swimming in it (or drinking it) have standing to complain? Is Justice Scalia right that, under the majority's approach, "[i]f there are permit violations, and a member of a plaintiff environmental organization lives near the offending plant, it would be difficult not to satisfy today's lenient standard?"

4. *Laidlaw* appears to have been what we will call a "one polluter" case; there was no apparent contention that other sources of pollution may have been causing or contributing to the alleged harms being suffered by the plaintiff's affiants. When these allegations are present, they can pose interesting causation and redressability questions. If the plaintiff's alleged injury relates to seeing an oily sheen on the water, for example, how much proof should the courts require as to whether the defendant's oily discharges were in fact the source of the oil observed? If the defendant is one of a number of sources of the relevant oil, should the plaintiff be denied standing for want of redressability if it cannot show that the river will be observably less oily absent the defendant's discharges? In *Public Interest Research Group of New Jersey, Inc. v. Powell Duffryn Terminals Inc.*, 913 F.2d 64 (3d Cir. 1990), the Third Circuit concluded that all the plaintiff must show to demonstrate causation in multiple-polluter situations is that the defendant

> has 1) discharged some pollutant in concentrations greater than allowed by its permit 2) into a waterway in which the plaintiffs have an interest that is or may be adversely affected by the pollutant and that 3) this pollutant causes or contributes to the kinds of injuries alleged by the plaintiffs.

Id. at 72. With regard to redressability, the court found that "[p]laintiffs need not show that the waterway will be returned to pristine condition in order to establish the minimal requirements of Article III." Id. at 73. Do you agree with the Third Circuit on these fronts? Judge Aldisert concurred in *Powell-Duffryn*, but expressed his reservations in the following terms:

> Throughout my extensive preparation of this case including close attention at argument and discussion with my colleagues at conference, I was persuaded that the member/plaintiffs had failed to show an actual injury that was traceable to the permit violations. I am now willing to join my colleagues' view. But I feel somewhat like Lord Byron's fair maiden in Don Juan, c 1, dedication cxvii,

> A little more she strove, and much repented, And whispering "I will ne'er consent"—consented.

Id. at 83.

The Gaston Copper Saga

The impact of *Laidlaw* can perhaps best be seen in the effect it had on the Fourth Circuit in *Friends of the Earth, Inc. v. Gaston Copper Recycling Corp.*, 204 F.3d 149 (4th Cir. 2000). In that case, the plaintiffs' best standing affiant, Mr. Shealy, testified that South Carolina officials had tested his lake the year before the lawsuit was filed and had found copper, zinc, nickel, iron and PCBs, all of which pollutants the defendant's smelting facility had discharged in the past. As a result, he testified that he was injured in three ways: (1) he reduced his consumption of the fish from the lake; (2) he restricted his grandchildren's access to the water; and (3) his property value had diminished because the lake was known to be polluted.

Before *Laidlaw* was decided, the panel majority at the Fourth Circuit level found that the plaintiffs had not demonstrated that they were injured because:

> ... [N]o evidence was presented that established that Shealy's lake ... [was] in fact adversely affected by pollution.... Indeed, there were no toxicity tests, or tests or studies of any kind, performed on waters from Shealy's lake.... Further, none of the members even testified that there was an observable negative impact on the waters that they used or on the surrounding ecosystem of such water. Their concerns were based on mere speculation as to the presence of pollution without any evidence to support their fears or establish the presence of pollutants in the allegedly affected waters.

179 F.3d 107, 113–114 (4th Cir. 1999).

Upon rehearing after *Laidlaw*, the *en banc* panel of the Fourth Circuit unanimously reversed course, determining that Mr. Shealy was "a classic example of an individual who has suffered an environmental injury in fact fairly traceable to a defendant's conduct." 204 F.3d at 155. The majority opinion at the *en banc* level was written by Chief Judge Wilkinson, who had dissented from the original panel opinion. Perhaps unsurprisingly (given the fact that he thought the panel was wrong in the first place), his opinion does not place much reliance on *Laidlaw*.

More interesting are the three concurring opinions. Judge Luttig, with Judge Niemeyer concurring, wrote that:

> I concur in the judgment of the court, but not in its opinion. Through no fault of this court, the Supreme Court's recent decision in [*Laidlaw*], has rendered much of the discussion in today's opinion not merely unnecessary, but affirmatively confusing. Rather than persist in the fiction (as we do in the court's opinion) that Laidlaw was part of the fabric of standing jurisprudence at the time of argument in this case, or worse (as we also do) that that decision

was merely an unexceptional reaffirmation of the Court's previous precedents, I would simply reverse the district court's judgment on the specific reasoning of the Supreme Court in *Laidlaw* and say little else. The unfortunate implication left by the court's failure to address the significant change in environmental standing doctrine worked by the Supreme Court's recent decision in *Laidlaw* (and by the court's comfortable, but mistaken, assumption that the Supreme Court's decisions prior to Laidlaw themselves dictated the conclusion we reach today), is that the district court seriously erred in its application of the standing doctrine extant at the time that it ruled—which it did not.

Id. at 164–165. Judge Niemeyer also wrote separately:

Before the Supreme Court's recent decision in [*Laidlaw*], I would have affirmed the district court in this case because the plaintiffs, who expressed only a subjective belief of injury, have not shown that they "personally [have] suffered some actual or threatened injury as a result of the putatively illegal conduct of the defendant and that the injury fairly can be traced to the challenged action." *Valley Forge Christian College v. Americans United for Separation of Church and State, Inc.*, 454 U.S. 464, 472 (1982). . . .

As my concurrence in Judge Luttig's opinion indicates, I believe that the decision in Laidlaw represents a sea change in constitutional standing principles, and in view of that decision I agree that we are now required to reverse.

Id. at 164. And finally, Judge Hamilton lamented that:

The Supreme Court's decision in [*Laidlaw*] has unnecessarily opened the standing floodgates, rendering our standing inquiry "a sham," (Scalia, J., dissenting). However, being bound by [*Laidlaw*]., I concur in the court's judgment reversing the district court's judgment and remanding the case for a determination as to whether Gaston Copper has discharged pollutants in excess of its permit limits.

Id. at 165.

The panel majority in *Gaston Copper* had also found that the plaintiffs had failed to demonstrate causation. Cobbling together the facts from the various opinions, one is left with the following:

1. Gaston Copper discharged into Lake Watson, which flowed into the Boggy Branch, which, in turn, was a tributary of Bull Swamp Creek, which eventually flowed into the North Fork of the Edisto River. The distance from Lake Watson to the North Fork of the Edisto River was at least 10 miles (and maybe as many as 16.5 miles).

2. Mr. Shealy's lake was four miles downstream from Watson Lake and was fed in part by Bull Swamp Creek; however, there were 31 ponds between Gaston Copper and Mr. Shealy's lake, and three other tributaries fed into Mr. Shealy's lake;

3. The South Carolina Department of Health and Environmental Control (DHEC) had identified the same heavy metals and PCBs in Mr. Shealy's lake as were contained in the plant's discharges. Apparently, none of the parties submitted evidence regarding the existence of other potential sources of these contaminants (or the lack thereof); and

4. In response to a question raised during the comment period for Gaston Copper's permit, DHEC had indicated the "runoff" from Gaston Copper's discharges would "go to Boggy Branch to Bull Swamp to the Edisto River." Unfortunately, none of the relevant opinions indicated whether Gaston Copper's pollutants would have had to travel through Mr. Shealy's lake to get to the Edisto River. The opinions do not preclude the possibility that, while the Bull Swamp Creek fed into Mr. Shealy's lake, it could have been a side channel that did not feed back into either the Creek or the Edisto River.

The *en banc* panel in *Gaston Copper* rejected the panel majority's causation analysis, finding traceability as a matter of law. 204 F.3d at 161–162. It did so, however, without any reference to *Laidlaw*, which is perhaps unsurprising given that *Laidlaw* did not address the causation element of the standing test. Interestingly, the two judges in the panel majority (Judges Hamilton and Williams) must have read *Laidlaw* as undermining their earlier analysis on this front as well, or they presumably would have dissented from the *en banc* result.

Do you agree that *Laidlaw* should have affected even the causation analysis in *Gaston Copper*? Do you think the plaintiffs put on enough evidence to support a finding of causation even if *Laidlaw* is deemed irrelevant?

3. The *Gwaltney* Doctrine

As the Supreme Court mentions in the first case below, there is little doubt that the Government can bring penalty actions with respect to violations to "wholly past" violations; that is, violations that have ceased prior to the commencement of the enforcement action. In the citizen suit context, however, the question whether citizens may bring or maintain actions after the violation has ceased can raise a host of issues regarding statutory interpretation, redressability and mootness. Because these issues are closely intertwined, we treat them together under the general rubric of the *Gwaltney* doctrine. We begin with the case that gives the doctrine its name:

GWALTNEY OF SMITHFIELD, LTD., v. CHESAPEAKE BAY FOUNDATION, INC.

Supreme Court of the United States, 1987.
484 U.S. 49, 108 S.Ct. 376, 98 L.Ed.2d 306.

Justice MARSHALL delivered the opinion of the Court.

In this case, we must decide whether § 505(a) of the Clean Water Act confers federal jurisdiction over citizen suits for wholly past violations.

... The holder of a federal NPDES permit is subject to enforcement action by the Administrator for failure to comply with the conditions of the permit. The Administrator's enforcement arsenal includes administrative, civil, and criminal sanctions. § 1319. The holder of a state NPDES permit is subject to both federal and state enforcement action for failure to comply. §§ 1319, 1342(b)(7). In the absence of federal or state enforcement, private citizens may commence civil actions against any person "alleged to be in violation of" the conditions of either a federal or state NPDES permit. § 1365(a)(1). If the citizen prevails in such an action, the court may order injunctive relief and/or impose civil penalties payable to the United States Treasury. § 1365(a).

The Commonwealth of Virginia established a federally approved state NPDES program administered by the Virginia State Water Control Board (Board). In 1974, the Board issued a NPDES permit to ITT–Gwaltney authorizing the discharge of seven pollutants from the company's meat-packing plant on the Pagan River in Smithfield, Virginia. The permit, which was reissued in 1979 and modified in 1980, established effluent limitations, monitoring requirements, and other conditions of discharge. In 1981, petitioner Gwaltney of Smithfield acquired the assets of ITT–Gwaltney and assumed obligations under the permit.

Between 1981 and 1984, petitioner repeatedly violated the conditions of the permit by exceeding effluent limitations on five of the seven pollutants covered. These violations are chronicled in the Discharge Monitoring Reports that the permit required petitioner to maintain. The most substantial of the violations concerned the pollutants fecal coliform, chlorine, and total Kjeldahl nitrogen (TKN). Between October 27, 1981, and August 30, 1984, petitioner violated its TKN limitation 87 times, its chlorine limitation 34 times, and its fecal coliform limitation 31 times. Petitioner installed new equipment to improve its chlorination system in March 1982, and its last reported chlorine violation occurred in October 1982. The new chlorination system also helped to control the discharge of fecal coliform, and the last recorded fecal coliform violation occurred in February 1984. Petitioner installed an upgraded wastewater treatment system in October 1983, and its last reported TKN violation occurred on May 15, 1984.

Respondents Chesapeake Bay Foundation and Natural Resources Defense Council ... sent notice in February 1984 to Gwaltney, the Administrator of EPA, and the Virginia State Water Control Board, indicating respondents' intention to commence a citizen suit under the Act based on petitioner's violations of its permit conditions. Respondents proceeded to file this suit in June 1984, alleging that petitioner "has violated ... [and] will continue to violate its NPDES permit." Respondents requested that the District Court provide declaratory and injunctive relief, impose civil penalties, and award attorney's fees and costs....

... Gwaltney moved in May 1985 for dismissal of the action for want of subject-matter jurisdiction under the Act. Gwaltney argued that the language of § 505(a), which permits private citizens to bring suit against any person "alleged to be in violation" of the Act, requires that a defendant be violating the Act at the time of suit. Gwaltney urged the District Court to adopt the analysis of the Fifth Circuit in *Hamker v. Diamond Shamrock Chemical Co.*, 756 F.2d 392 (1985), which held that "a complaint brought under [§ 505] must allege a violation occurring at the time the complaint is filed." *Id.*, at 395. Gwaltney contended that because its last recorded violation occurred several weeks before respondents filed their complaint, the District Court lacked subject-matter jurisdiction over respondents' action.

The District Court rejected Gwaltney's argument, concluding that § 505 authorizes citizens to bring enforcement actions on the basis of wholly past violations. The District Court found that "[t]he words 'to be in violation' may reasonably be read as comprehending unlawful conduct that occurred solely prior to the filing of the lawsuit as well as unlawful conduct that continues into the present." In the District Court's view, this construction of the statutory language was supported by the legislative history and the underlying policy goals of the Act. The District Court held in the alternative that respondents satisfied the jurisdictional requirements of § 505 because their complaint alleged in good faith that Gwaltney was continuing to violate its permit at the time the suit was filed.

The Court of Appeals affirmed, expressly rejecting the Fifth Circuit's approach in *Hamker* and holding that § 505 "can be read to comprehend unlawful conduct that occurred only prior to the filing of a lawsuit as well as unlawful conduct that continues into the present." The Court of Appeals concluded that its reading of § 505 was consistent with the Act's structure, legislative history, and purpose. Although it observed that "[a] very sound argument can be made that [respondents'] allegations of continuing violations were made in good faith," the Court of Appeals declined to rule on the District Court's alternative holding, finding it unnecessary to the disposition of the case.

Subsequent to the issuance of the Fourth Circuit's opinion, the First Circuit also had occasion to construe § 505. It took a position different from that of either the Fourth or the Fifth Circuit, holding that jurisdiction lies under § 505 when "the citizen-plaintiff fairly alleges a continuing likelihood that the defendant, if not enjoined, will again proceed to violate the Act." *Pawtuxet Cove Marina, Inc. v. Ciba–Geigy Corp.*, 807 F.2d 1089, 1094 (1986). The First Circuit's approach precludes suit based on wholly past violations, but permits suit when there is a pattern of intermittent violations, even if there is no violation at the moment suit is filed. . . .

It is well settled that "the starting point for interpreting a statute is the language of the statute itself." *Consumer Product Safety Comm'n v. GTE Sylvania, Inc.*, 447 U.S. 102, 108 (1980). The Court of Appeals concluded that the "to be in violation" language of § 505 is ambiguous, whereas petitioner asserts that it plainly precludes the construction adopted below. We must agree with the Court of Appeals that § 505 is not a provision in which Congress' limpid prose puts an end to all dispute. But to acknowledge ambiguity is not to conclude that all interpretations are equally plausible. The most natural reading of "to be in violation" is a requirement that citizen-plaintiffs allege a state of either continuous or intermittent violation—that is, a reasonable likelihood that a past polluter will continue to pollute in the future. Congress could have phrased its requirement in language that looked to the past ("to have violated"), but it did not choose this readily available option.

Respondents urge that the choice of the phrase "to be in violation," rather than phrasing more clearly directed to the past, is a "careless accident," the result of a "debatable lapse of syntactical precision." But the prospective orientation of that phrase could not have escaped Congress' attention. Congress used identical language in the citizen suit provisions of several other environmental statutes that authorize only prospective relief. [Citing the Clean Air Act, RCRA, and TSCA]. Moreover, Congress has demonstrated in yet other statutory provisions that it knows how to avoid this prospective implication by using language that explicitly targets wholly past violations.[2]

Respondents seek to counter this reasoning by observing that Congress also used the phrase "is in violation" in § 309(a) of the Act, which authorizes the Administrator of EPA to issue compliance orders. That language is incorporated by reference in § 309(b), which authorizes the Administrator to bring civil enforcement actions. Because it is little questioned that the Administrator may bring enforcement actions to recover civil penalties for wholly past violations, respondents contend, the parallel language of § 309(a) and § 505(a) must mean that citizens, too, may maintain such actions.

Although this argument has some initial plausibility, it cannot withstand close scrutiny and comparison of the two statutory provisions. The Administrator's ability to seek civil penalties is not discussed in either § 309(a) or § 309(b); civil penalties are not mentioned until § 309(d), which does not contain the "is in violation" language. This Court recently has recognized that § 309(d) constitutes a separate grant of enforcement authority:

> "Section 1319 [§ 309] does not intertwine equitable relief with the imposition of civil penalties. Instead each kind of relief is separably authorized in a separate and distinct statutory provision. Subsection

---

2. For example, [RCRA] was amended in 1984 to authorize citizen suits against any "past or present" generator, transporter, owner, or operator of a treatment, storage, or disposal facility "who has contributed or who is contributing" to the "past or present" handling, storage, treatment, transportation, or disposal of certain hazardous wastes. 42 U.S.C. § 6972(a)(1)(B) (1982 ed., Supp. III). Prior to 1984, [RCRA] contained language identical to that of

§ 505(a) of the Clean Water Act, authorizing citizen suits against any person "alleged to be in violation" of waste disposal permits or standards. 42 U.S.C. § 6972(a)(1). Even more on point, the most recent Clean Water Act amendments permit EPA to assess administrative penalties without judicial process on any person who "has violated" the provisions of the Act. Water Quality Act of 1987, § 314, Pub.L. 100-4, 101 Stat. 46.

(b), providing injunctive relief, is independent of subsection (d), which provides only for civil penalties."

Tull v. United States, 481 U.S. 412, 425 (1987). In contrast, § 505 of the Act does not authorize civil penalties separately from injunctive relief; rather, the two forms of relief are referred to in the same subsection, even in the same sentence. The citizen suit provision suggests a connection between injunctive relief and civil penalties that is noticeably absent from the provision authorizing agency enforcement. A comparison of § 309 and § 505 thus supports rather than refutes our conclusion that citizens, unlike the Administrator, may seek civil penalties only in a suit brought to enjoin or otherwise abate an ongoing violation.

Our reading of the "to be in violation" language of § 505(a) is bolstered by the language and structure of the rest of the citizen suit provisions in § 505 of the Act. These provisions together make plain that the interest of the citizen-plaintiff is primarily forward-looking.

One of the most striking indicia of the prospective orientation of the citizen suit is the pervasive use of the present tense throughout § 505. A citizen suit may be brought only for violation of a permit limitation "which is in effect" under the Act. 33 U.S.C. § 1365(f). Citizen-plaintiffs must give notice to the alleged violator, the Administrator of EPA, and the State in which the alleged violation "occurs." § 1365(b)(1)(A). A Governor of a State may sue as a citizen when the Administrator fails to enforce an effluent limitation "the violation of which is occurring in another State and is causing an adverse effect on the public health or welfare in his State." § 1365(h). The most telling use of the present tense is in the definition of "citizen" as "a person . . . having an interest which is or may be adversely affected" by the defendant's violations of the Act. § 1365(g). This definition makes plain what the undeviating use of the present tense strongly suggests: the harm sought to be addressed by the citizen suit lies in the present or the future, not in the past.

Any other conclusion would render incomprehensible § 505's notice provision, which requires citizens to give 60 days' notice of their intent to sue to the alleged violator as well as to the Administrator and the State. If the Administrator or the State commences enforcement action within that 60-day period, the citizen suit is barred, presumably because governmental action has rendered it unnecessary. It follows logically that the purpose of notice to the alleged violator is to give it an opportunity to bring itself into complete compliance with the Act and thus likewise render unnecessary a citizen suit. If we assume, as respondents urge, that citizen suits may target wholly past violations, the requirement of notice to the alleged violator becomes gratuitous. Indeed, respondents, in propounding their interpretation of the Act, can think of no reason for Congress to require such notice other than that "it seemed right" to inform an alleged violator that it was about to be sued.

Adopting respondents' interpretation of § 505's jurisdictional grant would create a second and even more disturbing anomaly. The bar on citizen suits when governmental enforcement action is under way suggests that the citizen suit is meant to supplement rather than to supplant governmental action. The legislative history of the Act reinforces this view of the role of the citizen suit. The Senate Report noted that "[t]he Committee intends the great volume of enforcement actions [to] be brought by the State," and that citizen suits are proper only "if the Federal, State, and local agencies fail to exercise their enforcement responsibility." S.Rep. No. 92–414, p. 64 (1971), *reprinted in* 2 A Legislative History of the Water Pollution Control Act Amendments of 1972, p. 1482 (1973) (hereinafter Leg.Hist.). Permitting citizen suits for wholly past violations of the Act could undermine the supplementary role envisioned for the citizen suit. This danger is best illustrated by an example. Suppose that the Administrator identified a violator of the Act and issued a compliance order under § 309(a). Suppose further that the Administrator agreed not to assess or otherwise seek civil penalties on the condition that the violator take some extreme corrective action, such as to install particularly effective but expensive machinery, that it otherwise would not be obliged to take. If citizens could file suit, months or years later, in order to seek the civil penalties that the Administrator chose to forgo, then the Administrator's discretion to enforce the Act in the public interest would be curtailed considerably. The same might be said of the discretion of state enforcement authorities. Respondents' interpretation of the scope of the citizen suit would change the nature of the citizens' role from interstitial to potentially intrusive. We cannot agree that Congress intended such a result.

Our conclusion that § 505 does not permit citizen suits for wholly past violations does not necessarily dispose of this lawsuit, as both lower courts recognized. The District Court found persuasive the fact that "[respondents'] allegation in the complaint, that Gwaltney was continuing to violate its NPDES permit when plaintiffs filed suit[,] appears to have been made fully in good faith." On this basis, the District Court explicitly held, albeit in a footnote, that "even if Gwaltney were correct that a district court has no jurisdiction over citizen suits based entirely on unlawful conduct that occurred entirely in the past, the Court would still have jurisdiction here." The Court of Appeals acknowledged, also in a footnote, that "[a] very sound argument can be made that [respondents'] allegations of continuing violations were made in good faith," but expressly declined to rule on this alternative holding. Because we agree that § 505 confers jurisdiction over citizen suits when the citizen-plaintiffs make a good-faith allegation of continuous or intermittent violation, we remand the case to the Court of Appeals for further consideration.

Petitioner argues that citizen-plaintiffs must prove their allegations of ongoing noncompliance before jurisdiction attaches under § 505. We cannot agree. The statute does not require that a defendant "be in violation" of the Act at the commencement of suit; rather, the statute requires that a defendant be "alleged to be in violation." Petitioner's construction of the Act reads the word "alleged" out of § 505. As petitioner itself is quick to note in other contexts, there is no reason to believe that Congress' drafting of § 505 was sloppy or haphazard. We agree with the Solicitor General that "Congress's use of the phrase 'alleged to be in violation' reflects a conscious sensitivity to the practical difficulties of detecting and proving chronic episodic violations of environmental standards." Our acknowledgment that Congress intended a good-faith allegation to suffice for jurisdictional purposes, however, does not give litigants license to flood the courts with suits premised on baseless allegations. Rule 11 of the Federal Rules of Civil Procedure, which requires pleadings to be based on a good-faith belief, formed after reasonable inquiry, that they are "well grounded in fact," adequately protects defendants from frivolous allegations.

Petitioner contends that failure to require proof of allegations under § 505 would permit plaintiffs whose allegations of ongoing violation are reasonable but untrue to maintain suit in federal court even though they lack constitutional standing. Petitioner reasons that if a defendant is in complete compliance with the Act at the time of suit, plaintiffs have suffered no injury remediable by the citizen suit provisions of the Act. Petitioner, however, fails to recognize that our standing cases uniformly recognize that allegations of injury are sufficient to invoke the jurisdiction of a court. In *Warth v. Seldin*, 422 U.S. 490, 501 (1975), for example, we made clear that a suit will not be dismissed for lack of standing if there are sufficient "allegations of fact"—not proof—in the complaint or supporting affidavits. This is not to say, however, that such allegations may not be challenged. In *United States v. SCRAP*, 412 U.S. 669, 689 (1973), we noted that if the plaintiffs' "allegations [of standing] were in fact untrue, then the [defendants] should have moved for summary judgment on the standing issue and demonstrated to the District Court that the allegations were sham and raised no genuine issue of fact." If the defendant fails to make such a showing after the plaintiff offers evidence to support the allegation, the case proceeds to trial on the merits, where the plaintiff must prove the allegations in order to prevail. But the Constitution does not require that the plaintiff offer this proof as a threshold matter in order to invoke the District Court's jurisdiction.

Petitioner also worries that our construction of § 505 would permit citizen-plaintiffs, if their allegations of ongoing noncompliance become false at some later point in the litigation because the defendant begins to comply with the Act, to continue nonetheless to press their suit to conclusion. According to petitioner, such a result would contravene both the prospective purpose of the citizen suit provisions and the "case or controversy" requirement of Article III. Longstanding principles of mootness, however, prevent the maintenance of suit when " 'there is no reasonable expectation that the wrong will be repeated.' " *United States v. W.T. Grant Co.*, 345 U.S. 629, 633, (1953). In seeking to have a case dismissed as moot, however, the defendant's burden "is a heavy one." 345 U.S., at 633. The defendant must demonstrate that it is "absolutely clear that the allegedly wrongful behavior could not reasonably be expected to recur." *United States v. Phosphate Export Assn., Inc.*, 393 U.S. 199, 203 (1968). Mootness doctrine thus protects defendants from the maintenance of suit under the Clean Water Act based solely on violations wholly unconnected to any present or future wrongdoing, while it also protects plaintiffs from defendants who seek to evade sanction by predictable "protestations of repentance and reform." *United States v. Oregon State Medical Society*, 343 U.S. 326, 333 (1952).

Because the court below erroneously concluded that respondents could maintain an action based on wholly past violations of the Act, it declined to decide whether respondents' complaint contained a good-faith allegation of ongoing violation by petitioner. We therefore remand the case for consideration of this question. The judgment of the Court of Appeals is vacated, and the case is remanded for further proceedings consistent with this opinion.

Questions and Notes

1. How persuasive was the Court's statutory analysis in *Gwaltney*? Do you agree that any other reading would render incomprehensible § 505's requirement that the plaintiff give notice to the alleged violator, in addition to the EPA and the state? Interestingly, the legislative histories of both § 505 and its predecessor provision in the Clean Air Act (§ 304) are silent as to why Congress required notice to the alleged violator. Are there any other possible explanations as to why Congress may have done so? In writing for the majority, Justice Marshall also relied in part on the fact that § 505(b)(1)(B) bars citizen suits when either EPA or the State undertakes diligent enforcement action. Does this bar support the Court's interpretation? In answering this question, keep in mind that "diligent prosecution" does not necessarily result in immediate compliance–there are some situations in which even aggressive enforcement actions will result in compliance schedules that may have yet to have run their course when a citizens group files its action. In such situations, shouldn't the bar apply? On the other hand, might not there be some situations in which a prior governmental enforcement action might be deemed to be non-diligent, even though the violation might be wholly past–such as, for example, a situation in which a State imposes no fine for several flagrant and serious (though wholly-past) hazardous waste disposal events? If these things are true, does this undermine the Court's conclusion that the presence of the bar sheds light on the "wholly past" violation issue? As we will see in our consideration of these bar provisions, below, Justice Marshall's paragraph on this dynamic in *Gwaltney* has had a significant effect on how some courts have interpreted those provisions.

2. Regardless of what one thinks of some of the issues raised in the previous note, the Supreme Court's holding in *Gwaltney* clearly reflects a defensible reading of § 505(a)(1) itself. The ultimate test the Court established has two parts. First, at the time of filing the plaintiff must make "a good faith allegation of continuous or intermittent violation." Second, so long as the plaintiff submits enough evidence to survive a motion for summary judgment, "the case proceeds to trial on the merits, where the plaintiff must prove the allegations to prevail." How does this differ from the test that the petitioner advanced? What is the practical effect of this

distinction? How should a court determine whether the plaintiff's allegations were made in good faith?

3. The *Gwaltney* majority did not address with any specificity how plaintiffs should go about proving the required continuous or intermittent violations at trial. In his concurrence, Justice Scalia offered the following:

> ... The phrase in § 505(a), "to be in violation," unlike the phrase "to be violating" or "to have committed a violation," suggests a state rather than an act—the opposite of a state of compliance. A good or lucky day is not a state of compliance. Nor is the dubious state in which a past effluent problem is not recurring at the moment but the cause of that problem has not been completely and clearly eradicated. When a company has violated an effluent standard or limitation, it remains, for purposes of § 505(a), "in violation" of that standard or limitation so long as it has not put in place remedial measures that clearly eliminate the cause of the violation. It does not suffice to defeat subject-matter jurisdiction that the success of the attempted remedies becomes clear months or even weeks after the suit is filed. Subject-matter jurisdiction "depends on the state of things at the time of the action brought"; if it existed when the suit was brought, "subsequent events" cannot "ous[t]" the court of jurisdiction.

> Thus, I think the question on remand should be whether petitioner had taken remedial steps that had clearly achieved the effect of curing all past violations by the time suit was brought....

484 U.S. at 69–70 (citations omitted). On remand, the Fourth Circuit determined that the plaintiffs could prevail by either "(1) by proving violations that continue on or after the date the complaint is filed, or (2) by adducing evidence from which a reasonable trier of fact could find a continuing likelihood of a recurrence in intermittent or sporadic violations." *Chesapeake Bay Found., Inc. v. Gwaltney of Smithfield, Ltd.*, 844 F.2d 170, 171–172 (4th Cir. 1988). This test has been universally embraced by other courts. See, e.g., *Atlantic States Legal Found., Inc. v. Stroh Die Casting Co.*, 116 F.3d 814, 825 (7th Cir. 1997).

4. Most lower courts have concluded that they should analyze *Gwaltney* issues on a "parameter-by-parameter" basis; that is, they should recognize that a facility may have solved some problems but not others by the time the complaint is filed, and that should treat each problem separately for purposes of determining whether the relevant violations were in wholly past. In *Gwaltney*, for example, the Fourth Circuit ultimately determined that the company had solved its chlorine problems, but not its TKN problems, before the complaint was filed. Thus, the court determined that it should uphold that portion of the penalty relating to the TKN violations ($289,822), but reverse that portion relating to the chlorine issues ($995,500). *Chesapeake Bay Found., Inc. v. Gwaltney of Smithfield, Ltd.*, 890 F.2d 690, 687–698 (4th Cir. 1989). Do you agree that this is the proper mode of analysis?

In the penultimate paragraph of his majority opinion in *Gwaltney*, Justice Marshall noted that the petitioner raised Article III questions regarding the plaintiffs' ability to continue to press their lawsuit if the violations ceased. This contention invoked both redressability and mootness concerns. This is perhaps unsurprising given that, as noted in the continuation of

Laidlaw below, the Supreme Court has often described the doctrine of mootness as "the doctrine of standing set in a time frame: The requisite personal interest that must exist at the commencement of the litigation (standing) must continue throughout its existence (mootness)." *Arizonans for Official English v. Arizona*, 520 U.S. 43, 68, n.22, 117 S.Ct. 1055, 137 L.Ed.2d 170 (1997). On the redressability front, the theory is that, at least in situations in which there is no ongoing violation, the plaintiffs receive no Constitutionally-cognizable benefit from penalties paid to the Treasury. While this might be a pure standing argument in situations in which the defendant eliminated the violations before the lawsuit was filed, it morphs into a mootness argument where the purported solution occurs during the pendency of the suit.

The petitioner in *Gwaltney* was apparently hedging its bets, arguing that it had solved all of its problems before the suit was filed, while at the same time raising concerns about whether the lawsuit should continue if it solved them during its pendency. Interestingly, even the first of these theories posed standing issues. Despite that, however, the majority addressed the effect of the allegedly wholly-past nature of the violations solely on statutory grounds. Indeed, the Court's only mention of standing is in its mootness discussion in the second-to-last paragraph.

The fact that the Supreme Court resolved the primary issue in *Gwaltney* solely on statutory grounds raised the question of whether Congress could "fix" the *Gwaltney* result by amending the citizen suit provisions to specifically authorize citizen actions with respect to wholly past violations. Indeed, Congress moved to do essentially that when it amended the Clean Air Act in 1990, allowing suits against those alleged "to have violated" the relevant CAA standards, at least in situations in which the violations were not one-time events. See 42 U.S.C. § 7004(a)(1). Before too long, however, the Supreme Court returned to "wholly past violation" issue in *Steel Co. v. Citizens for a Better Environment*, 523 U.S. 83, 118 S.Ct. 1003, 140 L.Ed.2d 210 (1998).

Steel Co. involved a situation in which the plaintiff, before filing suit, had sent the defendant a notice letter under the Emergency Planning and Community Right–To–Know Act of 1986, 42 U.S.C. § 11001 et seq. (EP-CRA). In its notice, the plaintiff alleged that Steel Co. had violated the statute for seven years by failing to submit the required chemical inventory forms. During the 60–day notice period, the defendant submitted all of the required forms, and, when the suit was filed, argued that the plaintiffs could not maintain an action for wholly past violations. Ultimately, the Seventh Circuit held that they could, determining that EPCRA's citizen-suit provision (42 U.S.C. § 11046) was worded sufficiently differently from § 505 of the CWA so as to call for a contrary result. *Citizens for a Better Environment v. Steel Co.*, 90 F.3d 1237 (7th Cir. 1996). This created a split in the Circuits. Compare *Atlantic States Legal Found., Inc. v. United Musical Instruments, U.S.A., Inc.*, 61 F.3d 473 (Sixth Cir. 1995) (deeming *Gwaltney* applicable).

When *Steel Co.* reached the Supreme Court, Justice Scalia, writing for the majority, did not even address the statutory question. Instead, he resolved the case on standing grounds, finding that, absent ongoing violations, penalties payable to the Treasury do not provide sufficient redressability to support standing under Article III. 523 U.S. at 107. In response to Justice Stevens' argument that the deterrent effect that penalties would have on Steel Co. should suffice, id. at 127 (dissenting), Justice Scalia responded as folllows:

> Justice Stevens thinks it is enough that respondent will be gratified by seeing petitioner punished for its infractions and that the punishment will deter the risk of future harm. . . . Obviously, such a principle would make the redressability requirement vanish. By the mere bringing of his suit, every plaintiff demonstrates his belief that a favorable judgment will make him happier. But although a suitor may derive great comfort and joy from the fact that the United States Treasury is not cheated, that a wrongdoer gets his just deserts, or that the nation's laws are faithfully enforced, that psychic satisfaction is not an acceptable Article III remedy because it does not redress a cognizable Article III injury. Relief that does not remedy the injury suffered cannot bootstrap a plaintiff into federal court; that is the very essence of the redressability requirement.

Id. at 106–107.

Steel Co. essentially constitutionalized the *Gwaltney* doctrine; that is, it established that Article III precludes Congress from "solving" the "*Gwaltney* problem" simply by making clear its desire that citizen plaintiffs be able to pursue penalties payable to the Treasury for wholly-past violations. Additionally, the Court's view that penalties payable to the Treasury yield citizen plaintiffs only "psychic satisfaction" raised the question whether such citizens should ever be able seek this form of relief, even where there are ongoing violations.

At the same time that these issues were percolating, the Courts of Appeals were wrestling with the mootness issues posed by *Gwaltney*. How difficult would it be for a citizen-suit defendant to show that it was "absolutely clear that the allegedly wrongful behavior could not reasonably be expected to recur?" And what was the effect of such a showing, if made? Did it result in the mooting only of any claims for injunctive relief, or did it moot the entire case, including the claims for penalties for past violations (both pre-and post-complaint)?

Most court resolved these issues in ways that favored the plaintiffs, emphasizing the difficulty of establishing mootness in the "voluntary cessation" context, and limiting its effect when demonstrated to claims for injunctive relief. See, e.g., *Atlantic States Legal Foundation, Inc. v. Pan Am. Tanning Corp.*, 993 F.2d 1017, 1019–1021 (2d Cir. 1993); *Chesapeake Bay Foundation, Inc. v. Gwaltney of Smithfield, Ltd.*, 890 F.2d 690, 696–697 (4th Cir. 1989); *Atlantic States Legal Foundation, Inc. v. Stroh Die Casting Co.*, 116 F.3d 814, 820 and 822 (7th Cir.), *cert. denied*, 522 U.S. 981, 118 S.Ct. 442, 139 L.Ed.2d 379 (1997); *Natural Resources Defense Council v. Texaco Refining & Mktg., Inc.*, 2 F.3d 493, 502–504 (3d Cir. 1993) (on the penalty issue); and *Atlantic States Legal Foundation, Inc. v. Tyson Foods, Inc.*, 897 F.2d 1128, 1134–1137 (11th Cir. 1990) (same); compare *Comfort Lake Assn. v. Dresel Contracting, Inc.*, 138 F.3d 351, 356 (8th Cir. 1998) (agreeing with the above cases, but applying different rules where the case was mooted by regulatory enforcement actions).

The most discordant opinion was the Fourth Circuit's in *Friends of the Earth, Inc. v. Laidlaw Environmental Services (TOC), Inc.*, 149 F.3d 303 (4th Cir. 1998). There, the court relied on *Steel Co.* in finding the case to be moot because the lower court had denied the plaintiffs' claim for injunctive relief. The court reasoned that, if penalties were all that was at issue, they would provide no redress to the plaintiffs and thus could not provide a basis for ongoing jurisdiction in the case. Id. at 306–307.

This set the stage for the Supreme Court's consideration in *Laidlaw*, the injury portion of which we already have considered. We now present those portions of *Laidlaw* addressing the redressability and mootness issues:

FRIENDS OF THE EARTH, INC. v. LAIDLAW ENVIRONMENTAL SERVICES

Supreme Court of the United States, 2000.

528 U.S. 167, 120 S.Ct. 693, 145 L.Ed.2d 610.

Laidlaw argues next that even if FOE had standing to seek injunctive relief, it lacked standing to seek civil penalties. Here the asserted defect is not injury but redressability. Civil penalties offer no redress to private plaintiffs, Laidlaw argues, because they are paid to the government, and therefore a citizen plaintiff can never have standing to seek them.

Laidlaw is right to insist that a plaintiff must demonstrate standing separately for each form of relief sought. But it is wrong to maintain that citizen plaintiffs facing ongoing violations never have standing to seek civil penalties.

We have recognized on numerous occasions that "all civil penalties have some deterrent effect." *Hudson v. United States*, 522 U.S. 93, 102 (1997). More specifically, Congress has found that civil penalties in Clean Water Act cases do more than promote immediate compliance by limiting the defendant's economic incentive to delay its attainment of permit limits; they also deter future violations. This congressional determination warrants judicial attention and respect. "The legislative history of the Act reveals that Congress wanted the district court to consider the need for retribution and deterrence, in addition to restitution, when it imposed civil penalties. ...[The district court may] seek to deter future violations by basing the penalty on its economic impact." *Tull v. United States*, 481 U.S. 412, 422–423 (1987).

It can scarcely be doubted that, for a plaintiff who is injured or faces the threat of future injury due to illegal conduct ongoing at the time of suit, a sanction that effectively abates that conduct and prevents its recurrence provides a form of redress. Civil penalties can fit that description. To the extent that they encourage defendants to discontinue current violations and deter them from committing future ones, they afford redress to citizen plaintiffs who are injured or threatened with injury as a consequence of ongoing unlawful conduct.

The dissent argues that it is the availability rather than the imposition of civil penalties that deters any particular polluter from continuing to pollute. This argument misses the mark in two ways. First, it overlooks the interdependence of the availability and the imposition; a threat has no deterrent value unless it is credible that it will be carried out. Second, it is reasonable for Congress to conclude that an actual award of civil penalties does in fact bring with it a significant quantum of deterrence over and above what is achieved by the mere prospect of such penalties. A would-be polluter may or may not be dissuaded by the existence of a remedy on the books, but a defendant once hit in its pocketbook will surely think twice before polluting again.

Laidlaw contends that the reasoning of our decision in *Steel Co.* directs the conclusion that citizen plaintiffs have no standing to seek civil penalties under the Act. We disagree. *Steel Co.* established that citizen suitors lack standing to seek civil penalties for violations that have abated by the time of suit. We specifically noted in that case that there was no allegation in the complaint of any continuing or imminent violation, and that no basis for such an allegation appeared to exist. In short, *Steel Co.* held that private plaintiffs, unlike the Federal Government, may not sue to assess penalties for wholly past violations, but our decision in that case did not reach the issue of standing to seek penalties for violations that are ongoing at the time of the complaint and that could continue into the future if undeterred.[4]

Satisfied that FOE had standing under Article III to bring this action, we turn to the question of mootness.

The only conceivable basis for a finding of mootness in this case is Laidlaw's voluntary conduct—either its achievement by August 1992 of substantial compliance with its NPDES permit or its more recent shutdown of the Roebuck facility. It is well settled that "a defendant's voluntary cessation of a challenged practice does not deprive a federal court of its power to determine the legality of the practice." [*City of Mesquite v. Aladdin's Castle*, 455 U.S. 283, 289 (1982)]. "[I]f it did, the courts would be compelled to leave '[t]he defendant . . . free to return to his old ways.'" Id., at 289, n. 10. In accordance with this principle, the standard we have announced for determining whether a case has been mooted by the defendant's voluntary conduct is stringent: "A case might become moot if subsequent events made it absolutely clear that the allegedly wrongful behavior could not reasonably be expected to recur."

---

4.   . . . [T]he dissent's . . . charge that citizen suits for civil penalties under the Act carry "grave implications for democratic governance" seems to us overdrawn. Certainly the federal Executive Branch does not share the dissent's view that such suits dissipate its authority to enforce the law. In fact, the Department of Justice has endorsed this citizen suit from the outset, submitting amicus briefs in support of FOE in the District Court, the Court of Appeals, and this Court. As we have already noted, the Federal Government retains the power to foreclose a citizen suit by undertaking its own action. 33 U.S.C. § 1365(b)(1)(B). And if the Executive Branch opposes a particular citizen suit, the statute allows the Administrator of the EPA to "intervene as a matter of right" and bring the Government's views to the attention of the court. § 1365(c)(2).

United States v. Concentrated Phosphate Export Assn., 393 U.S. 199, 203 (1968). The "heavy burden of persua[ding]" the court that the challenged conduct cannot reasonably be expected to start up again lies with the party asserting mootness. Ibid.

The Court of Appeals justified its mootness disposition by reference to *Steel Co.*, which held that citizen plaintiffs lack standing to seek civil penalties for wholly past violations. In relying on *Steel Co.*, the Court of Appeals confused mootness with standing. The confusion is understandable, given this Court's repeated statements that the doctrine of mootness can be described as "the doctrine of standing set in a time frame: The requisite personal interest that must exist at the commencement of the litigation (standing) must continue throughout its existence (mootness)." *Arizonans for Official English*, 520 U.S., at 68, n. 22.

Careful reflection on the long-recognized exceptions to mootness, however, reveals that the description of mootness as "standing set in a time frame" is not comprehensive. As just noted, a defendant claiming that its voluntary compliance moots a case bears the formidable burden of showing that it is absolutely clear the allegedly wrongful behavior could not reasonably be expected to recur. By contrast, in a lawsuit brought to force compliance, it is the plaintiff's burden to establish standing by demonstrating that, if unchecked by the litigation, the defendant's allegedly wrongful behavior will likely occur or continue, and that the "threatened injury [is] certainly impending." [*Whitmore v. Arkansas*, 495 U.S. 149, 158 (1990)]. Thus, in *Lyons*, as already noted, we held that a plaintiff lacked initial standing to seek an injunction against the enforcement of a police chokehold policy because he could not credibly allege that he faced a realistic threat arising from the policy. 461 U.S., at 105–110. Elsewhere in the opinion, however, we noted that a citywide moratorium on police chokeholds—an action that surely diminished the already slim likelihood that any particular individual would be choked by police—would not have mooted an otherwise valid claim for injunctive relief, because the moratorium by its terms was not permanent. Id., at 101. The plain lesson of these cases is that there are circumstances in which the prospect that a defendant will engage in (or resume) harmful conduct may be too speculative to support standing, but not too speculative to overcome mootness.

Laidlaw also asserts, in a supplemental suggestion of mootness, that the closure of its Roebuck facility, which took place after the Court of Appeals issued its decision, mooted the case. The facility closure, like Laidlaw's earlier achievement of substantial compliance with its permit requirements, might moot the case, but—we once more reiterate—only if one or the other of these events made it absolutely clear that Laidlaw's permit violations could not reasonably be expected to recur. The effect of both Laidlaw's compliance and the facility closure on the prospect of future violations is a disputed factual matter. FOE points out, for example—and Laidlaw does not appear to contest—that Laidlaw retains its NPDES permit. These issues have not been aired in the lower courts; they remain open for consideration on remand.

Justice STEVENS, concurring.

. . . [P]etitioners' claim for civil penalties would not be moot even if it were absolutely clear that respondent's violations could not reasonably be expected to recur because respondent achieved substantial compliance with its permit requirements after petitioners filed their complaint but before the District Court entered judgment. As the Courts of Appeals (other than the court below) have uniformly concluded, a polluter's voluntary post-complaint cessation of an alleged violation will not moot a citizen-suit claim for civil penalties even if it is sufficient to moot a related claim for injunctive or declaratory relief. [Citations]. This conclusion is consistent with the structure of the Clean Water Act, which attaches liability for civil penalties at the time a permit violation occurs. 33 U.S.C. § 1319(d) ("Any person who violates [certain provisions of the Act or certain permit conditions and limitations] shall be subject to a civil penalty . . .") . . . .

Justice KENNEDY, concurring.

Difficult and fundamental questions are raised when we ask whether exactions of public fines by private litigants, and the delegation of Executive power which might be inferable from the authorization, are permissible in view of the responsibilities committed to the Executive by Article II of the Constitution of the United States. The questions presented in the petition for certiorari did not identify these issues with particularity; and neither the Court of Appeals in deciding the case nor the parties in their briefing before this Court devoted specific attention to the subject. In my view these matters are best reserved for a later case. With this observation, I join the opinion of the Court.

Justice SCALIA, with whom Justice THOMAS joins, dissenting.

. . . Only last Term, we held that such penalties do not redress any injury a citizen plaintiff has suffered from past violations. *Steel Co.*, 523 U.S. 83, 106–107 (1998). The Court nonetheless finds the redressability requirement satisfied here, distinguishing *Steel Co.* on the ground that in this case the petitioners allege ongoing violations; payment of the penalties, it says, will remedy petitioners' injury by deterring future violations by Laidlaw. It holds that a penalty payable to the public "remedies" a threatened private harm, and suffices to sustain a private suit.

That holding has no precedent in our jurisprudence, and takes this Court beyond the "cases and controversies" that Article III of the Constitution has entrusted to its resolution. Even if it were appropriate, moreover, to allow Article III's remediation requirement to be satisfied by the indirect private consequences of a public penalty, those consequences are entirely too speculative in the present case. The new standing law that the Court makes—like all expansions of standing beyond the traditional constitutional limits—has grave implications for democratic governance. . . .

The Court recognizes, of course, that to satisfy Article III, it must be "likely," as opposed to "merely speculative," that a favorable decision will redress plaintiffs' injury, [*Lujan*, 504 U.S. at 561] .... It concludes, however, that in the present case "the civil penalties sought by FOE carried with them a deterrent effect" that satisfied the "likely [rather than] speculative" standard. Ibid. There is little in the Court's opinion to explain why it believes this is so.

The Court points out that we have previously said "all civil penalties have some deterrent effect." That is unquestionably true: As a general matter, polluters as a class are deterred from violating discharge limits by the availability of civil penalties. However, none of the cases the Court cites focused on the deterrent effect of a single imposition of penalties on a particular lawbreaker. Even less did they focus on the question whether that particularized deterrent effect (if any) was enough to redress the injury of a citizen plaintiff in the sense required by Article III. They all involved penalties pursued by the government, not by citizens.

If the Court had undertaken the necessary inquiry into whether significant deterrence of the plaintiffs' feared injury was "likely," it would have had to reason something like this: Strictly speaking, no polluter is deterred by a penalty for past pollution; he is deterred by the fear of a penalty for future pollution. That fear will be virtually nonexistent if the prospective polluter knows that all emissions violators are given a free pass; it will be substantial under an emissions program such as the federal scheme here, which is regularly and notoriously enforced; it will be even higher when a prospective polluter subject to such a regularly enforced program has, as here, been the object of public charges of pollution and a suit for injunction; and it will surely be near the top of the graph when, as here, the prospective polluter has already been subjected to state penalties for the past pollution. The deterrence on which the plaintiffs must rely for standing in the present case is the marginal increase in Laidlaw's fear of future penalties that will be achieved by adding federal penalties for Laidlaw's past conduct.

I cannot say for certain that this marginal increase is zero; but I can say for certain that it is entirely speculative whether it will make the difference between these plaintiffs' suffering injury in the future and these plaintiffs' going unharmed. In fact, the assertion that it will "likely" do so is entirely farfetched....

Article II of the Constitution commits it to the President to "take Care that the Laws be faithfully executed," Art. II, § 3, and provides specific methods by which all persons exercising significant executive power are to be appointed, Art. II, § 2. As Justice Kennedy's concurrence correctly observes, the question of the conformity of this legislation with Article II has not been argued—and I, like the Court, do not address it. But Article III, no less than Article II, has consequences for the structure of our government, and it is worth noting the changes in that structure which today's decision allows.

By permitting citizens to pursue civil penalties payable to the Federal Treasury, the Act does not provide a mechanism for individual relief in any traditional sense, but turns over to private citizens the function of enforcing the law. A Clean Water Act plaintiff pursuing civil penalties acts as a self-appointed mini-EPA. Where, as is often the case, the plaintiff is a national association, it has significant discretion in choosing enforcement targets. Once the association is aware of a reported violation, it need not look long for an injured member, at least under the theory of injury the Court applies today. And once the target is chosen, the suit goes forward without meaningful public control.[2] The availability of civil penalties vastly disproportionate to the individual injury gives citizen plaintiffs massive bargaining power—which is often used to achieve settlements requiring the defendant to support environmental projects of the plaintiffs' choosing. Thus is a public fine diverted to a private interest.

To be sure, the EPA may foreclose the citizen suit by itself bringing suit. 33 U.S.C. § 1365(b)(1)(B). This allows public authorities to avoid private enforcement only by accepting private direction as to when enforcement should be undertaken—which is no less constitutionally bizarre. Elected officials are entirely deprived of their discretion to decide that a given violation should not be the object of suit at all, or that the enforcement decision should be postponed.[3] This is the predictable and inevitable consequence of the Court's allowing the use of public remedies for private wrongs.

Questions and Notes

1. As mentioned, *Steel Co.* makes clear that Congress cannot "solve" the "*Gwaltney* problem" simply by making clear its desire that citizen plaintiffs be able to pursue penalties payable to the Treasury for wholly-past violations. What if Congress provides the possibility of other forms of relief. In 1990, for example, Congress amended the Clean Air Act to specifically allow up to $100,000 of any penalty imposed in a CAA citizen suit to be diverted to "beneficial mitigation projects" (which are presumably similar to what EPA refers to as a "supplemental environmental project" in its SEP Policy). 42 U.S.C. § 7604(g)(2). Recall that Congress also amended the CAA to allow citizen suits for at least some wholly-past violations. See 42 U.S.C. § 7604(a)(1). Should the potential availability of these mitigation projects provide the required redressability? If so, should it also citizens to seek additional penalty amounts payable to the Treasury?

2. The Court points out that the government is allowed to intervene in a citizen suit, but this power to "bring the Government's views to the attention of the court," is meager substitute for the power to decide whether prosecution will occur. Indeed, according the Chief Executive of the United States the ability to intervene does no more than place him on a par with John Q. Public, who can intervene—whether the government likes it or not—when the United States files suit. § 1365(b)(1)(B).

3. The Court observes that "the federal Executive Branch does not share the dissent's view that such suits dissipate its authority to enforce the law," since it has "endorsed this citizen suit from the outset." Of course, in doubtful cases a long and uninterrupted history of presidential acquiescence and approval can shed light upon the constitutional understanding. What we have here—acquiescence and approval by a single Administration—does not deserve passing mention.

2. Note the starkness of the argument Laidlaw was advancing regarding penalties. If it had succeeded in establishing the citizens cannot seek penalties payable to the Treasury even where there are ongoing violations, it may (subject to the potential qualifications in note 1, above) have been the death knell for citizen penalty actions.

3. What did you make of the debate between Justice Ginsburg and Justice Scalia regarding whether the impact of penalties on a violator's future behavior should be an adequate basis for finding redressability? Do you agree that "a defendant once hit in its pocketbook will surely think twice before polluting again?" Or is it "entirely speculative" as to whether the actual imposition of fines for past violations (as distinct from the threat thereof for new violations) will make such a difference?

4. In *Steel Co.*, eight Justices (all but Justice Stevens) concurred in the majority's redressability analysis. Two years later, with the composition of the Court unchanged, seven Justice's (all but Justice's Scalia and Thomas) concurred in the *Laidlaw* redressability analysis. Were you convinced by the distinction the *Laidlaw* Court drew between the two cases? Why is it that penalties provide sufficient redressability in situations in which there are ongoing violations, but not where, as in *Steel Co.*, the defendant brought itself into (temporary?) compliance by filing all of the required reports?

5. Do you understand the nature of the burden shifting the Court discusses in its mootness analysis? Note that the combined effect of *Gwaltney*, *Steel Co.* and *Laidlaw* places enormous significance on whether the defendant allegedly eliminates the root cause of the violations before or after the filing of the complaint. If its potentially curative actions were taken before filing, the plaintiff will bear the burden of showing that there is an ongoing violation. On the other hand, if it completes those same steps the day after filing, the defendant will bear the burden of showing that it is "absolutely clear that the allegedly wrongful behavior could not reasonably be expected to recur." Does this make sense?

6. Does *Laidlaw* shed any further light on the difficulty of making the required mootness showing? The post-*Laidlaw* case law suggests that the courts continue to consider this analysis as requiring a fact-specific inquiry, with the results being varied thus far. Compare *Puerto Rico Campers' Ass'n v. Puerto Rico Aqueduct & Sewer Auth.*, 219 F.Supp.2d 201 (D.P.R. 2002), and *San Francisco Baykeeper, Inc. v. Tosco Corp.*, 309 F.3d 1153 (9th Cir. 2002) (neither finding mootness), with *Ailor v. City of Maynardsville, Tenn.*, 368 F.3d 587 (6th Cir. 2004), and *Mississippi River Revival, Inc. v. City of Minneapolis*, 319 F.3d 1013, 1016 (8th Cir. 2003) (both finding mootness).

7. What should the effect be if a defendant makes the required mootness demonstration? Thus far, the lower courts seem to be reading *Laidlaw* as indicating that such showings result in the mooting not only of claims for injunctive relief, but also of those for penalties. See, e.g., *Mississippi River Revival*, 319 F.3d at 1016. Do you agree? In answering this question, keep in mind that penalties were the only thing at issue in *Laidlaw*; that is, the plaintiffs had not appealed the district court's denial of their claim for injunctive relief. At the same time, consider the implications of allowing defendants to moot claims for penalties at any time during the course of the lawsuit. If they can do so, how much fear will prospective defendants have of

citizen suits if they are confident that they can conclusively resolve their compliance problems during the pendency of any such suits? In such situations, would the plaintiffs at least be entitled to an award of attorney fees? We will address this question in our discussion of fee awards, below.

8. Justices Kennedy and Scalia both hinted at lurking Article II issues in their opinions in *Laidlaw*. As alluded to by Justice Scalia, these issues hinge on what are referred to as the "Take Care" and "Appointments" clauses in Article II. What did you think of Justice Scalia's points and Justice Ginsburg's responses in footnote 4 of the majority opinion? Cf. *Riley v. St. Luke's Episcopal Hospital*, 252 F.3d 749 (5th Cir. 2001) (rejecting an Article II challenge to the False Claims Act).

9. We close this section with a song that one of the authors wrote in response to the Court's opinion in *Laidlaw*, to be sung to the tune of Eric Clapton's "Layla" (originally recorded by Clapton's band Derek and the Dominos, on the album "Layla and Other Assorted Love Songs").

Laidlaw

by
Craig N. Johnston
adapted from Layla (by Eric Clapton and Jim Gordon)

What do we do when we get sued now

If the Court's not on our side?

If we can't rely on standing constraints

Do they expect us to comply?

Laidlaw! What are these non-use injuries?

Laidlaw! Based on subjectivity

Laidlaw! Antonin please ease our worried minds

Defenders gave us consolation

And *Steel Co.* made us paint the town

But like fools, we put our faith in you

You and C.T. got voted down

Laidlaw! What about these penalties?

Laidlaw! Where's the redressability?

Laidlaw! Antonin please ease our worried minds

Let's make the best of the situation

Article II's our last resort

Please don't say we'll never find a way

To keep these plaintiffs out of court

Laidlaw! What was it Sandra didn't see?

Laidlaw! Where were the Chief and Kennedy?

Laidlaw! Antonin please ease our worried minds

Laidlaw! We miss the old majority

Laidlaw! How can we pay these penalties?

Laidlaw! Antonin please ease our worried minds

4.   The Effect of Prior Governmental Enforcement Actions

The environmental citizen suit provisions typically contain express provisions addressing the preclusive effect of prior governmental enforcement actions. These provisions tend to fall into one of two categories. Virtually all of the statutes have a provision precluding citizens from filing suit if either EPA or the State "has commenced" and "is diligently prosecuting" an action "in a court" to require compliance with the relevant standard. See, e.g., 33 U.S.C. § 1365(b)(1)(B), 42 U.S.C. § 6972(b)(1)(B), and 42 U.S.C. § 7604(b)(1)(B). Second, a few statutes, notably including the CWA, have an additional provision specifically governing the preclusive effect of administrative-penalty actions. See, e.g., 33 U.S.C. § 1319(g)(6).

Let us first address the more common preclusion provisions. Given that most statutes do not have separate provisions addressing the preclusive effect of administrative actions, as a threshold matter it becomes important to know whether such actions can every qualify as actions "in a court;" if not, administrative actions will never preclude citizen suits under those statutes. Despite the oddness of this result from a policy perspective (does it really make sense to allow for follow-up citizen suits in situations in which EPA may have imposed multi-million dollar administrative penalties under RCRA?), the vast majority of Circuits have determined that Congress meant what it said–i.e, that only judicial enforcement actions may give rise to the bar under these "in a court" formulations. See, e.g., *Texans United for a Safe Economy Education Fund v. Crown Central Petrol. Corp.*, 207 F.3d 789 (5th Cir. 2000) (and cased cited therein). Even the Third Circuit, which is the only Circuit that has diverged from the majority view, established a demanding "substantial equivalence" test that few administrative schemes would ever meet. See, e.g., *Student Public Interest Research Group of New Jersey, Inc. v. Fritsche, Dodge & Olcott, Inc.*, 759 F.2d 1131 (3d Cir. 1985).

In situations in which either EPA or the State either is pursuing or has completed a judicial enforcement action, the key question becomes whether the "diligence" standard has been met. Here also, the courts appear to be of two views. The district court's opinion in *Laidlaw* is indicative of the approach that most courts have taken. There, the court described its approach and its view the tensions inherent in its inquiry in the following terms:

First, the citizen-plaintiffs bear the burden of proving that the state agency's prosecution was not diligent. This burden is a heavy one because diligence on the part of the enforcement agency is presumed. As several courts have recognized, "the state [enforcement] agency must be given great deference to proceed in a manner it considers in the best interests of all parties involved." *Arkansas*

Wildlife Fed'n v. ICI Americas Inc., 842 F.Supp. 1140, 1147 (E.D.Ark.1993), aff'd, 29 F.3d 376 (8th Cir.1994), cert. denied, ___ U.S. ___.

Deference to governmental enforcement agencies is appropriate because the CWA delegates the primary enforcement responsibility to designated state and federal agencies. For example, the requirement in section 505(b)(1)(A) that a citizen must file a notice letter sixty days before bringing a private enforcement suit clearly was designed to give the governmental agencies the "first shot" at enforcement. As the Supreme Court stated in *Gwaltney*, "the citizen suit is meant to supplement rather than to supplant governmental action." 484 U.S. at 60. Appropriate limitations on citizen suits generally "allow for smoother operation of ordinary enforcement mechanisms" and encourage out-of-court settlements between agencies and polluters. *Connecticut Coastal Fishermen's Ass'n v. Remington Arms Co.*, 777 F.Supp. 173, 179, 186 (D.Conn.1991), aff'd in part, rev'd in part, 989 F.2d 1305 (2d Cir.1993).

On the other hand, Congress certainly intended to provide private citizens with significant opportunities to participate in the enforcement of the CWA. As the United States Court of Appeals for the Second Circuit stated, "Congress made clear that citizen groups are not to be treated as nuisances or troublemakers but rather as welcomed participants in the vindication of environmental interests." *Friends of the Earth v. Consolidated Rail Corp.*, 768 F.2d 57, 63 (2d Cir.1985). In addition to authorizing citizen suits under section 505, the CWA provides several opportunities for citizens to participate in governmental enforcement activities. Indeed, as noted previously, the last phrase of section 505(b)(1)(B) provides that if a citizen suit is barred by the EPA's or the state's diligent prosecution of a judicial action, "in any such action in a court of the United States any citizen may intervene as a matter of right." 33 U.S.C. § 1365(b)(1)(B).

Thus, the issue presently before the court involves a delicate balance between the Act's preference for governmental enforcement efforts and the recognized policy of allowing private citizens to participate in the enforcement process. Of course, the overriding concern is to assure vigorous enforcement of the CWA to achieve the stated goals of the Act.

890 F.Supp. 470, 486–487 (D.S.C. 1995). With these points in mind, the court went on to engage in a searching review of the record, ultimately determining that South Carolina's enforcement action did not constitute diligent enforcement despite the fact that it resulted in the imposition of a $100,000 penalty. In so finding, the court relied on the fact that the State: (a) began its enforcement action only at the violator's request (to preempt the citizen suit), (b) negotiated the consent decree in record time (to beat the expiration of the notice period), (c) made no effort to even calculated the defendant's economic benefit, although it clearly was

substantially in excess of the penalty-amount; (d) waived penalties for future violations despite the fact that the decree lacked a definite date by which compliance would be achieved, and (e) allowed the citizen plaintiffs no effective opportunity to intervene before the consent decree was entered. *Id.*

The Seventh Circuit took a different approach in *Supporters to Oppose Pollution, Inc. v. The Heritage Group*, 973 F.2d 1320 (7th Cir. 1992) ("*Heritage Group*"). In writing for the majority, Judge Easterbrook, like the *Laidlaw* court, began by referring to Justice Marshall's "supplement" versus "supplant" discussion from *Gwaltney*. He went on, however, to draw a very different conclusion as to its implications for the "diligence" inquiry:

> ... An Administrator unable to make concessions is unable to obtain them. A private plaintiff waiting in the wings then is the captain of the litigation. And it makes no difference that this person chooses to sue another party....

> "Diligent" prosecution is all the statute requires. Although StOP wants a trial on the question whether the EPA's prosecution was "diligent," such follow-up inquiries are appropriate only when the agency loses its suit and the private litigant insists that the agency had not tried hard enough. RCRA permits a follow-on private suit if the public suit was not prosecuted diligently. But if the agency prevails in all respects, that is the end; § 6972(b)(1)(B) does not authorize a collateral attack on the agency's strategy or tactics....

Id. at 1324.

Which of these approaches do you think is correct? Cf. *Friends of Milwaukee's Rivers v. Milwaukee Metropolitan Sewerage District*, 382 F.3d 743 (7th Cir. 2004) (in which the Seventh Circuit, without expressly overruling *Heritage Group*, appears to embrace a more aggressive oversight role in evaluating diligence for purposes of analyzing privity in determining whether a citizen suit was barred by res judicata).

As mentioned, some statutes have specific provisions governing the preclusive effect of administrative-penalty actions. The most notable of these provisions, § 309(g)(6) of the CWA, is extremely complex and has given rise to a whole sub-universe of judicial opinions. While the issues are too numerous and complicated to deal with in an overview course, students at least should be aware that the area is a minefield and that the courts are badly split on many of the issues. Compare, e.g., *North & South Rivers Watershed Ass'n v. Scituate*, 949 F.2d 552 (1st Cir. 1991), with *Citizens for a Better Environment–California v. Union Oil Co. Of Calif.*, 83 F.3d 1111 (9th Cir. 1996).

5. Attorney Fees

The environmental citizen suit provisions, like many other statutes adopting the private-attorney-general model, provide for the award of attorney fees and costs to successful plaintiffs. These amounts are to be paid by the defendants. The intent, of course, is to promote citizen enforcement by enabling would-be plaintiffs to retain competent counsel.

The attorney fee aspects of these citizen-suit provisions have been the subject of much litigation. The Supreme Court's most extensive treatment of these issues was in *Hensley v. Eckerhart*, 461 U.S. 424, 103 S.Ct. 1933, 76 L.Ed.2d 40 (1983), a civil rights case. There, Justice Powell included in his majority opinion what is essentially a primer on both what it takes to qualify as a "prevailing party" and how fees should be calculated. We include this portion of the opinion, below. We also include the Court's much more recent opinion in the *Buckhannon* case. This latter case addresses the much more controversial question of whether a plaintiff should be deemed to have "prevailed" if its lawsuit prompts the defendant to come into compliance, but if the defendant does so during the pendency of the case in a way that renders the suit moot.

HENSLEY v. ECKERHART

Supreme Court of the United States, 1983.

461 U.S. 424, 103 S.Ct. 1933, 76 L.Ed.2d 40.

Justice Powell delivered the opinion of the Court:

A plaintiff must be a "prevailing party" to recover an attorney's fee under [42 U.S.C. § 1988]. The standard for making this threshold determination has been framed in various ways. A typical formulation is that "plaintiffs may be considered 'prevailing parties' for attorney's fees purposes if they succeed on any significant issue in litigation which achieves some of the benefit the parties sought in bringing suit." *Nadeau v. Helgemoe*, 581 F.2d 275, 278–279 (CA1 1978). This is a generous formulation that brings the plaintiff only across the statutory threshold. It remains for the district court to determine what fee is "reasonable."

The most useful starting point for determining the amount of a reasonable fee is the number of hours reasonably expended on the litigation multiplied by a reasonable hourly rate. This calculation provides an objective basis on which to make an initial estimate of the value of a lawyer's services. The party seeking an award of fees should submit evidence supporting the hours worked and rates claimed. Where the documentation of hours is inadequate, the district court may reduce the award accordingly.

The district court also should exclude from this initial fee calculation hours that were not "reasonably expended." S.Rep. No. 94–1011, p. 6 (1976). Cases may be overstaffed, and the skill and experience of lawyers vary widely. Counsel for the prevailing party should make a good faith effort to exclude from a fee request hours that are excessive, redundant, or otherwise unnecessary, just as a lawyer in private practice ethically is obligated to exclude such hours from his fee submission. "In the private sector, 'billing judgment' is an important component in fee setting. It is no less important here. Hours that are not properly billed to one's client also are not properly billed to one's *adversary* pursuant to statutory authority." *Copeland v. Marshall*, 641 F.2d 880, 891 (1980) (en banc).

The product of reasonable hours times a reasonable rate does not end the inquiry. There remain other considerations that may lead the district court to adjust the fee upward or downward, including the important factor of the "results obtained." This factor is particularly crucial where a plaintiff is deemed "prevailing" even though he succeeded on only some of his claims for relief. In this situation two questions must be addressed. First, did the plaintiff fail to prevail on claims that were unrelated to the claims on which he succeeded? Second, did the plaintiff achieve a level of success that makes the hours reasonably expended a satisfactory basis for making a fee award?

In some cases a plaintiff may present in one lawsuit distinctly different claims for relief that are based on different facts and legal theories. In such a suit, even where the claims are brought against the same defendants—often an institution and its officers, as in this case— counsel's work on one claim will be unrelated to his work on another claim. Accordingly, work on an unsuccessful claim cannot be deemed to have been "expended in pursuit of the ultimate result achieved." *Davis v. County of Los Angeles*, 8 E.P.D. P 9444 (CD Cal.1974). The congressional intent to limit awards to prevailing parties requires that these unrelated claims be treated as if they had been raised in separate lawsuits, and therefore no fee may be awarded for services on the unsuccessful claim.

It may well be that cases involving such unrelated claims are unlikely to arise with great frequency. Many civil rights cases will present only a single claim. In other cases the plaintiff's claims for relief will involve a common core of facts or will be based on related legal theories. Much of counsel's time will be devoted generally to the litigation as a whole, making it difficult to divide the hours expended on a claim-by-claim basis. Such a lawsuit cannot be viewed as a series of discrete claims. Instead the district court should focus on the significance of the overall relief obtained by the plaintiff in relation to the hours reasonably expended on the litigation.

Where a plaintiff has obtained excellent results, his attorney should recover a fully compensatory fee. Normally this will encompass all hours reasonably expended on the litigation, and indeed in some cases of exceptional success an enhanced award may be justified. In these circumstances the fee award should not be reduced simply because the plaintiff failed to prevail on every contention raised in the lawsuit. Litigants in good faith may raise alternative legal grounds for a desired outcome, and the court's rejection of or failure to reach certain grounds is not a sufficient reason for reducing a fee. The result is what matters.[11]

11. We agree with the District Court's rejection of "a mathematical approach comparing the total number of issues in the case with those actually prevailed upon."

If, on the other hand, a plaintiff has achieved only partial or limited success, the product of hours reasonably expended on the litigation as a whole times a reasonable hourly rate may be an excessive amount. This will be true even where the plaintiff's claims were interrelated, nonfrivolous, and raised in good faith. Congress has not authorized an award of fees whenever it was reasonable for a plaintiff to bring a lawsuit or whenever conscientious counsel tried the case with devotion and skill. Again, the most critical factor is the degree of success obtained.

Application of this principle is particularly important in complex civil rights litigation involving numerous challenges to institutional practices or conditions. This type of litigation is lengthy and demands many hours of lawyers' services. Although the plaintiff often may succeed in identifying some unlawful practices or conditions, the range of possible success is vast. That the plaintiff is a "prevailing party" therefore may say little about whether the expenditure of counsel's time was reasonable in relation to the success achieved. In this case, for example, the District Court's award of fees based on 2,557 hours worked may have been reasonable in light of the substantial relief obtained. But had respondents prevailed on only one of their six general claims, ... a fee award based on the claimed hours clearly would have been excessive.

There is no precise rule or formula for making these determinations. The district court may attempt to identify specific hours that should be eliminated, or it may simply reduce the award to account for the limited success. The court necessarily has discretion in making this equitable judgment. This discretion, however, must be exercised in light of the considerations we have identified.

A request for attorney's fees should not result in a second major litigation. Ideally, of course, litigants will settle the amount of a fee. Where settlement is not possible, the fee applicant bears the burden of establishing entitlement to an award and documenting the appropriate hours expended and hourly rates. The applicant should exercise "billing judgment" with respect to hours worked and should maintain billing time records in a manner that will enable a reviewing court to identify distinct claims.

We reemphasize that the district court has discretion in determining the amount of a fee award. This is appropriate in view of the district court's superior understanding of the litigation and the desirability of avoiding frequent appellate review of what essentially are factual matters. It remains important, however, for the district court to provide a concise but clear explanation of its reasons for the fee award. When an adjustment is requested on the basis of either the exceptional or limited

---

Such a ratio provides little aid in determining what is a reasonable fee in light of all the relevant factors. Nor is it necessarily significant that a prevailing plaintiff did not receive all the relief requested. For example, a plaintiff who failed to recover damages but obtained injunctive relief, or vice versa, may recover a fee award based on all hours reasonably expended if the relief obtained justified that expenditure of attorney time.

nature of the relief obtained by the plaintiff, the district court should make clear that it has considered the relationship between the amount of the fee awarded and the results obtained.

BUCKHANNON BOARD AND CARE HOME, INC. V. WEST VIRGINIA DEPARTMENT OF HEALTH AND HUMAN RESOURCES

Supreme Court of the United States, 2001.

532 U.S. 598, 121 S.Ct. 1835, 149 L.Ed.2d 855.

CHIEF JUSTICE REHNQUIST delivered the opinion of the Court.

Numerous federal statutes allow courts to award attorney's fees and costs to the 'prevailing party.' The question presented here is whether this term includes a party that has failed to secure a judgment on the merits or a court-ordered consent decree, but has nonetheless achieved the desired result because the lawsuit brought about a voluntary change in the defendant's conduct. We hold that it does not.

Buckhannon Board and Care Home, Inc., which operates care homes that provide assisted living to their residents, failed an inspection by the West Virginia Office of the State Fire Marshal because some of the residents were incapable of 'self-preservation' as defined under state law. On October 28, 1997, ... [Buckhannon and others (petitioners)] brought suit in the United States District Court for the Northern District of West Virginia against the State of West Virginia, two of its agencies, and 18 individuals (hereinafter respondents), seeking declaratory and injunctive relief that the 'self-preservation' requirement violated the Fair Housing Amendments Act of 1988 (FHAA), 42 U. S. C. § 3601 et seq., and the Americans with Disabilities Act of 1990 (ADA), 42 U. S. C. § 12101 et seq.

... In 1998, the West Virginia Legislature enacted two bills eliminating the 'self-preservation' requirement, and respondents moved to dismiss the case as moot. The District Court granted the motion, finding that the 1998 legislation had eliminated the allegedly offensive provisions and that there was no indication that the West Virginia Legislature would repeal the amendments.

Petitioners requested attorney's fees as the 'prevailing party' under the FHAA, 42 U. S. C. § 3613(c)(2), and ADA, 42 U. S. C. § 12205. Petitioners argued that they were entitled to attorney's fees under the 'catalyst theory,' which posits that a plaintiff is a 'prevailing party' if it achieves the desired result because the lawsuit brought about a voluntary change in the defendant's conduct. Although most Courts of Appeals recognize the 'catalyst theory,'[3] the Court of Appeals for the

---

3. See, e.g., Stanton v. Southern Berkshire Regional School Dist., 197 F. 3d 574, 577, n. 2 (CA1 1999); Marbley v. Bane, 57 F. 3d 224, 234 (CA2 1995); Baumgartner v. Harrisburg Housing Authority, 21 F. 3d 541, 546–550 (CA3 1994); Payne v. Board of

Fourth Circuit rejected it in *S–1 and S–2 v. State Bd. of Ed. of N. C.*, 21 F. 3d 49, 51 (1994) (en banc). The District Court accordingly denied the motion and, for the same reason, the Court of Appeals affirmed....

In the United States, parties are ordinarily required to bear their own attorney's fees—the prevailing party is not entitled to collect from the loser. Under this 'American Rule,' we follow 'a general practice of not awarding fees to a prevailing party absent explicit statutory authority.' *Key Tronic Corp. v. United States*, 511 U. S. 809, 819 (1994). Congress, however, has authorized the award of attorney's fees to the 'prevailing party' in numerous statutes in addition to those at issue here....[4]

In designating those parties eligible for an award of litigation costs, Congress employed the term 'prevailing party,' a legal term of art. Black's Law Dictionary 1145 (7th ed. 1999) defines 'prevailing party' as '[a] party in whose favor a judgment is rendered, regardless of the amount of damages awarded <in certain cases, the court will award attorney's fees to the prevailing party>.—Also termed successful party.' This view that a 'prevailing party' is one who has been awarded some relief by the court can be distilled from our prior cases.[5]

In *Hanrahan v. Hampton*, 446 U. S. 754, 758 (1980), we reviewed the legislative history of § 1988 and found that 'Congress intended to permit the interim award of counsel fees only when a party has prevailed on the merits of at least some of his claims.' Our '[r]espect for ordinary language requires that a plaintiff receive at least some relief on the merits of his claim before he can be said to prevail.' *Hewitt v. Helms*, 482 U. S. 755, 760 (1987). We have held that even an award of nominal damages suffices under this test. See *Farrar v. Hobby*, 506 U. S. 103 (1992).

In addition to judgments on the merits, we have held that settlement agreements enforced through a consent decree may serve as the basis for an award of attorney's fees. See *Maher v. Gagne*, 448 U. S. 122 (1980). Although a consent decree does not always include an admission of liability by the defendant, it nonetheless is a court-ordered 'chang[e] [in] the legal relationship between [the plaintiff] and the defendant.' *Texas State Teachers Assn. v. Garland Independent School Dist.*, 489 U. S. 782, 792 (1989). These decisions, taken together, establish that

Ed., 88 F. 3d 392, 397 (CA6 1996); Zinn v. Shalala, 35 F. 3d 273, 276 (CA7 1994); Little Rock School Dist. v. Pulaski Cty. School Dist., #1, 17 F. 3d 260, 263, n. 2 (CA8 1994); Kilgour v. Pasadena, 53 F. 3d 1007, 1010 (CA9 1995); Beard v. Teska, 31 F. 3d 942, 951–952 (CA10 1994); Morris v. West Palm Beach, 194 F. 3d 1203, 1207 (CA11 1999).

4. We have interpreted these fee-shifting provisions consistently, see *Hensley v. Eckerhart*, 461 U. S. 424, 433, n. 7 (1983), and so approach the nearly identical provisions at issue here.

5. We have never had occasion to decide whether the term 'prevailing party' allows an award of fees under the 'catalyst theory' described above. Dicta in Hewitt v. Helms, 482 U. S. 755, 760 (1987), alluded to the possibility of attorney's fees where 'voluntary action by the defendant ... affords the plaintiff all or some of the relief ... sought,' but we expressly reserved the question, see id., at 763 ('We need not decide the circumstances, if any, under which this 'catalyst' theory could justify a fee award')....

enforceable judgments on the merits and court-ordered consent decrees create the 'material alteration of the legal relationship of the parties' necessary to permit an award of attorney's fees.

We think, however, the 'catalyst theory' falls on the other side of the line from these examples. It allows an award where there is no judicially sanctioned change in the legal relationship of the parties. Even under a limited form of the 'catalyst theory,' a plaintiff could recover attorney's fees if it established that the 'complaint had sufficient merit to withstand a motion to dismiss for lack of jurisdiction or failure to state a claim on which relief may be granted.' Brief for United States as Amicus Curiae 27. This is not the type of legal merit that our prior decisions, based upon plain language and congressional intent, have found necessary. Indeed, we held in *Hewitt* that an interlocutory ruling that reverses a dismissal for failure to state a claim 'is not the stuff of which legal victories are made.' 482 U. S., at 760. A defendant's voluntary change in conduct, although perhaps accomplishing what the plaintiff sought to achieve by the lawsuit, lacks the necessary judicial imprimatur on the change. Our precedents thus counsel against holding that the term 'prevailing party' authorizes an award of attorney's fees without a corresponding alteration in the legal relationship of the parties.

The dissenters chide us for upsetting 'long-prevailing Circuit precedent.' But, as Justice Scalia points out in his concurrence, several Courts of Appeals have relied upon dicta in our prior cases in approving the 'catalyst theory.' Now that the issue is squarely presented, it behooves us to reconcile the plain language of the statutes with our prior holdings.... While urging an expansion of our precedents on this front, the dissenters would simultaneously abrogate the 'merit' requirement of our prior cases and award attorney's fees where the plaintiff's claim 'was at least colorable' and 'not ... groundless.' We cannot agree that the term 'prevailing party' authorizes federal courts to award attorney's fees to a plaintiff who, by simply filing a nonfrivolous but nonetheless potentially meritless lawsuit (it will never be determined), has reached the 'sought-after destination' without obtaining any judicial relief.

Petitioners nonetheless argue that the legislative history of the Civil Rights Attorney's Fees Awards Act supports a broad reading of 'prevailing party' which includes the 'catalyst theory.' We doubt that legislative history could overcome what we think is the rather clear meaning of 'prevailing party'—the term actually used in the statute. Since we resorted to such history in *Garland*, 489 U. S., at 790, *Maher*, 448 U. S., at 129, and *Hanrahan*, 446 U. S., at 756–757, however, we do likewise here.

The House Report to § 1988 states that [t]he phrase 'prevailing party' is not intended to be limited to the victor only after entry of a final judgment following a full trial on the merits, H. R. Rep. No. 94–1558, p. 7 (1976), while the Senate Report explains that 'parties may be considered to have prevailed when they vindicate rights through a consent judgment or without formally obtaining relief,' S. Rep. No. 94–

1011, p. 5 (1976). Petitioners argue that these Reports and their reference to a 1970 decision from the Court of Appeals for the Eighth Circuit, *Parham v. Southwestern Bell Telephone Co.*, 433 F. 2d 421 (1970), indicate Congress' intent to adopt the 'catalyst theory.'[9] We think the legislative history cited by petitioners is at best ambiguous as to the availability of the 'catalyst theory' for awarding attorney's fees. Particularly in view of the 'American Rule' that attorney's fees will not be awarded absent 'explicit statutory authority,' such legislative history is clearly insufficient to alter the accepted meaning of the statutory term. *Key Tronic*, 511 U. S., at 819.

Petitioners finally assert that the 'catalyst theory' is necessary to prevent defendants from unilaterally mooting an action before judgment in an effort to avoid an award of attorney's fees. They also claim that the rejection of the 'catalyst theory' will deter plaintiffs with meritorious but expensive cases from bringing suit. We are skeptical of these assertions, which are entirely speculative and unsupported by any empirical evidence (e.g., whether the number of suits brought in the Fourth Circuit has declined, in relation to other Circuits, since the decision in *S–1 and S–2*).

Petitioners discount the disincentive that the 'catalyst theory' may have upon a defendant's decision to voluntarily change its conduct, conduct that may not be illegal. 'The defendants' potential liability for fees in this kind of litigation can be as significant as, and sometimes even more significant than, their potential liability on the merits,' *Evans v. Jeff D.*, 475 U. S. 717, 734 (1986), and the possibility of being assessed attorney's fees may well deter a defendant from altering its conduct.

[Moreover,] it is not clear how often courts will find a case mooted: 'It is well settled that a defendant's voluntary cessation of a challenged practice does not deprive a federal court of its power to determine the legality of the practice' unless it is 'absolutely clear that the allegedly wrongful behavior could not reasonably be expected to recur.' *Friends of Earth, Inc. v. Laidlaw Environmental Services (TOC), Inc.*, 528 U. S. 167, 189 (2000). If a case is not found to be moot, and the plaintiff later procures an enforceable judgment, the court may of course award attorney's fees. Given this possibility, a defendant has a strong incentive to enter a settlement agreement, where it can negotiate attorney's fees and costs.

9. Although the Court of Appeals in *Parham* awarded attorney's fees to the plaintiff because his 'lawsuit acted as a catalyst which prompted the [defendant] to take action . . . seeking compliance with the requirements of Title VII,' 433 F. 2d, at 429–430, it did so only after finding that the defendant had acted unlawfully, see id., at 426 ('We hold as a matter of law that [plaintiff's evidence] established a violation of Title VII '). Thus, consistent with our holding in *Farrar*, *Parham* stands for the proposition that an enforceable judgment permits an award of attorney's fees. And . . . the Court of Appeals in *Parham* ordered the District Court to 'retain jurisdiction over the matter for a reasonable period of time to insure the continued implementation of the appellee's policy of equal employment opportunities.' 433 F. 2d, at 429. Clearly *Parham* does not support a theory of fee shifting untethered to a material alteration in the legal relationship of the parties as defined by our precedents.

JUSTICE SCALIA, with whom JUSTICE THOMAS joins, concurring.

The dissent distorts the term 'prevailing party' beyond its normal meaning for policy reasons, but even those seem to me misguided. They rest upon the presumption that the catalyst theory applies when 'the suit's merit led the defendant to abandon the fray, to switch rather than fight on, to accord plaintiff sooner rather than later the principal redress sought in the complaint.' As the dissent would have it, by giving the term its normal meaning the Court today approves the practice of denying attorney's fees to a plaintiff with a proven claim of discrimination, simply because the very merit of his claim led the defendant to capitulate before judgment. That is not the case. To the contrary, the Court approves the result in *Parham v. Southwestern Bell Tel. Co.*, 433 F. 2d 421 (CA8 1970), where attorney's fees were awarded 'after [a] finding that the defendant had acted unlawfully.' What the dissent's stretching of the term produces is something more, and something far less reasonable: an award of attorney's fees when the merits of plaintiff's case remain unresolved—when, for all one knows, the defendant only 'abandon[ed] the fray' because the cost of litigation—either financial or in terms of public relations—would be too great. In such a case, the plaintiff may have 'prevailed' as Webster's defines that term—'gain[ed] victory by virtue of strength or superiority.' But I doubt it was greater strength in financial resources, or superiority in media manipulation, rather than superiority in legal merit, that Congress intended to reward.

It could be argued, perhaps, that insofar as abstract justice is concerned, there is little to choose between the dissent's outcome and the Court's: If the former sometimes rewards the plaintiff with a phony claim (there is no way of knowing), the latter sometimes denies fees to the plaintiff with a solid case whose adversary slinks away on the eve of judgment. But it seems to me the evil of the former far outweighs the evil of the latter. There is all the difference in the world between a rule that denies the extraordinary boon of attorney's fees to some plaintiffs who are no less 'deserving' of them than others who receive them, and a rule that causes the law to be the very instrument of wrong—exacting the payment of attorney's fees to the extortionist.

The dissent points out that petitioners' object in bringing their suit was not to obtain 'a judge's approbation,' but to 'stop enforcement of a [West Virginia] rule.' True enough. But not even the dissent claims that if a petitioner accumulated attorney's fees in preparing a threatened complaint, but never filed it prior to the defendant's voluntary cessation of its offending behavior, the wannabe-but-never-was plaintiff could recover fees; that would be countertextual, since the fee-shifting statutes require that there be an 'action' or 'proceeding,' see 42 U. S. C. § 3613(d); § 1988(b)—which in legal parlance (though not in more general usage) means a lawsuit. Does that not leave achievement of the broad congressional purpose identified by the dissent just as unsatisfactorily incomplete as the failure to award fees when there is no decree? ... My point is not that it would take no more twisting of language to produce prelitigation attorney's fees than to produce the decreeless attorney's fees that the dissent favors. My point is that the departure from normal usage that the dissent favors cannot be justified on the ground that it establishes a regime of logical even handedness. There must be a cutoff of seemingly equivalent entitlements to fees—either the failure to file suit in time or the failure to obtain a judgment in time. The term 'prevailing party' suggests the latter rather than the former. One does not prevail in a suit that is never determined.

Justice Ginsburg, with whom Justice Stevens, Justice Souter, and Justice Breyer join, dissenting.

Prior to 1994, every Federal Court of Appeals (except the Federal Circuit, which had not addressed the issue) concluded that plaintiffs ... could obtain a fee award if their suit acted as a 'catalyst' for the change they sought, even if they did not obtain a judgment or consent decree. The Courts of Appeals found it 'clear that a party may be considered to have prevailed even when the legal action stops short of final ... judgment due to ... intervening mootness.' Interpreting the term 'prevailing party' in 'a practical sense,' federal courts across the country held that a party 'prevails' for fee-shifting purposes when 'its ends are accomplished as a result of the litigation.'

In 1994, the Fourth Circuit en banc, dividing 6–to–5, broke ranks with its sister courts. The court declared that, in light of *Farrar v. Hobby*, 506 U. S. 103 (1992), a plaintiff could not become a 'prevailing party' without 'an enforceable judgment, consent decree, or settlement.' *S–1 and S–2 v. State Bd. of Ed. of N. C.*, 21 F. 3d 49, 51 (1994). As the Court today acknowledges, the language on which the Fourth Circuit relied was dictum. . . .

After the Fourth Circuit's en banc ruling, nine Courts of Appeals reaffirmed their own consistently held interpretation of the term 'prevail.'

The array of federal court decisions applying the catalyst rule suggested three conditions necessary to a party's qualification as 'prevailing' short of a favorable final judgment or consent decree. A plaintiff first had to show that the defendant provided 'some of the benefit sought' by the lawsuit. Under most Circuits' precedents, a plaintiff had to demonstrate as well that the suit stated a genuine claim, i.e., one that was at least 'colorable,' not 'frivolous, unreasonable, or groundless.' Plaintiff finally had to establish that her suit was a 'substantial' or 'significant' cause of defendant's action providing relief. In some Circuits, to make this causation showing, plaintiff had to satisfy the trial court that the suit achieved results 'by threat of victory,' not 'by dint of nuisance and threat of expense.' One who crossed these three thresholds would be recognized as a 'prevailing party' to whom the district court, 'in its discretion,' could award attorney's fees.

Developed over decades and in legions of federal-court decisions, the catalyst rule and these implementing standards deserve this Court's respect and approbation.

The Court today detects a 'clear meaning' of the term prevailing party that has heretofore eluded the large majority of courts construing those words. 'Prevailing party,' today's opinion announces, means 'one who has been awarded some relief by the court.' The Court derives this 'clear meaning' principally from Black's Law Dictionary, which defines a 'prevailing party,' in critical part, as one 'in whose favor a judgment is rendered' (quoting Black's Law Dictionary 1145 (7th ed. 1999)).

One can entirely agree with Black's Law Dictionary that a party 'in whose favor a judgment is rendered' prevails, and at the same time resist . . . any implication that only such a party may prevail. In prior cases, we have not treated Black's Law Dictionary as preclusively definitive; instead, we have accorded statutory terms, including legal 'term[s] of art,' a contextual reading. Notably, this Court did not refer to Black's Law Dictionary in *Maher v. Gagne*, 448 U. S. 122 (1980), which held that a consent decree could qualify a plaintiff as 'prevailing.' The Court explained:

> 'The fact that [plaintiff] prevailed through a settlement rather than through litigation does not weaken her claim to fees. Nothing in the language of [42 U. S. C.] § 1988 conditions the District Court's power to award fees on full litigation of the issues or on a judicial determination that the plaintiff's rights have been violated.' Id., at 129.

. . . In everyday use, 'prevail' means 'gain victory by virtue of strength or superiority: win mastery: triumph.' Webster's Third New International Dictionary 1797 (1976). There are undoubtedly situations in which an individual's goal is to obtain approval of a judge, and in those situations, one cannot 'prevail' short of a judge's formal declaration. In a piano competition or a figure skating contest, for example, the person who prevails is the person declared winner by the judges. However, where the ultimate goal is not an arbiter's approval, but a favorable alteration of actual circumstances, a formal declaration is not essential. Western democracies, for instance, 'prevailed' in the Cold War even though the Soviet Union never formally surrendered. Among television viewers, John F. Kennedy 'prevailed' in the first debate with Richard M. Nixon during the 1960 Presidential contest, even though moderator Howard K. Smith never declared a winner.

A lawsuit's ultimate purpose is to achieve actual relief from an opponent. Favorable judgment may be instrumental in gaining that relief. Generally, however, 'the judicial decree is not the end but the means. At the end of the rainbow lies not a judgment, but some action (or cessation of action) by the defendant . . . .' *Hewitt v. Helms*, 482 U. S. 755, 761 (1987). . . .

Under a fair reading of the FHAA and ADA provisions in point, I would hold that a party 'prevails' in 'a true and proper sense,' when she achieves, by instituting litigation, the practical relief sought in her complaint. The Court misreads Congress, as I see it, by insisting that, invariably, relief must be displayed in a judgment, and correspondingly that a defendant's voluntary action never suffices. . . .

Under the catalyst rule that held sway until today, plaintiffs who obtained the relief they sought through suit on genuine claims ordinarily qualified as 'prevailing parties,' so that courts had discretion to award them their costs and fees. Persons with limited resources were not impelled to 'wage total law' in order to assure that their counsel fees would be paid. They could accept relief, in money or of another kind, voluntarily proffered by a defendant who sought to avoid a recorded decree. And they could rely on a judge then to determine, in her equitable discretion, whether counsel fees were warranted and, if so, in what amount.

The concurring opinion adds another argument against the catalyst rule: That opinion sees the rule as accommodating the 'extortionist' who obtains relief because of 'greater strength in financial resources, or superiority in media manipulation, rather than superiority in legal merit.' This concern overlooks both the character of the rule and the judicial superintendence Congress ordered for all fee allowances. The catalyst rule was auxiliary to fee-shifting statutes whose primary purpose is 'to promote the vigorous enforcement' of the civil rights laws. [*Christiansburg Garment Co. v. EEOC*, 434 U. S. 412, 422 (1978)]. To that end, courts deemed the conduct-altering catalyst that counted to be the substance of the case, not merely the plaintiff's atypically superior financial resources, media ties, or political clout. And Congress assigned responsibility for awarding fees not to automatons unable to recognize extortionists, but to judges expected and instructed to exercise 'discretion.' So viewed, the catalyst rule provided no berth for nuisance suits. . . .

Questions and Notes

1.   In *Hensley*, the Court embraced the First Circuit's conclusion that "plaintiffs may be considered 'prevailing parties' for attorney's fee purposes if the succeed on any significant issue in litigation which achieves some of the benefit the parties sought in bringing suit." Interestingly, elsewhere in *Hensley* the Court cited *Christiansburg Garment Co. v. EEOC*, 434 U.S. 412, 421, 98 S.Ct. 694, 700, 54 L.Ed.2d 648 (1978) for the proposition that prevailing defendants are entitled to fee awards only "where the suit was vexatious, frivolous, or brought to harass or embarrass the defendant." *Hensley*, 461 U.S., at 429 n.2, 103 S.Ct., at 1937. While there is legislative history supporting this dichotomy, see *Christiansburg*, 434 U.S., at 420, 98 S.Ct., at 699–700, one must wonder whether this unequal treatment is supportable in statutory schemes that simply provide for fee awards to "prevailing parties." Cf. *Fogerty v. Fantasy, Inc.*, 510 U.S. 517, 525–539, 114 S.Ct. 1013, 1034–1034 127 L.Ed.2d 455 (1994) (Thomas, concurring).

2.   Few if any environmental statutes use the same "prevailing party" formulations that were litigated in *Hensley* and *Buckhannon*. Instead, the environmental statutes tend to fall into two camps. Some, like the Clean Water Act and RCRA, provide for fee awards to any "prevailing or substan-

tially prevailing party." 33 U.S.C. § 1365(d), 42 U.S.C. § 6772(a). Others, such as the Endangered Species Act and the Clean Air Act, don't use either the "prevailing party" or "substantially prevailing party" formulations. Instead, they authorize a fee awards "whenever the court determines such an award is appropriate." See 16 U.S.C. § 1540(g)(4), and 42 U.S.C. § 7604(d). Putting mootness issues aside for the moment, should the threshold requirements for awards be the same under these different formulations? In *Ruckelshaus v. Sierra Club*, 463 U.S. 680, 103 S.Ct. 3274, 77 L.Ed.2d 938 (1983), the Supreme Court has determined that, despite the CAA's "whenever appropriate" phraseology, courts cannot award fees to losing parties. See also *Marbled Murrelet v. Babbitt*, 182 F.3d 1091 (9th Cir. 1999) (deeming the *Christiansburg* test applicable to prevailing defendants under the ESA).

3. What did you think of the Supreme Court's statutory analysis in *Buckhannon*? Do you find the statutory language to be clear? Do you find the legislative history to be ambiguous? What did you think of the policy arguments advanced by the various Justices?

4. How, if at all, should the different statutory formulations under statutes such as the CWA ("prevailing or substantially prevailing") or the CAA ("whenever appropriate") affect the application of *Buckhannon*? Thus far, the Circuit Courts have been unanimous in determining that *Buckhannon* applies under statutes that use the "substantially prevailing" formulation. See, e.g., *Sierra Club v. City of Little Rock*, 351 F.3d 840 (8th Cir. 2003) ("*Little Rock*") (assuming without discussion that *Buckhannon* applies under the CWA); see also *Oil, Chem. & Atomic Workers Int'l Union v. Department of Energy*, 288 F.3d 453, 455 (D.C. Cir. 2002), and *Union of Needletrades, Industrial and Textile Employees v. U.S. INS*, 336 F.3d 200, 207–210 (2d Cir. 2003) (both under the Freedom of Information Act, 5 U.S.C. § 552). At the same time, they have been similarly unanimous in concluding that they may still apply the catalyst theory under statutes with the "where appropriate" standard. See, e.g., *Sierra Club v. Environmental Protection Agency*, 322 F.3d 718 (D.C. Cir. 2003) (CAA), and *Association of Calif. Water Agencies v. Evans*, 386 F.3d 879 (9th Cir. 2004), and *Loggerhead Turtle v. County Council of Volusia County, Fla.*, 307 F.3d 1318 (11th Cir. 2002) (both under the ESA). Do you agree with these results?

5. Short of a consent decree, what, if anything, do you think should constitute a sufficient "judicial imprimatur" under *Buckhannon*? What if, for example, the court has endorsed the plaintiff's legal theories in denying the defendant's motion for summary judgment, but has reserved final judgment until it has a chance to review the defendant's discharge monitoring reports to determine the total number of violations? How much discretion does the court have to control whether or when it generates the necessary imprimatur? What if, when the defendant moves for a finding of mootness, the plaintiff asks the court to pass on whether violations have been committed and whether its lawsuit was the catalyst for the defendant's coming into compliance? Can the court pass on these questions at that point in time? If it can and does, would that be a sufficient imprimatur? See *Little Rock*, 351 F.3d 840 (denying fees for want of an imprimatur despite the fact that the lower court had found liability, without asking whether the plaintiff's lawsuit had triggered the defendant's compliance). If the court can do so, must it?

6. Even if courts may continue to apply the catalyst theory under statutes (such as the ESA) using the "where appropriate" test, the court still must find that the plaintiff's lawsuit led to the defendant's compliance. This is not always a foregone conclusion. Compare *Center for Biological Diversity v. Norton*, 262 F.3d 1077 (10th Cir. 2001), with *Association of Calif. Water Agencies v. Evans*, 386 F.3d 879 (9th Cir. 2004).

7. How will *Buckhannon* affect the decisions of plaintiffs' lawyers as to whether to take on particular citizen suits? How will it affect both plaintiffs' and defendants' incentives during the course of the lawsuits? Does it create any conflict of interest problems for plaintiffs' lawyers?

8. In later cases, the Supreme Court has established a "strong presumption" that what it refers to as the "lodestar" figure (that is, the product of reasonable hours times a reasonable rate) represents the "reasonable" fee. See, e.g., *City of Burlington v. Dague*, 505 U.S. 557, 562, 112 S.Ct. 2638, 2641, 120 L.Ed.2d 449 (1992). It has also determined that these fees cannot be increased to account for the risk of failure in particular cases (so-called "contingency enhancements"). Id. at 566–567, 112 S.Ct., at 2643–2644. Under what circumstances should courts award prevailing plaintiffs less than the lodestar? See *Little Rock*, 351 F.3d 840.

9. If courts deem full fee awards appropriate, they generally determine the reasonable hourly rate by the prevailing market rates for lawyers of similar skill in the relevant community, regardless of whether the plaintiff is represented by private or nonprofit counsel. See, e.g., *Blum v. Stenson*, 465 U.S. 886, 895, 104 S.Ct. 1541, 79 L.Ed.2d 891 (1984), and *Public Interest Research Group of New Jersey, Inc. v. Windall*, 51 F.3d 1179 (3d Cir. 1995). Does this create the possibility of a windfall to the plaintiff in some situations?

Chapter 7

COMPREHENSIVE ENVIRONMEN-
TAL RESPONSE, COMPENSA-
TION AND LIABILITY ACT

I. CERCLA

A. Overview and Jurisdiction

Congress first passed the Comprehensive Environmental Response, Compensation and Liability Act ("CERCLA") in 1980, 42 U.S.C. §§ 9601–9675, Pub. L. No. 96–510, 94 Stat. 2767 (1980), in response to the discovery of infamous sites such as Love Canal in Niagara Falls, New York, and the "Valley of the Drums" in Shepardsville, Kentucky. Since then, Congress has comprehensively amended CERCLA once, through the Superfund Amendments and Reauthorization Act ("SARA"), Pub. L. 99–499, 100 Stat. 1615 (1986). Additionally, it has tinkered with the statute on several occasions since, most notably through the Small Business Liability Relief and Brownsfields Revitalization Act ("Brownsfields Amendments"), Pub. L. 107–118, Stat. 2356 (2002).

From its inception, CERCLA has had a very different cast than the other pollution-control statutes we have considered in this course. Unlike statutes such as the Clean Water Act and RCRA, it is not a traditional "command and control" statute. It imposes very few regulatory obligations. Instead, it is a remedial program, giving EPA and others the tools they need to address contamination and to impose liability for past actions associated with it, even if those actions were consistent with all then-existing laws and standards of care. While "command and control" programs are primarily forward looking, CERCLA is backward looking. It doesn't tell companies how they have to run their businesses to minimize the risk of contamination; instead, it merely imposes responsibility for such contamination should it occur.

CERCLA provides EPA with four basic options for responding to contamination problems. First, it may in investigate or clean up a site itself § 104 and then seek reimbursement from any potentially responsible parties ("PRPs") under § 107. If EPA chooses this option, it draws upon the Superfund ("Fund") to front load its investigatory and/or cleanup expenses. The amount of money in the Fund has varied over time, from a high-water mark of $8.5 billion in 1986 to an annual appropriation of $1.25 billion in 2005. Second, EPA may seek to compel any PRP (or group of PRPs) to conduct any necessary investigations or cleanup activities by initiating a judicial action seeking a court order under § 106. Third, it may issue one or more PRPs a unilateral order requiring them to conduct the same activities, also under § 106. And finally, it may negotiate a settlement with some or all of the PRPs under which they agree to undertake any necessary response actions. See 42 U.S.C. § 9622.

EPA tends to focus its attention on sites that are on what is referred to as National Priorities List ("NPL"). Roughly speaking, this is a list of the most contaminated sites in the country, as determined by EPA. There were 1,245 sites on this list as of July 22, 2004. When EPA is drawing upon the Fund, it can only undertake full-blown "remedial actions," as distinct from short-term steps know as "removals," if the site is on NPL. 40 C.F.R. § 300.425(b); see also 42 U.S.C. § 101(23) and (24) (definitions of removal and remedial action). While EPA is not similarly restricted under its other response options, it seldom seeks the full range of CERCLA-type relief at non-NPL sites.

CERCLA also provides states, Indian tribes, and even private parties with the ability to seek cost recovery from PRPs for any costs incurred in the cleanup process (although, as will be seen, would-be private-party plaintiffs face some additional constraints). 42 U.S.C. § 9607(a)(4)(A) and (B). The vast majority of these non-EPA lead cleanups occur at sites that are not on the NPL. Additionally, § 113(f)(1) and (3) supplement the private-party cost-recovery authority by allowing PRPs to bring claims for contribution in certain situations in which they allege that they have paid more than their fair share of any necessary cleanup costs.

The basic elements of CERCLA jurisdiction consist of three requirements: (1) a release or substantial threat of a release; (2) of a hazardous substance; (3) from a facility. See §§ 104(a)(1), 106(a), and 107(a)(4). There are other elements that apply to CERCLA's enforcement mechanisms. If a CERCLA plaintiff is suing for cost-recovery, for example, it must show that it has expended funds on cleanup, and it must demonstrate that the defendants are liable under § 107. 42 U.S.C. § 9607(a). Alternatively, if EPA is ordering the PRPs to do the work, § 106 requires it to have determined that the site "may" present "an imminent and substantial endangerment to public health or welfare or the environment." 42 U.S.C. § 9606. But it is the breath of CERCLA three key jurisdictional terms that give the statute its remarkable sway. If an otherwise-eligible plaintiff is confident that these elements are present, it will be confident that CERCLA provides it with a powerful tool to induce those responsible to either undertake, fund, or contribute to cleanup efforts.

CERCLA's most important jurisdictional element is established through its definition of the term "hazardous substance." Section

101(14) defines this term primarily through a process of incorporation, using both Congress's and EPA's prior efforts in classifying contaminants of concern under other environmental programs. Specifically, the realm of CERCLA hazardous substances is defined to include:

i. Any toxic pollutants or hazardous substances designated pursuant to the Clean Water Act;

ii. Any listed or characteristic hazardous wastes under RCRA;

iii. Any hazardous air pollutants under the Clean Air Act; and

iv. Any imminently hazardous chemical substances or mixtures with respect to which EPA has taken action under § 7 of the Toxic Substances Control Act.

Additionally, EPA can specifically designate any substance as a hazardous substance specifically for purposes of the CERCLA program. CERCLA § 102.

The entire list of hazardous substances is found at 40 C.F.R. Part 302, Table 302.4. In addition to contaminants such as trichloroethylene ("TCE") and dioxin, it includes substances as ubiquitous as lead, copper, chlorine, and fluorine. Additionally, neither the statutory definition nor EPA's list contains any quantity or concentration requirements. The presence of these substances in any amount or concentration will satisfy this jurisdictional element.

The only significant restraint in CERCLA's definition of "hazardous substance" inheres in what is known as the "petroleum exclusion." Specifically, Section 101(14) excludes "petroleum, including crude oil and any fraction thereof which is is not otherwise specifically listed or designated as a hazardous substance ..." from the ambit of the CERCLA program. This exclusion is not scientifically based; petroleum-based waste frequently contains toxic constituents at levels that would qualify them as hazardous wastes under RCRA. Instead, the petroleum exclusion originated from the circumstances surrounding the enactment of CERCLA. At the time Congress was considering CERCLA, it also was considering a parallel oil spill bill (H.R. 85) that would have comprehensively addressed petroleum-based contamination. Releases of hazardous substances were to be addressed under one bill and releases of oil under the other. At the last minute, however, the Senate failed to move forward on H.R. 85, leaving the problem of land-based petroleum contamination unaddressed except in relatively rare instances where it poses an accompanying threat to the navigable waters.

The precise contours of the petroleum exclusion have been subject to considerable litigation. At least two general principles have emerged. On the one hand, there is consensus that petroleum will not lose its exempt status where hazardous substances such as benzene, ethylbenzene, toluene, and lead are added to it during the refining process. See, e.g., *Wilshire Westwood Assoc. v. Atlantic Richfield Corp.*, 881 F.2d 801 (9th Cir.1989). On the other hand, there is also agreement that the exclusion does not encompass oil which through use has become contaminated with other hazardous substances. See *United States v. Alcan Aluminum Corp.*, 964 F.2d 252 (3d Cir.1992).

CERCLA defines the term "release" to mean "any spilling, leaking, pumping, pouring, emitting, emptying, discharging, injecting, escaping, leaching, dumping, or disposing into the environment...." CERCLA § 101(22). Giving effect to the breadth of this language, the courts have determined that any uncontrolled movement of contaminants in the environment qualifies as a release. CERCLA also authorizes response and imposes liability for actions taken in response to "threatened release[s]." See §§ 104(a)(1), 106(a), and 107(a)(4). While undefined in the statute, the courts have indicated that a "threatened release" may be established by (1) evidence of the presence of hazardous substances at a facility; (2) together with evidence of the unwillingness of any party to assert control over the substances. *United States v. Northernaire Plating Co.*, 670 F.Supp. 742, 747 (W.D.Mich.1987), *aff'd sub nom. United States v. R.W. Meyer, Inc.*, 889 F.2d 1497, 1507 (6th Cir.1989), *cert. denied*, 494 U.S. 1057, 110 S.Ct. 1527, 108 L.Ed.2d 767 (1990); *see also New York v. Shore Realty Corp.*, 759 F.2d 1032, 1045 (2d Cir.1985)(a facility's lack of expertise in handling hazardous waste or its failure to comply with licensing requirements may, by itself, constitute a threatened release).

The final jurisdictional requirement common to all of CERCLA's options is that the release or threatened release be from a "facility." See §§ 106(a) and 107(a)(4). However, this term imposes almost no substantive limitation on the scope of the program. Section 101(9) defines it to include "any site or area where a hazardous substance has ... come to be located." In line with this definition, courts have recognized that this definition includes far more than what typically would be considered to be hazardous waste facilities. See, e.g., *United States v. Ward*, 618 F.Supp. 884, 895 (D.N.C.1985) (roadsides where hazardous waste had been dumped); and *New York v. General Electric Co.*, 592 F.Supp. 291 (N.D.N.Y.1984) (a dragstrip where PCB–contaminated oils had been applied as a dust suppressant). Moreover, the relevant "facility" need not correspond to or be coextensive with property boundaries. In some cases, it can be broader; in others, narrower.

B. EPA Response

As mentioned, EPA has four options in responding to the actual or threatened contamination when these jurisdictional elements are satisfied. It may: (1) investigate or clean up the site and then seek cost recovery; (2) commence a judicial abatement action; (3) issue a unilateral administrative order requiring investigation or cleanup; or (4) negotiate a settlement under which the PRPs agree to perform the necessary actions. In all four of these contexts, EPA's cleanup methodology is delimited by the National Contingency Plan ("NCP"), which Congress tasked EPA with creating in § 105 of CERCLA. See 40 C.F.R. §§ 300.400–300.440. The NCP serves as the blueprint for response, regardless of which of the four enforcement option EPA pursues, and regardless of who is to perform the relevant investigatory or cleanup activities.

Many students reasonably assume that EPA typically pursues the first of the above options; i.e., that it cleans up the relevant sites and then sues for cost recovery. In fact, this is not the case. While EPA often uses its § 104 authorities to begin its investigations and/or to implement some preliminary response measures, at most sites it relies on the PRPs undertake the bulk of the necessary investigations and/or cleanup activities, albeit subject to EPA oversight. Typically, this happens pursuant to consent decrees, pursuant to which the PRPs "voluntarily" agree to take the lead on these required activities. In order to understand why the PRPs agree to do this (often at the cost of tens of millions of dollars), one must understand a bit about the leverage that EPA has in these settlement negotiations.

EPA's general enforcement strategy in the CERCLA context is to promote settlement by relying on its unilateral order authority in situations in which negotiations fail. See, e.g., EPA, Enforcement First for Remedial Action at Superfund Sites (Sept. 20, 2002), www.epa.gov/compliance/resources/policies/cleanup/superfund/enffirst-mem.pdf. In order to understand why this strategy is so effective, one must understand the power of EPA's unilateral order authority. Again, § 106 gives EPA the power to issue unilateral orders compelling PRPs to implement any required investigations or cleanup activities. In order to do so, EPA need only determine that the basic statutory elements are present and that the site "may" present an "imminent and substantial endangerment." 42 U.S.C. § 9606(a). Moreover, the statute explicitly precludes the courts from reviewing the legality of these orders of a pre-enforcement basis. 42 U.S.C. § 9613(h). Further, § 107(c)(3) allows EPA to seek punitive damages of up to three times the cost of cleanup if the recipient of such an order fails to comply therewith and its noncompliance is deemed to be "without sufficient cause." Given the threat of these sanctions, it is hardly surprising that most PRPs choose to proceed via consent, rather than face the threat of receiving such an order.

As a prelude to negotiation, EPA of course must identify those parties it deems to be liable under § 107. Additionally, if it is seeking to impose joint and several liability, it must determine whether that doctrine applies given the facts of the particular case. As such, we now turn to those issues:

1. Liable Parties

The elements of liability under CERCLA are straightforward. In governmental enforcement actions, EPA (or the State or Indian tribe) must show three things in order to establish liability:

1. That there has been a release or threatened release of a hazardous substance from a facility;

2. That the government or other authorized party incurred response costs because of the release or threatened release; and

3. That the party being sued falls into one of the four classes of PRPs under § 107.

See CERCLA § 107(a).

Section 107 imposes liability on four classes of "persons." These include (1) the present owner and operator of the site; (2) anyone who owned or operated the site at a time when hazardous substances were disposed of there; (3) anyone who "arranged for disposal or treatment" of such substances at the site; and (4) any transporters who selected the site. In practice, the vast majority of PRPs will fit within one of three groups—the current owner or operator of the site, the company that contaminated the site or allowed the contamination to occur (owner/operator at the time of disposal), or the generators who arranged to have their materials disposed of at the site. Hence, our discussion will focus on owner/operator and generator liability.

a. Owner/Operator Liability

i. *Ownership Liability*

The combined effect of § 107(a)(1) and (2) is to impose strict liability on both the current owner of the contaminated site and anyone who owned it during any periods of prior disposal. The seminal "current owner" liability case is *New York v. Shore Realty Corp.*, 759 F.2d 1032 (2d Cir.1985):

NEW YORK v. SHORE REALTY CORP.

United States Court of Appeals, Second Circuit, 1985.
759 F.2d 1032.

OAKES, CIRCUIT JUDGE

[Shore Realty ("Shore") agreed to purchase a piece of property at which a hold-over tenant was storing approximately 700,000 gallons of hazardous chemicals in a group of above-and below-ground tanks. Upon learning of the potential for contamination, Shore sought a waiver from the State of New York regarding any potential liability it might incur as the purchaser of the property. Despite being denied this waiver, Shore took title "and obtained certain rights over against the tenants," whom it shortly evicted. Despite the prompt eviction, however, tenants had added nearly 90,000 gallons of chemicals to the tanks during Shore's ownership period.]

Shore argues that it is not covered by section 9607(a)(1) because it neither owned the site at the time of disposal nor caused the presence or the release of hazardous waste at the facility. While section 9607(a)(1) appears to cover Shore, Shore attempts to infuse ambiguity into the statutory scheme, claiming that section 9607(a)(1) could not have been intended to include all owners, because the word "owned" in section 9707(a)(2) would be unnecessary since an owner "at the time of disposal" would necessarily be included in section 9607(a)(1). Shore claims that

Congress intended that the scope of section 9607(a)(1) be no greater than that of section 9607(a)(2) and that both should be limited by the "at the time of disposal" language. By extension, Shore argues that both provisions should be interpreted as requiring a showing of causation. We agree with the State, however, that section 9607(a)(1) unequivocally imposes strict liability on the current owner of a facility from which there is a release or threat of release, without regard to causation.

Shore's claims of ambiguity are illusory; section 9607(a)'s structure is clear. Congress intended to cover different classes of persons differently. Section 9607(a)(1) applies to all current owners and operators, while section 9607(a)(2) primarily covers prior owners and operators. Moreover, section 9607(a)(2)'s scope is more limited than that of section 9607(a)(1). Prior owners and operators are liable only if they owned or operated the facility "at the time of disposal of any hazardous substance"; this limitation does not apply to current owners, like Shore....

Shore's causation argument is also at odds with the structure of the statute. Interpreting section 9607(a)(1) as including a causation requirement makes superfluous the affirmative defenses provided in section 9607(b), each of which carves out from liability an exception based on causation. Without clear congressional command otherwise, we will not construe a statute in any way that makes some of its provisions surplusage....

Our interpretation draws further support from the legislative history. Congress specifically rejected including a causation requirement in section 9607(a). The early House version imposed liability only upon "any person who caused or contributed to the release or threatened release." H.R. 7020, 96th Cong., 2d Sess. § 3071(a), 126 Cong. Rec. 26,779. The compromise version, to which the House later agreed, imposed liability on classes of persons without reference to whether they caused or contributed to the release or threatened release....

Furthermore, as the State points out, accepting Shore's arguments would open a huge loophole in CERCLA's coverage. It is quite clear that if the current owner could avoid liability merely by having purchased the site after chemical dumping had ceased, waste sites certainly would be sold, following the cessation of dumping, to new owners who could avoid the liability otherwise required by CERCLA. Congress had well in mind that persons who dump or store hazardous waste sometimes cannot be located or may be deceased or judgment proof.... We will not interpret section 9607(a) in any way that apparently frustrates the statute's goals, in the absence of a specific congressional intention otherwise....

Notes and Questions

1. Why do you think Shore framed its argument in terms of whether it fit within the scope of § 107(a)(1), instead of directly addressing the standard of liability issue?

2. CERCLA itself says little about the standard of liability it imposes. Section 101(32) merely indicates that the term "liability" under the statute

"shall be construed to be the standard of liability which obtains under [§ 311 of the Clean Water Act]." Interestingly, § 311 itself does not specify any standard of liability. This has not posed any serious problems, however. Numerous courts had previously interpreted that section as imposing strict liability. See *United States v. Chem–Dyne Corp.*, 572 F.Supp. 802, 805 (S.D. Ohio 1983) (and cases cited therein). In his testimony on the Senate floor, Senator Randolph, one of CERCLA's sponsors, indicated that Congress was aware of these decisions: "We have kept strict liability in the compromise, specifying the standard of liability under section 311 of the [CWA]; that is, strict liability." 126 Cong. Rec. S14,964 (daily ed. Nov. 24, 1980). As a result, the courts have been unanimous in determining that CERCLA imposes strict liability. *Shore Realty* is considered the seminal case in this regard. Indeed, it is the most frequently-cited CERCLA decision of all time.

3. It is one thing to hold that a statute imposes strict liability. It is another to determine that it imposes liability without respect to causation. Do you understand the distinction between the two? Were you persuaded by the *Shore Realty* court's causation analysis? Does it go beyond traditional notions of fairness to impose strict liability on the current owners of contaminated land regardless of whether they played any part in causing the relevant contamination? If so, is the new leap justified? Did you find satisfactory the *Shore Realty* court's justification that imposing strict liability was necessary to prevent a sale of the property to new owners who would "avoid the liability otherwise required by CERCLA?"

4. In the last paragraph you have from this excerpt from *Shore Realty*, the court emphasized that it would not interpret § 107 "in any way that apparently frustrate's the statute's goals, in the absence of a specific congressional intention otherwise." Many courts have expressed similar sentiments in interpreting CERCLA, noting, for example, that "a liberal judicial interpretation is consistent with CERCLA's 'overwhelmingly remedial' statutory scheme." *United States v. Aceto Agricultural Chemicals Corp.*, 872 F.2d 1373, 1380 (8th Cir. 1989); see also *Florida Power & Light Co. v. Allis Chalmers Corp.*, 893 F.2d 1313, 1317 (11th Cir. 1990). Other courts, such as the Seventh Circuit, have disagreed. In *Edward Hines Lumber Co. v. Vulcan Materials Co.*, 861 F.2d 155 (7th Cir. 1988), Judge Easterbrook responded to the invocation of this "remedial purpose" argument in the following terms:

> ... To the point that courts could achieve "more" of the legislative objectives by adding to the lists of those responsible, it is enough to respond that statutes have not only ends but also limits. Born of compromise, laws such as CERCLA and SARA do not pursue their ends to their logical limits. A court's job is to find and enforce stopping points no less than to implement other legislative choices.

861 F.2d at 157. Which approach do you think is correct? Why?

5. CERCLA liability is not only strict and causation-free, the courts unanimously have determined that it is also retroactive. They have reached this conclusion despite the fact that the statute contains no explicit statement regarding its retroactive application. In so holding, the courts have relied on the fact that: (1) Section 107(a)(2) imposes liability on those who owned contaminated properties at the time the disposal activities occurred; (2) Section 103(c) required those who owned certain sites where disposal had

occurred to notify EPA within 180 days after the CERCLA's passage, and penalized those who failed to do so by depriving them of any defenses to which they may otherwise have been entitled; and (3) CERCLA's legislative history indicates that one of CERCLA's central purposes is to impose the costs of cleanup on those who caused the relevant contamination. See *United States v. Olin Corp.*, 107 F.3d 1506 (11th Cir. 1997). Are you persuaded? The courts have been similarly unanimous in determining that the imposition of this retroactive liability is not unconstitutional. In the leading case of *United States v. Monsanto Co.*, 858 F.2d 160 (4th Cir. 1988), cert. denied, 490 U.S. 1106, 109 S.Ct. 3156, 104 L.Ed.2d 1019 (1989), the Fourth Circuit relied on the Supreme Court's earlier decision in *Usury v. Turner Elkhorn Mining Co.*, 428 U.S. 1, 96 S.Ct. 2882, 49 L.Ed.2d 752 (1976), in which the Court upheld the retroactive operation of the Black Lung Benefits Act of 1972. The *Monsanto* court further noted that:

> ... CERCLA does not exact punishment. Rather it creates a reimbursement obligation on any person judicially determined responsible for the costs of remedying hazardous conditions at a waste disposal facility. The restitution of cleanup costs was not intended to operate, nor does it operate in fact, as a criminal penalty or a punitive deterrent....

858 F.2d at 174–175. More recent decisions have held that this analysis survives the Supreme Court's more recent decision in *Eastern Enterprises v. Apfel*, 524 U.S. 498, 118 S.Ct. 2131, 141 L.Ed.2d 451 (1998). See, e.g., *United States v. Alcan Aluminum*, 315 F.3d 179, 188–190 (2d Cir. 2003) (and cases cited therein).

6. Since *Shore Realty*, Congress has established two significant, but still relatively narrow, defenses to current landowner liability. First, when it passed SARA in 1986, Congress created what is referred to as the "innocent landowner defense." See 42 U.S.C. § 9601(35)(A). Second, when Congress passed the Brownfields Amendments in 2002, it created the "prospective purchaser" exclusion, which shields some parties who knowingly purchase contaminated sites. 42 U.S.C. § 9607(r). We will discuss these provisions in more detail in subpart B.3 of this chapter, below.

7. Another interesting issue under § 107(a) involves the liability of so-called "interim owners." Imagine a situation in which A contaminated land and then sold it to B, who, without having added to the contamination, then sold the land to C, the current owner. A and C are clearly liable under § 107(a); but what about B? Most courts have held that such parties are not liable, determining that the passive migration of hazardous substances within soils and/or groundwater does not make parties like B owners "at the time of disposal" within the meaning of § 107(a)(2). See, e.g., *United States v. CDMG Realty Co.*, 96 F.3d 706 (3d Cir. 1996) (noting that while CERCLA's definition of "disposal"–which it incorporates from RCRA through reference—includes leaking, it does not include "leaching"); cf. *Nurad, Inc. v. William E. Hooper & Sons Co.*, 966 F.2d 837 (4th Cir.), cert. denied sub nom *Mumaw v. Nurad, Inc.*, 506 U.S. 940, 113 S.Ct. 377, 121 L.Ed.2d 288 (1992) (holding an interim owner liable where there was an ongoing leak from underground storage tank during its period of ownership).

ii. Operator Liability

In addition to imposing liability on owners, § 107(a)(1) and (2) impose liability on both the current operator of the facility and anyone who operated the facility at the time of disposal. In many cases, these operators will be obvious: they will be the entities who are or were doing business on the property; to the extent that they are distinct from the owners, they will typically have been lessees.

More difficult questions arise, however, when one considers the extent to which entities such as parent corporations or individuals such as corporate officers or employees may qualify as "operators" under CERCLA. In these contexts, two separate questions can be raised: First, does the relevant entity or individual bear "direct" liability under the statute by virtue of being an "operator" in its own right; and second, is "piercing the corporate veil" appropriate such that the relevant entity or individual can be deemed to be derivatively liable for the sins of the relevant subsidiary or employer. Consider the following case:

UNITED STATES v. BESTFOODS

Supreme Court of the United States, 1998.
524 U.S. 51, 118 S.Ct. 1876, 141 L.Ed.2d 43.

Justice Souter delivered the opinion of the Court.

In 1957, Ott Chemical Co. (Ott I) began manufacturing chemicals at a plant near Muskegon, Michigan, and its intentional and unintentional dumping of hazardous substances significantly polluted the soil and ground water at the site. In 1965, respondent CPC International Inc. incorporated a wholly owned subsidiary to buy Ott I's assets in exchange for CPC stock. The new company, also dubbed Ott Chemical Co. (Ott II), continued chemical manufacturing at the site, and continued to pollute its surroundings. CPC kept the managers of Ott I, including its founder, president, and principal shareholder, Arnold Ott, on board as officers of Ott II. Arnold Ott and several other Ott II officers and directors were also given positions at CPC, and they performed duties for both corporations.

In 1972, CPC sold Ott II to Story Chemical Company, which operated the Muskegon plant until its bankruptcy in 1977. Shortly thereafter, when respondent Michigan Department of Natural Resources (MDNR) examined the site for environmental damage, it found the land littered with thousands of leaking and even exploding drums of waste, and the soil and water saturated with noxious chemicals. MDNR sought a buyer for the property who would be willing to contribute toward its cleanup, and after extensive negotiations, respondent Aerojet–General Corp. arranged for transfer of the site from the Story bankruptcy trustee in 1977. Aerojet created a wholly owned California subsidiary, Cordova Chemical Company (Cordova/California), to purchase the property, and Cordova/California in turn created a wholly owned Michigan subsidiary,

Cordova Chemical Company of Michigan (Cordova/Michigan), which manufactured chemicals at the site until 1986.

By 1981, [EPA] had undertaken to see the site cleaned up, and its long-term remedial plan called for expenditures well into the tens of millions of dollars. To recover some of that money, the United States filed this action under § 107 in 1989, naming five defendants as responsible parties: CPC, Aerojet, Cordova/California, Cordova/Michigan, and Arnold Ott. (By that time, Ott I and Ott II were defunct.) . . .

[In the liability phase, the district court found CPC directly liable as an operator under § 107(a)(2), finding it "particularly telling that CPC selected Ott II's board of directors and populated its executive ranks with CPC officials, and that a CPC official, G.R.D. Williams, played a significant role in shaping Ott II's environmental compliance policy."

An en banc panel of the Sixth Circuit ultimately reversed on this point (7 judges to 6), holding that parent corporations could be liable as "operators" only where they essentially operate the facility either in the stead of their subsidiaries or as joint venturers alongside their subsidiaries. In either event, the en banc panel determined that their must be an abuse the corporate form to an extent that would give rise to piercing the corporate veil under traditional, state-law tests. Applying this analysis, the decided that under Michigan veil-piercing law CPC was not liable for controlling the actions of its subsidiaries, since the parent and subsidiary corporations maintained separate personalities and CPC did not utilize the subsidiary corporate form to perpetrate fraud or subvert justice.]

It is a general principle of corporate law deeply "ingrained in our economic and legal systems" that a parent corporation (so-called because of control through ownership of another corporation's stock) is not liable for the acts of its subsidiaries. Douglas & Shanks, Insulation from Liability Through Subsidiary Corporations, 39 Yale L. J. 193 (1929) (hereinafter Douglas) [and other citations]. Thus it is hornbook law that "the exercise of the 'control' which stock ownership gives to the stockholders . . . will not create liability beyond the assets of the subsidiary. That 'control' includes the election of directors, the making of by-laws . . . and the doing of all other acts incident to the legal status of stockholders. Nor will a duplication of some or all of the directors or executive officers be fatal." Douglas 196. Although this respect for corporate distinctions when the subsidiary is a polluter has been severely criticized in the literature, nothing in CERCLA purports to reject this bedrock principle, and against this venerable common-law backdrop, the congressional silence is audible. The Government has indeed made no claim that a corporate parent is liable as an owner or an operator under § 107 simply because its subsidiary is subject to liability for owning or operating a polluting facility.

But there is an equally fundamental principle of corporate law, applicable to the parent-subsidiary relationship as well as generally, that the corporate veil may be pierced and the shareholder held liable for the corporation's conduct when, inter alia, the corporate form would otherwise be misused to accomplish certain wrongful purposes, most notably fraud, on the shareholder's behalf. Nothing in CERCLA purports to rewrite this well-settled rule, either. CERCLA is thus like many another congressional enactment in giving no indication "that the entire corpus of state corporation law is to be replaced simply because a plaintiff's cause of action is based upon a federal statute," and the failure of the statute to speak to a matter as fundamental as the liability implications of corporate ownership demands application of the rule that "[i]n order to abrogate a common-law principle, the statute must speak directly to the question addressed by the common law." The Court of Appeals was accordingly correct in holding that when (but only when) the corporate veil may be pierced,[9] may a parent corporation be charged with derivative CERCLA liability for its subsidiary's actions.[10]

If the act rested liability entirely on ownership of a polluting facility, this opinion might end here; but CERCLA liability may turn on operation as well as ownership, and nothing in the statute's terms bars a parent corporation from direct liability for its own actions in operating a facility owned by its subsidiary. As Justice (then-Professor) Douglas noted almost 70 years ago, derivative liability cases are to be distinguished from those in which "the alleged wrong can seemingly be traced to the parent through the conduit of its own personnel and management" and "the parent is directly a participant in the wrong complained of." Douglas 207, 208. In such instances, the parent is directly liable for its own actions. The fact that a corporate subsidiary happens to own a polluting facility operated by its parent does nothing, then, to displace the rule that the parent "corporation is [itself] responsible for the wrongs committed by its agents in the course of its business," *Mine Workers v. Coronado Coal Co.*, 259 U. S. 344, 395 (1922), and whereas the rules of veil-piercing limit derivative liability for the actions of another corporation, CERCLA's "operator" provision is concerned primarily with direct liability for one's own actions. It is this direct liability that is properly seen as being at issue here.

Under the plain language of the statute, any person who operates a polluting facility is directly liable for the costs of cleaning up the pollution. This is so regardless of whether that person is the facility's

9. There is significant disagreement among courts and commentators over whether, in enforcing CERCLA's indirect liability, courts should borrow state law, or instead apply a federal common law of veil piercing. [Citations]. Since none of the parties challenges the Sixth Circuit's holding that CPC and Aerojet incurred no derivative liability, the question is not presented in this case, and we do not address it further.

10. Some courts and commentators have suggested that this indirect, veil-piercing approach can subject a parent corpora-

tion to liability only as an owner, and not as an operator. See, e.g., *Lansford-Coaldale Joint Water Auth. v. Tonelli Corp.*, supra, at 1220; Oswald, Bifurcation of the Owner and Operator Analysis under CERCLA, 72 Wash. U. L. Q. 223, 281–282 (1994) (hereinafter Oswald). We think it is otherwise, however. If a subsidiary that operates, but does not own, a facility is so pervasively controlled by its parent for a sufficiently improper purpose to warrant veil piercing, the parent may be held derivatively liable for the subsidiary's acts as an operator.

owner, the owner's parent corporation or business partner, or even a saboteur who sneaks into the facility at night to discharge its poisons out of malice. If any such act of operating a corporate subsidiary's facility is done on behalf of a parent corporation, the existence of the parent-subsidiary relationship under state corporate law is simply irrelevant to the issue of direct liability.

This much is easy to say; the difficulty comes in defining actions sufficient to constitute direct parental "operation." Here of course we may again rue the uselessness of CERCLA's definition of a facility's "operator" as "any person ... operating" the facility, 42 U. S. C. § 9601(20)(A)(ii), which leaves us to do the best we can to give the term its "ordinary or natural meaning." In a mechanical sense, to "operate" ordinarily means "[t]o control the functioning of; run: operate a sewing machine." American Heritage Dictionary 1268 (3d ed. 1992); see also Webster's New International Dictionary 1707 (2d ed. 1958) ("to work; as, to operate a machine"). And in the organizational sense more obviously intended by CERCLA, the word ordinarily means "[t]o conduct the affairs of; manage: operate a business." American Heritage Dictionary, supra, at 1268; see also Webster's New International Dictionary, supra, at 1707 ("to manage"). So, under CERCLA, an operator is simply someone who directs the workings of, manages, or conducts the affairs of a facility. To sharpen the definition for purposes of CERCLA's concern with environmental contamination, an operator must manage, direct, or conduct operations specifically related to pollution, that is, operations having to do with the leakage or disposal of hazardous waste, or decisions about compliance with environmental regulations.

With this understanding, we are satisfied that the Court of Appeals correctly rejected the District Court's analysis of direct liability. But we also think that the appeals court erred in limiting direct liability under the statute to a parent's sole or joint venture operation, so as to eliminate any possible finding that CPC is liable as an operator on the facts of this case.

By emphasizing that "CPC is directly liable under section 107(a)(2) as an operator because CPC actively participated in and exerted significant control over Ott II's business and decision-making," the District Court applied the "actual control" test of whether the parent "actually operated the business of its subsidiary," as several Circuits have employed it.

The well-taken objection to the actual control test, however, is its fusion of direct and indirect liability; the test is administered by asking a question about the relationship between the two corporations (an issue going to indirect liability) instead of a question about the parent's interaction with the subsidiary's facility (the source of any direct liability). If, however, direct liability for the parent's operation of the facility is to be kept distinct from derivative liability for the subsidiary's own operation, the focus of the enquiry must necessarily be different under the two tests. "The question is not whether the parent operates the subsidiary, but rather whether it operates the facility, and that operation is evidenced by participation in the activities of the facility, not the subsidiary. Control of the subsidiary, if extensive enough, gives rise to indirect liability under piercing doctrine, not direct liability under the statutory language." Oswald 269. The District Court was therefore mistaken to rest its analysis on CPC's relationship with Ott II, premising liability on little more than "CPC's 100–percent ownership of Ott II" and "CPC's active participation in, and at times majority control over, Ott II's board of directors." [*CPC Int'l, Inc. v. Aerojet–General Corp.*, 777 F.Supp. 549, 572, 575 (W.D.Mich.1991)]. The analysis should instead have rested on the relationship between CPC and the Muskegon facility itself.

In addition to (and perhaps as a reflection of) the erroneous focus on the relationship between CPC and Ott II, even those findings of the District Court that might be taken to speak to the extent of CPC's activity at the facility itself are flawed, for the District Court wrongly assumed that the actions of the joint officers and directors are necessarily attributable to CPC. The District Court emphasized the facts that CPC placed its own high-level officials on Ott II's board of directors and in key management positions at Ott II, and that those individuals made major policy decisions and conducted day-to-day operations at the facility. . . .

In imposing direct liability on these grounds, the District Court failed to recognize that "it is entirely appropriate for directors of a parent corporation to serve as directors of its subsidiary, and that fact alone may not serve to expose the parent corporation to liability for its subsidiary's acts."

This recognition that the corporate personalities remain distinct has its corollary in the "well established principle [of corporate law] that directors and officers holding positions with a parent and its subsidiary can and do 'change hats' to represent the two corporations separately, despite their common ownership." Since courts generally presume "that the directors are wearing their 'subsidiary hats' and not their 'parent hats' when acting for the subsidiary," it cannot be enough to establish liability here that dual officers and directors made policy decisions and supervised activities at the facility. The Government would have to show that, despite the general presumption to the contrary, the officers and directors were acting in their capacities as CPC officers and directors, and not as Ott II officers and directors, when they committed those acts. . . . [13]

---

13. We do not attempt to recite the ways in which the Government could show that dual officers or directors were in fact acting on behalf of the parent. Here, it is prudent to say only that the presumption that an act is taken on behalf of the corporation for whom the officer claims to act is strongest when the act is perfectly consistent with the norms of corporate behavior, but wanes as the distance from those accepted norms approaches the point of action by a dual officer plainly contrary to the interests of the subsidiary yet nonetheless advantageous to the parent.

In sum, the District Court's focus on the relationship between parent and subsidiary (rather than parent and facility), combined with its automatic attribution of the actions of dual officers and directors to the corporate parent, erroneously ... treated CERCLA as though it displaced or fundamentally altered common law standards of limited liability. [If such were the case, there] would in essence be a relaxed, CERCLA-specific rule of derivative liability that would banish traditional standards and expectations from the law of CERCLA liability. But, as we have said, such a rule does not arise from congressional silence, and CERCLA's silence is dispositive.

We accordingly agree with the Court of Appeals that a participation-and-control test looking to the parent's supervision over the subsidiary, especially one that assumes that dual officers always act on behalf of the parent, cannot be used to identify operation of a facility resulting in direct parental liability. Nonetheless, a return to the ordinary meaning of the word "operate" in the organizational sense will indicate why we think that the Sixth Circuit stopped short when it confined its examples of direct parental operation to exclusive or joint ventures, and declined to find at least the possibility of direct operation by CPC in this case.

In our enquiry into the meaning Congress presumably had in mind when it used the verb "to operate," we recognized that the statute obviously meant something more than mere mechanical activation of pumps and valves, and must be read to contemplate "operation" as including the exercise of direction over the facility's activities. The Court of Appeals recognized this by indicating that a parent can be held directly liable when the parent operates the facility in the stead of its subsidiary or alongside the subsidiary in some sort of a joint venture. We anticipated a further possibility above, however, when we observed that a dual officer or director might depart so far from the norms of parental influence exercised through dual officeholding as to serve the parent, even when ostensibly acting on behalf of the subsidiary in operating the facility. Yet another possibility, suggested by the facts of this case, is that an agent of the parent with no hat to wear but the parent's hat might manage or direct activities at the facility.

Identifying such an occurrence calls for line drawing yet again, since the acts of direct operation that give rise to parental liability must necessarily be distinguished from the interference that stems from the normal relationship between parent and subsidiary. Again norms of corporate behavior ... are crucial reference points. Just as we may look to such norms in identifying the limits of the presumption that a dual officeholder acts in his ostensible capacity, so here we may refer to them in distinguishing a parental officer's oversight of a subsidiary from such an officer's control over the operation of the subsidiary's facility. "[A]c-tivities that involve the facility but which are consistent with the parent's investor status, such as monitoring of the subsidiary's perform-ance, supervision of the subsidiary's finance and capital budget decisions, and articulation of general policies and procedures, should not give rise to direct liability." Oswald 282. The critical question is whether, in degree and detail, actions directed to the facility by an agent of the parent alone are eccentric under accepted norms of parental oversight of a subsidiary's facility.

There is, in fact, some evidence that CPC engaged in just this type and degree of activity at the Muskegon plant. The District Court's opinion speaks of an agent of CPC alone who played a conspicuous part in dealing with the toxic risks emanating from the operation of the plant. G.R.D. Williams worked only for CPC; he was not an employee, officer, or director of Ott II, and thus, his actions were of necessity taken only on behalf of CPC. The District Court found that "CPC became directly involved in environmental and regulatory matters through the work of . . . Williams, CPC's governmental and environmental affairs director. Williams . . . became heavily involved in environmental issues at Ott II." 777 F. Supp., at 561. He "actively participated in and exerted control over a variety of Ott II environmental matters," ibid., and he "issued directives regarding Ott II's responses to regulatory inquiries," id., at 575.

We think that these findings are enough to raise an issue of CPC's operation of the facility through Williams's actions, though we would draw no ultimate conclusion from these findings at this point. Not only would we be deciding in the first instance an issue on which the trial and appellate courts did not focus, but the very fact that the District Court did not see the case as we do suggests that there may be still more to be known about Williams's activities. Indeed, even as the factual findings stand, the trial court offered little in the way of concrete detail for its conclusions about Williams's role in Ott II's environmental affairs, and the parties vigorously dispute the extent of Williams's involvement. Prudence thus counsels us to remand, on the theory of direct operation set out here, for reevaluation of Williams's role, and of the role of any other CPC agent who might be said to have had a part in operating the Muskegon facility.

Notes and Questions

1. Under what circumstances did the Supreme Court determine that CPC might bear direct liability in *Bestfoods*? Did it require that CPC be found to have participated in the pollution-causing activities? That it was involved in environmental decision-making at the underlying facility? That it exercised a more general form of operational control over activities at the underlying facility? That it exercised some degree of operational supervision over Ott II in general (even if not with respect to the day-to-day activities at the relevant facility)? That it had the capacity to control either the operations or the environmental decisions at the underlying facility? Did you agree with the Court's approach? Why or why not?

2. If *Bestfoods* requires some degree of involvement in one of the above categories of activities, how much involvement is required? Is mere participation enough? Or does the parent's representative have to have issued directives or exercised decision-making authority? Why did the Supreme

Court determine that a remand was necessary? On remand, the lower court found these facts with respect to Mr. Williams:

> ... Williams was a lawyer who coordinated air and water pollution programs for CPC. From 1966 through 1972, he drafted or was copied on numerous CPC environmental documents. Beginning in 1966, he was involved with the Muskegon facility of Ott II, upon the recommendation of dual-director Harold Hellman.

> While Williams never visited the site, he consulted with Ott II officers concerning Ott II's responses to environmental agency surveys. In September 1966, he attended one meeting with the Michigan Water Resource Commission, together with Ott II officials. Prior to that meeting, Williams advised Ott II representatives not to tell the MWRC about the opinion of Ott II's engineering consultants that a biological treatment facility may be required in future. Williams generally advised Ott II to delay as much as possible the making of capital expenditures.

> The record reflects, however, that, despite Williams' recommendations, Ott II officials shared with the MWRC the recommendations of their engineering consultants shortly after the September meeting. The report was discussed at the November 10, 1966 meeting with the MWRC. Thereafter, on November 18, 1966, the Ott II board approved $375,000 for completion of the first phases of the engineering plan and so advised the MWRC, contrary to the recommendation of Williams, who sought to delay all expenditures until 1968. Since none of Ott II's engineers recommended biological treatment or additional incinerators or deep well in 1966, Ott's decision not to seek or approve funds for such treatment in 1966 cannot be viewed as being caused by Williams' advice.

> Taken together, the record reflects that while Williams may have advocated that Ott II delay implementation of waste treatment plans, his advice was rejected. Although delays in discharge compliance eventually occurred, and although the biological treatment facility was never built, those delays are not shown to have resulted from any influence Williams may have had on Ott II at the September 1966 meeting. Instead, they reflect the Ott II decision to connect to the county waste water treatment system, and the record contains no evidence that Williams was involved in that decision.

Bestfoods v. Aerojet–General Corp., 173 F.Supp.2d 729, 749 (W.D. Mich. 2001). Based on these findings, the court found the record "far too thin to conclude that Williams was responsible for any delays in compliance," *id.* at 750, and that "his limited involvement with the MWRC in 1966 is not consistent with the control of Ott II," *id.* The court went on to conclude that the government had not established that CPC's activities gave rise to "operator" status.

For purposes of comparison, in *United States v. Kayser–Roth Corp.*, 272 F.3d 89 (1st Cir. 2001), the First Circuit reaffirmed its finding of parent liability upon determining that the parent's representative "played a central role in decisions about environmental compliance" at the relevant facility. Id. at 104. And in *City of Wichita, Kansas v. Trustees of the APCO Oil Corp. Liquidating Trust*, 306 F.Supp.2d 1040, 1055 (D.Kan. 2003) (*City of Wichita*), the court found that "an operator ... must make the relevant decisions on a frequent, typically day-to-day basis." The court found this standard satisfied where there was uncontroverted testimony that the relevant corporate president was present at weekly management meetings at which environmental compliance issues were discussed, and that no decisions were made at those meetings without the president's approval. Id. at 1055–1056. Are these decisions consistent with each other? If not, which do you find to be more in line with *Bestfoods*?

3. Is the Supreme Court's discussion of operator liability relevant to entities other than parent corporations? In *City of Wichita*, the court assumed the *Bestfoods* approach also applies to individuals such as corporate officers. See also *Browning–Ferris Indus. of Illinois, Inc. v. Ter Maat*, 195 F.3d 953 (7th Cir. 1999) (accord). If *Bestfoods* indicates that corporate officers will only bear CERCLA liability if they involve themselves in environmental decision-making, does the Court's opinion bear the risk of encouraging these officers to delegate all such decisions to their underlings? Is this sound policy?

4. The issue of individual liability under CERCLA appears to have arisen mostly (perhaps solely) in the context of a closely-held corporations. Is CERCLA's text limited to imposing liability only upon officers or employees of closely-held firms? Are the policy justifications for imposing liability enhanced in this context? Why do you think there is little or no case law involving entities such as General Electric's vice-president in charge of environmental operations, its environmental compliance managers, or its environmental supervisors at each G.E. facility? At a pragmatic level, the most significant difference between these situations and those involving closely-held corporations is that, assuming liability, companies like G.E. are likely to be both willing and able to assume whatever share of liability they are deemed to be "responsible" for at any given site. But is there a legal difference? If you represented G.E.'s compliance manager, how would you assess his or her exposure under CERCLA for the liabilities G.E. has incurred based upon activities occurring during his or her tenure in that position? Would your assessment vary if bankruptcy of the corporation was a potential concern? Would in-house lawyers who give legal advice be immune from liability? What about outside counsel? Assume now that you represent EPA. Is there any reason, even outside the bankruptcy context, why you might want to sue some officers or mid-level managers from large corporations? If you did, might it discourage capable and environmentally-concerned individuals from accepting such positions? Is this enough of a reason not to do so?

5. What instructions did the Supreme Court provide for how lower courts should address the so-called "dual officer" problem, where the same individual might be an officer for both the parent corporation and its subsidiary? Is this approach satisfactory?

6. What application would the Supreme Court's approach to "operator" liability have, if any, with respect to someone who operated or is currently operating a completely non-polluting business on a contaminated site? Is there such thing as a business that never engages in environmental decision-making? Imagine, for example, that a bookstore leases a contaminated site. Assuming it played no role in causing the contamination, would it

qualify as a current "operator" under § 107(a)(1)? If not, does this suggest a problem with the Court's analysis? Alternatively, does the term "operator" itself provide a basis for distinguishing between some types of lessees and others with regard to the extent to which they may be subject to causation-free liability under § 107(a)(1)?

7. What if EPA had written a rule specifying the situations in which it felt that parent corporations and corporate officers or employees should bear "direct" operator liability under CERCLA? Is this a situation in which EPA's views would be entitled to deference? The D.C. Circuit addressed this question in *Kelley v. EPA*, 15 F.3d 1100 (D.C. Cir. 1994), in which the State of Michigan challenged EPA's authority to issue regulations purporting to govern the situations in which lenders would bear liability under CERCLA. The court determined that "Congress meant the judiciary, not EPA, to determine liability issues." It further explained that:

> ... "A precondition to deference under *Chevron* is a congressional delegation of administrative authority." [*Adams Fruit Co. v. Barrett*, 494 U.S. 638, 649 (1990)]. *Chevron*, which sets forth the reigning rationale for judicial deference to agency interpretation of statutes, is premised on the notion that Congress implicitly delegated to the agency the authority to reconcile reasonably statutory ambiguities or to fill reasonably statutory interstices. Where Congress does not give an agency authority to determine (usually formally) the interpretation of a statute in the first instance and instead gives the agency authority only to bring the question to a federal court as the "prosecutor," deference to the agency's interpretation is inappropriate....

Id. Interestingly, EPA did not seek Supreme Court review of the *Kelley* decision. Moreover, it does not appear to have written any rules since then interpreting CERCLA's liability provisions. Why do you think EPA has acquiesced (at least implicitly) in the *Kelley* result? Should EPA have the authority to promulgate legislative rules interpreting § 107? What other ambiguities in that section would EPA have been able to address through rulemaking if it had prevailed in *Kelley*? Would EPA be able to "correct" any adverse judicial opinions on an after-the-fact basis? In the mid–1990s, EPA sought a legislative "fix" regarding the scope of its rulemaking authority under CERCLA in the Superfund Reauthorization process. Some of the bills Congress considered in 1994 provided EPA with the authority that the D.C. Circuit found lacking in *Kelley*.

8. Before *Bestfoods* there was a split of sorts in the Circuits regarding whether courts should look to state or federal common law in resolving veil-piercing issues. Most courts had determined that they should apply principles of federal common law, see, e.g., *Lansford–Coaldale Joint Water Auth. v. Tonolli Corp.*, 4 F.3d 1209, 1221 (3d Cir. 1993) (in the context of parent liability), and *B.F. Goodrich v. Betkoski*, 99 F.3d 505, 519 (2d Cir. 1996), *cert. den. sub nom Zollo Drum Co., Inc. v. B.F. Goodrich Co.*, 524 U.S. 926, 118 S.Ct. 2318, 141 L.Ed.2d 694 (1998) and *Louisiana–Pacific Corp. v. Asarco, Inc.*, 909 F.2d 1260, 1263 (9th Cir. 1990) (both in the context of successor liability), but at least two Circuits had found that it would look to principles of state law, *Donahey v. Bogle*, 129 F.3d 838, 843 (6th Cir. 1997), *vacated on other grounds*, 524 U.S. 924, 118 S.Ct. 2317, 141 L.Ed.2d 692 (1998),

reinstated 16 Fed.Appx. 283 (6th Cir. 2000) (successor liability), and *Redwing Carriers, Inc. v. Saraland Apartments*, 94 F.3d 1489, 1500–1502 (11th Cir. 1996) (limited partnership). What, if anything, did the Supreme Court indicate about this issue? How should lower courts react to the Court's opinion in this regard?

9. Note that, in footnote 10, the Court specifically recognized that veil-piercing may transcend the "ownership" liability realm. There, the court speaks (in *dicta*) to parent corporations that pervasively control subsidiaries that would only qualify as "operators" under CERCLA. Would the same logic apply to the parents of those subsidiaries that qualify as "arrangers for disposal" under § 107(a)(3)? See *Carter-Jones Lumber Co. v. Dixie Distributing Co.*, 166 F.3d 840, 846 (6th Cir. 1999). As the *Bestfoods* Court points out in context of operator liability, this is a different question than would be posed if we were asking whether the parent qualified as an "arranger" in its own right. Do you understand the distinction?

10. The issue of lender liability under CERCLA, mentioned in note 7 above, had a controversial life for some time, but has receded in the wake of legislative changes. From the outset, CERCLA's definition of definition of "owner or operator" has provided an exemption for those who own property to protect their security interests, so long as they refrain from "participat[ing] in the management" of those facilities. 42 U.S.C. § 9601(20). As originally drafted, however, the statute left key questions unresolved. Two issues in particular proved vexing: What types of lender oversight would be deemed to constitute the type of "participat[ion] in ... management" that voided the defense? And second, under what circumstances, if any, could a lender foreclose on its security interest without losing its statutory protection? Notably, in *United States v. Fleet Factors Corp.*, 901 F.2d 1550 (11th Cir. 1990), the Eleventh Circuit determined that lenders could incur liability "by participating in the financial management of a facility to a degree indicating a capacity to influence the corporation's treatment of hazardous wastes." *Id.* at 1557. It further opined that "a secured creditor will be liable if its involvement with the management of the facility is sufficiently broad to support the inference that it could affect hazardous waste disposal decisions if it so chose." *Id.* at 1558. This decision created a backlash, resulting first in EPA's efforts to back-pedal by writing a lender-friendly rule, which the D.C. Circuit then invalidated in *Kelley*. Ultimately, however, Congress essentially codified EPA's rule by passing the Asset Conservation, Lender Liability, and Deposit Insurance Protection Act of 1996 as a rider to the Omnibus Consolidated Appropriations Act. Pub. L. No. 104–208, §§ 2501–2505. Lenders will rarely face direct liability under these new provisions. See 42 U.S.C. § 9601(20)(E) and (F).

b. Arrangers for Disposal or Treatment

As previously mentioned, § 107(a)(3) imposes liability on those who "arranged for disposal or treatment" of any hazardous substances at the relevant facility. Most typically, this provision serves to impose liability on the so-called "generators" of the waste; that is, the companies that generated the particular substances that came to be located at the relevant site. The following case, while decided quite early in the

CERCLA era, contains what probably remains the best treatment to date of the elements of generator liability under § 107(a)(3):

UNITED STATES v. WADE

United States District Court, Eastern District of Pennsylvania, 1983.

577 F.Supp. 1326.

NEWCOMER, DISTRICT JUDGE

[This case involved the "Wade" site in Chester, Pennsylvania. In addition to suing the property owner and others, the government also sought reimbursement of the costs incurred and to be incurred in cleaning up the site from Apollo Metals, Inc., Congoleum Corporation, Gould, Inc. and Sandvik, Inc. ("generator defendants").]

The generator defendants ... argue that the government has not and cannot establish the requisite causal relationship between their wastes and the costs incurred by the government in cleaning up the site.

In a nutshell, the generator defendants' causation argument is as follows. To establish liability under the Act the government must prove a link, or more specifically a causal nexus, between costs incurred in clean-up and a given generator's waste. The argument is based on traditional tort concepts of proximate causation. The generator defendants first argue that the government has no admissible evidence that their wastes were in fact disposed of at the Wade site. The government agrees that actual dumping of a defendant's waste at the Wade site is an element of its case but urges that its evidence on this issue is not only admissible but also dispositive.

[The court first determined that the issues regarding whether each generator's wastes in fact wound up at the Wade site would have to be resolved at trial.]

Even assuming the government proves that a given defendant's waste was in fact disposed of at the Wade site, the generator defendants argue it must also prove that a particular defendant's actual waste is presently at the site and has been the subject of a removal or remedial measure before that defendant can be held liable. In the alternative, the generator defendants argue that at a minimum the government must link its costs incurred to waste of the sort created by a generator before that generator may be held liable. This argument in part overlaps the defendants' argument pertaining to recoverable damages. Based on my reading of the Act, I must reject both causation requirements urged by the generator defendants.

The liability provision of CERCLA provides in relevant part as follows:

Notwithstanding any other provision or rule of law, and subject only to the defenses set forth in subsection (b) of this section— ...

(3) Any person who by contract, agreement, or otherwise arranged for disposal or treatment or arranged with a transporter
for transport for disposal or treatment of hazardous substances
owned or possessed by such person, by any other party or
entity, at any facility owned or operated by another party or
entity and containing *such* hazardous substances ... (4) ...
from which there is a release, or a threatened release which
causes the incurrence of response costs, of *a* hazardous substance, shall be liable for—

(A) All costs of removal or remedial action incurred by the
United States Government or a state not inconsistent with the
national contingency plan."

42 U.S.C. § 9607(a)(emphasis added). At one extreme the Act could be
read to impose liability on certain parties who merely arrange for
transport of their waste but never actually do so. I do not understand
the government to urge such a construction and would reject it. I
mention the possibility only to underscore the lack of precision with
which the statute was drafted.

Part of the generator defendants' argument revolves around the use
of the word "such" in referring to the "hazardous substances" contained
at the dump site or "facility." It could be read to require that the facility
contain a particular defendant's waste. On the other hand it could be
read merely to require that hazardous substances like those found in a
defendant's waste must be present at the site. The legislative history
provides no enlightenment on this point. I believe that the less stringent
requirement was the one intended by Congress.

The government's experts have admitted that scientific technique
has not advanced to a point that the identity of the generator of a
specific quantity of waste can be stated with certainty. All that can be
said is that a site contains the same kind of hazardous substances as are
found in a generator's waste. Thus, to require a plaintiff under CERCLA
to "fingerprint" wastes is to eviscerate the statute. Given two possible
constructions of a statute, one which renders it useless should be
rejected. Generators are adequately protected by requiring a plaintiff to
prove that a defendant's waste was disposed of at a site and that the
substances that make the defendant's waste hazardous are also present
at the site.

Besides eviscerating the statute the generator defendant's contention would lead to ludicrous results. For example, assuming wastes could
be "fingerprinted," once all the hazardous substances in a generator's
waste had migrated from the "facility" the generator could no longer be
held liable. In fact, one generator makes this argument.

I turn now to the generator defendants' contention that the government must link its costs incurred to wastes of the sort created by them.

A reading of the literal language of the statute suggests that the
generator defendants read too much into this portion of its causation

requirement. Stripping away the excess language, the statute appears to impose liability on a generator who has (1) disposed of its hazardous substances (2) at a facility which now contains hazardous substances of the sort disposed of by the generator (3) if there is a release of that or some other type of hazardous substance (4) which causes the incurrence of response costs. Thus, the release which results in the incurrence of response costs and liability need only be of "*a*" hazardous substance and not necessarily one contained in the defendant's waste. The only required nexus between the defendant and the site is that the defendant have dumped his waste there and that the hazardous substances found in the defendant's waste are also found at the site. I base my disagreement with defendants' reading in part on the Act's use of "such" to modify "hazardous substance" in paragraph three and the switch to "a" in paragraph four.

Additional support for my reading may also be found in the legislative history of the Act. The original House Committee bill imposed liability on "any person who caused or contributed to the release." H.R. 7020, 96th Cong., 2d Sess., § 3071(a)(1), 126 Cong. Rec. at H9459 (daily ed. September 23, 1980). Although the committee bill was changed in several important respects by the full House, this language was also contained in the final House-passed version. Id. at H9479. This language clearly requires a causal nexus between a generator and the release causing the incurrence of response costs, and the House Committee understood it to do so[. Citing an early House Report]. The problem with the generator defendants' reliance on this report, however, is that the liability provision which was ultimately enacted bears no real resemblance to the House-passed bill to which the report refers. Instead, the legislation enacted specifies certain groups which will be held liable when a release of a hazardous substance causes the incurrence of clean-up costs. One of those groups is those who have disposed of hazardous substances at the site if hazardous substances of that sort are present at the site.

Deletion of the causation language contained in the House-passed bill and the Senate draft is not dispositive of the causation issue. Nevertheless, the substitution of the present language for the prior causation requirement evidences a legislative intent which is in accordance with my reading of the Act.

Notes and Questions

1. What did the *Wade* court mean when it required, as its first element of generator liability, that CERCLA plaintiffs establish that a given generator's wastes were in fact "disposed of" at the site? Do plaintiffs need to show that each generator's wastes were in fact dumped or otherwise disposed of onto the ground? Alternatively, may a given generator be held liable without any showing that its wastes were part of the release that triggered the need for cleanup? Or even that its wastes came into contact with any soils or groundwater? What if a generator can show that none of its drums ever leaked or otherwise caused any releases. Cf. CERCLA § 107(b)(3).

2. Restating its holding slightly, the *Wade* court essentially determined that CERCLA plaintiffs must establish four elements in order to impose liability on a given generator. They must show (1) that the relevant generator has arranged for the disposal or treatment of hazardous substances (2) at a facility which now contains hazardous substances of a type similar to those sent by the generator (3) and that there is a release or threatened release of that or some other type of hazardous substance (4) which causes the incurrence of response costs. Do you agree with the court's determination that CERCLA plaintiffs need not even establish that there are wastes like those of the generator in the release at issue? What is the effect of this ruling?

3. Is the *Wade* interpretation the most defensible reading of the statute, or was the court overly influenced by the difficulties of proof that would pertain under any other causation test? At least two appellate courts have agreed with the *Wade* causation analysis. *United States v. Monsanto*, 858 F.2d 160, 167–69 (4th Cir.1988), *cert. denied*, 490 U.S. 1106, 109 S.Ct. 3156, 104 L.Ed.2d 1019 (1989); *United States v. Alcan Aluminum Corp.*, 964 F.2d 252, 264–66 (3d Cir.1992). Should the standard change if science advances to the point where the government is able to "fingerprint" wastes with more precision?

4. What should be required before a given generator is found to have "arrange[d] for disposal . . . at any facility . . . containing such substances?" Should EPA be required to show that the defendant selected the relevant site? The courts universally have determined that a given generator need not have selected the relevant site in order to be held liable if its wastes wound up there. Can this result be squared with the statutory language? Why have the courts been so adamant on this point? See *United States v. Ward*, 618 F.Supp. 884, 895 (E.D.N.C.1985)("To [require a showing of such knowledge] would allow generators of hazardous waste to escape liability under CERCLA by closing their eyes to the method in which their wastes were disposed of"). Is this logic compelling?

5. At a minimum, *Wade* appears to require EPA to demonstrate that each particular generator's wastes in fact arrived at the relevant facility. What if hundreds of generators send their waste to one facility, which then sporadically commingles the wastes and redirects them to numerous other facilities? Will each of the original generators be jointly and severally liable for cleanup at all of the "remote" sites? Is there some preliminary showing EPA should be required to make regarding the likelihood of each particular generator's wastes having wound up at each remote site, as a precondition to imposing liability? See *United States v. Bliss*, 667 F.Supp. 1298 (E.D.Mo. 1987) (holding the generators liable for each remote site on the theory that at least trace amounts of their waste were likely in the mixtures delivered to each site). What if the wastes were not physically commingled, but the operator of the original facility distributed the wastes to the remote sites without keeping any records of whose wastes were going where? Should the same rule obtain?

6. How should the issue of "direct" liability for parent corporations and individuals play out in the context of "arranger" liability under § 107(a)(3)? In a pre-*Bestfoods* case, the Eighth Circuit determined that

CERCLA imposes different liability tests regarding parent corporations in the "operator" and "arranger for disposal" contexts:

> ... The critical distinction between operator liability under [§ 107(a)(2)] and arranger liability under [§ 107(a)(3)], for purposes of this parent corporation liability analysis, is that subsection (a)(2) requires only that the person operate the facility where disposal occurs at the time of disposal; by contrast, subsection (a)(3) requires that the person arrange for the disposal, treatment, or transportation for disposal or treatment. Therefore, while a parent corporation need only have the authority to control, and exercise actual or substantial control, over the operations of its subsidiary in order to incur direct liability for the subsidiary's on-site disposal practices, we believe that, in order for a parent corporation to incur direct arranger liability for a subsidiary's off-site disposal practices, there must be some causal connection or nexus between the parent corporation's conduct and the subsidiary's arrangement for disposal, or the off-site disposal itself.

United States v. TIC Investment Corp., 68 F.3d 1082, 1091–92 (8th Cir.1995) Does this distinction make sense? Does it survive *Bestfoods*?

7. Under what circumstances, if any, should the sale of a hazardous substance, or of a material or product containing hazardous substances, be deemed to constitute an "arrange[ment] for disposal" under § 107(a)(3)? There seem to be two lines of cases in this area. First, there are cases in which a company sells something that has been through its primary intended use, but which may have residual value to someone else (e.g., a recycler). In these cases, the court have typically deemed these sales to be arrangements for disposal. See, e.g., *Catellus Development Corp. v. United States*, 34 F.3d 748 (9th Cir.1994) (defendant sold spent automotive batteries to a lead reclamation facility), and *New York v. General Electric Co.*, 592 F.Supp. 291 (N.D.N.Y.1984) (defendant sold contaminated waste oil to a drag strip for use as a dust suppressant). In 1999, Congress passed a rider exempting certain recycling transactions from the scope of § 107(a)(3). See 42 U.S.C. § 9627. Take a look at that provision. Does it strike an appropriate balance? See also *Pneumo Abex Corp. v. High Point, Thomasville and Denton Railroad Co.*, 142 F.3d 769 (4th Cir. 1998). The second line of cases involves situations in which someone sells a virgin product that they know will at some point release hazardous substances into the environment. The leading case here is *Florida Power & Light Co. v. Allis Chalmers Corp.*, 893 F.2d 1313 (11th Cir. 1990). While declining to establish a per se rule of non-liability, the Eleventh Circuit in that case found that the plaintiffs had "not met their burden of demonstrating that the transactions involved anything more than a mere sale" in a situation in which the defendants had sold transformers that one of the plaintiffs had used for 40 years before disposing of them. Id. at 1319. Are there situations in which the initial sale of a manufactured product should give rise to liability? What if a timber company sells railroad ties impregnated with pentachlorophenol, creosote and other hazardous substances, knowing that these substances are likely to leach out into the environment? Compare CERCLA § 107(i) (exempting the application of registered pesticides from CERCLA's liability scheme).

8. The Eighth Circuit issued perhaps the most far-reaching "arranger" liability case to date in *United States v. Aceto Agricultural Chemicals Corp.*, 872 F.2d 1373 (8th Cir. 1989). In that case, the court determined that EPA had stated a claim upon which relief could be granted when it sued six pesticide manufacturers who had hired another company to formulate their technical grade pesticides into commercial grade pesticides. The court found it particularly relevant that the manufacturers retained title to the pesticides throughout the formulation process, and that the generation of waste was inherent in the process. It rejected the defendants' arguments that they hired the formulator to formulate, not to dispose, and that had no ability to control the formulator's operational or disposal activities. Do you agree with this result? Interestingly, almost as an afterthought, the Eight Circuit indicated that the district court had not erred in applying the common law "abnormally dangerous activities" doctrine as a basis for imposing vicarious liability on the manufacturers. Should this doctrine have any sway under CERCLA? If so, what are its implications?

2. Scope of Liability

We already have seen that the courts have interpreted CERCLA as imposing both strict and retroactive liability, despite the Act's silence on those points. We now turn to the scope of the liability CERCLA imposes. Here also, the statute is silent on its face. Despite this silence, however, the courts have had little difficulty in determining that CERCLA generally imposes joint and several liability, though it does not mandate its imposition in all cases. We begin our discussion of when and how the doctrine applies under CERCLA with the two leading cases in this area:

UNITED STATES v. CHEM–DYNE CORP.

United States District Court, Southern District of Ohio, 1983.
572 F.Supp. 802.

CARL B. RUBIN, Chief Judge.

... In order to expedite discovery and trial preparation, the defendants have moved for an early determination that they are not jointly and severally liable for the cleanup costs at Chem–Dyne.

The liability section lists the classes of persons potentially liable under the Act for the costs incurred by government removal or remedial action. In contrast to plaintiff's assertion that joint and several liability is clear from the express statutory language, the Court finds the language ambiguous with regard to the scope of liability. Consequently, in an attempt to discern the Congressional intent, the Court will review and weigh the legislative history of the Act.

As background, two different superfund bills proceeded simultaneously through the House and Senate. On November 24, 1980, the Senate made its final amendment to its bill, thereby eliminating the term strict, joint and several liability from its provisions. Subsequently, on December 3, 1980, the House struck the language in its bill and substituted the language of the Senate bill, which was later enacted. The defendants quote at length from Senator Helms' speech:

> Retention of joint and several liability in S. 1480 received intense and well-deserved criticism from a number of sources, since it could impose financial responsibility for massive costs and damages awards on persons who contributed only minimally (if at all) to a release or injury. Joint and several liability for costs and damages was especially pernicious in S. 1480, not only because of the exceedingly broad categories of persons subject to liability and the wide array of damages available, but also because it was coupled with an industry-based fund. Those contributing to the fund will frequently be paying for conditions they had no responsibility in creating or even contributing to. To adopt a joint and several liability scheme on top of this would have been grossly unfair.

> The drafters of the Stafford Randolph substitute have recognized this unfairness, and the lack of wisdom in eliminating any meaningful link between culpable conduct and financial responsibility. Consequently, all references to joint and several liability in the bill have been deleted ...

> It is very clear from the language of the Stafford Randolph substitute itself, from the legislative history, and from the liability provisions of section 311 of the Federal Water Pollution Control Act, that now the Stafford Randolph bill does not in and of itself create joint and several liability.

This view of statutory construction is at odds with the guidelines provided by the Supreme Court. Senator Helms was an opponent of the bill. Accordingly, his statements are entitled to little weight in construing the statute.

Senator Stafford, sponsor of the bill, succinctly noted that there was an elimination of the term joint and several liability as well as an elimination of the scope of liability. Senator Randolph, sponsor, explained the significance of these modifications:

> We have kept strict liability in the compromise, specifying the standard of liability under section 311 of the Clean Water Act, but we have deleted any reference to joint and several liability, relying on common law principles to determine when parties should be severally liable ... The changes were made in recognition of the difficulty in prescribing in statutory terms liability standards which will be applicable in individual cases. The changes do not reflect a rejection of the standards in the earlier bill.

* * *

> It is intended that issues of liability not resolved by this act, if any, shall be governed by traditional and evolving principles of common law. An example is joint and several liability. Any reference to these terms has been deleted, and the liability of joint tortfeasors will be determined under common or previous statutory law.

[The court also quoted similar statements from Representatives Florio and Waxman.]

Statements of the legislation's sponsors are properly accorded substantial weight in interpreting the statute, although the remarks of a single legislator are not controlling. The fact that the term joint and several liability was deleted from a prior draft of the bill or that the term liability refers to the standard under 33 U.S.C. § 1321, in and of itself, is not dispositive of the scope of liability under CERCLA. . . . A reading of the entire legislative history in context reveals that the scope of liability and term joint and several liability were deleted to avoid a mandatory legislative standard applicable in all situations which might produce inequitable results in some cases. The deletion was not intended as a rejection of joint and several liability. Rather, the term was omitted in order to have the scope of liability determined under common law principles, where a court performing a case by case evaluation of the complex factual scenarios associated with multiple-generator waste sites will assess the propriety of applying joint and several liability on an individual basis.

Because the legislative history evinces the intent that the scope of liability under [§ 107] be determined from traditional and evolving principles of common law, the next issue becomes whether state or federal common law should be applied. In situations where, as here, there is a lack of an express statutory provision selecting state or federal law, the inevitable incompleteness presented by all legislation means that interstitial federal lawmaking is a basic responsibility of the federal courts. . . .

State law as a rule of decision is not mandated under the *Erie* doctrine in this case because it falls within the exception provided for federal laws. 28 U.S.C. § 1652; *Erie v. Tompkins*, 304 U.S. 64, (1938). Although *Erie* eliminated the power of federal courts to create federal general common law, the power to fashion federal specialized common law remains untouched when it is "necessary to protect uniquely federal interests."

The improper disposal or release of hazardous substances is an enormous and complex problem of national magnitude involving uniquely federal interests. Typically, an abandoned waste site will consist of waste produced by companies in several states within the area or region. The pollution of land, groundwater, surface water and air as a consequence of this dumping presents potentially interstate problems. A driving force toward the development of CERCLA was the recognition that a response to this pervasive condition at the state level was generally inadequate. . . . Additionally, the superfund monies expended, for which the United States seeks reimbursement, are funded by general revenues and excise taxes. The degree to which the United States will be able to protect its financial interest in the trust fund is directly related to the scope of liability under CERCLA and is in no way dependent upon the laws of any state. When the United States derives its authority for reimbursement from the specific Act of Congress passed in the exercise of a constitutional function or power, its rights should also derive from federal common law. In conclusion, the rights, liabilities and responsibilities of the United States under [§ 107] are governed by a federal rule of decision.

The question now becomes whether the scope of liability should be interpreted according to the incorporated state law of the forum state or a federally created uniform law. This determination is a matter of judicial policy dependent upon a variety of considerations relevant to the nature of the specific governmental interests and to the effects upon them of applying state law. Federal programs that by their nature are and must be uniform in character throughout the nation necessitate the formulation of federal rules of decision. CERCLA is such a federal program.... A liability standard which varies in the different forum states would undermine the policies of the statute by encouraging illegal dumping in states with lax liability laws. There is no good reason why the United States' right to reimbursement should be subjected to the needless uncertainty and subsequent delay occasioned by diversified local disposition when this matter is appropriate for uniform national treatment.

Finding, then, that the delineation of a uniform federal rule of decision is consistent with the legislative history and policies of CERCLA and finding further that no compelling local interests mandate the incorporation of state law, a determination of the content of the federal rule is the final step in the analysis. Federal statutes dealing with similar subject matter are a prime repository of federal policy on a subject and a starting point for ascertaining federal common law. Neither statutes nor decisions of a particular state can be conclusive when fashioning federal law.

Typically, as in this case, there will be numerous hazardous substance generators or transporters who have disposed of wastes at a particular site. The term joint and several liability was deleted from the express language of the statute in order to avoid its universal application to inappropriate circumstances. An examination of the common law reveals that when two or more persons acting independently caused a distinct or single harm for which there is a reasonable basis for division according to the contribution of each, each is subject to liability only for the portion of the total harm that he has himself caused. Restatement (Second) of Torts §§ 433A, 881 (1976). But where two or more persons cause a single and indivisible harm, each is subject to liability for the entire harm. Furthermore, where the conduct of two or more persons liable under [§ 107] has combined to violate the statute, and one or more of the defendants seeks to limit his liability on the ground that the entire harm is capable of apportionment, the burden of proof as to apportionment is upon each defendant. These rules clearly enumerate the analysis to be undertaken when applying [§ 107] and are most likely to advance the legislative policies and objectives of the Act.

The question of whether the defendants are jointly or severally liable for the clean-up costs turns on a fairly complex factual determination. Read in the light most favorable to the plaintiff, the following facts illustrate the nature of the problem. The Chem–Dyne facility contains a variety of hazardous waste from 289 generators or transporters, consisting of about 608,000 pounds of material. Some of the wastes have commingled but the identities of the sources of these wastes remain unascertained. The fact of the mixing of the wastes raises an issue as to the divisibility of the harm. Further, a dispute exists over which of the wastes have contaminated the ground water, the degree of their migration and concomitant health hazard. Finally, the volume of waste of a particular generator is not an accurate predictor of the risk associated with the waste because the toxicity or migratory potential of a particular hazardous substance generally varies independently with the volume of the waste.

Because there are genuine issues of material fact concerning the divisibility of the harm and any potential apportionment, the defendants are not entitled to judgment as a matter of law.

O'NEIL v. PICILLO

United States Court of Appeals, First Circuit, 1989.

883 F.2d 176, *cert. denied*, 493 U.S. 1071, 110
S.Ct. 1115, 107 L.Ed.2d 1022 (1990).

COFFIN, SENIOR CIRCUIT JUDGE

[In 1977, the Picillo family agreed to allow part of their pig farm in Coventry, Rhode Island to be used as a disposal site for drummed and bulk waste. Thousands of barrels of hazardous waste were dumped on the farm, culminating in a major fire caused by the improper storage of incompatible wastes. In 1979, the state and EPA jointly undertook to clean up the area. What they found, in the words of the district court, were massive trenches and pits "filled with free-flowing, multi-colored, pungent liquid wastes" and thousands of "dented and corroded drums containing a veritable potpourri of toxic fluids."

The State of Rhode Island sued to recover the cleanup costs it incurred between 1979 and 1982 and to hold the responsible parties liable for all future costs associated with the site. The state's complaint originally named thirty-five defendants, all but five of whom eventually entered into settlements totalling $5.8 million, the money to be shared by the state and EPA. After a month-long bench trial, the district court found three of the remaining five companies jointly and severally liable for all past costs not covered by the settlement agreements, as well as for all future cleanup costs. Two of the three generators held liable at trial, American Cyanamid and Rohm and Haas, appealed, contending that their contribution to the disaster was insubstantial and that it was, therefore, unfair to hold them jointly and severally liable for all of the state's past expenses not covered by settlements.]

It is by now well settled that Congress intended that the federal courts develop a uniform approach governing the use of joint and several liability in CERCLA actions. The rule adopted by the majority of courts, and the one we adopt, is based on the Restatement (Second) of Torts: damages should be apportioned only if the defendant can demonstrate that the harm is divisible.

The practical effect of placing the burden on defendants has been that responsible parties rarely escape joint and several liability, courts regularly finding that where wastes of varying (and unknown) degrees of toxicity and migratory potential commingle, it simply is impossible to determine the amount of environmental harm caused by each party. It has not gone unnoticed that holding defendants jointly and severally liable in such situations may often result in defendants paying for more than their share of the harm. Nevertheless, courts have continued to impose joint and several liability on a regular basis, reasoning that where all of the contributing causes cannot fairly be traced, Congress intended for those proven at least partially culpable to bear the cost of the uncertainty.

In enacting [SARA], Congress had occasion to examine this case law. Rather than add a provision dealing explicitly with joint and several liability, it chose to leave the issue with the courts, to be resolved as it had been—on a case by case basis according to the predominant "divisibility" rule first enunciated by the *Chem–Dyne* court. Congress did, however, add two important provisions designed to mitigate the harshness of joint and several liability. First, the 1986 Amendments direct the EPA to offer early settlements to defendants who the Agency believes are responsible for only a small portion of the harm, so-called *de minimis* settlements. See § 122(g). Second, the Amendments provide for a statutory cause of action in contribution, codifying what most courts had concluded was implicit in the 1980 Act. See § 113(f)(1). Under this section, courts "may allocate response costs among liable parties using such equitable factors as the court determines are appropriate."

While a right of contribution undoubtedly softens the blow where parties cannot prove that the harm is divisible, it is not a complete panacea since it frequently will be difficult for defendants to locate a sufficient number of additional, solvent parties. Moreover, there are significant transaction costs involved in bringing other responsible parties to court. If it were possible to locate all responsible parties and to do so with little cost, the issue of joint and several liability obviously would be of only marginal significance. We, therefore, must examine carefully appellants' claim that they have met their burden of showing that the harm in this case is divisible.

Appellants begin by stressing that the state's past costs involved only surface cleanup. They then argue that because it was possible to determine how many barrels of waste they contributed to the site, it is also possible to determine what proportion of the state's removal expenses are attributable to each of them simply by estimating the cost of excavating a single barrel. . . .

The state's removal efforts proceeded in four phases, each phase corresponding roughly to the cleanup of a different trench. The trenches were located in different areas of the site, but neither party has told us the distance between trenches. Appellants contend that it is possible to apportion the state's removal costs because there was evidence detailing (1) the total number of barrels excavated in each phase, (2) the number of barrels in each phase attributable to them, and (3) the total cost associated with each phase. In support of their argument, they point us to a few portions of the record, but for the most part are content to rest on statements in the district court's opinion. Specifically, appellants point to the following two sentences in the opinion: (1) "I find that [American Cyanamid] is responsible for ten drums of toxic hazardous material found at the site;" and (2) as to Rohm and Haas, "I accept the state's estimate [of 49 drums and 303 five-gallon pails]." Appellants then add, without opposition from the government, that the ten barrels of American Cyanamid waste discussed by the district court were found exclusively in Phase II, and that the 303 pails and 49 drums of Rohm and Haas waste mentioned by the court were found exclusively in Phase III. They conclude, therefore, that American Cyanamid should bear only a minute percentage of the $995,697.30 expended by the state during Phase II in excavating approximately 4,500 barrels and no share of the other phases, and that Rohm and Haas should be accountable for only a small portion of the $58,237 spent during Phase III in removing roughly 3,300 barrels and no share of the other phases. We disagree.

The district court's statements concerning the waste attributable to each appellant were based on the testimony of John Leo, an engineer hired by the state to oversee the cleanup. We have reviewed Mr. Leo's testimony carefully. Having done so, we think it inescapably clear that the district court did not mean to suggest that appellants had contributed only 49 and 10 barrels respectively, but rather, that those amounts were all that could be *positively attributed* to appellants.

Mr. Leo testified that out of the approximately 10,000 barrels that were excavated during the four phases, only "three to four hundred of the drums contained markings which could potentially be traced." This is not surprising considering that there had been an enormous fire at the site, that the barrels had been exposed to the elements for a number of years, and that a substantial amount of liquid waste had leaked and eaten away at the outsides of the barrels. Mr. Leo also testified that it was not simply the absence of legible markings that prevented the state from identifying the overwhelming majority of barrels, but also the danger involved in handling the barrels. Ironically, it was appellants themselves who, in an effort to induce Mr. Leo to lower his estimate of the number of barrels attributable to each defendant, elicited much of the testimony concerning the impossibility of accurately identifying all of the waste.

In light of the fact that most of the waste could not be identified, and that the appellants, and not the government, had the burden to account for all of this uncertainty, we think it plain that the district court did not err in holding them jointly and severally liable for the state's past removal costs. Perhaps in this situation the only way appellants could have demonstrated that they were limited contributors would have been to present specific evidence documenting the whereabouts of their waste at all times after it left their facilities. But far from doing so, appellants deny all knowledge of how their waste made its way to the site. Moreover, the government presented evidence that much of Rohm and Haas' waste found at the site came from its laboratory in Spring House, Pennsylvania and that during the relevant years, this lab generated over two thousand drums of waste, all of which were consigned to a single transporter. Under these circumstances, where Rohm and Haas was entrusting substantial amounts of waste to a single transporter who ultimately proved unreliable, we simply cannot conclude, absent evidence to the contrary, that only a handful of the 2,000 or more barrels reached the site.

Notes and Questions

1. Did you agree with the *Chem-Dyne* court's determination that CERCLA imposes joint and several liability in situations in which its application would be consistent with the common law? *Picillo* is typical of the post-*Chem-Dyne* case law in its assumption that this is the case.

2. Both the *Chem-Dyne* and *Picillo* courts determined that they develop uniform federal rules in determining whether joint and several liability applies in individual cases. Recall that in *Bestfoods* the Supreme Court, while declining to resolve the question, seemed skeptical as to whether the courts should apply federal rules of decision in analyzing questions of parent-corporation liability under CERCLA. In *United States v. Kimbell Foods, Inc.*, 440 U.S. 715, 99 S.Ct. 1448, 59 L.Ed.2d 711 (1979), identified three factors courts should look to in resolving whether they should apply state or federal rules of decision in filling in the interstices of federal programs:

> (1) whether the federal program by its nature must be uniform, (2) whether application of state law would frustrate special objectives of the federal program, and (3) the extent to which application of a federal rule would disrupt commercial relationships predicated on state law.

Id. at 728–729. What rationales did the *Chem-Dyne* court determine supported the application of federal rules of decision in resolving issues relating to the imposition of joint and several liability? Were you persuaded? Are the dynamics different in the joint and several liability context than they might be in the context of piercing the corporate veil?

3. What test does the *Chem-Dyne* court apply for when joint and several liability should be imposed? Do you agree with this test? How is it likely to apply in most contexts? Why did the court impose joint and several liability regarding the removal costs in *Picillo*? To the extent that the court rested its indivisibility finding on the problems of proof posed by inadequate records regarding the generators of each drum, *Picillo* appears to be the only

appellate decision in which a court has applied joint and several liability based upon indivisibility problems other than those posed through the commingling of waste. Why did the defendants bear the burden of accounting for the uncertainty regarding all unlabeled drums? Does this result make sense? Could EPA apply this same theory if a transporter distributed wastes from numerous customers to various sites without keeping records of whose wastes went where?

4.   EPA raised an alternative "averted harm" theory in *Picillo* based on the idea that even if it were possible to determine what proportion of the state's removal costs were attributable to the appellants, joint and several liability still would have been proper because the appellants' drums would have led to an indivisible harm had not the government intervened. The court expressed reservations about this theory, but chose not to directly address it in reaching its decision. Do you agree with the court's reservations? Why or why not?

5.   Under what circumstances should PRPs be able to avoid joint and several liability under CERCLA? Section 433A(1) of the Restatement (Second) of Torts states that:

(1) Damages for harm are to be apportioned among two or more causes where

(a) there are distinct harms, or

(b) there is a reasonable basis for determining the contribution of each cause to a single harm.

The first of these scenarios is easy to apply. Assume, for example that a given site has two separate contaminated areas, with one containing PCB-contaminated soils, and the other solvent-based soil and groundwater contamination. If a given PRP could show that it sent only PCBs to the site, and that there are no PCB or PCB-derivatives in the second area, it would be able to establish divisibility as a matter of law.

6.   Can you envision any circumstances in which the Restatement's second scenario might come into play? In *In the Matter of Bell Petroleum Services, Inc.*, 3 F.3d 889 (5th Cir. 1993), all of the parties (including EPA) seemed to assume that courts can apportion liability as a matter of law in situations in which multiple parties contribute known quantities of the same contaminant (in that case, chromium) to the same commingled mass. In that case, the dispute was over whether the relevant defendant had made an adequate showing with respect to the volumes discharged. The Fifth Circuit determined that it had, declaring that "evidence sufficient to permit a rough approximation is all that is required under the Restatement." Id. at 904 n. 19. Additionally, in two cases involving Alcan Aluminum Corp., the Second and Third Circuits determined that, in multi-waste cases, the government could not overcome apportionment arguments merely by demonstrating that the defendant's wastes have commingled with others and that the resulting mixture required investigation or remediation. *United States v. Alcan Aluminum Corp.*, 964 F.2d 252, 270 (3d Cir. 1992); *United States v. Alcan Aluminum Corp.*, 990 F.2d 711, 722 (2d Cir. 1993). In both cases, the courts remanded to the district court to give Alcan the opportunity to prove that its "emulsion did not or could not, *when mixed with other hazardous wastes*,

contribute to the release and the resultant response costs...." 964 F.2d at 271 (emphasis in original); 990 F.2d at 722. The courts determined that, if Alcan could make this showing, it would not only result in apportionment, but in fact its apportionable share would be zero. Do you agree with these decisions, and with the assumption that EPA was willing to buy into in *Bell Petroleum*? How much of a swath do they cut from the general rule of joint and several liability? We should perhaps note that Alcan was ultimately unable to make the showing required by the courts in either of the *Alcan* cases. See *United States v. Alcan Aluminum Corp.*, 892 F.Supp. 648, 655 (M.D.Pa. 1995); and *United States v. Alcan Aluminum Corp.*, 315 F.3d 179, 187 (2d Cir. 2003).

7. Where it applies, joint and several liability allows EPA, in theory, to sue any one of perhaps several hundred generators for the entire cost of cleanup at a given site. In its efforts to dismantle the joint and several liability scheme, industrial advocates frequently have raised the specter of EPA imposing the entire cost of cleanup at a given site upon a so-called "one-drum generator." In practice, however, EPA has been much more moderate, typically trying to negotiate settlements with all identified PRPs. Given the transaction costs and delays involved with CERCLA–scale multiparty negotiations, why do you think EPA has pursued this course?

8. In practice, EPA tends to use joint and several liability for at least three purposes. First, it uses the threat of joint and several liability as an inducement to settlement. Second, it frequently uses the doctrine to reallocate what are referred to as "orphan shares" (the liability shares, for example, of parties who cannot be located or who may be bankrupt or have dissolved) among the remaining solvent parties. And third, if negotiations break down and EPA is left in the position of either issuing a unilateral order or commencing a cost-recovery action, it may use joint and several liability as a means of limiting the number of PRPs to whom it will issue an order or against whom it will commence a law suit. Are all of these purposes appropriate? Are there others that you would add?

9. As noted by the *Picillo* court, the SARA amendments "soften[ed] the blow" of joint and several liability by providing an explicit contribution right in § 113(f). Do you share the court's perception that this right is only of limited benefit to PRPs that have been subjected to more than their proportionate share of liability? Why?

10. If EPA or, perhaps more accurately, the Department of Justice chooses to sue fewer than the full range of potential defendants in a multiparty case, should the named defendants be entitled to join any unnamed PRPs as third-party defendants? Would you expect EPA to resist such efforts? Why or why not?

3. Defenses

Section 107(b) of CERCLA establishes three narrow defenses to liability. Additionally, in passing the Brownfields Amendments, Congress added a series of new exclusions to liability to § 107 which function like defenses in that, generally speaking, they impose on defendants the burden of demonstrating that they qualify thereunder. CERCLA § 107(*o*), (p), (q) and (r). In this section, we provide a brief overview of

the three most significant carve-outs from the CERCLA liability scheme:
the "traditional" third-party defense under § 107(b)(3), the "innocent
landowner defense" under that same section, and the "prospective
purchaser exclusion" under § 107(r).

Section 107(b)(3) provides a "third-party" defense that applies if a
party not in contractual privity with the person asserting the defense
was the sole cause of the relevant release or threatened release and the
resulting damages. Specifically, § 107(b)(3) requires that the party who
caused the release or threatened release be neither an employee nor an
agent of the defendant, nor "one whose act or omission occurs in
connection with a contractual relationship, either directly or indirectly,
with the defendant ..." Additionally, it requires that the defendant
establish that:

> (a) he exercised due care with respect to the hazardous substance
> concerned, taking into consideration the characteristics of such
> hazardous substance, in light of all relevant facts and circumstances,
> and (b) he took precautions against foreseeable acts or omissions of
> any such third party and the consequences that could foreseeably
> result from such acts or omissions ...

CERCLA § 107(b). In its "traditional" (and only pre-SARA) application,
one who has status liability (e.g., the current owner of a site) may
establish this defense if an unrelated third party caused the relevant
release. This would be the case, for example, if the contamination was
caused by a vandal or other "midnight dumper." It might also be the
case if contamination from an upgradient parcel seeped down onto his or
her property (although to this extent, § 107(b)(3) would now seem to
overlap with the new defense in § 107(q)). In either event, the relevant
party would also have to establish that it meets § 107(b)(3)'s "due care"
requirements.

The innocent landowner defense is actually a subset of the
§ 107(b)(3) defense. As EPA has noted, before SARA was passed EPA
"took the position that a real estate deed represented a contractual
relationship within the meaning of § 107(b)(3), thus eliminating the
availability of the third party defense for a landowner in the chain of
title with a party who had caused or contributed to the release." EPA
Guidance on Landowner Liability under Section 107(a)(1) of CERCLA,
De Minimis Settlements under Section 122(g)(1)(B) of CERCLA, and
Settlements with Prospective Purchasers of Contaminated Property,
June 6, 1989, at p. 9–10 ("Innocent Landowner Guidance"). Congress
appeared to confirm this interpretation in 1986, making explicit in
§ 101(35)(A) that deeds and other land contracts give rise to the type of
"contractual relationship" that can defeat the § 107(b)(3) defense. At
the same time, however, Congress created an exception to this general
rule for those purchasers that, before acquiring title, diligently investigate the potential existence of contamination and find none, so long as,
after having purchased the property, they act appropriately if and when
they become aware that there was preexisting contamination. These so-

called "innocent landowners" are deemed not to have had a "contractual relationship" with the person causing the release for purposes of § 107(b)(3). CERCLA § 101(35)(A)(I).

The million dollar question in the innocent landowner context involves the degree of investigation that purchasers must have undertaken before they bought the relevant property. In this regard, § 101(35)(A)(i) requires the defendant to show that it "did not know and had no reason to know" of the relevant contamination. In order to demonstrate this, § 101(35)(B) requires it to establish that it made "all appropriate inquiry into the previous ownership and uses of the property consistent with good commercial or customary practice...." As originally passed, SARA required the court to take the following factors into account in determining whether "all appropriate inquiry" has been made:

1. Any specialized knowledge or experience on the part of the landowner;

2. The relationship of the purchase price to the value of the property if uncontaminated;

3. Commonly known or reasonably ascertainable information about the property;

4. The obviousness of the presence or likely presence of contamination on the property; and

5. The ability to detect such contamination by appropriate inspection.

See CERCLA Section 101(35)(B)(iv).

Over the years, these standards proved unacceptably vague. Neither EPA nor the courts developed clear guidelines for what constitutes "all appropriate inquiry" under differing factual circumstances. Absent this guidance, the private sector of necessity began to work out for itself what it thought was necessary to establish the defense. Soon, a series of industry practices emerged. In most transactions involving commercial or industrial property, the would-be purchaser would begin its analysis with what became known a "phase 1" site assessment. This typically consisted of a site visit and walk-around, interviews with past and present employees, title searches, file reviews at both the facility and the relevant regulatory agencies, and a review of aerial photographs, if available. This assessment was intended to determine the potential existence of contamination. If this inquiry didn't raise any "red flags," most would-be purchasers felt comfortable proceeding with the purchase. In 1997, the American Society for Testing and Materials ("ASTM") developed standardized guidelines for these "phase 1" assessments. See ASTM Standard E–1527–97, Standard Practices for Environmental Site Assessment: Phase 1 Site Assessment, Process.

When it passed the Brownfields Amendments in 2002, Congress returned to this issue, establishing a three-tiered scheme for resolving "all appropriate inquiry" questions. In short, Congress charged EPA with writing rules fleshing out these requirements, which will be binding upon the courts when issued with respect to investigations performed after that time. CERCLA § 101(35)(B)(iii). Congress did not intend, however, for these new rules to have retroactive effect. Instead, the revised § 101(35)(B) contemplates that the courts will continue to apply the original five factors set out in SARA to questions about the validity of any investigations performed before May 31, 1997. Additionally, Congress codified the ASTM standards as the appropriate measuring stick for pre-purchase investigations conducted between May 31, 1997, and the date when EPA promulgates the new standards. CERCLA Section 101(35)(B)(iv)(I) and (II). Thus, we now have the following framework:

1. For purchases before May 31, 1997, the courts are to apply the original five statutory factors, now set out in § 101(35)(B)(iv)(I);

2. For purchases between May 31, 1997, and the date when EPA promulgates its new rules, the courts are to apply the ASTM standards; and

3. Once EPA promulgates its rules, the courts are to apply them.

In the Brownfields Amendments, Congress also created the "prospective purchaser exclusion" to address another perceived flaw in the preexisting scheme. For the first 21 years of CERCLA's existence, those who purchased property knowing it was contaminated were strictly liable and, generally speaking, had no defenses. Perhaps obviously, the specter of this liability served to discourage investments in contaminated land. Oftentimes, would-be buyers walked away from deals at the first indication of potentially significant contamination issues, choosing to shift their development focus from previously-developed industrial properties (denominated "brownfields") to hitherto undeveloped land (denominated "greenfields"). Other developers simply set their sights on greenfields in the first place, choosing to avoid the headaches associated with even beginning to analyze the environmental risks at previously developed sites. At the macroscopic level, these dynamics served to stifle the redevelopment or urban, industrial areas, pushing new growth outside of the industrial core areas and, frequently, into the suburbs. In turn, this posed social justice issues, as industrial flight tended to take the associated jobs farther and farther from inner-city populations, leaving only scarred land at former industrial sites.

Beginning in late 1980s, EPA began to grapple with this problem by creating what were referred to as "prospective purchaser agreements" ("PPAs"). See Innocent Landowner Guidance. EPA moved even more aggressively in this direction in 1995, issuing a new Guidance on Settlements with Prospective Purchasers of Contaminated Property, together with a model agreement. 60 Fed.Reg. 34792 (1995) ("Prospective Purchaser Guidance"). Still, from the perspective of would-be purchasers, these relief valves were seen to be too limited. Most significantly, due to resource constraints EPA limited the availability of PPAs to facilities at which EPA action had been taken, was undergoing, or was anticipated to be taken. 60 Fed. Reg. at 34793. As EPA explained, this criterion was meant "to ensure that EPA [did] not become unnecessarily involved in purely private real estate transactions or expend its limited resources in negotiation which [were] unlikely to produce a sufficient benefit to the public." Id. While this was understandable from an Agency resources standpoint, it placed severe limitations on the availability of PPAs. As we have seen, the specter of CERCLA liability far transcends any list of sites at which EPA is or is likely to become involved. As previously mentioned, EPA tends to focus its attention on site that are or are likely to be on the NPL. Currently, just over 1,200 sites are on the NPL. See www.epa.gov/superfund. By contrast, the U.S. Conference of Mayors has estimated that there are more than 450,000 brownfield sites. S.Rep. No. 107–2, 107th Cong., 1st Sess., p.1 (March 12, 2001). Under EPA's then-existing approach, the benefits of the PPA program were simply unavailable if a particular site was not on EPA's radar screen.

In the Brownfields Amendments, Congress fundamentally altered the CERCLA liability scheme as it relates to prospective purchasers. In the new Section 107(r), Congress provided an exclusion for "bona fide prospective purchaser[s]." This exclusion is available only to those whose potential liability would be based solely on their ownership or operation. CERCLA § 107(r). Moreover, the term "bona fide prospective purchaser" is defined in a way that makes clear that the exclusion is prospective only; i.e. it only applies to those who acquired their interest in the relevant facility after the date of the Brownfields Amendments (January 11, 2002). CERCLA § 101(40). Additionally, the definition requires the owner to establish the following elements:

A. It must have acquired the property after "[a]ll disposal of hazardous substances;"

B. It must have satisfied the "all appropriate inquiry" standard before acquiring the property;

C. It must make all legally required notices with regard to the discovery or release of any hazardous substances;

D. It must exercise appropriate care with respect to any hazardous substances found, including taking reasonable steps to stop any continuing releases, prevent any threatened releases, and prevent or limit exposure to existing releases;

E. It must provide full cooperation, assistance and access to anyone authorized to conduct response actions;

F. It must be in compliance with any land use restrictions that are part of the response action, and it must not have impeded the effectiveness of any institutional controls;

G. It must have complied with all EPA information requests under § 104(e); and

H. It must not be potentially affiliated with anyone with is potentially liable (e.g., through a familial or corporate relationship).

Id. If these conditions are met, however, there is no longer any need for the owner to enter into a PPA. The relevant owner simply bears no liability under CERCLA. There is one caveat, however: Section 107(r)(2) allows EPA to impose a lien on the property to cover any unrecovered response costs if its cleanup increased the value of the property. The amount of the lien cannot exceed the increase in value attributable to the response. CERCLA § 107(r)(4)(A).

Notes and Questions

1.　What kinds of contractual relationships should preclude the application of the traditional § 107(b)(3) defense? Should all land sale agreements do so? Should a landowner be deemed to have a disqualifying "indirect" contractual relationship with all prior owners in the chain of title. Compare *New York v. Lashins Arcade Co.*, 91 F.3d 353 (2d Cir. 1996), with *Lefebvre v. Central Maine Power Co.*, 7 F.Supp. 2d 64, 68 n.3 (D.Me. 1998), *Goe Eng'g Co. v. Physicians Formula Cosmetics*, 1997 WL 889278, at *10 n.7 (C.D.Cal. 1997), and *Bangor v. Citizens Communication Co.*, 2004 WL 483201 (D.Me. 2004); see also Johnston, Current Landowner Liability Under CERCLA: Restoring the Need for Due Diligence, 9 Fordham Env'l Law Journal 401 (1998). Should a lessor have a disqualifying relationship with all of its tenants, or all of its subtenants? See *Bedford Affiliates v. Sills*, 156 F.3d 416, 425 (2d Cir. 1998), *United States v. A & N Cleaners*, 788 F.Supp. 1317 (S.D.N.Y.1992), and *United States v. Northernaire Plating Co.*, 670 F.Supp. 742 (W.D.Mich. 1987). Even if lessors might otherwise be eligible for a § 107(b)(3) defense, what kinds of precautions should they be required to undertake to meet the requirements of § 107(b)(3) when they are aware that their sublessees are operating businesses like dry cleaning establishments? What if they are unaware to the types of businesses to which their lessees may be subleasing the properties? Should they have a duty to inform themselves of the nature of these businesses and their work practices? Should they be able to pass any such obligations on to their lessees by contract? See *United States v. A & N Cleaners and Launderers, Inc.*, 854 F.Supp. 229, 243–244 (S.D.N.Y. 1994).

2.　What should the "due care" obligation entail when a property owner who otherwise has a valid defense under § 107(b)(3) becomes aware of contamination on his or her property? Should it be enough merely to contact either State authorities or EPA? Should it matter whether these authorities are actively responding to the relevant contamination? Compare *Kerr–McGee Chemical v. Lefton Iron & Metal Co.*, 14 F.3d 321 (7th Cir.1994); *New York v. Lashins Arcade Co.*, 91 F.3d 353 (2d Cir. 1996); *United States v. 150 Acres of Land*, 204 F.3d 698, 706 (6th Cir. 2000); *Franklin County Convention Facilities Auth. v. American Premier Underwriters, Inc.*, 240 F.3d 534, 548 (6th Cir. 2001); and *United States v. DiBiase Salem Realty Trust*, 1993 WL 729662 (D.Mass. 1993). It may be one thing to expect an otherwise non-liable landowner to remove some corroded drums, or to fence off a contaminated area. But is it reasonable to require such a landowner to undertake extensive removal or remedial measures? Do courts need to be leery about requiring landowners to act like liable parties in order to preserve their defenses? See *Kalamazoo River Study Group v. Rockwell International*, 3 F.Supp.2d 799, 807–807 (W.D.Mich. 1998), *rev'd on other grounds*, 228 F.3d 648 (6th Cir.

2000) (riparian landowners were not required to take affirmative actions to address contaminated sediments in the Kalamazoo River); see also EPA's Final Policy Toward Owners of Property Containing Contaminated Aquifers, 60 Fed. Reg. 34790, 34791 (1995) (stating EPA's view that if a landowner otherwise has a valid § 107(b)(3) defense, its failure to conduct groundwater monitoring or to install groundwater remediation systems should not, in the absence of exceptional circumstances, be deemed a failure to exercise "due care").

3. The innocent landowner defense (like the prospective purchaser defense) applies only to pre-existing contamination. CERCLA § 101(35)(A). If a particular case involves disposal during the owner's period of ownership, that owner must find comfort, if at all, in CERCLA's other defenses (e.g., the traditional § 107(b)(3) defense).

4. In the innocent landowner context, should the amount of money at issue in a given transaction be relevant to the degree of inquiry required? This factor could cut either way in different factual settings. Should someone buying a small business (e.g., an auto repair shop) be expected to spend up to 50% or more of the purchase price on environmental investigations? Will the market bear this degree of investigation? Should those who purchase such businesses effectively be rendered unable to establish an innocent landowner defense? At the other extreme, should a company undertaking a $100 million corporate acquisition be able to rely on a $5,000 "phase 1" site assessment even if that assessment reveals no evidence of contamination?

5. Should "no inquiry" ever constitute "all appropriate inquiry?" The Government has consistently argued that, at a minimum, a visual inspection should be required in order to establish the defense. See, e.g., Innocent Landowner Guidance, supra, at 12 n. 11. Several courts have rejected this absolutist position, requiring at a minimum some evidence regarding the customary due diligence practices under the circumstances. See *United States v. 150 Acres of Land*, 204 F.3d 698, 707 (6th Cir. 2000); *United States v. Serafini*, 706 F.Supp. 346, 353 (M.D.Pa.1988); and *United States v. Pacific Hide & Fur Depot*, 716 F.Supp. 1341, 1348–49 (D.Idaho 1989). Not surprisingly, however, in some contexts courts have deemed the lack any pre-purchase investigations to be fatal to any attempts to establish an innocent landowner defense. See, e.g., *Foster v. United States*, 922 F.Supp. 642, 655–56 (D.D.C. 1996) (finding the innocent landowner defense unavailable where the purchaser undertook no environmental investigation before buying the site in 1985); *United States v. Taylor*, 1993 WL 760996 (W.D.Mich.1993) (deeming the defense unavailable with respect to a purchase in 1986 where "[a]ny diligence would have revealed problems"); and *United States v. Rohm and Haas Co.*, 790 F.Supp. 1255, 1264 (E.D.Pa. 1992), aff'd 2 F.3d 1265 (3d Cir. 1993) (landowner did not meet test where it offered no evidence of having investigated the prior uses or previous ownership of the property). In one of the most defendant-friendly innocent landowner cases to date, the court in *Goe Engineering Co., Inc. v. Physicians Formula Cosmetics*, 1997 WL 889278 (C.D.Cal. 1997), found that the purchaser met the all appropriate inquiry standard where it had inspected the property prior to purchasing it in 1985, even though it apparently had undertaken no sampling despite having seen oil staining on the floor and some 50-gallon drums outside, and its having been aware of the fact that the prior owner had operated a

machine shop using underground storage tanks (UST's) at the site. The court found that the plaintiffs had failed to offer "any legal or scientific authority for their contention that the presence of oil stains, barrels, or UST's should put a purchaser on notice that the property may be contaminated with hazardous substances." Id. at *13.

6. Congress may have caught some landowners off guard by imposing the ASTM standards retroactively for the five year period between 1997 and 2002. During that period, many consulting firms looked to those standards for guidance, but may have deviated from them somewhat on the theory that what they were doing was still "appropriate" under the then-existing statutory standards. Many of those investigations may now be deemed to be defective as a matter of law according to the ASTM standards.

7. EPA issued proposed rules fleshing out the "all appropriate inquiry" requirements in August of 2004. 65 Fed.Reg. 52542 (Aug. 26, 2004).

A Note on the Brownfields Program

As we have seen, Congress provided targeted liability relief when it passed the Brownfields Amendments. At the same time, Congress sought to further promote the redevelopment of brownfield sites by creating a grant program primarily for the benefit of local governments, States and Indian tribes. This program has two key features. First, Congress authorized the appropriation of $50 million per year for each of the fiscal years 2002 through 2006, for a grant program, administered by EPA, to encourage States and Indian tribes to establish or enhance their response programs. CERCLA § 128. Second, Congress authorized the appropriation of $200 million per year for each of those same years for direct grants to local governments, States, Indian tribes and even nonprofit groups, to be used inventory, characterize, assess and remediate brownfield sites. CERCLA § 104(k). The term "brownfield site" is defined broadly to mean any site at which actual or potential contamination may be complicating the expansion, redevelopment or reuse of the property, but is qualified by several exclusions, including actual or proposed NPL sites and other sites being addressed under either CERCLA or RCRA. CERCLA § 101(39).

To be eligible for State program grants, State or tribal programs must have either entered into a Memorandum of Agreement (MOA) with EPA or established a program containing the following elements: (1) a survey and inventory of brownfield sites; (2) oversight and enforcement authorities to ensure that response actions will be appropriate; (3) mechanisms and resources to provide meaningful opportunities for public participation; and (4) mechanisms for approval of cleanup plans, and a requirement for certification regarding the completion of any necessary response activities. CERCLA § 128(a)(1)(A) and (2). In addition to using these grants to establish or enhance their response programs, States and tribes can use them either (1) to capitalize revolving loan funds for brownfields remediation, or (2) to purchase insurance or develop other risk sharing mechanisms as a funding source for response actions. CERCLA § 128(a)(1)(B).

There are actually three types of brownfield-specific grants under § 104(k). First, EPA can award grants of up to $200,000 (or, in some cases, up to $350,000) per site to either States, tribes, or various local governmental authorities (collectively denominated "eligible entities") to inventory, characterize and assess brownfield sites. CERCLA § 104(k)(1), (2)(A) and (B), and (4)(A)(i). Second, EPA can provide grants of up to $200,000 to either eligible entities or non-profit organizations for the remediation of sites owned by those entities. CERCLA § 104(k)(3)(A)(ii). And third, EPA can award grants of up to $1 million to eligible entities for the purpose of capitalizing revolving loan funds, and can supplement these grants in later years. CERCLA § 104 (3)(A)(i) and (4)(A)(ii). In turn, eligible entities can use these funds to award loans to site owners or developers, or to award grants to either other eligible entities or non-profit organizations. CERCLA § 104(k)(3)(B)(i) and (ii). The statute also provides criteria to guide these granting decisions. See, CERCLA § 104(k)(3)(C) (relating to site remediation), (k)(4)(A)(ii) (relating to supplemental loan fund grants), and (k)(5)(C) (general criteria).

Three other aspects of the Brownfields Amendments are worth noting. First, the new Section 105(h) provides that, upon request of the States, EPA should generally defer listing certain sites, called "eligible response sites," on the NPL so long as the States are either conducting response actions or pursuing or overseeing private-party responses. "Eligible response sites" correlate generally, but not precisely, with brownfield sites; they specifically do not include sites that EPA has determined are eligible for placement on the NPL. See CERCLA § 101(41). Second, Congress sought to remove where possible a perceived impediment to brownfields redevelopment; i.e., the rigorousness of the NCP. In this vein, Section 104(k)(5)(A)(i)(II) limits EPA's ability to condition grants on compliance with the NCP to those situations where EPA determines that a particular requirement of the NCP is relevant and appropriate. Third, Section 128(b) now generally bars EPA from bringing an action under either § 106 or § 107 at an "eligible response site" if someone is conducting or has completed a response action under a State cleanup program. There are exceptions that apply when the State asks EPA to get involved, when EPA determines that the site may still present an imminent and substantial endangerment, or when new information indicates that the site still presents a threat. CERCLA § 128(b).

4. A Quick Overview of the Cleanup Process

The topic of CERCLA cleanups is quite complex. We will only treat it briefly here. Students should be aware that the discussion below is intended to provide only a brief overview and is in many ways oversimplified.

Statutorily, § 104(a)(1) authorizes EPA to act, consistent with the NCP, to provide for both removal and remedial actions. Section 121 establishes the applicable cleanup standards. EPA has integrated both of these provisions through the NCP, which is found at 40 C.F.R. §§ 300.400–300.440.

The NCP requires that CERCLA cleanup decisions be made through a prolonged process that includes several different steps and provides opportunities for involvement on behalf of both the affected state and local governments and the public generally. The procedure may include the following components:

1. The preliminary assessment and site investigation ("PA/SI");

2. The decision to implement removal action;

3. The decision regarding whether the site merits placement on the NPL;

4. The remedial investigation and feasibility study ("RI/FS"); and

5. The issuance of a proposed plan, the provision of an opportunity for public comment, and the issuance of a record of decision ("ROD").

In short, the PA/SI has two primary purposes: (1) to determine the need for removal action; and (2) to generate the information necessary to determine whether the site warrants placement on the NPL. While both the statute and the NCP define the term "removal" broadly, CERCLA § 101(22) and 40 C.F.R. § 300.5, these measures are best conceptualized as short term steps that either stabilize releases, abate threatened releases, or mitigate near-term threats. 53 Fed.Reg. 51411 (Dec. 21, 1988). At the same time EPA is considering or implementing these actions, it is trying to determine whether the site warrants placement on the NPL. EPA evaluates sites for potential listing on the NPL based primarily on a ranking system known as the Hazard Ranking System ("HRS"). See 40 C.F.R. § 300.425(c); and 40 C.F.R. Part 300, Appendix A. EPA feeds data from observed or potential releases of hazardous substances into the HRS to derive a numeric score indicating EPA's preliminary assessment of the perceived risk associated with the site and comparing it with perceived risks at other sites. Currently, the magic number is 28.5; any site scoring higher than that number under the HRS qualifies for listing on the NPL. 55 Fed.Reg. 51,559 (Dec. 14, 1990).

The remedial investigation and feasibility study ("RI/FS") is at the heart of the CERCLA remedy selection process. As stated at 40 C.F.R. § 300.430(a)(2), the purpose of the RI/FS is "to assess site conditions and evaluate alternatives to the extent necessary to select a remedy." Conceptually, the two components of the RI/FS can be separated. The purpose of the remedial investigation is to gather sufficient data to characterize the conditions at the site for the purpose of developing and evaluating effective remedial alternatives. 40 C.F.R. § 300.430(d). The RI assesses the physical characteristics of the site, the nature and extent of the contamination, and the actual and potential pathways of exposure to the surrounding population. The feasibility study, by contrast, develops and analyzes alternatives for appropriate response. It is important to note, however, that in practice the RI and FS "are not sequential but rather concurrent processes." 55 Fed.Reg. 8712 (March 8, 1990). Thus, the very first step in the RI/FS process—the "scoping" stage—includes the identification of both "likely response scenarios and potentially applicable technologies ... that may address site problems" and "the type, quality, and quantity of data that will be collected during the RI/FS to support decisions regarding remedial response activities." 40 C.F.R. § 300.430(b).

Ultimately, the most important function of the RI/FS is to set the stage for remedy selection by zeroing in on a preferred alternative. To do this, the RI/FS must encompass both a risk assessment and a process for determining the desired level of risk reduction–this latter part being frequently referred to as the "how clean is clean" question. Both of these undertakings are both complex and controversial. On the latter front, the relevant provisions of § 121 establish at least five requirements that CERCLA remedial actions must meet:

1.   They must attain a degree of cleanup that assures protection of human health and the environment (§ 121(b)(1));

2.   With regard to hazardous substances that will remain after completion, they must, in most circumstances, meet all "applicable" and/or "relevant and appropriate" requirements under federal and state law ("ARARs") (§ 121(d)(2)) (these include, for example, Safe Drinking Water Act standards if the groundwater at the site is a potential source of drinking water);

3.   They must utilize permanent solutions and alternative treatment technologies or resource recovery technologies to the maximum extent practicable (§ 121(b)(1));

4.   They must provide for cost-effective response, taking into account the total long-and short-term costs of such actions (including operation and maintenance costs)(§ 121(a) and (b)(1)); and

5.   They must be in accordance with the NCP to the extent practicable (§ 121(a)).

As if to underscore the Congressional desire for permanent remedies, § 121(b)(1) establishes two specific statutory preferences. First, it provides that remedies that emphasize "treatment which permanently and significantly reduces the volume, toxicity or mobility of the hazardous substances ... are to be preferred over remedial actions not involving such treatment." It further states that "[t]he offsite transport and disposal of hazardous substances or contaminated materials without such treatment should be the least favored alternative remedial action where practicable treatment technologies are available." CERCLA § 121(b).

SARA added two provisions addressing state and community involvement in the remedy-selection process. Section 121(f) required EPA to promulgate regulations "providing for substantial and meaningful involvement by each State in initiation, development, and selection of remedial actions to be undertaken in that State." Section 117 requires

EPA both to "[p]rovide a reasonable opportunity for submission of written and oral comments and an opportunity for a public hearing at or near the facility at issue" regarding the contemplated remedy, and to respond "to each of the significant comments, criticisms, and new data submitted . . ." CERCLA § 117(a) and (b).

EPA sought to implement these mandates, some of which (e.g., the preference for permanence versus the insistence on cost-effectiveness) appear to conflict with each other, in the 1990 NCP. It did this by establishing nine criteria according to which potential remedies are to be evaluated during both the FS alternatives analysis and the ultimate remedy-selection process. The criteria include:

1. Overall protection of human health and the environment;

2. Compliance with ARARs;

3. Long-term effectiveness and permanence;

4. Reduction of toxicity, mobility, or volume through treatment;

5. Short-term effectiveness;

6. Implementability;

7. Cost;

8. State acceptance; and

9. Community acceptance.

40 C.F.R. § 300.430(e)(9) and (f)(1).

These criteria are not given equal weight in the remedy-selection process. EPA has identified the first two criteria (protectiveness and ARAR–compliance) as "threshold criteria" that each alternative must meet in order to be eligible for selection, unless a specific ARAR is waived (see below). 40 C.F.R. § 300.430(f)(1)(i)(A). The next five criteria (long-term effectiveness and permanence; reduction of toxicity, mobility, and volume through treatment; short-term effectiveness; implementability; and cost) are deemed "primary balancing criteria" and are used to weigh major tradeoffs between alternative cleanup strategies. 40 C.F.R. § 300.430(f)(1)(i)(B); see also 53 Fed.Reg. 51428 (Dec. 21, 1988). Finally, the last two criteria, state and community acceptance, are referred to as "modifying criteria," primarily because the information necessary to fully consider them typically will not be complete until after the official public comment period. 40 C.F.R. § 300.430(f)(1)(i)(C); see also 55 Fed. Reg. 8730 (March 8, 1990).

We conclude our discussion of remedy selection with some brief consideration of how EPA defines "protectiveness" under this program. In the absence of ARARs specifying a more stringent result, EPA assesses protectiveness primarily in terms of toxicity and carcinogenicity. For systemic toxicants, EPA's regulations provide that "acceptable exposure levels shall represent concentration levels to which the human population, including sensitive subgroups, may be exposed without adverse effect '"""' 40 C.F.R. § 300.430(e)(2)(i)(A)(1). For known or suspected carcinogens, EPA takes the view that the appropriate risk range for CERCLA sites is between "10^{-4}" to "10^{-6}," with the 10^{-6} level serving as the point of departure. 40 C.F.R. § 300.430(e)(2)(i)(A)(2). A 10^{-6} cancer risk indicates that if 1,000,000 people were exposed to the contamination over the course of a lifetime, using predetermined exposure and carcinogenicity assumptions, the exposure theoretically would result in one additional cancer case. The 10^{-4} risk level would indicate that, theoretically, 100 out of those same 1,000,000 people would develop cancer, again assuming certain levels of exposure and toxicity. In the preamble to the 1990 NCP, EPA explained the point of departure concept in the following terms:

> Where the aggregate risk of contaminants based on existing ARARs exceeds 10^{-4} or where remediation goals are not determined by ARARs, EPA uses 10^{-6} as a point of departure for establishing preliminary remediation goals. This means that a cumulative risk level of 10^{-6} is used as the starting point ... for determining the most appropriate risk level that alternatives should be designed to attain. The use of 10^{-6} expresses EPA's preference for remedial actions that result in risks at the more protective end of the risk range, but this does not reflect a presumption that the final remedial action should attain such a risk level. Factors related to exposure, uncertainty and technical limitations may justify modification of initial cleanup levels that are based on the 10^{-6} risk level. The ultimate decision on what level of protection will be appropriate depends on the selected remedy, which is based on the [nine remedy-section criteria].

55 Fed.Reg. 8718 (March 8, 1990); *see also Id.* at 8717.

5. Settlement

We conclude our discussion of EPA response with an overview of the approaches EPA uses to promote settlement under CERCLA. As mentioned at the outset, EPA long has exhibited a preference for resolving CERCLA cases through the negotiation of settlements under which PRPs perform the necessary investigatory and/or remedial activities. Congress embraced this approach when it passed SARA in 1986, creating a specific provision promoting and establishment guidelines for settlement. Section 122(a) urges EPA to enter into settlements whenever it determines that they are in the public interest and consistent with the NCP. If EPA decides not to pursue settlement in a particular case, the same section requires it to explain to the PRPs in writing why it has chosen to forsake such an approach. (Note, however, that any decision by EPA not to pursue settlement is not subject to judicial review.)

EPA usually begins the settlement process as quickly as it can once it has determined who might bear potential liability for a particular site. EPA notifies PRPs of their potential liability through what are known as "notice letters." EPA's policy is to send out notice letters to all or virtually all parties for whom there is sufficient evidence to make a preliminary determination of potential liability. EPA may begin informal negotiations with the PRPs as soon as they receive their notice letters. Often, EPA will hold a "PRP meeting" to explicitly begin the negotiation process. At some sites, there may be just a handful of PRPs; at others, these meetings can involve dozens or even hundreds of parties. Not surprisingly, in these cases EPA is reluctant to engage in negotiations with individual PRPs. Instead, it seeks to negotiate with the PRP community collectively, or at least with all of those PRPs who are willing to negotiate in good faith.

In multi-party cases, EPA's first order of business generally is to seek to reach agreement with the *de minimis* parties. Section 122(g) requires EPA to enter into settlements with *de minimis* PRPs as promptly as possible whenever such settlements are practicable and in the public interest. Section 122(g)(1)(A) defines the universe of *de minimis* generators as including those whose contribution to the site is minimal both in the amount and toxicity of the substances involved. In practice, EPA usually further defines this group as including any generator who sent less than 1% of the overall volume of waste to the site.

One of the clear Congressional goals underlying § 122(g) was to eliminate *de minimis* parties from CERCLA cases as quickly and with as much finality as possible. As a result, EPA provides *de minimis* settlors with a degree of finality that is unavailable to other parties. In order to understand the distinction here, it is necessary to have a broader understanding of how settlement works generally. EPA has two major "carrots" it can offer to PRPs as inducements to settlement. First, it can provide both major and *de minimis* parties with "covenants not to sue" warranting that the government will not, as a general matter, seek any further relief from the settling parties. CERCLA § 122(f) and (g)(2). Second, it can provide either group of parties with "contribution protection" protecting them from potential suits by other PRPs through which they otherwise might seek to impose further liability on the settling parties regarding the site at issue. CERCLA §§ 113(f)(2) and 122(g)(4) and (h)(4). At least under the first of these two inducements, the protection that EPA provides to *de minimis* settlors is more absolute. As will be discussed below, major party settlements generally contain "reopeners" allowing EPA to pursue settling PRPs anew if conditions that were unknown at the time of the settlement subsequently are discovered, if new information later reveals that the remedy was not protective of human health or the environment, or if, in an EPA–lead cleanup situation, there are significant cost overruns. *De minimis* settlements, by contrast, typically include none of these reopeners; instead, they tend to include a reopener covering only situations in which new information comes to light indicating that a given party should not have qualified for *de minimis* status in the first place.

In exchange for this enhanced degree of finality, EPA typically extracts from *de minimis* settlors what it refers to as a "premium" payment designed to account for the uncertainties that they are avoiding by being allowed to settle without the more broad types of reopeners. EPA notes that:

> ... The premium charged should be in addition to the *de minimis* party's *pro rata* share of the site response costs. The premium should be sufficient to compensate the Agency for the risks associated with: (1) Settling at a site where the future response action has not been chosen; (2) possible cost overruns for a remedy not yet selected and; (3) potential inability to recover response costs from other sources.

Early *De Minimis* Waste Settlement Guidance, 57 Fed.Reg. at 29318 (July 1, 1992).

Once the *de minimis* negotiations are far enough along, EPA turns its attention to the major parties. Here, the dynamics are much more complex. For one thing, there is much more money at stake. Additionally, if there are to be any battles as to what the appropriate remedy should be, this is where they typically play out. Moreover, it is here that EPA and the PRPs must sort through the difficult issues regarding which PRPs are to pay how much, an issue that can get complicated, for example, when trying to determine the appropriate shares of the major generators as compared to owner/operators. And finally, because EPA typically asks the major parties to perform the necessary investigatory and/or remedial activities, it is during these negotiations that the PRPs must determine (generally as a group) whether they are willing to sign a consent decree or, alternatively, whether they would prefer to run the risk of having EPA issue them a unilateral order.

Depending on where EPA is on the technical side of the case, EPA may offer the major parties the opportunity to perform the RI/FS. EPA views negotiations concerning the RI/FS differently from those regarding cleanup. While the Agency is interested in having PRPs conduct RI/FSs, it is not inclined to spend long periods of time negotiating these agreements. Accordingly, EPA requires that PRPs meet three conditions as a precondition to negotiations regarding who will perform the RI/FS: they must (1) organize quickly into a group representing enough parties to assume full responsibility for conducting the RI/FS; (2) agree to follow EPA's scope of work for the RI/FS (although some minor negotiation may be allowed); and (3) demonstrate to the Agency their capability of adequately carrying out the RI/FS. EPA, "Participation of Potentially Responsible Parties in Development of Remedial Investigations and Feasibility Studies Under CERCLA," dated May 20, 1984.

Regardless of whether EPA is negotiating regarding the RI/FS or the ultimate remedy, it has at its disposal a procedural device wherein, at its option, it can invoke a formalized framework imposing rigid time constraints on the negotiation process. Under this process, known as "special notice," EPA sends out what in most circumstances will be a second notice letter prior to the RI/FS ("RI/FS special notice") and a third notice letter prior to the initiation of the remedial action ("RD/RA special notice"). To the extent the information is available, these notices are to provide each PRP with the names and addresses of the other PRPs, the volume and nature of the substances contributed by each PRP, and a volumetric ranking. See CERCLA § 122(e)(1). Under § 122(e)(2), the PRPs receiving the notice letter then have 60 days to coordinate and make a proposal for either undertaking the cleanup or financing a governmental cleanup. EPA must abstain from commencing any response actions under § 104(a), any RI/FS activities under § 104(b), or an action under § 106 during this 60-day period. If EPA determines that the PRPs submit a "good faith offer" within the 60-day period, it shall not commence any RI/FS activities for 30 more days, or any cleanup activities under § 104(a) or enforcement actions under § 106 for 60 more days.

Perhaps obviously enough, these moratoria are intended to provide for periods of negotiation between EPA and the PRPs. EPA, however, cleverly has interpreted these moratoria not only as a "floor" on the necessary negotiation period, but also a "ceiling." That is, EPA interprets the 90–and 120–day timeframes as placing a cap on the period of its negotiations with the PRPs. The current Agency position is that if the relevant negotiations are not concluded within the relevant timeframe, EPA generally will exercise its option to issue a unilateral order under § 106. Thus EPA has transformed the special notice device into a tool that permits it to invoke rigid "drop dead" dates at a moment's notice during the negotiations, instilling a clear sense of urgency in the negotiations.

As mentioned, the primary benefits EPA can confer to encourage settlement are a covenant not to sue and contribution protection. See CERCLA §§ 122(f), 113(f), and 122(h)(4). As also mentioned, EPA insists upon broader reopeners here than in the *de minimis* context. One is statutorily based: § 122(f)(6) provides that, in most situations, any covenant not to sue for future liability must include a reopener allowing EPA to pursue the settling PRPs for conditions that were unknown at the time EPA certified that the remedial action was complete. Additionally, § 122(f)(6)(C) authorizes EPA to include in any reopener such other terms as it deems necessary to protect human health and the environment. EPA's current policy is to include a reopener covering all situations where new information reveals that the remedy is not protective of human health and the environment. In cost-recovery settlements, it also frequently imposes a reopener addressing the possibility of cost-over-runs.

The major-party negotiations frequently founder not upon fights between EPA and the PRPs, but on those between warring factions among the PRPs themselves. Interestingly, EPA is often a disinterested observer in exactly how these battles play out, being much more interested in simply whether they are resolved on a timely basis. What role should EPA play in resolving any of these questions? Interestingly, at many sites EPA in the end acts almost as a facilitator or mediator because there tends to be a collective assumption among EPA and the PRPs that EPA will be made whole; the only question is how much each

PRP is going to have to pay. In fact, § 122(e)(3)(A) contemplates such a role in authorizing EPA to provide the PRPs with what is called a "nonbinding preliminary allocation of responsibility" (or—in acronym-speak—an "NBAR") allocating percentages of the total cost among the PRPs if it determines that such a step would expedite settlements and remedial action. While EPA seldom formally invokes the NBAR process, its very existence speaks to the odd neutral-party role that EPA frequently assumes in CERCLA negotiations.

A further significant question that PRPs may face in CERCLA negotiations involves whether to enter into a consent decree on EPA's terms or to risk the alternatives—either a unilateral order or an EPA-lead cleanup. In multi-party cases, the choice may not be available. If some subset of the PRPs are going to enter into a decree, the others may have to choose simply between signing on or being left out in the cold as non-settlors (whom EPA pejoratively refers to as "recalcitrants"). (The harshness of this dichotomy will be considered further below.) In other cases, however, the PRPs collectively may have the power to determine at least the method through which their poison will be administered. While settlement may offer the benefits of a covenants not to sue and contribution protection, it also has its costs. Most notable among these are the various one-sided provisions EPA insists upon including in its consent decrees. These include, for example, the accrual of stipulated penalties not only during periods of clear noncompliance, but also in situations where the respondents may have raised legitimate but ultimately unsuccessful arguments regarding the implementation of the decree during a dispute resolution process. See EPA's Revised Model RD/RA Consent Decree, 60 Fed.Reg. 38817 (July 28, 1995), at paragraphs 68 and 77.

How much liability, if any, should EPA reserve for non-settlors in the negotiation process? From one perspective, it can be argued that EPA should impose all remaining liabilities, after any *de minimis* settlements, on the settling major parties. Under this route, the government bears no further risk and the settling parties can file suit against the non-settlors for contribution. This approach does have some drawbacks, however. To the extent that it imposes on settling parties the transaction costs of pursuing the non-settlors, it tends to discourage proactive behavior (i.e., settling) on the part of those parties that would like to step forward and assume their cleanup obligations. Conversely, it tends to reward those who "lie in the weeds," by increasing the chance that they will never be sued—given the transaction costs, the settling PRPs may not find it to be in their best interest to pursue all non-settlors.

In the *Cannons* case (set forth below), EPA chose to tier its settlement offers in a way that would encourage early settlement and thus necessarily, given the combined effects of joint and several liability and contribution protection, impose any resulting shortfalls on the remaining non-settlors. See CERCLA § 113(f)(2) (settlement with one PRP "reduces the potential liability of the others by the amount of the settlement"). After raising approximately $13.5 million through the *de minimis* settlement, which was entered administratively, EPA negotiated a settlement with the major parties that resulted in their commitment to commit approximately $34 million to the past and future cleanup efforts, with appropriate reopeners. This, however, left 37 nonsettlors—all of whom were *de minimis* parties—exposed to almost $11 million in unresolved liability.

Prior to the finalization of the major party decree, many of the nonsettling *de minimis* parties began to recognize that they might be left bearing disproportionate amounts of liability. They therefore sought to be included in the major-party settlement, agreeing to be bound by its terms including the various reopeners. EPA declined to allow them to participate in this decree. Why do you think EPA did so? After having been rebuffed in their efforts to join in the major-party settlement, these non-settlors then asked EPA if it would negotiate another *de minimis* settlement on the same terms as the first. EPA declined, but did put forward a second *de minimis* offer with an enhanced premium of 160%, thus allowing these generators to settle only if each agreed to pay 260% of its volumetric share of the total projected response costs. The first *de minimis* settlement had been based upon a premium of 60 percent. Thus, EPA's tiering methodology resulted in a penalty of 100% of the base volumetric share due to the nonsettlors' failure to have accepted its first *de minimis* proposal. Perhaps surprisingly, twelve *de minimis* parties accepted this offer, contributing an aggregate total of another $792,000 to the cleanup effort, but still leaving more than $10 million in liability for the non-settlors. When EPA moved to enter the decrees, the nonsettling parties objected to EPA's negotiating tactics. This litigation eventually resulted in the following First Circuit opinion:

UNITED STATES v. CANNONS ENGINEERING CORP.

United States Court of Appeals, First Circuit, 1990.

899 F.2d 79.

SELYA, CIRCUIT JUDGE.

Our starting point is well defined. [SARA] authorized a variety of types of settlements which the EPA may utilize in CERCLA actions, including consent decrees providing for PRPs to contribute to cleanup costs and/or to undertake response activities themselves. See 42 U.S.C. § 9622 (1987). SARA's legislative history makes pellucid that, when such consent decrees are forged, the trial court's review function is only to "satisfy itself that the settlement is reasonable, fair, and consistent with the purposes that CERCLA is intended to serve." H.R.Rep. No. 253, Pt. 3, 99th Cong., 1st Sess. 19 (1985), *reprinted in* 1986 U.S.Code Cong. & Admin.News 3038, 3042. Reasonableness, fairness, and fidelity to the statute are, therefore, the horses which district judges must ride.

That said, we are quick to concede that these three steeds are all mutable figures taking on different forms and shapes in different factual settings. Yet, the concepts' amorphous quality is no accident or quirk of fate. We believe that Congress intended, first, that the judiciary take a broad view of proposed settlements, leaving highly technical issues and relatively petty inequities to the discourse between parties; and second, that the district courts treat each case on its own merits, recognizing the wide range of potential problems and possible solutions. When a court considers approval of a consent decree in a CERCLA case, there can be no easy-to-apply check list of relevant factors.

We agree with the district court that fairness in the CERCLA settlement context has both procedural and substantive components. To measure procedural fairness, a court should ordinarily look to the negotiation process and attempt to gauge its candor, openness, and bargaining balance.

In this instance, the district court found the proposed decrees to possess the requisite procedural integrity and appellants have produced no persuasive reason to alter this finding. It is clear the district court believed that the government conducted negotiations forthrightly and in good faith, and the record is replete with indications to that effect. Most of appellants' contrary intimations are vapid and merit summary rejection. But their flagship argument—that the procedural integrity of the settlement was ruptured because appellants were neither allowed to join the [major party (MP)] decree nor informed in advance that they would be excluded—requires comment.

Appellants claim that they were relatively close to the 1% [volumetric contribution] cutoff point [for being treated as *de minimis* parties], and were thus arbitrarily excluded from the major party settlement, avails them naught. Congress intended to give the EPA broad discretion to structure classes of PRPs for settlement purposes. We cannot say that the government acted beyond the scope of that discretion in separating minor and major players in this instance, that is, in determining that generators who had sent less than 1% of the volume of hazardous waste to the Sites would comprise the [*de minimis* classification (DMC)] and those generators who were responsible for a greater percentage would be treated as major PRPs. While the dividing line was only one of many which the agency could have selected, it was well within the universe of plausibility. And it is true, if sometimes sad, that whenever and wherever government draws lines, some parties fall on what they may perceive as the "wrong" side. There was no cognizable unfairness in this respect. Moreover, having established separate categories for different PRPs, the agency had no obligation to let defendants flit from class to class, thus undermining the rationale and purpose for drawing lines in the first place.

Nor can we say that appellants were entitled to more advance warning of the EPA's negotiating strategy than they received. At the time de minimis PRPs were initially invited to participate in the administrative settlement, the EPA, by letter, informed all of them, including appellants, that:

The government is anxious to achieve a high degree of participation in this de minimis settlement. Accordingly, the terms contained in this settlement offer are the most favorable terms that the government intends to make available to parties eligible for de minimis settlement in this case.

[*United States v. Cannons Engineering Corp.*, 720 F.Supp. 1027, 1033 (D.Mass.1989)]. Appellants knew, early on, that they were within the DMC and could spurn the EPA's proposal only at the risk of paying more at a later time. Although appellants may have assumed that they could ride on the coattails of the major parties and join whatever MP decree emerged—the government had, on other occasions, allowed such cafeteria-style settlements—the agency was neither asked for, nor did it give, any such assurance in this instance. As a matter of law, we do not believe that Congress meant to handcuff government negotiators in CERCLA cases by insisting that the EPA allow polluters to pick and choose which settlements they might prefer to join. And as a matter of equity, we think that if appellants were misled at all, it was by their own wishful thinking.

The district court found the consent decrees to have been the product of fair play. Given that the decrees were negotiated at arm's length among experienced counsel, that appellants ... had an opportunity to participate in the negotiations and to join both the first and the second de minimis settlements, and that the agency operated in good faith, the finding of procedural fairness is eminently supportable.

Substantive fairness introduces into the equation concepts of corrective justice and accountability: a party should bear the cost of the harm for which it is legally responsible. The logic behind these concepts dictates that settlement terms must be based upon, and roughly correlated with, some acceptable measure of comparative fault, apportioning liability among the settling parties according to rational (if necessarily imprecise) estimates of how much harm each PRP has done.

Even accepting substantive fairness as linked to comparative fault, an important issue still remains as to how comparative fault is to be measured. There is no universally correct approach. It appears very clear to us that what constitutes the best measure of comparative fault at a particular Superfund site under particular factual circumstances should be left largely to the EPA's expertise. Whatever formula or scheme EPA advances for measuring comparative fault and allocating liability should be upheld so long as the agency supplies a plausible explanation for it, welding some reasonable linkage between the factors it includes in its formula or scheme and the proportionate shares of the settling PRPs. Put in slightly different terms, the chosen measure of comparative fault should be upheld unless it is arbitrary, capricious, and devoid of a rational basis.

Not only must the EPA be given leeway to construct the barometer of comparative fault, but the agency must also be accorded flexibility to diverge from an apportionment formula in order to address special factors not conducive to regimented treatment. While the list of possible variables is virtually limitless, two frequently encountered reasons warranting departure from strict formulaic comparability are the uncertainty of future events and the timing of particular settlement decisions. Common sense suggests that a PRP's assumption of open-ended risks may merit a discount on comparative fault, while obtaining a complete release from uncertain future liability may call for a premium. By the same token, the need to encourage (and suitably reward) early, cost-effective settlements and to account inter alia for anticipated savings in transaction costs inuring from celeritous settlement can affect the construct. Because we are confident that Congress intended EPA to have considerable flexibility in negotiating and structuring settlements, we think reviewing courts should permit the agency to depart from rigid adherence to formulae wherever the agency proffers a reasonable good-faith justification for departure.

We also believe that a district court should give the EPA's expertise the benefit of the doubt when weighing substantive fairness—particularly when the agency, and hence the court, has been confronted by ambiguous, incomplete, or inscrutable information. In settlement negotiations, particularly in the early phases of environmental litigation, precise data relevant to determining the total extent of harm caused and the role of each PRP is often unavailable. Yet, it would disserve a principal end of the statute—achievement of prompt settlement and a concomitant head start on response activities—to leave matters in limbo until more precise information was amassed. As long as the data the EPA uses to apportion liability for purposes of a consent decree falls along the broad spectrum of plausible approximations, judicial intrusion is unwarranted—regardless of whether the court would have opted to employ the same data in the same way.

In this instance, we agree with the court below that the consent decrees pass muster from a standpoint of substantive fairness. They adhere generally to principles of comparative fault according to a volumetric standard, determining the liability of each PRP according to volumetric contribution. And, to the extent they deviate from this formulaic approach, they do so on the basis of adequate justification. In particular, the premiums charged to de minimis PRPs in the administrative settlement, and the increased premium charged in the DMC decree, seem well warranted.

The argument that the EPA should have used relative toxicity as a determinant of proportionate liability for response costs, instead of a strictly volumetric ranking, is a stalking horse. Having selected a reasonable method of weighing comparative fault, the agency need not show that it is the best, or even the fairest, of all conceivable methods. The choice of the yardstick to be used for allocating liability must be left primarily to the expert discretion of the EPA, particularly when the PRPs involved are numerous and the situation is complex. We cannot reverse the court below for refusing to second-guess the agency on this score.

Appellants' next asseveration—that the decrees favor major party PRPs over their less culpable counterparts—is a gross distortion. While the DMC and MP decrees differ to some extent in application of the volumetric share formula, requiring lower initial contributions under the latter, the good-faith justification for this divergence is readily apparent. In return for the premium paid, de minimis PRPs can cash out, thus obtaining two important benefits: reduced transaction costs and absolute finality with respect to the monetization of their overall liability. The major PRPs, on the other hand, retain an open-ended risk anent their liability at three of the Sites, making any comparison of proportionate contributions a dubious proposition. At the very least, assumption of this unquantifiable future liability under the MP decree warranted some discount—and the tradeoff crafted by the government's negotiators seems reasonable. Indeed, the acceptance of the first and second DMC settlement offers by so many of the de minimis PRPs is itself an indication of substantive fairness toward the class to which appellants belong. On this record, the district court did not misuse its discretion in ruling that the decrees sufficiently tracked the parties' comparative fault.

The last point which merits discussion under this rubric involves the fact that the agency upped the ante as the game continued, that is, the premium assessed as part of the administrative settlement was increased substantially for purposes of the later DMC decree. Like the district court, we see no unfairness in this approach. For one thing, litigation is expensive—and having called the tune by their refusal to subscribe to the administrative settlement, we think it not unfair that appellants, thereafter, would have to pay the piper. For another thing, rewarding PRPs who settle sooner rather than later is completely consonant with CERCLA's makeup.

Although appellants berate escalating settlement offers as discriminating among similarly situated PRPs, we think that the government's use of such a technique is fair and serves to promote the explicit statutory goal of expediting remedial measures for hazardous waste sites. That the cost of purchasing peace may rise for a laglast is consistent with the method of the statute; indeed, if the government cannot offer such routine incentives, there will be little inducement on the part of any PRP to enter an administrative settlement. Of course, the extent of the differential must be reasonable and the graduation neither unconscionable nor unduly coercive, but these are familiar subjects for judicial review in a wide variety of analogous settings. We believe that the EPA is entitled to make use of a series of escalating settlement proposals in a CERCLA case and that ... the serial settlements employed in this instance were substantively fair.

In the SARA Amendments, Congress explicitly created a statutory framework that left nonsettlors at risk of bearing a disproportionate amount of liability. The statute immunizes settling parties from liability for contribution and provides that only the amount of the settlement— not the pro rata share attributable to the settling party—shall be subtracted from the liability of the nonsettlors.[5] This can prove to be a substantial benefit to settling PRPs—and a corresponding detriment to their more recalcitrant counterparts.

Although such immunity creates a palpable risk of disproportionate liability, that is not to say that the device is forbidden. To the exact contrary, Congress has made its will explicit and the courts must defer. Disproportionate liability, a technique which promotes early settlements and deters litigation for litigation's sake, is an integral part of the statutory plan.

In a related vein, appellants assail the district court's dismissal of their cross-claims for contribution as against all settling PRPs. They contend, in essence, that the district court failed to appreciate that they would potentially bear a greater proportional liability than will be shouldered by any of the settling parties. They claim this result to be both unfair and inconsistent with the statutory plan.

... Congress plainly intended non-settlors to have no contribution rights against settlors regarding matters addressed in settlement. Thus, the cross-claims were properly dismissed; Congress purposed that all who choose not to settle confront the same sticky wicket of which appellants complain.

The statute, of course, not only bars contribution claims against settling parties, but also provides that, while a settlement will not discharge other PRPs, "it reduces the potential liability of the others by the amount of settlement." 42 U.S.C. § 9613(f)(2)(1987). The law's plain language admits of no construction other than a dollar-for-dollar reduction of the aggregate liability.... This clear and unequivocal statutory mandate overrides appellants' quixotic imprecation that their liability should be reduced not by the amount of settlement but by the equitable shares of the settling parties. In a very real sense, the appellants' arguments are with Congress, not with the district court.[6]

On a similar note, appellants bemoan the dismissal of their cross-claims for indemnity against the settling PRPs. We are unmoved. Although CERCLA is silent regarding indemnification, we refuse to read into the statute a right to indemnification that would eviscerate § 9613(f)(2) and allow non-settlors to make an end run around the statutory scheme.

---

5. The statute provides:

A person who has resolved its liability to the United States or a State in an administrative or judicially approved settlement shall not be liable for claims for contribution regarding matters addressed in the settlement. Such settlement does not discharge any of the other potentially liable persons unless its terms so provide, but it reduces the potential liability of the others by the amount of the settlement.

42 U.S.C. § 9613(f)(2)(1987).

6. The veiled constitutional argument sponsored principally by Kingston–Warren does not withstand scrutiny. There is no federal common law right to contribution, *Texas Indus., Inc. v. Radcliff Materials, Inc.*, 451 U.S. 630, 641–42 (1981); *Northwest Airlines, Inc. v. Transport Workers Union*, 451 U.S. 77, 90–91 (1981), and hence, no deprivation of any constitutionally protected interest.

Appellants allege no contractual basis for indemnification. Their noncontractual indemnity claim, by definition and extrapolation, "is in effect only a more extreme form of [a claim for] contribution." *Drake v. Raymark Industries, Inc.*, 772 F.2d 1007, 1011 n. 2 (1st Cir.1985), *cert. denied*, 476 U.S. 1126 (1986). Clearly, if appellants' claims for partial contribution can validly be barred in the course of implementing a CERCLA settlement, their claims for total contribution, i.e., indemnity, can likewise be foreclosed.

The appellants also contend that the government's negotiating strategy must be an open book. We disagree. Congress did not send the EPA into the toxic waste ring with one arm tied behind its collective back. Although the EPA may not mislead any of the parties, discriminate unfairly, or engage in deceptive practices, neither must the agency spoon feed PRPs. In the CERCLA context, the government is under no obligation to telegraph its settlement offers, divulge its negotiating strategy in advance, or surrender the normal prerogatives of strategic flexibility which any negotiator cherishes. In short, contrary to the objectors' thesis, the EPA need not tell de minimis PRPs in advance whether they will, or will not, be eligible to join ensuing major party settlements.

Notes and Questions

1. As mentioned, the premium payment in the first *de mimimis* settlement in *Cannons* was 60%, resulting in a multiplier of 1.6 over that amount which the *de minimis* generators would have paid in the absence of such a premium. Do you think this is an appropriate amount? How do you think it was determined?

2. Should the government be under an obligation to "telegraph its settlement offers" or "divulge its negotiating strategy in advance?" Should it be able to penalize non-settlors in the way that the *Cannons* court appears to bless? In *Cannons*, one of the *de minimis* nonsettlors—Olin Hunt—was able to show that, while its base volumetric share of the overall liability would have been $370,000 (without any premiums), it was now facing liabilities in excess of $2 million because its share comprised 20 percent of the total volumetric share of non-settling defendants. Thus, EPA's tactics had increased Olin Hunt's overall exposure to more than three times what it would have paid had it accepted EPA's first settlement offer ($592,000 versus $2,000,000). Does this seem appropriate? How did the court address the constitutional arguments raised by Kingston–Warren? What are the lessons of this case for those involved in CERCLA negotiations?

3. Did you agree with the court's treatment of the appellants' indemnity claims? Presuming this claim was based on a state-law theory, should Congress be able to take such rights away? Does § 113(f)(2) clearly do so? On the other hand, would the effect of this section be nullified if state law contribution or indemnity claims were allowed to survive?

C. Private Party Cost–Recovery and Contribution

As previously mentioned, CERCLA's cost recovery authority is not limited to governmental entities. While § 107(a)(4)(A) creates a right of cost-recovery in the Federal Government, the states, and Indian Tribes, § 107(a)(4)(B) creates a substantially similar right in private parties, albeit with one additional requirement. Unlike the sovereigns, private parties bear the burden of demonstrating that any costs incurred were consistent with the NCP. Additionally, § 113(f)(1) and (f)(3)(B) supplement § 107(a)(4)(B) by authorizing contribution actions for PRPs under specified circumstances.

These provisions have the effect of dramatically expanding the scope of the CERCLA program. Over the years, an ever-increasing percentage of the judicial opinions addressing liability issues have been issued in the context of private-party actions. Moreover, private-party CERCLA actions are significant not only for the numbers of cases they generate, but also for the nature of the problems addressed in those cases. As we already have seen, EPA's primary emphasis under CERCLA is on sites qualifying for the NPL; indeed, EPA may perform "remedial" activities only at NPL sites. While states and Indian tribes are not so limited, as sovereigns they face the ever-present need to focus their attention on their highest-priority sites. Those with potential private-party claims, by contrast, may be limited only by the minimal statutory elements, the bounds of their reason, and their ability to locate PRPs.

At first blush, Sections 107(a)(4), 113(f)(1) and 113(f)(3)(B) appear to establish a clear dichotomy pursuant to which one who cleans up a site on her own initiative would have a claim under § 107(a)(4), whereas one who does so in response to governmental prodding (or who reimburses the government for a government-lead cleanup) would have a claim under one of the subparts of § 113(f). Upon closer examination, however, the statutory waters are seen to be muddier than they first appear. One question is whether those who themselves may be liable may bring cost-recovery claims under § 107(a)(4) against other PRPs. This question can come up in a host of different circumstances. In some cases, the plaintiff's liability may be obvious (e.g., where it admits to having played a role in causing the contamination); in others, it may be less so (e.g., in situations in which it owns the relevant property but may have an argument as to whether it qualifies for either the innocent landowner or prospective purchaser defense). Should this make a difference? The pre-complaint legal dynamics may also vary. In some cases, for example, the plaintiff may have cleaned up the site without any governmental edict requiring it to do so (a so-called "voluntary" cleanup). In others, it may have done pursuant to an EPA-induced consent decree or an EPA-issued administrative order. In still others, the State may have compelled it to clean up a site pursuant to State law. Take a close look at the language of § 107(a)(4) and § 113(f)(1) and (f)(3)(B). Do these provisions clearly resolve the circumstances under which a plaintiff has a claim under either each provision? Are there circumstances in which it may have a claim under more than one of them, or none of them? Even if we assume that one who cleans up a site should generally have a claim under at least one of these provisions (which, as we will see, may or may not be a safe assumption), what effect, if any, would the source of the claim have on the nature of the recovery that the PRP might be able to obtain?

Consider these issues as you read the following decisions from the Second Circuit and the Supreme Court:

BEDFORD AFFILIATES v. SILLS

United States Court of Appeals, Second Circuit, 1998.

156 F.3d 416.

CARDAMONE, Circuit Judge:

[Bedford Affiliates (Bedford) owned a piece of property in Glen Cove, New York, that was subleased to RonGlen Cleaners (RonGlen) for use as a dry cleaning establishment. Richard Sills was RonGlen's sole officer, director and shareholder. In 1990, after RonGlen had vacated the premises, Bedford learned that RonGlen had been responsible for at least three significant releases of tetrachloroethylene, a dry cleaning solvent also known as "perc." Bedford ultimately entered into a series of consent orders with the New York State Department of Environmental Conservation (DEC) to study and clean up the site. It then filed suit against Sills and Harvey and Beverly Manheimer (Manheimers), the latter two of whom were co-trustees of a trust that held the leasehold interest for part of the relevant period, and were the direct leaseholders for the rest of it.

The district court held that Bedford could seek contribution under § 113(f)(1), but could not proceed under § 107(a)(4). It went on to apportion 95% of the liability to Sills. Sills appealed, and Bedford cross-appealed, arguing (among other things) that it should have been allowed to seek cost-recovery under § 107(a)(4). We deal here only with Bedford's cross appeal.]

The original CERCLA legislation enacted in 1980 created the cost recovery scheme under § 107(a).... Potentially responsible persons are held strictly liable for, among others, necessary cleanup costs "incurred by any other person consistent with the national contingency plan." CERCLA § 107(a)(4)(B). Where the environmental harm is indivisible, multiple responsible persons will be jointly and severally liable for cleanup costs.

In its original form, CERCLA lacked a specific provision permitting a potentially responsible person that had incurred cleanup costs to seek contribution from other liable parties. Numerous district courts, in response, interpreted CERCLA § 107(a) to imply such a cause of action. *See Key Tronic Corp. v. United States,* 511 U.S. 809, 816 (1994). With the 1986 enactment of SARA, Congress added CERCLA § 113(f)(1) as an express authorization of claims for contribution. CERCLA § 113(f)(1) states "[a]ny person may seek contribution from any other person who is liable or potentially liable under [CERCLA § 107(a)]" for response costs. To resolve § 113(f)(1) contribution claims, "the court may allocate response costs among liable parties using such equitable factors as the court determines are appropriate." *Id.*

The district court in the present case properly held that Bedford could not pursue a § 107(a) cost recovery claim against Sills and the Manheimers due to its status as a [PRP]. Section 107(a) holds a potentially responsible person liable for costs incurred by "any other person" during an environmental cleanup. As noted earlier, where multiple parties are responsible, joint and several liability attaches. Consequently, one potentially responsible person can never recover 100 percent of the response costs from others similarly situated since it is a joint tortfeasor—and not an innocent party—that ultimately must bear its *pro rata* share of cleanup costs under § 107(a).

To bring a derivative action to recoup the portion of costs exceeding a potentially responsible person's equitable share of the overall liability, however, is a quintessential claim for contribution, where a party seeks to apportion liability for an injury for which it is also directly liable.

CERCLA § 113(f) plainly governs such contribution actions. *See* 42 U.S.C. § 9613(f)(1) (permitting "any person" to seek contribution from "any other person" potentially liable under CERCLA § 107; *see also* H.R.Rep. No. 99–253(I), at 79 (1985), *reprinted in* 1986 U.S.C.C.A.N. 2835, 2861 (enunciating that a principal goal in passing CERCLA § 113 was to "clarif[y] and confirm [] the right of a person held jointly and severally liable under CERCLA to seek contribution from other potentially liable parties, when the person believes that it has assumed a share of the cleanup or cost that may be greater than its equitable share under the circumstances.").

Our decision today to limit the recovery of a potentially responsible person to contribution under § 113(f) not only is in keeping with the holdings of other Circuits, but also gives CERCLA its full intended effect. In contrast to § 113(f)(1), which apportions liability based on equitable considerations and has a three-year statute of limitations, *see* 42 U.S.C. § 9613(g)(3), § 107(a) has a six-year statute of limitations, *see* 42 U.S.C. § 9613(g)(2). Were we to permit a potentially responsible person to elect recovery under either § 107(a) or § 113(f)(1), § 113(f)(1) would be rendered meaningless. A recovering liable party would readily abandon a § 113(f)(1) suit in favor of the substantially more generous provisions of § 107(a).

We decline to interpret § 107(a) so broadly that § 113(f)(1) would become a nullity. The language of CERCLA suggests Congress planned that an innocent party be able to sue for full recovery of its costs, *i.e.,* indemnity under § 107(a), while a party that is itself liable may recover only those costs exceeding its *pro rata* share of the entire cleanup expenditure, *i.e.,* contribution under § 113(f)(1).

COOPER INDUSTRIES, INC. v. AVIALL SERVICES, INC.

Supreme Court of the United States, 2004.

___ U.S. ___, 125 S.Ct. 577, 160 L.Ed.2d 548.

Justice THOMAS delivered the opinion of the Court.

Section 113(f)(1) of [CERCLA] allows persons who have undertaken efforts to clean up properties contaminated by hazardous substances to seek contribution from other parties liable under CERCLA. Section 113(f)(1) specifies that a party may obtain contribution "during or following any civil action" under CERCLA § 106 or § 107(a). The issue we must decide is whether a private party who has not been sued under § 106 or § 107(a) may nevertheless obtain contribution under § 113(f)(1) from other liable parties. We hold that it may not.

After CERCLA's enactment in 1980, litigation arose over whether § 107, in addition to allowing the Government and certain private parties to recover costs from PRPs, also allowed a PRP that had incurred response costs to recover costs from other PRPs. More specifically, the question was whether a private party that had incurred response costs, but that had done so voluntarily and was not itself subject to suit, had a cause of action for cost recovery against other PRPs. Various courts held that § 107(a)(4)(B) ... authorized such a cause of action.

After CERCLA's passage, litigation also ensued over the separate question whether a private entity that had been sued in a cost recovery action (by the Government or by another PRP) could obtain contribution from other PRPs. As originally enacted in 1980, CERCLA contained no provision expressly providing for a right of action for contribution. A number of District Courts nonetheless held that, although CERCLA did not mention the word "contribution," such a right arose either impliedly from provisions of the statute, or as a matter of federal common law. That conclusion was debatable in light of two decisions of this Court that refused to recognize implied or common-law rights to contribution in other federal statutes. See *Texas Industries, Inc. v. Radcliff Materials, Inc.,* 451 U.S. 630, 638–647 (1981); *Northwest Airlines, Inc. v. Transport Workers,* 451 U.S. 77, 90–99 (1981).

Congress subsequently amended CERCLA in [SARA] to provide an express cause of action for contribution, codified as CERCLA § 113(f)(1):

Any person may seek contribution from any other person who is liable or potentially liable under section 9607(a) of this title, during or following any civil action under section 9606 of this title or under section 9607(a) of this title. Such claims shall be brought in accordance with this section and the Federal Rules of Civil Procedure, and shall be governed by Federal law. In resolving contribution claims, the court may allocate response costs among liable parties using such equitable factors as the court determines are appropriate. Nothing in this subsection shall diminish the right of any person to bring an action for contribution in the absence of a civil action under section 9606 of this title or section 9607 of this title. *Id.,* at 1647, as codified in 42 U.S.C. § 9613(f)(1).

SARA also created a separate express right of contribution, § 113(f)(3)(B), for "[a] person who has resolved its liability to the United States or a State for some or all of a response action or for some or all of the costs of such action in an administrative or judicially approved settlement." In short, after SARA, CERCLA provided for a right to cost recovery in certain circumstances, § 107(a), and separate rights to contribution in other circumstances, §§ 113(f)(1), 113(f)(3)(B).[3]

This case concerns four contaminated aircraft engine maintenance sites in Texas. Cooper Industries, Inc., owned and operated those sites until 1981, when it sold them to Aviall Services, Inc. Aviall operated the four sites for a number of years. Ultimately, Aviall discovered that both it and Cooper had contaminated the facilities when petroleum and other hazardous substances leaked into the ground and ground water through underground storage tanks and spills.

Aviall notified the Texas Natural Resource Conservation Commission (Commission) of the contamination. The Commission informed Aviall that it was violating state environmental laws, directed Aviall to clean up the site, and threatened to pursue an enforcement action if Aviall failed to undertake remediation. Neither the Commission nor the EPA, however, took judicial or administrative measures to compel cleanup.

Aviall cleaned up the properties under the State's supervision, beginning in 1984. Aviall sold the properties to a third party in 1995 and 1996, but remains contractually responsible for the cleanup. Aviall has incurred approximately $5 million in cleanup costs; the total costs may be even greater. In August 1997, Aviall filed this action against Cooper in the United States District Court for the Northern District of Texas, seeking to recover cleanup costs. The original complaint asserted a claim for cost recovery under CERCLA § 107(a), a separate claim for contribution under CERCLA § 113(f)(1), and state-law claims. Aviall later amended the complaint, combining its two CERCLA claims into a single, joint CERCLA claim. That claim alleged that, pursuant to § 113(f)(1), Aviall was entitled to seek contribution from Cooper, as a PRP under § 107(a), for response costs and other liability Aviall incurred in connection with the Texas facilities. Aviall continued to assert state-law claims as well.

[The District Court granted Cooper's motion for summary judgment, determining that Aviall had abandoned its § 107 claim and did not have a valid contribution claim under § 113(f)(1) because it had not been sued

---

3. In *Key Tronic Corp. v. United States,* 511 U.S. 809 (1994), we observed that § 107 and § 113 created "similar and somewhat overlapping" remedies. *Id.* at 816. The cost recovery remedy of § 107(a)(4)(B) and the contribution remedy of § 113(f)(1) are similar at a general level in that they both allow private parties to recoup costs from other private parties. But the two remedies are clearly distinct.

under CERCLA § 106 or § 107. Having dismissed Aviall's federal claim, the court declined to exercise jurisdiction over the state-law claims.

After a divided panel of the Fifth Circuit affirmed, an en banc panel of the Fifth Circuit reversed, again by a divided vote. The en banc panel concluded that § 113(f)(1) allows a PRP to obtain contribution from other PRPs regardless of whether the PRP has been sued under § 106 or § 107. 312 F.3d 677 (2002).] The court held that "[s]ection 113(f)(1) authorizes suits against PRPs in both its first and last sentence[,] which states without qualification that 'nothing' in the section shall 'diminish' any person's right to bring a contribution action in the absence of a section 106 or section 107(a) action." *Id.,* at 681. The court reasoned in part that "may" in § 113(f)(1) did not mean "may only." *Id.,* at 686–687. . . .

III

A

Section 113(f)(1) does not authorize Aviall's suit. The first sentence, the enabling clause that establishes the right of contribution, provides: "Any person *may* seek contribution . . . *during or following* any civil action under section 9606 of this title or under section 9607(a) of this title," 42 U.S.C. § 9613(f)(1) (emphasis added). The natural meaning of this sentence is that contribution may only be sought subject to the specified conditions, namely, "during or following" a specified civil action.

Aviall answers that "may" should be read permissively, such that "during or following" a civil action is one, but not the exclusive, instance in which a person may seek contribution. We disagree. First, as just noted, the natural meaning of "may" in the context of the enabling clause is that it authorizes certain contribution actions—ones that satisfy the subsequent specified condition—and no others.

Second, and relatedly, if § 113(f)(1) were read to authorize contribution actions at any time, regardless of the existence of a § 106 or § 107(a) civil action, then Congress need not have included the explicit "during or following" condition. In other words, Aviall's reading would render part of the statute entirely superfluous, something we are loath to do. Likewise, if § 113(f)(1) authorizes contribution actions at any time, § 113(f)(3)(B), which permits contribution actions after settlement, is equally superfluous. There is no reason why Congress would bother to specify conditions under which a person may bring a contribution claim, and at the same time allow contribution actions absent those conditions.

The last sentence of § 113(f)(1), the saving clause, does not change our conclusion. That sentence provides: "Nothing in this subsection shall diminish the right of any person to bring an action for contribution in the absence of a civil action under section 9606 of this title or section 9607 of this title." 42 U.S.C. § 9613(f)(1). The sole function of the sentence is to clarify that § 113(f)(1) does nothing to "diminish" any cause(s) of action for contribution that may exist independently of

§ 113(f)(1). In other words, the sentence rebuts any presumption that the express right of contribution provided by the enabling clause is the exclusive cause of action for contribution available to a PRP. The sentence, however, does not itself establish a cause of action; nor does it expand § 113(f)(1) to authorize contribution actions not brought "during or following" a § 106 or § 107(a) civil action; nor does it specify what causes of action for contribution, if any, exist outside § 113(f)(1). Reading the saving clause to authorize § 113(f)(1) contribution actions not just "during or following" a civil action, but also before such an action, would again violate the settled rule that we must, if possible, construe a statute to give every word some operative effect.

Our conclusion follows not simply from § 113(f)(1) itself, but also from the whole of § 113. As noted above, § 113 provides two express avenues for contribution: § 113(f)(1) ("during or following" specified civil actions) and § 113(f)(3)(B) (after an administrative or judicially approved settlement that resolves liability to the United States or a State). Section 113(g)(3) then provides two corresponding 3–year limitations periods for contribution actions, one beginning at the date of judgment, § 113(g)(3)(A), and one beginning at the date of settlement, § 113(g)(3)(B). Notably absent from § 113(g)(3) is any provision for starting the limitations period if a judgment or settlement never occurs, as is the case with a purely voluntary cleanup. The lack of such a provision supports the conclusion that, to assert a contribution claim under § 113(f), a party must satisfy the conditions of either § 113(f)(1) or § 113(f)(3)(B).

Each side insists that the purpose of CERCLA bolsters its reading of § 113(f)(1). Given the clear meaning of the text, there is no need to resolve this dispute or to consult the purpose of CERCLA at all. As we have said: "[I]t is ultimately the provisions of our laws rather than the principal concerns of our legislators by which we are governed." *Oncale v. Sundowner Offshore Services, Inc.,* 523 U.S. 75, 79 (1998). Section 113(f)(1) authorizes contribution claims only "during or following" a civil action under § 106 or § 107(a), and it is undisputed that Aviall has never been subject to such an action.[5] Aviall therefore has no § 113(f)(1) claim.

B

Aviall [contends] that, in the alternative to an action for contribution under § 113(f)(1), Aviall may recover costs under § 107(a)(4)(B) even though it is a PRP. The dissent would have us so hold. We decline to address the issue. Neither the District Court, nor the Fifth Circuit panel, nor the Fifth Circuit sitting en banc considered Aviall's § 107 claim. In fact, as noted above, Aviall included separate § 107 and § 113 claims in its original complaint, but then asserted a "combined" § 107/§ 113 claim in its amended complaint. The District Court took

---

5. Neither has Aviall been subject to an administrative order under § 106; thus, we need not decide whether such an order would qualify as a "civil action under section 9606 . . . or under section 9607(a)" of CERCLA. 42 U.S.C. § 9613(f)(1).

this consolidated claim to mean that Aviall was relying on § 107 "not as an independent cause of action," but only "to the extent necessary to maintain a viable § 113(f)(1) contribution claim." Consequently the court saw no need to address any freestanding § 107 claim. [Likewise, at the Fifth Circuit level neither the three-judge panel nor the en banc panel addressed this claim.]

"We ordinarily do not decide in the first instance issues not decided below." *Adarand Constructors, Inc. v. Mineta,* 534 U.S. 103, 109 (2001). Although we have deviated from this rule in exceptional circumstances, the circumstances here cut *against* resolving the § 107 claim. Both the question whether Aviall has waived this claim and the underlying § 107 question (if it is not waived) may depend in part on the relationship between §§ 107 and 113. That relationship is a significant issue in its own right. It is also well beyond the scope of the briefing and, indeed, the question presented, which asks simply whether a private party "may bring an action seeking contribution pursuant to CERCLA Section 113(f)(1)." The § 107 claim and the preliminary waiver question merit full consideration by the courts below.

Furthermore, the parties cite numerous decisions of the Courts of Appeals as holding that a private party that is itself a PRP may not pursue a § 107(a) action against other PRPs for joint and several liability. To hold here that Aviall may pursue a § 107 action, we would have to consider whether these decisions are correct, an issue that Aviall has flagged but not briefed. And we might have to consider other issues, also not briefed, such as whether Aviall, which seeks to recover the share of its cleanup costs fairly chargeable to Cooper, may pursue a § 107 cost recovery action for some form of liability other than joint and several. We think it more prudent to withhold judgment on these matters.

In view of the importance of the § 107 issue and the absence of briefing and decisions by the courts below, we are not prepared—as the dissent would have it—to resolve the § 107 question solely on the basis of dictum in *Key Tronic.* We held there that certain attorney's fees were not "necessary costs of response" within the meaning of § 107(a)(4)(B). 511 U.S., at 818–821. But we did not address the relevance, if any, of Key Tronic's status as a PRP or confront the relationship between §§ 107 and 113.... Aviall itself recognizes the need for fuller examination of the § 107 claim; it has simply requested that we remand for consideration of that claim, not that we resolve the claim in the first instance.

C

In addition to leaving open whether Aviall may seek cost recovery under § 107, we decline to decide whether Aviall has an implied right to contribution under § 107. Portions of the Fifth Circuit's opinion below might be taken to endorse the latter cause of action, 312 F.3d, at 687; others appear to reserve the question whether such a cause of action exists, *id.,* at 685, n. 15. To the extent that Aviall chooses to frame its

§ 107 claim on remand as an implied right of contribution (as opposed to a right of cost recovery), we note that this Court has visited the subject of implied rights of contribution before. See *Texas Industries,* 451 U.S., at 638–647; *Northwest Airlines,* 451 U.S., at 90–99. We also note that, in enacting § 113(f)(1), Congress explicitly recognized a particular set (claims "during or following" the specified civil actions) of the contribution rights previously implied by courts from provisions of CERCLA and the common law. Nonetheless, we need not and do not decide today whether any judicially implied right of contribution survived the passage of SARA . .

* * *

We hold only that § 113(f)(1) does not support Aviall's suit. We therefore reverse the judgment of the Fifth Circuit and remand the case for further proceedings consistent with this opinion . .

Justice GINSBURG, with whom Justice STEVENS joins, dissenting.

In [*Key Tronic,* 511 U.S. at 818], all Members of this Court agreed that § 107 . . . "unquestionably provides a cause of action for [potentially responsible persons (PRPs)] to seek recovery of cleanup costs." The Court rested that determination squarely and solely on § 107(a)(4)(B), which allows *any* person who has incurred costs for cleaning up a hazardous waste site to recover all or a portion of those costs from any other person liable under CERCLA.

The *Key Tronic* Court divided, however, on the question whether the right to contribution is implicit in § 107(a)'s text, as the majority determined, or whether § 107(a) expressly confers the right, as the dissenters urged. The majority stated: Section 107 *"implies*—but does not expressly *command*—that [a PRP] may have a claim for contribution against those treated as joint tortfeasors." 511 U.S., at 818, and n. 11 (emphasis added). The dissent maintained: "Section 107(a)(4)(B) states, as clearly as can be, that '[c]overed persons . . . shall be liable for . . . necessary costs of response incurred by any other person.' Surely to say that A shall be liable to B is the *express* creation of a right of action." *Id.,* at 822. But no Justice expressed the slightest doubt that § 107 indeed did enable a PRP to sue other covered persons for reimbursement, in whole or part, of cleanup costs the PRP legitimately incurred.

In the Fifth Circuit's view, § 107 supplied the right of action for Aviall's claim, and § 113(f)(1) prescribed the procedural framework. 312 F.3d 677, 683, and n. 10 (2002) (stating that § 107 "impliedly authorizes a cause of action for contribution" and § 113(f) "govern[s] and regulate[s]" the action). Notably, Aviall expressly urged in the Court of Appeals that, were the court to conclude that § 113(f)(1)'s "during or following" language excluded application of that section to this case, Aviall's suit should be adjudicated independently under § 107(a).

I see no cause for protracting this litigation by requiring the Fifth Circuit to revisit a determination it has essentially made already: Federal courts, prior to the enactment of § 113(f)(1), had correctly held that

PRPs could "recover [under § 107] a proportionate share of their costs in actions for contribution against other PRPs," 312 F.3d, at 687;[2] nothing in § 113 retracts that right. Accordingly, I would not defer a definitive ruling by this Court on the question whether Aviall may pursue a § 107 claim for relief against Cooper.

Notes and Questions

1. As indicated in both *Bedford* and *Cooper*, the Courts of Appeals have been virtually unanimous in holding that PRPs cannot bring "pure" § 107 actions (seeking to impose joint and several liability) against other PRPs. In addition to *Bedford*, see *United Technologies Corp. v. Browning–Ferris Industries, Inc.*, 33 F.3d 96, 98–103 (1st Cir. 1994); *New Castle County v. Halliburton NUS Corp.*, 111 F.3d 1116, 1120–1124 (3d Cir. 1997); *Axel Johnson, Inc. v. Carroll Carolina Oil Co., Inc.*, 191 F.3d 409, 415 (4th Cir. 1999); *Centerior Service Co. v. Acme Scrap Iron & Metal Corp.*, 153 F.3d 344, 350 (6th Cir. 1998); *Akzo Coatings, Inc. v. Aigner Corp.*, 30 F.3d 761, 764–765 (7th Cir. 1994); *Control Data Corp. v. S.C.S.C. Corp.*, 53 F.3d 930, 934–935 (8th Cir. 1995); *The Pinal Creek Group v. Newmont Mining Corp.*, 118 F.3d 1298, 1301 (9th Cir. 1997); *Sun Co., Inc. v. Browning–Ferris, Inc.*, 124 F.3d 1187, 1190–1193 (10th Cir. 1997); and *Redwing Carriers, Inc. v. Saraland Apartments*, 94 F.3d 1489, 1496 and n. 7 (11th Cir. 1996). In *Bedford*, the Second Circuit appeared to identify three rationales for this outcome: (1) that otherwise the plaintiff would be able to recover 100% of its costs under a theory of joint and several liability; (2) that an action by one liable party against another is a "quintessential claim for contribution;" and (3) that a contrary ruling would render § 113(f)(1) a nullity because such plaintiffs would always choose "the substantially more generous provisions of § 107(a)." We will consider each of these points below.

2. In order to put the first of the *Bedford* court's rationales into perspective, imagine a site to which four parties have sent equal amounts of the exact same pollutant, all of which are commingled in the release. Imagine further that these are the only four PRPs, that they are equally culpable, and that two of them are insolvent. Assume that if all four of these parties were before the court in an EPA-lead action, and that if insolvency were not an issue, the court would be likely to allocate responsibility equally among the parties, with each paying 25% of the cleanup costs. Cf. CERCLA § 113(f)(1). If we assume that the cleanup costs are $20,000,000, each party would wind up paying $5,000,000. What would happen, though, if one of the two solvent parties spent the $20,000,000 cleaning up the site on a voluntary basis and then sued the other? One possibility, of course, is that the plaintiff would have no CERCLA claim whatsoever, a point to which we will return below. If we were to assume that the plaintiff would be entitled to at least some form of partial recovery, however, there would presumably be four possibilities as to how the cleanup costs could be divvied up between the two

---

2. The cases to which the Court refers, *Texas Industries, Inc. v. Radcliff Materials, Inc.*, 451 U.S. 630 (1981), and *Northwest Airlines, Inc. v. Transport Workers*, 451 U.S. 77 (1981), do not address the implication of a right of action for contribution under CERCLA. *Texas Industries* concerned the Sherman and Clayton Acts; *Northwest Airlines*, the Equal Pay Act and Title VII. A determination suitable in one statutory context does not necessarily carry over to a different statutory setting.

solvent parties. (1) we could hold the defendant jointly and severally responsible for all of the response costs, resulting in a 100% recovery for the plaintiff; (2) we could require the defendant to bear the burden of the so-called "orphan shares" (that is, the equitable shares of the two insolvent parties), resulting in its ultimately bearing 75% of the cleanup costs; (3) we could compel the plaintiff to bear those shares, resulting in its ultimately absorbing 75% of the cleanup costs; or (4) we could require them to each bear responsibility for half of the orphan shares (in addition to their own shares), resulting in each party's having to bear 50% of the cleanup costs. The *Bedford* court appeared to assume that allowing the plaintiff to proceed under § 107(a)(4) would compel the first of these outcomes. Do you agree?

3. In *Pinal Creek* (referred to in note 1), the plaintiffs ("the Pinal Group") had engaged in a voluntary cleanup. As a result, they argued that they had § 107 claims against the defendants, while at the same time acknowledging that the defendant might have viable § 113(f)(1) contribution counterclaims against them. 118 F.3d at 1298. In setting up their argument this way, they urged that, even if the court ultimately deemed them liable (a point which they appeared to concede), the defendants should be required to bear the orphan shares, as in the second example in note 2, above. Id. In rejecting this approach, the Ninth Circuit identified both procedural and substantive concerns. On the procedural front, the court determined that the Pinal Group's approach "would guarantee inefficiency, potential duplication, and prolongation of the litigation process." Id. at 1303. Do you agree? Is there any reason why the defendants would have been unable to assert their contribution claims in the same action, presumably by way of an affirmative defense under FRCP 8(c)? Substantively, the court appeared convinced that if it treated the claims in the manner advocated by the plaintiffs (i.e., cost-recovery claims buffered by the possibility of contribution counterclaims), the result would be that the defendants would bear all of the orphan shares. Are you convinced that this would be the case?

4. The Pinal Group may have compromised its cost-recovery claim by conceding its members' liability. What if there had been a real dispute as to whether they were liable? Even absent a serious question as to whether a particular CERCLA plaintiff is liable, shouldn't the court presume that it is not, and that it therefore has a right to file a pure § 107 claim, until the plaintiff either concedes its own liability or the defendant demonstrates it? This, of course, raises issues regarding the burden of both pleading and proof. In tort law, the defendant generally bears the burden of both pleading and proof with respect to defenses such as contributory and comparative negligence. Dobbs, The Law of Torts, § 198, p. 493 (West, 2000). Should this same principle apply under CERCLA? If the plaintiff should generally be presumed to be blameless until the defendant shows otherwise, what does this suggest as to the nature of the plaintiff's claim?

5. Turning to the *Bedford* court's second rationale, Black's Law Dictionary defines the term "contribution" as the "[r]ight of one who has discharged a common liability to recover of another also liable, the aliquot portion of which he ought to pay or bear." Black's Law Dictionary 328 (6th Ed. 1990). Given that Bedford had entered into a series of consent orders with the New York DEC, it is easy to see how the court regarded this as a "quintessential" claim of contribution. Indeed, although the court did not

focus on it, Section 113(f)(3)(B) appears to give parties such as Bedford an express statutory right of contribution where they have entered into administrative settlements with States. What if Bedford had voluntarily cleaned up the site on its own, without any governmental order, decree or agreement (again, a so-called "voluntary" cleanup)? Would this still be such a "quintessential" claim? Cf. Restatement (Second) Torts § 886(a), cmt. b. (contribution "applies in favor of a tortfeasor who has paid more than his equitable share of the common liability in settlement, without any judgment or even suit against him"). Even if it might be (which is quite debatable), should that control over the express language of § 107(a)(4)?

6. As mentioned in the note 1, above, the *Bedford* court also felt that allowing PRP plaintiffs to frame their claims under § 107(a)(4) would render § 113(f)(1) a nullity. Do you agree? Is there any other way (besides the innocent party/PRP dichotomy) to harmonize § 107(a)(4) with the contribution provisions in § 113(f)(1) and (f)(3)(B), giving each of them sway in appropriate circumstances? Remember that Bedford may very well have had a claim under § 113(f)(3)(B). Would the Second Circuit have been on firmer ground if it had simply said no one who has an express claim under either § 113(f)(1) or (f)(3)(B) can avoid the relevant provision (and the attendant statutes of limitation in § 113(g)(3)) by seeking to frame its claim under § 107(a)(4)? Would this approach have changed the outcome in *Bedford*?

7. Other courts have identified a fourth reason for restricting PRPs to contribution claims: at least in circumstances where some of the defendants may have resolved their liability to the government, allowing plaintiffs to frame their claims in cost-recovery might allow them to avoid the contribution protection provisions in § 113(f)(2). See, e.g., *United Technologies*, 33 F.3d at 102–103. Is this a concern? Should this be dispositive? Should it affect the analysis in situations in which the government has had no involvement at the site?

8. If PRPs cannot bring § 107 actions, what non-governmental entities can? The very existence of § 107(a)(4) indicates that Congress intended for some private parties to have cost-recovery claims. Although there does not appear to be any significant case law to date, one obvious candidate for this category would be the truly innocent purchaser; i.e., the landowner that has a valid defense under § 107(b)(3) of the statute (or for that matter, under any portion of § 107(b)). Others might include cleanup contractors whose contracting entities have gone bankrupt, or good samaritans who choose to clean up sites that they do not own. Compare *OHM Remediation Services v. Evans Cooperage Co., Inc.*, 116 F.3d 1574, 1579–1580 (5th Cir. 1997) (indicating that cleanup contractors may pursue a § 107(a)(4) claim despite the lack of any "protectable interest" in the property) with *Pennsylvania Urban Development Corp. v. Golen*, 708 F.Supp. 669 (E.D.Pa.1989) (holding that a subsequent purchaser did not have such a claim for cost associated with its pre-purchase investigations due to the absence of any protectable interest). More controversially, the Seventh Circuit appears to have determined that some "blameless" landowners (in which category it appeared to include any that did not actively contribute to contamination) can pursue claims under § 107(a)(4) even if they do not meet the requirements of the innocent purchaser defense (or any other statutory defense). See, e.g., *Rumpke of Ind., Inc. v. Cummins Engine Co., Inc.*, 107 F.3d 1235, 1240–1241 (7th Cir. 1987).

Moreover, the *Rumpke* court appeared to contemplate that such landowners might be entitled to allowed to make full use of joint and several liability in appropriate circumstances. 107 F.3d at 1240; but see *Bedford*, 156 F.3d at 424–425, and *Western Properties Service Corp. v. Shell Oil Co.*, 358 F.3d 678, 689–690 (9th Cir. 2004) (both declining to follow *Rumpke* on this point). Assuming that all of these parties can bring claims under § 107(a)(4), does it seem likely that this is the entire universe of potential plaintiffs that Congress intended to empower under that section?

9. The above notes raise questions regarding the correctness of the Second and Ninth Circuits' blanket assertions (and those of virtually every other Circuit) that PRPs can never have cost-recovery claims against other PRPs under § 107. The Fifth Circuit and the D.C. Circuit appear to be the only Circuits that have not yet issued similar edicts (any implication in *Geraghty and Miller* on this point was dicta, see 234 F.3d at 924). How do you think the Fifth Circuit is likely to address this issue on remand in *Cooper*? How do you think other Circuits are likely to respond to *Cooper*? Should the Supreme Court have taken the state of the law in these other Circuits into account in deciding whether to address this question? When considering these questions, keep in mind that many of the decisions cited in note 1 are like *Bedford* in that, while they have broad language about the inability of PRPs to proceed under § 107(a)(4), they could have been decided on the narrower ground suggested in note 6 because they involved plaintiffs who appeared to have claims under either § 113(f)(1) or (f)(3)(B). See, e.g., *United Technologies v. Browning-Ferris Industries, Inc.*, 33 F.3d 96 (1st Cir. 1994). Should the question of whether those who engage in voluntary cleanups (such as Aviall or the Pinal Group) have a cost-recovery claim be considered to be an open one in those Circuits?

10. Turning to the ability of those who have engaged in voluntary cleanups (such as Aviall or the Pinal Group) to file claims under § 113(f), what did you think of the Supreme Court's analysis in *Cooper*? Do you agree that § 113(f) provided no independent basis for the contribution claim in that case? In finding that § 113(f) provided for such a claim, the en banc panel of the Fifth Circuit relied on combined effect of the "may seek contribution" language in § 113(f)'s enabling clause together with the breadth of its savings clause. 312 F.3d at 681 and 686–687. Is this approach tenable? Did it attract any votes at the Supreme Court level? What are the implications of *Cooper*, if any, for § 113(f)(3)(B) actions in *Bedford*-type situations, where the plaintiffs have entered into administrative agreements with State officials? See *Pfohl Brothers Landfill Site Steering Committee v. Allied Waste Systems, Inc.*, 255 F.Supp.2d 134, 154 (W.D.N.Y 2003) (a pre-*Cooper* case). Assuming that such actions are still valid, what would the relevant statute of limitations be? See CERCLA § 113(g)(3). What about a situation in which EPA has unilaterally ordered a PRP to clean up a site under § 106? What type of claim, if any, would that party have? See footnote 5 in *Cooper*; see also § 113(f)(1) and (f)(3)(B).

11. Prior to the Supreme Court's decision in *Cooper*, a number of Circuits had embraced "hybrid" claims under some combination of §§ 107 and 113 in situations in which PRP claims did not fall squarely within the meaning of § 113(f)'s enabling clause. While not all of these decisions were clear regarding precisely how the courts' viewed these provisions as working

together, the better-articulated decisions appeared to treat the claims as implied claims for contribution originating under § 107, with § 113(f) governing the mechanics of how the liability was to be allocated among the various PRPs. See, e.g,., *Pinal Creek*, 118 F.3d at 1301–1306, *New Castle County v. Halliburton NUS Corp.*, 111 F.3d 1116, 1122 (3d Cir. 1997), and *Sun Co., Inc. v. Browning–Ferris, Inc.*, 124 F.3d 1187, 1191–1192 (10th Cir. 1997). As the discussions in the majority and dissenting opinions in *Cooper* demonstrate, the Fifth Circuit itself has been somewhat ambiguous on this point when one considers the combined effect of *Geraghty and Miller* and *Aviall Services*. How would you predict that the Fifth Circuit will resolve the implied contribution theory upon remand in *Cooper*? What impact do you think *Cooper* will have in Circuits that have previously embraced implied contribution claims?

12.   As noted in notes 3 and 11, above, the *Pinal Creek* court rejected the Pinal Group's argument that it had a "pure" § 107(a)(4) claim (subject to its being buffered by the defendants' potential counterclaims), but found instead that it had a "hybrid" claim under §§ 107 and 113(f). Under this approach, the court determined that any orphan shares would be distributed equitably among all of the PRPs, both plaintiff and defendants, as in the fourth example in note 2, above. 118 F.3d at 1303. Could the court have reached this same result under the Pinal Group's preferred approach? If so, it the distinction between the two approaches just one of semantics?

13.   Prior to *Cooper,* every single Circuit that had touched on these issues had held that liable parties who voluntarily cleaned up sites had some type of CERCLA claim against other PRPs, whether they framed them as "pure" contribution claims under § 113(f) or hybrid claims under §§ 107 and 113(f) (again, no court had recognized "pure" § 107 claims). Absent Congressional action, where do you think the case law will be on these issues ten years from now?

14.   Finally, it is worth noting that three Circuits have determined that CERCLA preempts state law contribution claims in at least some situations. See *Bedford*, 156 F.3d, at 427; *In re Reading Co.*, 115 F.3d 1111, 1117 (3d Cir. 1997); and *PMC v. Sherwin–Williams Co.*, 151 F.3d 610, 617–618 (7th Cir. 1998). Do these decisions survive *Cooper*?

15.   If we assume that *Cooper* is not the death of private party actions under § 107(a)(4) (and it certainly is not with respect to non-PRP plaintiffs), it is worth considering some of the other dynamics presented thereunder. Unlike governmental entities, private-party plaintiffs bear the burden of demonstrating that their costs were consistent with the NCP. See § 107(a)(4). As we have seen, the NCP imposes both procedural and substantive requirements that guide the remedy-selection process. The burden of establishing consistency with its terms poses two significant concerns for would-be private-party plaintiffs. First, they must determine whether the game is worth the candle; that is, they must determine whether the prospect of recovering some or all of their response costs justifies assuming the significant procedural burdens imposed by the NCP. In situations where the total cleanup costs are likely to be moderate, or where the prospects for significant recovery are dim, potential plaintiffs may determine that the advantages of any potential claims are offset by the burdens of compiling an

RI/FS or going through a public comment process. Second, in many instances the NCP is vague concerning the ultimate question of "how clean is clean;" that is, what degree of cleanup will be deemed to be sufficiently protective of human health and the environment while still comporting with competing concerns such as the need to ensure some degree of cost-effectiveness. Private parties bear a significant burden as a result of this uncertainty. Although there has not been much litigation in this area to date, it is easy to foresee controversy concerning whether a particular plaintiff could have achieved a similar level of protection at less cost through the implementation of alternative remedies that may be permissible under the NCP, such as institutional remedies (e.g., precluding access to the site or imposing deed restrictions) and/or natural attenuation. The mere prospect of such controversy is likely to impose a throttle on the degree of cleanup achieved in these private-party cases. The rational potential plaintiff may realize that, in a cost-recovery case, it is unlikely to ever be challenged for not having gone far enough.

16. In promulgating the revised NCP in 1990, EPA sought to afford some relief on the points discussed in the prior note by indicating that "substantial compliance" with the NCP suffices with respect to its procedural and public participation requirements. EPA still requires a strict showing that the end result was a "CERCLA–quality cleanup." See 40 C.F.R. § 300.700(c)(3)(I). While the NCP does not define what constitutes "substantial compliance" on the procedural front, the preamble to the final rule provides the following elaboration on the rationale underlying the new standard:

> EPA's decision to require only "substantial" compliance with potentially applicable requirements is based . . . on the recognition that providing a list of rigid requirements may serve to defeat cost recovery for meritorious cleanup actions based upon a mere technical failure by the private party that has taken the response action.

55 Fed.Reg. at 8793 (March 8, 1990). The preamble goes on to provide two examples of situations where technical failure to fully comply with the listed requirements should not be deemed to preclude recovery: (1) where the private party affords ample opportunity for public comment but does not provide a public hearing; and (2) where it may have been difficult to judge which NCP requirements apply (e.g., determining whether a "focused" feasibility study makes more sense that a full analysis of alternative remedial options). On the substantive side, the NCP also fails to define the term "CERCLA–quality cleanup." Again, however, the preamble provides more specificity:

> In order to achieve a "CERCLA–quality cleanup," the action must satisfy the three basic remedy selection requirements of CERCLA section 121(b)(1)—i.e., the remedial action must be "protective of human health and the environment," utilize "permanent solutions and alternative treatment technologies or resource recovery technologies to the maximum extent practicable," and be "cost-effective"—attain applicable and relevant and appropriate requirements (ARARs)(CERCLA section 121(d)(4)), and provide for meaningful public participation (section 117).

55 Fed.Reg. at 8793 (March 8, 1990). Should EPA's view regarding what constitutes compliance with the NCP be binding in the context of wholly-private actions? Does the statute provide clear authority for this sort of legislative rule? See CERCLA §§ 105 and 115; see also Executive Order 12,580, 52 Fed.Reg. 2923 (January 29, 1987)(delegation from President to EPA under § 115); and 55 Fed.Reg. at 8795 (March 8, 1990)(expressing EPA's view that it has the authority to write such a rule). Would EPA have the authority to establish a "substantial compliance" test with regard to its own procedural compliance with the NCP? If so, why has it not done so? Assuming that EPA has the authority to address these issues, do you agree with the balance it has struck? Why should private parties receive a more relaxed standard than EPA? On the other hand, is it really necessary to insist that private parties provide for "meaningful public participation" in selecting remedies at sites that EPA has determined do not warrant federal attention?

Chapter 8

PROTECTION OF PARTICULAR NATURAL RESOURCES

In some of the previous chapters, we have covered pollution prevention. By preventing or reducing pollution, we protect the natural resources of the air, water, and land. In this chapter we deal with federal laws protecting particular natural resources: endangered species, wetlands, and areas affected by surface coal mining.

I. THE ENDANGERED SPECIES ACT OF 1973

The Endangered Species Act (ESA), 16 U.S.C. §§ 1531 *et seq.*, has frequently been called the pit bull of environmental law. Under the ESA, the Supreme Court held that in order to safeguard the endangered snail darter, a three-inch fish with no known economic or ecological value, indistinguishable from 130–odd other species of darters except to the trained ichthyologist, the government could not close the gates to impound water behind a dam on which $150 million had already been spent.[1] *TVA v. Hill,* 437 U.S. 153, 98 S.Ct. 2279, 57 L.Ed.2d 117 (1978). Largely without regard to its economic consequences, Congress passed the ESA as an affirmation of the importance of preserving species. In retrospect it is difficult to imagine how such a radical law could pass by a unanimous vote in the Senate and near unanimous vote in the House and be signed by President Richard Nixon. While those legislators may have voted for the law to protect wolves, grizzly bears, whales, and eagles, its effect has been to protect not only those mega fauna, but also flower loving flies, blind salamanders, cave cockroaches, and a wide variety of other exotic plant and animal species certainly unknown to members of Congress.

For whatever reason, people usually do not demand some instrumental basis for preserving bears, whales, eagles, and similar species. We marvel at them, probably most often on television or in the movies, but

---

1. Not that it was well spent. As the lawyer for the snail darter has taken pains to explain, the dam was an economic mistake and environmental disaster even without regard to the snail darter. *See, e.g.,* Zygmunt Plater, *Law and the Fourth Estate: Endangered Nature, the Press, and the Dicey Game of Democratic Governance,* 32 ENV. L. 1, 4 *et seq.* (2002).

nevertheless we feel they are unquestionably important to us. Beetles, spiders, flies, and similar species do not have the same cachet. It is often difficult to explain why it is important to preserve such species. The ESA itself states that species are to be protected because of their esthetic, ecological, educational, historical, recreational, and scientific value to the Nation. 16 U.S.C. § 1531(a)(3). But for many of these species it is not clear which, if any, of these values they represent. Nevertheless, the Endangered Species Act remains popular with people. At the same time, experience with its administration has left both environmentalists and persons adversely affected by species' protection with many complaints. With thirty years of experience, it would probably be impossible to pass the ESA today, but it would be equally impossible to repeal it. For better or for worse, for many species it remains the last legal hope against extinction.

A. Outline of the Act

The Endangered Species Act is, of course, designed to protect endangered species, so the first objective of the Act is to establish the procedure and standards for determining which species should be protected and how much of their habitat needs to be protected in order to protect the species. Section 4, 16 U.S.C. § 1533, performs this function. Once the appropriate species and habitat for protection are determined, the ESA operates to protect the affected species in two separate ways. Section 7 of the Act, 16 U.S.C. § 1536, imposes both procedural and substantive duties on federal agencies whose actions may jeopardize the protected species or adversely affect their habitat. It was Section 7 that stopped the Tellico Dam to protect the snail darter. Section 9 of the Act, 16 U.S.C. § 1538, prohibits anyone from engaging in certain actions that might harm threatened or endangered species. Section 10, 16 U.S.C. § 1539, provides a mechanism for persons to avoid the absolute prohibitions of Section 9, and Section 11, 16 U.S.C. § 1540, specifies the civil and criminal penalties to which a person is subject if they violate Section 9, and it provides a citizen suit provision for enforcing the Act.

B. Section 4

The Endangered Species Act is unusual in that it assigns responsibility for implementing the Act generally to two different agencies–the Department of Interior and the Department of Commerce. Interior is responsible for terrestrial species; Commerce is responsible for marine species. Exclusively fresh water fish are considered terrestrial species, but fish species that live in both fresh and salt water, such as salmon, are generally considered marine species. Marine mammals, such as sea lions, are marine species. The Secretary of Interior has delegated Interior's duties to the United States Fish and Wildlife Service, and the Secretary of Commerce has delegated Commerce's duties to the National Marine Fisheries Service (NMFS), a subunit of the National Oceanic and Atmospheric Administration in Commerce, sometimes known as NOAA Fisheries.

1. Listing

a. Endangered or Threatened

The respective secretaries are to list a "species" as endangered if it is "in danger of extinction throughout all or a significant portion of its range." 16 U.S.C. § 1532(6). An exception is made for insects constituting a pest whose protection would present great risk to humans. *Id.* A "species" is to be listed as threatened if it is "likely to become an endangered species within the foreseeable future throughout all or a significant portion of its range." 16 U.S.C. § 1532(20). Under the Act, the listing is only supposed to occur if the threat or endangerment is caused by one or more of five listed factors: impacts on the species' habitat; overuse of the species, such as by hunting or fishing; disease or predation; the inadequacy of existing regulations; or any other factor affecting its continued existence. 16 U.S.C. § 1533(a)(1). As a practical matter, these factors would seem to be all inclusive, so any endangerment or threat thereof would seem to require listing.

Today, human caused impacts on species' habitat is overwhelmingly the largest threat to species' existence. This can occur through urban development and the conversion of undeveloped land to agricultural use. For example, the threatened destruction of vernal pools (small seasonal ponds largely in California) that are the unique habitat of three species of fairy shrimp and a vernal pool tadpole shrimp led to the listing of the fairy shrimp as endangered and the tadpole shrimp as threatened. Or the habitat can be altered through timber cutting, which led to the listing of the Northern Spotted Owl as threatened. Or a combination of factors can together degrade the habitat of a species, placing it under significant strain. This is the situation for most listed salmon species, where the combination of dams impeding their migration to and from the ocean and timber and grazing practices at headwaters resulting in increased water temperature and sediment are believed to be the most significant factors causing reduced numbers of wild salmon.

Gathering the scientific evidence of the current status of a species, as well as the stresses under which it is laboring, is a substantial undertaking, and if the Fish & Wildlife Service or NMFS fails to do a good job, there is a high degree of likelihood that either concerned environmentalists or concerned development, agricultural, logging, or grazing interests will sue to overturn the decision. Judicial review of a listing decision (either for or against) will be under the Administrative Procedure Act, and unless the listing agency violates some procedural requirement, *see, e.g., Alabama–Tombigbee Rivers Coalition v. Department of Interior*, 26 F.3d 1103 (11th Cir. 1994)(enjoining the FWS from using information obtained in violation of the Federal Advisory Committee Act's procedural requirements), the review is likely to be under the APA's "arbitrary and capricious" standard. This standard, while deferential to the agency, especially when the agency is operating on the edges of scientific knowledge, requires a "thorough, probing in-depth review" of the agency action. *See, e.g., Alsea Valley Alliance v. Evans*,

161 F.Supp.2d 1154 (D. Or. 2001)(finding NMFS listing of west coast coho salmon arbitrary and capricious); *Northern Spotted Owl v. Hodel*, 716 F.Supp. 479 (W.D. Wash. 1988)(finding FWS decision not to list the owl arbitrary and capricious).

Notes and Comments

1. The determination of whether a species is endangered or threatened is a classic case of risk assessment, which is supposed to be performed by objective scientists, and the Endangered Species Act reflects that in its requirement that a species listing of endangered or threatened is to be based "solely on the basis of the best scientific and commercial data available."[2] 16 U.S.C. § 1533(b)(1)(A). However, neither the Act nor the agencies' regulations provide any further guidance on what might constitute endangerment of extinction or its threat. The risk of extinction necessarily involves at least two variables: time and probability. Probability, of course, refers to the likelihood of extinction. Is a species in "danger of extinction" if there is merely some chance of extinction, perhaps 5%? Or does it take some higher degree of likelihood? More probable than not? Nothing in the agencies' policies answers these questions. There is also the question of time. That is, we are all going to be extinct at some point, perhaps when the sun burns out, maybe earlier. On the other hand, even species under significant pressures are rarely likely to become extinct within only a few years. If there is virtually no danger of extinction within ten years, but a 60% probability within 100 years, is that in "danger of extinction"? Again, the agencies' documents provide no clue. The requirement for "threatened species" is that "in the foreseeable future" the species will become in danger of extinction. What is the foreseeable future? We see into the future with different levels of certainty. That is, we can predict a species' status next year with a high degree of certainty, but its status a hundred years from now, much less 500 years, while certainly foreseeable to some degree, involves a high degree of uncertainty. Again, the agencies' regulations do not help us (or them) in answering these questions.

2. Obviously, the answers to these questions cannot be answered by science. Rather, the answers are value-laden determinations that may be made by scientists in the course of their supposedly neutral scientific determination of endangerment or may be made by policymakers reviewing the scientists' work. In essence, they reflect the degree of protectiveness desired. That is, if you want to be "protective," then a 40% chance of extinction in 100 years may be unacceptable, but if you do not want to be protective, then a 40% chance of extinction in 100 years simply is not "in danger" of extinction. In any case, the determinations are non-transparent, based upon considerations undisclosed and unknown to the public. *See, e.g.*, Daniel J. Rohlf, *Section 4 of the Endangered Species Act: Top Ten Issues for the* Next *Thirty Years*, 34 Envtl. L. 483, 501–507 (2004).

3. Interestingly, the issue of these underlying questions has not come up in litigation, which, when it focuses on the validity of a listing (or failure

---

2. The reference to "commercial data" means that where the threat to the species is from commercial use of the species, then the extent of that commercial use should be determined by the best available commercial data. It does not suggest any consideration of the economic impact of the listing of a species.

to list), usually involves questions of fact, such as the remaining numbers of the species, the rate of decline, the cause of the decline, the extent of existing habitat, etc. If closing the gates of the Tellico dam will within 3 months totally eliminate the habitat of the snail darter, there may be little question as to its "danger of extinction," but if the indefinite continuation of existing (but unsustainable) timber practices on public lands would lead to a 0.7% annual decline in the Northern Spotted Owl population, the "danger of extinction" is much less clear.

4. There is also the question of the reliability of the data used by scientists. Attempts to count the number of members of a species which naturally tries to hide from humans is difficult to say the least. Computer models that make predictions from data may provide a false sense of certainty. But, as the adage goes, garbage in, garbage out. "One model of Steller sea lion population dynamics, for example, predicted a 100 percent probability of extinction within 100 years when applied to data collected from 1985 to 1994, but only a 10 percent probability of extinction if the data were limited to the period from 1989 to 1994." Holly Doremus, *Listing Decisions Under the Endangered Species Act: Why Better Science Isn't Always Better Policy*, 75 Wash. U.L.Q. 1029, 1120 (1997). Who's to say which years to use?

5. An important issue in deciding whether a species is in danger of extinction, or likely to become so, is how to assess possible future conservation efforts. For example, if a state, seeking to avoid having a species listed, states that it will take various actions to protect the habitat of the species, should FWS or NMFS accept that at face value, assess the probability that the state will indeed do what it says, or ignore it. If taken at face value, the proposed state actions might well end the perceived decline in the species, but will the state really follow through? Even if it follows through, will its actions be successful? Perhaps its proposed actions are to organize a voluntary program by landowners to set aside habitat for the species. Will the landowners actually participate? In several cases the listing agencies have accepted state (and federal) plans, cooperative agreements, memoranda of agreement, and the like as a basis for predicting that a population decline will be arrested. And in 2003, FWS and NMFS adopted their PECE policy, Policy for Evaluation of Conservation Efforts When Making Listing Decisions, 68 Fed. Reg. 15,100 (Mar. 28, 2003). Generally, however, courts have been skeptical. "Courts have specifically and repeatedly interpreted this provision to mean that an agency may not rely upon future actions to justify a decision not to list a species as threatened or endangered." *Center for Biological Diversity v. Badgley*, 2001 WL 844399 (D.Or. 2001)(citing *Oregon Natural Resources Council v. Daley*, 6 F.Supp.2d 1139, 1153–54 (D.Or. 1998)); *Friends of Wild Swan, Inc. v. United States Fish and Wildlife Serv.*, 945 F.Supp. 1388, 1399 (D.Or.1996); *Biodiversity Legal Found. v. Babbitt*, 943 F.Supp. 23, 26 (D.D.C.1996); *Southwest Center for Biological Diversity v. Babbitt*, 939 F.Supp. 49, 52 (D.D.C.1996). Similarly, most courts have held that actions that are voluntary should not be considered. *See, e.g., ONRC v. Daley*, 6 F.Supp.2d 1139 (D.Or. 2001). But the results are not unanimous. *See, e.g., Defenders of Wildlife v. Babbitt*, 1999 WL 33537981 (S.D.Cal. 1999). Generally, courts have upheld listing agencies' reliance on legally binding regulations requiring conservation efforts. *See, e.g., id.* Recall that Section 4

specifically includes as one of the five factors to be considered in a listing decision "the inadequacy of existing regulatory mechanisms." 16 U.S.C. § 1533(a)(1)(D). This certainly suggests that "existing" (i.e., not future, anticipated) "regulatory" (i.e., not voluntary) mechanisms *might* be adequate to protect species. Section 4 also states that a listing determination is to be made "after taking into account those efforts, if any, being made by any State, or foreign nation, or any political subdivision of a State or foreign nation, to protect such species." 16 U.S.C. § 1533(b)(1)(A). This too seems to focus on the present activities, but it is not stated so as to exclude voluntary activities. If determinations as to endangerment or its threat is all about predicting the future, why should agencies be precluded from considering predictable future activities by states or other federal agencies?

b. "A Significant Portion of its Range"

Contrary to what most lay people consider to be extinction, the ESA refers to "extinction" of a species (or the foreseeable threat thereof) "throughout all or a significant portion of its range." Precisely what this means is unclear.

DEFENDERS OF WILDLIFE v. NORTON

United States Court of Appeals, Ninth Circuit, 2001.
258 F.3d 1136.

BERZON, Circuit Judge:

[After proposing to list the Flat–Tailed Horned Lizard as a threatened species, the Secretary of Interior's final decision was to withdraw the proposed rule on the basis that although the lizard was subject to substantial habitat loss on private lands, "[b]ecause of the large amount of flat-tailed horned lizard habitat located on public lands within the United States and the reduction of threats on these lands ..., threats due to habitat modification and loss do not warrant listing of the species at this time." This decision was challenged by the Defenders of Wildlife, arguing that the species needed to be listed because the destruction of its habitat on private lands would likely result in its extinction in the foreseeable future throughout a significant portion of its range.]

* * *

Standing alone, the phrase "in danger of extinction throughout ... a significant portion of its range" is puzzling. According to the Oxford English Dictionary, "extinct" means "has died out or come to an end.... Of a family, class of persons, a race of species of animals or plants: Having no living representative." Thus, the phrase "extinc[t] throughout ... a significant portion of its range" is something of an oxymoron....

1. THE SECRETARY'S EXPLANATION

The Secretary's explanation of this odd phraseology is of no assistance in puzzling out the meaning of the phrase, since her interpretation simply cannot be squared with the statute's language and structure. The Secretary in her brief interprets the enigmatic phrase to mean that a species is eligible for protection under the ESA if it "faces threats in enough key portions of its range that the *entire species* is in danger of extinction, or will be within the foreseeable future." She therefore assumes that a species is in danger of extinction in "a significant portion of its range" only if it is in danger of extinction everywhere....

2. DEFENDERS' EXPLANATION

Defenders' interpretation of the phrase "extinction throughout . . . a significant portion of its range" is similarly unsatisfactory. Defenders takes a more quantitative approach to the phrase, arguing that the projected loss of 82% of the lizard's habitat in this case constitutes "a substantial portion of its range." Appellants then cite to other cases in which courts found listing of species warranted after the loss of even smaller amounts of habitat. *Federation of Fly Fishers v. Daley*, Civ. No. 99–981–SI (N.D.Cal. Oct. 25, 2000), Slip Op. at 17–18 (finding listing of the steelhead trout warranted despite protections covering 64% of its range); *ONRC v. Daley*, 6 F.Supp.2d 1139, 1157 (D.Or.1998) (finding the coho salmon in danger of extinction despite federal forest land protections extending over 35% of its range); 45 Fed.Reg. 63,812, 63,817–18 (Sept. 25, 1980) (listing the Coachella Valley fringe-toed lizard as a threatened species although 50% of its historical habitat remained).

There are two problems with Defenders' quantitative approach. First, it simply does not make sense to assume that the loss of a predetermined percentage of habitat or range would necessarily qualify a species for listing. A species with an exceptionally large historical range may continue to enjoy healthy population levels despite the loss of a substantial amount of suitable habitat. Similarly, a species with an exceptionally small historical range may quickly become endangered after the loss of even a very small percentage of suitable habitat....

In the absence of a fixed percentage, Defenders' suggested interpretation of the phrase begins to look a lot like the faulty definition offered by the Secretary, i.e., "a substantial portion of its range" means an amount of habitat loss such that total extinction is likely in the near future. As noted above, this reading does not comport with the other terms of the statute.

3. INSIGHT FROM THE LEGISLATIVE HISTORY

The legislative history of the ESA suggests an entirely different meaning of the inherently ambiguous phrase "extinction throughout . . . a significant portion of its range." . . .

It appears that Congress added this new language in order to encourage greater cooperation between federal and state agencies and to allow the Secretary more flexibility in her approach to wildlife management. The case of the American alligator, which was frequently cited during the Senate debate, illustrates this likely intent:

In 1973, the range of the alligator stretched from the Mississippi Delta in Louisiana to the Everglades of Florida. Its distribution over that range, however, varied widely. While habitat loss had pushed the species to the verge of extinction in Florida, conservation efforts had resulted in an overabundance of alligators in Louisiana, such that harvesting was required to keep the alligators from overrunning the human population. In order to address problems such as this, the Act allows the Secretary to "list an animal as 'endangered' through all or a portion of its range." Senator Tunney explained:

> An animal might be "endangered" in most States but overpopulated in some. In a State in which a species is overpopulated, the Secretary would have the discretion to list that animal as merely threatened or to remove it from the endangered species listing entirely while still providing protection in areas where it was threatened with extinction. In that portion of its range where it was not threatened with extinction, the States would have full authority to use their management skills to insure the proper conservation of the species.

Id. In describing this provision as "perhaps the most important section of this bill," *id.,* Senator Tunney also noted that

> The plan for Federal–State cooperation provides for much more extensive discretionary action on the part of the Secretary and the State agencies. Under existing law [(namely, the Endangered Species Conservation Act of 1969)], a species must be declared "endangered" even if in a certain portion of its range, the species has experienced a population boom, or is otherwise threatening to destroy the life support capacity of its habitat. Such a broad listing prevents local authorities from taking steps to insure healthy population levels.

Id.

The historical application of the Act is consistent with this interpretation of the statute, not with the interpretation suggested by the Secretary in her briefs in this case. Grizzly bears, for example, are listed as threatened species within the contiguous 48 states, but not in Alaska. Similarly, only the California, Oregon and Washington populations of the marbled murrelet, whose range in North America extends from the Aleutian Archipelago in Alaska to Central California, are listed as threatened. . . .

We conclude, consistently with the Secretary's historical practice, that a species can be extinct "throughout . . . a significant portion of its range" if there are major geographical areas in which it is no longer viable but once was. Those areas need not coincide with national or state political boundaries, although they can. The Secretary necessarily has a wide degree of discretion in delineating "a significant portion of its range," since the term is not defined in the statute. But where, as here, it is on the record apparent that the area in which the lizard is expected to survive is much smaller than its historical range, the Secretary must at least explain her conclusion that the area in which the species can no longer live is not a "significant portion of its range."

* * *

Notes and Comments

1.   Can you decipher what the difference is between the three different interpretations of "extinction throughout a significant portion of its range"? The Secretary seems to be saying that the whole species is to be listed if the species will be extinct in enough of its range to be in danger of extinction everywhere, and here there is no need to list the species because there is enough protected public land remaining to preserve the species. The Defenders of Wildlife seem to be saying much the same thing, except that it wants to establish by a percentage of the whole range the amount of range which, if the species were to become extinct there, would require listing of the whole species. Here, it is arguing that because 82% of the lizard's range is on private property, where it is likely to go extinct, that is enough to require listing of the whole species. The court, however, distinguishes between the whole species and that portion of the species that exists (or did exist) on the significant portion of its range. It is this portion of the species that the court suggests should be listed. Do you think the court is right? If it is, how does this relate to the definition of species to include a "distinct population segment," which is discussed below?

   c.   "Species" includes "subspecies"

Even when one understands what is endangerment or its threat, one must still understand what constitutes a "species." It is only when a "species" is endangered or threatened that it becomes listed and protected. Under the Act, the term is defined to include not only "species" but also "any subspecies of fish or wildlife or plants, and any distinct population segment of any species of vertebrate fish or wildlife which interbreeds when mature."

For those whose biology is rusty, the general taxonomic classifications are:

- Phylum (e.g., Chordata or vertebrates)
- Class (e.g., Mammalia or mammals)
- Order (e.g., Carnivora or carnivores)
- Family (e.g., Ursidae or bears, including pandas, sloth bears, black bears, brown bears, etc.)
- Genus (e.g., Ursus or brown, black, polar, and Asiatic black bears)
- Species (e.g., Ursus Arctos or Brown Bear)
- Subspecies (e.g., Ursus Arctos Horribilis or Grizzly Bear)

The general rule is that members of the same species can interbreed in the wild and produce fertile offspring, so Grizzly bears and Kodiak bears (Ursus Arctos Middendorfi), different subspecies of the species

Ursus Arctos, can interbreed, but Grizzly bears and Polar bears (Ursus Maritimus), different species, do not.

These classifications and which plants and animals fit into them where, however, are a continuing issue among scientists. For example, during the controversial listing of the Northern Spotted Owl, interests opposed to the listing argued that the Northern Spotted Owl and the California Spotted Owl were not different subspecies of the species Spotted Owl, but merely "clinal" variations of the same subspecies. That is, the subtle differences in appearance between the two owls were really a difference in appearance related to where they lived, rather than to any taxonomic or genetic differentiation. They supported this argument with an early twentieth century study reaching that conclusion and the fact that genetic testing did not reveal any difference between the two types of owls. At the same time, the 1957 edition of the Checklist of North American Birds, published by the American Ornithological Union, the oldest and largest private organization in the New World devoted to the scientific study of birds, listed the two types of owls as separate subspecies, and the AOU's Committee on Classification and Nomenclature decided in 1989 not to reclassify the owls on the basis of the testing showing no genetic difference, because "present techniques for exposing genetic variation examine only a tiny fraction of the genome." The FWS and NMFS joint regulations state that the agencies will "rely on standard taxonomic distinctions and the biological expertise of the Department and the scientific community concerning the relevant taxonomic group." 50 CFR § 424.11(a). Accordingly, the FWS followed the AOU's direction and concluded that they were different subspecies. *See* Determination of Threatened Status for the Northern Spotted Owl, 55 Fed. Reg. 26114, 26130 (June 26, 1990).

These debates are not just academic. Those opposed to listing the Northern Spotted Owl wanted it combined with the Califonia Spotted Owl as all one species, because then the population and dispersal of the Northern/California Spotted Owl would be sufficiently large to suggest that it need not be listed at all. Indeed, in a later decision, the FWS decided that listing the California Spotted Owl was not warranted. *See* 12 Month Finding for a Petition to List the California Spotted Owl, 68 Fed. Reg. 7580 (Feb. 14, 2003). The exercise involved in this example is played out in numerous controversies over whether to list a species as threatened or endangered, with those who desire listing attempting to define the "species" as restrictively as possible, to minimize its range and population and therefore its ability to survive indefinitely, while those who oppose listing attempting to define the species as broadly as possible, to maximize its range and population and therefore its ability to survive indefinitely.

d.   "Species" includes Distinct Population Segments

The concept of "distinct population segment" is easy to understand at one level. Above, in the *Defenders of Wildlife v. Norton* case, the court noted that grizzly bears are listed as threatened species in the lower 48 states, but not in Alaska, where you can legally hunt them for sport. However, the grizzlies in Yellowstone National Park, for example, cannot interbreed with those in Alaska; they are totally isolated from those grizzlies. The Endangered Species Act, especially with its authors' focus on mega-fauna, was intended to protect such isolated populations of fish and vertebrate wildlife. Grizzlies may be easy, but what about some other species? Here the FWS and NMFS have adopted guidance to give further clarification. However, that clarification still leaves a lot of questions.

NATIONAL ASSOCIATION OF HOME BUILDERS v. NORTON

United States Court of Appeals, Ninth Circuit, 2003.

340 F.3d 835.

The National Association of Home Builders, the Southern Arizona Home Builders Association, and the Home Builders Association of Central Arizona (collectively, "Home Builders") appeal the district court's decision upholding the designation of a population of cactus ferruginous pygmy-owls in Arizona as a distinct population segment ("DPS") pursuant to the Fish and Wildlife Service's ("FWS") *Policy Regarding the Recognition of Distinct Vertebrate Population Segments Under the Endangered Species Act,* 61 Fed.Reg. 4722 (Feb. 7, 1996) ("*DPS Policy*").....

The cactus ferruginous pygmy-owl (*Glaucidium brasilianum cactorum*) is a small bird, about 6.75 inches in length, that can be reddish-brown or gray. *Determination of Endangered Status for the Cactus Ferruginous Pygmy Owl in Arizona,* 62 Fed.Reg. 10,730, 10,730 (Mar. 10, 1997) (codified at 50 C.F.R. § 17.11(h)) ("Listing Rule"). It is one of four subspecies of the ferruginous pygmy-owl. *Id.* The range of the cactus ferruginous pygmy-owl ("pygmy-owl") extends "from lowland central Arizona south through western Mexico, to the States of Colima and Michoacan, and from southern Texas south through the Mexican States of Tamaulipas and Nuevo Leon." The pygmy-owls in Arizona represent the northernmost edge of the subspecies' range.

... By the FWS' estimates, pygmy-owls were once common to Arizona prior to the mid–1900s, but only between 20 and 40 pygmy-owls remain in Arizona.

... After a notice and comment period, the FWS issued a final rule listing the Arizona pygmy-owls as endangered (but not listing the Texas pygmy-owls as threatened).

In the Listing Rule, the FWS designated the Arizona pygmy-owls as a DPS. The ESA permits the FWS to designate a population of a species as a DPS and to list it as an endangered species. To designate a DPS under the *DPS Policy,* the FWS must find that a population is discrete "in relation to the remainder of the species to which it belongs" and significant "to the species to which it belongs." 61 Fed.Reg. at 4725. In making this designation in the Listing Rule, the FWS first found that the pygmy-owl populations in the east (southeast Texas south through northeastern Mexico) and west (central Arizona south through northwestern Mexico) are (1) discrete "based on geographic isolation, distribution and status of habitat, and potential morphological and genetic distinctness," and (2) significant because the loss of either population would create a significant gap in the range of the subspecies.

Next, the FWS further subdivided the western pygmy-owl DPS into an Arizona population and a northwestern Mexico population. According to the Listing Rule, the Arizona pygmy-owls are discrete from the northwestern Mexico pygmy-owls because they are "delimited by international boundaries" and "the status of the species in Arizona is different from that in Sonora [Mexico], with records currently indicating a higher number of individuals in Sonora." ...

Home Builders sued to vacate the Listing Rule and the designation of critical habitat. The district court granted summary judgment to the FWS....

On appeal, Home Builders argue that the FWS violated the *DPS Policy* by designating the Arizona pygmy-owls as a DPS.

... Home Builders do not contest the designation of the eastern and western pygmy-owls as DPSs, only the subdivision of the western pygmy-owls into the Arizona DPS and the northwestern Mexico population. Thus, the question we must decide is whether the FWS violated its *DPS Policy* by finding that the Arizona pygmy-owls are a discrete and significant population.

... Since the ESA does not define the term "distinct population segment,"[8] the FWS and the National Marine Fisheries Service jointly promulgated the *DPS Policy* to ensure consistency in their respective DPS designations. Under the *DPS* Policy, a DPS must be discrete "in relation to the remainder of the species to which it belongs" and significant "to the species to which it belongs." 61 Fed.Reg. at 4725. A DPS must be both discrete and significant, because "[t]he interests of conserving genetic diversity would not be well served by efforts directed at either well-defined but insignificant units or entities believed to be significant but around which boundaries cannot be recognized." *Id.* at 4724.

A. *The FWS Did Not Arbitrarily and Capriciously Find That the Arizona Pygmy–Owl Population is Discrete*

The purpose of the discreteness standard is to ensure that a DPS is "adequately defined and described," allowing for the effective administration of the ESA. *DPS Policy,* 61 Fed.Reg. at 4724.... A population is discrete if (1) "[i]t is markedly separated from other populations of the same taxon as a consequence of physical, physiological, ecological, or behavioral factors"; or (2) "[i]t is delimited by international governmen-

---

8. The term "distinct population segment" is "not commonly used in scientific discourse." DPS Policy, 61 Fed.Reg. at 4722.

tal boundaries within which differences in control of exploitation, management of habitat, conservation status, or regulatory mechanisms exist that are significant in light of section 4(a)(1)(D) of the Act." *Id.* at 4725. Although the use of international borders "may introduce an artificial and non-biological element" into the discreteness standard, "it appears to be reasonable for national legislation ... to recognize units delimited by international boundaries when these coincide with differences in the management, status, or exploitation of a species." *Id.* at 4723.

In the Listing Rule, the FWS found that the Arizona pygmy-owls are discrete from the northwestern Mexico pygmy-owls because the international border divides the two populations and significant differences in conservation status exist between those populations. . . .

Comparing the "conservation status" of pygmy-owls across the border, the FWS found that pygmy-owls were abundant in parts of northwestern Mexico but were rare and declining in Arizona. Home Builders challenge the FWS' assertion that pygmy-owls were once common in Arizona but have been declining in number since the mid 1900s due to habitat modification and destruction. Home Builders contend that the pygmy-owls were never numerous in Arizona, because their numbers have always fluctuated as a peripheral population at the edge of the subspecies' range. . . .

This case presents exactly the type of informed agency discretion to which we must defer. After examining all the evidence, including the comments and studies cited by Home Builders, the FWS found that the declining numbers of Arizona pygmy-owls were due to habitat destruction and modification, not fluctuations in a peripheral population. . . . The FWS' finding that pygmy-owls were "extremely limited in distribution" in Arizona but existed in greater numbers in northwestern Mexico was an adequate exercise of agency expertise. Thus, we hold that the FWS did not arbitrarily find that the differences in the conservation status of pygmy-owls across the border satisfied the discreteness element of the *DPS Policy.*

B. *The FWS Has Not Demonstrated a Rational Basis in the Listing Rule For its Finding That the Arizona Pygmy Owl Population is Significant to its Taxon*

If a population is discrete, the FWS then considers the "biological and ecological significance" of the population to the taxon to which it belongs. *DPS Policy,* 61 Fed.Reg. at 4724, 4725. The purpose of the significance element is "to carry out the expressed congressional intent that this authority [to list DPSs] be exercised sparingly as well as to concentrate conservation efforts undertaken under the Act on avoiding important losses of genetic diversity." *Id.* at 4724; *see also* S.Rep. No. 96–151, at 7 ("[T]he committee is aware of the great potential for abuse of this authority [to list DPSs] and expects the FWS to use the ability to list populations sparingly and only when the biological evidence indicates that such action is warranted."). The FWS determines the significance of a discrete population by considering the following non-exclusive factors:

1. Persistence of the discrete population segment in an ecological setting unusual or unique for the taxon,

2. Evidence that loss of the discrete population segment would result in a significant gap in the range of a taxon,

3. Evidence that the discrete population segment represents the only surviving natural occurrence of a taxon that may be more abundant elsewhere as an introduced population outside its historic range, or

4. Evidence that the discrete population segment differs markedly from other populations of the species in its genetic characteristics.

DPS Policy, 61 Fed.Reg. at 4725.

In the Listing Rule, the FWS found that the discrete population of Arizona pygmy-owls is significant because

> [s]hould the loss of either the Arizona or Texas populations occur, the remaining population would not fill the resulting gap as the remaining population would not be genetically or morphologically identical, and would require different habitat parameters. The loss of either population also would decrease the genetic variability of the taxon and would result in a significant gap in the range.

The FWS argues that it found the Arizona pygmy-owl population to be significant to its taxon in the Listing Rule based on the second and fourth significance factors.

1. *The Second Significance Factor*

In the Listing Rule, the FWS concluded that the loss of the Arizona pygmy-owls "would result in a significant gap in the range" of their taxon. The question, then, is whether the FWS arbitrarily determined that the loss of the discrete Arizona pygmy-owl population would cause a gap in the range of its taxon and that such a gap would be significant.

a. *Whether the Loss of the Arizona Pygmy Owl Population Would Cause a Gap in the Range of the Taxon*

The FWS noted in the Listing Rule that the Arizona pygmy-owls "represent the northernmost portion of the pygmy-owl's range." The parties disagree over whether the loss of a peripheral population (*i.e.,* a population at the edge of a species' range) could create a gap in the range of a taxon. . . .

We defer to the FWS' interpretation of a "gap at the end of the fence" because it is not plainly erroneous. Even the loss of a peripheral population, however small, would create an empty geographic space in the range of the taxon. . . .

b. *Whether the Gap Would be Significant*

Since the loss of the Arizona pygmy-owls would create a gap in the range of the taxon, we now consider whether that gap is significant. The *DPS Policy* intended the term "significant" to have its "commonly understood" meaning, which is "important." . . .

In the Listing Rule, the FWS did not clearly explain why the gap that would be caused by the extirpation of the Arizona pygmy-owls is significant....

The FWS argues that it found the gap to be significant in the Listing Rule because the loss of the Arizona pygmy-owls would (1) decrease the genetic variability of the taxon; (2) reduce the current range of the taxon; (3) reduce the historic range of the taxon; and (4) extirpate the western pygmy-owls from the United States....

(1) Decrease the Genetic Variability of the Taxon

In the Listing Rule, the FWS found that the loss of the Arizona pygmy-owl population would "decrease the genetic variability of the taxon." On appeal, the FWS contends that peripheral populations like the Arizona pygmy-owls "may have more genetic divergence than central populations, making them more important to the survival of the species, particularly in response to adaption to environmental change." Thus, since the peripheral Arizona pygmy-owl population might be genetically distinct from the central population of pygmy-owls in northwestern Mexico, the loss of the Arizona population could impair the survival of the northwestern Mexico population in a crisis....

Nowhere in the Listing Rule, however, does the FWS mention the existence of any genetic differences between the pygmy-owls in Arizona and northwestern Mexico, nor does the record provide any evidence to that effect.... We cannot defer to the FWS' argument on appeal that the Arizona pygmy-owls are genetically distinct from and important to the central population of northwestern Mexico pygmy-owls because the FWS did not make such a finding in the Listing Rule. Since the Listing Rule does not contain evidence of genetic variability between the Arizona and northwestern Mexico pygmy-owls, the argument that the loss of the Arizona population is significant because it would "decrease the genetic variability of the taxon" appears to be a *post hoc* rationalization. While the FWS can draw conclusions based on less than conclusive scientific evidence, it cannot base its conclusions on no evidence. *See Bennett v. Spear,* 520 U.S. 154, 176, 117 S.Ct. 1154, 137 L.Ed.2d 281 (1997) ("The obvious purpose of the requirement that each agency 'use the best scientific and commercial evidence available' is to ensure that the ESA not be implemented haphazardly, on the basis of speculation or surmise.").

(2) Reduce the Current Range of the Taxon

The FWS argues that the gap would be significant because the loss of the Arizona pygmy-owls would reduce the current range of its taxon. In other listing rules, the FWS has found two ways in which the loss of a discrete population could reduce the current range of its taxon.

First, the loss of a discrete population could reduce the geographic size of the taxon's range. [Citations to listing rules where this was true are omitted] These listing rules suggest that finding a gap significant based on the curtailment of a taxon's current range requires the loss of a geographic area that amounts to a substantial reduction of a taxon's range. The FWS found in the Listing Rule, however, that the Arizona pygmy-owls represented only "a small percentage" of the total range of the western pygmy-owls. It did not find that the loss of this "small percentage" of the western pygmy-owls' current range would substantially curtail that range.

Second, the loss of a discrete population that is numerous and constitutes a large percentage of the total number of taxon members could be considered a significant curtailment of a taxon's current range. Here, the FWS found that the Arizona pygmy-owls number between 20 and 40 individuals. The FWS did not find, however, that the loss of these 20 to 40 individuals would significantly curtail the western pygmy-owls' current range, which consists mostly of the more-numerous northwestern Mexico pygmy-owl population.

(3) Reduce the Historic Range of the Taxon

The FWS argues that the gap would be significant because the loss of the Arizona pygmy-owls would reduce the historical range of its taxon. Other listing rules have found a gap to be significant on these grounds.

The issue here is whether the FWS provided a rational basis in the Listing Rule for its conclusion that the loss of the Arizona pygmy-owl population would significantly reduce the historical range of its taxon.... Although "the 'significant gap in the range' analysis required for a DPS" is not the same as "the 'significant portion of the range' analysis required for a listing decision for the entire species," the two analyses are similar.... By analogy, the historical range of a taxon would be reduced "if there are major geographical areas in which it is no longer viable but once was."

While the loss of pygmy-owls in Arizona would mean that western pygmy-owls were no longer viable where they once were, the question arises as to whether Arizona is a "major geographic area" in the historical range of the western pygmy-owls....

While the Arizona range might possibly be significant to its taxon's historic range despite its existence as a stable population at the periphery of that range, the FWS did not articulate a reasoned basis in the Listing Rule as to why that is so....

(4) Extirpation of the Western Pygmy Owl from the United States

Finally, the FWS argues that the gap would be significant because it would deprive the United States of its portion of the western pygmy-owl's range....

This argument misconstrues the second significance factor. In designating a DPS under the *DPS Policy,* the FWS must find that a discrete population is significant to its taxon as a whole, not to the United States. *See* 61 Fed.Reg. at 4725. Extirpation of the western pygmy-owl from the United States is certainly significant to the United States, but that does not mean that the loss of the Arizona pygmy-owl population is significant to its taxon....

In other listing rules, the FWS has found a gap to be significant due to the loss of the United States range of a population only where some additional significance to the taxon as a whole also existed. In the case at bench, it is true that the loss of the Arizona pygmy-owls would move the western pygmy-owl range beyond the borders of the United States. Yet, apart from the significance of that loss to the United States, the FWS did not give any additional reason in the Listing Rule why the gap caused by the loss of the Arizona population would also be significant to its taxon as a whole.

In sum, we conclude that the FWS did not articulate a reasoned basis in the Listing Rule for finding that the gap created by the loss of the discrete Arizona pygmy-owl population would be significant to the taxon as a whole.

2. *The Fourth Significance Factor*

A discrete population can be significant to its taxon based on evidence that it "differs markedly from other populations of the species in its genetic characteristics." *DPS Policy,* 61 Fed.Reg. at 4725....

In the Listing Rule, the FWS divided the Arizona pygmy-owls and the northwestern Mexico pygmy-owls into separate populations. Therefore, under the plain language of the fourth significance factor, the FWS needed to show that the Arizona pygmy-owls differed markedly in their genetic characteristics from the northwestern Mexico pygmy-owls. Yet neither the Listing Rule nor the record presented any evidence of marked genetic differences between the pygmy-owls in Arizona and northwestern Mexico....

The FWS promulgated the *DPS Policy* consistently to designate DPSs "in light of Congressional guidance ... that the authority to list DPS's [sic] be used ' ... sparingly' while encouraging the conservation of genetic diversity." 61 Fed.Reg. at 4725.... As such, to meet this fourth significance factor, the FWS must find significance to the taxon as a whole, not just to the United States. It did not do so in this case.

We conclude, therefore, that the FWS did not articulate a rational basis in the Listing Rule for its finding that the discrete Arizona pygmy-owl population is significant to its taxon as a whole under either the second or fourth significance factor.

... The judgment of the district court is reversed and the case is remanded to the district court for further proceedings consistent with this opinion.

Notes and Comments

1. The court remands the case to the district court for further proceedings consistent with this opinion. What further proceedings might there be? Must the district court set aside the agency rule? Could it remand the rule to the agency without setting aside the rule, to enable the agency to better articulate its explanation of why the discrete population was significant? In some circumstances courts do that. *See, e.g.,* Ronald Levin, *"Vacation" at*

Sea: Judicial Remedies and Equitable Discretion in Administrative Law, 53 Duke L.J. 291 (2003). Even if the court sets the rule aside, can the FWS merely reinstate it by better articulating their rationale? Or, do you think that their conclusion that the Arizona ferruginous pygmy-owl is a distinct population segment cannot be justified?

2. How does the justification for a distinct population segment differ from a determination that a species may become extinct throughout a significant portion of its range? In *NAHB* the FWS argued that the Arizona owl was a distinct population segment because, if it became extinct, there would be a significant reduction in its historic range. The court analogized this argument to the requirement in *Defenders of Wildlife*, excerpted earlier, that in order to say that a species was in risk of becoming extinct throughout a significant portion of its range, the affected range must involve a "major geographic area." Because the FWS had not shown that the range of the Arizona owl was a major geographic area, the court held that the FWS had not shown that the effect of the Arizona owl's extinction would be significant.

3. Why does the court think it is not sufficient to establish that this discrete population, if made extinct, would deprive the United States of this subspecies altogether? The court states that the important issue is the impact on the entire taxon. What leads the court to believe this is the critical issue? Is there anything in the findings, purposes, or policy of the Endangered Species Act that the FWS could refer to support its case that eliminating the owls from the United States should be sufficient in itself to justify listing? Consider 16 U.S.C. § 1531(a). More broadly, why do you think we *should* protect species? What purpose should the ESA serve?

4. A particular problem with regard to distinct population segments involves anadromous fish. These are fish that are born in the headwaters of rivers, but then they migrate downstream to the ocean, where they live their adult life until they return to the headwaters where they were born in order to spawn and then die. Because the fish from the headwaters of one river do not generally interbreed with the fish from adjacent headwaters, each of these different stocks of fish might be considered a distinct population segment. Prior to the FWS and NMFS joint adoption of the DPS Policy in 1996, however, NMFS had on its own adopted a particular distinct population segment policy regarding Pacific Salmon to address this issue. Policy on Applying the Definition of Species Under the Endangered Species Act to Pacific Salmon, 56 Fed. Reg. 58,612 (1991). This policy used the term, Evolutionarily Significant Unit, to describe the distinct population segments for Pacific Salmon, and hence has come to be known as the ESU Policy. Under the ESU Policy, in order for a Salmon stock to be an ESU, (1) it must be substantially reproductively isolated from other conspecific population units, and (2) it must represent an important component in the evolutionary legacy of the species. The first criterion can be measured by movements of tagged fish, recolonization rates of other populations, and the efficacy of natural barriers. The second criteria is concerned with "ecological/genetic diversity" of the species as a whole, so NMFS looks to see if the population is genetically distinct from other conspecific populations, occupies an unusual or distinctive habitat, or shows evidence of unusual or distinctive adaptation to its environment. How, if at all, is this different from the criteria for DPS?

5. Recall that listing is supposed to be a scientific determination. Is determining the significance of a particular population segment a scientific determination, or is it one of those embedded value determinations hidden within the scientific process? What would you say the *Home Builders* case suggests?

6. An interesting problem involves invasive aliens or exotics, in other words, species that humans have intentionally or unintentionally introduced outside their natural range and that lacking natural predators have mushroomed in population. Such species include the kudzu vine, zebra mussels, and the starling. We would like to extirpate some of these species because of the harm they do, but does the ESA stand in the way? Nothing in the ESA limits its protections to species in their "natural" habitats. For the most part, this question is largely academic, because despite our best efforts, these invasive aliens are not in danger of being eradicated. Indeed, Congress has passed certain laws intended to help counter alien invasives. *See* Nonindigenous Aquatic Nuisance Prevention and Control Act of 1990, as amended, 16 U.S.C. 4701 *et seq.*; Federal Noxious Weed Act of 1974, as amended, 7 U.S.C. 2801 *et seq. See also* Invasive Species, E.O. 13112, 64 Fed. Reg. 6183 (Feb. 3, 1999). There are, however, some situations in which the question is real. For example, in the Olympic Mountains in the Olympic National Park there is a population of mountain goats, a beautiful and majestic creature (but is that relevant?). Because these mountain goats harm the rare (but not listed) alpine and sub-alpine plants, the National Park Service has proposed to extirpate the goat population by hiring professional hunters in helicopters to shoot all the goats. The NPS believes that these goats are not native to the Olympic Mountains but were introduced in the 1920s for sport hunting purposes. Others, however, believe that the goats are endemic to the Olympic Mountains, citing reports of early expeditions and Native American artifacts in the area made from mountain goat wool and horns. This population of mountain goats would certainly seem to be a distinct population segment, isolated as it is from other populations. What difference should it make under the Endangered Species Act whether the mountain goat has been in the Olympic Mountains for 80 years, 280 years, or 800 years?

2. Critical Habitat

Section 4 generally requires FWS or NMFS, when they list a species as endangered or threatened, concurrently to designate "critical habitat" for the species. 16 U.S.C. § 1533(a)(3)(A). Critical habitat is a defined term. It includes those areas occupied by the species at the time of listing that provide "those physical or biological features (I) essential to the conservation of the species and (II) which may require special management considerations or protection." 16 U.S.C. § 1532(5)(A)(i). In addition, it includes those areas outside area occupied by the species at the time of listing that the FWS or NMFS determines are essential for the conservation of the species. 16 U.S.C. § 1532(5)(A)(ii). Thus, only areas "essential to [or for] the conservation of the species" can be critical habitat. "Conservation" is also a defined term. It means to do what is necessary "to bring any endangered species or threatened species to the point at which the [protections of the ESA] are no longer necessary." 16 U.S.C § 1532(3). In other words, to conserve the species means not just to preserve the species from extinction but to bring it to the point at which it is no longer likely to become endangered in the foreseeable future absent the protections of the Act.

Like the listing determinations, the FWS and NMFS are supposed to make the determination of whether areas are necessary for conservation of the species "on the basis of the best scientific data available." 16 U.S.C. § 1533(b)(2). However, unlike the listing determinations, that is only the first step. After determining what areas are necessary for conservation of the species, the FWS and NMFS are also to consider "the economic impact, the impact on national security, and any other relevant impact, of specifying any particular area as critical habitat." *Id.* Then those agencies may exclude areas from critical habitat if the benefits of exclusion outweigh the benefits of inclusion, so long as the exclusion will not result in the extinction of the species. *Id.* This exclusion power, for example, was used to exclude approximately one-third of the habitat of the Northern Spotted Owl that otherwise would have been deemed critical, and it has been used to exclude area within military training areas.

To qualify for critical habitat, an area must be necessary for conservation of the species and may also require special management considerations or protection. That is, if an area does not need special management, then it does not qualify for critical habitat designation. Presumably, the concept behind this requirement is that if the habitat in its natural and unregulated state is adequately providing the necessary habitat for the species, there is no need for critical habitat designation. This is unlikely to be the case when the threat to the species comes from habitat destruction or degradation, the source of most risks to threatened and endangered species. The FWS, however, has interpreted this requirement also to exclude areas that are already under management to protect the habitat. For example, the FWS excluded tribal lands of two Native American tribes from the critical habitat designation of the Mexican Spotted Owl because those lands were subject to owl management plans. This exclusion was challenged, however, and the reviewing court found this exclusion "nonsensical." In its view, the fact that there was already an owl management plan in place was proof that the area might need special management. *See Center for Biological Diversity v. Norton*, 240 F.Supp.2d 1090, 1098 (D. Az. 2003).

As might be imagined, the designation of critical habitat is a difficult determination both scientifically and practically. Listing is difficult enough, but at least that decision is polar; that is, the services either list or not. Either the evidence supports the listing or not. Critical habitat designation is more open-ended. Lines must be drawn on a map, and where those lines are drawn must be supportable. Moreover, Section 4 makes clear that the listing decision is to be made without regard to the economic or social impacts listing might have. This at least theoretically insulates the services from much outside pressure from those impacted by the listing. The explicit need to consider such impacts in designating critical habitat, however, means the services must deal with those pressures and respond to them in a coherent manner. As a result of all these difficulties, the resources necessary for critical habitat designation are generally much greater than those necessary for listing a species. At the same time, critical habitat designation is not as vital to a species protection as its listing. That is, even absent a critical habitat designation, a listed species cannot be "jeopardized" by government action and endangered fish and wildlife species cannot be "taken" by anyone. The critical habitat designation only provides additional protection for listed species when government action may adversely affect that habitat. This combination of the need for increased resources to make the designation and its perception that the designation's additional protections were not significant led the FWS over the years to attempt to avoid having to make critical habitat designations to the extent possible.

Section 4 requires a designation of critical habitat "to the maximum extent prudent and determinable." 16 U.S.C. § 1533(a)(3)(A). Difficulty in the determinability of critical habitat provides a basis for delaying its designation for a year, but not a basis for avoiding it altogether. *See* 16 U.S.C. § 1533(b)(6)(C)(ii). However, if it is not "prudent" to designate critical habitat, then the services are excused from designating it altogether. "Prudent" is not a defined term, and the legislative history indicates that it was a narrow concept. For example, it might not be beneficial to designate critical habitat, if, as might be the case for parrots or certain kinds of medicinal plants, their very rarity made them valuable, because such designation would identify on publicly available maps where the species could be found, thereby increasing the risk of predation. However, the services have not so limited their definition of the term. In their regulations, they include the original concept but then also include a more general concept: any time designation of critical habitat "would not be beneficial to the species." 50 CFR § 424.12(a)(1)(ii).

Relying on this provision, the FWS, in particular, has refused to designate critical habitat in a number of cases, arguing that designating critical habitat simply would not increase any protection of the species that does not automatically accrue from its being a listed species. Assessing the merits of this claim requires an understanding of what protections the ESA provides for critical habitat, protections that are specified in Section 7 of the Act, and then comparing them to the protections afforded listed species, protections afforded by both Section 7 and Section 9. As described in the introductory paragraph outlining the ESA, Section 7 only protects against federal government action, not private or state action that might harm endangered species or their habitat. Accordingly, FWS maintains, designating critical habitat on private land would be meaningless because it would have little to no effect other than upset the landowners, who might actually be moved to destroy the habitat—an action that the critical habitat designation would not preclude. On federal land, FWS argues, critical habitat designation does not benefit the species either, because federal actions that harm the species, whether through habitat destruction or otherwise, are prohibited by Section 7. We will postpone a full discussion of these claims and the counterarguments until the discussion of Section 7, but at this point it should be noted that the basis for these claims has been uniformly rejected by the courts. *See, e.g., New Mexico Cattle Growers Ass'n v. USFWS*, 248 F.3d 1277 (10th Cir. 2001); *Sierra Club v. USFWS*, 245 F.3d 434 (5th Cir. 2001); *NRDC v. USDOI*, 113 F.3d 1121 (9th Cir. 1997). Nevertheless, FWS has not given up on this issue.

3. Recovery

In addition to requiring FWS or NMFS to list endangered and threatened species and to designate their critical habitat, Section 4 also requires the services to "develop and implement" recovery plans for the conservation of the listed species, unless such a plan would not promote the conservation of the species. 16 U.S.C. § 1533(f). Recall that the term "conservation" means to bring the species to the point that it need not be listed anymore. Thus, recovery plans are intended not only to keep the species from extinction but to recover it to a point that it can be delisted. These plans are supposed to be specific, describing site-specific management actions, objective, measurable criteria, which if met, would enable delisting, and timetables and budgets for achieving recovery. 16 U.S.C. § 1533(f)(1)(B).

Although there is no requirement for when recovery plans must be developed, the FWS adopted a policy of adopting plans within 2½ years of a listing decision. Attempts by environmental groups to force the development of recovery plans through litigation have been generally unsuccessful, as courts have held that decisions as to when to adopt recovery plans is at the discretion of the agency, so long as it does not abandon the attempt altogether. *See, e.g., ONRC v. Turner*, 863 F.Supp. 1277 (D. Or. 1997).

A major issue with respect to recovery plans is their legal status; that is, do they require agencies to comply with their terms, or are they merely "guidance"? The position of FWS is that they are merely guidance, or, as it has sometimes characterized them, they are like a menu from which agencies are free to choose. The lack of enforceability as well as underfunding by Congress has led commentators to conclude that the recovery process does not come close to achieving its objectives. *See, e.g.,* Federico Cheever, *The Road to Recovery: A New Way of Thinking About the Endangered Species Act*, 23 Ecology L.Q. 1 (1996).

4. The Procedures

Section 4 spells out a detailed procedure by which species can become listed or delisted. While a species can be considered for listing or delisting on the initiative of one of the services, Section 4 also provides that an interested person can petition for a species to be listed or delisted. 16 U.S.C. § 1533(b)(3)(A). Increasingly, this has become the method by which new species have been considered for listing. Section 4 requires the service receiving the petition to decide whether the petition presents "substantial scientific or commercial information" indicating that listing "may be warranted." This decision is to be made "to the extent practicable, within 90 days after receiving the petition." *Id.* If the service finds the petition is meritorious, the species is denominated a "candidate species," a denomination that affords no protection to the species, but which triggers the next procedural requirement.

"Within 12 months of receiving a [meritorious] petition," the service is to make a finding whether in fact the petitioned action is warranted or not and promptly to publish its finding. 16 U.S.C. § 1533(b)(3)(B). If the decision is that the petitioned action is warranted, the published finding must either include a notice of proposed rulemaking proposing the species for listing or a determination that such a notice is precluded at this time because of other pending proposals and "expeditious progress" is being made with respect to adding and deleting species to the lists. *Id.* If a proposal is currently precluded, the service has an additional year within which to make the finding again. 16 U.S.C. § 1533(b)(3)(C)(i). However, at the end of that year, the service may again make the "warranted but precluded" determination and thereby recycle these petitions on a year-to-year basis, never proposing the species for listing. In this way the services can devote their rulemaking resources to those species with the greatest need for listing. Indeed, the FWS has developed a priority system to decide which species should be considered first. *See* Endangered and Threatened Wildlife and Plants; Final Listing Priority Guidance for Fiscal Year 2000, 64 Fed. Reg. 57114 (October 22, 1999).

The rulemaking generally follows the procedures for notice-and-comment rulemaking in the Administrative Procedure Act, but within one year the service must adopt the rule listing the species, make a finding that there is insufficient evidence to justify listing, or that there is substantial controversy over the evidence and additional time is required to gather more evidence. 16 U.S.C. § 1533(b)(6)(A). In the last case, the service may extend the one-year period for not longer than six months. 16 U.S.C. § 1533(b)(6)(B)(i).

As described earlier, critical habitat designations are to be made in the same rulemaking as the listing determination, unless the critical habitat is not then determinable, in which case the service can take not more than one additional year in order to designate the critical habitat. 16 U.S.C. § 1533(b)(6)(C)(ii). Given the FWS priorities, the FWS almost never designates critical habitat concurrently with a listing.

Since its original passage, the FWS has had difficulty making listing decisions, critical habitat designations, and recovery plans in a reasonable period of time. For the most part this has been due to inadequate appropriations combined with the inherent difficulty in making the requisite determinations. The current detailed and prescriptive time periods were a response to this earlier failure to list species and designate critical habitat in a timely fashion under earlier provisions of the ESA. This response, however, was not an effective solution. Inadequate funding, reflecting congressional ambivalence with the ESA, and the one-year ban on spending any funds to list a species as threatened or endangered or to designate critical habitat, *see* Emergency Supplemental Appropriations and Rescissions for the Department of Defense to Preserve and Enhance Military Readiness Act of 1995, Pub. L. No. 104–6, 109 Stat. 73 (1995), reflecting congressional hostility to the Act, have stymied any real attempt to make listing and critical habitat determinations on a current and timely basis. Consequently, the FWS took the position that it simply need not respond to petitions for listing, because the 90–day requirement was limited by the phrase "to the extent practicable," and that the 12–month period to decide whether to undertake a rulemaking only began to run after the petition had been acted upon. These arguments have apparently now been rejected by the courts. *See, e.g., Biodiversity Legal Found. v. Badgley*, 309 F.3d 1166 (9th Cir. 2002). As a result, these statutory time periods have provided a handle whereby environmental groups can sue the services to force decisions. Thus, currently, most listing decisions seem to be driven by litigation brought by environmental groups seeking listings for their particular purposes.

This, however, hardly solves the basic problem of too much to do with too little resources. Thus, today, after thirty years, the services have listed 990 endangered species and 275 threatened species in the United States. While in the decade of the 90's, the services were averaging about 67 listings a year, in the past four years, the average has dropped down to about 6 per year. In 2004, there were currently 24 species proposed for listing, but there were also 280 candidate species. Thus, at current rates, there is already a forty-year backlog of listing decisions, even if no new petitions for listing were filed.

The services assign priorities to the candidate species and the "warranted but precluded" species, so that at least in theory the most endangered species can be put at the front of the line and the least threatened at the back. In addition, the Act does provide an emergency procedure, if a service finds there is "any emergency posing a significant risk to the well-being of any species." 16 U.S.C. § 1533(b)(7). This procedure allows a service to avoid all the aforementioned procedural requirements, as well as the requirements of the APA, and immediately list a species or designate critical habitat, if it explains the reasons why the immediate action is necessary. This emergency regulation, however, can only be effective for 240 days. *Id.* The idea is that during that period the service could undertake a rulemaking using the normal procedures to supplant the emergency rule.

Notes and Comments

1. The listing process, including the designation of critical habitat, has been fraught with difficulties since the inception of the ESA. While the technicalities of the law have at least temporarily provided avenues for delay for administrations so inclined, the system is widely perceived as dysfunctional. The problem is that there is no consensus on the nature of the problem, much less how to fix it. To some, the current ESA is viewed as

misguided in its attempt to save all species without regard to their role in the ecosystem or the value to humankind. To others, the process of listing and critical habitat designation unnecessarily strives for amassing overwhelming evidence in support of determinations, rather than following a precautionary principle, resulting in delay in listings and inadequate critical habitat designations. Obviously, the solutions proposed by those with these different views would be very different. What do you think is the problem? How would you fix it?

2.   There has been a question as to what role NEPA should play in the listing and critical habitat decisions. The services have always maintained that these decisions are not subject to NEPA. Although it is usually environmental groups arguing for greater use of NEPA, with respect to the ESA environmentalists have opposed applying NEPA to ESA decisionmaking. They perceive, rightly, that requiring EA's or EIS's would slow the process even more, which is precisely why property owners and development interests here favor a greater use of NEPA. The courts have generally sided with environmentalists on this issue, holding uniformly that listing decisions are not subject to NEPA, *see, e.g., Pacific Legal Found. v. Andrus*, 657 F.2d 829 (6th Cir. 1981), and the circuits have split on whether NEPA applies to critical habitat designations. *Compare Catron County Bd. of Commissioners v. USFWS*, 75 F.3d 1429 (10th Cir. 1996)(NEPA applies) *with Douglas County v. Babbitt*, 48 F.3d 1495 (9th Cir. 1995), *cert. denied*, 516 U.S. 1042, 116 S.Ct. 698, 133 L.Ed.2d 655 (1996)(NEPA does not apply).

3.   The requirement for the services to create recovery plans, plans designed not just to keep the species from the brink of extinction but to enable them to become a healthy species no longer needing the protections of the ESA, is a potentially powerful tool. In practice, however, they have not been very successful. Thus, while over 1000 of the listed species are covered by recovery plans, only 15 have been "recovered" so that they could be delisted. Is this a failure that can be remedied, such as by providing for judicial enforcement, or is this the inevitable consequence of expanded population and economic growth?

4.   The statistics on the number of species listed differ dramatically between the Clinton administration and the George W. Bush administration, just as they had between the Carter administration and the first four years of the Reagan administration. Why would Democratic administrations be more likely to list species than Republican administrations?

C. Section 7

Section 7 of the ESA imposes three different sets of obligations on federal agencies. The first obligation is to "utilize their authorities in furtherance of the purposes of this chapter by carrying out programs for the conservation of [listed] species...." 16 U.S.C. § 1536(a)(1). Their second obligation is to consult with the FWS or NMFS if their actions are likely to affect listed species. 16 U.S.C. § 1536(a)(2). Their final obligation is to insure that their actions are not "likely to jeopardize the continued existence of any endangered species or threatened species or result in the destruction or adverse modification of [critical] habitat...." 16 U.S.C. § 1536(a)(2).

1. The Affirmative Obligation

By its terms, Section 7(a)(1) imposes an affirmative obligation on all agencies to carry out programs for the conservation of listed species by utilizing their existing authorities in furtherance of the ESA. Recall that the term "conservation" means to recover a species to the point that it no longer needs to be listed. 16 U.S.C. § 1532(3). The FWS and NMFS in particular are required to utilize all the programs they administer to further the purposes of the ESA. 16 U.S.C. § 1536(a)(1). What this means to agencies in their everyday activities, however, is open to question. For example, is the United States Forest Service to abandon all its timber harvesting and recreational authorities and manage its forests to recover species at the expense of all of its other goals? Are the military departments to manage their ranges and practice areas for the benefit of species without regard to their mission to prepare and train military personnel?

In practice, agencies have all but ignored Section 7(a)(1)'s mandate. They have argued that they need to conserve species only to the extent consistent with the accomplishment of their primary goals. In other words, if an action to conserve species would interfere at all with their primary goals, they need not take the action to conserve a species. Lawsuits brought to try to enforce a more rigorous requirement have been generally unsuccessful. Courts have recognized the statutory obligation, but in light of its general language the courts have held that how agencies fulfill that mandate is subject to their discretion, which is subject only to arbitrary and capricious review. There is apparently only one court of appeals case that actually directed an agency to take any action under Section 7(a)(1). *See Sierra Club v. Glickman*, 156 F.3d 606 (5th Cir. 1998). And in that case the court only directed the Department of Agriculture to adopt a plan, not to take a specific action. More common is the outcome in *Pyramid Lake Paiute Tribe of Indians v. U.S.D.O.N.*, 898 F.2d 1410 (9th Cir. 1990), where the court recognized the mandate to conserve but interpreted Section 7(a)(1) to give discretion to the agency in determining how to fulfill that mandate in light of its other statutory obligations.

Perhaps the most cited case under Section 7(a)(1) is *Carson-Truckee Water Conservancy Dist. v. Clark*, 741 F.2d 257 (9th Cir. 1984). There, the Bureau of Reclamation withheld water in its dammed reservoir, that it ordinarily would have sold for irrigation purposes, in order to conserve the endangered cui-ui fish. The irrigation district desiring the withheld water sued to require the Bureau to release the water, but the court upheld the Bureau's action, relying on Section 7(a)(1)'s mandate to conserve listed species. This mandate, the court said, authorized the agency to give preference to the ESA over its ordinary contractual obligations to release the water to the irrigation district.

These cases have led commentators to characterize Section 7(a)(1) in practice as an agency shield, rather than an environmentalist's sword.

2. The Procedural Requirements

Section 7(a)(2)-(4) requires agencies to engage in certain inquiries and consultations when they take actions that may affect listed species. As under NEPA, the trigger in Section 7(a)(2) is agency action, which includes not only direct agency action but also agency funding of someone else's action or agency permitting of someone else's action. For example, if the Federal Highway Administration pays for a portion of an interstate highway to be built by a state, that would be a federal agency action, which, if the road were to affect a listed species, would require consultation with the FWS. Similarly, if the Corps of Engineers permits a person to fill a wetland under Section 404 of the Clean Water Act, and the fill would affect a listed species, then the Corps would have to consult with the FWS.

The overall purpose of the procedural requirement to consult is to provide sufficient information to the action agency to assure that it will not violate the substantive command of Section 7 that federal agencies not jeopardize a listed species or adversely affect critical habitat. The process to assure this is somewhat complicated.

- First the agency must decide whether its action is "likely to affect" a listed species or designated critical habitat.

  - In order to make that decision, the agency must determine whether a listed species is present in the area to be affected by the action. The agency may know this on its own, in which case it provides this information to the applicable service for confirmation; otherwise it must request information from the services in order to make that determination. *See* 16 U.S.C. § 1536(c)(1).

    - If no such species or critical habitat is in the area, then that is end of the matter.

  - If a species or critical habitat is in the area, and the action would have physical impacts on the environment sufficient to require an Environmental Impact Statement (EIS) under the National Environmental Policy Act (NEPA), then the agency must make a "biological assessment." *See* 50 CFR § 402.12 and § 402.02 (definition of "major construction activity"). The BA is to assess whether the agency action will likely affect the listed species.

    - If the agency concludes in the BA that its action will not likely have an adverse effect on the species or critical habitat, and the service agrees, that is the end of the matter.

  - If a BA is not required, the agency may engage in "informal consultation," which is designed to determine whether "formal consultation" is required.

    - As under the BA, if at the conclusion of "informal consultation" the agency determines and the service concurs that the agency's action will not likely have an adverse effect on the species or critical habitat, that is the end of the matter.

- If, however, there is no negative finding at the conclusion of either the BA or the informal consultation, then the agency must engage in formal consultation with the appropriate service. Formal consultation requires the agency to supply the appropriate service with a full description of the proposed action, the best scientific information available concerning the possible effects on the species and habitat, and any other relevant data to enable the service to determine the extent of the effect on the species or habitat.

- The conclusion of the formal consultation results in a "biological opinion" from the relevant service to the action agency.

- The BO can have one of three possible conclusions:

  - the proposed agency action will jeopardize the species or result in the adverse modification of critical habitat, but these effects can be avoided through "reasonable and prudent alternatives,"

  - the proposed agency action will jeopardize the species or result in adverse modification to critical habitat, and these effects cannot be avoided, or

  - the proposed agency action will not jeopardize the species or result in the adverse modification of critical habitat.

- As part of the BO, the service can approve the "incidental take" of certain of the listed species, subject to conditions in the BO. The purpose of the incidental take statement is to provide an exemption from Section 9 of the ESA which makes the "take" of any endangered (and in some cases threatened) fish or wildlife species unlawful. But for the incidental take statement, the action agency (or the person using the federal funds or acting under the federal permit) would be acting unlawfully if even a single member of the species was harmed.

- The agency then determines for itself, informed by the BO, whether its action will jeopardize the species or have an adverse effect on critical habitat.

- During the period of consultation, neither the agency nor any permit applicant may make "any irreversible or irretrievable commitment of resources ... which has the effect of foreclosing ... any reasonable and prudent alternative measures." The purpose of this limitation is to assure that agencies or applicants will not commit resources to try to influence the jeopardy outcome by making the cost of a jeopardy finding very great.

Under Section 7(a)(4), 16 U.S.C. § 1536(a)(4), species proposed for listing, but not yet listed, receive a similar procedural protection, although it is called "conferring" rather than "consulting." No biological assessment is required, however, and even if a proposed species or proposed critical habitat is present in the action area, a conference is only required if the agency action is "likely to jeopardize the continued existence" of the species or "result in the destruction or adverse modification of critical habitat proposed to be designated." Under the services' regulation all that is required in the conference is "informal discussions" of ways to minimize the impact on the species or habitat, but if the proposed listing becomes final before the agency action is completed, the agency will need to engage in the formal consultation process. Agencies may request the services actually to make a biological opinion as part of the conference, which then become the formal biological opinion if the listing becomes final. There is no prohibition on the commitment of resources during the conference period.

Section 7(a)(3), 16 U.S.C. § 1536(a)(3), provides the basis for what the services call "early consultation." *See* 50 CFR § 402.11 (2003). The purpose of this procedure is to enable applicants for government permits or licenses to discover before they actually apply for their permits or licenses whether the ESA will stand in their way. In essence, the formal consultation takes place as above except that its results are called "preliminary" determinations. These preliminary determinations can become final determinations after the applicant actually files his application.

As may be seen, these procedural requirements for consultation constitute hurdles that must overcome before an agency takes an action that may adversely affect listed (or even proposed) species. Failure to comply with these procedures, if someone challenges the proposed action in court, may result in the agency action being blocked until the agency has complied with the requisite requirements. There are essentially two ways in which compliance may be lacking: the required consultation may not take place at all (perhaps because the agency or service thinks it is not applicable for one or more reasons), or the consultation that did take place is deemed inadequate and therefore not in compliance with the ESA.

The following cases provide examples.

THOMAS v. PETERSON

United States Court of Appeals, Ninth Circuit, 1985.

753 F.2d 754.

SNEED, Circuit Judge:

Plaintiffs sought to enjoin construction of a timber road in a former National Forest roadless area. The District Court granted summary judgment in favor of defendant R. Max Peterson, Chief of the Forest Service, and plaintiffs appealed. . . .

We conclude that: . . . The Endangered Species Act (ESA) requires the Forest Service to prepare a biological assessment to determine whether the road and the timber sales that the road is designed to facilitate are likely to affect the endangered Rocky Mountain Gray Wolf, and construction of the road should be enjoined pending compliance with the ESA.

I.

STATEMENT OF THE CASE

... Plaintiffs—landowners, ranchers, outfitters, miners, hunters, fishermen, recreational users, and conservation and recreation organizations—challenge actions of the United States Forest Service in planning and approving a timber road in the Jersey Jack area of the Nezperce National Forest in Idaho. The area is adjacent to the Salmon River, a congressionally-designated Wild and Scenic River, and is bounded on the west by the designated Gospel Hump Wilderness and on the east by the River of No Return Wilderness. The area lies in a "recovery corridor" identified by the U.S. Fish & Wildlife Service for the Rocky Mountain Gray Wolf, an endangered species....

The plaintiffs filed this action, challenging the Chief's decision, on June 30, 1982. Their three principal allegations are:

(1) NEPA, and regulations issued by the Council on Environmental Quality (CEQ), require the Forest Service to prepare an EIS that analyzes the combined effects of the proposed road and the timber sales that the road is designed to facilitate.

(2) The decision to build the road is inconsistent with the National Forest Management Act, 16 U.S.C. §§ 1600–1614, because the cost of the road will exceed the value of the timber that it will access.

(3) The road is likely to affect the Rocky Mountain Gray Wolf, an endangered species, and the Forest Service has failed to follow procedures mandated by the Endangered Species Act, 16 U.S.C. §§ 1531– 1543.

II.

THE NEPA CLAIM

[The court found that NEPA did not allow the Forest Service to engage in this action having only prepared an Environmental Assessment. It agreed with the plaintiffs that an EIS was required.]

III.

THE NATIONAL FOREST MANAGEMENT ACT CLAIM

[The court upheld the decision of the Forest Service under the National Forest Management Act, rejecting the plaintiffs' claim.]

IV.

THE ENDANGERED SPECIES ACT CLAIM

The plaintiffs' third claim concerns the Forest Service's alleged failure to comply with the Endangered Species Act (ESA) in considering the effects of the road and timber sales on the endangered Rocky Mountain Gray Wolf.

The ESA contains both substantive and procedural provisions. Substantively, the Act prohibits the taking or importation of endangered species, *see* 16 U.S.C. § 1538, and requires federal agencies to ensure that their actions are not "likely to jeopardize the continued existence of any endangered species or threatened species or result in the destruction or adverse modification" of critical habitat of such species, *see* 16 U.S.C. § 1536(a)(2).

The Act prescribes a three-step process to ensure compliance with its substantive provisions by federal agencies. Each of the first two steps serves a screening function to determine if the successive steps are required. The steps are:

(1) An agency proposing to take an action must inquire of the Fish & Wildlife Service (F & WS) whether any threatened or endangered species "may be present" in the area of the proposed action. *See* 16 U.S.C. § 1536(c)(1).

(2) If the answer is affirmative, the agency must prepare a "biological assessment" to determine whether such species "is likely to be affected" by the action. *Id.* The biological assessment may be part of an environmental impact statement or environmental assessment. *Id.*

(3) If the assessment determines that a threatened or endangered species "is likely to be affected," the agency must formally consult with the F & WS. *Id.* § 1536(a)(2). The formal consultation results in a "biological opinion" issued by the F & WS. *See id.* § 1536(b). If the biological opinion concludes that the proposed action would jeopardize the species or destroy or adversely modify critical habitat, *see id.* § 1536(a)(2), then the action may not go forward unless the F & WS can suggest an alternative that avoids such jeopardization, destruction, or adverse modification. *Id.* § 1536(b)(3)(A). If the opinion concludes that the action will not violate the Act, the F & WS may still require measures to minimize its impact. *Id.* § 1536(b)(4)(ii)-(iii).

Plaintiffs first allege that, with respect to the Jersey Jack road, the Forest Service did not undertake step (1), a formal request to the F & WS. The district court found that to be the case, but concluded that the procedural violation was insignificant because the Forest Service was already aware that wolves may be present in the area. The court therefore refused to enjoin the construction of the road. Plaintiffs insist, based on *TVA v. Hill,* 437 U.S. 153, 98 S.Ct. 2279, 57 L.Ed.2d 117 (1978), that an injunction is mandatory once any ESA violation is found. . . .

We need not reach this issue. The Forest Service's failure goes beyond the technical violation cited by the district court, and is not *de minimis.*

Once an agency is aware that an endangered species may be present in the area of its proposed action, the ESA requires it to prepare a biological assessment to determine whether the proposed action "is likely to affect" the species and therefore requires formal consultation with the F & WS. *See supra.* The Forest Service did not prepare such an assessment prior to its decision to build the Jersey Jack road. Without a biological assessment, it cannot be determined whether the proposed project will result in a violation of the ESA's substantive provisions. A failure to prepare a biological assessment for a project in an area in which it has been determined that an endangered species may be present cannot be considered a *de minimis* violation of the ESA.

The district court found that the Forest Service had "undertaken sufficient study and action to further the purposes of the ESA," Memorandum Decision at 1149, E.R. 103. Its finding was based on affidavits submitted by the Forest Service for the litigation.[7] *See* Memorandum Decision at 1148, E.R. 99. These do not constitute a substitute for the preparation of the biological assessment required by the ESA.

Given a substantial procedural violation of the ESA in connection with a federal project, the remedy must be an injunction of the project pending compliance with the ESA. . . .

Our cases repeatedly have held that, absent "unusual circumstances," an injunction is the appropriate remedy for a violation of NEPA's procedural requirements. . . . We see no reason that the same principle should not apply to procedural violations of the ESA.

The Forest Service argues that the procedural requirements of the ESA should be enforced less stringently than those of NEPA because, unlike NEPA, the ESA also contains substantive provisions. We acknowledge that the ESA's substantive provisions distinguish it from NEPA, but the distinction acts the other way. If anything, the strict substantive provisions of the ESA justify *more* stringent enforcement of its procedural requirements, because the procedural requirements are designed to ensure compliance with the substantive provisions. The ESA's procedural requirements call for a systematic determination of the effects of a federal project on endangered species. If a project is allowed to proceed without substantial compliance with those procedural requirements, there can be no assurance that a violation of the ESA's substantive provisions will not result. The latter, of course, is impermissible.

The district court, citing *Palila v. Hawaii Dept. of Land and Natural Resources,* 639 F.2d 495 (9th Cir.1981), held that "[a] party asserting a violation of the Endangered Species Act has the burden of showing the proposed action would have some prohibited effect on an endangered species or its critical habitat," and found that the plaintiffs in this case had not met that burden. This is a misapplication of *Palila.* That case concerned the ESA's prohibition of the "taking" of an endangered species, 16 U.S.C. § 1538(a)(1)(B), not the ESA's procedural requirements. Quite naturally, the court in *Palila* found that a plaintiff, in order to establish a violation of the "taking" provision, must show that

---

7. The district court relied on the Forest Service's assertion that it had worked in "close cooperation" with the F & WS, but that assertion is undermined by letters in the record from the F & WS indicating that the Forest Service had not consulted with the F & WS on the impact of the road and the timber sales on the gray wolf, and that the F & WS felt that the Forest Service was not giving the wolf adequate consideration. See E.R. 55–58.

such a "taking" has occurred. The holding does not apply to violations of the ESA's procedural requirements. A plaintiffs' burden in establishing a procedural violation is to show that the circumstances triggering the procedural requirement exist, and that the required procedures have not been followed. The plaintiffs in this case have clearly met that burden.

The Forest Service would require the district court, absent proof by the plaintiffs to the contrary, to make a finding that the Jersey Jack road is not likely to affect the Rocky Mountain Gray Wolf, and that therefore any failure to comply with ESA procedures is harmless. This is not a finding appropriate to the district court at the present time. Congress has assigned to the agencies and to the Fish & Wildlife Service the responsibility for evaluation of the impact of agency actions on endangered species, and has prescribed procedures for such evaluation. Only by following the procedures can proper evaluations be made. It is not the responsibility of the plaintiffs to prove, nor the function of the courts to judge, the effect of a proposed action on an endangered species when proper procedures have not been followed.

We therefore hold that the district court erred in declining to enjoin construction of the Jersey Jack road pending compliance with the ESA. . . .

LANE COUNTY AUDUBON SOCIETY v. JAMISON

United States Court of Appeals, Ninth Circuit, 1992.

958 F.2d 290.

SCHROEDER, Circuit Judge:

In June of 1989, the United States Fish & Wildlife Service (FWS) proposed listing the northern spotted owl as a threatened species under the Endangered Species Act, 16 U.S.C. §§ 1531 et seq. (ESA). In addition, in October of 1989, the Interagency Scientific Committee to Address the Conservation of the Northern Spotted Owl (the ISC) was formed to "develop a scientifically credible conservation strategy for the northern spotted owl." In May of 1990, the ISC issued its Final Report, concluding that the lack of a consistent planning strategy has resulted in a high risk of extinction for the owl. In June of 1990, the FWS listed the northern spotted owl as a threatened species pursuant to the ESA. The FWS based its decision to list the owl on its finding that "[e]xisting regulatory mechanisms are insufficient to protect either the northern spotted owl or its habitat."

In response to these events, the Bureau of Land Management (BLM), which manages approximately 1,149,954 acres of the remaining old growth forests suitable for spotted owl habitat in western Oregon, promulgated a document entitled "Management Guidelines for the Conservation of the Northern Spotted Owl, FY 1991 through FY 1992", commonly known as the "Jamison Strategy" ("the Strategy"). In this Strategy, the BLM essentially sets forth the criteria for selection of land for logging in the millions of acres administered by the BLM in Washington, Oregon and California. The BLM described the Jamison Strategy as "a four-phase plan ... which will direct BLM management of western forest lands into FY 1994 and beyond." The Strategy contains management guidelines for fiscal years 1991 and 1992, including a program to offer 750 million board feet of timber for sale each year. The Strategy was designed to be implemented immediately.

On December 4, 1990, Lane County Audubon Society and various environmental groups (Lane County), filed the requisite 60–day notice of their intention to file an ESA citizen suit to challenge the BLM's failure to consult with the FWS on the Strategy pursuant to 16 U.S.C. § 1536 ("Section 7") of the ESA. *See* 16 U.S.C. § 1540(g)(2)(A)(i). In January of 1991, the BLM submitted about 174 proposed timber sales to be conducted in fiscal 1991 to the FWS for consultation pursuant to section 7 of the ESA, but did not submit the Jamison Strategy itself.

Lane County then filed this action in United States District Court for the District of Oregon seeking an injunction barring the conduct of any sales until the Jamison Strategy had undergone the consultation process. The district court agreed with Lane County that the Jamison Strategy is an "action" within the meaning of section 7 of the ESA and held that the BLM had violated that section by failing to consult with the FWS to obtain that agency's biological opinion regarding the effects of the Strategy on the northern spotted owl before implementing the Strategy. The district court on April 4, 1991, enjoined the BLM from implementing the Strategy pending compliance with section 7, but stated in its order that the 1991 sales were not affected by its order. At the time of the district court's order, the FWS had reviewed 174 of the proposed 1991 sales and had declared that 122 of these would not be likely to jeopardize the owls' habitat, provided the remaining 52, the so called "jeopardy sales," would take place only within the strict limitations provided for in the FWS' biological opinion. In reviewing the 1991 sales, FWS had before it the Jamison Strategy and found its criteria insufficient to protect owl habitat. It applied instead the criteria recommended in the ISC Final Report.

Lane County now appeals the district court's refusal to enjoin the 1991 timber sales. It seeks an injunction, pending completion of consultation on the Jamison Strategy, prohibiting all future sales on BLM lands in the affected area, including the 1992 sales and the remaining 1991 sales that have not yet been awarded.

The BLM cross-appeals the district court's order holding that the Jamison Strategy is "agency action" and requiring the BLM to submit the Strategy for consultation. The BLM contends that the Jamison Strategy is not an "action" requiring consultation and that it is merely a voluntarily created "policy statement." Moreover, the BLM contends that it has in fact substantially complied with the ESA by submitting the individual 1991 sales for section 7 consultation, and so, an injunction is unwarranted.

We hold that the district court correctly declared the Jamison Strategy itself to be an agency action and correctly enjoined its implementation pending consultation. We further hold that all future sales the BLM proposes to conduct are also "agency actions" and should not go forward until consultation is satisfactorily completed on the sales and on the Jamison Strategy itself or on another functionally similar plan establishing the governing criteria for sale site selections on BLM land. We enjoin, pending completion of such consultation, the award of any sales that may be announced in the future. The status of the remaining announced, but not yet awarded, 1991 sales is somewhat different, since those sales have already been submitted to the FWS. We remand to the district court for reconsideration of whether the award of those sales should also be enjoined based upon our holding today.

I

We turn first to the Jamison Strategy itself. It is intended to establish interim timber management standards to replace standards set forth in the old Timber Management Plans (TMPs) pending issuance of new TMPs.... The TMPs are 10–year plans that "designate commercial forest land under BLM management in [each] district for one of several uses." *Id.* at 1234. TMPs do not designate specific timber-sale boundaries, or require that any particular area be harvested. *Id.* at 1235. Rather, they decide land-use allocation and set the "annual allowable harvest" for each district. *See id.*

The BLM itself described its Jamison Strategy as an "interim strategy" to be carried out while new management plans are prepared. The Strategy outlines in detail the various criteria that will be used to develop the 1991 and 1992 timber sales. It develops a "detailed management strategy" to be carried out in four phases to cover fiscal years 1990 through 1994 "and beyond." Like the TMPs, it establishes total annual allowable harvests. The impact of each individual sale on owl habitat cannot be measured without reference to the management criteria established in the TMPs and the Jamison Strategy.

Section 7(a)(2) of the ESA requires the Secretary of the Interior to ensure that an action of a federal agency is not likely to jeopardize the continued existence of any threatened or endangered species. To this end, section 7(b) sets out a process of consultation whereby the agency with jurisdiction over the protected species issues to the Secretary a "biological opinion" evaluating the nature and extent of jeopardy posed to that species by the agency action. 16 U.S.C. § 1536(b). In order to maintain the status quo, section 7(d) forbids "irreversible or irretrievable commitment of resources" during the consultation period. *Id.* § 1536(d).

Section 7 specifically provides that a federal agency (the "action" agency) *shall* "in consultation with ... the Secretary [of the Interior], insure that any action authorized, funded, or carried out by such agency

... is not likely to jeopardize the continued existence of any endangered species or threatened species...." *Id.* § 1536(a)(2) (emphasis added).

Procedural guidelines for complying with this consultation requirement are codified at 50 C.F.R. Part 402. The FWS implementing regulations under the ESA require agencies to review their action "at the earliest possible time to determine whether any action may affect listed species." *Id.* § 402.14(a). The FWS defines agency "action" broadly to include "all activities or programs of any kind authorized, funded, or carried out, in whole or in part, by Federal agencies...." *Id.* § 402.02. Examples include but are not limited to:

(a) actions intended to conserve listed species or their habitat;

* * * * *

(d) actions directly or indirectly causing modifications to the land, water, or air.

Id.

This court also interprets the term "agency action" broadly. *Conner v. Burford,* 848 F.2d 1441, 1452 (9th Cir.1988), *cert. denied sub nom Sun Exploration & Prod. Co. v. Lujan,* 489 U.S. 1012, 109 S.Ct. 1121, 103 L.Ed.2d 184 (1989) (citing *TVA v. Hill,* 437 U.S. 153, 173 & n. 18, 98 S.Ct. 2279, 2291 & n. 18, 57 L.Ed.2d 117 (1978) (Supreme Court held that Congress had explicitly foreclosed the exercise of discretion by courts faced with a violation of section 7 of the ESA)).

We agree with the district court that "without a doubt," the Jamison Strategy as announced was to be an agency action "authorized, funded or carried out by the BLM." Moreover, the Jamison Strategy is action that "may affect" the spotted owl, since it sets forth criteria for harvesting owl habitat. It falls squarely within the definition of agency action set forth in 50 C.F.R. § 402.02. Accordingly, the BLM must submit the Jamison Strategy to the FWS for consultation before the Jamison Strategy can be implemented through the adoption of individual sale programs. In implementing the Jamison Strategy before consultation with the FWS, the BLM has violated the ESA. The district court properly enjoined implementation of the Strategy.

II

This brings us to Lane County's appeal regarding sales. Lane County asks that all sales be enjoined pending consultation on the Jamison Strategy. The government acknowledges that sales are "actions" under section 7 and require ESA consultation. The government contends, however, that despite the district court's injunction against implementation of the Jamison Strategy, individual sales may nevertheless go forward under the TMPs promulgated between 1979 and 1983 rather than the Jamison Strategy. The TMPs were, of course, not submitted for consultation at the time they were promulgated, because the owl was not listed as a threatened species until 1990. The government argues that the sales may go forward because Lane County has not challenged the TMPs under the ESA.

This is not a tenable position, for if the Jamison Strategy is an "action" requiring consultation, then clearly the BLM's reinstatement of the TMPs would also constitute such action. The two documents serve the same function with respect to sales. Moreover, in adopting the Jamison Strategy in the first place, the government recognized that a new, interim underlying strategy was necessary after the owls were listed pursuant to the ESA, because the old TMPs were inadequate to meet the requirements of that Act....

In sum, neither the underlying TMPs nor the Jamison "interim management strategy" has ever been submitted to FWS for consultation pursuant to the mandate of the ESA. Accordingly, the individual sales cannot go forward until the consultation process is complete on the underlying plans which BLM uses to drive their development.

The district court's order, however, did not make it clear that pending the completion of the consultation process, the BLM should be enjoined from conducting any new sales. Such an injunction is necessary because until consultation is satisfactorily concluded with respect to the Jamison Strategy, or indeed any other conservation strategy intended to establish the criteria under which sites for sales are to be selected, the sales cannot lawfully go forward. The ESA prohibits the "irreversible or irretrievable commitment of resources" during the consultation period. 16 U.S.C. § 1536(d). The sales are such commitments.

NEWTON COUNTY WILDLIFE ASSOCIATION v. ROGERS

United States Court of Appeals, Eighth Circuit, 1998.

141 F.3d 803.

LOKEN, Circuit Judge.

Newton County Wildlife Association, the Sierra Club, and certain individuals (collectively "the Wildlife Association") sued the United States Forest Service and four of its employees (collectively the "Forest Service") to enjoin or set aside four timber sales in the Ozark National Forest....

I. BACKGROUND.

... In the early 1990's, the Forest Service proposed four timber sales in "general" areas of the Buffalo Ranger District (areas administered under the Plan to yield a high level of timber). The proposed sales—Sand Gap, Round Hill, Junction, and Sandy Springs—involve timber harvesting on a total of 3,011 acres of forest and require 13.64 miles of logging road reconstruction and 5.08 miles of new road. For each proposed sale, the Forest Service mailed notices to affected and interested members of the public, including the Wildlife Association, describing the proposal and soliciting comments. After receiving responses, the

Forest Service studied site-specific environmental effects and developed Environmental Assessments ("EAs") evaluating the environmental impacts of various sale alternatives, including the "no action" alternative. Biological evaluations were prepared analyzing likely effects on species known to inhabit the Forest. The District Ranger circulated the EAs with requests for public comment prior to issuing Decision Notices.

The Forest Service issued Decision Notices for Sand Gap and Round Hill on May 27, 1994. Administrative appeals were rejected by September 1994, and the sales took place that fall. Purchasers commenced road construction and logging in the spring of 1995. The Forest Service issued Decision Notices for Junction and Sandy Springs on June 19 and May 22, 1995, and rejected administrative appeals in the fall of 1995. The Wildlife Association filed this lawsuit on December 20, 1995. The second amended complaint alleges that plaintiffs "seek judicial review of final agency action in approving" the four timber sales. Counsel for the Forest Service advised at oral argument that approximately three-fourths of road work and timber harvesting in the four sale areas is now completed. . . .

F.   Endangered Species Act. The Endangered Species Act requires federal agencies to consult with the appropriate federal fish and wildlife agency when their actions "may affect" an endangered or threatened species. *See* 16 U.S.C. § 1536(a)(2); 50 C.F.R. § 402.14(a). The Wildlife Association argues the Forest Service was arbitrary and capricious in approving the sales before the United States Fish and Wildlife Service determined whether the logging might significantly affect any listed species. The Forest Service prepared a detailed biological "evaluation" for each sale and found there was no effect on any listed or endangered species. A finding of no effect obviates the need for consultation with the Fish and Wildlife Service. *See* 50 C.F.R. § 402.14. The Wildlife Association argues the Forest Service was required to prepare biological "assessments" to decide whether to consult with the Fish and Wildlife Service. *See* 16 U.S.C. § 1536(c). However, a biological assessment is only required for "major construction activities." 50 C.F.R. § 402.12. Finally, the Wildlife Association argues the Forest Service failed to make an adequate assessment of whether the sales would affect the bald eagle. However, the biological evaluations and the EAs specifically considered impacts on the bald eagle and its habitat and determined that the sales would have no effect. Accordingly, nothing in the administrative record establishes that the Forest Service was arbitrary or capricious in carrying out its ESA obligations regarding these sales.

We have carefully considered all other arguments made by the Wildlife Association and conclude they are without merit.

Questions and Comments

1.   What are the differences that lead the courts in *Thomas v. Peterson* and *Newton County* to come out so differently? Why did the court believe a biological assessment was necessary in *Thomas* but not in *Newton County*?

Note that in *Thomas* there was no need for the plaintiff to show any adverse effect on the wolf in order to obtain an injunction.

2.   In *Thomas* the court says that the ESA's substantive provisions call for more stringent enforcement of the ESA's procedural requirements. Why is that? Why if the substantive provisions are themselves enforceable is there any need to enforce the procedural requirements?

3.   In *Lane County* what was the Forest Service's error? How does the Jamison strategy affect the owls separate from the timber sales? That is, if the timber sales themselves are concededly subject to consultation requirements, what benefit is there is to subjecting the Jamison strategy to consultation as well?

4.   Why in *Lane County*, if the Forest Service has already consulted on the individual 1991 timber sales and the Fish and Wildlife Service has either declared them not to jeopardize the owl or has specified conditions in its Biological Opinion to prevent jeopardy, does the court enjoin those sales as well as those for which there has been no consultation?

5.   In *Lane County* the court stresses the broad understanding of what can constitute an agency "action." There are a number of courts and cases making the same point. One of the more dramatic cases involved a determination that EPA's registrations of pesticides under the Federal Insecticide, Fungicide and Rodenticide Act was an action requiring consultation because the application of pesticides has been shown to affect listed salmon. *See Washington Toxic Coalition v. EPA*, No. 01–132C (W.D. Wash. July 2, 2002).

6.   As appears in both *Thomas* and *Newton County*, there is often a relationship between and agency's responsibilities under the National Environmental Policy Act and under the ESA. This is often the case and is not surprising in that the responsibilities of each is triggered by agency action. In *Thomas* the agency is found to have failed both those responsibilities, and in *Newton County* the court finds the agency satisfied both responsibilities. The ESA itself specifies that a biological assessment may be undertaken as part of the agency's NEPA compliance. *See* 16 U.S.C. § 1536(c)(1). Thus, even if an agency does not identify an analysis as a biological assessment, if it performs the same functions as part of an Environmental Impact Statement, this can satisfy the ESA requirement. *See Sierra Club v. U.S.A.C.O.E.*, 295 F.3d 1209, 1219 (11th Cir. 2002).

7.   Just as there is a requirement for supplemental EIS's under NEPA, the services' regulations require reinitiation of consultation if the incidental take limits are exceeded, if a new species is listed or critical habitat designated that might be affected by the action, if new information develops relevant to the effect on the species or critical habitat, or the action is subsequently modified in a way that would result in an effect not already considered. 50 CFR § 402.16. *See Sierra Club v. Marsh*, 816 F.2d 1376 (9th Cir. 1987)(Corps violated requirement to reinitiate consultation because mitigation efforts were delayed and might not take place at all).

8.   Also similar to NEPA implementation, consultation can be on a programmatic basis, rather than limited to a particular action. Consultation on the Jamison strategy, for example, would likely be deemed programmatic consultation. Still following the NEPA model, these programmatic consulta-

tions can be "tiered" when site-specific effects cannot yet be adequately determined. This kind of programmatic BO would not include incidental take authorizations. Only when later site-specific BOs are prepared would any incidental take be authorized.

9. Recently the services have adopted two so-called "counterpart" regulations. Counterpart regulations are regulations that substitute for the normal consultation regulations with respect to particular matters. 50 CFR § 402.04. One was adopted in 2003 and relates to implementing the National Fire Plan, an executive plan for managing wildfires on national lands. 50 CFR Part 402, Subpart C. The other was adopted in 2004 and relates to EPA's implementation of the consultation requirements in registering pesticides. 50 CFR Part 402, Subpart D. Both are intended to streamline the consultation process while maintaining the same overall degree of protection for species, but precisely because they do streamline the process, they raise concerns among environmental groups.

3. The Substantive Requirements

Separate from, but obviously connected to, the procedural requirement to engage in consultation, Section 7 also imposes substantive requirements. Specifically, Section 7(a)(2) prohibits federal agencies from taking any action if it is "likely to jeopardize the continued existence of any [listed species] or result in the destruction of or adverse modification of [critical habitat]." The Act does not define "jeopardize the continued existence," but the services' regulations do:

> "Jeopardize the continued existence of" of means to engage in an action that reasonably would be expected, directly or indirectly, to reduce appreciably the likelihood of both the survival and recovery of a listed species in the wild by reducing the reproduction, numbers, or distribution of that species.

50 CFR § 402.02 (2004). By requiring an action to adversely affect *both* the survival *and* the recovery of the species the regulation would appear to add a requirement not contained in the statute. However, it is difficult to imagine a circumstance in which, if the survival of a species is put at risk, its recovery will not likewise be put at risk. Thus, while the regulation literally requires the likelihood of both to be reduced, as a practical matter only the effect on survival is relevant.

Because the action agency normally relies on the biological opinion that results from consultation, much of the litigation challenging an action agency's decision is actually an attack on adequacy of the biological opinion. Often the litigation regarding jeopardy to a species involves challenges to the methodology of the biological opinion. For example, in *Gifford Pinchot Task Force v. USF & WS*, 378 F.3d 1059 (9th Cir. 2004), the environmental plaintiffs challenged the use of impacts on the species' habitat as a proxy for impacts on the species itself. The court rejected the challenge, calling it a close case, concluding that "the habitat models used here reasonably ensure that owl population projections from the habitat proxy are accurate." In *Pacific Coast Federation of Fishermen's Ass'n v. National Marine Fisheries Service*, 265 F.3d 1028

(9th Cir. 2001), the court found the no-jeopardy determination arbitrary and capricious because NMFS failed to consider the short-term effects of logging measurable at smaller than watershed level. In *National Wildlife Federation v. Coleman*, 529 F.2d 359 (5th Cir. 1976), the court held that, while the Department of Transportation adequately considered the effects on the Mississippi Sand Hill crane of the actual loss of habitat occasioned by the right-of-way for a highway, it failed to consider the indirect effects resulting from construction impacts and the commercial and residential development expected to result from the highway construction.

The other half of the substantive requirement—that the agency action not "result in the destruction of or adverse modification of [critical habitat]"—also is not amplified in the statute, but the services' regulations define "destruction or adverse modification" to mean:

> a direct or indirect alteration that appreciably diminishes the value of critical habitat for both the survival and recovery of a listed species. Such alterations include, but are not limited to, alterations adversely modifying any of those physical or biological features that were the basis for determining the habitat to be critical.

50 CFR § 402.02 (2004). This definition has been a source of some contention.

GIFFORD PINCHOT TASK FORCE v. UNITED STATES

United States Court of Appeals, Ninth Circuit, 2004.

378 F.3d 1059.

GOULD, Circuit Judge:

This is a record review case in which the Appellants, an assortment of environmental organizations, challenge six biological opinions (BiOps) issued by the United States Fish and Wildlife Service (USFWS or FWS) pursuant to the Endangered Species Act (ESA). The BiOps in question allowed for timber harvests in specified Northwest forests and also authorized incidental "takes" of the Northern spotted owl (spotted owl), a threatened species under the ESA. . . .

I

A

We begin by explaining the legal regime created by the ESA. For any federal action that may affect a threatened or endangered species (or its habitat), the agency contemplating the action (the action agency) must consult with the consulting agency to ensure that the federal action is not likely to jeopardize "the continued existence of" an endangered or threatened species and that the federal action will not result in the "destruction or adverse modification" of the designated critical habitat of the listed species. These consultations are known as "Section 7" consultations. The action agency typically makes a written request to the consulting agency, and, after formal consultation, the process concludes with the consulting agency issuing a biological opinion. The BiOp should address both the jeopardy and critical habitat prongs of Section 7 by considering the current status of the species, the environmental baseline, the effects of the proposed action, and the cumulative effects of the proposed action.

If the BiOp concludes that jeopardy is not likely and that there will not be adverse modification of critical habitat, or that there is a "reasonable and prudent alternative" to the agency action that avoids jeopardy and adverse modification, the FWS can issue an Incidental Take Statement (ITS) which, if followed, exempts the action agency from the prohibition on takings found in Section 9 of the ESA. . . .

III

The Appellants challenge the six BiOps on both the jeopardy analysis and the critical habitat requirements of a Section 7 consultation. . . .

A

[The court rejected the challenge to the jeopardy analysis.]

B

We next turn to the critical habitat portion of the challenged BiOps. It is here that the picture is complicated by error and, on our analysis, becomes less rosy for the FWS.

1

Appellants first argue that the FWS's interpretation of "adverse modification," 50 C.F.R. § 402.02, is unlawful. ESA Section 7 consultations require that in every biological opinion, the consulting agency (here the FWS) ensure that the proposed action "is not likely to jeopardize the continued existence of" an endangered or threatened species and that the federal action will not result in the "destruction or adverse modification" of the designated "critical habitat" of the listed species.

The FWS, in turn, defined "destruction or adverse modification" as:

[A] direct or indirect alteration that appreciably diminishes the value of critical habitat for both the survival and recovery of a listed species. Such alterations include, but are not limited to, alterations adversely modifying any of those physical or biological features that were the basis for determining the habitat to be critical.

50 C.F.R. § 402.02. This regulation requires a close reading to grasp its import. Appellants argue that the regulatory definition sets the bar too high because the adverse modification threshold is not triggered by a proposed action until there is an appreciable diminishment of the value of critical habitat for both survival and recovery.[6]

---

6. This claim, which challenges the FWS regulation, is reviewed under the familiar Chevron U.S.A., Inc. v. Natural Resources Defense Council, Inc., 467 U.S. 837, 104 S.Ct. 2778 (1984), framework.

We agree. Here, the FWS has interpreted "destruction or adverse modification" as changes to the critical habitat "that appreciably diminish[ ] the value of critical habitat for *both* the survival *and* recovery of a listed species." This regulatory definition explicitly requires appreciable diminishment of the critical habitat necessary for survival before the "destruction or adverse modification" standard could ever be met. Because it is logical and inevitable that a species requires more critical habitat for recovery than is necessary for the species survival, the regulation's singular focus becomes "survival." Given this literal understanding of the regulation's express definition of "adverse modification," we consider whether that definition is a permissible interpretation of the ESA.

To answer that question, there is no need to go beyond *Chevron's* first step in analyzing the permissibility of the regulation; the regulatory definition of "adverse modification" contradicts Congress's express command. As the Fifth and Tenth Circuits have already recognized, the regulatory definition reads the "recovery" goal out of the adverse modification inquiry; a proposed action "adversely modifies" critical habitat if, and only if, the value of the critical habitat for *survival* is appreciably diminished. *See N.M. Cattle Growers Ass'n v. United States Fish and Wildlife Serv.,* 248 F.3d 1277, 1283 & n. 2 (10th Cir.2001); *Sierra Club v. United States Fish and Wildlife Serv.,* 245 F.3d 434, 441–42 (5th Cir.2001). The FWS could authorize the complete elimination of critical habitat necessary only for recovery, and so long as the smaller amount of critical habitat necessary for survival is not appreciably diminished, then no "destruction or adverse modification," as defined by the regulation, has taken place. This cannot be right. If the FWS follows its own regulation, then it is obligated to be indifferent to, if not to ignore, the recovery goal of critical habitat.

The agency's controlling regulation on critical habitat thus offends the ESA because the ESA was enacted not merely to forestall the extinction of species (i.e., promote a species survival), but to allow a species to recover to the point where it may be delisted. *See* 16 U.S.C. § 1532(3) (defining conservation as all methods that can be employed to "bring any endangered species or threatened species to the point at which the measures provided pursuant to this [Act] are no longer necessary"). The ESA also defines critical habitat as including "the specific areas ... occupied by the species ... which are ... essential to the *conservation* of the species" and the "specific areas outside the geographical area occupied by the species ... that ... are essential for the *conservation* of the species...." By these definitions, it is clear that Congress intended that conservation and survival be two different (though complementary) goals of the ESA. *See* 16 U.S.C. § 1533(f)(1) ("The Secretary shall develop and implement plans ... for the *conservation* and *survival* of endangered species and threatened species.") (emphasis added). Clearly, then, the purpose of establishing "critical habitat" is for the government to carve out territory that is not only necessary for the species' survival but also essential for the species' recovery.

Congress, by its own language, viewed conservation and survival as distinct, though complementary, goals, and the requirement to preserve critical habitat is designed to promote both conservation and survival. Congress said that "destruction or adverse modification" could occur when sufficient critical habitat is lost so as to threaten a species' recovery even if there remains sufficient critical habitat for the species' survival. The regulation, by contrast, finds that adverse modification to critical habitat can only occur when there is so much critical habitat lost that a species' very survival is threatened. The agency's interpretation would drastically narrow the scope of protection commanded by Congress under the ESA. To define "destruction or adverse modification" of critical habitat to occur only when there is appreciable diminishment of the value of the critical habitat for both survival *and* conservation fails to provide protection of habitat when necessary only for species' recovery. The narrowing construction implemented by the regulation is regrettably, but blatantly, contradictory to Congress' express command. Where Congress in its statutory language required "or," the agency in its regulatory definition substituted "and." This is not merely a technical glitch, but rather a failure of the regulation to implement Congressional will.

The Fifth Circuit reached this same conclusion in *Sierra Club.* . . . The court bolstered its conclusion from the legislative history where Congress had considered an earlier critical habitat regulation that required effects on both recovery and survival and had rejected such an interpretation. We agree with the Fifth Circuit, and with the Tenth Circuit's analogous reasoning, and hold that the regulatory definition of "adverse modification" gives too little protection to designated critical habitat. . . .

Notes and Comments

1. Earlier, in the discussion of Section 4's requirement for designating critical habitat, we noted the services' reluctance to undertake critical habitat designations, finding instead that designation was not "prudent," because designation would not increase protections for the species beyond the protection afforded by listing alone. Given the services' definition of "destruction or adverse modification," one might understand how the services made those findings.

2. The Ninth Circuit notes that both the Fifth and Tenth Circuits had earlier found the services' definition improper. Nevertheless, despite three different circuits' rulings, the services' regulation remains on the books and there is no acknowledged intent to change it. Why do you suppose that is?

3. Another issue in the *Gifford Pinchot Task Force* case was a claim by the FWS that, because there was substantial suitable habitat for the owls outside the designated critical habitat, the proposed timber sales would not have any significant adverse effect on the owls' overall habitat. The court

rejected the FWS argument, holding that the statute refers only to the adverse modification of critical habitat. If there is other, suitable habitat available to the owls, the agency could by rule modify the critical habitat designation, the court said, and then perhaps the proposed timber sale's effect on the redesignated critical habitat might not be meaningful.

4. To avoid jeopardy determinations, the services have often tried to rely on various agreements or undertakings from action agencies that would mitigate the effects of the action agency's proposed action, or the action agencies have tried to rely on agreements or undertakings from third persons to mitigate the effects of the agencies' actions . This is not unlike action agencies attempting to mitigate out of significance for purposes of NEPA. Litigation challenging these mitigation agreements also has tended to reflect the same considerations as the NEPA litigation. *See, e.g., Selkirk Conservation Alliance v. Forsgen*, 336 F.3d 944 (9th Cir. 2003)(FWS could rely upon legally enforceable conservation agreement between Forest Service and private timber company to lower threats to grizzly bears); *National Wildlife Federation v. NMFS*, 254 F.Supp.2d 1196 (D. Or. 2003)(NMFS no jeopardy determination deemed unlawful because it relied on mitigation measures for which there was no funding, for which the agencies lacked authority, and which were not reasonably certain to occur because of the lack of binding agreements); *Center for Biological Diversity v. Rumsfeld*, 198 F.Supp.2d 1139 (D.Ariz. 2002)(Dept. of Army MOA with FWS inadequate to assure no jeopardy).

4. Exemptions

When the Tellico Dam was halted by the snail darter, the ESA contained no exemptions from the prohibition on agency actions that jeopardize a listed species. The Supreme Court's enforcement of the literal terms of the ESA in those circumstances led to Congress enacting an exemption process in 1979. 16 U.S.C. § 1536(e)-(*o*).

This process begins with application for exemption when a service has rendered a biological opinion concluding that the agency action would likely jeopardize a listed species or destroy or adversely modify critical habitat. The application may be made by the action agency, the permit or license applicant when the action in question would be granting that license or permit, or the governor of the state in which the action would occur. 16 U.S.C. § 1536(g)(1). The application is made to the Secretary of the Interior, who makes a determination whether the action agency and applicant have engaged in the required Section 7 assessments and consultations in good faith, have made a responsible effort to adopt modifications or alternatives that would not violate the ESA, and have not made any irreversible or irretrievable commitment of resources after initiating consultations. 16 U.S.C. § 1536(g)(3). If the Secretary makes a positive determination, the Secretary is to undertake a formal adjudication under the Administrative Procedure Act in order to prepare a report to be submitted to the Endangered Species Committee, which has the authority to grant the exemption. 16 U.S.C. § 1536(g)(4).

The Endangered Species Committee is a unique entity and its composition and operation are not designed to facilitate granting exemptions. The committee, popularly entitled the God Squad, because of its ability to decide to jeopardize a species, is comprised of at least seven members: the Secretary of the Interior, who chairs the committee; the Secretary of Agriculture; the Secretary of the Army; the Chair of the Council of Economic Advisors; the Administrator of EPA; the Administrator of NOAA; and a person appointed by the President from each affected state after receiving recommendations from the governors of the affected states. 16 U.S.C. § 1536(e). The committee also is supposed to be governed in its consideration of the application by the formal adjudication provisions of the APA, and it takes at least five members (or their representatives) to constitute a quorum. 16 U.S.C. § 1536(g)(5) & (6). When it comes to voting, however, the members are not allowed to have representatives; they must be present and vote themselves. To grant an application, at least five members must vote in person to grant the exemption upon a finding based on the record that: there are no reasonable and prudent alternatives; the benefits of the action with its adverse effects on the species clearly outweigh the benefits that would be available from an action without such adverse effects; the action is of regional or national significance; and there were no irretrievable or irreversible commitment of resources made after initiation of consultation. 16 U.S.C. § 1536(h)(1)(A). If the committee grants the exemption, it must establish mitigation and enhancement measures to minimize the adverse effects on the species. 16 U.S.C. § 1536(h)(1)(B). No exemption can be granted if the Secretary of State informs the committee that to do so would violate a United States treaty or other international obligation. 16 U.S.C. § 1536(i). However, if the Secretary of Defense finds an exemption is necessary for national security purposes, the committee is required to grant the exemption. 16 U.S.C. § 1536(j). If the exemption is granted, Section 9's prohibition on taking endangered species does not apply to actions pursuant to the exemption. 16 U.S.C. § 1536(o).

Despite the relative lax standard for filing an application and for its referral to the Endangered Species Committee, only three applications have made it to the committee. The first two were specifically mentioned in the legislation creating the exemption. One involved the Tellico Dam, but the committee denied the exemption in that case, finding the dam not cost effective even without considering the snail darter. The other involved the Greylocks Dam on the Platte River, which had been found to jeopardize whooping cranes. In this case the committee granted the exemption, but subject to such mitigation and enhancement measures that the result was supported by environmental groups. The third application was not until 1992, when the Secretary of Interior (on behalf of the Bureau of Land Management) sought exemptions for a number of timber sales in Oregon. While the committee by a vote of 5–2 approved a limited number of the requested exemptions, subject to significant mitigation and enhancement requirements, before the approval could take place, the new Secretary of the Interior (in the new administration) withdrew the application.

Notes and Comments

1.   Although the Endangered Species Committee refused an exemption for the Tellico Dam, Congress took the matter into its own hands and passed a rider to an appropriations act in 1979 directing that notwithstanding the Endangered Species Act the dam should be completed and operated. The completion of the dam and the filling of the reservoir destroyed the entire habitat of the only known location of the snail darter. However, subsequently other small populations of snail darters were found in the Tennessee River watershed, resulting in the snail darter's being reclassified as threatened, rather than endangered. Is there any lesson to be learned from this?

2.   Consider the composition of the Endangered Species Committee. Why do you suppose these specific officers were chosen to be members? And why do you suppose the legislation required these busy, high level officials personally to be present for any vote?

3.   The Endangered Species Act has generated significant controversy precisely because in various situations plants or animals of seemingly little worth have appeared to frustrate significant economic undertakings. *See,* *e.g.,* David Klinghoffer, What Suckers!, National Review Online, September 10, 2001, www.nationalreview.com/comment/comment-klinghoffer091001.shtml, last visited on 9/1/2004 (describing as "idiotic verging on sadistic" the logic of the ESA saving suckers by depriving farmers of needed water). Why is it then that so few applications for exemptions have been filed, when any any applicant for a permit, any governor of an affected state, or any action agency can file an application for an exemption? And why is it that obtaining an exemption is viewed as very difficult when the committee essentially can grant an application simply if the benefits greatly outweigh the benefits of the alternatives, so long as the action has at least regional significance? That is, if the economic benefits of a particular action purportedly stymied by the ESA are so great, why is the exemption process not a solution?

Problem

The Corps of Engineers administers a federal dam that impounds water for flood control in Georgia. The resulting lake is a center for water oriented recreation, especially fishing. Recently, however, an alien invasive plant has begun to grow in the lake, covering much of shoreline and many of the best fishing areas. Moreover, by crowding out the native water plants, the invasive is changing the nature of the lake's ecosystem. Attempts to cut the plant back have been unsuccessful, so the Corps is considering poisoning the plant. Necessarily, this will mean poison in the lake, killing non-invasive plants and perhaps some fish and amphibians. Complicating the matters is the fact that a threatened species of frog lives in the lake, which is designated critical habitat for the frog. Assess the procedural steps and substantive limitations on the Corps' plan to poison the invasive plants.

D. Section 9

Whereas Section 7 of the ESA only applies when there is federal government action, as in NEPA, Section 9 has no such limitation. It applies to any person, including federal and state actors. It prohibits the sale, delivery, or transport in interstate or foreign commerce, including the importation into or the export from the United States, of any *endangered* species. 16 U.S.C. § 1538(a)(1)(A), (E), (F) & (2)(A), (C), (D). It also makes unlawful the "take" of any *endangered* species of fish or wildlife. *Endangered* species of plants are only protected under Section 9 if they are in areas under Federal jurisdiction or if the person harming them does it in violation of a state trespass law or in knowing violation of any other state law or regulation. Finally, *threatened* species only receive protection to the extent provided by regulations adopted by the Secretary of Interior or the Secretary of Commerce.

While Section 7 speaks of jeopardizing a listed species or harming habitat needed by listed species, Section 9 does not directly speak about habitat, and its most frequently operative term is to "take" a species. "Take" is a defined term, meaning: "to harass, harm, pursue, hunt, shoot, wound, kill, trap, capture, or collect, or attempt to engage in such conduct." The question this definition raises is whether destruction of habitat upon which an endangered species relies is included within the prohibited acts. By regulation, the services have interpreted the word "harm" to include certain significant habitat destruction. In a noteworthy case, the Supreme Court assessed the validity of this regulation.

BABBITT v. SWEET HOME CHAPTER OF COMMUNITIES FOR A GREAT OREGON

Supreme Court of the United States, 1995.

515 U.S. 687, 115 S.Ct. 2407, 132 L.Ed.2d 597.

Justice STEVENS delivered the opinion of the Court.

The Endangered Species Act of 1973 (ESA or Act) contains a variety of protections designed to save from extinction species that the Secretary of the Interior designates as endangered or threatened. Section 9 of the Act makes it unlawful for any person to "take" any endangered or threatened species. The Secretary has promulgated a regulation that defines the statute's prohibition on takings to include "significant habitat modification or degradation where it actually kills or injures wildlife." This case presents the question whether the Secretary exceeded his authority under the Act by promulgating that regulation.

I

Section 9(a)(1) of the Act provides the following protection for endangered species:

Except as provided in sections 1535(g)(2) and 1539 of this title, with respect to any endangered species of fish or wildlife listed pursuant to section 1533 of this title it is unlawful for any person subject to the jurisdiction of the United States to— . . .

(B) take any such species within the United States or the territorial sea of the United States.

Section 3(19) of the Act defines the statutory term "take": "The term 'take' means to harass, harm, pursue, hunt, shoot, wound, kill, trap, capture, or collect, or to attempt to engage in any such conduct."

The Act does not further define the terms it uses to define "take." The Interior Department regulations that implement the statute, however, define the statutory term "harm":

> "*Harm* in the definition of 'take' in the Act means an act which actually kills or injures wildlife. Such act may include significant habitat modification or degradation where it actually kills or injures wildlife by significantly impairing essential behavioral patterns, including breeding, feeding, or sheltering."

This regulation has been in place since 1975.

A limitation on the § 9 "take" prohibition appears in § 10(a)(1)(B) of the Act, which Congress added by amendment in 1982. That section authorizes the Secretary to grant a permit for any taking otherwise prohibited by § 9(a)(1)(B) "if such taking is incidental to, and not the purpose of, the carrying out of an otherwise lawful activity." . . .

Respondents in this action are small landowners, logging companies, and families dependent on the forest products industries in the Pacific Northwest and in the Southeast, and organizations that represent their interests. They brought this declaratory judgment action against petitioners, the Secretary of the Interior and the Director of the Fish and Wildlife Service, in the United States District Court for the District of Columbia to challenge the statutory validity of the Secretary's regulation defining "harm," particularly the inclusion of habitat modification and degradation in the definition. . . .

Respondents advanced three arguments to support their submission that Congress did not intend the word "take" in § 9 to include habitat modification, as the Secretary's "harm" regulation provides. First, they correctly noted that language in the Senate's original version of the ESA would have defined "take" to include "destruction, modification, or curtailment of [the] habitat or range" of fish or wildlife, but the Senate deleted that language from the bill before enacting it. Second, respondents argued that Congress intended the Act's express authorization for the Federal Government to buy private land in order to prevent habitat degradation in § 5 to be the exclusive check against habitat modification on private property. Third, because the Senate added the term "harm" to the definition of "take" in a floor amendment without debate, respondents argued that the court should not interpret the term so expansively as to include habitat modification. . . .

[The court of appeals found for the respondents.] Although acknowledging that "[t]he potential breadth of the word 'harm' is indisputable," *id.,* at 1464, the majority concluded that the immediate statutory context in which "harm" appeared counseled against a broad reading; like the other words in the definition of "take," the word "harm" should be read as applying only to "the perpetrator's direct application of force against the animal taken.... The forbidden acts fit, in ordinary language, the basic model 'A hit B.'"The majority based its reasoning on a canon of statutory construction called *noscitur a sociis,* which holds that a word is known by the company it keeps....

The Court of Appeals' decision created a square conflict with a 1988 decision of the Ninth Circuit that had upheld the Secretary's definition of "harm." See *Palila v. Hawaii Dept. of Land and Natural Resources,* 852 F.2d 1106 (1988) (*Palila II*).... We granted certiorari to resolve the conflict. Our consideration of the text and structure of the Act, its legislative history, and the significance of the 1982 amendment persuades us that the Court of Appeals' judgment should be reversed.

II

Because this case was decided on motions for summary judgment, we may appropriately make certain factual assumptions in order to frame the legal issue. First, we assume respondents have no desire to harm either the red-cockaded woodpecker or the spotted owl; they merely wish to continue logging activities that would be entirely proper if not prohibited by the ESA. On the other hand, we must assume, *arguendo,* that those activities will have the effect, even though unintended, of detrimentally changing the natural habitat of both listed species and that, as a consequence, members of those species will be killed or injured....

The text of the Act provides three reasons for concluding that the Secretary's interpretation is reasonable. First, an ordinary understanding of the word "harm" supports it. The dictionary definition of the verb form of "harm" is "to cause hurt or damage to: injure." In the context of the ESA, that definition naturally encompasses habitat modification that results in actual injury or death to members of an endangered or threatened species.

Respondents argue that the Secretary should have limited the purview of "harm" to direct applications of force against protected species, but the dictionary definition does not include the word "directly" or suggest in any way that only direct or willful action that leads to injury constitutes "harm."[10] Moreover, unless the statutory term "harm" en-

---

10. Respondents and the dissent emphasize what they portray as the "established meaning" of "take" in the sense of a "wildlife take," a meaning respondents argue extends only to "the effort to exercise dominion over some creature, and the concrete effect of [sic] that creature." This limitation ill serves the statutory text, which forbids not taking "some creature" but "tak[ing] any [endangered] species"—a formidable task for even the most rapacious feudal lord. More importantly, Congress explicitly defined the operative term "take" in the ESA, no matter how much the dissent wishes otherwise, thereby obviating the need for us to probe its meaning as we must probe the meaning of the undefined subsidiary term "harm." Finally, Congress' definition of "take" includes several words—most obviously "harass," "pursue," and

compasses indirect as well as direct injuries, the word has no meaning that does not duplicate the meaning of other words that § 3 uses to define "take." A reluctance to treat statutory terms as surplusage supports the reasonableness of the Secretary's interpretation.[11]

Second, the broad purpose of the ESA supports the Secretary's decision to extend protection against activities that cause the precise harms Congress enacted the statute to avoid. In *TVA v. Hill,* we described the Act as "the most comprehensive legislation for the preservation of endangered species ever enacted by any nation." Whereas predecessor statutes enacted in 1966 and 1969 had not contained any sweeping prohibition against the taking of endangered species except on federal lands, the 1973 Act applied to all land in the United States and to the Nation's territorial seas. As stated in § 2 of the Act, among its central purposes is "to provide a means whereby the ecosystems upon which endangered species and threatened species depend may be conserved. . . ."

In *Hill,* we construed § 7 as precluding the completion of the Tellico Dam because of its predicted impact on the survival of the snail darter. Both our holding and the language in our opinion stressed the importance of the statutory policy. "The plain intent of Congress in enacting this statute," we recognized, "was to halt and reverse the trend toward species extinction, whatever the cost. This is reflected not only in the stated policies of the Act, but in literally every section of the statute." Although the § 9 "take" prohibition was not at issue in *Hill,* we took note of that prohibition, placing particular emphasis on the Secretary's inclusion of habitat modification in his definition of "harm." In light of that provision for habitat protection, we could "not understand how TVA intends to operate Tellico Dam without 'harming' the snail darter." Congress' intent to provide comprehensive protection for endangered and threatened species supports the permissibility of the Secretary's "harm" regulation.

Respondents advance strong arguments that activities that cause minimal or unforeseeable harm will not violate the Act as construed in the "harm" regulation. Respondents, however, present a facial challenge to the regulation. Thus, they ask us to invalidate the Secretary's understanding of "harm" in every circumstance, even when an actor knows

"wound," in addition to "harm" itself—that fit respondents' and the dissent's definition of "take" no better than does "significant habitat modification or degradation."

11. In contrast, if the statutory term "harm" encompasses such indirect means of killing and injuring wildlife as habitat modification, the other terms listed in § 3—"harass," "pursue," "hunt," "shoot," "wound," "kill," "trap," "capture," and "collect"—generally retain independent meanings. Most of those terms refer to deliberate actions more frequently than does

"harm," and they therefore do not duplicate the sense of indirect causation that "harm" adds to the statute. In addition, most of the other words in the definition describe either actions from which habitat modification does not usually result (e.g., "pursue," "harass") or effects to which activities that modify habitat do not usually lead (e.g., "trap," "collect"). To the extent the Secretary's definition of "harm" may have applications that overlap with other words in the definition, that overlap reflects the broad purpose of the Act.

that an activity, such as draining a pond, would actually result in the extinction of a listed species by destroying its habitat. Given Congress' clear expression of the ESA's broad purpose to protect endangered and threatened wildlife, the Secretary's definition of "harm" is reasonable.[13]

Third, the fact that Congress in 1982 authorized the Secretary to issue permits for takings that § 9(a)(1)(B) would otherwise prohibit, "if such taking is incidental to, and not the purpose of, the carrying out of an otherwise lawful activity," strongly suggests that Congress understood § 9(a)(1)(B) to prohibit indirect as well as deliberate takings. The permit process requires the applicant to prepare a "conservation plan" that specifies how he intends to "minimize and mitigate" the "impact" of his activity on endangered and threatened species, making clear that Congress had in mind foreseeable rather than merely accidental effects on listed species. No one could seriously request an "incidental" take permit to avert § 9 liability for direct, deliberate action against a member of an endangered or threatened species, but respondents would read "harm" so narrowly that the permit procedure would have little more than that absurd purpose.... Congress' addition of the § 10 permit provision supports the Secretary's conclusion that activities not intended to harm an endangered species, such as habitat modification, may constitute unlawful takings under the ESA unless the Secretary permits them....

We need not decide whether the statutory definition of "take" compels the Secretary's interpretation of "harm," because our conclusions that Congress did not unambiguously manifest its intent to adopt respondents' view and that the Secretary's interpretation is reasonable suffice to decide this case. See generally *Chevron U.S.A. Inc. v. Natural Resources Defense Council, Inc.*...

III

Our conclusion that the Secretary's definition of "harm" rests on a permissible construction of the ESA gains further support from the legislative history of the statute. The Committee Reports accompanying the bills that became the ESA do not specifically discuss the meaning of "harm," but they make clear that Congress intended "take" to apply broadly to cover indirect as well as purposeful actions....

Two endangered species bills, S. 1592 and S. 1983, were introduced in the Senate and referred to the Commerce Committee. Neither bill

---

13. The dissent incorrectly asserts that the Secretary's regulation (1) "dispenses with the foreseeability of harm" and (2) "fail[s] to require injury to particular animals." As to the first assertion, the regulation merely implements the statute, and it is therefore subject to the statute's "knowingly violates" language, and ordinary requirements of proximate causation and foreseeability. Nothing in the regulation purports to weaken those requirements. To the contrary, the word "actually" in the regulation should be construed to limit the liability about which the dissent appears most concerned, liability under the statute's "otherwise violates" provision. The Secretary did not need to include "actually" to connote "but for" causation, which the other words in the definition obviously require. As to the dissent's second assertion, every term in the regulation's definition of "harm" is subservient to the phrase "an act which actually kills or injures wildlife."

included the word "harm" in its definition of "take," although the definitions otherwise closely resembled the one that appeared in the bill as ultimately enacted. Senator Tunney, the floor manager of the bill in the Senate, subsequently introduced a floor amendment that added "harm" to the definition, noting that this and accompanying amendments would "help to achieve the purposes of the bill." Respondents argue that the lack of debate about the amendment that added "harm" counsels in favor of a narrow interpretation. We disagree. An obviously broad word that the Senate went out of its way to add to an important statutory definition is precisely the sort of provision that deserves a respectful reading.

The definition of "take" that originally appeared in S. 1983 differed from the definition as ultimately enacted in one other significant respect: It included "the destruction, modification, or curtailment of [the] habitat or range" of fish and wildlife. Respondents make much of the fact that the Commerce Committee removed this phrase from the "take" definition before S. 1983 went to the floor. We do not find that fact especially significant. The legislative materials contain no indication why the habitat protection provision was deleted. That provision differed greatly from the regulation at issue today. Most notably, the habitat protection provision in S. 1983 would have applied far more broadly than the regulation does because it made adverse habitat modification a categorical violation of the "take" prohibition, unbounded by the regulation's limitation to habitat modifications that actually kill or injure wildlife. The S. 1983 language also failed to qualify "modification" with the regulation's limiting adjective "significant." We do not believe the Senate's unelaborated disavowal of the provision in S. 1983 undermines the reasonableness of the more moderate habitat protection in the Secretary's "harm" regulation.[19]

---

19. Respondents place heavy reliance for their argument that Congress intended the § 5 land acquisition provision and not § 9 to be the ESA's remedy for habitat modification on a floor statement by Senator Tunney:

"Many species have been inadvertently exterminated by a negligent destruction of their habitat. Their habitats have been cut in size, polluted, or otherwise altered so that they are unsuitable environments for natural populations of fish and wildlife. Under this bill, we can take steps to make amends for our negligent encroachment. The Secretary would be empowered to use the land acquisition authority granted to him in certain existing legislation to acquire land for the use of the endangered species programs.... Through these land acquisition provisions, we will be able to conserve habitats necessary to protect fish and wildlife from further destruction.

"Although most endangered species are threatened primarily by the destruction of their natural habitats, a significant portion of these animals are subject to predation by man for commercial, sport, consumption, or other purposes. The provisions in S. 1983 would prohibit the commerce in or the importation, exportation, or taking of endangered species...."

Similarly, respondents emphasize a floor statement by Representative Sullivan, the House floor manager for the ESA:

"For the most part, the principal threat to animals stems from destruction of their habitat.... H.R. 37 will meet this problem by providing funds for acquisition of critical habitat.... It will also enable the Department of Agriculture to cooperate with willing landowners who desire to assist in the protection of endangered species, but who are understandably unwilling to do so at excessive cost to themselves.

"Another hazard to endangered species arises from those who would capture or kill

The history of the 1982 amendment that gave the Secretary authority to grant permits for "incidental" takings provides further support for his reading of the Act.... Indeed, Congress had habitat modification directly in mind: Both the Senate Report and the House Conference Report identified as the model for the permit process a cooperative state-federal response to a case in California where a development project threatened incidental harm to a species of endangered butterfly by modification of its habitat. Thus, Congress in 1982 focused squarely on the aspect of the "harm" regulation at issue in this litigation. Congress' implementation of a permit program is consistent with the Secretary's interpretation of the term "harm."

IV

When it enacted the ESA, Congress delegated broad administrative and interpretive power to the Secretary.... The proper interpretation of a term such as "harm" involves a complex policy choice. When Congress has entrusted the Secretary with broad discretion, we are especially reluctant to substitute our views of wise policy for his....

Justice O'CONNOR, concurring.

My agreement with the Court is founded on two understandings. First, the challenged regulation is limited to significant habitat modification that causes actual, as opposed to hypothetical or speculative, death or injury to identifiable protected animals. Second, even setting aside difficult questions of scienter, the regulation's application is limited by ordinary principles of proximate causation, which introduce notions of foreseeability. These limitations, in my view, call into question *Palila v. Hawaii Dept. of Land and Natural Resources,* 852 F.2d 1106 (CA9 1988) (*Palila II*), and with it, many of the applications derided by the dissent. Because there is no need to strike a regulation on a facial challenge out of concern that it is susceptible of erroneous application, however, and because there are many habitat-related circumstances in which the regulation might validly apply, I join the opinion of the Court.

In my view, the regulation is limited by its terms to actions that actually kill or injure individual animals. Justice SCALIA disagrees, arguing that the harm regulation "encompasses injury inflicted, not only upon individual animals, but upon populations of the protected species." At one level, I could not reasonably quarrel with this observation; death to an individual animal always reduces the size of the population in which it lives, and in that sense, "injures" that population. But by its

them for pleasure or profit. There is no way that Congress can make it less pleasurable for a person to take an animal, but we can certainly make it less profitable for them to do so."

Each of these statements merely explained features of the bills that Congress eventually enacted in § 5 of the ESA and went on to discuss elements enacted in § 9. Neither statement even suggested that § 5

would be the Act's exclusive remedy for habitat modification by private landowners or that habitat modification by private landowners stood outside the ambit of § 9. Respondents' suggestion that these statements identified § 5 as the ESA's only response to habitat modification contradicts their emphasis elsewhere on the habitat protections in § 7.

insight, the dissent means something else. Building upon the regulation's use of the word "breeding," Justice SCALIA suggests that the regulation facially bars significant habitat modification that actually kills or injures *hypothetical* animals (or, perhaps more aptly, causes potential additions to the population not to come into being). Because "[i]mpairment of breeding does not 'injure' living creatures," Justice SCALIA reasons, the regulation *must* contemplate application to "*a population* of animals which would otherwise have maintained or increased its numbers."

I disagree. As an initial matter, I do not find it as easy as Justice SCALIA does to dismiss the notion that significant impairment of breeding injures living creatures. To raze the last remaining ground on which the piping plover currently breeds, thereby making it impossible for any piping plovers to reproduce, would obviously injure the population (causing the species' extinction in a generation). But by completely preventing breeding, it would also injure the individual living bird, in the same way that sterilizing the creature injures the individual living bird. To "injure" is, among other things, "to impair." Webster's Ninth New Collegiate Dictionary 623 (1983). One need not subscribe to theories of "psychic harm," to recognize that to make it impossible for an animal to reproduce is to impair its most essential physical functions and to render that animal, and its genetic material, biologically obsolete. This, in my view, is actual injury.

In any event, even if impairing an animal's ability to breed were not, *in and of itself,* an injury to that animal, interference with breeding can cause an animal to suffer other, perhaps more obvious, kinds of injury. The regulation has clear application, for example, to significant habitat modification that kills or physically injures animals which, because they are in a vulnerable breeding state, do not or cannot flee or defend themselves, or to environmental pollutants that cause an animal to suffer physical complications during gestation. Breeding, feeding, and sheltering are what animals do. If significant habitat modification, by interfering with these essential behaviors, actually kills or injures an animal protected by the Act, it causes "harm" within the meaning of the regulation. In contrast to Justice SCALIA, I do not read the regulation's "breeding" reference to vitiate or somehow to qualify the clear actual death or injury requirement, or to suggest that the regulation contemplates extension to nonexistent animals.

There is no inconsistency, I should add, between this interpretation and the commentary that accompanied the amendment of the regulation to include the actual death or injury requirement. Quite the contrary. It is true, as Justice SCALIA observes, that the Fish and Wildlife Service states at one point that "harm" is not limited to "direct physical injury to an individual member of the wildlife species." But one could just as easily emphasize the word "direct" in this sentence as the word "individual." Elsewhere in the commentary, the Service makes clear that "section 9's threshold does focus on individual members of a protected species." Moreover, the Service says that the regulation has no application to speculative harm, explaining that its insertion of the word "actually" was intended "to bulwark the need for proven injury to a species due to a party's actions." That a protected animal could have eaten the leaves of a fallen tree or could, perhaps, have fruitfully multiplied in its branches is not sufficient under the regulation. Instead, as the commentary reflects, the regulation requires demonstrable effect (*i.e.,* actual injury or death) on actual, individual members of the protected species.

By the dissent's reckoning, the regulation at issue here, in conjunction with 16 U.S.C. § 1540(a)(1), imposes liability for any habitat-modifying conduct that ultimately results in the death of a protected animal, "regardless of whether that result is intended or even foreseeable, and no matter how long the chain of causality between modification and injury." Even if § 1540(a)(1) does create a strict liability regime (a question we need not decide at this juncture), I see no indication that Congress, in enacting that section, intended to dispense with ordinary principles of proximate causation. Strict liability means liability without regard to fault; it does not normally mean liability for every consequence, however remote, of one's conduct. I would not lightly assume that Congress, in enacting a strict liability statute that is silent on the causation question, has dispensed with this well-entrenched principle. In the absence of congressional abrogation of traditional principles of causation, then, private parties should be held liable under § 1540(a)(1) only if their habitat-modifying actions proximately cause death or injury to protected animals....

Proximate causation is not a concept susceptible of precise definition. It is easy enough, of course, to identify the extremes. The farmer whose fertilizer is lifted by a tornado from tilled fields and deposited miles away in a wildlife refuge cannot, by any stretch of the term, be considered the proximate cause of death or injury to protected species occasioned thereby. At the same time, the landowner who drains a pond on his property, killing endangered fish in the process, would likely satisfy any formulation of the principle.... Proximate causation depends to a great extent on considerations of the fairness to impose liability for remote consequences....

In my view, then, the "harm" regulation applies where significant habitat modification, by impairing essential behaviors, proximately (foreseeably) causes actual death or injury to identifiable animals that are protected under the Endangered Species Act. Pursuant to my interpretation, *Palila II*—under which the Court of Appeals held that a state agency committed a "taking" by permitting mouflon sheep to eat mamane-naio seedlings that, when full grown, might have fed and sheltered endangered palila—was wrongly decided according to the regulation's own terms. Destruction of the seedlings did not proximately cause actual death or injury to identifiable birds; it merely prevented the regeneration of forest land not currently sustaining actual birds....

Justice SCALIA, with whom THE CHIEF JUSTICE and Justice THOMAS join, dissenting.

I think it unmistakably clear that the legislation at issue here (1) forbade the hunting and killing of endangered animals, and (2) provided federal lands and federal funds *for the acquisition of private lands,* to preserve the habitat of endangered animals. The Court's holding that the hunting and killing prohibition incidentally preserves habitat on private lands imposes unfairness to the point of financial ruin—not just upon the rich, but upon the simplest farmer who finds his land conscripted to national zoological use. I respectfully dissent.

I

[T]he regulation has three features which, for reasons I shall discuss at length below, do not comport with the statute. First, it interprets the statute to prohibit habitat modification that is no more than the cause-in-fact of death or injury to wildlife. *Any* "significant habitat modification" that in fact produces that result by "impairing essential behavioral patterns" is made unlawful, regardless of whether that result is intended or even foreseeable, and no matter how long the chain of causality between modification and injury.

Second, the regulation does not require an "act": The Secretary's officially stated position is that an *omission* will do....

The third and most important unlawful feature of the regulation is that it encompasses injury inflicted, not only upon individual animals, but upon populations of the protected species. "Injury" in the regulation includes "significantly impairing essential behavioral patterns, including breeding." Impairment of breeding does not "injure" living creatures; it prevents them from propagating, thus "injuring" *a population* of animals which would otherwise have maintained or increased its numbers....

None of these three features of the regulation can be found in the statutory provisions supposed to authorize it. The term "harm" in § 1532(19) has no legal force of its own. An indictment or civil complaint that charged the defendant with "harming" an animal protected under the Act would be dismissed as defective, for the only *operative* term in the statute is to "take." If "take" were not elsewhere defined in the Act, none could dispute what it means, for the term is as old as the law itself. To "take," when applied to wild animals, means to reduce those animals, by killing or capturing, to human control. This is just the sense in which "take" is used elsewhere in federal legislation and treaty. And that meaning fits neatly with the rest of § 1538(a)(1), which makes it unlawful not only to take protected species, but also to import or export them; to possess, sell, deliver, carry, transport, or ship any taken species; and to transport, sell, or offer to sell them in interstate or foreign commerce. The taking prohibition, in other words, is only part of the regulatory plan of § 1538(a)(1), which covers all the stages of the process by which protected wildlife is reduced to man's dominion and made the object of profit. It is obvious that "take" in this sense—a term of art deeply embedded in the statutory and common law concerning wildlife—describes a class of acts (not omissions) done directly and intentionally (not indirectly and by accident) to particular animals (not populations of animals).

The Act's definition of "take" does expand the word slightly (and not unusually), so as to make clear that it includes not just a completed taking, but the process of taking, and all of the acts that are customarily identified with or accompany that process ("to harass, harm, pursue, hunt, shoot, wound, kill, trap, capture, or collect"); and so as to include attempts. § 1532(19). The tempting fallacy—which the Court commits with abandon, see *ante,* at 2413, n. 10—is to assume that *once defined,* "take" loses any significance, and it is only the definition that matters. The Court treats the statute as though Congress had directly enacted the § 1532(19) definition as a self-executing prohibition, and had not enacted § 1538(a)(1)(B) at all. But § 1538(a)(1)(B) *is* there, and if the terms contained in the definitional section are susceptible of two readings, one of which comports with the standard meaning of "take" as used in application to wildlife, and one of which does not, an agency regulation that adopts the latter reading is necessarily unreasonable, for it reads the defined term "take"—the only operative term—out of the statute altogether.

That is what has occurred here. The verb "harm" has a *range* of meaning: "to cause injury" at its broadest, "to do hurt or damage" in a narrower and more direct sense.... To define "harm" as an act or omission that, however remotely, "actually kills or injures" a population of wildlife through habitat modification is to choose a meaning that makes nonsense of the word that "harm" defines—requiring us to accept that a farmer who tills his field and causes erosion that makes silt run into a nearby river which depletes oxygen and thereby "impairs [the] breeding" of protected fish has "taken" or "attempted to take" the fish. It should take the strongest evidence to make us believe that Congress has defined a term in a manner repugnant to its ordinary and traditional sense.

Here the evidence shows the opposite. "Harm" is merely one of 10 prohibitory words in § 1532(19), and the other 9 fit the ordinary meaning of "take" perfectly. To "harass, pursue, hunt, shoot, wound, kill, trap, capture, or collect" are all affirmative acts (the provision itself describes them as "conduct," see § 1532(19)) which are directed immediately and intentionally against a particular animal—not acts or omissions that indirectly and accidentally cause injury to a population of animals.... What the nine other words in § 1532(19) have in common—and share with the narrower meaning of "harm" described above, but not with the Secretary's ruthless dilation of the word—is the sense of affirmative conduct intentionally directed against a particular animal or animals.

I am not the first to notice this fact, or to draw the conclusion that it compels. In 1981 the Solicitor of the Fish and Wildlife Service delivered a legal opinion on § 1532(19) that is in complete agreement with my reading:

> "The Act's definition of 'take' contains a list of actions that illustrate the intended scope of the term.... With the possible exception of 'harm,' these terms all represent forms of conduct that are directed against and likely to injure or kill *individual* wildlife. Under the principle of statutory construction, *ejusdem generis,* ... the term 'harm' should be interpreted to include only those actions that are directed against, and likely to injure or kill, individual wildlife." Memorandum of Apr. 17, reprinted in 46 Fed.Reg. 29490, 29491 (1981) (emphasis in original)....

So far I have discussed only the immediate statutory text bearing on the regulation. But the definition of "take" in § 1532(19) applies "[f]or the purposes of this chapter," that is, it governs the meaning of the word *as used everywhere in the Act.* Thus, the Secretary's interpretation of "harm" is wrong if it does not fit with the use of "take" throughout the Act. And it does not. In § 1540(e)(4)(B), for example, Congress provided for the forfeiture of "[a]ll guns, traps, nets, and other equipment ... used to aid the taking, possessing, selling, [etc.]" of protected animals. This listing plainly relates to "taking" in the ordinary sense. If environmental modification were part (and necessarily a major part) of taking, as the Secretary maintains, one would have expected the list to include "plows, bulldozers, and backhoes." As another example, § 1539(e)(1) exempts "the taking of any endangered species" by Alaskan Indians and Eskimos "if such taking is primarily for subsistence purposes"; and provides that "[n]on-edible byproducts of species taken pursuant to this section may be sold ... when made into authentic native articles of handicrafts and clothing." ...

III

[One] point the Court stresses in its response [to this dissent] seems to me a belated mending of its holding. It apparently *concedes* that the statute requires injury *to particular animals* rather than merely to populations of animals. The Court then rejects my contention that the regulation ignores this requirement, since, it says, "every term in the regulation's definition of 'harm' is subservient to the phrase 'an act which actually kills or injures wildlife.' "[T]his reading is incompatible with the regulation's specification of impairment of "breeding" as one of the *modes* of "kill[ing] or injur[ing] wildlife."[5]

---

5. Justice O'CONNOR supposes that an "impairment of breeding" intrinsically injures an animal because "to make it impossible for an animal to reproduce is to impair its most essential physical functions and to render that animal, and its genetic material, biologically obsolete." This imaginative construction does achieve the result of extending "impairment of breeding" to individual animals; but only at the expense of also expanding "injury" to include elements beyond physical harm to individual animals. For surely the only harm to the individual animal from impairment of that "essential

But since the Court is reading the regulation and the statute incorrectly in other respects, it may as well introduce this novelty as well—law à la carte. As I understand the regulation that the Court has created and held consistent with the statute that it has also created, habitat modification can constitute a "taking," but only if it results in the killing or harming of *individual animals,* and only if that consequence is the direct result of the modification. This means that the destruction of privately owned habitat that is essential, not for the feeding or nesting, but for the *breeding,* of butterflies, would not violate the Act, since it would not harm or kill any living butterfly. I, too, think it would not violate the Act—not for the utterly unsupported reason that habitat modifications fall outside the regulation if they happen not to kill or injure a living animal, but for the textual reason that only action directed at living animals constitutes a "take."

* * *

The Endangered Species Act is a carefully considered piece of legislation that forbids all persons to hunt or harm endangered animals, but places upon the public at large, rather than upon fortuitously accountable individual landowners, the cost of preserving the habitat of endangered species. There is neither textual support for, nor even evidence of congressional consideration of, the radically different disposition contained in the regulation that the Court sustains. For these reasons, I respectfully dissent.

Notes and Questions

1. After *Sweet Home,* it is clear that the services' regulation is valid on its face, but is it clear how it can be applied? In the *Palila* case, described in *Sweet Home,* the Ninth Circuit had found a violation of Section 9 in the destruction of habitat that was necessary for the *recovery* of a species, but not for its survival. Justice O'Connor says that the *Sweet Home* decision is inconsistent with *Palila.* What do you think? The regulation says that significant habitat modification qualifies as "harm," if "it actually kills or injures wildlife by significantly impairing essential behavioral patterns, including breeding, feeding, or sheltering." Does this mean that *any* significant impairment of "essential behavioral patterns" necessarily kills or injures wildlife, or does it mean that *when* significant impairment of "essential behavioral patterns" actually kills or injures wildlife, only then does habitat modification become "harm"? If the latter, how do you determine the causal connection between the impairment and actual harm? Draining the pond so that all the endangered fish die is an easy case. A more likely scenario is the cutting of trees which are habitat to endangered birds. There is other habitat available to them, but their total habitat has been reduced, putting them under greater stress. Do you need to find a dead bird? How about expert testimony by wildlife biologists that such habitat destruction

function" is not the failure of issue (which harms only the issue), but the psychic harm of perceiving that it will leave this world with no issue (assuming, of course, that the animal in question, perhaps an endangered species of slug, is capable of such painful sentiments)....

would "injure or kill wildlife"? *See, e.g., Marbeled Murrelet v. Babbitt*, 83 F.3d 1060 (9th Cir. 1996)(significant impairment of breeding and sheltering is a take). How should the FWS interpret its regulation? Under a Republican President? Under a Democratic President?

2. Whatever the intentions of the original drafters of Section 9, it is fairly clear that the amendments in 1982 to Section 10, providing for the Secretary to grant an incidental take permit to private persons who obtain an approved conservation plan, understood that Section 9 "takes" could include results of habitat modification. This, of course, is not surprising, because the FWS regulations had always so provided, and there were some development projects blocked by assertions of the FWS that they would result in habitat modification violating Section 9. These assertions gained some publicity and were an important cause of the amendments providing for permits. How should that later congressional understanding affect the interpretation of the original language?

3. The introductory material on Section 9 noted that its prohibitions are broader with respect to fish and wildlife than to plants. Thus, any "take" of endangered fish and wildlife is prohibited, but harm to endangered plants is prohibited only if the plants are on federal property or the activity would violate state law. Why do you suppose the ESA provides such limited protection to plants compared to fish and wildlife, especially because most hopes for new drugs identify plants as possible sources? Would the explanation for this different treatment support the dissent's view of the meaning of "take" in *Sweet Home*?

4. The introductory material on Section 9 also emphasized that the statute itself only provides Section 9 protections to *endangered* species. However, Section 4(d) requires the Secretary to adopt "such regulations as he deems necessary and advisable to provide for the conservation of [threatened] species," and Section 9 prohibits any person from violating those regulations. While the original conception behind Section 4(d) was probably to tailor protections to the particular needs of a newly listed threatened species, traditionally the FWS has by general regulation extended all the protections afforded endangered species to threatened species. NMFS, on the other hand, has adopted species specific Section 4(d) protections. In recent years there has been increasing interest in using the threat of extending Section 4(d) regulations to newly listed threatened species as an incentive to obtain state and private conservation measures, that if undertaken, would justify the services to find that it is not necessary to adopt the full range of Section 4(d) protections to the species.

5. Section 9 clearly prohibits government action that itself takes an endangered fish or wildlife species, and courts have also routinely held that government action that authorizes private action, which in turn would take an endangered fish or wildlife species, likewise is prohibited by Section 9. *See, e.g., Defenders of Wildlife v. EPA*, 882 F.2d 1294 (8th Cir. 1989)(finding EPA's registration of certain pesticides violated Section 9 because those pesticides were causing the death of endangered species). Courts have not distinguished between federal and state actors in this regard, *see, e.g., Loggerhead Turtle v. County Council of Volusia County*, 148 F.3d 1231 (11th Cir. 1998)(failure of county to ban beach driving and beachfront lighting

during loggerhead sea turtle mating season constituted take). There may, however, be a problem in the latter regard. Recall from Chapter 1 that the Supreme Court has interpreted the Tenth Amendment to prohibit the federal government from in effect requiring states to administer federal laws, or as the Court put it, from commandeering state governments. By interpreting the ESA in the *Loggerhead Turtle* case to require the county to regulate beachfront lighting to protect the turtles, however, the Eleventh Circuit, which did not discuss the issue, would seem to be running afoul of that constitutional limitation. *See also Strahan v. Coxe*, 127 F.3d 155 (1st Cir. 1997)(Massachusetts permitting of lobster pot and gillnet fishing violated Section 9 with respect to northern right whales). The irony in *Strahan* is that if Massachusetts abandoned its issuance of permits for lobster pot and gillnet fishing, which it regulates to protect lobster and certain fish species, it would not be engaged in the permitting of the activities that cause the harm to the endangered species. In other words, extending Section 9 liability to states and counties for permitting activities that may harm endangered species might lead states and counties simply to abandon their permitting schemes, which would not increase protection for endangered species, but which could undermine other environmental protection. In Oregon, for example, there was a lawsuit against the state board of forestry under Section 9 for issuing permits for steep slope timber cutting, which allegedly increases siltation of streams, adversely affecting listed salmonids. This permit scheme was adopted to protect against logging that results in dangerous landslides, but in response to the lawsuit, the board rescinded its regulation requiring a permit, thereby allowing steep slope timber cutting without any permit.

E. Section 10

Section 10 of the ESA, 16 U.S.C. § 1539, provides exceptions to the prohibitions of Section 9. We have already seen two exceptions to Section 9 arising out of Section 7: incidental take statements contained in Biological Opinions and takings pursuant to an exception granted by the Endangered Species Committee. Section 10 contains several additional exceptions. The first provides for the Secretary to permit takes for scientific purposes or to enhance the species. 16 U.S.C. § 1539(a)(1)(A). Thus, for example, the Secretary can adopt regulations providing for the capture of endangered species for research or breeding purposes. Another provides an exemption for persons that entered into a contract with respect to a species before it was listed, if they would suffer "substantial economic hardship" as a result. 16 U.S.C. § 1539(b). There is also a general exemption for Alaskan natives and residents in Alaskan native villages who take species for subsistence purposes. 16 U.S.C. § 1539(e). The Secretary, however, may adopt specific regulations governing and limiting such subsistence takings. *Id.*

The most significant exception was added in the 1982 amendments and allows the Secretary to grant an incidental take permit when a person obtains approval of a habitat conservation plan (HCP). 16 U.S.C. § 1539(a)(2). Like the incidental takes authorized in biological opinions under Section 7 when there is a federal action, Section 10 provides a procedure whereby private persons may also obtain an exemption from Section 9 for takes incidental to other economic activity, e.g., development projects and timber harvesting. In order to obtain approval of an HCP, a person files an application that identifies what the impacts of the project will be, what steps the applicant will take to minimize and mitigate those impacts, what alternatives the applicant considered that would have less impacts and why those alternatives are not feasible, and such other information as the Secretary requires. Because granting the permit is a federal action, consideration of the proposed HCP requires consultation under Section 7 of the ESA and NEPA analysis. In addition, the process includes public involvement and comment on the proposed HCP. In short, the process is extensive and expensive for the applicant. Approval is granted if the Secretary finds that the HCP will be carried out, including the minimization and mitigation of incidental takes and the inclusion of any measures required by the Secretary, and that as implemented the take will "not appreciably reduce the likelihood of the survival and recovery of the species in the wild." 16 U.S.C. § 1539(a)(2)(B).

The substantial commitment of time and resources to the development and approval of an HCP has been a major disincentive for private persons to seek these permits, especially for limited projects. Indeed, by 1992, only 14 HCPs had been approved, and most of these involved large undertakings, sometimes initiated by state or local planning agencies. Nevertheless, environmentalists have insisted upon the full process in light of the potential effects of an HCP, which may run as long as 50 to 100 years. Suits have been brought by environmental groups challenging the approval of HCPs, and courts have been vigilant in their reviews. *See, e.g., Gerber v. Norton*, 294 F.3d 173 (D.C. Cir. 2002)(HCP for housing subdivision affecting an endangered squirrel overturned).

The Clinton administration made a number of efforts to facilitate the HCP process and most controversially to create additional incentives for persons to seek them. It adopted what it called the "No Surprises" rule, which in essence provided that, so long as the permittee complied with the HCP, the federal government would not impose additional financial requirements or additional land use restrictions on the permittee, *even if new information was developed indicating the insufficiency of the original HCP.* Instead, the government would undertake the financial commitments necessary to overcome any insufficiency in the HCP. This policy had an immediate effect, resulting in hundreds of new HCPs.

Environmental groups sued, alleging that this policy had been enacted without following the proper procedures and that it violated the ESA. A district court in the District of Columbia agreed that the proper procedures had not been followed and enjoined the "no surprises" rule until the government went through a new notice-and-comment procedure. *Spirit of Sage Council v. Norton*, 294 F.Supp.2d 67 (D.D.C. 2003). The government was supposed to conclude its rulemaking by the end of 2004.

Section 10 also contains a provision governing the treatment of experimental populations introduced into areas beyond the current range of the species. 16 U.S.C. § 1539(j). This has been most notable and controversial with respect to the reintroduction of wolves into areas they historically occupied but from which they have been extirpated. The Secretary is authorized to release populations of endangered or threatened species into areas outside their current range if the Secretary finds that such release will further the conservation of the species. Before making the release, the Secretary must determine whether the population to be released is "essential to the continued existence" of the species. 16 U.S.C. § 1539(j)(2)(B). Experimental populations have been controversial both from an environmental and ranching perspective. Environmentalists have concerns about experimental populations, because members of these populations are not entitled to all the protections afforded members of the same species that are not members of an experimental population. For example, all experimental populations are treated as threatened, even though the species might be endangered. 16 U.S.C. § 1539(j)(2)(C). In addition, in order to make experimental populations politically acceptable, further allowances may be granted, such as allowing the harassment of wolves found on private land and even killing of wolves injuring or killing livestock. At the same time, ranchers are concerned about wolves attacking their livestock, and while they are allowed to kill wolves injuring or killing livestock, the regulations require the rancher to be able to provide proof in the form of an injured animal to justify such takes.

One of the requirements for the introduction of an experimental population is that it be "wholly separate geographically from nonexperimental populations of the same species." 16 U.S.C. § 1539(j)(1). The purpose of this requirement was to ensure that members of the species naturally in an area would not effectively have their protection diminished because they would be intermingled with and indistinguishable from the experimental population. This requirement led to claims from those opposing introductions that there were members of the species already present in the area. The FWS regulation, however, interpreted the term "population" to mean a self-sustaining group in common spatial arrangement, not just individual interlopers. Both the Tenth and Ninth Circuits have found that interpretation reasonable. *See Wyoming Farm Bureau Federation v. Babbitt*, 199 F.3d 1224 (10th Cir. 2000); *United States v. McKittrick*, 142 F.3d 1170 (9th Cir. 1998).

F. Section 11

Section 11 of the ESA provides the penalties and enforcement mechanisms for violations of the Act. While environmental enforcement issues are dealt with separately in Chapter 6, it is worth noting here that the ESA has a full panoply of enforcement mechanisms, ranging from injunctive relief and administratively imposed civil penalties to criminal penalties. In addition, the ESA has one of the broadest ranging citizen suit provisions, allowing "any person" to bring suit against "any person" alleged to be in violation "of any provision" of the ESA. 16 U.S.C. § 1540(g). Section 11 even has a provision authorizing the payment of rewards to persons to provide information leading to an arrest, conviction, or civil penalty. 16 U.S.C. § 1540(d).

A recurring issue in the enforcement of the ESA is what knowledge the person violating Section 9 must have. The statute refers to a person "who knowingly violates" the statute or regulations. 16 U.S.C. § 1540(a)(1) & (b)(1). The original statute used the phrase "willfully violates." As a result, the courts have uniformly interpreted the "knowingly" requirement to mean only that the person knows he or she is killing or harming an animal; the person need not know that killing the animal is unlawful or that the animal is a member of a listed species.

Problem

A rancher in Montana would like to subdivide some of his 7000 acre ranch into "ranchette" parcels with log cabin McMansions and sell them to wannabe cowboys from the East and California. A surveyor he hires discovers a number of isolated Spaldings Catchfly, a threatened species of plant, on the properties surveyed for ranchettes. A county official mentions to the rancher that the Canada Lynx, a threatened wildlife species, famous for its unwillingness to share habitat with humans, has been sighted in the area. The rancher has heard horror stories about the Endangered Species Act, including that another Montana rancher was convicted and sentenced to six months in prison for killing a wolf. He contacts you in a panic, wondering if his retirement plans have been scuttled by "them damn burricats in Washington DC!"

Assess what further information you need, what the impacts will be on his plans depending upon that information, and what alternatives he might have.

II. PROTECTING WETLANDS

It is only relatively recently that we have come to believe that there is a need to protect wetlands. Throughout much of our history wetlands were viewed at best as worthless. For example, in argument to the Supreme Court in 1829 a wetland was described as "one of those sluggish reptile streams, that do not run but creep, and which, wherever it passes, spreads its venom, and destroys the health of all those who inhabit its marshes." *See* Wilson v. Black–Bird Creek Marsh Co., 27 U.S. (2 Pet.) 245, 7 L.Ed. 412 (1829). Moreover, because wetlands are particularly fertile, being one of the most productive ecosystems in the world, when they are drained they make wonderful farmland. Thus, it is not surprising that until recently government policy at all levels encouraged the draining of wetlands. Of the approximately 221 million acres of wetlands that existed in the 1780s in what is now the lower 48 states, today there are only about 105 million acres, 95% of which are freshwater wetlands. In the beginning years of federal regulation there were an average of 260,000 acres a year more lost, almost all of them from freshwater wetlands. Today the estimated losses are down to about 60,000 acres a year, which is significant improvement, but still short of the "no net loss" of wetlands pledged by the first President Bush in 1989.

We now recognize the important role that wetlands play in the environment. As stated by EPA:

> Wetlands play an integral role in the ecology of the watershed. The combination of shallow water, high levels of nutrients, and primary productivity is ideal for the development of organisms that form the base of the food web and feed many species of fish, amphibians, shellfish, and insects. Many species of birds and mammals rely on wetlands for food, water, and shelter, especially during migration and breeding. Wetlands' microbes, plants, and wildlife are part of global cycles for water, nitrogen, and sulfur. Furthermore, scientists are beginning to realize that atmospheric maintenance may be an additional wetlands function. Wetlands store carbon within their plant communities and soil instead of releasing it to the atmosphere as carbon dioxide. Thus wetlands help to moderate global climate conditions.

http://www.epa.gov/owow/wetlands/vital/nature.html (visited on December 10, 2004). More than one-third of the United States' threatened and endangered species live only in wetlands, and nearly half use wetlands at some point in their lives. http://www.epa.gov/owow/wetlands/fish.html (visited on December 10, 2004). In addition, wetlands can act as buffers against flooding, because they slow the velocity of the water heading toward rivers during spring thaws or after heavy rains, and against shoreline erosion caused by wave action. Wetlands also act as filters for runoff, capturing pollutants and sediment that otherwise would end up in rivers, lakes, and the ocean. A 1990 study reported by EPA indicated that the Congaree Bottomland Hardwood Swamp in South Carolina performed filtering functions equivalent to a $5 million waste water treatment plant. Many of the species that live in or are dependent on wetlands are significant economic resources. For example, muskrats live in wetlands, and the nation's harvest of muskrat pelts alone is worth over $70 million annually. Wetlands are also an important site for recreation, especially for fishers, birdwatchers, and hunters.

Beginning in the 1970s and with greater emphasis added in the 1980s, the federal government began to regulate the destruction of wetlands. Two laws in particular are involved: Section 404 of the Clean Water Act and the Swampbuster provisions of the Food Security Act of 1985. The first and most important is Section 404. 33 U.S.C. § 1344.

A. Section 404 of the Clean Water Act

Recall from the portion on the Clean Water Act from Chapter 3 that that Act prohibits the discharge of any pollutant by any person without a permit. There we discussed the NPDES program under Section 402, whereby persons can obtain a permit from EPA (or an authorized state) to discharge pollutants under certain restrictions and standards. Section 404 provides a different permit for a specified subset of pollutants–"dredged or fill material." That is, if the pollutant involved is either dredged or fill material, the discharger needs a permit under Section 404 rather than under Section 402. The 404 permit is granted by the Corps of Engineers (or an authorized state). The differing treatment of dredged and fill material under the Act reflected the Corps' long history both with respect to dredging and the permitting of obstructions to navigation under Sections 9 and 10 of the Rivers and Harbors Act of 1899. 33 U.S.C. §§ 403 and 407.

While the CWA does not define either "dredged material" or "fill material," the Corps of Engineers in its regulations have defined "dredged material" as "material that is excavated or dredged from waters of the United States," 33 CFR § 323.2(c), and "fill material" as "material placed in waters of the United States where the material has the effect of: (i) Replacing any portion of a water of the United States with dry land; or (ii) Changing the bottom elevation of any portion of a water of the United States," but not including trash or garbage. 33 CFR § 323.2(e).[3] While one might imagine that the purpose of Section 404 in light of its history together with these definitions was to continue to assure the navigability of the Nation's waters by restricting the placement of dredge spoil (the material taken from the bed of a water as a result of dredging) or any other material that might affect the depth or width of a body of water, Section 404 has become the primary regulatory protection of the nation's wetlands.

1. What Waters are Covered?

Earlier, in the chapter on pollution prevention under the Clean Water Act, we found that the coverage of the Act depends upon whether something is a "navigable water," for only discharges into "navigable waters" are regulated by the Act. The term "navigable waters" actually has quite a history. It was used at least as long ago as 1899 in the Rivers and Harbors Act, which historically was the forerunner to the Clean Water Act. In that Act, for example, persons could not deposit refuse in any navigable water of the United States without the permission of the Secretary of the Army (as the head of the Corps of Engineers, the agency responsible for maintaining the navigability of waters). 33 U.S.C. § 407. The Corps and judicial interpretation had evolved a working definition of navigable waters as "those waters of the United States which are subject

---

3. Earlier the regulation had excluded "waste" from fill material, rather than "trash or garbage." This led to environmentalists challenging the Corps' ability to permit the discharge of mining overburden from mountaintop removal mining into valleys and headwaters of various streams. The intent of the litigation was to require EPA to be the permitting agency under the NPDES program, rather than the Corps under the 404 program, because of a perception that EPA would be more environmentally protective. The Corps' interpretation of "waste" as limited to garbage and trash and not including "mining waste" was upheld in *Kentuckians for Commonwealth, Inc. v. Rivenburgh*, 317 F.3d 425 (4th Cir. 2003). In any case, the Corps and EPA amended their regulations to specify the exception was limited to trash and garbage. Thus, the Corps is the permitting agency for such valley fills.

to the ebb and flow of the tide, and/or are presently, or have been in the past, or may be in the future susceptible for use for purposes of interstate or foreign commerce.''

In enacting the CWA, however, Congress was less than precise in describing the extent of that Act's jurisdiction. Earlier versions of the bill that became the Act defined the term ''navigable waters'' as ''navigable waters of the United States,'' precisely the term used by the Corps under the Rivers and Harbors Act, but the legislative history is clear that Congress wanted the CWA's jurisdiction to reach waters that the Corps had not historically regulated under the Rivers and Harbors Act. After all, the CWA was not about navigation; it was about water quality. Thus, the final bill that became law simply dropped the word ''navigable'' from the definition, leaving the definition of ''navigable waters'' as ''the waters of the United States.'' 33 U.S.C. § 1362(7). The Corps did not distinguish this definition from its historical term, and its initial regulation under the CWA simply imported its historical definition from the Rivers and Harbors Act to the CWA. EPA, however, read the statute differently and adopted a broader definition to which the Corps acceded in 1975. Their regulations then both defined ''navigable waters'' to include not only waters navigable in fact but also tributaries of such waters, interstate waters and their tributaries, nonnavigable intrastate waters whose use or misuse could affect interstate commerce, and wetlands adjacent to the above waters. The extension of jurisdiction to wetlands was controversial, especially because it interfered with the traditional practice of filling wetlands for both industrial, commercial, and residential development as well as for expanding acreage for farming.

As a result, there were attempts by some in Congress to amend the CWA to limit coverage of wetlands in the Act. That attempt failed, and instead in 1977 Congress amended the Act to exempt certain activities (such as ''normal farming, silviculture, and ranching activities''), rather than certain areas. Nevertheless, the controversy did not go away, and in 1985 the issue reached the Supreme Court.

UNITED STATES v. RIVERSIDE BAYVIEW HOMES, INC.

Supreme Court of the United States, 1985.

474 U.S. 121, 106 S.Ct. 455, 88 L.Ed.2d 419.

Justice WHITE delivered the opinion of the Court.

This case presents the question whether the Clean Water Act (CWA), together with certain regulations promulgated under its authority by the Army Corps of Engineers, authorizes the Corps to require landowners to obtain permits from the Corps before discharging fill material into wetlands adjacent to navigable bodies of water and their tributaries.

I

... After initially construing the Act to cover only waters navigable in fact, in 1975 the Corps issued interim final regulations redefining "the waters of the United States" to include not only actually navigable waters but also tributaries of such waters, interstate waters and their tributaries, and nonnavigable intrastate waters whose use or misuse could affect interstate commerce. More importantly for present purposes, the Corps construed the Act to cover all "freshwater wetlands" that were adjacent to other covered waters. A "freshwater wetland" [is] defined ... as follows: "The term 'wetlands' means those areas that are inundated or saturated by surface or ground water at a frequency and duration sufficient to support, and that under normal circumstances do support, a prevalence of vegetation typically adapted for life in saturated soil...."[2]

Respondent Riverside Bayview Homes, Inc. (hereafter respondent), owns 80 acres of low-lying, marshy land near the shores of Lake St. Clair in Macomb County, Michigan. In 1976, respondent began to place fill materials on its property as part of its preparations for construction of a housing development. The Corps of Engineers, believing that the property was an "adjacent wetland" under the 1975 regulation defining "waters of the United States," filed suit in the United States District Court for the Eastern District of Michigan, seeking to enjoin respondent from filling the property without the permission of the Corps.

[The District Court enjoined the filling, but the Court of Appeals reversed.] The court construed the Corps' regulation to exclude from the category of adjacent wetlands—and hence from that of "waters of the United States"—wetlands that were not subject to flooding by adjacent navigable waters at a frequency sufficient to support the growth of aquatic vegetation.... The court also expressed its doubt that Congress, in granting the Corps jurisdiction to regulate the filling of "navigable waters," intended to allow regulation of wetlands that were not the result of flooding by navigable waters. Under the court's reading of the regulation, respondent's property was not within the Corps' jurisdiction, because its semiaquatic characteristics were not the result of frequent flooding by the nearby navigable waters. Respondent was therefore free to fill the property without obtaining a permit.

We granted certiorari to consider the proper interpretation of the Corps' regulation defining "waters of the United States" and the scope of the Corps' jurisdiction under the Clean Water Act, both of which were called into question by the Sixth Circuit's ruling. We now reverse.

II

The question whether the Corps of Engineers may demand that respondent obtain a permit before placing fill material on its property is primarily one of regulatory and statutory interpretation: we must deter-

---

2. The regulations also cover certain wetlands not necessarily adjacent to other waters. These provisions are not now before us.

mine whether respondent's property is an "adjacent wetland" within the meaning of the applicable regulation, and, if so, whether the Corps' jurisdiction over "navigable waters" gives it statutory authority to regulate discharges of fill material into such a wetland. [On the question of regulatory interpretation, the Court concluded that the Corps' interpretation of its regulation was correct, and there was no need under the regulation for the water in the wetland to come from flooding as opposed to saturation. Accordingly,] if the regulation itself is valid as a construction of the term "waters of the United States" as used in the Clean Water Act, a question which we now address, the property falls within the scope of the Corps' jurisdiction over "navigable waters" under § 404 of the Act.

IV

A

An agency's construction of a statute it is charged with enforcing is entitled to deference if it is reasonable and not in conflict with the expressed intent of Congress. Accordingly, our review is limited to the question whether it is reasonable, in light of the language, policies, and legislative history of the Act for the Corps to exercise jurisdiction over wetlands adjacent to but not regularly flooded by rivers, streams, and other hydrographic features more conventionally identifiable as "waters."[8]

On a purely linguistic level, it may appear unreasonable to classify "lands," wet or otherwise, as "waters." Such a simplistic response, however, does justice neither to the problem faced by the Corps in defining the scope of its authority under § 404(a) nor to the realities of the problem of water pollution that the Clean Water Act was intended to combat. In determining the limits of its power to regulate discharges under the Act, the Corps must necessarily choose some point at which water ends and land begins. Our common experience tells us that this is often no easy task: the transition from water to solid ground is not necessarily or even typically an abrupt one. Rather, between open waters and dry land may lie shallows, marshes, mudflats, swamps, bogs—in short, a huge array of areas that are not wholly aquatic but nevertheless fall far short of being dry land. Where on this continuum to find the limit of "waters" is far from obvious.

Faced with such a problem of defining the bounds of its regulatory authority, an agency may appropriately look to the legislative history and underlying policies of its statutory grants of authority. Neither of these sources provides unambiguous guidance for the Corps in this case, but together they do support the reasonableness of the Corps' approach of defining adjacent wetlands as "waters" within the meaning of § 404(a). Section 404 originated as part of the Federal Water Pollution

---

8. We are not called upon to address the question of the authority of the Corps to regulate discharges of fill material into wetlands that are not adjacent to bodies of open water, and we do not express any opinion on that question.

Control Act Amendments of 1972, which constituted a comprehensive legislative attempt "to restore and maintain the chemical, physical, and biological integrity of the Nation's waters . ." This objective incorporated a broad, systemic view of the goal of maintaining and improving water quality: as the House Report on the legislation put it, "the word 'integrity' . . . refers to a condition in which the natural structure and function of ecosystems is [are] maintained." Protection of aquatic ecosystems, Congress recognized, demanded broad federal authority to control pollution, for "[w]ater moves in hydrologic cycles and it is essential that discharge of pollutants be controlled at the source."

In keeping with these views, Congress chose to define the waters covered by the Act broadly. Although the Act prohibits discharges into "navigable waters," the Act's definition of "navigable waters" as "the waters of the United States" makes it clear that the term "navigable" as used in the Act is of limited import. In adopting this definition of "navigable waters," Congress evidently intended to repudiate limits that had been placed on federal regulation by earlier water pollution control statutes and to exercise its powers under the Commerce Clause to regulate at least some waters that would not be deemed "navigable" under the classical understanding of that term.

Of course, it is one thing to recognize that Congress intended to allow regulation of waters that might not satisfy traditional tests of navigability; it is another to assert that Congress intended to abandon traditional notions of "waters" and include in that term "wetlands" as well. Nonetheless, the evident breadth of congressional concern for protection of water quality and aquatic ecosystems suggests that it is reasonable for the Corps to interpret the term "waters" to encompass wetlands adjacent to waters as more conventionally defined. Following the lead of the Environmental Protection Agency, the Corps has determined that wetlands adjacent to navigable waters do as a general matter play a key role in protecting and enhancing water quality:

> The regulation of activities that cause water pollution cannot rely on . . . artificial lines . . . but must focus on all waters that together form the entire aquatic system. Water moves in hydrologic cycles, and the pollution of this part of the aquatic system, regardless of whether it is above or below an ordinary high water mark, or mean high tide line, will affect the water quality of the other waters within that aquatic system.

> For this reason, the landward limit of Federal jurisdiction under Section 404 must include any adjacent wetlands that form the border of or are in reasonable proximity to other waters of the United States, as these wetlands are part of this aquatic system.

We cannot say that the Corps' conclusion that adjacent wetlands are inseparably bound up with the "waters" of the United States—based as it is on the Corps' and EPA's technical expertise—is unreasonable. In view of the breadth of federal regulatory authority contemplated by the Act itself and the inherent difficulties of defining precise bounds to regulable waters, the Corps' ecological judgment about the relationship between waters and their adjacent wetlands provides an adequate basis for a legal judgment that adjacent wetlands may be defined as waters under the Act.

This holds true even for wetlands that are not the result of flooding or permeation by water having its source in adjacent bodies of open water. The Corps has concluded that wetlands may affect the water quality of adjacent lakes, rivers, and streams even when the waters of those bodies do not actually inundate the wetlands. For example, wetlands that are not flooded by adjacent waters may still tend to drain into those waters. In such circumstances, the Corps has concluded that wetlands may serve to filter and purify water draining into adjacent bodies of water, and to slow the flow of surface runoff into lakes, rivers, and streams and thus prevent flooding and erosion. In addition, adjacent wetlands may "serve significant natural biological functions, including food chain production, general habitat, and nesting, spawning, rearing and resting sites for aquatic ... species." In short, the Corps has concluded that wetlands adjacent to lakes, rivers, streams, and other bodies of water may function as integral parts of the aquatic environment even when the moisture creating the wetlands does not find its source in the adjacent bodies of water. Again, we cannot say that the Corps' judgment on these matters is unreasonable, and we therefore conclude that a definition of "waters of the United States" encompassing all wetlands adjacent to other bodies of water over which the Corps has jurisdiction is a permissible interpretation of the Act. Because respondent's property is part of a wetland that actually abuts on a navigable waterway, respondent was required to have a permit in this case.[9]

Notes and Comments

1. *Riverside Bayview* settled the question whether wetlands could be "waters" of the United States, and it upheld the Corps' interpretation that adjacent wetlands could be covered by the Act. Nevertheless, the decision left a number of questions unsettled.

2. For example, in *Riverside Bayview Homes*, the Court mentions that the Corps and EPA regulations defining "waters of the United States" included "isolated wetlands and lakes, intermittent streams, prairie potholes, and other waters that are not part of a tributary system to interstate waters or to navigable waters of the United States, the degradation or destruction of which could affect interstate commerce." The regulations gave

---

9. Of course, it may well be that not every adjacent wetland is of great importance to the environment of adjoining bodies of water. But the existence of such cases does not seriously undermine the Corps' decision to define all adjacent wetlands as "waters." If it is reasonable for the Corps to conclude that in the majority of cases, adjacent wetlands have significant effects on water quality and the aquatic ecosystem, its definition can stand. That the definition may include some wetlands that are not significantly intertwined with the ecosystem of adjacent waterways is of little moment, for where it appears that a wetland covered by the Corps' definition is in fact lacking in importance to the aquatic environment—or where its importance is outweighed by other values—the Corps may always allow development of the wetland for other uses simply by issuing a permit.

three examples of such waters, which, if harmed, could affect interstate commerce: those which are or could be used by interstate or foreign travelers for recreational or other purposes, those from which fish or shellfish are or could be taken and sold in interstate or foreign commerce, and those which are used or could be used for industrial purposes by industries in interstate commerce. In 1986, the Corps issued a notice interpreting its regulation, which provided four additional examples of isolated, nonnavigable waters whose harm could affect interstate commerce. This notice, popularly known as the Migratory Bird Rule, was challenged in a number of cases, in all but one of which the courts eventually ruled in favor of the validity of the Rule, but in 2000 the Supreme Court granted certiorari in one of the cases. Its decision follows.

SOLID WASTE AGENCY OF NORTHERN COOK COUNTY v. UNITED STATES ARMY CORPS OF ENGINEERS

Supreme Court of the United States, 2001.

531 U.S. 159, 121 S.Ct. 675, 148 L.Ed.2d 576.

Chief Justice REHNQUIST delivered the opinion of the Court.

Section 404(a) of the Clean Water Act (CWA or Act) regulates the discharge of dredged or fill material into "navigable waters." The United States Army Corps of Engineers (Corps) has interpreted § 404(a) to confer federal authority over an abandoned sand and gravel pit in northern Illinois which provides habitat for migratory birds. We are asked to decide whether the provisions of § 404(a) may be fairly extended to these waters, and, if so, whether Congress could exercise such authority consistent with the Commerce Clause. We answer the first question in the negative and therefore do not reach the second.

Petitioner, the Solid Waste Agency of Northern Cook County (SWANCC), is a consortium of 23 suburban Chicago cities and villages that united in an effort to locate and develop a disposal site for baled nonhazardous solid waste. The Chicago Gravel Company informed the municipalities of the availability of a 533–acre parcel, bestriding the Illinois counties Cook and Kane, which had been the site of a sand and gravel pit mining operation for three decades up until about 1960. Long since abandoned, the old mining site eventually gave way to a successional stage forest, with its remnant excavation trenches evolving into a scattering of permanent and seasonal ponds of varying size (from under one-tenth of an acre to several acres) and depth (from several inches to several feet).

The municipalities decided to purchase the site for disposal of their baled nonhazardous solid waste. [B]ecause the operation called for the filling of some of the permanent and seasonal ponds, SWANCC contacted federal respondents (hereinafter respondents), including the Corps, to determine if a federal landfill permit was required under § 404(a) of the CWA.

Section 404(a) grants the Corps authority to issue permits "for the discharge of dredged or fill material into the navigable waters at specified disposal sites." The term "navigable waters" is defined under the Act as "the waters of the United States, including the territorial seas." The Corps has issued regulations defining the term "waters of the United States" to include

"waters such as intrastate lakes, rivers, streams (including intermittent streams), mudflats, sandflats, wetlands, sloughs, prairie potholes, wet meadows, playa lakes, or natural ponds, the use, degradation or destruction of which could affect interstate or foreign commerce...." 33 CFR § 328.3(a)(3) (1999).

In 1986, in an attempt to "clarify" the reach of its jurisdiction, the Corps stated that § 404(a) extends to intrastate waters:

"a. Which are or would be used as habitat by birds protected by Migratory Bird Treaties; or

"b. Which are or would be used as habitat by other migratory birds which cross state lines; or

"c. Which are or would be used as habitat for endangered species; or

"d. Used to irrigate crops sold in interstate commerce."

This last promulgation has been dubbed the "Migratory Bird Rule."

[A]fter the Illinois Nature Preserves Commission informed the Corps that a number of migratory bird species had been observed at the site, the Corps ... asserted jurisdiction over the balefill site pursuant to subpart (b) of the "Migratory Bird Rule." The Corps found that approximately 121 bird species had been observed at the site, including several known to depend upon aquatic environments for a significant portion of their life requirements. Thus, on November 16, 1987, the Corps formally "determined that the seasonally ponded, abandoned gravel mining depressions located on the project site, while not wetlands, did qualify as 'waters of the United States' ... based upon the following criteria: (1) the proposed site had been abandoned as a gravel mining operation; (2) the water areas and spoil piles had developed a natural character; and (3) the water areas are used as habitat by migratory bird [sic] which cross state lines." ...

Petitioner filed suit under the Administrative Procedure Act in the Northern District of Illinois challenging both the Corps' jurisdiction over the site and the merits of its denial of the § 404(a) permit. [Both the district court and the Seventh Circuit affirmed the Corps' determination, and the petitioner sought certiorari.]

We granted certiorari and now reverse.

Congress passed the CWA for the stated purpose of "restor[ing] and maintain[ing] the chemical, physical, and biological integrity of the Nation's waters." In so doing, Congress chose to "recognize, preserve, and protect the primary responsibilities and rights of States to prevent, reduce, and eliminate pollution, to plan the development and use (including restoration, preservation, and enhancement) of land and water resources, and to consult with the Administrator in the exercise of his authority under this chapter." Relevant here, § 404(a) authorizes respondents to regulate the discharge of fill material into "navigable waters," which the statute defines as "the waters of the United States, including the territorial seas." Respondents have interpreted these words to cover the abandoned gravel pit at issue here because it is used as habitat for migratory birds. We conclude that the "Migratory Bird Rule" is not fairly supported by the CWA.

This is not the first time we have been called upon to evaluate the meaning of § 404(a). In *United States v. Riverside Bayview Homes, Inc.*, we held that the Corps had § 404(a) jurisdiction over wetlands that actually abutted on a navigable waterway. In so doing, we noted that the term "navigable" is of "limited import" and that Congress evidenced its intent to "regulate at least some waters that would not be deemed 'navigable' under the classical understanding of that term." But our holding was based in large measure upon Congress' unequivocal acquiescence to, and approval of, the Corps' regulations interpreting the CWA to cover wetlands adjacent to navigable waters. We found that Congress' concern for the protection of water quality and aquatic ecosystems indicated its intent to regulate wetlands "inseparably bound up with the 'waters' of the United States."

It was the significant nexus between the wetlands and "navigable waters" that informed our reading of the CWA in *Riverside Bayview Homes*. Indeed, we did not "express any opinion" on the "question of the authority of the Corps to regulate discharges of fill material into wetlands that are not adjacent to bodies of open water...." In order to rule for respondents here, we would have to hold that the jurisdiction of the Corps extends to ponds that are *not* adjacent to open water. But we conclude that the text of the statute will not allow this.

Indeed, the Corps' *original* interpretation of the CWA, promulgated two years after its enactment, is inconsistent with that which it espouses here. Its 1974 regulations defined § 404(a)'s "navigable waters" to mean "those waters of the United States which are subject to the ebb and flow of the tide, and/or are presently, or have been in the past, or may be in the future susceptible for use for purposes of interstate or foreign commerce." The Corps emphasized that "[i]t is the water body's capability of use by the public for purposes of transportation or commerce which is the determinative factor." Respondents put forward no persuasive evidence that the Corps mistook Congress' intent in 1974.[3]

---

3. Respondents refer us to portions of the legislative history that they believe indicate Congress' intent to expand the definition of "navigable waters." Although the Conference Report includes the statement that the conferees "intend that the term 'navigable waters' be given the broadest possible constitutional interpretation," neither this, nor anything else in the legislative history to which respondents point, signifies that Congress intended to exert anything more than its commerce power over navigation. Indeed, respondents admit that the legislative history is somewhat ambiguous.

Respondents next contend that whatever its original aim in 1972, Congress charted a new course five years later when it approved the more expansive definition of "navigable waters" found in the Corps' 1977 regulations.... Respondents argue that Congress was aware of this more expansive interpretation during its 1977 amendments to the CWA. Specifically, respondents point to a failed House bill, H.R. 3199, that would have defined "navigable waters" as "all waters which are presently used, or are susceptible to use in their natural condition or by reasonable improvement as a means to transport interstate or foreign commerce." ... The failure to pass legislation that would have overturned the Corps' 1977 regulations and the extension of jurisdiction in § 404(g) to waters "other than" traditional "navigable waters," respondents submit, indicate that Congress recognized and accepted a broad definition of "navigable waters" that includes nonnavigable, isolated, intrastate waters.

Although we have recognized congressional acquiescence to administrative interpretations of a statute in some situations, we have done so with extreme care.... Because "subsequent history is less illuminating than the contemporaneous evidence," respondents face a difficult task in overcoming the plain text and import of § 404(a).

We conclude that respondents have failed to make the necessary showing that the failure of the 1977 House bill demonstrates Congress' acquiescence to the Corps' regulations or the "Migratory Bird Rule," which, of course, did not first appear until 1986....

We thus decline respondents' invitation to take what they see as the next ineluctable step after *Riverside Bayview Homes:* holding that isolated ponds, some only seasonal, wholly located within two Illinois counties, fall under § 404(a)'s definition of "navigable waters" because they serve as habitat for migratory birds. As counsel for respondents conceded at oral argument, such a ruling would assume that "the use of the word navigable in the statute ... does not have any independent significance." We cannot agree that Congress' separate definitional use of the phrase "waters of the United States" constitutes a basis for reading the term "navigable waters" out of the statute. We said in *Riverside Bayview Homes* that the word "navigable" in the statute was of "limited import" and went on to hold that § 404(a) extended to nonnavigable wetlands adjacent to open waters. But it is one thing to give a word limited effect and quite another to give it no effect whatever. The term "navigable" has at least the import of showing us what Congress had in mind as its authority for enacting the CWA: its traditional jurisdiction over waters that were or had been navigable in fact or which could reasonably be so made.

Respondents—relying upon all of the arguments addressed above— contend that, at the very least, it must be said that Congress did not address the precise question of § 404(a)'s scope with regard to nonnavigable, isolated, intrastate waters, and that, therefore, we should give deference to the "Migratory Bird Rule." We find § 404(a) to be clear, but even were we to agree with respondents, we would not extend ... deference here.

Where an administrative interpretation of a statute invokes the outer limits of Congress' power, we expect a clear indication that Congress intended that result. This requirement stems from our prudential desire not to needlessly reach constitutional issues and our assumption that Congress does not casually authorize administrative agencies to interpret a statute to push the limit of congressional authority. This concern is heightened where the administrative interpretation alters the federal-state framework by permitting federal encroachment upon a traditional state power. Thus, "where an otherwise acceptable construction of a statute would raise serious constitutional problems, the Court will construe the statute to avoid such problems unless such construction is plainly contrary to the intent of Congress."

Twice in the past six years we have reaffirmed the proposition that the grant of authority to Congress under the Commerce Clause, though broad, is not unlimited. Respondents argue that the "Migratory Bird Rule" falls within Congress' power to regulate intrastate activities that "substantially affect" interstate commerce. They note that the protection of migratory birds is a "national interest of very nearly the first magnitude," *Missouri v. Holland,* 252 U.S. 416, 435, 40 S.Ct. 382 (1920), and that, as the Court of Appeals found, millions of people spend over a billion dollars annually on recreational pursuits relating to migratory birds. These arguments raise significant constitutional questions. For example, we would have to evaluate the precise object or activity that, in the aggregate, substantially affects interstate commerce. This is not clear, for although the Corps has claimed jurisdiction over petitioner's land because it contains water areas used as habitat by migratory birds, respondents now, *post litem motam,* focus upon the fact that the regulated activity is petitioner's municipal landfill, which is "plainly of a commercial nature." But this is a far cry, indeed, from the "navigable waters" and "waters of the United States" to which the statute by its terms extends.

These are significant constitutional questions raised by respondents' application of their regulations, and yet we find nothing approaching a clear statement from Congress that it intended § 404(a) to reach an abandoned sand and gravel pit such as we have here. Permitting respondents to claim federal jurisdiction over ponds and mudflats falling within the "Migratory Bird Rule" would result in a significant impingement of the States' traditional and primary power over land and water use. Rather than expressing a desire to readjust the federal-state balance in this manner, Congress chose to "recognize, preserve, and protect the primary responsibilities and rights of States ... to plan the development and use ... of land and water resources...." 33 U.S.C. § 1251(b). We thus read the statute as written to avoid the significant constitutional and federalism questions raised by respondents' interpretation, and therefore reject the request for administrative deference.

We hold that 33 CFR § 328.3(a)(3) (1999), as clarified and applied to petitioner's balefill site pursuant to the "Migratory Bird Rule" exceeds the authority granted to respondents under § 404(a) of the CWA. The judgment of the Court of Appeals for the Seventh Circuit is therefore

Reversed.

Justice STEVENS, with whom Justice SOUTER, Justice GINSBURG, and Justice BREYER join, dissenting.

In 1969, the Cuyahoga River in Cleveland, Ohio, coated with a slick of industrial waste, caught fire. Congress responded to that dramatic event, and to others like it, by enacting the Federal Water Pollution Control Act (FWPCA) Amendments of 1972, commonly known as the Clean Water Act (Clean Water Act, CWA, or Act). The Act proclaimed the ambitious goal of ending water pollution by 1985. The Court's past interpretations of the CWA have been fully consistent with that goal. Although Congress' vision of zero pollution remains unfulfilled, its pursuit has unquestionably retarded the destruction of the aquatic environment. Our Nation's waters no longer burn. Today, however, the Court takes an unfortunate step that needlessly weakens our principal safeguard against toxic water.

It is fair to characterize the Clean Water Act as "watershed" legislation. The statute endorsed fundamental changes in both the purpose and the scope of federal regulation of the Nation's waters. In § 13 of the Rivers and Harbors Appropriation Act of 1899 (RHA), Congress had assigned to the Army Corps of Engineers (Corps) the mission of regulating discharges into certain waters in order to protect their use as highways for the transportation of interstate and foreign commerce; the scope of the Corps' jurisdiction under the RHA accordingly extended only to waters that were "navigable." In the CWA, however, Congress broadened the Corps' mission to include the purpose of protecting the quality of our Nation's waters for esthetic, health, recreational, and environmental uses. The scope of its jurisdiction was therefore redefined to encompass all of "the waters of the United States, including the territorial seas." That definition requires neither actual nor potential navigability.

The Court has previously held that the Corps' broadened jurisdiction under the CWA properly included an 80–acre parcel of low-lying marshy land that was not itself navigable, directly adjacent to navigable water, or even hydrologically connected to navigable water, but which was part of a larger area, characterized by poor drainage, that ultimately abutted a navigable creek. *United States v. Riverside Bayview Homes, Inc.* Our broad finding in *Riverside Bayview* that the 1977 Congress had acquiesced in the Corps' understanding of its jurisdiction applies equally to the 410–acre parcel at issue here. Moreover, once Congress crossed the legal watershed that separates navigable streams of commerce from marshes and inland lakes, there is no principled reason for limiting the statute's protection to those waters or wetlands that happen to lie near a navigable stream.

In its decision today, the Court draws a new jurisdictional line, one that invalidates the 1986 migratory bird regulation as well as the Corps' assertion of jurisdiction over all waters except for actually navigable waters, their tributaries, and wetlands adjacent to each. Its holding rests on two equally untenable premises: (1) that when Congress passed the 1972 CWA, it did not intend "to exert anything more than its commerce power over navigation"; and (2) that in 1972 Congress drew the boundary defining the Corps' jurisdiction at the odd line on which the Court today settles.

As I shall explain, the text of the 1972 amendments affords no support for the Court's holding, and amendments Congress adopted in 1977 do support the Corps' present interpretation of its mission as extending to so-called "isolated" waters. Indeed, simple common sense cuts against the particular definition of the Corps' jurisdiction favored by the majority.

I

The significance of the FWPCA Amendments of 1972 is illuminated by a reference to the history of federal water regulation, a history that the majority largely ignores. [Justice Stevens then provided such a history, noting that] [d]uring the middle of the 20th century, the goals of federal water regulation began to shift away from an exclusive focus on protecting navigability and toward a concern for preventing environmental degradation....

The shift in the focus of federal water regulation from protecting navigability toward environmental protection reached a dramatic climax in 1972, with the passage of the CWA. The Act, which was passed as an amendment to the existing FWPCA, was universally described by its supporters as the first truly comprehensive federal water pollution legislation.... This Court was therefore undoubtedly correct when it described the 1972 amendments as establishing "a comprehensive program for controlling and abating water pollution." *Train v. City of New York,* 420 U.S. 35, 37, 95 S.Ct. 839 (1975).

Section 404 of the CWA resembles § 13 of the RHA, but, unlike the earlier statute, the primary purpose of which is the maintenance of navigability, § 404 was principally intended as a pollution control measure.... Strikingly absent from its declaration of "goals and policy" is *any* reference to avoiding or removing obstructions to navigation. Instead, the principal objective of the Act, as stated by Congress in § 101, was "to restore and maintain the chemical, physical, and biological integrity of the Nation's waters." Congress therefore directed federal agencies in § 102 to "develop comprehensive programs for preventing, reducing, or eliminating the pollution of the navigable waters and ground waters and improving the sanitary condition of surface and underground waters." The CWA commands federal agencies to give "due regard," not to the interest of unobstructed navigation, but rather to "improvements which are necessary to conserve such waters for the protection and propagation of fish and aquatic life and wildlife [and] recreational purposes."

Because of the statute's ambitious and comprehensive goals, it was, of course, necessary to expand its jurisdictional scope. Thus, although Congress opted to carry over the traditional jurisdictional term "navigable waters" from the RHA and prior versions of the FWPCA, it broadened the *definition* of that term to encompass all "waters of the United States." Indeed, the 1972 conferees arrived at the final formulation by specifically deleting the word "navigable" from the definition that had originally appeared in the House version of the Act. The majority today undoes that deletion.

The Conference Report explained that the definition in § 502(7) was intended to "be given the broadest possible constitutional interpretation." The Court dismisses this clear assertion of legislative intent with the back of its hand.... The activities regulated by the CWA have nothing to do with Congress' "commerce power over navigation." Indeed, the goals of the 1972 statute have nothing to do with *navigation* at all.

As we recognized in *Riverside Bayview*, the interests served by the statute embrace the protection of " 'significant natural biological functions, including food chain production, general habitat, and nesting, spawning, rearing and resting sites' "for various species of aquatic wildlife. For wetlands and "isolated" inland lakes, that interest is equally powerful, regardless of the proximity of the swamp or the water to a navigable stream. Nothing in the text, the stated purposes, or the legislative history of the CWA supports the conclusion that in 1972 Congress contemplated—much less commanded—the odd jurisdictional line that the Court has drawn today....

II

As the majority correctly notes, when the Corps first promulgated regulations pursuant to § 404 of the 1972 Act, it construed its authority as being essentially the same as it had been under the 1899 RHA.[8] The reaction to those regulations in the federal courts, in the Environmental Protection Agency (EPA), and in Congress convinced the Corps that the statute required it "to protect water quality to the full extent of the [C]ommerce [C]lause" and to extend federal regulation over discharges "to many areas that have never before been subject to Federal permits or to this form of water quality protection." ... The Corps' broadened

---

8. The Corps later acknowledged that the 1974 regulations "limited the Section 404 permit program to the same waters that were being regulated under the River and Harbor Act of 1899." Although refusing to defer to the Corps' present interpretation of the statute, the majority strangely attributes some significance to the Corps' initial reluctance to read the 1972 Act as expanding its jurisdiction. But, stranger still, by construing the statute as extending to non-navigable tributaries and adjacent wetlands, the majority reads the statute more broadly than the 1974 regulations that it seems willing to accept as a correct construction of the Corps' jurisdiction. As I make clear in the text, there is abundant evidence that the Corps was wrong in 1974 and that the Court is wrong today.

reading of its jurisdiction provoked opposition among some Members of Congress. As a result, in 1977, Congress considered a proposal that would have limited the Corps' jurisdiction under § 404 to waters that are used, or by reasonable improvement could be used, as a means to transport interstate or foreign commerce and their adjacent wetlands. A bill embodying that proposal passed the House but was defeated in the Senate. The debates demonstrate that Congress was fully aware of the Corps' understanding of the scope of its jurisdiction under the 1972 Act.... The net result of that extensive debate was a congressional endorsement of the position that the Corps maintains today....

Even if the majority were correct that Congress did not extend the Corps' jurisdiction in the 1972 CWA to reach beyond navigable waters and their nonnavigable tributaries, Congress' rejection of the House's efforts in 1977 to cut back on the Corps' 1975 assertion of jurisdiction clearly indicates congressional acquiescence in that assertion....

IV

Because I am convinced that the Court's miserly construction of the statute is incorrect, I shall comment briefly on petitioner's argument that Congress is without power to prohibit it from filling any part of the 31 acres of ponds on its property in Cook County, Illinois. The Corps' exercise of its § 404 permitting power over "isolated" waters that serve as habitat for migratory birds falls well within the boundaries set by this Court's Commerce Clause jurisprudence.

In *United States v. Lopez,* this Court identified "three broad categories of activity that Congress may regulate under its commerce power": (1) channels of interstate commerce; (2) instrumentalities of interstate commerce, or persons and things in interstate commerce; and (3) activities that "substantially affect" interstate commerce. The migratory bird rule at issue here is properly analyzed under the third category. In order to constitute a proper exercise of Congress' power over intrastate activities that "substantially affect" interstate commerce, it is not necessary that each individual instance of the activity substantially affect commerce; it is enough that, taken in the aggregate, the *class of activities* in question has such an effect.

The activity being regulated in this case (and by the Corps' § 404 regulations in general) is the discharge of fill material into water.... There can be no doubt that, unlike the class of activities Congress was attempting to regulate in *United States v. Morrison* ("[g]ender-motivated crimes") and *Lopez* (possession of guns near school property), the discharge of fill material into the Nation's waters is almost always undertaken for economic reasons.

Moreover, no one disputes that the discharge of fill into "isolated" waters that serve as migratory bird habitat will, in the aggregate, adversely affect migratory bird populations. Nor does petitioner dispute that the particular waters it seeks to fill are home to many important species of migratory birds, including the second-largest breeding colony of Great Blue Herons in northeastern Illinois and several species of waterfowl protected by international treaty and Illinois endangered species laws.[16]

In addition to the intrinsic value of migratory birds, it is undisputed that literally millions of people regularly participate in birdwatching and hunting and that those activities generate a host of commercial activities of great value.[17] The causal connection between the filling of wetlands and the decline of commercial activities associated with migratory birds is not "attenuated," it is direct and concrete.

Finally, the migratory bird rule does not blur the "distinction between what is truly national and what is truly local." Justice Holmes cogently observed in *Missouri v. Holland* that the protection of migratory birds is a textbook example of a *national* problem. The destruction of aquatic migratory bird habitat, like so many other environmental problems, is an action in which the benefits (*e.g.,* a new landfill) are disproportionately local, while many of the costs (*e.g.,* fewer migratory birds) are widely dispersed and often borne by citizens living in other States. In such situations, described by economists as involving "externalities," federal regulation is both appropriate and necessary. . . .

The power to regulate commerce among the several States necessarily and properly includes the power to preserve the natural resources that generate such commerce. Migratory birds, and the waters on which they rely, are such resources. . . .

Notes and Comments

1. The next to last sentence of the Court's opinion in *SWANCC* concludes that paragraph (3) of Section 328.3(a) of the Corps' regulations (the paragraph that includes isolated waters within the definition of "waters of the United States" if an adverse effect on them could affect interstate commerce) "as clarified and applied" according to the Migratory Bird Rule exceeds the Corps authority. What precisely does this mean? If you were in the Corps of Engineers General Counsel's office after the *SWANCC* decision, how would you advise the various Corps offices across the nation with respect to the Corps' jurisdiction? Are all four examples of covered waters included in the Migratory Bird Rule (waters used as habitat by birds protected by Migratory Bird Treaties, waters used as habitat by other migratory birds which cross state lines, waters used as habitat for endangered species, and waters used to irrigate crops sold in interstate commerce) beyond the Corps' jurisdiction, or only those involving migratory birds? How

---

16. Other bird species using petitioner's site as habitat include the Great Egret, Green-backed Heron, Black-crowned Night Heron, Canada Goose, Wood Duck, Mallard, Greater Yellowlegs, Belted Kingfisher, Northern Waterthrush, Louisiana Waterthrush, Swamp Sparrow, and Red-winged Blackbird.

17. In 1984, the U.S. Congress Office of Technology Assessment found that, in 1980,

5.3 million Americans hunted migratory birds, spending $638 million. More than 100 million Americans spent almost $14.8 billion in 1980 to watch and photograph fish and wildlife. Of 17.7 million birdwatchers, 14.3 million took trips in order to observe, feed, or photograph waterfowl, and 9.5 million took trips specifically to view other water-associated birds, such as herons like those residing at petitioner's site.

about the examples of covered isolated waters in paragraph (3) itself (those which are or could be used by interstate or foreign travelers for recreational or other purposes, those from which fish or shellfish are or could be taken and sold in interstate or foreign commerce, and those which are used or could be used for industrial purposes by industries in interstate commerce) that are unrelated to the Migratory Bird Rule? If otherwise isolated waters are connected hydrologically through underground aquifers to navigable waters, do they have a sufficient nexus to navigable waters to be within the CWA's jurisdiction? Or are all isolated nonnavigable waters beyond the Corps' jurisdiction? And if so, what about nonnavigable tributaries of navigable waters?

2. Following *SWANCC*, the Corps and EPA issued an Advance Notice of Proposed Rulemaking, 68 Fed. Reg. 1991 (Jan. 15, 2003), for the purpose of asking for public comment on possible approaches to redefining "waters of the United States" in light of *SWANCC* and to give notice of their interim guidance to agency field offices. It appears that the rulemaking proceeding has been abandoned, but the interim guidance remains in effect. That guidance concludes that no field office should attempt to exercise jurisdiction over any isolated nonnavigable water on the basis of any of the factors included in the Migratory Bird Rule. Moreover, in the Fourth Circuit, no field office should assert jurisdiction over any isolated, nonnavigable water, because that circuit had earlier ruled that the Corps' regulation asserting jurisdiction over such waters was beyond its authority, *see United States v. Wilson*, 133 F.3d 251 (4th Cir. 1997). Finally, in all the other circuits, because of the questions raised by *SWANCC* with respect to isolated, nonnavigable waters, the guidance directs field offices to "seek formal project-specific Headquarters approval prior to asserting jurisdiction over such waters." Do you agree with this guidance? As an already overworked staff member in a field office, do you think that the need to seek formal headquarters approval for the exercise of jurisdiction over a nonnavigable isolated water on the basis of, say, its potential effect on recreational use by interstate travellers, while requiring no such approval for a denial of jurisdiction, is likely to affect your decision?

3. Both the majority and dissent in *SWANCC* limit their discussion of the reach of "waters of the United States" to the Corps and Section 404, but the term they are interpreting, "navigable waters," as defined by Section 502, 33 U.S.C. § 1362(7), to mean "waters of the United States, including the territorial seas," applies to the whole CWA, not just Section 404. Accordingly, any limitation on the Corps' jurisdiction by reason of the definition of waters will equally restrict EPA's jurisdiction under the NPDES program and states' jurisdiction under Section 401 to check federal permitting that may affect states' water quality. Moreover, because the Oil Pollution Act, 33 U.S.C. 2701, *et seq.*, has the same jurisdictional reach as the CWA, the ability of EPA and the Coast Guard to obtain cleanups of oil spills and to pursue enforcement against those who spill oil would also be affected.

4. It is often difficult to measure the effects of court decisions, but commentators have suggested that *SWANCC* likely has devastating effects on a wide range of isolated wetlands that provide habitat for various species.

Some states have amended their laws to cover such wetlands, but most states have not, including some states likely to be most affected.

5. Prior to *SWANCC*, it was not very important to determine if a wetland was adjacent to a navigable water or not, because there was almost invariably evidence of use of the wetland by migratory fowl. With the invalidation of the Migratory Bird Rule, however, and the suspicion that all isolated waters might likewise be beyond the CWA's jurisdiction, there is a premium on finding a wetland to be "adjacent." The Corps' regulation defines "adjacent" as "bordering, contiguous, or neighboring. Wetlands separated from other waters of the United States by man-made dikes or barriers, natural river berms, beach dunes and the like are 'adjacent wetlands.'" Bordering and contiguous seem pretty clear, but neighboring might be construed to be a little broader, such as "in the neighborhood." Even if we understand what "adjacent" means, the question then becomes: adjacent to what? In *SWANCC* Chief Justice Rehnquist's opinion for the Court characterizes *Riverside Bayview* at one point as upholding jurisdiction over a wetland that "actually abutted on a navigable waterway" and at another point as upholding jurisdiction over a wetland adjacent to "open water." And it is true that both these phrases occur in *Riverside Bayview*. Such a reading would seem to limit adjacent wetlands to those directly adjacent to actually navigable waters. Nevertheless, it is possible to read *Riverside Bayview* more liberally, for example, to approve CWA jurisdiction over wetlands adjacent to any other water within the Corps' definition of waters of the United States, including tributaries that ultimately feed into actually navigable waters. The lower courts that have faced this question since *SWANCC* have split on the issue, although most have taken the more liberal approach. *Compare In re Needham*, 354 F.3d 340 (5th Cir. 2003)(denying CWA jurisdiction to tributaries that are neither navigable themselves nor adjacent to truly navigable waters) *with United States v. Deaton*, 332 F.3d 698 (4th Cir. 2003)(upholding CWA jurisdiction over a wetland adjacent to a roadside ditch whose waters eventually reached a navigable water 8 miles away); *United States v. Rapanos*, 339 F.3d 447 (6th Cir. 2003)(same for a ditch 11 miles upstream from the actually navigable waterway); *and Headwaters, Inc. v. Talent Irrigation Dist.*, 243 F.3d 526 (9th Cir. 2001)(irrigation canal that exchanged water with natural streams and at least one lake was subject to CWA).

6. In some of these cases the government has put more effort into characterizing the wetland not as adjacent to navigable waters but as itself a tributary, because of a hydrological connection whereby water drains from the wetland through ditches and/or creeks ultimately into an actually navigable water. In this regard the government has stressed the language in *SWANCC* suggesting that CWA jurisdiction extends to waters that have a "substantial nexus" with an actually navigable water. Which do you think is the stronger approach?

7. While *SWANCC* requires us to ask which wetlands are covered by the CWA, there is also a question as to what is a "wetland." It is not a term generally used in the CWA—its one appearance is in Section 404(g)(1), which exempts wetlands adjacent to traditional navigable waters from state administration pursuant to an EPA delegation—much less defined there. Since 1977 the Corps and EPA have defined "wetlands" in their regulations as: "those areas that are inundated or saturated by surface or ground water at a

frequency and duration sufficient to support, and that under normal circumstances do support, a prevalence of vegetation typically adapted for life in saturated soil conditions. Wetlands generally include swamps, marshes, bogs, and similar areas." 33 CFR 328.3(b); 40 CFR § 230.3(t). The devil, however, is in the details. In order to provide guidance to its field offices and hopefully to achieve some consistency in administration, the Corps in 1987 adopted a Wetlands Delineation Manual, essentially describing how one went about establishing the elements of a wetland so that wetlands could be identified and their boundaries established. EPA, however, was not satisfied with the Manual, and there were two other agencies identifying wetlands on the ground that each had their own method—the Department of Agriculture's Natural Resources Conservation Service is responsible for enforcing the Swampbuster law described later in this chapter, and the Department of Interior's Fish and Wildlife Service is charged with mapping the nation's wetlands. An interagency task force in 1989 came up with a new Manual, the effect of which was to reduce the number of criteria needed to find an area to be a wetland. In other words, the new manual effectively enlarged the areas subject to wetlands regulation by a more inclusive form of identifying wetlands. This effect resulted in substantial opposition from the usual suspects—farmers and developers generally—in part because the new manual had been adopted without public notice and comment. As consequence, a new interagency task force under the leadership of then-Vice President Dan Quayle was created. In August 1991, the new task force published a proposed manual for public notice and comment. The comment was devastating. Whatever enlargement of regulated wetlands was the effect of the 1989 manual, the 1991 proposed manual would have undone, and wetlands jurisdiction would have been so difficult to establish that it appeared that the Florida Everglades would no longer be protected. At this point, Congress stepped in and directed that the 1987 manual be the basis for Section 404 jurisdiction until such time as the National Academy of Sciences could make a study of the issue, which could then form the basis for any further action. The Academy issued its report in 1995, generally confirming the validity of the methods used in both the 1987 and 1989 manuals, but recommending that one manual be used by all agencies. The 1987 manual is still in use today by the Corps. Even if the same manual were used, however, different agencies might still reach different results in terms of the boundaries of a wetland because of the inevitable exercise of judgment the manual requires. For persons subject to regulation by more than one agency, such disparate results did not engender confidence. To improve matters, during the Clinton administration, the Natural Resources Conservation Service was made the lead agency for identifying and delineating wetlands in "agricultural areas," although it would continue to use its delineation manual rather than the Corps',and the Corps was made the lead agency for identifying and delineating wetlands in all other areas. Thus, only one agency would generally be making the delineation, so conflicts between agencies should occur less frequently.

2.   What Activities are Covered?

Just as the CWA only protects "navigable waters," defined as "waters of the United States, including the territorial seas," it only protects those waters from a "discharge of any pollutant," and "a discharge of a pollutant" is defined as "the addition of any pollutant from a point source." 33 U.S.C. § 1352(12). In the discussion of the NPDES program, we discovered that there could be some problems in interpreting what the "addition" of a pollutant means. For example, the recent case of *South Florida Water Management Dist. v. Miccosukee Tribe of Indians*, 541 U.S. 95, 124 S.Ct. 1537, 158 L.Ed.2d 264 (2004), concluded that the taking of waters from one water body and returning them unaltered to the same water body could not be the "addition of any pollutant." Section 404's application has also raised questions about the meaning of "addition."

Recall that Section 404 provides for a permit for the addition of two types of pollutants—fill material and dredged material. Clearly, if a dump truck full of dirt backs up to a covered wetland and dumps the dirt into the water, there has been an "addition of any pollutant from a point source," either fill material or dredged material, if the material had earlier been taken out of waters. On the other hand, if someone sinks a well near to the wetland and pumps ground water out of the ground, resulting in a covered wetland's water disappearing, it seems difficult to find any "addition" of anything, even though the wetland has been destroyed just as if dry fill had been trucked in and dumped into the wetland. *See Save Our Community v. U.S. EPA*, 971 F.2d 1155 (5th Cir. 1992). Between those two extremes, however, there is a vast gray area.

A relatively early case, *Avoyelles Sportsmen's League v. Marsh*, 715 F.2d 897 (5th Cir. 1983), held that mechanized landclearing and leveling that involved bulldozing of high spots into low spots of a wetland constituted a redeposit of soil and, therefore, an addition of a pollutant. Developers and farmers retaliated by digging channels or ditches in wetlands to drain wetlands, but "sidecasting," in which the material dug out of the ditch in the wetland is placed alongside the ditch, was then also considered the redeposit of soil, or the addition of a pollutant. While this approach was generally accepted by other courts, some questioned whether the mere redeposit or moving of soil from one place in a wetland to another constituted an "addition" of a pollutant. *See, e.g., United States v. Wilson,* 133 F.3d 251, 258–260 (4th Cir. 1997)(Opinion of Niemeyer for himself).

Nevertheless, if developers or farmers took the expense of trucking away the material dug out of the ditch, the Corps initially believed that they escaped regulation. In response to a suit by environmentalists, however, the Corps reconsidered its position and adopted a regulation, known as the Tulloch Rule, after the name of the case that inspired it. This regulation effectively subjected all mechanical digging or earth movement in a wetland to be the addition of a pollutant, which led to the following case.

NATIONAL MINING ASSOCIATION v. U.S. ARMY CORPS OF ENGINEERS

United States Court of Appeals, District of Columbia Circuit, 1998.

145 F.3d 1399.

STEPHEN F. WILLIAMS, Circuit Judge:

[I]n 1986 the Corps issued a regulation defining the term "discharge of dredged material," as used in § 404, to mean "any addition of dredged material into the waters of the United States," but expressly excluding "*de minimis,* incidental soil movement occurring during normal dredging operations." In 1993, responding to litigation, the Corps issued a new rule removing the *de minimis* exception and expanding the definition of discharge to cover "any addition of dredged material into, *including any redeposit of dredged material within,* the waters of the United States." (emphasis added). Redeposit occurs when material removed from the water is returned to it; when redeposit takes place in substantially the same spot as the initial removal, the parties refer to it as "fallback." In effect the new rule subjects to federal regulation virtually all excavation and dredging performed in wetlands.

The plaintiffs, various trade associations whose members engage in dredging and excavation, mounted a facial challenge to the 1993 regulation, claiming that it exceeded the scope of the Corps's regulatory authority under the Act by regulating fallback. The district court agreed and granted summary judgment for the plaintiffs ... We affirm....

The 1993 rulemaking under challenge here was prompted by a lawsuit, *North Carolina Wildlife Federation v. Tulloch* (E.D. N.C.1992), concerning a developer who sought to drain and clear 700 acres of wetlands in North Carolina. Because the developer's efforts involved only minimal incidental releases of soil and other dredged material, the Corps's field office personnel determined that, under the terms of the 1986 regulation, § 404's permit requirements did not apply. Environmental groups, concerned by what they viewed as the adverse effects of the developer's activities on the wetland, filed an action seeking enforcement of the § 404 permit requirement. As part of the settlement of the *Tulloch* case (a settlement to which the developer was not a party), the two administering agencies agreed to propose stiffer rules governing the permit requirements for landclearing and excavation activities. The result—the regulation at issue here—has come to be called the "*Tulloch* Rule."

As mentioned above, the *Tulloch* Rule alters the preexisting regulatory framework primarily by removing the *de minimis* exception and by adding coverage of incidental fallback. Specifically, the rule defines "discharge of dredged material" to include "[a]ny addition, *including any redeposit,* of dredged material, including excavated material, into waters of the United States which is incidental to any activity, including mechanized landclearing, ditching, channelization, or other excavation."

The *Tulloch* Rule does have its own *de minimis* exception, but it is framed in terms of the Act's overall goals. A permit is not required for "any incidental addition, including redeposit, of dredged material associated with any activity that does not have or would not have the effect of destroying or degrading an area of waters of the United States." Persons engaging in "mechanized landclearing, ditching, channelization and other excavation activity," however, bear the burden of proving to the Corps that their activities would not have destructive or degrading effects. Degradation is defined as any effect on the waters of the United States that is more than *de minimis* or inconsequential. Thus, whereas the 1986 rule exempted *de minimis* soil movement, the *Tulloch* Rule covers all discharges, however minuscule, unless the Corps is convinced that the *activities with which they are associated* have only minimal adverse effects. In promulgating the new rule the Corps "emphasize[d] that the threshold of adverse effects for the *de minimis* exception is a very low one."

It is undisputed that by requiring a permit for *"any* redeposit" (emphasis added), the *Tulloch* Rule covers incidental fallback. According to the agencies, incidental fallback occurs, for example, during dredging, "when a bucket used to excavate material from the bottom of a river, stream, or wetland is raised and soils or sediments fall from the bucket back into the water." (There is no indication that the rule would not also reach soils or sediments falling out of the bucket even *before* it emerged from the water.) Fallback and other redeposits also occur during mechanized landclearing, when bulldozers and loaders scrape or displace wetland soil, as well as during ditching and channelization, when draglines or backhoes are dragged through soils and sediments. Indeed, fallback is a practically inescapable by-product of all these activities. In the preamble to the *Tulloch* Rule the Corps noted that "it is virtually impossible to conduct mechanized landclearing, ditching, channelization or excavation in waters of the United States without causing incidental redeposition of dredged material (however small or temporary) in the process." As a result, the *Tulloch* Rule effectively requires a permit for all those activities, subject to a limited exception for ones that the Corps in its discretion deems to produce no adverse effects on waters of the United States.

The plaintiffs claim that the *Tulloch* Rule exceeds the Corps's statutory jurisdiction under § 404, which, as we have noted, extends only to "discharge," defined as the "addition of any pollutant to navigable waters." It [*sic*] argues that fallback, which returns dredged material virtually to the spot from which it came, cannot be said to constitute an *addition* of anything. Therefore, the plaintiffs contend, the *Tulloch* Rule conflicts with the statute's unambiguous terms and cannot survive even the deferential scrutiny called for by *Chevron U.S.A., Inc. v. NRDC....*

The agencies argue that the terms of the Act in fact demonstrate that fallback may be classified as a discharge. The Act defines a discharge as the addition of any pollutant to navigable waters, and defines "pollutant" to include "dredged spoil," as well as "rock," "sand," and "cellar dirt." The Corps in turn defines "dredged material" as "material that is excavated or dredged from waters of the United States," a definition that is not challenged here. Thus, according to the agencies, wetland soil, sediment, debris or other material in the waters of the United States undergoes a legal metamorphosis during the dredging process, becoming a "pollutant" for purposes of the Act. If a portion of the material being dredged then falls back into the water, there has been an addition of a pollutant to the waters of the United States. Indeed, according to appellants National Wildlife Federation *et al.* ("NWF"), who intervened as defendants below, this reasoning demonstrates that regulation of redeposit is actually *required* by the Act.

We agree with the plaintiffs, and with the district court, that the straightforward statutory term "addition" cannot reasonably be said to encompass the situation in which material is removed from the waters of the United States and a small portion of it happens to fall back. Because incidental fallback represents a net withdrawal, not an addition, of material, it cannot be a discharge.... The agencies' primary counterargument—that fallback constitutes an "addition of any pollutant" because material becomes a pollutant only upon being dredged—is ingenious but unconvincing. Regardless of any legal metamorphosis that may occur at the moment of dredging, we fail to see how there can be an addition of *dredged material* when there is no addition of *material*. Although the Act includes "dredged spoil" in its list of pollutants, Congress could not have contemplated that the attempted removal of 100 tons of that substance could constitute an addition simply because only 99 tons of it were actually taken away....

NWF complains that our understanding of "addition" reads the regulation of dredged material out of the statute. They correctly note that since dredged material comes from the waters of the United States, any discharge of such material into those waters could technically be described as a "redeposit," at least on a broad construction of that term. The Fifth Circuit made a similar observation fifteen years ago: " '[D]redged' material is by definition material that comes from the water itself. A requirement that all pollutants must come from outside sources would effectively remove the dredge-and-fill provision from the statute." *Avoyelles Sportsmen's League v. Marsh.* But we do not hold that the Corps may not legally regulate some forms of redeposit under its § 404 permitting authority. We hold only that by asserting jurisdiction over "*any* redeposit," including incidental fallback, the *Tulloch* Rule outruns the Corps's statutory authority. Since the Act sets out no bright line between incidental fallback on the one hand and regulable redeposits on the other, a reasoned attempt by the agencies to draw such a line would merit considerable deference. But the *Tulloch* Rule makes no effort to draw such a line, and indeed its overriding purpose appears to be to expand the Corps's permitting authority to encompass incidental fallback and, as a result, a wide range of activities that cannot remotely be said to "add" anything to the waters of the United States....

Perhaps the strongest authority for the agencies' position is *Ryba-chek v. EPA*, 904 F.2d 1276 (9th Cir.1990). There the Ninth Circuit found that the Act permitted EPA to regulate placer mining, a process in which miners excavate dirt and gravel in and around waterways, and, after extracting the gold, discharge the leftover material back into the water. *Rybachek* held that the material separated from gold and released into the stream constituted a pollutant, and, to the extent that "the material discharged originally comes from the streambed itself, [its] resuspension [in the stream] may be interpreted to be an addition of a pollutant under the Act." *Rybachek* would help the agencies if the court had held that imperfect extraction, i.e., extraction accompanied by inci-dental fallback of dirt and gravel, constituted "addition of a pollutant," but instead it identified the regulable discharge as the discrete act of dumping leftover material into the stream after it had been pro-cessed....

In a press release accompanying the adoption of the *Tulloch* Rule, the White House announced: "Congress should amend the Clean Water Act to make it consistent with the agencies' rulemaking." While remark-able in its candor, the announcement contained a kernel of truth. If the agencies and NWF believe that the Clean Water Act inadequately pro-tects wetlands and other natural resources by insisting upon the pres-ence of an "addition" to trigger permit requirements, the appropriate body to turn to is Congress. Without such an amendment, the Act simply will not accommodate the *Tulloch* Rule. The judgment of the district court is *Affirmed*.

Notes and Comments

1. The court says it is not holding that the Corps and EPA cannot regulate *some* redeposits as additions, just that they cannot regulate all redeposits, including incidental fallback. What redeposits do you think the Corps and EPA can still regulate?

2. After the *National Mining* case, the Corps and EPA undertook a rulemaking to address the court's injunction against enforcing the Tulloch Rule. The outcome of that rulemaking was to exempt incidental fallback from the definition of "discharge of dredged material," but to add a new paragraph to the definition as follows: "The Corps and EPA regard the use of mechanized earth-moving equipment to conduct landclearing, ditching, channelization, in-stream mining or other earth-moving activity in waters of the United States as resulting in a discharge of dredged material unless project-specific evidence shows that the activity results in only incidental fallback." 33 CFR § 323.2 (d)(2)(i). How is this different from the Tulloch Rule in its coverage? This new rule was immediately challenged by the same interests that challenged the Tulloch Rule, but that suit has been indefinite-ly stayed.

3. Although the court in *National Mining* does not raise the issue, is there any problem with the fact that, even if the incidental fallback could be considered an "addition of a pollutant," the fallback or redeposit of dredged material is not what causes the damage to the wetland? Rather, it is the

ditch that drains the water out. Compare that to the facts in the *Rybachek* case, where it was the discharge of the left over material taken out of the water for mining purposes that affected the quality of the water. Should Section 404 regulate redeposits of dredged material when the redeposit does not cause harm to the wetlands but the associated activity (ditching and draining) does? By its terms, the CWA requires permits (either NPDES or 404) whenever there is a discharge of a pollutant, whether or not the discharge adversely affects the waters. Indeed, if the discharge does not adversely affect the waters, that would be a basis for granting the permit.

4. *National Mining* was not the last word on the "addition" question by any means. In 2000, the Fourth Circuit confirmed that the Corps could regulate sidecasting in the case of *United States v. Deaton*, 209 F.3d 331, 335–36 (4th Cir. 2000), saying:

> The Deatons seize on the word "addition" in the phrase "addition of any pollutant" in the statutory definition of discharge. They argue that the "ordinary and natural meaning of 'addition' means something added, i.e., the addition of something not previously present." Thus, according to the Deatons, no pollutant is discharged unless there is an "introduction of new material into the area, or an increase in the amount of a type of material which is already present." Wilson, 133 F.3d at 259 (op. of Niemeyer, J.). Because sidecasting results in no net increase in the amount of material present in the wetland, the Deatons argue, it does not involve the "addition" (or discharge) of a pollutant. See National Mining Ass'n v. U.S. Army Corps of Engineers, 145 F.3d 1399, 1404 (D.C.Cir.1998) ("[W]e fail to see how there can be an addition of dredged material when there is no addition of material."). We are not convinced by this argument.

> Contrary to what the Deatons suggest, the statute does not prohibit the addition of material; it prohibits "the addition of any pollutant." The idea that there could be an addition of a pollutant without an addition of material seems to us entirely unremarkable, at least when an activity transforms some material from a nonpollutant into a pollutant, as occurred here. In the course of digging a ditch across the Deaton property, the contractor removed earth and vegetable matter from the wetland. Once it was removed, that material became "dredged spoil," a statutory pollutant and a type of material that up until then was not present on the Deaton property. It is of no consequence that what is now dredged spoil was previously present on the same property in the less threatening form of dirt and vegetation in an undisturbed state. What is important is that once that material was excavated from the wetland, its redeposit in that same wetland added a pollutant where none had been before. Thus, even under the definition of "addition" (that is, "something added") offered by the Deatons, sidecasting adds a pollutant that was not present before.

Can *Deaton* be reconciled with *National Mining*, or does this represent a split in the circuits?

5. The Ninth Circuit, in *Borden Ranch Partnership v. U.S. Army Corps of Engineers*, 261 F.3d 810 (9th Cir. 2001), a split decision, followed the logic of *Deaton* with regard to a practice known as "deep ripping." The dissent

would have followed and extended *National Mining*. In *Borden Ranch* the Partnership wanted to destroy the wetlands on its ranch to make the land suitable for vineyards. The wetlands existed because of a restrictive layer of soil, which prevented the surface water from penetrating deeply into the soil. Deep ripping involves the dragging of four-to seven-foot long metal prongs through the soil behind a tractor or a bulldozer. The ripper gouges through the restrictive layer, disgorging soil that is then dragged behind the ripper. This then allows the surface water to drain away into the ground. The court said:

> In this case, the Corps alleges that Tsakopoulos has essentially poked a hole in the bottom of protected wetlands. That is, by ripping up the bottom layer of soil, the water that was trapped can now drain out. While it is true, that in so doing, no new material has been "added," a "pollutant" has certainly been "added." Prior to the deep ripping, the protective layer of soil was intact, holding the wetland in place. Afterwards, that soil was wrenched up, moved around, and redeposited somewhere else. We can see no meaningful distinction between this activity and the activities at issue in Rybachek and Deaton.

261 F.3d at 815. The court then added a footnote:

National Mining Assoc. v. U.S. Army Corps of Eng'rs, upon which [the Partnership] heavily relies, does not persuade us to the contrary. That case distinguished "regulable redeposits" from "incidental fallback." Here, the deep ripping does not involve mere incidental fallback, but constitutes environmental damage sufficient to constitute a regulable redeposit.

Do you think "deep ripping" is like "sidecasting"?

6. That was not the end of the story, however. The Supreme Court granted certiorari in the case and then affirmed by an equally divided Court, when Justice Kennedy recused himself. Why do you think the Court granted certiorari? When the Court affirms by a split vote, it has no precedential value; no opinion is written; and no notation is made as to how the Justices voted. Court watchers feel confident that the Chief Justice and Justices O'Connor, Scalia, and Thomas voted to reverse, with Justices Stevens, Souter, Breyer, and Ginsburg voting to affirm. One must wonder whether *Borden Ranch* is a harbinger of things to come in a case where Justice Kennedy will cast a deciding vote.

7. An issue that has not received the same attention as the "addition" requirement is what constitutes a "point source." It is, after all, only additions of a pollutant "from any point source" that trigger a permit requirement under either the NPDES program or the 404 program. Recall that "point source" is a defined term in the CWA, 33 U.S.C. § 1362(14), that means: "any discernible, confined and discrete conveyance, including but not limited to any pipe, ditch, channel, tunnel, conduit, well, discrete fissure, container, rolling stock, concentrated animal feeding operation, or vessel or other floating craft, from which pollutants are or may be discharged." The list of items are said to be "included" within the meaning of a "discernible, confined and discreet conveyance"—the basic definition of "point source." Most of the listed items do not seem applicable to the discharge of dredged and fill material. Obviously, the dump truck emptying its load is a discerni-

ble, confined, and discrete conveyance, even if it is not clearly a listed item. However, most of the pieces of heavy equipment used for moving earth to destroy wetlands, such as bulldozers, backhoes, and deep ripping machines, are not so obviously "conveyances" at all. However, it might be said that heavy equipment is a "conveyance" to the extent that it moves (conveys) the earth from one place to another. Neither EPA nor the Corps has attempted a regulatory definition that goes beyond the statutory definition.

3. Exceptions from the Permit Requirement

Section 404(f), 33 U.S.C. § 1344(f), specifically exempts some activities from Section 404, even though they may involve the addition of dredged or fill material to jurisdictional waters. The most controversial exceptions are for: "normal farming, silviculture, and ranching activities such as plowing, seeding, cultivating, minor drainage, harvesting for the production of food, fiber, and forest products." 33 U.S.C. § 1344(f)(1)(A). On its face, this language might suggest that one could destroy wetlands so long as one was engaged in "normal farming." Indeed, the Partnership in *Borden Ranch* made that argument in its case. Paragraph (2) of the same subsection, however, known as the "recapture provision," limits the "normal farming" exception by stating that:

> Any discharge of dredged or fill material into the navigable waters incidental to any activity having as its purpose bringing an area of the navigable waters into a use to which it was not previously subject, where the flow or circulation of navigable waters may be impaired or the reach of such waters be reduced, shall be required to have a permit under this section.

To destroy wetlands (at least wetlands that are within the statutory requirement of being waters of the United States) necessarily reduces the reach of those waters, so to destroy wetlands for the purpose of expanding one's farming (or silvicultural or ranching) activities does not obtain the benefit of the exception. In *Borden Ranch*, the Partnership wanted to change the wetlands, which had been used as pasture, into a vineyard, and this it could not do under the exception.

4. The 404 Permit

Under Section 404 the Corps can either issue individual permits for individual discharges of dredged or fill material, or it can issue general permits covering a category of discharges. Individual permits are issued by one of the 38 Corps districts. General permits are issued by Corps headquarters, by Corps divisions, or by Corps districts, depending on their nature. The Corps is required to provide "notice and opportunity for public hearings" before issuing either type of permit, 33 U.S.C. § 1344(a) & (e)(1), but by regulation the Corps has stated that normally there will be no public hearing unless the Corps believes that a hearing is "needed for making a decision." 33 CFR § 327.4 (a). Persons desiring a public hearing must convince the Corps that the hearing is needed.

Because the Corps issuance of a permit is a federal agency action, the Corps must perform the analysis required by NEPA, and if an endangered species may be present, the biological assessment required by the ESA. In addition, if the activity takes place in a coastal area, the Corps must receive a determination from the state that the action is consistent with the state's Coastal Zone Management Plan under the Coastal Zone Management Act, 16 U.S.C. § 1456, and if the activity might affect a historical site, the Corps must coordinate with the State Historic Preservation Office pursuant to the National Historic Preservation Act, 16 U.S.C. § 470f. Because the Corps' action is likely to affect the quality of waters, the Corps must also engage in consultation with the Fish & Wildlife Service under the Fish and Wildlife Coordination Act, 16 U.S.C. §§ 661–666c, and obtain a Section 401 certification from the state that the activity will not impair the state's water quality, 33 U.S.C. § 1341(a). Federal agencies that disagree with the Corps' proposed decision may request that the decision be "elevated" from the District level to the Assistant Secretary of the Army for Civil Works.

The issuance of permits depends on meeting two different substantive standards: the 404(b)(1) Guidelines developed by EPA and the "public interest" evaluation imposed by the Corps on itself. Section 404(b)(1), 33 U.S.C. § 1344(b)(1), requires that proposed permits should be assessed by the Corps according to guidelines developed by EPA in conjunction with the Corps. These guidelines were to be based on similar criteria to those used in setting guidelines for the disposal of pollutants in the ocean, *see* 33 U.S.C. § 1343(c). The ocean discharge criteria listed in the statute generally require the application of an alternatives analysis, and this is the essence of the 404(b)(1) Guidelines, *see* 40 CFR. § 230.10.

Finally, before the Corps may issue a 404 permit, EPA must have the opportunity to review it. Under Section 404(c), 33 U.S.C. § 1344(c), EPA has the authority to veto any permit issuance if EPA finds that it would have "an unacceptable adverse effect on municipal water supplies, shellfish beds and fishery areas (including spawning and breeding areas), wildlife, or recreational areas." Courts have interpreted this veto power broadly and have rejected attempts to require EPA to determine the unacceptability of the adverse effects by balancing them against the social and economic benefits of granting the permit. *See, e.g., James City County, Va. v. EPA*, 12 F.3d 1330 (4th Cir. 1993). EPA rarely needs to exercise this authority, however, because its potential use provides EPA with significant influence on the Corps' decision.

Section 404 does provide for a limited version of "cooperative federalism," *see* 33 U.S.C. § 1344(g). If a state provides assurances to EPA that under its state law it can administer a program in accordance with the requirements of Section 404, EPA authorizes the state to issue individual and general permits in lieu of the Corps. However, only two states, New Jersey and Michigan, have applied and been authorized to issue 404 permits in lieu of the Corps. There are two primary reasons for the lack of state interest. First, the state authorization is very limited. States cannot displace the Corps' authority to issue the 404 permits with respect to traditional navigable waters and their adjacent wetlands. Even before *SWANCC*, this did not leave many waters subject to state permitting; after *SWANCC* it would seem to leave only nonnavigable tributaries. Even with respect to those waters, EPA retains a veto authority over the state's permits. Second, unlike the NPDES program, states do not receive federal funds if they become authorized states. Whereas EPA does not have the infrastructure actually to administer in the states either the Clean Air Act or the NPDES program under the Clean Water Act, the Corps does have the infrastructure to administer Section 404, because of its historic and continuing permitting responsibility under the Rivers and Harbors Act and its residual permitting authority under Section 404 for traditionally navigable waters. That is, under the NPDES program, EPA needs states to administer the program; under the 404 Program, the Corps does not have that need. As with other pollution control statutes, Section 404 does not preclude states from providing protection beyond that in federal law. Many states have enacted laws to protect their wetlands, and the Court's decision in *SWANCC* provided an incentive for more to do so.

a. The 404(b)(1) Guidelines and the Public Interest Review

The substantive standards governing the decision whether a 404 permit should be issued are to be found in the 404(b)(1) Guidelines and the Corps' Public Interest review standards. The basic requirement of the Guidelines is that: "no discharge of dredged or fill material shall be permitted if there is a practicable alternative to the proposed discharge which would have less adverse impact on the aquatic ecosystem, so long as the alternative does not have other significant adverse environmental consequences." 40 CFR § 230.10(a). If the activity is not "water dependent," a practicable alternative to siting the activity in a special aquatic area (e.g., a wetland) is presumed to exist, but the permit applicant can rebut the presumption. That is, if the activity does not *need* to be near or on water, then it is presumed that there is alternative to filling a wetland or waters for the activity. Moreover, if there is a practicable alternative not located in a special aquatic area, its environmental effects are presumed to be less adverse than the its effects would be in the special aquatic area. Thus, for example, if a developer already owns a parcel that includes a wetlands, and he wishes to develop it for a strip mall and associated parking lot, there will be a presumption that there is an available alternative and practicable site not involving a wetlands, because the development is not wetlands dependent, and that such alternative would be less harmful to the environment.

Under the Guidelines, an alternative is "practicable" if "it is available and capable of being done after taking into consideration cost, existing technology, and logistics in light of overall project purposes." 40 CFR § 230.10(a)(2). Thus, cost and feasibility are factored into whether the discharge should be allowed. In our strip mall example, for instance, the developer may rebut the presumption that there is a non-wetlands alternative by showing that given the market area he proposes to serve and which would support stores that would locate in the strip mall, there is no other feasible location, perhaps because other locations are either too small or too expensive to make his project feasible. If he establishes these facts, then he will have satisfied the Guidelines requirement. The fact that he already owns the proposed site does not foreclose consideration of other possible sites, but the additional cost of purchasing one of those sites might make the alternative impracticable. If the developer came to the area with the intent to develop a strip mall and bought the property in question that contains the wetlands, while passing up the other sites, EPA maintains that the alternatives analysis should proceed from the time he entered the market, not the time he seeks the 404 permit. In other words, the analysis would assume he did not own any property and would consider whether the non-wetlands alternatives were practicable from that perspective. In the case of *Bersani v. U.S. EPA*, 850 F.2d 36 (2d Cir. 1988), the court upheld EPA's position.

As was the case with NEPA analyses, the applicant's project purposes must be respected, but they cannot be framed in too narrow a manner. For example, in our strip mall hypothetical, if the applicant had stated that his purpose was to create a strip mall with 37 stores and 370 parking places, this might be too restrictive. The proper analysis would be whether a profitable strip mall could be developed at an alternative site. If this only required 34 stores and 340 parking places, then a practicable alternative would be presumed to exist unless the developer demonstrated that there was no available site that would accommodate such a strip mall. On the other hand, the Corps' acceptance of a developer's claim, that in order to create a successful alpine destination resort (for skiing in the winter) it was necessary to have an associated 18–hole golf course (for the summer), was upheld in *Sylvester v. U.S. Army Corps of Engineers*, 882 F.2d 407 (9th Cir. 1989). This is an area in which the Corps' judgment, if reasonably explained, is likely to be upheld.

In any case, under the alternatives analysis, it is possible that a permit applicant could show that there was no practicable alternative to filling a wetland to build a strip mall and associated parking lot, but the Guidelines have a safety net: "no discharge of dredged or fill material shall be permitted which will cause or contribute to significant degradation of the waters of the United States." 40 CFR § 230.10(c). What constitutes a "significant degradation," nevertheless, is a matter of judgment, and there is little case law clarifying the concept. Again, this is an area where the Corps' judgment, if reasonably explained, is likely to be upheld.

Under the 404(b)(1) Guidelines, whenever a permit is granted, the permittee must provide for compensatory mitigation for any destruction to wetlands. In practice, this means that, for example, if an acre of wetlands were to be destroyed by the discharge, the permittee would have to restore or create more than an acre of similar wetlands in the area. For a period, it was not clear whether a permit applicant could avoid the alternatives analysis by promising compensatory mitigation, as one can avoid a "significant impact" decision under NEPA by compensatory mitigation actions. However, in 1980, the Corps and EPA entered a Memorandum of Agreement on the the so-called sequence of mitigation. First, the applicant must attempt to avoid impacts on wetlands to the extent practicable (the alternatives analysis); second, the applicant must minimize the impacts on wetlands; and only then, for whatever effects on wetlands remain, the applicant must provide compensatory mitigation.

For the past ten years there has been an attempt to encourage the creation of "mitigation banks," wetlands restored and recreated as an investment, which could then be used as a market from which developers could purchase mitigation credits to satisfy their compensatory mitigation requirements. The idea was to create a financial incentive for creating new or restoring formerly destroyed wetlands in light of an anticipated market demand for needed compensatory mitigation. While the jury is still out on the idea, it certainly did not achieve the success that was hoped for. First, creating and restoring wetlands has turned out to be harder than thought, and initial attempts that failed set a bad precedent. Second, in order for compensatory mitigation to compensate for losses, the new or restored wetlands must serve the same functions as the destroyed wetlands. Usually, although not always, this requires the compensation to be at least near the site of the destroyed wetlands, which severely limits the the potential market for wetlands banks.

The second substantive standard governing the Corps' issuance of 404 Permits is its "public interest" review. *See* 33 CFR § 320.4(a). This review only comes into play after consideration of the 404(b)(1) Guidelines, so that if a permit is to be denied under the Guidelines, there would be no public interest review. The Corps' "public interest" review traces its history to the Corps' administration of the Rivers and Harbors Act, where the statute had provided no meaningful standard for decision and the Corps invented the "public interest" review as the basis for decisions whether to issue permits under that statute. Because Section 404, through the mandated 404(b)(1) Guidelines, does provide a standard for decision, the legal basis for a separate, distinct review is unclear. Nevertheless, the Corps regulation provides one public interest review applicable to all Corps permit actions, whether under Section 404 or the Rivers and Harbors Act. It provides that:

> The decision whether to issue a permit will be based on an evaluation of the probable impacts, including cumulative impacts, of the proposed activity and its intended use on the public interest. Evaluation of the probable impact which the proposed activity may have on the public interest requires a careful weighing of all those factors which become relevant in each particular case. The benefits which reasonably may be expected to accrue from the proposal must be balanced against its reasonably foreseeable detriments.

33 CFR § 320.4(a)(1). The regulation then provides a list of more than 20 factors that should go into the balancing process. At least one lower court has held that the Corps does not have the authority under Section

404 to consider economic costs and benefits unrelated to the activity's effect on the environment. *Mall Properties, Inc. v. Marsh*, 672 F.Supp. 561 (D.Mass. 1987), *appeal dismissed*, 841 F.2d 440 (1st Cir. 1988). For most practical purposes, however, the factors stress environmental protection as in the public interest and the destruction of wetlands as contrary to the public interest, so the public interest review rarely adds much to the 404(b)(1) Guidelines analysis.

The following is a typical case applying the Guidelines.

FUND FOR ANIMALS, INC. v. RICE

United States Court of Appeals, Eleventh Circuit, 1996.

85 F.3d 535.

DUBINA, Circuit Judge:

The Plaintiffs–Appellants ("the Plaintiffs"), seek to prevent the construction of a municipal landfill on a site in Sarasota County, Florida.... The Plaintiffs bring this case before us to challenge the district court's grant of summary judgment in favor of the Defendants–Appellees ("the Defendants"). The district court's challenged judgment has thus far allowed Sarasota County to proceed with construction of the landfill. For the reasons stated below, we affirm the district court's judgment.

I. BACKGROUND

* * *

B. *The Landfill*

On November 22, 1989, the United States Army Corps of Engineers ("the Corps") received an application from Sarasota County, Florida ("Sarasota County" or "the County") for a permit under Section 404 of the Clean Water Act ("CWA"). The proposed project for which Sarasota County sought a permit consists of constructing an 895–acre landfill and required ancillary structures on a 6,150–acre site known as the "Walton Tract." The Walton Tract is located in west central Sarasota County, north of the Caloosahatchee River, west of the Myakka River, and just southwest of the Myakka River State Park. According to current projections, the fill material for the landfill will impact approximately seventy-four acres of isolated wetlands. The project also includes construction of a roadway extension ("the Knights Trail Road extension"), consisting of approximately 2.5 miles of new road and impacting 0.47 acres of wetlands.

During June of 1990, the Corps dispersed notice of Sarasota County's application to government agencies, private organizations, and other interested persons. The notice invited public comment on the landfill proposal. [T]he Environmental Protection Agency ("the E.P.A.") recommended denial of the permit under Section 404(b)(1) of the guidelines promulgated pursuant to the Clean Water Act. At that time, Sarasota County projected that the landfill would affect 120 acres of wetlands.

The following year, Sarasota County submitted an alternative analysis, which included modifications of the project calculated to reduce the prospective effect on wetlands. Four sites, labeled D, E, F (the Walton Tract), and G, were proposed for the landfill. During September of 1993, Sarasota County submitted a revised plan that would reduce the landfill's effect on wetlands from 120 acres to approximately seventy-four acres. In February of 1994, the E.P.A. notified the Corps that it no longer objected to the issuance of the permit.

At the end of May 1994, the Corps completed an Environmental Assessment and Statement of Findings, determining that no environmental impact statement was required. In addition, the Corps announced that a public hearing would not benefit the decision-making process. After nearly five years of administrative review, the Corps approved the requested permit on June 3, 1994. On August 10, 1994, the Corps verified the applicability of Nationwide Permit No. 26 to Sarasota County's proposal to fill 0.47 acre of wetlands as part of the Knight's Trail Road extension project.

On June 17, 1994, the Plaintiffs submitted a sixty-day notice of intent to sue. The Plaintiffs alleged violations of the Clean Water Act and the Endangered Species Act ("ESA"). Two months later, the F.W.S. requested resumption of § 7 consultation under the ESA to allow consideration of any potential effect on the Florida Panther and the Eastern Indigo Snake. In October of 1994, the F.W.S. issued its first Biological Opinion addressing concerns regarding the Florida Panther and the Eastern Indigo Snake. The Opinion concluded that the project was unlikely to jeopardize further the existence of either the Florida Panther or the Eastern Indigo Snake. However, it did include an "incidental take" statement for the Eastern Indigo Snake and recommendations for Florida Panther conservation, wetland preservation, and a monitoring program. The Corps incorporated the F.W.S.'s recommendations and modified Sarasota County's permit on November 14, 1994. Two weeks later, the Plaintiffs commenced an action in federal district court against the Corps, the F.W.S., the E.P.A., and the Sarasota County Administrator.

In response to the suit, the F.W.S. requested that the Corps resume § 7 consultation on the permit. The Corps suspended Sarasota County's permit the next day, and on February 7, 1995, the Corps also suspended its verification of coverage for discharge of fill associated with the Knight's Trail Road extension project. In April of 1995, the F.W.S. issued to the Corps its second Biological Opinion addressing concerns regarding the Florida Panther and the Eastern Indigo Snake. The Opinion included both an "incidental take" statement for the Eastern Indigo Snake and conservation recommendations for the Florida Panther. This Opinion, which superseded the F.W.S.'s previous Biological Opinion, again concluded that the proposed project was unlikely to jeopardize the continued existence of either the Florida Panther or the Eastern Indigo Snake.

On April 12, 1995, the Plaintiffs submitted comments to the Corps on the F.W.S.'s new Biological Opinion. The next day, the Corps determined, based on the F.W.S.'s Biological Opinion and the Corps' independent environmental assessment, that reinstatement of the permit to dredge and fill seventy-four acres of wetlands with additional modifications was in the public interest. Thus, the modified permit was reinstated on April 13, 1995.

Following final issuance of the permit, the Plaintiffs filed their Second Amended Complaint, which raised claims under the Clean Water Act, the Endangered Species Act, and the National Environmental Policy Act ("NEPA"). The complaint requested declaratory and injunctive relief. . . .

On October 12, 1995, the district court granted summary judgment in favor of Sarasota County and denied the Plaintiffs' contingent request for discovery. The Plaintiffs filed a notice of appeal and asked this court to grant an emergency injunction prohibiting Sarasota County from commencing construction of the new facility until resolution of the appeal. This court denied the Plaintiffs' emergency motion for an injunction pending appeal in an order dated October 26, 1995, and set an expedited briefing schedule.

II. STATEMENT OF THE ISSUES

(1) Whether the district court erred in finding that the Corps did not act arbitrarily or capriciously in making the following . . . decision[]:

A.   to grant a permit to fill seventy-four acres of wetland on the Walton Tract for a county landfill. . . .

B.   not to hold its own public hearing on the project.

III. STANDARDS OF REVIEW

The standard of review applicable to the main issues in this case is provided by the Administrative Procedure Act ("APA"), 5 U.S.C. § 706, which states that a court may set aside agency action that is "arbitrary, capricious, an abuse of discretion, or otherwise not in accordance with law." . . .

IV. DISCUSSION

* * *

A. Challenges Under The Clean Water Act.

The CWA prohibits the discharge of pollutants, including dredged spoil, into the waters of the United States, except in compliance with various sections of the CWA, including Section 404. Section 404(a) authorizes the Secretary of the Army, acting through the Corps, to issue permits for the discharge of dredge or fill material into waters of the

United States. The Corps may issue individual permits on a case-by-case basis, or it may issue general permits on a state, regional, or nationwide basis.

The Plaintiffs allege that the Corps violated the substantive and procedural requirements of the CWA in three ways: (1) by not choosing an alternative site where the landfill would have a less adverse impact on wetlands; (2) by not considering the cumulative impact of the permitting decision; and (3) by not giving notice and an opportunity for a public hearing on the permit. We consider each of these contentions in turn.

1. *Alternative Sites*

The Plaintiffs' primary argument is that the Corps ignored alternative sites where the landfill would have had less of an impact on the aquatic ecosystem. Under applicable Section 404 guidelines, a discharge of dredge or fill will not be permitted if, among other things, there is a "practicable alternative" to the proposed discharge that would have a less adverse impact on the aquatic ecosystem. 40 C.F.R. § 230.10(a). An alternative is considered practicable if "it is available and capable of being done after taking into consideration cost, existing technology and logistics in light of overall project purposes." 40 C.F.R. § 230.10(a)(2). The guidelines create a rebuttable presumption that practicable alternatives are available where the activity associated with a proposed discharge would occur on a wetland and is not water dependent. 40 C.F.R. § 230.10(a)(3). If the Corps finds that the permit complies with the Section 404(b)(1) guidelines, the permit "will be granted unless the district engineer determines that it would be contrary to the public interest." 33 C.F.R. § 320.4(a)(1). The public interest review evaluates "the probable impacts, including cumulative impacts, of the proposed activity and its intended use on the public interest." *Id.*

According to the Plaintiffs, Sarasota County itself identified three such practicable alternatives, and use of any of these sites would result in less harm to the environment than use of the Walton Tract. The Plaintiffs rely heavily on a particular section of a 1991 study performed by Sarasota County in which the County considered alternatives to the Walton Tract. As part of this study, Sarasota County assigned a numerical "environmental score" to each of the four potential sites. The scoring system was designed to give higher scores to those sites most suited for a landfill. As the following point totals illustrate, the Walton Tract received the lowest numerical score of the four tracts in the analysis: Site D—39 points; Site E—39 points; Site F (the Walton Tract)—34 points; and Site G—41 points.

Nonetheless, the Plaintiffs' argument that an alternative to the Walton Tract should have been chosen is meritless for two reasons. First, the ranking was done by Sarasota County and not the Corps, and the Corps is not bound by an applicant's ranking system. In fact, the Corps conducts its own independent evaluation, and its practicable alternative analysis is not susceptible to numerical precision, but instead requires a balancing of the applicant's needs and environmental concerns.

Second, the Corps and Sarasota County point to numerous reasons to explain why, although the Walton Tract received the lowest environmental score, it was nonetheless the most suited for placement of a landfill. Specifically, our review of the record persuades us that the Corps did not act contrary to, but instead adhered to, the sequencing preference expressed in the CWA regulations: (1) avoidance, (2) minimization, and (3) compensatory mitigation. See 33 C.F.R. § 320.4(r); 40 C.F.R. § 230.10.

As its first task, the Corps determined that there was no alternative site available that would avoid any impact on wetlands. Had a suitable upland site existed, such a site would have been entitled to a presumption that it was a practical alternative. See 40 C.F.R. § 230.10(a)(3). Each of the four highest ranking sites contain scattered, isolated wetlands: Site D is 19% wetlands, Site E is 22% wetlands, Site G is 13% wetlands, and the Walton Tract is 22% wetlands. A landfill of 895 acres in Sarasota County would involve impacts on aquatic ecosystems (i.e., filling of wetlands) and raise the same Section 404 permitting concerns no matter which of the four sites was chosen. Since the Plaintiffs have not identified an 895–acre parcel of contiguous uplands in all of Sarasota County, it is not clear that the presumption established by 40 C.F.R. § 230.10(a)(3) would ever apply in this case.

The absence of a suitable upland site required the Corps to analyze all suitable alternatives. In this case, each of the alternative sites poses its own environmental problems which led the Corps to determine that it was less suitable for the landfill than the Walton Tract. Site D contains wetlands across its southern boundary, including the headwaters for a stream know as South Creek. The site contains ninety-two acres of wetlands, which is eighteen more acres of wetlands than would be filled by the project if done on the Walton Tract. Most notably, Site D is confirmed to be a nesting site for the Bald Eagle (Haliaeetus leucocephalus). Site E borders the Myakka River State Park and contains two large wetland systems that drain to both the Myakka River and a waterway called the Cow Pen Slough. Site E contains sixty-one acres of wetlands. Presence of a state listed species, the Florida Sandhill Crane (Grus canadensis), was confirmed on the site. Moreover, any landfill located on Site G would have been within the Myakka River watershed. The Corps noted the probable presence of the Eastern Indigo Snake on Site G, and Site G was also designated a "Priority 1 Florida Panther habitat."

By contrast, the Walton Tract possesses characteristics that the Corps considered to be significant environmental advantages. Each of the other sites is considerably smaller than the Walton Tract: Site D is 2,130 acres, Site E is 3,360 acres, and Site G is 2,100 acres. The Walton Tract is 6,150 acres. Thus, the site is large enough to provide a broad natural vegetative buffer around all sides of the landfill. The large size of the tract also allows a substantial buffer between the landfill and adjoining areas. Sarasota County has zoned approximately 2,971 acres on the site as a conservation area, which includes the most valuable areas of upland wetland habitat on the Walton Tract and adjoins other preserve areas off-site. These preserved lands combine with adjacent properties to form a continuous unit of potentially suitable Florida Panther habitat and serve as a barrier between the Myakka River ecosystem and further development from the west.

Where, as here, filling of wetlands cannot be avoided, then "appropriate and practicable steps" must be taken to minimize the potential adverse impacts of the discharge on wetlands. 40 C.F.R. § 230.10(d). While the original design of the landfill would have impacted approximately 120 acres, Sarasota County subsequently scaled down the project so that wetland impacts would be reduced to approximately seventy-four acres. Furthermore, although the project will eliminate approximately seventy-four acres of isolated wetlands, the large size of the Walton Tract allows on-site mitigation. Sarasota County is replacing the lost acreage with approximately seventy acres of wet prairie habitat in the northeast corner of the tract and enhancing and restoring an additional 262 acres of wetlands. While wetlands will be lost, a greater acreage of higher quality wetlands will be restored and enhanced, resulting in no net loss of wetland resources.

In discussing the alternatives analysis, the district court did not suggest, nor do we, that practicable alternatives may be ignored because of the mitigation potential of a site, as the Plaintiffs claim. To the contrary, the district court recognized, as do we, that the Corps had taken into account all the considerations which factor into the alternatives analysis. There is no substantial question as to whether Sarasota County needs a new landfill, because the County's current landfill must close in 1999. Sarasota County, the Corps, the F.W.S., and the E.P.A. all scrutinized the project for over five years, and all agree that the Walton Tract is the most suitable site for the new landfill. Accordingly, insofar as the CWA practicable alternatives analysis is concerned, we hold that the Plaintiffs failed to demonstrate that the Corps acted arbitrarily and capriciously in granting a permit to fill seventy-four acres of wetlands on the Walton Tract....

3. *Public Hearings*

The Plaintiffs' third argument under the CWA is that the Corps violated requirements by failing to provide the public "any hearings" on the landfill project and by failing to provide the public with information regarding possible effects of the project on the Florida Panther and the Eastern Indigo Snake. The CWA mandates an "opportunity for public hearings." However, the statute does not state that the Corps itself must hold its own public hearings regardless of how many other hearings have been held on a project. The applicable regulations provide the Corps discretion to hold hearings on permit applications on an "as needed" basis. 33 C.F.R. § 327.4. If the Corps determines that it has the information necessary to reach a decision and that there is "no valid interest to

be served by a hearing," the Corps has the discretion not to hold one. Id.
§ 327.4(b).

Here, the Corps recognized that two public hearings on the project
had already been conducted under the state process. Given the information generated from these hearings and the voluminous written information submitted to the Corps by opponents of the project, including the
Plaintiffs, the Corps concluded that holding its own additional public
hearing was unlikely to generate any new information that was not
already in the Corps' possession. Moreover, the Plaintiffs point to no
such information. Under these circumstances, we are persuaded that the
Corps did not act arbitrarily or abuse its discretion in deciding to forego
further public hearings on the matter. . . .

AFFIRMED.

Notes and Comments

1.   Edited from this case is the challenge to the permit based upon the
Endangered Species Act, in which the Fund for Animals alleged that the
Fish and Wildlife Service's Biological Opinion was arbitrary and capricious
in finding the landfill would not jeopardize the very rare and endangered
Florida Panther ("one of the most endangered large mammals in the world")
and the threatened Eastern Indigo Snake ("Measuring up to 8 1/2 feet, this
docile, nonpoisonous snake is the longest found in North America"). The
plaintiffs lost on that issue as well, but first their threat to bring a lawsuit
and then their filing of the lawsuit resulted in the Fish and Wildlife Service
taking a closer look and imposing conservation requirements regarding the
Panther and an incidental take statement for the snake that would not
otherwise have been included. Considering the alternative possible locations
for the landfill, do you think the plaintiffs were really concerned about the
wetlands or about the significant acreage involved at the Walton site?

2.   The court refers to the Walton Tract as involving "isolated wetlands." This case, of course is pre-*SWANCC*. After *SWANCC*, would Sarasota County even have needed to involve any of the Federal agencies before
using the Walton Tract as a landfill?

3.   How did the County rebut the presumption that a nonwater dependent activity has a practicable alternative?

4.   What about the Corps' denial of a public hearing on its permit? Do
you think Congress intended that a county's public hearing regarding the
siting of a landfill would satisfy the "opportunity for a public hearing"
requirement in Section 404? Does it not seem likely that the public hearing
opportunity called for in Section 404 was intended to address Section 404
issues, which probably would not be the focus of a county hearing? On the
other hand, if the plaintiffs cannot show any harm from being denied the
hearing, what would be the point. Perhaps the court's best response would
have been to have found the denial of a public hearing to be harmless error
in the circumstances. *See* 5 U.S.C. § 706. Nevertheless, the court's analysis
is typical of what other courts have held. *See, e.g., Friends of the Payette v.
Horseshoe Bend Hydroelectric Co.*, 988 F.2d 989, 996–97 (9th Cir. 1993). If a
hearing were to be held, what kind of hearing should it be? The Corps, when

it provides a hearing, always provides a legislative-type hearing, not a trial-type hearing.

5. In the course of the opinion, the court affirms the Corps' use of a nationwide permit to authorize the filling of .47 acres for road access to the land fill. The use of nationwide permits is discussed below.

b. General Permits and Alternative Procedures

While most of the focus of litigation has been on individual permits, most discharges actually take place under General Permits of one form or another. In FY 2002, for example, there were roughly 4000 individual 404 permits issued, but there were roughly 75,000 activities occurring under General Permits. General Permits are adopted after notice and comment and are good for up to five years. According to Section 404, a General Permit can be issued only if "the activities in such category are similar in nature, will cause only minimal adverse environmental effects when performed separately, and will have only minimal cumulative adverse effect on the environment." 33 U.S.C. § 1344(e)(1). The Corps by regulation seems to have expanded the statutory standard by adding an additional definition of "general permit" that eliminates the requirement that the activities subject to the permit be "similar in nature" but adds the requirement that the general permit would result in avoiding unnecessary duplication of regulatory control exercised by another Federal, state, or local agency. 33 CFR 323.2(h). There are three General Permits and one "alternative procedure" worth mentioning: Nationwide Permits, Regional Permits, State Programmatic General Permits, and Letters of Permission.

i. Nationwide Permits

Nationwide Permits (NWPs), issued by Corps headquarters, are probably the most important form of General Permit. *See generally* 33 CFR Part 330. In FY 2002, approximately 35,000 activities were authorized under NWPs. The current list of NWPs was adopted in 2002 and contains 44 NWPs. Until 2002 NWPs were published in the Code of Federal Regulations, but the Corps maintains that NWPs are permits, not rules, so it has ceased their publication in the CFR. They are available online. www.usace.army.mil/inet/functions/cw/cecwo/reg/ nationwide_permits.htm. Despite the Corps' insistence that the NWPs are not rules, the Corps adopts them after notice-and-comment, and the NWPs act in the nature of rules. That is, the NWPs establish on a generic basis that certain types of activities, if carried out in accordance with the terms in the NWPs, are permitted. Moreover, these NWPs are subject to general conditions. For example, persons must assure that state water quality certifications under Section 401, if required, have been obtained before the NWP is effective as to their activity. For discharges likely to have any effect on wetlands or water quality, the Corps requires Preconstruction Notification (PCN) to the District Engineer. This enables the District Engineer to review the particular proposed activity, including the proposed mitigation, to determine whether it raises environmental questions—in particular, whether the activity would have a significant adverse effect on waters or wetlands. The District Engineer is authorized to suspend, modify, or revoke any NWP if he determines that concerns for the environment make the NWP inappropriate in a particular case. If the NWP is revoked for a particular case, the person may still seek an individual 404 permit.

Some NWPs are uncontroversial. For example, NWP 36 authorizes the discharge of dredged and fill material for the creation of boat ramps, so long as the discharge does not exceed 50 cubic yards of an approved material and no discharge occurs in a wetland. NWP 29 authorizes natural persons to fill up to one-quarter acre of non-tidal waters for a single family residence.

There are several, however, that are controversial. Historically, NWP 26 generally authorized discharges to wetlands associated with isolated waters or headwaters so long as the discharge did not adversely affect more than a certain area. Originally, the area was 10 acres, which was reduced to 3 acres in 1996. Because the Corps required Preconstruction Notification (PCN) for discharges affecting greater than 1 acre originally and one-third acre in 1996, which notification could provide a basis for the Corps to remove the activity from the NWP and require an individual permit, the Corps believed the NWP was sufficiently protective. Nonetheless, environmentalists believed this NWP was a significant loophole, and the Corps promised to and did delete it in 2002. However, it replaced it with five new NWPs (NWPs 39, 41–44) that are activity specific: Residential, Commercial, and Institutional Developments; Reshaping Existing Drainage Ditches; Recreational Facilities; Stormwater Management Facilities; and Mining Activities. Because these new NWPs, especially the first, in essence recreate in most respects NWP 26 with slightly different area limitations, this change was opposed by environmentalists. At the same time, developers were not particularly pleased with the change either, because it did not loosen restrictions and in some ways tightened them. For example, developers cannot adversely affect more than one-half acre of non-tidal waters (including wetlands) or more than 300 linear feet of a stream and must provide a PCN if the activity affects more than one-tenth of an acre of non-tidal waters or causes the loss of any open waters.

Another NWP that is controversial is NWP 21, Surface Coal Mining Activities. This NWP originally authorized discharges associated with surface coal mining, so long as the coal mining was authorized by the Department of Interior or an approved state under the Surface Mining Control and Reclamation Act (SMCRA). This NWP has been the authorization for filling valleys with mining overburden associated with mountain-top removal mining. That is, the mining company literally removes the top of a mountain to obtain open access to the coal seam, and the mountain top is dumped into the adjoining valley, invariably covering streams and watersheds. This led to law suits challenging the Corps' authority to permit such activities, which concluded with a settlement agreement in 1998 that in West Virginia the NWP would not authorize valley fills burying a stream draining more than 250 acres and that the Corps and other federal agencies would undertake a Programmatic Environmental Impact Statement regarding mountain-top and valley-fill mining, an analysis that had not previously been done, and, at least of the date of this writing, yet to be completed. One can imagine why environmentalists were and are concerned.

The Corps has defended the concept of its NWP on the grounds that it is unnecessary bureaucratic duplication for it to review what has been reviewed and approved by a federal or state agency under SMCRA. Its latest NWP 21, however, issued in 2002, reflects an increased sensitivity to the issue. First, the NWP requires preconstruction notification to the District Engineer in all cases, and it further requires the District Engineer to determine that the adverse environmental effects of the activity are minimal both individually and cumulatively and must notify the project sponsor of this determination in writing before the activity may commence. Finally, the District Engineer must determine on a case-by-case basis the necessary mitigation to assure that effects to aquatic systems are minimal. In short, according to its NWP and implementing guidance, the Corps seems to engage in virtually the same review under NWP 21 as it would if it were an application for an individual permit.

Even were this so, it would not quell the fears of environmentalists. This is due to the procedural differences between an individual permit action and Corps review pursuant to a preconstruction notification under a NWP. The former requires notice and an opportunity for a public hearing, as well as triggering NEPA and other federal statutory provisions because the action is "federal agency action." The latter, however, does not involve public notice or comment. The issuance of the NWP itself was subject to notice, comment, and a public hearing. Because the "permit" has been issued, the Corps believes no further public participation is required in its review pursuant to the NWP. Moreover, the Corps maintains that its review after a preconstruction notification is not "federal agency action," triggering NEPA and other statutory requirements. Thus, in a sense, the Corps can have its cake and eat it too. That is, it can retain the ability to review actions to determine whether they should receive intensive review (i.e., individual permit treatment) without all the procedural requirements attendant to individual permit actions. If the Corps believes the action has no significant effect, the Corps can let it go forward with little resource demand on the Corps. When the Corps' review is only as to whether the activity should qualify for treatment under a NWP or should be handled as an individual permit action, the theory that this is not a separate agency action might be well founded. However, when the Corps is making substantive determinations, such as the requisite mitigation to require, its theory becomes more tenuous.

ii. Other General Permits and Letters of Permission

Nationwide Permits are not the only form of General Permit. Another form of General Permit is the Regional Permit, which is issued by Division or District Engineers. *See* 33 CFR § 325(e)(2). These are like NWPs except they are tailored for activities that are more regional or localized in nature. The concept, however, is the same; the Regional Permit authorizes a class of activities, and if an activity is within the terms of the Regional permit and complies with any condition placed on it, the activity may go forward without an individual permit. In FY 2002, there were approximately 38,000 activities authorized by Regional Permits.

Still another form of General Permit is the State Programmatic General Permit (SPGP). This is the Corps' preferred alternative to authorizing states to issue 404 Permits under Section 404(g). This permit relies on the additional definition of a General Permit in the Corps regulations because it is justified by a state having a regulatory program in place that makes the Corps permitting process an unnecessary duplication of regulatory control. If a state establishes to the Corps' satisfaction that its regulatory program operates in a fashion duplicative of the Corps' program, then the Corps can grant a SPGP covering all or some of the activities regulated by the state.

In theory at least, the Corps could in essence delegate its entire Section 404 authority to a state if it was convinced that the state would assure that no permit would individually or cumulatively have more than a minimal adverse effect on the environment. Because of the legal questions this would raise—in particular, the apparent evasion of the statutory procedure and limitation on state authorization to issue 404 permits and the difficulty of justifying the SPGP under the statutory requirement that general permits be for activities "similar in nature"— the Corps in practice has limited its SPGPs to activities of very limited effect. For example, in Vermont, one of the relatively few states with an SPGP, fills of under 1 acre are generally authorized if they comply with the state regulatory procedure. Many, if not most, of these activities are subject to PCNs to the Corps, however, and fills in certain specified waters or wetlands are only authorized if less than 5000 square feet are affected.

"Letters of Permission" (LOP) are in the Corps' terminology an alternative procedure for receiving an individual permit through abbreviated procedures and not involving publication of notice of the particular activity, but including coordination with appropriate federal and state agencies. *See* 33 CFR § 325.2(e)(1). In FY 2002, approximately 3000 LOPs were issued. Despite the Corps' characterization, which would raise serious questions under Section 404, which provides no authorization for such an alternative procedure, the Corps' practice makes LOPs look more like a form of general permit. That is, in order for a District Engineer to issue an LOP, the District Engineer must first, in coordination with federal and state wildlife agencies, develop a list of categories of activities proposed for authorization by LOP. The District Engineer must then publish that list and provide an opportunity for a public hearing and comment. An LOP can only be issued for an activity after the state has given any required 401 certification and CZMA consistency determination. On the face of the regulation there is no requirement that the adverse effect of the activity will be minimal, but before LOPs were authorized for Section 404, the Corps had issued them under Section 10 of the Rivers and Harbors Act, and the implementing regulations there specify that LOPs under Section 10 are authorized only when, in the opinion of the district engineer, the proposed work would be minor, would not have significant or cumulative impacts on environmental values, and should encounter no appreciable opposition. 33 CFR § 325.2(e)(1)(i). Why the same requirement is not made for Section 404 LOPs is unknown, but one might imagine that the Corps treats the two LOPs similarly.

Notes and Comments

1. As may be seen, the Corps approach to its Section 404 responsibilities has in many respects been informed (or distorted) by its experience under the Rivers and Harbors Act as well as the frequent overlap between Section 404 permits involving discharges of dredged and fill material and Section 10 Permits under the Rivers and Harbors Act involving obstructions to navigation. The geographic jurisdiction and the focus of the regulatory review is different between the two provisions, but there has perhaps been a tendency to treat them alike. In particular, the extension of the Corps' public interest review and the use of LOPs for Section 404 permitting, both developed under the Rivers and Harbors Act, are examples of such a tendency.

2. A recurrent theme in the Corps' handling of its permitting responsibilities is the attempt to streamline the procedural requirements while maintaining overall control of the process. The use of general permits of one sort or another combined with PCN requirements enables the Corps to deal with what it believes are routine and minor activities in a summary manner, even as it retains the discretionary authority to impose particular conditions or even to require individual permitting in individual cases the Corps deems appropriate. Because these summary procedures generally shortcut certain analyses and public procedures, environmentalists view them with significant skepticism, worrying that the Corps has been captured by agricultural or development interests.

3. Persons who have been denied permits (or offered permits upon conditions they find unacceptable or believe are unlawful) or who dispute a Corps determination that it has regulatory jurisdiction over a water body or wetland may file an administrative appeal with the Corps. *See* 33 CFR Part 331. Interested third persons, such as environmental groups or neighboring land owners, cannot administratively appeal any Corps determination. This is a relatively new procedure, adopted in 2000, after a five year rulemaking proceeding. Unlike most intra-agency review procedures, the review is not de novo. The reviewing official is to overturn the original decision only if on some relevant matter it was arbitrary, capricious, an abuse of discretion, not supported by substantial evidence in the administrative record, or plainly contrary to a requirement of law, regulation, an Executive Order, or officially promulgated Corps policy guidance. 33 CFR § 331.9(b). The reviewing official is one level higher than the deciding official, but the reviewing official

is not an independent administrative law judge. An issue that may be administratively appealed must be administratively appealed before the person may seek judicial review.

4. Enforcement of Section 404 generally occurs under the same provisions as enforcement of the NPDES program, including citizens suits, and is dealt with in the chapter on enforcement. There are a couple of idiosyncracies involved with respect to Section 404 enforcement, however, that deserve mention here. First, under the CWA the Administrator of EPA is given the authority for taking actions against persons who unlawfully discharge without a permit, whether the discharge involves dredged or fill material or any other pollutant. See 33 U.S.C. § 1319. The Corps (actually the Secretary of the Army, under the statute) is only responsible for enforcement against persons who violate the terms of the permit they receive under Section 404. See 33 U.S.C. § 1344(s). In 1989, the Corps and EPA entered into a Memorandum of Agreement relating to the division of enforcement responsibilities for Section 404. While it reflects the statutory division of responsibilities, by making EPA the lead agency for unpermitted discharges and the Corps the lead agency for permit violations, it recognizes the Corps' greater field resources and accordingly generally gives the Corps the lead responsibility for investigating possible unpermitted discharges and making initial determinations whether a permit was required. In addition, the MOA purports to allow EPA to enforce against permit violations when the Corps declines and the Corps to enforce against unpermitted discharges in more minor cases. Second, the citizen suit provision of the CWA allows for suits against persons who violate "an effluent standard or limitation" or an order by the Administrator or a state with respect to such a standard or limitation. 33 U.S.C. § 1365(a)(1). There is no mention of an order by the Secretary of the Army (or the Corps). "Effluent standard or limitation" is a defined term in the citizen suit provision, and it expressly includes a permit or condition thereof under Section 402 (the NPDES program) but does not include permits or conditions thereof under Section 404. See 33 U.S.C. § 1365(f). This perhaps suggests that citizens suits cannot be brought to enforce against Section 404 permit violations (as opposed to failures to get permits), but there is no case discussing the issue.

B. The Swampbuster Program

As indicated earlier, it was long the policy of the United States Government to encourage the filling of wetlands to increase agricultural acreage. Indeed, even after passage of the CWA in 1972, the Department of Agriculture was still encouraging the draining of wetlands for agricultural purposes. In 1985, however, Congress passed the Food Security Act of 1985, Pub. L. No. 99–198, 99 Stat.1504 (1985), which included a number of provisions intended to stop the conversion of wetlands to agricultural land. Primary among these was a portion of the Act known as the Swampbuster program. 16 U.S.C. §§ 3801, 3821–3824.

The Swampbuster program denies to farmers certain agricultural subsidies if they produce agricultural commodities on converted wetland. 16 U.S.C. § 3821. Because the agricultural subsidies are often critical to financial survival of farms, the possibility of withholding such subsidies can be as threatening as a potentially large civil penalty.

Until recently, there has not been much attention given to the Swampbuster program by environmentalists. However, because Swampbuster is subject neither to the jurisdictional limitation of "navigable waters" nor to the limitation that only "discharges" are prohibited, Swampbuster is becoming increasingly important as a protection for wetlands. At the same time, as government farm policy has turned toward restricting, if not eliminating, price supports for commodity crops, the government's leverage to induce protection of wetlands by farmers will be reduced.

Swampbuster is administered by two separate agencies in the Department of Agriculture. The Natural Resources Conservation Service (NRCS), formerly the Soil Conservation Service, is responsible for making wetland delineations after consultation with the Fish and Wildlife Service. As a result of a Memorandum of Agreement in 1994 between NRCS, the Corps, EPA, and the Fish and Wildlife Service, the NRCS's wetlands delineations in agricultural areas also govern Section 404 determinations. In making these delineations, the NRCS uses its own delineation manual, rather than the Corps 1987 Manual. In addition, the NRCS is responsible for other biological or geological determinations in administering Swampbuster. The Farm Service Agency (FSA), formerly the Agricultural Stabilization and Conservation Service (ASCS), acting through local committees, enforces Swampbuster by determining when a person has engaged in an act that violates Swampbuster. *See generally* 7 CFR Part 12, Subpart A.

Swampbuster does have its own limitations. First, it only applies to farmers producing an "agricultural commodity," which is defined as sugarcane or a commodity planted and produced by annual tilling of the soil. 16 U.S.C. § 3801(a)(1). While this probably covers most farm acreage, it does not include all of it by any means. The Department of Agriculture reports that only 30% of all farms produce traditional commodity crops. Second, it only applies to "converted wetlands," which is defined as wetlands that have been impaired for the purpose or having the effect of agricultural commodity production, if the land could not have been farmed but for the conversion. 16 U.S.C. § 3801(a)(6). Thus, wetlands that are able to be farmed without any action by the farmer to impair the wetlands are not considered to be converted. This is, in a sense, consistent with the "normal farming" exception from Section 404's permit requirement, but unlike that exception there is no prohibition in Swampbuster to bringing new areas into production so long as the farmer merely farms the wetland, rather than manipulates the wetland in order to farm it. Nevertheless, bringing such wetlands into new production would still violate Section 404. *See United States v. Brace*, 41 F.3d 117 (3d Cir. 1994)(farmers activities that did not violate Swampbuster violated Section 404 by bringing new areas into production).

Moreover, there are a number of exemptions from the prohibition. The most important exemption is that Swampbuster does not apply to any conversion that was commenced before December 23, 1985. 16 U.S.C. § 3822(b)(1)(A). While for a number of years there were disputes as to what constituted "commencing," which spawned a number of court cases, the mere passage of time and an amendment in 1990 barring new conversions, see 16 U.S.C. § 3821(c), have effectively ended that litigation. Lands actually converted before December 23, 1985, known as "prior converted croplands," and lands converted after December 23, 1985 (and before 1995), but the conversion of which commenced before that date, known as "commenced conversion croplands," are both exempt from Swampbuster; they are distinguished from "farmed wetlands," those wetlands not subject to Swampbuster because they have not been "converted" at all. Farmers are entitled to have their land certified as prior converted or commenced conversion croplands.

For years the exemption of prior converted and commenced conversion croplands from Swampbuster but not from Section 404 caused confusion to farmers. The Corps regulations were amended in 1993 in an attempt to reduce conflicts by excluding "prior converted croplands" from the definition of "waters of the United States," and hence the jurisdiction of the Corps. 33 CFR § 328.3(a)(8). The Corps' rationale was that normally the conversion destroyed the wetlands characteristics of the land in question and therefore protection of that land was unnecessary. However, the regulatory change does not eliminate all confusion over what is excluded from both Swampbuster and Section 404. First, the Corps uses the term "prior converted cropland" and does not reference "commenced conversion cropland," while both are excluded from Swampbuster. Second, the regulation explicitly states that other agencies' determinations of an area being prior converted croplands do not necessarily govern, because for purposes of the CWA, the final authority resides with EPA. This reservation of EPA authority also exists in the MOA between NRCS, EPA, the Corps, and F & WS as to delineations on agricultural land. As a practical matter, EPA rarely, if ever, exercises this retained authority, but the mere insistence of the retention does not provide confidence to farmers that a NRCS delineation will be respected by EPA.

Unlike Section 404, Swampbuster has a number of "farmer friendly," or some might say "fairness," provisions, mitigating potential harshness. For example, as a result of amendments, a violation of Swampbuster does not automatically mean a total loss of crop subsidies. Rather, the amount of the penalty is to be "proportionate to the severity of the violation." 16 U.S.C. § 3821(a)(2). In addition, there is both a de minimis and a good faith exemption from loss of subsidies, see 16 U.S.C. § 3822(f)(1) & (h). Moreover, if a farmer fully restores the wetlands characteristics destroyed or otherwise mitigates for the harm, then in subsequent years his subsidies can be restored. See 16 U.S.C. § 3822(i). There is also an exception for converting wetlands that were voluntarily created or restored by the farmer after having originally converted them prior to December 23, 1985. *See* 16 U.S.C. § 3822(b)(1)(H). And perhaps most importantly, if a farmer who commenced his conversion before December 23, 1985, neglects to maintain the drainage or manage the land, so the land returns to a wetland, he may again convert the wetland without violating Swampbuster. *See* 16 U.S.C. § 3822(b)(1)(G).

In light of these various provisions, many of which were passed in 1996, the environmental protection afforded by Swampbuster has perhaps been diminished, but its overall directive that farmers not destroy wetlands for agricultural commodity production remains intact.

III. THE SURFACE MINING CONTROL AND RECLAMATION ACT OF 1977

The Surface Mining Control and Reclamation Act of 1977 (SMCRA), 30 U.S.C. § 1201 *et seq.*, was another of the many environmental laws passed in the 1970s in response to a widely perceived need for federal regulation to protect the environment. It regulates the surface mining of coal, as well as some of the surface disturbances caused by underground coal mining. Today, almost 60% of all coal produced in the United States comes from surface mining. Because SMCRA, like the other statutes covered in this chapter, regulate the use of land, it also has been highly controversial, at least in coal mining states, and it has led to a large number of court cases, including several cases claiming compensation for regulatory takings under the Fifth Amendment and the only Supreme Court cases addressing the constitutionality of an environmental law. SMCRA shares some of the characteristics of the other 1970 laws, in particular the presence of a citizen suit provision and the reliance on a cooperative federalism model for administration of the Act.

A. Background

Surface mining of coal involves removing overlying soil and rock in order to expose the coal, which typically is 30–90 feet underground. Compared to underground coal mining, surface mining generally costs less, is safer for miners, and usually results in more complete recovery of the coal. However, it also results in much more extensive disturbance of the land.

Surface mining, often called strip mining, is either of two types. One, called area surface mining, occurs on rather flat land, in which case the land is excavated to reach the coal seam and a very large hole results. This occurs generally in the west. The other, called contour mining, occurs in hilly or mountainous areas, generally in Appalachia. First, a cut is made in the hillside above a coal seam and the coal is further exposed as the overburden is removed. The mine is then enlarged by successive cuts that follow the coal seam around the side of the hill. The mining extends into the hill to the point where the overburden is too thick to make further exposure of the coal economic. Auger mining often is used at this stage to maximize coal recovery.[4] In either case, the

---

4. Auger mining is a method of surface mining whereby a large mechanical screw penetrates a coal seam and turns to extract the coal.

overburden, the soil and rock removed to reach the coal, must be disposed of in some way.

Historically, when the coal seam was played out in area mining, a giant pit of exposed rock and one or more huge piles of overburden were left . *See* Figure 1. In contour mining, the overburden was simply pushed down the mountain, and when the mining was completed, cliff-like excavated faces of exposed rock, known as a highwall, were left on the hillside. *See* Figure 2.

Surface mining became more widespread in the 1930s, and some states passed laws to deal with its effects, but the laws were uneven, not very rigorous, and not strictly enforced. As a result, as described by the Office of Surface Mining in its 25th Anniversary of SMCRA Report:

> Mining pits were not backfilled. Dangerous highwalls were left exposed. Trees and other vegetation were buried by waste material that was simply dumped down the slopes below mines. Topsoil was buried or allowed to wash away. Landslides formed on unstable hillsides. Slopes eroded rapidly because of the lack of vegetation. Polluted water collected in mine pits. Streams became clogged with sediment. Streams and rivers were frequently polluted by acid mine drainage.

The 1970s, with the energy crisis associated with the OPEC petroleum embargo, saw another significant expansion of surface mining, at the same time as there was a growing awareness of and concern for the environment.

Figure 1
Area Surface Mining Before SMCRA

Key

1. Overburden from the initial mining is dumped in a heap at the edge of the operation. Top soil has been buried beneath the heap or mixed in with the rock overburden. Without topsoil grasses and trees do not grow and the overburden pile is exposed to natural elements. The wind blows dust throughout the surrounding area and each rain storm causes the steep sides of the pile to erode.

2. Sediment that is running off the overburden pile has clogged roadside ditches and culverts and is polluting nearby streams. Before the Surface Mining Law was passed, this off site impact was not the responsibility of the mine operator.

3. The dragline removes both the topsoil and overburden from the coal seam in one operation. If acid-forming rock is encountered it is mixed with the overburden and will cause acid mine drainage in the future.

4. Overburden cast by the dragline forms a hill and dale character that will be left when the mining operation is completed. This rough topography eliminates future use of the land.

5. A backhoe digs a diversion that will reroute the stream that is in the way of the mining operation. This keeps the water out of the pit during mining; but, will result in long term bank erosion, downstream flooding, and water pollution. The stream will not be reclaimed.

6. A tributary stream is already being mine through, resulting in some back flow into the pit. As the mine progresses this stream tributary will be permanently eliminated.

7.   A drill rig is preparing holes for explosives used to blast the overburden loose. With uncontrolled blasting rock is cast long distances causing damage and potential safety hazards. In addition, extensive blasting has disrupted the groundwater flow and nearby springs and farm wells have become unreliable.

8.   This resident living next to the mining operation has had his house hit by large rocks from the blasting, lost his long time natural source of water and has been awaken in the middle of the night by blasting very close to his house. He is afraid to sit in his backyard since he does not know when the blasting will occur and without reclamation of the land his property value will be reduced.

9.   In areas where the overburden contains acid forming rock, pools of acid mine drainage begin to collect. In addition, this unrestored land results in permanent loss of farmland and will continue to erode and be a source of sediment and acid drainage to nearby streams for years after the mining is completed.

10.   The maintenance yard and refuse dump will be left after the mining operation. This will cause an eyesore and a safety nuisance to both the neighbors and anyone driving along the road.

Figure 2

Contour Mining Before SMCRA

Key

1.   Bulldozers push trees, shrubs, topsoil, subsoil, and overburden over the down-slope with no intention of reclaiming the land. Mixing the trees, soil, and rock together eliminate the chance for plants to grow and create a highly erodible condition that will last for many years in the future.

2.   This corn field has been greatly impacted by a landslide caused by the mining. Large streams of water now rush down across the field carrying rock and sediment from the mine. This common problem associated with contour mines before the Surface Mining Law will continue to damage the farmers land and he will eventually have to abandoned the field.

3.   A drilling rig bores blast holes and blasts consolidated overburden. Without any blasting regulations the mine operator scatters rock for long distances any time day or night. The nearby farmhouse has been damaged by flying rock and the resident is afraid to let his children play outside.

4.   This farm has been using a spring for its water supply for over 100 years. The mining above the house has destroyed the spring and left the resident without water for his family and livestock.

5.   A bulldozer works together with a shovel removing the remainder of the overburden and exposing the coal. Rock spoil is pushed over the slope and crashes down the hillside. When mining is complete the cliff-like highwall behind the mine and the eroded overburden will remain. This exposed material will continue to erode and cause streams in the valley to clog and be polluted.

6.   A front-end loader digs coal and loads trucks which use a haul road located on a previously mined bench. Rainfall accumulating on the bench runs off and cuts deep gullies in the slope as it pours down the hillside.

7.   Auger mining is in progress removing additional coal from the exposed outcrop. Without reclamation acid mine drainage will pour from these holes and run into nearby streams killing all plant and animal life in the water.

B.   SMCRA's Provisions

The D.C. Circuit has had a lot of experience with SMCRA, because challenges to SMCRA regulations, as well as certain other types of SMCRA cases, must be brought in the District Court for the District of Columbia, see 30 U.S.C. § 1276. In one of those cases the court provided a good summary of the law.

> In brief, the Act is intended to protect the environment from the adverse effects of surface coal mining while ensuring an adequate supply of coal to meet the nation's energy requirements. 30 U.S.C. § 1202(a), (f). Section 501(b) directs the Secretary to promulgate regulations establishing regulatory procedures and performance standards "conforming to the provisions of" the Act (30 U.S.C. § 1251(b)). Section 515 contains detailed "environmental protection performance standards" applicable to "all surface coal mining and reclamation operations." 30 U.S.C. § 1265. Through the Office of Surface Mining Reclamation and Enforcement ("OSMRE"), the

Secretary is to take steps "necessary to insure compliance with" the Act. 30 U.S.C. § 1211(a), (c)(1). The states too have a significant role to play. After an interim period of federal regulation, states had the option of proposing plans for implementing the Act consistent with federal standards on non-federal lands. When the Secretary approved the programs submitted by the states, those states became primarily responsible for regulating surface coal mining and reclamation in the non-federal areas within their borders. 30 U.S.C. § 1253. In states not having an approved program, the Secretary implemented a federal program. 30 U.S.C. § 1254(a), (b). The "permanent program" regulations issued under section 501(b) set standards for federally-approved state programs and for the federal program that takes effect when a State fails to "implement, enforce, or maintain" its program. 30 U.S.C. § 1254(a). Enforcement is carried out by the "regulatory authority," that is, the state agency administering the federally-approved program, the Secretary administering a federal program, or OSMRE conducting oversight of state programs. *See* 30 C.F.R. § 700.5.

The primary means of ensuring compliance is the permit system established in sections 506 through 514 and section 515(a). 30 U.S.C. §§ 1256–1264, 1265(a). [Generally, a] permit is required for "any surface coal mining operations." 30 U.S.C. § 1256. Summaries of applications for permits must be published, and objections may be submitted by local agencies or by "any person having an interest which ... may be adversely affected" by a proposed operation. 30 U.S.C. § 1263. Each application must include a reclamation plan. Section 507(d), 30 U.S.C. § 1257(d). A reclamation plan describes the present use of the land, proposed and possible post-mining uses of the land, and what steps the operator will take to ensure the viability of the latter. Among other things, the plan must show how the operator will achieve soil reconstruction and revegetation of the mined area.[4] Section 508, 30 U.S.C. § 1258. A permit application can only be approved if it demonstrates that "all requirements" of the Act have been satisfied and that "reclamation as required by [the Act] ... can be accomplished." 30 U.S.C. § 1260.

Section 509 requires the operator to post a performance bond in an amount sufficient to secure completion of reclamation. The operator and the surety remain liable under the bond for the duration of the surface mining and reclamation operation and until the end of the "revegetation period" (5 or 10 years) prescribed by section 515(b)(20). 30 U.S.C. § 1259(b). At that time, the operator may petition the regulatory authority for release of the bond. The petition must be published, and is subject to the same opportunities for

---

4. The revegetation standards require that an operator establish "a diverse, effective and permanent vegetative cover" over the area after mining has ceased. 30 U.S.C. § 1265(b)(19). By the terms of the Act, the operator "assume[s] the responsibility" for success of the revegetation program for 5 years (10 years in the arid Western states) after the revegetation standard is first met. 30 U.S.C. § 1265(b)(20).

comment and hearing as the permit application. 30 C.F.R. § 800.40(a)(2), (b)(2). Further, "[n]o bond shall be fully released . . . until reclamation requirements of the Act and the permit are fully met." *Id.* § 800.40(c)(3).

National Wildlife Fed. v. Lujan, 950 F.2d 765 (D.C. Cir. 1991).

Notes and Comments

1.   After the initial federal program period, virtually all the states with active coal mining did apply for and obtain authorization (termed "primacy") to regulate surface mining in their states in lieu of the federal program. Today, of the 36 states with some coal resource, 25 states have active coal production. Twenty-four of these have approved state programs. Tennessee, which previously had an approved program, repealed its program in 1984. There are federal programs not only for Tennessee and the eleven other states with coal resources but no active mining program, but also for four Indian tribes that produce coal on their reservations, as well as for coal production on federal lands.

2.   The "environmental protection performance standards" of 30 U.S.C. § 1265 provide detailed requirements both for how the surface mining shall take place and for reclamation after the mining has terminated. Generally, reclamation is required to re-establish the "approximate original contours" (AOC) of the land, 30 U.S.C. § 1265(b)(3); to restore topsoil, 30 U.S.C. § 1265 (b)(6); to establish native plant communities, 30 U.S.C. § 1265(b)(19); all to restore to the extent possible the land to its original uses, 30 U.S.C. § 1265(b)(2). There are special requirements for mining on "prime farm lands," which are promulgated by the Secretary of Agriculture, 30 U.S.C. § 1265(b)(7), and there are special requirements for mining on steep slopes, 30 U.S.C. § 1265(d). Surface mining is prohibited on certain types of lands, such as National Parks and other federal lands where surface mining would be incompatible with their primary uses, within 100 feet of a public right-of-way, and within 300 feet of an occupied dwelling. 30 U.S.C. 1272(e). State plans are required to identify equivalent prohibited areas of state concern and provide a system by which persons may petition for additional prohibited areas to be added. 30 U.S.C. § 1272(a) & (c).

3.   In addition to regulating new and existing coal mines, SMCRA also contains provisions relating to the reclamation of coal mines abandoned before passage of SMCRA. *See* 30 U.S.C. §§ 1231–1243. To pay for this reclamation, fees are levied on currently mined coal. If the state has an approved state reclamation program, half the fees go to the state from which the fees originate.

4.   Despite its title, SMCRA is not limited to the regulation of surface mining. Section 516, 30 U.S.C. § 1266, specifically requires the Secretary of the Interior to promulgate rules "directed toward the surface effects of underground coal mining operations," and it makes the provisions of the Act "relating to State and Federal programs, permits, bonds, inspections and enforcement, public review, and administrative and judicial review" applicable to surface operations and surface impacts incident to underground

mining.[5] The Secretary's rules, however, are to take account of the "distinct difference" between underground and surface mining. Section 516 also requires "each permit [issued pursuant to a state or federal program under SMCRA] and relating to underground coal mining" to include various specific requirements to protect the environment. Underground coal mining actually can cause many of the same adverse environmental effects as surface mining, such as the placement of overburden and acid or toxic drainage from mines. The one unique potential adverse effect of underground coal mining is subsidence, whereby the land over the underground mine literally sinks to fill in the mined out area. As a result, the federal regulations governing minimum state program requirements are largely identical for both underground and surface mining, except that there are special and detailed requirements for underground mining to avoid subsidence to the extent feasible and to reclaim land that does subside, to the extent feasible.

C. Issues

1. Federalism Issues

While the CWA, the CAA, and RCRA, like SMCRA, all follow a cooperative federalism model for administration of the statute, SMCRA uses a unique word to characterize the state's jurisdiction if it qualifies for authorization—"exclusive" jurisdiction. 30 U.S.C. § 1253(a). In addition, the Congressional findings outlined in SMCRA reinforce the concept of exclusive jurisdiction:

> [B]ecause of the diversity in terrain, climate, biologic, chemical, and other physical conditions in areas subject to mining operations, the primary governmental responsibility for developing, authorizing, issuing, and enforcing regulations for surface mining and reclamation operations subject to this chapter should rest with the States.

30 U.S.C. § 1201(f). Moreover, unlike EPA's authority under the CWA and CAA to review and object to state permitting decisions, SMCRA has no such provision. Consequently, it may not be surprising that the relationship between a state with primacy and the federal government has been described by one court as follows:

> The Surface Mining Control and Reclamation Act of 1977 ("SMCRA") was enacted to strike a balance between the nation's interests in protecting the environment from the adverse effects of surface coal mining and in assuring the coal supply essential to the nation's energy requirements. See 30 U.S.C. § 1202(a), (d), (f); see also *Hodel v. Va. Mining & Reclamation Ass'n*, 452 U.S. 264, 268–69, 101 S.Ct. 2352, 69 L.Ed.2d 1 (1981). The Act accomplishes these purposes through a "cooperative federalism," in which responsibility for the regulation of surface coal mining in the United States is

---

5. The D.C. Circuit, however, upheld an interpretive rule that excluded underground mining from the prohibitions in 30 U.S.C. § 1272(e), banning surface coal mining operations from various places, including within 300 feet of an occupied dwelling, terming the interpretation reasonable and not precluded by the statute. *See* Citizens Coal Council v. Norton, 330 F.3d 478 (D.C.Cir. 2003).

shared between the U.S. Secretary of the Interior and State regulatory authorities. Under this scheme, Congress established in SMCRA "minimum national standards" for regulating surface coal mining and encouraged the States, through an offer of exclusive regulatory jurisdiction, to enact their own laws incorporating these minimum standards, as well as any more stringent, but not inconsistent, standards that they might choose. 30 U.S.C. § 1255(b).

To implement this cooperative federalism, SMCRA directs the U.S. Secretary of the Interior to develop a "federal program" of regulation that embodies the minimum national standards and to consider for approval any "State programs" that are submitted to it for approval. To obtain approval of its program, a State must pass a law that provides for the minimum national standards established as "requirements" in SMCRA and must also demonstrate that it has the capability of enforcing its law. *See* 30 U.S.C. § 1253(a). Once the Secretary is satisfied that a State program meets these requirements and approves the program, the State's laws and regulations implementing the program become operative for the regulation of surface coal mining, and the State officials administer the program, *see id.* § 1252(e), giving the State "exclusive jurisdiction over the regulation of surface coal mining" within its borders, *id.* § 1253(a). If, however, a State fails to submit a program for approval, or a program that it submits is not approved, or approval of a State's program is withdrawn because of ineffective enforcement, then the federal program becomes applicable for the State, and the Secretary becomes vested with "exclusive jurisdiction for the regulation and control of surface coal mining and reclamation operations taking place [in the] State." *Id.* § 1254(a).

Thus, SMCRA provides for either State regulation of surface coal mining within its borders or federal regulation, but not both. The Act expressly provides that one or the other is exclusive, see 30 U.S.C. §§ 1253(a), 1254(a), with the exception that an approved State program is always subject to revocation when a State fails to enforce it, see *id.* §§ 1253(a); 1271(b). Federal oversight of an approved State program is provided by the Secretary's obligation to inspect and monitor the operations of State programs. *See id.* §§ 1267, 1271. Only if an approved State program is revoked, as provided in § 1271, however, does the federal program become the operative regulation for surface coal mining in any State that has previously had its program approved. *See id.* §§ 1254(a), 1271....

As we have noted, under SMCRA Congress intended to divide responsibility for the regulation of surface coal mining between the federal government and the States. But characterizing the regulatory structure of SMCRA as "cooperative" federalism is not entirely accurate, as the statute does not provide for shared regulation of coal mining. Rather, the Act provides for enforcement of either a federal program or a State program, but not both. Thus, in contrast to other "cooperative federalism" statutes, SMCRA exhibits extraordinary deference to the States. The statutory federalism of SMCRA is quite unlike the cooperative regime under the Clean Water Act.... Under SMCRA, in contrast, Congress designed a scheme of mutually exclusive regulation by either the U.S. Secretary of the Interior or the State regulatory authority, depending on whether the State elects to regulate itself or to submit to federal regulation....

Bragg v. West Virginia Coal Assn., 248 F.3d 275, 288–89, 293 (4th Cir. 2001).

This description, however, may be somewhat misleading. As early as 1979, Interior issued a rule providing that OSMRE could issue Notices of Violation (NOV) to mine operators acting in violation of the Act, the state program requirements, or their permit conditions, notwithstanding that the alleged violation occurred in a primacy state and Interior had not instituted proceedings to withdraw or declare the state program administration inadequate. This rule was challenged by the coal industry in 1988, when Interior refused its petition for rulemaking to rescind the rule authorizing the NOVs. The coal industry maintained that once a state had primacy, OSMRE could only issue NOVs incident to withdrawal of a state's authorization or upon a determination that a state was not enforcing part of its program. According to the industry, the agency's issuance of NOVs in primacy states effectively placed OSMRE in the position of enforcing its view of the state-issued permit requirements in opposition to the state agency charged with enforcing the permit conditions. This was said to create confusion in the industry and conflict between federal and state agencies.

The D.C. Circuit upheld the rule, but only on the grounds that the industry could not challenge a SMCRA rule after the 60–day period provided in the statute, *see* 30 U.S.C. § 1276(a)(1). *National Min. Ass'n v. U.S. Dept. of Interior*, 70 F.3d 1345 (D.C.Cir. 1995). Nevertheless, the lower court's opinion, which decided the merits against the industry, and aspects of the D.C. Circuit's opinion strongly suggested that Interior did have the authority directly to enforce the Act, the state programs, and individual permit conditions.

The characterization of primacy states having exclusive jurisdiction has also caused problems under SMCRA's citizen suit provision, 30 U.S.C. § 1270. Compare the following two cases.

HAYDO v. AMERIKOHL MINING, INC.

United States Court of Appeals, Third Circuit, 1987.

830 F.2d 494.

MANSMANN, Circuit Judge.

This appeal presents the question of whether there is subject matter jurisdiction in the federal district court to hear a claim for damages arising from an alleged violation by an operator of the Surface Mining Control and Reclamation Act ("SMCRA"), where a state has submitted and the Secretary of the Interior has approved a program for state regulation as contemplated by the Act. We find that there is no federal jurisdiction, and we will affirm the district court's dismissal of the action.

I.

Donald and Patricia Haydo brought this action for damages for the loss of a water well allegedly due to the coal exploration program of the defendant, Amerikohl Mining, Inc. . . .

II.

The Haydos complained that the defendant's exploratory drilling adversely affected their water supply and violated the environmental protection standards prescribed by Section 515 of the SMCRA, 30 U.S.C. § 1265. The complaint alleged that the Commonwealth of Pennsylvania, administering the SMCRA under a program approved by the Secretary of the Interior, promulgated regulations pursuant to Section 515 of the SMCRA, 30 U.S.C. § 1265, concerning the reclamation of the prevailing hydrologic balance. The plaintiffs alleged that the defendant's operations contravened both the state regulations and the SMCRA. . . .

V.

We turn now to the question of whether the district court had jurisdiction over the subject matter of this action. The complaint alleged violations of the Pennsylvania regulatory plan and of the SMCRA itself and asserted subject matter jurisdiction in the district court under ... Section 520 of the SMCRA.

A.

[S]ection 520 of the SMCRA, in pertinent part, confers jurisdiction on the federal district courts to hear citizen suits to compel compliance with the SMCRA against the United States or any other governmental instrumentality or agency for violations both of the SMCRA and of any rule, regulation, order or permit issued pursuant thereto. 30 U.S.C. § 1270(a)(1). Section 520 also permits a citizen enforcement action against "any other person who is alleged to be in violation of *any rule, regulation, order or permit issued pursuant to this subchapter.*" *Id.* (emphasis added). The act also permits a damage action by "[a]ny person who is injured in his person or property through the violation by any operation *of any rule, regulation, order, or permit issued pursuant to this chapter.*" 30 U.S.C. § 1270(f) (emphasis added).

While citizen suits against state and federal governmental defendants may be predicated directly upon violations of the provisions of the SMCRA, Section 520 does not provide for an action against individual defendants for violations of the act itself. The principal purpose of the citizen suit provision was to provide "a practical and legitimate method of assuring the *regulatory authority's* compliance with the requirements of the act."

The jurisdictional basis for a citizen suit against a nongovernmental defendant, either to compel compliance or for damages, is an alleged violation of "any rule, regulation, order or permit issued pursuant to this subchapter." The defendant argues that the district court lacked subject matter jurisdiction in this case because the complaint alleged only violations of the SMCRA itself and of the *state* regulatory plan and Section 520 confers federal jurisdiction only over alleged violations of *federal* regulations.

The defendant argues that Section 520 must be read in conjunction with Section 503 of the SMCRA which provides that a regulatory plan may be submitted for approval by "[e]ach state.... which wishes to assume *exclusive jurisdiction* over the regulation of surface coal mining and reclamation operations," 30 U.S.C. § 1253 (emphasis added). The defendant argues that because Pennsylvania's regulatory plan has been approved by the Secretary, jurisdiction over the alleged violations of the state statute and regulations lies exclusively in the courts of Pennsylvania. We agree.

The plaintiffs urge us to interpret Section 520 to include state rules, regulations, orders or permits as among those "issued pursuant to this subchapter," at least where the state regulation is one required by the SMCRA. 30 U.S.C. § 1270(a)(1), (f). However, Section 520* offers "exclusive" jurisdiction to states obtaining approval of a regulatory plan. The obvious and usual meaning of the word "exclusive" is plain enough, and the plaintiffs suggest no other meaning for this language. The plaintiffs cite us to numerous cases involving citizen suits filed under similar jurisdictional provisions in other environmental protection statutes. However, the issues in all of those cases involve questions of the *primacy* of the jurisdiction of administrative agencies or state courts. The plaintiffs have cited us to no other statute where, as in the SMCRA, the state is expressly offered "exclusive" jurisdiction to enforce its regulatory program. We have encountered nothing in the statute or the legislative history which leads us to believe that anything other than the ordinary meaning of "exclusive" was intended by the enactors of the SMCRA.

Congress found that "effective and reasonable regulation of surface coal mining operations by the States and by the Federal Government in accordance with the requirements of this chapter is an effective and necessary means to minimize so far as practicable the adverse social, economic, and environmental effects of such mining operations." 30 U.S.C. § 1201(e). However, the statute does not provide for concurrent jurisdiction in the states and federal government. When a state fails to submit, implement, enforce or maintain an acceptable state regulatory program, the Secretary is required to prepare, promulgate and implement a federal program for the state. 30 U.S.C. § 1254(a). Promulgation and implementation of a federal program for a state preempts and supersedes any inconsistent state law and "vests the Secretary with

---

* So in the original. It should probably say "Section 503." [editor's note].

exclusive jurisdiction for the regulation and control of surface coal mining and reclamation operations" taking place within the state. *Id.*

Congress found the imposition of minimum nationwide environmental protection standards necessary to prevent a state from allowing competitive advantage to its own operators through possible production cost savings due to inadequate environmental protection standards. However, Congress recognized that "because of the diversity in terrain, climate, biologic, chemical, and other physical conditions in areas subject to mining operations, primary governmental responsibility for developing, authorizing, issuing, and enforcing regulations for surface mining and reclamation operations subject to this chapter should rest with the States." 30 U.S.C. § 1201(f). In order to allow the individual states to retain this primary responsibility, the statute provided for state jurisdiction over its own operators to be exclusive once the state plan has been approved.

Interpreting Section 520 to afford federal jurisdiction in this case would render meaningless the Congressional offer in Section 503 of "exclusive" jurisdiction to states obtaining approval of a regulatory plan. Therefore we find that there is no federal jurisdiction under the SMCRA over suits such as this against operators who are alleged to be in violation of an approved state plan.

MOLINARY v. POWELL MOUNTAIN COAL COMPANY

United States Court of Appeals, Fourth Circuit, 1997.
125 F.3d 231.

HAMILTON, Circuit Judge:

In this appeal, we consider whether § 520(f) of the Surface Mining Control and Reclamation Act of 1977 (SMCRA), 30 U.S.C. § 1270(f), provides a federal cause of action for the recovery of damages resulting from violation of state regulations that are a part of the state's surface coal mining and reclamation regulatory program approved by the United States Secretary of the Interior pursuant to § 503 of SMCRA, 30 U.S.C. § 1253. We hold that it does.

I.

In this suit, Jo D. Molinary represents a class of persons, known as the "Pruitt heirs" (Pruitt Heirs), who own more than a 99% undivided interest in the surface estate of a fifty-acre tract of land located in Lee County, Virginia (the Pruitt Tract).... Prior to Congress' enactment of SMCRA in 1977, a three-acre portion of the Pruitt Tract (the Three Acre Tract) was strip mined for coal by parties unrelated to [The Powell Mountain Coal Company (Powell Mountain)]....

In February 1990, Powell Mountain submitted a permit application to the Division of Mined Land Reclamation for the Commonwealth of Virginia (the DMLR), seeking permission to auger mine the Three Acre Tract for coal that still remained. In its permit application, Powell

Mountain listed itself and the "Pruitt Heirs" as cosurface owners, but did not list each heir by name.... Without further submissions from Powell Mountain, the DMLR issued the permit. Powell Mountain then extracted 4423.51 tons of coal from the Three Acre Tract by the auger mining method....

After receiving complaints about the permit's issuance, the DMLR determined that Powell Mountain's permit application did not comply with certain state permitting regulations.... As a result, the DMLR revoked Powell Mountain's permit, issued a cessation order, and ordered Powell Mountain to reclaim the Three Acre Tract.

Subsequently, this class action was filed in the United States District Court for the Western District of Virginia under SMCRA's citizen suit provision, § 520(f) of SMCRA. *See* 30 U.S.C. § 1270(f). Section 520(f) of SMCRA provides that "[a]ny person who is injured in his person or property through the violation by any operator of any rule, regulation, order, or permit issued pursuant to [SMCRA] may bring an action for damages (including reasonable attorney and expert witness fees)...." *Id.* ...

Powell Mountain moved to dismiss the complaint for lack of subject matter jurisdiction. In its motion to dismiss, Powell Mountain argued that federal courts lack subject matter jurisdiction over citizen suits in states whose regulatory and enforcement programs have been approved by the Secretary of the Interior (the Secretary) pursuant to § 503 of SMCRA. Rejecting this argument as inconsistent with the plain language of § 520(f) of SMCRA, the district court denied the motion....

Powell Mountain noted a timely appeal. On appeal, Powell Mountain challenges: (1) the district court's denial of its motion to dismiss for lack of subject matter jurisdiction....

II.

Before we address Powell Mountain's challenge to the district court's denial of its motion to dismiss for lack of subject matter jurisdiction, we briefly set forth some background information about SMCRA and Virginia's federally approved version of SMCRA. Congress enacted SMCRA in 1977 to "establish a nationwide program to protect society and the environment from the adverse effects of surface coal mining operations." 30 U.S.C. § 1202(a). Section 201 of SMCRA, 30 U.S.C. § 1211, "creates the Office of Surface Mining Reclamation and Enforcement (OSM), within the Department of the Interior, and the Secretary of the Interior (Secretary) acting through OSM, is charged with primary responsibility for administering and implementing [SMCRA] by promulgating regulations and enforcing its provisions."

To achieve its goals, SMCRA relies on "a program of cooperative federalism that allows States, within limits established by federal minimum standards, to enact and administer their own regulatory programs, structured to meet their own particular needs." Any state "wish[ing] to assume exclusive jurisdiction over the regulation of surface coal mining and reclamation operations" on nonfederal lands within its borders must submit a proposed program to the Secretary for approval. 30 U.S.C. § 1253(a). A state program must include a permitting system that incorporates SMCRA's environmental protection standards and is in accordance with SMCRA's enforcement and procedural requirements. . . .

[Since December 1981] Virginia has had "exclusive jurisdiction over the regulation" of surface coal mining and reclamation within its borders. . . .

III.

. . . As previously stated, the Pruitt Heirs brought this action in the United States District Court for the Western District of Virginia pursuant to SMCRA's citizen suit provision, § 520(f) of SMCRA. Section 520(f) of SMCRA provides:

Any person who is injured in his person or property through the violation by any operator of any rule, regulation, order, or permit issued pursuant to [SMCRA] may bring an action for damages (including reasonable attorney and expert witness fees) only in the judicial district in which the surface coal mining operation complained of is located. Nothing in this subsection shall affect the rights established by or limits imposed under State Workmen's Compensation laws.

30 U.S.C. § 1270(f). This provision creates a federal cause of action for the recovery of damages resulting from the violation of "any rule, regulation, order, or permit issued pursuant to [SMCRA]." *Id.* The dispute here centers on whether the statutory phrase "issued pursuant to [SMCRA]," includes state-promulgated regulations that comprise a federally approved state surface mining and reclamation program. More precisely for purposes of this case, the issue is whether the Virginia regulations allegedly violated by Powell Mountain were issued "pursuant to" SMCRA, such that the district court had subject matter jurisdiction over the complaint under § 520(f). Powell Mountain contends that the Virginia regulations were not issued pursuant to SMCRA, while the Pruitt Heirs contend that they were. The Secretary, who has submitted an amicus brief in this case, espouses the same interpretation as the Pruitt Heirs.

Congress has not directly spoken on this precise issue through a provision in SMCRA or its legislative history. Because Congress has not "directly spoken to the precise question at issue," we must sustain the Secretary's interpretation so long as it is "based on a permissible construction of the statute." *Chevron U.S.A., Inc. v. Natural Resources Defense Council, Inc.,* 467 U.S. 837 (1984). . . . For the following reasons, we conclude that the interpretation espoused by the Secretary is a permissible construction of § 520(f) of SMCRA.

First, the language at issue is certainly broad enough to support the Secretary's interpretation. It may reasonably be said that once the Secretary approves a state surface coal mining and reclamation program, the rules, regulations, orders, and permits issued under that program are "issued," in the language of § 520(f), "pursuant to" SMCRA.

Second, creating a federal cause of action so that citizens may redress violations of state surface coal mining and reclamation regulations in federal court is consistent with Congress' goal of establishing "a nationwide program to protect society and the environment from the adverse effects of surface coal mining operations." 30 U.S.C. § 1202(a).

Third, as the Secretary points out in its *amicus* brief, when Congress referred to permits issued by either state or federal regulatory authorities elsewhere in SMCRA, it used the phrase,"permit issued pursuant to this chapter." *See, e.g.,* 30 U.S.C. §§ 1256(d)(1), 1261(b), 1272(a)(6). By contrast, when Congress intended to limit the application of a provision to permits or orders issued pursuant to a federal program, it did so expressly. *See, e.g.,* 30 U.S.C. §§ 1268(e)-(f) ("permit issued pursuant to a Federal program"); 1273(b) ("permit ... issued by the Secretary"); 1275(a)(1) & (c) ("notice or order" issued "pursuant to Federal Program").

Fourth and finally, as the Secretary also points out, its interpretation is consistent with the operation of § 520(a)(1) of SMCRA, which provides for citizen suits to ensure compliance with the "provisions of [SMCRA] or of any rule, regulation, order or permit issued pursuant thereto," 30 U.S.C. § 1270(a)(1), in conjunction with the operation of § 520(b) of SMCRA, which places limits on the initiation of such suits. Section § 520(b)(1)(B) of SMCRA states that a suit may not be commenced under § 520(a)(1) if "the Secretary or the State" is already "diligently prosecuting a civil action ... to require compliance." 30 U.S.C. § 1270(b)(1)(B). Because a state would only prosecute a compliance action if it were a primacy state, the language of these subsections shows that Congress contemplated that federal citizen suits for compliance would be brought in primacy states. Considering that the key language in § 520(a)(1) of SMCRA is virtually identical to the key language in § 520(f) of SMCRA, it follows that Congress intended § 520(f) of SMCRA to provide for federal citizen suits for damages in primacy states.

The Secretary's interpretation does not conflict, as Powell Mountain suggests, with the federal grant of "exclusive regulatory jurisdiction over the regulation of surface coal mining and reclamation operations" in § 520(f) of SMCRA to states with federally approved surface coal mining and reclamation programs. *See* 30 U.S.C. § 1253(a). Exclusive regulatory jurisdiction simply does not encompass exclusive adjudicatory jurisdiction. Common sense dictates that a government's acts in regulating a subject are distinctly different than its acts in adjudicating a party's rights related to the subject.[5]

---

5. In Haydo v. Amerikohl Mining, Inc., 830 F.2d 494 (3d Cir.1987), the Third Circuit refused to make this distinction. In that case, the court concluded that reading the language of § 503(a) of SMCRA in conjunction with § 520(f) of SMCRA compelled the conclusion that a state regulation connected to a federally approved regulatory

Because Congress has not specifically assigned jurisdiction over § 520(f) suits elsewhere, we conclude the district court possessed subject matter jurisdiction. . . .

Notes and Comments

1. What do you think about the contrary arguments between the *Haydo* and *Molinary* courts? These are apparently the only two cases dealing with the question whether the SMCRA citizen suit provision authorizes suits against persons who violate state rules, regulations, or permits in primacy states. Note that the extended selection from *Bragg v. West Virginia Coal Assn.*, that began this Federalism issue, was also from the Fourth Circuit, subsequent to the *Molinary* decision. Some courts have read *Bragg* to have abrogated or cast in doubt the *Molinary* decision. *See Pennsylvania Federation of Sportsmen's Clubs, Inc. v. Hess*, 297 F.3d 310, 318 n.7 (3d Cir. 2002). Of course, the Third Circuit is the *Haydo* circuit. The *Bragg* court itself, however, cited positively to *Molinary*: "It is now settled that 30 U.S.C. § 1270 confers on federal district courts subject matter jurisdiction over at least some sorts of claims. *See Molinary v. Powell Mtn. Coal Co.*, 125 F.3d 231, 235–37 (4th Cir.1997)." The Fourth Circuit includes two major coal producing states with primacy—Virginia and West Virginia, whereas the Third Circuit includes only Pennsylvania.

2. The citizen suit provision explicitly limits suits against states to those permitted by the Eleventh Amendment. This would preclude actions for damages (and attorneys fees) in the normal course. Under the doctrine of *Ex parte Young*, 209 U.S. 123, 28 S.Ct. 441, 52 L.Ed. 714 (1908), it would not normally preclude actions against a state officer for prospective injunctive relief, where the claim is based upon a continuing violation of federal law. *See, e.g., NRDC v. California Dept. of Transportation*, 96 F.3d 420 (9th Cir. 1996)(citizen suit under the CWA). However, given SMCRA's unique character, the Eleventh Amendment can preclude citizen suit actions to compel state compliance in primacy states. In *Bragg v. West Virginia Coal Assn.*, quoted and discussed above, the court barred a citizen suit seeking to prohibit the Director of the West Virginia Division of Environmental Protection (WVDEP) from issuing permits for mountaintop-removal mining, alleging that such permits violated SMCRA. The court, relying on its conclusion that in primacy states the applicable law to be enforced was state law, not federal law, found that the *Ex parte Young* exception to the Eleventh Amendment did not apply. Can the conclusion that in primacy states regulated entities are only subject to state, not federal law, be squared with the same court's holding in *Molinary* or the D.C. Circuit's dicta in *National Min. Ass'n v. U.S. Dept. of Interior*, 70 F.3d 1345 (D.C.Cir. 1995)?

2. Mountaintop-removal/Valley fill mining

In the section of this chapter dealing with Section 404, we discussed the Corps' Nationwide Permit 21 authorizing valley fills with mining

program was not "issued pursuant to [SMCRA]," in the language of § 520(f) of SMCRA. As the district court in the present case correctly recognized, the holding in Haydo ignores the fact that the word "exclusive" in § 503(a) modifies the phrase "regulatory jurisdiction," and nothing more. The Third Circuit is the only federal appellate court that has addressed the scope of the phrase "issued pursuant to [SMCRA]," as found in § 520(f) of SMCRA.

overburden associated with mountaintop removal mining. Mountaintop removal mining is an extreme form of contour mining. As described in OSMRE regulations, "Mountaintop removal mining means surface mining activities, where the mining operation removes an entire coal seam or seams running through the upper fraction of a mountain, ridge, or hill ... by removing substantially all of the overburden off the bench and creating a level plateau or a gently rolling contour...." 30 CFR § 785.14(b). "Valley fills are constructed from and used to dispose of the spoil or coal mine waste material generated during mining operations." *West Virginia Coal Ass'n v. Reilly*, 728 F.Supp. 1276, 1280 (S.D.W.Va. 1989), *aff'd.* 932 F.2d 964, 1991 WL 75217 (4th Cir.1991) (unpublished). In other words, the rubble from the top of the mountain is placed in the adjacent valley. "When valley fills are permitted in intermittent and perennial streams, they destroy those stream segments. The normal flow and gradient of the stream is now buried under millions of cubic yards of excess spoil waste material, an extremely adverse effect. If there are fish, they cannot migrate. If there is any life form that cannot acclimate to life deep in a rubble pile, it is eliminated. No effect on related environmental values is more adverse than obliteration. Under a valley fill, the water quantity of the stream becomes zero. Because there is no stream, there is no water quality." *Bragg v. Robertson*, 72 F.Supp.2d 642 (S.D.W.Va. 1999), *rev'd sub nom. Bragg v. West Virginia Coal Ass'n*, 248 F.3d 275 (4th Cir. 2001). Recall that the Corps tried to justify its Nationwide Permit on the grounds that, if the mining process had been approved by a regulatory authority under SMCRA, for the Corps then to engage in individual permitting actions would be duplicative and confusing.

It is fairly clear that mountaintop removal mining is not prohibited by SMCRA. It is specifically included as an example of "surface coal mining operations" in the definition of that term. *See* 30 U.S.C. § 1291(28)(A). It is not as clear that valley fills are permitted. After all, among other things, the environmental protection performance standards required to be included in state or federal programs include requirements that excess spoil not be placed in natural water courses, 30 U.S.C. § 1365(b)(22)(D), and that waivers from the Approximate Original Contours requirement not allow any damage to natural watercourses. *But see Kentuckians for Commonwealth, Inc. v. Rivenburgh*, 317 F.3d 425, 442 (4th Cir. 2003)("It is apparent that SMCRA anticipates the possibility that excess spoil material could and would be placed in waters of the United States").

Two major law suits have been brought by environmental groups challenging the practice of mountaintop removal/valley fill mining, especially prevalent in West Virginia. The first, *Bragg v. Robertson*, was brought against the Director of West Virginia's Department of Environmental Protection, alleging that he had approved mountaintop removal/valley fill mining permits in violation of both SMCRA and the state program approved under SMCRA, and against the Corps of Engineers, alleging it had violated the Clean Water Act, NEPA, and the Administrative Procedure Act.

In the trial court, all but two counts of the complaint were settled through a consent decree that required the Corps and the WVDEP, as well as EPA, OSMRE, and the Fish and Wildlife Service, none of whom had been parties to the suit, to prepare a programmatic EIS on mountop-removal/valley fill mining. *See Bragg v. Robertson*, 83 F.Supp.2d 713 (S.D.W.Va. 2000), *aff'd sub nom. Bragg v. West Virginia Coal Ass'n*, 248 F.3d 275 (4th Cir. 2001). As of this writing, the federal agencies have published a draft EIS but have not published a final EIS. In addition, the Corps agreed to require individual permits for any fill in West Virginia that would result in more than a minimal adverse effect on waters of the United States, with any fill of waters draining a watershed of greater than 250 acres conclusively presumed to have a greater than minimal adverse effect. *Id.*

The two counts that were not settled related to a West Virginia regulation, intended to conform with a federal regulation, known as the Stream Buffer Zone rule (SBZ), that established 100–foot buffer zones around perennial and intermittent streams. The district court held that the state had been violating those requirements and enjoined the state from placing any excess spoil in such streams. *Bragg v. Robertson*, 72 F.Supp.2d 642 (S.D.W.Va. 1999). On appeal, the Fourth Circuit reversed, finding that the Eleventh Amendment precluded the suit against the Director of the WVDEP. *Bragg v. West Virginia Coal Ass'n*, 248 F.3d 275 (4th Cir. 2001). Nevertheless, in 1999, as a result of the lawsuit, EPA, the Corps, OSMRE, and the WVDEP entered into a Memorandum of Understanding (MOU) to clarify the meaning of the SBZ rule.

The second law suit challenging mountaintop/valley fill removal mining was *Kentuckians for Commonwealth Inc. v. Rivenburgh*, 317 F.3d 425 (4th Cir. 2003). In that case, an environmental group sued the Corps, asserting that valley fill disposal of excess spoil in streams was not the discharge of "fill" within the meaning of Section 404. If correct, this would mean that EPA would be the permitting authority under Section 402 and the NPDES program, rather than the Corps. Although the district court agreed with the plaintiffs, the Fourth Circuit reversed, holding that the Corps' (and EPA's) interpretation was reasonable. Accordingly, the Corps remains the permitting authority under Section 404 for valley fill disposal of excess spoil.

Neither of the cases were against OSMRE. Indeed, in *Bragg* the plaintiffs relied on OSMRE's SBZ rule to attack West Virginia's permitting actions, and the Department of Justice, representing the Corps, indicated agreement with the plaintiffs' interpretation of the SBZ rule. However, OSMRE essentially agreed with West Virginia and not with the Department of Justice as to the meaning of its rule. It was this lack of agreement and coordination that created the need for the MOU to clarify the meaning of the rule. The MOU concluded that, if a valley fill was not inconsistent with the 404(b)(1) Guidelines under Section 404, the fill would not be deemed to violate the SBZ rule. This MOU, however, was held by the district court in *Bragg* to be inconsistent with SMCRA, but this aspect of the district court's decision was overruled on jurisdictional grounds under the Eleventh Amendment.

In *Rivenburgh*, although the suit was against the Corps, asserting it did not have permitting authority for valley fills under the CWA, both the district court and appellate decisions expressed interpretations of SMCRA and the SBZ rule.

As a result of all these actions, OSMRE undertook to clarify the SBZ Rule and SMCRA's treatment of valley fills in a new rulemaking. *See* 69 Fed. Reg. 1036 (January 7, 2004)(Proposed Rule). [As of this writing, the agency has not promulgated a final rule.] The current, unamended SBZ rule applicable to state programs states:

(a) No land within 100 feet of a perennial stream or an intermittent stream shall be disturbed by surface mining activities, unless the regulatory authority specifically authorizes surface mining activities closer to, or through, such a stream. The regulatory authority may authorize such activities only upon finding that—

(1) Surface mining activities will not cause or contribute to the violation of applicable State or Federal water quality standards, and will not adversely affect the water quantity and quality or other environmental resources of the stream; and

(2) If there will be a temporary or permanent stream-channel diversion, it will comply with § 816.43.

(b) The area not to be disturbed shall be designated as a buffer zone, and the operator shall mark it as specified in § 816.11.

30 CFR 816.57. On its face, this would seem to prohibit valley fills, because, as the district court in *Bragg* noted, filling a stream with excess spoil adversely affects the stream by destroying it. However, intermittent streams are defined generally as streams that drain a watershed of at least one square mile, *see* 30 CFR 701.5. Streams draining smaller watersheds, OSMRE maintains, are simply not protected by the SBZ Rule, 69 Fed. Reg. 1036, 1042 (2004), even though perennial streams are not defined by the size of their drainage but simply as streams that flow continuously throughout the year. Thus, this provision allows fill to totally destroy a stream that does not drain at least a one square mile watershed, although OSMRE recognizes that many of these non-qualifying streams "support biological communities or serve as fish spawning areas." *Id*. Moreover, OSMRE indicates that it has always interpreted the SBZ Rule not to actually prohibit stream fills in the mining area, because waivers could be granted to fill streams so long as there were no adverse effects within 100 feet downstream of the fill. *See* 69 Fed. Reg. 1036, 1041 (2004). Under this interpretation, even large streams may be destroyed if they are within the mining area, so long as 100 feet from the mining area the stream is not adversely affected.

Its proposed rule, OSMRE says, is intended to make this idea more clear. It would provide:

(a) No land within 100 feet of a perennial stream or an intermittent stream shall be disturbed by surface mining activities, unless the regulatory authority specifically authorizes such activities closer to or through the stream. The regulatory authority may authorize such activities only upon finding that the activities will, to the extent possible, using the best technology currently available—

(1) Prevent additional contributions of suspended solids to the stream section within 100 feet downstream of the surface mining activities, and outside of the area affected by surface mining activities; and

(2) Minimize disturbances and adverse impacts on fish, wildlife, and other related environmental values of the stream.

Notes and Comments

1. One of the changes in the proposed rule is to require the prevention of additional contributions of suspended solids (silt) and the minimization of disturbance and adverse impacts only "to the extent possible, using the best technology available." The preamble to the proposed rule does not indicate what the best technology available might be, or to what extent it is possible to avoid the adverse effects identified in paragraphs (1) and (2). Indeed, the preamble says that "It is virtually impossible to conduct mining activities within 100 feet of an intermittent or perennial stream without causing some adverse impacts." 69 Fed. Reg. 1036, 1043 (2004).

2. The preamble states that "[w]e believe SMCRA recognizes that an absolute standard of 'no adverse impacts' is unattainable. This is reflected in the fact that SMCRA in most cases requires the mining operation to minimize, rather than completely prevent, adverse environmental impacts." *Id.* For example, 30 U.S.C. § 1265(b)(24) mandates that state and federal programs require mining operations to "minimize disturbances and adverse impacts on fish, wildlife, and related environmental values...." "to the extent possible using the best technology currently available." However, there is no attempt to relate the SBZ Rule to 30 U.S.C. § 1265(b)(22)(D), that requires state and federal programs to flatly prohibit placement of excess spoil material in an area containing "springs, natural water courses or wet weather weeps unless lateral drains are constructed...." Thus, even if the proposed rule more accurately captures OSMRE's interpretation of the original SBZ Rule, does it then square with the requirements of SMCRA?

3. Enforcement Issues

SMCRA was deemed necessary because coal mining states were unable, in the face of both coal industry (think Republican) and union (think Democratic) pressures, to muster sufficient political will to regulate mining themselves. SMCRA, however, still offers states "exclusive jurisdiction" if they have approved state programs. Because a state program, reflecting the state's laws and regulations, will have been approved by OSMRE in a public process with the input of EPA, Agriculture, and other federal agencies, the state's laws and regulations are usually not the problem. The problem is state administration and enforcement. Here, largely out of the view of the public, the same political pressures that historically affected coal regulation in major coal states continue to have substantial effects. In *Bragg* the plaintiffs alleged that the WVDEP routinely issued permits in violation of its own regulations, and in *Molinary* there was testimony from the permitting officer of the Virginia Division of Mined Land Reclamation that he routinely approved permit applications without requiring that all the regulatory requirements were met.

The statute provides for the withdrawal of a state's primacy, in whole or in part, for failing to enforce its laws effectively. *See* 30 U.S.C. § 1271(b). *See also* 30 U.S.C. § 1254(b) (allowing OSMRE, when a state is not enforcing "any part" of its program, to "provide for the federal enforcement, under [§ 1271], of that part of the State program"). And OSMRE has been willing to utilize this authority. In 1984 it instituted direct federal enforcement of the inspection provisions of Oklahoma's and Tennessee's programs. And in 2003 it instituted direct federal enforcement of inspection, enforcement, permitting, and bonding activities in Missouri. While this authority, which EPA has under the CWA, the CAA, and RCRA, may be adequate for OSMRE to ensure general adequacy of a state program, it provides no safety net of enforcement for individual, even serious, violations of state laws or regulations.

SMCRA does provide some safety net, but its extent depends on how some of its provisions are interpreted. First, if, "on the basis of any Federal inspection," conditions or practices are found to exist that cause an imminent danger to health or safety of the public, OSMRE may issue orders to cease mining operations and to take other actions necessary to abate the danger. 30 U.S.C. § 1271(a)(2). This provision, however, only comes into play if the violation is found incident to a federal inspection, and in primacy states federal inspections under SMCRA are only explicitly authorized in two situations. One is "to evaluate the administration of approved programs," not to discover violations or imminent danger conditions, 30 U.S.C. § 1267(a), although if conditions causing imminent danger are then found, the order provision comes into play. The other situation in which a federal inspection is authorized is when, "on the basis of any information available to him, including receipt of information from any person," OSMRE believes that any person is "in violation of any requirement of [SMCRA] or any permit condition required by [SMCRA]." 30 U.S.C. § 1271(a)(1). When the information provided to OSMRE is "adequate proof" that an imminent danger of significant environmental harm exists and that the state has failed to take appropriate action, the inspection may take place immediately. *Id.* Otherwise, before the inspection may take place in a primacy state, OSMRE must give the state regulatory authority 10–days notice, during which time the state regulatory authority may avoid the federal inspection by taking appropriate action or showing good cause why it has not. *Id.* There is an argument, based on the characterization of the violation as a "violation of any requirement of [SMCRA] or any permit condition required by [SMCRA]," that in primacy states an operator is simply incapable of violating SMCRA or a permit condition required by SMCRA, because in primacy states the operative regulatory law is state law, not SMCRA. The language in *Bragg* and the rationale in *Haydo* probably might support this argument. However, OSMRE does not accept this interpretation and its regulations explicitly authorize inspections upon receiving information regarding violations of state program requirements and state-issued permits. *See* 30 CFR § 842.11.

In the absence of an imminent danger, SMCRA may also provide some federal safety net. OSMRE adopted a regulation providing that, if a federal inspection in a primacy state reveals a violation of a state program requirement or permit condition that does not amount to an imminent danger, OSMRE may issue a notice of violation to the violator, requiring it to come into compliance within a reasonable time. 30 CFR § 843.12. If the inspection was not pursuant to enforcing a state program because the failure of a state to enforce that part of its program, *see* 30 U.S.C. 1254(b), OSMRE provides notice of the violation first to the state regulatory authority and allows it 10 days in which to take appropriate action or show good cause why it has not. 30 CFR § 843.12(a)(2). The coal industry challenged this regulation as beyond OSMRE's statutory authority, but its challenge was dismissed as barred by SMCRA's time limit of 60 days in which to challenge a regulation, 30 US.C. 1276(a)(1). *See National Min. Ass'n v. U.S. Dept. of Interior*, 70 F.3d 1345 (D.C.Cir. 1995).

The above discussion has focused on OSMRE being the safety net for enforcing requirements stemming from SMCRA not being adequately enforced by primacy states. Is OSMRE itself reliable? The Department of Interior traditionally has been more "political" than EPA, with its Secretaries reflecting the ideologies of their Presidents, and OSMRE has been affected by those politics. Its rulemakings expand or contract the protections provided by SMCRA depending upon the party in power. What about its enforcement actions? There is little empirical evidence upon which to base a conclusion, but its willingness on a few occasions to institute direct federal enforcement in place of the state regulatory authority, the number of contested enforcement actions reported in cases, and the number of Fifth Amendment takings cases from prohibitions against mining in certain areas, all suggest that OSMRE is a credible enforcement branch.

Perhaps the final safety net is the citizen suit by a person adversely affected to compel compliance with SMCRA. Some of the particular federalism problems as they affect SMCRA citizen suits were addressed earlier. Otherwise, the SMCRA citizen suit provision shares many similarities with other citizen suit provisions in environmental laws, which are discussed at length in the chapter on enforcement. There are two unique aspects to SMCRA's citizen suit provision. First, there is no provision for the citizen suit to result in civil penalties for the violator. Second, perhaps in place of civil penalties, there is provision for a damages action by any person injured in his person or property through the violation by any operator of "any rule, regulation, order, or permit issued pursuant to [SMCRA]." It was this part of the citizen suit provision that was in issue in both *Haydo* and *Molinary*.

Appendix

SUBMITTED COMMENTS OF LAW PROFESSORS[1]

80290   Federal Register / Vol. 67, No. 251 / Tuesday, December 31, 2002 / Proposed Rules

ENVIRONMENTAL PROTECTION AGENCY

40 CFR Parts 51 and 52

[FRL–7414–6; Docket A–2002–4]

RIN 2060–AK28

Prevention of Significant Deterioration (PSD) and Non-attainment New Source Review (NSR): Routine Maintenance, Repair and Replacement

AGENCY: Environmental Protection Agency (EPA).

ACTION: Proposed rule.

SUMMARY: The EPA is proposing revisions to the regulations governing the NSR programs mandated by parts C and D of title I of the Clean Air Act (CAA). These proposed changes reflect the EPA's consideration of the President's National Energy Policy (NEP), EPA's Report to the President on the impact of NSR pursuant to the NEP, and EPA's recommended changes to NSR based on the Report findings and discussions with various stakeholders including representatives from industry,

State and local governments, and environmental groups. The proposed changes provide a future category of activities that would be considered to be routine maintenance, repair and replacement (RMRR) under the NSR program. The changes are intended to provide greater regulatory certainty without sacrificing the current level of environmental protection and benefit derived from the program. We believe that these changes will facilitate the safe, efficient, and reliable operation of affected facilities.

DATES: *Comments.* Comments must be received on or before March 3, 2003.

Public Hearing. If anyone contacts us requesting to speak at a public hearing by January 21, 2003, we will hold a public hearing approximately 30 days after publication in the Federal Register.

ADDRESSES: *Comments.* Comments may be submitted electronically, by mail, by facsimile, or through hand delivery/ courier. Follow the detailed instructions as provided in section I.C. of the **SUPPLEMENTARY INFORMATION** section.

Public Hearing. The public hearing, if requested, will be held at the EPA's facilities at 109 TW Alexander Drive, Research Triangle Park, NC 27709 or at an alternate facility nearby. The EPA will not hold a hearing if one is not requested. Please check EPA's web page at *http://www.epa.gov/ttn/nsr/ whatsnew.html* on January 21, 2003 for the announcement of whether the hearing will be held.

FOR FURTHER INFORMATION CONTACT: Mr. Dave Svendsgaard, Information Transfer and Program Integration Division (C339–03), U.S. Environmental Protection Agency, Research Triangle Park, NC 27711, telephone (919) 541– 2380, or electronic mail at svendsgaard.dave@epa.gov.

SUPPLEMENTARY INFORMATION:

I. General Information

A. What Are the Regulated Entities?

Entities potentially affected by this proposed action include sources in all industry groups. The majority of sources potentially affected are expected to be in the following groups.

Industry group	SEC[a]	NAICS[b]
Electric Services	491	221111, 221112, 221113, 221119, 221121, 221122
Petroleum Refining	291	32411
Chemical Processes	281	325181, 32512, 325131, 325182, 211112, 325998, 331311, 325188
Natural Gas Transport	492	48621, 22121
Pulp and Paper Mills	261	32211, 322121, 322122, 32213
Paper Mills	262	322121, 322122
Automobile Manufacturing	371	336111, 336112, 336712, 336211, 336992, 336322, 336312, 33633, 33634, 33635, 336399, 336212, 336213
Pharmaceuticals	283	325411, 325412, 325413, 325414

[a] Standard Industrial Classification
[b] North American Industry Classification System. Entities potentially affected by this proposed action also would include State, local, and tribal governments that are delegated authority to implement these regulations.

B. How Can I Get Copies of This Document and Other Related Information?

1. Docket. EPA has established an official public docket for this action under Docket ID No. A–2002–04. The official public docket consists of the documents specifically referenced in this action, any public comments received, and other information related to this action. Although a part of the official docket, the public docket does not include Confidential Business Information (CBI) or other information whose disclosure is restricted by statute. The official public docket is the collection of materials that is available for public viewing at the EPA Docket Center, (Air Docket), U.S. Environmental Protection Agency, 1301 Constitution Ave., NW., Room: B108, Mail Code: 6102T, Washington, DC, 20004. The EPA Docket Center Public

Reading Room is open from 8:30 a.m. to 4:30 p.m., Monday through Friday, excluding legal holidays. The telephone number for the Reading Room is (202) 566–1742. A reasonable fee may be charged for copying.

2. Electronic Access. You may access this **Federal Register** document electronically through the EPA Internet under the "Federal Register" listings at *http://www.epa.gov/fedrgstr/.*

An electronic version of the public docket is available through EPA's electronic public docket and comment system, EPA Dockets. You may use EPA Dockets at *http://www.epa.gov/edocket/* to submit or view public comments, access the index listing of the contents of the official public docket, and to access those documents in the public docket that are available electronically. Once in the system, select "search,"

then key in the appropriate docket identification number.

Certain types of information will not be placed in the EPA Dockets. Information claimed as CBI and other information whose disclosure is restricted by statute, which is not included in the official public docket, will not be available for public viewing in EPA's electronic public docket. EPA's policy is that copyrighted material will not be placed in EPA's electronic public docket but will be available only in printed, paper form in the official public docket. To the extent feasible, publicly available docket materials will be made available in EPA's electronic public docket. When a document is selected from the index list in EPA Dockets, the system will identify whether the document is available for viewing in EPA's electronic public docket. Although not all docket materials may

---

1. From Victor Flatt, Michael M. O'Hear, Mark Squillace, and Robert R.M. Verchick, *Let the People Speak: Notice-and-Comment Rulemaking (Lessons from the Controversial New Source Review Proposal of the Clean Air Act),* 34 ELR 10115 (February 2004).

Federal Register / Vol. 67, No. 251 / Tuesday, December 31, 2002 / Proposed Rules   80291

be available electronically, you may still access any of the publicly available docket materials through the docket facility identified in section I.B.1. EPA intends to work towards providing electronic access to all of the publicly available docket materials through EPA's electronic public docket.

For public commenters, it is important to note that EPA's policy is that public comments, whether submitted electronically or in paper, will be made available for public viewing in EPA's electronic public docket as EPA receives them and without change, unless the comment contains copyrighted material, CBI, or other information whose disclosure is restricted by statute. When EPA identifies a comment containing copyrighted material, EPA will provide a reference to that material in the version of the comment that is placed in EPA's electronic public docket. The entire printed comment, including the copyrighted material, will be available in the public docket.

Public comments submitted on computer disks that are mailed or delivered to the docket will be transferred to EPA's electronic public docket. Public comments that are mailed or delivered to the Docket will be scanned and placed in EPA's electronic public docket. Where practical, physical objects will be photographed, and the photograph will be placed in EPA's electronic public docket along with a brief description written by the docket staff.

For additional information about EPA's electronic public docket visit EPA Dockets online or see 67 FR 38102, May 31, 2002.

C. How and to Whom Do I Submit Comments?

You may submit comments electronically, by mail, by facsimile, or through hand delivery/courier. To ensure proper receipt by EPA, identify the appropriate docket identification number in the subject line on the first page of your comment. Please ensure that your comments are submitted within the specified comment period. Comments received after the close of the comment period will be marked "late." EPA is not required to consider these late comments. If you wish to submit CBI or information that is otherwise protected by statute, please follow the instructions in section I.D. Do not use EPA Dockets or e-mail to submit CBI or information protected by statute.

1. Electronically. If you submit an electronic comment as prescribed below, EPA recommends that you include your name, mailing address, and an e-mail address or other contact information in the body of your comment. Also include this contact information on the outside of any disk or CD ROM you submit, and in any cover letter accompanying the disk or CD ROM. This ensures that you can be identified as the submitter of the comment and allows EPA to contact you in case EPA cannot read your comment due to technical difficulties or needs further information on the substance of your comment. EPA's policy is that EPA will not edit your comment, and any identifying or contact information provided in the body of a comment will be included as part of the comment that is placed in the official public docket, and made available in EPA's electronic public docket. If EPA cannot read your comment due to technical difficulties and cannot contact you for clarification, EPA may not be able to consider your comment.

a. EPA Dockets. Your use of EPA's electronic public docket to submit comments to EPA electronically is EPA's preferred method for receiving comments. Go directly to EPA Dockets at *http://www.epa.gov/edocket*, and follow the online instructions for submitting comments. To access EPA's electronic public docket from the EPA Internet Home Page, select "Information Sources," "Dockets," and "EPA Dockets." Once in the system, select "search," and then key in Docket ID No. A–2002–04. The system is an "anonymous access" system, which means EPA will not know your identity, e-mail address, or other contact information unless you provide it in the body of your comment.

b. E-mail. Comments may be sent by electronic mail (e-mail) to *a-and-r-docket@epamail.epa.gov*, Attention Docket ID No. A–2002–04. In contrast to EPA's electronic public docket, EPA's e-mail system is not an "anonymous access" system. If you send an e-mail comment directly to the Docket without going through EPA's electronic public docket, EPA's e-mail system automatically captures your e-mail address. E-mail addresses that are automatically captured by EPA's e-mail system are included as part of the comment that is placed in the official public docket, and made available in EPA's electronic public docket.

c. Disk or CD ROM. You may submit comments on a disk or CD ROM that you mail to the mailing address identified in section I.C.2. These electronic submissions will be accepted in WordPerfect or ASCII file format. Avoid the use of special characters and any form of encryption.

2. *By Mail.* Send two copies of your comments to: U.S. Environmental Protection Agency, EPA West (Air Docket), 1200 Pennsylvania Ave., NW, Room: B108, Mail code: 6102T, Washington, DC, 20460, Attention Docket ID No. A–2002–04.

3. *By Hand Delivery or Courier.* Deliver your comments to: EPA Docket Center, (Air Docket), U.S. Environmental Protection Agency, 1301 Constitution Ave., NW., Room: B108, Mail Code: 6102T, Washington, DC, 20004., Attention Docket ID No. A–2002–04. Such deliveries are only accepted during the Docket's normal hours of operation as identified in section I.B.1.

4. *By Facsimile.* Fax your comments to the EPA Docket Center at (202) 566–1741, Attention Docket ID. No. A–2002–04.

D. How Should I Submit CBI to the Agency?

Do not submit information that you consider to be CBI electronically through EPA's electronic public docket or by e-mail. Send or deliver information identified as CBI only to the following address: Mr. David Svendsgaard, c/o OAQPS Document Control Officer (C339–03), U.S. Environmental Protection Agency, Research Triangle Park, NC 27711, Attention Docket ID No. A–2002–04. You may claim information that you submit to EPA as CBI by marking any part or all of that information as CBI. (If you submit CBI on disk or CD ROM, mark the outside of the disk or CD ROM as CBI and then identify electronically within the disk or CD ROM the specific information that is CBI.) Information so marked will not be disclosed except in accordance with procedures set forth in 40 CFR Part 2.

In addition to one complete version of the comment that includes any information claimed as CBI, a copy of the comment that does not contain the information claimed as CBI must be submitted for inclusion in the public docket and EPA's electronic public docket. If you submit the copy that does not contain CBI on disk or CD ROM, mark the outside of the disk or CD ROM clearly that it does not contain CBI. Information not marked as CBI will be included in the public docket and EPA's electronic public docket without prior notice. If you have any questions about CBI or the procedures for claiming CBI, please consult the person identified in the **FOR FURTHER INFORMATION CONTACT** section.

80292 Federal Register / Vol. 67, No. 251 / Tuesday, December 31, 2002 / Proposed Rules

E. What Should I Consider as I Prepare my Comments for EPA?

You may find the following suggestions helpful for preparing your comments.

• Explain your views as clearly as possible.

• Describe any assumptions that you used.

• Provide any technical information and/or data you used that support your views.

• If you estimate potential burden or costs, explain how you arrived at your estimate.

• Provide specific examples to illustrate your concerns.

• Offer alternatives.

• Make sure to submit your comments by the comment period deadline identified.

• To ensure proper receipt by EPA, identify the appropriate docket identification number in the subject line on the first page of your response. It would also be helpful if you provided the name, date, and **Federal Register** citation related to your comments.

F. How Can I Find Information About a Possible Public Hearing?

Persons interested in presenting oral testimony or inquiring as to whether a hearing is to be held should contact Ms. Pamela J. Smith, Integrated Implementation Group, Information Transfer and Program Integration Division (C339–03), U.S. Environmental Protection Agency, Research Triangle Park, NC 27711, telephone number (919) 541–0641, at least 2 days in advance of the public hearing. Persons interested in attending the public hearing should also contact Ms. Smith to verify the time, date, and location of the hearing. The public hearing will provide interested parties the opportunity to present data, views, or arguments concerning these proposed emission standards.

G. Where Can I Obtain Additional Information?

In addition to being available in the docket, an electronic copy of this proposed rule is also available on the WWW through the Technology Transfer Network (TTN). Following signature by the EPA Administrator, a copy of the proposed rule will be posted on the TTN's policy and guidance page for newly proposed or promulgated rules at *http://www.epa.gov/ttn/oarpg*. The TTN provides information and technology exchange in various areas of air pollution control. If more information regarding the TTN is needed, call the TTN HELP line at (919) 541–5384.

H. How is This Preamble Organized?

The information presented in this preamble is organized as follows:

I. General Information
  A. What are the regulated entities?
  B. How can I get copies of this document and other related information?
  C. How and to whom do I submit comments?
  D. How should I submit CBI to the Agency?
  E. What should I consider as I prepare my comments for EPA?
  F. How can I find information about a possible public hearing?
  G. Where can I obtain additional information?
  H. How is this preamble organized?
II. Purpose
III. Background
  A. How does the process of using the RMRR exclusion currently work?
  B. Why is the specification of categories of RMRR activities appropriate?
  C. Process Used to Develop This Rule
IV. Overview of Recommended Approaches for RMRR
  A. Annual Maintenance, Repair and Replacement Allowance
  B. Equipment Replacement Provision
V. Legal Basis for Recommended Approaches
VI. Discussion of Issues Under Annual Maintenance, Repair and Replacement Allowance Approach
  A. Appropriate Time Period for a Maintenance, Repair and Replacement Allowance
  B. Cost Basis
  C. Basis for Annual Allowance—Stationary Source vs Process Unit
  D. Basis for Annual Maintenance, Repair and Replacement Allowance Percentage
  E. How to Calculate Costs
  F. Applicability Safeguards
  G. Timing of Determination
VII. Discussion of Issues under the Equipment Replacement Approach
  A. Replacement of Existing Equipment with Identical or Functionally Equivalent Equipment
  B. Defining "Process Unit" for Evaluating Equipment Replacement Cost Percentage
  C. Miscellaneous Issues
  D. Quantitative Analysis
VIII. Other Options Considered
  A. Capacity-Based Option
  B. Age-Based Option
IX. Administrative Requirements for this Proposed Rulemaking
  A. Executive Order 12866—Regulatory Planning and Review
  B. Executive Order 13132—Federalism
  C. Executive Order 13175—Consultation and Coordination with Indian Tribal Governments
  D. Executive Order 13045—Protection of Children from Environmental Health Risks and Safety Risks
  E. Paperwork Reduction Act
  F. Regulatory Flexibility Act (RFA), as Amended by the Small Business Regulatory Enforcement Fairness Act of 1996 (SBREFA), 5 U.S.C. 601 *et seq.*
  G. Unfunded Mandates Reform Act of 1995
  H. National Technology Transfer and Advancement Act of 1995

I. Executive Order 13211—Actions Concerning Regulations That Significantly Affect Energy Supply, Distribution, or Use
X. Statutory Authority

II. Purpose

We are proposing a change to the NSR program to provide specific categories of activities that EPA will consider RMRR in the future. We are seeking comment on all aspects of our proposed approaches to specifying categories of RMRR activities under the NSR program, and on other options considered. These approaches would be voluntary, in that owners or operators could opt to continue using the current procedures for determining what activities constitute RMRR at their facilities. This proposal seeks public comments in accordance with section 307(d) of the CAA and should not be used or cited in any litigation as the final position of the Agency.

III. Background

A. How Does the Process of Using the RMRR Exclusion Currently Work?

Under the changes promulgated today to 40 CFR parts 51 and 52, "major modification" is defined as any physical change in or change in the method of operation of a major stationary source that would result in: (1) A significant emissions increase of a regulated NSR pollutant; and (2) a significant net emissions increase of that pollutant from the major stationary source. Owners/operators of major stationary sources are required to obtain a major NSR permit prior to beginning actual construction of a modification that meets this definition. The regulations exclude certain activities from the definition of "major modification." One such exclusion is for RMRR activities. The regulations do not define this term. (See 40 CFR 51.165(a)(1)(v)(C)(*1*), 51.166(b)(2)(iii)(*a*), 52.21(b)(2)(iii)(*a*) and 52.24(f)(5)(iii)(*a*).)

Under our current approach, the RMRR exclusion is applied on a case-by-case basis. In interpreting this exclusion, we have followed certain criteria. The preamble to the 1992 "WEPCO Rule" (57 *FR* 32314) and applicability determinations made to date describe our current approach to assessing what activities constitute RMRR. These applicability determinations are available electronically from the Region 7 NSR Policy and Guidance Database (*http://www.epa.gov/Region7/programs/artd/air/nsr/nsrpg.htm*).

To summarize these documents, to determine whether proposed work at a facility is routine, EPA makes a case-by-case determination by weighing the nature, extent, purpose, frequency, and the cost of the work as well as other relevant factors to arrive at a common sense finding. WEPCO at 910. None of these factors, in and of itself, is conclusive. Instead, a reviewing authority should take account of how each of these factors might apply in a particular circumstance to arrive at a conclusion considering the project as a whole. If an owner or operator is uncertain whether he or she is applying the NSR regulations correctly, we encourage the owner or operator to consult the appropriate reviewing authority for assistance.

B. Why Is Specification of Categories of RMRR Activities Appropriate?

There has been some debate over the years as to the case-by-case approach and the types of activities that qualify as RMRR under our current case-by-case approach. The case-specific approach works well in many respects. For example, it is a flexible tool that accommodates the broad range of industries and the diversity of activities that are potentially subject to the NSR program.

However, the case-by-case approach has certain drawbacks. Unless an owner or operator seeks an applicability determination from his or her reviewing authority or from EPA, it can be difficult for the owner or operator to know with certainty whether a particular activity constitutes RMRR. Applicability determinations can be costly and time consuming for reviewing authorities and industry alike. If a source proceeds without a determination and is later proven to have made an incorrect determination, that source faces potentially serious enforcement consequences. Moreover, under the current case-by-case approach, State and local reviewing authorities must devote scarce resources to making complex determinations and consult with other agencies to ensure that any determinations are consistent with determinations made for similar circumstances in other jurisdictions and/or that EPA or other reviewing authorities would concur with the conclusion.

On the other hand, if a source foregoes or defers activities that are important to maintaining its plant when the activities in question are in fact within scope of the exclusion, that can have adverse consequences for the source's reliability, efficiency, and safety. Finally, the source may install less efficient or less modern equipment in order to be more certain that it is within the regulatory bounds, or it may

agree to limit its hours of operation or capacity. Any of these approaches will make the source less productive than it would be otherwise. In fact, we concluded in our recent report to the President on the impacts of NSR on the energy sector that there have been cases in which uncertainty about the exclusion for RMRR resulted in delay or cancellation of activities that would have maintained and improved the reliability, efficiency, and safety of existing energy capacity. Such discouragement results in lost capacity and lost opportunities to improve energy efficiency and reduce air pollution.

We believe that these problems would be significantly reduced by adding to our current RMRR provision specific categories of activities that will be considered to be RMRR in the future. Such categories would remove disincentives to undertaking RMRR activities and provide more certainty both to source owners and operators who could better plan activities at their facilities, and to reviewing authorities who could better focus resources on activities outside these RMRR categories. Accordingly, the establishment of categories of activities as RMRR is consistent with the central purpose of the CAA, "to protect and enhance the quality of the Nation's air resources so as to promote the public health and welfare and the productive capacity of its population." CAA section 101.

It should be noted that there may be some activities which, while fitting within the ambit of the RMRR exclusion could, if implemented, violate other applicable CAA requirements. As has always been the case, compliance with NSR requirements is not a license to violate any of the other applicable CAA requirements such as title V permitting requirements.

C. Process Used To Develop This Rule

In the 1992 "WEPCO Rule" preamble, we indicated that we planned to issue guidance on the subject of RMRR. In 1994, as part of our meetings with the Clean Air Act Advisory Committee, we developed, for discussion purposes only, a document on how RMRR could be defined. We received a substantial volume of comments on this document. We subsequently decided not to include a definition of RMRR in our 1996 NSR proposed rulemaking.

In 2001, the President's NEP Report [1] directed EPA in consultation with the

[1] Reliable, Affordable, and Environmentally Sound Energy for America's Future, Report of the National Energy Policy Development Group, May 17, 2001.

Department of Energy (DOE) and other federal agencies to review the impact of NSR on investment in new utility and refinery generation capacity, energy efficiency and environmental protection. The release of the report in May 2001 triggered a review of the impacts of NSR rules. EPA's Report to the President underscored the desirability of specifying certain categories of activities that qualify as RMRR. In parallel with this review, we renewed our exploration of recommendations for improving the NSR program. Recommended improvements suggested during this time represented a continuation of discussions on NSR issues that had taken place during the 1990's, as well as new ideas.

The process of discussing possible improvements to the NSR program included significant interagency consultation, including meetings with representatives from the DOE, the Department of the Interior, and the Office of Management and Budget. Building on what we heard, we held conference calls with various stakeholders during October 2001 (including representatives from industry, State and local governments, and environmental groups) to discuss new ideas that were raised. During many of these meetings, we discussed ideas for how to define RMRR in order to create more certainty for the industry and reviewing authorities. Today's proposed rule is an outgrowth of ideas discussed in those meetings.

IV. Overview of Recommended Approaches for RMRR

Ever since EPA's promulgation of its original Prevention of Significant Deterioration (PSD) regulations in 1980, EPA has defined "modification" in its NSR regulations to include common-sense exclusions from the "physical or operational change" component of the definition, including an exclusion for RMRR. Today, we are proposing two categories of activities that will in the future be considered RMRR activities: activities within an annual maintenance, repair and replacement allowance and replacements that meet our equipment replacement provision criteria.

Under the proposal, when an activity falls within either of these categories, it would be considered RMRR and a source's owners or operators would know that the activity was excluded from NSR without regard to other considerations. When an activity did not fall within one of these categories, then it still could qualify as routine maintenance, repair, and replacement under the case-by-case test.

A. Annual Maintenance, Repair and Replacement Allowance

First, we are proposing to add new language to the RMRR exclusion at 40 CFR 51.165 (a)(1)(v)(C)(*1*), 40 CFR 51.166 (b)(2)(iii)(*a*), 40 CFR part 51, Appendix S (A)(5)(iii)(*a*), 40 CFR 52.21(b)(2)(iii)(*a*), and 40 CFR 52.24 (f)(5)(iii)(*a*).This proposal would allow certain activities engaged in to promote the safe, reliable and efficient operation of a facility-that is, those that involve relatively small capital expenditures compared with the replacement cost of the facility—to be excluded from NSR provided that total costs did not exceed the annual maintenance, repair and replacement allowance. The annual maintenance, repair and replacement allowance and the rules for calculation and summation of activities under the allowance would be defined in new provisions at 40 CFR 51.165(a)(1)(xxxxii), 40 CFR 51.166(b)(53), 40 CFR 52.21(b)(55), and 40 CFR 52.24(f)(25).

Under our proposed approach, a calendar year maintenance, repair and replacement allowance would be established for each stationary source. The owner or operator may elect to use a fiscal year period instead of a calendar year if financial records are typically kept for a period other than calendar year at a facility.[2] Although the proposal contemplates a one-year allowance, in recognition of the fact that maintenance cycles in many industries extend for more than 1 year, we also seek comment on whether a stationary source should have the option of a multi-year allowance, such as over 5 years.

Under our 1-year allowance proposal, an owner or operator would sum the costs of the relevant activities performed at the stationary source during the fiscal or calendar year (from the least expensive to the most expensive) to get a yearly cost. For activities taking more than 1 year to complete, costs associated with those activities would be included in the cost calculations for the year that the costs were incurred (using an accounting method consistent with that used for other purposes by the stationary source). If the total costs for all activities undertaken for these purposes came within the annual maintenance, repair and replacement allowance, these activities would all be considered RMRR activities. Other than documentation of the results of this assessment, the owner or operator

would not have to do anything further with respect to those activities for purposes of major NSR.

Where total yearly costs for all activities undertaken for these purposes at a source exceed the annual maintenance, repair and replacement allowance, the activities would be reviewed as follows.

• The owner or operator would subtract activities from the total yearly cost, starting with the most expensive activity, until the remainder is less than or equal to the annual maintenance, repair and replacement allowance.

• The owner or operator would evaluate on a case-by-case basis in accordance with EPA's case-by-case test any activities that did not come within the allowance and that are not otherwise excluded, in order to determine whether they are RMRR. If uncertain about a particular activity the owner or operator could seek an applicability determination.

• If an owner or operator concluded that any such activity was not RMRR, he or she would then have to determine whether it constitutes a "major modification" that requires an NSR permit.

The annual maintenance, repair and replacement allowance would be equal to the product of the replacement cost of the source and a specified maintenance, repair and replacement percentage. (See §§ 51.165(a)(1)(xxxxii), 51.166(b)(53), 52.21(b)(55) and 52.24(f)(25) of proposed rules.) EPA intends to set this percentage on an industry-specific basis. There are several ways in which the percentage could be established. One way is to set the threshold so as to cover the RMRR capital and non-capital costs that an owner or operator incurs to maintain, facilitate, restore, or improve the safety, reliability, availability, or efficiency of the source. We are also requesting comment on other approaches. For example, we could apply a discount factor to the typical costs in order to account for variability within an industry. We also ask for comment on how to determine typical costs for particular industries. We are considering using the Internal Revenue Service "Annual Asset Guideline Repair Allowance Percentages" (AAGRAP), which we use for an exclusion under the New Source Performance Standard (NSPS) program for increases in production. See also could rely on industry specific data for choosing an appropriate threshold, such as the North American Electric Reliability Council Generating Availability Data System (NERC/GADS) database or standard industry reference manuals.

The replacement cost used in the calculation described above would be an estimate of the total capital investment necessary to replace the stationary source. The accounting procedures used to document eligibility under this rule should conform to the accounting procedures used for other purposes at a facility. Where several accounting procedures are used at a facility (*e.g.*, methods for tax accounting and for setting rates often are different), the most appropriate procedures should be used for the purpose of determining costs pursuant to this regulation.

EPA also seeks to standardize practices for estimating this investment, along the lines described in the *EPA Air Pollution Control Cost Manual*, excluding the costs for installing and maintaining pollution control equipment. See section V.E. of this document for further information on our recommended approach to calculating costs. The control cost manual is available electronically via the internet at *http://www.epa.gov/ttn/catc/dir1/ c_allchs.pdf*. We acknowledge that this manual is geared toward cost calculations for add-on control equipment but believe the basic concepts can be applied to process equipment as well. These concepts are taken from work done by the American Association of Cost Engineers to define the components of cost calculations for all types of processes, not just emission control equipment. We seek comment on whether this manual or other reference documents or tools provide the best approach for standardizing estimation of these costs, whether different methods should be provided, and whether provision should be made in the form of a requirement or an assurance that if a method is used, we will accept it.

Our recommended approach will contain safeguards to help ensure that activities that should be considered a physical change or change in the method of operation under the regulations are ineligible for exclusion from NSR under the annual maintenance, repair and replacement allowance. We are proposing to exclude the following from use of the annual allowance.

• The construction of a new "process unit," which is a collection of structures and/or equipment that uses material inputs to produce or store a completed product. See discussion below at section VII for further information regarding process units.

• The replacement of an entire process unit

• Any change that would result in an increase in the source's maximum

Federal Register / Vol. 67, No. 251 / Tuesday, December 31, 2002 / Proposed Rules   80295

achievable hourly emissions rate of any regulated NSR pollutant, or in the emission of any regulated NSR pollutant not previously emitted by the stationary source.

If an owner or operator uses the annual maintenance, repair and replacement allowance to determine that certain activities at a stationary source are RMRR, all relevant activities performed at that source must be included in the annual cost calculations unless the owner or operator elects to obtain a major NSR permit for the activity. In other words, an owner or operator may not select which activities to review case-by-case and which to include in the cost calculations when using the annual maintenance, repair and replacement allowance to determine RMRR activities. This is because, assuming the threshold is set to approximate the total amount that an owner or operator would typically be expected to spend on RMRR activities (or a discounted portion of this value selected to account for variability within an industry), the fact that a given activity's cost comes within the allowance can only reasonably assure that it is RMRR if all other relevant activities also are included. If the owner

or operator could pick and choose among activities that he or she wished to include in the allowance, such an approach might allow the owner or operator to include large, atypical activities that do not constitute RMRR within the allowance, while applying the case-by-case test to smaller activities that quite clearly constitute RMRR under that test. The rule that all relevant activities must be included in the calculation and that lowest cost activities would be counted first should provide sufficient protection against this risk.

Owners or operators electing to use the annual maintenance, repair and replacement allowance to determine RMRR activities will be required to submit an annual report to the appropriate reviewing authority within 60 days after the end of the year over which activity costs have been summed. The report will provide a summary of the estimated replacement value of the stationary source, the annual maintenance, repair and replacement allowance for the stationary source, a brief description of all maintenance, repair and replacement activities undertaken at the stationary source, and the costs associated with those

activities. If the costs of activities in question exceed the annual maintenance, repair and replacement allowance for a stationary source, the report must identify the activities included within the allowance and the activities that fell outside the allowance. The procedures set out in 40 CFR part 2 are available for confidential and business-sensitive information submitted as part of this report.

The following provides an example of how the process would work. Assume the source's annual maintenance, repair and replacement allowance equals $2,000,000. During a given year, the owner or operator spends $1,000,000 on running maintenance activities, and implements five other discrete maintenance activities at the source with costs as follows in Table 1 (none of these activities involves the construction of a new process unit, replacement of an existing process unit, or an increase in the maximum achievable hourly emissions rate of a regulated NSR pollutant or in the emission of any regulated NSR pollutant not previously emitted by the stationary source).

TABLE 1.—EXAMPLE SUMMARY OF ACTIVITIES COMMENCED DURING YEAR

Change	Month	Cost
Activity 1	January	$200,000
Activity 2	March	600,000
Activity 3	April	360,000
Activity 4	July	150,000
Activity 5	November	250,000

The sum of costs incurred during the year is $2,560,000, $560,000 above the annual maintenance, repair and replacement allowance. The most expensive activity commencing during the year was the $600,000 activity commencing in March. The source must evaluate on a case-by-case basis whether this activity is RMRR. When the cost of Activity 2 is subtracted from the total annual cost, the remainder is $1,960,000, less than the annual maintenance, repair and replacement allowance. The remaining activities (Activities 1, 3, 4, and 5) are considered to be RMRR.

We note that this example is framed as if the owner or operator would make these calculations for the first time at the end of the year. In reality, however, an owner or operator who is considering relying on the maintenance, repair and replacement allowance as the basis for his or her conclusion that a particular activity is RMRR is likely to make these

calculations before beginning construction on any activity. This is because the owner or operator would know that he or she will only be able to rely on the allowance if the costs of the activity in question, when added with the costs of other activities to assure the safe, efficient, and reliable operation of the plant that the owner or operator is planning for the year, will in fact be within the allowance.

B. Equipment Replacement Provision

In addition to our proposed annual maintenance, repair and replacement allowance, today we are also soliciting comment on an additional approach to be used in the future for those replacement activities that should qualify without regard to other considerations as RMRR. Specifically, we are soliciting comment on whether replacing existing equipment with equipment that serves the same function and that does not alter the basic design

parameters of a unit should also qualify without regard for other considerations for RMRR treatment provided the cost of the replacement equipment does not exceed a certain percentage of the cost of the process unit to which the equipment belongs. While we believe the annual maintenance, repair and replacement provisions described above will significantly improve implementation of the RMRR exclusion, we recognize that the allowance may apply only to a subset of the activities that appropriately fall within the exclusion and that are susceptible of being identified as categorically constituting RMRR.[3]

---

[3] Of course, as noted earlier, the traditional case-by-case approach to administering the RMRR exclusion will continue to apply to activities that do not qualify under the annual maintenance, repair and replacement allowance approach described above, but for the reasons noted earlier, we believe that approach would be improved on by the identification of activities that may be found to
Continued

Accordingly, today we are soliciting comment on an additional approach to be used in the future for determining that certain replacement activities whose costs fall below a specified threshold qualify as RMRR without regard for other considerations. Under this approach, EPA would establish a percentage of the replacement value of a process unit as a threshold for applying the equipment replacement provision. If the replacement component is functionally equivalent to the replaced component, does not change the basic design parameters of the process unit, and does not exceed the cost threshold, it would constitute RMRR. This approach should enable the owner or operator to streamline the RMRR analysis and make this determination more readily and should further alleviate some of the problems noted above. We are soliciting comment on whether this approach would serve to streamline the RMRR determination process for activities that involve the replacement of existing equipment with identical new equipment and the replacement of existing equipment with functionally equivalent equipment. We are also soliciting comment on whether this approach should be adopted along with the annual maintenance, repair and replacement allowance described above, or whether this approach is preferred over the other such that we should only offer the equipment replacement provision in the final rule.

We also solicit comment on what provisions might be needed to clarify and facilitate implementation of a combined approach. For example, should the costs of activities that qualify as an excluded equipment replacement count toward the annual maintenance, repair and replacement allowance? And, if so, how should they be counted? We are also soliciting comment on whether any other category of activity undertaken for these purposes should be excludable by the owner or operator from the annual maintenance, repair and replacement allowance. For example, activities undertaken to address unanticipated forced outages or catastrophic events such as fires or explosions may be the kind of unforeseeable expenditure that an owner or operator should not have to include because it is not possible to plan for it. Also, the absence of an exclusion for such activities might be a disincentive for maintaining and ensuring safe operation. If excluded from the maintenance, repair and replacement allowance, these activities

constitute RMRR without requiring case-by-case consideration of this type.

could still qualify for RMRR status under the equipment replacement provision of this rule if they meet the criteria for that allowance or under the case-by-case analysis.

Finally, we are soliciting comment on other approaches that might be effective in streamlining the RMRR determination process.

V. Legal Basis for Recommended Approaches

The modification provisions of the NSR program in parts C and D of title I of the CAA are based on the broad definition of modification in section 111(a)(4) of the CAA. The term "modification" means "any physical change in, or change in the method of operation of, a stationary source which increases the amount of any air pollutant emitted by such source or which results in the emission of any air pollutant not previously emitted." That definition contemplates that you will first determine whether a physical or operational change will occur. If so, then you proceed to determine whether the physical or operational change will result in an emissions increase over baseline levels.

The expression "any physical change * * * or change in the method of operation" in section 111(a)(4) of the CAA is not defined. We have recognized that Congress did not intend to make every activity at a source subject to the major NSR program. As a result, we have previously adopted nine exclusions from what may constitute a "physical or operational change." One of these is an exclusion for routine maintenance, repair, and replacement. Today's rulemaking proposes two provisions that will improve and help carry out the purposes of this exclusion.

VI. Discussion of Issues Under Annual Maintenance, Repair and Replacement Allowance Approach

The following provides a discussion of the key issues we considered in developing our preferred approaches to addressing RMRR under the NSR program. We are requesting comment on all alternatives considered and any other viable alternatives. We are also interested in the impact the use of a cost-based approach such as the annual maintenance, repair and replacement allowance will have on reviewing authorities, such as the need for staff knowledgeable in cost estimation, and are requesting comment on this issue.

A. Appropriate Time Period for a Maintenance, Repair and Replacement Allowance

In developing a maintenance, repair and replacement allowance, we considered setting an allowance based on either a calendar or fiscal year or a multi-year limit. We believe that a limit applied over a specified period of time is more appropriate than an activity-based limit. We are proposing an annual limit, but we also believe that a multi-year limit is worthy of serious consideration as a possible option that could be chosen by owners or operators with multi-year maintenance cycles.

Under NSR, to determine applicability, the owner or operator of a major source must determine whether an activity performed at a source is a physical change or change in the method of operation that results in a significant emissions increase and a significant net emissions increase. NSR may apply to a single physical change or operational change at a single process unit, to several physical or operational changes at a single process unit, or to multiple changes across multiple process units, each of which changes can vary widely in scope and cost. Developing a maintenance, repair and replacement allowance on an activity basis would be consistent with this framework. However, the variability in the scope of such activities makes it difficult to establish an appropriate cost allowance for individual activities based on data currently available to us. On the other hand, the majority of information that is currently available to us does provide a reasonable basis for developing facility-wide, annual maintenance, repair and replacement cost estimates. In addition to the difficulty in establishing an activity cost limit, maintenance budgets are typically set on an annual basis rather than an activity basis, making an annual allowance more consistent with industry financial practices.

In choosing between an annual versus a multi-year limit, there are considerations pointing in both directions. The most important argument in favor of a multi-year option is that in a number of industries, maintenance cycles extend over multiple years. For example, petroleum refineries conduct regularly scheduled maintenance, referred to as a "turnaround," in cycles that can be as long as 8 years depending on the type of units and equipment involved and the particulars of the unit's operations. During a turnaround, all or part of the refinery is shut down, and the owner or operator undertakes numerous

Federal Register / Vol. 67, No. 251 / Tuesday, December 31, 2002 / Proposed Rules **80297**

maintenance, repair and/or replacement activities during the shutdown.

Similarly, the power generation sector performs regularly scheduled maintenance, inspections, and repair on varying cycles, which, depending on the equipment involved, can range from 12 months to a number of years. Like refineries, power generation facilities must conduct much of the inspection, maintenance, repair and replacement work when the units are shut down, and to minimize the frequency of scheduled outages, the owner or operator will undertake numerous activities during a given shutdown to minimize maintenance costs, minimize the need for replacement power, and maximize the availability of the units. As a result, for industries of this type, the cost of maintenance will vary significantly from year to year and may be distributed across several years.

An annual allowance for industries of this type may be unworkable if the allowance is set at the average of their maintenance costs during their maintenance cycle. But setting the level higher than the average runs the risk of sweeping in non-routine activity. In addition, an annual allowance might lead owners or operators in such industries to engage in more outages than is efficient in order to make sure that they were not losing a portion of their allowance. This could increase energy costs and reduce energy availability to consumers.

If a multi-year allowance were used, the same principles of summing the costs of activities from least to most costly and excluding the most costly activities from the allowance and instead subjecting them to case-by-case scrutiny would continue to apply.

This approach also may have its difficulties. For example, as the cycle gets longer, it is harder for owners or operators to project their costs for safeguarding the safety, reliability and efficiency of their plants farther into the future. This, in turn, may contribute to a rule that is more difficult to implement and enforce. If, through the after the fact case-by-case review, it is determined that certain activities should have been subject to the NSR program, all parties may be placed in the difficult situation of implementing a preconstruction review program for an activity that was begun or completed significantly prior to the applicability determination. This difficulty may arise to some extent even with a 1-year allowance period. But extending the period beyond 1 year increases both the possibility for this occurrence and the potential difficulties of an after-the-fact applicability determination for older

activities. Thus, while using a single year as the time period will reduce the flexibility for some owners or operators, we believe it will help to reduce the likelihood that an after-the-fact NSR review will be required. For these reasons, we are proposing the annual maintenance, repair and replacement allowance approach, but will also be giving serious consideration to the multi-year approach of up to 5 years. We are requesting comments on the approaches discussed above.

We are also proposing that the time period for the annual maintenance, repair and replacement allowance should be a calendar or fiscal year. If the owner or operator of a major stationary source uses a fiscal year that differs from a calendar year for accounting purposes, the proposed rule would allow the stationary source to elect to use that fiscal year for purposes of applying the annual maintenance, repair and replacement allowance. As proposed, once the choice is made, the choice is permanent. (See § 51.165(a)(1)(xxxxii)(A)(*1*), § 51.166(b)(53)(i)(*a*), § 52.21(b)(55)(i)(*a*), and § 52.24(f)(25)(i)(*a*) of proposed rules.) We specifically ask for comment on this aspect of the proposal.

B. Cost Basis

Under our proposal, the replacement cost of a source would be multiplied by the maintenance percentage established by rule to determine the annual maintenance, repair and replacement allowance. (See § 51.165(a)(1)(xxxxii), § 51.166(b)(53), § 52.21(b)(55), and § 52.24(f)(25) of proposed rules.) In developing the proposal, we also considered using an invested cost basis adjusted for inflation.

There can be advantages to using invested cost. The most obvious advantage is that knowledge of cost estimation is not necessary, because actual cost data would be used. However, complete invested cost information may no longer exist for older stationary sources, or it may not have been provided to the buyer when a source was purchased. As a result, we would still need to provide for an alternative for situations where invested cost data were not available.

In addition, even when adjusted for inflation, there could be inequities between facilities if an invested cost basis was used. Adjustment for inflation between sources will not likely take into account variations in site-specific costs such as land, labor, and materials, among others. Use of replacement cost, which takes into account site-specific factors to a greater degree, will put all regulated entities on a more equitable

footing. Moreover, most decisions regarding maintenance, repair and replacement are more likely to take into consideration the cost of replacement rather than the original invested cost.

We are proposing to use source replacement cost; however, we are requesting comment on other potentially appropriate bases for source cost, including invested cost, invested cost adjusted for inflation or any other viable methodology.

C. Basis for Annual Allowance— Stationary Source vs Process Unit

We are considering two approaches for administering the annual maintenance, repair and replacement allowance—the allowance could be established at either an entire stationary source (source) or at the process unit level. A comprehensive discussion of the term "process unit," along with a proposed definition, is set forth in section VII, below. If we opt for the "process unit" approach, we would use the definition and concepts proposed in section VII. We are proposing the stationary source approach but seeking comment on both.

If the annual maintenance, repair and replacement allowance is established for the entire stationary source, the owner or operator would only have to track compliance with a single annual maintenance, repair and replacement allowance and would have greater flexibility in decision making with respect to maintenance, repair and replacement activities. It is our understanding that accounting of maintenance activities is most often performed at the facility level and, consequently, managing the RMRR annual maintenance, repair and replacement allowance from a facility-wide standpoint is more consistent with current industry practices. In large, complex manufacturing facilities such as refineries, several major processes are constantly being maintained but larger maintenance activities may be rotated throughout the plant during different years to accommodate fiscal and operating cycles. Requiring these facilities to divide their plants into separate process units for maintenance accounting would create disincentives to the source in administering the allowance. A source-wide approach also may be more sensible to account for situations in which shared services (*e.g.*, electrical distribution, wastewater treatment) cannot be attributed to a single process at a facility.

On the other hand, setting the annual maintenance, repair and replacement allowance at the source-wide level presents the possibility that an owner or

80298   Federal Register / Vol. 67, No. 251 / Tuesday, December 31, 2002 / Proposed Rules

operator could forego maintenance at some process units and engage in activities at others that are not truly RMRR and seek to use the maintenance, repair and replacement allowance as a shield for these activities. Setting the annual maintenance, repair and replacement allowance at the process unit level would help to alleviate this concern.

On balance, however, we are not persuaded that this concern is well-founded. If the allowance level is set correctly, the only way an owner or operator could attempt the kind of misuse of the allowance described above would be to forego maintenance, repair and replacement activities at other process units—activities that are important to keep those other process units in good working order. It seems unlikely that an owner or operator would think that a prudent or sensible course.

Finally, we note that it likely is more difficult to develop reliable estimates of what it typically costs an owner or operator to maintain a process unit. That being the case, the most likely way a process-unit-based allowance would be developed would be by taking the numbers that would underlie a source-wide allowance and allocating them to process units. This approach could present its own opportunities for gaming the system.

We are proposing to set the annual maintenance, repair and replacement allowance at the source-wide level. (See § 51.165(a)(1)(v)(C)(*1*), § 51.166(b)(2)(iii)(*a*), § 52.21(b)(2)(iii)(*a*), and § 52.24(f)(5)(iii)(*a*) of proposed rules.) We believe that this approach is, on balance, easier to implement for both the reviewing authorities and the industry and is more consistent with current industry maintenance and financial practices. We specifically request comment on the use of a source-wide limit, a process unit limit, or any other means of applying a cost threshold. In addition, as noted in section VII, we request comment on our proposed definition of process unit.

D. Basis for Annual Maintenance, Repair and Replacement Allowance Percentage

The proposed annual maintenance, repair and replacement allowance for each source would be determined by multiplying the replacement cost of the source by an annual maintenance, repair and replacement allowance percentage specified by rule. (See § 51.165(a)(1)(xxxxii), § 51.166(b)(53), § 52.21(b)(55), and § 52.24(f)(25) of proposed rules.) As stated previously, the goal of this portion of the rule is to

provide a clear exclusion for the activities whose total costs fall below specified thresholds. We intend to set these thresholds on an industry-specific basis, and believe the following sources of information should be useful in establishing these thresholds: the IRS AAGRAP, standard engineering reference manuals, and actual industry data available to the EPA.

The IRS AAGRAP is the value used in an exclusion under the NSPS for increases in production. The IRS AAGRAP values provide repair allowance percentages for specific industries in order to reflect differing maintenance needs. These percentages range from 0.5 percent to 20 percent of invested cost. For instance, the aerospace industry has an AAGRAP value of 7.5 percent, electric utility steam generation has a value of 5 percent, and cement plants have a value of 3 percent. There is good reason to think that the industry-specific basis and the specific percentages are appropriate in the RMRR context. For example, the AAGRAP values have been used for over 20 years in the NSPS program, so they are time-tested and appear to work well in that context. Moreover, because the values were developed in the first instance to differentiate between costs that should be capitalized for tax accounting purposes and costs that properly should be expensed, the values should be well suited to distinguishing maintenance, repair and replacement from non-routine activities in the NSR context.

However, the AAGRAP is based on the invested cost of the facility, not the replacement cost, which may or may not require us to make some adjustments. Also, there are some industries for which an AAGRAP is not available. The policy reasons behind the use of AAGRAP in the tax context also may not be the same as those we need to consider in the NSR context, notwithstanding the fact that the AAGRAP has been used in the NSPS context. Finally, the IRS has moved to other approaches. We solicit comment on the extent to which the AAGRAP, or some derivative of the AAGRAP, may appropriately be employed if we determine that a safe harbor based on replacement cost is preferable.

There are also standard reference manuals that provide cost estimation information that is considered to be up to date. *Plant Design and Economics for Chemical Engineers,* by Peters and Timmerhaus, and *Perry's Chemical Engineer's Handbook,* by Perry and Green, are two widely used resources. They provide a range of annual maintenance and repair costs from 2

percent to 10 percent of the fixed capital investment of the stationary source. These two resources, however, are limited to the chemical process industry and may not have broader applicability to other industry sectors (although there may be comparable resources for other industries). Based on information contained in the resources mentioned above, the appropriate annual maintenance percentages would be in the range of 0.5 percent to 20 percent, depending on the industry.

To the extent that we have data, we intend in the final rule to set different percentages for specific industry categories. In selecting appropriate industry-specific percentages, it would be helpful if further information is made available to us during the public comment period for this proposal; therefore, we are requesting that information relating to types of maintenance, repair and replacement activities undertaken and costs associated with those activities be provided during the public comment period on this proposed rule. For example, relevant information for the electric utility industry might be available from the NERC/GADS database, the Federal Energy Regulatory Commission, or the Integrated Environmental Control Model maintained by the Energy and Environmental Center at Carnegie-Mellon University. Commenters should provide actual source, company or industry information, as well as any other data underlying summaries. Substantiated claims and estimates will be given greater consideration than information not supported by actual data. If there is a lack of information with which to set industry specific percentages, we may elect to set a default value. We are seeking comment on the appropriate default percentage to be used, and/or methods available to determine that percentage.

E. How To Calculate Costs

In order for a cost-based approach to be equitable, all owners or operators must include the same categories of expenses in both the replacement cost and the cost sought to be covered by the allowance. Therefore, we believe it may be appropriate to require that costs be calculated using an approach along the lines set out as the elements of Total Capital Investment as defined in the *EPA Air Pollution Control Cost Manual* (*http://www.epa.gov/ttn/catc/dir1/ c_allchs.pdf*). While the manual contains basic concepts that could be used to estimate total capital investment at a process unit, it is geared toward cost calculations for add-on control

Federal Register / Vol. 67, No. 251 / Tuesday, December 31, 2002 / Proposed Rules 80299

equipment. On the other hand, the underlying concepts are taken from work done by the American Association of Cost Engineers to define the components of cost calculations for all types of processes, not just emission control equipment.

We invite comment on whether we should use the manual as the mechanism for standardizing these calculations, whether we should use other manuals, or whether it might make sense to give sources a range of manuals whose approach to this question we believe may be appropriate for their circumstances. We also invite comment on whether EPA should require use of the manuals identified or simply provide assurance that if methods in an identified manual are used, EPA will accept them.

Under the EPA Manual, Total Capital Investment includes the costs required to purchase equipment, the costs of labor and materials for installing the equipment (direct installation costs), costs for site preparation and buildings, and certain other indirect installation costs. However, any costs associated with the installation and maintenance of pollution control equipment would be excluded from the cost calculation. For the purposes of this maintenance, repair and replacement allowance, we believe that equipment that serves a dual purpose of process equipment and control equipment (that is, combustion equipment used to produce steam and to control Hazardous Air Pollutant emissions, exhaust conditioning in the semiconductor industry, etc.) should be considered process equipment. We ask for comment on this point.

Direct installation costs include costs for foundations and supports, erecting and handling the equipment, electrical work, piping, insulation, and painting. Indirect installation costs include such costs as engineering costs; construction and field expenses (that is, costs for construction supervisory personnel, office personnel, rental of temporary offices, etc.); contractor fees (for construction and engineering firms involved in the activity); startup and performance test costs; and contingencies.

We are also considering whether or not to exclude costs associated with the unanticipated shutdown of equipment, due to component failure or catastrophic failures such as explosions or fires, from the costs that must be included in the allowance. If costs associated with unanticipated outages are excluded, these activities would be subjected to a case-by-case review of NSR applicability. We request comment on whether or not repairs and replacements resulting from the unanticipated shutdown of equipment, or of an entire source, should be included in the annual maintenance, repair and replacement allowance calculations.

F. Applicability Safeguards

We are proposing to include some safeguards in our rules. There are some relatively inexpensive activities that can be undertaken at a facility that we believe should not be included within the maintenance, repair and replacement allowance because, due to their very nature, they may significantly alter the design of the source or they may result in significantly greater emissions. Ineligibility for the allowance does not mean that the activities will necessarily be subject to NSR. These activities will still be eligible for treatment as RMRR under a case-by-case review, may qualify for other exclusions, may not require a major NSR permit because of emissions limitations in a synthetic minor limitation, or may be netted out of NSR applicability. We are proposing to include three such safeguards. (See § 51.165(a)(1)(xxxxii)(B), § 51.166(b)(53)(ii), § 52.21(b)(55)(ii), and § 52.24(f)(25)(ii) of proposed rules.)

The first of the safeguards is that no new process unit may be added under the annual maintenance, repair and replacement allowance. The addition of a new process unit is not maintenance, repair or replacement of existing equipment at a stationary source in order to ensure continued safe and reliable operation and hence should not qualify for the allowance.

The second safeguard is that an owner or operator may not use the maintenance, repair and replacement allowance to replace an entire process unit. We do not believe that replacement of an entire process unit should qualify for the allowance. Because of their nature, wholesale exchanges of a process unit should be subject to greater scrutiny in determining NSR applicability than use of the maintenance, repair and replacement allowance would entail.

The third safeguard is not allowing any activity that results in an increase in maximum achievable hourly emissions rate of a regulated NSR pollutant at the stationary source or in the emission of any regulated NSR pollutant not previously emitted to be excluded under the annual maintenance, repair and replacement allowance. Such activities are more likely to result in possible significant emissions increases and, therefore, should not be excluded from NSR on the basis that they fall within the maintenance, repair and replacement allowance. We request comment on the appropriateness and adequacy of these proposed safeguards or any additional safeguards that may be appropriate.

G. Timing of Determination

Under the annual maintenance, repair and replacement allowance as proposed, an owner or operator will sum the costs of maintenance, repair and replacement activities from least to most expensive to determine which activities are excluded pursuant to the allowance. Actual activity costs will not be known until activities are underway or completed. We have considered two options for the timing of the decision regarding qualification of activities under the annual maintenance, repair and replacement allowance when summing activities in this manner. The first is to require application of the allowance prior to construction based on planned activities and estimated costs. The second is to perform an end-of-year reconciliation after the activity costs are known.

If an end-of-year reconciliation is used, actual costs incurred would be known. However, if costs exceed the annual maintenance, repair and replacement allowance, some activities that have already been started or completed will have to be evaluated on a case-by-case basis unless already excluded from major NSR on some other basis. If it is determined that the activity is not RMRR and does not qualify for another exclusion, and it results in a significant emissions increase and a significant net emissions increase, and it is consequently subject to the requirements of NSR, the owner or operator would be in violation of the CAA for failure to obtain the necessary permit prior to commencing construction. In addition, if in a nonattainment area, the owner or operator could be required to obtain offsets, which may not be readily available in the area. The owner or operator may also be faced with penalties for constructing without a permit.

In practice, however, we do not believe this scenario is likely to occur. We expect that an owner or operator who intended to rely on the annual maintenance, repair and replacement allowance would have planned the year's activities accordingly and would be tracking activities throughout the year in order to avoid this situation.

We believe requiring an end-of-year reconciliation strikes a reasonable balance, since it will lead owners or operators to make preconstruction

80300 Federal Register / Vol. 67, No. 251 / Tuesday, December 31, 2002 / Proposed Rules

estimates of activities and costs in order to determine qualification for the exclusion but will not require them to become involved in permitting-type actions with respect to excluded activities. Finally, it is not possible for an owner or operator to plan all maintenance, repair and replacement needs, so there will be inaccuracies in any estimation no matter how diligent an owner or operator may be in seeking to plan these activities.

We have considered two other possible ways to address this situation. The first is to allow any unplanned activity to undergo a case-by-case determination of RMRR. However, this method might create an incentive to omit smaller, less expensive activities from the preconstruction estimation in order to avoid a case-by-case review on larger activities. The second is to make ineligible for the use of the maintenance, repair and replacement allowance any activity that was not included in the preconstruction estimation. But that seems unreasonable, since as noted above actual activity costs may be unintentionally underestimated or omitted, resulting in actual activity costs exceeding the annual maintenance, repair and replacement estimates.

After considering the options, we believe that an evaluation based on actual data rather than estimates is preferable. Careful planning by an owner or operator should reduce the likelihood that the annual allowance is exceeded for activities that the owner believes will come within the allowance. Moreover, a prudent owner or operator who believes his RMRR activities will be close to exceeding the allowance will determine whether more costly activities are otherwise excluded, evaluate them under the case-by-case test, or seek an applicability determination or a permit to assure compliance with NSR requirements. Therefore, we are proposing to determine qualification for the exclusion through an end-of-year reconciliation. (See § 51.165(a)(1)(xxxxii)(A)(5), § 51.166(b)(53)(i)(e), § 52.21(b)(55)(i)(e), and § 52.24(f)(25)(i)(e) of proposed rules).

One other possible approach to this question would be to sum costs in the order they occur, rather than from least expensive to most expensive.

Under that approach, an owner or operator would maintain a running total of maintenance, repair and replacement costs and could determine before beginning construction on a subsequent activity if there was room under the

annual maintenance, repair and replacement allowance. However, this process might encourage an owner or operator to delay less costly activities in order to use the annual maintenance, repair and replacement allowance for activities that are both larger and more atypical and, therefore, might not qualify for RMRR treatment.

Maintaining the least expensive to most expensive methodology discussed above, we could address the issue through an expedited case-by-case review of larger activities. An owner or operator would be responsible for obtaining a case-by-case determination from the reviewing authority for larger activities to ensure that an activity would still be considered RMRR if it is later found that the activity could not be accommodated under the annual maintenance, repair and replacement allowance. This, however, is inconsistent with our intent that owners or operators be able to use these provisions without obtaining an advance determination from the reviewing authority.

Finally, rather than establishing an annual cost threshold to define what activities fit within the allowance, we could establish a threshold per activity. Activities whose costs fell below the threshold could proceed as RMRR. Activities with costs above the threshold would be ineligible to use the allowance, and thus could only constitute RMRR if they either fell within the portion of the RMRR exclusion for equipment replacements or constitute RMRR upon an application of the case-by-case test. We are proposing a similar approach for replacement of equipment with functional equivalents. But we believe that any broader activity-based approach would have the undesirable consequence of forcing industry and the reviewing authorities to address potentially complex questions about how to define whether activities are truly separate and hence below the threshold or whether they are part of some larger activity that exceeds the threshold.

To summarize, at this time we are proposing an annual maintenance, repair and replacement allowance; to sum activities from least expensive to most expensive to determine eligibility; and an end-of-year review and report. We request comment on each of these aspects of the proposal and any additional approaches that commenters wish to recommend.

VII. Discussion of Issues Under the Equipment Replacement Approach

We recognize that there are numerous occasions when, to maintain, facilitate, restore, or improve efficiency, reliability, availability, or safety within normal facility operations, facilities replace existing equipment with either identical equipment or equipment that serves the same function. Such replacements may be conducted immediately after component failure or they may be conducted preventively to assure a source's continued safe, reliable and efficient operation. We believe that many such replacements typically should be considered RMRR activities. But, allowing replacement of equipment with "functionally equivalent" or "identical" equipment to qualify as RMRR, if unbounded, could theoretically allow replacement of an entire production line or utility boiler. Thus, there must also be some reasonable bound to equipment replacements that qualify.

The following discussion addresses key considerations in determining the appropriate boundary for the types of replacement activities that should be excluded under the equipment replacement provision of the RMRR exclusion.

A. Replacement of Existing Equipment With Identical or Functionally Equivalent Equipment

One of today's proposals deals with replacing equipment with identical or functionally equivalent equipment. This proposal is based on our view that most replacements of existing equipment that are necessary for the safe, efficient, and reliable operation of practically all industrial operations are not of regulatory concern and should qualify for the RMRR exclusion. Industrial facilities are constructed with the understanding that equipment failures are common and ongoing maintenance programs are routine. Delaying or foregoing maintenance could lead to failure of the production unit and may create or add to safety concerns.

When such equipment replacement occurs and the replacement is identical, the replacement is inherent to both the original design and purposes of the facility, and ordinarily will not increase emissions. For example, if a pump associated with a distillation column fails and is replaced with an identical new pump, we believe that such a common activity is and should be considered an excluded replacement. We believe that activities like such pump replacements are routine and should not trigger NSR permitting requirements.

We also recognize that this principle extends beyond the replacement of equipment with identical equipment. When equipment is wearing out or breaks down, it often is replaced with equipment that serves the same purpose or function but is different in some respect or improved in some way in comparison to the equipment that is removed. For example, when worn out pipes are replaced in a chemical process plant, the replacement pipes sometimes are constructed of new or different materials to help reduce corrosion, erosion, or chemical compatibility problems.

Moreover, the technology employed in certain types of equipment is constantly changing and evolving. When equipment of this sort needs to be replaced, it often is simply not possible to find the old-style technology. Owners or operators may have no choice but to purchase and install equipment reflecting current design innovations. Even if it is possible to find old-style equipment, owners or operators have obvious incentives for wanting to use the best equipment that suits the given need when replacements must be installed.

A good example was presented to us by the forest products industry during our review of the NSR program's impacts on the energy sector. A company in that sector needed to replace outdated analog controllers at a series of six batch digesters. The original controllers were no longer manufactured. The new digital controllers, costing approximately $50,000, are capable of receiving inputs from the digester vessel temperature, pressure, and chemical/steam flow. The new controllers would have more precisely filled and pressurized digesters with chips, chemicals, and steam, thus bringing a batch digester on line faster. The source determined that this activity would not be considered routine under today's NSR rules and decided not to proceed with the project.

The limiting principle here is that the replacement equipment must be identical or functionally equivalent and must not change the basic design parameters of the affected process unit (for example, for electric utility steam generating units, this would mean maximum heat input and fuel consumption specifications). Efficiency, however, should not be considered a basic design parameter, as NSR should not impede industry in making energy and process efficiency improvements which, on balance, will be beneficial both economically and environmentally.

This should address the concern and perception that the NSR program serves as a barrier to activities undertaken to facilitate, restore, or improve efficiency, reliability, availability, or safety of a facility.

We also note, however, that taken to the extreme, even without a change in basic design parameters, an identical or functionally equivalent replacement activity can still go beyond the bounds of the RMRR exclusion. For example, instead of replacing a pump, what if a chemical manufacturing facility replaced an entire production unit? Even if the replacement was identical, we likely would not consider the activity to be an excluded replacement. Such an activity effectively constitutes construction of a new process unit in much the same way the construction of an entirely new process unit at an existing stationary source could not constitute RMRR. This is not the kind of activity that sources typically engage in to maintain their plants, and it is the kind of activity that would likely be a logical point for owners or operators to install state-of-the-art controls.

We recognize that it may sometimes be difficult to determine where to draw the line between an activity that should be treated as an excluded replacement activity and one that should be viewed as a physical change that might constitute a major modification when the replacement of equipment with identical or functionally equivalent equipment involves a large portion of an existing unit. At the same time, we believe it is important to provide some clear parameters for making this determination.

To that end, we are soliciting comment on an equipment replacement cost approach based on the NSPS program to determine whether identical or functionally equivalent replacement activities constitute RMRR without regard to other considerations. Under the NSPS program, a project at an existing affected source triggers any applicable NSPS when the cost of the project exceeds 50 percent of the fixed capital cost that would be required to construct a comparable entirely new unit—that is, the current capital replacement value of the existing affected source. 40 CFR 60.15(b). In essence, such a "reconstruction" is tantamount to new construction and, therefore, triggers any applicable NSPS even if the project would otherwise be excluded.

We recognize that, in some respects, an equipment replacement cost threshold such as the NSPS reconstruction test may be viewed as the proper tool to be used in the future for

distinguishing between routine and non-routine identical and functionally equivalent replacements under the NSR program. As noted above, we do not believe it is reasonable to exclude from NSR activities that involve the total replacement of an existing entire process unit. By extension, it is therefore logical and consistent to conclude that activities which, based on their cost, effectively constitute replacement of the process unit should not qualify as RMRR. Thus, we believe that the 50 percent capital replacement threshold used under the NSPS might constitute an appropriate limitation on when identical or functionally equivalent replacements should qualify as RMRR under the equipment replacement provision without regard to other considerations.

We also recognize, however, that there are other considerations pointing in favor of a threshold lower than the 50 percent reconstruction threshold that may be appropriate to bound the equipment replacement provision. For example, since under NSPS half of the capital replacement value of an existing affected facility effectively constitutes construction of a new unit, it could be argued that some percentage less than the 50 percent reconstruction threshold might be a suitable line of demarcation in determining whether identical replacements constitute a modification of an existing unit.

We are soliciting comment on whether the proposed approach is workable, whether the capital replacement percentage should be 50 percent or another lesser percentage, and whether different percentages should apply to different industrial groupings or different types of industrial processes. For example, it may be appropriate to set a higher percentage for process operations that involve heat and corrosive compounds. Such processes may require more expensive replacements, and a greater degree of maintenance activities than other types of processes. In addition, we solicit comment on whether this equipment replacement provision should be implemented on a component-by-component basis, or some other reasoned basis such as applying the percentage to components that are replaced collectively over a fixed period of time.

We recognize that there are widely divergent views as to how expansive the RMRR exclusion should be. From our perspective, the most important thing we can do to improve air quality in the United States with respect to stationary sources is to make substantial reductions in NO_x and SO_2 emissions from facilities in the utility sector. Our current view, however, is that if the rules clearly establish a narrow RMRR exclusion and set out to require permits for replacement of larger components or the replacement of components with more efficient ones, owners or operators will comply with these rules but will find ways to make the replacements without having to obtain permits and install state-of-the-art controls. As a result, such rules will not achieve significant reductions in NO_x or SO_2 on a prospective basis. As discussed below, these owners or operators will likely avoid having to make such reductions through one of several ways plainly permissible under NSR.

For example, when a power plant operator plans to undertake an activity that the operator believes may not qualify as RMRR and is assessing compliance alternatives, that operator is faced with three options: (1) Proceed with the activity pursuant to an NSR permit, which could require more than $100 million to be spent on air pollution controls; (2) forego the activity, which likely would result in a permanent reduction in capacity or utilization of the facility or might reduce efficiency and increase emissions per unit of product manufactured or energy produced; or (3) proceed with the activity, but take steps to limit future emissions such that the activity would not result in a significant net emissions increase.

We also believe that few owners or operators would choose the first option. This option would make economic sense only in circumstances where the current capacity and utilization of the facility are so low that the major investment in air pollution controls would provide an incrementally better payback than the option of investing the same money in other assets or in the development of a new power plant.

We also believe that few owners or operators would elect the second option. It makes no sense in most cases for the owners or operators of costly power plants to let these assets significantly deteriorate over time, because the value of the asset will eventually be lost.

We believe that most owners or operators would select the third option. We note that industry commenters during our review of the impact of NSR on the energy sector argued that this option would, over time, result in a substantial reduction in the capacity of their facilities. For example, the Tennessee Valley Authority reported that, over the last 20 years, it would have lost 32 percent of its coal system's energy capability if it had capped

emissions under a "narrow" routine maintenance exclusion. In similar analyses, Southern Company estimated that it would have experienced an energy shortfall of 57.5 million MW-hr, and First Energy estimated that it would have lost 39 percent of its coal-fired generating capacity between 1981 and 2000. West Associates, the Western System Coordinating Council, and the National Rural Electric Cooperative Association reported similar results.

Notwithstanding these assessments, we believe that most owners or operators would proceed with activities and take emissions limitations. To the extent that such limitations might curtail full utilization of the facility, incremental control measures of modest cost would likely be taken to recover the "lost" utilization. For example, use of a slightly lower sulfur coal could produce the marginally lower SO_2 emissions that would be needed to recapture some capacity. Likewise, various types of relatively low-cost combustion or process control modifications could be employed to reduce NO_x emissions.

Thus, it is not probable that owners or operators would respond to a narrow exclusion by installing state-of-the-art controls every time they need to replace a major component. At the same time, a narrow RMRR exclusion of this type would not allow in many cases the replacement of equipment with equipment that improves process efficiency. This would cause owners or operators to forego replacements that would improve air quality because they would allow greater efficiency.

For these reasons, a narrow RMRR exclusion that is clearly established is not expected to achieve significant reductions in historic emissions levels, and might even lead to area wide emissions increases. Most facilities would take lawful steps to avoid having to obtain an NSR permit that would impose strict limitations, even when replacements would be found under this narrow exclusion to be non-routine.

B. Defining "Process Unit" for Evaluating Equipment Replacement Cost Percentage

In this section, we discuss issues related to what collection of equipment should be considered in applying the equipment replacement approach. We are proposing the term "process unit" as the appropriate collection. A definition of process unit currently is included in 40 CFR 63.41. We have built upon that definition to accommodate the intended coverage of activities under the equipment replacement approach. The purpose of this term is, as best as possible, to align implementation of the

provision with generally accepted and practical understandings of what constitutes a discrete production process. The general definition would read as follows:

Process unit means any collection of structures and/or equipment that processes, assembles, applies, blends, or otherwise uses material inputs to produce or store a completed product. A single facility may contain more than one process unit.

Our primary goal in defining this term is to encompass integrated manufacturing operations that produce a completed product rather than smaller pieces of such operations.

To help illustrate these concepts, we developed and have included in the proposed rules some industry-specific examples of how this definition might be applied. The examples are drawn from a few selected industry categories—electric utilities, refineries, cement manufacturers, pulp and paper producers, and incinerators. Because of the centrality of the "process unit" concept to the usefulness of the equipment replacement provision, it is our desire to include a version of these examples in the final rule to make sure sources have a benchmark against which they can evaluate with greater confidence whether a particular replacement comes within the equipment replacement provision of the RMRR exclusion. We also request comment on whether associated pollution control equipment should typically not be considered part of the process unit. We are proposing to exclude such equipment from the definition.

• For a steam electric generating facility, the process unit would consist of those portions of the plant that contribute directly to the production of electricity. For example, at a pulverized coal-fired facility, the process unit would generally be the combination of those systems from the coal receiving equipment through the emission stack, including the coal handling equipment, pulverizers or coal crushers, feedwater heaters, boiler, burners, turbine-generator set, air preheaters, and operating control systems. Each separate generating unit would be considered a separate process unit. Components shared between two or more process units would be proportionately allocated based on capacity.

• For a petroleum refinery, there are several categories of process units: those that separate and distill petroleum feedstocks; those that change molecular structures; petroleum treating processes; auxiliary facilities, such as boilers and hydrogen production; and those that load, unload, blend or store products.

• For a cement plant, the process unit would generally consist of the kiln and equipment that supports it, including all components that process or store raw materials, preheaters, and components that process or store products from the kilns, and associated emission stacks.

• For a pulp and paper mill, there are several types of process units. One is the system that processes wood products, another is the digester and its associated heat exchanger, blow tank, pulp filter, accumulator, oxidation tower, and evaporators. A third is the chemical recovery system, which includes the recovery furnace, lime kiln, storage vessels, and associated oxidation processes feeding regenerated chemicals to the digester.

• For an incinerator, the process unit would consist of components from the feed pit or refuse pit to the stack, including conveyors, combustion devices, heat exchangers and steam generators, quench tanks, and fans.

We solicit comment on the proposed definition of "process unit" and whether another approach might be more effective. We also solicit comment on the particular process units identified in specific industries, whether there are better ways of identifying those process units in those industries, and whether other process units should be specifically identified as part of the rule.

Finally, today's proposed approaches for replacement of existing equipment with identical or functionally equivalent equipment rely on the concept of a process unit, but it is possible that it is not appropriate for replacement of non-emitting components because such replacements may not have emissions consequences in the first place and hence would not warrant scrutiny under NSR. Similarly, it is possible that maintenance, repair and replacement activities performed on non-emitting units should not be included in the activities that would have to be accounted for under the annual maintenance, repair and replacement allowance provision of the RMRR exclusion. We solicit comment on how these various activities should be handled in the context of today's proposal, bearing in mind that forthcoming proposed NSR rules for future activities involving debottlenecking will specifically address changes made at non-emitting units that affect emissions at other process units at a stationary source among other issues. However, we request comment on limiting today's proposed approaches to changes made at emitting units or modifying them so as to differentiate between changes

made at emitting versus non-emitting units.

C. Miscellaneous Issues

In addition to the issues noted above, we also request comment on the following matters. First, we solicit comments on the topic of basic design parameters. Our proposal states that maximum heat input and fuel consumption specifications (for electric utility steam generating units) and maximum material/fuel input specifications (for other types of units) are basic design parameters. We solicit comment on whether that provides sufficient definition of this term, whether further definition is appropriate, or whether there are industry-specific considerations that should be taken into account.

Second, in calculating costs, we propose that owners or operators should use the same principles and guidelines as discussed above with respect to calculating costs for the maintenance, repair and replacement allowance. We request comment on whether these same principles and requirements are applicable and workable for the equipment replacement provision.

Third, in addition to soliciting comment on the approaches described above, we are also soliciting comment on whether the maintenance, repair and replacement allowance and this equipment replacement provision should both be adopted or whether just the equipment replacement provision is sufficient? In addition, if we assume that both approaches are adopted, how should they work together? Should an RMRR activity that is excluded under the equipment replacement provision also count against your annual maintenance, repair and replacement allowance? We are soliciting comment on whether to adopt any or all of these approaches and how they might fit together.

Lastly, EPA strongly supports efforts to improve energy efficiency at existing power plants. These activities reduce the amount of criteria pollutants (SO_2 and NO_X) emitted per unit of electricity generated and also reduce greenhouse gas emissions. During our study of the impact of NSR on the energy sector, we received information concerning a number of instances where activities that would have improved energy efficiency were not implemented because they would have resulted in significant annual emission increases that would have triggered NSR. Some have commented that any activity that produces any improvement in energy efficiency should be exempt from NSR. However, given the continuing

improvement in materials and design, almost any component replacement can be expected to have some beneficial impact on the energy efficiency of the unit and, left unbounded, this approach could result in the replacement of an entire boiler with a new, more efficient boiler without state-of-the-art pollution controls. As mentioned above, however, we do not think replacement of an entire boiler is properly viewed as routine. We also do not believe that the need to install state-of-the-art controls on new boilers will deter sources from installing new boilers if they are otherwise prepared to do so.

These issues prompt EPA to solicit comment in several areas. To the extent that an activity is the replacement of existing equipment that serves the same function as the equipment replaced, does not alter the basic design parameters of the process unit, and otherwise meets the provisions of our proposed equipment replacement approach, described above, it would be excluded from NSR under the proposal. There may, however, be rare instances where activities do not involve replacing existing equipment, are not otherwise excluded from NSR, and nevertheless promote energy efficiency. Is there a need for a separate "stand-alone" exclusion for such activities? If so, should there be other limitations on the scope of such activities? Are there activities that result in a minor improvement in efficiency but a very large increase in annual emissions? If so, what are the characteristics of such activities and how should EPA treat them? Today, we solicit comment broadly on the impact of the NSR program on decisions to proceed with activities that produce net benefits to human health and the environment, including, but not limited, to energy efficiency activities. We also solicit comments on the extent to which our proposals can promote energy efficiency while preserving the benefits of the NSR program.

D. Quantitative Analysis

We have attempted to analyze quantitatively the possible emissions consequences of the range of different approaches to the RMRR exclusion described above to evaluate if our policy conclusions are correct. Our analysis was conducted using the Integrated Planning Model (IPM). This analysis was done for electric utilities because we have a powerful model to perform such an analysis that we do not have for other industries. We think the results for the electric utilities accurately reflects the trends we would see in other industries. This model and technical information describing it can be found in the docket. The analysis included several relevant scenarios. In the first scenario, we assumed that efficiency and capacity of relevant units modestly decrease over time. This scenario was intended to reflect the consequences of a new rule with a relatively "narrow" RMRR exclusion, under which we would assume that there would be slow and steady deterioration of relevant generating assets. As explained above, we do not actually believe that such a trend would occur under such a new RMRR exclusion, because plants would take steps to limit emissions and perhaps implement incremental controls to recapture lost capacity. Nevertheless, we believe that this scenario offers a bounding analysis for seeing whether a narrow RMRR exclusion can have significant emissions benefits because our model assumes well controlled and highly efficient new generating assets rather than recaptured capacity from incrementally better controlled existing units.

In the other scenarios, we assumed that utilization, efficiency, or capacity of relevant units modestly increases over time. These scenarios were intended to reflect the consequences of a new rule with a "broader" RMRR exclusion, which would allow facility availability and/or output over time without triggering major NSR. These scenarios present various combinations of assumptions on possible incremental changes to relevant operational parameters and are intended to encompass the range of possible operational outcomes that might be associated with the proposed RMRR exclusion.

The IPM analyses of these scenarios proves the point made above, that the breadth of the RMRR exclusion would have no practical impact on, let alone being the controlling factor in determining, the emissions reductions that will be achieved in the future under the major NSR program. The analyses show that emissions of SO_2 are essentially the same under all scenarios. This stands to reason because nationwide emissions of SO_2 from the power sector are capped by the title IV Acid Rain Program. For NO_X, these analyses show modest relative decreases in some cases and modest relative increases in other cases. These predicted changes represent only a modest fraction of nationwide NO_X emissions from the power sector, which hover around 4.3 million tons per year (tpy). At this time, we do not have adequate information to predict with confidence which modeled scenario is

most likely to occur if the options under consideration are adopted. What these analyses indicate, however, is that regardless of which scenario is closest to what comes to pass, none of the proposed provisions related to the RMRR exclusion will have a significant impact on emissions from the power sector.

The DOE also attempted to analyze quantitatively the possible emissions consequences of the range of different approaches to the RMRR exclusion described above. Using the National Energy Modeling System (NEMS), a variety of changes in energy efficiency and availability were evaluated, as well as the effect on emissions resulting from these changes. This analysis concluded that efficiency improvements resulting from increased maintenance are expected to decrease emissions, whereas availability improvements are expected to increase emissions. In the cases represented in this analysis, the impacts of the assumed reductions in heat rates tend to dominate the corresponding effects of the assumed availability increases.

Data regarding the emissions reductions that are achieved under other CAA programs further illustrate the relative limits of the major NSR program as a tool for achieving significant emissions reductions. For example, the title IV Acid Rain Program has reduced SO_2 emissions from the electric utility industry by more than 7 million tpy and will ultimately result in reductions of approximately 10 million tpy. The Tier 2 motor vehicle emissions standards and gasoline sulfur control requirements will ultimately achieve NO_X reductions of 2.8 million tpy. Standards for highway heavy-duty vehicles and engines will reduce NO_X emissions by 2.6 million tpy. Standards for non-road diesel engines are anticipated to reduce NO_X emissions by about 1.5 million tpy. The NO_X "SIP call" will reduce NO_X emissions by over 1 million tpy. Altogether, these and other similar programs achieve emissions reductions that far exceed those attributable to the major NSR program and dwarf any possible emissions consequences attributable to future promulgation of a rule based on today's proposal.

A copy of our IPM analysis and the DOE NEMS analysis are included in the docket for this rulemaking. We ask for comment on all aspects of these analyses and on the policy discussion provided above.

VIII. Other Options Considered

In addition to the cost-based approaches discussed above, we are considering two additional options for

addressing RMRR. These options are discussed below, and we are requesting comment on these options. We are also interested in other possible alternatives.

A. Capacity-Based Option

We are considering the alternative option of developing an RMRR provision based on the capacity of a process unit. Under such an approach, an owner or operator could undertake any activity that did not increase the capacity of the process unit. Such an approach would require safeguards similar to those in the proposed cost-based approaches in order to ensure that activities that should be subject to the NSR program are not inappropriately excluded. These safeguards would exclude the construction of a new process unit, the replacement of an entire process unit, and activities that result in an increase in maximum achievable hourly emissions rate of a regulated NSR pollutant from use of the exclusion or the emission of any regulated NSR pollutant not previously emitted by the stationary source.

Basing RMRR on capacity is appealing for several reasons. The primary objective of RMRR is to keep a unit operating at capacity and/or availability. In addition, the linkage between capacity and environmental impact is more apparent than cost and environmental impact. Finally, this type of approach might, in principle, be easier to use before beginning actual construction than the cost-based approaches.

The difficulty with using a capacity-based approach is defining the capacity of a process unit. Capacity may be defined based on input or output. Nameplate capacity of a process unit may vary greatly from the capacity at which the process unit may be able to operate. It may be more appropriate in some industries to measure capacity based on input while in others on output. As an example, in a review of promulgated and proposed Maximum Achievable Control Technology standards, six of eleven standards measured capacity based on unit output while five based capacity on input. In fact, the NSPS exclusion for increases in production rate at 40 CFR 60.14(e) originally was dependent upon the "operating design capacity" of an affected unit. In proposed revisions to the NSPS program published on October 15, 1974, we state (39 FR 36948):

The exemption of increases in production rate is no longer dependent upon the "operating design capacity." This term is not easily defined, and for certain industries the "design capacity" bears little relationship to the actual operating capacity of the facility.

Federal Register / Vol. 67, No. 251 / Tuesday, December 31, 2002 / Proposed Rules 80305

We are requesting comment on this capacity-based option, as well as comments on possible methods to address any of the issues relating to implementation of such an option.

B. Age-Based Option

Under an age-based approach, any process unit under a specified age could undergo any activity that does not increase the capacity of a process unit on a maximum hourly basis without triggering the requirements of the major NSR program. However, the activities could not constitute reconstruction of the process unit; that is, their cost could not exceed 50 percent of the cost of a replacement process unit. The age of the process unit would likely be in the range of 25–50 years. An owner or operator would have to become a Clean Unit as defined at 40 CFR 51.165(c)(3), 51.166(t)(3), and 52.21(x)(3), once the age of a process unit exceeds the age threshold.

Such an approach would provide an owner or operator a clear understanding of RMRR for an extended period of time. It also may provide the owner or operator greater flexibility than under the current system for a limited period of time. Like the capacity-based approach, this approach would, in principle, allow for a fairly simple preconstruction determination of applicability.

We see several difficulties in developing this type of approach. The first is defining capacity. The second is establishing the age cut-off for the exclusion. The useful life of equipment is difficult to establish and may vary greatly. The third is that some of the activities that would be allowed at newer sources do not fit within any ordinary meaning of RMRR and some of the activities that would be forbidden at older facilities would come within that meaning. Fourth, some sources may consciously, and appropriately, engage in aggressive RMRR as a method of maximizing the life span of its process units, and an age-based approach would discriminate against them.

We are requesting comment on this age-based option, as well as comments on possible methods to address the issues raised above with respect to this option.

IX. Administrative Requirements for This Proposed Rulemaking

A. Executive Order 12866—Regulatory Planning and Review

Under Executive Order 12866 [58 FR 51,735 (October 4, 1993)], we must determine whether the regulatory action is "significant" and therefore subject to

review by the Office of Management and Budget (OMB) and the requirements of the Executive Order. The Executive Order defines "significant regulatory action" as one that is likely to result in a rule that may:

(1) Have an annual effect on the economy of $100 million or more or adversely affect in a material way the economy, a sector of the economy, productivity, competition, jobs, the environment, public health or safety, or State, local, or tribal governments or communities;

(2) Create a serious inconsistency or otherwise interfere with an action taken or planned by another agency;

(3) Materially alter the budgetary impact of entitlements, grants, user fees, or loan programs, or the rights and obligations of recipients thereof; or

(4) Raise novel legal or policy issues arising out of legal mandates, the President's priorities, or the principles set forth in the Executive Order.

Pursuant to the terms of Executive Order 12866, OMB has notified us that it considers this an "economically significant regulatory action" within the meaning of the Executive Order. We have submitted this action to OMB for review. Changes made in response to OMB suggestions or recommendations will be documented in the public record. All written comments from OMB to EPA and any written EPA response to any of those comments are included in the docket listed at the beginning of this notice under **ADDRESSES**. In addition, consistent with Executive Order 12866, EPA consulted extensively with the State, local and tribal agencies that will be affected by this rule. We have also sought involvement from industry and public interest groups.

B. Executive Order 13132—Federalism

Executive Order 13132, entitled "Federalism" (64 FR 43255, August 10, 1999), requires us to develop an accountable process to ensure "meaningful and timely input by State and local officials in the development of regulatory policies that have federalism implications." "Policies that have federalism implications" are defined in the Executive Order to include regulations that have "substantial direct effects on the States, on the relationship between the national government and the States, or on the distribution of power and responsibilities among the various levels of government."

This proposed rule does not have federalism implications. Nevertheless, in developing this rule, we consulted with affected parties and interested stakeholders, including State and local authorities, to enable them to provide

timely input in the development of this rule. A summary of stakeholder involvement appears above in section III.C. of today's proposed rule. It will not have substantial direct effects on the States, on the relationship between the national government and the State and local programs, or on the distribution of power and responsibilities among the various levels of government, as specified in Executive Order 13132. While this proposed rule will result in some expenditures by the States, we expect those expenditures to be limited to $580,160 for the estimated 112 affected reviewing authorities. This figure includes the small increase in burden imposed upon reviewing authorities in order for them to revise the State's State Implementation Plan (SIP). However, this revision provides sources permitted by the States greater certainty in application of the program, which should in turn reduce the overall burden of the program on State and local authorities. Thus, the requirements of Executive Order 13132 do not apply to this rule.

C. Executive Order 13175—Consultation and Coordination With Indian Tribal Governments

Executive Order 13175, entitled "Consultation and Coordination with Indian Tribal Governments" (65 FR 67249, November 6, 2000), requires EPA to develop an accountable process to ensure "meaningful and timely input by tribal officials in the development of regulatory policies that have tribal implications." EPA believes that this proposed rule does not have tribal implications as specified in Executive Order 13175. Thus, Executive Order 13175 does not apply to this rule.

The purpose of today's proposed rule is to add greater flexibility to the existing major NSR regulations. These changes will benefit reviewing authorities and the regulated community, including any major source owned by a tribal government or located in or near tribal land, by providing increased certainty as to when the requirements of the NSR program apply. Taken as a whole, today's proposed rule should result in no added burden or compliance costs and should not substantially change the level of environmental performance achieved under the previous rules.

The EPA anticipates that initially these changes will result in a small increase in the burden imposed upon reviewing authorities in order for them to be included in the State's SIP. Nevertheless, these options and revisions will ultimately provide greater operational flexibility to sources

80306   Federal Register / Vol. 67, No. 251 / Tuesday, December 31, 2002 / Proposed Rules

permitted by the States, which will in turn reduce the overall burden on the program on State and local authorities by reducing the number of required permit modifications. In comparison, no tribal government currently has an approved Tribal Implementation Plan (TIP) under the CAA to implement the NSR program. The Federal government is currently the NSR reviewing authority in Indian country. Thus, tribal governments should not experience added burden, nor should their laws be affected with respect to implementation of this rule. Additionally, although major stationary sources affected by today's proposed rule could be located in or near Indian country and/or be owned or operated by tribal governments, such affected sources would not incur additional costs or compliance burdens as a result of this rule. Instead, the only effect on such sources should be the benefit of the added certainty and flexibility provided by the rule.

The EPA recognizes the importance of including tribal consultation as part of the rulemaking process. Nonetheless, to this point we have not specifically consulted with tribal officials on this proposed rule. We are committed to work with any tribal government to resolve any issues that we may have overlooked in today's proposed rules and that may have an adverse impact in Indian country. As a result, today we are announcing our intention to develop and implement a consultation process with tribal governments to ensure that the concerns of tribal officials are considered before finalizing this proposed rule. EPA specifically solicits additional comment on this proposed rule from tribal officials.

D. Executive Order 13045—Protection of Children From Environmental Health Risks and Safety Risks

Executive Order 13045, "Protection of Children from Environmental Health Risks and Safety Risks" (62 *FR* 19885, April 23, 1997) applies to any rule that (1) is determined to be "economically significant" as defined under Executive Order 12866, and (2) concerns an environmental health or safety risk that EPA has reason to believe may have a disproportionate effect on children. If the regulatory action meets both criteria, we must evaluate the environmental health or safety effects of the planned rule on children and explain why the planned regulation is preferable to other potentially effective and reasonable alternatives that we considered.

This proposed rule is not subject to Executive Order 13045, because we do not have reason to believe the

environmental health or safety risks addressed by this action present a disproportionate risk to children. We believe that this package as a whole will result in equal or better environmental protection than currently provided by the existing regulations, and do so in a more streamlined and effective manner.

E. Paperwork Reduction Act

The EPA prepared an Information Collection Request (ICR) document (ICR No. 1713.04). You may obtain a copy from Sandy Farmer by mail at the U.S. Environmental Protection Agency, Office of Environmental Information, Collection Strategies Division (2822), 1200 Pennsylvania Avenue, NW., Washington, DC 20460–0001, by e-mail at *farmer.sandy@epa.gov,* or by calling (202) 260–2740. A copy may also be downloaded from the internet at *http://www.epa.gov/icr.*

The information that ICR No. 1713.04 covers is required for EPA to carry out its required oversight function of reviewing preconstruction permits and assuring adequate implementation of the program. In order to carry out its oversight function, EPA must have available to it information on proposed construction and modifications. This information collection is necessary for the proper performance of EPA's functions, has practical utility, and is not unnecessarily duplicative of information we otherwise can reasonably access. We have reduced, to the extent practicable and appropriate, the burden on persons providing the information to or for EPA. The collection of information is authorized under 42 U.S.C. 7401 *et seq.*

According to ICR No. 1713.04, the first 3 years of this proposed rulemaking will potentially incur a burden of 17,400 hours and 1,305,000 dollars to affected sources, and 2,906 hours and 107,522 dollars for the Federal government, and 15,680 hours and 580,160 hours for reviewing authorities. These costs are based upon an estimated number of 1,450 affected sources.

Burden means the total time, effort, or financial resources expended by persons to generate, maintain, retain, or disclose or provide information to or for a Federal agency. This includes the time needed to review instructions; develop, acquire, install, and utilize technology and systems for the purpose of responding to the information collection; adjust existing ways to comply with any previously applicable instructions and requirements; train personnel to respond to a collection of information; search existing data sources; complete and review the

collection of information; and transmit or otherwise disclose the information.

An agency may not conduct or sponsor, and a person is not required to respond to, a collection of information unless it displays a currently valid OMB control number. The OMB control numbers for EPA's regulations are listed in 40 CFR part 9 and 48 CFR chapter 15. We will continue to present OMB control numbers in a consolidated table format to be codified in 40 CFR part 9 of the Agency's regulations, and in each CFR volume containing EPA regulations. The table lists the section numbers with reporting and record keeping requirements, and the current OMB control numbers. This listing of the OMB control numbers and their subsequent codification in the CFR satisfy the requirements of the Paperwork Reduction Act (44 U.S.C. 3501 *et seq.*) and OMB's implementing regulations at 5 CFR part 1320.

F. Regulatory Flexibility Act (RFA), as Amended by the Small Business Regulatory Enforcement Fairness Act of 1996 (SBREFA), 5 U.S.C. 601 et seq.

The RFA generally requires an agency to prepare a regulatory flexibility analysis of any rule subject to notice and comment rulemaking requirements under the Administrative Procedure Act or any other statute unless the agency certifies that the rule will not have a significant economic impact on a substantial number of small entities. Small entities include small businesses, small organizations, and small governmental jurisdictions. For purposes of assessing the impacts of today's rule on small entities, small entity is defined as: (1) Any small business employing fewer than 500 employees; (2) a small governmental jurisdiction that is a government of a city, county, town, school district or special district with a population of less than 50,000; and (3) a small organization that is any not-for-profit enterprise which is independently owned and operated and is not dominant in its field.

After considering the economic impacts of today's proposed rule on small entities, I certify that this action will not have a significant economic impact on a substantial number of small entities. In determining whether a rule has a significant economic impact on a substantial number of small entities, the impact of concern is any significant *adverse* economic impact on small entities, since the primary purpose of the regulatory flexibility analyses is to identify and address regulatory alternatives "which minimize any significant economic impact of the proposed rule on small entities." 5 U.S.C. 603 and 604. Thus, an agency may certify that a rule will not have a significant economic impact on a substantial number of small entities if the rule relieves regulatory burden, or otherwise has a positive economic effect on all of the small entities subject to the rule. Today's proposed rule will not have a significant economic impact on a substantial number of small entities because it will decrease the regulatory burden of the existing regulations and have a positive effect on all small entities subject to the rule. This rule improves operational flexibility for owners and operators of major stationary sources and clarifies applicable requirements for determining if a change qualifies as a major modification. We have therefore concluded that today's proposed rule will relieve regulatory burden for all small entities. We continue to be interested in the potential impacts of the proposed rule on small entities and welcome comments on issues related to such impacts.

G. Unfunded Mandates Reform Act of 1995

Title II of the Unfunded Mandates Reform Act of 1995 (UMRA), Public Law 104–4, establishes requirements for Federal agencies to assess the effects of their regulatory actions on State, local, and tribal governments and the private sector. Under section 202 of UMRA, we generally must prepare a written statement, including a cost-benefit analysis, for proposed and final rules with "Federal mandates" that may result in expenditures to State, local, and tribal governments, in the aggregate, or to the private sector of $100 million or more in any one year. Before promulgating an EPA rule for which a written statement is needed, section 205 of the UMRA generally requires us to identify and consider a reasonable number of regulatory alternatives and adopt the least costly, most cost-effective or least burdensome alternative that achieves the objectives of the rule. The provisions of section 205 do not apply when they are inconsistent with applicable law. Moreover, section 205 allows us to adopt an alternative other than the least costly, most cost-effective, or least burdensome alternative if the Administrator publishes with the final rule an explanation why that alternative was not adopted.

Before we establish any regulatory requirements that may significantly or uniquely affect small governments, including tribal governments, we must have developed under section 203 of the UMRA a small government agency plan.

The plan must provide for notifying potentially affected small governments, enabling officials of affected small governments to have meaningful and timely input in the development of our regulatory proposals with significant Federal intergovernmental mandates, and informing, educating, and advising small governments on compliance with the regulatory requirements.

We believe the proposed rule changes will actually reduce the regulatory burden associated with the major NSR program by improving the operational flexibility of owners and operators and clarifying the requirements. Because the program changes provided in the proposed rule are not expected to result in any increases in the expenditure by State, local, and tribal governments, or the private sector, we have not prepared a budgetary impact statement or specifically addressed the selection of the least costly, most cost-effective, or least burdensome alternative. Because small governments will not be significantly or uniquely affected by this rule, we are not required to develop a plan with regard to small governments. Therefore, this proposed rule is not subject to the requirements of section 203 of the UMRA.

H. National Technology Transfer and Advancement Act of 1995

Section 12(d) of the National Technology Transfer and Advancement Act of 1995 (NTTAA), Public Law No. 104–113, section 12(d) (15 U.S.C. 272 note) directs us to use voluntary consensus standards (VCS) in our regulatory activities unless to do so would be inconsistent with applicable law or otherwise impractical. VCS are technical standards (for example, materials specifications, test methods, sampling procedures, and business practices) that are developed or adopted by voluntary consensus standards bodies. The NTTAA directs us to provide Congress, through OMB, explanations when the Agency decides not to use available and applicable VCS.

Although this rule does involve the use of technical standards, it does not preclude the State, local, and tribal reviewing agencies from using VCS. Today's proposed rulemaking is an improvement of the existing NSR permitting program. As such, it only ensures that promulgated technical standards are considered and appropriate controls are installed, prior to the construction of major sources of air emissions. Therefore, we are not considering the use of any VCS in today's rulemaking.

I. Executive Order 13211—Actions Concerning Regulations That Significantly Affect Energy Supply, Distribution, or Use

This proposed rule is not a "significant energy action" as defined in Executive Order 13211, "Actions Concerning Regulations That Significantly Affect Energy Supply, Distribution, or Use" (66 FR 28355 (May 22, 2001)) because it is not likely to have a significant adverse effect on the supply, distribution or use of energy.

Today's proposed rule improves the ability of sources to maintain the reliability of production facilities, and effectively utilize and improve existing capacity.

X. Statutory Authority

The statutory authority for this action is provided by sections 101, 111, 114, 116, and 301 of the CAA as amended (42 U.S.C. 7401, 7411, 7414, 7416, and 7601). This rulemaking is also subject to section 307(d) of the CAA (42 U.S.C. 7407(d)).

List of Subjects in 40 CFR Parts 51 and 52

Environmental protection, Administrative practice and procedure, Air pollution control, Intergovernmental relations, Reporting and recordkeeping requirements.

Dated: November 22, 2002.

Christine Todd Whitman,

Administrator.

For the reasons set out in the preamble, title 40, chapter I of the Code of Federal Regulations is proposed to be amended as follows:

PART 51—[AMENDED]

1. The authority citation for part 51 continues to read as follows:

Authority: 23 U.S.C. 101; 42 U.S.C. 7401–7671q.

Subpart I—[Amended]

2. Section 51.165 is amended:
a. By revising paragraph (a)(1)(v)(C)(*1*).
b. By adding paragraphs (a)(1)(xliii) through (xlvii).
The revision and additions read as follows:

§ 51.165 Permit requirements.

(a) * * *
(1) * * *
(v) * * *
(C) * * *

(*1*) Routine maintenance, repair and replacement, which shall include but not be limited to the activities set out in paragraphs (a)(1)(v)(C)(*1*)(*i*) and (*ii*) of

80308   **Federal Register** / Vol. 67, No. 251 / Tuesday, December 31, 2002 / Proposed Rules

this section. Without regard to other considerations, the activities specified in paragraphs (a)(1)(v)(C)(1)(i) and (ii) shall constitute routine maintenance, repair and replacement:

(*i*) Activities performed at a stationary source in order to maintain, facilitate, restore or improve the efficiency, reliability, availability or safety of that stationary source, whose total cost, when added together with the total costs of all previous activities performed at the same stationary source in the same year in order to maintain, facilitate, restore or improve the efficiency, reliability, availability or safety of that stationary source, does not exceed that stationary source's annual maintenance, repair and replacement allowance. "Annual maintenance, repair and replacement allowance" is defined in paragraph (a)(1)(xliii) of this section. Rules for calculation and summation of costs are provided in paragraph (a)(1)(xliii)(A) of this section. A stationary source may elect to calculate an annual maintenance, repair and replacement allowance for either all or none, but not some, of the maintenance, repair, and replacement activities performed at the stationary source.

(*ii*) The replacement of components of a process unit with identical or functionally equivalent components, provided that: The fixed capital cost of the components does not exceed [x] [1] percent of the fixed capital cost that would be required to construct an entirely new process unit; and the replacement does not change the basic design parameters of the process unit. The basic design parameters for electric utility steam generating units are maximum heat input and fuel consumption specifications. For non-utilities, basic design parameters are the maximum fuel or material input specifications to the process unit. An improvement in efficiency does not change a process unit's basic design parameters. "Functionally equivalent components" and "fixed capital cost" are defined in paragraphs (a)(1)(xlv) and (a)(1)(xlvi) of this section, respectively.

*   *   *   *   *

(xliii) *Annual maintenance, repair and replacement allowance* means a dollar amount calculated according to the following equation: (Industry sector percentage) × (replacement cost of the stationary source) where "industry sector percentage" is drawn from Table 1 of this section.

[1] EPA has not determined this value.

TABLE 1 OF § 51.165(A)(1)(XLIII).— INDUSTRY SECTOR PERCENTAGES

Industry sector	Industry sector percentage
Electric Services	
Petroleum Refining	
Chemical Processes	
Natural Gas Transport	
Pulp and Paper Mills	
Paper Mills	
Automobile Manufacturing	
Pharmaceuticals	
Other	

(A) A stationary source's annual maintenance costs shall be calculated and summed according to the following rules:

(*1*) The owner or operator may choose to sum costs over either a calendar year or initially specified fiscal year. The initially specified fiscal year must remain in use unless other accounting procedures at the stationary source subsequently change to a different fiscal year.

(*2*) Costs incurred for all activities performed at the stationary source in order to maintain, facilitate, restore or improve the efficiency, reliability, availability or safety of that stationary source that are not excluded under paragraph (a)(1)(xliii)(B) of this section, or that have not been issued a preconstruction permit, shall be tracked chronologically and summed at the end of the year.

(*i*) At the end of the year, these costs shall be listed and summed in order from least cost to highest cost.

(*ii*) All activities prior to the point on the cost-ordered list at which the sum of activity costs exceeds the annual maintenance, repair and replacement allowance shall automatically qualify as routine maintenance, repair, or replacement.

(*3*) Costs associated with maintaining or installing pollution control equipment shall not be included in the calculation and summation of costs for routine maintenance, repair, and replacement. Costs shall remain included if they are associated with maintaining or installing equipment that serves a dual function as both process and control equipment.

(*4*) The owner or operator shall provide an annual report to the reviewing authority containing complete information on all maintenance, repair and replacement costs and process unit replacement cost estimates at the stationary source. The report shall be provided within 60 days after the end of the year over which activity costs have been summed.

(B) An activity otherwise eligible for inclusion in the annual maintenance, repair and replacement allowance shall not be eligible to be included in the allowance if it:

(*1*) Results in an increase in the maximum achievable hourly emissions rate of the stationary source of a regulated NSR pollutant, or results in emissions of a regulated NSR pollutant not previously emitted;

(*2*) Constitutes construction of a new process unit; or

(*3*) Removes an entire existing process unit and installs a different process unit in its place.

(xliv)(A) In general, *process unit* means any collection of structures and/or equipment that processes, assembles, applies, blends, or otherwise uses material inputs to produce or store a completed product. A single stationary source may contain more than one process unit.

(B) The following list identifies the process units at specific kinds of stationary sources.

(*1*) For a steam electric generating facility, the process unit would consist of those portions of the plant which contribute directly to the production of electricity. For example, at a pulverized coal-fired facility, the process unit would generally be the combination of those systems from the coal receiving equipment through the emission stack, including the coal handling equipment, pulverizers or coal crushers, feedwater heaters, boiler, burners, turbine-generator set, air preheaters, and operating control systems. Each separate generating unit would be considered a separate process unit. Components shared between two or more process units would be proportionately allocated based on capacity.

(*2*) For a petroleum refinery, there are several categories of process units: those that separate and distill petroleum feedstocks; those that change molecular structures; petroleum treating processes; auxiliary facilities, such as boilers and hydrogen production; and those that load, unload, blend or store products.

(*3*) For a cement plant, the process unit would generally consist of the kiln and equipment that supports it, including all components that process or store raw materials, preheaters, and components that process or store products from the kilns, and associated emission stacks.

(*4*) For a pulp and paper mill, there are several types of process units. One is the system that processes wood products, another is the digester and its associated heat exchanger, blow tank, pulp filter, accumulator, oxidation tower, and evaporators. A third is the

Federal Register / Vol. 67, No. 251 / Tuesday, December 31, 2002 / Proposed Rules   80309

chemical recovery system, which includes the recovery furnace, lime kiln, storage vessels, and associated oxidation processes feeding regenerated chemicals to the digester.

(5) For an incinerator, the process unit would consist of components from the feed pit or refuse pit to the stack, including conveyors, combustion devices, heat exchangers and steam generators, quench tanks, and fans.

(xlv) *Functionally equivalent component* means a component that serves the same purpose as the replaced component.

(xlvi) *Fixed capital cost* means the capital needed to provide all the depreciable components. "Depreciable components" refers to all components of fixed capital cost and is calculated by subtracting land and working capital from the total capital investment, as defined in paragraph (a)(1)(xlvii) of this section.

(xlvii) *Total capital investment* means the sum of the following: all costs required to purchase needed process equipment (purchased equipment costs); the costs of labor and materials for installing that equipment (direct installation costs); the costs of site preparation and buildings; other costs such as engineering, construction and field expenses, fees to contractors, startup and performance tests, and contingencies (indirect installation costs); land for the process equipment; and working capital for the process equipment.

*   *   *   *   *

3. Section 51.166 is amended:
a. By revising paragraph (b)(2)(iii)(a).
b. By adding paragraphs (b)(53) through (57). The revision and additions read as follows:

§51.166 Prevention of significant deterioration of air quality.

*   *   *   *   *

(b) *   *   *
(2) *   *   *
(iii) *   *   *
(a) Routine maintenance, repair and replacement, which shall include but not be limited to the activities set out in paragraphs (b)(2)(iii)(a)(1) and (2) of this section. Without regard to other considerations, the activities specified in paragraphs (b)(2)(iii)(a)(1) and (2) shall constitute routine maintenance, repair and replacement:

(1) Activities performed at a stationary source in order to maintain, facilitate, restore or improve the efficiency, reliability, availability or safety of that stationary source, whose total cost, when added together with the total costs of all previous activities performed at the same stationary source in the same year in order to maintain,

facilitate, restore or improve the efficiency, reliability, availability or safety of that stationary source, does not exceed that stationary source's annual maintenance, repair and replacement allowance. "Annual maintenance, repair and replacement allowance" is defined in paragraph (b)(53) of this section. Rules for calculation and summation of costs are provided in paragraph (b)(53)(i) of this section. A stationary source may elect to calculate an annual maintenance, repair and replacement allowance for either all or none, but not some, of the maintenance, repair, and replacement activities performed at the stationary source.

(2) The replacement of components of a process unit with identical or functionally equivalent components, provided that:

(i) The fixed capital cost of the components does not exceed [x][1] percent of the fixed capital cost that would be required to construct an entirely new process unit; and

(ii) The replacement does not change the basic design parameters of the process unit. The basic design parameters for electric utility steam generating units are maximum heat input and fuel consumption specifications. For non-utilities, basic design parameters are the maximum fuel or material input specifications to the process unit. An improvement in efficiency does not change a process unit's basic design parameters. "Functionally equivalent components" and "fixed capital cost" are defined in paragraphs (b)(55) and (b)(56) of this section.

*   *   *   *   *

(53) *Annual maintenance, repair and replacement allowance* means a dollar amount calculated according to the following equation: (Industry sector percentage) × (replacement cost of the stationary source) where "industry sector percentage" is drawn from Table 1 of this section.

TABLE 1 OF §51.166(B)(53).—
INDUSTRY SECTOR PERCENTAGES

Industry sector	Industry sector percentage
Electric Services	
Petroleum Refining	
Chemical Processes	
Natural Gas Transport	
Pulp and Paper Mills	
Paper Mills	
Automobile Manufacturing	
Pharmaceuticals	
Other	

[1] EPA has not determined this value.

(i) A stationary source's annual maintenance costs shall be calculated and summed according to the following rules:

(a) The owner or operator may choose to sum costs over either a calendar year or initially specified fiscal year. The initially specified fiscal year must remain in use unless other accounting procedures at the stationary source subsequently change to a different fiscal year.

(b) Costs incurred for all activities performed at the stationary source in order to maintain, facilitate, restore, or improve the efficiency, reliability, availability, or safety of that stationary source that are not excluded under paragraph (b)(53)(ii) of this section, or that have not been issued a preconstruction permit, shall be tracked chronologically and summed at the end of the year.

(1) At the end of the year, these costs shall be listed and summed in order from least cost to highest cost.

(2) All activities prior to the point on the cost-ordered list at which the sum of activity costs exceeds the annual maintenance, repair and replacement allowance shall automatically qualify as routine maintenance, repair, or replacement.

(c) Costs associated with maintaining or installing pollution control equipment shall not be included in the calculation and summation of costs for routine maintenance, repair, and replacement. Costs shall remain included if they are associated with maintaining or installing equipment that serves a dual function as both process and control equipment.

(d) The owner or operator shall provide an annual report to the reviewing authority containing complete information on all maintenance, repair and replacement costs and process unit replacement cost estimates at the stationary source. The report shall be provided within 60 days after the end of the year over which activity costs have been summed.

(ii) An activity otherwise eligible for inclusion in the annual maintenance, repair and replacement allowance shall not be eligible to be included in the allowance if it:

(a) Results in an increase in the maximum achievable hourly emissions

80310   Federal Register / Vol. 67, No. 251 / Tuesday, December 31, 2002 / Proposed Rules

rate of the stationary source of a regulated NSR pollutant, or results in emissions of a regulated NSR pollutant not previously emitted;

(b) Constitutes construction of a new process unit; or

(c) Removes an entire existing process unit and installs a different process unit in its place.

(54)(i) In general, *process unit* means any collection of structures and/or equipment that processes, assembles, applies, blends, or otherwise uses material inputs to produce or store a completed product. A single stationary source may contain more than one process unit.

(ii) The following list identifies the process units at specific kinds of stationary sources.

(a) For a steam electric generating facility, the process unit would consist of those portions of the plant which contribute directly to the production of electricity. For example, at a pulverized coal-fired facility, the process unit would generally be the combination of those systems from the coal receiving equipment through the emission stack, including the coal handling equipment, pulverizers or coal crushers, feedwater heaters, boiler, burners, turbine-generator set, air preheaters, and operating control systems. Each separate generating unit would be considered a separate process unit. Components shared between two or more process units would be proportionately allocated based on capacity.

(b) For a petroleum refinery, there are several categories of process units: those that separate and distill petroleum feedstocks; those that change molecular structures; petroleum treating processes; auxiliary facilities, such as boilers and hydrogen production; and those that load, unload, blend or store products.

(c) For a cement plant, the process unit would generally consist of the kiln and equipment that supports it, including all components that process or store raw materials, preheaters, and components that process or store products from the kilns, and associated emission stacks.

(d) For a pulp and paper mill, there are several types of process units. One is the system that processes wood products, another is the digester and its associated heat exchanger, blow tank, pulp filter, accumulator, oxidation tower, and evaporators. A third is the chemical recovery system, which includes the recovery furnace, lime kiln, storage vessels, and associated oxidation processes feeding regenerated chemicals to the digester.

(e) For an incinerator, the process unit would consist of components from the feed pit or refuse pit to the stack, including conveyors, combustion devices, heat exchangers and steam generators, quench tanks, and fans.

(55) *Functionally equivalent component* means a component that serves the same purpose as the replaced component.

(56) *Fixed capital cost* means the capital needed to provide all the depreciable components. "Depreciable components" refers to all components of fixed capital cost and is calculated by subtracting land an working capital from the total capital investment, as defined in paragraph (b)(57) of this section.

(57) *Total capital investment* means the sum of the following: all costs required to purchase needed process equipment (purchased equipment costs); the costs of labor and materials for installing that equipment (direct installation costs); the costs of site preparation and buildings; other costs such as engineering, construction and field expenses, fees to contractors, startup and performance tests, and contingencies (indirect installation costs); land for the process equipment; and working capital for the process equipment.

*   *   *   *   *

Appendix S—[Amended]

4. In Appendix S to Part 51 Section II is amended:

a. By revising paragraph A.5(iii) (a).

b. By adding paragraphs A.21 through 25.

The revision and additions read as follows:

Appendix S to part 51—Emission Offset Interpretative Ruling

*   *   *   *   *

II. Initial Screening Analyses and Determination of Applicable Requirements

A. *   *   *

5. *   *   *

(iii) *   *   *

(a) Routine maintenance, repair and replacement, which shall include but not be limited to the activities set out in paragraphs A.5 (iii)(a)(1) and (2) of this section. Without regard to other considerations, the activities specified in paragraphs A.5 (iii)(a)(1) and (2) shall constitute routine maintenance, repair and replacement:

(1) Activities performed at a stationary source in order to maintain, facilitate, restore or improve the efficiency, reliability, availability or safety of that stationary source, whose total cost, when added together with the total costs of all previous activities performed at the same stationary source in the same year in order to maintain, facilitate, restore or improve the efficiency, reliability, availability or safety of that stationary source, does not exceed that stationary source's annual maintenance, repair and replacement allowance. "Annual maintenance, repair and replacement allowance" is defined in paragraph A.21 of this section. Rules for calculation and summation of costs are provided in paragraph A.21 (i) of this section. A stationary source may elect to calculate an annual maintenance, repair and replacement allowance for either all or none, but not some, of the maintenance, repair, and replacement activities performed at the stationary source.

(2) The replacement of components of a process unit with identical or functionally equivalent components, provided that:

(i) The fixed capital cost of the components does not exceed [x] [1] percent of the fixed capital cost that would be required to construct an entirely new process unit; and

(ii) The replacement does not change the basic design parameters of the process unit. The basic design parameters for electric utility steam generating units are maximum heat input and fuel consumption specifications. For non-utilities, basic design parameters are the maximum fuel or material input specifications to the process unit. An improvement in efficiency does not change a process unit's basic design parameters. "Functionally equivalent components" and "fixed capital cost" are defined in paragraphs A.23 and A.24 of this section, respectively.

*   *   *   *   *

21. *Annual maintenance, repair and replacement allowance* means a dollar amount calculated according to the following equation: (Industry sector percentage) × (replacement cost of the stationary source) where "industry sector percentage" is drawn from Table 1 of this section.

TABLE 1. OF SECTION II.A.21.—
INDUSTRY SECTOR PERCENTAGES

Industry sector	Industry sector percentage
Electric Services	
Petroleum Refining	
Chemical Processes	
Natural Gas Transport	
Pulp and Paper Mills	
Paper Mills	
Automobile Manufacturing	
Pharmaceuticals	

[1] EPA has not determined this value.

Federal Register / Vol. 67, No. 251 / Tuesday, December 31, 2002 / Proposed Rules 80311

TABLE 1. OF SECTION II.A.21.—INDUS-
TRY SECTOR PERCENTAGES—Continued

Industry sector	Industry sector percentage
Other	

(i) A stationary source's annual maintenance costs shall be calculated and summed according to the following rules:

(a) The owner or operator may choose to sum costs over either a calendar year or initially specified fiscal year. The initially specified fiscal year must remain in use unless other accounting procedures at the stationary source subsequently change to a different fiscal year.

(b) Costs incurred for all activities not performed at the stationary source in order to maintain, facilitate, restore or improve the efficiency, reliability, availability or safety of that stationary source that are not excluded under A.21 (ii) of this section, or that have not been issued a preconstruction permit, shall be tracked chronologically and summed at the end of the year.

(1) At the end of the year, these costs shall be listed and summed in order from least cost to highest cost.

(2) All activities prior to the point on the cost-ordered list at which the sum of activity costs exceeds the annual maintenance, repair and replacement allowance shall automatically qualify as routine maintenance, repair, or replacement.

(c) Costs associated with maintaining or installing pollution control equipment shall not be included in the calculation and summation of costs for routine maintenance, repair, and replacement. Costs shall remain included if they are associated with maintaining or installing equipment that serves a dual function as both process and control equipment.

(d) The owner or operator shall provide an annual report to the reviewing authority containing complete information on all maintenance and replacement costs and process unit replacement cost estimates at the stationary source. The report shall be provided within 60 days after the end of the year over which activity costs have been summed.

(ii) An activity otherwise eligible for inclusion in the annual maintenance, repair and replacement allowance shall not be eligible to be included in the allowance if it:

(a) Results in an increase in the maximum achievable hourly emissions rate of the stationary source of a regulated NSR pollutant, or results in emissions of a regulated NSR pollutant not previously emitted;

(b) Constitutes construction of a new process unit; or

(c) Removes an entire existing process unit and installs a different process unit in its place.

22. (i) In general, *process unit* means any collection of structures and/or equipment that processes, assembles, applies, blends, or otherwise uses material inputs to produce or store a completed product. A single stationary source may contain more than one process unit.

(ii) The following list identifies the process units at specific kinds of stationary sources.

(a) For a steam electric generating facility, the process unit would consist of those portions of the plant which contribute directly to the production of electricity. For example, at a pulverized coal-fired facility, the process unit would generally be the combination of those systems from the coal receiving equipment through the emission stack, including the coal handling equipment, pulverizers or coal crushers, feedwater heaters, boilers, burners, turbine-generator set, air preheaters, and operating control systems. Each separate generating unit would be considered a separate process unit. Components shared between two or more process units would be proportionally allocated based on capacity.

(b) For a petroleum refinery, there are several categories of process units: those that separate and distill petroleum feedstocks; those that change molecular structures; petroleum treating processes; auxiliary facilities, such as boilers and hydrogen production; and those that load, unload, blend or store products.

(c) For a cement plant, the process unit would generally consist of the kiln and equipment that supports it, including all components that process or store raw materials, preheaters, and components that process or store products from the kilns, and associated emission stacks.

(d) For a pulp and paper mill, there are several types of process units. One is the system that processes wood products, another is the digester and its associated heat exchanger, blow tank, pulp filter, accumulator, oxidation tower, and evaporators. A third is the chemical recovery system, which includes the recovery furnace, lime kiln, storage vessels, and associated oxidation processes feeding regenerated chemicals to the digester.

(e) For an incinerator, the process unit would consist of components from the feed pit or refuse pit to the stack, including conveyors, combustion devices, heat exchangers and steam generators, quench tanks, and fans.

23. *Functionally equivalent component* means a component that serves the same purpose as the replaced component.

24. *Fixed capital cost* means the capital needed to provide all the depreciable components. "Depreciable components" refers to all components of fixed capital cost and is calculated by subtracting land and working capital from the total capital investment, as defined in paragraph A.25 of this section.

25. *Total capital investment* means the sum of the following: all costs required to

purchase needed process equipment (purchased equipment costs); the costs of labor and materials for installing that equipment (direct installation costs); the costs of site preparation and buildings; other costs such as engineering, construction and field expenses, fees to contractors, startup and performance tests, and contingencies (indirect installation costs); land for the process equipment; and working capital for the process equipment.

* * * * *

PART 52—[AMENDED]

1. The authority citation for part 52 continues to read as follows:

Authority: 42 U.S.C. 7401, *et seq.*

Subpart A—[Amended]

2. Section 52.21 is amended:
a. By revising paragraph (b)(2)(iii)(a).
b. By adding paragraphs (b)(55) through (59).
The revision and additions are revised to read as follows:

§ 52.21 Prevention of significant deterioration of air quality.

* * * * *

(b) * * *
(2) * * *
(iii) * * *

(a) Routine maintenance, repair and replacement, which shall include but not be limited to the activities set out in paragraphs (b)(2)(iii)(a)(1) and (2) of this section. Without regard to other considerations, the activities specified in paragraphs (b)(2)(iii)(a)(1) and (2) shall constitute routine maintenance, repair and replacement:

(1) Activities performed at a stationary source in order to maintain, facilitate, restore or improve the efficiency, reliability, availability or safety of that stationary source, whose total cost, when added together with the total costs of all previous activities performed at the same stationary source in the same year in order to maintain, facilitate, restore or improve the efficiency, reliability, availability or safety of that stationary source, does not exceed the stationary source's annual maintenance, repair and replacement allowance. "Annual maintenance, repair and replacement allowance" is defined in paragraph (b)(55) of this section. Rules for calculation and summation of costs are provided in paragraph (b)(55)(i) of this section. A stationary source may elect to calculate an annual maintenance, repair and replacement allowance for either all or none, but not some, of the maintenance, repair, and replacement activities performed at the stationary source.

(2) The replacement of components of a process unit with identical or

APPENDIX

749

functionally equivalent components, provided that:

(i) The fixed capital cost of the components does not exceed [x][1] percent of the fixed capital cost that would be required to construct an entirely new process unit; and

(ii) The replacement does not change the basic design parameters of the process unit. The basic design parameters for electric utility steam generating units are maximum heat input and fuel consumption specifications. For non-utilities, basic design parameters are the maximum fuel or material input specifications to the process unit. An improvement in efficiency does not change a process unit's basic design parameters. "Functionally equivalent components" and "fixed capital cost" are defined in paragraphs (b)(57) and (b)(58) of this section.

* * * * *

(55) *Annual maintenance, repair and replacement allowance* means a dollar amount calculated according to the following equation: (Industry sector percentage) x (replacement cost of the stationary source) where "industry sector percentage" is drawn from Table 1 of this section.

TABLE 1 OF § 52.21(B)(55).—
INDUSTRY SECTOR PERCENTAGES

Industry sector	Industry sector percentage
Electric Services	
Petroleum Refining	
Chemical Processes	
Natural Gas Transport	
Pulp and Paper Mills	
Paper Mills	
Automobile Manufacturing	
Pharmaceuticals	
Other	

(i) A stationary source's annual maintenance costs shall be calculated and summed according to the following rules:

(a) The owner or operator may choose to sum costs over either a calendar year or initially specified fiscal year. The initially specified fiscal year must remain in use unless other accounting procedures at the stationary source subsequently change to a different fiscal year.

(b) Costs incurred for all activities not performed at the stationary source in order to maintain, facilitate, restore or improve the efficiency, reliability, availability or safety of that stationary source that are not excluded under paragraph (b)(55)(ii) of this section, or

[1] EPA has not determined this value.

that have not been issued a preconstruction permit, shall be tracked chronologically and summed at the end of the year.

(1) At the end of the year, these costs shall be listed and summed in order from least cost to highest cost.

(2) All activities prior to the point on the cost-ordered list at which the sum of activity costs exceeds the annual maintenance, repair and replacement allowance shall automatically qualify as routine maintenance, repair, or replacement.

(c) Costs associated with maintaining or installing pollution control equipment shall not be included in the calculation and summation of costs for routine maintenance, repair, and replacement. Costs shall remain included if they are associated with maintaining or installing equipment that serves a dual function as both process and control equipment.

(d) The owner or operator shall provide an annual report to the reviewing authority containing complete information on all maintenance, repair and replacement costs and process unit replacement cost estimates at the stationary source. The report shall be provided within 60 days after the end of the year over which activity costs have been summed.

(ii) An activity otherwise eligible for inclusion in the annual maintenance, repair and replacement allowance shall not be eligible to be included in the allowance if it:

(a) Results in an increase in the maximum achievable hourly emissions rate of the stationary source of a regulated NSR pollutant, or results in emissions of a regulated NSR pollutant not previously emitted;

(b) Constitutes construction of a new process unit; or

(c) Removes an entire existing process unit and installs a different process unit in its place.

(56) (i) In general, *process unit* means any collection of structures and/or equipment that processes, assembles, applies, blends, or otherwise uses material inputs to produce or store a completed product. A single stationary source may contain more than one process unit.

(ii) The following list identifies the process units at specific kinds of stationary sources.

(a) For a steam electric generating facility, the process unit would consist of those portions of the plant which contribute directly to the production of electricity. For example, at a pulverized coal-fired facility, the process unit would generally be the combination of those systems from the coal receiving

equipment through the emission stack, including the coal handling equipment, pulverizers or coal crushers, feedwater heaters, boiler, burners, turbine-generator set, air preheaters, and operating control systems. Each separate generating unit would be considered a separate process unit. Components shared between two or more process units would be proportionately allocated based on capacity.

(b) For a petroleum refinery, there are several categories of process units: those that separate and distill petroleum feedstocks; those that change molecular structures; petroleum treating processes; auxiliary facilities, such as boilers and hydrogen production; and those that load, unload, blend or store products.

(c) For a cement plant, the process unit would generally consist of the kiln and equipment that supports it, including all components that process or store raw materials, preheaters, and components that process or store products from the kilns, and associated emission stacks.

(d) For a pulp and paper mill, there are several types of process units. One is the system that processes wood products, another is the digester and its associated heat exchanger, blow tank, pulp filter, accumulator, oxidation tower, and evaporators. A third is the chemical recovery system, which includes the recovery furnace, lime kiln, storage vessels, and associated oxidation processes feeding regenerated chemicals to the digester.

(e) For an incinerator, the process unit would consist of components from the feed pit or refuse pit to the stack, including conveyors, combustion devices, heat exchangers and steam generators, quench tanks, and fans.

(57) *Functionally equivalent component* means a component that serves the same purpose as the replaced component.

(58) *Fixed capital cost* means the capital needed to provide all the depreciable components. "Depreciable components" refers to all components of fixed capital cost and is calculated by subtracting land and working capital from the total capital investment, as defined in paragraph (b)(59) of this section.

(59) *Total capital investment* means the sum of the following: all costs required to purchase needed process equipment (purchased equipment costs); the costs of labor and materials for installing that equipment (direct installation costs); the costs of site preparation and buildings; other costs such as engineering, construction and field expenses, fees to contractors, startup and performance tests, and

Federal Register / Vol. 67, No. 251 / Tuesday, December 31, 2002 / Proposed Rules   **80313**

contingencies (indirect installation costs); land for the process equipment; and working capital for the process equipment.

* * * * *

3. Section 52.24 is amended:

a. By revising paragraph (f)(5)(iii)(*a*).

b. By adding paragraphs (f)(25) through (29).

The revision and additions read as follows:

§ 52.24 Statutory restriction on new sources.

* * * * *

(f) * * *

(5) * * *

(iii) * * *

(*a*) Routine maintenance, repair and replacement, which shall include but not be limited to the activities set out in paragraphs (f)(5)(iii)(*a*)(*1*) and (*2*) of this section. Without regard to other considerations, the activities specified in paragraphs (f)(5)(iii)(*a*)(*1*) and (*2*) shall constitute routine maintenance, repair and replacement:

(*1*) Activities performed at a stationary source in order to maintain, facilitate, restore or improve the efficiency, reliability, availability or safety of that stationary source, whose total cost, when added together with the total costs of all previous activities performed at the same stationary source in the same year in order to maintain, facilitate, restore or improve the efficiency, reliability, availability or safety of that stationary source, does not exceed that stationary source's annual maintenance, repair and replacement allowance. "Annual maintenance, repair and replacement allowance" is defined in paragraph (f)(25) of this section. Rules for calculation and summation of costs are provided in paragraph (f)(25)(i) of this section. A stationary source may elect to calculate an annual maintenance, repair and replacement allowance for either all or none, but not some, of the maintenance, repair, and replacement activities performed at the stationary source.

(*2*) The replacement of components of a process unit with identical or functionally equivalent components, provided that:

(*i*) The fixed capital cost of the components does not exceed [x] [1] percent of the fixed capital cost that would be required to construct an entirely new process unit; and

(*ii*) The replacement does not change the basic design parameters of the process unit. The basic design parameters for electric utility steam generating units are maximum heat

input and fuel consumption specifications. For non-utilities, basic design parameters are the maximum fuel or material input specifications to the process unit. An improvement in efficiency does not change a process unit's basic design parameters. "Functionally equivalent components" and "fixed capital cost" are defined in paragraphs (f)(27) and (f)(28) of this section, respectively.

* * * * *

(25) *Annual maintenance, repair and replacement allowance* means a dollar amount calculated according to the following equation: (Industry sector percentage) x (replacement cost of the stationary source) where "industry sector percentage" is drawn from Table 1 of this section.

TABLE 1 OF § 52.24(F)(25).—
INDUSTRY SECTOR PERCENTAGES

Industry sector	Industry sector percentage
Electric Services	
Petroleum Refining	
Chemical Processes	
Natural Gas Transport	
Pulp and Paper Mills	
Paper Mills	
Automobile Manufacturing	
Pharmaceuticals	
Other	

(i) A stationary source's annual maintenance costs shall be calculated and summed according to the following rules:

(*a*) The owner or operator may choose to sum costs over either a calendar year or initially specified fiscal year. The initially specified fiscal year must remain in use unless other accounting procedures at the stationary source subsequently change to a different fiscal year.

(*b*) Costs incurred for all activities not performed at the stationary source in order to maintain, facilitate, restore or improve the efficiency, reliability, availability or safety of that stationary source that are not excluded under paragraph (f)(25)(ii) of this section, or that have not been issued a preconstruction permit, shall be tracked chronologically and summed at the end of the year.

(*1*) At the end of the year, these costs shall be listed and summed in order from least cost to highest cost.

(*2*) All activities prior to the point on the cost-ordered list at which the sum of activity costs exceeds the annual maintenance, repair and replacement allowance shall automatically qualify as routine maintenance, repair, or replacement.

(*c*) Costs associated with maintaining or installing pollution control equipment shall not be included in the calculation and summation of costs for routine maintenance, repair, and replacement. Costs shall remain included if they are associated with maintaining or installing equipment that serves a dual function as both process and control equipment.

(*d*) The owner or operator shall provide an annual report to the reviewing authority containing complete information on all maintenance, repair and replacement costs and process unit replacement cost estimates at the stationary source. The report shall be provided within 60 days after the end of the year over which activity costs have been summed.

(ii) An activity otherwise eligible for inclusion in the annual maintenance, repair and replacement allowance shall not be eligible to be included in the allowance if it:

(*a*) Results in an increase in the maximum achievable hourly emissions rate of the stationary source of a regulated NSR pollutant, or results in emissions of a regulated NSR pollutant not previously emitted;

(*b*) Constitutes construction of a new process unit; or

(*c*) Removes an entire existing process unit and installs a different process unit in its place.

(26) (i) In general, *process unit* means any collection of structures and/or equipment that processes, assembles, applies, blends, or otherwise uses material inputs to produce or store a completed product. A single stationary source may contain more than one process unit.

(ii) The following list identifies the process units at specific kinds of stationary sources.

(*a*) For a steam electric generating facility, the process unit would consist of those portions of the plant which contribute directly to the production of electricity. For example, at a pulverized coal-fired facility, the process unit would generally be the combination of those systems from the coal receiving equipment through the emission stack, including the coal handling equipment, pulverizers or coal crushers, feedwater heaters, boiler, burners, turbine-generator set, air preheaters, and operating control systems. Each separate generating unit would be considered a separate process unit. Components shared between two or more process units would be proportionately allocated based on capacity.

(*b*) For a petroleum refinery, there are several categories of process units: those that separate and distill petroleum

---

[1] EPA has not determined this value.

feedstocks; those that change molecular structures; petroleum treating processes; auxiliary facilities, such as boilers and hydrogen production; and those that load, unload, blend or store products.

(c) For a cement plant, the process unit would generally consist of the kiln and equipment that supports it, including all components that process or store raw materials, preheaters, and components that process or store products from the kilns, and associated emission stacks.

(d) For a pulp and paper mill, there are several types of process units. One is the system that processes wood products, another is the digester and its associated heat exchanger, blow tank, pulp filter, accumulator, oxidation tower, and evaporators. A third is the chemical recovery system, which

includes the recovery furnace, lime kiln, storage vessels, and associated oxidation processes feeding regenerated chemicals to the digester.

(e) For an incinerator, the process unit would consist of components from the feed pit or refuse pit to the stack, including conveyors, combustion devices, heat exchangers and steam generators, quench tanks, and fans.

(27) *Functionally equivalent component* means a component that serves the same purpose as the replaced component.

(28) *Fixed capital cost* means the capital needed to provide all the depreciable components. "Depreciable components" refers to all components of fixed capital cost and is calculated by subtracting land and working capital from the total capital investment, as

defined in paragraph (f)(29) of this section.

(29) *Total capital investment* means the sum of the following: all costs required to purchase needed process equipment (purchased equipment costs); the costs of labor and materials for installing that equipment (direct installation costs); the costs of site preparation and buildings; other costs such as engineering, construction and field expenses, fees to contractors, startup and performance tests, and contingencies (indirect installation costs); land for the process equipment; and working capital for the process equipment.

*   *   *   *   *

[FR Doc. 02–31900 Filed 12–30–02; 8:45 am]

BILLING CODE 6560-50-P

Comment of Professor Flatt

February 26, 2003

U.S. Environmental Protection Agency
EPA West (Air Docket)
1200 Pennsylvania Ave., NW
Room B108, Mail code: 6102T
Washington, DC 20460
Attn: Docket ID #A–2002–04
OAR–2002–068

Ladies and Gentlemen:

My name is Victor B. Flatt, and I am the A.L. O'Quinn Chair in Environmental Law at the University of Houston. I teach and do research in the area of environmental law, and in particular the area of environmental administration. Due to my area of expertise, and my duties as a public servant, I wanted to submit a comment on the proposed EPA rule defining Routine Repair and Maintenance (RRAM) for purposes of New Source Review (NSR) of existing air pollution sources which undergo alterations. As a law professor who has studied these issues over time, I believe that some of my comments might be germane to the viability and legality of this proposed rule.

Under Secs. 165(a), 172, and 173 of the Clean Air Act, annotated at 42 U.S.C. Secs. 7475(a), 7502, and 7503, major new sources or major modifications of existing sources of criteria air pollutants must submit to review as a new source and are required to install pollution control equipment which represent the Best Available Control Technology (BACT) for sources in attainment areas, and Lowest Achievable Emissions Rate in non-attainment areas. 42 U.S.C. Secs. 7475(a)(4) and 7503(a)(2). A "new source" is defined in the Clean Air Act to include already existing sources which are modified after the effective date of these acts. 42 U.S.C. Sec. 7411(a)(2). In pertinent part, a "modification" occurs if "any physical change" or "change in method of operation . . . increases the amount of any air pollutant emitted by such source." In general, a major source is defined as capable of emitting 100 tons of a regulated pollutant annually. 42 U.S.C. Sec. 7602(j). With respect to the non-attainment program, "major" is defined as those sources which can emit or have the potential to emit either 100 tons or 250 tons (depending upon the type of source) of certain pollutants. 42 U.S.C. Sec. 7479(1).

On December 31, 2002, the EPA announced its final rule defining "major modification" for purposes of NSR, to be set out in 40 CFR, parts 50 and 51. This rule attempts to define "major modification" as a result of "significant" emissions increase of a regulated NSR pollutant. This rule specifically exempted routine repair and maintenance (RRAM) from activities which would trigger NSR for existing sources. RRAM is the subject of this rulemaking, and is what these comments address.[2]

The definition of modification in 42 U.S.C. Sec. 7411 in many ways is quite explicit and clear. However, there are some questions as to what constitutes a source for application or what activities cause emissions increases. Historically, the EPA has not defined RRAM for purposes of triggering NSR for alterations of existing sources, preferring to work on a case by case basis. In making its determination, the EPA has considered the nature, extent, purpose, frequency, and the cost of the work. Those regulated entities that are unsure whether or not NSR and its accompanying technological requirements are triggered, may consult the reviewing authority for assistance in making the determination.

This proposal seeks to create classes of categories, defined by total expenditures as a percentage of capital cost, which would uniformly be considered RRAM.

My comments address two major considerations: 1) the need for this "clarification," and 2) substantive and procedural problems with the proposal.

I. THE NEED FOR A CLARIFICATION OF RRAM.

According to the call for comments, the EPA has undertaken this rulemaking because industry believes that the current approach is too uncertain, proving costly since industry may not undertake needed repair and maintenance because of uncertainty about what changes might be allowed without triggering NSR requirements. According to the call for comments, the option of requesting an applicability determination is considered too costly by some in industry. Such applicability determinations also require time and resources from the EPA as well.

If it is possible to avoid sacrificing legitimate NSR while introducing more specific guidelines to define RRAM, then it would make sense to do so and would not be inconsistent with the legislation that requires NSR for certain modifications of existing sources. The problem is that the large diversity of industries and situations makes it almost impossible to avoid a case by case approach without making the definition of RRAM both over and under-inclusive. Indeed, the current proposal does not

---

2. The final rule defining major modification has already been challenged in court, but the overturning of that rule will not affect the process governing this rule. Thus my comments will address this rule as a self contained proposal.

truly eliminate the uncertainty of the procedure. The current proposal posits that an owner or operator "would evaluate on a case-by-case test any activities that did not come within the allowance and that are not otherwise excluded, in order to determine whether they are RMRR." Furthermore, the proposal might exempt certain kinds of replacement or maintenance activity or other activity that is not legitimately considered a RRAM, even if it comes within the yearly budget allowance.

The truth is that there is no real way to categorically define all of the activities that could or could not be considered routine repair and maintenance. If that were possible, then Congress would have made that determination itself. Similarly, it could have chosen some percentage expenditure, but it did not. Instead, where Congress has explicitly spoken on the issue, it has stated that the term "modification" means an increase in the amount of "*any* air pollutant," 42 U.S.C. Sec. 7411(a)(4), and that with respect to certain non-attainment areas, there shall be *no* de minimis exception for increases of volatile organic compounds from existing sources unless it is less than 25 tons over five years. 42 U.S.C. 7511a(c)(6). (emphasis added).

Essentially then, the proposed rule would simply exclude certain activities that fall under a specific budget, while still leaving uncertainty as to those activities beyond that budget or activities in which there is any question whether the activity is routine repair and maintenance. However, this does nothing to eliminate the current uncertainty which the purported rule addresses. This is because the "exception" to the annualized budget is no different than the current situation. Under the current regulations, an owner or operator would only need to seek applicability review if the activity is not clearly routine repair and maintenance. The definition of RRAM is not connected to the expense of the project, but rather the nature of the project, and presumably whether it would operate as an increase to emissions. The new proposal does nothing to eliminate that. If there is uncertainty whether an activity which falls within the annual budget is not really RRAM but instead an upgrade or major modification forbidden by the statute, then applicability review is still required. The only change is that there will now be created a situation in which there is a safe harbor of activities (those under a certain budget) which will not trigger routine scrutiny as opposed to the current situation in which all activities might trigger such scrutiny. Assuming that owners and operators follow the letter of the regulation then virtually all activities that are currently in question will still be in question under the proposed new rules. Therefore the effect of the new rules is simply to allow larger investments in upgrades without scrutiny, subverting the purpose of the statute. This brings us to part II.

II. SUBSTANTIVE AND PROCEDURAL PROBLEMS WITH THE RRAM

The proposed rule also suffers from substantive and procedural problems in that its implementation may be inconsistent with the Clean Air Act and the Administrative Procedures Act.

Secs. 165 and 173 of the C.A.A. specifically note that any change in pollution levels from an existing source triggers NSR and accompanying technological upgrades. Nothing in the proposed definition based on cost of changes or maintenance address this clear language of Congress.

Moreover, this proposed definition of routine repair and maintenance would essentially exempt any modifications of the need to go through NSR. That is because it allows for upgrades that will indefinitely keep existing sources in service without ever having to upgrade to new source requirements.

This problem is recognized in the proposal, which notes that replacement of "existing process units" (which presumably would be an "upgrade" as opposed to a "routine maintenance") would not qualify for the RRAM exceptions. However, it does allow that "some partial replacements [of existing process units] would qualify for the proposed RRAM exclusion." But partial replacements over time can easily have the same effect as an entire replacement of an "existing process unit" which the proposal notes would not be RRAM. Under its own terms then, the proposed rule allows changes over the course of years to occur which it supposedly would not allow to occur in one year. Either an activity is routine repair and maintenance or it is not; it should be immaterial if the activity occurs in the course of one year or five years. It is true that many "partial replacements" may not be disguised upgrades but RRAM, but the only way to determine if piece by piece alterations are not cumulative upgrades is to have case by case analysis, which this proposal seeks to eliminate as routine procedure.

The proposed rule is also in direct violation of the enabling statute in noting that changes that would increase "efficiency" of the unit do not automatically qualify as a major modification. This flies directly in the face of the words and spirit of the Clean Air Act, and cannot withstand analysis.

As the proposal itself points out, RRAM would usually be expected to encompass simple replacement of parts with identical ones. This proposal seeks to expand this by allowing replacements of similar units or equipment, even if the use of an "improved" version increases the life or preserves the efficiency of the affected unit. (Section VII. A.)

The purpose of allowing existing sources to avoid the imposition of the pollution control equipment for new sources was to recognize the already fixed costs that had been incurred prior to the passage of the Clean Air Act. However, it is clear from all contemporaneous debates that this was not meant to be a permanent situation. It was believed that eventually as the older plants reached the end of their useful life, they would be replaced by new plants or significantly upgraded so that new state of the art, pollution control equipment would be installed. If they were not eventually phased out or upgraded, there would not only still be dirty air, but it would also make new, pollution controlling plants, comparably inefficient. Under the Clean Air Act, then, even allowing for one to one replacement of parts might be problematic. The only justification for allowing even this is that eventually new plants, parts, and machines would be so much more efficient, that simply substituting one old fashioned part for another in an existing plant, would eventually cease to be economically logical, even when including the costs of significant pollution control upgrades.

The current proposal effectively eliminates the possibility of an existing plant ever having an economic incentive to upgrade by allowing these plants to install replacement equipment that is more efficient. This means that existing plants can continue to modernize, bringing in comparable efficiencies to new plants while at the same time not being required to upgrade pollution control equipment. As noted in the proposal itself (Section VII. B.),:

> "almost any component replacement can be expected to have some beneficial impact on the energy efficiency of the unit and, left unbounded, this approach could result in the replacement of an entire boiler with a new, more efficient boiler without state of the art pollution controls."

This proposal admits that the "replacement" of an entire boiler should not be considered "routine," and thus should trigger NSR, but the proposal notes that by allowing replacement of parts with more efficient and newer parts, that in fact this could occur. Thus the proposal itself recognizes that it might be allowing "major modifications" under the proposed rule without triggering NSR, in violation of the enabling statute. Any elimination of pollution control equipment upgrades for existing sources must be undertaken through the legislative process, and not implemented in the guise of an administrative change.

The problem is exacerbated by the lack of specificity in the proposal. The proposal notes that RRAM allowance should be defined as a certain percentage of capital cost per year, but it fails to set out what that percentage will be or how "overall capital cost" will be determined. In this case, the devil is truly in the details. Depending upon how "capital cost" is determined and depending on what percentage is allowed, the number of activities that will qualify for RRAM could vary enormously, even to the point where almost any activity, not excluded as "major modification" by the owner itself will qualify under this "exception." In addition to the increasing scope with which this would allow more activities that should be considered "major modification" to avoid NSR, it also is procedurally problematic.

In order for this proposal to be implemented in final form, it first must be circulated as a draft in substantially the same form as it will appear as final. Without this, there can be no effective comment as required by the APA, 5 U.S.C. Sec. 553, nor effective due process to those who will be affected by the rule. Without sufficient detail, any movement to final rule implementation without more specificity regarding the calculation of "capital costs," determination of percentage allowance, and determination of time event horizon for calculation would be an APA violation.

III. CONCLUSION

This lack of specificity frames exactly what is wrong with the proposal. The proposal is being put forward to supposedly solve the problem of uncertainty with respect to what will trigger NSR for repair and maintenance activities. However, its effect cannot be evaluated without more detail as to how any annual allowance would be calculated. Moreover, the proposal has not indicated how it would actually eliminate uncertainty since it still retains an exception for activities which are "not to be considered RRAM." Since the proposal does not effectively demonstrate how it will be an efficiency improvement over the current case by case analysis, but does indicate the likely possibility of currently regulated activities escaping NSR, its implementation must be considered arbitrary and capricious and an abuse of discretion, and thus a violation of the APA. The only substantive proposal, that which anticipates allowing efficiency upgrades to occur with RRAM, violates the spirit and letter of the CAA. Thus, this proposal should not be implemented. The EPA should continue with the current case by case approach which is the only solution to analyzing the diversity of air pollutant sources which may trigger NSR.

Very truly yours,

Victor B. Flatt
A.L. O'Quinn Chair in Environmental Law
University of Houston Law Center
713–743–2155; vflatt@central.uh.edu

Comment of Professor O'Hear

March 2, 2003

U.S. Environmental Protection Agency
EPA West (Air Docket)

Room: B108
Mail Code: 6102T
Washington, DC 20460

Re: Docket ID No. A–2002–04

Dear Sir or Madam:

These comments are addressed to the proposed rule for routine maintenance, repair, and replacement ("RMRR"). I am a professor at Marquette University Law School, where my teaching responsibilities include Environmental Law, Natural Resources, and Legislation.[3]

---

3. Please note that these comments are mine alone, and do not necessarily reflect the views of my academic institution.

Summary

The proposed rule is inconsistent with the statutory purposes of New Source Review ("NSR"). Specifically, the Agency has proposed two new categories of activities that would be treated as RMRR per se, and hence shielded from the Agency's traditional case-by-case approach to NSR. The first category encompasses activities within a new annual maintenance, repair, and replacement allowance. The second encompasses the replacement of existing equipment within certain cost limitations. Taken together, the two proposed exclusions from NSR would allow many grandfathered air polluters to operate indefinitely without installing state-of-the-art pollution control equipment. This would contravene the purpose of NSR, which is to ensure that grandfathered facilities eventually do improve their environmental performance.

Loopholes in the proposed rule would provide ample opportunity for sources to construct major modifications without adopting new pollution control technology. Changes to the proposed rule might reduce the scope of some of the loopholes, but a more fundamental objection would remain: cost-based approaches, as the Agency here proposes, distract attention from more important considerations. In particular, NSR should focus on whether a contemplated activity (whatever its cost) represents a suitable opportunity for concurrent improvements in pollution control technology.

If the Agency nonetheless decides to proceed with one or both of its cost-based exclusions, the Agency should also consider an additional cost-based safeguard: a lifetime cap on expenditures that are treated as RMRR per se.

Analysis

Purposes of NSR and RMRR

In structuring the Clean Air Act, Congress chose to impose different environmental performance standards on new and existing sources of air pollution. This decision stemmed from the recognition that "[b]uilding control technology into new plants at time of construction will plainly be less costly [than] requiring retrofit."[4] However, Congress did not intend that the grandfathered existing facilities would forever be exempt from enhanced pollution control requirements. Congress thus chose to apply the new source standards to old sources when they underwent "modifications."[5] The logic was obvious: While a pollution control retrofit might be unduly burdensome for a facility busily engaged in productive activities, the same retrofit might be far less costly and intrusive if performed in conjunction with other activities that significantly interrupted production and involved restructuring of equipment and workflows.[6] Existing

---

4. H.R. Rep. No. 294, 95th Cong., 1st Sess. 185, *reprinted in* 1977 U.S. Code Cong. Admin. News at 1264.

5. *See* 42 U.S.C. § 7411(a)(2) (defining "new source" to include modifications).

6. *See* Wisconsin Electric Power Co. v. Reilly, 893 F.2d 901, 909 (7th Cir. 1990) (discussing purpose of "modification" rule). Indeed, the Agency makes much the same point in a portion of its explanation for the

plants, with deteriorating and increasingly obsolete equipment, would inevitably either shut down or undergo modification, thus triggering a duty to install state-of-the-art pollution control technology.

In order to implement this scheme, the Agency chose to create a safe harbor for "routine maintenance, repair, and replacement." Unfortunately, RMRR has from the beginning presented a subtle risk of distraction: the standard invites regulators (and industry) to focus on the semantics of "routine"–a term found nowhere in the statute and only tangentially related to the real objective, namely, ensuring that all existing facilities enhance their environmental performance at some time when it is relatively less burdensome for them to do so. Indeed, with clever engineering and an aggressive interpretation of "routine," a facility may dramatically lengthen its productive life without ever adopting stringent pollution control measures.

The subtle risks implicit in RMRR have become quite explicit in the present proposed rule. Where the original RMRR rule only suggested that grandfathered sources might retain their favored status indefinitely, the new proposal plainly codifies the policy. Step by the step, the question for environmental protection shifts from "when" to "if."

Criteria for Evaluation

Any proposed reform of RMRR should be evaluated under at least three criteria: (1) consistency with statutory text; (2) consistency with statutory purposes; and (3) consistency with the spirit of RMRR. As to text, the Clean Air Act indicates that NSR should be triggered by the "modification" of any stationary source. "Modification," in turn, is defined broadly as "<u>any</u> physical change" that increases air emissions.[7]

As to purposes, while Congress chose to grandfather existing sources in light of the costs of retrofitting old plants, Congress's implicit intent in adopting NSR was to ensure that the old plants would eventually adopt new controls at an opportune time.

Finally, while the Agency is not bound by existing regulations in the same way that it is bound by statutory text and purpose, the Agency should be sensitive to the fact that the proposed rule has been offered as an elaboration on the concept of RMRR. Thus, in the interests of candor and informed public discussion, the proposed rule should not reach beyond the scope of what can plausibly be considered "routine maintenance, repair, and replacement."

As detailed below, both aspects of the proposed rule (the annual allowance and the equipment replacement provision) fail with regard to all three criteria. The proposed rule potentially shields from NSR many activities that would normally be considered "modifications" or are otherwise plainly not "routine." In so doing, the proposed rule invites

---

proposed rule . . . 67 Fed. Reg. 80301 (2002) (concluding that activity should be excluded from RMRR protection because "it is the kind of activity that would likely be a logical point for owners or operators to install state-of-the-art controls").

7. 42 U.S.C. § 7411(a)(4) (emphasis added).

sources to replace and even upgrade equipment indefinitely without implementing new pollution controls.

Annual Allowance

The annual allowance proposal uses expenditures as a proxy for determining what is "routine." The Agency's approach is subject to manipulation and might allow many major modifications to escape NSR. A few specific concerns are highlighted below.

1. A source's annual maintenance allowance is not based on that source's actual maintenance needs. The allowance is calculated based on (1) the source's replacement cost, and (2) a uniform industry-wide "maintenance percentage." However, there is no reason to believe that sources within an industry have any uniformity in their actual maintenance needs. Indeed, needs likely vary considerably based on such factors as age, prior maintenance history, intensity of use, raw materials used in production processes, climate, and local labor costs. Many sources will thus likely have excess allowances, which may be used to shield from NSR significant equipment upgrades and other physical changes that are not in any conventional sense "routine."

2. Calculating allowances on an annual basis invites manipulation of expenditures. A source wishing to shield a major equipment upgrade from NSR in one year might crowd genuine routine maintenance into a prior or subsequent year. Granted, if the source exceeded its annual allowance in the "maintenance year," then its activities that year might be subject to case-by-case NSR. However, because the reviewed activities would be genuine routine maintenance, the activities would not likely trigger heightened performance standards. Meanwhile, the real changes that might actually fail NSR would never even be reviewed (assuming they cost less than the annual allowance).

3. Quite apart from manipulation, the Agency itself notes that multi-year maintenance cycles are routine in some industries, with major maintenance activities concentrated in just one year.[8] For some petroleum refineries, for instance, major maintenance activities are conducted once every eight years.[9] If allowances are calculated on an annual basis, then such sources would be expected to have significant excess allowances seven out of every eight years.

4. Costs are attributed to the year in which they are incurred, even if they arise from a multiyear activity. A source may thus shield a major modification from NSR by dividing the project into discrete components such that the costs are incurred over more than one year.[10] If the

---

8. 67 Fed. Reg. 80296 (2002).

9. *Id.*

10. If the timing were planned carefully, this might not even result in any meaningful delay in implementing a modification. For instance, for a source using a calendar year system, new equipment might be purchased in December and labor costs for installing the equipment incurred in January. Separately, the two pieces might each squeeze under the applicable annual allowance, even though they might not if conducted over any other two-month period during the year.

source's allowance exceeds its actual maintenance expenses over the time period, case-by-case review might never be triggered. Even if case-by-case review were triggered in a given year, the modification might still escape review if the project's costs in that year were lower than any of the source's routine maintenance expenses. (This is because, under the Agency's proposal, case-by-case review is conducted from most-expensive to least-expensive.)

5. Because the allowance is determined on a source-wide basis, sources may trade off expenses across process units. A source planning a major modification at one process unit might, in effect, acquire excess allow-ances by discontinuing routine maintenance at another process unit. This might eventually lead to the deterioration and closure of the undermaintained process unit, but a source might find the loss of one process unit to be an acceptable price for an NSR-shielded major upgrade at another.

The foregoing concerns all arise from a fundamental weakness of the Agency's proposal: generic expenditure standards can serve as only a very crude proxy for "routine maintenance" (or "major modification"). Some of the specific concerns may be marginally ameliorated by better tailoring allowances to the realities on the ground (e.g., developing a multiyear allowance for industries with multiyear maintenance cycles; determining allowances on a process unit, instead of a source-wide, basis). But adopting such changes would make the proposal considerably more difficult to develop and administer, and might undermine some of the transparency and flexibility objectives that the proposal is intended to advance.

Equipment Replacement

The equipment replacement proposal also misdirects the NSR inquiry, likewise potentially allowing sources to operate indefinitely without installing state-of-the-art pollution controls. At least three concerns merit particular consideration.

First, through careful planning, a source may over time replace an entire process unit, piece by piece, without ever triggering NSR. The source would only need to take care that the unit's "basic design parameters" remain unchanged and that no particular project costs more than 50% of the unit's overall replacement cost.[11] At the end of the replacement period, the source would, in effect, have a brand-new process unit without the pollution controls that would normally be expected of a new process unit. Yet, as the Agency's proposal itself recognizes, replacement of a process unit (even with an identical new unit) is, in fact, "the kind of activity that would likely be a logical point for owners or operators to install state-of-the-art controls."[12] There is no apparent reason to treat

---

11. This assumes the Agency adopts 50% as the applicable standard, as the Agency suggests it may do. 67 Fed. Reg. 80301 (2002). A lower percentage might make it marginally more difficult for a source to achieve this result, but the basic concern remains the same.

12. *Id.*

differently the source that replaces a process unit all at once and the source that divides total replacement into smaller discrete projects over time.

Second, while the proposal suggests treating equipment replacement costing up to half the value of an entire process unit as RMRR, it is hard to believe that such projects would commonly fit anyone's understanding of "routine." Indeed, other regulations promulgated by the Agency characterize 50% of the replacement cost as the expenditure threshold for what constitutes "reconstruction."[13] Surely, some significant range of costs must separate "reconstruction" from "routine." At a minimum, more study is needed to determine a lower, more realistic replacement cost percentage on an industry-by-industry basis, reflecting practices that are, in fact, routine.

Third, the proposal makes no distinction for replacement activities that represent an ideal opportunity for upgrading pollution controls. For instance, when equipment is replaced that is directly connected to pollution control equipment, or that otherwise imposes limits on the source's ability to implement new control technologies, a retrofit might be especially timely. In such circumstances, the NSR process should not be artificially constrained by cost-based safe harbors, or by other extra-statutory concepts like "routine" and "functionally equivalent."

Lifetime Cap on Cost–Based Exclusions

The Agency should reject cost-based safe harbors from NSR because, among other things, the inquiry into cost issues misses the real point of NSR. Cost-based exclusions raise at least two overlapping risks, both of which have been noted above: (1) such exclusions may allow sources to avoid a pollution control retrofit even at those times that a retrofit could be performed with minimal disruption; and (2) such exclusions may allow sources to operate indefinitely without implementing state-of-the-art control technology. Both of these eventualities would contravene the underlying objectives of NSR.

If the Agency nonetheless decides to adopt one or both of its proposed cost-based exclusions, the Agency should consider an additional safe-guard: a lifetime cap on expenditures that qualify for the cost-based protections. The cap might be set on any of a number of potential bases. For instance, the cap might be determined by multiplying an annual maintenance allowance (calculated as the Agency has suggested in the present proposal) by the number of years representing a process unit's expected useful life. Alternatively, the cap might be based directly on a process unit's replacement cost.

However calculated, when a process unit exceeds its lifetime cap, it should no longer qualify for special cost-based exclusions. By that time, the process unit will be presumptively beyond the realm of routine maintenance, repair, and replacement, and instead presumptively engaged in extraordinary life-extending measures. Subsequent expendi-

---

13. 40 C.F.R. 60.15(b).

tures might still be treated as RMRR after case-by-case review, but should be subject to at least a rebuttable presumption that they are not RMRR.

A lifetime cap would emphasize that RMRR is a finite concept and that grandfather status should not last forever. This, in turn, might encourage sources to look for the optimal time for a retrofit, knowing that a retrofit (or shutting down) will eventually be required.

A lifetime cap would reduce incentives for some of the types of manipulation discussed above. For instance, under the annual allowance proposal, sources might spread the costs of a major modification over a period of several years in order to avoid NSR. The incentives for doing so might be lessened if all of those costs would be counted against the source under a lifetime cap, potentially drawing closer the day of reckoning under NSR.

Conclusion

For the foregoing reasons, the Agency should reconsider its annual allowance and equipment replacement proposals, and, more generally, its cost-based approaches to NSR. If the Agency does proceed with one or both of the cost-based proposals, the Agency should refine the proposals so as to minimize the likelihood that major modifications and other nonroutine activities will be conducted under the guise of RMRR. As an additional safeguard, the Agency should also consider implementing a lifetime cap on expenditures that qualify for the cost-based exclusions.

Thank you for the opportunity to comment on the pending proposal.

Glossary of Acronyms

AAPCC:	American Association of Poison Control Centers
ADA:	Americans with Disabilities Act
AEC:	Atomic Energy Commission
ADEC:	Alaska Department of Environmental Conservation
ALJ:	Administrative Law Judge
AMC:	American Mining Congress
AOU:	American Ornithological Union
APA:	Administrative Procedure Act
API:	American Petroleum Institute
ARAR:	Applicable or Relevant and Appropriate Requirement
ASCS:	Agricultural Stabilization and Conservation Service
ASTM:	American Society for Testing and Materials
BA:	Biological Assessment
BACT:	Best Available Control Technology
BADT:	Best Available Demonstrated Control Technology
BART:	Best Available Retrofit Technology
BAT:	Best Available Control Technology that is Economically Achievable
BiOp:	Biological Opinion
BLM:	Bureau of Land Management
BMP:	Best Management Practice
BO:	Biological Opinion
BOD:	Biochemical Oxygen Demand
BPJ:	Best Professional Judgment
BPT:	Best Practicable Control Technology
BTU:	British Thermal Unit
CAA:	Clean Air Act
CAFO:	Concentrated Animal Feeding Operation
CBE	Citizens for a Better Environment
CEGs:	Conditionally-Exempt Generators
CEQ	Council on Environmental Quality
CEQA:	California Environmental Quality Act
CERCLA:	Comprehensive Environmental Response, Compensation, and Liability Act
EA:	Environmental Assessment
EDF:	Environmental Defense Fund
EGU:	Electric Generating Unit
EIS:	Environmenta Impact Statement
ELR:	Environmental Law Reporter
EMS:	Environmental Management Systems

EPCRA:	Emergency Planning and Community Right-to-know Act
ESA:	Endangered Species Act
ESECA:	Energy Supply and Environmental Coordination Act
ESU:	Evolutionary Significant Unit
FAA:	Federal Aviation Administration
FDF:	Fundamentally Different Factors
FEC:	Federal Election Commission
FEIS:	Final Environmental Impact Statement
FERC:	Federal Energy Regulatory Commission
FHAA:	Fair Housing amendments Act
FHWA:	Federal Highway Administration
FIFRA:	Federal Insecticide, Fungicide, and Rodenticide Act
FIP:	Federal Implementation Plan
FLPMA:	Federal Land Policy and Management Act
FONSI:	Finding of no Significant Impact
FPC:	Federal Power Commission
FR:	Federal Register
FSA:	Farm Service Agency
FWPCA:	Federal Water Pollution Control Act
FWS:	Fish and Wildlife Service
GAO:	General Accounting Office
GPM:	Grams Per Mile
HAP:	Hazardous Air Pollutant
HCP:	Habitat Conservation Plan
HDE:	Heavy-Duty Engines
HRS:	Hazard Ranking System
HSWA:	Hazardous and Solid Waste Amendments
IG:	Inspector General
IPM:	Integrated Planning Model
ISC:	Interagency Scientific Committee
LAER:	Lowest Achievable Emission Rate
LDT:	Light-Duty Trucks
LDV:	Light-Duty Vehicles
LLC:	Limited Liability Company
LOP:	Letters of Permission
LULUs:	Locally Unwanted Land Uses
MACT:	Maximum Achievable Control Technology
MIR:	Maximum Individual Risk
MOU:	Memorandum of Understanding
MP:	Major Party
MPG:	Miles Per Gallon
MY:	Model Year

NAAQS: National Ambient Air Quality Standards
NAHB: National Association of Home Builders
NAMF: National Association of Metal Fisheries
NAPAP: National Acid Precipitation Assessment Program
NRCS: National Resources Conservation Service
NRDC: National Resources Defense Council
NSPS: New Source Performance Standard
NSR: New Source Review
NWF: National Wildlife Federation
NWP: Nationwide Permit

OIG: Office of Inspector General
OIRA: Office of Information and Regulatory Affairs
OMB: Office of Management and Budget
ONDA: Oregon National Desert Association
OPEC: Organization of the Petroleum Exporting Countries
OSM: Office of Surface Mining
OSMRE: Office of Surface Mining Reclamation and Enforcement

PA/SI: Preliminary Assessment and Site Investigation
PCN: Preconstruction Notification
PECE: Policy for Evaluation of Conservation Efforts
PM: Particle Matter
POTW: Publicly Owned Treatment Work
PPA: Prospective Purchaser Agreement
PRP: Potentially Responsible Party
PSD: Prevention of Significant Deterioration
PUD: Public Utility District

RACT: Reasonably Available Control Technology
RCRA: Resource Conservation Recovery Act
RD/RA: Remedial Design/Remedial Action
RHA: Rivers and Harbors Appropriation Act
RI/FS: Remedial Investigation and Feasibility Study
RMRR: Routine Maintenance, Repair, and Replacement
RRAM: Routine Repair and Maintenance

SARA: Superfund Amendments and Reauthorization Act
SBZ: Stream Buffer Zone
SCR: Selective Catalytic Reduction
SEIS: Supplementary Environmental Impact Statement
SEP: Supplemental Environmental Project
SEQRA: State Environmental Quality Review Act
SIPs: State Implementation Plans
SMCRA: Surface Mining and Reclamation Act
SPGP: State Programmatic General Permit
SQG: Small Quantity Generator

SRLPTF:	Small Refiner Lead Phase-down Task Force
SUV:	Sport Utility Vehicle
SWANCC:	Solid Waste Agency of Northern Cook County
TCE:	Trichloroethylene
TKN:	Total Kjeldahl Nitrogen
TLCP:	Toxicity Characteristic Leachate Procedure
TMDL:	Total Maximum Daily Load
TMP:	Timber Management Plan
TRI:	Toxic Release Inventory
TSD:	Treatment, Storage and Disposal Facility
TSS:	Total Suspended Solids
UAA:	Use Attainability Analysis
UNCED:	United Nations Conference on Environment and Development
USFWS:	United States Fish and Wildlife Service
UST:	Underground Storage Tank
VMT:	Vehicle Miles Traveled
VOC:	Volatile Organic Compound
WEPCO:	Wisconsin Electric Power Company
WHITEX:	Winter Haze Intensive Tracer Experiment
WHO:	World Health Organization
WQS:	Water Quality Standard
WVDEP:	West Virginia Department of Environmental Protection

Index

References are to Pages

404(b)(1) Guidelines, Clean Water Act, 686–695

A

Ability to Pay, Penalty Calculations, 454
Acid Rain Control, Clean Air Act, 381–385
Addition of a Pollutant, Clean Water Act, 132–138
Adler, Robert, 202–203
Administrative Adjudication, Generally, 71–72
Administrative Enforcement, 424, 439–455
Administrative Hearings, 445, 454, 466
Administrative Orders, 439–444, 522, 582
Administrative Penalties, 445–455, 502, 504
Air Quality Related Values Protection, Clean Air Act, 328–329
Alternatives Analysis, NEPA, 121–123
Ambient Air Quality Criteria, 239
Antidegradation Policy, Clean Water Act, 180, 181–182, 184, 191, 192, 193, 197
ARARs, CERCLA, 562, 563–564
Article II, U.S. Constitution, 497–499, 501
ASTM Standards, 554–559
Attorney Fees, 504–517
Authorization, RCRA, 467
Authorization Requirements, Clean Water Act, 151–157, 465
Authorization Status, Clean Water Act, 151

B

Best Available Demonstrated Control Technology, Clean Water Act, 163, 174, 176
Best Available Control Technology, Clean Air Act, 283, 284
Best Available Control Technology, Clean Water Act, 163, 168, 172, 173–174, 175–176, 428
Best Available Retrofit Technology, Clean Air Act, 283
Best Practicable Control Technology, Clean Water Act, 163, 164–173, 175–176, 428

Best Professional Judgment, Clean Water Act, 159–162
Brownfields, 555, 559–560
Brownfields Amendments, the, 518, 526, 554, 555
Bubble Policy, Clean Air Act
Bush, George W., 319
Bush Administration, 126, 319, 372

C

California Environmental Quality Act, 126
California Mobile Source Standards, 376–378
Cap and Trade Regulations, 7–8
Catalyst Theory, 508–517
Categorical Exclusions, NEPA, 85–89
Causation, CERCLA, 524, 525
Causation, Standing, 480, 482–483
Characteristic Waste, RCRA, 404–406
Chevron Deference, 80, 133, 141, 142, 172, 194, 199, 211–212, 395, 396, 398–399, 536
Citizen Suits, 153, 472–517, 655–656, 701, 726
Civil Enforcement in Court, 424–439
Civil Penalties, 432–439, 486–487
Clapton, Eric, 501
Clean Skies Initiative, 319
Climate Change, 252–255
Closed–Loop Exception, RCRA, 394, 398
Closure Requirements, RCRA, 417–421
Command and Control Regulations, 6, 518
Commerce Clause, U.S. Constitution, 37–48
Common Law, State, 3–5
"Comparison Factors," Clean Water Act, 167–168, 172
Conditionally–Exempt Generators, RCRA, 408
Conservationism, 2–3
"Consideration Factors," Clean Water Act, 168, 172
Consultation, Endangered Species Act, 618–631
Contribution, CERCLA 519, 548, 575–591
Contribution Protection, CERCLA, 565, 567, 574–575

Cooperative Federalism, see Federal/State
    Relationship
Cost–Benefit Analysis, 15–20, 169, 562–563
Cost–Benefit Regulations, 6
Council of Environmental Quality, 83
Covenants Not to Sue, CERCLA, 565, 567
Criminal Enforcement, 424–425, 455–465,
    656
Criteria Pollutants, Clean Air Act, 234–248
Critical Habitat, Endangered Species Act,
    610–613

D

De Minimis Settlements, CERCLA, 548,
    565–566, 569–570, 575
Defenses, CERCLA, 524, 526, 552–559
Derived From Rule, RCRA, 406, 407
Design Standards, 7
Designated Uses, Clean Water Act,
    179–180, 195–197, 199–200, 202
Diligent Prosecution, 502–504
Discharge, Clean Water Act, 198, 200–201
Discharge Monitoring Reports, 423
Discharge of a Pollutant, Clean Water Act,
    131, 426, 686–695
Distinct Population Segments, Endangered
    Species Act, 601–610
Donora, Pennsylvania, 219–231
Dormant Commerce Clause, U.S. Constitu-
    tion, 56–58

E

Economic Benefit, Penalty Calculations,
    433–438, 451–452
Economic Incetives, 385–388
Ehrlich, Paul, 25
Eleventh Amendment, U.S. Constitution,
    49–50
Endangered Species Committee (God
    Squad), 636–638
Environmental Assessments, NEPA, 89
Environmental Audit Policy, 455
Environmental Impact Statements, NEPA,
    84, 89–91, 112–127
EPA Review of State–Issued Permits, Clean
    Water Act, 158–162
EPA Review of State Water Quality Stan-
    dards, Clean Water Act, 178–180, 181
Effluent Limitation Guidelines, Clean Wa-
    ter Act, 163
Emission Controls, Automobiles, Clean Air
    Act, 376–381
Environmental Justice, 32–35, 555
Environmental Management Systems, 9
Equitable Discretion, 425–432
Ethics, Environmental, 30–32
Exhaustion, 77–78
Existing Uses, Clean Water Act, 179
Expanded Characteristic Option, RCRA,
    407

F

Facility, CERCLA, 521
Federal/State Relationship, 9–10, 150–162,
    202, 685–686, 711–720, 724–726
Federal Implementation Plans, Clean Air
    Act
FERC Licenses, Applicability of Water
    Quality Certification Requirements,
    201, 202
Finality, 75–77
Financial Responsibility Requirements,
    RCRA, 421
Fishable/swimmable goal, Clean Water Act,
    130, 179
Free Market Environmentalism, 5, 14
Fundamentally Different Factors Variance,
    Clean Water Act, 175

G

General Mining Act of 1872, 2, 13
General Permits, Clean Water Act, 696–700
Generator Liability, CERCLA, 537–543
Generator Requirements, RCRA, 408–412
Governmental Preclusion of Citizen Suits,
    see Preclusion
Groundwater Monitoring Requirements,
    RCRA, 413–417, 420–421
Gwaltney Doctrine, 473, 483–502

H

Habitat Conservation Plans, Endangered
    Species Act, 653–655
Hazard Ranking System, CERCLA 561
Hazardous Air Pollutants, Clean Air Act,
    367–372
Hazardous Substance, CERCLA, 519–520
Hazardous Waste, RCRA, 389–390, 404–408
Houck, Oliver, 130, 171, 178
Household Waste, RCRA, 406
How Clean is Clean, CERCLA, 562–564
HSWA, 389

I

Imminent and Substantial Endangerments,
    486, 519, 522
Incidental Takes, Endangered Species Act,
    619, 653–654
Injunctive Relief, 425–432, 486–487
Injury in Fact, 474–482, 489
Innocent Landowner Defense, CERCLA,
    526, 553–559
Interference, Clean Water Act, 177
Interim Owners, CERCLA, 526
Interim Status, RCRA, 413
Interstate Transport, Clean Air Act,
    259–275
Investigations, 422–423

J

Jeopardy, Endangered Species Act, 631–636
Joint and Several Liability, CERCLA, 543–552
Judicial Review, Generally, 73–81
Judicial Review of Administrative Orders, 439–444, 522
Judicial Review of Administrative Penalties, 454
Judicial Review of Consent Decrees, 569–575
Judicial Review of Permits, 162
Judicial Review of Rules, 398, 401
Jurisdiction, CERCLA, 519–521
Jurisdiction, Clean Water Act, 131–150, 686–695
Jurisdiction, RCRA, 389–407

L

Land Ban, RCRA, 409, 421
Layla, Derek and the Dominos, 501
Lender Liability, CERCLA, 537
Lenity, the Rule of, 145, 147–148, 149–150
Leopold, Aldo, 30–32
Letters of Permission, Clean Water Act, 699–700
Liable Parties, CERCLA, 522–543
Listed Waste, RCRA, 404–406
Listing, Endangered Species Act, 593–610, 613–616
Lomborg, Bjorn, 25–26
Lowest Achievable Emission Rate, Clean Air Act, 283
Love Canal, 518

M

Major Federal Actions, NEPA, 101–105
Market Forces, Clean Air Act, 385–388
Minnesota Environmental Protection Act, 126
Mitigation Under NEPA, 123–125
Mixing Zones, Clean Water Act, 189–190
Mixture Rule, RCRA, 406, 407
Mobile Sources, Clean Air Act, 373–381
Mootness, 489–490, 491–492, 493–502
Mountaintop-removal/Valley-fill Mining, 720–724
Muir, John, 2

N

Narrative Permit Conditions, Enforceability Thereof, Clean Water Act, 184, 190–191
National Ambient Air Quality Standards, 239–253
National Contingency Plan, CERCLA, 521–522, 560–564, 576, 589–591

National Pollutant Discharge Elimination System, 130–192
National Priorities List, CERCLA, 519, 561, 576
Nationwide Permits, 696–698
Navigable Waters, Clean Water Act, 138–143, 658–676
Necessary and Proper Clause, U.S. Constitution, 37
New Source Performance Standards, Clean Air Act, 282, 289
New Source Performance Standards, Clean Water Act, see Best Available Demonstrated Control Technology
New Source Review, Clean Air Act, 289–298
New York State Environmental Quality Review Act, 126
Nonbinding Preliminary Allocation of Liability, CERCLA, 568
Nonpoint Pollution, Clean Water Act, 146–147, 202–203, 205–212
Normal Farming Exemption, Clean Water Act, 684
Notice Letters, CERCLA, 564–565, 566–567
Notice Requirements, Citizen Suits, 473, 487, 490
NPDES, Jurisdictional Elements, 131

O

Office of Information and Regulatory Affairs, 15, 72–73
Office of Management and Budget, 15, 17, 19–20, 72–73
Operator Liablity, CERCLA, 527–537
Overfiling, 351–367, 466–472
Ownership Liability, CERCLA, 523–526

P

Parent Corporations, Liability thereof Under CERCLA, 527–537
Pass Through, Clean Water Act, 177
Performance Standards, Clean Air Act, 281–284
Pinchot, Gifford, 2
Pedersen, William, 171–172
Permit Shield Doctrine, 158
Permitting Requirements, RCRA, 413
Personnel Training, RCRA, 411
Petroleum Exclusion, CERCLA, 520–521
Piercing the Corporate Veil, CERCLA, 527, 528–529
Point Source, Clean Water Act, 143–150
Pollutant, Clean Water Act, 132, 135–137, 148
Polluter Pays Principle, 24
Potentially Responsible Parties, CERCLA, see Liable Parties
Precautionary Principle, 26–30
Preclusion, 487–488, 490, 502–504
Preemption, 36

References are to Pages

Preenforcement Review, 439–444, 522

Preliminary Investigation and Site Assessment, CERCLA, 561

Premium Payments, CERCLA, 565–566

Preservationism, 2

Presidential Oversight, 72–73

Pretreatment, Clean Water Act, 163, 176–178

Prevention of Significant Deterioration, Clean Air Act, 289, 321–328

Private Party Cleanup and Cost Recovery, CERCLA, 519, 575–591

Privatization, 13–15

Project XL, 8–9

Property Clause, U.S. Constitution

Prospective Purchaser Exclusion, CERCLA, 526, 555–557

Protectiveness, CERCLA, 563–564

Public Goods, 11–15

Public Welfare Offense Doctrine, 458–465

Publicly Owned Treatment Works, Clean Water Act, 163, 176–177

R

RCRA Civil Penalty Policy, 445–454

Recovery, Endangered Species Act, 613

Reasonably Available Control Technology, Clean Air Act, 283

Redressability, 480–481, 491–493, 493–502

Release, CERCLA, 521

Remedial Action, CERCLA, 519

Remedial Investigation and Feasibility Study, CERCLA, 561–564, 566–567

Remedial Purpose Canon, 525

Removal Action, CERCLA, 519, 561, 576

Removal Credits, Clean Water Act, 177–178

Res Judicata, 471

Retroactivity, CERCLA, 525–526

Ripeness, 78–79

Risk Analysis, 20–24

Rulemaking, 70–71

S

Sanctions for Failure to Produce Adequate SIP, Clean Air Act, 279–280

Seminole Rock Deference, 80–81, 142, 211–212

Settlement, CERCLA, 522, 564–575

Skidmore Deference, 80, 133, 211–212

Small Handles Problem, NEPA, 101

Small Quantity Generators, RCRA, 408

Solid Waste, RCRA, 390–404

Speculative Accumulation, RCRA, 393

Spending Clause, U.S. Constitution

Standing to Sue, 58–59, 474–483

State Environmental Policy Acts, 125–127

State Implementation Plans, Clean Air Act, 255–259, 276–277, 279–280

Statute of Limitations, 438–439, 455, 578, 587

Strict Liability, CERCLA, 524–525

Superfund, the, CERCLA, 518–519

Supplemental Environmental Projects, 455

Sustainable Development, 24–26

Swampbuster Program, 701–704

T

Takings, Endangered Species Act, 639–653

Takings Clause, U.S. Constitution, 50–54

Technology–Based Standards, Clean Water Act, 163

Tenth Amendment, U.S. Constitution, 48–49

Third–Party Defense, CERCLA, 553

Thoreau, Henry, 2

Threatened Release, CERCLA, 521

Title V Permit Program, Clean Air Act, 341–351

Total Maximum Daily Loads, Clean Water Act, 183, 187, 203–212

Toxicity Characteristic, RCRA, 405–406

Toxicity Characteristic Leachate Procedure, 405–406

Trading, Clean Air Act, 382–383, 387

Tragedy of the Commons, 11–15

Treatment, Storage and Disposal Facilities, RCRA, 412–421

U

Unilateral Orders, see Administrative Orders

Unitary Waters Theory, Clean Water Act, 137

Used Oil, RCRA, 399

V

Visibility Protection, Clean Air Act, 329–340

Voluntary Cleanup, CERCLA, 576, 579–591

W

Waste Determination Requirement, RCRA, 409

Water Quality–Based Permit Conditions, Clean Water Act, 163, 166, 182–192

Water Quality Certification, Clean Water Act, 192–202

Water Quality Criteria, Clean Water Act, 178, 179–180, 181, 196

Water Quality Standards, Clean Water Act, 178–182

Waters of the United States, Clean Water Act, see Navigable Waters

Wetland Delineation, Clean Water Act, 675–676

Z

Zone of Interests, 74–75

†